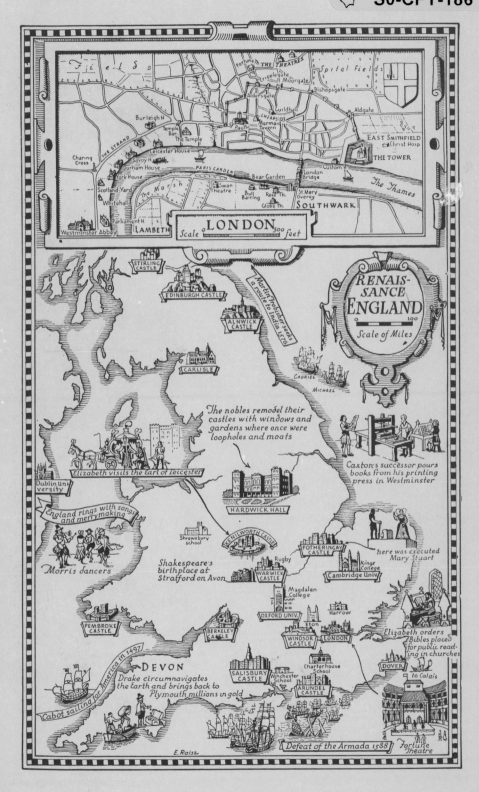

LONDON Scale 500 feet

Fields — THE THEATRES — *Spital Fields* — Fortune Th. — Cripplegate — Moorgate — Bishopsgate — Aldersgate — Aldgate — Guildhall — CHEAPSIDE — Marmaid Tavern — Pauls — Burleigh H. — Temple Bar — The Temple — EAST SMITHFIELD — Christ Hosp. — THE TOWER — Leicester House — THE STRAND — Charing Cross — Savoy Ho. — Durham House — York House — PARIS GARDEN — London Bridge — Custom — Scotland Yard — The Marsh — Swan Theatre — Bear Garden — Bull Baiting — Rose Th. — St Mary Overey — The Thames — Whitehall — Globe Th. — SOUTHWARK — Parliament H. — Westminster Abbey — LAMBETH

RENAISSANCE ENGLAND Scale of Miles 100

STIRLING CASTLE

EDINBURGH CASTLE

ALNWICK CASTLE

Martin Frobisher seeks a route to India 1576

CARLISLE

GABRIEL

MICHAEL

The nobles remodel their castles with windows and gardens where once were loopholes and moats

Caxton's successor pours books from his printing press in Westminster

Elizabeth visits the Earl of Leicester

Dublin University

HARDWICK HALL

England rings with songs and merrymaking

Shrewsbury school

KENILWORTH CASTLE

FOTHERINGAY CASTLE

here was executed Mary Stuart

Morris dancers

Shakespeare's birthplace at Stratford on Avon

Rugby

WARWICK CASTLE

Kings College

Cambridge Univ.

Magdalen College

PEMBROKE CASTLE

BERKELEY CASTLE

OXFORD UNIV.

Eton

Harrow

WINDSOR CASTLE

LONDON

Elizabeth orders Bibles placed for public reading in churches

DEVON

Drake circumnavigates the Earth and brings back to Plymouth millions in gold

SALISBURY CASTLE

Winchester school

Charterhouse School

DOVER

to Calais

Cabot sailing for America in 1497

ARUNDEL CASTLE

E. Raisz

Defeat of the Armada 1588

Fortune Theatre

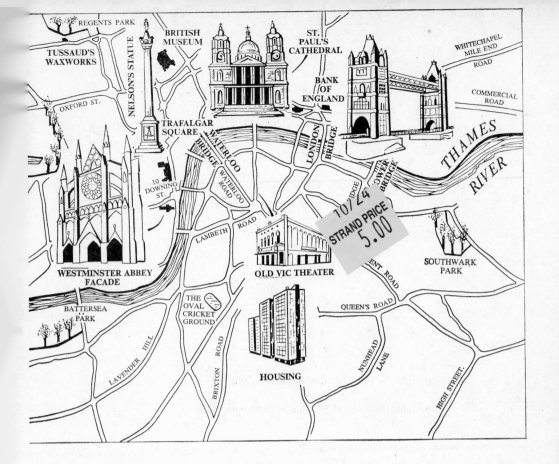

A History of England

THIRD EDITION

CHARLES SCRIBNER'S SONS, NEW YORK

TO THE MEMORY
OF
CARL L. BECKER

Preface

TO write a history of England is bound to be a troublesome task. Every historian knows how difficult it is to capsule and correlate material to meet the needs of the general reader and the student. Mindful of both readers, I have attempted throughout this book to maintain a just proportion and perspective in showing the direction, strength, and significance of the major forces and trends in the history of England. Knowing from experience that many readers will not read beyond this general history I have also tried to explain in readable prose the ideas behind the events and the reasons why men acted as they did. For the guidance of those who may wish to read further I have included at the end of the volume a rather extensive bibliography of books and articles that are of special value.

The expert reader will doubtless discover inaccuracies or omissions in the field of his special competence. Learned articles and monographs, born of careful scholarship, appear at a disconcertingly rapid pace. No author can hope to read them all or to avoid errors of fact and interpretation. For my errors and my purely private heresies I ask indulgence.

It is a special pleasure to record my appreciation of the unsparing assistance given me by Professor Arthur C. Bining, the editor of the series. His meticulous craftsmanship and wide knowledge have saved me from many ambiguities of expression and errors of fact. In writing this book I have also been particularly indebted to Professor Conyers Read of the University of Pennsylvania. Every chapter of the manuscript profited from his patient and detailed criticism.

My ideas through the years have been influenced by many scholars. I cannot hope to acknowledge my debt to all of them. Some of my associates, past and present, have patiently explained their ideas to me and thus helped me to form my own. My sincerest thanks are especially due to C. W. de Kiewiet, Provost of Cornell University;

vii

to Professor George H. Sabine, Professor F. G. Marcham, and Professor Carl Stephenson, also of Cornell University; to Professor George Cuttino of Swarthmore College; to Professor Ernest P. Kuhl, Professor Harry G. Plum, and Dr. William H. Seiler, my friends and former colleagues at the State University of Iowa; to Professors Walter Balderston, Arthur G. Dorland, Fred Landon and Hartley M. Thomas of the University of Western Ontario; to Professor Charles F. Mullett of the University of Missouri; to Professor Francis D. Wormuth of the University of Utah; to Professors W. Stull Holt and Solomon Katz of the University of Washington and Professor Lyle Shelmidine of the College of Puget Sound, who were responsible for producing a Seattle summer and ideal conditions for writing several chapters of this book; to my admirable colleagues at Wayne University; to Miss Veva Cox, Mrs. Velma Farrar, Mrs. Sylvia Goodman and Miss Lillian Benson, who gave me valuable help with the manuscript; and to the many others upon whose stores of knowledge and kindness I have so freely drawn.

In the preparation of the second revised edition I have been aided by Professor Willson H. Coates of the University of Rochester whose suggestions were wise and welcome. I also appreciate the interest and assistance of Professor John C. Galbraith of the University of California at Los Angeles and the numerous acts of kindness and courtesy of Professor A. C. Cooke, Professor Margaret Ormsby, Professor W. N. Sage, and Professor W. H. Soward of the University of British Columbia.

For advice and assistance in preparing the third revised edition I am particularly grateful to Dr. T. K. Derry of Marylebone Grammar School, London, England, Professor E. J. Knapton of Wheaton College, Norton, Massachusetts, Professor Willson H. Coates of the University of Rochester, and Mrs. Annette Riley, Miss Helen J. Jankowska, and Mrs. Marilynn Lystad of Wayne State University. I am also indebted to the numerous teachers and students who have written to me through the years offering valuable suggestions and advice. To my colleagues I renew my thanks for their invaluable criticism and unfailing patience.

GOLDWIN SMITH

Wayne State University
Detroit, Michigan

Contents

Appendices and Indices

A History

of ENGLAND

Chapter I

THE BEGINNINGS

TIME AND TIDE

LONG before our planet was suitable for mankind, the relentless forces of nature were making mountains and valleys, seas and continents. The globe that once had been a ball of molten matter continued to spin through space as hot and moist centuries spawned the first animal life. Lush tropical plant growth laid down the world's coal beds. Over large areas rolled the masses of great glaciers. Then they retreated, leaving behind the evidence of their power in ripped and reshaped land. They came many times, and at last withdrew to the silent and icy polar caps. Thus in the vast immensities of astronomical space and geological time the physical world as we know it was prepared.

On the western edge of Europe the sea slowly wore broad channels through soft chalk; it swept over the marshes and invaded river valleys; wide areas of land were submerged. In time the British Isles were separated from the Continent. Through succeeding centuries this separation was important not only to the people of Britain but to the whole world. Geography is more than the handmaiden of history. The plain man, who is not a professional archaeologist, geographer, or historian, might wonder why such closely allied subjects are usually studied in isolation.

The early hazards and difficulties of sea transport meant that European invaders never came to Britain in large numbers at once. They arrived in driblets. Hence no single continental cultural, political, or economic influence ever stretched over from Europe to remain strong or stable in Britain. Successive waves of influence, varying in power and length of dominance, flowed into eastern England and to a lesser extent into Scotland, Wales, Cornwall, and Ireland. Through the centuries the result was a mingling of populations, a layering of several strata of cultures and political habits. Deep in the core of

1

English history lie the twin facts that Englishmen live on an island and are sprung from the fusion of many stocks.

The shaping importance of geography is easily recognized as a general truth and often overlooked in a particular application. Many chapters of the history of men in Britain have been written because highlands, lowlands, downs, and rivers exist in certain places. The highland zones of England rise to the north and west; the lowland areas lie in the south and east. It was therefore the lowlands that were nearest to the early invaders. These strangers usually landed on the flat Channel coasts opposite France or on the long eastern shore. The rivers were easily navigable; the lowland plains were habitable, fertile, and easy to seize. At the same time the Welsh mountains, the Pennines, and Scottish mountains held up the invading Romans, Saxons, Danes, and Normans. Thus the highland west and north were blocked by their own natural barriers from contact with Europe.

The ancient differences between hillsmen and plainsmen, highlanders and lowlanders, were nourished by the facts of geography. The highland areas, particularly in Scotland and Wales, did not welcome alien intruders. Fixed in their ancient ways, they did not easily embrace change or novelty. Many pages of British history contain drama and color because of the vigorously distinct characteristics of men long separated by forests, rivers, moorlands, marshes, and mountains. The difficulties of internal communication and complete conquest were to delay the achievement of national unity and to prolong the power of local patriotism. The economic revolution rising in the eighteenth century helped to pull millions of workers towards the factories clustered about the twin magnets of iron and coal. Nevertheless, this partial redistribution of population did not completely reverse the continuous tide of differing cultures, language, and attitude in Scotland, Wales, and England. Often in the history of nations the important political, social, and economic facts are mainly geographical ones.

THE EMERGENCE OF MAN

Over half a million years ago *Pithecanthropus Erectus,* the Erect Ape Man, leaped from the leafy stalks of the prehistoric jungles. Only in the last 6,000 years has the story of human advance been recorded in written evidence. All the rest is prehistory.

The first stage of man's advance was the stone age, distinguished by various kinds of stone tools. This period has been divided by archaeologists into several phases including the eolithic (the dawn of stone), the paleolithic (old stone age) and the neolithic (new stone age). The stone age in Britain seems to have developed continuously through the long eolithic and paleolithic ages from nearly 500,000 years ago to about 8000 B.C. In the later paleolithic period men still

8000 - 3000 BC   Neolithic culture came mainly from Spain + Brittany

lived, as earlier, in caves, or in pit dwellings; they painted on the walls of their caves. In the years between 8000 B.C. and 3000 B.C. the neolithic phase of stone culture began to appear.

The invaders who brought the neolithic culture came mainly from Spain and Brittany; a smaller number came from the Baltic regions. Succeeding generations of neolithic men made finely polished

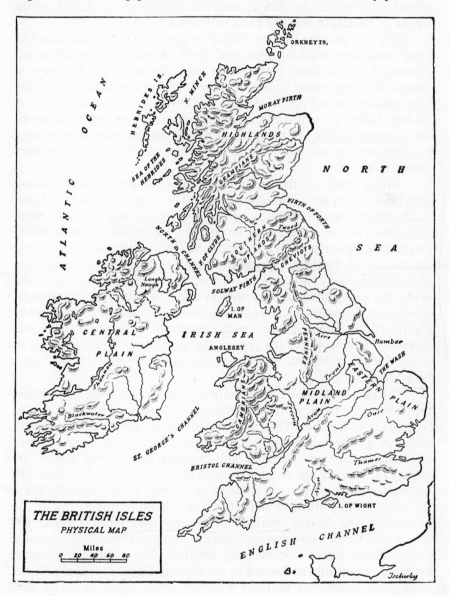

THE BRITISH ISLES
PHYSICAL MAP

Miles
0 20 40 60 80

weapons and tools; they made pottery; they domesticated a number of animals, including the horse and the dog. It seems probable that they tilled the soil and grew crops. Like most of their predecessors, neolithic men tended to live on the uplands. They inhabited huts and developed a primitive community life on a fairly large scale. They worked the flint mines to an increasing extent and engaged in widespread domestic trade. Their scattered settlements stretched northwards to Yorkshire and the Firth of Forth.

The pivotal area was the Wiltshire plateau. Out of Wiltshire ran great trackways reaching from the York moors to Cornwall, crisscrossing England from the Humber and the Wash to Anglesea in Wales. The long green fingers of these trackways probed through the hilly country, avoiding the forests and swamps of the lowlands. A modern expert has called this coordinated network of communications the "nervous system" of the great stone culture. Its nerve centers were concentrated on massive temples and stone circles such as Avebury and Stonehenge.

About 2000 B.C. the neolithic age merged slowly into the bronze age. Once again new immigrants arrived in England. These peoples came chiefly from the Rhine and Danube regions bringing with them their own cultures. There was no marked gap between the neolithic and bronze ages; the immigrants from the Rhineland and the neolithic inhabitants of England possessed similar customs; the two peoples intermingled easily; no wave of warfare or destruction swept over the land. The great advance was now in the production of metal tools. Mines and foundries increased in number. Tin was exported to the Continent. Britain's import trade, particularly in ornaments, was extended. The people of the bronze age wove cloth. Their methods of tilling the soil improved. As their standard of living rose their life span lengthened.

During the thousand years before Julius Caesar arrived in Britain the Celts began to sweep from Europe over the seas to England, Wales, Scotland, and Ireland. When the Roman legions came and conquered, probably all the inhabitants of the British Isles spoke Celtic. Gradually the bronze age elements and customs faded away before the impact of the iron age culture brought from Europe by the Celts. In the western and northern highlands, of course, the villages far from the main arteries of travel and settlement carried on their ways of life unchanged. As always, periods of culture overlapped. Where the streams of Celtic immigration brought particular types of iron age culture there was a considerable advance. Metal objects, such as brooches beautifully decorated in the flowing Celtic curvilinear style, have been discovered in large numbers. New types of metal and wooden tools appeared. Remains of carts, looms, spoons, tubs, and pottery testify to the general prosperity. Wooden floors and doors were put into the houses. The men used razors, the women cosmetics. Agricultural improvements continued. Mining developments increased. Various commodities, including tin, grain, cattle, gold, and silver were exported to the Continent. Large communities arose, such as the famous lake-village of Glastonbury.

Exports from Britain to Continent

The Celts were divided into turbulent and rival tribes, ruled by

THE ENGLISH COUNTIES

chiefs or kings. In the Celtic society there were nobles, freemen, and slaves. Each tribe apparently had several gods; some important gods were worshipped by a number of tribes. There was a considerable body of rites, symbols, and magical observance, now lost in the clouds of time. A priesthood of druids formed an influential and respected class. They were the feared medicine men, the teachers, the magistrates, the magicians. It was they who preserved the traditions, the lore, and the sacred cults of their tribes.

After the Roman and Anglo-Saxon conquests the remnants of the Celtic race remained in the Welsh mountains, behind the Grampians, across the seas in Ireland, in the western lowlands of Scotland, and in the hills of Devonshire and Cornwall. They held fast to several dialects, their Celtic customs and characteristics. These differences, protected by highlands and seas, were to play a momentous part in the political history of the British Isles. They combined with differences of religion, mistaken policy, and evil chance to produce through the centuries such results as the Anglo-Scottish wars, the long agitation for Welsh disestablishment, and the deep and vicious Irish ulcer.

THE ROMAN INVASIONS

In the first three chapters of Edward Gibbon's *The Decline and Fall of the Roman Empire* is described the prosperous condition of the Empire when it was at its height and "comprehended the fairest part of the earth, and the most civilized portion of mankind." At the dawn of the Christian era the Roman legions had conquered both Greeks and Carthaginians and subdued the larger part of Europe. Roman civilization and Roman trade were everywhere protected by watchful and efficient soldiers. Roman rule meant almost universal law, order, and peace. Throughout all the Empire there was the Roman culture, the Roman institutions, the Latin language. Far frontiers were guarded by the legions of Rome. "The terror of the Roman arms added weight and dignity to the moderation of the emperors. They preserved peace by a constant preparation for war."

Between 58 and 50 B.C. Julius Caesar completed a series of great campaigns that added all Gaul to the Empire. This he accomplished with six legions, comprising about 30,000 men. At the same time he lunged across the Channel against England. The relative insulation of Britain was at an end. The British Isles emerged into the light of history.

In August, 55 B.C. Julius Caesar embarked from Boulogne with a force of about 10,000 men. British charioteers, cavalry, and infantry gathered on the downs above Dover to throw back the threatened attack from the sea. Caesar's legionaries were victorious, but a gale dashed anchored Roman transports on the shore. In the following year, Caesar left his fleet anchored "off a gentle open beach." Again a gale hammered his ships. Forty vessels were destroyed. Meanwhile the

Romans were harassed by mobile groups of Celts. In the end Caesar won because he destroyed the fortress of the enemy and developed a method of dealing with the British charioteers. The first step in the conquest of Britain had been taken. But Gaul was not yet fully pacified; and Caesar had an appointment in the senate-house on the Ides of March, 44 B.C.

For nearly a century no further attempts were made to conquer Britain. The legions of Rome were busy elsewhere on frontiers of the Empire. By A.D. 43, however, the Emperor Claudius gathered about 40,000 men and invaded Britain. Slowly the Britons were driven back and Roman authority established. There were several rebellions, including the great revolt led by the Celtic Queen Boudicca in A.D. 61. Her destruction of London was complete. "To this day, men digging in the city still find everywhere the layer of ashes which is all that was left when her men had done their work." Roman vengeance was horrible and thorough, and Roman power steadily advanced. Agricola, a fine leader and father-in-law of Tacitus, was governor of Britain from A.D. 78 to A.D. 85. He finished the conquest of Wales. Then he turned northwards against the Caledonian tribes. Before he was recalled to Rome his legions had driven far beyond the Clyde.

When Agricola returned to Rome Caledonia slipped out of the grasp of the legions. Rome did not again attempt the conquest of Scotland. Probably in 122 the Emperor Hadrian began the building of a wall across the island from the Tyne to the Solway. It was finished about 127. This wall was a continuous rampart ten Roman feet thick and twenty feet high, protected by a ditch thirty feet wide and garrisoned by troops housed in forts along its line. To dig the ditch it was necessary to move nearly two million cubic yards of soil, subsoil, and solid rock. The wall itself, mainly stone and mortar, contained over two million cubic yards of material. Often the stone had to be carried from distant quarries. It was a tremendous achievement. Beyond the wall, Scotland remained unconquered.

TOWN AND VILLA

To England the Roman Empire brought law and order, town life, roads; and the roads, as the saying is, all led to Rome. For three hundred years England had peace; she was not to have it again so completely until the twelfth century.

The machinery of Roman government varied in different parts of the Empire. For example, there were two classes of provinces, the one group controlled by the senate, the other by the emperor. Britain was one of the latter class, an imperial province ruled by a governor who was the legate, or representative, of the emperor. This official, like all imperial governors, normally held his post for a term of not less than three years, and not more than five. He was responsible for civil administration. He was also commander-in-chief of the military forces of the province.

Within the broad structure of the provincial political, military, and financial system there was considerable opportunity for local self-government by the inhabitants of Britain. The development of local autonomy was particularly strong in the towns where Roman ways of life had been widely adopted. In the internal affairs of towns called *coloniae*, which were settlements of retired legionaries, and the *municipia*, communities of Roman citizens or those who enjoyed the franchise without full citizenship, the governor seldom interfered. The municipal government of both *coloniae* and *municipia* was modelled after Rome. We know of four *coloniae* in Britain: Lincoln, Colchester, Gloucester, and York. So far as we are aware Verulam was the only *municipium*. Beyond these organized and chartered towns there were wide degrees of autonomy. The Roman system was very flexible; in proportion as various parts of Britain became Romanized they obtained varying powers of self-government.

The Mediterranean world believed that man's spiritual needs could be satisfied only by the town. "The town was at once the symptom and the symbol of all that was highest and most precious in human life, all that raises man above the beasts of the field." Because this was so, the Romans tried to supply Britain with towns. In the lowlands they were successful in creating urban units, large and small, as centers of Roman culture. These settled areas normally had regular chessboard street plans, a forum, a market square surrounded on three sides by shops and flanked on the fourth by a town hall; there were public baths and temples. The townspeople usually came to speak Latin and to live in a Roman way. It has been estimated that the small tribal capitals had an average of one or two thousand inhabitants; places like Verulam had about five thousand, London about fifteen thousand.

In the third century a rapid decay of city life occurred throughout the Roman Empire. Professor Rostovtzeff has shown that the foundations of urban civilization were destroyed by the predatory Emperor Septimius Severus. This grim African plundered towns by taxation to strengthen the army. Perhaps the underprivileged and envious peasantry assisted in the new policy. In any event, the wealth of urban aristocracy was dissipated; people fled from the cities. City life, upon which the process of provincial Romanization was so dependent, was now almost entirely wrecked.

By far the largest part of the inhabitants of Roman Britain lived in the country, either in villages or in country houses called villas. The village was a group of Celtic stone huts, usually one-roomed and circular, clustered inside a fence or ditch; outside were small enclosed fields; there was usually little evidence of Roman influence. On the other hand, the villas were residences of Romans or Romanized Britons who ran their own estates, presumably by slave labor, and lived until the late fourth century in increasing prosperity. These villas were either large or small; some of the most magnificent had mosaics, frescoes, hot air furnaces. Most had bathrooms, courtyards and rectangular, walled farmyards in which stood barns, stables, and quarters for the workers.

Villas were always self-sufficient; about them were the large open

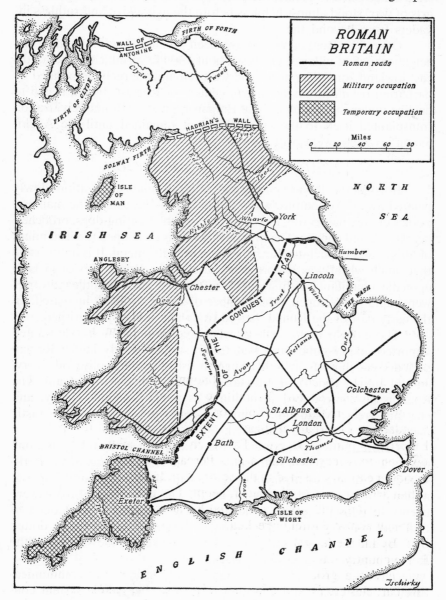

fields of the owners' estates. The Roman peace was so complete that no moats or walls stood about these great farmhouses. The legions were ready to defend those who were untrained to fight. Forty thousand legionaries, based on fortresses such as York and Chester, protected Britain from the turbulent Picts and Scots. In the days when the legions were called back to Rome, the people of Britain, unaccustomed to the arts of war, stood almost helpless before the aggressive and ruthless invaders from beyond the seas.

Over 500 Roman villas have been located, few of them in the neighborhood of villages. Of these about 450 are sprinkled in the southeast lowland zone. The north and west remained largely dominated by barbarian tribalism. As the urban centers of Roman Britain began to decline under the assaults of the Emperor Severus, Roman civilization transplanted itself to the villas. There it remained until the Anglo-Saxon invaders swept over the coast.

TRADE, ROADS, AND RELIGION

Beyond the towns, cities, and villas Roman civilization slowly petered away. Agriculture was still the leading industry. The main exports were textiles, cattle, hides, slaves, oysters, hunting-dogs, brooches, pearls, tin, and copper. The practical Romans developed the iron mines of Sussex and Gloucestershire; they exported the metal. It is improbable that much wheat was exported because of the Roman levies in kind upon the inhabitants. Strong glassware, pottery, brick, and tile industries were rapidly developed. The number of foreign traders increased. In the early part of the Roman period trade and industry flourished.

Those of the highest classes who lived in the Roman style wanted imported luxury goods and that traffic swelled. Early in the Roman period these imports included Spanish fish-sauce and olive oil, ivory, amber, Italian wine, and red-glazed Samian pottery from Gaul. The Romans also introduced such things as poplar, walnut, cherry, and chestnut trees. Meanwhile domestic commerce increased as rustic markets and town fairs multiplied.

Before the Roman conquest the chief paths of travel were along the ancient roads and old ridgeways like the Ichnield Way of the Berkshire and Chiltern escarpment. The Romans built a system of imperial military highways 5,000 miles in length. The main arterial roads were twenty to twenty-five feet wide, usually gravelled and kept open to traffic all the year round. This amazing system of radial roads, dotted by forts and legion garrisons, was the major key to the success of the Roman military conquest and government.

Thus there spread over England a great gridiron of communication between towns and guardian fortresses. The whole system converged on London. That city was the great supply base. It was the great trading center, the little Rome of England, an ideal port. Continental commerce came up the Thames to London Bridge; one half of the major highways radiated north and west from it. London's commercial greatness, behind the Roman walls, was assured despite the trade shrinkage of the Saxon period.

More important in English history than these developments in government, commerce, industry, and communication was the coming of Christianity. In the beginning, the motley varieties of the Celtic religion, purged of their nationalistic Druidism, were left alone by the Romans. The Celts had over forty jealous gods and godlings. The fact that in their kaleidoscopic and fissiparous religions the Celts had no single God reflected the disunity that has marked the long course of Celtic history. The Roman and British religions usually blended freely. Jupiter, Mars, and Mercury were easily identified with Celtic gods. Eastern faiths also came in with the soldiers and traders. Rome put no shackles on any religion that did not challenge the state.

We are not sure when Christianity first reached Britain. Tradition declared that St. Paul and St. Peter had visited the British Isles; that Joseph of Arimathea had brought the Gospel and the Holy Grail to Glastonbury where he planted the sacred thorn from Christ's crown of thorns. Certainly by the early years of the third century Christianity was gathering momentum in Britain. The Christian leaders preached a dynamic and expansive faith. They declared all Roman and Celtic gods false. Because it was a political offense to insult the official deities the Christians were intermittently persecuted, mainly under Diocletian in the early part of the fourth century. At this time there were probably about 10,000,000 Christians in the Empire's total population of 100,000,000. One martyr in Britain was the Roman Alban, who was slain at Verulam; when Verulam later fell and crumbled there rose on its ruins the new town of St. Albans.

The waves of persecution levelled off and Christianity advanced. Three British bishops attended the Council of Arles in 314 to represent the Christian communities in Britain. In the fifth century Celtic Christianity was planted widely among the Picts by the evangelical Ninian; in Ireland by St. Patrick; in Wales, Cornwall, and Devon by St. Illtyd, a disciple of St. Germanus, and the constellation of his missionaries. It is probable that St. Illtyd was a teacher of St. David.

The Emperor Constantine was probably converted to Christianity by a mystical revelation. He abandoned sun-worship himself and gave the Christians toleration throughout the Empire by the famous Edict of Milan in 313. It is often inaccurately stated that Constantine made Christianity the state religion. In his day the ancient prerogatives of the old cults were still left untouched. It remained for a later generation to proscribe the gods of Caesar.

When Constantine died in 337 the Empire was already beginning to shrink and tremble. Soon the legions went home from Britain, one by one. In their wake the fearful scuttled to security. The Christian missionaries remained behind in Britain. Their cause was greater than that of the Roman Empire.

THE END OF ROMAN BRITAIN

The proud Roman conquerors would forge no new provinces. Gently and irrevocably, the Empire flickered to its death. The black chaos that came with the utter collapse of civilization was almost an aftermath and an anticlimax. In Britain and Gaul there is unassailable evidence that many men did not suspect that the end was at hand, even in a world where disintegration became each year more insistent.

In the fourth century Rome organized a fleet and built about a dozen forts to defend the southeastern Saxon Shore, from Lincoln-shire to the Isle of Wight, against the raids of the Saxons from across the sea. Similar forts were built in Wales to discourage Irish attacks. Some people returned to Rome. Archaeologists still find treasures buried by fugitives who never returned. Others stayed on in Britain. In 410 Rome itself was sacked. The hosts of the Vandals, Goths, and Lombards were in the heart of the dying Empire.

Gildas, a sixth century monk, passionate, rhetorical, and usually unreliable, has left dramatic tales of the barbarian attacks and "the groans of the Britons." In 446, states Gildas, the Britons appealed in despair to the Roman consul Aetius, then commanding the Roman forces in Gaul: "The barbarians drive us to the sea; the sea drives us back to the barbarians; we are either slaughtered or drowned." Aetius gave no help. Other Roman generals were then fully occupied in defending Rome against the vast hosts of the tribes from the north and east. The Britons had to fend for themselves. The Irish and Scots struck at the west coast; the Picts broke over the Roman walls on the north; the Saxons beached their ships on the east coast. The Roman Empire in the west was at an end. It was astounding that it had achieved so much and lasted so long.

Chapter 2

ANGLO-SAXON ENGLAND

COMING OF THE INVADERS

THE Anglo-Saxon invasions of England were a part of the general movements against the collapsing Roman Empire, beginning strongly in the fifth century. The bold barbarians cracked the Rhine-Danube frontier of the Romans and swept over all the Western Empire. As the Burgundians, Franks, Goths, and Vandals plunged southward towards Rome, the sea-rover Angles, Saxons, Jutes, and the rest of the mingled peoples who lived in the northeast area of Europe began to swoop over the sea to England. First the marauders raided irresponsibly. Then, about 450, they began to move their families across the sea in their small boats; to clear forests; to settle, particularly in Essex, Kent, Surrey, Sussex, and Hampshire. There they made their hamlets of wooden huts amid shaggy trees and brushwood, downs and marshes, their trackways meandering through the forest. They spread out their areas of settlement from the great radiation points of the Anglo-Saxon immigration, the river systems of eastern England.

In the end they conquered and held the larger part of what is now England. They were no more successful than the Romans in overrunning the upland districts of Wales. They were held below the Forth River in Scotland. They did not penetrate Devon, Cumberland, Somerset, or Cornwall. West Yorkshire and Lancashire long remained Celtic, safe behind the Pennines. During the long period of the conquest the Anglo-Saxons fought hard; but the view that they exterminated the Britons, even in the east and south, cannot wisely be held today. Where the Anglo-Saxons conquered, the Celts were sometimes killed; more often they became serfs or craftsmen or were forced to flee to the ancient fortresses of Wales or Cornwall; although many went across the seas to Brittany, it is unlikely that they went as a direct result of Saxon pressure.

Sometimes they did not flee, and there was some intermingling of races even in eastern England. There were several pockets of Britons

13

left in the Anglo-Saxon regions. The fusion of races in Wessex appears to have been considerable. "There can be little doubt," runs an authoritative anthropological opinion, "that the physical inheritance of a great proportion of the present population of the country is derived from its pre-Roman inhabitants who were already of so many breeds established side by side."

Until recently it was believed that the Jutes, Angles, and Saxons, the tall, long-headed, and fair-haired invaders who arrived in their long boats to conquer England, came from distinct continental areas and were divided into separate, well-organized tribes. There is now a growing body of evidence to support the conclusion that the tribes who came over were somewhat mingled together, and poured over the sea "with a common purpose but little unity of command." It is only roughly accurate, therefore, to say that the Jutes settled in the Kent area of the southeast; the Saxons in the southeastern regions around Kent, in Essex, Sussex, and Wessex; the Angles in territories north from Essex, in Anglia, Mercia, and Northumbria. The term "Saxon" itself was apparently used by the Romano-British as a general term of abuse; it included all the invaders.

As the scattered forces of the Anglo-Saxons moved inland it was clear that they preferred to live away from the large towns built by the Romans or the camps deserted by the fleeing legions. The newcomers were lovers of the open field and woodland. Many of the Roman towns were left unoccupied for some time. Not only was there a real break in the continuity of urban life; the whole structure of rural society was shattered and reformed. The Roman villas were completely abandoned. The gigantic Roman roads were allowed to deteriorate; the bridges fell in from neglect. At first there was but a small trade with the Continent; England's chief export was slaves. In their new frontiers the Anglo-Saxons lived mainly by hunting and agriculture. Theirs was a true barbaric culture; to the Roman world they were indeed "outer barbarians."

The Anglo-Saxons were certainly as pagan as in the days of Tacitus. Their religion was a religion of warfare and destruction, with a paradise of alternate wassail and combat. Some of the present days of the week are derived from the names of their nature gods. For example, Wednesday is the day of Woden, god of war. Thursday is the day of Thunor, hammer-god of weather. Friday is the day of Frig, goddess of fertility. The name of Easter comes from the Anglo-Saxon goddess Eostre, who returned in April to greet the spring. The work of modern scholars on English place-names has yielded much information about Anglo-Saxon heathenism. Many modern customs, such as the use of holly and the burning log at Christmas, have descended from the Anglo-Saxon Yuletide celebrations. When the old gods succumbed to Christianity they left in these things, and in fairy tales and legends, the traces of their reign.

The poetic literature of the Anglo-Saxons is characterized by a sense of harsh reality and a sense of reverence. Most students of English history have read the heroic and vigorous verse of *Widsith*, perhaps the oldest of English poems, the *Phoenix*, the *Battle of Maldon*, *The Wanderer*, and *The Seafarer*. One of the famous singers of the seventh century was Caedmon, a Northumbrian cowherd and later a lay brother in the Abbey of Whitby. It may be that *Caedmon's Hymn*, "Now we must hymn the Master of heaven," was the first piece of literature composed on English soil (665). The poems of Cynewulf, who wrote in the eighth century, were gems of sparkling workmanship.

There were also the early religious poems by unknown authors, such as *The Dream of the Rood, Genesis, Exodus,* and *Daniel;* and there were the verses with which the peasants entertained one another, the Old English alliterative riddles, of which nearly a hundred survive. Most of the early English poetry from the seventh to the ninth century that has come down to us has been preserved in the contents of four manuscript volumes. It is a fortunate accident of English literary history that none of these four great collections has been destroyed; for the poetry that they contain is the authentic voice of Anglo-Saxon England.

Beowulf, the oldest English epic, is a series of episodes about the hero of the people living to the south of the great lakes of Sweden. It is the only survivor in a completed form of the many epics known to have existed. Sometime before the ninth century this long poem was composed from several old lays and chants, sifted through many versions and forms. The earliest manuscript now extant is written in West Saxon and dates from the tenth century. Those who had travelled on the sea, " 'Mid the terrible rolling of waves, habitations of sorrow," would doubtless have listened with sympathy and understanding to the minstrel describing the terrors of the sea, or the great dragon of *Beowulf*, or praising the foremost Anglo-Saxon virtue, which was constant courage. England has always kept its interest in heroic tradition and something, perhaps, of the soul of the northern seafarers.

THE RETURN OF CHRISTIANITY

Slowly the number of petty Anglo-Saxon tribal units decreased, until at last there emerged the seven great kingdoms of the Anglo-Saxon heptarchy: Northumbria, Mercia, East Anglia, Essex, Wessex, Kent, and Sussex. Into a territory thus divided among strong and ambitious kings there came the unifying force of Christianity.

When the Anglo-Saxons came to conquer and colonize, Christianity had been wiped out except among the Celtic Christians in Ireland and Wales. These Celtic Christians were at first almost out of touch with the Saxons, with Europe, with Rome. Then the fog slowly lifted. St. Patrick, born in Britain, was taken as a youth to Ireland, where he was a slave. He escaped, travelled to Europe, and entered a monastery. Later he returned as a missionary to Ireland.

For centuries the Irish churchmen had been great scholars; now they increased their missionary work. They founded monasteries in Italy, Switzerland, Wales, Cornwall, and on the island of Iona, off the coast of Scotland. St. Columba, an Irish Scot, who founded the monastery at Iona about 590, converted many heathen Scotsmen and Picts. Thus, along the western fringe of Britain, the Celtic monks and missionaries kept Celtic Christianity alive.

From 560 to 616 Ethelbert ruled as king of Kent; soon he controlled all England south of the Humber. Sometime before 588 Ethelbert married Bertha, daughter of the powerful Frankish king ruling at Paris. Frankish priests came over with the new queen. In 597 Gregory the Great, deeply influenced by the ideals of St. Benedict, and determined to make Rome once more the spiritual capital of Europe, sent his friend Augustine and forty monks to begin the conversion of England. Ethelbert convinced himself of the honesty of Augustine at a famous interview at Thanet. He gave the Roman missionaries a dwelling-place at Canterbury, provided food, and permitted them to preach their religion. Shortly afterwards, Ethelbert accepted Christianity, gave a grant of land in Canterbury to Augustine, and began to build new churches and repair old ones. Augustine was soon consecrated archbishop of Canterbury.

Many Kentishmen were baptized, though not so many as tradition has declared. Slowly Christianity spread into East Anglia and Northumbria. The important question was now the conflict between Roman and Celtic Christianity. On many points the habits of the Celtic Christians, so long separated from Rome and Europe, differed from the prevailing customs of the Roman Christians. There were Celtic peculiarities of ritual, liturgy, Irish asceticism, penitential discipline, the organization of ecclesiastical districts, the shape of the tonsure. Finally, the Celtic system of computing the date of Easter was fundamentally different from that followed in churches under Roman influence. The date of the chief Christian festival seemed a matter of considerable importance to devout and passionate churchmen.

In 664, at the Synod of Whitby, the representatives of rival Celtic and Roman missions debated before Oswy of Northumbria the questions at issue. What was most important was the problem of Christian unity in the British Isles. Would the Celtic Christians turn aside from the Roman Christians of all Europe? "To fight against Rome," said a debater at Whitby, "is to fight against the world." Oswy decided in favor of the usages of Rome and the Pope sent the Greek Theodore of Tarsus, the city of St. Paul, to organize a new hierarchy, a united English church under the dominion of Canterbury. Theodore was a great ecclesiastical statesman. "This was the first archbishop whom all the English church obeyed." Theodore increased the number of dioceses, precisely defined the duties of bishops, undertook parish reforms, and generally improved the efficiency and organization of the church. In 735 the archbishopric of York was established. It was to hold jurisdiction north of the Humber.

Through these years, the temporal power of the church increased as more wealth passed into its hands. Anglo-Saxon kings and nobles endowed bishoprics and monasteries with land to save their souls; the nobles attached chaplains to their halls, soon to become the parsons of the parish. To the devout Anglo-Saxon, God was ever present, ready to reward and punish; the eternal life of the next world was surely more important than the brief tale of this. All men could see that many Anglo-Saxon clergymen were martyrs for their faith; many became saints. Anglo-Saxon Christians tended to remember that in the midst of life men might be in death.

Throughout the vital years of Anglo-Saxon rule the moral force and strength of the church, in diocese, parish, and monastery, was steadily extended. The churchmen stood, in an age of faith, as mediators between God and man; they alone controlled the means of salvation, the holy sacraments. The learned men of the age were almost all churchmen. With courage and tenacity the churchmen helped to stimulate a national literature; some created a part of it; and many beautiful things, such as the manuscript art of the Lindisfarne Gospels and the Book of Kells, came out of their cloistered monasteries.

The church developed schools, often giving their students a training equal to the best in Europe. Apart from the palace schools, the church maintained all the schools and libraries in England. Churchmen also took an active part in government and diplomacy. They stimulated commerce and agriculture, industrial crafts and arts. They promoted the development of art and architecture. They brought more music to the people and music tightened the bonds of Christianity. They built churches of stone in place of the structures of timber and reeds; squared and chiselled stones were often at hand for building in the shells of Roman villas and towns. "The Conversion, more truly than the age of the Renaissance, gave Englishmen a new heaven and a new earth."

ANGLO-SAXON SOCIETY

It is always difficult to reduce a complex piece of history to a formula; in the case of Anglo-Saxon England it is perhaps impossible. The records show that Anglo-Saxon society was aristocratic rather than democratic. There was, indeed, very little that can properly be called democratic in the Anglo-Saxon conception of social organization. All Anglo-Saxons seem to have been very sensitive to diversities in rank. For example, the institution of slavery was a part of the earliest English law. The Anglo-Saxon freeman was usually a slave owner. In their agrarian routine, and in the principles by which their society was ordered, the Anglo-Saxons never departed from the aristocratic order. They first came to England, mainly a peasantry composed of essentially free men. Then, slowly, many free men lost their economic and personal independence. The general drift of the mass of the Anglo-Saxons before the Normans came was from freedom towards subordination and servitude.

The slimness of an average peasant's resources, the dangers of a cattle plague or bad harvests, the Danish invasions, the king's food-rents, account in part for the fact that many freemen were compelled to put themselves under the protection and at the disposal of lords who could give them food and security. In return, a peasant, bound by personal ties to his lord, performed customary service, almost invariably agricultural and not military. The ceorl, or freeman, may have fought in the *fyrd* of his own shire, though not on distant expeditions, for some time. "Different scholars have come to very different opinions about the military value of the ceorl."

In any event, despite the later romantic tradition of an Anglo-Saxon village as composed of free warrior-peasants, the evidence shows that to an increasing extent as the centuries passed the position of the peasant was essentially servile. Throughout the Anglo-Saxon period, therefore, there occurred considerable changes in the ranks of a society that was not static, but fluid. Any attempt to describe succinctly various shifting aspects of Anglo-Saxon society through several centuries in the form of a fixed chart must fail from the weight of its own inaccuracy.

When the Anglo-Saxons came to England they were roughly divided into nobles, freemen, partially free men, serfs, and slaves. Movements up and down the scale were easy and frequent. In the early stages of the conquest the nobility, who were a nobility of blood, were called eorls. These eorls were gradually replaced by a new nobility of service and wealth, called thegns or gesiths. The military associates of the king, his main household servants, formed the nucleus of this class. Although custom varied in different kingdoms the nobles usually received large grants of land from the king. In the later Saxon period any man who obtained sufficient land might become a thegn. As a holder of large estates, the thegn had lordship over other men. His oath in court was worth six times that of a freeman. He was protected by a *wergeld*, his valuation in terms of money to be paid by the guilty party if he should be slain; this was six times that of a freeman. The higher offices in church and state went to men of his class. Many sat in the witan, or great council of the kingdom.

The non-noble freeman, or ceorl, lived in the villages; in the later Anglo-Saxon period, as described earlier, the freemen sank in large numbers into unfree classes, dependent upon local lords. Usually the holding of a freeman was about one hide of land, or 120 acres. Below the freemen were the various classes of men who were only partially free, or who were serfs, economically dependent. The serf still had a small *wergeld;* his lord could not sell him or mistreat him; he could marry; he worked for the lord and he paid the lord in part in produce for the land he held. Finally, there were the slaves, mere chattels, who could be bought and sold as livestock. This class was small; many were

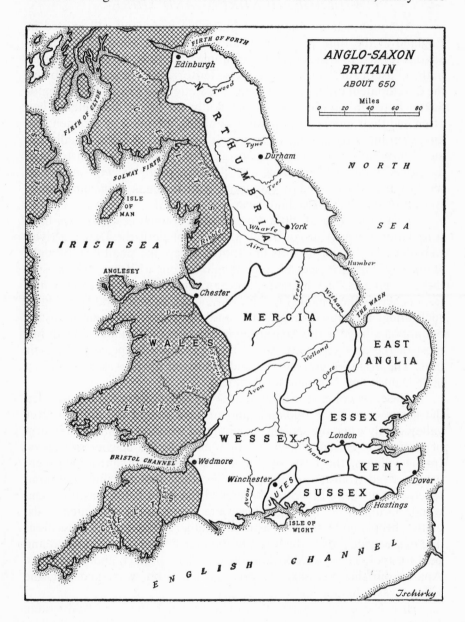

freed from full slavery in later Anglo-Saxon days and became serfs. On the eve of the Norman Conquest the small thegnage aristocracy was the most important class in society; there were fewer slaves and free-men; and the various grades of unfree serfs had greatly increased.

VILLAGE, HUNDRED, AND SHIRE

Although a large amount of unbroken woodland still existed in England at the time of the Norman Conquest in 1066 most Anglo-Saxons tended to live together in innumerable tuns, or small villages, in the midst of rural agricultural areas. Historians have warmly debated the development of larger units, called boroughs or towns. Such Anglo-Saxon boroughs as there were had really no urban character. They often had their moots, or popular assemblies, attended by freemen; the king appointed royal officials to watch over market sales, usually the most important aspect of borough life; many boroughs seem to have developed their own practices and customs, probably with an eye to the fact that their concern was more with business than agriculture. But all of this was on a small scale.

There was, indeed, little Anglo-Saxon commerce and hence little stimulation towards urban development. Not until the Danes arrived were there any major imports or exports, except the small flow brought about by the pilgrimages of some Anglo-Saxons to Rome, the trips of the missionaries, the limited shuttlecock movements of Continental traders across the Channel seeking slaves, tin, or wool and bringing in such things as gems, trinkets, silk, and oil. There was some industry, but not on a large scale. Artisans in metal were particularly skilled; but most of the arts and crafts were those practised by peasants in their huts. The origin of commercial and industrial towns was essentially a later Danish and Norman development.

The early colonists, struggling for existence, seem to have avoided the heavy clay of the midlands and to have sought the alluvial river valleys. Only when the settlers accumulated working capital in the form of ploughs, oxen, and slaves did they move to the heavier soil areas. In the villages, the basis of Anglo-Saxon social organization, there usually lived from ten to thirty families, their thatched huts clustered together. Out from the village stretched the open fields, pastures, and woods. Grain, fruit, and vegetables were grown in the cultivated fields; cattle, sheep, and hogs were pastured together in the untilled grass areas and in the woods; from the forest or the marsh were obtained wood and peat for fuel. There were local smiths, millers, potters, and carpenters. Apart from the necessary imports, such as iron, wax, and salt, the village was self-sufficient.

It is easy to exaggerate the extent to which the open field system formed the framework of agrarian life. A large part of England never came under the open field system at all. It was not found, for example, in the far north, the northwest, Devon, or along the Welsh border. When the open fields existed, the arable unenclosed land was not divided into blocks, one to each villager. It was divided into strips, usually separated by unploughed turf. A villager might have several strips, scattered in different parts of the great open field.

In some areas it is probable that all the large arable field was itself subdivided into two fields, one of which could lie fallow each year. The pasture and the woodland were shared by the villagers in common, and they often cut their hay from a common meadowland. In free villages the villagers had individual ownership of the land they cultivated; there is no evidence of communal ownership. In the unfree villages, where the villagers depended upon a lord who owned all of the land, the men of the village cultivated the part of the open field not used by their lord and paid the lord in rents and services. On the eve of the Norman Conquest, as described earlier in this chapter, most of the villages had ceased to be free.

About the government of the villages, historians do not agree, mainly because the evidence is so slender, the contemporary language so vague. One famous historian has ascribed considerable importance to the meetings of the villagers in a "village moot" in terms of later local government developments. A second has doubted that there was any assembly of villagers at all for economic, judicial, or political purposes. A third has contented himself with stating that village agricultural policy was probably determined in an annual meeting. It is certain that in the twelfth century a reeve, a priest, and four men attended some of the local hundred courts to represent village interests; but it is not at all clear when this development began.

It is also true that "from the earliest phase of permanent settlement the need must have arisen for local assemblies." And yet the historian must make his conclusion about village assemblies by inference, and inferences vary. In writing about the difficult problems of local Anglo-Saxon courts and assemblies the greatest of modern authorities on the period has stated a fact that those who have argued brilliantly by inference have sometimes forgotten: "One of the anomalies of Anglo-Saxon history is the extreme rarity of early reference to these fundamental institutions."

Above the village and the borough, the smallest units in Anglo-Saxon England, was the hundred, in the north of England known by the Danish name "wapentake." The origin of this institution is one of the most difficult problems in Anglo-Saxon history. Only bare rudiments of the territorial divisions forming the bases of the hundred system have been identified before the reign of Alfred (871–900); the name itself has not been found before the reign of Edgar (959–975). Recently scholars have tended to the view that the hundred was deliberately developed as an administrative, financial, and judicial unit intermediate between the meeting of the large folkmoot and a village community. It was, in their opinion, "a deliberate remodelling of administrative geography," at least in the midland regions where the hundreds were rather neatly divided and symmetrical. The hundred usually contained about 100 hides, or 12,000 acres, of land in the midlands; elsewhere the size varied considerably, from less than 20 to more than 150 hides.

The hundred had a court that met every four weeks to administer customary law and settle local pleas; it punished thieves and those who had been slack in their pursuit; it checked upon recalcitrant or delinquent taxpayers and adjusted taxation. The king's reeve presided over, but did not control, the deliberations of the freemen learned in the customary law. The hundred court, attended by all free landholders, was the most active and popular of the local organs of Anglo-Saxon government.

The largest Anglo-Saxon administrative division in the local government system was known as the shire, later called a county, after the Norman equivalent *comté*. The practice of creating counties probably began in Wessex, and was extended to the eastern and western midlands. In each shire was a shire court, a public assembly that met twice a year; in the later Anglo-Saxon period it was usually attended only by the large landholders. This shire court was presided over by the ealdorman, who was always a noble, the head of the shire community, the commander of the militia. The ealdorman was often the representative of the king. He was also the official head of the local judicial system. In the latter part of the Anglo-Saxon period the ealdorman came to be called by a Danish name, the earl. His social status and his income were alike high.

A second royal official in the shire was the shire reeve, or sheriff. The sheriff's office probably began in the tenth century. He was the guardian of the king's interests in the shire; he stood for the executive power of the crown even within the territory of the greatest lords; he was the effective link between the crown and the local districts. As the king's financial agent, it was his task to maintain the king's peace in the shire and to collect the royal revenues, such as rents from the royal estates and fines, the profits of justice, imposed by the shire and hundred courts. The king also expected the sheriff to see that the courts' decisions were carried out.

The sheriff was often instructed to execute specific royal orders in the shire. Through the years the correspondence from the royal court to the shire steadily rose in volume. When, in a later day, the authority of the ealdormen or earls began to extend over more than one county many of their tasks within single counties fell to the sheriffs, who became increasingly more important in shire administration. By the side of the ealdorman and the sheriff in the shire court sat the bishop, who declared ecclesiastical law. These three men were the pillars of government and law in the shires.

KING, WITAN, AND LAW

The king was the highest executive authority in Anglo-Saxon England. It was he who maintained order and peace, and protected his kingdom against enemies without and within; he commanded the kingdom's military forces; he appointed the main officers of the kingdom; he summoned and presided over the great council; he controlled the appointment of many higher officials in the church. Meanwhile the power of strong kings was often increased by the teachings of the clergy; for they brought to the king's service the concepts of the Roman law regarding the might of the royal prerogative.

The highest assembly in the Anglo-Saxon kingdoms was the witan, or the witenagemot, the council of the wise and great of the realm. It had no fixed membership although there were certain essential members, such as the gesiths or thegns, the ealdormen or earls. The ecclesiastical element in the council, the archbishops, bishops, and abbots, became very important in the later Anglo-Saxon period. Attendance at a normal council can be determined today only by a study of a list of witnesses with which royal charters end; but the length of a list of witnesses was decided by the length of the parchment on which the charter was written. Thus there are few full lists of those attending the witan. It was apparently the duty of the witan to meet at the king's command and to advise him on any important problems of state. To what extent it had formal powers and definite privileges has been a matter of controversy.

This council also acted as a court for the trial of great men and of cases important to the kingdom. It chose the king, usually from the royal family. It assisted in making important laws. It shared in the king's responsibility for many public acts: the imposition of taxes; negotiations with foreign powers; defense measures; prosecution of traitors; royal gifts of estates; ecclesiastical patronage. A strong king dominated the witan. A weak king bowed before the magnates who sat about him. No king could afford to ignore the witan. It kept alive the principle that the king must govern with advice.

Besides the customary law mainly administered by the local courts there slowly arose a body of law declared by various kings and witans. The existing fragments of written Anglo-Saxon laws, or dooms, span five centuries, beginning with the enactments of Ethelbert, first Christian king of Kent, and ending with those of Canute. These dooms, together with the various charters issued by the kings, form a most valuable source for students of Anglo-Saxon institutions.

In a primitive society it was inevitable that most of the dooms were about crimes of violence or theft. For serious crimes the punishment was mutilation, such as the loss of a hand or a foot. A thief caught in the act might be slain on the spot without trial. Imprisonment was seldom used as a method of punishment. Usually the penalties took the form of fines. By this procedure the injured party obtained compensation; the compensation for injuries was a *bot*, carefully calculated. For example, by the dooms of Ethelbert it was provided that compensation for minor injuries should be as follows: one eye, 50 shillings; one ear, 12 shillings; a front tooth, 6 shillings; a big toe, 10 shillings.

In case of violent death the relatives of the dead man were compensated by a *wergeld*, supposed to represent the value of a man's life; it has earlier been explained that a ceorl's *wergeld* was usually about 200 shillings, and a thegn's about 1200; the higher a man's position in society, the higher was his *wergeld*. There was in addition a fine called the *wite*, paid to the king, partly because the state, as well as an individual, had been sinned against.

The main local courts in Anglo-Saxon England were the shire and hundred courts described earlier in this chapter. The judgment in a case was reached by the men assembled in the courts. That judgment merely settled upon the method by which the innocence or guilt of an accused man should be determined. There were several ways of doing this. One commonly used was called compurgation.

Compurgation meant proof by the aid of oath-helpers. At the beginning, the plaintiff or the defendant would take an oath that his charge or denial was true. Such oaths had to be delivered in a set form with verbal accuracy and without stammering. The Anglo-Saxons felt that if a man faltered God was pointing to his guilt. And if a man took a false oath he imperilled his soul. In a religious age such a procedure was a solemn affair.

After this preliminary proceeding the court awarded the proof to one of the contesting parties whose task it then was to obtain a sufficient number of oath-helpers or compurgators, who would swear that his story was true. Fear of God's punishment was supposed to make men reluctant to swear in support of a bad or doubtful character. Where a man could not produce a sufficient number of oath-helpers the case went against him. Usually a man making proof in this fashion was asked to produce six, twelve, or twenty-four oath-helpers. The value of an oath varied according to a man's rank in society; the oath of a thegn, as noted earlier, was equal to the oaths of six ceorls.

There was also the ordeal, usually used in serious crimes. This, again, was an appeal to God to show where the guilt lay. There were several kinds of ordeals, each used only after solemn religious ceremonies conducted by the priest and ending with "a prayer to God Almighty that He disclose the fullness of truth." In the ordeal of hot iron a man carried a piece of hot iron in his hand a certain number of feet, the distance usually varying with the seriousness of the charge.

The hand was then bound up and sealed. "And after the third day it shall be inspected to see whether within the sealed wrapping, it is foul or clean." If the hand was healing cleanly, the man was innocent; if not, he was guilty.

In the ordeal of hot water a man was required to pick a stone out of a pot of boiling water; then his hand was bound up and the same procedure followed as in the case of the ordeal by hot iron. Another type of ordeal was by cold water. An accused man was bound and thrown into a pool blessed by a priest. If he sank in the consecrated water, he was innocent; if he floated he was guilty, the pure water having refused to accept him.

Such methods of determining guilt or innocence may appear in a later century to be quite irrational. And yet, in the Anglo-Saxon age, there were probably few guilty men who would refuse to confess their guilt when the alternative appeared to be a direct challenge to God or the eternal damnation of their souls through a combination of guilt and perjury.

ALFRED AND THE DANES

In the eighth century the tale of Northumbria was one of bloodshed, war, and the assassination of her kings. Mercia then became supreme over all England south of the Humber. Offa II of Mercia (757–796) drove back the Welsh and made the west country from Cumberland to Devon part of England. After Offa died Wessex conquered Mercia (825). King Egbert of Wessex (802–839) began the supremacy of his kingdom that was to last until 1066 and the Norman Conquest. He conquered Cornwall; even the Northumbrians acknowledged him as their overlord. At last the long wars among the Anglo-Saxon kingdoms ended. They ended because the Danes came in waves of invasion. The *Anglo-Saxon Chronicle* recorded the "harrowing inroads of the heathen men." Wessex alone survived their attacks.

The Danes, or vikings, came from Norway and Denmark, seeking food and fortune as pirates, warriors, and traders. They were of the same Nordic race as the Anglo-Saxons. Like the Anglo-Saxons they were hardy seamen, probably the first Europeans to reach America. These Northmen raided the coasts of Europe. An expansive energy shot them down through Russia to found the city of Kiev on the Volga; some reached Constantinople to serve in the eastern emperor's bodyguard. They settled in the Orkneys and the Hebrides; they founded the city of Dublin in Ireland; they landed in Spain; they were soon to settle in Sicily; they moved across the seas and colonized Iceland; they put up villages on the Isle of Man; they raided and ravaged the shores of England, splitting the skulls of monks with battle-axes, killing and stealing, burning the monasteries, loading their long ships with gold and gems, booty from ill-guarded shrines.

The Danes first appeared from "the land of robbers" to attack England in a small raid in 787. Then there were more raids, and larger ones. By 850 the Danes were bent on conquest. When Alfred became king of Wessex in 871 the Danes had almost completely conquered Northumbria, Mercia, and East Anglia. They set up an operational base at Reading, looped down into Dorset, joined the Cornishmen, and attacked Wessex. After several defeats, Alfred drove back the Danes. By the Treaty of Wedmore (878) the Danish king Guthrum divided England with Alfred. Guthrum's part, called the Danelaw, was north and east of London, along a line running roughly from London through Bedford to Chester. Guthrum also agreed to make no more war and to be baptized a Christian. Wessex was free, and apparently safe.

Alfred was more than a warrior. He issued his famous dooms, or laws, as a basis for the law and order he wished to see. A man of natural intellectual curiosity, Alfred was also convinced that "a life without knowledge or reflection is unworthy of respect." He labored steadily for the restoration of learning, so disturbed by years of war. He assembled the best scholars he could find and established a palace school. He aided in the revival of the monasteries. He translated several "necessary works." He encouraged the industrial arts. The *Anglo-Saxon Chronicle* was probably begun at his command.

Alfred was buried at Winchester, where he died in the year 900, at the age of fifty-two. There is still something magnificent about the personality of this English Charlemagne, reaching out to us across a thousand years.

THE SUCCESSORS OF ALFRED

Alfred's son was Edward the Elder (900–925); after Edward came Ethelstan (925–940), Edmund (940–946), and Edred (946–955). All four of these kings fought against the Danes, hoping to conquer the Danelaw. Edward the Elder did succeed in overrunning the Danelaw up to the Humber. Ethelstan pushed his power still farther north and called himself "King of Britain." His brother Edmund was killed by a thief in his own banqueting hall. Only slowly did the Danelaw yield to the pressure of Wessex. The last great Danish rebellion was in 954. Then political unity became complete. Gradually the process of assimilation went on; the blood of Saxon and Dane began to flow in one stream. The Danish contributions were certainly traceable, or almost so, in the stirring of commerce north of the Humber, in the trading, industrial, and maritime skill for which men of the northern shires have long been praised.

After Edred died in 955 his nephew Edwig came to the throne to reign for only four years. These were years of internal warfare, the usual result of centrifugal forces made stronger by the weakness of a king. In 959 began the reign of Edgar the Peaceful, in whose rule of sixteen years there were no wars. His quiet and competent government is mainly notable because of the work of his chief adviser, the ecclesiastical counsellor <u>Dunstan</u>, who was the first of the great clerical statesmen of England. Born the son of a thegn, Dunstan had served in the court of Ethelstan and had then entered Glastonbury Abbey to be a monk. He became abbot of Glastonbury; under Edgar he was appointed bishop of Worcester and, later, bishop of London. In 960 he became archbishop of Canterbury. Dunstan, a man of power, was responsible for a series of important monastic reforms in England.

All the monasteries were brought under the strict discipline of the rule of St. Benedict. The monks, called the "regular" clergy because they lived by a "regula" or rule, sought behind the monastery walls seclusion from the slow stain of the contaminating world. In suppressing the physical, material, worldly, and baser parts of their natures they hoped to develop more fully their spiritual life. The "secular" clergy, on the other hand, went out into the world as fishers of men. Under the control of Dunstan the Benedictine rule, strictly enforced, compelled the monks to take an oath of poverty, chastity, and obedience. Renouncing the outside world, they performed their seven divine services a day; they spent four hours daily in studies, six hours in physical work. The monastic revival in England, parallelled by a similar revival on the Continent, was of particular importance in the advancement of learning and the general lifting of morality.

In 975 Edgar died and was succeeded by his son Edward the Martyr. Edward's brief reign was marked by disorder. There was a halt to the endowment of monasteries. Many thegns and ealdormen were shocked at the drift of land into the hands of the church; they were anxious to stop the growth of great monastic holdings with the consequent weakening of their own local influence. In 978 Edward was treacherously murdered in Dorset and his young half brother Ethelred, only ten years of age, became king. Edward had been murdered by those who wanted to see Ethelred on the throne. The new ruler could not escape the consequences of that event. The circumstances under which he became king overcast all his reign. "He behaved like a man who is never sure of himself." In everything, it seemed, Ethelred was so weak and ineffective that he was called the "redeless" (lacking in counsel). Factions of nobles quarrelled. The Danes began to raid from the restless north. Everywhere disaster fell upon English arms.

In 991 Ethelred tried to buy off the invading Danes by paying them tribute, collected by a direct tax on the people called the Danegeld. This tax was levied six times in Ethelred's reign and paid to the blackmailing Danes; the total amount handed over was about 160,000 pounds of silver. England lacked a leader; Ethelred shifted courses and changed plans; in all he failed. Until 1013 the defences of England slowly disintegrated. Then Sweyn, king of Denmark, forced Ethelred to flee to Normandy, where he died in 1016. Most of England submitted to Sweyn.

Upon Sweyn's death his son Canute sought to complete the conquest of all England. The war continued. Edmund Ironside, son of Ethelred, fought so successfully that Canute agreed to a partition of England similar to that agreed upon between Alfred and Guthrum in 878. Late in 1016 Edmund Ironside died. The English had no leader, and the witan chose Canute as king of all England.

The reign of Canute (1016–1035) began with a series of murders. Having dealt with his opponents, Canute sent his troops home and kept only a bodyguard of 3,000 men. To his Danish advisers he added Englishmen. He declared that he would maintain English law, and he published a great code. He became such a friend of the church that the clerical writer of the *Anglo-Saxon Chronicle* referred to Canute as "the illustrious king." Canute also strengthened his position by marrying Ethelred's widow. For the first time in many years England had peace and prosperity. Canute gave safety to the common man, security to trading. He was soon fairly certain of the loyalty of his English subjects.

Norway, Denmark, and England were held together by Canute's power. Through the geographical position of his dominions he controlled the entrance to the Baltic, the North Sea, the sea trade lines reaching up from the Bay of Biscay. Conrad, the Holy Roman Emperor, hoped for an alliance with him. In 1027 Canute travelled to Rome to attend the coronation of Conrad and to visit the Pope, "the teacher of kings." He also obtained concessions from the European princes who had set up toll stations on the main road to Italy travelled by English traders and pilgrims.

In 1035 Canute died and his empire fell apart. Norway had already slipped from the control of his family. Denmark went to Canute's only legitimate son, Harthacanute. This son would also have become king of England had not the danger of a Norwegian attack on Denmark made him reluctant to leave his country long enough to take up his inheritance in England. The English witan decided to make Harold, illegitimate son of Canute, the regent of England until Harthacanute could leave Denmark. Harold soon succeeded in making himself king; but he died in 1040 and Harthacanute came over to claim his kingdom. Two years later Harthacanute himself collapsed and died "as he stood at his drink." There were no heirs; the line of Canute was dead; the English turned to the Saxon family of Alfred. On Easter Day, 1043, Edward, son of Ethelred the Redeless and Emma of Normandy, was crowned at Winchester.

Edward, soon called "the Confessor" because of his piety, had spent much of his life in Normandy, his mother's country. When he came to the English throne at the age of thirty-seven, Edward was not familiar with England. He had few English friends. It was natural that he should bring to England Normans to hold office in his household, to be priests in his chapel, to be wine merchants. It was also natural that Anglo-Danish nobles should resent the Norman invasion of the court. The great earls, accustomed to power and place, were particularly angry at their failure to control the grants of royal patronage. Edward the Confessor, despite his asceticism and his essential weakness as a king, was able to keep his Norman favorites about him mainly because of the divisions and jealousies of the Anglo-Danish earls.

So far as the competing English groups could be said to have had a leader, that leader was Earl Godwin of Wessex, most prominent and powerful of all the mighty nobles. Godwin's earldom extended along the south coast from Kent to Cornwall. His daughter was married to the king. His two disreputable sons and a nephew were given earldoms by Edward. It was not surprising that the earl of Mercia and the rest of Godwin's noble rivals resented the apparent increase of the proud earl's power, which may have been exactly what Edward the Confessor intended. In any event, the enemies of Godwin increased.

When the townsmen of Dover became involved in a fracas in which several Normans were killed, Edward ordered Earl Godwin to punish the offending community. Godwin refused to obey the king's explicit order, an action that was dangerously close to rebellion. The earls of Mercia and Northumbria stood by the king and Godwin and his sons were forced to flee from England in 1051.

Edward's patronage of individual Normans continued. He took their advice; he gave them lands and in other ways strengthened their influence in the English state. These foreigners, who "promoted injustice, gave unjust judgments, and counselled folly," became increasingly hateful to the English. Earl Godwin was soon remembered as the great opponent of Norman influence seeping into the country. In 1052 Godwin's return was welcomed by the earls and thegns when a military and naval enterprise against the king brought the house of Godwin back into power.

The witan at once revoked the sentence of outlawry against Godwin and his sons, gave Godwin back his earldom, and restored all that had been taken from him and his family. The Normans in England were reduced to political insignificance. Most of the Frenchmen who had recently arrived were outlawed or sent home. The Norman archbishop of Canterbury was ousted and Stigand, an English supporter of Earl Godwin, was called to take his place. Legally, however, the Norman archbishop could not be removed except by the Pope. The Pope, for his part, refused to recognize Stigand, whom he regarded as a usurper.

The Holy See could not get rid of Stigand so long as Earl Godwin supported him. Nevertheless, the Pope could bring heavy political pressure to bear from other quarters, with dark consequences for the house of Godwin.

Earl Godwin died on April 15, 1053. The earldom of Wessex then passed to his son Harold, who also became the main adviser of the king. On January 5, 1066, following a nasty revolt in Northumbria, Edward the Confessor died, eight days after the first Westminster Abbey, which he built, was consecrated. As Edward had no children, the witan at once decided to place Godwin's son Harold upon the throne. The hour was dark; speed was important.

Harold's brother Tostig, the exiled earl of Northumbria, was threatening to invade England because, as he bitterly said, Harold had betrayed him to his enemies. In any conflict the king of the Scots would probably support Tostig. There were stirrings in restless Norway, a possible prelude to a sudden attack. Most dangerous of all, Harold's cousin William, Duke of Normandy, was an ambitious candidate for the English throne, a strong ruler and a mighty robber.

Had Harold been wrecked in 1064 off the coast of Normandy and taken to William's court? Had Harold, to obtain his liberty, sworn an oath to be William's vassal, or to support his claim to the English throne? There were many assertions about the nature of William's claim to England's crown. The Bayeux tapestry stated that "Harold took an oath to Duke William." Several Norman writers asserted that Harold once swore to help William to obtain the English throne. Whatever the facts may have been, William began to prepare for the invasion of England.

Chapter 3

THE NORMANS

WILLIAM THE CONQUEROR

A S WILLIAM, Duke of Normandy, prepared to attack and depose Harold the fleet of the king of Norway was moving against England. Tostig, Harold's brother, joined the Norwegian forces, vowing that he would recover the earldom of Northumbria and punish Harold for betraying him. On September 25, 1066, Harold defeated and killed both the Norwegian king and Tostig at the battle of Stamford Bridge, despite the fact that many of the English soldiers had earlier been disbanded to harvest the ripening grain.

Three days later William of Normandy landed on an undefended shore in the south; the banners that snapped in the wind had been blessed by the Pope. Harold's enemy was a man familiar with all the devices of Continental warfare. To be a successful ruler in Normandy it was necessary to be a master of war. The Norman state, founded by Danes and Norsemen, was filled with restless men, grandchildren of the fiord, their love of adventure and conflict unabated by the passage of time. Against the old Anglo-Danish national tactics William brought these Normans, trained in the new skills of the Continent. His army supply system was efficient; his discipline in a miscellaneous force of feudal tenants and loot-seeking foreign adventurers was admirable. The core of William's army was an array of mailed horsemen; the infantry was a subsidiary arm. Harold's force, on the other hand, was mainly infantry, designed to fight with spear, axe, and shield. The English army probably numbered about 7,000 men, ranging from thegns to ill-armed peasants. William's force was probably smaller; but all his men were picked troops.

Harold moved swiftly southwards. On October 13 he massed his army on the brow of a steep hill, "at the grey apple tree" near Hastings. To protect his front line he dug a ditch and threw up a fence of stakes and wattled boughs; he hoped this device would help to hold back the charge of the Norman horsemen. The center of the crowded

31

hill was held by the well-equipped thegns who locked their shields together to form a shield wall. On the flanks and in the rear were the levies of the shires, a motley crowd armed with spears, axes, swords, and clubs. Harold's only chance of victory was in the possibility that his army could fight a protracted defensive engagement until the Norman forces had exhausted themselves in attack.

In the dawn of October 14, 1066, William prepared to strike. Placed in the first rank were his archers, slingers, and crossbowmen; in the second were the heavily armed infantrymen; in the third were the feudal horsemen, the Bretons on the left, the Normans in the center, the French mercenaries on the right.

The battle lasted all day. Once the Norman lines gave way; it was William himself who rallied his forces. Afterwards the Normans were able to cut off and destroy some of their Anglo-Saxon pursuers. Later the Normans carried out several pretended flights with the same results. Norman arrows shot perpendicularly into the air killed many Englishmen within the shield wall. Nevertheless, the shrunken English lines held throughout the daylight hours. At last Harold fell; his brothers were already dead. In the dusk the leaderless English army broke and fled along the darkening trackways; and the Frenchmen held the place of slaughter.

This battle decided the fate of a nation. For five days William rested; then he moved slowly to Romney, Dover, and Canterbury. After he had encircled London the English leaders formally surrendered and the witan accepted William as king. On Christmas Day, 1066, William was crowned in Westminster Abbey by a Saxon prelate. During the coronation ceremony the Norman knights outside the Abbey misunderstood the shouting inside and thought the crowd was attacking William. In a panic they set fire to some neighboring buildings. The flames lit up the coronation scene, symbolic of the events that had brought William to the throne.

All England was not conquered. Could a few thousand armored Normans hold more than a million and a half Englishmen in subjection? In 1067, when William was absent in Normandy, there were anti-Norman uprisings in Exeter and York. In 1069 a general war developed out of a bloody Northumbrian conflict. The king of Denmark sent many troops to help the insurgent Englishmen. York fell under their attacks. When William appeared, the rebels retreated and remained inert. Before the Norman power resistance soon collapsed. Risings in Dorset, Cornwall, Somerset and elsewhere were swiftly crushed. Only the Lincolnshire thegn, Hereward the Wake, held out for several months on the Isle of Ely. He was to be a hero of song and legend through later centuries, a name still remembered as a symbol of resistance to William.

In the sullen north William carried out a systematic devastation of the country in a campaign of sustained ferocity. Domesday Book, written seventeen years later, shows that many ravaged areas were still ghastly and derelict then. The Durham and Yorkshire region did not really recover from the disaster until the Pennine slopes were turned into great sheep farms by the Cistercian monks in the next century. The object of "the harrying of the north" was to make certain that Mercia, Northumbria, and the other northern shires would never revolt again. As a further guard against rebellion the logical William built great castles at strategic points in England and along the Welsh border. South Wales and the border countries of Hereford, Monmouth, and Shropshire still reveal a large number of Norman castles; but the Welsh were never easy to keep in subjection. In northern England, the great castle of Durham arose above the charred villages and wasted dales.

The castle, called by the English historian Freeman "the vulture's nest upon the crag," played as important a part in English history as the Norman heavily armed cavalry. Early Norman castles were often built on the edge of a cliff overlooking a river; one side was therefore impregnable. A castle constructed to command a borough, such as those at Chester and York, was usually built on the borough walls, or immediately outside. In the event of siege a borough could thus communicate more easily with a relieving army; the castle was some distance from the houses of the borough in case it should be fired by the enemy. In the country the builders of castles showed that they were alive to the facts of local geography. The castles they built usually commanded the landscape for miles around.

Most early Norman castles of the eleventh century were made of timber; the main exception was the stone White Tower of London. The strength of wooden castles lay in the height of the earthwork, or mound, upon which they were built and the depth of the ditches surrounding them. Most had small garrisons; the total number of knights in England in the late eleventh century was probably about 5,000. Wooden castles could be built rapidly, and in years of turbulence speed of construction was important. When the time factor declined in value during the twelfth century kings and barons began to build almost impregnable citadels of stone. They erected square towers with walled enclosures, or "baileys"; the walls were very thick because the mortar was poor. These rectangular keeps, or donjons, were so strong that they were capable of holding out for long periods in silent passive defense. They often became hubs of population because they gave protection to those who settled near their walls. It was quite natural that a king should insist that a royal license be obtained before any one of his barons raised a private fortress. Of course, the main weakness of a Norman castle was that it was essentially a defensive instrument; its garrison could effect little harm on the enemy unless the castle gates were opened to let it sally forth.

NORMAN FEUDALISM

A modern scholar has stated that by 1087, with about six exceptions, every temporal lord in England was a Norman. William I confiscated all the lands of those who had fought against him. Part of the seized estates he distributed among his glutted Norman noble followers, lay and clerical. In the church, no Englishman was appointed to any English see; when William died there were only two English bishops and two English abbots. The main members of the royal household were Normans. Only a few sheriffs were Englishmen. A new order, a social revolution, came into existence in England. In describing this revolution Professor F. M. Stenton has expressed the opinion that "it is still difficult to find a better definition" than is stated in the familiar sentences attributing most changes to "the introduction of feudalism into England." The fabric of Anglo-Saxon England had a few signs of an approach to some feudal arrangements, as in the practice of "commendation." But there was no nation-wide tenurial and social organization in which, for example, the terms of a tenant's obligation were defined with precision.

Like all proliferating organic growths, feudalism varied in form from country to country and from age to age. It is a mistake to think that feudal arrangements ever stood still. One fairly constant and basic fact was that few men could give protection and land to those who wanted both. On the other hand, thousands could give loyalty and service to a lord or king. At the height of feudalism society was organized according to a man's relation to the land, then the chief source of wealth and power.

In Norman times the king kept a large part of the confiscated lands for his own use. For example, William I and his immediate successors maintained about seventy forests, estimated at nearly a third of the whole area of England. In the great acreage of the forest, the forest laws, forerunners of the later obnoxious game laws, were enforced by special courts, odious to the people. Under William I a king's subject who killed a deer was blinded; under his successors the penalty was death.

Under feudalism all other land was in theory held of the king. Holders of land directly of the king, the tenants-in-chief, held by a feudal tenure according to which they swore that they would render military and other services to the king in return for the use of the land. Their degree of ownership of the land was thus limited by their obligations.

Usually a tenant-in-chief let out a large part of his holdings to other men, lesser or mesne tenants, who in turn pledged their specified services to the tenant-in-chief. This subletting, or subinfeudation, continued downwards through the social strata, from the great baron who held a hundred manors to the knight who held but one; Domesday Book listed about 8,000 subtenants. England was thus partitioned among a foreign aristocracy. Most of the manors were held by some kind of military tenure, the knight-service tenure idea brought over by the Normans. The feudal baronage somehow must supply knights for William; that was their responsibility.

A man who held land, or a fief, from another became his vassal; the man from whom he held was his lord, to whom he owed allegiance and did homage. Often, however, a man held land from several lords; in such cases he acknowledged one of the lords as his liege lord; then the tenant could swear allegiance and do homage to the other lords only in so far as he did not violate his oaths to his liege lord. Feudal tenurial arrangements frequently became a very complicated web. But there was everywhere reasonable stability and cohesion. Every medieval man was another man's vassal; all land had its lord.

Each tenant received both a fief and personal protection; and each owed personal loyalty to his immediate lord and his overlord. Both lord and vassal had rights and duties that had to be fulfilled. Honorable feudal services varied according to the specific contractual terms of the agreement. A vassal usually promised, for example, to provide a specified number of soldiers, usually for forty days' service a year. At certain times of the year a vassal was required to go to his lord's court to help in the administration of justice. On some occasions a vassal was obliged to pay certain feudal "aids" to his lord "for the ransoming of our body, for the making of our eldest son a knight and for the once marrying of our eldest daughter."

When the heir of a deceased vassal wished to succeed to his father's estate he paid a sum of money called a "relief." This custom was based upon the theory that the regranting of land was only an act of grace on the part of the lord and hence to be paid for. The lord also had the right of wardship for minor heirs, in which case he took all the returns from the lands until the heir could render all the military service called for under the feudal contract. If a vassal died without heirs the land reverted by escheat to his lord. If a vassal was convicted of felony his land was forfeit to his lord. If a vassal broke his contract the land might also go back to his lord.

Many of the customary obligations varied according to time and place. The feudal "system" must not be considered as always clear, fixed, and immutable. On the contrary, it was lively and flexible. Not all vassal's oaths were kept; not all lords gave their vassals protection.

Nevertheless, this arrangement does not deserve to be called, as it has been, "legalized anarchy." The words suggest that feudalism did not possess much controlled efficiency. It should not be easy to forget that for more than two centuries feudalism worked with considerable success. One of the main reasons for its long acceptance was the active idea it contained of the mutual obligation of all men to all men by custom. Everybody was responsible to someone else; nobody was entirely free. In the feudal arrangements the custom was the community custom, and no man had a right to change it. The task of courts was mainly to discover and decide custom; and, in these days, custom and right were usually held to be synonymous.

The Normans were a harsh and violent race. William I, who was one of them, determined to remain the political master of his world. He saw to it that he controlled the great redistribution of land among his greedy barons; there was no scramble for territory. William distributed the land so that there were few large compact territorial units; most of the holdings of his tenants-in-chief consisted entirely of isolated manors or groups of manors widely scattered over England. In some cases this was probably due less to policy than to accident. In any event, William did not revive the great earldoms of Wessex and Northumbria. The crown was the strongest landholder in every county. William would not have his lords behaving like the semi-independent nobles of France. There the Capets were "overshadowed by the tall trees of the feudal forest." William, as king of England, checked rigorously the powers of his baronage and the natural feudal tendencies towards regionalism. To this end he kept the old Anglo-Saxon national levy or *fyrd*. In 1075 he used it against a small group of revolting barons.

William also maintained the local shire courts and hundred courts under royal authority so that the feudal lords would not possess too great control over the local administration of justice. The nominated sheriffs, like the similar *viscomtes* of Normandy, were under William's direct control. The post of these local pillars of royal authority was not hereditary. William also compelled all the lower tenants to swear a feudal oath of allegiance to him superior to that given to their immediate lords. The vassal in England, unlike the Continental vassal, could not "legally" support his lord against the king. So long as William ruled England there was small chance of feudal disorder. The confusion of the era of migrations was ended, for a time. One of the foundations of the relative stability of the Middle Ages was the coherent and logical work of William the Conqueror.

Throughout the medieval centuries the normal unit of land division for purposes of feudal landholding was called the manor. The manor was an agricultural estate, usually containing a village, pastures, fields, and woods; in most respects it closely resembled the nearly self-sufficient Anglo-Saxon village system. The lord of the manor kept part of the estate for his own use, and that portion of the total manor land was called the demesne. It usually included the manor house, the house of the lord or his agent; the orchard, garden, and barn areas; and a part of the arable land of the great fields, where the lord's strips ran alongside those of his tenants. The lord also shared with his tenants the meadows and the woodland.

All the lords, to whom the king had granted one or more manors, controlled the tenants living on them by a system of rigid economic feudalism. The land outside the lord's demesne was held by the tenants. They lived in a village of thatched chimneyless huts. The huts were usually divided into two parts; the tenants inhabited one part, the domestic animals the other. Each hut had a small yard where meager garden crops could grow. Every tenant pastured his few cattle in the meadowland and tilled his strips of arable land.

Most of the freemen or ceorls still clinging to freedom in 1066 were swiftly forced into the great mass of unfree villeins. Those few who did remain legally free held various amounts of land in permanent tenure, for which they paid rents of money or produce. They could sell or alienate their holdings; they seldom owed the lord any servile, or "base," labor. So long as the freeman kept up the specified payments and services due the lord he could not be ousted. He took part in the business of the local hundred and shire courts. He served as a juror in the royal courts. He could move to another manor if he wished. He was eligible for military service in the *fyrd*. His descendants were the tough yeomen infantry later so important in English history when the life of feudalism was ebbing away.

The largest group of workers on the manor were the villeins. A villein usually held about thirty acres of land in the arable open field. In return for his holding he did heavy "base" services, or *week work*, on the land of his lord; this was usually two or three days a week. In ploughing or harvesting he did extra, or "boon" work. He was also required to make payments of rent, usually in kind, to his lord. He had to pay a fee for using the lord's mill, bridges, and oven. These fees were often excessive; it is no accident that the miller is always a rogue in medieval literature.

The villein also had to pay heavy tallages and fees on certain special occasions. For example, when he died his heir had to give the best ox, or some other valuable gift, to the lord as a *heriot*, corresponding to the relief in higher feudal society. When a villein's daughter married he had to pay another fee to his lord, called the *merchet*. The villein was also "bound to the soil"; he could not leave the village or even get married without his lord's permission. For justice he depended on the manor court, controlled by the lord's steward and operating under the local "custom of the manor" stretching back into the mists of the past.

Below the villeins were the cottars and the bordars, whose holdings were sometimes five acres, often only a hut and a garden plot. They, too, owed labor services and payments to the lord. Occasionally there were men of lower status still, the bondsmen who held no land but who did chores for the lord of the manor or worked as swineherds or beekeepers.

All of these tenants had a core of rights, protected by the royal courts and by national and local law. The lord's power was not absolute. However, the bailiffs and stewards, the lord's chief administrative officers, were frequently harsh and ruthless, hated by all the tenants. The lives of most of the people of England were poor and short. Seventy-nine per cent of the heads of families in the rural population were listed in Domesday Book as unfree; only twelve per cent were freemen. The remainder were great and small vassals, including the lords of the manors; the manorial officials; some members of the clergy; the landless wage laborers; merchants, craftsmen and others who escaped the net of the Domesday inquest.

In 1085 and 1086 William set up a royal commission and sent agents on circuit to compile the record known as Domesday Book. He wanted to know the essential facts about his kingdom, particularly the operation of Anglo-Saxon economic feudal arrangements in rural England. He was also anxious to obtain detailed information about national economic conditions so that a heavier Danegeld might be assessed. He wanted to have a collection of facts useful in settling outstanding pleas. The Domesday survey, so called because none could escape its judgment, was an extraordinary record, one of the most valuable documents in English history. "So narrowly did he cause the survey to be made," wrote a monk at Peterborough in the *Anglo-Saxon Chronicle*, "that there was not one single hide nor rood of land, nor—it is shameful to tell but he thought it no shame to do—was there an ox, cow, or swine that was not set down in the writ."

The perambulating inquisitors of the king, with the authority of royal justices, collected the facts. William and his agents did not want the inquiry to degenerate into an accumulation of useless information. In the final abstract of the original returns the statistical details obtained in the survey were drastically curtailed. The condensed and rearranged remainder was divided into the two volumes of Domesday Book. One volume was devoted to Essex, Norfolk, and Suffolk; the second to the rest of England.

Probably no other ruler of this age could have extorted such a comprehensive mass of information from a reluctant people. When Domesday Book was completed it remained as an ordered and permanent record of England's national economic resources, the royal rights over them, the social conditions of Englishmen in the eleventh century. Nothing similar to it appeared in any part of Europe. The success of William's agents indicated the power that "the stark, stern, and wrathful" Norman held in the England he had conquered two decades earlier.

NORMAN GOVERNMENT

The immense and flexible developments of a feudalism transplanted from Normandy were parallelled by other important changes in the face of England. The Normans, vigorous and capable, were able to import new ideas from Europe. England was no longer an island on the edge of the Continent, but more closely connected with Normandy and, through Normandy, with European habits and culture.

Typical of the general attitude of William I is the legislation that has come down to us. Early in his reign William made a vague grant to the Londoners in the form of a charter. He declared that he wanted both French and English "to enjoy all the rights that you enjoyed in the days of King Edward." Among the ordinances of the Conqueror was one setting up certain procedures to be followed by both Normans and Anglo-Saxons in cases of trial by combat, compurgation, and ordeal. The document containing the "Ten Articles" attributed to William I is apparently an unofficial compilation of a summary of several decrees made by him. One decree declared that no person should be slain or hanged for any offence; the most severe punishment was henceforth to be mutilation. A second decree provided that the land laws of Edward's day should be kept; a third that lesser freemen should be organized into groups of ten; within each group the members were to be held mutually responsible for the good behavior of one another; this was the Norman system of frankpledge.

These acts of William were practical measures designed to meet the needs of the hour. They were not striking innovations. As William moved towards the increased centralization of his government he was probably not at all conscious that what he was doing had important implications for future centuries. For example, the council of the king was not at first essentially different from the Anglo-Saxon witan either in membership or functions. It contained the great temporal and spiritual nobles. However, when feudal principles prevailed, the council came to include only the tenants-in-chief, over which William presided as England's great feudal lord.

By the application of feudal theory to an existing institution the king's council became the king's court, the *curia regis*. Membership was now based upon landholding, not upon the criterion of personal importance, as in the Anglo-Saxon witan. William kept the powers of an Anglo-Saxon king; he added to them his authority as a mighty feudal landlord. He could summon up a feudal army from his vassals;

he could also call out the Anglo-Saxon *fyrd*. He collected feudal dues; at the same time he gathered the taxes owed his Anglo-Saxon predecessors.

The *curia regis* usually met three times a year. All the tenants-in-chief, called barons, were expected to attend, including abbots and bishops, who were legally barons for feudal purposes. The total number of those expected to be present was about 500. Not all attended in William's day; twenty years later only the upper baronage, numbering about 170, were specially summoned to the king's feudal court.

Some of the earlier functions of the Anglo-Saxon witan were now lost by the *curia regis*. For example, it was no longer necessary to obtain the consent of the nobles to the alienation of royal lands. The king might ask the court, or council, to endorse his decrees, particularly the financial ones; but he was under no obligation to do so. The judicial functions of the *curia regis* increased tremendously; they too, were under the control of the king. The great feudal court, or council, thus found its advisory, legislative, and judicial burdens steadily mounting as Norman government became more centralized.

There was a smaller, permanent council in constant attendance upon the king. Its powers were apparently identical with those of the great feudal council and it was called by the same name as the larger assembly, the *curia regis*. In the following pages, for the sake of convenient reference, a purely arbitrary distinction will be made between the two bodies: the full feudal assembly will be called the great council and the smaller group will be referred to as the *curia regis*. The *curia regis*, or small council, was composed of the tenants-in-chief who were attending the king and the permanent officials of the royal household. Anglo-Saxon kings had often asked for advice and assistance from household servants when the witan was not in session. William I not only continued that practice but gave the household officials more administrative and executive tasks in government affairs.

The centralization of government meant an increase in routine business; household officials such as the royal butler and steward found themselves busy executive officers of the king. They were, so to speak, the predecessors of the modern civil servants. Edward the Confessor had earlier taken over from Norman practice the official known as the chancellor, or king's secretary, whose main duty it was to prepare and issue royal documents. In time the king's chancellor became the Lord Chancellor, today the highest officer of the crown. William I added another official, called the justiciar. This officer was not technically a member of the royal household at all, but a special agent who was the king's chief administrative and legal assistant; he was head of the royal judicial system, and usually served as regent in the king's absence. This office of justiciar was continued until the late thirteenth century.

By the addition of the chancellor and the justiciar to the *curia regis* the efficiency of that body was increased. As state business grew, it was inevitable that still more officials would be needed to assist the members of the royal household and their clerks. The *curia regis*, as later chapters will show, grew into a body of permanent and trained officials carrying on the work of government until they gradually went "out of court" to become the forerunners of the modern departments of government.

In local government institutions William made few changes. As noted earlier, he kept the shire and hundred courts under royal authority and appointed sheriffs responsible to him alone; these sheriffs remained for a century the most powerful district officers in England. The earls, once so important in local administration, saw their powers steadily whittled away. Most of the great earldoms disappeared completely. The earldom of Wessex went down with the house of Godwin and reappeared only in the novels of Thomas Hardy; Mercia, Northumbria, and East Anglia soon toppled. Only in the restless borderlands were the strong earldoms of Chester, Shrewsbury, and Durham left to keep England's guard strong against the Scotsmen and the Welsh. Elsewhere the earldoms became offices great in prestige, almost barren of power.

WILLIAM AND THE CHURCH

When William I had invaded England in 1066, he had promised the Pope that he would oust Stigand from the archbishopric of Canterbury. The moral support of the church had been valuable to William in his attack upon Harold and the Anglo-Saxons. After the conquest was completed Stigand was deposed. As has been noted earlier, Norman churchmen, learned and energetic, replaced most of the Anglo-Saxon bishops. The successor to Stigand was the famous theologian and lawyer Lanfranc, an Italian from Pavia who had been prior of the Norman abbey of Bec and later the abbot responsible for important reforms at the monastery of St. Stephen's at Caen, earlier built by William. Lanfranc, William's friend and supporter, united with his king to undertake a reformation of the church in England.

In 1078 the militant and powerful monk Hildebrand became Pope Gregory VII. Throughout continental Europe the zealous Gregory swiftly increased the power and claims of the papacy. Under his control the government of the church became more centralized; he saw the see of Rome as an instrument for uniting Christendom more effectively than ever before. According to the extreme claims of Gregory VII every temporal ruler should obey the orders of the papacy. Within the church the Pope should be an absolute monarch; all roads must lead to Rome. In the church hierarchy the chain of command should reach downwards from Pope to parish priest.

In England, William the Conqueror was quite prepared to assist Lanfranc in carrying out vital church reforms. William had noted the excellent results of Gregory's campaign to purge away many evils among the secular clergy in Normandy. The widespread corruption of the regular clergy had also declined considerably as the Cluniac reform movement swept over Europe. Despite the earlier achievements of Dunstan and Edgar, the Anglo-Saxon church was corrupt, slovenly, decadent, wordly, somnolent. William and Lanfranc therefore set out to enforce clerical celibacy, to purify monastic life, to raise the level of intellectual activity, to abolish simony, to do all that the reforming zeal of Gregory had achieved in Europe.

Under the command and inspiration of Pope, king, and archbishop, church councils were summoned in 1070 to begin the papal reform program. Cathedral chapter government was reorganized. A new and stricter discipline began to be enforced among the secular clergy. The rules of the monasteries were tightened and made effective. Schools and monasteries multiplied. Lanfranc, sober and vigorous, showed himself an efficient administrative officer, an excellent ecclesiastical statesman. The best of the new spirit of Rome and Cluny poured across the Channel.

At the same time William separated the church councils or synods from lay assemblies so that the legislative independence of the church was increased in matters purely ecclesiastical. He completely separated the church courts from the ordinary lay courts. No longer was the bishop to preside with the earl or sheriff over the shire court for the purpose of jointly administering justice to layman and cleric. Nor were churchmen to appear in the hundred court. Henceforth the bishop or his officers in the new church courts set up by William would deal with all cases involving clergymen or the great tracts of problems covered by the canon law. This separation of lay and ecclesiastical courts helped to prepare the way for conflict between church and state throughout the later Middle Ages.

To the larger claims of Gregory VII William would not agree. When the Pope boldly demanded an oath of fealty as a formal acknowledgment that England was a fief of Rome William refused to give it. "I have refused to do fealty, and I do refuse, because neither did I promise it, nor, as I find, did my predecessors do fealty to your predecessors." When Gregory decreed that the papacy should control the appointment of bishops and abbots William replied by insisting that all bishops and abbots should be elected in his presence; to the end of his reign he continued to invest them with the symbols of their ecclesiastical offices. This problem of "lay investiture" was later to cause many bitter quarrels between church and state.

William also refused to allow English churchmen to acknowledge any Pope without royal consent. He commanded that no papal letters or legates should come into England unless he permitted it. In temporal matters the Pope's orders must yield to the authority of the king. William insisted that he should have the power of vetoing any legislation made by an English ecclesiastical synod. He refused to permit any appeals to papal courts without his consent. He ordered that none of his tenants-in-chief should be excommunicated by the Pope unless William agreed to it. In such things there must be no papal pressure upon the royal councillors and, through them, upon the secular arm of the state.

The suspicious king watched narrowly the claims of the papacy and stood adamant against them. William would reform the church; but he intended to remain king of England, with his sovereign rights unimpaired. A strong king and a strong Pope had reached a stalemate.

NORMAN CULTURE

It is obvious that the Norman Conquest opened the gateways of England to new influences from Europe. The leading members of the church and state were now Normans; many held their Norman estates; and most of them were in frequent touch with the Continent from France to Rome. New avenues of Anglo-Continental trade were opened up, although the flow of goods was in fact smaller than is usually supposed. English and Norman soldiers fought together across the Channel; English and Norman clerics found posts on the Continent. The bursting intellectual revival of Europe, the prelude to the renaissance of the next century, was soon mirrored in England, where Norman churchmen led the way in founding English schools.

French became the language of the court, the law, the government. Educated men spoke and wrote both French and Latin. Exiled from hall, court, and cloister, English remained almost entirely a spoken tongue for about three centuries. Anglo-Saxon, as a submerged peasant's jargon, slowly lost its clumsy inflections, its seven strong and two weak verbs, its elaborate genders; there were no grammarians to protest. The English tongue gained the suppleness and grace that are among its chief merits today. At the same time it was enriched by French words and ideas, particularly those that had to do with hunting, cooking, art, religion, politics, justice, war. In the fourteenth century English again entered polite and learned society in the works of Geoffrey Chaucer, John Wycliffe, and their fellows. Then its long and unconscious underground growth had left it improved and flexible, ready to develop into the language of Shakespeare.

Most writers in the Norman age used Latin. Songs and tales in Norman French had little influence upon authors in England until the late twelfth century. Soon after 1066 several monks began to record for posterity the events of their world. What they wrote filled many volumes. Among them was William of Malmesbury, the best of the chroniclers of the Norman period. He planned to write a connected history of England, filled with variety and anecdotes. Although he never finished his task he left many manuscript pages, filled with sparkle and interest.

It was not in literary works but in architecture that the Normans achieved most nobly. In the full flood tide of the ecclesiastical revival the landscape was transformed by Norman churches, huge and magnificent, rising beside the castles. God was to be glorified in splendid ceremonial and massive building, symbols of His power and majesty. About 300 churches were constructed, some of them the largest of their kind in Europe. The floor area of four of England's churches exceeded 60,000 square feet (Bury St. Edmund's, St. Paul's, St. Swithin's, St. Albans); in these years only two churches built in Europe were comparable in size (Spiers and Cluny). As a part of the monastic revival there soon arose the abbeys and priories of the Cistercian monks, who first came to England in 1128, especially to Yorkshire; the Benedictine houses; the nine Carthusian monasteries; a few Cluniac strongholds.

Norman architecture, like Anglo-Saxon, was a type of the earth-clinging Romanesque, characterized by round arches, thick walls, small windows, massive pillars. The Normans, with their skilled craftsmen, improved upon the Saxons in terms of technique and variety. In the rugged early Anglo-Norman architecture the walls and pillars were very low and thick. The sculpture work about the churches was done with an axe; it was plain, rude, and shallow. About 1130, the sculptors began to use the chisel. In the masonry of early Norman walls, as in the Saxon, there was an abundance or mortar, few stones. Early in the twelfth century the walls and pillars became higher and flat buttresses were used at points of strain and pressure. Doors and windows were deeply recessed; the solid towers suggested strength and repose. New forms of decoration appeared: the zigzag, the triangular dog-tooth, the scallop, the beak, the signs of the zodiac. The masonry of the walls became short-jointed as the blocks of stone were carefully cut and less mortar was used. Hundreds of workmen chiselled and carved in stone the gargoyles and capitals in great cathedrals, elaborate monastic buildings, small parish churches.

Norman bishops transferred their residences to the most important towns in their dioceses, such as Chester, Lincoln, Durham, and Norwich. There the new cathedrals rose; the noble sternness of Durham Cathedral, with its adjacent castle to guard against the Scots, is probably the best illustration in England of the Norman Romanesque achievement. The silent majesty of Durham stands as a symbol of the worship of a mighty God, suggesting by its solidity the attitude of medieval man towards the Christian religion.

WILLIAM II

In 1072 William the Conqueror pushed over the border of Scotland and received the homage of the Scottish leaders. He thrust westward into Wales, went on a pilgrimage to St. David's, and built a castle at Cardiff. In 1073 he conquered Maine, southwest of Normandy. Philip I of France, long jealous of William's power, joined in a factious cabal to intrigue against his overmighty vassal and helped William's rebellious son Robert fight against his father. Finally, in 1087, open warfare arose between the two kings.

William raided up the Seine valley from Normandy, set fire to the town of Nantes. As he was riding through the ruins his horse stumbled and threw him from the saddle. The injury proved fatal. William died at Rouen, the Norman capital, on September 9, 1087; he was buried at St. Stephen's, his own magnificent church in Caen.

William I left Normandy to his eldest son Robert, a weakling; England to his second son William Rufus (William II); and 5,000 pounds of silver to his youngest son Henry. The Norman barons in England would have preferred Robert as their ruler; those who had territories in both Normandy and England dreaded the possible results of divided allegiance. The majority rebelled, led by Bishop Odo, the brother of William the Conqueror, who had been released from prison. William II put down the rebellion; the nobles, thoroughly cowed, stayed quiet.

William Rufus appears to have been thoroughly wicked, a coarse and debased likeness of his father. It was said, on a later day, that he "made hell fouler by his coming." He had almost no sense of decency or justice. His feudal levies on his tenants were extortionate. Lanfranc, who had tried to hold a tight rein on William and had given him wise advice, died in 1089. For four years William left the archbishopric unfilled, collecting the revenues of the see for himself. There were several vacant bishoprics and William's treasurer, the unscrupulous shyster clerk Ranulf Flambard, shamelessly diverted their incomes to the royal coffers. Soon Flambard was appointed to the rich bishopric of Durham. Later he became the king's justiciar.

Suddenly, in 1093, William became ill and illness brought repentance. "The devil a saint would be." Fearing death, William forced Anselm, saintly Italian abbot of the monastery at Bec and famous theologian and scholar, to fill the vacant archbishopric. Anselm, consummate fisher of men, was a quiet, pious man with no desire to be an archbishop. Was he, "a weak old sheep," to be yoked to "that fierce young bull, the king of England"?

When William unexpectedly recovered, he found out that the mild Anselm was prepared to fight about the plundering of church lands by the king. He also discovered that Anselm believed strongly in the extreme papal claims to power over temporal rulers. On this point Anselm was inflexible; he refused to accept the pallium, symbol of his new office, from the scandal-stained hands of William and he asked permission to go to Rome to receive it from the Pope himself. At that time, however, there were two rival Popes in Christendom and William had accepted neither. He claimed that no Pope could be recognized without his consent. He saw no reason why Anselm should go to Rome. "You have committed no sin needing absolution, and as for advice, you are better able to give it to the Pope than the Pope is to give it to you." In 1097 Anselm finally succeeded in obtaining William's permission to go into voluntary exile. Alone of the king's subjects he had dared to resist.

All the territory his father bequeathed him, William kept. He took Cumberland from the Scots and made it an English county. He was nursing ambitions to take over Aquitaine when the fates decided otherwise. On August 2, 1100, William was hunting in the great New Forest his father had made in Hampshire. There he was shot through the heart, perhaps by accident. Some foresters took his body up to Winchester on a cart. Without religious rites, William was laid in a tomb in Winchester. "Anselm, who is said alone to have wept, would feel that he had lost a soul." William's younger brother Henry, who had been in the fateful hunting party, had ridden at once to Winchester and seized the royal treasure. Robert, the immediate heir, was far away in the Holy Land on a crusade.

HENRY I AND STEPHEN

Henry had seized the royal treasure; then he seized the throne. His older brother's claim by right of primogeniture could not be enforced from distant Jerusalem. The shrewd Henry at once sought popular support by marrying a Saxon princess, daughter of the king of Scotland. He imprisoned the rapacious justiciar, Ranulf Flambard, in the Tower. Anselm was recalled with honor. To many it must have seemed that the "lion of justice" foretold by Merlin had come.

Then Henry issued a coronation charter in which he vaguely promised to redress all grievances and "bad customs"; to restore the good laws of Edward the Confessor; and to keep "firm peace" in England. This declaration was to be read in every shire court. Probably it was never intended that the charter would be enforced. In any event, the document is mainly important because it did become the basis for the greatest of all medieval royal charters obtained by the barons from John in 1215. Henry I had recognized, by implication at least, that the king was subject to the law. By such means Henry strengthened his precarious hold on the throne. A chronicler wrote of Henry's eyes being "soft and mild," strange adjectives to describe a king who was calculating and cold-blooded. Perhaps the chronicler had forgotten, or did not know, that Henry had once pushed a foe off the top of a tower, had ordered blinded a minstrel who satirized him.

In 1101 Robert returned from Jerusalem and invaded England, claiming the crown as his birthright. Several English barons supported Robert; but Henry persuaded his brother to withdraw in return for an annual pension of three thousand marks. Henry then turned against the barons who had backed Robert's claims; he confiscated their lands and forced many of them into exile. Over in Normandy the weakness of Robert soon brought chaos. At the invitation of several Norman barons the strong Henry crossed the Channel in 1106; he defeated Robert at the battle of Tinchebrai, annexed Normandy, imprisoned his brother in Cardiff Castle. Not even the Pope was able to open the prison door of the crusader. Robert stayed a prisoner until he died in 1134.

Meanwhile Henry began to quarrel with Anselm, now restored as archbishop of Canterbury. Henry offered to return all the arch-episcopal lands seized by William II provided that Anselm rendered the customary homage as a tenant-in-chief. Once more the problems of royal and spiritual power grew into conflict. A great church council of 1099, filled with the militant doctrines of Gregory VII, had forbidden any churchmen to do homage to a layman. Anselm had attended that council. He obstinately refused to do homage to Henry I for the fief he held.

There was a second major difficulty. Gregory VII had decreed that investiture, the formal presentation to an elected archbishop or bishop of the ring and staff symbolic of the transfer of office to them, could only be performed by a churchman. There must be no "lay investiture." This decision of Gregory, repeated by the church council of 1099, apparently meant that kings could no longer control appointments to spiritual offices. Thus the power of the state within the church would be greatly reduced. When Anselm steadily refused to allow royal investiture Henry I seized the church lands and exiled Anselm.

The archbishop was about to excommunicate Henry when a compromise was proposed. In 1107 it was accepted by all parties to the dispute. The final agreement provided that churchmen should render homage for their fiefs, thus admitting that they were feudally vassals of the king. Henry I, for his part, surrendered his claim to invest with their symbols of office the churchmen elected by the cathedral clergy. This so-called compromise was in fact a triumph for Henry I. Through the cathedral chapters Henry and his successors could control the elections of churchmen to vacant offices. When the king's candidates were almost invariably chosen as prelates the control of the investiture ceremony was actually of little consequence. But the controversy was ended, for a time. Until he died at the age of seventy-six, Anselm ruled his church in peace.

The reign of Henry I won him the title of "the lion of justice." His exactions were heavy, but not so bad as baronial pillage. In the years of this successful reign there were several important developments in governmental procedure. The wretchedly assembled and often inaccurate compilation of the "Laws of Henry I" provides some information, particularly about the legal history of Henry's day. Such documents as the pipe rolls, the writs concerning feudal tenure, the charters granted to boroughs, and the records of the king's household have enabled scholars to trace many significant tendencies in the thirty-five years of Henry's reign.

Under Henry I the exchequer probably first appeared in roughly the same form that it held until its reorganization under Henry II. The small council, or *curia regis*, sitting with a staff of clerks for financial business, came to be called the exchequer court, probably because of the chequered cloth covering the table of accounts. Twice a year the exchequer court audited the returns of the sheriffs, who collected most of the king's revenues in feudal incidents, dues, taxes, and fines. The accounts of a sheriff were set up by means of a modified abacus reckoning of columns and counters on the chequered table of accounts. The exchequer court provided a careful check upon sheriffs and other local royal officials; it also made certain that the king obtained all the revenues to which he was entitled. Later in the century the exchequer moved still further towards the modern system of English financial administration. This development is described in the next chapter.

The growth of commerce and towns led to another event of considerable later consequence. Wealthy towns, such as London, could afford to buy valuable privileges from the king. The charter given by Henry I to London sometime between 1130 and 1135 was a grant, the earliest known, of a borough in fee-farm to the burgesses, by which the citizens were permitted such privileges as the collection of the revenues of London and Middlesex and the installation of a sheriff of their own choosing, in return for a rent of £300 payable to the royal exchequer. Similar charters were sold to other boroughs, a process that reached its crest later in the twelfth century.

At the same time we can discern the beginnings of the system of itinerant justices, who travelled out from the *curia regis* to the shire courts to do royal business, particularly financial and judicial tasks. The regular jurisdiction of the *curia regis* properly extended to all suits in which tenants-in-chief were involved, to pleas of the crown, or cases involving serious crimes such as murder or felony, and to certain other fields. The *curia regis* might also decide to deal with a specific case which would be taken out of a local hundred, shire, or feudal court by a royal command called a writ. Royal justice, reasonably impartial, became popular. It was difficult, however, for the king's subjects to follow the *curia regis* as it travelled about with the king. So Henry I sometimes sent itinerant justices, members of the *curia regis*, out into the counties to hold local sessions of the king's court in the county courts and to do other local judicial and administrative business. This practice was only beginning in the days of Henry I. Later in the century, during the reign of Henry II, the use of royal itinerant justices became constant and regular; the idea of "national justice" began to grow. This further extension of the activity of the king's court is described in the next chapter.

Henry had hoped to bequeath his throne to his son William; but William was drowned in 1120. Henry then asked the English barons to recognize his daughter Matilda as his heiress. No woman had yet ruled over all England. Could Matilda perform the heavy tasks of a Norman ruler? In 1125, Matilda, the widow of the Holy Roman Emperor Henry V, married Geoffrey, son of the count of Anjou. The barons swore oaths of fealty to Matilda despite her sex, her unpopular Angevin marriage, and her silly arrogance.

In 1135 Henry I died. The barons at once broke faith with Matilda and gave the crown to Stephen of Blois, son of William the Conqueror's daughter Adela. Stephen was supported by his brother Henry, bishop of Winchester and papal legate. London, populous and powerful, acclaimed him as a popular choice. He was crowned king by the archbishop of Canterbury.

As a man, Stephen was a gallant knight, energetic and conscientious. As a ruler he was weak. Nothing prospered under him. Law and justice collapsed. He could not manage the turbulent barons. They began to throw off the royal authority. Lacking common sense, Stephen squandered the royal treasure in a desperate attempt to purchase loyalty. The barons fought intermittently among themselves, pillaging the lands of their neighbors. One of the last sad entries of the *Anglo-Saxon Chronicle* soberly related a story of rapine, pestilence, and general disruption. "Men said openly that Christ and His saints slept."

Stephen quarrelled with Roger, bishop of Salisbury, and put him in prison. The king's violence cost him the wavering support of the clergy. Even Henry, bishop of Winchester, turned against his brother Stephen. In 1139, amidst the mounting anarchy of private warfare, Matilda landed in England to claim the throne. The bishops declared Matilda queen; but she was driven from London when she tried to collect a tax. Several years of indecisive civil war followed.

Matilda's husband, Geoffrey of Anjou, conquered Normandy. When he died in 1151, Matilda left her claim to the English throne to her son Henry, who landed in England in 1152. The supporters of Stephen now saw the youthful Henry, master of Anjou, Maine, and Normandy, gathering strong forces. Meanwhile Stephen's only son had died. Stephen was broken-spirited, weary of war.

In such circumstances Henry, bishop of Winchester, "half soldier and half monk," aided by Theobald, archbishop of Canterbury, succeeded in arranging a peace to end the war of succession. It was agreed that Stephen should reign unopposed for the rest of his life. Henry of Anjou was recognized as the heir to the English throne. Unlicensed castles built after 1135 were to be razed; their number was reckoned at over a thousand. Crown lands seized by the barons were to be restored. Foreign mercenaries were to be sent home. The principle of election was again set aside by a dynastic treaty.

In 1154 Stephen died. The horrible confusion of his reign had shown once more how dangerous it was to have a "soft and good" man for a king. Unchecked feudalism meant anarchy and bloodshed, tortured peasants and depopulated villages. It was fortunate that Stephen's successor was Henry II, one of the greatest monarchs of the Middle Ages.

Chapter 4

THE AGE OF HENRY II
FIRST OF THE ANGEVINS

HENRY II was a remarkably able ruler, thoroughly capable of curbing the barons who had broken loose from royal control in Stephen's reign. As a result of matrimonial diplomacy Henry held more territory in France than the king of France himself. His father, Geoffrey, count of Anjou and Maine, had conquered Normandy. Henry inherited all his father's lands in 1151. Then, in 1152, he had married Eleanor of Aquitaine. Her dowry, added to his own French possessions, gave him control of all western France. When he succeeded Stephen as king of England his territories reached from Scotland to the Pyrenees.

The personality of Henry counted for much in his age; it was one of the reasons why he left his mark forever upon England and her laws. Henry was twenty-one years old in 1154, scholarly, efficient, intelligent, practical, with an essentially legal turn of mind. His energy was demonic. Courtiers were amazed by this king who seemed never to grow weary. Henry was a skilled politician, preferring the tools of diplomacy to those of force and war. He was also particularly shrewd in selecting able servants. Industrious and determined, Henry tolerated no slackness in others. With him all seemed to move upon a heroic scale. On occasion he burst into almost incredible fits of anger, rolling in the rushes on the floor. Likewise, his fits of remorse often carried him into almost psychopathic troughs of depression.

With Henry the business of kingship was an absorbing passion. He would do all his grandfather Henry I had done, and more. He, too, would be a "lion of justice." He would make England a model state. There would be no anarchy among the barons while Henry was king, for Henry intended to be master of his realm. This vitality and unswerving determination made him one of the greatest men in English medieval history. He restored order and reorganized the central government; he suppressed the baronage; he extended the power of the

51

central royal courts; he increased the use of writs and itinerant justices; he introduced the jury system as a normal part of royal court procedure; he added much to the coral reef of the common law. Wherever he met objection or defiance he pounced swiftly and hard. The day of feudal anarchy was ended. For thirty-five years Henry II drove on towards his goals, relentless and almost unimpeded.

Henry II and his ministers shaped many legal and administrative procedures and determined the direction of their growth in later centuries. The power of the central government was soon felt at the shoulder of every Englishman. A strong monarch, working through improved and impartial government machinery, Henry contributed much to the popular welfare. At the same time, the steady unification of government and law helped to create a civic solidarity that formed one basis for the later growth of national consciousness.

THE CENTRAL GOVERNMENT

For several years the main task of Henry II was to recover the order shattered in the chaos of Stephen's reign. Henry promised to restore the lost efficiency of the Norman monarchy. Shortly after his coronation he sent home the foreign mercenaries Stephen had hired. He ordered the destruction of all castles that had been built by the barons without the king's license. He revoked a number of royal grants of lands and offices made by Stephen. He also selected men to help him rebuild the machinery of the central government on the foundation laid by his grandfather Henry I.

A major task was the reorganization of the exchequer courts set up under Henry I to deal with the financial affairs of the kingdom. This body was the first clear division or offshoot of the *curia regis*, the smaller king's council from which were to grow and break off so many administrative departments and sets of royal courts. Most men engaged in royal business met at the exchequer board. In these years, too, the whole *curia regis* came to have more judicial business. Because it contained several lawyers and the great council was mainly composed of laymen it was quite natural that most cases should not be tried before the great council at all, but before the smaller *curia regis*, or a part of it. With some exceptions, only cases in which the king or the barons had a major interest continued to be tried before the great council. The *curia regis* was thus coming slowly to be considered as a body whose work was mainly judicial. Thus a division of functions between the great council and the *curia regis* was beginning to develop.

At the same time there appeared a division of functions within different parts of the *curia regis* itself. The exchequer court, for example, was clearly both a judicial and a financial body. The justiciar presided over the exchequer; other members were the chancellor, the treasurer, the chamberlain, the constable, the marshal, all principal officers of the royal household. These men, who were also important members of the *curia regis*, gradually concluded that there was no need for them to attend the exchequer; most of their functions could be adequately performed by clerks. Hence the clerks in fact became the exchequer and that body really parted from the parent stem of the *curia regis* because no members of the *curia regis* sat in it.

The pipe rolls, containing the permanent annual financial reports of the kingdom, appeared in a continuous series after the second year of Henry's reign. Much information about the financial administration of England is contained in them. There was also a remarkable essay in Latin called the *Dialogue on the Exchequer* attributed to Richard Fitz-Nigel, treasurer of the exchequer and bishop of London. This work described minutely the proceedings of the royal exchequer. It was also lightened by chapters of Nigel's experience as a higher civil servant. He recorded, for example, how many peasants came to court offering him their idle ploughs in token of the decay of husbandry. Professor F. W. Maitland once remarked that "agrarian history becomes more catastrophic as we trace it backwards."

The tendency that later resulted in the emergence of still more sets of separate courts and departments in the amoeba divisions of the *curia regis* was vividly shown in 1178. In that year Henry II set up a special group of five barons from the *curia regis* who were to sit permanently at Westminster to transact judicial business, other than that covered by exchequer jurisdiction. Thus the remaining members of the *curia regis* would be left free for other work, except when important judicial problems called for consideration by the whole *curia regis,* perhaps even by the great council. This new court was a permanent central court, later known as the Court of Common Pleas.

The growth of centralization was further aided by the rise of royal revenues and the continued decline of baronial power. The income from the royal estates, the feudal incidents, and the administration of justice increased almost steadily during the reign of Henry II. Henry allowed the collection of Danegeld to be abandoned but he imposed "shield money" or scutage taxes by which feudal magnates paid money to the king instead of sending military aid. Thus Henry II was able to hire mercenaries who would be loyal to him and not to the barons. There were also extraordinary levies of the tallage. This was an arbitrary levy upon "the king's demesnes and lands which were then in the king's hands" and upon the boroughs.

There were several other significant measures. In 1170 Henry held an inquiry into the behavior of sheriffs with the object of deposing feudal lords from the sheriffdoms and putting efficient agents of the exchequer in their places. After the reports were gathered, Henry saw to it that few barons remained as sheriffs; the new sheriffs were usually better tax collectors. In 1166 Henry placed a small income tax upon his subjects to aid in the recovery of Jerusalem from the Moham- medans. In 1188 the Saladin tithe was levied. This famous ordinance provided that "Every one shall give in alms for this year's aid of the land of Jerusalem a tenth of his rents and movables."

In 1181 the assize of arms ordered all freemen in England to furnish themselves with arms and armor according to their means. "Whoever possesses one knight's fee shall have a shirt of mail, a hel- met, a shield, and a lance." Thus Henry in fact revived the Anglo- Saxon *fyrd* or national army, a useful bulwark against foreign invasion or feudal rebellion. In the case of the assize of arms and the Saladin tithe the assessment was to be made by local juries, a step to be fol- lowed in later years. At the same time, as peace slowly began to con- vert the barons into country gentlemen, the local gentry began to develop a tradition of responsibility and service, a silent process of great importance.

ROYAL JUSTICE AND COMMON LAW

By steps such as those described above Henry II made himself the most powerful king England had yet seen. His most desirable re- forms were in the fields of judicial procedure. Under Henry the law became more comprehensive, equal, and reasonable. The story of many of Henry's achievements was told in a famous treatise on the laws and customs of England, the *Tractatus de Legibus et Consue- tudinibus Regni Angliae,* probably written by Ranulf Glanville, Henry's justiciar. The book of Glanville was the first of a long series of massive works recording and interpreting the English law. His name stands beside such great jurists as Bracton, Littleton, Coke, and Blackstone.

Early in his reign Henry began to send out royal justices to the counties to investigate and report upon local conditions, to check upon the sheriffs, and to see that justice was done. Henry I had used this machinery in a fitful and spasmodic manner. Henry II, on the other hand, made it his normal procedure. In doing so he extended the authority of the king's courts and thus reduced the power of private baronial jurisdictions. The royal or itinerant justices went down regularly to every county. Their presence in a county court turned it into a royal court. The travelling justices were "the *curia regis* on the march." They used the freeholders assembled in the county court to help them in judicial, financial, and administrative business. Such a procedure was one of the many ways in which traditions of service and cooperation were developed, useful chapters in the background of the growth of local self-government.

The itinerant justices not only brought surer justice to the coun- ties; they also helped to spread a knowledge of the legal principles used by the *curia regis* and its branches. In the long development of a reasoned system of law this slow process was important. The cumbersome and formal customary law that had grown up in various local areas through Anglo-Saxon days varied from district to district. Although the feudal law brought by the Normans was similar throughout England it was concerned with the conditions of landholding and little else. As the itinerant justices moved about England they began to make a national, common law for the whole kingdom, declaring the principles and practice of the central courts at Westminster and absorbing the best of the local law.

The result, slowly achieved, was a uniform law for all England, a living growth, rooted like an oak in the soil and unshattered by the storms of centuries. In France and Germany local differences existed in variegated provincial customs. Those countries at last had to adopt large parts of Roman law to obtain a uniform national code. England had no need for the reception of Roman law because both accident and policy had already produced an English common law, "the common engagement of the republic." As common law hardened into fixed forms it did not always provide remedies or protect rights; it sometimes worked injustice. Then it was the right and duty of the king to intervene with his prerogative power to secure justice and to see that right was done. Justice not allowed by the forms of the law could thus be obtained by royal interference. This was the beginning of the great system of law known as equity.

It may be that we have been taught to overstress the coherence of the common law and its utility as an instrument of national cohesion. In later centuries the common law lawyers, like Sir John Fortescue and Sir Edward Coke, probably exaggerated the "dangers" from the civil law of Rome. In many respects, too, the English common law was a mixture of Roman and feudal law, as well as Anglo-Saxon. For example, the contribution of the feudal idea of "immunities" and "liberties" was of some importance, even to those who blindly believed that the central principle of Roman law was to be found in absolutism. Under feudalism the ancient custom of the local community was the law of the fief. In the case of England it might be held that the whole kingdom was the "community" and strong kings and feudalism combined to preserve the Anglo-Saxon customs, now fixed in the common law.

THE JURY AND THE WRIT

Henry II made few discoveries or inventions in law or government. The body of laws issued in his reign was not large. His supreme achievement was that he made certain procedures regular and normal. One of these was the rise of the jury system.

The principle of the jury can be traced back to the sworn inquest. In the inquest a number of neighbors were placed upon oath (juré) and ordered to answer certain questions truthfully. The Roman emperors obtained information by using this inquest procedure. It was later employed by many kings and nobles who wanted specific information. William the Conqueror had used the sworn inquest or jury to ascertain the rights of the crown and whatever else he wished to know. Domesday Book is an excellent example of the use of the inquest on a national scale. The successors of William also used the inquest as a means of obtaining information, usually about the administrative or fiscal rights of the crown. In England nobody but the king was permitted to use the jury or inquest unless royal permission was granted. The jury was regarded as a purely prerogative institution.

It has been noted how Henry II, with his genius for order and detail in administration, instructed his justices to go about the counties at regular intervals to inquire into the king's rights; to assess taxes; to examine and report on the work of the sheriffs; to inspect the barons' courts and ward off the growth of excessive power there; to preside over the county courts. "The justices were quite as busy collecting the king's revenues as enforcing the king's peace." In 1166 the assize of Clarendon, expanded in 1176 by the assize of Northampton, ordered this practice to be maintained, so that the local machinery of the shire and hundred might continue in close relationship with Westminster. The twenty-two clauses of the assize, so called because it was a royal decree issued in an "assize," or sitting, of notables, provided also for the use of the jury system in certain types of cases appearing before the itinerant justices.

By the assize of Clarendon, Henry II ordered that there should be present at each full meeting of the shire court to meet the itinerant justices "twelve of the more lawful men of each vill" who were to be put "on oath to tell the truth, whether in their hundred or in their vill there is any man accused or publicly known as a robber or murderer or thief, or anyone who has been a receiver of robbers or murderers or thieves, since the lord king has been king."

The accusing or presenting jury, the antecedent of the modern grand jury, aided in the enforcement of criminal law. The members of the jury presented to the king's justice the names of those suspected of crimes. When the presenting jury was used, all the long preliminary forms employed in the older forms of trial, such as oath-taking, were eliminated. Under the second clause of the assize of Clarendon, the accused was to go at once to the ordeal of water. Accused men, "publicly and shamefully denounced," who were found innocent by the ordeal still had to "abjure the lands of the king so that they shall cross the sea within eight days unless they are detained by the wind." They were forbidden to return to England.

The jurors were "lawful men," reputedly honest individuals, neighbors who knew one another; they were chosen because they were well-informed about local conditions, such as the number of ploughs someone possessed, the last owner of a piece of land, the number and nature of the crimes committed in the neighborhood. These presenting jurors were, in a modern sense, sworn witnesses. They "indicted," or spoke against, the suspected persons. They were not under the immediate control of either the presiding judge on the one hand or of the accused and his friends on the other. In later days, the jury system worked well mainly because the bench was stronger than the bar.

It has been noted earlier that the king's courts alone could use this prerogative institution of the jury. A suspect accused by the jury-men could be tried only in the king's courts. Hence nobles who owned private courts with criminal jurisdiction lost that jurisdiction in the case of a man accused by a jury. The use of the presentment jury drove wedges into the power of those who held private jurisdictions and helped to increase the royal authority. It was obvious, too, that the justice brought by the jury system was superior to that achieved under earlier methods. It was reasonably efficient and swift. By the use of the accusing jury public responsibility for the detection and punishment of criminals was increased. As the number of criminal cases, or pleas of the crown, slowly grew in the king's courts, there was a corresponding advance in the royal revenues from fines and other profits of justice. The whole machinery of orderly government, local and central, reflected the effective enforcement of the law.

It was also clear that the jury system offered a reasonably impartial and satisfactory manner of settling civil cases, or common pleas, as well as criminal. If a private freeman wanted to get the facts in his case before a jury, he had to pay the king for the privilege of using the royal court, the king's justice, and the jury, which was a royal judicial instrument. This permission was given, for a price, in a royal writ. The writ described the civil case and authorized the royal justice to try it. Here began the common law principle that every case must open with a writ, the original writ. For the payment of money, part of the king's machinery of justice was thus thrown open to the nation.

Most civil cases in the twelfth century fell into rather clearly defined categories. For each case of a kind frequently occurring a special writ was developed. By a series of royal ordinances, called assizes, Henry II classified judicial actions and multiplied the types of writs. The word "assize" was carried over from the enactments setting up new forms of action and used to describe the actions themselves. Thus, the actions were also called "assizes."

There were three forms of possessory assizes, or assizes used to decide disputes over possession or ownership of land. In each of these a jury studied the case and gave a verdict. Like the presentment jury, the trial jury had Continental origins. The use of the trying jury was confined in Henry's reign almost solely to assize cases. Together these assizes draw a large body of civil litigation regarding land claims over from feudal courts to the royal courts. A weak freeman was protected by the assizes against the strong-arm methods of overmighty neighbors. He could not be forced to defend himself by judicial combat because there was jury trial. He could never be dispossessed of his freehold without a royal court judgment against him; and that judgment could be reached only as a result of a summons to court by a writ.

The first possessory assize was *novel disseisin* (recent dispossession); the purchase of a *novel disseisin* writ entitled the purchaser to have a jury decide as to whether A recently dispossessed B of a piece of land, or a cow, or any other real property. If the jury decided in the affirmative, the property in question was to be restored to B's possession (seisin) at once. The second possessory assize was *mort d'ancestor,* used by heirs who had been prevented from obtaining possession of lands which they claimed as their just inheritance. The third was *darrein presentment* (last presentment) designed to settle disputes over appointments, or presentments, of clergymen to church livings. Quarrels about advowson rights, or rights to appoint parsons, were numerous.

Among other important writs for real actions was the writ of right. This writ recognized the right of the plaintiff's feudal lord to try in his own feudal court a specific case about the ownership of a piece of land; it commanded the feudal lord to do justice to the plaintiff, and implied that if he did not, the king's justice would interfere. Closely related to this writ was the writ *praecipe*, which went further than the writ of right. It ignored the feudal court and instructed the sheriff to command the defendant to restore to the plaintiff the land in dispute or appear in a royal court to answer for his refusal. These writs, and others such as the real property writ of entry, marked definite steps in the royal encroachment upon the jurisdiction of the feudal baronial courts.

There were several other important writs of the reign of Henry II, particularly those for personal, as opposed to real, actions. Throughout the reign of Henry II, the forms of action increased; the number of writs multiplied; the law developed steadily as men sought writs that exactly fitted their needs. The obvious advantages of the trying jury were such that it soon came to be used in most civil actions in the king's courts; at first it had been used only in the assizes.

The ordeal by cold water was still employed in criminal trials after the accusing juries had presented their indictments. In 1215, the fourth Lateran Council at Rome prohibited priests from taking any further part in ordeals; thus, from one point of view, the ordeal was henceforth valueless. It seemed reasonable that jury trial should now be used in all cases. One obstacle, however, stood formidably against that procedure: an accused person might not be tried by the human means of jury trial without his consent.

After having been indicted by a presenting jury, many accused persons felt, and rightly, that they had small chance of acquittal by a trying jury. If they were convicted, all their property was forfeit to the king. Hence, many refused to submit to jury trial. To persuade such recalcitrant persons to consent to be tried by jury, weights and stones were loaded upon them; they were frequently given no food. As a result of this treatment, called *peine forte et dure,* many died. How-ever, as they died legally unconvicted of any crime their families in-herited their property.

HENRY II AND THE CHURCH

In the fourth century, the church had entered European politics as a new institution. There was henceforth the idea of two powers, spiritual and temporal, a dual authority governing the lives of men. Every European had two loyalties, one to the church and one to the state; he was to render some things to his temporal rulers, some to the papacy. There was one church, one revelation, one spiritual domination of the church universal. Europe was Christendom; and the spiritual center of Christendom was at Rome.

In this single universal society, men lived under one principle of life, expounded in the last resort by the Pope. The church main-tained that there could be no end to the validity of the natural law. "All custom and all written law which is adverse to natural law is to be accounted null and void." Kings who moved against the papacy found that the pervasive and immutable natural law, in the eyes of the church, was identical with the law of Christ. There was no gainsaying the voice of Rome. *"Si Roma locuta sit causa finita sit."*

Of course, the church in fact regulated human life by a careful accommodation of the ideal principle and the actual tendency. Never-theless, the two loyalties to church and state imposed upon medieval man were potentially incompatible. They caused many disputes be-tween lay rulers and the papacy. English kings, as described earlier, had frequent quarrels about the lines of demarcation between papal and royal jurisdiction. Not until the sixteenth century did there arise the new idea that Christian doctrines could be divided by national boundaries. The concept would have been unintelligible to men of the Middle Ages.

Under Henry II, the conflict between church and state arose once more. During the dislocation of Stephen's reign, the clergy had made deep inroads into the powers of the king. Stephen had issued a charter granting privileges to the church that Henry II would have abruptly denied. Bishops had obeyed the commands of the Pope and ignored the orders of Stephen. The claims of ecclesiastical jurisdiction were being steadily defined and broadened by church lawyers who had profited from the increased study of Roman law.

Church courts handled extensive areas of law. Clerics in orders could be tried for crimes only in the church courts, where no penalty involving the shedding of blood could be imposed. For example, a murderer convicted in a church court could not be executed. He might be punished by penance or unfrocked and degraded from his clerical office. Henry said that "it took two crimes to hang a priest." The "criminous clerks" who thus escaped severe sentences were a public scandal. Almost every scoundrel who had a smattering of education or any connection with a church might call himself a "clerk." Hence, he might demand "benefit of clergy," which included the right to be tried in a church court. Monks, priests, students, sextons, and many others were all "clerks." Over these subjects, the royal courts of Henry II had no jurisdiction. Appeals to Rome made further gaps in the royal power.

No open breach occurred between Henry and his churchmen in the early years of his reign; but the legal mind of Henry was troubled; he wanted to end the immunity of the church from lay jurisdiction and to bring it under the control of the royal courts. The masterful Henry was bending the barons to the royal will. Could he not make the churchmen subject to the king's law?

In 1161, Theobald, the archbishop of Canterbury, died. Henry selected as archbishop his friend, confidant, and chancellor Thomas Becket. Becket was a brilliant son of a London merchant; he had studied in England, France, and Italy; he had been a clerk and close associate of Theobald. In 1154, Henry had made Becket chancellor. The king apparently felt that Becket as archbishop would continue to cooperate with the crown. In that assumption, Henry was mistaken.

When Thomas Becket became archbishop in 1162, he abandoned the roads of luxury he had followed as courtier and chancellor; he adopted an ascetic way of life. Nor did he remain a friend and loyal servant of the king and the state. Becket was now determined to be a champion of the church. He resigned from the chancellor's office because he felt that an archbishop could not serve two masters.

The main clash between king and archbishop arose about the question of "criminous clerks," which in turn involved the basic question of the relations between church and state. In a council held at Clarendon in 1164, Henry stated that he intended to return to the customs of the time of Henry I. These "ancient customs" were included in a statement of the rules Henry wanted the church to accept. The rules were listed in the sixteen sections of a document called the Constitutions of Clarendon, a "record and recognition of a certain portion of the customs and liberties and rights," of Henry II's ancestors, "which ought to be observed and held in the kingdom."

The third clause of the Constitutions of Clarendon required that "clerks," or clergymen, should be accused in a royal court, tried in an ecclesiastical court and, if found guilty, unfrocked and sent back to the royal court for sentence and punishment. There were also clauses that restated the feudal position of the bishop as baron; declared that the king had the right to control the election of bishops; prohibited appeals from ecclesiastical courts to Rome without royal permission; asserted that no subject of the king might be excommunicated without the king's consent; and extended the jurisdiction of the royal courts in several directions. Becket, under heavy pressure, agreed to accept the rules included in the king's list of "ancient customs." He later asserted that his promise conflicted with the "liberties of the church" and obtained a papal dispensation releasing him from any obligation to observe customs contrary to ecclesiastical interests.

Becket at last refused to put the archbishop's seal on any document containing the king's proposals. At Northampton he again refused to submit to Henry. Fearing the royal wrath, he fled to Rome. Henry then seized the revenues of the see of Canterbury; Becket replied by excommunicating the king and all his ministers.

After six years of broken negotiations, the king and the archbishop reached an uneasy compromise. Becket returned to England in December, 1170. But there was to be no peace. In Becket's absence, the archbishop of York had crowned Henry II's son Henry as the royal heir. Becket resented the impertinence of the archbishop of York and the bishops who had assisted in the coronation. He excommunicated three of the bishops and denounced the archbishop of York.

The news of Becket's aggressive action roused Henry's terrible Angevin wrath. Cursing his archbishop as a "turbulent priest," he apparently shouted that the royal servants would eat the king's bread but would not rid him of Becket. Four knights, fired by Henry's hasty words, crossed the Channel and killed the archbishop in Canterbury Cathedral. Becket had become a martyr. Miracles were to be wrought at the tomb of St. Thomas of Canterbury. Over the old road of the pilgrims' way, men and women were to trudge and ride from every shire "the holy blisful martir for to seke, that hem hath holpen whan that they were seke." It was the popular voice that canonized Becket. In later centuries, he was to become a symbol of political protest. His name was invoked in many a national crisis by the commonalty. Prayers and pilgrimages to Canterbury became a habit, long continued. Had not Becket the martyr suffered in the popular cause?

All Christendom was shaken by the news of the murder in the Cathedral. Henry II immediately despatched his ambassadors to Rome to assure the Pope that he had known nothing of the plans of the assassins. The Pope refused to grant absolution until Henry had promised to allow appeals to Rome. Henry agreed, on condition that such appeals did not encroach upon the royal prerogative; he insisted that he had to have some safeguards against disloyal subjects.

Henry was also forced to permit "criminous clerks" to be tried and punished by the church. He did succeed in his demand that such clerks who "pled their clergy" must give proof of their status in the royal courts. Despite this papal concession, there were still to be criminals that public justice could not reach. The royal principles of the Constitutions of Clarendon had not been destroyed by the papal wrath; but they had been greatly weakened. In his death Becket had triumphed. Appeals to Rome increased; papal authority mounted with them.

The king rode out the storm of obloquy that clerical fury and public horror had raised. In 1173, faced by a rebellion led by the barons and his undutiful sons, Henry found his middle classes loyal. Although he had made peace with the church, he carried out a spectacular public act of contrition. The simple and great folk of England saw their king, warrior, and statesman on his knees before the tomb of St. Thomas of Canterbury, his back scarred with weals of penance.

SCHOLARS AND IDEAS

Thus the church administered a check to Henry II. Of its expanding power there was much evidence. Scores of monasteries were built in the twelfth century. The Cistercian movement, for example, gave an added impulse to monasticism, particularly in the north of England. At the same time, both royal court and holy monastery produced more scholars than England had yet seen. For instance, several Englishmen were interested in science; some of them travelled in the Near East to learn from the Moslems. Among the royal justices was Roger of Hoveden, one of the best-known medieval chroniclers. Walter Map, a clever satirist, was also a royal servant. The work of the monk William of Newburgh, who wrote a history covering the twelfth century, is still regarded with respect; it was a balanced and sensible achievement. Other scholars and writers left to posterity a mass of manuscripts about the England they knew when Henry II was king.

There was one man who produced a romantic work in Latin called the *History of the Britons*. He was Geoffrey of Monmouth, a Welshman who drew upon Welsh legends and the freely flowing springs of his own imagination for his text. His book is mainly about the misty Celtic hero King Arthur and the magician Merlin. Geoffrey's work was one of the sources of the Arthurian romance tales and legends that grew through later centuries. His robustly imaginative book is the most famous piece of nationalistic historiography of the Middle Ages. William of Newburgh called Geoffrey an impudent liar.

More famous in his own age than any of these was John of Salisbury, who finished his *Polycraticus*, or *Statesman's Book,* in 1159. This book, written in the confident and creative years of the medieval Christian polity, was the only important political treatise written in

Europe before the western world recovered and used Aristotle's *Politics*. Inspired by the concepts of the Roman Empire and the Old Testament theocracy, John of Salisbury tried to find a basis for the cooperation of church and state, to him the first requirement of any harmonious social system. By steps that were logically magnificent John of Salisbury endeavored to explain the respective roles of church and state in the medieval world. To him the church, as the embodiment of righteousness, was the supreme ruler of men.

IRELAND, SCOTLAND, WALES

The fame of the indefatigable Henry II springs more from what he did in his island kingdom of England than from his deeds beyond its borders. Nevertheless, Henry claimed and held at sword's point wide areas of the British Isles. In Ireland, Scotland, and Wales the exploits of Henry and his servants were always dramatic and usually profitable. In the fields and bogs of southern and eastern Ireland his predatory vassals advanced his power and their own. Henry asserted his feudal lordship over the moors of Scotland and the hills of Wales. The result was war and the harvest of war was a steady extension of royal authority.

In 1166 one of the Irish kings was driven into exile. He asked Henry II to restore him to his kingdom. Henry, occupied with the Becket controversy and with difficulties in France, could do no more than grant permission to the Irishman to ask the Norman-English barons for help. One of these nobles was Richard de Clare, earl of Pembroke, usually called Strongbow. He agreed to invade Ireland. Strongbow obtained many recruits from among the border barons of the Welsh marches and led an army across the Irish Sea in 1170. Papal endorsement was obtained for the Irish adventure.

Irish resistance was swiftly overcome; the Irishmen were divided by tribal jealousies and had no body armor. Henry II, fearful of the creation of an independent state across St. George's Channel and the Irish Sea, visited Ireland for a few months and obtained recognition as overlord. He planted three royal garrisons along the coast, appointed a justiciar to rule in his name, and set up a colony of English and Welsh traders in Dublin. In a region extending about twenty-five miles around Dublin English control and administration were reasonably effective. This district was later called the Pale. In the regions immediately beyond the Pale the Anglo-Norman barons were not inclined to respect the authority of the justiciar appointed by Henry. They tried to carve out estates for themselves, and plundered and fought at will.

During the anarchy of Stephen's reign Scotland had obtained the counties of Cumberland, Northumberland, and Westmorland from northern England. Henry, then a fighting candidate for the English throne and anxious for Scottish good-will, had agreed to confirm Stephen's cession of the three counties. But when Henry became king of England he could afford to change his mind and seized the first chance to repudiate his concessions. Malcolm, the boy-king of a Scotland divided by civil conflict, was forced to hand back the counties when Henry threatened war.

In 1173 the Scottish king joined a rebellion against Henry and was captured, quite by chance, when he lost his way in an English fog. He obtained his release only by agreeing to render homage to the English king "as the other men of my lord the king are wont." He also promised that the prelates and barons of Scotland would do homage and that the Scottish church should be subordinate to the see of York. To Henry II he surrendered, as a guarantee of his good faith, five Scottish castles to be garrisoned by English troops. Henry II fully exercised his feudal rights and the Scottish king found that he was in fact, as well as in name, a tenant-in-chief of a fief held of the English crown.

In Wales the disturbances of Stephen's reign had given the native Welsh princes of the south an opportunity to rise against the Norman marcher lords whose land and language wedged into Wales from the border counties. The marches west of the Wye were ravaged by Welsh fire and sword. In the knotted uplands of the north the Welsh chieftains were still almost independent, despite the attempts of succeeding English kings to surround and subdue them. Under Stephen they had been particularly successful in bulging out their holdings down the valleys from Snowdon. Henry II repaired the English fortresses west of the Conway and conducted three campaigns in Wales. When the English expeditions came home the prince of North Wales had pledged his homage, for what it was worth, to England's Henry II.

To the south, the lands of the marcher lords were still flanked on the east by orderly English counties and on the west by seething, primitive Welsh principalities. But for the rest of Henry's reign they stayed in nominal subjection to him. Over in southern Wales the natives prudently gave lip-service to the royal authority of Henry II and awaited a time when the leaven of ancient grievance might begin to work again. It was hoped that the Welsh might be able, in an hour of England's weakness, to obliterate the alien marcher lords and roll back English influence from the lands of Celtic tradition. The conquest of Wales by the armies of Henry II was far from complete.

HENRY II AND FRANCE

The fortunes of Henry II in the British Isles were not matched by his achievements across the English Channel. Henry II, the ruler of what is sometimes called the Angevin Empire, controlled a vast and hybrid collection of territories. From his father, Geoffrey Plan-

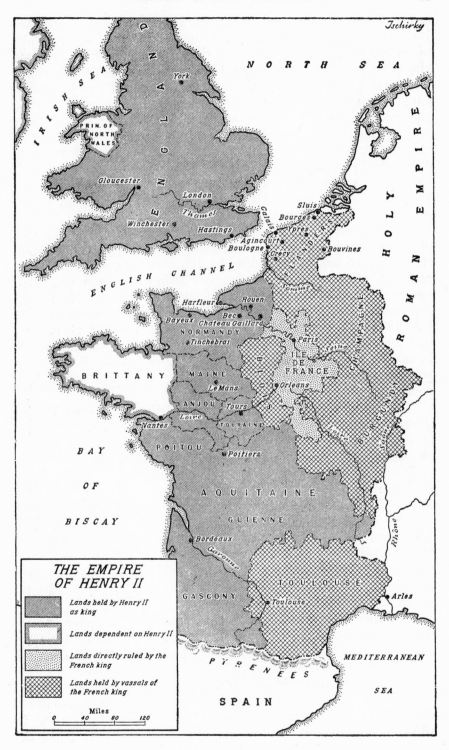

Tschirky

NORTH SEA

IRISH SEA

ENGLAND

York

PRIN. OF
NORTH
WALES

Gloucester

London
Thames
Winchester
Hastings

Calais
Sluis
Bourges
Ypres
Agincourt
Boulogne
Crecy
Bouvines

FLANDERS

HOLY ROMAN EMPIRE

ENGLISH CHANNEL

Harfleur
Rouen
Bayeux
Bec
Chateau Gaillard
NORMANDY
Tinchebrai

Paris

ILE
DE
FRANCE

Orleans

CHAMPAGNE

BRITTANY

MAINE

Le Mans

ANJOU
Tours
Loire
Nantes
TOURAINE

BURGUNDY

BAY

OF

BISCAY

POITOU

Poitiers

AQUITAINE

GUIENNE

Bordeaux
Garonne

Rhône

TOULOUSE

GASCONY
Toulouse
Arles

MEDITERRANEAN

PYRENEES

SEA

SPAIN

THE EMPIRE OF HENRY II

Lands held by Henry II as king

Lands dependent on Henry II

Lands directly ruled by the French king

Lands held by vassals of the French king

Miles
0   40   80   120

tagenet, count of Anjou, and his mother, Matilda, Henry inherited Anjou, England, Maine, Normandy, Touraine, and an unsettled claim to the overlordship of Brittany, the origin of running feuds with the king of France. In 1152 the pious Louis VII of France had persuaded the church to annul his marriage with the flirtatious Eleanor of Aquitaine. She had turned immediately to Henry of Anjou and married him, bringing with her hand Auvergne, Guienne, and the broad duchy of Aquitaine. Thus, as vassal to the Capetian king of France, Henry II held a composite belt of dominions stretching southward from Flanders to the Pyrenees and the borders of Navarre and Aragon and westward from the Bay of Biscay almost to the Rhone. Ambitious Henry was soon to marry his son Geoffrey to the heiress of Brittany and to construct strong alliances in Germany, Sicily, and Spain.

The strange and heterogeneous character and discrepant interests of Henry's feudal holdings in France made administration difficult. Henry's feudal lands were divided by differences in culture, language, and race. Their economic and political desires were quite dissimilar. Before the birth of French national feeling these men of Normandy, Aquitaine, and the other provinces had no common bonds to unite their interest or enthusiasm. By accident, and accident alone, they were all ruled by Henry II of England. Henry, in turn, was responsible, in varying feudal relationships, to the king of France. Beyond that political and feudal fact there was no unity in Henry's vast French domain.

To an increasing extent the kings of France coveted English territory. Amidst defiant ambition and jealousies they were prepared to seize every chance to dislodge Englishmen from a county here, a city there, and to round off and knit up the royal lands of the kingdom of France at the expense of their alien feudatories as well as their French rivals. The envenomed Continental duel between England and France began when William of Normandy conquered England and the destinies of the two states athwart the Channel became intertwined. It was not to end until Mary Tudor suffered the staggering loss of Calais nearly five hundred years later. What began as essentially a French civil war became a war between states. Out of this protracted struggle two nations emerged, clearly distinguished in their religious, social, and political structure.

It is not difficult to see how the problems of his French provinces occupied much of Henry's time. He had to keep his vassals submissive, his French rivals thwarted. These were days when feudal bonds could easily be cut in the night. Henry's Continental schemes and claims were steadily directed to retaining and extending his French possessions. For example, Eleanor, Henry's queen, had a flimsy claim to Toulouse. Henry seized upon it; his ferocious and fertile legalism saw a way in which the weak claim could be nursed to strength. He therefore declared war upon Toulouse and marched south from Normandy in 1159. When he reached Toulouse he found that Louis VII, king of France and his feudal suzerain, had arrived first and was safely within the city walls. Henry would not step outside the feudal law and openly attack his lord. He retreated, made peace with Toulouse, and planned vengeance upon Louis VII.

Louis himself was not an aggressive king. His temperament was placid; his resources were insignificant. "Your lord, the king of England," he once remarked, "has gold and silk and jewels and good things in abundance. We of France have only bread and wine and gaiety." Louis was aware that his kingdom was weak and disjointed and that he could not afford to gamble his inheritance by open battle with the menacing Henry II. He preferred to rest upon his legal claims and to stir up Henry's restless and unscrupulous vassals to strike against their English master. He could also shake the throne of his too powerful vassal by plotting with Eleanor, Henry's queen, and with Henry's four legitimate sons.

Between Henry and his queen a hatred burned steadily, fanned by the king's roving loves. Eleanor was powerful in Aquitaine; Henry was not. It was through Aquitaine that Eleanor struck most strongly at her royal husband and the weapons she used were their sons. There were four of them: Henry, Richard, Geoffrey, and John. Henry and Geoffrey died before their father; Richard and John were to succeed him upon the throne. Perhaps because of his deep affection for his sons Henry never restrained them. The harsh and ungentle methods he employed to curb other men were not used upon his children. The princes did not become either dutiful youths or gentlemen. One of the sons declared that in the Plantagenet family brother always strove against brother and son against father. "From the devil we came; to the devil we return," said Richard, the best of the four.

Henry II was anxious that his vast dominions should not fall apart when he died or be the cause of battle and bitterness among his turbulent sons. He wanted to be quite sure that each of "the lion's brood" would succeed to a prescribed inheritance. Accordingly, he had Henry, the eldest, crowned in 1170 as his successor to the throne of England and the heir to Anjou, Maine, and Normandy. To Richard, his second son, he assigned Aquitaine, which Richard would hold as a fief directly of the king of France. Geoffrey, his third son, had married the heiress of Brittany; Henry therefore assigned Brittany to Geoffrey, who was to hold that duchy of his older brother Henry. John, the fourth son, was only five years old. He was called "Lackland" because he was not covered by these preliminary partitions. When he was eight years old he was given the lordship of Ireland. He was nineteen when he led an ill-fated expedition to his restless domain.

All of these arrangements were undertaken by Henry II to show

how he wanted the Angevin dominions to be divided when he died. He had no intention of surrendering any of his power so long as he lived. His sons saw their inheritances dangling before them but still beyond their grasp. Despite their nominal dignity they stood, discontented and impotent, waiting for the great king to die. In such circumstances the youths easily listened to the intriguing Louis VII and, above all, to their mother, Eleanor.

In 1173 Henry, Geoffrey, and Richard led revolts against their father in the eastern counties of England, in Normandy, and in Brittany. Several of the great Anglo-Norman barons seized the chance to rebel against the king who had done so much to curtail their power. The Scotsmen under William the Lion came down from the north. The king of France, supported by the strong counts of Boulogne and Flanders, invaded Normandy. Thus the conspiracy of the princes grew into a dangerous coalition of all the king's enemies. But Henry was not easily overcome. In England the strength of his government showed itself; there would be no return to the days of Stephen. The middle and lower classes detested the prospect of a baronial oligarchy influenced by the tempers and whims of Henry's sons. They stood by the king who had given England strong and sound government. The royalist forces triumphed everywhere. It was the peasants of Suffolk who used pitchforks and flails to wipe out the Flemish mercenaries of the rebelling earl of Leicester. The proud earl was taken captive and submitted to the king he had hoped to dethrone. The king of Scotland, as noted earlier in this chapter, became Henry's prisoner. The revolt in Normandy collapsed.

When the last skirmishes were ended Henry II promised the rebel princes an annual revenue, but nothing more. He still refused to share his sovereign power. To John, his favorite son, he gave lands and castles in Anjou, Normandy, and England. The first rebellion had failed and Henry, for the time, was secure and unchallenged. But the king knew that the peace could not last. In 1175 he sent Richard to administer the duchy of Aquitaine and trouble started again. Richard's envious brothers intrigued against him. When Richard encroached upon Anjou, the fief of his elder brother Henry, war began between the two brothers. Henry was soon joined by Geoffrey. Then Henry II intervened and the brothers turned against the father. When Prince Henry lay ill with dysentery in 1183 it is said that in an agony of remorse he begged his father to visit his deathbed. Henry II, fearing treachery, refused to come but sent his ring in token of his forgiveness and affection.

The brief interval of peace that followed Prince Henry's death was used to advantage by Philip Augustus, who had succeeded Louis VII as king of France in 1180. Wary, hard, suspicious, and able, Philip Augustus was determined to redeem his father's errors. He would drive his English vassals out of France and he would not be scrupulous about the means he used. He began by plotting with Geoffrey of Brittany, Henry II's third son. When Richard and his father were fighting about the disposal of Aquitaine Geoffrey died. Then Philip turned to Richard. In the summer of 1189 Richard defeated his father and forced him to accept a series of humiliating demands. Henry II was prematurely old, broken by labor, disease, and sorrow; he came to the formal conference with Richard and Philip Augustus a dying man.

All of Henry's sons, he believed, had betrayed him but John, and John was far away. When he left the conference Henry knew that the name of John, the son he had trusted, led the list of the conspirators for whom amnesty had been demanded. At Chinon, in its summer beauty, the agony of defeat mingled with the delirium of disease. In the shadows of treachery and humiliation Henry II died on July 6, 1189, at the age of fifty-six. He did not know what great things he had done. Few rulers of the Middle Ages had achieved so much.

Chapter 5

KINGS AND BARONS
RICHARD I

THE SUCCESSOR of Henry II was Richard I; the statesman had been followed by the soldier. A man of adventure, fiery and reckless, Richard is chiefly remembered as the romantic hero of a dying age of chivalry. When the new king came to the English throne in 1189 he was thirty-two years old. Only twice had he visited England. The rest of the time he had lived and fought on the Continent. The government remained in the hands of his ministers, particularly the able Hubert Walter, later archbishop of Canterbury and justiciar.

Richard himself was not interested in statecraft but in war. He was not really an Englishman at heart. To him England was useful mainly as a source of gold to finance his projects abroad. To obtain money he sold bishoprics, abbacies, offices of state, and a number of charters to English towns. He sold the earldom of Northumberland. He sold heiresses who were royal wards as brides to the highest bidders. He sold the sovereignty of Scotland to its king. He dismissed sheriffs and they paid for their restoration. His half brother, Geoffrey, handed over three thousand pounds after he became archbishop of York. The relation between romantic chivalry and common honesty is not always clear.

In 1189 Richard of England, greatest of knight-errants, the aged Frederick Barbarossa, Holy Roman Emperor, and Philip Augustus of France stood pledged to start for Palestine on the third crusade. The enthusiasm of those who took the Cross was contagious. A vast movement born of piety, honor, curiosity, adventure, greed, and many other mingled emotional experiences swept over Europe, engulfing thousands of men who mustered together to battle in a holy war on the sands and pink hills of Palestine. Energetic western Christendom was thrusting outward towards the East.

Richard came to England for his coronation and at once set about collecting revenue to finance his share in the crusade. He tried to protect himself against the ambitions of his brothers in his absence. John and Geoffrey swore that they would not enter England when Richard was busy with his holy enterprise; such oaths were worthless. To John was given the effective lordship of Ireland, the control of a dozen counties and several castles in England, and the hand of the heiress to the Gloucester earldom. Geoffrey, as noted earlier, obtained election to the archbishopric of York. For these arrangements Richard's brothers were not grateful; they wanted more.

The Emperor Frederick Barbarossa was drowned as he tried to make his way overland to Syria. During July, 1190, Richard sailed from Marseilles and his ally Philip Augustus sailed from Genoa. In Richard's passage there were several delays, during which Richard first sacked the Sicilian city of Messina, then paused to conquer Cyprus and marry the beautiful Berengaria of Navarre. At last Richard reached the Holy Land, where he found that Philip Augustus had laid siege to Acre, the best harbor in Palestine. Despite the sickness, petty discords, and paralyzing spite that hampered the crusaders the attack upon Acre was pressed home. On July 12 the city surrendered and the banner of the Cross floated over its gate.

When Saladin, suspecting the good faith of the Christians, delayed the ransoming of his soldiers, Richard ordered a general massacre; on one day over 2,500 Moslem prisoners were slain. Meanwhile, feuds were breaking out among the crusaders. Between Leopold, duke of Austria, and Richard an open quarrel developed, born of long ill-will. Philip Augustus was jealous of the exploits of the English king, who had shown by his courage and leadership that his prowess was as great as his fame. In August, 1192, Philip, pleading ill-health, departed for France. Richard suspected that Philip would not be too ill to begin operations against some of the Angevin inheritance in France while his English ally carried on alone against Saladin.

Richard intended to march down the coast of Jaffa and then over-land to Jerusalem. Upon that barren land the sun beat like fire; there was almost no fodder for the horses. The soldiers were fed from the baggage train and the fleet that followed them along the coast. Saladin's army, moving southward farther inland, jabbed continuously at Richard's forces. In early September, 1192, the crusading host won the battle of Arsuf and reached Jaffa. It had taken them three weeks to travel the sixty miles from Acre. Saladin was yet unbeaten in the field. Difficulties and discords among the crusaders increased. Should they advance at once in a winter attack upon Jerusalem? Could the city be taken? If so, could it be held? A truce was finally signed with Saladin, who promised Christian pilgrims free access to the Holy Sepulchre in Jerusalem. Jaffa, Acre, Tyre, and certain other coastal ports were to stay in Christian hands. This was the conclusion of the crusade whose prelude had been so dramatic and ambitious. On October 9, 1192, Richard sailed from Palestine for England.

Richard had planned to return home by an overland journey from Marseilles. Consequently he sent his main fleet in advance. Then he received news that one of his enemies, the count of Toulouse, was waiting to capture him if he approached the shores of France. Richard decided to try to land at the head of the Adriatic and make his way through Europe disguised as a merchant. The Emperor Henry VI watched his ports and roads; the king of England would be an excellent prize. As he passed through Vienna Richard was betrayed and imprisoned. Philip Augustus and Richard's brother John tried to persuade the emperor to keep Richard in prison. Early in 1194 the English king was released when his vassals gathered a feudal aid to provide a part of the ransom of 100,000 pounds demanded by the imperial brigand.

When Richard at last reached England he found his kingdom had been disturbed by rivalries among the barons within and without his council. His faithless brother John had been intriguing with Philip Augustus. Richard contemptuously pardoned John. Then he turned to prepare for a war with Philip Augustus in defence of the imperilled Angevin possessions in France. Such a project required money, and Richard once more sold sheriffdoms, castles, and anything else that could command a market. In May, 1194, he departed from England for the last time.

Richard now began a sporadic war with Philip Augustus. He built the famous fortress of Chateau Gaillard to guard the Norman border by commanding the Seine and the approach to Rouen. Few results attended his desultory military operations against Philip and they were suddenly interrupted when Richard was lured into Aquitaine by the tale that one of his vassals had treasure-trove hidden at Chaluz. Richard meant to have it. He demanded the treasure and, when he was refused, laid siege to his vassal's castle. In April, 1199, he was wounded by a crossbow. A few days later Richard died in his tent outside the castle walls.

Had the principle of primogeniture been then in force, Arthur, the young son of John's elder brother Geoffrey, would have been Richard's successor on the throne. But the rule was not yet clear and it was widely held that the uncle was the legal heir. Moreover, Richard had designated John as his successor. The man was still preferred to the boy.

Although John was crowned king of England there was much dissent in Anjou, Brittany, and Maine. Philip Augustus seized the chance to recognize Arthur as the rightful holder of these fiefs and to accept his homage for them. John refused to yield his claims and carried on the war that Richard had begun. The result of that conflict was a major disaster to British arms.

THE LOSS OF NORMANDY

In 1200 Philip Augustus made a treaty of peace with John. John won several advantages in the peace arrangements. It was unfortunate that he was soon to throw them all away. Late in 1199 John had obtained an annulment of his marriage to the Gloucester heiress and thus had offended the powerful Gloucester family. He then sent an embassy to Portugal to sue for the hand of the sister of the Portuguese king. After his envoys left, the capricious John suddenly decided that his second bride should be the thirteen-year-old Isabella of Angouleme, beautiful daughter of one of his Poitevin vassals. There was one obstacle in the king's way: Isabella was already betrothed to Hugh the Brown, another of John's vassals in Aquitaine. In the thirteenth century a precontract agreement was nearly as final and binding as the marriage contract itself. Nevertheless, John pressed his suit and Isabella's father did not demur. In August, 1200, the marriage took place. John had overridden the rights of his vassal Hugh the Brown. His action was a morally indefensible violation of the feudal code.

The insulted Hugh immediately obtained strong support among his friends in Poitou. A rebellion against John blazed suddenly, and Hugh the Brown carried his grievance to Philip Augustus, his overlord. By 1202 disputes had multiplied in France, always a focus of feudal mutiny. Many Norman barons were deserting John and joining Philip. The French king, as John's suzerain, ordered him to appear in a French feudal court to explain his actions. John insolently refused to come. Philip then declared all of John's French fiefs forfeit because he had trampled on the rights of Hugh the Brown and had broken his feudal contract with his lord. The treaty of 1200 had collapsed. Philip once again gave Arthur, John's nephew, all the disputed French fiefs except Normandy, which he intended to seize for himself. In the early months of the new war John lost several allies by his savage treatment of prisoners. Meanwhile, however, he succeeded in capturing his nephew Arthur of Brittany. Arthur soon disappeared. Rumor said that John had murdered his nephew at Rouen; and rumor was probably right.

The ugly suspicion that John had been responsible for Arthur's death drove many angry Bretons and Angevins into the camp of Philip Augustus. John was progressively alienating vassals who had previously been faithful to him. In the meantime, Philip was steadily pressing his attacks and by the end of 1203 almost all of John's lands were in danger. He could get almost no revenue or military assistance. As his supporters and supplies declined, John's earlier energy seemed to be drained away. "Let it be, let it be," a contemporary quoted him as saying. "One day I shall win it all again." But in December, 1203, John secretly returned to England, leaving his depleted forces to get along as best they could.

Soon many of John's French territories were gathered into Philip's eager hands: Normandy, Maine, Anjou, Touraine, and Brittany. It seemed that the English might be driven from all of France. But the lands south of the Loire, partly for economic reasons, refused to yield to Philip. If Philip had ousted the English from Aquitaine, a profitable wine trade would have been endangered.

The severance from Normandy was an important step in the growth of an English sense of nationality. As a result of the humiliating reverse of English arms Englishmen also found that they no longer paid heavy and profitless taxes to defend English territories in France against the assaults and intrigues of Frenchmen. In the fourteenth century, when England moved into the Hundred Years' War, the attempt to recoup the losses of John's day proved costly enough. It was only possible for Englishmen of a later age to conclude that territories held under the British flag in Europe were a liability and colonies planted abroad were citadels of power and fountains of profit.

THE STRUGGLE WITH ROME

Scarcely had the curtain fallen on the drama in Normandy than a new struggle began, this time between John and Pope Innocent III, militant and able defender of papal authority. The quarrel arose out of events attending the election of an archbishop of Canterbury to succeed Hubert Walter, who died in 1205.

The archbishop of Canterbury was customarily elected by the monks of the cathedral chapter who were sometimes aided by the bishops of the province. From the days of Henry I and Anselm a candidate approved by the king had always been chosen. Shortly after Hubert Walter's death several monks of the cathedral chapter loudly opposed the participation of the provincial bishops in the election process. They insisted that the monks of Christchurch, Canterbury, and they alone, possessed the right to choose the archbishop. Under canon law their position was sound; neither the bishops nor the king had any legal right to interfere in the election.

The bishops, and probably a majority of the monks, were willing to accept John's candidate, the complaisant politician John de Grey, bishop of Norwich. But some of the younger monks met at night, elected their sub-prior Reginald to be the successor to Hubert Walter, and sent him to Rome to receive the pallium from Innocent III. As Reginald passed through Flanders he boasted of his new elevation and the news leaked back to John and the bishops. When the angry John confronted the monks of Canterbury they hastened to join with the bishops in choosing John's candidate. Commissioners were sent to Rome asking that the second claimant be confirmed.

Innocent III, the strongest Pope since Gregory VII, decisively refused to accept either candidate. He declared both elections irregular and persuaded the monks of Canterbury who were in Rome to elect Stephen Langton, a distinguished English cardinal then resident at the court of Rome and once a lecturer at the University of Paris. There could be no doubt that in bestowing the pallium upon Langton Innocent III had made a wise choice. The new archbishop was a famous scholar, theologian, and poet, an honest man and a devoted servant of the church. Nevertheless, the election of Innocent III's nominee was as irregular as the two previous contests held at Canterbury. Only the Canterbury monks present at Rome had taken part in the third election; it was not a "free" election in the sense prescribed by the canon law; and it broke the custom by which the king controlled the choice of archbishops and bishops.

John angrily refused to recognize the appointment. He threatened to stop the papal revenues flowing from England to Rome. He said he knew nothing of Langton, except that he had lived in France, the worst enemy of England. Heedless of menacing allusions to Thomas Becket, John took over the estates of Canterbury, forced several monks into exile, and defied the Pope. John apparently forgot, or did not know, that he was pitting himself against a veteran fighter whose agility was as formidable as his power. The biography of Innocent III is a long tale of superlative skill in diplomacy and successive chapters of political conquest. Against such a Pope, John had little chance of winning the contest.

In March, 1208, after futile parleys, Innocent placed an interdict upon England. All public church services were suspended; the bells were silent; no sacraments were given except the baptism of infants, extreme unction and, under certain restrictions, baptism, confirmation, and penance. The dead were buried in unconsecrated ground without the services of a priest. Marriages were performed only at the church porch; sermons were preached only in the churchyard. In an age of faith the interdict was a powerful weapon; the laymen of the land upon which it was imposed may well have felt that they ran the risk of damnation when they were forbidden to take part in the rites of the church and many of the sources of spiritual life were cut off.

John hastened to retaliate. Raging like a hunted boar, he showed his Angevin fire and obstinacy. He ordered all tenants of the crown to renew their homage; from the barons he suspected of being disloyal he took hostages. He seized the lands of the regular and secular clergy who obeyed the interdict, allowing them only a pittance for their daily food. The king's orders were executed zealously by royal officers. John publicly denounced, and privately connived at, the persecution of churchmen. Most of the bishops, having pronounced the interdict, fled from the kingdom. A few clergymen agreed to disobey the Pope, but not enough to lighten the weight of the interdict. At the same time, the seizure of church property enabled John to decrease taxation; the collection of aids and scutages temporarily ceased, a cause of widespread satisfaction. Among laymen, often resentful of papal interference, there was at first no strong opposition to the king's policy.

[handwritten notes in margin: 1209 / John Ex-communicated]

After two years the Pope warned John, his "dear son," that the papal bow was fully bent. In November, 1209, the arrow flew. Innocent III excommunicated the king. The fearful sentence cut John off from the services and sacraments of the church and damned his soul if he died before the curse was removed. Many of the king's supporters were filled with panic because the decree of excommunication meant that anybody who remained loyal to John was thereby placing his own soul in jeopardy. John was not cowed; he did not yield. His policy was to discourage others from surrendering to the Pope by increasing their fear of the king. From his tenants he took new oaths of homage and more hostages. Means were found to persuade the waverers. John's mercenaries were increased; their wages were paid from the spoils of the church, the Cistercian wool, the tallage from the towns, the coffers of the Jews. John's officers were faithful to his gold; and they would remain so, while the gold lasted.

By such means John stifled open doubt and objection among his subjects. But these expedients could be used only for a short time. Violence and terror invited opposition. Slowly the surging domestic discontent grew into an underground movement and this, in turn, was to become an open revolt. Public anger was not by any means solely the result of John's battle with the church. It came from scores of sources. John arbitrarily used his despotic power to override justice and morality. He condoned gross maladministration in his government and his courts. He made exorbitant financial demands upon every class. As the tyranny tightened disaffection ran through all classes, from baron to peasant.

John saw the gathering clouds of baronial conspiracy when he called the feudal levies to deal with a Welsh rebellion in 1212. Suddenly aware of his danger, the king abandoned the Welsh expedition, dismissed his English troops, and sent abroad for more mercenaries. He hanged twenty-eight prisoners he had seized from the Welsh chieftains. He forced the English barons he suspected of treasonable inclinations to surrender their children into his hands as hostages. To gain support among the lower classes John promised to reduce the severity of the forest laws. He set up royal commissions to hear grievances; he cut down the tolls collected by the plundering sheriffs. Despite these gestures, the tide of public hostility continued to roll heavily against the king. A mad hermit prophesied that John had less than a year to reign. From castle to cottage rumors raced through England that the royal cause was desperate.

At this point the shrewd Innocent III struck again. He declared John deposed, released his subjects from their allegiance, and gave his kingdom to Philip Augustus of France. The rapacious Philip answered with alacrity to the papal request that he carry out the sentence of deposition by invading England. The wily Innocent III never intended

Philip to conquer England; the union of the two crowns would diminish papal power in both countries. Innocent's purpose was to frighten John. Philip, however, took the Pope's proposal in good faith. He began to gather an army for the invasion of England. A papal legate slipped across the Channel to tell John that the French invasion force was growing more formidable every hour.

In April, 1213, John, seeing that the game was up, changed his tactics. He surrendered to Innocent III and consented to accept Langton as archbishop of Canterbury; to restore all church property; to pay compensation to all those he had despoiled; to recall the exiled monks and bishops; to give an amnesty to all the lesser clergy; and to take part in a future crusade. John, probably at his own suggestion, made over his kingdom of England and Ireland to the papacy and then received it back as a fief, for which he agreed to pay a tribute of 1,000 marks a year. The homage was really of small importance, for John in fact incurred no obligations beyond the annual payments of 1,000 marks. The arrangement was not a novelty in Europe: five other European rulers had earlier become vassals of the Pope. For John it was a wise move on the chessboard. He now had the papal support against his barons; and the dismayed Philip Augustus would certainly not be permitted to invade a fief of the papacy.

When the humiliating surrender was complete John was released from the excommunication by Stephen Langton. A year later, after John had satisfied the Pope by carrying out the terms of his capitulation, the interdict was removed. The bells rang out and the services of the church were performed once more.

John had lost Normandy. He had been worsted in his protracted struggle against the Pope. With Philip Augustus and Innocent III he had made an ignominious peace. But peace had not been made with his subjects. Opposition to the king was rising, and for good reason. The last years of John's reign showed his utter failure to placate the wrath of his barons. And most important of all, the domestic disaffection produced Magna Carta, the first major attempt of embattled tenants-in-chief to keep the king within the limits of the feudal law.

MAGNA CARTA

There is no doubt that John was guilty of numerous vices and crimes, of vicious and arbitrary acts. On the other hand, John was active and able, a hard and calculating king in a turbulent age. His royal demesne was small. The country's income was growing and John could not tap it. His royal expenses were rising and he could not stamp them down. Hence he tried new, ingenious, and often unscrupulous expedients to raise money.

The English barons refused to go to wage war in France because they saw no hope of winning back the lost Angevin possessions. They were also determined to check their king and compel him to adhere to feudal custom. John sailed for France with mercenary troops and left the barons behind. When he returned without victory to England he tried in vain to attack and smash baronial opposition. In January, 1215, his recalcitrant vassals presented a series of demands. John asked them to wait until Easter and seized the intervening weeks to gather support. But the support he gained was not enough. On June 15, 1215, the king met his barons at Runnymede beside the Thames and placed his seal to a provisional list of the baronial demands. During the next few days the details of a final document were discussed and settled. The result was the sixty-three clauses of Magna Carta.

Magna Carta proclaimed no abstract principles. It simply redressed wrongs. The significant thing is that the wrongs were substantially those of all bad government in any age and the principles of redress have altered little through the centuries. Each clause was directed to a specific problem. The language was simple and direct, the language of practical men. John was forced to agree to many things in Magna Carta. The church was to have "its rights entire and its liberties inviolate." There was to be no more overriding of feudal law and custom by force or chicanery in the collection of aids and reliefs. No scutage or aid, except those provided by feudal law, were to be levied without the consent of the great council. John also agreed to stop plundering the fiefs that fell under his wardship. The merchants were to be protected. Abuses of the forest laws and all "bad customs" were to be ended. Several clauses referred to the law and the law courts. "To no one will we sell, to no one will we deny or delay right or justice," ran the famous Clause 40. "No freeman shall be captured or imprisoned or disseised or outlawed or exiled or in any way destroyed, nor will we go against him or send against him, except by the lawful judgment of his peers and by the law of the land," stated the celebrated Clause 39 about which historians have engaged in so much controversy, discussion, and skilled speculation and scholarship.

The sanctions by which it was hoped to enforce the charter were important. The barons knew that John must be restrained by the threat of coercion into keeping his promises. The king was to return all hostages; discharge several unpopular officials; restore all property he had seized and all illegal fines; grant a general pardon; discharge all his mercenaries. By the terms of Clause 61 the barons were to elect twenty-five of their number to whom complaints could be made about any violations of the charter. Any four could call the king's attention to such transgressions, and if no remedial steps were taken with forty days, the four barons were to report the delinquency of the king to the committee of twenty-five. "And those twenty-five barons, together with the community of the entire country, shall distress and injure us in all ways possible . . . until they secure redress according to their own decision . . . and when redress has been made they shall be as obedient to us as they were before." The humiliated John also promised to make his subjects swear obedience to the mandates of the twenty-five barons.

In 1215 the barons could think of no constitutional method of checking John. Hence they adopted the clumsy expedient of legalizing the general right of insurrection and civil war. It was a crude way of protecting Magna Carta; but in 1215 there was no conception of any other effective method. In any event, the meaning and intention of the barons was clear enough. They were determined to enforce upon the king what they considered to be the essential principles of the "fundamental law" of their day.

Most nineteenth century scholars believed and asserted that Magna Carta was a golden milepost on the road to national liberty. They were right about some things, wrong about others. Magna Carta was reissued in 1216 and again in 1217, each time with many revisions. Under succeeding kings it was frequently confirmed, as in the famous Confirmation of the Charters of 1297. It became a symbol and a precedent because it contained the idea that there were certain things a king might not do. The concept of royal responsibility was to be carried over to the modern state. Long after almost everything else in feudalism had fallen into ruins, the contract principle continued to relate the sovereign to his subjects and became a part of the origin of limited monarchy.

The principle that John was bound by what the barons considered a feudal contract became expanded into the broader idea that in some directions any king is bound by law. He must respect the rights of his subjects, although those "rights" were not easily defined. If the king violates these laws and rights, said the expanded principle, he may be compelled by force to observe them. Magna Carta in 1215 was a feudal document and record. It contained almost no new law and asserted no new liberties. It was really a rather conservative product of baronial labors.

Probably nobody expected the charter settlement to be anything but a truce. The northern barons hurried home to prepare for war against the king. John summoned French mercenaries and freebooters and sent messengers to Rome to ask the Pope to pronounce the agreement invalid. Innocent III was anxious to have John go on a crusade. He had no desire to have the strength of his vassal king sapped by recalcitrant and factious barons. In August, 1215, he declared that Magna Carta was unjust, unlawful, and void. Both sides mustered their forces. A friendly Philip Augustus sent the barons siege guns and promised more later. In October, 1215, civil war broke out.

At first John was fairly successful. Then several barons offered the English throne to Louis, son of Philip Augustus. Thousands of

Englishmen allied themselves with the French forces that began to flow across the Channel. That fact alone showed the level of fear and hatred roused by the name of John. When Innocent III died in July, 1216, even the future support of Rome for the king's cause was uncertain.

In October, 1216, disaster overtook John. He lost much of his baggage and treasure when his forces were caught by the quicksands and rushing tide of the sea arm called the Wash. A few days later John died at Newark. He was buried at Worcester. The French burial place of his house belonged to his house no more.

THE MINORITY OF HENRY III

Within a few days John's nine-year-old son was crowned Henry III at Gloucester in the presence of four bishops and a few barons. The thankless office of regent of England was held three years by the aged William Marshal, earl of Pembroke. The able and experienced Marshal had faithfully served England for twenty years. He was honest, blunt, and universally respected. As soon as Marshal took control of affairs he set out with his usual energy to restore order. Several administrative, financial, and judicial reforms were undertaken to conciliate the disaffected and strengthen the disjointed royalist party. On land and sea the French were defeated. In September, 1217, France made peace and the last of the French invaders left English soil.

In 1219 Marshal died and with his death his power was divided. Marshal himself committed the young king to the care of the papal legate, Pandulph, who was devoted to Henry III and the royal interests. Pandulph, attempting to wield the full authority of regent, failed to overcome the power and hostility of Hubert de Burgh, the justiciar, and the crafty Peter des Roches, the Poitevin bishop of Winchester and tutor of the king. The pervasive spirit of disorder was not easily repressed in the government. Baronial jealousies often threatened to disrupt the weak machinery of the regency. The hostility between Stephen Langton, archbishop of Canterbury, and Pandulph, the papal legate, grew bitter. Hubert de Burgh and Peter des Roches hated each other. Each waited for an hour to come when he might destroy his enemy.

After Pandulph was recalled to Rome, Peter des Roches and Hubert de Burgh began to quarrel more violently. Stephen Langton, archbishop of Canterbury, was the ally of Hubert. Peter des Roches, for his part, was the leader and outstanding representative of the foreigners he had brought over from Poitou. His nephew, for example, held the office of sheriff in sixteen counties and pocketed the income from each. Peter was also close to the young king Henry III. This enemy of Hubert de Burgh was a soldier turned churchman for preferment, slow at the Gospel, quick at financial accounts, and a tricky politician.

Hubert's policies continued to arouse the anger of some English barons. The justiciar, for example, insisted that those who had unlawfully seized or fraudulently taken over lands, castles, and sheriffdoms should hand them back to the rightful owners. When some of the noble brigands defied Hubert's authority and even the king's writ, they were sharply brought to heel by punitive expeditions. Stephen Langton helped with bell, book, candle, and threats of excommunication against those who resisted the royal power and added to the disaffection of the realm. The earl of Chester, for example, was summarily forced to disgorge three castles and three sheriffdoms at one time. The dangers of organized rebellion by the baronial cliques were checked only by forthright action and ceaseless vigilance on the part of Hubert de Burgh and his allies.

THE YEARS OF MISRULE

In 1227 the council formally declared Henry III free from all the restrictions imposed upon him during his minority. The new king was devout, artistic, refined, a patron of art and letters. He had none of the evil characteristics of his father. At the same time, Henry was amiable, vain, capricious, a poor judge of men. Physically, he was not wanting in courage: he proved it on the battlefield. Morally, he was feeble. A contemporary said that Henry's heart was as easily molded as wax and it was a pity that those who set themselves to mold it were often evil men. Henry adored Edward the Confessor and went far beyond the Confessor in superstition. The best part of his piety was his taste for church art, which he displayed to advantage in rebuilding Westminster Abbey. Dante put him in the part of purgatory reserved for children and simpletons. Weak, easily bullied, and impractical, Henry was still obstinate and fond of his prerogative. Nor did he ever forget that the church had protected him in his minority.

Henry III was certain that he could recover the lost provinces in France. In 1229 he called upon his vassals to go with him to Aquitaine. Despite the strong opposition of Hubert de Burgh, who wanted no English blood and treasure spent in France, Henry had planned a great campaign. When the troops gathered at Portsmouth, there were not enough ships to transport them to France. Henry blamed his justiciar for failing to provide the necessary ships. He called Hubert a traitor, accused him of being in the pay of France, and rushed upon him with drawn sword. The invasion of France was postponed until the spring of 1230. All of the campaign was frightfully mismanaged. In September Henry claimed that his health made his return to England necessary and his army soon followed. Henry's grand design had collapsed.

Henry III and his justiciar also quarreled about papal taxation. The devout Henry wanted to pay all the levies imposed by the Pope.

Hubert de Burgh, his policy always insular and national, opposed both Pope and king. There was also widespread public anger at the papal appointment of Italian clergymen directly to English benefices. Several riots broke out against "beneficed aliens." A papal courier was slain near Dover. Hubert de Burgh was accused of conniving at these outrages and he probably did.

Henry III made a series of charges against Hubert de Burgh and dismissed him. For Hubert there was wide popular sympathy. Had he not stood up for the rights of Englishmen against the flood of foreigners? Peter des Roches had returned from a long visit to Rome and was restored to power in the royal household. Alien parasites swarmed over the Channel from Poitou, ravenous for place and plunder. Poitevin mercenary troops were imported to guard the court and the king. On these foreigners were lavished favors, honors, castles, gold, offices, profitable marriages, and the like. It seemed to make no difference that the English treasury was running low.

The baronage demanded that the foreigners should be sent home. In 1234 a baronial league, supported by revolting Welshmen, forced Henry to pack the Poitevins home. Peter des Roches went to Italy. Henry then began an experiment in personal rule. Wishing to imitate Continental methods of arbitrary government, he tried, to an increasing extent, to get along without baronial advisers. In the midst of fumbling activity the capricious Henry took another step. In 1236 he married Eleanor of Provence. The splendid ceremony lowered the level of the exchequer still more. Then the relatives and compatriots of the new queen descended like locusts from across the Channel. One of the queen's uncles was created the earl of Richmond; another became archbishop of Canterbury. Henry III's mother had married Hugh the Brown of Poitou after John's death and now Henry's four half brothers found spoils in England. The English barons complained that they were being treated as lackeys in their own land.

The domain of the crown continued to be reduced by improvident grants. By 1254 the royal debts of Henry III stood at about £235,000, many times his annual income. Foreign churchmen were drawing out of England about £47,000 annually, a sum greater than the regular royal revenue. There were loud objections to the financial exactions of the Pope. Because of Henry III's subservience to Rome the antipapal leaders could obtain no satisfaction from him. They had to look elsewhere.

In 1254 the Pope offered to confer the empty honor of the disputed crown of Sicily upon Edmund of Lancaster, Henry's second son. The Pope claimed that as suzerain of Sicily he could dispose of the crown. True, he was not in possession of Sicily and was, in fact, fighting the occupant of the throne. The Sicilian crown still had to be won. If Henry III wanted the prize for his son, he might have it, provided he could conquer Sicily. Henry, fresh from an unsuccessful campaign against the Welsh, welcomed the Pope's proposal, an offer that had already been twice rejected by Henry III's brother, Richard of Cornwall.

The uncautious Henry agreed to pay £90,000 to compensate the Pope for the expenses he had earlier incurred in fighting for Sicily; he also promised to find and equip an army to win Sicily for his son Edmund. In 1255 both the great council and the clergy refused to grant any money for this silly enterprise. Soon there was more disturbance in Wales. An abortive campaign in 1257 resulted in an inglorious retreat by Henry from the borderlands. The tide of public indignation mounted.

In April, 1258, the great council met, angry and turbulent. Henry feared Rome more than the barons and asked for a subsidy to help him pay an instalment due on the £90,000 he owed the Pope. The barons refused, and plainly told Henry that redress must precede supply. They announced that they intended to end the excesses of the royal administration. Henry, they asserted, must dismiss the aliens. He must sanction the appointment of a reform committee that would have complete control over the exchequer and full authority to reform the government. Knights of the shire were in attendance at this assembly and joined with the barons in presenting their demands to the king. Henry III, alarmed at the turn of events, submissively agreed to accept whatever was proposed. A reform committee, composed of twelve members of the king's party and twelve of the baronial group, was appointed to prepare a report for submission to the great council in June, 1258. The experiment in personal rule was at an end. Once again, as so often in the feudal age, royal power was to give way to baronial oligarchy.

THE PROVISIONS OF OXFORD

Leader of the rebelling barons was Simon de Montfort, earl of Leicester. His earldom had been inherited from his English grandmother; all the rest of his family were French. In 1230 he came to England and soon became a counsellor of Henry III and governor of Gascony. He was, it seemed, only another alien interloper. When de Montfort married the king's sister Eleanor in 1238 there was wide indignation among the more truly English barons. Soon, however, the inconstant Henry III began to quarrel with his brother-in-law, mainly about money. In 1240 de Montfort went on a crusade. Upon his return he joined the baronial opposition to the king.

In 1248 de Montfort was sent to restore order in Gascony. Many complaints about his arbitrary actions in France easily persuaded Henry III to bring him to public trial in 1252. The angry earl was acquitted and returned to Gascony to complete his task of defeating the king's Gascon enemies. When the suspicious Henry made a visit to

Gascony and added to the confusion by his arbitrary interference de Montfort's contempt increased. Early in 1254 the earl returned to England. There he became active once more in the baronial movement for reform. It was de Montfort who stood forward as leader of the barons in the critical days of April, 1258.

When the great council met at Oxford in June, 1258, they considered the "articles of complaint" against Henry III and passed the Provisions of Oxford, mainly prepared by the committee of twenty-four barons appointed in April. The political reforms set forth in the Provisions of Oxford in fact put the kingship into commission. A series of committees and commissions were appointed and all were responsible, not to the king but to the great council acting in the name of the king. The royal prerogative, it seemed, was to rest in the hands of the barons. All important administrative officials, such as the chancellor, justiciar, and treasurer, were to be appointed by and responsible to the barons; so, too, were the local officials, such as the sheriffs.

"For the common good of the whole kingdom," fifteen barons, including nine from the barons' party led by Simon de Montfort, were to form a standing committee, or permanent council, to supervise all divisions of the government. "And they shall have the power of advising the king in good faith concerning the government of the kingdom and concerning all matters that pertain to the king or the kingdom; and of amending and redressing everything they shall consider in need of amendment or redress." Even the king's ministers were responsible to the committee of fifteen. A second body of twelve, representing the great council, was ordered to meet with the fifteen barons three times a year to consult and join with them in exercising the functions of the great council; the great council itself might be called at any time. Twenty-four additional barons were appointed to consider the problem of aid to the king. The Provisions of Oxford, the work of the feudal baronage, was in fact the first stage of a new experiment in baronial government. The king submitted, for a time. Most of his foreign favorites went home.

The actual operation of the Provisions of Oxford was not successful. The barons disagreed among themselves. Some argued that no reforms should affect their own relations with their tenants. Others, including de Montfort, insisted that the welfare of all classes should be considered. In 1259 the Provisions of Westminster finally contained a list of reluctant concessions and supplementary reforms of particular value to the third estate. For example, the judicial powers of landlords were decreased; they were deprived of half their suitors.

In 1261 the Pope, Urban IV, was persuaded to absolve Henry III from his oath to obey the Provisions of Oxford. Henry asserted that there were only "a few malicious schemers" and he would deal with them. He gathered foreign mercenaries and dismissed the committee of fifteen. In January, 1264, Louis IX of France agreed to arbitrate the quarrel between Henry III and his barons. In the famous Mise of Amiens the saintly Louis decided in favor of Henry III. Simon de Montfort and the barons allied with him refused to accept the decision of Louis IX. The result of the French king's award was civil war in England.

THE BARONIAL WARS

To support the rebel army of de Montfort came numerous recruits from the liberal edges of society: younger nobles, commoners from the main cities of England, ecclesiastical reformers, many Oxford and Cambridge students, and the like. They were enthusiastic, but they were usually not trained soldiers. Even the London city militiamen, hastening to join the antiroyalist forces, were not very efficient in a military sense. On May 14, 1264, de Montfort, himself the greatest soldier in England, moved into Sussex and outwitted the king's commanders at the battle of Lewes. The position of Henry III and his son Prince Edward was hopeless and they surrendered. "Now England breathes in the hope of liberty," ran a poem of the day; "the English were despised like dogs, but now they have lifted up their heads and their foes are vanquished."

By the terms of a new capitulation, usually called the Mise of Lewes, a government similar to that set up by the Provisions of Oxford was again established. A baronial council of nine replaced the council of fifteen. The new council was headed by Simon de Montfort. Aware of the weakness and dissension always to be found in baronial ranks, de Montfort set out at once to gain the support of the country gentry and the burgesses of the towns. There is no doubt that his interest in the welfare of the middle class was sincere. To the meetings of the great council, or Parliament, summoned under the auspices of de Montfort in 1265 came two representatives from every shire and two burgesses from every city and borough that supported the baronial cause. Representatives of the middle class from the shires had been summoned to earlier sessions of the great council; but it is almost certain that representatives of the towns had never been called before. In de Montfort's assembly of 1265 they were present to give strength to his cause. Only those twenty-three barons who had consistently supported de Montfort were summoned to this packed and partisan meeting of the great council. The barons were generally opposed to sharing their political power with the middle classes. This aristocratic point of view was not easily changed; it was clearly stated nearly six hundred years later during the debates on the reform bill of 1832.

The liberal actions of de Montfort drove several barons, alarmed at his impetuous, radical tendencies, over to the royalist camp. They could not share de Montfort's enthusiasm for political reform. Several nobles were also lost to de Montfort's cause because they were alienated by his arrogant and arbitrary temper. Consequently Simon was followed by far fewer barons in 1265 than had served under his banners in 1264. To the royalist nobles who had refused to lay down their arms after Lewes were now added the conservative barons who had deserted de Montfort. In May, 1265, Prince Edward escaped from his captors and joined his father's rising forces.

The position of de Montfort was precarious. On August 1, his son was defeated at Kenilworth by Prince Edward. On the night of August 3 de Montfort's forces camped at Evesham, a town near Worcester enclosed on three sides by the curving river Avon. There was only one bridge across the river. In the morning Prince Edward's soldiers blocked the bridge and threw a superior force across the neck of land north and northwest of the town. The experienced Simon saw that he had been outwitted. "By St. James," he is said to have exclaimed, "they come on bravely; but it was from me that they learned this order." The royalist forces, far superior in numbers, withstood a desperate attempt of de Montfort to break through their lines. Before he fell, stabbed in the back, Simon's two-handed sword killed many of the king's men. But with his death the cause of the rebelling barons who followed his flag was lost. Those who survived the butchery of the three-hour battle scattered to safety.

The partisan and transient baronial controls established by the Provisions of Oxford and the Mise of Lewes collapsed at Evesham. The king's appointees went back to their jobs. The avenging royalists hunted down the supporters of de Montfort. The Londoners, always loyal to de Montfort's cause, were fined; for a short time the city charter was taken away. Campaigns against the barons who continued heavy resistance at Kenilworth and Ely prolonged the rebellion; not until 1267 were the last flames of revolt extinguished. In that year, by the terms of the Statute of Marlborough, several of the Provisions of Westminster were confirmed, mainly because of the power of the earl of Gloucester. But the limitations imposed upon the king by the Provisions of Oxford were not restored. Once again the tradition of baronial opposition to the crown had been renewed; another chapter in the growth of the background and idea of limited monarchy had been added to the accumulating precedents. The events of 1265 were signposts; in themselves they accomplished little.

Simon de Montfort was widely regarded by the people as a patriot and an idealist, a martyr in the cause of freedom. For many years he was worshipped as a saint, a custom encouraged by his allies the friars. "He had been the special friend of those who were powerless to help their friends." Impatience, perhaps, was mainly responsible for his downfall. He violently broke the law; he alienated the timid; he offended those who had vested interests. Simon and his fellows went beyond Magna Carta and took almost all power away from the king, failing to appreciate the importance of the royal prerogative controls, particularly as a balancing factor in the stage of political evolution attained in the thirteenth century. Thus, instead of a royal despotism England was faced with the threat of a revolutionary dictatorship of barons.

Simon himself would have admitted the middle class to a part in the government; but the barons associated with him refused to share their power with men of lower birth and lesser substance. They wanted the king to govern in accordance with the wishes of their class, and their class alone. As the reader has noted, there were other causes of jealousies and discords. Many barons broke with de Montfort and his vision seemed to perish with him at Evesham. Only slowly did the evolution of Parliament permit the representation of interests other than those of the barons. It was fortunate that Prince Edward, who had learned so much from de Montfort, was to be England's next king because Edward was "one of those people whom revolutions teach." He was also to profit by the fact that the administrative machine set up by Henry II had operated successfully even in the disordered days of Henry III.

Prince Edward, whom Henry III had named for Edward the Confessor, bore most of the burdens of state before he left upon a crusade in 1270. His father, the frail but victorious champion of absolutism, was weary with age and battle. He would probably have made a good priest; he was a poor king. On November 16, 1272, as Henry lay dying at Westminster, the Londoners rioted outside: the poor were battling with the rich about the election of a new mayor. The dispute was prophetic of a new age in which Simon de Montfort would probably have been more content than Henry III.

Chapter 6

THE EARLY MIDDLE AGES
THE GOOD SOCIETY

IN DIFFERENT chapters of their history men have held various concepts about what is the "highest good," the *summum bonum*, for individuals and for states. Hence the expression of ideas in institutionalized forms has changed from age to age. The "highest good" of the Middle Ages became something far different, for example, in the eighteenth century, when God the Mathematician often replaced God the Heavenly Father. Human beings have frequently shown a disconcerting tendency to ascribe to God the attributes that they themselves value most highly at a particular moment in the time scale. Our own age, with its varieties of religions and political experience, its mass production of automobiles and neuroses, its conquests of Nature, has developed climates of opinion and a series of values that would have been quite unintelligible to medieval man.

In the Middle Ages the conception of a good society was one of a unified and hierarchical social and political structure in which a man was in his "proper station" as an archbishop or yeoman. The good for any individual was not deemed to be in equality with all other men. The ideal was rather in the finding of the niche that was best in terms of a man's peculiar abilities. Despite this emphasis upon the blessings of hierarchy and order, the economic aspect of English medieval life was marked by considerable individualism. Guilds and local crafts produced largely for local consumption. The hierarchical chains that existed there were mainly self-imposed and local. The organic communal idea of hierarchy in state and society thus existed side by side with a high degree of varying local economic and political freedom. That is one of the reasons why the smaller units of the parishes and counties were later so important as fountainheads of British democracy.

In such restless years as those of the late fourteenth century or the nineteenth, the social order changed swiftly. The twelfth and thirteenth centuries, on the contrary, were reasonably stable. There was economic

89

expansion, confidence, and prosperity; faith in the church and its teaching; increasing security in this world and the bright certainty of salvation for the sons of the church in the next. For all of Europe the ninth and tenth centuries had been at the bottom of an economic decline that had begun in the first century. Out of the great depression came recovery. In the late eleventh century Europeans stood at the beginning of a period of increasing prosperity. The Saracens and vikings had cut the life lines of the Roman Empire. In the twelfth century the Italian cities began a counteroffensive and led in the revival of commerce which came with the Crusades. In the north the pace of economic life began to quicken.

Population increased steadily. Prices rose. The great cathedrals of Europe were not built by a poor society or by men decadent and slothful. Late in the twelfth century, for example, the chronicle of Jocelin of Brakeland, afterwards so useful to Thomas Carlyle, recorded the work of the Benedictine Abbot Samson at Bury St. Edmunds: "Abbot Samson restored the old halls and the ruined halls through which the kites and crows flew; and he built chapels and constructed inner rooms and upper stories in many places where there had been no buildings, except barns. . . . He made many clearings and brought land into cultivation. . . . He built barns and cattle sheds, being anxious above all things to dress the land for tillage. . . . The abbot further appeared to prefer the active to the contemplative life and praised good officials more than good monks."

It is against this background that the early medieval panorama moved; and it is only in terms of these mingling cross-currents of stability and change that the pattern of the early Middle Ages can be explained and understood.

VILLAGE AND TOWN

The anatomy of rural society changed little from the eleventh to the fourteenth centuries. So long as feudalism prevailed the manor remained the unit of community organization. The word "manor" is still convenient and its meaning is still vague; there was no such thing as a "typical" manor. Energetic scholars have brought forth few solid conclusions about the origin of the manor, and the historian must admit some degree of inaccuracy when seeking for general characteristics to aid in definition. In any event, the manorial practices, described earlier, remained almost unchanged from generation to generation. On occasion the three-field system of field rotation was replaced by a two-field rotation. Otherwise there was small alteration in the habits of father and son.

The village community within the manor doubtless became more coherent and active as seigneurial ties were loosened in the fourteenth century and later as the lord's demesnes were consolidated and leased out; but in the twelfth and thirteenth centuries the seigneurial control over the open-field processes was probably as complete as it had been in the days of William the Conqueror. The commutation of services in labor to rents in money was a slow process, hardly beginning until the fourteenth century. When the rental of lands for money did become a common practice the whole basis of the manorial economic structure was, of course, undermined. As the villeins were emancipated in the fourteenth century and later, the economic form of the medieval world slowly began to collapse.

Before the stirrings of the fourteenth century the village inhabitants seldom moved far afield from their homes; usually they lived and died on the same manor. "Nothing is more noticeable in the early Middle Ages than the utter passivity of the mass of the people . . . their silence may be heard." A modern scholar as aptly remarked that "customs did not so change in the Middle Ages that what went on in one year necesarily did not go on one hundred years later." To his conclusion that the medieval years were "not wholly a Gothic idyll or a wretched state of poverty and oppression," the same writer added a wise comment: "Certainly the physical conditions of a husbandman's life were hard, but nothing is more commonplace or more often forgotten than the words 'Man does not live by bread alone.' "

The increase of population, as noted earlier, was considerable. In 1066 probably about 2,000,000 people lived in England and Wales. By about 1340 the total had risen to more than 4,000,000. The main reason for this increase was a fuller use of the soil. The magnates of church and state reclaimed much waste land. For example, the monks of Canterbury made large pastures for sheep and cattle by embankments protecting the mud flats. They drained and dried large areas of the great triangle of Romney Marsh, rescued from the sea in Roman times. Rivers were embanked in many parts of England; forests were cleared away. These steps added to the production of food; as the means of subsistence increased, the tide of population rose.

Earlier in this chapter it was remarked that English towns shared in the expansion of European commerce, and they profited by it. The increased stability brought by a stronger central government usually protected their trade, even in the days of baronial turbulence. London, with a population of about 40,000, grew steadily larger; it combined the advantages of an inland center and a seaport. The Thames estuary tides enabled ships to move up and down without long delays. Great roads thrust out their fingers to the north, west, and south. London was the center of government, more important as the Normans and Angevins increased the power and business of the crown. It obtained successive instalments of liberties, such as those granted in the famous charters of William I and Henry I.

Bristol, with a population of about 12,000 and second only to

London, had easy access to the sea. A great bridge over the Avon opened a fine road eastward. In the north, York was the main commercial city. Of the 200 towns in 1300, ranging in population from 1,000 to 5,000, several were blessed by particularly fortunate locations. Portsmouth, Yarmouth, Plymouth, and Southampton had good harbors. Such towns as Gloucester, Oxford, and Stratford were on rivers, important in inland trade. Other towns were near monasteries or castles, always good centers for commerce.

At first the English towns had usually been dominated by the king or by lesser feudal lords, subject to feudal burdens. Then, slowly, the townsmen began to bargain for special privileges, such as those earlier described in the case of London. Most English towns were on the royal demesne and hence negotiated directly with the king. The royal exchequer was always hungry, and for a sum of money the king granted charters of freedom. Henry II and Richard I sold many charters; John, the great "charter-monger," granted most of all. These charters usually gave the towns the right to pay a lump sum, the *firma burgi,* to the king instead of various taxes, rents, and tolls; local town authorities collected these dues from the inhabitants and the king's sheriff had no right to interfere. Many towns also obtained the right to hold a town court for all cases outside royal jurisdiction. Several held the right to elect local officials; to set up an independent merchant guild to regulate the town trade; to be exempted from paying certain restrictive tolls levied by some lords in return for the privilege of trading in their feudal estate areas.

Towns not in the royal demesne usually obtained similar privileges by paying the local lords. Those on church lands often had a more difficult time because the church was always reluctant to sell its privileges; and it was, of course, a perpetual corporation. The struggles between town and monastery were particularly bitter and there were often serious riots. In 1327, for example, the townsmen of Bury invaded the monastery of Bury St. Edmunds and put the abbots and the monks in prison. Then they "mowed the meadows, felled the trees, and fished the ponds of the abbey, taking away the grass, trees, and fish."

The government of the towns, under charter rights, was usually vested in a few officials elected by the burgesses. The burgesses were originally those who had met certain qualifications, such as the ownership of land, or a dwelling within the city walls (burgage) and the payment of local taxes. In the beginning most town dwellers were burgesses and the local government was therefore quite democratic. By 1300, however, the control of government in several towns was beginning to pass into the hands of a few men. This oligarchical development continued to such an extent that by the end of the fifteenth century most town councils had ceased to be democratic at all. The members of these small councils, chosen by a restricted group of electors, ran municipal affairs, usually to the advantage of themselves and their friends. Not until 1835 were any major steps taken to loosen the tight structure of the municipal corporations.

Many churches were built in these early medieval towns. Norwich, for example, once had over fifty. Town builders and artisans, filled with local pride, raised beautiful structures to glorify God and to stand as evidence of their skill. The great guildhalls, the public or community buildings of the towns, were often magnificently constructed and decorated. Medieval artisans had no need to hurry. No age of speed or swelling profit motives had as yet forced them to hasten overmuch. They were often not greatly concerned with becoming; they were content to be.

The darker side of medieval life is often exaggerated. In the midst of disease, stagnant filth, and poverty there was still some laughter and beauty. Through noisy, stinking, and narrow streets the merchants, housewives, vagabonds, and ruffians swarmed about their business. To our descendants the conditions of the twentieth century may seem somewhat less than satisfactory. Arrogant in our achievements, and proud of our historical hindsight, it is easy for us to stress the evils of the early Middle Ages. It is likewise good sense to remember that human beings in any age have shown themselves remarkably adaptable creatures; the general nature of Western mankind in the mass has remained fairly constant; the man of the thirteenth century did not know what amenities of civilization lay unborn in the womb of time; therefore he made the most of what he had. Knowing nothing about modern sanitation, for example, he did not bewail its absence.

GUILDS, TRADE, FINANCE

Behind the strength of their wealth and their walls, medieval townsmen were often suspicious and jealous of "foreigners" from outside. The "foreign" trader had to pay a toll to be admitted through the town gates. In most early medieval towns, the trade was controlled by an organization known as the merchant guild. Private capitalism and local politics were inextricably mingled. In the merchant guild were all the merchants, the buyers and sellers of goods, who wanted to hold a monopoly of the internal trade of their town. They often stood together to obtain special privileges from the king or the noble or churchman in whose demesne the town stood. The merchant guilds usually had codes of law by which all members were rigidly controlled. The regulation of community prices, for example, was very strict. The seller must not make excessive profits. There were also royal controls. For instance, the "assize" of bread and the "assize" of ale set a "just" price, based upon the market price of wheat and barley.

Men who violated such guild or "assize" rules or who were proved guilty of fraudulent practices were punished severely. The central and municipal government and the guilds cooperated in attempting to establish and maintain a sound and nationally uniform system of weights and measures. Both king and guildsmen tried to stop engrossing, or the buying of a crop before it was harvested; forestalling, or the "cornering" of a market by speculators who bought up goods before they reached the market so that prices would be forced up; regrating, or buying in the market in order to sell at a higher price. The guilds also protected their members, so far as was possible, from being badly used in other towns. Several guilds resembled modern "clubs" and "brotherhoods" in their charitable activities; they often visited the sick, looked after the indigent families of deceased members, attended in a full assembly the funeral of a merchant "brother," and distributed charity to the poor. They were rather conservative bodies, not inclined to encourage initiative or invention.

In the thirteenth century there grew up alongside the merchant guilds the craft guilds, composed of all men engaged in one particular craft or "mystery." For example, the masons, weavers, carpenters, goldsmiths, ironmongers, tanners, fishmongers, and shoemakers all had their own craft guilds to regulate the affairs of their trade. Each guild included all the workers in the town who practised its craft. No man could engage in any particular craft until he became a member of the guild. As the years passed it became increasingly difficult to obtain membership. The guilds later developed the general rule that a period of apprenticeship had to be served before a man could enter a trade. After an apprentice had worked under contract with a master of a trade for a definite term, usually seven years, he became a journeyman. In time, if he could accumulate enough money to start a shop of his own, he might become a master craftsman.

The artisans of the craft guilds regulated the size and quality of their products. They supervised many other things. For example, a butcher was forbidden to sew the fat from good meat on lean to deceive his customers. For the welfare of the craft they fixed wages, hours of labor, quantity of production, and sometimes prices. They tried to keep a monopoly of the market for their goods. Many of the craft guilds were also benevolent, religious, and social organizations similar to the merchant guilds. They had patron saints and processions on holy days. They provided money for masses for dead members. They looked after the brethren of the trade who were ill, aged, poor, or in trouble.

These guilds, or "companies," also aided in education and founded several grammar schools. They frequently performed religious plays for the entertainment of the town and themselves. These plays, often presented annually, were usually prepared with considerable care and enthusiasm. In the larger towns, such as Coventry, Chester, and York, the beginnings of the English drama were in part traceable to these events. From the "cycles" of mystery and morality plays and the later interludes played in a presentation of a craft guild or in tavern courts or churchyards it was not a long step to the "plays" of comedy and tragedy in the sixteenth century.

In the late fourteenth century, as the interest of masters and journeymen began to diverge, separate journeymen's guilds, or "yeomen's guilds," arose. In some respects this event marked the beginning of the great division between employers and artisans that foreshadowed the final separation of capital and labor interests characteristic of a later industrial age. Meanwhile, the English workers who belonged to no guilds, such as the miners, moved into similar types of organizations. For example, the tin miners belonged to "stannary" associations, usually rather completely under the control of the mine owners. Here, as in the case of the craft and merchant guilds, a later day brought a labor and capital division within the associations on a basis quite unfamiliar to the Middle Ages.

Almost every town had weekly markets. On "market day" the farmers brought their produce to sell to the townsmen. With the money they got for their eggs or hogs they bought goods and groceries from the shops. Once or twice a year a "fair" was held when traders from other localities in England and from foreign lands came to exchange goods and ideas. These fairs were held under a special permit from the king, usually outside the town in the "fair grounds." Booths and stalls were erected; the voices of hawkers and barkers rose above the chatter of the crowds. These fairs were almost always held under the monopoly control of a private person, usually a lord or a bishop, who had paid for the royal permit and had to realize a profit by charging a sales tax and rental fees for the booths and stalls.

In the main wholesale centers of England and Europe the fairs were huge assemblies; merchant traders came from many countries; the volume of business sales and wholesale contract delivery arrangements was large. Many of the greater English fairs were arranged to fall on different dates so that the traders, as well as the moving swarm of jugglers and other sideshow artists, could travel from place to place. The large fair at Stourbridge opened on September 18 and lasted for three weeks. It controlled the trade of the eastern counties and much of the export-import trade of the Baltic Sea region. Winchester, lying between London and Southampton, held its great fair for the southeast from August 31 to September 16. These fairs, and others such as those at St. Ives and Northampton, attracted foreign and native import and export merchants, local businessmen, the bailiffs of manors seeking a mass-purchase supply of goods for the coming year, and all the lesser fair-following individuals hungry for profit and pleasure.

To deal speedily with disputes, petty cases of thievery, and general misdemeanors, the proprietor of the fair held a rather informal court called the "pie powder" court, a corruption of the French phrase "pied poudré" or dusty foot. In this court dusty-footed peddlers, pickpockets, and respectable but disputing merchants received summary disposal of their cases on a basis of equity and the "law merchant" developed as an international customary code through the centuries.

The flow of English exports inevitably increased as the volume of domestic and foreign trade expanded. As was earlier noted, the twelfth and thirteenth centuries marked a period of almost constant prosperity except for the darkness brought by the famine of 1257–1259. In foreign trade the great cargoes of English wool led the list of English exports. Most of the wool went to the looms of the skilled weavers of Flanders. Hides, lead, tin, grain, salt meats, coarse cloths, iron, and sheepskins were also exported in increasing quantities. The nobles and the wealthy bourgeoisie, their interest in trade with the Near East quickened by the crusades, imported spices, dyes, wax, drugs, wines, silks, and jewels. From the Baltic regions came furs, tar, silver, and fish through the trade arteries of the Hanseatic league. The wines of Gascony and the Rhineland were found on many an upper class English table.

Most of this foreign trade was looked upon as being between towns rather than between nation states. For example, the merchants of London traded directly with the merchants of Paris. The central governments of France and England seldom interfered. To a Plymouth merchant a trader from Bristol was in many ways as much a "foreigner" as a trader from Lisbon. This local or municipal idea of foreign and domestic trade was long in dying. Only slowly, too, did the export trade of England pass into the hands of Englishmen. In the twelfth and thirteenth centuries most English exports, despite the improvement of England's shipping position, were sent out of England by foreign wholesale merchants who came over to England and bought and exported the goods they wanted.

Many of the alien Hanseatic, Flemish, and Gascon merchants, as well as the Bardi Society of Florence and the Lucca Society, obtained through negotiation important and formidable concessions from English kings in return for money payments. They were sometimes permitted to live in a separate guild or corporate hanse, to have their own warehouses, to be freed from payment of certain tolls, to trade throughout England, and even to dabble in retail trade. The Hanseatic League men, for example, had a great *kontor,* or fortified headquarters, in London, on the spot where the Cannon Street station now stands.

Late in the thirteenth century a number of English merchants stood together to advance their business interests by obtaining a monopoly on the export of wool, hides, and tin. They were called the Merchants of the Staple, the oldest of English trading corporations. Here began the monopolistic trading company, particularly characteristic in a later age. In medieval England the name "staple" meant a designated town where certain goods were to be bought and sold, a steady market. Thus, for a long time, England's Calais was the "staple" port through which all wool must come to be sold, the mart for European buyers. In 1297 Edward I set up certain "staple" ports within England so that the royal revenue taxes could be collected more easily. Specified "staple" commodities, such as wool, hides, and tin, moved through these "staple" ports.

Foreigners in England controlled the financial side of business. In the Middle Ages the lending of money at interest was called *usury* usury, and usury was called a sin. It was "a false and abominable contract, under colour and cover of good and lawful trading," which "ruins the honour and soul of the agent, and sweeps away the goods and property of him who appears to be accommodated." Christians were forbidden to lend money. The Jews, however, were quite willing to do it. Many had come to England in the wake of William the Conqueror. They were not citizens; they lived in segregated areas by themselves; they did not usually enter into agriculture or business enterprises in the towns. In the years before the development of anything similar to modern credit or banking operations the alien Jews became the great moneylenders. Where kings permitted them to carry on their lending the Jews profited because money was scarce and they could command high interest rates. The Norman and Angevin rulers often taxed the accumulated wealth of the Jews, "the king's sponges," very heavily. Riots against the Jews, particularly during the years of the crusades, were frequent. In 1290 Edward I ordered about 16,000 of them to leave England. Until the days of Oliver Cromwell few Jewish feet touched English soil.

Even before the Jews had gone the Italians had commenced operations to break the Jewish strangle hold. They were skilled in the new procedures of deposit and credit developed in Italy as a result of the availability of liquid capital. These Italians, with their knowledge of bills of exchange and insurance and the like, were more than moneylenders, "usurious Christians." They were also approaching many modern banking methods. Several great Italian companies soon had representatives in England. Many were from Lombardy and hence the area of their operations was to be called Lombard Street, still a financial center of London. It was not long before a number of English financiers appeared; they later helped to finance the Hundred Years' War and the Wars of the Roses. In the sixteenth century, as the new age of commercial capitalism dawned, Englishmen were reaching towards control of their own high finance and money market.

THE RISE OF THE UNIVERSITIES

From these shaping changes in the economic pattern of England there was slowly emerging a formidable challenge to the feudal order.

In the reasonably quiet and stable days of the twelfth and thirteenth centuries several other silent movements arose, prophetic of the age of unrest in the fourteenth century. One of these was the appearance and growth of the universities.

Before the twelfth century renaissance of learning and thought, the monasteries and the collegiate and cathedral schools of the church had maintained the flickering lamps of learning. In western Christendom there was not much education outside the church. Intellectual life was not, and could not be, widely diffused. The monks trained their novices; the secular clergy instructed other boys not intended for the cloister. In the twelfth century and later several new schools were established, particularly by the merchant and craft guilds. These were called grammar schools because Latin grammar was studied more than any other subject. Logic and rhetoric were combined with Latin grammar to form what was called the _trivium_. The more advanced _quadrivium_ included arithmetic, astronomy, geometry, and music. In the late eleventh and early twelfth centuries there occurred an expansion of the study of the _trivium_ and _quadrivium_ to include with grammar much classical literature; with rhetoric much more law; with logic considerable philosophy and theology.

The teaching and the intellectual pabulum of the early Middle Ages was based upon one point of view, that of the church. It was dogmatic, authoritative. Nevertheless, within certain limits teachers and students might think independently; and that is what they often proceeded to do. Young men then, as in any age, were repelled by being ordered to accept the dogmatic assertions of their elders. They wanted to ask questions, a custom that has since continued. The increase of wealth, safety, and mobility had quickened intellectual life. The crusades to the Holy Land had stimulated interest and wonder. The advance of trade and industry and the extraordinary growth of the town population throughout Europe gave men, particularly young men, a chance to gather in taverns, streets, and roominghouses to argue and talk. Out in the wild stretches of rural ignorance youths might be isolated and lonely. In the towns it was different, for the towns had many people, many experiences; there was life, action, energy, and the ferment of ideas.

In northern Europe there arose a widespread interest in philosophy and theology. Could the logical conclusions of reason be reconciled with the dogma and doctrine of the church? Out of attempts to answer that question grew the unique intellectual triumph of the mighty system of thought called scholasticism. Knowledge, asserted the scholastic philosophers, was to be obtained and used only to bulwark faith. Reason was to be considered as a buttress to the authority of the church, nothing more. Faith had its foundations in truth; but the truth was declared by authority; therefore men must not try to ask questions beyond the limits prescribed by the church. "I know," said the great Abelard, "in order that I may believe." Reason must be tethered to and reconciled with authority.

Where inquiring minds travelled too far afield, as in discussing problems of science, the church moved in to silence them, because it was felt that faith might be endangered by searching for things it was not good for curious man to know. That is one reason why the modern scientific ability to separate the true and the false was seldom found in the Middle Ages. Many men sought to discover what the ancient authorities said and repeated them as truths of science. The medieval natural sciences were therefore a strange compound of morals, fables, and some rather excellent practical ideas; there was never anything approaching a scientific synthesis of logical and experimental methods with the teachings of the past. Barren dialectic and logic-chopping often took the place of learning.

The scholastic method enhanced the prestige of formal logic; it trained and subtilized the minds of men to handle philosophical material. Theology was the "queen of the sciences." In the great work of medieval logic and scholasticism original thought was not under an interdict; but it was confined to certain channels of inquiry. The church would not permit her sons to debate or discuss certain propositions considered heretical, such as "There never was a creation" or "All sin is not forbidden" or "Matter cannot be created." Men must not reason to conclusions that conflicted with dogma; they must not discuss questions that might lead them to such conclusions.

With the gradual recovery of the long-lost works of Aristotle in the twelfth and thirteenth centuries his influence began to sweep over Europe. The first task of the theologians and philosophers was to reconcile Aristotle's teachings with those of the church. St. Thomas Aquinas made a monumental synthesis of the works of Aristotle and the teachings of the church; he showed that in many respects Aristotle was not in opposition to Rome. Where there was an obvious conflict, Aristotle was condemned. When St. Thomas finished his impressive *Summa Theologica* it took its place as the most important theological and philosophical contribution of the Middle Ages, combining sacred and profane learning into one harmonious system. Of course, it was not the *Summa* but popular works to instruct the layman that had the widest circulation. For example, the *Bible of the Poor* and the famous *Mirror of Human Salvation* had great popularity, like the later *Art of Dying* of the fifteenth century. There were many illustrations of the "drifting down, into the popular consciousness, of the definitions of high and abstract thought."

Meanwhile Italian scholars were much more concerned with the law than with philosophy or theology or the invading scientific and mathematical genius of Arab culture. In the twelfth century the codification of Roman law made by Justinian was carefully studied and many commentaries or glosses were written. At the same time more attention was given to canon law. The study of both civil and canon law soon began to increase all over Europe. Kings and princes sought the services of those skilled in Roman law. A profitable career was opened to young men who were willing to study law. Many became legal and administrative servants of the state in a day when the complex life brought by towns, wealth, and commerce made the local manorial customary laws obsolescent. The world was becoming a world of practical men, and lawyers were often more highly regarded than teachers of theology or liberal arts.

It was in the midst of such intellectual stirrings in the twelfth century that the first universities appeared, a great event in the history of the world. The universities were typical of the medieval tendency to give corporate expression to an idea. They arose in much the same way as many of the earlier schools. Throughout Europe free-lance teachers were meeting wandering scholars, ambitious and greedy for adventure and knowledge. Both students and teachers lectured and quizzed by the roadside, in upper rooms, in any convenient place. In some towns several famous teachers settled down and attracted tramping students from distant places. At Bologna, under the influence of Gratian, arose a famous law school. At Salerno there grew up a medical school.

These schools, and others later, soon formed learned guilds of masters and scholars for the purpose of regulating their affairs. Each cooperative guild association was under a rector and the university operated according to a set of rules drawn up by the guild. The universities also began to obtain special charters or privileges from the Pope, emperor, or king. Under these the scholars were usually granted the universal protection given to clerics and pilgrims; therefore they had the right to be tried either in church courts or special university courts. The degrees of master or doctor granted by an acceptable and chartered university gave the holder the right to teach anywhere. Every university degree was originally a teaching license or certificate, a *licentia docendi*. To the bachelor, the master, and the doctor, certain specific rights and privileges were given.

The medieval universities had at first no campus, no buildings. The lecturers usually talked in hired halls. The students lived wherever they could find a place to sleep. They ate what they could buy cheaply, or what they could steal. The "ancient and honourable company of scholars" often came into dispute with townspeople, who frequently sought to overcharge and profiteer or to infringe upon university rights. Then the university authorities could, if they wished, merely stop the lectures, and the whole university would go somewhere else. The threat that the university would leave the town usually helped to bring the townspeople to heel; it was better for the local tradesmen and renters to have some income from the students and professors than none at all.

In the thirteenth century, universities were founded throughout Europe. Among the famous schools in Italy there appeared the universities of Padua and Naples. In France the great medical school at Montpellier outranked all medical centers on the Continent. At Paris, mother of the northern universities, three separate colleges attracted great teachers and thousands of students. Life was hard in these early universities. Many students were young, far from home, light of heart. They quarrelled among themselves. In northern universities, for example, there were different national groups that very easily fell into bloody battle. The students also had financial troubles. In 1220 one young man stated in a letter to his father that he was "studying with the greatest diligence" but that he lacked money. "You know that without clothes and food and wine your son grows cold."

England had been rather closely associated with the intellectual tides of the Continent after the Norman Conquest. The University of Oxford probably developed from a local school into a university in consequence partly of a royal edict of Henry II issued in 1167. The king of France favored Becket, and Henry recalled all English students from abroad, especially from France. "Let all clerks who have revenues in England be warned to come back to England, as they love their revenues, there to enjoy the same." Many English-speaking scholars migrated with their books and their songs to the royal borough of Oxford. The number of scribes, bookbinders, and students increased so steadily that by 1300 there were as many students as townsmen. In 1248 Henry III gave the university a royal charter.

Most of the early students at Oxford were sons of yeomen and craftsmen, "the chartered beggars of learning." They lived in the *hospicia,* which were large boarding houses. Because of the dangers of permitting the students too much freedom for rowdiness there were usually faculty members resident in the *hospicia* to watch over the welfare of the young men. In 1231 Henry III ordered that every student at Oxford must be in charge of a master. At Oxford, as on the Continent, frequent disputes arose between the university and the townsmen. These "town and gown" feuds sometimes assumed serious proportions. Oxford was also troubled by battles between the students from the north and south of England, the Tweed being the rough boundary. These struggles, similar to those between the nations in European universities, were often long and bloody. In 1383, for example, one fray lasted for three days. The students expelled from Oxford after the brawl suffered the disaster of having to go to Cambridge. They had "blackened the fair manners, the famous learning, and the sweet fragrant report of the University of Oxford."

Oxford, like nearly all English universities, was in time made up of halls and later colleges. Most halls developed into colleges; thus University Hall became University College. St. Edmund Hall, however, still remains, its name unchanged. About 1264 Walter de Merton, bishop of Rochester and once chancellor of England, founded Merton College, one of the first of the modern colleges. Merton was built on the pattern of a quadrangle; the students who lived in the college were under the direction of a warden; they observed the laws set down by the founder; they attended the lectures conducted by the university. Sometime between 1261 and 1266 Sir John de Balliol founded Balliol College. In the late thirteenth and fourteenth centuries several other colleges were established.

About 1209, if the word of the chronicler Roger of Wendover be accepted, a student at Oxford killed a woman and fled. Three of his companions, probably innocent of any major crime, were caught and hanged by the townsmen. King John, then under sentence of excommunication by the Pope, not only did nothing to help the students but perhaps sided with the citizens of Oxford. Thus the ecclesiastical liberties of the students had been violated by the secular authorities. A number of masters and students left Oxford in alarm and went to Reading and Cambridge, among the eastern fens. Although this migration may not in fact be the beginning of Cambridge University there certainly were large numbers of students at Cambridge a few years later and the organization of Oxford's sister university was well begun. In England Oxford retained an undisputed supremacy until the sixteenth century. Then Cambridge pulled even and soon took the lead in mathematics and science.

THE COMING OF THE FRIARS

It is difficult for many modern minds to comprehend and appreciate the medieval concern with the progress of the human soul in this world and the next. In the Middle Ages the last judgment was a vivid, real, and imminent event. "Men's minds were haunted by the Apocalypse and the more dismal chapters of the Prophets." The famous *Dies Irae,* written by the Franciscan Thomas of Celano in the thirteenth century, shows very clearly, like several hymns in medieval breviaries and missals, the prevailing interest in the day of judgment. Unfortunately, in the late twelfth and thirteenth centuries both the secular and regular clergy had begun to enter upon a period of decline. The flame of the mighty monastic revival was burning less brightly. Hospitality declined; learning and education suffered; monasteries were no longer attracting many able men.

Many monastic orders, such as the Cluniacs and Benedictines, were sinking into spiritual degeneracy. They had become such busy and wealthy landlords that their discipline and ideals had slipped from their once high spiritual level. Even the Cistercians, whose influence was powerful for good in the twelfth century, began to show signs of increasing worldliness. The ideals of monasticism were fading because the material world was too much with the monks and abbots. Although England was "swarming with clerics" and it has been estimated that about one man in fifty was a churchman, the harsh fact remained that the zealous, crusading fires were banked. Parish priests were often ignorant; some were absentees. The bishops, with a few exceptions, were not active Christian soldiers. Many Englishmen saw and noted Rome's political ambitions and the flood of papal taxes to Italy. Many also resented the rising worldliness and lethargy of the regular and secular clergy.

There was much evidence of an increasingly secularized perspective. One churchman said that a morally good man who cared for the common weal and did not strive for possessions too much ought not to be hindered from growing rich since he brought benefits to the community. The author of *Aucassin and Nicolette* lightly wrote: "Into Paradise . . . go those aged priests, and those old cripples, and the maimed, who all day long and all night cough before the altars . . . with them I have nought to do. But in Hell will I go. For to Hell go the fair clerks and the fair knights . . . there go the fair and courteous ladies who have friends, two or three, together with their wedded lords. And there pass the gold and silver, the ermine and all rich furs, harpers and minstrels, and the happy of the world."

The dismal prospect soon altered. At the opening of the thirteenth century there began the new orders of the mendicant friars. The first was founded in 1216 by the Spaniard Dominic Guizman, who had seen the wholesale butchery of the Albigensian heretics and the desolation of lovely Provence. The Preaching Brothers of the Dominican order at first numbered sixteen men. They were to go from town to town in poverty, like Christ's first disciples. Their task was to convert the sinners, fight heresy, awaken the spiritually drowsy. The monks could flee from the world and save their own souls. The crusading Dominicans, on the contrary, would be fishers of men. "Zeal must be met by zeal, lowliness by lowliness, false sanctity by real sanctity, preaching lies by preaching truth."

In 1220 thirteen Dominicans, or "Black Friars," landed in England, following Peter des Roches, bishop of Winchester and favorite of Henry III. In 1221, the year the order was recognized by the Pope, the Dominicans had one house at Oxford; by 1300 they had over fifty houses in England and Wales. These humble friars, who possessed no personal property, were the prophets and missionaries of a new spiritual and intellectual awakening.

St. Francis of Assisi, the son of a merchant, became weary of the vapid maundering of his bourgeois society friends. After a serious illness he began to give so much money to charity that his father was alarmed. The frescoes of Giotto and the verse of Dante tell how St. Francis "took Poverty for his bride." To him the words of the Gospel were clear: "As ye go, preach, saying, the kingdom of heaven is at hand. Heal the sick, cleanse the lepers, raise the dead, cast out devils; freely ye have received, freely give. Provide neither gold, nor silver, nor brass in your purses, nor scrip for your journey, neither two coats, neither shoes, nor yet staves: for the workman is worthy of his meat." With their coarse gray robes and girdles of rope the Franciscans, the "begging friars" who followed St. Francis, preached the word of God and did good works. "They are the true doctors who, with the meekness of wisdom, show forth good works for the edification of their neighbors." In 1223 nine Franciscans landed in England.

The friars brought a great revival, like the Christians of the later Puritan, Wesleyan, and Salvation Army movements. "Three things," said a Franciscan, "have chiefly exalted our order: bare feet, mean garments, and the refusal of money." St. Francis, of course, believed that poverty was more important than preaching; that the Franciscans should lead humble lives that would be examples. St. Dominic, on the other hand, stressed the missionary element of evangelical preaching. The Dominicans were at first much more learned and intellectual than the more mystical Franciscans, for St. Francis had forbidden his order to read books. Later the Franciscans followed the Dominicans in their search for knowledge, and produced some outstanding scholars.

Throughout Europe the good Samaritans of both orders did not pass by on the other side. They sought out the poor, the neglected, and the sick. They filled the stomachs of the hungry. They preached the teachings of Christ and His apostles. They offered salvation to all, in the name of the Saviour. Above all, perhaps, the friars spoke a language all understood; what they said was intelligible because it was as simple as the Gospels. They spoke with enthusiasm; to them religion was a way of life, not a form. "Woe to those who die in mortal sin," says St. Francis' beautiful Italian *Canticle of the Sun.* "Praise ye and bless my Lord, and give Him thanks, and serve Him with great humility."

Long after the institutions of the mendicant orders survived the fires of the apostolic spirit had sunk into embers. Until the fourteenth century the Dominicans and Franciscans were the leading exponents of the Christian faith; then they fell upon evil days. They came to enforce their discipline but laxly. They were wealthy corporations, increasingly careless about the things of the spirit; and they had many enemies. The secular clergy, for example, hated the friars for carrying off so many flocks and fees. The followers of John Wycliffe picked up the torch of crusading zeal when the friars dropped it. Geoffrey Chaucer and others laughed at the hypocrisy of the begging brothers and the various signs of their degeneration. Many perhaps forgot that once, in a crisis of religion, the friars had indeed followed in the footsteps of the Master.

IDEAS IN BOOKS AND STONE

In the early Middle Ages one of the outstanding scholars was the Franciscan friar Roger Bacon. From Oxford Bacon went to Paris, where he gained a wide reputation as a brilliant and original scientist. Many of his ideas were so strongly opposed to the prevailing climate of opinion that he ran into heavy trouble with both church and state authorities. Bacon did accept many current assumptions; he believed in astrology; he believed that all truth was in the Scriptures; he thought the circle could be squared. On the other hand, the fiery Bacon sturdily opposed many of the ideas of the scholastic leaders, particularly the giant St. Thomas Aquinas. He pointed out that a parade of formal logic could not contribute much towards finding out the secrets of nature. He thought it was absurd to accept Aristotle blindly, particularly through translations that had quite probably distorted Aristotle's meaning. He also drew attention to the fact that the schoolmen were far removed from Aristotle when they neglected nature. Why did they not study nature themselves, in the manner of their master Aristotle?

About 1267 Bacon wrote his famous *Opus Majus*. His later *Opus Minus* and *Opus Tertium* were really summaries of the *Opus Majus* with some additions on alchemy and chemistry. In almost all his works Bacon stressed the importance of using the inductive, experimental method in seeking knowledge. "Experimental science controls the conclusions of all the other sciences; it reveals truths which reasoning from general principles would never have discovered; finally, it starts us on the way to marvellous inventions that will change the face of the world." Bacon was a man of many interests; he not only wrote about theology and grammar but he also experimented in chemistry, optics, and mathematics; he worked with gunpowder; he revised Ptolemy's geography.

In 1277 the bishop of Paris condemned 219 current "errors" of liberal thought. Bacon was imprisoned, a powerless and unpopular victim of the tide of prejudice in his age. He may have been released from prison in 1290; he may have remained there until 1292, probably the year of his death. Of himself he wrote: "I recognized my own littleness, my stammering speech and my scratching pen." At the same time he revealed his pride in the work he had done: "It is well known that no man hath laboured in so many languages and sciences as I, nor hath laboured so hard therein." About the state of the world around him Bacon had much to say, mainly in words of despair.

A second scholar of the thirteenth century was the Franciscan Robert Grosseteste, who was a widely ranging student and teacher of mathematics, natural science, law, and medicine. He became chancellor of Oxford, bishop of Lincoln, and a famous administrative servant of Henry III. A third outstanding figure of the age was the jurist Henry de Bracton, a royal justice who wrote a comprehensive study of the substance and operation of the laws of England. His work, in which he analyzed hundreds of case decisions, was of great significance both in the study of jurisprudence and in the actual development of English law.

At the end of the thirteenth century the Franciscan Duns Scotus became so famous for his thoroughgoing logic that he was called "the Subtle Doctor." Duns Scotus was perhaps less concerned than some of his fellows with diverting his thought to plausible conclusions. Nevertheless, his acute and careful logical patterns were so delicately refined that he helped to bring scholasticism into disrepute a century later. Most of his work was negative. For example, he demonstrated, to his satisfaction at least, that God was an arbitrary Supreme Being, without the usual attributes of reason and goodness. In his numerous attacks upon the work of St. Thomas Aquinas, Scotus gained several followers. Those who stood by St. Thomas came to be called Thomists; those who supported Duns Scotus were called by his scornful opponents Dunces, a name that has stayed fixed in the language.

Meanwhile the writing of chronicles continued apace, adding to the knowledge made available to the historian by government documents such as the charters and the close and patent rolls, the cartularies of the monasteries, the manorial and borough records. The most famous chroniclers of the period lived at St. Albans, thirty miles from London. One of them, Roger of Wendover, wrote an excellent chronicle, the *Flowers of History;* it was lively and complete. When he died in 1236 his work was carried on by Matthew Paris, who continued the chronicle until his own death in 1259. Matthew Paris was the greatest of medieval historiographers, despite his errors, his fervent prejudices, and his somewhat less than perfect Latin. He was, above all, a master storyteller. An excellent example of dramatic writing in his *Historia Major* is the description of the battle in 1250 between the canons of St. Bartholomew's Priory at Smithfield and the archbishop of Canterbury.

Most of the vernacular literature of the early Middle Ages in England was in Norman French. The new chivalry of the age produced the troubadours, the epic *chansons de geste*, like the earlier *Song of Roland,* and later the courtly and often mystical metrical romances. There were also the moralizing beast fables, the political and romantic ballads, the religious poems, and the coarse tales of the *fabliaux*. At the same time, the Celtic legends about Arthur and Merlin, so important to Geoffrey of Monmouth earlier, appeared in both English and Norman French versions and merged in scores of folk tales. The Arthurian legend was well launched on its prolific and amazing career.

About 1205 a parish priest from the west Severn district named Layamon wrote a rhymed chronicle called *Brut,* based on an earlier Anglo-Norman work and the widespread legend that the Britons were descended from the Trojan Brutus, one of whose ancestors was Aeneas. After Layamon several metrical chronicles appeared side by side with translations and imitations of the French. There were also a few fragments of verse in Middle English, among which was the earliest known English lyric, the lovely "Sumer is icumen in, Lhude sing cuccu!" Here was the creativeness of Anglo-Saxon and Norman fusion. The bone structure of the English language had changed; it was almost ready for Geoffrey Chaucer and John Wycliffe.

There were also major changes in architecture. In the late twelfth century the massive and robust Norman Romanesque began to yield to the influence of the graceful Gothic. The great cathedrals of Europe, such as Rheims, Amiens, and Chartres, marked the highest expression of the Gothic development in Europe. In Gothic construction the roof was supported on interlaced and soaring pointed arches called vaults; the arches were held in place by buttresses outside the building; the heavy supporting pillars of the Romanesque construction were replaced by slender groups of columns. Because the walls themselves carried little weight and stress there was an opportunity to use large multicolored glass windows, thus adding to the effect of lightness and airy grace already achieved by the vertical lines of construction.

The early English Gothic, extending from about 1170 to 1280, can be recognized by the delicate tracery and geometrical patterns of the pointed lancet windows. Early English Gothic in most features of their construction are the choir of Lincoln Cathedral, rebuilt about 1200; Westminster Abbey, rebuilt by Henry III; Wells Cathedral in Somerset; and Canterbury Cathedral. Salisbury Cathedral, finished about 1258, is throughout a magnificent example of pure early English Gothic. From about 1280 to 1380 there appeared the fantastic traceries of the broad-windowed and decorated Gothic. An excellent example of decorated Gothic architecture is Exeter Cathedral. From about 1380 to 1500 the so-called perpendicular Gothic exhibited a blunting of the pointed arches, the tracery usually reduced to a series of vertical straight lines, and squarish towers. These characteristics are perhaps best shown in perpendicular additions made to Gloucester Cathedral in the fourteenth century. In scores of cathedral and parish churches the restrained and noble beauty wrought by medieval builders still excites the wonder and admiration of modern man.

Naturally these profound changes in the social, economic, and intellectual history of England were not without their parallels and repercussions in the forward movements that characterized political history. During the reign of Edward I the work of the state-building Norman and Angevin kings reached its height. His reign saw important

chapters in the development of the institution of Parliament, effective
centralized government, the beginning of statute law and modern land
law, broader political education. All of these were capital events in
English history. Edward I was one of the greatest of the thirty-nine
monarchs who have reigned in England since the Norman Conquest.
The next chapter traces the story of his achievements.

Chapter 7

THE REIGN OF EDWARD I
STATUTE LAW AND COMMON LAW COURTS

EDWARD I, who came to the throne in 1272, was a man of sense and action. He wanted no civil war like that of his father's reign. One of the strongest and most dynamic of England's medieval kings, he reorganized the system of government; he codified existing laws and made numerous new ones. In all that he did the hard-working Edward was efficient and thorough. "His head was round, the abiding-place of great wisdom and the special sanctuary of high counsel," runs the fulsome comment of a contemporary. "No one had a keener wit in counsel, a greater fluency in speaking, coolness in danger, restraint in success, constancy in failure." Over six feet in height, strong in body and personality, Edward intended to have results when he acted. The results that he obtained in legislation and administration were so remarkable that their consequences have flowed through the centuries to the present day.

When Henry III died Edward was in the Holy Land on the last great crusade. He did not return to his kingdom until 1274. Upon his arrival in England he began an extensive series of enactments designed to satisfy the strict requirements of his passion for efficiency and order. Most of this legislation was not done by means of a royal ordinance in council but usually with the assent of the great council or of full Parliaments. Such pieces of legislation, intended to be permanent, were beginning to be called statutes, although the word was still vague, being generally used to describe any very formal statement of law. The statutes of the realm, or acts of Parliament, were soon to be considered superior to customs or to common law. They were to be the law of all the land.

In the making of this large body of legislation Edward was aided by a few professional and expert lawyers and ministers. To carry the laws into execution the shrewd king needed a more efficient administrative system than the one he had inherited. With characteristic energy he housecleaned the civil service offices. Many dullards and loafers were dismissed. Mainly from the wardrobe, the chancery, and the exchequer Edward chose able and loyal servants for promotion to higher administrative ranks. Most of these individuals were not of noble birth. They were men of the middle class. With them the civil service was a career and they became increasingly loyal to a king to whom they owed their jobs and who rewarded work and merit.

The sharp vision of Edward recognized that in his day a good government must be centralized. The centripetal tendencies of feudalism had resulted in many evils when feudal barons got out of hand, as in his father's reign. Shortly after Edward returned to England he ordered itinerant justices to ask juries throughout each hundred in England about baronial exemptions and "liberties" possibly prejudicial to royal authority and the execution of justice. Four years later the Statute of Gloucester required the barons to show by what authority (*quo warranto*) they held private courts and enjoyed several other privileges. Thus Edward hoped to stop the nobles from exercising feudal rights for which they could not show a royal warrant, grant, or charter. The barons were incensed. One declared his sword was his title-deed. Edward finally agreed that uninterrupted possession of exemptions and other privileges from the first year of the reign of Richard I was sufficient warrant for continued exercise of them. The year 1189–1190 was thus fixed as the limit of English legal memory, the time "whereof the memory of man runneth not to the contrary."

Although the frontal attack upon the barons had not been entirely successful a series of flank assaults by the persistent king progressively narrowed the scope of private jurisdictions. By the end of his reign a few manorial courts were still disposing of petty cases in which villeins were involved. Elsewhere the encroachments of royal justice had left the once powerful baronial courts conquered and silent.

The important enactments of Edward I were so numerous, their character so varied, that it is possible in these pages to record and describe only a few of the statutes upon which his massive reputation rests. In the field of land law, for instance, the influence of Edward's legislation reaches into the twentieth century. One of the most important of his land laws was an enactment of 1285 usually called the Second Statute of Westminster (*de donis conditionalibus*). This law was made for several reasons, all of them strong in the thirteenth century. Many barons had been distressed by the efforts of royal courts to permit free alienation of land. The barons, for their part, usually attempted to attach conditions to the disposition of fee simple holdings in their families. Most prominent landlords wanted to find some way of ensuring that their wide fields would remain in the possession of their descendants. They did not want their heirs to leave or lose the land that to them meant wealth and power.

In the late thirteenth century, as suggested earlier, the economic side of feudalism was becoming increasingly important as the military and political aspects diminished in meaning and value. All landlords, including the king, wanted to keep the economic incomes from a feudal tenure system. Any transfer of property was unwelcome if it reduced the income from such feudal sources as reliefs, escheats, and wardships. The Second Statute of Westminster provided that land should descend through the generations in the order set forth in the original charter, so that nobody, even a spendthrift or a black sheep, could ever alienate so much as a single acre. This practice of entail, then and later, was designed to keep estates intact; the successive heirs had only a life use of their holdings. Despite various legal devices later developed to break entails the Second Statute of Westminster was a major reason for the maintenance of large estates in England through several centuries. Not until 1925 was the creation of new entails prohibited.

In 1290, by another important land law, Edward I struck heavily at the feudal power of his barons. The Third Statute of Westminster (*quia emptores*) forbade further subinfeudation. Before 1290, many leading barons had "sold" part of their lands to men who technically became subvassals, or mesne vassals. From this practice of subinfeudation the barons had derived profitable incomes. Under the new statute all buyers became direct vassals or tenants of the seller's overlord, who was very often the king. The seller lost all his feudal rights over the land. Edward justified this law by asserting that the practice of subinfeudation had been depriving the original lords of their feudal rights. As the years passed, more and more intermediate lords died without heirs or were found guilty of felony or treason. Thus, in time, almost every landlord held his land directly of the king.

The clear-headed Edward continued his plans to diminish baronial power by still further reducing the military significance of feudalism. Through the use of writs for "distraint of knighthood," issued in 1278, he commanded all men having lands worth twenty pounds a year to accept knighthood, for which they paid. As members of England's militia, every man holding the rank of knight was required to keep himself ready for mounted service by supplying himself with the necessary equipment, which was expensive. Infantrymen, of lesser rank, could be more easily obtained than knights. Thus Edward increased the cavalry power of the militia, diminished the need for hiring foreign mercenaries, and made himself less dependent upon his barons for military support. The militiamen of England were summoned by the king's agents armed with royal commissions.

Such were a few of the steps taken by Edward I to alter the land law and reduce or prune away some swollen baronial powers. There were other measures calculated to encourage and strengthen the merchants. In 1283, for instance, the Statute of Merchants, or Acton

Burnell, provided that a man might be legally imprisoned for debt. This law was particularly welcome to the rising commercial classes. Under the terms of the statute the movable goods of a debtor, or even his land, might be sold by the mayor and the clerk of London, York, or Bristol in order to satisfy the legitimate demands of creditors.

Many acts in the mass of Edward I's prolific legislation were passed to increase the social stability of the state and the general observance of law. For example, the Statute of Winchester of 1285 stated that as "robberies, murders, and arsons be more often used than they have been heretofore" penalties were to be imposed on individuals who protected or concealed criminals; the gates of towns were to be closed at night; the people dwelling in each county were to be answerable for robberies and damages done within their borders; hedges and underbrush along the highways, apt to shelter lurking highwaymen, were to be cut; the men of England were to keep themselves armed according to their rank and be prepared to join in the "hue and cry" for suspected criminals. Other statutes carefully defined the duties and authority of royal officials, specified the amount of the fees to be charged by the king's officers, and prohibited the demanding of excessive feudal aids.

Meanwhile the vigor and initiative of Edward I and his servants brought extensive changes in the judicial system. From the days of Henry II, whose labors in extending royal judicial power have been described in Chapter 4, the central royal courts had steadily expanded the scope of their jurisdiction and the volume of their business. This advance had been accomplished by the invasion of many functions previously performed by the free and public hundred and shire courts. Where outright invasion and seizure had not occurred, many local powers had been eaten away by a protracted process of nibbling, particularly by ingenious extensions of the common law by royal judges. For example, the Statute of Gloucester of 1278 ordered that no case should be heard in the king's courts where the amount involved was less than forty shillings. The royal judges interpreted this as meaning that no case where more than forty shillings was in dispute should be tried in a county tribunal. The sheriff's tourn, a royal court of record, absorbed the criminal work of the hundred court. As England moved into the fourteenth century the once great authority of the hundred and shire courts had dwindled to a petty civil and criminal jurisdiction.

The scope and weight of the work performed by the royal judicial agents was becoming very heavy. In order to increase efficiency and speed it was natural that shrewd men should develop machinery and methods to cope with the rising burden of their tasks. That is exactly what happened. In Henry II's day it was easy for an itinerant justice on mission to do many kinds of judicial and administrative work on his rounds through the counties. By the thirteenth century it was impossible. To meet the needs of a new age several groups of justices were sent out to the counties; to the members of each group was usually assigned the duty of trying one particular class of cases. For example, justices of assize usually tried civil suits. Justices holding commissions of jail delivery were ordered to try all prisoners in certain jails and thus empty them. Royal judges under commissions of *oyer* and *terminer* heard and settled criminal cases. Such commissions were not always general. Sometimes they were even limited to a certain kind of crime, or to a single court.

Such developments were already well in progress when Edward I came to the throne. So far as the operations of the itinerant justices were concerned Edward's work was one of organization and improvement rather than creation. His main achievement in the field of judicial affairs was the integration of the itinerant justice system with the royal central common law courts.

In the thirteenth century there became fully separated from the *curia regis* two common law courts: the court of exchequer and the court of common pleas. The exchequer court really broke away from the *curia regis* in the reign of Henry III. From the days of Henry I the exchequer in its judicial capacity had been expanding its jurisdiction. By 1235 a separate set of plea rolls began. After the separation from the *curia regis* the jurisdiction of the exchequer was still closely connected with the financial administration of the government and particularly concerned with all cases involving the royal revenue. The court procedure was speedy and effective. The tradition of swift and ruthless collection of government revenue was not born in Edward's day; but it became stronger then, and it has never died. Private creditors were permitted, for a price, to use this royal court for the collection of their debts.

The second great central court that had clearly emerged by the thirteenth century was the court of common pleas, set apart for the trial of cases between private citizens. In 1178 Henry II had appointed five members of the royal household section of the *curia regis* to deal with ordinary cases. During the next thirty-five years Englishmen grew weary of following the king about on his travels in order to get their cases heard. They wanted a stationary royal court to which they could easily go. Article 17 of Magna Carta stated that common pleas were not to follow the court of the king but were to be held in a definite place. In 1234 the court of common pleas gained the right to keep its own separate records in the *de banco* rolls. In 1272 a chief justice was appointed. For the next six centuries the separate court of common pleas remained chiefly concerned with what are now called civil cases, or suits between subjects of the king.

After the courts of common pleas and exchequer had left the parent household of the *curia regis* there naturally remained in the *curia regis* all of the jurisdictional powers not possessed by either common pleas or exchequer. As a judicial body the *curia regis* exercised its residual jurisdiction, particularly in the supervision of difficult or important cases in the lesser courts. It was therefore natural that a number of men skilled in solving knotty legal problems should still be summoned to the *curia regis*. In 1268 a chief justice was appointed. The pleas were no longer heard in the presence of the king (*coram rege*). Thus occurred further steps in the growth of a third central common law body: the court of king's bench. By the time of Edward I it had not yet sharply emerged as a separate court; the cleavage was still incomplete; but the movement was steady and the direction sure. It was soon to be a court fully separated from the mother *curia regis* and mainly concerned with criminal cases, or pleas of the crown.

These, then, were the three great central courts of common law, each with increasingly specialized functions. Until 1873 they remained essentially unchanged and the foundation of the whole national judicial system.

PARLIAMENT

The growth of the English Parliament is one of the capital facts of modern civilization. The Parliaments summoned by Edward I were national assemblies called to deal with national questions, particularly problems of finance. It was practically convenient to vote supplies and handle petitions in a full gathering of representatives from the borough and shire as well as the nobles of the great council. The idea of political representation had already been used in the organization of county government in the county court. It was also important in the convocation of the church and in such organizations as the Dominican order. From such sources easily came the idea of political representation in the new national Parliament. In Edward I's day the normal and official Parliament included two burgesses chosen in each borough and two knights chosen in each county court.

Public policy was steadily expanding in its scope; trade and commerce swelled in every port and borough; the demands of the royal administration, of justice and police, grew apace. These new enterprises cost money; and the best way for Edward I to obtain a national revenue was through the expedient of calling Parliament. Edward I could not live upon his income from the royal demesne, from feudal incidents supplemented by court fees, fines, occasional tallage or scutage levies, and other hereditary revenues. The more extensive use of customs duties greatly eased the royal needs. This was particularly true after 1275, when Parliament granted Edward, as a part of his regular permanent revenue, specified export duties on wool and leather hides to be collected at export points in England, Wales, and Ireland *development of the constitution — point tradition & precedent* [handwritten marginalia]

"for the use of our said lord the king." Import duties of two shillings were also levied on each tun, or cask, of foreign wine and each pound of merchandise. Such duties were soon called "tunnage and poundage."

In addition to the hereditary revenues and certain specified customs duties Edward I requested and received nine separate subsidy grants from Parliament of a total value of about £450,000. These grants were in the form of direct taxes, similar to the Saladin tithe which Henry II had imposed in 1188 upon all individuals who were not going on the crusade. Such levies were usually in the form of percentage taxes on movable goods, a uniform levy on the personal property of all classes. The feudal lords and the burgesses in Parliament normally granted "a tenth and a fifteenth," or ten per cent from the townsmen and about seven per cent from the landowners. The churchmen made their own separate grants of "free gifts." This granting of money was important; it was a part of the national revenue; and it was done by a national Parliament growing in importance and power.

The activities of Parliament in Edward's reign were by no means solely concerned with financial affairs. Members of Parliament discussed local grievances and redressed private wrongs. Petitions submitted to Parliament were usually disposed of swiftly. As the highest court of justice was still the *curia regis* the judges of the council and the lawyers in the lower ranks of Parliament were busy disposing of petitions involving legal questions or cautiously drafting statutes and treaties. Matters of finance were usually referred to the exchequer. In a meeting of Parliament a huge and miscellaneous body of business had to be transacted. As pressures increased, machinery grew. Constitutional laws, customs, and usages multiplied. Political tradition and precedent hardened.

Although the structure of Parliament remained fluid and uncertain for a long time, its essential form was finally established in the reign of Edward I. Under his strong hand Parliament became the usual instrument for the transaction of public business. Edward has some claim to be called the father of Parliament as well as the English Justinian. His impressive work in developing the institution of Parliament is probably his greatest title to fame. When he died in 1307 a long step had been taken towards the creation of a permanent and national assembly that would one day represent the mind and will of the British people.

essential form of Parliament established in Ed. I reign [handwritten marginalia]

To understand the importance of Edward I's experiments we must remember that Parliament began in the deliberations of the King's central *magnum concilium,* or great council. The council was not only the parent of the common law courts and the possessor of all jurisdiction not sloughed off and given to those law courts; it still remained the highest court in the land, the king's court, the "high court of Parliament." Many cases, either within or without the cognizance of the courts of common law, were tried before it. Difficult problems were often sent up to the council by the common law courts. Appeals from the decisions of itinerant justices or the court of common pleas were settled in the council sitting as a court. By virtue of its residual jurisdiction its work was heavy and remained so, especially where questions of equity, as distinct from the statute or common law, were involved.

At the same time, the council was the most important administrative body in the kingdom, particularly in its reduced form as a small council, which was already beginning to separate into what are now the various departments of government. The great council was also the body most competent to advise and consult with the king. It was inevitable that the functions of the council should increase tremendously in the thirteenth century as the burdens of royal government administration increased, particularly in areas where no governmental departments, such as the exchequer or the chancery, had yet been developed.

The members of the council included several lords spiritual and temporal, the influential ministers of the crown, and such important individuals as judges and clerks. Many of the lesser barons stayed away, anxious to avoid the expensive journey to court. Sometimes the council was expanded by the summoning of more barons, prelates, royal officials, and others. The king in his council had a higher legal, political, and moral authority than the king alone. When the full council met mainly for judicial purposes it was usually called a Parliament in the reign of Edward I. Sometimes the smaller permanent council alone sat in the Parliament. Sometimes, too, the council settled cases when Parliament was not in session at all. The sessions of the council to deal with petitions for the remedying of grievances and injustice were usually called Parliaments. These facts are mentioned here to show that in the late thirteenth century Parliament was a growing and a changing body. Nothing in its composition or procedure was as yet fixed or final.

For certain purposes the council was expanded greatly before it sat as a Parliament. Besides the presenting of petitions and the trying of cases most Parliaments quite properly carried on the council duty of advising the king on matters of government policy, especially about projected laws or proposed taxes. In the reign of Edward I Parliament became a more comprehensive body, largely because of the calculated introduction of new representative elements. These new elements were added to the council for many reasons, including the powerful one that it was necessary to obtain their support for royal taxation programs. Representatives of the rural and town middle class were called to attend meetings of the great council in Parliament. It was less cumbersome and awkward to summon representatives of the knights and burgesses to Parliament than it was to do business about taxes and aids through itinerant justices or other royal agents in the local communities. John had summoned the representatives of the shires to the great council in 1213; Henry III had repeated the step in 1254. Henry III had occasionally called burgesses from the main towns. Simon de Montfort had done so in 1265.

It slowly became the policy of Edward I to call to a central assembly the knights and burgesses representing the "communities" of shire and borough. In later days the house of commons of Parliament did not take its name from the fact that it represented "the common people," but from the fact that it represented the organized communities, the towns, and counties. Edward summoned knights and burgesses to the Parliaments of 1273 and 1275. In the following twenty years he never completely abandoned the practice of having some middle class representatives attending the full meetings of the great council in Parliament. More and more frequently, the wealthy merchants and moneyed men of the middle class were consulted by the king on matters of policy, finance, or taxation.

In 1295 Edward I summoned a full Parliament, the like of which England had not seen before. This so-called Model Parliament included the great council and representatives of the shires and towns. The bishops had been instructed to bring with them the heads of their cathedral chapters, their archdeacons, one procurator for the clergy of each cathedral and two for the clergy of each diocese. The cathedral and parochial clergy soon preferred to attend their own purely ecclesiastical assemblies, the convocations of Canterbury and York. They wanted to deal with the crown separately, and they did so. The clergy, for example, continued to tax themselves in convocation until 1664, when they decided at last to be taxed by Parliament. Thus the lower clergy withdrew from Parliament and failed to become an important element in what was one day to be the sovereign power in England. England's Parliament was to be a national assembly quite unlike the French concourse of estates.

In the words of the king's writ the members of the Model Parliament were summoned in 1295 to deal with "certain arduous affairs touching us and our kingdom" and "to consider the said affairs and to give us your counsel." Edward was at war with France and a series of disasters had imperilled England. He wanted money grants to wage war, and he wanted them from all classes of his subjects. In the sessions of the Model Parliament the knights acted with the barons and granted a tax of an eleventh on their goods; the burgesses acted alone and granted a seventh; the clergy granted a tenth. Only later did the knights gradually decide to act with the townsmen, who were of an inferior social position. Until that decision the knights of the shire worked with their fellow feudal landlords, the barons. The union of the knights and the burgesses was to give the house of commons, an institution destined to appear in the next century, a substance and strength of massive importance in its later march to power. The social prestige of the knights united with the money power of the burgesses to create a political firmness that the unorganized middle class groups did not possess in Edward's day and which only a clear-visioned prophet could then have foreseen. We can now see what Edward and his people were doing because we know what happened afterwards. They could not know the final result and certainly cannot be said to have planned or intended it.

There is no doubt that the importance of the Model Parliament can easily be stressed too strongly. It determined nothing. It made nothing necessary. Indeed, twelve of the twenty Parliaments called after 1295 by Edward I contained no representatives of the counties and towns. Only three followed the model of 1295. The Model Parliament was a step, and a long one, in the line of precedent and practice that gradually established the custom of consulting the middle class in Parliament. Had later events turned England's political and economic history in another direction, then the functions and features of the modern parliamentary system would obviously not have emerged in their present form. It is wise to remember that Parliament, in its final structure, was not the result of careful planning or deliberate organization but rather the result of time, chance, and constant compromise.

In the reign of Edward I, for example, the powers and spheres of action of the middle class representatives were narrow and circumscribed. Only the council received petitions and dealt with them. The representatives of the shires and towns played but a small part in the work of Parliament, which remained primarily judicial. The king consulted them about proposed taxation programs, about the state of public opinion in their local areas, sometimes about statutes that were being drafted. When that had been done, the knights and townsmen usually went home, leaving the king and his council to accept or reject their advice.

One thing the middle class representatives were able to do, and that was significant. They might present petitions. It was by means of this right that they were gradually able to take part in the making of law. The knights and burgesses could petition the king, with or without the support of the great barons of the council, for a redress of general or specific grievances. If the petition was accepted by the king, the council might prepare a statute providing for the enactment into law of the measures proposed in the petition. In this manner the representative elements in Parliament could work with the king and his council. As the years passed, the judicial character of Parliament became less important, although the house of lords still remains the highest court in the United Kingdom. With the decline of judicial and administrative functions there was more than a corresponding increase in the legislative functions. Parliament was to become primarily a maker of laws, a representative assembly with broad powers of legislation. In Edward's time this development was still in the future; but the conditions for its growth had been created.

Two years after the famous assembly of 1295 an event occurred of considerable importance in the later chapters of the growth of Parliament. In 1297 Edward desperately needed money for military operations in France and Scotland. When he demanded heavy taxes he encountered strong opposition. At a Parliament held at Salisbury there were violent scenes as a baronial group defied the royal orders about the war campaign in Gascony and Flanders. Many barons were angered at the successive taxes levied upon them. The clergy had been ordered by Boniface VIII to refuse payment of taxes without papal permission. The merchants were furious at Edward's placing of an irregular exaction, or maltote, on their export wool; his tax amounted to a forty shilling levy on each sack of wool.

During Edward's absence on the Continent Parliament forced the reissuance of Magna Carta, the Charter of the Forests, and other concessions earlier made by the crown. The liberties guaranteed in the past were "to be observed without impairment in all their particulars." In November, 1297, the king reluctantly accepted the "Confirmation of the Charters." In doing so he agreed, under Clause 6 of the document, that in the future he would not levy "aids, taxes, and prises except by the common assent of the whole kingdom and for the common benefit of the same kingdom, saving the ancient aids and prises due and accustomed."

Historians are not in general agreement as to whether or not the words "aids, taxes, and prises" (prises being requisitions or customs charges) meant non-feudal taxes of the type levied by Edward I before 1297. Nor do they agree that "the common assent of the whole kingdom" necessarily meant the approval of a representative body such as a Parliament in which non-noble townsmen and knights participated. The weight of learned opinion inclines to accept the conclusion that the Confirmation of the Charters in Clauses 6 and 7 in fact promised to the knights and townsmen in Parliament at least a share in controlling the amount and incidence of non-feudal taxes levied upon personal property.

Although Edward I did not strictly keep his promise, the significance of this event was twofold. In the first place, it was henceforth necessary that representatives of the middle class be summoned to all Parliaments where any extraordinary or non-feudal taxation proposals were to be discussed. Secondly, a fact of great importance, the control of the purse, limited through it may have been in some respects, was to provide a power that Parliament frequently used to persuade the king to grant concessions. One reason for the steady extension of the legal power and the political liberties and privileges of Parliament was that it grasped the power of the purse. The positive and negative poles of constitutional development were to be concession, or redress of grievances, on the one hand and the granting of supply on the other. Through succeeding centuries the king was to press for more than his normal income. Parliament was to press for more than its normal powers.

EDWARD I AND THE CHURCH

In the long struggles between the opposed claims of church and state the reign of Edward I does not form a chapter as violent and dramatic as that of William II, Henry I, Henry II, or John. The papal demands, so precisely formulated by Innocent III, that militant Pope and excellent canon law lawyer, were never relaxed or abandoned by the church in the thirteenth century. During the years of Henry III the power of the clergy had grown stronger in England; the privileges and exemptions of churchmen had increased; their property holdings broadened. Edward I was as determined to block clerical invasions of what he regarded as his proper sphere of authority as he was to check the baronial claims to excessive power.

The relations of Edward and the papacy never deteriorated to the level of, say, the years of John's reign. Edward was a devout son of the church. As king of England, he wanted no papal claims to press into the field of his temporal jurisdiction. At the same time, he was anxious to avoid open and unfriendly struggles with the papacy. The tides of English popular opinion were running strongly against Rome, mainly because the papal taxes were increasing in number and quantity. Edward was sharply aware of the widespread opposition to clerical exactions; but he also realized that the loss of papal friendship had always proved costly to his predecessors.

Edward knew how the taxes imposed upon the clergy swelled the exchequer funds. He would not cut off that source of royal income unless very strong reasons compelled him to do so. Moreover, the church had frequently been friendly and cooperative. Early in Edward's reign, for instance, the Pope had requested the English clergy to make a large grant to help defray the costs of the crusade undertaken by Edward and his brother in the Holy Land. Reasons of profit, policy, religion, and gratitude thus combined to persuade the king to maintain friendly relations with the church.

Nevertheless, several chapters of Edward I's legislation were unpopular in Rome. Among these was the Statute of Mortmain of 1279. This law was made because both king and barons were troubled by the fact that large amounts of land had passed under ecclesiastical control. The possessions of the church, said the Hildebrandine tradition, were sacred; they were not to be touched by lay hands, even those of a king. Through the centuries many landlords had left broad acres to the

Mortmain –
Ecclesiastical Tenure

church, some of them in the hope that such gifts would pave the way to paradise. Land acquired by the church seldom returned to the king. The church was a great corporation. It always had heirs. Thus it never lost its lands by escheat; nor did it lose them by being found guilty of felony or treason. The clenched hand of the church was as strong and unrelaxed as that of a dead man. Hence ecclesiastical tenure, under frankalmoign or similar arrangements, was often called mortmain.

The Statute of Mortmain was enacted to prevent future transfers of property to the church without royal permission. The words of the statute pointed out that despite earlier prohibitions in 1217 and 1259 "men of religion have nevertheless entered upon the fiefs of others as well as their own, appropriating them and buying them, and sometimes receiving them as gifts of others whereby the services that are due from such fiefs and which were originally provided for the defense of the kingdom are wrongfully withdrawn and the chief lords do lose their escheats." In the future, the statute declared, no "man of religion" should "buy or sell" or receive by "donation, lease, or any other title" any lands or tenements, "or presume by any craft or device to appropriate them in any way whatsoever." It was hoped that this law would help to protect the income of lay landlords, including the king, by stopping the alienation of more land to the church. The Statute of Mortmain was not wholly successful because legal fictions and devices were swiftly developed to evade the intent of the law and the church was able to have the use and benefit of many new grants and gifts.

Edward I also refused to permit the collection of a number of new clerical taxes that Rome proposed to levy. He made it clear that he would not allow any papal interference in the election of bishops. This firm policy of the king roused no open opposition in Rome until the election of Boniface VIII as Pope in 1294. Boniface VIII, arrogant, learned in the civil and canon law, was vigorous and eloquent in pressing extreme papal claims. He quarreled with Phillip IV of France, failing to see that the rising tide of national developments in Europe had placed the papacy in a weaker position than it had held in the eleventh century when Gregory VII could bring Henry IV to the snows at Canossa.

When Edward I and Philip IV were battling over the possession of certain lands in France Boniface VIII ordered both of them to submit to his arbitration. They refused to obey and Boniface issued in 1296 the famous bull *Clericis laicos,* which forbade the clergy to pay taxes or make gifts to laymen without papal consent. Boniface asserted the complete immunity of the clergy from taxation by the state. The laity, declared *Clericis laicos,* "press with unbridled presumption to things unlawful." In referring to taxation of the clergy by the state the bull asserted that the Pope intended "utterly to repudiate this so horrible abuse of the secular power."

In England the clergy, heavily hit by Edward's recent taxes, hastened to obey Boniface VIII. They refused to accede to the royal demand for a fifth in 1296. In France Philip IV prohibited the export of money without royal consent, cutting off French contributions to Rome. In England Edward I outlawed the clergy, placing them outside the protection of the lay law. Boniface, misled by the religious enthusiasm occasioned by the famous year of Jubilee in 1300, at first refused to modify *Clericis laicos*. In 1301 he issued the bull *Ausculta filii,* reasserting the papal power over kings and kingdoms. In 1302 he continued his offensive with the bull *Unam sanctam*, declaring in extreme form that the Pope held both the temporal and spiritual swords and was the supreme authority on earth in spiritual and temporal matters. It was all to no avail. The aged Boniface was seized by the agents of Philip IV and, though soon freed, he died a month later from shame and shock.

In England most of the clergy paid the fifth Edward demanded. The goods of those who refused to do so were confiscated. Boniface VIII was forced to retreat. He permitted the clergy to make "gifts" to the king in lieu of taxes. When Clement V became Pope in 1305 relations between England and Rome at once improved. Clement quashed the offending decrees of Boniface VIII and ordered the English clergy to pay Edward I a tenth for seven years. Edward then permitted the papacy to increase the papal revenues by the collection of a new tax from the English clergy. This tax, called annates, was to be the full returns from the first year's occupancy of any ecclesiastical office, paid by all clergymen appointed to benefices in the British Isles.

In 1307, the Parliament of Carlisle petitioned Edward to stop the flow of annates and other new papal taxes to Rome. The Carlisle Parliament, angered by the fiscal policy of the church, also forbade the papal collector to gather the new impositions ordered by the Pope. After the Parliament was dissolved Edward I commanded the gathering of the annates but upheld the parliamentary prohibition regarding the collection of any other payments not previously made to Rome. Later in the century the changing spirit of the age was clearly shown when successive Parliaments passed anti-papal laws of considerable significance in the long history of the relations between England and Rome. The Pope was soon to go into "captivity" at Avignon, in the south of France. The Hundred Years' War was approaching and Englishmen were not likely to respect or hearken to a papacy that many considered a French institution.

WALES, FRANCE, SCOTLAND

Shortly after Edward I came to the throne he was challenged by Wales, always a turbulent land. Two centuries before, several Norman barons had conquered and held estates in the borderlands of southern

Wales and southwestern England. These "marcher lords" built strong castles and tried to maintain peace in the territories they had seized. To the west and the north the wild Welsh tribes of the hills and valleys fought among themselves and raided England. Through two centuries the private armies of the marcher lords, sometimes with royal aid, beat back the Welsh invaders. This history of the borderlands was a tale of violence and massacre, raids and reprisals, the alternate advance and withdrawal of the English frontier and influence. Behind the border areas, in the fortresses or the hills, the distinctively Welsh habits, language, music, and folklore remained undisturbed, passing through the generations the fierce Celtic pride of tradition and race.

In the thirteenth century Wales almost became united under a prince of northern Wales, Llewellyn the Great, who joined the baronial party against John and later widely extended his power in the early part of the reign of Henry III. His grandson, also called Llewellyn, was betrothed to the daughter of Simon de Montfort and supported de Montfort in his struggle against Henry III. In return for homage to the English king Llewellyn was finally recognized by Henry III and the English as head of a principality that included almost all Wales except part of the marcher lands. This agreement was confirmed by the Treaty of Montgomery in 1267.

Five years later Llewellyn refused to do homage to Edward I as his overlord, to attend his coronation, or to pay the indemnity he had promised. It was a foolish step. In 1277 Edward led a large expedition from Worcester into Wales to punish the Welshman.

The swift drive of Edward cut off southern Wales from the north, and the southern lords, never strongly loyal to Llewellyn, threw off their allegiance to him. Llewellyn was then forced back into the fastnesses of the northwest. Edward moved into Chester and seized the region to the west. At the same time an English fleet from the Cinque Ports moved in from the sea to capture the island of Anglesey, upon which all northern Wales depended for its grain supply. Llewellyn, who had moved into the rugged mountains of Snowdon, was thus blocked by land and sea. Faced with starvation, he surrendered. Under the terms of his submission in 1277 Llewellyn had to pay a large indemnity and lost all his holdings except a small region in north Wales around Snowdon for which he promised to render homage to Edward. He also agreed that upon his death the title "Prince of Wales" would revert to the English crown.

In the areas of Wales that had been ceded to England the agents of Edward I attempted to substitute English law for Welsh tribal custom. They also tried to set up a local administrative organization based upon the English shire system. In 1282 the angered Welsh revolted under the leadership of Llewellyn's brother David. Llewellyn himself soon joined the rebels and swept over the Conway to pillage and slay. Edward I moved once more against Wales. This time Llewellyn was killed. His brother David was condemned to death as a traitor by a Parliament called at Shrewsbury.

Edward I at once built a girdle of strong castles in northern Wales, wise insurance against Welsh rebellion. At the new castle of Carnarvon a son was born to Edward and his queen. When this child was seventeen years old the title "Prince of Wales" was revived and bestowed upon him; it has since been borne by the eldest sons of England's kings. About the formidable castles towns grew up and English settlers came to live in them. Merchants flooded up the valleys and one aspect of English civilization at last broke upon the remote Celtic settlements. Another consequence of the Welsh war was Edward's reform of the English army. He began to use more light-armed troops, especially infantrymen carrying longbows. The wisdom of this step was later to be seen in the triumph of English arms abroad.

In 1284 the Statute of Wales, or Rhuddlan, provided that the Welsh territories formerly subject to Llewellyn were to be formally annexed to the English crown and divided into counties. With the exception of certain specified Welsh laws and customs English law was to prevail in the newly annexed areas of the native principality of Wales. Not all Welshmen tamely accepted this settlement. There was a strong revolt in 1294 and discontent was long in dying.

In the strongholds of the marcher lords there was little change. The barons there continued to rule their lands as private jurisdictions, subject to the king only in the sense that he was their feudal lord. Their old powers remained relatively untouched until the sixteenth century. They fought among themselves and slew and pillaged at will. Henry VIII was to end their chronic disorders by incorporating all Wales with England in 1536 and executing a number of marcher lords whom he found undesirable.

Meanwhile Edward I had become involved in a war with France. It will be recalled that under the terms of the Treaty of Paris, negotiated between Henry III and Louis IX in 1259, Henry had renounced all claims to the former Angevin possessions in France except Aquitaine and had agreed to render homage to the French king for that fief. Louis IX had also promised to restore to Aquitaine some territories that had been taken from it. This treaty settlement really provided no basis for permanent peace because strong French kings like Philip Augustus and Philip IV were steadily extending royal control over the great feudal fiefs into which France had so long been divided. It was inevitable that Philip IV, powerful, wealthy, and anxious to continue the process of centralization, should seek to seize Aquitaine. As the consolidation of France moved forward by conquest, marriage, escheat and forfeiture, Philip IV and his successors were aided by stirrings of what may be called, even in the thirteenth century, an increasing national feeling.

An excuse for conflict was easily found. Sailors from Philip's Normandy frequently clashed with Gascon sailors from Edward's Aquitaine. In 1293 an English and Gascon merchant fleet fought a sea battle with Norman ships and defeated them. Philip summoned Edward I, as Duke of Aquitaine and Philip's vassal, to answer for the actions of the men of Gascony. Edward agreed to surrender temporarily a part of Gascony as a guarantee that he would investigate the charge against the Gascon sailors and punish them if the evidence warranted it. French troops thereupon proceeded to seize all of Gascony and Philip declared the territory forfeit. In 1294 Edward I went to war against France.

In 1294 and 1296 English forces were sent across the Channel. Edward was not able to equip and dispatch large armies because he was then in the midst of his conflicts with Wales and Scotland. Philip IV, for his part, was occupied with a struggle against Flanders. In these years, too, both Philip and Edward were engaged in their difficult struggle with the papacy. In 1297 Edward made an alliance with Flanders, so important to England's wool trade, and sent a third expedition to France. It achieved nothing. In 1303 the two kings, each with many tasks elsewhere, agreed to make peace. Philip IV restored Gascony to England and awaited a more propitious time to seize it again.

During the first eighteen years of Edward's reign England and Scotland were at peace. Edward I took no steps to press his claim to the overlordship of Scotland until 1290, when Alexander III of Scotland fell over a cliff and left his kingdom without a male heir. Alexander's daughter had married the king of Norway and had died in childbirth, leaving an infant daughter. This child, Margaret, the Maid of Norway, was proclaimed queen of Scotland. When the Scots had finally agreed to Edward's proposal that his son be betrothed to Margaret and thus bring about the amicable union of England and Scotland tragedy intervened. Margaret died on the voyage from Norway to Scotland.

There were now thirteen claimants to the Scottish throne. John Balliol and Robert Bruce had the best claims. Soon the Scottish nobles became divided into several factions and the unhappy country moved to the edge of civil war. A few nobles and churchmen asked Edward to settle the question of the disputed succession. This approach was welcomed by the English king, who had already insisted upon his right to decide the quarrel because, he asserted, he was overlord of Scotland. It was true that Henry II had received homage from the kings of Scotland for the whole Scottish realm; but what Henry II had extorted Richard I had sold back. Before the Norman Conquest certain Scottish kings had apparently been in a position of legal dependence upon the English crown. On occasion Scottish kings had rendered homage, probably only for the fiefs they held across the border in England.

Consequently the claim of Edward was not a sound one. Nevertheless, Scotland could not afford to reject Edward's demand. The alternative was a certain civil war in Scotland and a probable war with England.

In 1291 Robert Bruce and John Balliol met Edward I at Norham Castle on the Tweed. After they had taken an oath of homage Edward referred the claims to a court selected by himself and the two rivals. This court, consisting of eighty Scotsmen and twenty-four Englishmen, finally decided in favor of John Balliol and Edward accepted their report. In 1292 he received homage and fealty for the fief of Scotland and handed the government over to Balliol, the new king of Scots.

To the anger and resentment of Scotsmen Edward I took the oath of homage quite seriously. He insisted that appeals from the courts of Scotland should be made to him. In 1294 he demanded that his vassal Balliol should provide troops to fight in England's war against Philip IV of France. It was not surprising that in 1295 the Scottish nobles apparently forced Balliol to make a defensive alliance with France, the beginning of nearly three hundred years of Scottish-French arrangements directed against England. English estates in Scotland were confiscated. Scottish raiders plunged over the English borders.

Edward at once called the Model Parliament to obtain money to punish Scotland and to invade France. In 1296 he seized and sacked the border town of Berwick and routed the resisting Scots at Dunbar. Balliol was forced to abdicate and Edward took over the government, appointing three English commissioners to rule in his absence. He took back to London Scotland's sacred coronation stone, the Stone of Scone; it now forms the seat of the coronation chair in Westminster Abbey.

Within a year Scotland was ablaze with revolt. Many had refused to take the oath of allegiance to Edward I. Those who had bowed before England's might and tried to make the most of a bad situation soon regretted it. In 1297 appeared William Wallace, a popular leader from the laird, or lower gentry, class. He was an outlaw, a dashing underground leader. After some delay, even a few Scottish nobles joined the forces led by this redoubtable fellow. Most of his followers, fired by anti-English patriotism, were solid men of the peasant and lower gentry class. Led by Wallace, the Scotsmen defeated the English at Stirling Bridge in 1297. The battle was lost by the stupidity of the English commander, who madly sent his men in a double file order over a long and narrow bridge when he might have used a broad ford not far away. When a third of the English force was across the river the Scotsmen struck swiftly. Those who had crossed the bridge were killed; those on the other side fled southwards.

In 1298 Edward himself marched into Scotland and defeated Wallace at Falkirk. There the Scottish pikemen held back the English cavalry until the accurate English longbowmen lengthened the Scottish casualty list with nearly every shot. Then the Scottish pikemen faltered, the English cavalry charged, and all was over. This was the weapon and the method Englishmen were soon to use in France. From their enemies the Welsh the English had learned a lesson with which to defeat the Scotsmen and the French.

After the success at Falkirk it was unfortunate that disputes between Edward and his barons forced the English to withdraw. For six years Edward tried to subdue Scotland. At last, in 1305, Wallace was betrayed and handed over to the English. He was executed for treason and other crimes charged against him; but his spirit did not die. Many Scotsmen who had bled and fought with Wallace were prepared to go on fighting until they found either victory or a gory bed in battle.

There soon arose a new leader, Robert Bruce, grandson of the claimant of 1290. In the eyes of some Scotsmen the royal Bruce had tarnished his name by earlier dealings with the English. However, after he stabbed his cousin, a rival claimant to the throne, Bruce was an outlaw. In the circumstances he decided to gamble everything and stand with those who were fighting the English. He had himself crowned at Scone and proclaimed himself national leader of the resistance movement.

In 1306 Edward's forces drove Bruce into exile. In 1307, however, the tale took a different turn. Edward was ill, but he started north at the head of an English army. Almost within sight of the Scottish border he died. His son, Edward II, whose tragic life will be described in the next chapter, abandoned the projected invasion and went back to London. In 1310, making a pitiful attempt to remedy the results of his incompetence and apathy, Edward led an army against Robert Bruce. The expedition failed completely. Meanwhile Bruce was conquering English garrisons and seizing English castles in Scotland. In 1314 he laid siege to Stirling, one of the last castles still held by the English. Edward II raised an army from England, Wales, and Gascony and invaded Scotland once again, planning to defeat the Scotsmen and raise the siege of Stirling.

Two miles south of Stirling castle the opposing forces met at Bannockburn. The English found themselves badly hampered by marshes, a large ravine, and woods; they were weary from long forced marches. The Scotsmen, on the other hand, were fresh. They held a good position on rising ground behind the stream that gave the battlefield its name. The English outnumbered the Scots three to one; but their organization and command were deplorable. Soon after action began a large number of English troops got caught in a bog. Scottish cavalry attacked the English archers on the flank. Scottish pikemen threw back the first charge of the English horsemen. English reserves could not get into the battle. A feinted flank attack by some Scottish camp followers turned confusion into a rout. Thousands of Edward's army were slain. The rest, including the king himself, fled to an inglorious safety.

Scotland was free. It was still independent when James VI inherited the throne of England in 1603. Only in 1707 did Scotland join England to form the kingdom of Great Britain. Had the policy of Edward I not brought forth Wallace and Bruce and a flaming Scottish nationalism the union he wanted to achieve might have come to pass in his own day.

Edward II, who came to the throne of England in 1307, was a hollow counterfeit of his father. His reign was to be short, and his fate tragic.

Chapter 8

THE FOURTEENTH CENTURY:
POLITICAL AND FOREIGN AFFAIRS
EDWARD II

EDWARD II was unlike his mighty father in almost everything but name. When he came to the throne in 1307 he showed himself to be thoroughly weak. His dilatory and incompetent part in the Scottish conflict has already been described. At home, the restless baronage, recalling their golden hours in the reign of the incapable Henry III, were anxious to check the royal power and to increase their own. They felt that under Edward I they had been denied their proper and legitimate place in government. With the accession of Edward II it seemed that the awaited chance to alter that state of affairs had at last arrived.

The new king was handsome, tall, strong, athletic, a hard drinker and a spendthrift. He was not greatly interested in either politics or war; his inclinations lay in other directions. As the barons noted his manifest inability to grasp and hold the reins of power they grew bolder. Their general annoyance was increased by the fact that Edward soon dismissed several of his father's ministers and replaced them by personal favorites who were frequently devoid of political knowledge or skill and were regarded by the barons as objectionable upstarts. One of these friends of the king was Piers Gaveston, a dashing Gascon whom Edward I had exiled because he did not want him associating with his son. Edward II recalled Gaveston and made him earl of Cornwall. Gaveston and other favorites, such as Hugh Despenser and his son, infuriated the barons by their arrogant assumption of power. In 1310 the barons forced Edward II to send Gaveston into exile again: he became governor of Ireland. In 1312 he came back, at Edward's insistence. This time his enemies, led by the earl of Warwick, treacherously seized and beheaded him without trial.

Meanwhile, in 1310, the barons came to Parliament with armed retainers and compelled Edward II to submit to baronial control. A reform commission of twenty-one lay and ecclesiastical magnates, the

129

so-called "Lords Ordainers," forced Edward to accept their rules for the reform of the royal household and the government. The "Ordinances of London," completed in 1310 and confirmed by Parliament in 1311, were reminiscent of the Provisions of Oxford that had humiliated Henry III in 1258. The forty-one clauses of the ordinances of 1311 declared that Edward II's favorites, particularly the two Despensers, father and son, should be dismissed: "We ordain that all the evil councillors shall be put out and utterly removed." The way would thus be open for "fit persons," such as the barons, to advise the king. Edward II was forbidden to make any major appointments to the royal household or administration without the consent of the barons in Parliament.

The ordinances of 1311 also specifically declared that "the customs of the kingdom shall be received and kept by men of the kingdom itself, and not by aliens." Nor was Edward permitted to "go out of the kingdom or to undertake an act of war against anyone without the common assent of his baronage and that in parliament." Several other clauses further limited the royal power in order to redress the situation declared to exist in the preamble to the ordinances: "Through bad and deceitful counsel, our lord the king and all his men have everywhere been dishonoured and his crown in many ways has been debased and ruined."

Thus Edward's bosom favorites were ousted and the king, it seemed, was to be checked and guided by the barons. All might have turned out as the magnates planned but for two facts. In the first place, the new "Lords Ordainers" showed themselves as greedy as Edward's friends had been, and no more competent; they were "swollen by the pride of birth"; and they could not give the necessary steady application to the business of government. Secondly, Edward was able to use competent and loyal members of the large and complicated royal household to outwit, to "dive underground," and to circumvent the nobles set about him. The permanent household officials, trained and skilled, could quietly handle the specialized business of government to the king's advantage—and their own. Fools or scoundrels, in rank far over the heads of civil servants, could never carry on the king's government well; that was a task for experts.

The baronage, led by Edward's cousin Thomas, earl of Lancaster, showed their lack of concern for the national welfare by refusing to help Edward II against the Scots; the result was the battle of Bannockburn. They proved unable to make effective use of the power they had wrested from the king. There was widespread internal disorder; taxes were high, and rising still; the Scottish clansmen were raiding from their northern lairs. The barons began to fall apart, divided by rivalries in the scrambles for power. In 1322 Edward decided that the hour for revenge had come. He struck swiftly, in a momentary flash of his father's energy, and defeated the barons in a short campaign in Yorkshire. The Duke of Lancaster was captured and beheaded. Several other barons were hanged or exiled. A Parliament held at York revoked the ordinances of 1311, thus confirming the king's victory and the failure of the baronial experiment in coercion. The putting of the crown into commission had proved unwise.

Edward at once turned to his favorites, particularly the two Hugh Despensers, father and son. The jealous and impotent barons watched resentfully. In 1325 Edward's queen, Isabella, was sent to negotiate with her brother, the king of France, about the future of Aquitaine. Already offended at the activities of one of Edward's odious favorites in London the queen joined several exiled English barons to plot against her husband. Of one of them, Roger Mortimer, earl of March, she became the mistress. So scandalous was her conduct that her brother ordered her out of France. Accompanied by several disaffected and intriguing exiles, Isabella went to Flanders, where she stopped at the court of the count of Hainault. There she obtained soldiers after agreeing to a marriage between her son Edward and Philippa, daughter of the count. In 1326 the conspirators and their forces landed in England.

Many Englishmen, weary of Edward's misrule, swarmed towards the banners of Isabella. Edward found himself deserted, detested, and friendless. The jackals whom his bounty had fed scented danger and disappeared. The two Despensers were caught; both were summarily hanged. In vain Edward sought support. At last he fled frantically southwestward to Devonshire. From there he sailed for Lundy's Isle; but the wind drove his ship ashore on the Welsh coast. There he was captured and brought a prisoner to the dungeon of Kenilworth Castle.

Pressed by the lords of Parliament, Edward II abdicated in favor of his son, Prince Edward, then thirteen years of age. In January, 1327, articles of accusation against Edward II declared that he was "incompetent to govern in person." In the name of the young Edward III Isabella and Mortimer ruled. Before the close of 1327 the deposed Edward II was taken to Berkeley Castle in Gloucestershire. There he was murdered by means more horrible than those used by the assassins in Christopher Marlowe's *Edward II*.

EDWARD III

For three years after the deposition of Edward II, Roger Mortimer and Isabella ruled and plundered England. Mortimer, always fearful of his enemies, brought about the execution of Edward III's uncle, the earl of Kent, in 1330. Another relentless foe of the usurper was the earl of Lancaster, who proposed to Edward III that Mortimer be pulled from power. Late in 1330 the young king suddenly acted. Mortimer was arrested, tried for high treason, and executed. Edward's mother, Isabella, was hurried into retirement. The unpopular regency was ended.

Edward III was energetic, ambitious, and popular, particularly among the nobles. The long conflicts between royal and baronial policies almost disappeared. Edward's spectacular court, filled with tournaments and pomp, delighted Englishmen in the last bright hours of chivalry and feudalism. By freely granting petitions, by numerous concessions, by his charming grace and courtesy, Edward III soon won a high place in the hearts of many of his subjects. His main interest, however, was in war. War was the sport of kings.

The young monarch first turned against Scotland. In 1332 Edward Balliol had seized the Scottish throne; the house of Robert Bruce objected and the resulting civil war tempted Edward III to follow in the footsteps of his grandfather, Edward I. In 1333 he sent an army to support Balliol and defeated the forces backing the cause of the Bruce factions. But Balliol was unpopular in Scotland, especially after he demeaned himself in the eyes of Scotsmen by rendering homage to Edward III. In 1334 the English forces tried in vain to check the flames of resistance to Balliol's rule. Edward III was finally compelled to withdraw his soldiers because of worsening relations between England and France. Then, in 1342, David Bruce overthrew Edward Balliol. Scotland was soon at peace and once more free from English control.

Meanwhile, under her martial king, England moved towards war with France. A hasty treaty, made in 1303 between Philip IV and Edward I, had left Gascony, the southwest section of Aquitaine, in English hands. Thus England controlled the shipbuilding of Bayonne and the wine trade of Bordeaux. However, it was not to be expected that the aggressive French kings would meekly surrender their ambition to drive the English out of all France. Late in the reign of Edward II another war had resulted in further French conquests. After Edward II's deposition in 1327 Mortimer and Isabella had signed a treaty conceding to France almost all the territories her armies had seized. This peace was as unstable as all the ones that had preceded it. For two hundred years there had been intermittent conflict between England and France because England's kings held great fiefs in France over which the French kings, busy building a centralized nation state, wanted to obtain control. The age-long conflict could come to an end only when England surrendered her possessions in France. This simple fact was the fundamental cause of the long conflict usually called the Hundred Years' War which began when Edward III declared war against France in 1337.

There were many sources of friction. In the war Edward had begun against Scotland, France had consistently aided the Scots; the French king had given asylum to the exiled David Bruce. English and French sailors, always rivals, were raiding the Channel ports, committing open acts of piracy, waging spasmodic warfare in the narrow seas. The French continued to interfere, openly and secretly, in the affairs of Gascony. There were knotty difficulties about the question of homage for Gascony, about boundaries, about interpretation of the treaty terms. The French were again threatening Flanders and consequently the English wool trade. The pro-French count of Flanders prohibited trade between his country and England. Edward III thereupon forbade the export of raw wool to Flanders or the import of woven commodities to England. The economic results of Edward's action proved too heavy a burden for the Flemish weavers and merchants of Bruges, Ghent, and Ypres to endure. In 1338 they revolted against their count and persuaded Edward to rescind his orders on the understanding that Flanders would remain neutral in the Anglo-French conflict. In a later hour, the Flemish merchants were to force the count of Flanders into war on the English side. Meanwhile the channels of the wool trade remained open.

During these years of undeclared hostilities Edward sought allies in Europe. He formed several agreeable alliances with ambitious German and Dutch princes to the northeast of France. His father-in-law, the count of Hainault, also pledged his armed support. Such was the explosive character of Anglo-French relations when Edward III determined upon war in the autumn of 1337. The actual outbreak of conflict occurred when the aggressive Edward claimed the throne of France.

The law of primogeniture ruled the succession to the French throne. It had also been decided that a woman could not inherit the crown. Could a woman transmit a claim to her son? To that question there was no clear answer. When the last of the three sons of France's Philip IV died in 1328 without a male heir the problem of the succession at once arose. Isabella, the mother of Edward III of England, was the daughter of Philip IV. Edward III was still a minor; but English claims were put forward in his name for the throne of France because he was the grandson of Philip IV. A French court, naturally reluctant to have the English Edward III as king of France, declared that the French crown could not descend to Edward III through Isabella because a woman could have no claim and could transmit none. To justify their action the French lawyers invoked an ancient tribal custom of the Salian Franks, which was called the "Salic law"; this old custom in fact had nothing to do with the national principle established in 1328.

As a result of the French court decision, Philip of Valois, the nephew of Philip IV, became king of France as Philip VI. For several years Edward III rendered homage for the fief of Gascony to Philip VI. In 1337, seeking a pretext and a rallying slogan for war, Edward reasserted his claim to the French throne. At Ghent, in 1340, he declared himself king of France, quartered his arms with the French lilies. The kings of England continued to call themselves kings of France until the reign of George III. Meanwhile, the merchants of Flanders ousted their count and recognized Edward's right to the French throne. Their ships joined with the English to keep the Channel open. The wool trade, first foundation of England's commercial greatness and source of disposable wealth, largely financed the Hundred Years' War; it also dictated the alliance between the Low Countries and England, long a feature of British foreign policy.

By his entrance into war Edward III hoped to retain Gascony, perhaps to build again the great Angevin Empire; to exclude the French from Flanders and bind the Flemings to England's wool trade; to subjugate the Scots after he had defeated their French allies. In England the war was widely popular among all classes, particularly the knights and the yeomen, already famous for their skill with the yew longbows. The lure of adventure, the prospects of plunder, conquest, and glory, shone brightly as Englishmen went forth to war and the wind stood fair for France.

THE HUNDRED YEARS' WAR

The spasmodic and spectacular Hundred Years' War produced several results of significance in English history. Apart from its purely military aspects, the long conflict was important in one phase of the growth of English national feeling. Through the centuries this national consciousness in England proceeded mainly from below, being encouraged by the royal policy neatly described by a modern scholar as "self-government at the king's command." Professor G. P. Cuttino has shown that the rise of the national awareness of England as a kingdom, a separate entity, was closely connected in the thirteenth and fourteenth centuries with the increasing participation of "lesser folk" in public affairs. In tracing the growth of anti-foreign feeling Professor Cuttino has remarked that "fear, and later hatred, of the foreigner was a fear and hatred of the Frenchman born of bitter experience on the part of English officials who were responsible for the conduct of foreign affairs."

The attitude of both Henry III and Edward I was in most respects characterized by a medieval feudal cosmopolitanism. Their specialists and advisers attempted to stress the importance and necessity of anti-foreign elements in English national policy, but without much success. After 1307 the inadequacy of Edward II was to the advantage of the civil service officials so completely opposed to France. In this respect the brief reign of Edward II was a period of transition. When Edward III moved towards the Hundred Years' War he had fully accepted the xenophobian aspect of national consciousness.

Thus another component was added to the already lusty sense of

England as a separate kingdom. "It was a new consciousness of England as a political entity opposed to a similar political entity." A solid basis for the later nationalism of the nation state was almost completely laid. The English victories in the war were to provide bright chapters of tradition and hope for the future. There were, of course, many other reasons why the flickering light of nationalism began to shine more brightly in the fourteenth century. Several of the tides and crosscurrents of this restless age are described in the following chapter. In any event, it was inevitable and natural that England should cease being merely the recipient of foreign influence and should begin to move from the defensive to the aggressive in both spirit and action. Such stirrings were in the air of the age.

In 1339, Edward III invaded France from the northeast; he laid waste wide areas but did not encounter the forces of Philip VI. The next year, Edward saw the first great naval battle in English history. Off Sluys, near Ostend, an English army transport fleet of two hundred ships met and destroyed or captured the vessels of a larger French fleet. This victory ended the danger of French raids on English ports and secured English communication with the Flemish towns; the mastery of the Channel was henceforth the main aim of English naval policy.

After Edward undertook a fruitless invasion of Brittany in 1342, there was a truce until 1346. In that year, the French attacked Gascony and Edward gathered about 12,000 men to invade France once more. In July, 1346, the army sailed from Portsmouth and landed in Normandy. Edward then marched eastward, captured Caen, and moved towards Paris. Then he crossed the Seine and headed northwards, hoping to join his Flemish allies. The pursuing French army beat the English to the Somme and nearly pushed Edward into a pocket between the Somme and the sea. Through good fortune, the English were able to ford the river and draw up their forces at Crecy, a few miles north of Abbeville. The English flanks were protected by a stream and a forest. On the crest of a hill, three battalions of knights, infantry, and dismounted cavalry formed a curved front line, its end thrust forward. Edward divided his 3,000 archers and stationed them on the flanks of each battalion. It was their task to break the charge of the French cavalry before it reached the English lines.

At the battle of Crecy the French outnumbered the English two to one. Because the French nobility did not regard the bow as a gentleman's weapon, Philip VI had hired Genoese crossbowmen, who advanced about five o'clock in the afternoon to fire upon the English lines. The whole French army was tired; the uncovered Genoese bowstrings had been dampened by a shower. The English, with the sun at their backs, could see better than the enemy archers. Crossbows had to be stretched with a rack; the longbows could fire arrows at the rate of five or six a minute; and their range was longer than that of the crossbow. Many Genoese were slain before they had shot one arrow. The Genoese, whose hearts were not in the battle, were soon confused, and the impatient French knights charged through them towards the English.

In a famous passage, the chronicler Froissart wrote that the English let fly their arrows "with such force and quickness that it seemed as if it snowed." The ranks of the mail-clad feudal horsemen were broken; few reached the English lines. As darkness fell, the English swept down the hill and the battle was ended. What was left of Philip's army retreated to Abbeville. Behind, slaughtered on the battlefield, were fifteen hundred French nobles and knights and ten thousand men of lesser rank. The archers had conquered the mailed horsemen. Edward I would have been pleased at the work of his royal grandson and his army, lords and commoners, Englishmen all, fighting side by side. It was a lesson the French had yet to learn.

Edward III at once marched upon Calais, the nearest French port to England. For nearly a year the inhabitants of that city refused to surrender. Only when their food was gone did they open their gates. Soon English merchants began to settle and the colony they planted steadily grew. For over two hundred years Calais remained a valuable port for English trade with the Continent, a commercial rival to the towns of Flanders and a useful base for military invasion.

Meanwhile David II of Scotland had unwisely listened to the French king, who had urged him to strike at England when so many Englishmen were busy in France. David moved across the borders and was captured by the northern militiamen at Neville's Cross. Everywhere Edward's arms were triumphant. In both Gascony and Brittany the armies and cities of Philip VI were yielding before the tide of English power.

A truce agreed upon in 1347 did not end all hostilities; there were several spasmodic bursts of pillaging and fighting before 1355, the year when Edward III decided to invade France with overwhelming force and thus end the war. From Edward's point of view nothing went well. He could not muster enough power to carry out his plans, partly because the Black Death, to be described in the following chapter, had reduced the number of men available for military service. Meanwhile, however, Edward III's eldest son, called the Black Prince, was successfully leading several devastating raids against the French out of his headquarters at Bordeaux. It was said that his men destroyed more than five hundred towns and villages in two months, a feat worthy of note in the fourteenth century, if not in later chapters of European disorder. The darker aspects of the age of chivalry are often overlooked by the writers of romance. For example, the chivalrous Black Prince himself, "inflamed with ire" at the town of Limoges, was responsible in 1370 for the callous slaughter of 3,000 men, women, and children.

In 1356 the Black Prince led an army of about 6,000 men north-

[handwritten margin note: Battle of Poitiers]

wards towards Tours. His path was blocked at Poitiers by John II, the gallant, courteous, and incompetent king who had come to the French throne in 1350. John II had a force of over 20,000 men gathered to rescue Languedoc from the Black Prince. His strategy, or that of his advisers, soon cut the Black Prince off from the sea and the south; the stage was ready for a French victory and an English disaster. But the French victory never came. The Englishmen were drawn up in a strong defensive position on a hill, as they had been at Crecy ten years before. Repeating the tactics of Crecy, the English archers and dismounted knights won a battle against heavy odds. Thousands of Frenchmen died in the arrow storm and the captured French king was sent over the seas to England. Poitiers sped the decline of chivalry. For France it was a catastrophe.

Nevertheless, the English victory did not end the war. Royal authority collapsed in France. A series of truces had no practical effect. Wandering bands, or "free companies," of English marauders harassed and plundered the desperate French peasants. Mercenaries of both sides lived off the country. At last, raided by the English and ravaged by the French tax collectors, the French peasants rose in the famous unorganized and brief rebellion called the Jacquerie. The rebels, quickly crushed by several feudal forces, were savagely punished; but the national misery continued. An exhausted France could not keep up the war. Finally, in May, 1360, Edward III imposed upon his enemies the treaty of Bretigny, or Calais. By the terms of this agreement Edward obtained complete sovereignty over an Aquitaine enlarged to include Poitou, Gascony, and most of the other territories it had embraced in the days of Henry II. Edward also received Calais and Ponthieu, an area around Crecy a few miles south of Calais. Edward, for his part, abandoned his claim to the French throne and his alliance with Flanders. The French temporarily gave up their alliance with Scotland. France also agreed to pay a ransom of 500,000 pounds to effect the release of John II. When it was later found impossible to meet the first payment of the ransom John chivalrously went back to captivity in England.

[handwritten margin note: Jacquerie — French peasant Rebellion]

Once more a peace treaty failed to end the war. The French nobles of Aquitaine refused to surrender their castles to the arms and trumpets of Edward III and the Black Prince. French and English freebooters waged their local battles. The increase of English territories in France widened the original causes of the Anglo-French conflict. Meanwhile France, divided and shattered, slowly began to mend. When John II died in captivity in 1364 his able son, Charles V, aided by his talented constable, the ugly and famous Breton warrior Bertrand du Guesclin, almost completely reorganized the French government and administration. At the same time, Charles V and du Guesclin prepared to drive the English out of France.

In Normandy and Brittany there had really been no effective peace in the years after the treaty of 1360. In 1367 the French and English widened their areas of dispute by supporting rival candidates for the Spanish throne of Castile. Edward, the Black Prince, led an English army into Spain and won several battles; but disease killed thousands of English soldiers. When the Black Prince returned from his bootless adventures to resume his position as governor of Aquitaine he was already suffering from the tuberculosis that was to kill him a few years later. In 1369 he tried to collect taxes in the duchy of Aquitaine to pay for sending the English forces to Spain. English rule was already widely unpopular, and this step made it more so.

At this stage the shrewd Charles V of France ordered the Black Prince to answer in a feudal court to the charges of tyranny made against him by some nobles of Aquitaine. The treaty of 1360 had denied to the French kings the right to exercise such powers and Charles knew it. "I will come," the Black Prince is said to have replied, "but with 60,000 men at my back." The French demand and the English answer meant that Charles V and Edward III were once again formally at war. For Edward it was not a fortunate event. He was sixty-two years old, surrounded by conspiracies and corruption, and swayed by the demands and rewards of his mistress, Alice Perrers. The Black Prince was ill; he was to return to England in 1372 and to die a few years later. England had few competent military leaders; her treasury and her energy were low.

Charles V, on the other hand, was younger than Edward, energetic, and intelligent. By his side Bertrand du Guesclin soon reorganized the French army; it was no longer the undisciplined and cumbersome feudal levy of the days of Crecy and Poitiers, doomed by its own blindness and pride. The new commander made no attempt to defeat the English in pitched battles; he saw that the English army would always win when the French attacked it in position. The Frenchman preferred to use sieges and guerrilla tactics to wear down English forces far removed from their bases of supply.

In the last years of Edward III England lost most of Aquitaine. Ponthieu was seized by the French. England's allies in Normandy and Brittany were defeated. Several English expeditions failed, notably one led by John of Gaunt in 1373. In 1372 an English fleet was almost destroyed off Rochelle by the naval forces of France's ally, the king of Castile. When the weary and desperate English agreed to the treaty of Bruges in 1375 they held only Calais, Bordeaux, and Bayonne with a narrow coastal strip of land between the two latter towns.

The skies grew darker. When the young Richard II came to the throne in 1377 the French renewed the war and attacked the English coast, poorly defended since the heavy English losses in the naval battle of 1372. The raiding Frenchmen burned Rye and Hastings; they thrust up the Thames estuary and as far inland as Lewes; they set fire to several towns on the Isle of Wight. Ineffective English expeditions against France cost money and lost men and gave rise to loud complaint. So far as England was concerned it was fortunate that both Bertrand du Guesclin and Charles V died in 1380. Charles VI, the new king of France, was a minor, and the French regency was as divided and as weak as the regency in England. In such circumstances it seemed foolish to prolong the war.

In 1394 a truce was agreed upon. Two years later the truce grew into a peace arrangement. England's Richard II married Isabella, the eight-year-old daughter of Charles VI of France. Both kings formally promised to wage no war before 1426. Each nation was to hold inviolate whatever territories it possessed in 1396. For England this meant that Richard II kept what had been left when the treaty of Bruges had been signed in 1375: Bayonne, Bordeaux, Calais, and a narrow ribbon of the Gascon coast. It was not much for England to salvage from the conquests marked by the treaty of Calais in 1360. The triumphs of Edward III and the Black Prince at Sluys, Crecy, and Poitiers were not forgotten; the magic names told of the harvest of glory; but the lands that the armies had won had been lost again.

THE POWERS OF PARLIAMENT

It is never possible, when discussing the fourteenth century, to make any separation between what might be called parliamentary affairs on the one hand and the affairs of the crown and council on the other. Parliament, all through the century, meant a special meeting of the king and those who were summoned to counsel him, including the lords spiritual and temporal, some permanent royal advisers and servants of the household, and the deputies of the commons. Most of the Parliaments of the fourteenth century lasted only a few days or weeks. In 1328, for example, there were four Parliaments; in 1340 there were three. The procedure of keeping the same Parliament in existence for a long period and calling it from time to time into "sessions" was probably not invented until the reign of Richard II, who "packed" his Parliaments and wanted to hold on to a friendly body once he had it.

Parliament rolls, statutes, and ordinances, the best sources for the constitutional history of the fourteenth century, show many significant developments. The thirteenth century Parliament had been in many respects a vague and formless body. It remained for the fourteenth century to witness the emergence of a Parliament legally defined and constituted. Under Edward II the changes in organization and function were not to contemporaries prophetic of major changes. Parliament seemed to remain chiefly a meeting of the king's great council or court. The main elements in Parliament were still the official peerages of England. In the fourteenth century it was the magnates, and they alone, who heard pleas and generally provided remedies.

Nevertheless, the knights and burgesses were summoned to Parliament in almost every year of Edward III's reign. A precedent, useful for the future, was being established. During the Parliaments of 1339–1341 the knights and burgesses united to form what was to become the house of commons. The lower clergy had withdrawn to their own convocation, as earlier described, and hence were now outside Parliament. The commons and lords still met in full sessions; but they separated to debate and decide most questions among themselves, especially those set before the full Parliament in the king's speech. The lords usually stayed in the Parliament chamber; slowly the council in Parliament was to become the house of lords in a bicameral parliamentary system. This gradually happened when the council in Parliament came to be composed only of a fixed hereditary element of lay and ecclesiastical lords and the royal officials of the council disappeared from Parliament and took no part in its work.

The knights and burgesses met in the precincts of Westminster Abbey. They had their own clerk. They soon elected a speaker to speak for them to the full sessions in the Parliament chamber. The speakership was to become an important institution in later centuries. Presiding over the house of commons, it is the speaker's duty to maintain the dignity of the house; to ensure free and courteous debate; with indisputable impartiality to apply and interpret the formidable body of precedent that now constitutes Parliamentary law.

The first main advance of the power of Parliament in the fourteenth century came through the increased control of national finance. The costs of the Hundred Years' War were so great that Edward III was compelled to ask for large and numerous sums of money. The representatives in the commons seized the chance to demand concessions from the king in return for money grants to him. They had experimented with that procedure a few times earlier in the century. For example, on two occasions in Edward II's reign the commons had asked for a redress of grievances before they granted taxes on personal property. In each case the substance of their petition was approved and enacted into statutes by the king and the lords.

By Edward III's day it was becoming quite customary to attach conditions to money grants. To obtain the one the king had to grant the other. Here was the beginning of the modern system of parliamentary appropriations. Parliamentary committees were set up to audit the royal accounts. There were frequent complaints about royal expenditures. Parliament often insisted that money granted should be spent for certain specific purposes, and no others. In the Parliament of 1376, for example, a knight of the south country asserted that "all we have given to the war for a long time we have lost because it has been badly wasted and falsely expended."

The second main extension of parliamentary power was in the field of legislation. The house of commons had no right of initiative except by starting the process of legislation through common petitions, as distinct from the petitions of individuals, to the king and the council. These petitions might not be accepted. They might be changed by the king and his ministers before they were enrolled as statutes. This was a problem of considerable importance in the fourteenth and fifteenth centuries.

There was a further difficulty: the king and his council might still make ordinances and proclamations which were as much laws as statutes. How could the older method of legislation by king and council be eliminated and all legislation be limited to the new system of parliamentary petition procedure? Only very slowly was it tacitly agreed that ordinances were to be considered temporary measures; statutes, on the other hand, were part of the permanent law of the land. At the end of the fourteenth century the vexed problems of legislative dominance were not finally solved. It remained for the next age to develop the new pressures, privileges, and procedures to be described later.

Besides strengthening its position with respect to national finance and legislation Parliament made a series of lesser gains in a third field. It frequently sought to influence the policy of the government. In earlier days the royal administration had often been checked or persuaded by the growth of a baronial opposition to its policy. Parliament could also refuse money grants and thus force the king, through his financial dependence, to yield to their wishes. However, in the latter part of the fourteenth century, Parliament used another process, very effective and direct. This was the weapon of impeachment, useful in controlling the king and his ministers, particularly because it involved less danger of revolution and civil war. As a result of the use of the impeachment process a minister of the king could be held directly responsible to Parliament for his official acts. A charge against a king's minister would not be liable to provoke a civil war, whereas a charge against the king himself was always dangerous. Hence the principle: a king can do no wrong; but his ministers can.

The impeachment process was a criminal trial. The house of lords has always kept the judicial functions of the old great council; it was, and is, the highest court of law in the land. The house of commons, by acting as a grand or accusing jury, could present ministers or other servants of the king before the house of lords for trials for serious offenses, such as felony or treason. If the upper house found the accused guilty of the charges against him, the penalty might be death. Aware of the consequences of giving bad advice or obeying bad orders, the royal servants might well tread warily; to do otherwise was risky. In such circumstances, irresponsible or arbitrary rulers might expect to have difficulty in finding able or loyal ministers. The house of commons in the "Good Parliament" of 1376, moving against John of Gaunt's political machine, impeached Richard Lyons, a merchant and customs officer, together with others who had used their offices for illegal purposes "which would have been a horrible matter to rehearse in full." This was the first time the weapon of impeachment was used; it was by no means the last.

By such slow processes the powers of Parliament grew stronger and more numerous. Meanwhile, as Parliament invaded new judicial and legislative fields the functions of the king's council were diminished. Several government departments and royal courts were also unconsciously striking out in new directions. Every gain they made meant a corresponding decrease in the powers and jurisdiction of the council. For example, the court of chancery was slowly becoming differentiated from the council proper; as it developed procedural methods not used in the council, fewer members of the council attended. In the fifteenth century the chancellor found that his court had become almost entirely separate from the council.

As it moved towards independence the chancery took with it a large part of the business formerly performed by the council in the area of civil jurisdiction. Most of the cases that came up to chancery were not covered by either common or statute law and thus the chancery slowly became the main equity court of the realm. In the next century the chancery finally developed a court jurisdiction completely separate from that of the council. Twelve assistants, called masters in chancery and headed by a master of the rolls, were appointed to aid the chancellor. The separate jurisdiction of the chancery, founded upon the equitable and prerogative residual powers of the council, was gradually expanded; and with the expansion the body of equity jurisprudence was consequently enlarged.

RICHARD II ~ 1376

Edward, the famous Black Prince, eldest son of Edward III and pattern of European chivalry, died in 1376. A year later death ended the long reign of Edward III and Richard, son of the Black Prince, came to the throne. He was only eleven years old. Because Richard II was a minor England was governed by a regency. The years of the regency marked a period of widespread social and economic discontent, so important in the history of England that they will be discussed in the following chapter. The results of the maladministration of England's armies abroad heightened public unrest. Parliament tried eagerly, and without success, to control the government of the regency. Under Parliament's watchful guidance the council members did try to manage national affairs adequately; they were prevented from doing so by their factional disputes and their own incompetence.

When Richard II was seventeen years old he began to gather about him several friends who were willing to aid the impetuous youth in his plans to end the control of Parliament in governmental affairs.

Richard's chancellor, appointed in 1384, was Michael de la Pole, whom Richard made earl of Suffolk. A second important minister was the young Robert de Vere, earl of Oxford. The advice of these two councillors, and others like them, helped to convince Richard that the power of the great nobles, particularly his uncles, should be diminished; that England should make peace with France; and that the powers of a presumptuous Parliament should be curbed. Against Richard and his ministers stood several jealous nobles, led by the king's uncle, the ambitious and unscrupulous Thomas of Woodstock, Duke of Gloucester.

The turbulent Gloucester itched for greater power; some contemporaries thought he even aspired to the throne itself. John of Gaunt, also Richard's uncle, was busily waging a private war in Spain, claiming the Spanish crown. A third uncle, Edmund, Duke of York, did not seriously concern himself about the bickerings in council and Parliament. Gloucester alone was ready to cause trouble for Richard.

In 1385 Richard stubbornly refused to yield to Parliament's request that he dismiss several of his ministers. At the same time he became involved in long disputes with the house of commons about the expenses of the royal household. Richard was always in need of money. In 1386 there were some ugly scenes in Parliament, in part the work of the malcontent barons. Meanwhile the French were threatening to invade southern England. Gloucester and his followers took advantage of the general turmoil to attack the earl of Suffolk and four other ministers of the king. Gloucester and his allies were called the "Lords Appellant" because they "appealed," or accused, Suffolk and his courtier colleagues of treason.

In 1387 Richard prepared for civil war. But Gloucester and his fellow magnates had already gathered forces and the result was a heavy defeat for the king's supporters under the command of Robert de Vere, earl of Oxford. The five accusers were supported by a Parliament anxious to see effective parliamentary control established once more over the restless king. Suffolk and the other defendants were swiftly found guilty of the charges advanced by the Lords Appellant. The so-called "Merciless Parliament," backed by Gloucester, ordered the execution of many of the king's friends, including the lord chief justice, the mayor of London, and even Richard's harmless tutor. Suffolk and Oxford luckily escaped to France.

Richard was compelled, for a time, to submit to the unquiet ambition of the five Lords Appellant. After the oligarchy had ruled for a year in unchallenged triumph Richard suddenly declared that he would take the reins of government into his own hands. He asserted that he would govern in harmony with the advice of Parliament. John of Gaunt had returned from Spain and his friendly presence probably gave Richard courage to defy the gang of men who had set themselves about him. Richard knew that the Lords Appellant were divided by jealous rivalries and had no loyalty to one another. When he took his bold step he met no resistance.

For eight years Richard ruled well; he tactfully used his power with moderation and abstained from reprisals. As described earlier in this chapter, he made peace with France in 1396; by this peace policy he estranged many nobles. He pacified Ireland, for a time. England was prosperous, secure, and quiet. Richard apparently wanted no trouble; he even kept some of the Lords Appellant in his council.

Meanwhile, however, the king was silently introducing a larger element of courtier support into his council and placing loyal and expert followers in strategic places in the royal administration. The foundations of despotism were being prepared. In 1397 the quiet rule of Richard suddenly ended. The "constitutional" monarch became an unfettered despot. Some contemporaries believed that Richard had been made impatient by continued objections on the part of Parliament to his extravagance. Parliament was always liberal with criticism and chary of supplies. Others have attributed the startling change in the king's attitude and actions to the death of his first wife, Anne of Bohemia, who had restrained his violent passions. Still others have contented themselves by saying that Richard's autocratic temper could brook restraint no longer. In any event, the king burst the bonds tied about him by Parliament and turned to revenge himself upon the Lords Appellant, who had slain his friends nine years before.

Richard himself subdued and arrested a startled Duke of Gloucester who was taken to Calais and murdered. Two other Lords Appellant were charged with treason; one died under the headsman's axe; the other had all his property confiscated. Several friends and relatives of these men were executed, exiled, or imprisoned. Richard did not strike at the two remaining Lords Appellant, Thomas, earl of Nottingham, and Henry, earl of Derby, because they were supporting him in 1397. Instead, he rewarded them for their services, creating Nottingham Duke of Norfolk and his cousin Derby Duke of Hereford. It seemed that he had forgiven or forgotten their share in the events of 1388. But events proved otherwise. When Norfolk and Hereford quarrelled in 1398 Richard II exiled Norfolk for life and Hereford for six years. Apparently the vengeance of Richard was complete; the last of the five Lords Appellant had been punished. But the final lines of the chapter had not been written. The exiled Henry Bolingbroke, Duke of Hereford, was the son of John of Gaunt, Duke of Lancaster. Hence Hereford was heir to the vast Lancastrian estates. He was the really formidable and inveterate enemy who would one day oust Richard from his throne.

In 1398 a Parliament, adjourned from Westminster to Shrewsbury, packed with the king's men and watched by thousands of his archers, voted Richard a life income. It committed political suicide by permitting several of its powers to be exercised by a committee of eighteen members, submissive creatures of the king. New treason laws expanded the definition of treason and wrapped it up in such ambiguous language that any opposition to the king might be called treason. Richard arbitrarily imprisoned men who spoke against tyrannical acts. Law after law was broken by the royal commands. Richard imposed and collected forced loans; he also embroiled himself with the Percy family, whose earldom of Northumberland was a petty kingdom in the north. It was rash of the king to antagonize and defy the wrath of so many of his subjects, all at the same time. He sold charters of pardon to the Gloucester adherents; he recklessly interfered with the courts of law and justice. All the checks that Parliament and baronage had been able to impose upon the monarchy were broken and cast aside by armed force and legal chicanery. No man's life or property was safe. Richard was king indeed.

In February, 1399, John of Gaunt died and Richard seized all of the property of the house of Lancaster. "Think what you will; we seize into our hands His plate, his goods, his money and his lands." That step was not Richard's last mistake; but it was one of his greatest.

THE REVOLUTION OF 1399

Early in 1399 Richard II allowed himself to be lured to Ireland to deal with rebellious Irishmen who had murdered his deputy. In his absence his cousin, the banished Henry Bolingbroke, now Duke of Lancaster and heir of John of Gaunt, landed in Yorkshire to claim the estates that Richard had arbitrarily seized. Thousands of Englishmen, including the earl of Northumberland, mightiest magnate of the north, flocked to serve under Henry's banners. Richard, long stormbound in Ireland, returned to Wales too late. When he landed at Milford Haven he found that nearly the whole of England not only supported Bolingbroke's claim to the confiscated lands but also wanted Bolingbroke to be king. Even the troops that Richard had brought back from Ireland began to melt away. Richard made every possible mistake at the crisis. Helpless, he surrendered and abdicated.

The Parliament of 1399 accepted Richard's abdication and a commission was appointed to draw up the final document of deposition. "Those statements of his crimes and defaults were notoriously sufficient for deposing the same king," declared the Parliament roll of 1399, "considering also his own confession with regard to his incompetence." Like James II, three centuries later, Richard II was denounced above all on the ground that he had broken the fundamental laws of England. He was formally charged with the crime of having declared the laws to be "in his own heart." Richard, with all his vagaries, had finally aimed at making himself an absolute monarch; the result was revolution and the establishment of the Lancastrian dynasty.

Scholars have discovered that almost all happenings in the reign of Richard II are intricate and ill-reported. "The revolution of 1399 is perhaps as fully documented as any event of equal importance in medieval history," a modern student has written, "yet the main trend of events remains in obscurity." Most of the witnesses were divided into different camps. Many contemporaries, carefully recording the story for posterity, were Lancastrian propagandists, anxious to describe the deeds and motives of Henry of Lancaster in as gentle a manner as possible. For example, the St. Alban's Chronicle and Adam of Usk rapidly slurred over the abdication of Richard. The official Lancastrian apologists and the French royalists have baffled honest historians of later centuries in their search for answers to some crucial questions. Almost all of the contemporary evidence is tainted and partisan. A recent scholar has shown, for example, that on three points the official Parliament roll has either distorted or suppressed the truth.

Despite the obscuring fogs of prevarication and ignorance that have drifted over more than five centuries of time there is no doubt about the importance of the swift revolution of 1399. Richard II was not only the last direct Plantagenet; he was perhaps the last truly medieval king of England. In some respects the reign of this unhappy prince, sick and prematurely old at the age of thirty, was a culminating point in English medieval history. Richard II was the last king of England to rule by strict hereditary right. In 1327 Parliament had deposed Edward II. In 1399 Parliament not only deposed Richard II but chose his successor.

An act of Parliament changed the succession by selecting the cheerless Henry, Duke of Lancaster, as king. It will be recalled that the new ruler, Henry IV, was the son of John of Gaunt, fourth son of Edward III. Parliament passed over the infant Edmund Mortimer, the great-grandson of Lionel, Duke of Clarence and third son of Edward III. Against the direct claims of Edmund Mortimer the shrewd Henry of Lancaster could not show the dimmest pretence of hereditary right. Nevertheless, Henry became king by the twin facts of conquest and of Parliamentary approval. The Lancastrians ruled by Parliamentary title. Henceforth in the royal administration the baronial ministers would not easily be displaced or circumvented by any group of favorites about the king. Henry IV and his successors, proclaimed the events of 1399, were to rule only if they heeded the limitations imposed upon them by Parliament and the laws of England.

A king who consistently failed to satisfy Parliament could not long expect to keep his crown, even if the issue had to be settled by civil war, as it was in the age of the Stuarts. Edward II had been deposed because he governed too little, Richard II because he tried to govern too much. Astute, wily, and unscrupulous, the successor of Richard II was determined to hold his throne against all challenge.

Chapter 9

THE AGE OF UNREST

THE BLACK DEATH

IN OCTOBER, 1347, Edward III had returned to England in triumph. "A new sun seemed to have arisen over the people," wrote a chronicler, "in the perfect peace, in the plenty of all things, and in the glory of such victories." Then, in the summer of 1348, England was struck by a plague of the most virulent kind. It had swept along the trade routes to Europe from some mysterious fountainhead of disease in the East. The Black Death, as it was called, rolled from the west of England into London during the winter. Then it leaped up the east coast and spent itself in Scotland and Ireland in 1349. Many authorities today believe that this disease was some type of the deadly bubonic plague. Wherever it struck there was terror and death.

Henry Knighton of Leicester wrote of "the fell death" that "broke forth on every side with the course of the sun." Far away in Florence, Giovanni Boccaccio later described the plague as it swept over his city: "No physician's council, no virtue of medicine whatsoever seemed to have an effect or profit against this sickness—it spread no less rapidly than fire will spread to dry or oily things that lie close at hand." In some English villages nearly all the inhabitants died. Through the filthy medieval streets of the larger towns the deadly infection raced unhindered. The manor rolls, episcopal registers, and parish and borough records tell a frightful story. In the diocese of Norwich 800 parishes lost their priests; whole families died; many areas were so depopulated that they reverted to waste land. Full statistics are, of course, not available for the fourteenth century but sober estimates set the mortality at from twenty-five to twenty-eight per cent.

The social and economic results were immediate and important. It is true that the Black Death merely hastened changes it was formerly thought to have originated; but the speed at which those changes occurred after 1350 gave tremendous impetus to the decline of feudalism,

147

to servile emancipation, and to the whole tide of economic and social discontent among the lower classes. After the Black Death England was never the same again. The smaller society that survived was upset; agriculture, trade, religion, government administration, all were disrupted. The monasteries had lost so many monks that they could hardly carry on; their medieval greatness and influence was shattered forever. The secular clergy struggled to recruit reasonably able men for the priesthood; but it was not easy.

In view of the decreased labor supply it was inevitable that the hired rural and town workers in England should demand and get higher wages. The villeins who had survived the plague insisted upon their freedom. They did not want to perform any more compulsory labor; they wanted wages. The few tenants replacing those who had died wanted easier terms. The income of the landlords went down as their tenants decreased in number; their overhead costs kept going up. Craft and merchant guilds could often pass their increased expenses on to the consumer in the form of higher prices; the landowner could not easily force up the prices of grain and meat, particularly when the number of Englishmen to be fed had diminished so much. Meanwhile laborers were gliding from manor to manor to find an employer who would pay them well. Landlords were in despair. How could their ripe and rotting crops be harvested? How could their cattle, dying of neglect, be cared for? It is often asserted that landlords made a wholesale substitution of sheep pasture for arable farming after the Black Death. A few years ago it was proved conclusively that such statements do not fit the facts. The evidence points, on the contrary, to "a serious drop in sheep-farming" caused in part by the war and war taxation and by the quasi-monopolistic practices of the staple system.

Could the manorial system be propped up by an act of Parliament? The landowners attempted to put back the clock by passing the Statute of Labourers in 1351, based on an ordinance made by the king and his council in 1349. The ordinance of 1349, said the statute of 1351, had been passed "to curb the malice of servants who after the pestilence were idle and unwilling to serve without securing excessive wages." Despite the law, continued the statute, "to suit their ease and their selfish desires" these servants "refrain from serving the lords or other men unless they receive double or triple that which they were accustomed to have—to the great danger of the lords and the impoverishment of all men of the said commons." All workmen were ordered to accept the wage rate customary before the plague. Employers who paid higher wages were to be fined; workers who accepted them were to be imprisoned. Prices were to be held stable; if prices did not rise, workers did not need higher wages. No alms were to be given to sturdy beggars.

Enactment and enforcement were different things. In 1357 and 1360 further statutes were passed to control wages and to stop the price rise. The workers refused to accept lower wages. Masters and land-lords had to have help, and most of them yielded to the demands of the laborers. Many lords of the manors could not work their own de-mesnes; then they leased out their lands for money rents to tenant farmers. They were becoming "landlords" of the modern type. To a greater extent than ever before the lords began to commute the feudal services required of villeins into straight money payments; the villeins, too, were becoming rural wage earners. Cash was replacing kind and physical services in the manorial economy. The basis of the feudal manorial system was being rapidly destroyed; and the pace increased every year.

THE PEASANTS' REVOLT, 1381

In the thirty years following the Black Death the spirit of unrest mounted as the working class sought to make still further gains. The social malaise is described at length in *The Vision of William Concerning Piers the Plowman*, an earnest and sincere poem written in the vernacular of the fourteenth century and usually attributed to William Langland. Based in part upon some contemporary sermons, this long alliterative poem denounced in allegorical passages the vice and folly of the rich and preached the glory of the honest worker placing his hardened hands on the plow stilts. When nine men out of ten were tillers of the soil the peasant was a proper object of sympathy. Langland warned the rich men not to deal harshly with the country worker: "Though he be thine underling now, well may hap in Heaven that he be worthier set and with more bliss than thou." Wrote Langland: "In a summer season, when soft was the sun . . . I slumbered in a sleeping, it rippled so merrily, And I dreamed marvellously." The sleeper dreamed about the society of his day, the peasants, the townsmen, the frairs, the nobles, all the violence and the injustice. The first part of his poem was a satirical and protesting picture of his world; the second described the kind of world it would be if Christian ethics prevailed.

The life of the rural worker was always hard. His hours of toil were long. His cattle were few and scrawny; there was little manure for the soil. The crops were carefully protected. Under the harvest by-laws no one might go into the fields at night "between bell and bell" lest he steal some of his neighbor's grain. Only the young boys and the old men and women were permitted to glean; the able-bodied men were to do the heavy work. The landless laborers worked hard, ate their cabbage, peas, beans, and bacon, drank their beer. In the fourteenth century, unlike their ancestors, they were bitterly discontented with their lot. They had tasted power, and they were ambitious. They wanted higher wages, lower rents, better working conditions. Those who had fought in France knew that an arrow could bring down a gentleman as well as a peasant.

Meanwhile the Hundred Years' War was devastating France and exhausting England. Over all Europe the economic expansion slowed down in the latter fourteenth century. By the early fifteenth century England was to move into a period of agricultural stagnation. Long before that dark chapter of depression and poverty arrived serious disturbances had broken out among the English rural workers, filled with a spirit of disorderly freedom. The peasants, chafing under real and fancied social and economic grievances, began to talk vaguely about equal rights for all men. There were many preaching reformers, including some of the coarser and more violent disciples of John Wycliffe and some wandering friars and parish priests. Against a background of primitive Christian communism they were telling the peasants that no man was born to be any man's inferior.

One of the most widely known of these preachers was the clerical demagogue John Ball, who stumped the country around the London district. His blunt oratory added fuel to the flaming discontent of the peasants. Jean Froissart, the vivacious chronicler and sporting reporter, saw everything from the point of view of the nobility and was therefore not kind to John Ball or to any other radicals. One of the communistic harangues of Ball was recorded, probably with reasonable accuracy, by Froissart: "Ah, ye good people, the matter goeth not well to pass in England, nor shall not do so till everything be common. . . . We be all come from one father and one mother Adam and Eve; whereby can they say or show that they be greater lords than we be, saving by that they cause us to win and labour for what they dispend . . . we will have it otherwise, or else we will provide us with some remedy, either by fairness or otherwise." Froissart added that the people "would murmur one with another in the fields and in the ways as they went together, affirming as how John Ball said truth." There was a miscellaneous alliance of general and local elements in peasant discontent, the prelude of a social storm.

To the economic and social reasons for the approaching rebellion was soon added another, mainly political. After 1369 England had entered upon a period of military disaster and economic exhaustion. In order to pay part of the expenses of the war Parliament decided in 1377 to levy a graduated poll tax upon almost every adult in England. A schedule provided that the tax should be determined by a man's social and economic position; it might be as little as fourpence or as much as £5; for a duke it was even more. In 1379 and 1380 further poll taxes were levied; the one of 1380 demanded a shilling for every man and woman in England over fifteen years of age. Such direct exactions fell heavily upon the poor, some of whom had never been subject to any tax before; a shilling was roughly equivalent to the wage of a skilled laborer for a week's work. In some communities the methods of collection were particularly annoying to the already incensed peasants. Thousands evaded the tax. False returns streamed in from every county.

Early in 1381 the government appointed commissioners to investigate the evasions and to collect unpaid taxes from the delinquents. In May, 1381, one menacing commissioner was driven out of an Essex village. An abrupt explosion shook the whole county as messengers rode to rouse the people. In the first days of June there was a major rebellion in Kent. Soon all southeastern England was in a blaze of revolt and the fire was spreading to the north and west. Unpopular landlords were murdered. Manor houses were pillaged and manorial rolls and title deeds, containing the records of the villein services, were burned. A definite revolutionary organization had carefully planned the revolt all over the country. When the moment arrived cryptic messages sped from village to village: "Jack Trueman doth you to understand that falseness and guyle have reigned too long." One messenger ordered the peasants "to stand together in God's name, and biddeth Piers Plowman goe to his werke and chastise well Hob the Robber."

In the years when Edward III was in his dotage and Richard II was a child the government had fallen into the hands of greedy nobles, of whom John of Gaunt, Duke of Lancaster and fourth son of Edward III, was typical. John of Gaunt's wealth was colossal; his manors were popularly said to cover a third of England. Gaunt and his fellow machine politicians were widely hated for their corruption and blamed for the shameful reverses of English arms in the war. It did not matter that Gaunt himself was probably an amiable nonentity of no special attainments except a low kind of political cunning; he had become a symbol of greed and incompetence and the rising tempers of the rebels seized and tugged upon that idea and refused to let it go. They had seen much and suspected more about the intrigues of the magnates, the futilities of the French conflict, the collection of the poll tax; these streams of anger mingled with the desire for freedom from servitude, with a muddled anti-clericalism, with a general detestation of landlords, lawyers, and aliens.

The Peasants' Revolt in 1381 was the first uprising of the submerged classes in England on a large scale, the first fumbling attempt of "John Nameless, John the Miller and John the Carter and John Trewman and all his fellows" to act for themselves. In Kent the rebels seized Rochester, Maidstone, and Canterbury. At Maidstone John Ball was released from prison to share with the resourceful Wat Tyler the leadership of the advancing peasants. Froissart, of course, called Tyler "a bad man and a great enemy to the nobility." Shortly after Ball's release a concerted march on London began. On June 12 one army of peasants encamped on Blackheath; others approached from the north and east. Inside London the rebels had many supporters, especially among the journeymen, the apprentices, and the numerous runaway villeins. On Thursday, June 13, the London sympathizers, including some aldermen, opened London Bridge and the Aldgate and the peasants, probably numbering about 60,000, poured into the city.

At once the rebels broke open the prisons and released the prisoners. They pillaged and burned the Savoy, John of Gaunt's beautiful palace in the Strand. Its owner was in Scotland; he was safe. His servants and many of his supporters were slaughtered. The Temple, headquarters of the lawyers, and Marshalsea prison were burned. At first the leaders of the peasants were successful in keeping them from undiscriminating pillage. Then the mob spirit broke loose and London was a city of anarchy.

Many Flemish traders, popularly blamed for stealing England's wealth, were killed. Richard II and his ministers fled to the Tower. On June 14 the king agreed to meet the rebels. In a conference at Mile End Richard granted the major demands of Wat Tyler and his fellows. Not all the rebels were united in their wishes because some wanted the church disendowed, the free use of the forests, and the abolition of the game laws and outlawry. Richard promised that the villeins would be made "free forever" and that the rents paid in place of customary services should be reduced to fourpence an acre. He promised charters and "upwards of thirty secretaries drew up letters as fast as they could." Many rebels, having received their parchment charters, went home.

Meanwhile London was terrorized by hooligan elements among the peasants and the urban slum dwellers. The Tower of London was stormed and taken. Sir Robert Hales, the treasurer, and the unpopular Simon of Sudbury, chancellor and archbishop of Canterbury, were seized in the chapel of the White Tower, taken to Tower Hill, and executed. "We must judge them by their works," wrote a contemporary, "for they slew the father of the whole clergy, the head of the English church, the Archbishop of Canterbury."

On June 15, Richard II, not yet fifteen years old, again met the rebels on the market square at Smithfield. It is impossible to tell exactly what happened at that meeting because the accounts of men who reported it conflict considerably. For some reason, now obscure, Wat Tyler drew his dagger and was struck down and killed by the mayor of London and a royal guard. The savage and masterless rebels were about to fire upon the king and his small band when Richard rode calmly forward and promised that he would be their leader. The day was saved. Several thousand citizens soon rushed out from London to rescue the king. Richard II was a brave lad, not the pitiful neurotic he was later to become.

Almost all the rebels who had remained about London now went home, clutching the royal promises of freedom and pardon. They had been duped, but most of them did not know it then. Up in Norfolk the rebellion collapsed; the battles between Yarmouth and Grimsby about the fishing trade guttered out. Meanwhile Richard II and his ministers had resolved upon vengeance. Richard himself accompanied the Lord Chief Justice about the assizes. The charters of liberation were revoked. Many peasants were slaughtered in a bloody progress of the army through the countryside. When the peasants at Waltham objected they were brutally answered: "Villeins ye are and villeins ye will remain." The Peasants' Revolt was crushed in a strong and cruel reaction.

Nevertheless, the revolt was not a complete failure. The upper classes had been badly scared. The poll tax of 1382 was levied only upon the landowners. An attempt to keep wages at the old level was abandoned when Parliament authorized justices of the peace to fix wages in their district in accordance with the prevailing prices. Commutation went on steadily. Real wages tended to rise. The economic tendencies of the period made it profitable for the landlord to lease out his surplus lands for rent payments in money. In some regions compact, small farms gradually began to replace the open field system. By the fifteenth century most of the peasantry were free wage earners or yeomen farmers. Indeed, the fifteenth century was to be in many ways the day of the small man. "Whoever was enclosing in the last part of the century it was not the old landlord." In a new age of labor fluidity men were moving more freely as workers about the land; as sailors over the seas; or as soldiers in foreign wars. "The world was all before him where to choose." Thus, in these long years, the economic causes working towards the disappearance of villeinage and serfdom rolled on their relentless way.

MEN OF THE MIDDLE CLASS

In the fourteenth century the slow disintegration of the feudal system was marked not only by several steps in the economic emancipation of the lower classes but also by a steady increase in the importance of the merchants and knights. Foreign commerce rose in volume and value, and the merchants and other men of business profited. In the twelfth and thirteenth century the English exporters had been overshadowed by foreigners, especially the Flemings and Italians. Then, slowly, the English began to prevail. In Parliament the merchants became more powerful. Edward III not only borrowed from the Italians in England and foreign bankers abroad but also from English merchants. One of the Florentine banking houses in England failed and the English took over its business. They also increased their activity at the great fairs and in foreign markets.

Several merchants intermarried with the nobility. Some of them were rising to high rank because of their own ability. Michael de la Pole, made earl of Suffolk by Richard II, was the son of a Hull merchant. Richard Whittington was a mercer who made a fortune by trading and became three times lord mayor of London. The importance of men such as these is clearly shown in their almost complete control of municipal affairs and in the number of steps taken by king and Parliament to regulate commerce in the interests of the English traders and the national welfare of England. For example, the watchful townsmen forced Edward III and Richard II to abandon almost completely the earlier practice of granting special privileges to foreign merchants.

The influence of the commons on early legislation, particularly the new capitalist class, is also shown in the fact that to a greater extent than in any previous century the merchants and other businessmen from the boroughs loudly complained about things they did not like. They found fault with the state of the king's account books; they repeatedly called attention to the need of governing the royal household with "good moderation of expenses"; they did not wish to see so much money spent outside England. Foreign merchants were excluded from retail trade in England. The export of bullion was curtailed so that there would be more cash in circulation at home.

The Navigation Act of 1381 required Englishmen to use English ships to export or import goods. The statute was not enforceable because there were too few ships; the law was therefore altered to read that English ships should be used whenever they were available. These regulations, and others, bore witness to the new and strongly national point of view. Some mercantilist practices appeared occasionally before mercantilist maxims were clearly formulated. The so-called navigation policy, however, never developed with any consistency before the reign of Elizabeth.

In the total tide of exports first place was still held by wool in the fourteenth century. English wool was shipped to the great Flemish cloth cities such as Ghent, Bruges, Ypres. Almost all this exportation continued to be through the Merchants of the Staple, whose operations have been earlier explained. In 1313 the staple system was reorganized and the monopoly position of the Merchant Staplers still further strengthened. In 1340, when Edward III was forming an alliance with the Flemings, he made Bruges the staple town for wool. Later, in 1353, he yielded to the complaints of English merchants and made ten English towns staple points. A decade later, however, the advantages of Calais as an English port across the Channel that was readily accessible to Continental merchants became so obvious that the staple was shifted to Calais, where it stayed almost continuously until England finally lost Calais in 1558.

Meanwhile more and more English wool was exported in the form of cloth. The weavers' guilds prospered. Edward invited skilled Flemish weavers to come to England. In 1331 John Kemper and his workmen settled in Norwich, which soon became the greatest center of weaving; a near-by village called Worsted gave its name to one kind of cloth. After 1337 the central government placed heavy taxes on exported wool to aid in financing the war with France. This step also helped to stimulate the production and export of wool in the form of cloth.

The home market increased with the growth of native cloth manufacturing and the woolman who was not a Stapler had his hands full with the domestic demand. About 35,000 sacks of wool had been exported in the year 1310; by 1450 only about 8,000 sacks were sent out of England. Meanwhile the great race of speculative financiers among the wool merchants, similar to the Italian merchant princes of another age, slowly petered out. "They were succeeded by the smaller, very substantial, but essentially middle class woolmen of the fifteenth century who if they quit their wool became not peers or bankrupts, but squires and begetters of squires."

ENGLAND AND THE CHURCH

It was inevitable that the tide of nationalist feeling in the fourteenth century should result in a clash between England and the papacy. All over Europe the sense of medieval unity was departing. Anti-papal and anti-clerical sentiment swelled to new levels, particularly after the Popes took up their seventy years' residence at Avignon, across the Rhone from France. In these years of the "Babylonian Captivity" the Popes and the majority of the papal court were French. After Englishmen began the Hundred Years' War with their long-time enemy it was natural that they should look with suspicion upon the French influence at "the sinful city" of Avignon.

English opposition to papal authority and papal taxation, always an important factor in the relations of church and state, became steadily stronger. Were the taxes paid to the Pope finding their way into the moneychests of the French kings to be used in the war against England? In *Piers Plowman* William Langland opposed the shipment of gold to Avignon:

> "Till Rome-runners carry no silver over sea
> Graven or ungraven, for the robber pope of France."

The suspicion of Rome and the lowering of papal prestige was increased by the "Great Schism" from 1378 to 1415 when two Popes, each denouncing the other, divided the church. It was a sight at once pathetic and ridiculous.

The anti-papal temper of the age was evident in the enactments of Parliament. In 1343 Parliament forbade anyone to bring in letters from Avignon that might be prejudicial to the interests or rights of the king. The clergymen of England must not divide their allegiance between king and Pope. In 1351 the first Statute of Provisors, extended in 1390, was designed to prevent the Pope from giving any English benefices to his followers. The act declared that any persons accepting papal appointments to English benefices should be imprisoned until they paid fines and had surrendered their newly acquired benefices. The statutes of Provisors apparently had small effect. Kings continued to secure the appointment of their chosen men to bishoprics through the Popes, who were usually obliging enough; elections by cathedral chapters were often quibbling and troublesome. Lesser benefices were usually conferred by the Pope, despite the provisions of the laxly enforced statutes.

In 1353, as a result of "clamours and grievous complaints," the first Statute of Praemunire, reissued and strengthened in 1365 and 1393, forbade appeals from English courts to the papal courts "in cases of which the cognizance pertains to the court of our lord the king." It provided that any person who appealed to Rome in contempt of the crown would be called to stand trial and would be subject to the penalty of outlawry and forfeiture of goods. It is probable that neither the statutes of Provisors nor Praemunire were intended to be strictly enforced. Nevertheless, they stand as clear expressions of anti-papal feeling in the fourteenth century. In 1366 the prevailing attitude was revealed even more sharply when Englishmen refused the Pope's demand for the 1,000 marks of annual tribute John had promised to pay in the previous century. England was then about thirty years in arrears; after 1366 she paid no more.

The church no longer claimed the respect or reverence of the laity. In *Piers Plowman* Langland wrote of the religious decadence and the bishops, pardoners, and friars acting "in deceit of the people." Accumulated legacies in the hands of the monks and higher churchmen had made them more worldly statesmen than humble disciples of Christ. Chaucer's easygoing monk

> "gave not of that text a pulled hen
> That saith that hunters be not holy men
> Nor that a monk, when that he is reckless,
> Is likened to a fish that is waterless . . .
> Why should he study and make himself wood, [mad]
> Upon a book in cloister always to pore . . .?"

Chaucer's lines reflected the spirit of his time. Even the friars were skilled in strolling knavery.

> "A friar there was, a wanton and a merry . . .
> He was an easy man to give penance . . .
> He knew the taverns well in every town
> For there was he not like a cloisterer
> With threadbare cope, as is a poor scholar . . ."

Modern writers have frequently exaggerated the uniformity of

*Laity disrespect &
attack on church*

the medieval faith, particularly in the later Middle Ages. By the fourteenth century many thoughtful and plain-spoken men were seriously disturbed about problems of both practice and doctrine. At the same time the monopoly of education by the clergy had been broken; a new non-clerical learned profession had arisen in the persons of the lawyers. Hence the fourteenth century produced a large group of secular writers trained in the Roman law. As these men wrote on the serious level characteristic of lawyers other men were producing more popular paragraphs for a wider public. The attack on the church became general.

lawyers

Before the fourteenth century England was but slightly affected by the heresies that swarmed on the Continent. The pre-Reformation church was opposed to an "open Bible" that all men might read in English. Conscientious translators had many difficulties because there were often things the church wanted kept in the Latin tongue. Was there not a danger that the vulgarization of the Latin might lead to heretical questions and answers? Until the late Middle Ages the ordinary Englishman was rather apathetic about speculative unorthodoxy. By the fourteenth century, however, there were appearing heretical doctrines born of the independent thought of the market place and the tavern, the preaching of new evangelists, and the pervasive and restless anticlericalism. For example, in 1355 the bishop of Exeter denounced the heresies of a certain deacon, especially his denial of transubstantiation. "O detestable tongue, more poisonous than that of any mad dog, which should be cut away by the physicians of the church and by the king's ministers, and cut into small pieces . . . since it knoweth not to speak rightly and learneth not to refrain from uttering so execrable a heresy." Heretics should be "cast into the outer darkness wherein is weeping and gnashing of teeth, where the fire is not quenched, nor shall the worm of conscience die."

Meanwhile the intellectual vigor of the universities continued until the latter part of the fourteenth century; then a decline set in and much of England's academic prestige vanished. Before the days of this university stagnation several outstanding scholars appeared, particularly at Oxford where sharp speculation challenged the best brains of the educated world. One of these was the Franciscan nominalist William of Ockham who obtained a European reputation before his death about 1349. Ockham, called "the invincible doctor," was probably the most important of the scholastic philosophers and theologians after St. Thomas Aquinas.

The Franciscan order defended the idea of clerical poverty. Pope John XXII opposed it. William of Ockham entered vigorously into the quarrel. Like Marsiglio of Padua William stood steadfast against the claims of papal sovereignty, insisting that the position of the Pope was not Christian. "What would you do if you had an heretical Pope?"

William asserted that it was possible for the Pope to be in error. If the Pope should be wrong, there was no reason why he should be obeyed.

William's theory of resistance to the papacy was mainly devised to support Ludwig of Bavaria, elected emperor in 1314, in his long struggle against Pope John XXII. William and Ludwig agreed that the Pope was a heretic. None of the arguments of William differed much from the later ideas used to prove that it was right to resist tyrannical kings. Although William's strategic theories were not so neatly developed as those of Marsiglio of Padua his propositions continued to be subjects of lively debate until the Reformation. He asserted that the Scriptures were the sole source of law. He attacked canon law, the legalism of medieval Christianity, the hierarchy in the church. Canon law, he declared, was valid only as an interpretation of the Scriptures; it was an administrative device, nothing more. William also claimed that the church was really the whole body of Christian people and that the Pope never did possess the authority to speak for all the church. He insisted that the rules of faith were the rules of the whole community of the faithful. A council of churchmen was more likely to be right than the Pope. The anti-clerical pen of William of Ockham remained busy until his death and his influence stretched down the years towards the Reformation.

The spirit of anti-clericalism reached its climax in the teachings of John Wycliffe, born in Yorkshire about 1320. Wycliffe became a famous teacher at Oxford, was made a fellow, master of Balliol, and later chaplain to Edward III. He was very much concerned about the evil of the church and launched several attacks upon clerical wealth and immorality. Wycliffe, insisting on "apostolic poverty," defended the claim of the crown to tax and secularize ecclesiastical property. Wycliffe also supported the king in advancing strong arguments against the demands of the papacy for tribute from the English crown. The church, declared Wycliffe, should be as poor as it had been when Christ and the apostles spread the Gospel.

In the interests of the state Wycliffe continued to preach loudly against clerical ownership of property. The civil authority, Wycliffe argued, had the duty and the power to take away the property of all clerics who had betrayed their trust by failing in their duties, abusing their authority, or falling from grace. Many nobles saw an advantage in confiscating church property, particularly if some of it should fall into their hands. John of Gaunt, Duke of Lancaster, gave Wycliffe his strong support. The nationalistic and evangelical crusader began to preach to the laymen from the London pulpits. In London the tide of anti-clericalism was already running high and Wycliffe's words fell upon receptive ears.

Wycliffe was convinced that in all temporal matters the king was

superior to the clergy. Influenced by the ideas of Marsiglio of Padua
and William of Ockham, he vigorously advanced his theories about the
relations of church and state in several pamphlets, most famous of
which were two, *On Civil Dominion* and *On Divine Dominion*. In all
of his writings Wycliffe exalted the state at the expense of the church. *Divine Right*
Kings, he held, ruled by divine right. Both priestly power and royal
power came from divine appointment; the church and state should
cooperate with each other. Christ was the head of the church, not the
Pope. Wycliffe foreshadowed Jean Bodin and Thomas Hobbes in his
conception of a national church subordinate to a national state. Of sinful mankind in general Wycliffe had a rather low opinion; his writings
were essentially aristocratic, in some respects an interesting combination of Plato's philosopher king and the judges of the Old Testament.

In 1377 Wycliffe was called before an ecclesiastical court at St.
Paul's to answer for his public outcries against the clergy. John of
Gaunt strongly supported him, particularly attracted by Wycliffe's ideas
about the confiscation of the church lands. When the bishop of London
joined in a quarrel with John of Gaunt a London mob, hostile to
Gaunt, broke into the trial and everything ended in confusion. Then
the Pope ordered several bishops to try Wycliffe at Lambeth. When
they attempted to do so the queen mother ordered the bishops to pronounce no sentence against Wycliffe. Again the mob interfered and
raided the courtrooms; the bishops were forced to interrupt their sitting,
and the court never met again.

Wycliffe now began to write several "heretical and depraved"
pamphlets and other works in English. In a series of lashing rebukes he
denounced bishops, monks, parish priests, church courts; he denied
the temporal authority of the clergy; and he again demanded the confiscation of church property. Thus far Wycliffe had said nothing specific
about the teachings of his church. After his trial in 1378 he developed
revolutionary and heretical doctrinal ideas. As the Great Schism arose
in the papacy Wycliffe questioned the spiritual authority of the Pope.
He asserted that the church was nothing more than a purely religious
association of all men predestined to salvation. He declared that
the main source of spiritual authority was the Scriptures, not the
Pope.

Wycliffe also stated that a good life was more important than sacraments. "Each man that shall be damned shall be damned by his own
guilt, and each man that is saved shall be saved by his own merit." He
wrote rather vaguely about the sovereignty of God and the equality of
man. Either Wycliffe or his followers translated the Bible from the
Latin of the Vulgate into English. "The gospel pearl is cast abroad,"
complained a churchman, "and trodden upon by swine." Wycliffe also
founded the Lollards, a word meaning mumblers or lazy folk. These
"poor priests" were to go in pairs about England, barefoot and in

brown gowns, to preach the Gospel and the Franciscan idea of poverty. The Lollards spread everywhere their founder's hatred of the papacy and the property-owning clergy.

Finally, in 1381, Wycliffe attacked the citadel of the church by denouncing the doctrine of transubstantiation. He said that Christ was really present in the sacrament of the Eucharist but not as a result of any words or action of the priest. This departure shocked and alienated many of those who had hitherto supported him. John of Gaunt, for example, would have nothing to do with a man who assaulted the doctrines of the church. Early in 1382 the archbishop of Canterbury commanded the chancellor of Oxford to expel all heretics. Several of Wycliffe's followers were forced to leave. Some were tried for heresy; everyone recanted or escaped. Under Richard II the Lollards were not heavily persecuted. Even if the royal family had been opposed to the Lollards the anti-clerical feeling among Englishmen was so strong that the church could not hope to obtain the aid of the state for any purpose, even the suppressing of heresy. It was through the household of the queen, Anne of Bohemia, that the teachings of Wycliffe were carried to Europe. In Prague, Wycliffe's mighty disciple John Huss spread abroad the new ideas from England until he was burned at the stake in 1415.

Wycliffe was allowed to live out his days in peace. He retired to his rectory at Lutterworth in Leicestershire where he continued to write tracts against the "Caesarean papacy" and to direct his Lollard missionaries, who won many converts. When Henry IV seized the throne in 1399 the clergy in convocation complained about the increase of Lollards and Henry, anxious for clerical support, started to persecute Wycliffe's poor preachers. In 1401 the statute *De Haeretico Comburendo* placed the secular arm of the state at the service of church justice. There were not many martyrs.

Henry V carried on the persecution; in 1414 he attacked the greatest Lollard in all England, Sir John Oldcastle. Oldcastle escaped, later led a rebellion against Henry and was finally captured and executed. Throughout Henry V's reign the attacks upon Wycliffe's followers continued. The Lollards dwindled steadily in the fifteenth century; but they never entirely disappeared. They may have survived in sufficient underground strength to link up with the English Reformation. In the early sixteenth century Erasmus wrote to the Pope: "Once the party of the Wyclifites was overcome by the power of kings; but it was overcome and not extinguished."

Wycliffe, who was solemnly condemned by Gregory XI for teaching "the ignorant doctrine of Marsiglio of Padua of accursed memory," himself influenced John Huss, as was noted earlier. Huss, in turn, influenced Martin Luther. Hence the remarkable Wycliffe was in truth a prophet and forerunner of the Protestant Reformation.

In 1384 Wycliffe died, and his body was buried at Lutterworth. Thirty-one years after his death the Council of Constance declared vengeance upon Wycliffe's remains: "In obedience hereunto Richard Fleming, bishop of Lincoln, sent his officers to ungrave him accordingly. To Lutterworth they come, take what is left out of the grave and burn them to ashes; and cast them into Swift, a neighbouring brook running hard by. Thus this brook hath conveyed his ashes into Avon, Avon into Severn, Severn into the narrow seas, they into the main ocean. And thus the ashes of Wycliffe are the emblem of his doctrine, which is now dispersed all the world over."

LITERATURE AND ARCHITECTURE

In this age of nationalism and unrest there came a swift surge of advance in literature and architecture. Native music lagged behind the other arts, despite the European fame of the composer John Dunstable and the rise of a good school of counterpoint in England. Most impressive were the events in literature. There appeared a great many sermons, hymns, poems, carols, ballads, chronicles, and miracle plays. The upper classes were now beginning to speak English. In the next century Henry V was to use it in his official correspondence. In 1362 Edward III ordered English to be used in all the law courts. French was being replaced by English in the schools. Not only *Piers Plowman* and some of Wycliffe's prose works but also scores of anonymous poems and tracts were being written in English. For example, one of the popular dream and allegory poems of the fourteenth century was the *Pearl*, by an unknown author. The writer was sad because his daughter, the pearl, had died. In a vision he saw her again and took comfort in the knowledge that she was happy and safe. "Pensive, broken, forpined am I; but thou hast reached a life of joy, in the strifeless home of Paradise."

The Kentish John Gower, probably a Southwark merchant, wrote his first poems in French and Latin; then he turned to English. Thomas Occleve, who was born in 1368 and whose death date is unknown, had intended to be a priest but instead spent long years in the privy seal office. His poems and dialogues were in English; he translated several works from Latin. John Lydgate, born about 1372, carried on the stream of English prose into the next century. The products of Occleve and Lydgate were pedestrian; they showed little promise of the later fine work of Sir Thomas Malory and John Skelton. Nevertheless, it was through the work of such men that the long submerged English language came swiftly into its own. When it appeared again in polite society it was supple and taut; the old inflections were gone; the vocabulary had become larger, its main flood enriched by tributary streams from many sources, especially French and Danish. The speech of the eastern midlands, of London, Oxford, Cambridge, and of

John Wycliffe and Geoffrey Chaucer was to be the "standard" English language.

Geoffrey Chaucer was the first of the great English poets, England's "morning star of song." He was born about 1340 and died about 1400. The bourgeois son of a wine merchant, the nimble, eager, and clear-eyed Chaucer crowded a great many activities into the sixty years of his life. His literary work was not the creation of art for the sake of art alone but the result of experience, shrewd observation, travel, and work. In his youth Chaucer was a page in the household of Lionel, Duke of Clarence; then he fought for his king in the French wars and was taken prisoner; he was later sent on secret diplomatic missions to Flanders and Italy.

For a time Geoffrey Chaucer was controller of the customs at the Aldgate. He was once clerk of the king's works at Windsor. He was thus a successful diplomat and civil servant. Chaucer was also the first English poet to sit in Parliament, the literary defender of Henry IV's claims to the throne, and "the first example of an illustrious lay servant of the state and man of letters to be buried in Westminster Abbey." It was not surprising that such a man sensed and saw and wrote about the new forces stirring in a restless age. Geoffrey Chaucer did not see life solely "through the stained glass of literature."

After Chaucer was released from prison in France he brought back a copy of the French *Romance of the Rose* which he began to translate in the court at Westminster, a favorite rendezvous of men of arts and letters. His work, strongly influenced by French literature, soon took second place to none in England. Attracted by Italian writers, particularly Boccaccio, Dante, and Petrarch, Chaucer's nimble and nosing curiosity led him to experiment in new poetic forms and techniques. All this was part of the apprenticeship of the man who gave the world *The Canterbury Tales*.

Over five hundred years after it was written the Prologue of *The Canterbury Tales* stirs men to wonder and admiration. In the swiftly moving camera lines of the Prologue, Chaucer precisely described the thirty pilgrims who met at the Tabard Inn in Southwark to begin their pilgrimage to the shrine of St. Thomas of Canterbury, "the holy blisful martir for to seke." The mixed company of the pilgrims included typical people from many classes, English to the core. There was the perfect and gentle knight, with his coat of mail; the friendly host, with his strong wine; the gross shipman and the indecent miller. There was the man of law; the lisping prioress; the five burgesses; the ploughman; the brawny, hunt-loving monk; the wanton friar; the rich doctor of physic; the hollow-cheeked "clerk of Oxenford"; the money-grabbing pardoner with his wallet on his lap full of his relics and his pardons "come from Rome all hot."

There was the buxom and amazing Wife of Bath who had been

on many pilgrimages and had had five husbands: "Three of them were gode and two were badde." There was also the poor parson:

"A good man was ther of religioun
And was a poore Persoun of a toun
But rich he was of holy thoght and werk."

There was the merchant with his forked beard; the franklin, or small businessman: "Well loved he in the morn a sop in wine. . . . It snowed in his house of meat and drink"; the yeoman with his bow and his coat and hood of green. As the pilgrims moved at a slow pace over the rough road of the "Pilgrims' Way" to Canterbury their tales revealed what they thought about the world they knew in fourteenth century England. The tellers of the tales also told many other things about themselves. In every page of *The Canterbury Tales* there stands forth the shrewd poetic temper of Geoffrey Chaucer, his dramatic power, his gentle satire, his genial tolerance, and the universality of his sympathy.

It has been claimed that what Chaucer did for the English language Henry Yevele did for architecture. This prolific and versatile individual helped to develop a more truly national style in the new perpendicular Gothic architecture that replaced the decorated and curvilinear design in the fourteenth century. It was Henry Yevele who aided master architects such as William Ramsey, William Hurley, and John Spondee in carrying the perpendicular Gothic to Gloucester in the west and Ely in the east. In the fourteenth century there was also a great development in the science of timber roofing and the construction of lierne vaults, such as the crypt of St. Stephens' Chapel in Westminster Palace. The special character, altogether national, that Yevele gave to English architecture reached its height in his brilliant artistic achievements, splendid in massing and proportion, completed during the late fourteenth century, particularly in the ten years of the reign of Richard II.

Yevele reconstructed Westminster Hall, a huge building 238 feet long and 70 feet wide erected by William Rufus about 1098. He built the Abbot's House and the Palace Clock Tower at Westminster; the tomb of John of Gaunt in St. Paul's; parts of London Bridge, including St. Thomas's chapel; the nave, the west cloister, and the tomb of Richard II in Westminster Abbey; the nave and the Black Prince's Chantry in Canterbury Cathedral; the West Gate at Canterbury; part of the tomb of Blanche of Lancaster in St. Paul's. The name of Henry Yevele, long almost forgotten, has only recently been restored to a place of high honor among the master architects of England. In him English Gothic art reached the last of its successive phases of beauty.

The effect of the profound changes discussed in this chapter was not immediately apparent during the century that followed. In England the fifteenth century was almost wholly barren and sterile, a startling contrast to the vigor of the age of Wat Tyler, Chaucer, and Wycliffe. The fifteenth century was a distracted period of almost disastrous foreign and dynastic warfare, a story of faction, intrigue, cabal, and treachery. The lingering rays of the sun of Crecy died away. In the carnival of crime and blood there were only a few bright chapters: the continued advance of the middle classes; the premature constitutionalism in government; the glory of Agincourt. At the end of the age of Lancaster and York a new king, Henry VII, who can with diligence and care be linked up genealogically to the Lancastrian family, seized the throne. It was an hour that marked the end of medieval England. In the bloody and convulsive Wars of the Roses feudalism was to fall upon its own sword.

Section I

BRITON–SAXON–NORMAN

THE BEGINNINGS
TO THE END OF THE MIDDLE AGES

Remains of a Roman fortified camp in Gloucestershire.

Portion of a Roman wall, part of the foundation of a modern London building.

This mosaic pavement covered the series of flues which warmed a Roman bath.

Above, portion of a page from the *Anglo-Saxon Chronicle;* at right, part of the poem *The Dream of the Rood* attributed to Cynewulf, from a manuscript in the Cathedral library, Vercelli, Italy. It is possible that the manuscript was left at Vercelli by English pilgrims on their way to Rome.

The battle of Hastings from the Bayeux Tapestry, an almost contemporary document.

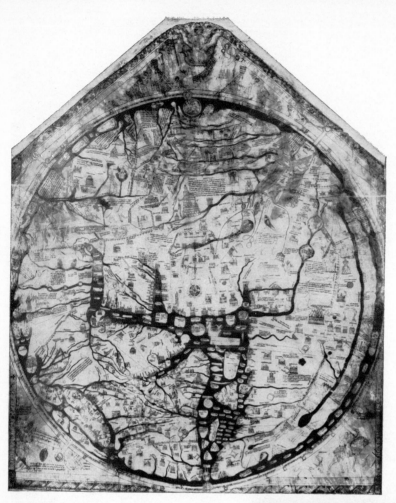

The world as Richard of Haldingham conceived of it, A.D. 1280. The British Isles appear at the lower left.

An English Crusader. The funeral effigy of William Longespée, Earl of Salisbury.

Norman military architecture. The keep of the Tower of London shown in a late 15th Century manuscript.

Below, ". . . the earth-clinging Romanesque, characterized by round arches, thick walls, small windows and massive pillars." Choir of the Church of St. Bartholomew the Great, Smithfield, London, *circa* A.D. 1150.

Caernarvon Castle, begun for Edward I in A.D. 1284.
The town walls to the north of the castle are still intact
although the castle is a ruin.

"Durham Cathedral, with its adjacent Castle to guard against the Scots . . ."

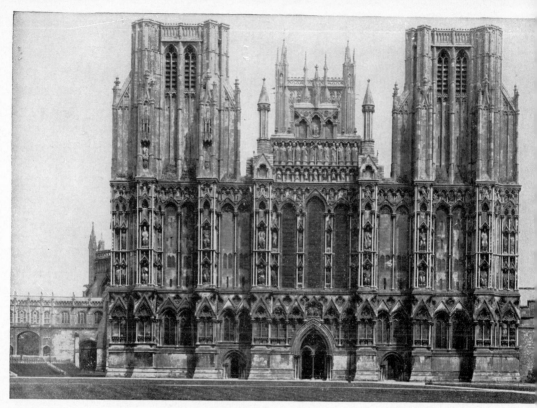

Wells Cathedral, the west facade, a glory of 13th Century English architecture and sculpture.

Canterbury Cathedral, a view down the nave. "In Gothic construction, the roof was supported on interlaced and soaring pointed arches called vaults . . . the heavy supporting pillars of the Romanesque construction were replaced by slender groups of columns."

Nuns in choir, *circa* A.D. 1450.

Pilgrim,
14th Century.

Surgeon at work, early 12th Century.

Leper woman ringing her bell.

Garden Party, 15th Century.

Reeve and Manor laborers,
early 14th Century.

In this 15th Century picture of the battle of Crécy, the English archers are shown attacking the Genoese crossbowmen in the French service, while at the upper left King Philip VI of France seeks refuge in a castle.

Richard the Second, A.D. 1390.

Geoffrey Chaucer.

Contemporary, but idealized, view of John Ball leading a mob. "His blunt oratory added fuel to the flaming discontent of the peasants."

Herbert

Nevill

DeVere

Coats of Arms
of the principal leaders in the
Wars of the Roses.

Richard III

Percy

Guildmaster judging journeymen's work.

Market house in Chipping Campden, Gloucestershire.

Court of King's bench in session, early 15th Century.

Making beds in a
15th Century inn.

A play of Terence is being
acted on a Medieval stage.
Note the masked actors in the
foreground at top.

Haddon Hall, Derbyshire. The earliest portions of this house are Norman, the banqueting-hall dates from the 14th Century, and the long gallery is Elizabethan.

Chapter 10

LANCASTER AND YORK
PREJUDICE AND PROMISE

THE fifteenth century was an age of paradox and contrast. Feudalism was steadily declining; its long death agonies came with the Wars of the Roses. On the other hand, in the midst of a generally dreary scene there was a real increase in the prosperity of the mass of people through the century. Domestic trade and industry, despite the merchants' laments, did advance slowly. Abroad, however, the English were still unable to break the formidable monopoly of the Hanseatic League. The Hansa merchants gained notably at the expense of the English. Some further steps were taken in parliamentary government. It is true that the gangster methods of the nobles, so vividly described, for example, in the famous Paston letters, were adding to the difficulties of the transition from a feudal to a bourgeois society. Nevertheless, the dramatic aspects of the nobles' feuds has probably resulted in too much emphasis upon their total importance. Not all the great barons were coroneted brigands or uncultured barbarians. The noble Humphrey, Duke of Gloucester and brother of Henry V, gave the first important contribution of books and manuscripts to Oxford University in 1435 and brought Italian humanists to teach in England.

It is sometimes stated that the fifteenth century was a period of intellectual stagnation in the schools and universities. This is not quite true. The universities had certainly fallen from their high estate of the fourteenth century, especially after the teachings of Wycliffe were suppressed at Oxford and scholasticism degenerated into mutterings and mumbles. And yet there was not the complete collapse often suggested by later writers who brighten the glories of the Renaissance noonday sun by making the night that preceded it darker than it really was. In the fifteenth century new Oxford colleges were being founded: Lincoln, All Souls, and Magdalen. Cambridge was expanding. In the midst of the trumpets of war there were over two hundred students in each of the inns of court: Lincoln's Inn, Gray's Inn, the Inner and Middle Temple. Secularized elementary education spread as the facilities for it increased. Grammar school foundations multiplied. Such slow changes, silent and often not clearly perceived by later generations, must not be overlooked or forgotten. The story of the fifteenth century is more than the tale of charging knights at Towton and murder in the Tower of London. Some of the most important events did not happen on the battlefield. There were signs of promise even in the dark hours of national humiliation and civil war. We shall get a false picture of fifteenth century England if we visualize it merely as being "futile, bloody and immoral" and the cockpit of contending disasters.

As England moved into the fifteenth century the government extended its areas of control in commerce by a long series of regulations. When the locust years of the war with France drained the royal treasury the king's broad powers enabled him to draw thousands of pounds from the pockets of the merchants. Despite this source of revenue the French war was too costly for the government to finance successfully. The feudal monarchy, weakened by poverty, gradually allowed power to slip from its fingers and the noble families began to fight among themselves. Defeated barons often had their land confiscated by the king, who still remained strong enough to seize the estates of a weakened noble. The general disorder in England was rising steadily by the middle of the century and many nobles were finding that the larger magnates were trying bravely to subdue their lesser neighbors and to create local territorial sovereignties almost independent of the king's control.

The war with France and the baronial disorders were clearly opposed to the interests of the commercial classes. In the confused reign of Henry VI, to be described later, one contemporary document expressed in exaggerated language the anger and dismay of the merchants. "His law is lost, his commerce destroyed, the sea is lost; himself is made so poor that he hath not pay for his meat and drink; he oweth more and is greater in debt than ever was king of England." The merchants wanted a strong king who would keep England united and safe for peaceful and profitable commerce. The navy was neglected under Henry VI and the French raided the English coast; the Hanseatic League became aggressive, its pirates swept unchecked over the North Sea. The Merchant Adventurers claimed that they were treated harshly by the Dutch and complained that the English government gave them no support.

Meanwhile the Irish trade was expanding into the Icelandic fishing trade. The Danes, for their part, wanted to keep Englishmen out of the Icelandic fishery. Henry VI prohibited English ships from going to Iceland and getting into trouble; but they went. The earlier Biscayan trade in wine and salt was growing into the Castilian and Portuguese traffic. Welsh and English traders wanted to break the Mediterranean monopoly of the Italians and Catalans, but the English kings could not aid them. The English merchants were at a serious disadvantage. Nevertheless, they held on. Master mariners of the fifteenth century were not troubled by delicacy or scruple.

It was against this background that an anonymous author, possibly Adam de Moleyns, bishop of Chichester, wrote in 1436 *The Libelle of English Policy*, demanding a strong navy and the encouragement of trade. "Cherish merchandise, keep the Admiralty, that we be masters of the Narrow Sea." This "manual of statesmanship in rude verse" set forth a series of mercantilist views about England's foreign trade and its regulation. Throughout the long tract the author stressed the importance of commerce in the destiny of England. His heroes were the great merchants. "And in worship now think I on the son of merchandy, Richard of Whittington, That lode-star and chief chosen flower." The strongly nationalist language of the poem was particularly evident in the prejudiced descriptions of the Flemings, whose country the author felt was little more than a land of commercial exchange. If the English merchants were rich, "then in prosperity shall be our land, lordes and commonalty." The safety of England lay in "king, ship, and sword, and power of the sea." One despairing line of the *Libelle* must have been repeated by many merchants: "Where been our ships? Where been our swords become?" Fifty years were to pass before Henry VII, first of the Tudors, provided an answer to that question.

The author of the *Libelle* was one of the best of the writers of poetry in the early fifteenth century. John Lydgate and Thomas Occleve were still producing numerous poems, usually long, flat, elaborate, and faulty in verse structure. Their themes were orthodox, almost always about romance, morals, or religion. Other poets, and of these there were many, were at once prolific, careless, wandering in barren mazes. They turned out hundreds of pages of haphazard and dreary verse, without depth or surface sparkle. When they tried to imitate Chaucer they failed; and such was their mediocrity that they had even less chance of success when they attempted to write something entirely their own. In England the fire of genius had gone out of her literature; almost every poem was turbid and sluggish. There was perhaps only one exception in the trumpet call of the Song of Agincourt: "Our king went forth to Normandy With grace and might of chivalry." In Scotland it was different; some very good poetry was written there.

In prose the picture was brighter. Most of the monastic chronicles dwindled away; but there were appearing a large number of town chronicles, such as the great chronicles of London. These were written in English. History was no longer being recorded by cloistered monks in Latin but by the burghers of the towns for the literate middle class.

The fifteenth century also witnessed a great increase in private correspondence, resulting in part from the widening use of linen paper in place of the costlier parchment. "No person of any rank or station in society above mere labouring men seems to have been wholly illiterate." Modern scholars have done considerable research in the important collections of private letters that have come down from the fifteenth century. Finest and largest of these is the Paston collection. The vivacious and fluent Paston letters were written by three generations of a middle class Norfolk family. Like the great volumes of family diaries and memoirs of a later age the fascinating Paston letters described not only family affairs but the political, social and economic conditions of Norfolk and, to a lesser extent, of the whole kingdom of England.

One of the outstanding prose works of the age was the conservative Sir Thomas Malory's lively *Morte d'Arthur*, a fine piece of romantic writing based on the great Arthurian legend. In this last and splendid version of the Arthur saga Malory looked back upon a civilization that was dying as the knights and barons tumbled like the tall trees of the forest and the feudal order ended. In the past Malory found ideals that he hoped would not perish as commerce and civil war destroyed so much that he admired. "Oh ye knights of England. Where is the custom and usage of noble chivalry that was used in those days . . .? Alas! What do you do but sleep and take ease and are all disordered from chivalry?"

Another writer of distinction was Reginald Pecock, bishop of St. Asaph, who quarrelled loudly with the Lollards, the Yorkist clergy, and the London mobs. In *The Repressor of Overmuch Blaming of the Clergy* and other works Pecock led the way in ecclesiastical controversy. His sharp treatises were well written and widely read. Pecock's vigorous prose stood by the side of Malory's work as an example of the achievements to come in the next century.

In the latter part of the Lancastrian and Yorkist age there were two important writers in the field of law and political philosophy. The first was Sir Thomas Littleton whose treatise on the land law, usually called the *Tenures,* passed through more than seventy editions by the seventeenth century. The second was Sir John Fortescue, who became Governor of Lincoln's Inn in 1425 and Chief Justice of the King's Bench in 1442. Fortescue was later an active supporter of the Lancastrians in the Wars of the Roses. He went into exile with them in 1461. After 1471 he became a Yorkist and served in the council of Edward IV until his death about 1476.

Sometime between 1461 and 1463 Fortescue wrote his *De Natura Legis Naturae* which was a long anti-Yorkist tract explaining how the Lancastrian claim to the English throne was justified by the laws of nature. Between 1468 and 1470 the *De Laudibus Legum Angliae* was prepared for the edification of Prince Edward. This book, written in the form of a dialogue, described the English law, the courts, the jury system, and the Inns of Court. It was a remarkable and reasoned defense of the laws of England. Fortescue explained how statute law was wise because it was based on the consent of the whole kingdom. It provided the people with justice and "for want of justice the human race would have tore itself to pieces in mutual slaughter."

In the English political system, called by Fortescue a *dominium politicum et regale*, the king was not an absolute monarch. "The king makes not the laws, nor imposes subsidies without the consent of the three estates of the realm." Even judges, though commanded by the king, were bound by oath not to render decisions against the law of the land. It was far otherwise in France, as Fortescue frequently insisted, because there the civil law and the Roman principles were diligently followed; there the king was absolute. The English Fortescue disliked both the French and their system of law and government; and he lost no chance to say so. The English lawyers of the seventeenth century, as well as opponents of the civil law in all later centuries, inherited and employed the principles of Fortescue. The *De Laudibus* was published four times in the sixteenth century and three times in the eighteenth.

In the *De Laudibus* and the later *Monarchia* or *Governance of England* Fortescue also analyzed some of the faults, as he saw them, of the English method of government and put forward some concrete proposals for reform. Fortescue wanted a strong executive such as that the Tudors later developed. "The law, not Parliament," asserted Fortescue, "should limit royal absolutism." This idea occurred in all of Fortescue's works. He once proposed, for example, that the royal council should prepare legislation for Parliament. In later years propagandists for the cause of Parliament against the king used Fortescue's theory of the distinction between *jus regale* and *jus politicum et regale* for their own purposes. In doing so, they badly warped Fortescue's ideas. Apparently they conveniently overlooked his comments about the subordinate position of Parliament and his plans for conciliar reform. Fortescue, like Sir Edward Coke later, would have been as much opposed to the absolutism of Parliament as to the absolutism of the king.

HENRY IV AND HENRY V

In 1399 the energetic and unscrupulous Henry IV had easily ousted Richard II from the throne. Henry had been made king by Parliament and the Lancastrian dynasty was thus legally established. The direct royal line was excluded from the throne until its claims were later acquired and asserted by the Yorkists. Despite these events, Henry knew that a parliamentary title alone would not adequately defend him from the assaults of his enemies and he set about to obtain further support. He turned first to the church. In the previous chapter reference was made to the statute *De Haeretico Comburendo*. This law of 1401 provided for the burning of Lollards and other heretics who "against the law of God and of the church usurping the office of preaching, do perversely and maliciously in divers places under the cover of dissembled holiness, preach and teach these days openly and privily divers new doctrines and wicked heretical and erroneous opinions." Convicted heretics were to be burned "before the people in a high place; that such punishment may strike fear in the minds of others." The clergy had long sought such legislation against heretics and applauded Henry's support of it. At the same time the new king made a series of important concessions to Parliament and studiously courted the house of commons. That stern necessity in fact compelled Henry to attend to the wishes of Parliament did not diminish the popularity he obtained by doing it.

Such steps were not enough to quell disaffection. "Uneasy lies the head that wears a crown." There were four rebellions in the first nine years of Henry's reign. The first revolt was led by Richard II's half brothers. After it was crushed, Richard II, who had been imprisoned by Henry IV, was murdered. We can hardly doubt, though Pomfret Castle has kept its secret well, that it was by the order of Henry IV that Richard died. Meanwhile the Welshmen were inspired by the magnetic Owen Glendower to assert their ancient claims to independence under the golden dragon banner of Wales. Soon the French began to send aid to the rebels. Glendower was joined in 1402 by Sir Edmund Mortimer, uncle of Edmund, the young earl of March. Mortimer proclaimed his nephew king as the rightful heir of the childless Richard II, the last direct Plantagenet. As was earlier explained, the earl of March did possess a better hereditary claim to the throne than Henry IV, for he was the great-grandson of Edward III's third son, Lionel, Duke of Clarence. Henry IV was the son of Edward III's fourth son, John of Gaunt.

In 1403 the powerful northern Percy family decided to ally themselves with Glendower and Mortimer. The chief of the Percy clan was the earl of Northumberland, who had once adhered to Henry's cause and had been described by Shakespeare's Richard II as the "ladder wherewithal the mounting Bolingbroke ascends my throne." The son of Northumberland was Henry, usually called "Hotspur." In 1402 the two Percies, holding the border against the Scots, had captured several Scotsmen in battle, including the Scottish nobleman Earl Douglas. Henry IV had insisted that the captives be handed over to him. The Percies refused to obey because they wanted to claim the ransom money. They had already become dissatisfied with their meager reward for loyally helping Henry. They were also annoyed at Henry's treatment of the family of the young earl of March, who was related to Hotspur's wife. Thus they deserted the king, raised the Cheshire archers, and set out to join forces with the Celtic insurgent Glendower.

Hotspur marched towards the forces of Glendower, then in the south of Wales. Before he could reach his ally he found his road blocked by Henry IV and his son "Prince Hal" at Shrewsbury. In the resulting battle Hotspur was defeated and killed. Northumberland was captured and imprisoned for six months, then released and pardoned. The redoubtable Glendower resisted for several years before his forces were finally rolled back and scattered by English arms.

After "Harry Percy's spur was cold" there were other rebellions. One was led by the intriguing earl of Nottingham and Scrope, the archbishop of York. It was crushed and the leaders executed after a mock trial. No moral earthquake followed Scrope's death; the age of Thomas Becket was long past. In the north the earl of Northumberland rose again in 1405; he saved himself by fleeing to Scotland. In 1408 he tried a third revolt and died in battle. Two years earlier James Stuart, heir to the Scottish throne, was captured by English pirates and handed over to Henry. The chronic wars with Scotland were ended, for a time. In 1407 the French, beset by internal disputes, made a truce with the English. England was finally at peace and the Lancastrian throne secure.

Henry IV was exhausted by the arduous demands of war and business. During the last five years of his life he suffered from an illness that was popularly believed to be leprosy. His council was torn by personal and factional strife. His son Henry, portrayed by Shakespeare as a wild and dissolute madcap, added to the heavy cares of the ill and unsteady king. Harassed and unloved, Henry IV died in 1413, at the age of forty-six. The crown passed to a hard and intense son whose early life had been most disorderly but whose character, in Shakespeare's words, gave "some sparkle of a better hope."

When the young and vigorous Henry V came to the throne he at once intensified the persecution of the Lollards. In the previous chapter it was noted that even the wealthy and learned Sir John Oldcastle was seized and sent to the flames at Smithfield. Many lesser Lollards perished at the hands of a king who was determined to burn heretics and hang traitors. Nevertheless, Henry was more interested in glorifying the house of Lancaster by winning wars than by hunting heretics. He had decided to reconquer the lost heritage of the Angevins and in 1415 he renewed the Hundred Years' War against France.

In the years when the war had languished the French kingdom had suffered a calamity. The son and heir of the strong Charles V was Charles VI (1380–1422), thoroughly incompetent and intermittently insane. Two factions at the French court struggled for power; one was led by the king's brother Louis, Duke of Orleans; the other by his uncle, Philip the Bold, Duke of Burgundy, a powerful and aggressive prince. When Philip died in 1404 his son John the Fearless brought about the murder of the Duke of Orleans and a bloody and paralyzing civil war broke out between the Burgundians and Orleanists. France was in a desperate situation when Henry V of England allied himself with the Burgundians, persuaded Parliament to grant him money, pawned the crown jewels to help finance an expeditionary army, and energetically prepared to cross the Channel.

On August 9, 1415, Henry V's army of about 30,000 men, including 8,000 archers, embarked at Portsmouth in 1,500 ships. From August 17 to October 7 the English besieged Harfleur where they used artillery for the first time in a siege operation. After the costly capture of that city Henry's army moved up the coast towards Calais, swinging inland along the Somme to a convenient crossing point near Nesle. Astride the Calais road stood Charles VI's French army, numbering about 60,000 men.

On October 25 the English forces, now thinned by disease and casualties to 12,000, met the French at Agincourt. Against the redoubtable missile troops of Henry V the French used the same feudal tactics as their forefathers had employed at Crecy seventy years before. The English mobility, the firepower of quick-shooting longbows in the skilled hands of cloth-clad archers, stood them in good stead against the crossbowmen and the heavily armored chevaliers of France. English historical estimates placed the English losses at 500, the French at 7,000. French historical estimates set English losses at 1,600, the French at 10,000. It was a great English victory on St. Crispin's Day.

After the battle of Agincourt Henry returned to England. In 1417 he came back to France and began to reduce the fortresses of Normandy. Meanwhile the Burgundians had driven their rivals out of Paris and taken over the government. John the Fearless, Duke of Burgundy, was almost persuaded to join the Orleanists in order to expel the English from France. But that threat to the English designs never ripened. When the Duke of Burgundy met the king's son to discuss common action against Henry V he was murdered by an Orleanist. His son Philip at once actively allied himself with the English in order to avenge his father's death. By the terms of the treaty of Troyes, signed in 1420 between Charles VI and Henry V, Henry agreed to marry Katherine, daughter of the French king, to seal the new Anglo-French settlement. This treaty, largely the work of Philip of Burgundy, also disinherited the son of Charles VI and provided that on the death of the French king the throne of France should go to Henry of England. Two years later Henry V died. His son and heir was Henry VI.

THE HUNDRED YEARS' WAR: LAST PHASE

In accordance with the instructions of Henry V his younger brother John, Duke of Bedford, became regent of France on the death of Charles VI, late in 1422. Bedford was efficient and shrewd, a skilled administrator and a capable soldier. A second brother, Humphrey, Duke of Gloucester, was made regent of England during the minority of the infant Henry VI. Gloucester was unsteady, unpredictable, and quarrelsome; he battled with several of his councillors who persuaded Parliament to limit his powers. Opposition to Gloucester was headed by his half-uncle, Henry, Cardinal Beaufort, who was chancellor. Beaufort, sublimely slandered by Shakespeare, was one of the four sons born out of wedlock to John of Gaunt and his mistress, Catherine Swynford. Gaunt had eventually made Catherine his third wife and two acts of Parliament had declared the Beaufort branch of the royal line legitimate (1392) although debarred from succession to the throne (1407). The factional strife between the Gloucester and Beaufort forces in the council continued for many years to disrupt the deteriorating machinery of government at home and to weaken the war effort abroad. On several occasions the Duke of Bedford was compelled to come over from France to quiet the bitter squabbles.

For nearly seven years, in cooperation with the Burgundians, the vigorous armies of Bedford strove successfully against the disinherited son of Charles VI who refused to recognize the Treaty of Troyes and called himself Charles VII. Bedford and his allies finally occupied nearly all of the country north of the Loire. In 1428 they laid siege to Orleans, the key to southeastern France, where the uncrowned and befuddled Charles VII was still in control. The surrender of famished Orleans seemed at hand when Joan of Arc, an illiterate peasant girl, "black and swart," from the village of Domremy on the Lorraine border dramatically claimed that she had been called by God to save France.

Mystical voices heard by the passionate Joan had instructed her to raise the siege of Orleans. She went to the court of Charles VII. An amazing episode followed. Convinced of Joan's divine mission, Charles placed her at the head of his army and the French advanced towards Orleans. A queer mixture of masculine and feminine attributes, sincere and confident, Joan of Arc roused a new patriotic fervor and courage among the French soldiers. The English fell back from Orleans, muttering that the white-armored woman who led the French was a devil or a witch.

Joan helped Charles VII to defeat his enemies in several battles. She cleared the road to Rheims, where Charles was at last crowned king. She declared that she would expel the demoralized English from "the whole kingdom of France." Although Charles signed a truce with the Burgundians, the Maid of Orleans, convinced of her sacred mission, refused to stop fighting. She was wounded during an attack on Paris and in 1431 she was captured by the Burgundians. Charles VII did not offer to ransom her, and the Burgundians sold her to the English.

In the eyes of the English Joan was clearly a witch. Bedford had her tried at Rouen by a special court of French clergy. In May, 1431, they declared her guilty of heresy, and handed her over to the secular authorities to be burnt in the market place at Rouen. It is said that the secretary of England's Henry VI exclaimed: "We are lost; we have burned a saint."

The war continued and the inspiration of Joan of Arc lived on. The French, filled with a new pugnacity, steadily advanced. In 1435 the Burgundians deserted the English and joined Charles VII in return for the province of Picardy. Then Bedford died and there was no competent Englishman to succeed him. Charles VII recovered Paris in 1436. Soon the French threatened Normandy and Gascony and the English cause in northern France seemed irretrievably lost. At home, the Duke of Gloucester wanted to wage the war with all of England's resources. His opponents, led by Cardinal Beaufort, wanted peace. Although Henry VI was declared of age in 1437, he was too weak to command the divided council. With Bedford's strong hand gone old quarrels broke out again. Finally, by 1443, William de la Pole, the earl of Suffolk, controlled the council. He was supported by John and Edmund Beaufort, nephews of the great cardinal.

A truce with France was arranged in 1445, mainly by Suffolk. The terms provided for a marriage between the young Henry VI and Margaret of Anjou, niece of the queen of France. It was also secretly agreed that England would cede Maine to France. A few years later war broke out again and a newly organized French army with strong artillery power began the conquest of Normandy. Charles VII completed that task late in 1450. In 1451 Gascony collapsed. Two years later an English expeditionary army was disastrously defeated at Castillon. Charles VII entered Bordeaux in triumph. Of all the English possessions in France only Calais remained. The Hundred Years' War had ended.

THE LANCASTRIAN COLLAPSE

In England the warring factions of Gloucester and the Beauforts had brought the nation to the edge of civil war. Law and order had been shattered. Bands of brigands roamed the roads and forests. Great lords gathered private armies of liveried retainers, oppressed and plundered their weaker neighbors and bickered and skirmished among themselves. Their forces grew larger as they recruited discharged veterans of the war in France. Royal itinerant justices and sheriffs were overawed or bribed by local magnates, many of whom were in the king's council. Justice staggered before unbridled and often conscienceless power, violence, and corruption. The ministers were hated and distrusted. Such was the disordered state of affairs that prevailed as disasters fell upon English arms in France.

When Henry VI was declared of age in 1437 the power of the

Beauforts rapidly grew. The weak Henry yielded to their demands. John and Edmund Beaufort and their friend the Duke of Suffolk not only controlled the council, as explained earlier, but also extended their influence in several other directions. John Beaufort became Duke of Somerset. When he died in 1444 his brother Edmund succeeded to the title. After Henry VI's marriage, Edmund and the Duke of Suffolk found a valuable ally in the new queen, Margaret of Anjou.

Margaret was able, ruthless and dominating, inclined to intrigue and jobbery. Shakespeare called her the "she-wolf of France" with a "tiger's heart wrapped in a woman's hide" and "stern, obdurate, flinty, rough, remorseless." Before his vixen queen the gentle Henry VI quailed and retreated. Henry was a scholarly man, devoted to religion and study; the domestic peace he longed for was seldom his. Nevertheless, he quietly triumphed in one respect, at least, for he founded Eton College and King's College, Cambridge, greater achievements in the end than those of his queen or his self-seeking barons.

Queen Margaret not only supported Suffolk and Somerset but she also plotted with them against Gloucester. In 1447 Gloucester was formally charged with treason in a Parliament held at Bury. He was widely popular, especially among those who supported and hoped for a vigorous prosecution of the war. A few days after the accusation in Parliament Gloucester was found dead in bed. Probably he was murdered. In any event, Suffolk, Somerset, and the violent queen were widely blamed for Gloucester's death. Public opinion also condemned the three for the successive disasters in France and the confusion, discontent, and maladministration at home.

The secret agreement of 1445 by which England had ceded Maine to France soon became known. Suffolk was denounced for handing over territory that France had not been able to conquer by her armies. When the English forces in Normandy, commanded by the incompetent Somerset, were defeated in 1449 and 1450 the popular temper exploded. Suffolk, the minister officially responsible for the management of the war, was impeached by an angry Parliament. Henry VI refused to permit the earl to be tried but advised him to flee the realm. On his way to France in May, 1450, Suffolk was murdered by his enemies. It was a symptom of the general disaffection and a bloody sign of the times. The financial situation was desperate. The government was foundering in a sea of national distrust. As Somerset took Suffolk's place by Margaret's side events moved to a crisis.

A disturbance broke out in Kent and Sussex, led by the Irish adventurer Jack Cade, who asserted that he was one of the Mortimers. Cade, like Wat Tyler, came out of Kent, but the springs of Cade's rebellion were different from those of the Kentish revolt of the peasants in 1381. The rebels of 1450 included several landed gentlemen and yeomen. Their manifesto demanded the dismissal of incompetent and possibly treacherous royal ministers; a reform of the royal government, the end of widespread interference with justice and packing of the house of commons by the great lords backed by their private armies of liveried servants; the protection of real and personal property against greedy and powerful robbers.

The royal armies sent against Cade mutinied. Soon after Henry VI had fled the rebels entered London. Once in the city they got out of hand. The result was a havoc of riot, pillage, and murder. Finally the two archbishops agreed to lay the demands of the invaders before Henry VI and promised royal pardon for all the rebels. Most of the marchers then went home. Although Cade was killed in London, he was later attainted of treason in Parliament for having "falsely and traitorously imagined the king's death, destruction and subversion of this realm, in gathering and levying a great number of the king's people, and them exciting to make insurrection against the king . . . and howbeit though he be dead and mischieved, yet by the law of the land not punished . . . our sovereign lord the king . . . to put such traitors in doubt so to do in time coming . . . hath ordained by the authority of the said Parliament, that he shall be of these treasons attainted."

In August, 1453, Henry VI went insane. Richard, Duke of York, was appointed regent. Richard was a man of moderate and cautious ambition. On his father's side he was descended from Edmund, Duke of York, the fifth son of Edward III. His mother was the great-granddaughter of Lionel, Duke of Clarence, the third son of Edward III. It will be recalled that the Lancastrian line of Henry VI was descended from John of Gaunt, the fourth son of Edward III, and that Henry IV owed his throne in 1399 to the decision of battle and an act of Parliament rather than to an indisputable hereditary claim. Richard, with his double descent from Edward III, was in a strong position, particularly because he was powerful and popular, and Henry VI was not. The Duke had been in Ireland and hence could not be blamed for the unhappy state of England's affairs. He had fought well in France. He had opposed Suffolk and Somerset. In 1452 he had threatened an armed attack upon the king and Somerset, and Henry VI had promised to dismiss Somerset. When Richard became regent, he put Somerset in prison. These aspects of the Duke of York's personal history added to his mounting popularity. He made no claim to supplant Henry VI but he was certainly hopeful of succeeding him.

Two events occurred to heighten the hostility between the Yorkists and Lancastrians. In October, 1453, a son was born to Henry VI and Margaret of Anjou, thus excluding Richard from the succession to the throne if the Parliamentary claim of the Lancastrians continued to prevail. Then, in 1454, Henry VI suddenly became quite sane again. His clever and vindictive wife now determined to dispose of the Yorkists as quickly as possible. Henry VI, acting on the prompting of Margaret and her friends, released Somerset, restored him to power, and completely excluded Richard and his followers from the government. Several of Richard's enemies spread the tale that he had earlier been a party to Cade's rebellion. The queen held a council "to provide for the safety of the king's person against his enemies." In 1455 Richard took arms, alleging that he did so to protect the Yorkists from the designs of the queen and Somerset. He made no open claim to the throne, although his adherents were asserting that the house of Lancaster was no longer capable of governing England.

Thus began the intermittent, civil and dynastic war later called the Wars of the Roses, from the true tradition that the white rose was the badge of the Yorkists and the romantic but mistaken idea that the red rose was the symbol of the Lancastrians. The red rose was used in the sixteenth century, but not before. Unlike the civil war of the Stuart age, the thirty-year conflict of the fifteenth century was not fought about ideals or contracts or theories of government. It was a factional struggle between two branches of the royal line and their supporters; and it was nothing more. The nobles, under the system of "livery and maintenance," hired large numbers of Englishmen and foreign mercenaries for their private armies which were further swelled by large numbers of tenants. Nobles such as the powerful Richard Neville, earl of Warwick and nephew of the Duke of York, had thousands of men in their forces, skilled in the use of bow and bill.

Most of the mass of English people viewed the outcome of the rough-and-tumble wars with indifference. Many of the nobles shifted sides from time to time as their interests changed and the wheel of fortune turned. There were no principles to desert. Most of the cities freely opened their gates to the forces of either side. The main concern of many rural Englishmen was the ruining of their crops by the passage of troops, carts, and horses across their lands. The majority of Englishmen were neutral and they did not suffer much. The weight of the war fell upon the nobles. Their numbers were greatly reduced by battle casualties and savage executions. Many were impoverished as a result of the ruthless confiscation of estates by both Yorkists and Lancastrians in turn in their hour of triumph. "The Wars of the Roses were a bleeding operation performed by the nobility upon their own body."

Several engagements of the wars were fought near London because each side wanted to hold the greatest city and the seat of government. At St. Albans, about twenty-five miles from London, occurred the first battle in 1455. The Duke of York won this brief encounter. His enemy Somerset was slain and Henry VI was captured. When another of Henry VI's periodic fits of insanity fell upon him, York again became regent. In 1456 the king recovered and the queen at once dismissed her enemy Richard. In 1459 she began to gather troops to lead the Lancastrians to victory. Richard found himself outnumbered and fled into exile with his son Edward and his nephew and ally Richard Neville, the earl of Warwick. Warwick went to Calais, where his fleet controlled the English Channel. Richard went to Ireland. A packed Lancastrian Parliament at Coventry passed a sweeping act of attainder declaring the Yorkist leaders guilty of treason.

In the summer of 1460 Richard and Warwick returned. Warwick won the battle of Northampton, captured Henry VI, and occupied London. At this point Richard claimed the crown; but Parliament obstinately refused to dethrone the saintly and pathetic Henry VI. It finally did agree to set aside Henry VI's son and Richard was recognized as the immediate heir to the throne. Queen Margaret, active as ever, was not prepared to accept a settlement that would exclude her son from the succession. She gathered forces swiftly and met Richard in December, 1460, in Yorkshire at Wakefield. In that battle Richard was killed and his army beaten. The queen's forces turned southwards and defeated Warwick at the second battle of St. Albans, where Henry VI was freed from the custody of the Yorkists.

The Lancastrians apparently did not consider themselves strong enough to seize London. At least there is no other satisfactory explanation for the fact that the queen and her army retreated northwards, laying waste the country as they marched. Behind them Edward, earl of March and eldest son of Richard, Duke of York, defeated the Welsh Lancastrian marcher lords, joined Warwick, and entered London. There, early in 1461, Warwick had Edward proclaimed king under the name of Edward IV. Then the new king marched northwards. Margaret had no able commanders. Edward, on the other hand, possessed a precocious genius for war. With him went Warwick, soon called "the kingmaker."

As the Yorkists advanced, their forces were swelled by numerous men made angry by the pillaging and plundering of the Lancastrian armies in a wide belt from London to York. Late in March, 1461, the Yorkists and Lancastrians met at Towton near York. The resulting struggle, fought in a snowstorm, was bloody and savage. It was a decisive victory for the Yorkists. Thousands of Lancastrians lay dead on the battlefield; many Lancastrian nobles who survived the battle were beheaded later. Henry VI, his queen, and his young son fled to Scotland.

Edward went back to London for his formal coronation. The country received the conqueror as king. Parliament had refused to give the throne to Richard of York in 1460; they recognized the title of his son in 1461. For sixty-two years England had lived under three Lancastrian rulers. During the next twenty-four years there were to be three Yorkist kings. They, in turn, were to give way to Henry VII, first of the Tudors.

THE RULE OF THE YORKISTS

The character of the young Edward IV was quite different from that of Henry VI, his mild and saintly predecessor. Edward was handsome, coarse, and cruel. His mental ability was considerable. He also had a remarkable gift for cultivating popularity, particularly among the rising commercial classes. Had he been willing to devote himself actively to the business of kingship he might have accomplished much more than he did. Unfortunately, his main interests did not lie in government and administration. He preferred eating, drinking, and numerous love affairs. That was one of the reasons why the disruptive power of the feudal lords remained uncrushed until the reign of Henry VII.

Richard Neville, earl of Warwick and "kingmaker," had helped to put his cousin Edward on the throne. Warwick was the most powerful of all the king's subjects; his estates were vast; his liveried retainers were numbered in thousands. Until 1464 he was the real ruler of England. In that year he stopped a further bid of the Lancastrians for the throne by defeating them at Hexham in the north of England. In 1465 Henry VI was captured in Yorkshire, and imprisoned in London. It was about this time that the influence of Warwick upon Edward IV began to grow weaker.

The first reason for the decline of Warwick's power resulted from the question of the king's marriage. Warwick wanted an alliance with France, arguing that such an agreement would strengthen the Yorkists against the still potentially dangerous Lancastrians. The crafty French King, Louis XI, had earlier supported Margaret of Anjou but by 1464 he naturally changed his mind and turned towards Edward IV. The Duke of Burgundy, bitter rival of Louis XI, also sought the support of an alliance with England. With Edward's apparent approval Warwick began negotiations pointing towards a marriage between Edward and the French queen's sister. Then, suddenly, Edward IV announced that he had been secretly married to Elizabeth Grey, the widow of a Lancastrian knight and daughter of the Lancastrian peer Richard Woodville, Lord Rivers. The Yorkists were disconcerted and furious. Warwick felt that he had been allowed to make a fool of himself by negotiating with the French when Edward was already married.

There was more to come. Edward, apparently weary and resentful of Warwick's tutelage and hectoring arrogance, began to seek ways of diminishing his cousin's power. He soon found one effective method. About him he gathered the Lancastrian relatives and friends of his queen. The queen had five brothers and seven sisters; she also had two sons by her first marriage; and there were numerous cousins. The Lancastrian Woodvilles scurried to the court where offices, honors, and noble marriages awaited them. Warwick's brother was ousted from the chancellorship. The queen's father became treasurer. Warwick and the Yorkists felt themselves in danger of being put completely outside. Nevertheless, Warwick held his peace, so anxious was he for the completion of an alliance with France.

Again Edward moved, this time in another direction. In 1467 he allied himself with Charles the Bold, Duke of Burgundy, the enemy of Louis XI. Despite the general hostility of Englishmen to France and the fact that Burgundy controlled Flanders, so important in England's wool trade, the alliance was unwise. The rash and changeable Duke of Burgundy could never be of much value as an ally. Edward also agreed that his sister, Margaret of York, would marry his Burgundian ally and that he would aid Burgundy in an assault upon Louis XI.

At this point Warwick left the court and began carefully to plot revenge. He found a partner in Edward's brother George, the Duke of Clarence, who had earlier married Warwick's daughter. Meanwhile, Edward IV was having trouble with Lancastrian plots, mainly fomented by an angry Louis XI. In 1469, to his surprise and alarm, there arose an open revolt led by Warwick and the Duke of Clarence. An aroused Yorkshire backed the bear and ragged staff, famous badge of Warwick's Neville family. Several of the king's leaders were defeated. The Woodville family suffered heavy casualties. Edward himself was captured.

In a few months Warwick apparently believed that he would be restored to his earlier posts of power in the court if he released Edward IV. If such was his belief, Warwick was soon undeceived. In 1470 Edward publicly declared both Warwick and Clarence traitors. Then Warwick fled to France, where he at last deserted the Yorkist camp and allied himself with his ancient enemy, Margaret of Anjou. Margaret's eldest son married Warwick's youngest daughter. Supported by Louis XI, Warwick invaded England and forced Edward IV to flee to Burgundy. Poor Henry VI, broken and imbecile, was released from the Tower and put back upon the throne by the "king-maker."

The restoration was brief. In 1471 Edward IV returned from Burgundy. The Duke of Clarence suddenly deserted Warwick. At the battle of Barnet Edward was victorious and Warwick was killed as he fled towards the woods. Edward then rushed upon the iron Margaret of Anjou, who had landed with a second army. He defeated her at Tewkesbury. In that battle Margaret was captured and Prince Edward, the son of Henry VI and Margaret, was slain, it was said, by the "false, fleeting, perjured" Duke of Clarence. Soon afterwards, the

*direct
Lancastrian
line
ended
only
Henry Tudor
Renewed*

demented Henry VI was murdered in the Tower. The direct line of the Lancastrians was ended and the last male Beaufort was dead. The only junior claimant to the Lancastrian inheritance was Henry Tudor, the earl of Richmond.

Triumphant and unchallenged, Edward IV proceeded to take a pitiless revenge upon those who had opposed him. There were many executions and widespread confiscations of property, windfalls to the crown. During the rest of his reign, Edward ruled with a strong hand. The weakness of the central government was changed to strength. Edward brooked no interference. For example, his ambitious brother, the despicable Duke of Clarence, began to dispute with his younger brother, the Duke of Gloucester, about certain lands of some destroyed Lancastrians. Edward secured from Parliament an act of attainder against Clarence in 1477. Soon Clarence died in the Tower. Rumor said that he had been murdered; that his enemies had drowned him in a butt of malmsey, his favorite wine.

At the same time, Edward brought quiet and security to an England so long troubled by intestine broils and distracted by conspiracy. Abroad, there were few disturbances of importance. In 1482 there occurred a short war with Scotland, from which the Duke of Gloucester emerged victorious, adding Berwick once more to England's northern territory as a key position on the Scottish border. In 1475 Edward invaded France as the ally of the Duke of Burgundy. He consented to withdraw in return for a cash payment of 75,000 crowns and a promise of 50,000 more. At home, Edward improved the administration of justice. He encouraged commerce. His wide popularity was based not only upon his robust geniality but upon some concrete results of his policies. If big, sensual Edward IV had not returned again to the vigorous pursuit of voluptuous and distracting pleasures the latter part of his reign might have shown more fruitful results.

In 1483 Edward IV died suddenly, at the age of forty-one. With his death the crown passed to his son, Edward, a child twelve years of age. After a last tragic scene the moral interregnum of the fifteenth century was to come to a sudden end.

THE EVOLUTION OF PARLIAMENT

When Henry IV came to the throne in 1399 he was dependent upon such support as he could win to hold his crown. He had to keep the good will of Parliament and he was compelled to ask Parliament frequently for money to finance his wars. When the members of Parliament, aware of their strong position, began to demand more privileges and powers Henry IV was forced to yield. His son, Henry V, depended upon Parliament for money to fight the Hundred Years' War. When he was absent in France his council and administrative officers often sought parliamentary approval for their actions. Henry VI was a minor when he came to the throne; he was pathological in his instability after he became of age. Until 1460 the authority of Parliament steadily expanded. It was the strongest factor in the nation. Thus the years before 1460 marked a period of almost unbroken constitutional government, "prematurely modern" in its nature. The habits and precedents of thought and action were important as a part of new and formative constitutional practices.

Before 1460 Parliament was greatly concerned about the privileges of the commons: freedom of debate; freedom of the members, to a certain extent, from arrest; the right of the house of commons, as distinct from the house of lords, to originate taxation and to determine the qualification of members; the determination of suffrage qualifications in the counties; the improvement of the legislative process. If the members of Parliament were denied freedom to speak without fear of reprisal, then they could not be independent of the king. If they were to be punished by the king for saying or doing things displeasing to him, then they could not check arbitrary government. Freedom of speech was a right fundamental to the power of Parliament, for without it Parliament might have no power at all.

The case of Thomas Haxey in 1397 had shown the importance of guarding against royal interference. Haxey, although not a member of Parliament, had prepared a petition that the commons had adopted and presented to the king. Richard II had imprisoned him for writing the petition. Before Henry IV came to the throne Haxey had been released, probably because he was in holy orders. In 1399 the house of lords approved a petition from Haxey for a reversal of the judgment against him. Later in the year the commons repeated the petition and again the house of the lords approved; this was equivalent to an action by the whole Parliament. Haxey was cleared of all shadow. In this case, at least, an important principle had been successfully defended: the king must not attempt to coerce Parliament by the arbitrary arrest or imprisonment of its members or its agents.

In 1400 the speaker of the house of commons said that certain members of Parliament had been in the habit of making reports to the king about matters on the agenda of the commons, "before the same had been described and agreed upon among the said commons by which the king might be incensed against them or some of them." The speaker asked the king to take no notice of such reports and to exert no royal pressure as a result of them. Henry acknowledged the right of the commons to debate freely and promised not to listen to unauthorized accounts of their activities.

In 1407 Henry IV proclaimed that the lords and commons might "commune among themselves in this present Parliament and in every other in time to come, in the absence of the king, of the estate of the realm and of the remedy necessary for the same." Four years earlier, Henry IV had formally recognized the privilege of members of Parliament to freedom from arrest on civil process during a session of Parliament and in going to or returning from one. This privilege was regulated and extended in the reign of Henry VII. Thus the bulwarks against royal influence in Parliament were being strengthened and the precedents were being created for assertions of Parliamentary privilege. On occasion, however, the Parliament could not maintain its claim of privileges. In 1453, for example, the Duke of York ordered the arrest of the Lancastrian speaker of the house of commons. Despite the protests of the commons the speaker was kept in prison.

In the late fourteenth century the practice of the separate taxation of each estate by its own representatives had come to an end, except in the case of the clergy. The commons kept control of the grant of taxation. In 1395 the grant to the king was made "by the commons with the advice and assent of the lords." In 1407 the king agreed that he would listen to reports about money grants only "by the mouth of the speaker of the commons." The right of the commons to originate taxation was a customary right, not one stated in a statute. The force of precedents was not, surely, so fully binding as it is sometimes believed to be. Nevertheless, the custom that grants of money should originate with the commons was not easily shaken. In 1407, for example, Henry IV failed when he tried to proceed first through the lords. The commons refused to accept such "a great prejudice and derogation of their liberties."

As the powers of Parliament grew under the watchful eyes of the knights, burgesses, and lawyers the problem of regulating representation increased. In the Middle Ages nobody was deeply concerned about the qualification of burgesses or the manner in which they were elected. The county representatives were "knights of the shire" or gentlemen born. In the late fourteenth century, however, there had been much interference in elections. Parliaments had often been packed as a result of the activities of the king and the nobles. Several men had been elected in the counties who were not in fact knights of the shire. The sheriffs had frequently made false election returns. Several steps were taken to check the defects and misdeeds of the sheriffs. For example, it was required that mayors, bailiffs, and sheriffs must make their election returns by sworn indentures, certified by some of the voters. For each false return a sheriff was to be fined £100. Persons aggrieved in fraudulent elections were given new legal remedies. In 1445 a statute formally required all those elected from the counties to be gentlemen born. In 1413, and again in 1430 and 1445, acts of Parliament required that all members should reside in the locality they represented, an enactment designed to check the sheriffs from reporting their own nominees, often from outside the county, as winners in the election. All the electors were also required to be resident in the county in which they voted.

Who are the "Electors"?
40 shilling freeholders
Limitation of franchise

　　　In 1429 it was provided by statute, later extended in 1432, that the right to vote in the counties should be limited. The statute recited the reasons for the decision: "in many counties the election of knights of the shires . . . have of late been carried out by too great and excessive a number of people dwelling within those same counties, of whom the larger part have been people of little substance or of no worth, each pretending to have the same voice in such elections as the most worthy knights or squires." Accordingly the new law provided that only the famous "forty shilling freeholder" class could henceforth be electors in the counties.

　　　One reason for the statute was declared to be the "homicides, riots, and assaults" at county elections held in the public county court sessions. Another reason was the fact that the limitation of the franchise reduced the interference of king and nobles in the elections. Hitherto the county members had been returned to Parliament by the vote of all who were freemen and above. The nobles had been using their numerous servants to swing elections. After the new statute this evil was ended. A man who owned enough freehold land to yield a clear profit of forty shillings a year was a moderately wealthy man. The general body of the freeman suitors in the county court no longer had a vote. These acts of 1429 and 1432 governed the franchise in the counties until the Reform Bill of 1832. No change was made in the system of election in the boroughs. They maintained their numerous and differing local procedures until the nineteenth century.

　　　Meanwhile Parliament extended its power in the control of government expenditures and the earmarking of appropriations of supply for particular purposes. Almost always it was stated that general taxes granted to the king were for national defense; a part of the custom on wool was to be for the maintenance of Calais; the tunnage and poundage tax, by this time usually granted to the king for life, was to be spent for such specific purposes as the navy and "the safeguarding of the sea and in no other way." The royal income was, as usual, to be used for the expenses of the royal household. In 1414 Parliament was also able to secure a definite royal pledge that statutes based on parliamentary petitions should not contain "either additions or subtractions which in any particular or particulars change the meaning and intent" of the petitions. Under Henry IV bills began to be substituted for petitions: the bill contained the statute asked for in exactly the form in which it was to be approved. Thus the king or his servants could not make changes in drafting the statute because it was already drafted in the bill.

Bill substituted for Petitions - conform exact statutes

　　　Before 1460 the Parliaments were able to control the royal council and household very effectively. Several officials of Henry IV's household were dismissed at the insistence of the commons. Both the household officials and the members of "the great and continual council" were named in Parliament. In the fifteenth century, of course, there was no constitutional way in which these royal servants could easily be made responsible to Parliament. In 1406 the council was almost completely reconstituted and "the wisest lords of the realm" were "to have the supervision of everything that should be done for the good government of the kingdom." All important documents issued by the king were to be approved by the council. Thus, for a time, the council was almost completely under parliamentary control.

When Henry V came to the throne Parliament lost some of its power over the council. The absence of Henry overseas left a large part of his executive power in the hands of the council members although the council, as noted earlier, did frequently seek parliamentary sanction for its actions. When Henry VI was a minor the council remained strong. Later, at the end of Henry VI's minority, and for a time under Edward IV, the council was in fact more powerful than Parliament itself. At other times, such as the years when the earl of Suffolk dominated the king, the council was almost powerless. After Suffolk was impeached in 1450 and fled into the hands of his murderers neither council nor Parliament could maintain control. In the middle of the century the council was merely the instrument of shifting baronial policies and the battleground of feuding noble factions.

Under the powerful Edward IV the strength of the council rose once more. It was the servant of the king and Parliament had no control over its composition. Edward IV eliminated many nobles from the council and increased the number of trained and expert administrative officials. The administrative and judicial functions of the council increased as it became the normal instrument for executing the king's commands. The civil jurisdiction of the council was almost completely handed over to the chancery court. Edward IV summoned only six Parliaments because he was less dependent than his predecessors upon money grants from the commons. An early Parliament granted him tunnage and poundage and several other customs grants for life. Edward also had the income from the royal lands and the forfeited estates of the Lancastrians.

There were other sources of revenue. From his wealthy subjects Edward collected forced gifts called benevolences. He gathered heavy fines from his courts. He made considerable profit from his activities as a trader. It will be recalled that in the latter part of his reign he received a large sum of money from the king of France. During these years the parliamentary power of the purse was almost without meaning. It was upon the council, not upon Parliament, that Edward IV depended for service and efficiency. The Tudors who followed after him were to view the council as the real organ of actual government acting for a stronger monarch. Such an instrument the council of the Tudors remained until the death of Elizabeth in 1603.

The spasmodic parliamentary control of the royal council in the fifteenth century was a premature chapter in constitutional history. It was an interesting event when Parliament expanded in the sunshine of its strength. With few exceptions, the precedents set in the days of Henry IV and in brief later moments were to remain largely forgotten until the seventeenth century. It was to be over two hundred years before the modern cabinet system made the royal ministers responsible to Parliament. The methods by which that responsibility was obtained were not to be impeachment, bills of attainder, or the uncertain machinery of the premature experiment of the Lancastrian age.

THE BATTLE OF BOSWORTH FIELD

When Edward IV died in 1483 his successor was his son, Edward V, twelve years of age. Elizabeth Woodville, widow of Edward IV and unpopular mother of Edward V, hoped to be regent of England while her son was a minor. Opposing Elizabeth and the Woodville family stood Richard, Duke of Gloucester and brother of Edward IV. With complete lack of mercy or scruple Richard seized and executed several of Elizabeth's relatives and supporters and forced the royal council to declare him regent and protector. He then secured custody of Edward V and his young brother, the Duke of York. Claiming that the sons of Edward IV were illegitimate and the queen mother was a witch, Richard packed Parliament with his supporters and had himself declared king. In July, 1483, he was crowned king as Richard III. Writers in the Tudor age stressed the fact that Richard was a hunchback, undersized, and had a withered arm. Shakespeare's unforgettable descriptions were suitable for a ruling house that hated the name of the Yorkist Richard III. In his own day Richard seems to have been reasonably popular, particularly in the strongly Yorkist northern counties. After he became king, his popularity waned, and for very good reason.

Richard's deformities may have been exaggerated, but hardly his crimes. The glittering bait of the crown was tempting. There appears to be no doubt that Edward V and his brother were murdered in the Tower and that Richard III was responsible for the deed. The bones of the boys were discovered in the Tower in the reign of Charles II. It is also probable that Richard had a hand in the murder of his wife, his brother Clarence, and Henry VI. Even in a callous and bloody age the vicious murder of the two princes by an uncle who had them in his trust shocked the nation. Many Yorkists joined the Lancastrians in rebellion against the villainous Richard. A premature revolt in 1484 was crushed. Soon, however, the opponents of Richard produced their candidate for the throne. He was Henry Tudor, earl of Richmond. His mother, Lady Margaret, was a Beaufort, descended from Edward III through the third marriage of John of Gaunt. His Welsh father, Edmund Tudor, was a son of Henry V's widow, Katherine of France, by a later marriage. Thus Henry Tudor had royal blood in his veins from both sides of his family. His remote hereditary right to the throne was dimmed by the fact that the Beauforts had been barred from the succession, as explained earlier, by an act of 1407. Nevertheless, he was the nearest male representative of the house of Lancaster. The earl of Warwick, son of Richard III's brother Clarence, was the obvious Yorkist claimant; but he was only a young boy.

Numerous enemies of Richard III hurried to join Henry Tudor. Many unhappy Yorkists were soothed by Henry's proposed marriage to Elizabeth, Edward IV's eldest daughter. In August, supported by troops and money given him by the French queen, Henry sailed from Brittany and landed in Pembrokeshire. His Welsh family connections joined him there. Bishop Morton of Ely, the Woodville family, and many powerful peers pledged their support. On August 22, 1485, the armies of Henry, flying the banners of Wales and England, met Richard's forces at Bosworth Field in Leicestershire, almost in the center of England.

In the battle several of Richard's soldiers deserted. Richard himself was slain, fighting bravely in the midst of treason. Tradition says that the crown Richard III had worn in the battle was found in a hawthorn bush and placed on the head of Henry Tudor by one of the barons who had craftily wavered and then betrayed Richard. Henry Tudor, by the fortune of battle and by act of Parliament, was to become Henry VII.

In the closing lines of Shakespeare's *Richard III*, Henry VII spoke of the new peace:

> "Abate the edge of traitors, gracious Lord
> That would reduce these bloody days again
> And make poor England weep in streams of blood."

The Wars of the Roses were ended. The house of Tudor had come to the throne. The first winds of the Renaissance spirit had swept lightly over the English Channel. The humanities had begun to reign and Aquinas and Duns Scotus were giving up their thrones to Plato and Cicero. "If medieval art still lingered it would not linger long." William Caxton had introduced printing into England in 1477. Feudal anarchy had wrecked itself. The main political force in England was the monarchy; and the Tudors kept it so.

Chapter 11

THE GREAT TRANSITION

NEW ROADS FOR OLD

[handwritten margin note: art of middle ages merged gradually into the modern era.]

T HE thrusts of continuity and change that we call history have been divided into periods usually described as ancient, medieval, and modern. This arbitrary division is an instrument of convenience, nothing more. Generations are born, live their allotted time, and die. Institutions grow and decay. In English history the medieval age did not end abruptly in 1485 when Henry VII ascended the throne. In some ways it was coming to an end many years before; in others it persisted for a long time after. The twentieth century still shows many lingering remants of the truly medieval. Historians, with the advantages of hindsight, have often described the close of the Middle Ages far more dramatically than contemporaries could have done. There was really no sharp cleavage with the past. What actually happened was that the world of the Middle Ages merged gradually into what we call the modern era.

The next few chapters are about the world of Englishmen in the sixteenth century. When Elizabeth, last of the Tudors, died in 1603 the transition to modern England was well advanced. In the great Tudor century a strong monarchy helped England towards the unity of a modern nation. Rival sovereignties within the state declined under rulers who, for a time, emancipated themselves from the control of fundamental law by taking advantage of the reasonable harmony of powers in court, crown, and Parliament. The strength of the feudal nobles was diminished. The sway of the Roman Catholic Church was ended. The astounding magnificence of the Renaissance spread its many-splendored colors through an age of power and versatility. The country gentry and the merchants of the middle class grasped new tools of power and wealth. Markets across distant seas called to English traders. New domestic markets were hungry for goods from abroad. "Englishmen above many others are worst able to live with a little." The ships of adventurers travelled to nearly every corner of the

189

earth. "Whosoever commands the sea," said Sir Walter Raleigh, "commands the trade; whosoever commands the trade commands the riches of the world, and consequently the world itself."

The generations who won such success were crowded with personality, talent, and force. In politics there were such men as Wolsey, Walsingham, and Burghley; in the church, Cranmer, Hooker, and Parker; in literature, Kyd, Marlowe, Shakespeare, Sidney, Spenser, and the lyric poets; in the steep ground of action, Drake, Frobisher, Gilbert, Hawkins. It was an acquisitive and superstitious age, at once ruthless and noble, an age of leaping action. "Energy," said an Elizabethan, "is an eternal delight." It was an aristocratic age, far from the theory or practice of equality. Despite the Tudor poor laws there were many of Shakespeare's "naked wretches" who moved with "loop'd and window'd raggedness" through the pelting economic storms of the sixteenth century.

In these days there was no mercy shown for heresy or treason; men were cruel to the enemies of the church and nation. They "burned witches, imprisoned debtors and imbeciles in foul cells, oppressed their weaker neighbours, robbed the state." The strong machine of the Tudor centralized monarchy could afford to tolerate no major challenge. Fallen courtiers, rebels, and old priests were marked for execution and carried in the Tyburn cart that climbed the heavy hill of Holborn. Part of what the Tudors did has survived, and part of it has not.

The Tudor century was filled with violent contrasts, kaleidoscopic shiftings of tumultuous patterns. Pure ideals and high thoughts were inextricably mingled with the base, the sordid, and the mean. The most important single achievement of the Tudor monarchs was that they gave England more order and peace than she had known for a century. To accomplish this was the first task of Henry VII.

1485 DECLINE OF THE OLD NOBILITY

When Henry VII won the battle of Bosworth Field on August 22, 1485, he was twenty-eight years old. He had successfully appealed to the judgment of battle against the "homicidal and unnatural tyrant" Richard III. The throne of England was his to take and hold. Henry VII was a cold, cautious, inscrutable, shrewd, Machiavellian individual, a man of clear and tenacious purpose. "What he minded, that he compassed." It was quite in keeping with his energetic character and methods that he summoned Parliament at once and set before it his claim to the throne on the grounds of conquest and heredity. "Heretofore it has always been an understood thing that he who lost the day lost the kingdom also."

On November 7, 1485, Parliament passed an Act of Succession granting Henry the crown. "In avoiding all ambiguities and questions" it was declared that the inheritance of the crown should "be, rest, remain, and abide in the most royal person of our now sovereign lord, King Henry VII." There was no mention of Henry's hereditary claim to the throne. Such frail title as Henry did possess came through his mother from the Beauforts and John of Gaunt. On the other hand, several descendants of Lionel, Duke of Clarence and older brother of John of Gaunt, had far better claims than Henry.

Henry VII knew that his position was really based on the victory title of battle and the political support of those who had power. In the knowledge that his hereditary claim was clouded he married Elizabeth of York, the eldest daughter of Edward IV and possessed of the best Yorkist claim to the throne as the most direct descendant from Lionel. Hence the houses of York and Lancaster were at last joined. When one son was born to Henry VII and Elizabeth in 1486 and a second in 1491 the future of the Tudor dynasty seemed assured. Thus one step had been taken towards the first object of Henry VII: to restore the authority of a monarchy weakened by the disorders of the previous age.

When Henry VII came to the throne England was being visited by the "sweating sickness" which lasted for more than a year. It was widely held to be an omen of "a stern rule and a troubled reign." In the Tudor and Stuart centuries the "plague" in its various forms struck frequently. In 1513 there were said to have been about 300 deaths in London daily. The plague came again in 1525, 1529, and 1532. It had been estimated that in 1551 about 5,000 died in London in three days. The court fled and the shops were shut. In Elizabeth's reign such epidemics raged several times. In the midst of a time of terror Philip Stubbs wrote one of the most beautiful prayers of his age: "The infection of the pestilence shall do us no great harm, if we withdraw ourselves from the infection of sin. Thou never forsakest them that put their trust in Thy goodness; under Whose protection, even they that die are safe."

Henry recognized that the soothsayers who foresaw a "troubled" reign would be proved true prophets unless he could obtain popular support. Like all the Tudors, Henry VII wanted the actualities of power. The administration of the law must be strengthened through the common law courts and through special prerogative bodies. The efficiency of the council must be increased. The disorder among the high and low must cease. The last fires of civil war must be quenched. Intrigue, lawlessness, and conspiracy must yield to the royal power. "Rebellion had become a habit, treason an occupation." Henry VII saw that the future of himself and his dynasty depended upon whether he could bring peace and prosperity to the farmers and merchants. Agriculture and commerce flourish best when there is no internal disorder and no foreign war.

One of the great centers of disturbance and threats to peace was the nobility. Against them Henry VII turned first. They had been the

Nobility = private armies used to defy Royal authority

leaders in the Wars of the Roses and their armies of liveried retainers had been used to defy the royal authority, to wage private wars, to molest the middle and lower classes, and to interfere with the administration of justice. Several of the greatest nobles had been killed in the wars; those who remained soon felt the heavy hand of the first grim Tudor. In the north of England, far from London, there were nests of aristocrats who thought themselves out of reach of the royal power. "It was marvellous necessary to repress the insolency of nobles or gentlemen who, being far from the king and the seat of justice, made almost, as it were, an ordinary war among themselves, and made force the law, binding themselves with their tenants and their servants to do or avenge an injury among themselves as they pleased."

Middle class supported Henry VII - v. nobility. Parlem. act against private liveried soldiers

The powerful middle class strongly approved when Henry VII moved against the "overmighty nobles" to force them to keep the law and the peace. The magnates who had rejoiced so long in the strength of military feudalism now reluctantly bowed before the strong king. In his first Parliament, Henry compelled the lords to take an oath that they would not maintain large bands of liveried men who might be used as servants one day and soldiers or robbers the next. In 1504 an act of Parliament referred to earlier legislation against the practice of liveries and maintenance and provided that "no person, of whatever degree or condition he be, . . . shall privily or openly give any livery or sign or retain any person, other than such as he giveth household wages unto without fraud or colour."

Tudors. Royal extended prerogative power / sought to strengthen existing institutions / both central + local to make them instruments of Royal power

Henry VII was not tyrannical in his methods, nor were any of his Tudor successors. It is true that the Tudors extended the royal prerogative power. It is also true that they usually depended upon the co-operation of their people in making their rule effective. They constantly sought to strengthen and invigorate existing institutions, central and local, making them instruments of royal power. They anxiously quoted and appealed to ancient customs, laws, and precedents to justify their actions. "If the king proposed to change any old established rule, it would seem to every Englishman as if his life were taken away from him." Everywhere the Tudors increased the efficiency of administration; they strengthened their council; they used Parliament when they wished its support. Where there was innovation they tried to legalize it by parliamentary statute. This judicious recognition of forms and precedents always tempered what is often called, not with entire justice, "the Tudor absolutism."

It was natural that Henry VII should use every possible agency to curb the powerful nobles. The common law courts had been seriously weakened during the chaotic years of civil war. Trial by jury had often mocked justice because the judges and juries were bribed or terrorized. Many criminals were never apprehended. The national disorder was only partially checked by acts aimed at punishing jurors for returning *important judicial reform* [handwritten margin note]

false verdicts and setting up machinery to determine their guilt or innocence. Townships which failed to discover and arrest murderers were fined heavily. Coroners who neglected to hold inquests were also punished. Such remedial measures were important. Nevertheless, their bright significance is dimmed when placed beside Henry VII's most important judicial reform: the effective use of the prerogative court of star chamber.

This court was not created by Henry. The royal council had a residual jurisdiction that it sometimes exercised itself and sometimes delegated to the chancellor. Such jurisdiction included the offenses of subjects too powerful to be tried and punished by the common law courts. In 1487 an act of Parliament designated certain members of the council who were to exercise criminal jurisdiction in the court of star chamber. The part of the council sitting as a court was ordered to have regular meetings for judicial purposes in a room in Westminster Palace that is supposed to have had starred walls and ceiling. Hence the name "star chamber" court.

The act of 1487 also gave the court statutory authority "to punish divers misdemeanors." It referred to the fact that "the policy and good rule of this realm is almost subdued . . . whereby the laws of the land in execution may take little effect, to the increase of robberies, perjuries, and insureties of all men living, and losses of their lands and goods, to the great displeasure of Almighty God." By the terms of the act the court of star chamber had authority to summon before it by writ or privy seal any "misdoers" and "to punish them after their demerits."

The court of star chamber was in fact an elastic law unto itself. There was no jury. Even the most powerful noble could not frighten or bribe the judges. The accused individual often did not see the witnesses against him; he was not permitted to cross-examine; he might be tortured; he might be sentenced to any kind of punishment except death. This court, and similar bodies such as the court of high commission, thus exercised court powers inherent in the central council of the king. Their members included individuals who were also members of the king's council. Such courts did not depend on the common law. Their authority and procedural methods were ultimately derived from the fountain of the royal prerogative, bulwarked on occasion by the statute law.

This star chamber court was an admirable and efficient instrument in the restoration of order and respect for the law. It could be used to strike at the most powerful lords in England. Those accused of such crimes as livery and maintenance, bribery, overawing the common law courts, and "undue demeaning of sheriffs" had short shrift before it. For example, the proud earl of Oxford paraded six hundred liveried retainers to honor his king. He was astounded when the court of star

chamber fined him £10,000 for violating the statute against the practice
of liveries and maintenance; he did not repeat the offense. As used by
Henry VII the court of star chamber swiftly put the fear of the law into
the turbulent nobles and brought them to heel. In later days, under the
Stuarts, this court became a vicious instrument of arbitrary and despotic power. But the Tudors did not abuse it; it enforced justice and
stopped proud lawbreakers from defying royal authority and trampling
on the rights of the king's subjects.

The strength of the old nobility was weakened by another practice.
"The benevolent mind of the rich sort was searched out and by their
open gifts the king would measure and search their benevolent hearts
and loving minds so that he who gave most should be judged his most
loyal friend and he who gave little be esteemed according to his gift."
Special agents, such as Archbishop John Morton, Sir Richard Empson,
and Edmund Dudley, helped reform the royal revenue apparatus and
collected forced loans and benevolences. If a noble lived well he was
informed that he could surely afford to make a gift to the king; if he
lived poorly he was told that he must be saving enough to do the same
thing. This dilemma was known as "Morton's fork."

As the old aristocracy declined in numbers and power Henry VII
turned for support and assistance to the solid and more easily controlled middle classes. Many men of the "new nobility," destined to be
outstanding statesmen of the Tudor era, were drawn from the ranks of
the country gentry or the city men of business. The Tudors wished to
see few powerful nobles. When a peerage died out there was no haste
to create a new one. Dukedoms were not easily obtained; the usual
reward of merit was a knighthood. From the middle classes Henry VII
showed his skill in selecting competent advisers and servants; into the
royal council came many an able middle class man whose loyalty to
the crown was increased by the fact that he held his position solely by
the royal will, and not by any blood title; and from the middle classes
were recruited the famous Yeomen of the Guard, the bodyguard of
the sovereign. At the same time Henry VII began the revival of the
medieval paternalism towards the humble workers, the poor, and
the sick in the state. There were many strong bases to a "popular
despotism."

DOMESTIC PLOTS AND FOREIGN QUARRELS

Despite the marriage of Henry VII and Elizabeth of York there
were several disgruntled Yorkists who plotted and raised rebellions.
Margaret of Burgundy, the sister of Edward IV, was a fierce Juno with
an undying hatred of the house of Lancaster. In a series of pertinacious
intrigues she supported the Yorkist leaders in England in their plans
for rebellion. Lambert Simnel, a handsome youth of low birth, was
persuaded to impersonate the earl of Warwick, son of the Duke of

Clarence and nephew of Edward IV. The real Warwick had earlier disappeared. When Simnel had been trained to act his part he was taken to Ireland, where he obtained strong support. In 1487 he landed in England with several thousand Irishmen and some German mercenaries hired by Margaret of Burgundy. In the resulting battle of Stoke Simnel was captured. Henry VII made him a scullion in the royal kitchen.

A second plot soon grew into action. In 1491 the Yorkists chose an adventurer by the name of Perkin Warbeck to masquerade as Richard, Duke of York, younger son of Edward IV. There had long been rumors that Richard III had not in fact murdered Edward V and his brother Richard in the Tower of London. If Richard still lived he had a stronger claim to the throne than Henry VII, Elizabeth of York, or the earl of Warwick. The Yorkists now asserted that Perkin Warbeck was indeed the long-vanished Richard.

Trained for his role at the court of Margaret of Burgundy, Warbeck expected to obtain considerable support from Charles VIII of France; from Maximilian, Duke of Burgundy; and from James IV of Scotland. But the promised aid was not forthcoming when Warbeck sailed for England in July, 1495, partly because the Italian warfare produced unexpected diplomatic alignments in Europe. Warbeck found the shores of Kent so strongly defended that his ships moved on to Ireland. The Irish were already angered by the passage of Poyning's law (1494) by which all the acts of the Irish Parliament had to be approved in advance by the English privy council. Hence Warbeck was assured of considerable Irish support. In 1496 the turbulent Scots launched an unsuccessful invasion of England. Far to the south the attempted collection of a subsidy in Cornwall started an ugly rebellion. "On a sudden," wrote a contemporary, "the people grew into a great mutiny."

Fortunately for Henry VII the fierce uprising among the miners of Cornwall was largely subdued before Warbeck landed in England. When the impostor did come to Cornwall in 1497 his forces were defeated and he was captured at the battle of Taunton. Warbeck explained that he had been duped by the Yorkists who "against my will made me learn English and taught me what I should do and say." At first Henry VII imprisoned the false Duke of York "so that he saw neither the sun nor moon." In 1498 Warbeck escaped. He was quickly recaptured and executed. At the same time Henry executed the genuine earl of Warwick; the people of England had been unaware that the earl had been Henry's prisoner for several years. Warwick was beheaded for no other reason than that he was the nephew of Edward IV. The fate of Simnel, Warbeck, Warwick, and others showed how unwise it was to question Henry VII's right to the throne.

Step by step, with his usual cold resolution, Henry VII was thus disposing of his enemies and buttressing his authority at home. In external affairs Henry also pursued a steady and consistent policy. He felt that his first task was to obtain the recognition of the Tudor dynasty by foreign powers. It was obvious that this might be accomplished by waging a successful war. To Henry war was not the answer. Foreign conflict was costly; the returns might be poor. Henry, always frugal, tried to keep his expenses as small as possible, for he believed that the king thrived best who had most gold in his purse. There were several ways of raising money. The rich could be fleeced. Parliaments could be asked for grants, but not too frequently. Henry called seven Parliaments in his reign, six of them before 1497; from these assemblies he asked only five grants of direct taxes. It was quite natural that such a king should determine to avoid the risks and costs of war provided that he could obtain what he wanted in some peaceful way.

Henry saw that much might be gained by marrying his son Arthur to a European princess. He found what he wanted in Spain, where the marriage of Ferdinand of Aragon and Isabella of Castile had created a united and powerful nation state. When Henry proposed that Arthur should marry Catherine of Aragon, daughter of Ferdinand and Isabella, the offer of a marriage alliance was accepted by Madrid. At the same time the Spanish sovereigns attached certain conditions to their acceptance of Henry's matrimonial project. Although Ferdinand and Isabella were already engaged in a war with the Moors in southern Spain, they wanted England's aid in an assault upon Charles VIII of France for the purpose of recovering two Spanish provinces seized a few years before by the predatory "spider king," Louis XI. The Spanish rulers therefore insisted that there would be a marriage alliance between Spain and England only if Henry VII would agree to invade France from the north, while Spain made an attack from the south. Henry, fearful lest his matrimonial schemes should collapse, finally agreed to attack Charles VIII of France. In 1489 the Treaty of Medina del Campo formally created an Anglo-Spanish alliance.

About these plans of Spain and England Charles VIII knew nothing. His greedy eyes were turned elsewhere. He soon attempted to conquer the hitherto independent duchy of Brittany. At the same time he supported the Flemings in their rebellion against Maximilian, Duke of Burgundy. It was at this point that Henry VII persuaded the English Parliament to grant him a large sum of money to invade France. Henry declared that he wanted to keep Brittany free, a reasonable objective. He was also making it clear to his subjects that England was not backing down before the ambitious Charles VIII. In striking at France Henry VII was keeping his treaty agreement with Spain. In 1489 England sent troops to the support of Maximilian and the Duchess of Brittany. Englishmen landed in France and laid siege to Boulogne.

The war did not last long. The Duchess of Brittany suddenly made peace with Charles VIII; Maximilian deserted his allies and made an alliance with the Flemings. Spain began secret peace negotiations with France. From this awkward situation the sharp-witted Henry VII escaped with considerable skill. Charles VIII was anxious to hurl his armies into Italy; the crown of Naples glittered and tempted him. If Henry VII would make peace and go home, then Charles could turn against Italy and beat back the Spaniards who were swarming like locusts into the Italian peninsula.

Henry VII, who had never wanted war, consented to be bought off at his own price by his "dearest cousin Charles." In November, 1492, the Treaty of Etaples ended the war between France and England. Henry went home for an immediate payment of about £180,000 and an annual pension of about £12,000. England merchants were to be permitted to trade without hindrance through French ports.

Thus Henry had obtained his marriage alliance with Spain and his son Arthur was betrothed to Catherine of Aragon. The conflict with France had been short and inexpensive. Henry had been well paid to get out of France and the barren war. The Frenchmen and the Spaniards were now preparing to slaughter one another in battles over the petty states of Italy. The French payments and the unspent parliamentary subsidies bulged the close-fisted Henry's purse. His throne was more secure than before. Among the princes of Europe respect for England and her king had risen again.

After long haggling about the dowry, Catherine of Aragon and Arthur were married in 1501. Five months later Arthur died. Henry VII, anxious not to lose the Spanish dowry, proposed that Catherine be betrothed to his second son, Henry. Ferdinand of Aragon and Henry VII were both crafty, cautious, and suspicious individuals, masters of the art of committing themselves to nothing. Their subtle webs of diplomacy were slowly spun again. In 1503 a papal dispensation permitted Prince Henry to marry his brother's widow. Though no man knew it then, an important step had been taken towards the English Reformation. In later years Henry VIII, husband of Catherine of Aragon, was to contend that the papal dispensation was invalid.

There was another important marriage, carefully planned. In 1499 Henry VII negotiated a treaty of peace with Scotland. In 1503 his eldest daughter, Margaret, was married to the Scottish king, James IV. One hundred years later the direct descendant of that marriage was James VI of Scotland. He became James I of England when the death of Elizabeth, the last Tudor, brought the house of Stuart to the English throne.

FINANCE AND COMMERCE

The victories of Henry VII were victories of peace. Henry was a successful king partly because he was a shrewd businessman. Francis Bacon said that Henry "could not endure to see trade sick." The germ of much of England's later development lay in that fact. Throughout his reign the first Tudor worked to advance the interests of the wealthy and influential middle class merchants and businessmen. Through them, above all, Henry sought the welfare of England and the Tudors. His aims of peace, security, and the prosperity of commerce and trade commended themselves to the middle class. What his biographer Bacon called "the considerations of plenty and the considerations of power" were always important to Henry VII. He wanted Englishmen to have a flourishing trade abroad, a greater share in the commerce of Europe. He wanted to restrict alien competition in England's domestic markets. He was also anxious to see his subjects contented with profitable employment. Henry VII knew that idle hands and brains often caused mischief in a state. "Idleness," said a contemporary, "is the cause and root of all evil, the parent of poverty and crime."

From the late fourteenth century English foreign trade in certain commodities had steadily risen in value and volume. About 1500 England was exporting sixteen times the amount of wool she had shipped abroad a hundred years before. Many merchants built their own ships and adventured all over the known world to market their goods and buy foreign commodities to sell in England. Plagued by pirates, harried by the ruthless jungle practices of business competitors, shot at by England's foes, kept out of many foreign markets by protective controls imposed by native merchants, these English traders needed the active intervention and support of the English government.

Why should the foreign Hanseatic League and the Italian city traders have such tight control of so many channels of trade within England itself? Abroad, the monopolies of the Hanseatic and Italian traders checked the English Merchants of the Staple and the newer Merchant Adventurers in many of their attempts to gain new markets. Why should foreign merchants and foreign ships carry English wool over the seas and bring back foreign goods to sell at huge profits for themselves? Could the English government adequately protect and extend the commercial privileges and rights of Englishmen? How could foreign competitors be met and held at bay?

All over Europe business was outgrowing its local character. The formation of new nation-state governments, such as those in France and Spain, made it possible for trade agreements to be negotiated directly between the national authorities. Henry VII struck at the Hanseatic League by making commercial treaties with Denmark and the port of Riga. Under the terms of these agreements English ships entered the stream of Baltic trade. The result was a considerable increase in England's commerce, particularly with Scandinavia and Iceland. Henry VII also made commercial agreements with several Italian states and more English merchant ships sailed into the Mediterranean. Englishmen moved down the Mediterranean coasts and even began to trade with Turkey, Egypt, and all the Levant.

Henry VII also declared that no foreign merchants should have special rights in England unless reciprocal privileges were given to Englishmen in the lands from whence the foreign merchants came. Everywhere the sagacious Henry supported and encouraged the Merchant Adventurers, especially those companies within the organization that were mainly engaged in the wool and cloth trade. Slowly the great monopolies of the Venetians and the Hanseatic League were whittled away and broken. In 1497 Henry made a famous commercial treaty with Flanders called the Intercursus Magnus by which the restrictions on the export of wool were removed and a market "without pass or license" was opened for English cloth. This was followed by the Intercursus Malus of 1506. Similar treaties were arranged with Venice.

During the political broils of the fifteenth century England had passed from being predominantly a producer of wool to being mainly a producer of cloth. The development of a capitalist textile industry, spreading out of Norwich and East Anglia, was easy and rapid. In 1354 about 5,000 pieces of cloth had been exported from England; in 1509 nearly 80,000 pieces were exported; in 1547, over 120,000 pieces. An important and continuous object of English policy was to find and maintain export markets for English cloth. Later in the century Richard Hakluyt wrote with more imagination than knowledge: "Because our chief desire is to find out ample vent of our woolen cloth, the natural commoditie of this our Realme, the fittest place which in all my readings and observations I find for that purpose are the manifold islands of Japan and the regions of Tartars next adjoining."

At last the years of England's exhaustion in foreign and civil wars had come to an end. Steadily her treasure by foreign trade increased. Waste and fraud in the customs collection were greatly reduced. The royal income from customs duties increased from about £32,000 a year in 1485 to about £42,000 in 1509. The king lent money to merchants to enable them to expand their operations. Protected and encouraged by the state, Englishmen prospered and their commercial empire grew.

Henry VII was active elsewhere. He increased the control of the central government over the craft guilds. This step hastened both the decline of the guilds and the further development of the domestic manufacturing system. Secondly, Henry saw that England must be made more independent in her shipping industry. To this end he built many large ships. Henry VII, and Henry VIII after him, laid the basis for a strong development of England's navy and merchant marine. Thirdly, a new Navigation Act of 1485 stated that Bordeaux wines imported into England were to be carried only in English ships manned by English, Welsh, or Irish sailors. Another act forbade foreign vessels in English ports to be loaded until all English ships had taken on their cargoes.

The Navigation Acts also strengthened the economic practice later called the mercantile system. This system aimed at making nation states powerful and self-sufficient through the regulation of trade. According to the mercantile theory, a nation should produce and export as much as possible. At the same time, it should keep its imports down to the lowest level consistent with national welfare. Hence all nations sought a so-called "favorable balance of trade." The difference between the total values of the exports and imports of a nation was paid by foreign countries in gold and silver. In the age of mercantilism the most important economic fact was held to be the accumulation of precious metals resulting from an excess of exports over imports. Money was considered to be the same thing as wealth. Commerce was slowly moving to a national basis. National governments were beginning to control, to regulate, and to encourage the world streams of trade in accordance with what they believed to be their own political and economic self-interest.

Thus the economic power of England increased. The national resources were husbanded. Native industry was fostered and protected. So far as numbers went, Henry VII made his navy the most efficient in the world. The *Regent* and the *Sovereign* were among the most powerful ships afloat. Henry built a great naval dock at Portsmouth. His shipyards constructed fine cargo vessels. "He kept his merchantmen protected and the sea clear of the Flemish and Bretagne corsairs and especially the Scotch, who, being very needy, observe neither peace nor truce."

DAWN OF THE ENGLISH RENAISSANCE

During these years of commercial activity England was swept into the current of the European Renaissance. The first waves of influence had been evident in the reign of Edward IV. After Henry VII brought a new degree of order and peace many of the ideals and practices of the Renaissance in northern and southern Europe moved in full flood across the English Channel.

Continental humanism had a long tradition that stressed training in religion and virtue, in letters and education, and in good works. Throughout the English intellectual revival of the sixteenth century there ran a constant emphasis upon the classical and humanistic ideal of civic responsibility and morality, and upon the importance of training men for the good life and for public service. The men of the Renaissance in Europe or England were not merely neo-pagans or immoral capitalists. In many ways the "typical" Renaissance man had

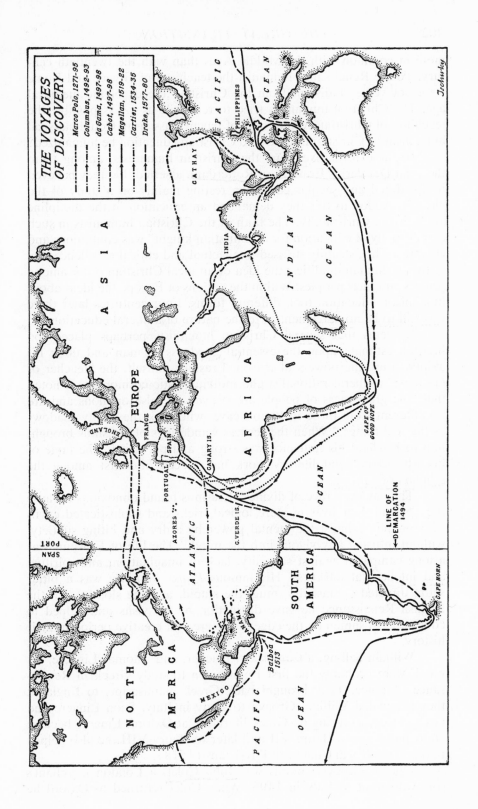

THE VOYAGES
OF DISCOVERY

Marco Polo, 1271-95
Columbus, 1492-93
da Gama, 1497-98
Cabot, 1497-98
Magellan, 1519-22
Cartier, 1534-35
Drake, 1577-80

more in common with the Middle Ages than with the twentieth century. To the Renaissance humanist the teachings of Greece and Rome were not very far distant from the Christian creeds of the medieval age. The Christian humanists tried to reconcile as far as possible the teachings of Christianity and those of pagan classicism. Could classical humanism be Christianized? Could Christian education be humanized?

In these formative years the Christian humanists, among them the great Desiderius Erasmus of Rotterdam, asserted that they believed in a rational and secular education resting mainly on a study of the classics. Added to this they demanded an education in the discipline and spirit of Christianity. The faith of the Christian humanists in such a philosophy of education for a "Christian knight" was continuous and effective. They steadily stressed intellectual and ethical excellence; the virtues of human qualities; the idea of an ideal Christian order among princes and their peoples. Within the nations of Europe the ideas about humanistic education took different forms. Four centuries later there was still to be no agreement as to the nature of a liberal education.

It seems that several Christian humanists perhaps placed too high an estimate upon the essential goodness of man and upon his ability to use the powers of reason. Erasmus himself, the "teacher of teachers," a liberal rationalist and individualistic cosmopolitan, noted that "the great mass of people are swayed by false opinions and are no different from those in Plato's cave, who took the empty shadows as the real things." When the restless wanderings of Erasmus brought him to England his influence was strong and pervasive. The fame of his educational and literary work had placed him first among the scholars of Europe.

The "modern race of divines" Erasmus found obnoxious because they "spend their lives in mere logical tricks and sophisticated cavils . . . for they exhaust the mental power by a dry and biting subtlety, without infusing any vigour into the mind." The life of Erasmus was a long campaign against stupidity, lack of imagination, and spiritual and intellectual darkness. His famous *Praise of Folly* was a bitter satire directed against the smug, the stupid, and the slothful. To the English Renaissance he gave distinction by his visits and helped to educate Englishmen on the edge of the greatest creative period in their history.

William Selling, a Canterbury teacher, and Thomas Linacre, his pupil, were probably the first Englishmen to study Greek in Renaissance Florence. They brought back Greek manuscripts to England; they persuaded William Grocyn to study in Italy. Soon Linacre and Grocyn were lecturing on Greek literature at Oxford. Linacre became court physician to Henry VII and later to Henry VIII; he also helped to found the Royal College of Physicians (1518).

One of Grocyn's pupils was John Colet, a London merchant's son, who went to Italy in 1496. When Colet returned to Oxford he began a course of lectures on St. Paul's Epistle to the Romans in which he discussed the meaning of the original Greek, setting aside the comments of the scholiasts and giving a humanist exposition of St. Paul's life and work. In 1510 he founded St. Paul's School, a free grammar school for boys; the first headmaster was William Lyly, the famed grammarian. In St. Paul's School the classical poets were to be studied in place of the medieval commentators.

Colet

For several years John Colet stood by the side of the mighty Erasmus in denouncing the schoolmen. He demanded a restoration of "that old and true theology which they have obscured by their subtleties"; he explained why the whole Christian church needed to be reformed from within, in the name of religion, morality, and scholarship. Soon he became Dean of St. Paul's and his words echoed over all England from that great cathedral.

Meanwhile Linacre and Grocyn extended their influence steadily. Sir Thomas More, great Catholic humanist and scholar, was a friend of Erasmus and Colet. The first book published in England had been published in 1477 by William Caxton in his Westminster shop. By the end of the century the classics that formed the textbooks of the Renaissance were appearing in large numbers in England. Meanwhile, too, the importation of books from Venice, Paris, and Cologne also increased. Patrons of the "new learning" became more numerous. Richard Foxe, bishop of Winchester and chancellor of Henry VII, founded Corpus Christi College at Oxford for the study of Greek, Latin, and Hebrew. Henry VII's mother, Lady Margaret Beaufort, founded two Cambridge colleges, Christ's and St. John's, and two Lady Margaret Professorships of Divinity, one at Oxford and one at Cambridge. Erasmus himself became Lady Margaret Professor of Divinity at Cambridge in 1511.

Thomas More

Thus the Oxford reformers had prepared the way for a Christian English Renaissance. These years were years of study and education. It was a time of preparation, not of creative achievement. Indeed, there had been little achievement in literature and learning for several decades. Foreign conflicts, domestic wars, the magnetic attractions of worldly gains in business and trade, the suppression of freedom of thought at the universities, had combined to discourage artistic and literary production. In the locust years of the fifteenth century, when Chaucer had readers, but no successors, only Sir Thomas Malory's *Morte d'Arthur* (1470) had stood forth as an admirable example of early English prose. In the dawn of the English Renaissance a new atmosphere was created; there appeared an unwonted interest in education, in literary and artistic activities, in critical scholarship, in religious reform. Several contemporaries have recorded small but significant facts such as the appearance of handbooks of travel talk, autograph albums, and polyglot manuals of all kinds.

In this new climate of opinion it was not surprising that the first literary work of the English reformers was Sir Thomas More's translation of an Italian biography of Pico della Mirandola, the Florentine Platonist (1510). Seven years later More's famous *Utopia* appeared, with consequences to be described later. Erasmus, the Samuel Johnson of his century, wrote of the England he saw on the eve of the golden age of the sixteenth century: "When I listen to my friend Colet it seems to me like listening to Plato himself. In Grocyn who does not admire the wide range of his knowledge? What could be more searching, deep and refined than the judgment of Linacre?"

The revival of interest in classical literature and the rise of humanism formed, of course, only one aspect of the many changes in the transition age of the Renaissance. Of massive significance in later English history were the geographical discoveries and the rise of maritime activity. Portugal and Spain began to open new sea routes and build their empires. Under the influence of their "Prince Henry the Navigator" the adventurers of compact Portugal pushed southwards along the coast of Africa. In 1487 Bartholomew Diaz reached the Indian Ocean, sailing around the southern point of Africa, soon to be called the Cape of Good Hope because it gave good hope of opening trade with the Far East. In 1497 Vasco da Gamma reached India and brought home a spice cargo. Mysterious Asia, the land of silks, pearls, perfumes, and incredible richness, now lay open by a direct sea route to the merchant ships of Europe. "Gold constitutes treasure," wrote Christopher Columbus, "and he who possesses it has all he needs in this world as also the means of rescuing souls from Purgatory and restoring them to the enjoyment of Paradise."

The Venetians and the Genoese had built huge fortunes trading with Asia through the Levant areas at the eastern end of the Mediterranean. Europe had long been weary of paying the high prices demanded by the Italians and other middlemen. Now stout English ships were plying in the eastern Mediterranean, backed by the ubiquitous diplomacy of Henry VII. It was yet to be nearly eighty years before the Plymouth keel of Sir Francis Drake furrowed the Indian Ocean. For a time eastern trade by direct water routes was left to Portugal and Spain.

The way to India by the Cape of Good Hope was long. Could there be a shorter route by the western seas? In 1492 the Genoese Christopher Columbus, backed by Isabella of Spain, sailed with three ships across the Atlantic, seeking eastern lands. The islands he found are still known as the West Indies; the descendants of the original inhabitants are still called Indians. Columbus found no spices. Although he made three more trips to the Caribbean area he discovered no lands like those of wealthy Asia, half a world away.

In 1497 the Venetian John Cabot obtained a charter from England's frugal and cautious Henry VII "for the discovery of new and unknown lands." With his three sons Cabot sailed in the *Matthew* from Bristol. He travelled by a more northerly route than Columbus and probably landed on or near Cape Breton Island. To the northeast, Cabot's "New Found Land" stood, bleak and desolate. "Here the soil is barren and yields little fruit, but it is full of white bears and stagges far greater than ours. The inhabitants of the island use to wear skinnes and have them in estimation as we have our finest garments." There were no spices, no Asiatic princes, no gold or pearls; but there were codfish. Very soon English ships were moving out of the western ports to "adventure" to the great banks off Newfoundland. Henry VII gave £10 to John Cabot, "hym that found the New Isle."

In 1498 John Cabot made a second voyage. This expedition disappeared with all hands. There are still many points of difference among scholars regarding the journeys of John Cabot and his sons across the Atlantic. In any event, the search for the Northwest Passage to the East had begun. "This enterprise would be the most glorious and most important, in all ages to come, of all others to make his name great and his fame immortall, farre more than can be done by all these great troubles and wars which daily are used in Europe among the miserable Christian people."

After John Cabot, great English sea captains of a later day came to search for the passage: Sir Martin Frobisher, John Davis, Sir Humphrey Gilbert, Henry Hudson. The bays and islands of the Canadian Arctic are the only memorials of many brave sailors. "Death was less a risk than a certainty for most of those who sailed." Meanwhile, too, men searched for a northeast passage; the Muscovy Company, formed in 1553, was particularly active. For this company, Richard Chancellor and Hugh Willoughby sailed round the north of Norway. Willoughby perished but Chancellor reached Archangel. He opened the sea road for English trade with Russia.

Englishmen did not lead or persist in the race for discoveries of new dominions beyond the seas. They were busied with the foreign policies of Henry VII and his son; the problems of the Reformation; the quest for trade. Portuguese and Spaniards raced for colonies; in Asia and Latin America their empires grew vast and wealthy. What their sailors discovered and their traders brought home meant much to all Europe. The Atlantic coast replaced the Mediterranean as a center of enterprise. The Mediterranean countries and their trade routes lost their ancient leadership. London and Antwerp were becoming great centers of commerce. Madrid and Lisbon were becoming capitals of empire. In a later day England, lying at the nodule of the shortest Atlantic crossings, France, and Holland commenced to trespass upon the Spanish and Portuguese monopolies. Active Englishmen of a later day studied geography and navigation to a greater degree than ever before. English colonies were first started on the American coastline and then, slowly, over all the world. England had one great advantage over Spain in America: Englishmen could always sell cloth in exchange for raw materials. When the Spaniards had exported their culture, their soldiers, priests, and colonists, they had almost nothing else to send over the Atlantic.

In April, 1509, Henry VII died. During the latter part of his reign he had become increasingly unamiable. He was surrounded by men he could command but could not trust. With advancing years an ungentle character hardened. This was the king who once helped to convert a Lollard at the stake; and left him to be burned in spite of his recantation. The financial methods of Henry's personal government grew more obnoxious. His servant Morton and his son Arthur were both dead. Henry remained a lonely, soured, enigmatic figure. He had amassed a fortune of nearly £2,000,000, a remarkable achievement. His Parliaments were submissive and his nobility subservient. The dangers and terrors of civil war were ended and those who had challenged Henry's right to the throne were all dead. A new period of growth, revolutionary change, adventure, and unified national achievement was at hand.

This calculating king who had never relaxed his labors had brought relative security, peace, and national prosperity. The pomp of Henry VII's funeral and the beauty of the Italian tomb in his chapel in Westminster Abbey betoken the power and majesty to which he had raised the throne. "So that he dwelleth more richly dead, in the monument of his tomb, than he did alive in Richmond or in any of his palaces."

Chapter 12

HENRY VIII: CHURCH AND STATE

THE RENAISSANCE SPIRIT

THE second son of Henry VII and Elizabeth of York was Henry VIII. When he came to the throne in 1509 at the age of eighteen John Skelton, famous poet and once a tutor of the young king, wrote: "The Rose both White and Rede In one Rose now dothe grow." The battles of York and Lancaster were ended forever. Henry VII had established order and security. "England was then called the golden world," wrote George Cavendish in 1557, "such grace and plenty reigned then within this realm." The rising middle class was naturally sympathetic with a monarchy to which they owed so much. Among almost all of his subjects Henry VIII was far more popular than the icy Henry VII had ever been. Throughout his reign the spell of his power was unbroken, the terror of his name unimpaired.

Henry VIII seemed to be a gracious Renaissance prince, generous and friendly, possessed of unusual gifts of personality and brains. He was a magnificent athlete, a musician, a poet, the living example of the Renaissance ideal of the versatile man. To his court came scholars from all over Europe to nourish and spread the spirit of the Renaissance. "The world is waking out of a long, deep sleep," wrote Erasmus. "The old ignorance is still defended with tooth and claw, but we have kings and nobles on our side. . . . Where in school or monastery will you find so many distinguished and accomplished men as at your English court? Shame on us all! The tables of priests and divines run with wine and echo with drunken noise and scurrilous jest, while in princes' halls is heard only grave and modest conversation on points of morals and knowledge."

Throughout the reign of Henry VIII the new views of the European Renaissance, earlier brought to England by such men as Thomas Linacre, William Grocyn, and John Colet, flourished at the royal court, at Oxford and Cambridge, and at several other important spots in England. New ideas about life and its meaning moved, by a kind of osmotic process, from the numerous schools and teachers down through several layers of society. Because they came to believe certain things Englishmen acted in certain ways. In the English Renaissance men of action were more numerous than men of letters until the blaze of the golden age of literature under Elizabeth.

At the same time the spirit of the Renaissance in English scholarship and writing was widely evident. Sir Thomas More's *Utopia* (1517) and his *Dialogue of Heresies* (1528) were criticisms of the social, religious, and political life of his day. More was a reformer in part because he was a Hellenist. "*Utopia* is an attempt to show whence springs the evils of states." Illustrations of the various literary activities inspired by the new learning can easily be multiplied. John Skelton, for example, condemned the new enthusiasm for classical studies as pedantry, even though he was no mean Latinist himself. The work of this versatile poet showed the strong native influence of Chaucer and Lydgate and the medieval makers of ballads. While Skelton was writing about Merry Margaret, Elinor Rumming, and Cardinal Wolsey, several young poets about the court of Henry VIII were following Italian models. These "Courtly Makers," led by the proud and violent Sir Thomas Wyatt and the earl of Surrey, were particularly interested in the Italian sonnet.

The widely ranging interests of writers and scholars in these years are also evident in such works as Sir Thomas Elyot's *Book of the Governor* (1531). Elyot was a public servant concerned about "the education of them that hereafter may be deemed worthy to be governors of the public weal." He thus preceded Roger Ascham as an educational reformer. Like most educational reformers he looked upon the existing system with horror. "Lord God! how many good and clean wits of children be nowadays perished by ignorant schoolmasters!" Elyot also wondered why noblemen in England were "not as excellent in learning as they were in old time among the Romans and Greeks." He concluded that the English nobles' learning had suffered because of their own pride and avarice and the negligence of their parents.

The *Book of the Governor* was thus a textbook in the art of government, similar to many others in the sixteenth century. "All ye readers that desire to have your children to be governors, or in any other authority to the public weal of your country, if ye bring them up and instruct them in such form as in this book is declared, they shall then seem to all men worthy to be in authority, honour and noblesse, and all that is under their governance shall prosper and come to perfection." Sir Thomas Elyot added that he intended not only to write a treatise on government and ethics, but "to augment our English tongue whereby men should . . . express more abundantly the thing that they conceived in their hearts, wherefore language was ordained."

It was against such a background in court and country that Henry VIII passed the years of his reign. He soon added to the popularity so freely given him when he ascended the throne. He pardoned nearly all of those who had been condemned near the end of his father's reign; he wiped out the debts of many who had been unjustly forced to pay money to the crown. He condemned several of his father's hated ministers, including Sir Richard Empson and Edmund Dudley, in trials that were void of justice and full of legality. All these acts strengthened his place in his subjects' hearts.

Then came his marriage to Catherine of Aragon, arranged by his father, Henry VII. The magnificent royal displays and celebrations provided bread and circuses for a delighted people. The treasure painfully accumulated by Henry VII melted away; but his son was popular and his throne secure. Sixteenth century Englishmen loved pageantry and splendor. When Henry VIII and Francis I of France met in 1520 on the famous Field of the Cloth of Gold near Calais a contemporary wrote of the pomp and circumstance: "Nor is it supposed that in our time a similar display was ever witnessed, or that the like will be seen for many a day to come." Henry's daughter Elizabeth shrewdly recognized that "in pompous ceremonies a secret of government doth much consist."

The personal element in monarchy was still very strong. It was true that feudal political arrangements were ceasing. Nevertheless, ideas lagged behind practice, and political sentiment remained largely feudal in the sixteenth century. The practice of government had not ceased to be personal and Henry VIII kept it so. For example, under Henry the royal council and the principal ministers could go for days without the touch of the king's hand; but that was only because Henry VIII permitted it. "His car of state might be allowed to run of its own momentum because he knew that its controls would instantly respond to the slightest inclination of the royal person."

Every minister drew his power from one source: the king's favor. Church and state, metropolis and province, politics and economics, all the varied workings of national life were watched over by the royal council; and behind the council stood the colossus of the king. "We will that none of our servants shall belong to any other person but to us," said Henry VIII.

EXTERNAL AFFAIRS

During the reign of Henry VII England began to recover from the effects of long and giddy years of foreign and domestic quarrels. When Henry VIII, ambitious and young, succeeded his canny father a new era of restless diplomacy began. England was not yet a first class power; but her status had risen so that European princes, most of them hoary and skilled intriguers, competed for her support.

In 1494 the lusty nation states of France and Spain had pounced upon the weak and divided peninsula of Italy. The result was a scramble for power. After he had twice outwitted France, Ferdinand VII of Spain finally filched control of Naples. France, for her part, seized and clung to Genoa and Milan.

In 1508 Pope Julius II, Louis XII of France, Maximilan, the Hapsburg Holy Roman Emperor, and Ferdinand VII of Spain united in the League of Cambrai to attack and dismember wealthy Venice. The Venetians found themselves almost friendless; their own unscrupulous policy through the years had left bitter memories in southern Europe. At that hour, of course, the discovery of America and new routes to the East had already sowed the seeds of the decline of Venetian commercial supremacy. When Venice was defeated by the League of Cambrai several concessions were wrung from her. After this victory the Italians decided to drive the French away from the Venetian banquet table. Pope Julius II thereupon allied himself with Venice in a Holy League against France. Ferdinand VII of Spain agreed to join the alliance. So did the Holy Roman Emperor Maximilian. At this point they asked Henry VIII to come in with them.

Henry was eager to shine in European affairs. England's hostility to France and her intellectual and commercial sympathy with Venice were alike natural and traditional. The military glory of Edward III and Henry V had been won in France, and Henry VIII felt that he, too, might burnish his sword in battle there. Hence he joined the Holy League. By doing so he pleased his queen, Catherine of Aragon, his father-in-law, Ferdinand VII, and Pope Julius II. The inexperienced Henry did not know that Ferdinand, Maximilan, and Pope Julius II, cunning and perfidious veterans of diplomacy, planned to use him as a catspaw. If they could bring Englishmen to bear the brunt of the battles in France it would not be difficult to drive the French out of Spanish Navarre and Italy.

In 1512 Ferdinand induced Henry to send an English army to southern France where it acted as a buffer and screen for the Spanish operations in Navarre. Discipline was relaxed among the restless English soldiers as the months passed and no enemy appeared. There was mutiny. The inactive forces came home without the king's permission. England's military reputation was tarnished. Henry's pride was hurt and his anger roused.

The Holy League had by now forced the French out of Italy and Navarre and had no further need of English arms. Nevertheless, Henry himself led an army into northeastern France in 1513. In August and September he captured two cities and won the Battle of the Spurs. England's military prestige rose again. Meanwhile, Henry's allies had deserted him and made peace with France. Henry could not continue to wage war alone. In 1514 it was agreed that Louis XII of France, then fifty-two years of age, would marry Henry VIII's sister Mary, aged seventeen. Louis promised to pay Henry an annual pension and Henry was to keep the town of Tournai as security for payment. Henry thus escaped neatly from the situation into which the chess players of Europe had maneuvered him.

Meanwhile the costly war with France had brought the Scots down upon England. Such Scottish invasions were traditional; this one would probably have occurred even if Scotland's James IV had not been under the influence of Louis XII of France. The Scots came along the east coast, crossed the Tweed, and were heavily defeated at the bloody battle of Flodden Field in September, 1513. "At Flodden hills," wrote John Skelton, "our bows and bills slew all the flower of their honour." James IV was killed.

In these years one man became outstanding as the most brilliant minister of the king. He was Thomas Wolsey, born in the middle class, educated at Oxford, and formerly a chaplain of Henry VII. Early in Henry VIII's reign Wolsey showed superb skill in planning the details of English military campaigns and in keeping army supplies moving forward. He was also largely responsible for the success of the peace negotiations with France in 1514. By 1515 Wolsey was archbishop of York and lord chancellor of England. He was shortly to be a cardinal and a papal legate. "I esteem him above my dearest friends," remarked Henry VIII, "and I can do nothing of importance without him."

Wolsey worked hard. Although the king spent much time in sport, dancing, and music Wolsey soon learned that Henry carefully kept himself informed of what was going on. Henry "would be obeyed, whoever spoke to the contrary." Wolsey's influence grew steadily. His self-confidence kept pace with his elevation. His arrogance and his unshared power made him widely unpopular and pointed for poets and prophets the moral of his fall. He was "the proudest prelate who ever breathed." He was "greedy of glory and covetous of praise." Many nobles felt that Wolsey was robbing them of titles and powers that were more properly theirs. The ill-concealed malice and envy of such men could be fatal if Wolsey ever fell from the favor of his king; and Wolsey knew it. As the years passed the lord chancellor also found that his master received the credit for popular policies. Wolsey was blamed for the unpopular ones. The poisoned arrows of men of ill-will flew against Wolsey, not against Henry VIII.

It was in the tortuous world of external affairs that Wolsey's chief work lay. For years he labored indefatigably to check the French and Spanish gambits. In 1515 Louis XII died and his young widow Mary was then secretly married to the Duke of Suffolk; Lady Jane Grey was to be a grandchild of that marriage. The new king of France was the twenty-one year old Francis I, of the house of Valois. In that year the Venetian ambassador recorded that Henry VIII queried him about the height and strength of Francis and then continued: "I am aware that his father, King Louis, was a bad man, though my brother-in-law. I know not what Francis may be. He is, however, a Frenchman, and so I cannot say how far you can trust him." Soon Henry VIII and Francis I came to "hate each other very cordially," especially after Francis threw Henry in a wrestling match in 1520 at the famous meeting in the Field of the Cloth of Gold.

These events occurred at a time of considerable public feeling against foreigners, especially Frenchmen, in England. "The multitude of strangers was so great about London," wrote Edward Hall, "that the poor English artificers could scarce get any living. And most of all, the strangers were so proud that they disdained, mocked, and oppressed the Englishmen." In 1517 there were ugly anti-foreign riots in London.

Francis I at once set about to buttress the weakened prestige of France. His armies surged into Italy and seized Milan again. Meanwhile, in 1516, Charles of Hapsburg succeeded Ferdinand VII as king of Spain. Charles was also Duke of Burgundy, with a long family tradition of hostility to France. Nevertheless, Charles made peace with Paris in order to improve his own position in Spain; but it was a fitful and feverish peace. The Hapsburg Charles V was as ambitious as the Valois Francis I. In 1519 Charles also inherited the broad lands of the Hapsburgs on the death of his grandfather Maximilan; soon he was elected as Holy Roman Emperor. Faced by such an increase in the power of Charles V, France prepared for war. In 1521 there began an armed Hapsburg-Valois conflict.

Before the outbreak of war both Charles V and Francis I had vied for the support of Henry VIII. In 1519 Charles visited England; then Henry visited Francis; later he was the guest of Charles in Flanders. After hostilities began in 1521 Henry VIII despatched an envoy to the Hapsburg court. Charles V proceeded to send ambassadors to request an English loan to aid him in the war. Henry was jealous of Francis I, resentful at French plotting in Scotland and rumors that some Englishmen in Europe had suffered at the hands of the French. The representatives of Charles V were received graciously. "The king sent for these ambassadors, and kept them to dine with him privately in his chamber with the Queen, a very unusual proceeding." Later there was a tournament in the lists near Hampton Court. "The king tilted eight times with the great Duke of Suffolk. After tiring one horse, the king would mount another." Wolsey soon travelled to Paris, ostensibly to mediate between France and Spain. He actually negotiated an offensive alliance with Charles V.

"The aim of the king of England is incomprehensible," wrote Pope Clement VII. "He may, perhaps, wish to revenge himself for the slights he has received from the king of France. He may want to win back a part of France for England." In fact, Henry VIII wanted the glory that might result from foreign conquest; he was also anxious to see his rival, Francis I, humbled. Wolsey, for his part, hoped that he might be able to advance himself further. His restless wishes towered to new heights. He wanted to be Pope. In this chapter of their diplomacy neither Henry VIII nor Wolsey acted upon the principle of the balance of power so important in centuries of English foreign policy. Instead of supporting the declining strength of France they added to the might of Charles V. They failed to recognize the fact that if Spain became too strong the security of all other European states, including England, would be threatened.

Two English expeditions to France failed to accomplish much. At home there was bitter and widespread opposition to the war. This hostility made it difficult to finance English military operations. Objections to Wolsey's demands for money became frequent and strong. A forced loan was raised in 1522. The next year Parliament was summoned and Wolsey asked for a large subsidy. The commons yielded only after long debate and then spread the subsidy payments over four years. Wolsey was angered at the publicity given to the proceedings of Parliament "for that nothing was so soon done or spoken therein but that it was immediately blown abroad in every ale house." At the same time both Henry VIII and his lord chancellor saw that the people were in no mood to support a costly conflict. After 1523 England played only a token part in the war.

Two years later Charles V won an overwhelming victory over the French at the battle of Pavia. Because England had not contributed much to the victory over France, Charles refused to divide the spoils. Francis I was his prisoner; the French army was shattered; Italy lay at the feet of the conqueror. By their spirited and mistaken foreign policy Henry VIII and Wolsey had helped to upset the European balance of power. The value of England's alliance had been reduced to a cipher. Charles V was master of Europe. The Hapsburg supremacy, so dangerous to England, had begun.

In 1526 England made peace with impotent France. Meanwhile Charles V turned against Italy. His armies ravaged the countryside and sacked the city of Rome. "Babylon the great has fallen, and become the habitation of devils, and the hold of every foul spirit." Faced by the Hapsburg march of victory, England now turned to make an offensive alliance with France against Charles.

The war had been at once ineffective and costly. In 1525 Wolsey tried to obtain an "amicable grant" which was in reality a forced loan. The royal council demanded that "the sixth part of every man's substance should without delay be paid, in money or in plate." The result was resistance. A rebellion broke out in Suffolk. It was impossible to collect the assessment. "All people cursed the Cardinal and his coadherents as subversors of the laws and liberties of England." In vain the government lobbied, cajoled, and compromised. On Wolsey, who was frequently accused of sending large sums of English money to Rome, fell the odium of the whole policy. Henry VIII himself withdrew the demand. "I will no more of this trouble," he wrote. "Let letters be sent to all shires that this matter no more be spoken of; I will pardon all them that have denied the demand, openly or secretly." Henry saw that he could not obtain the financial support of his subjects without which he could not go to war against Charles V.

Despite the importance of this rebuff to the royal policy, Henry VIII still remained in an excellent position to control capital. That fact was always a source of Tudor strength. In these early capitalist days many nobles owed the king money. He was usually able to borrow, provided that the sums were not too large. There were also being evolved several new devices for supplementing gold and silver with paper instruments. Above all, the creation of money was the king's monopoly. In 1526 the government suddenly began to overhaul the coinage, partly to equate the English metal values with those of foreign countries and partly to obtain a profit for the king. In later years, when Henry VIII found it no longer possible to grasp at easy revenue, he began a steady debasement of the gold and silver coins, with serious economic results.

THE MARRIAGE DILEMMA

Meanwhile other important problems had arisen. As early as September, 1514, it had been rumored in Rome that Henry VIII wished to have his marriage with Catherine of Aragon dissolved. As the church never granted divorces Henry could only obtain a dissolution of the marriage if the Pope agreed to recognize the union as originally invalid. Most historians avoid tedious circumlocutions by using the word "divorce" to describe the case of Henry VIII and Catherine of Aragon. The term, thus applied, is technically inaccurate; but it is brief and convenient.

Between 1509 and 1515 Catherine had borne Henry four sons and one daughter; all had died almost at birth. A daughter named Mary, born in 1516, survived. There followed successive miscarriages and a stillborn child. To secure the succession Henry felt that a son was vitally necessary. There was no precedent for a ruling queen. Matilda had never been crowned. If the strong Henry left only a daughter to succeed him, the result might be the end of the Tudor dynasty, a civil war like that of the fifteenth century, a national weakness tempting foreign foes.

Henry's affection for Catherine had declined for other reasons. For example, the queen was passionately attached to her native Spain and was indiscreet and unintelligent enough to reveal her feelings at the wrong moments. Nevertheless, Catherine was a kindly, religious, and courageous woman. Despite her birth and religion she was widely liked by Englishmen. "If not handsome, she is not ugly; she is somewhat short, and has always a smile on her countenance." It is arguable that Henry VIII might have taken no steps to obtain a divorce if the attraction of Anne Boleyn, one of the queen's attendants, had been less strong. On occasion Henry VIII fell short of the Renaissance ideal of the self-sufficient prince. "The gospel light first shone in Boleyn's eyes."

About the importance of another problem no historian can comment with certainty. Did Henry VIII have honest doubts about the validity of his marriage? In November, 1501, his elder brother Arthur had married Catherine; five months later Arthur died. In June, 1503, Catherine was betrothed to Henry, who was then twelve years old. The canon law said that a man might not marry his deceased brother's wife. True, Pope Julius II had issued a dispensation to permit the marriage of Henry and Catherine. Was the dispensation valid? Henry later contended it was not. Did the "curse of Leviticus" (XX.21) raise doubts in Henry's mind? In the book of Leviticus it was written that if a man marries his brother's widow "they shall be childless." In any event, scruples of conscience may have been a terrible reality to Henry VIII; and they may not.

In 1526 Henry was clearly nervous about the succession. His illegitimate son by Elizabeth Blunt was made Duke of Richmond and Lord High Admiral with precedence over all the nobility and even the Princess Mary. By 1527 Henry resolved to seek a divorce from Catherine. A contemporary records that "the king is studying the matter so diligently that I believe he knows more in this case than a great theologian and jurist." The papal legate Campeggio wrote that "an angel would not be able to persuade him otherwise." Embassy after embassy was sent to Pope Clement VII.

One massive obstacle stood in Henry's way. In 1527 the Emperor Charles V was in Rome. The Pope, an ally of Francis I, was the prisoner of Charles. Because Charles was the nephew of Catherine of Aragon it was not reasonable to expect that Henry would obtain a favorable hearing at the papal court. Henry's brother-in-law Suffolk and his sister Margaret of Scotland had been able to break their marriages. Henry's request was not unusual. However, it was difficult for Pope Clement VII to say that an emperor's aunt had been living in sin for eighteen years, especially when the emperor's soldiers streamed about the streets of Rome. Henry could not be accommodated.

Clement VII ordered the English Cardinal Wolsey and the Italian Cardinal Campeggio to try the case in England. At the same time he secretly instructed Campeggio to see that a decision was delayed. The court established by the two cardinals met at Blackfriars where Catherine made a piteous appeal. "If there can be any offense which can be alleged against me, I consent to depart with infamy; if not, then I pray you to do me justice." But Catherine could really expect no justice in England. Before a decision was reached, the case was called back to Rome; and Henry could expect no justice there.

Wolsey tried desperately to persuade Clement VII to find in Henry's favor. To the English envoys in Rome he declared: "A citation of the king to Rome, on threat of excommunication, is no more tolerable than the whole loss of the king's dignity. You must urge Clement therefore, to study how he can oblige the king, who is fully persuaded that his marriage is not good, and you shall urge that his desire to please the Emperor at all hazards will alienate this realm from the Holy See." A stream of such pleas and arguments failed to move Clement VII. The pressure of Charles V upon the papacy was sharp and heavy; the pressure of Henry VIII was mounting. Clement sent Campeggio to London to do his utmost "to restore mutual affection between the king and queen." Campeggio did his best. He tried without success to persuade Catherine to enter a nunnery. "If Henry's wishes are granted," wrote Clement VII to Campeggio, "and so great an injury done to the Emperor Charles the church cannot escape utter ruin."

In such a dilemma the Pope did not grant an annulment of the marriage. Could Henry VIII force Clement VII to yield, despite the baleful influence of Charles V? The attraction of Anne Boleyn joined with the demands of conscience and imperious egotism to spur Henry onwards. Anne Boleyn was not reluctant to accept the royal affection. She was the young daughter of a merchant, lady-in-waiting to Queen Catherine. The Venetian ambassador, who saw and wrote so much in these years, noted that "Madame Anne is not one of the handsomest women in the world; she is of middling stature, swarthy complexion, long neck, wide mouth. But her eyes are black and beautiful." To rid himself of Catherine, and to marry Anne Boleyn, Henry was prepared to go much further in his struggle with the papacy than an exchange of envoys and a formal suit to Rome.

EVE OF THE REFORMATION

The papal court had failed to meet Henry's wishes and the first to suffer was his servant Wolsey. Through the years Wolsey's arrogant accumulation of power had won him many enemies. William Roy's *Rede me and be not wrothe* is an excellent example of the outburst of destructive satirical literature against Wolsey and the Catholic church. "First as I said, there is a Cardinal, Which is the ruler principal, Through the realm in every part." John Skelton also attacked the clergy and the cardinal in his famous *Why come ye not to court?, The world nowadays,* and *Colin Clout.* When Wolsey ordered the burning of William Tyndale's translation of the Bible, Skelton called him a "miserable monster most malicious." Some men also felt that Wolsey had been too zealous for the preservation of the authority of the See Apostolic "because all his grandeur is connected with it."

About Wolsey his enemies gathered in the manner later described so finely in Dr. Samuel Johnson's *The Vanity of Human Wishes*. Denounced as the "patriarch of all wickedness," he was arrested in November, 1529, on a charge of high treason. It was alleged that he had traitorously corresponded with France and Rome and had violated the statute of praemunire. "It was never merry in England while we had cardinals among us," said one of his archenemies. Anne Boleyn, the Duke of Suffolk, and the Duke of Norfolk led the attacks upon him.

In December Parliament presented forty-four accusations against Wolsey under the signature of seventeen lords and councillors. No man then could see the tragic irony in the first signature, which was that of Sir Thomas More, who was soon to lose his life at the hands of Henry VIII. Nothing came of these proceedings in Parliament. In February, 1530, Wolsey resigned the bishopric of Winchester and the abbey of St. Albans and received £6,000, a royal pardon, and restoration to the archbishopric of York. In March he was ordered north; but even then he received "comfortable words" from the king. "Tell him that he shall not lack and bid him be of good cheer."

But Wolsey and his foes knew that his doom was sealed. "His face is dwindled to half its natural size," wrote the French ambassador. "In truth his misery is such that his enemies, Englishmen as they are, cannot help pitying him." In a year he was summoned back to London. Broken by his enormous labors, by grief, and by disease, he died on the journey southwards, reproaching the wrathful king who had given him over to his enemies.

The consequences that flowed from Wolsey's fall are worthy of several monographs in themselves. For example, the jurisdiction in equity, which had been so largely concentrated in chancery in Wolsey's day, now flowed back into the royal council. From thence it streamed into the common law courts. More obvious was the fact that Henry VIII now became the leader of those who insisted that the papal jurisdiction be limited or abolished and that the *regnum* must be maintained against the *sacerdotium*.

In books written about the events of the English Reformation the marriage problem has often assumed a place of improper importance, partly because of its clearly dramatic qualities. A reasonably adequate consideration of what happened in Henry's reign of consequence to the destinies of England must also stress the revival of the ancient question of royal and papal jurisdiction. In Tudor England political writers preached, with increasing frequency, the idea that absolute non-resistance to the king was essential for the security of the state. The authority claimed for the king was usually stated in rather vague terms; it was the later curse of the Stuarts that they tried to force the essence of king-worship into precise analyses and a fixed formula. The extreme form of the Tudor cult of authority perhaps appears in William Tyndale's *Obedience of a Christian Man*. The Protestant Tyndale asserted that "the king is, in this world, without law, and may at his lust do right or wrong, and shall give account to God only."

At the same time the growing English nationalism was coming to be more sharply personified by the king, particularly when opposed to the internationalism of the Catholic Church and the papacy. "I content myself with my own," said Henry VIII. "I only wish to command my own subjects; but, on the other hand, I do not choose anyone to have it in his power to command me, nor will I ever suffer it." When Henry declared that "England is an Empire" he was speaking the language of a defender of the sovereignty of a modern nation state.

Pressures of political nationalism cannot be separated from the religious aspects of the Reformation in Europe and England. Leaders of the European Reformation were mainly concerned with a revision of dogmas and the practices associated with them; but there were important political and economic consequences. On the other hand, the leaders of the early English Reformation were particularly occupied with the revisions of the relations between church and state. What should be the position of a clerical organization as part of a body politic? The English Reformation was thus at first primarily a political reconstruction; the reformed religion came later. Englishmen, in this age of rising nation states, were increasingly aware of their separateness from other nations. Their emotions were becoming more and more attached to the king and to England. Thus they turned less and less to Rome. The emotions that linked them to Rome or to the Christendom of the Holy Roman Empire had never been national ones, and the fires of nationalism were now burning brightly.

The medieval ideas of unity, order, hierarchy, and religion had earlier prevailed in the oneness of all Christian Europe. In the sixteenth century many of these ideas were lifted out of Europe and carried over to the small nation state of England. Later in the Tudor age the middle course of the Elizabethan religious compromise helped England to escape the bloody and retarding wars of religion that drained the energies of her European rivals. That compromise was partly the result of the English naturalization of medieval European ideas about unity, harmony, and order. The Anglican church devotion and sentiments were attached to England and to the crown, not to Rome or the Holy Roman Empire. At the same time the old local loyalties of men to their own towns, their guilds, and their landlords were becoming subordinate to loyalty to the king and the St. George of all England.

Henry VIII was theologically orthodox. In 1521 he had written a book about theology with the assistance of Sir Thomas More. This work defended the seven sacraments and attempted to refute Martin Luther's book about the Babylonian Captivity. Henry sent a copy to Pope Leo X and was rewarded with the title "Defender of the Faith." Despite the widespread opposition to heresy, of which Henry VIII's book is an illustration, there had long been waves of anti-clericalism in England. With the coming of the critical spirit of the Renaissance both scepticism and anti-papal feeling increased. Disputes multiplied about the corruption of the spiritual body of the church, the increase and degradation of relics, the decline of the practice of Christian virtues. John Colet preached fiery sermons of unusual boldness in which he demanded reform. "Pardon a man speaking out of zeal, a man sorrowing for the ruin of the church." As described earlier in this chapter, Sir Thomas More published his *Dialogue of Heresies* in 1528 in which he set forth and condemned a number of corruptions and muddles. He wanted reform from within.

Few of these reformers were schismatics; they were really scholars who opposed the evils in a church headed by such free living, warlike, and pagan Popes as the Borgia Alexander VI, Julius II, and Leo X. They wanted to end the degeneration of the monasteries, the profligacy of the higher churchmen, the decline of the mendicant orders, the abuses of benefit of clergy, the corruption of ecclesiastical courts. Hugh Latimer preached a famous "sermon on the plough" at St. Paul's in 1548. His words about prelates and priests left no doubt as to his opinion. "And how few of them there be throughout this realm that give meat to their flocks as they should do . . . too few, too few. The more is the pity, and never so few as now. . . . Cursed be he that doth the work of God negligently or guilefully. A sore word for them that are negligent in discharging their office, or have done it fraudulently; for that is the thing that maketh the people ill."

About the question of the church a large body of pamphlet literature arose. For example, London was flooded with copies of Simon Fish's *Supplication for Beggars* (1527). Fish had earlier been compelled to flee to Holland after he had ridiculed Wolsey. He died of the plague in 1531. In the *Supplication* Fish described the churchmen as an "idle, ravenous sort" who, like wolves, were devouring the flock. "Tie these holy thieves to the carts to be whipped naked about every market town till they will fall to labour." Sir Thomas More, who did not share the ideas of reform and overthrow proposed by Simon Fish, answered Fish in the *Supplication of Souls* (1529). Such pamphlets and antagonisms heightened the demands for reform. In the wake of Erasmus, More, and Colet came a flood of new men, some of them preaching the Protestant doctrines of Martin Luther.

In such a time of ferment it was natural that there would be popular objection to the endowed wealth of the church and the burden of church taxation. Many complained that the large sums of annates and Peter's pence collected from the people were shipped directly to the foreign city of Rome. Why should these funds be sent abroad? Why should they not remain in England? Everywhere the churchmen were gathering money. "The parson sheareth, the parish priest polleth, the friar scrapeth, and the pardoner pareth; we lack but a butcher to pull off the skin."

In 1529 the strong-willed Henry VIII called Parliament. He hoped that the state of public opinion would result in a Parliament sufficiently opposed to papal power in England to support the royal demands upon Clement VII. Henry knew how Englishmen resented the authority and exactions of the Pope. He also knew that the majority of those in the propertied classes would not shrink from plundering the churchmen, a wealthy and unpopular minority. So far as Henry VIII was concerned such a procedure would increase his income; it was also to be preferred to the more orthodox methods of direct taxation.

Where it was possible and convenient Henry used the royal influence to gain supporters in the new Parliament. Nevertheless, he did not pack that Parliament or browbeat the members. Almost at once the house of commons "began to commune of their griefs wherewith the spirituality had before time grievously oppressed them." In November, 1529, John Fisher, then bishop of Rochester, declared in the house of lords: "My lords, you see daily what bills come here from the common house and all is to the destruction of the Church; for God's sake see what a realm the kingdom of Bohemia was, and when the Church went down, then fell the glory of the kingdom; now with the commons is nothing but *down* with the Church!"

Would Pope Clement VII be coerced? Henry asserted that he was taking these steps "but only for the discharge of his conscience and the surety of the succession of his realm." There is no doubt that the Parliament of 1529 stood behind Henry VIII. Charges of servility, terror, or packing have frequently been made, and they remain unproved. Early in its sessions Parliament prohibited non-residence of the clergy and certain other obvious abuses. The papal jurisdiction next came under scrutiny. "Though from Christian charity we abhor retaliation yet we are not so preposterously patient to endure injuries with equanimity," declared Henry VIII. Clement VII wrote to Henry, "admonishing him in all benevolence and threatening excommunication."

In 1531 Henry accused the whole clergy of violating the acts of praemunire because they had recognized Wolsey as a papal legate. They voted in convocation to pay a fine of £100,000. They were also forced to acknowledge Henry VIII to be their "especial protector, single and supreme lord, and, as far as the law of Christ allows, even Supreme Head." The spirit of resistance was draining out of the clergy. Had not Henry VIII said that he "would not brook denial"?

Early in 1532 several acts were passed giving the king effective control of the clergy and ecclesiastical law. Among these was the Act in Conditional Restraint of Annates. This law stopped new incumbents of benefices from paying their first year's revenue to the Pope. These payments, called annates, were said to have totalled £2,000,000 in gold between 1485 and 1532. In Parliament their collection was called "a horrible and damnable custom." The restraint was at first declared to be "conditional" because if Clement VII agreed to meet Henry's wishes the payment of annates might be permitted.

Clement VII did not yield. Henry VIII, on the other hand, failed to see that a break with Rome, shattering the universal church, would open the floodgates to the waves of Reformation doctrines that were dashing over Europe. In England the deep and rooted resentment against the church united with the memory of the defeats that the papacy had inflicted upon kings like Henry II and John. Some Englishmen remembered the tradition of Wycliffe and the Lollards. There were also many who adopted and kept warm the Protestant ideas coming into England, mainly through the great eastern seaports. All over Europe the northern nations were revolting against the leadership of the south. The centers of commerce were shifting from the Mediterranean to the Atlantic. The centers of religious faiths were also moving into the north. They found a resting place in Wittenberg, Geneva, Canterbury; there they developed and grew strong in the nation states.

It was also in 1532 that Henry appointed Thomas Cranmer to the vacant archbishopric of Canterbury. Cranmer, earlier a chaplain in the Boleyn household, had long supported the king's desire for a divorce. Henry now had full control of the highest ecclesiastical court in England. At the same time he made it clear that his quarrel with the papacy had not weakened his loyalty to the teachings of the church. When Hugh Latimer was tried by convocation for his unorthodox views the king left no doubt as to his position. "Mr. Latimer, I am sure ye have good learning, and it were a pity but ye should hereafter preach much better than ye have, for you have been forced to recant and to be abjured, and I will not take upon me now to be a suitor to the bishops for you, unless you promise to do penance as ye have deserved, and never to preach any such things again. Ye shall else only get from me a faggot to burn you." Latimer acknowledged that he had "not erred only in discretion, but also in doctrine" and was received into favor again.

In January, 1533, Henry married Anne Boleyn. In February an act of Parliament forbade appeals to Rome. In April Cranmer announced that Henry's marriage to Catherine of Aragon had never been valid. In June Anne Boleyn was declared queen. In September the princess Elizabeth was born. The English ambassador was recalled from Rome. In 1534 Parliament passed an Act for the Submission of the Clergy, an Act Concerning Ecclesiastical Appointments, and an Act Concerning Peter's Pence and Dispensations.

All that had gone before was crowned in 1534 by the Act of

Supremacy, which declared that "the king, our sovereign lord, his heirs, and successors, kings of this realm, shall be taken, accepted, and reputed the only supreme head in earth of the Church of England . . . to the pleasure of Almighty God, the increase of virtue in Christ's religion, and for the conservation of the peace, unity, and tranquillity of this realm." The legal breach with the See Apostolic was complete.

Thus the issues between the rival powers of church and state were at last settled in England. The church was annexed to the state. Henry VIII was head of the state and head of the English national church. Parliament and convocation were now in a similar relationship to the crown. To all the steps taken by Henry VIII the Reformation Parliament gave legislative form and sanction. A national Parliament had placed itself at the side of the nation's king. Through the centuries civic interests had increasingly united more and more of the people for peaceful activities. As the classicism of the Renaissance stirred through Europe the national literatures of the Middle Ages were revived. The shaping ideas of national heroes and saints, of economic nationalism, of intellectual unity, and of national solidarity had been emerging more sharply into the full light of English history. What happened in 1534 was a natural chapter in a long process.

At the same time the first Act of Succession provided that the heirs of Henry VIII and Queen Anne should succeed to the throne. Secondly, the act declared it misprision of treason for a subject to make any oral statement slandering the marriage or the children born of it. Those who went further and by specific "writing, print, deed, or act" slandered the marriage were to be adjudged "high traitors" subject to execution. Thirdly, all subjects were required to take an oath to observe the statute.

A few Catholic consciences refused to take the prescribed oath. John Fisher, bishop of Rochester, and Sir Thomas More were sent to the Tower when they would not accept the Succession Act or acknowledge Henry VIII as supreme head of the church. "They were considering by what arguments," said an enemy, "in furtherance of their seditious purpose, they might, to the common hurt, elude, refute, and disturb the said laws." The real crime of More and Fisher was that they opposed the king's will. "It was a very hard thing," wrote More to his daughter, "to compel me to say, either precisely with it against my conscience to the loss of my soul, or precisely against it to the destruction of my body."

Both More and Fisher were executed in 1535. The prominence of these two men made it clear to all Europe that Henry VIII would tolerate no opposition. A new Act of Treason in 1534 had provided England with a broader definition of that crime. For example, the act provided that any "cankered or traitorous hearts" who called Henry VIII "a heretic, schismatic, tyrant, infidel, or usurper of the crown" were guilty of treason. Spies and informers plied their nefarious trades. Several executions testified to the determination of the king to crush all opposition.

Henry VIII now moved to seize the landed wealth of the church. In this task he was aided by his vicar-general, Thomas Cromwell, vicious, coarse, ruthless, and efficient. Cromwell undertook a visitation of the monasteries. In order to justify a dissolution his agents made exaggerated reports concerning the conditions they found. Many evils certainly existed in the monasteries; there was corruption, lack of discipline, immorality. More important was the fact that the monasteries, so important in the Middle Ages, had outlived their usefulness and their landed possessions were viewed with greedy eyes. The pretext for the dissolution of about 645 religious houses was supplied by Cromwell.

In 1536 the small monasteries, whose clear yearly income was valued at less than £200, were dissolved by an act of Parliament and their property was given to Henry VIII. "And in their time these were given unto the king by the consent of the great and fat abbots in the hope that their monasteries should have continued still; but even at that time one said in the parliament house that these were as thorns, but the great abbots were putrefied old oaks and they must needs follow."

By 1539 nearly all the remaining monasteries had been suppressed. Often the head of a monastic house would be attainted of treason and in consequence his institution would be confiscated. Sometimes the abbots would be frightened into signing a document of surrender to the king. Twenty-eight abbots dropped out of the house of lords in one year. Although it is impossible to identify "monastic lands" it is probable that about one-sixth of all the land in England passed into the king's hands.

Henry VIII gave away or sold the larger part of the monastic lands. Within a few years he had made 1,600 grants of property valued at £800,000. By 1547 Henry had alienated two thirds of the church land and leased the remaining third. The church was indeed the junior partner of the state. The power of the crown was tremendously increased. Henry used the wealth of the church to avoid asking Parliament for taxes; he built a strong fleet; he fortified the coasts; he waged another war with France. The propertied classes who shared in the plunder from the church were now more firmly bound to the house of Tudor and the repudiation of papal supremacy. A great economic revolution was beginning; it was not to end until the outbreak of the Civil War a century later.

The dissolution of the monasteries caused a rebellion in the northern counties called the Pilgrimage of Grace, an event that paralyzed Henry's government for several months. The steady progress of the enclosure movement, and the rapid rise of prices, rents, and fines had already caused discontent in the rural areas. There was bad weather and poor harvests. Added to these things were the tightening up of regulations on cloth manufacture and the suppression of a few local liberties and special jurisdictions, such as those of Durham. As the monasteries were dissolved rumors grew. It was said that "all church plate was to be seized"; that "no poor man could eat goose or capon or white bread"; that there was to be a "tax on every child and every chimney." Of such tales the clerics were often swift and eager carriers.

The chief demands of the pilgrim rebels were that the monasteries should be restored; that England should return to the papal fold; that the realm should be purged of heresy and such men as Cranmer, Latimer, and Cromwell should be dismissed and punished; that all who took part in the insurrection should be pardoned. Most of the rebels were peasants. Singing the sixteen verses of their "Pilgrims' Song," reciting the verse in the nineteenth chapter of Deuteronomy that says "Thou shalt not remove thy neighbour's landmark," they streamed through Lincolnshire, Norfolk, and Yorkshire.

But this movement really had no geographical cohesion; the rebels could not agree about their demands; the monks in the monasteries could not make up their minds to support such a rebellion. Meanwhile Henry VIII waited until he had gathered strength. Then he broke the temporizing Doncaster agreement and cruelly crushed the insurrection. In July, 1537, the leaders were executed. All over England those who were "led and seduced by the devil," whether the noble Lord Thomas Howard or the humble peasants of the north, found that their punishment was almost invariably the headsman's axe or the hangman's noose.

The great Reformation Parliament sat for the last time on July 18, 1536. The Speaker compared Henry VIII to the sun dispelling all noxious vapors and ripening all things good and necessary. Henry refused to accept the compliment and ascribed all the glory to God.

THE LAST YEARS, 1536–1547

In 1537 Henry VIII licensed the publication of an English translation of the Bible by John Rogers. This text was based on the earlier translations of the Protestant William Tyndale and Miles Coverdale. In 1539 Henry ordered a second edition to be printed and used in all the churches. As a result thousands of Englishmen could read the Scriptures and discuss religious problems and doctrines. Nevertheless, Henry VIII had no mind to tolerate Protestant ideas in his realm. Despite the creeping influence of Protestant voices from across the Channel, Henry VIII continued to be rigidly orthodox; the faith of Christendom was to be fully maintained within his kingdom. All doctrines and rituals were to be those of the church before the separation from Rome.

The Six Articles Act of 1539 provided that anyone denying

transubstantiation was to suffer the loss of life and property. The remaining five articles asserted the necessity of private masses, auricular confession, the obligation of vows of chastity, the celibacy of priests, and the doctrine that communion in both kinds was not necessary to salvation. Any individual denying one or more of these five articles was to be punished by the loss of liberty and property; a second denial meant death.

Henry VIII executed both the Roman Catholics who denied the royal supremacy and the heretics who denied the Catholic doctrines of the Six Articles. "It was wonderful to see adherents of the two opposing parties dying at the same time," said a contemporary, "and it gave offence to both." Henry was not lenient where matters of faith were concerned. For example, in 1540 a man was hanged in London for eating meat on Friday. The strong king saw that a national division on religion might bring the persecution and civil war that ravaged so many countries of Europe. "Never prince with more affection and with more charitable dexterity hath and daily doth persecute such ungracious persons as do preach and teach ill-learning." In 1543 the "King's Book" was published, with a royal preface by Henry VIII setting forth the main principles of anti-papal Catholicism "whereby all men may uniformly be led." A recent scholar has remarked that this volume was not only the "King's Book" but "it was also the Parliament's book; and the clergy's book; and the people's book."

Meanwhile Anne Boleyn had drifted to disaster. She had given Henry a daughter, Elizabeth, in 1533; but there was no male child. In January, 1536, Catherine of Aragon died; on the day of Catherine's funeral Anne Boleyn miscarried. With Catherine dead, nothing but Anne stood in the way of Henry's contracting a marriage that would be indisputable; and a third wife might provide a male heir to the throne.

In May, 1536, Anne was convicted of incest and adultery and immediately executed. The marriage of Henry VIII and Anne was declared invalid and both Mary and Elizabeth were now deemed illegitimate. An Act of Succession was passed by Parliament granting Henry the power to designate such persons as he chose to inherit the crown and the throne upon his death. The day after Anne Boleyn's execution Henry VIII was formally betrothed to Jane Seymour.

In 1537 the new queen died in childbirth; her son survived and later became Edward VI. After the death of his third wife Henry remained unwed for two years. Then the dangers of invasion from Catholic Europe seemed so great that Thomas Cromwell hastily negotiated a marriage alliance to join England with the Protestant princes of Germany. In January, 1540, Henry married Anne, the Lutheran sister of the German Duke of Cleves.

Henry VIII soon changed his mind about the German alliance. He did not relish being married to a policy and a woman of Thomas

Cromwell's choosing. Anne of Cleves lacked beauty and Henry could not forgive his minister for maneuvering him into an awkward matrimonial situation. Moreover, Cromwell's foreign diplomatic policy had failed. Erasmus had once remarked that in the days of Cromwell's villainous power men felt "as though a scorpion lay sleeping beneath every stone." Now, in June, 1540, Cromwell was charged with favoring heresy and its teachers; he was taken to the Tower, protesting his utter loyalty: "If it were in my power to make you live forever, God knows I would."

An act of attainder sent the broken minister to his death. Thomas Cranmer alone had the courage to say a word for Cromwell: "For who shall your grace trust hereafter, if you might not trust him?" On July 28, 1540, Thomas Cromwell was executed along with a member of the house of lords who had been convicted of harboring rebels and procuring conjurers who predicted the king's death. After Cromwell, Henry had no grand vizier, no confidant of all policy, no superintendent of all administration. Anne of Cleves was quietly divorced and given a generous alimony settlement.

Henry next married Catherine Howard, niece of the Duke of Norfolk and cousin of Anne Boleyn. Early in 1542 Catherine was justly convicted of adultery and executed. In 1543 Henry took his sixth and last wife, the twice-widowed Catherine Parr. She retained the affection of her royal husband and of his two daughters, Elizabeth and Mary; and Catherine Parr outlived Henry, in itself no mean achievement.

The matrimonial adventures of Henry VIII were accompanied by several significant developments in domestic and foreign affairs. In the first place, Henry crushed rebellion in Ireland; but more was needed than the conquest of rebels to make the English Reformation prevail across the Irish Sea. Secondly, Henry incorporated Wales into England; but more was needed than royal commands and acts of Parliament to destroy the Welsh language and culture. Men of Wales have always remained sharply aware of their national heritage from the days when history merged into the shaping magic of whispering Celtic legend. Thirdly, Henry maintained his alliance with France until 1536, despite the attempts of the papacy to unite Charles V and Francis I in a holy crusade against an England that had left the Roman Catholic church.

When Catherine of Aragon died Henry VIII and Charles V were reconciled. A threatened renewal of Hapsburg-Valois hostilities persuaded both Charles V and Francis I to seek Henry's support. In 1542 Henry, fearful of French plots in Edinburgh, attacked his nephew, James V of Scotland. The English defeated the Scots at Solway Moss (1542) and burned Edinburgh (1544). Henry VIII planned to marry his infant son Edward to the baby princess Mary, heiress to the

Scottish throne, thus uniting the crowns of England and Scotland; but the Scots would have none of it, and turned instead to the ancient alliance with France.

Meanwhile England joined Charles V to declare war upon Henry's rival, Francis I. In 1543 Henry invaded northeastern France and captured Boulogne. In 1544 Charles V made peace with Francis I and in 1546 Henry, too, signed a peace treaty under which France agreed to pay an indemnity to England.

This last war cost Henry over £2,000,000. From 1542 to 1547 the coinage was steadily debased. At the end of Henry's reign a silver coin contained roughly one part silver to two parts alloy. This myopic policy hastened a dangerous price rise. The king obtained a profit of about £900,000 from tinkering with his coinage.

In the last five years of Henry's reign the royal income from direct taxation was over £650,000. The total revenue from direct taxation during the twenty-four years of Henry VII's reign had totalled only £280,000. Henry had other ways of maintaining the gold level in his treasury. For instance, the ancient practice of "benevolences" was continued. An English knight, because he "would not agree to pay as they set him, was commanded on pain of death to make him ready to serve the king in his wars in Scotland." This knight did serve until he was taken prisoner; then he had to ransom himself. Such heavy financial demands combined with coinage debasement to contribute to the severe economic dislocation of the middle of the sixteenth century.

Men still debate about Henry VIII's political genius and monstrous iniquity. For good or ill, the actions of the second Tudor were always on a grand scale. Whatever may be said about his morals and his sins, the fact remains that Henry VIII had consolidated the Tudor power and strengthened England as a nation state. His safe and prudential Reformation had made the English church a national church in name and in fact. The strength of English arms was respected abroad. There were no challenges to the throne at home. Fifty-six years old, irascible, ill, corpulent, and suspicious, the king still at the end commanded the loyalty of his nation and his ministers of state.

The interests of the crown had become more closely identified with those of Englishmen. Henry kept a high degree of peace and prosperity at home. It was true that his acts were often arbitrary, cruel, unjust, and selfish; yet they touched but few men, and those that the king harmed were often not widely loved in England. With steady energy Henry VIII tried to make his subjects devoted to him. He created and courted public opinion and brought almost every major question to the floor of Parliament. He magnified Parliament for his own ends. Its competence and self-consciousness increased, even though Henry would have been startled at any proposal to encourage an approach to parliamentary independence. In all the great affairs of his reign Henry VIII tried to see to it that the Englishmen who sat in Parliament said the same thing as their king.

In January, 1547, Henry VIII died. His heir was a little boy, and two girls after him. The shocks and upheavals that followed the death of Henry are themselves evidence of his force and his power. He could ride the whirlwind; those who followed him could not.

Chapter 13

ROADS TO SALVATION
THE HEIRS OF HENRY VIII

THE will of Henry VIII had left the throne to his only son, Edward. If Edward had no heirs the crown was to go first to Henry's daughter Mary, then to his daughter Elizabeth. In 1547 Edward was only nine years of age, a sickly and precocious child. His father's strong hand had held many forces in iron control. Now men felt the grip of that hand no more. As in the days of the minority of Henry VI, Englishmen soon saw the flames of rebellion licking at the foundations of the state; through court and castle spread the slow poison of intrigue.

Henry VIII had named a regency council of sixteen individuals to govern England. He had chosen the council members with a view to creating a neat balance between those he called the "dull," or conservative, men and those who were "rash," or liberal. If neither group became too strong the government could be kept in a state of delicate equilibrium. It was perhaps too much to hope that the proposed arrangement would prove successful; and it was soon upset.

Leader of the council was the earl of Hertford, the brother of Jane Seymour and the uncle of Edward VI; he was strongly inclined towards the new Protestant doctrines in religion. After the council had appointed him lord protector he persuaded Edward VI to create him Duke of Somerset. Soon the young king also agreed to ignore his father's will and granted full power to Somerset and a council of twenty-six. The individuals who comprised the new council were ready to support the lord protector, at least for a time.

Somerset was an able soldier; he was neither a statesman nor a politician. Within his council were knots of men divided by doctrinal hatreds, by jealousies, by conflicting interests. Only a strong protector could have curbed the conspiracies of councillors greedy for profit and power; and Somerset was not strong. He was plagued by doubts. He vacillated. To be weak invited disaster.

229

The first problems that faced Somerset were difficult. Henry VIII had left an empty treasury and a heavy debt. France was anxious to recover Boulogne. Scotland, under French influence, was bitterly hostile. Somerset tried unsuccessfully to arrange a marriage between Edward VI and Mary, the infant queen of Scotland. When the tools of diplomacy broke in his hands Somerset launched an invasion of Scotland. His armies won the battle of Pinkie (1547), but the Scots thwarted Somerset's plans by sending their queen to France, where she was later betrothed to the heir to the French throne. So far as Scotland was concerned, Somerset's policy had failed completely.

When the protector returned from the north the first Parliament met. With the approval of Edward VI, Somerset proceeded to secure the passage of laws pointing towards Protestantism. The Treasons Act of Henry VIII was largely repealed. The Six Articles Act was rescinded. Various enactments against heresy were wiped away. Many of the church services were to be read in English. An act of Parliament permitted the clergy to marry. Protestant preachers came in from the Continent to explain the creeds of their reformed religions.

In 1549 the first Act of Uniformity was passed. It ordered a new prayer book to be used in the churches. The book contained the beautiful English liturgy prepared by Archbishop Cranmer, who was himself strongly influenced by Protestant doctrines. The prayer book was mainly an admirable translation from old Latin service books; but the Protestant tendencies in it were sharp and clear. The dignity and beauty of the new ritual rendered a priceless service to the national church. It gave complete and lasting expression to the changes of the sixteenth century.

At the same time the fact that the new prayer book and ritual stood as a compromise between the extremes of both Protestantism and Roman Catholicism served to anger all who did not like compromise, evasion, or obscurity. Among the people the use of a form of service strange to them produced considerable discontent; there were rebellions in Devon and Cornwall, serious disturbances in Oxfordshire. Once again, however, it was the central government of the state that had taken steps towards Protestantism. Legally, at least, national unity and uniformity were retained. Across the Channel the Reformation broke several countries asunder. Germany, for example, never fully recovered from the religious revolution of the sixteenth century and the later internecine wars.

Somerset and his pro-Protestant oligarchy also proceeded to carry further the confiscation of church property. Many chantries were dissolved and the proceeds went into the pockets of the king and the gentry. Hundreds of religious endowments, particularly those of the non-industrial guilds, were seized. Council members, eager for plunder, "gorged themselves with manors." Somerset himself built a great palace.

The council set out to destroy thousands of relics, images, and shrines. Priceless treasures of medieval art were knocked down, torn, or burned. Those who still walked in the old ways were horrified at the sacrilegious treatment of holy things and holy places. The argument that relics and shrines were breeding places for superstition satisfied some people; but the desecration certainly alienated many who had hitherto been lukewarm. The excesses of Protestant mobs increased the divisions of opinion. Throughout England squabbles multiplied and armed skirmishes often reddened the village greens.

Amidst such profanity and confusion the religious system maintained by Henry VIII seemed shattered beyond repair. Before the racing influence of the new religious ideas thousands of Englishmen were bewildered. Ecclesiastical order had nearly perished. In the chaos some priests hurled aside their surplices as superstitious. Gamekeepers were given benefices. All teaching of divinity ceased at Oxford and Cambridge. In these years there was but one splendid achievement, the foundation of several endowed grammar schools. One of the new institutions was the famous Christ's Hospital, still in our own day a monument to the virtues of charity and good will.

THE FALL OF SOMERSET

During the religious upheavals of the reign of Edward VI there occurred a profound economic disturbance. World markets and trade routes were being changed. Trade centers were shifting. The medieval structure of industry was everywhere collapsing. From the mines of Mexico and Peru a stream of precious metals flowed into Europe through the seaports of Spain. As the supply of gold and silver increased their value depreciated. Thus commodity prices rose. Widespread speculation increased the price disturbance. Wages lagged behind the mounting prices. As the cost of living increased and an uncontrolled inflation burst over Europe Englishmen began to complain and, finally, to rebel. Because they did not understand the basic causes of the price rise or the wage lag they blamed their troubles upon the evils they could see. They ascribed the hard times to such things as bad harvests, monopolies, and the luxury of the upper classes.

Few noted that the debasement of the coinage that had begun about 1543 was an important contributing factor in the economic troubles. Silver coins would not pass at their face values; gold coins had almost disappeared from circulation. Large quantities of gold were exported to Europe. Somerset could do nothing to restore the coinage; the national treasury, its gates so often open to pilferers, was empty.

Many Englishmen correctly claimed that one cause of the prevailing hardships in rural England was the enclosure by great landlords of many open fields and much common land. Earlier chapters have shown that in the medieval centuries land was used mainly to produce the means of livelihood for the people who lived upon it. There was only a small national export trade. Those who lived in the next county were "foreigners." The small fairs were the chief means of selling goods to itinerant merchants, their agents, or one's neighbors.

Then, as explained earlier, English merchants began to look abroad for export opportunities. New domestic markets began to appear when towns grew up. As the tides of commerce increased, one of the great demands was for wool, a commodity that could easily be transported to seaports and over the sea. Men began to invest money in land in order to be able to grow crops for profit. They were no longer mainly interested in producing agricultural goods merely to make an agrarian economy self-sufficient. They wanted to make money.

The growth of investment in land was hastened because the new commercial classes were heaping up larger and larger profits in trade. They had fluid capital; and they often joined the large landowners in capitalistic agricultural enterprise. The small tenants were accustomed to working their acres only for subsistence purposes. They could not force the land to produce its topmost yield, partly because they did not have the tools or the hired help, partly because open field arrangements prevented many improvements; nor could they raise large flocks of sheep. Only the great landowners could do these things. Those who had small holdings usually found it impossible to pay the increased commercial or "rack" rents. Many tenants were evicted and their tenements combined by the landowners into larger units; such was one of the results of "the inordinate enhancing of rents."

In the sixteenth century the main interest of the new agricultural capitalists was not in producing larger crops, although larger crops often did result from enclosures. The chief purpose of enclosures in the Tudor age was to provide broad ranges for sheep. Sheep raising was a decidedly profitable business. Sometimes arable land was turned into pasture land so that more sheep could be fed; this land was usually enclosed by a hedge. Frequently the "common" land surrounding the villages was seized by great private landowners. Such methods of enclosure had been used since the Black Death, but always on a small scale. In the Tudor age the profits of raising sheep sharply increased the number of enclosures. In fact, the enclosure movement was not to reach such a crest again until the great economic revolution of the eighteenth century; and then the enclosures were made for a different purpose. In the sixteenth century, as in the eighteenth, many evicted tenants found neither jobs nor homes.

The number of individuals involved in the unhappy results of this agrarian revolution has usually been exaggerated. Nevertheless, the sum total of human misery resulting from these and other economic upheavals was appalling and widespread. In the last Parliament of Henry VIII many bills in "poor men's causes" attacked the enclosures; but all such bills came to nothing. The literature of complaint and reform in books, sheep-tracts, pamphlets, supplications, and petitions grew large and bitter.

In his *Utopia* Sir Thomas More had earlier remarked upon "a certain conspiracy of rich men procuring their own commodities under the name and title of the commonwealth." Sir Thomas Elyot's *Book of the Governor* contained several allusions to the evils of enclosure. Further contemporary comments occur in such works as that of the London mercer Henry Brinkelow who published his *Complaynt of Roderyck Mors* in 1548. Another popular volume was *The Book of Husbandry,* probably written by Sir Anthony Fitzherbert and first printed in 1523; it went through ten editions before 1600. John Hales' *A Discourse of the Common Weal of this Realm of England* was written in manuscript in 1549 and printed in 1581.

The English people were also influenced by voices from the pulpit and platform. Archbishop Cranmer's sympathy for the suffering poor is evident in his "Prayer on Behalf of Landlords": "We heartily pray Thee to send Thy holy spirit into the hearts of men that possess the grounds, pastures, and dwelling places on the earth; that they, remembering themselves to be thy tenants, may not rack or stretch out the rents of their houses and lands; nor yet take unreasonable fines after the manner of covetous worldlings." In 1549 Hugh Latimer, bishop of Worcester, referred to the rural distress in a sermon before Edward VI. "But let the preacher preach till his tongue be worn to the stump," Latimer complained, "nothing is amended."

Somerset himself was prepared to aid the suffering poor. Despite strong opposition he secured the appointment of a commission to investigate the spread of enclosures; but the commission was fed false evidence by the enclosing landowners, the squires, the investing burgesses; everywhere there was pressure, secrecy, and deliberate fraud. The majority of the governing classes within and without Parliament sympathized with men of their own economic, political, and social level, not with the common people. Nor was Somerset able to enforce his proclamation ordering the existing laws against enclosures to be scrupulously observed. Most of his colleagues in the council were enclosing lands themselves; they looked upon the protector as a betrayer of his own class interests.

A rural revolt spread eastward in 1549 from Somerset through Gloucester and Dorset and the midland counties. In Norfolk about 15,000 peasants led by a tanner named Robert Kett captured Norwich, tore down enclosing hedges, and plundered the rich landowners. The rebels did not murder the gentry, nor were they guilty of any really black crimes; theirs was a rather orderly rebellion, and their grievances were certainly just. To aid the government in suppressing the revolt German mercenaries were used. They did their task well. Under the command of the earl of Warwick they joined the English soldiers to crush the rebellion. The lower classes watched the gathering shadows of despair, destitution, pauperism, and vagabondage. "Robert Kett, for struggling against economic destiny, swung in chains from the castle tower, while his brother William swung from the steeple of his parish."

All the Tudors and early Stuarts persistently opposed enclosures; their landed nobles did not. Although the liberal Somerset recognized the justice of the rebels' claims, his fellow councilmen felt that Kett's revolt clearly demonstrated the protector's folly in siding with the common people. Somerset was sincere in such things as his sympathy for the oppressed peasants, his Protestant principles, his ideas about more religious toleration. "Smithfield's fires remained unlit; the thumbscrew and the rack stood idle in the Tower." Somerset's major weakness was that he lost the support of his fluctuating council. "The Good Duke" at last found himself armed with little but good intentions. His friends in the lower classes were powerless to help him.

Led by the earl of Warwick, the son of Henry VII's unscrupulous servant Edmund Dudley, the enemies of Somerset stood together, and deposed him. In October, 1549, the fallen protector was sent to the Tower. In 1552 twenty Articles of Accusation charged him with an arbitrary use of power, with encouraging the people to rebellion, with seeking "to sow dissension between nobility, gentlemen, and commons." Somerset was found guilty of enough of the charges to ensure his execution; that was all his enemies wanted.

THE DUKE OF NORTHUMBERLAND

The earl of Warwick, now in complete control of the government, soon persuaded Edward VI to make him Duke of Northumberland. Northumberland was self-seeking and dishonest. He was determined to pursue his own selfish purposes by every means at his command. He increased the resources of the government by plundering the church in the name of Protestantism. He took away the sees of bishops who objected and seized the revenues of the vacant bishoprics; he sold church plate, crosses, candlesticks, chalices, and rich vestments. The spoils he distributed to the cliques about him. The pace of desecration quickened. Pictures on the walls of churches were painted out and texts took their places. Images and rood screens were wantonly smashed. Church festivals and "holy days" were forbidden. The England from which Henry VIII had tried to banish "diversity of opinions" was filled with the voices of "extreme" Protestantism. The child Edward VI is sometimes called a Protestant; Northumberland certainly was not.

In 1552 a new book of common prayer, "faithfully and godly perused and made fully perfect," was authorized by the second Act of

Uniformity. The use of this new service, suffused with Protestant language, was to be enforced in all churches. Priests who used other services were to be imprisoned. The communion service was no longer "commonly called the Mass." In 1553 the Forty-Two Articles, drawn up by Cranmer, summarized the doctrines of the new English Protestant church. Five of the seven medieval sacraments were abandoned. The Protestant doctrine of justification by faith was asserted; transubstantiation was denied.

The vigorous domestic policy of Northumberland left no doubt as to his position. Harsh treason laws were passed by a subservient Parliament. New enclosure legislation permitted landowners to enclose their commons provided they left enough land for their tenants. Of course, the landowners were left free to decide how much land their tenants needed, or whether there should be any tenants at all. The wool trade boomed; the sheepmen prospered; the poor grew poorer. Meanwhile the local gentry were ordered to raise troops of cavalry to keep down revolts among the lower classes.

Northumberland was less bold in the arena of external affairs. He wanted no entanglements abroad so that his hands might be free at home. Peace was made with France and Northumberland surrendered Boulogne for half of the sum the French had promised for it four years before. To Scotland Northumberland handed over all the Scottish strongholds held by English troops; for this he obtained no compensation. Nor did he object when Francis II of France and Mary, Queen of Scots, were betrothed, even though any observer knew that a marriage meant a close Franco-Scottish alliance. On every hand the reversal of Somerset's policy seemed complete.

Young Edward VI was completely under the baleful influence of Northumberland. However, by 1552 it was clear that Edward would not long survive the silent advance of tuberculosis. It was inevitable that Northumberland should cast about for some way of prolonging his own power. He knew that he was unpopular. Edward's death would leave him unprotected; his chances of keeping either his position or his life would then be faint indeed. The will of Henry VIII had provided that the throne should pass from Edward VI to Mary, Henry's daughter by Catherine of Aragon. If Catholic Mary came to the throne, then the head of Northumberland, who had paraded a belligerent Protestantism he did not feel, would surely roll. When Northumberland and his subservient council had vainly tried to convert Mary to Protestantism they sought ways to stop her from succeeding Edward VI.

Northumberland apparently found it an easy matter to convince Edward VI that the Catholic Mary might undo all his labors on behalf of Protestantism. The council had earlier agreed that it would not be necessary for every royal decision to be attested by at least six councillors. In 1553 Edward VI made a royal will to bestow the crown upon a Protestant. He "devised" the crown to his second cousin, Lady Jane Grey, and to her male heirs. The Protestant Lady Jane Grey was the daughter of the Duchess of Suffolk and granddaughter of Mary, the younger sister of Henry VIII. Under strong pressure the councillors signed the document, thus accepting the choice of Lady Jane Grey as England's next sovereign. Lady Jane Grey did not want the crown; but Northumberland would not let her refuse it.

Thus Mary Tudor, the real heiress, was to be excluded from the throne by the will of Edward VI. Northumberland proceeded to bulwark his own position by marrying his eldest son, Guildford Dudley, to Lady Jane Grey. He expected the Protestants in England to support the cause of a Protestant succession. He also hoped to obtain aid from abroad, perhaps from the Protestants in Germany who defeated Charles V in 1552. Meanwhile, France was again involved in war with Charles V. Mary Tudor was the cousin of Charles, and Henry II of France would certainly be opposed to having a relative of Charles upon the English throne. Northumberland may have felt that in a crisis Henry II might be persuaded to send military support to Lady Jane Grey and himself.

In July, 1553, Edward VI died. Lady Jane Grey, then only sixteen years of age, was proclaimed queen in London. Thus far all was well with the plans of Northumberland. Up in Norfolk Mary Tudor pointed to the fact that Parliament had sanctioned Henry VIII's right to settle the succession. The will of Edward VI, even though it might be genuine, was illegal. Mary issued a call to arms and her adherents moved towards her banners. Thousands came from the eastern counties where the hatred of Northumberland was sharp and strong; men remembered that it was Northumberland who had cruelly suppressed Kett's rebellion in the last days of Somerset's power. So Mary's forces grew stronger. Was there to be another War of the Roses?

Many Englishmen did not want a Catholic monarch. On the other hand, most men did not support the unpopular political adventurer, Northumberland; and they hated the idea of a civil war. Northumberland's army slowly moved northwards to meet Mary; but his soldiers deserted in increasing numbers. As he paused in Cambridge news came that his council and the city of London had pledged their support to Mary. Northumberland's clever schemes were over. A sordid chapter of greed and corruption had ended.

Mary entered London and was crowned queen. Northumberland begged abjectly for his life and insisted that he had always been a Roman Catholic. This public recantation of Protestantism did not save him from the axe on Tower Hill. Six months later, the modest and studious Lady Jane Grey, innocent victim of the Reformation at its vilest, followed Northumberland to the block.

MARY TUDOR

Queen Mary, daughter of Catherine of Aragon and Henry VIII, succeeded to the throne at the age of thirty-seven. Before she became queen her life had been one of almost unrelieved neglect and humiliation. She had been separated from her mother; she had been made miserable by the mean jealousy of Anne Boleyn; she had suffered from Henry VIII's cruel abuse of her mother and herself; she had been lucky to escape with her life when Northumberland tried to force her to abandon her Roman Catholic religion. It was not surprising that Mary Tudor was a worn and bitter woman in 1553, with a spirit made harsh and warped by brooding over her mother's religion and her mother's wrongs. She had grown up to be somber, stubborn, and unattractive, of limited intellectual power, wanting in judgment.

At the same time, Mary was personally kind, often magnanimous to her enemies. She was skilled in languages, dancing, and music; she loved magnificent clothes and jewels. Her injured Spanish mother had taught her to be a Roman Catholic and her faith was constant in the church. Through the years of danger and gloom she had clung stanchly to her religion; it had been her consolation and her refuge. Against it her enemies had not been able to prevail.

When Mary came to the throne in 1553 she was determined to bring Englishmen back to what she believed was the true way, the only religion that could save their souls. Mary's mission, as she saw it, was to restore the Roman Catholic church to its ancient power. She set about her task at once, resolute, dignified, indefatigable. Mary's double tragedy was to spring from her honest and passionate attachment to the church of Rome and to her Spanish husband at a time when Englishmen disliked both. Mary was the victim of her virtues as well as her weakness. She failed both as a woman and a queen. Nevertheless, this failure was not entirely Mary's fault. Hasty and generalized statements about her reign are often controversial, however conscientious the historians who make them attempt to be.

The return of England to the Roman allegiance began swiftly. Mary deprived the leading Protestant bishops of their sees. Latimer, Hooper, and Ridley were imprisoned in the Tower. The Catholic bishops Gardiner and Bonner were restored to their former bishoprics at Winchester and London. Gardiner, long a Catholic crusader, was made lord chancellor. Many Catholics who had been strongly opposed to the Protestant innovations in the reign of Edward VI now found themselves in the privy council. When Mary's first Parliament met in the autumn of 1553 she pressed at once for the restoration of the Roman Catholic church.

The new Parliament agreed to meet the queen's wishes up to a certain point. An Act of Repeal referred to the legislation and practices of Edward VI's reign "whereof has ensued amongst us, in a very short time, numbers of diverse and strange opinions and diversities of sects, and thereby grown great unquietness and much discord, to the great disturbance of the commonwealth of this realm, and in a very short time like to grow to extreme peril and utter confusion." The Act of Uniformity and eight other acts of the reign of Edward VI were "utterly repealed, void, and annihilated" with the result that Catholic doctrine and service were restored as they had stood at the end of the reign of Henry VIII.

The members of Parliament refused to go further. They declined to restore the papal authority by overthrowing the Act of Supremacy of 1534. Backed by strong vested interests, they declared that they would not return the church lands confiscated by acts of Parliament under Henry VIII. They refused to make public attendance at mass compulsory or to fine those who did not attend. If Mary had been willing to stop at the restoration of the Henrician system her settlement might have been permanent; but she obstinately insisted that England must return to the papal fold. Parliament, on the other hand, steadily refused to carry the nation any further towards Rome. The popular impulse, even in the rural areas where the old faith was still strong, was largely satisfied. It seems likely that most of the queen's subjects were no more sympathetic with her leanings towards Rome than they had been with the earlier violence of extreme Protestantism.

Long before Mary reached the throne she had been advised and aided by ambassadors and agents of her Spanish cousin the Emperor Charles V. The shrewd Charles was willing to help Mary advance her religious policy; but Mary, despite her reverence for him, ignored his sage advice: "Go slowly and be a good Englishwoman." Why should she listen to the Emperor Charles, when she heard the voice of God?

It was not politically wise to alarm England, as Mary did, by announcing her intention to marry Philip of Hapsburg, the son of her cousin Charles V and heir to all his father's holdings except the Hapsburg territories in Austria. The high-principled and bigoted Mary did not see, or at least was apparently untroubled by, the popular fear that England might become a Spanish province or that the English fleet and merchant marine might be controlled from Madrid. Mary felt that a Spanish alliance would help her bring England back to the Catholic church. Englishmen, with pride in their nation's growing strength, saw with despair and anger the prospects of foreign intervention in English affairs. Was England to be an adjunct or satellite of Spain? Bishop Gardiner warned the queen that her course would damage the Catholic cause; but Mary went ahead; she was in a hurry. The sentiment of nationality did not enter into her calculations.

Bishop Gardiner skilfully drew up the marriage contract with a special view to safeguarding English independence. Philip came to England and tried to be diplomatic and friendly. He could not make himself popular. Feeling against the marriage resulted in three rebellions. The most important was led by Sir Thomas Wyatt and arose in Kent. The purpose of the revolt was to dethrone Mary in favor of her half sister, Elizabeth. It came within an ace of success. The troops sent against Wyatt deserted the queen and joined the rebels. Had Wyatt marched immediately on London, Mary might have been captured. When the rebels delayed too long their cause was lost.

As Wyatt's forces at last penetrated London, Mary, who never lacked courage, appealed "with the voice of a man" for support. Wyatt's rebellion was suppressed. Several executions occurred in London. In Kent the gallows swiftly went up and many a peasant paid with his life for marching against his queen. Mary's half sister, Elizabeth had been sent to the Tower. The Spanish ambassador clamored in vain for her execution. When nothing could be proved against her she was released.

Mary was not dismayed. She went ahead with her plans for the Spanish marriage. When the members of her second Parliament met she asked them to repeal the Act of Supremacy and they refused. They also declined to revive the heresy acts or the Six Articles Act. They did agree to ratify the marriage treaty; then they were sent home. Mary called a third Parliament; she instructed the lords-lieutenant and sheriffs to ask the people to elect members "as the old laws require, and of the wise, grave, and Catholic sort." As a result of this packing, the third Parliament proved to be more submissive and pro-Catholic than the two before it.

Soon after the marriage of Philip and his doting Mary, the Pope sent Cardinal Pole to England. At a solemn session of the third Parliament he absolved England and admitted the English people once more to the union of the Catholic church. Parliament thereupon repealed most of the anti-papal laws of Henry VIII. Cardinal Pole, declared the second Act of Repeal, had been sent "to call us home again into the right way from whence we have all this long while wandered and strayed abroad." But Parliament did not hand back the spoils of the monasteries, chantries, and guilds. All who had profited in the redistributions of Henry VIII's reign were not to be deprived of their "great plunder." In fact, before repealing the Act of Supremacy Parliament had asked and obtained assurance that the Pope would not insist upon the return of the church lands. The lack of a real religious revival or a strong Catholic zeal was evident to any acute observer. The Venetian envoy wrote that "with the exception of a few most pious Catholics, none of whom are under thirty-five years of age, all the rest make this show of recantation, yet do not effectually resume the Catholic faith."

The third Parliament of Mary's reign also re-enacted the heresy acts "for the eschewing and avoiding of errors and heresies which of late have risen, grown, and much increased within this realm." Most Englishmen did not like either the Spanish marriage or the return to the jurisdiction of Rome. Nor did they like the heresy acts and the beginning of the Marian persecutions, so fatal to Catholicism in England. Mary declared that she wanted the heretics punished with caution, without passion, and in such a way that people might understand the justice of the sentences. Despite such declarations the burning of Protestants could not easily be explained or defended in England.

When Protestants were sent to the stake for their beliefs the cause for which Mary was battling so desperately was really lost. Probably not more than three hundred Protestant martyrs were burned in Mary's reign; far more died in the waves of death on the Continent. The queen does not deserve to be called "Bloody Mary." And yet her error was greater than she knew. Not long ago a famous Roman Catholic declared: "It is at least arguable that the saviour of the Protestant cause in England was this sour but not ignoble old maid who honestly and sincerely believed, and blindly believed, that her burnings would bring men back to the Church she loved."

Mary certainly expected that her persecution would weaken Protestantism. Here she miscalculated. The impression Mary created was indeed lasting, but it was the opposite of what she intended. The Protestant bishops Hooper, Latimer, and Ridley were burned at the stake. "Be of good comfort, Master Ridley," said Latimer. "We shall this day light such a candle by God's grace, in England, as I trust shall never be put out." Many people admired the courage of the martyrs and felt horror at the persecuting zeal of their queen. As her ill-judged severities increased, Mary's popularity shot downwards at a quickened pace. Her bright hopes tarnished, Mary kept on in flat disregard of her people's wishes.

In 1556 Thomas Cranmer was burned at Oxford. Before his death he repudiated his earlier recantation of Protestantism. "As for the Pope, I refuse him, as Christ's enemy and Antichrist, with all his false doctrine." In a last heroic gesture, so dramatically and bitterly described in John Foxe's *Book of Martyrs*, Cranmer's "unworthy right hand," which had offended in writing his recantation, was burned first. So the Protestant martyrs died as the Catholics More and Fisher had perished for their faith two decades before. The Reformation was sealed with the blood of martyrs, most of them humble folk.

THE FINAL TRAGEDY

Mary had hoped for an heir. In that hope, too, she was disappointed. Sterility is the keynote of her reign. As the sad results of her failure in the Catholic crusade at home became apparent her husband,

Philip, concluded that England would be of little use to the Catholic cause. In 1555 he left England; slighting his queen, he remained absent for nineteen months. Meanwhile, disease and famine sharpened the public discontent in England. There were riots and plots against the queen; there were ballads and pamphlets. Everywhere rose voices of anger and despair. In these lonely months the heart of Mary Tudor, brooding on things to come, must have grown cold at the thought that the future belonged to Elizabeth; and Elizabeth was not a crusading Roman Catholic.

In March, 1557, Philip, who had succeeded his father as king of Spain in 1556, returned to England. He found the faggots still burning about the Protestant martyrs. His wife, Mary, who loved him, was slowly dying of cancer. Philip stayed in London for about four months, long enough to persuade Mary to help Spain in a war against France. Mary sent troops and England was drawn into the conflict. It was perhaps love's crowning folly. Philip returned to Europe; Mary never saw him again.

The war had been started by the irascible Pope Paul IV, eighty years old, who hated Spain. He excommunicated Philip and joined with the French to drive the Spaniards out of Italy. Thus it was that the English soldiers of Mary Tudor, faithful daughter of the church, fought at the behest of her excommunicated husband against the troops of Pope Paul IV. For the devout Mary this was another bitter chapter in the dark book of her life tragedy.

Throughout England the war was very unpopular. In January, 1558, the French captured Calais, England's last link with Crecy. It was a heavy blow to the national pride. Englishmen felt that once again their island kingdom had suffered by a foreign marriage alliance. The dying queen also knew that such an event served to alienate Englishmen still further from her beloved church.

On November 6, 1558, the unfortunate queen was asked by her council to recognize Elizabeth as her successor. Mary did so, requesting pathetically that Elizabeth retain the Catholic religion. Would her half sister undo and ruin all her work? The reign of the honest and misguided Mary had been one of maladministration, discontent, disgrace, defeat, bloodshed, and persecution. Would the coming of Elizabeth bring better times? Would this daughter of Anne Boleyn solve the problems of a new age? Would the third and last of Henry VIII's children succeed where two of them had failed?

Mary died on November 17, 1558. It was in a way symbolic of the failure of the Catholic hopes in England that Cardinal Pole died twelve hours after his queen.

Chapter 14

QUEEN ELIZABETH I

THE LAST TUDOR: A PORTRAIT

ELIZABETH, daughter of Anne Boleyn and Henry VIII, ascended the throne in 1558 according to the provisions of her father's will and by virtue of extreme good fortune. Her early life had been filled with intrigues and dangers; in Mary's reign she had been close to execution; it was not far from the prison to the scaffold. In 1558 Elizabeth was twenty-five years of age, a Renaissance personality, young, vigorous, learned in languages and music, a graceful dancer, a good shot; she was self-confident, impetuous, proud, subject to furious fits of anger, delighting in splendor and pageantry, in dresses, jewels, and flattery. The hard school of experience had made her subtle, watchful, wise, sceptical, a queen with a peculiar political genius. Above all, her nature was essentially practical. She was well aware of what she could and could not do.

The intrigues and maneuvers of Elizabeth, her delight in "crooked ways," her evasions and delays, often shocked and confused those who dealt with her. Elizabeth could wait and finesse; when the time for action came she could move swiftly. Sir Francis Walsingham, one of her great ministers, complained bitterly that "Her Majesty counts much on Fortune. I wish she would trust more in Almighty God." All remonstrances were wasted upon her. "This queen is possessed of 100,000 devils," wrote the Spanish ambassador. To Elizabeth it was always wise to seek "an intellectual way of meeting a difficulty." Capricious as the surface of her nature might seem, the depths were usually steady and hard. Like her father before her, she craved power; and she knew that power must rest upon popular approval.

When Elizabeth came to the throne the nation supported her because the alternative was civil war. The popularity won for the Tudors by Henry VIII had been largely dissipated in the reigns of Edward VI and Mary. Most men saw the evils that would result if England should again be divided on the question of religion. Would

243

Elizabeth require the same professions of Roman Catholic religious zeal as Mary had demanded? Would Englishmen still constantly be "eating religion with their bread"? England had been defeated by France and Scotland. Her prestige abroad had fallen sharply in the currents and eddies of international politics. At home, the misgovernment of Mary had produced much discontent. The treasury had been drained by the expenses and plundering of the past decade. Economic dislocations had pressed heavily on the poorer classes. England's position, and the position of her queen, seemed hazardous.

"If ever any person had either the gift or the style to win the hearts of the people," wrote a contemporary, "it was this Queen, and if she ever did express this same it was in coupling mildness with majesty as she did, and in stately stooping to the meanest sort." Elizabeth knew and understood that public popularity was essential to the survival and strength of her throne. "She is much attached to the people and is very confident that they are on her side, which is indeed true," wrote the Spanish ambassador in London. Tactful and shrewd, with an increasing knowledge of men and affairs, Elizabeth paid careful heed to public opinion and often helped to create the kind of opinion she wanted. It had been the habit of Henry VIII to stoop to conquer; it was also the habit of his daughter.

As her reign progressed, Elizabeth became a symbol for the nation. The extreme homage of Edmund Spenser recorded in the dedication of the *Faerie Queene,* although filled with Elizabethan exaggerations and conceits, conveys a sense of the spirit of the age: "To the most high, mightie and magnificent Empress, renowned for piety, virtue and all gratious government, Elizabeth, by the grace of God, Queen of England, France and Ireland and of Virginia, Defender of the Faith, Her Most Humble Servant Edmund Spenser doth in all humilitie dedicate, present, and consecrate these his labours to live with the eternity of her fame." Throughout the forty-five years of her reign Elizabeth never lost sight of the fact that man is a political and patriotic animal. "Though I be a woman I have as good a courage answerable to my place as ever my father had. I am your anointed Queen. I will never be by violence constrained to do anything. I thank God I am endowed with such qualities that if I were turned out of the realm in my petticoat, I were able to live in any place in Christendom." The words of her speeches to Parliament rolled over England. "And though you have had, and may have many princes, more mighty and wise sitting in this state, yet you never had, or shall have, any that will be more careful and loving." Late in the century Gloriana was still touching familiar chords: "And though God has raised me high, yet this I count the glory of my crown, that I have reigned with your loves."

Elizabeth worked hard. She might be petulant, capricious, and vain, but these qualities had small place in state affairs. Politics was a hard and ruthless business. The tools of a successful monarch must be temperance, caution, good sense, a calm and critical intelligence. Most of these abilities Elizabeth showed when there was need for them. In all her great affairs she was aided, like her father and grandfather, by the fact that she was able to gather about her council table a group of able men. Of one of the rare occasions when Elizabeth herself sat in council, a contemporary remarked, "She interrupts not seldom." Another noted that "she is a haughty woman falling easily into rebuke." Her councillors were indeed her servants; and few rulers have been served so well. There were Leicester, Walsingham, Essex, Sir Nicholas Bacon, and many more. One of Elizabeth's greatest ministers was William Cecil, Lord Burghley, educated in the Renaissance atmosphere at Cambridge. There Burghley had learned Greek and Latin; he also absorbed the Renaissance political ideal: to worship at the shrine of the state, to believe that only by obedience to the national sovereign can the order of society be maintained. He remained by the queen's side until his death in 1598. Burghley's son, Sir Robert Cecil, served both Elizabeth and James I until 1612. Such a queen and such councillors heralded a new order in the making of modern England.

THE PROBLEM OF RELIGION

In dealing with the question of religion, Elizabeth moved circumspectly. The Roman Catholics waited and hoped. In the first public document of the new reign an "et cetera" was placed at the end of the royal titles where Henry VIII and Edward VI had written "Supreme Head of the Church." What did the alteration mean? "Let her highness etceterate herself. This will leave her hands free, and then afterwards she can explain the etceteration as occasion shall require. Suppose that sooner or later she must submit to the Pope, she can still say she has done no wrong." At first Elizabeth attended mass; she maintained her ambassador at Rome; she refused to permit any changes in the service; she kept the Roman Catholic bishops and clergy in their offices. The new queen wanted to avoid the hostility of Rome until her hold upon the throne was reasonably secure and Englishmen had become accustomed to her authority.

When the Spanish ambassador and others tried to learn the queen's intentions she did her shameless and clever best to confuse them. Elizabeth was illegitimate in the eyes of the church. The old and irascible Pope Paul IV was not kindly disposed towards her. Mary, Queen of Scots, great-granddaughter of Henry VII, was a dangerous Catholic candidate for the English throne. Her husband was the French king, Francis II. France backed Mary's claim and French power in Scotland was strong. If the church declared its opposition to Elizabeth there would be trouble with Roman Catholics in England and there might be war with France and Scotland. Elizabeth was fighting for time and she fought with consummate skill.

One European fact helped the English queen. The faithful Catholic Philip II of Spain did not want to see England lost to Catholicism. Nevertheless, he did not wish to see his rival France obtain control of the island kingdom, either by war or diplomacy. Meanwhile, at home, Elizabeth was winning the popular support she so desperately needed. In the matter of religion she favored the creation of a national church on a broad basis, a compromise church. Her great ministers, William Cecil and Sir Nicholas Bacon, were Protestants. Cecil had been the Duke of Somerset's secretary; but he had shrewdly gone to mass under Mary. He, too, favored a settlement of moderation and compromise. The majority of the queen's council seemed inclined to agree with Cecil and the queen.

Elizabeth made haste slowly. Many Protestants who had fled to Europe during Mary's reign were allowed to return. A Catholic bishop expressed the widespread Catholic alarm as the Marian refugee came back: "The wolves be coming out of Geneva and other places of Germany, and hath sent their books before, full of pestilent doctrines, blasphemy, or heresy, to infest the people." On Christmas Day, 1558, Elizabeth refused to permit the host to be elevated in her presence. Early in January, 1559, she forbade all preaching and teaching, thus silencing for a time both Protestant and Catholic zealots. Late in January, Parliament assembled. The measures placed before the members by the council were intended to establish the English church on a broad middle ground of doctrine and practice. The new state faith was to be a fiat religion, to which all must publicly conform.

The famous compromise settlement was swiftly effected. The Marian legislation that had brought England back into the Roman church was repealed. A new Act of Supremacy again abolished papal power in England. As has been noted earlier, Elizabeth avoided Henry VIII's title of Supreme Head of the Church of England; she soon became instead Supreme Governor, a title perhaps less offensive to Catholics. The acts of Henry VIII that had brought about the separation of the English church from Rome were revived. All who held church or state offices in England were required to take an oath acknowledging the queen as Supreme Governor and denying the spiritual jurisdiction of any "foreign prince, person, prelate, state, or potentate, spiritual or temporal."

The Act of Supremacy of 1559 enjoined the use of the Second Prayer Book of Edward VI in all churches. Alterations were made to provide a form of service acceptable to as many Englishmen as possible. Doctrinally much scope was left for varying shades of belief; precise doctrinal definition was carefully avoided. For example, the Catholic and Protestant doctrine were merged together in a chameleon communion service that could mean different things to different individuals. The completely contradictory words of Zwingli and the mass book on the sacrament were neatly compressed into one sentence.

Penalties for failure to use the new form of service in the Church of England were heavy. The religious settlement was thus uniform and compulsory. There was to be order and decency in the outer arrangements of the church. "All and every person within this Realm shall diligently and faithfully . . . resort to their parish church . . . upon every Sunday and Holy Days, and then and there to abide, orderly and soberly, during the time of the Common Prayer, Reading, and other services of God there to be ministered." However, the penalty for nonattendance was only a shilling a Sunday "for the maintenance of the poor." Nor was there anything in early Elizabethan legislation forbidding attendance at services held by groups outside the church.

In 1562 the convocation of the Church of England agreed upon certain changes in the doctrines of the church; these were enacted by Parliament in the Thirty-nine articles of 1571. This revision purged the Forty-two articles of Edward VI of their extreme Protestant elements. Thus the nation in Parliament decided the nature of the established church and the established religion. The court of high commission saw to it that the orders of Elizabeth and her Parliament were carried out. All Romanist bishops and about two hundred of the lower clergy were ousted from their livings.

Elizabeth hoped that this compromise settlement, tempered later by successive doses of toleration, would meet the wishes of the majority of her subjects. The queen preferred to have "controversial points involved in a wise obscurity." At the same time she determined to have outward conformity and complete royal supremacy. "God," she said to the bishops, "hath made me the Overlooker of the Church; if any schisms or errors heretical are suffered therein which you, my lords of the clergy, do not amend, I mean to depose you. Look you, therefore, well to your charges."

Elizabeth was aided in making the new settlement effective by Matthew Parker, her first archbishop of Canterbury. Parker, formerly dean of Lincoln, was a man without marked religious enthusiasm. He wanted to preserve a convenient peace in the church. "Experience doth teach," he once wrote, "that the world is much given to innovations, never content to stay and live well." So far as the church was concerned, Parker's chief desire was to see Englishmen "stay and live well." He did not want the church agog with spiritual excitement. Neither he nor his queen demanded unity of hearts or conviction. To "open windows into men's souls" was not their intention. They demanded only external conformity. On many questions of dogma and doctrine they were quite prepared to hedge; few governments were less swayed by purely religious motives. For the first decade of Elizabeth's reign there was very little persecution.

Soon, however, the religious wars in Europe increased in number and violence; the strength of the Counter-Reformation grew. Then the English government steadily attempted to reduce the number of Catholics in England and to make the people satisfied with the new settlement. All kinds of devices were used to achieve this end. For example, in 1559 John Foxe had published a book of over seven hundred pages in Latin about the Protestant saints and martyrs in the reign of Mary Tudor. In 1563 this book, the famous *Acts and Monuments,* was translated into English and five editions were published before 1603; four editions appeared in the seventeenth century. Convocation ordered copies to be put in all the cathedral churches.

At the same time, the importance of order and conformity was frequently stressed from the pulpits. A series of carefully prepared homilies was ordered to be read in the churches; they explained and praised the virtues of obedience and humility. "He that nameth rebellion," stated a homily of 1571, "nameth not a singular and one only sin, as is theft, robbery, murder, and such like; but he nameth the whole puddle and sink of all sins against God and man, against his prince, his country, his countrymen, his parents, his children, his kinsfolks, his friends and against all men universally; all sins, I say, against God and all men heaped together, nameth he that nameth rebellion."

As the years passed, the Anglican compromise was loudly opposed by two groups, the Catholics and the Puritans; the former rejected the Act of Supremacy; the latter demanded further Protestant reforms. For a hundred years these conflicts were to form a central theme of English history. Catholic opposition ranged from ballads and propaganda to active plots against the life of Elizabeth. The Catholic ballad "Winter Cold into Summer Hot" called Anglicanism "a bird of Calvin's broode." Catholics like the Lancashire priest William Allen, principal of St. Mary's Hall, Oxford, had fled across the Channel in 1559. Roman Catholic exiles at Louvain and elsewhere hoped and plotted for the rekindling of the Catholic faith, and for the overthrow of Elizabeth and her ecclesiastical system.

In 1568 an English Catholic seminary was founded at Douai to train missionaries to glide back and preach the old faith in England. Later English colleges were established at Rome and Rheims. The efficient Jesuits Edmund Campion and Robert Parsons came to England in the 1580's; Campion was tortured and hanged at Tyburn; he was as much a martyr as the Protestants who suffered death under Mary. A secret Catholic printing press was set up in Essex in 1581. In 1588, on the eve of the sailing of the Spanish Armada, the abusive "Admonition to the Nobility and People of England" was printed at

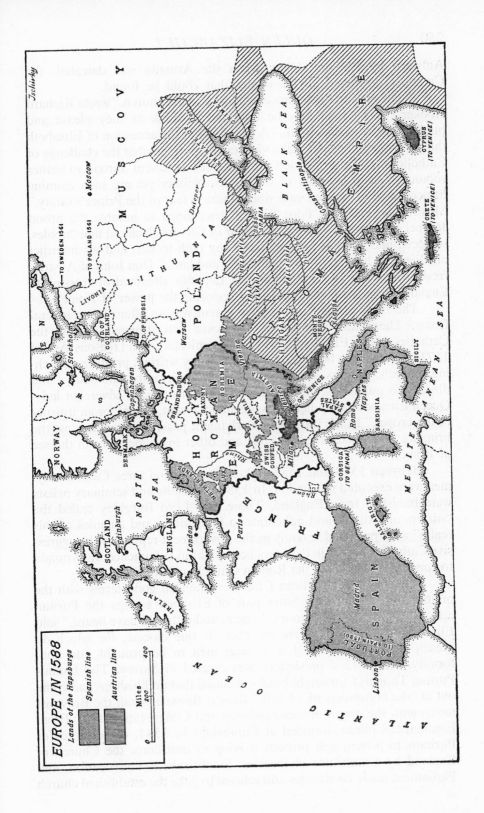

EUROPE IN 1588

Lands of the Hapsburgs

Spanish line

Austrian line

Miles
0   200   400

Antwerp by William Allen; when the Armada was defeated, the Catholics destroyed all the copies that could be found.

"Schisms and disturbances will arise in the church," wrote Richard Hooker, "if all men may be tolerated to think as they please and publicly speak as they think." A decade after the accession of Elizabeth the government began to take vigorous steps to combat the challenge of Catholicism. "To grope men's minds spies were sent abroad to gather rumours and to lay hold of words . . . Neither yet are such cunning devices to be accounted vain where there is fear of the Prince's safety." Meanwhile, in 1570, Pope Pius V determined to humble the proud Jezebel of England. The bull *Regnans in Excelsis* declared that "nobles, subjects, and peoples are free from any oath to her, and we interdict obedience to her monitions, mandates, and laws." Don John of Austria, fresh from victory over the Turks at Lepanto, dreamed of crossing to England from the Netherlands and restoring the power of Rome.

The reply of the English government was an offensive on several fronts. There was a series of repressive acts directed against the Catholics. After Elizabeth was excommunicated, the Treasons Act of 1571 declared it to be treason for anyone "by writing, printing, preaching, speech, express words or sayings, maliciously, advisedly, and directly to publish, set forth, and affirm that our said sovereign lady, Queen Elizabeth, is an heretic, schismatic, tyrant, infidel, or an usurper of the crown." In the same year Parliament passed "an act against the bringing in and execution of bulls and other instruments from the see of Rome."

Between 1578 and 1585 eighteen priests and three Catholic laymen were executed in London. In 1585 all Jesuits and seminary priests were banished from England. Those that Lord Burghley called the "stirrers of sedition and adherents to the traitors and enemies of this realm" were punished severely as the government replied to the aggressive Catholic crusade in the years before Philip II launched his Armada to conquer England for the Roman Church and for Spain.

Nor could the Anglican Church remain on good terms with the militant Puritans. In the latter part of Elizabeth's reign the Puritan attacks became steadily more vehement and bitter. "I have heard," said Elizabeth, "that there be six preachers in one diocese, the which do preach six sundry ways. I wish such men to be brought into conformity." In 1572 a presbytery was erected in Surrey. The famous Puritan Thomas Cartwright boldly declared that archbishops had come out of "the bottomless pit of hell." Robert Browne began the Brownist movement, the origin of Independency and Congregationalism. From Emmanuel College, founded at Cambridge in 1584, came scores of Puritans to preach and protest, striving to unbalance the Church of England by a multitude of theories; but Elizabeth, convocation, and Parliament made no changes and refused to yoke the established church to any more precise body of doctrine. The ambiguous and evasive words of Elizabeth, who did not greatly care, were sometimes embarrassing to her successors, who did.

Coarse and slashing attacks on the bishops and clergy became more frequent late in the century, prophetic of Stuart warfare. Such, for example, were the seven scurrilous Presbyterian tracts published at intervals during 1588 and 1589 under the pseudonym of Martin Marprelate. In these tracts the bishops were described as "false governors of the church; petty popes; proud, popish, profane, presumptuous, paltry, pestilent, pernicious prelates, and usurpers, enemies of God and the state." The clergy were condemned as "popish priests, ale hunters, drunkards, dolts, hogs, dogs, wolves, desperate and forlorn atheists, a crew of bloody soul murderers, sacrilegious church robbers." When Archbishop Whitgift replied to the tracts by establishing a strict censorship of the press and arresting leading Presbyterians in twenty counties the tide of assault subsided.

In 1593 Parliament passed "an act to retain the queen's subjects in obedience," directed against "the wicked and dangerous practices of seditious sectaries and disloyal persons" and providing for imprisonment of all offenders until they should conform. In the same year an act was passed "for the better discovering and avoiding of all such traitorous and most dangerous conspiracies and attempts as are daily devised and practised . . . by sending wicked and seditious persons . . . calling themselves Catholics." The result was an increase of persecution; many Puritans found themselves victims of the court of high commission. Some were put to death; other fled overseas, especially to Holland.

THE CHALLENGE OF MARY STUART

Throughout the early years of Elizabeth's reign ran the problem of her marriage. Among her many foreign suitors were Philip II of Spain, Prince Eric of Sweden, the Archduke Charles of Austria, and two brothers of Charles IX of France. Several English nobles about the court aspired to the queen's hand. All assumed Elizabeth would marry. When the Parliament of 1559 urged that step upon her she answered with her usual evasions. For two years Robert Dudley, son of the Duke of Northumberland, and later the earl of Leicester, seemed to hold her eye. When Amy Robsart, Dudley's wife, was found dead of a broken neck in the Dudley home near Oxford, Elizabeth returned to her inveterate virginity. Dudley remained her political adviser until his death in 1588.

Through several years a flood of petitions and pamphlets discussed the marriage of the queen, the question of an heir to the throne, and the problem of the succession. None of the protracted marriage negotiations came to anything. The queen fenced and dallied and the years went by. By leaving the question open so long Elizabeth kept on fairly good terms with France and Spain, which were both anxious to obtain her support.

Meanwhile, however, France was eager to aid Mary Stuart, Queen of Scots, in her plans to win the throne of England, which she claimed through her direct descent from Margaret, sister of Henry VIII. The youthful Mary was quartering the arms of England on her coat of arms and Elizabeth was quartering the lilies of France on hers. Mary was the focus of Catholic hopes. Mary's husband was Francis II of France and Mary of Guise, her mother, was regent of Scotland. France and Scotland were thus closely allied and the English feared a French invasion by land through Scotland.

It was at this point that the rigid Presbyterian John Knox left his master, Calvin, at Geneva to return to Scotland. There, in 1559, he became the leader of the Scottish Reformation. At the same time an anti-French section of the Scottish nobility joined together. Calling themselves the Lords of the Congregation, they appealed to John Knox for aid in driving the Catholic Frenchmen out of Scotland. Knox had once written an attack on Mary of England, Mary of Scotland, and Mary of Guise under the title *First Blast of the Trumpet against the Monstrous Regiment of Women*. Elizabeth had been deeply offended at what Knox had written about her sex. When Knox and the rebels sought her help against the French she hesitated, not because she disliked Knox, but because she was in a difficult position. If she helped the rebels against their legitimate ruler the precedent would be awkward. Then, too, Philip II of Spain might possibly join the French to make a Catholic crusade against England.

Elizabeth finally agreed to send help. Knox led his supporters against both the Frenchmen and the Catholic Church. English soldiers fought by the side of the roused Scotsmen. Mary, Queen of Scots, and her supporting Frenchmen were soon defeated. In 1560, by the Treaty of Edinburgh, France agreed to recall all but one hundred and twenty French soldiers from Scotland and to recognize Elizabeth as the lawful queen of England. The English troops were also withdrawn from Scotland and the land given over to the Lords of the Congregation and to John Knox. A grateful Knox apologized to Elizabeth for writing the *First Blast of the Trumpet*. A Scottish Parliament hastily summoned to Edinburgh abolished the papal power in Scotland. The monasteries were dissolved; the Scottish Kirk was established. Knox and his followers had none of the tepid Protestantism of Elizabeth.

In December, 1560, Francis II of France died. Mary Stuart, nineteen years of age, soon returned to Scotland to live in her native land as queen. Nevertheless, John Knox, who hated both Catholicism and France, was the real ruler of Scotland; and Mary's cousin, Elizabeth, had helped to put John Knox in power. What could be expected but inveterate enmity between Mary and Elizabeth? Mary Stuart had none of the sagacity of the English queen; she restored mass at Holyrood Palace; she antagonized John Knox.

The intrepid preacher bristled at Mary's Catholicism. "If there be not in her a proud mind, a crafty wit, and a hardened heart against God and His truth, my judgment failed me." Across the seas France was divided by civil wars between Catholics and Protestants. Mary could expect no aid from that quarter. In 1562 Elizabeth sent troops to help the French Protestants. As she did so, she laid claim to Calais, lost by her half sister, Mary. It was not a wise step. French Catholics and Protestants suddenly made peace, and forced the English soldiers to go home.

Mary Stuart now set about arranging a marriage with her Catholic cousin Lord Darnley, a grandson of Margaret Tudor by her second husband. This marriage, which took place in July, 1565, strengthened Mary's claim to the English throne. The Catholics of Europe were pleased. Elizabeth had tried to persuade Mary to wed a Protestant; but Mary had been suspicious. "This, of all her faults, is the greatest, that she conceives oft of evil where none is thought." Both Elizabeth and John Knox were angry about the Darnley marriage. "Whenever the nobility of Scotland," said Knox, "professing the Lord Jesus, consents that an infidel—and all Papists are infidels—shall be the husband of your Queen—ye in fact banish Jesus Christ from this realm."

During these years most of Europe was dividing into Protestant and Catholic camps. The Catholics were filled with the militant spirit of the Counter-Reformation. Some were certain that the great days of the Roman Church were returning. If a European war of religion arose, England would be the main enemy of the Catholic powers. If means could be found by war, diplomacy, or assassination, to replace Elizabeth by Mary Stuart, England might be brought back to the ancient faith. The devout Philip II of Spain saw with delight the reformed papacy, the crusades of the Jesuits, and the achievements of the Council of Trent (1545–1563). He was almost prepared to be the lay leader of the Counter-Reformation and to enter at once into armed conflict with England.

Several events occurred to prevent an attack upon England by Philip alone or by a Catholic Franco-Spanish alliance. In 1566 the Netherlands rebelled, led by the seven Calvinist northern provinces. Philip had to send troops to crush the revolt in this weak spot of his empire. Elizabeth sent aid secretly to the Dutchmen; in 1585 she sent troops openly, despairing of peace with Philip. She encouraged her great sailors to go on unofficial piratical expeditions against the ships and ports of Spain and the Spanish empire. France was again divided by a hideous Catholic-Protestant civil war, made dark and bloody by such chapters as the Massacre of St. Bartholomew (1572). Elizabeth sent money to the Protestant Huguenots of France. Harassed Spain and divided France were in no position to make war on England.

At this point disaster began to fall upon Mary, Queen of Scots. Her husband Darnley, "beardless and lady-faced," proved to be a contemptible character, lazy, drunken, vicious, arrogant, and jealous. "Woe worth the time whenever the Lord Darnley set his foot in this country," wrote Elizabeth's agent Thomas Randolph. Slowly Mary turned for advice to David Rizzio, her Italian Catholic secretary. The jealous Darnley, urged on by Protestant Scottish lords, murdered Rizzio, almost in the presence of the queen. Mary pretended reconciliation. Soon after this her son, the future James VI of Scotland and James I of England, was born.

Mary then turned to the earl of Bothwell, a man of loose tongue and morals, a foe of Knox and Protestantism, and widely hated in Scotland. Darnley was murdered, perhaps by Bothwell. If the famous "Casket Letters" are authentic Mary shared in Bothwell's guilt. Within two months Bothwell carried Mary off to Dunbar, divorced his wife, and then brought the queen back to Edinburgh, where he married her according to Protestant rites. The Protestant Scottish lords rose in rebellion. Bothwell escaped, but Mary was captured and forced to abdicate in favor of her infant son who was crowned king of Scotland as James VI. In 1568 Mary eluded her guards and fled to England.

Elizabeth was in an awkward position. She did not want to hand Mary, a queen who had fled to her for safety, over to her rebellious subjects. It was madness to permit her to go to France. On the other hand, Elizabeth could not support Mary's cause in Scotland. Even a court reception for Mary would have angered the Scots and perhaps driven them towards France. There were other difficulties. Mary Stuart was a danger in prison. She still remained the focus of Catholic hopes, the Catholic candidate for the throne of England.

Several English Catholics and malcontents, particularly from the more Catholic northern counties, wanted Mary to wed the Duke of Norfolk; then they would dispose of Elizabeth and place Mary and her husband on the throne. Their feeble rebellion, applauded by the Spanish ambassador, was swiftly crushed. Philip II of Spain did nothing more than "encourage with money and favour the Catholics of the north." About six hundred rebels were hanged; some fled to Holland. Elizabeth, like her father in the days of the Pilgrimage of Grace, took a harsh revenge. From Edinburgh, John Knox sounded a warning Elizabeth hardly needed: "If ye strike not at the root, the branches that appear to be broken will bud again, and that more quickly than men can believe." What should be done with Mary Stuart, "the root" of the Catholic conspiracies?

Catholic plotters crept about England after the Pope excommunicated Elizabeth in 1570. In 1571 Ridolfi, a papal agent masquerading as a Florentine banker, proposed that Elizabeth should be assassinated; Mary should wed the Duke of Norfolk; and the Duke of Alva should invade England from the Netherlands. Meanwhile, however, one of Lord Burghley's canny agents discovered the whole story. The ambassador was sent home and the Catholic Duke of Norfolk and several other nobles were executed, not because they were Catholics, but because they were traitors.

Many Englishmen were convinced that Mary Stuart should be put to death. While she lived, Elizabeth and England were in danger. The persecution of Catholics for treason increased. But Mary remained in safe custody. "There is an error crept into the heads of a number," remarked a contemporary, "that there is a person in this land whom no law can touch." Despite the fact that Elizabeth's difficulties with Spain and France increased, she refused to declare war against them. Instead she carried out a long flirtation with the French Duke of Anjou as a result of which France was for a time committed to support the Dutch against Philip II.

The military support sent by Elizabeth to the Dutch in 1585 helped to bring the struggle with Spain into the open. Philip II united with the powerful Catholic and pro-Spanish Guise family in France in preparing further plots for the murder of Elizabeth and the placing of Mary Stuart on the throne. When William of Orange was assassinated the English anger mounted against the Catholics and the Spanish. The climax of that anti-Spanish feeling was to come when the Spanish Armada sailed in 1588.

The last major plot was one led by Anthony Babington in 1586. This, like the earlier plots, was a plot to murder Elizabeth and to place Mary Stuart on the throne. Anthony Babington, the Jesuit Father Ballard, and several English Catholics were involved. Sir Francis Walsingham discovered all the details, placed the evidence before Elizabeth, and then arrested the plotters. Thirteen were executed. Mary Stuart, who was apparently aware of the plot, was brought to trial on a charge of treason. She was found guilty and Parliament petitioned for her early execution. The convocation of the Church of England declared that "the former Queen of Scotland hath heaped up together all the licentious sins of the sons of David" and stated that Elizabeth could proceed with the execution "with a white conscience."

Elizabeth finally signed the death warrant of "the monstrous and huge dragon." The council hastened to execute the warrant lest Elizabeth change her mind. When Mary was beheaded in February, 1587, Elizabeth blamed her secretary and had him brought to trial; he was ordered to pay a huge fine, which was later remitted. Elizabeth wrote to James VI of Scotland of "that miserable accident, far contrary to my meaning." All Europe was shocked by the execution of a queen.

One widespread view was perhaps well stated by a Flemish nobleman: "It had been better done to have poisoned her or to have choked her with a pillow, but not to have put her to so open a death."

Philip II of Spain now saw that England could not be brought back to the Roman Catholic Church except by war. Philip, who had long dreamed of a Catholic crusade, turned resolutely to a task he had begun earlier. The insolent islanders must be crushed. The ports of Spain stirred with preparations for a great Armada that would one day sail against the obstinate and heretical Englishmen. Perhaps the time had come when Philip's God would strike for His cause.

THE CHALLENGE OF SPAIN

Against the Spanish threat Elizabeth was able to mobilize the sea dogs of England, those adventuring sailors who had broken through the Catholic monopoly of America, sold Negroes, sacked Spanish treasure ships, and plundered Spanish settlements. In the name of Elizabeth and England, motivated by patriotic, personal, and religious interests, these mariners of England were anxious to enter into open war with Spain. They knew the importance of sea power; and they were eager to seize the trident of Neptune from the hands of Philip II.

In 1587 Sir Francis Drake struck suddenly at a part of the Armada assembled at Cadiz. Four vessels, well-handled, destroyed thirty-seven Spanish ships; the mobilization of the Spanish naval force was delayed for a year by this "singeing of the king of Spain's beard." Drake also seized a Spanish treasure vessel off the Azores and took its cargo, valued at over £100,000. He was anxious to continue these raids, so humiliating to Philip II; but Elizabeth, still hoping for peace, withheld her approval. By this time, most Englishmen were ready to echo the words of the doughty Sir John Hawkins: "It is not honourable for the Queen of England to be in any fear of the King of Spain."

In the summer of 1588 the "Invincible Armada" of Spain was ready to sail. Its commander was a Spanish grandee, a young and wealthy duke, a landsman who was innocent of any knowledge of naval strategy or tactics. In the Spanish fleet there were one hundred and thirty ships, totaling about 60,000 tons. They carried 8,000 sailors and 20,000 infantrymen; the excellent Spanish infantrymen carried on the "floating barracks" were to be used to repel any English attempts to board the Spanish galleons in a naval battle. Later they would aid in the land operations necessary for the conquest of England. Spain was a land power and looked upon a fleet as an army at sea. England was essentially a sea power and looked upon ships and seamen as more important than sea-borne soldiers.

Against the might of the Armada the English gathered one hundred and ninety-seven small ships totalling about 30,000 tons. Only thirty-four were royal navy vessels; the rest were supplied by private enterprise. These small ships, with the forecastle and poop cut down, could maneuver more swiftly and efficiently than the heavy Spanish galleons. The English admiral was the able Lord Howard of Effingham. Sir Francis Drake was vice-admiral; Sir John Hawkins was rear-admiral; Martin Frobisher was a captain. With such skilled and formidable advisers Lord Howard was well served. The English were better fighting sailors than the Spaniards; their confidence was high. "The Spaniards make much account of their beastly great ships, but any good English ship is able to combat them."

Late in July the Armada swept into the English Channel. The Spaniards planned to effect a junction with the Duke of Parma in the Netherlands; the Armada would then cover his crossing and support his troops by landing infantry forces carried from Spain. At Tilbury Elizabeth addressed the Englishmen gathered to repel the invaders. The queen had no doubts, she said, "but by your obedience to my general, by your concord in the camp, and your valour in the field we shall shortly have a famous victory over those enemies of my God, of my kingdom, and of my people."

The wind that drove the Spanish fleet towards the coast of England kept the English ships in Plymouth harbor. At last the English got their fleet out and in running fights began to hammer the Spanish galleons in swift, sharp attacks. The English avoided the traditional close-ranging and grappling action that the Spaniards had expected; there was no attempt to board the Spanish ships. The new naval tactics of the intrepid English sailors were terribly effective. Their numerous guns pounded the Spaniards from a distance; then the light but heavily armed English ships dashed in under the Spanish guns to rake the crowded decks of the galleons with terrific broadsides. This running fight, so admirably described in Garrett Mattingly's *The Armada,* lasted for six days. Six Spanish ships were sunk and 4,000 Spaniards killed.

Then the Armada, closely pursued by the English, moved into Calais. The English at once let loose fire ships among the Spanish vessels, most of which cut their anchor cables and straggled out to run before the heavy wind. They nearly ran ashore on the Flemish sand-banks but escaped into the North Sea. The storm finished the defeat of the Armada. Crippled and leaky Spanish ships rolled around the north of Scotland, down the coast of Ireland; many of them were wrecked on the inhospitable coasts. Only about fifty battered ships got back to Spain; only 10,000 men came home. Philip II was devoutly resigned to the disaster. "In God's actions reputations are neither lost nor gained. It is best not to talk of it." In England Lord Howard of Effingham wrote of the men he led out to meet the Armada: "God send me to see such company again, when need is."

The defeat of Spain hastened the decline of Spanish power throughout the world. For Englishmen the path lay open to world com-

merce and trade. North America was to be open to English colonization, a determining event in world history. English naval strength had
humbled the Catholic champion. All over Europe Protestants lifted up
their heads and took courage. The defeat of the Armada also increased
the national pride of Englishmen and contributed to the swelling tide
of the patriotism and aggressive enterprise of later years. Englishmen
were, it seemed, a chosen people; such an attitude could be felt in the
winds of opinion as the reign of Elizabeth drew to a close.

The war with Spain did not end with the defeat of the Armada.
It continued until 1604, the year after Elizabeth's death and six years
after the death of Philip II. Early in 1589 England took the offensive.
After many delays, an expedition was despatched to attack Spanish
ports and shipping. The expedition was a fiasco, and Drake was in
disgrace. Through the years continued raids were kept up on the
Spanish commerce. In 1591 occurred the magnificent achievement of
Sir Richard Grenville, who fought the whole Spanish fleet with Drake's
old ship, the *Revenge,* until he could fight no more.

Meanwhile Elizabeth helped the enemies of Spain in the Netherlands and in France. About 6,000 English soldiers still fought by
the side of the Protestant Dutchmen. In France the Catholic Guise
family, backed by Philip II, attempted to keep the Protestant Henry of
Navarre from succeeding to the French throne. In 1589 Henry appealed for help to Elizabeth, who sent 4,000 men to aid him, together
with arms and 22,000 pounds of English money in gold. Two years
later two expeditionary forces were sent from England to support
Henry's cause. In 1593, however, Henry abandoned Protestantism, for
state purposes, and was crowned king of France at Chartres in 1594.
Because he continued his war against Spain Elizabeth sent him further
aid, despite her annoyance at his conversion to Catholicism. When
Henry opened separate peace negotiations with Spain Elizabeth wrote
to him: "If there be any sin in this world against the Holy Ghost it is
ingratitude. Forsake not an old friend, for a new one will not be like
him." But Henry IV, now securely established on his throne, made
peace with Spain in 1598.

Meanwhile England fought on. In 1595 Hawkins and Drake
raided Spanish possessions in the West Indies. Both Hawkins and
Drake died in the Caribbean and were buried in the waters they knew
so well. In 1596 Lord Howard of Effingham, Sir Walter Raleigh, and
the earl of Essex led an expedition against the coasts of Spain. They
destroyed the shipping in Cadiz harbor. Essex took an army of 8,000
men ashore and burned a large part of the city. Philip II sent another fleet against England; it was destroyed by storms. In 1597 Essex
and Raleigh missed the Spanish treasure ships off the Azores in a
series of unlucky accidents. They quarrelled bitterly and returned to
face an angry Elizabeth. This was the last major effort of the war so far
as Elizabeth was concerned. In the succeeding years English privateers

continued to attack Spanish ships and inflicted heavy damage. Philip II died in 1598, leaving a bankrupt and crumbling empire.

THE LAST YEARS

As the reign of the great queen approached its end there were several problems besides those arising from the war against Spain. As described earlier, the Catholics and the Puritans were causing widespread disturbances and tension and Parliament passed several acts against them. Many Puritan doctrines were taking root, amidst bitter controversies, and persecution stimulated what it was designed to suppress. Late in Elizabeth's reign there also arose wide discontent about the question of monopolies. Grants of monopolies, the sole right to sell various articles, had often been made to favored nobles and businessmen. It was clearly an evil. There had been many petitions to the queen. Londoners were particularly resentful.

In 1601 Parliament became so incensed that Sir Robert Cecil lost control of the commons. Elizabeth knew when to yield. She revoked several monopolies and summoned the commons to hear her speech at Whitehall. It was a noble speech. "I have more cause to thank you all than you me; for, had I not received a knowledge from you, I might have fallen into a lap of an error only from lack of true information."

Meanwhile Ireland was in rebellion. The Irish were particularly angered by the imposition of taxes which were used by the English government to maintain troops in Ireland. In the sixteenth century there was added to ancient political, racial, and economic hatreds a religious element. The devout Irish Catholics had been systematically roused by the agents of the Pope to oppose Elizabeth and her ecclesiastical policy. In 1569 the first Irish revolt occurred, distinguished as usual by treachery and atrocity on both sides. The Pope and Philip II sent aid to the rebels and the Irish were able to keep up intermittent attacks on the English until 1583. In 1598 Philip II plotted with malcontent Irish leaders and the result was a widespread rebellion led by the O'Neills of Ulster and the Desmonds of the south. In the reign of Elizabeth the continued suppression of the Irish cost the English government about two million pounds.

In 1598 Elizabeth allowed the earl of Essex, stepson of Leicester, to lead an expedition against the Irish. The fiery Essex was young, handsome, and ambitious. He would have "no name so high as himself." When Essex was absent on the Cadiz expedition in 1596 William Cecil, Lord Burghley, had persuaded Elizabeth to confirm the appointment of his son, Robert Cecil, as principal secretary, and to pass over Sir Thomas Bodley, who was the nominee of Essex. In 1597, when Essex had been in Ireland, Lord Howard of Effingham was made earl of Nottingham and lord steward of the household. Lord Howard thus took precedence over Essex, and Essex retired in a tantrum from the court.

In his vehement contests for power Essex had made many enemies, especially Lord Burghley and his hunchbacked son, Sir Robert Cecil. The dashing Essex was no match for the careful Cecils. All about the court knew his impetuous ambition. When he pleaded for the renewal of his monopoly on sweet wines the queen remarked: "An unruly horse must be abated of his provender that he may be more easily managed."

Essex arrived in Ireland in March, 1599, with 16,000 men and 13,000 horses; one of his associates was the earl of Southampton, patron of Shakespeare. After a series of reverses, Essex made a truce with Hugh O'Neil, the earl of Tyrone, one of the main rebels. This Essex had not been authorized to do. From across the sea came scornful letters from the queen about the disasters that had befallen his forces. "If sickness of the army be the reason, why was not the action taken when the army was in a better state? If winter's approach, why were the summer months of July and August lost?"

Essex suddenly came home, leaving his army in Ireland. He was disgraced, deprived of his offices, imprisoned in his house. Essex was popular in London. Many attacks upon the Cecils appeared in a storm of pamphlets. Essex himself wrote violent letters of protest to the queen. "As if I were thrown into a corner like a dead carcass, I am gnawed at and torn by the basest creatures on earth." At last he foolishly entered into a mad plot to overthrow the government. He gathered a group of malcontents about him and led a rebellion. "A senseless ingrate," said Elizabeth, "hath at last revealed what has long been in his mind." Essex was executed for treason in February, 1601.

The great servants of the queen were dying, one by one: Leicester in 1588; Walsingham in 1590; Burghley in 1598. Early in 1603, when she was seventy years old, Elizabeth herself became ill. Sir John Harington tried to distract and divert her but his queen said: "When thou dost feel creeping time at the gate, these fooleries will please thee less." In March, 1603, Elizabeth died. Post horses carried the news northward to Scotland where James VI was waiting to hear that he had inherited the throne of England.

Section II

THE TUDORS AND THEIR TIMES

Henry VII.

The dockyards and fortified camp at Portsmouth, A.D. 1545. The attacking vessels are French.

Catherine of Aragon.

Henry VIII.

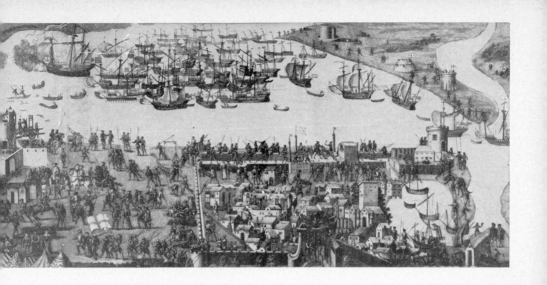

Cardinal Wolsey.

Anne Boleyn.

Holbein's original sketch for a painting of St. Thomas More and his Family.

Thomas Cromwell.

Sir Thomas Wyatt.

The ship *Jesus of Lubeck* in which Sir John Hawkins harried the Spaniard.

A page from Caxton's edition of the *Morte d'Arthur,* printed A.D. 1485.

Thomas Cranmer, Archbishop of Canterbury.

Elizabeth I, at 13 years of age.

Elizabeth the Queen.

Mary, Queen of Scots.

William Cecil, Baron Burghley.

John Knox.

The Spanish Armada in flight.

Hatfield House, Hertfordshire, a notable example of Jacobean architectural splendor.

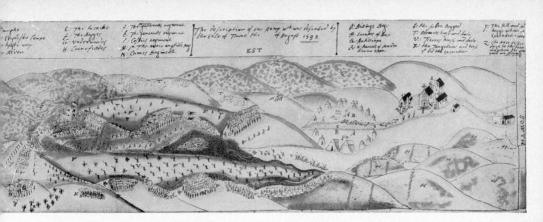

A contemporary sketch of the Irish campaign of 1598: Marshal Bagnal's English army defeated by Tyrone at the Yellow Ford of the Blackwater.

Burghley House, Northamptonshire—a monument to Cecil's success.

Compton Wynyates, on the borders of Oxfordshire and Warwickshire, a superb example of the so-called "Tudor" style.

A wedding, A.D. 1590, from a contemporary painting. Note the Tower of London across the river in the background.

CAP. XII.

odò verticitas exiſtit in ferro quouis excocto
magnete non excito.

Actenùs naturales & ingenitas cauſas, & acquiſitas
per lapidem potentias declarauimus: Nunc verò
& in excocto ferro lapide non excito, magnetica-
rum virtutum cauſæ rimandæ ſunt. Admirabiles
nobis magnes & ferrum promunt & oſtendunt ſub-
tilitates. Demonſtratum eſt anteà ſæpiùs, ferrum la-
excitum in ſeptentiones ferri & meridiem; ſed & habe-
itatem, id eſt proprias & ſingulares polares diſtinctiones,
modum magnes, aut ferrum magnete attritum. Iſtud qui-
is mirum & incredibile primùm videbatur: Ferri metallum
in fornace excoquitur, effluit ex fornace, & in magnâ maſ-
areſcit, maſſa illa diuiditur in magnis officinis, & in bacilla
tenditur, ex quibus fabri rurſus plurima componunt inſtru-
ferramenta neceſſaria. Ita variè elaboratur & in plurimas
ines eadem maſſa transformatur. Quid eſt igitur illud quod

SEPTENTRIO.

AVSTER

conſeruat

Magnetism induced in an iron bar
by a hammer stroke. A plate from
Gilbert's *De Magnete*, A.D. 1600.

THE PRINCIPALL
NAVIGATIONS,VOIA-
GES AND DISCOVERIES OF THE
English nation, made by Sea or ouer Land,
to the moſt remote and fartheſt diſtant Quarters of
the earth at any time within the compaſſe
of theſe 1500. yeeres: Deuided into three
ſeuerall parts, according to the po-
ſitions of the Regions whereunto they were directed.

The firſt, conteining the perſonall trauels of the Engliſh vnto *Indæa,Syria,A-
rabia,*the riuer *Euphrates, Babylon, Balsara,* the *Perſian* Gulfe, *Ormuz, Chaul,
Goa, India,*and many Iſlands adioyning to the South parts of *Aſia*: together with the like vnto *Ægypt,* the chiefeſt ports and places of *Africa* within and without the Streight of *Gibraltar,* and about the famous Promon-
torie of *Buona Eſperança.*

The ſecond, comprehending the worthy diſcoueries of the Engliſh towards
the North and Northeaſt by Sea, as of *Lapland, Scrikfinia, Corelia,* the Baie
of *S. Nicholas,* the Iſles of *Colgoieue, Vaigats,* and *Noua Zembla* toward the
great riuer *Ob,* with the mightie Empire of *Ruſſia,* the *Caſpian* Sea, *Georgia,
Armenia, Media, Perſia, Boghar* in *Bactria,* & diuers kingdoms of *Tartaria.*

The third and laſt, including the Engliſh valiant attempts in ſearching al-
moſt all the corners of the vaſte and new world of *America,* from 73.de-
grees of Northerly latitude Southward, to *Meta Incognita, Newfoundland,*
the maine of *Virginia,* the point of *Florida,*the Baie of *Mexico,* all the Inland of *Noua Hiſpania,* the coaſt of *Terra firma, Braſill,* the riuer of *Plate,*to
the Streight of *Magellan:* and through it, and from it in the South Sea to
Chili, Peru, Xaliſco, the Gulfe of *California, Noua Albion* vpon the backſide
of *Canada,* further then euer any Chriſtian hitherto hath pierced.

Whereunto is added the laſt moſt renowmed Engliſh Nauigation,
round about the whole Globe of the Earth.

*By Richard Hakluyt Maſter of Artes, and Student ſometime
of Chriſt-church in Oxford.*

Imprinted at London by GEORGE BISHOP
and RALPH NEWBERIE, Deputies to
CHRISTOPHER BARKER, Printer to the
Queenes moſt excellent Maieſtie.

1589.

Title-page of Hakluyt's collection of voyages.

*EXERCITATIO
ANATOMICA DE
MOTV CORDIS ET SAN-
GVINIS IN ANIMALI-
BVS,
GVILIELMI HARVEI ANGLI,
Medici Regii, & Profeſſoris Anatomiæ in Col-
legio Medicorum Londinenſi.

FRANCOFVRTI,
Sumptibus GVILIELMI FITZERI.
ANNO M. DC. XXVIII.

le-page of Harvey's
ok on the circulation of
blood.

THE FAERIE
QVEENE:

Diſpoſed into twelue books,
Faſhioning
XII. Morall vertues.

LONDON
Printed for William Ponſonbie.
1590.

Spenser's *Faerie
Queene,* A.D. 1590.

*FRANCISCI
DE VERVLAMIO,
Summi Angliæ
CANCELLARII
Inſtauratio*

Multi pertranſibunt & augebitur ſcientia

ANNO   1620

LONDINI
Apud Ioannem Billium Typo-
graphum Regium.

Title-page of Bacon's *Instauratio
Magna,* A.D. 1620.

Sir
Francis
Drake

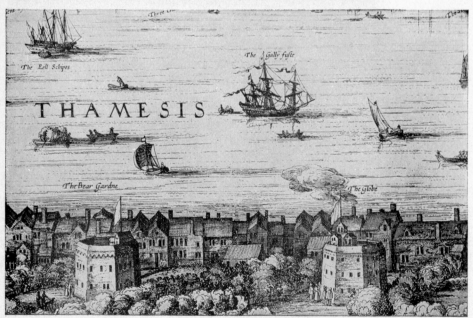

The Bear Garden and the Globe Playhouse, A.D. 1616.

Chapter 15

THE GOLDEN AGE
MEN AND IDEAS

"THE heavens themselves," wrote William Shakespeare, "the planets and this centre, Observe degree, priority, and place." The Tudor ideals of order and harmony, the links of a great chain of being, the inherent sinfulness of disorder and rebellion, all were stressed in places as far apart as the homilies and Lord Burghley's *Execution of Justice in England* (1583). "Every degree of people, in their vocation, calling, and office, hath appointed to them their duty and order. Some are in high places, some are in low. . . . Remove this divine order and there reigneth all abuse, carnal liberty, enormity, sin, and babylonical confusion." The whole Christian universe was conceived to be under divine ordinance. Chief Justice Catlin summarized a part of the temper of the times in 1572: "It is the chiefest point of the duty of every natural and reasonable man to know his prince and his head, to be true to his head and prince. . . . We must first look unto God, the high prince of all princes, and then to the Queen's Majesty."

At the same time, in an age of polemics and propaganda, every religious sect or minority was driven by the logic of the situation to state its will to live in terms of political right. In such sects and revolutions the ideas of freedom and equality, the New Testament principles, appeared in a brighter light. In the Middle Ages they had been obscured by Aristotle, St. Augustine, and the Roman law. Emerging slowly was the social dynamite of the idea that a natural state should be a commonwealth of free citizens.

In the reign of Elizabeth, alongside the "harmony and order" ideals of Sir Thomas Smith, the ministers of the government, the established church, and all the rest, were the new stirrings of a new age towards a challenge that was to shake and alter the whole concept of a man's relation to his prince, his church, and to his fellows in a free society. Shakespeare might write of "the ancient service of the antique

261

world, Which sweats for meed, not for promotion." The generation that followed him contained many men whose values were far different.

There were soon to be strangely confused and disruptive ideas about the destiny of England under a Protestant Jehovah. Was English imperialism a part of the divine plan? Should there be government of the church by Independent congregations? or by bishops? or by presbyters? Was the religion of Englishmen connected with the rise of capitalism? Was prosperity the barometer of godliness? Within and without the little island girt by its silver sea questions of this kind were shortly to be asked. The varying answers that were given were not calculated to contribute to harmony, order, or "the unity and married calm of states."

The Elizabethan years were years of energy, action, display. Many men of the upper and middle classes were not anxious to live "dully sluggardized" at home or to wear out their youth "with shapeless idleness." Some, said Shakespeare, went "to the warres to try their fortune there; some, to discover islands farre away; some, to the studious Universities." At a later day Robert Burton in the *Anatomy of Melancholy* wrote: "Peregrination charms our senses with such unspeakable and sweet variety . . . Pitty his case that from his cradle to his old age beholds the same still; still, still, the same, the same." The Elizabethans were eager to have new experiences, to buy new things, to see new sights. A large number toured the Continent "whence they bring home," wrote Samuel Purchas unkindly, "a few smattering terms, flattering garbes, foppish fancies, foolish guises and disguises, the vanities of neighbour nations without furthering their knowledge of God, the world, or themselves."

Commerce and industry provided the wealth that enabled Elizabethans to meet many of their desires. The nation, despite some sharp depressions, became increasingly prosperous. The government frequently interfered to regulate the economic and social affairs of England. In the years of a rising national state the local regulation of craft and industrial guilds was slowly replaced, or almost so, by central controls. The guilds had already been heavily hit by the confiscation of their religious and charitable funds under Henry VIII and Edward VI. They fought sturdily to salvage something of their power.

Local difficulties were frequent and considerable. The records of the Merchant Adventurers of Newcastle show that in January, 1564, an attempt was made to prevent the shipment of lead to London because "it hath in time past been a chief trade and living to the brethren of this Fellowship, and now of late the whole occupying and trade of the said commodity is growing into the hands of Londoners and other foreigners." The Newcastle defenders of the lead trade, aware of the "great hurt, decay and utter impoverishing" of their Fellowship that threatened, ordered that any brother of the Fellowship who bought up or shipped lead "for the use of the said foreigners," or otherwise helped them, would be dismissed from the freedom of the Fellowship. Newcastle members were all instructed to "let no houses, no cellars to Londoners, nor other strangers." Such attempts to impede economic destiny and large-scale capitalistic enterprise were almost always ineffective.

The advance of prosperity was hastened by a number of government measures. In 1560 Elizabeth struck at "the hideous monster of base money." In 1560 thousands of debased silver coins were called into a special mint and remade into coins of standard quality. Debased gold coins were also called in and the possessors were paid for the actual value of the gold in their coins. After a fixed date the debased money still in circulation ceased to be legal tender. Thus one of the great evils begun by Henry VIII was remedied.

Elizabeth's government also attempted to erase some evils in the labor situation. The enclosures had compelled many men to leave the rural areas; large numbers of artisans, fleeing from rigid guild controls in the towns, had remained to live unsupervised lives in the country. In 1563 the Statute of Artificers provided for "a uniform order, prescribed and limited, concerning the wages and other orders for apprentices, servants, and labourers," and stated that "there is good hope that it will come to pass that the same law, being duly executed, should banish idleness, advance husbandry, and yield unto the hired person both in the time of scarcity and in the time of plenty a convenient proportion of wages." This act was not repealed until 1813. Artisans were required to serve an apprenticeship for seven years. All physically fit men who were not apprentices or artisans were ordered to labor as agricultural workers when needed. The justices of the peace, supervised by the central privy council, were empowered to fix annually the wages for their locality in accordance with "the plenty or scarcity of the time."

Throughout the Tudor age much was said and written about the social and economic problems resulting from poverty. Voluntary charity and parish relief were alike inadequate. Several acts, particularly in the reign of Henry VIII, were passed to deal with rogues, beggars, and vagabonds. The monasteries and chantries no longer existed to give charity. In 1572 Elizabeth provided for the compulsory collection of poor rates, thus superseding the earlier voluntary alms system. Overseers of the poor were set up to administer poor relief.

In 1598 and in 1601 the mass of existing legislation was supplemented and codified. For example, the act of 1598 provided severe penalties for "jugglers, tinkers, and peddlers" and "seafaring men pretending the loss of their ships, . . . pretending themselves to be Egyptians . . . feigning themselves to have knowledge in physiognomy, palmistry, or other like crafty science." The act of 1601 provided that there should be overseers of the poor in each parish. They were given authority to levy a tax, or rate, on all property and owners to provide funds for the assistance of the poor. For physically fit paupers the overseers were to find work. Unemployed men who would not work were publicly whipped or shut up in houses of correction. This act remained essentially unchanged until 1834. Measures such as these helped to increase public order and security; they also improved the lot of those who were too ill or too old to help themselves.

An age throbbing with life, bold adventures, speculation, and politics brought both wealth and ruin. The themes of "fortune" and "mutability" were not in Elizabethan literature merely by chance. Tudor ideas about fortune were shaped by many factors. For example, the study of alchemy, astrology, sorcery, and witchcraft was widespread. In 1563 Parliament passed an "Act against Conjurations, Enchantments, and Witchcraft," at a time when England was witnessing a new agitation against witches. John Jewel, Elizabeth's new bishop of Salisbury, wrote in 1559 of the wicked work of the witches. "Your grace's subjects pine away even unto death. Their colour fadeth, their flesh rotteth, their speech is benumbed, their senses are bereft."

Superstition led to social disturbances when conjurers and others of their ilk prophesied Elizabeth's death. There was thus a political motive for persecution of simpleton peasant girls and daft old women. In London, the center of belief in witches, numerous chapbooks were published, describing notorious trials for witchcraft. Only a few men, such as Reginald Scott, who published in 1584 his *Discovery of Witchcraft,* opposed the superstition.

There was but small advance in natural science, which remained largely outside the universities. At the end of the sixteenth century William Gilbert published his researches on magnetism and Francis Bacon his *Advancement of Learning.* The slow and guarded investigations going forward on the Continent were not imitated or equalled in England. Nor was the influence of the Renaissance in the field of medicine in England immediately significant. The ferment caused upon the Continent by the work of the European physician Vesalius raised but feeble echoes, even in Oxford, Cambridge, and London. Little was known of Paracelsus but his name. The ancient authority of Galen's contributions to Greek medicine may have been weakened within a restricted circle, but to most physicians he still remained the "prince of physic" and the "lantern of surgeons." Before the achievements of Mayerne and Harvey, English medical advance lay largely in the field of preventive medicine in dealing with the plague. There were not many skilled and learned physicians and competent surgeons in Tudor England; among those of deserved reputation were Andrew Boorde, Thomas Vicary, William Clowes, Thomas Gale, and a very few others. Most of these depended for their skill and knowledge upon their experiences in the army or their studies in Padua, Leyden, Basel, Montpellier, and Heidelberg.

The suppression of the monasteries, guilds, and chantries had increased the need for public care of the afflicted poor, for in earlier days the monks had frequently maintained hospitals. With the dissolution of the religious houses and with the increase in enclosures the cripples, lepers, discharged soldiers, rogues, and beggars trekked desperately into London and other cities. Those with loathsome or contagious diseases were usually confined in the lazar-houses at Knightsbridge and Hammersmith and the warning clang of the leper's bell became daily more familiar. In London the hospitals were St. Bartholomew, Bridewell, St. Thomas's, Bethlehem, Christ's Hospital, and the Savoy. For the great city there were no more. St. Bartholomew could house only a hundred patients; Bridewell was in fact a prison hospital; St. Thomas's could accommodate only about two hundred aged and sick. In spite of the work the hospitals attempted to do, their success, in proportion to the need, was small.

The larger part of the practice of medicine was in the hands of men who possessed few pretensions to medical knowledge and, frequently, even fewer to respectability. Medical schools in England were still lamentably weak. The great bequest of Linacre had almost no immediate effect upon medical education in Oxford. In the period 1571–1600 Oxford gave only forty-seven medical degrees. The best published medical work came from the pens of men who had been in the army. It was from the army that Thomas Gale returned to write his *Treatise on Gunshot* (1548). The elder William Clowes, who produced some of the best surgical writings of his age, obtained most of his clinical experience serving with the English army in the Low Countries, where "bad surgeons slew more than the enemy."

At home, in England, it was difficult to eliminate ignorant and often rascally practitioners who deluded the sick and the sound. Andrew Boorde, in his *Breviary* (1542) raised a loud lament: "O Lord, what a great detriment is this to a noble science, that ignorant persons will enterprise to meddle with the ministrations of physic." Some were declared to be in league with the apothecaries who were accused in many an attack of selling "chalk for cheese" and "druggy baggage." Men were redrawing the map of the world, but the clinical study of disease was just beginning. When there was no English pharmacopeia and the apothecaries still had no charter to sell or purchase drugs, when the men of medicine guarded jealously their medieval secrets, the dawn of the medical Renaissance was slow in breaking.

More obvious to contemporaries than the slow, painful advances of medical knowledge were the achievements of their architects; the building of new dwelling houses and palaces; the outburst of energy among the middle class and the aristocracy. In the seventeenth century, as will be described later in Chapter 20, the English architects, led by Inigo Jones and Christopher Wren, were to blend the classical tradition with earlier English elements; thus was formed the Angloclassic style, balanced, unified, precise, and sometimes with the powerful simplicity that the hand of genius can alone create. The main Elizabethan treatise on architecture was published in 1563. This book, written by John Shute under the title *The First and Chief Grounds of Architecture,* was based on a treatise written by Vitruvius in the reign of the Roman Emperor Augustus. The manuscript of Vitruvius, discovered in the fifteenth century, became a manual for sixteenth century architecture, especially for the great Italian Palladio, who published in 1570 his *Four Books of Architecture.*

As greater wealth and rising standards of living came to Elizabethan England the new domestic architecture attempted to blend native and foreign elements. Classical influences were often strong, but no purely classical building appeared until Inigo Jones built the banqueting hall at Whitehall in the next century. In the dwelling houses the transitional note was particularly strong. Solid, comfortable structures sprang up. "Outrageous is the great and sumptuous building of our time," wrote a contemporary. "It consumeth all the great timber of the realm, which should serve to make us ships for our walls and defence, and within a while it will force us either to build our vessels in strange countries or else to yield ourselves for a prey to our enemies. Also it beggareth the greatest number of them that take pleasure therein and maketh them unable to serve their country; and there be many more great houses already than there be men of living able to uphold."

It was usual to build the larger Tudor houses in the form of a capital E or a capital H. The windows were large; the roofs were gabled and adorned with finials and chimneys. The main doorway was often surrounded by classical columns and decorated with Dutch scrolls and the owner's coat of arms. In the interior the ceilings were heavily molded, the woodwork richly carved; the fireplace dominated the main hall proudly. Everywhere was color, carving, ornament, decoration.

In music Elizabethan England led the world. Englishmen first translated the Italian madrigals; then they began to write their own music and their own words. The beautiful English madrigals excited the praise and delight of all Europe. Many of the most vivacious and electric lyric poems were written to be sung. Fine and rich church music carried on a long and splendid tradition. England was a nation interested in singing, composing, playing on musical instruments. There were no concert halls; but there were the parlors, the hearth, and the habit of song. The golden genius of William Byrd, greatest of English composers, of Thomas Tallis, of Orlando Gibbons, of Thomas Morley, would alone have placed London beyond challenge as the first and most exciting of the musical capitals of Europe. "The isle is full of noises, sounds and sweet airs, that give delight and hurt not."

LITERATURE

It is quite correct to describe the Elizabethan years as being comprehensive, disorderly, bubbling with a zest for life, extravagant, sensuous. Nevertheless, it is easy to give or to obtain a warped perspective, if nothing more is written or said. The crosscurrents of economic distress and prosperity; the patient quietness of those who tilled the fields and died; the sober parish priests whose headstones are now crumbled away; the political pressures that made men move swiftly, then as now, from the magnificent and the honest to the petty and the unclean—all these things, and many more, enter into the total of the life of any age. History is more than a section in the library.

The wide range of interests and activities of the Elizabethans is clearly revealed in the outburst of literature that made the age one of the greatest in the world's history. The vital springs of the Renaissance spirit, Christian and worldly humanism, the impulse of exploration and discovery, the soaring nationalism, the sense of rapidly expanding horizons, the training of the judgment through logic and rhetoric, formed a few of the stimulating wellsprings of literature. In the confused magnificence of the latter sixteenth century no common denominator can easily be found. The traffic and disturbance of ideas sometimes found expression in wheeling Ciceronian periods; sometimes in copious word-schemes; sometimes in the diction of common life. There was often a delight in language, words, and novelty of expression, in vigorous and energetic styles, or in the majestic dignity of a slow river of prose or poetry.

Ancient and foreign works were made available to a wide circle of Englishmen in a steady flow of translations. Early in the century the earl of Surrey proudly translated the *Aeneid*. In 1543 the Princess Elizabeth translated a mystical poem written by Queen Margaret of Navarre and presented it to her stepmother, Catherine Parr, as a New Year's gift. In 1548 John Bale printed it under the title *A Godly Meditation of the Christian Soul*. This poem pointed the way towards a new species of English mystical religious literature standing between the Platonic poetry of profane love and the writings of ordinary religious devotion. In 1593 Elizabeth translated Boethius' *Consolation of Philosophy*. In 1566 William Painter's *Palace of Pleasure,* a collection of stories translated from the French, Greek, Italian, and Latin, provided a rich source for Elizabethan dramatists. In 1579 Thomas North published a translation of a translation of Plutarch's *Lives*. George Chapman translated the *Iliad* (1598); Philemon Holland, "the translator general," put Pliny, Livy, and Suetonius into English. John Florio's translation of Montaigne's essays (1603) and Hoby's translation of Castiglione's *Courtier* still stand as works of art.

In English prose there was evident early in Elizabeth's reign much extravagance, pedantry, and aping of foreign models. Roger Ascham and others loudly protested: "He that will write well in any tongue must speak as the common people do, and think as wise men do. . . . Many English writers have not done so, but using strange words, as Latin, French, and Italian, do make all things dark." The height of this affectation was reached in John Lyly's *Euphues* (1579), whence arose the vogue of "Euphuism." In the reaction there was a marked advance towards clarity and brevity of expression, clearly seen, for example, in the devotional tracts, dialogues, and books of characters of Nicholas Breton, professional and prolific writer, courtier, and soldier.

The same pattern of change in style can be noted in the work of the wandering enthusiast George Gascoigne, whose exciting career as a courtier, lawyer, poet, and soldier embraces nearly all aspects of Elizabethan society. The writings of Thomas Lodge, who lived "under the tyranny of a gnawing sense of neglect," show similar phases. His romance *Rosalynde*, from which Shakespeare obtained the plot of *As You Like It*, was probably the best piece of prose fiction of Elizabeth's reign. An excellent illustration of the beginning of a transition from the cult of *Euphues* to the great prose of the last decade of the Tudor century can be found by contrasting Sir Philip Sidney's *Arcadia* with his *Defence of Poesie*.

The clenched fists of the writers of pamphlets and controversial literature also did much to hammer English prose into an effective instrument. To a lesser extent the long pages of the chronicles of the period aided in the development of narrative style. The discursive chroniclers have provided much information about the Tudor age, despite their frequent excursions into the dramatic and fanciful. Important among the mass of such works were Richard Hakluyt's *Principal Navigations*, first published in 1589; Edward Hall's vivid *Chronicles*, written in the reign of Henry VIII; Raphael Holinshed's *Chronicles* (1577), and John Stowe's *Annales* (1580) and his *Survey of London* (1598). William Camden's *Britannia* was a reasonably systematic survey of the antiquities of England, partly based upon the notes of John Leland, antiquary and librarian to Henry VIII. The delightful *Perambulations of Kent* of William Lambarde gave a remarkable picture of rural society under Elizabeth.

These writers, and many others, were writing to show Englishmen something of the greatness of England in an age of national pride and enthusiasm for queen and country. Their books were popular at a time when men were conscious of the new role their nation had taken in Europe and its manifest destiny in the new world of tomorrow.

The crowning achievements of the Elizabethan prose writers were Sir Francis Bacon's familiar *Essays* and Richard Hooker's *Laws of Ecclesiastical Polity,* the prose masterpiece of the age. Hooker's famous explanation and defense of the position of the Anglican church contained much of the Aristotelian and medieval conception of the universe and the state and man's place in both. Hooker's organic, hierarchical idea of the nature of a good state and a good individual was based on the theology of the Anglican church. His ideas have so deeply permeated English thought through recent centuries that today even Nonconformists tend sometimes to look upon the king as head of the Nonconformist churches. In many respects the work of Hooker still contains the basic political philosophy of the Anglican church and, to a lesser extent, of the modern Conservative political party.

Richard Hooker disliked the Puritan exaltation of the Scriptures as the sole rule of life. A constitutional monarchy, he declared, was "that most sweet rule of kingly government." Law, he asserted, was "the very soul of a politic body." In the comely paragraphs of his modulated prose Hooker described law as "the divine order of the universe." The seat of law "is in the bosom of God whose voice is the harmony of the world." To law all things in heaven and earth must do homage, for law is "the mother of their peace and joy." In the union of the prelacy and monarchy Hooker saw the happiness and stability of England. For him, "the commonwealth is like a harp or melodious instrument," a delicate preserver of public tranquillity.

In almost every page of Hooker's great work there was a reverence for England's historic past, an insistence upon the importance of continuity in the corporate life of the church and state, an emphasis upon the idea of balance and compromise in all aspects of political and religious life. When Richard Hooker identified the church and commonwealth as different aspects of the same system he was writing not only for the Tudor age but for some ends and ideals still widely held today. The foundation of morality, in the judgment of Hooker, was to be found in the religion of the state, in objective order and principle binding individuals together to themselves and to God.

The supreme achievements of the rich Elizabethan literature were in poetry and drama. The steadily swelling stream of sonnets, lyrics, epics, and pastorals reached its full flood late in Elizabeth's reign. It is impossible to do justice to these poets; they were so many, and they were so great. Sir Walter Raleigh's lovely "Walsingham" and "Give me my scallop-shell of quiet" stand side by side in beauty with the gems of Robert Southwell, Catholic poet martyred at Tyburn in 1595; and Southwell, in turn, is matched in the words of Thomas Nashe suggested by the plague year of 1593: "Beauty is but a flower . . . Dust has closed Helen's eye; I am sick, I must die. Lord, have mercy on us!" In the long parade of golden names there is recalled the gnomic lines of Fulke Greville; the voices of Ben Jonson, Thomas Dekker, and Thomas Ford on the edge of the Jacobean age; the *Astrophel and Stella* sonnets of Sir Philip Sidney: "With how sad steps, O moon, thou climb'st the skies! How silently, and with how wan a face!"

In 1579 Edmund Spenser published his *Shepherd's Calendar* and later his great epic the *Faerie Queene*. Spenser, the friend of Leicester, Raleigh, and Sidney, received an Irish estate from the queen in 1586. There he wrote the *Faerie Queene*. Elizabeth was pleased with the first three books, published in 1590, and gave Spenser a pension of fifty pounds a year. In 1596 Spenser published the second three books of his epic. Two years later he was forced to flee in the Tyrone rebellion; his house was sacked and burned. Three months afterwards he died in England. His body was buried by that of his master, Geoffrey Chaucer, in the south transept of Westminster Abbey.

Cast in the form of a medieval romance, the *Faerie Queene* is an elaborate allegorical defense of Protestantism and a glorification of Queen Elizabeth as England's champion against the falsehood and vice of Rome. Each character represents at the same time one living man or woman and one abstract virtue or vice. The first book of the *Faerie Queene* is the most successful, although there are many beautiful and graphic passages throughout the poem. One of the best is the description of the dragon before it is slain by the Red Cross Knight.

"For griefe thereof and divelish despight
From his infernall fournace forth he threw
Huge flames, that dimmed all the heaven's light
Enrold in duskisk smoke and brimstone blew;
As burning Aetna from his boyling stew
Doth belch out flames, and rockes in peeces broke,
And ragged ribs of mountains molten new
Enwrapt in coleblacke clouds and filthy smoke
That all the land with stench, and heaven with horror choke."

In the years before the Armada the English drama as yet gave small promise of the glory that was so swiftly to burst over the western world. Farces, masques, and interludes had developed early in the century. About 1541 Nicholas Udall, headmaster of Eton, had written the first English comedy, *Ralph Roister Doyster,* with much borrowed baggage from Latin models. In 1561 the first English tragedy, *Gorboduc,* written in blank verse by Thomas Norton and Thomas Sackville, was presented before Queen Elizabeth.

Strong impetus was given to the development of dramatic writing by the increase in the number of theatres. By 1574 several London inns had converted their yards into places of entertainment. Plays were licensed by the lord mayor and aldermen. In 1576 James Burbage, famous actor in the earl of Leicester's company, built a theatre in Holywell, on the edge of the city and outside the obnoxious control of the city authorities. In 1577 another playhouse, the Curtain, appeared; in 1587 the Rose was built in Southwark; in 1595 the Swan was erected near Blackfriars Bridge; and in 1599 the famous Globe was opened. These theatres became very popular, the meeting place of "silk and plush and all the wits."

Meanwhile a group of university men began to develop the new English drama, especially after the defeat of the Armada gave impetus to confidence and national spirit. The variety and range of that drama was astonishing; it moved all the way from the melodramatic and turbulent duels and suicides, from the numerous corpses in Thomas Kyd's *Spanish Tragedy* to the jolly and relaxed scenes of Thomas Dekker's *Shoemaker's Holiday*. Robert Greene's *The Honourable History of Friar Bacon and Friar Bungay* is an excellent example of the Elizabethan love of life, action, novelty: "Persia, down her Volga by canoes, Send down the secrets of her spicery."

One of the most original and vigorous of the university writers was Christopher Marlowe, author of many remarkable plays: *Tamburlaine* (1587), the *Tragical History of Doctor Faustus* (1588), the *Jew of Malta* (1593), and sections of the second and third parts of *Henry VI*, later finished by Shakespeare. Before the wilful and intellectual Marlowe died in a tavern brawl at the age of twenty-nine he had written many an unrestrained and soaring line; he stands among the world's great poets. Here, for example, is Dr. Faustus, who has sold his soul to the Devil, searching for what is forbidden to man, in the limbo between heaven and hell:

> "The stars move still, time runs, the clock will strike,
> The Devil will come, and Faustus must be damned.
> Oh, I'll leap up to my God! Who pulls me down?
> See, see where Christ's blood streams in the firmament!
> One drop would save my soul—half a drop . . . See
>   where God
> Stretcheth out his arm and bends his ireful brows.
> Mountain and hills, come and fall on me,
> And hide me from the heavy wrath of God!"

The awakening muse of the drama also produced William Shakespeare, without a peer in any age, in any language. Shakespeare was born in 1564, the son of a tradesman; he did not belong to the university group; his formal education had been obtained at the old grammar school of Stratford-on-Avon. When he came up to London there was nobody to know that he was to produce about forty plays, *Venus and Adonis, Lucrece,* and the sonnets.

About 1591 Shakespeare wrote *Love's Labours Lost.* After the early period of the influence of Marlowe the comedies began to appear: *The Merchant of Venice, A Midsummer Night's Dream, Twelfth Night,* and *As You Like It.* The great series of tragedies was written between 1599 and 1609: *Julius Caesar, Hamlet, Othello, King Lear.*

Then, at the end, came the new notes of *Cymbeline, A Winter's Tale, The Tempest.* Shakespeare's imperishable words, the immortal characters of Hamlet, Lear, Othello, Falstaff, Shylock, the scenes where Sir Toby Belch, champion of cakes and ale, speaks to the Malvolios of all time, these are among the highest reaches of human genius.

THE AGE OF ADVENTURE

Greatest of the Tudor writers who recorded the dramatic achievements of English sailors beyond the narrow seas was the clergyman and Anglo-Welsh graduate of Oxford, Richard Hakluyt the Younger. He spent much time and probably more money than he could afford in collecting, translating, and publishing everything he could discover about the voyages of Englishmen. The list of his works is long, but he is best known today for his *Principal Navigations, Voyages, and Discoveries of the English Nation,* mentioned earlier in this chapter. The first edition of the *Principal Navigations* appeared in 1589. Ten years later it was published in three volumes.

Hakluyt's *Principal Navigations* and his other works are filled with concrete arguments for new explorations and the advantages England would derive from them. There were also the constant threads of pride and patriotism. "Let me speak a word," runs a long sentence of the prose epic of the *Principal Navigations,* "of that just commendation which our nation doth indeed richly deserve; it cannot be denied but as in all former ages they have been men full of activity, stirrers abroad and searchers of the remote parts of the world, so in this most famous and peerless government of Her Most Excellent Majesty Queen Elizabeth, her subjects through the special blessing and assistance of God in searching the most opposite quarters and corners of the world, and to speak plainly, in compassing the vast globe of the earth more than once, have excelled all the nations and peoples of the earth." A contemporary of Hakluyt remarked: "History without that so much neglected study of Geography is sick of a half dead palsy."

From Richard Hakluyt historians have drawn much of their knowledge of the deeds of Englishmen who ranged along unknown coasts "further than any Christian passed." In the pages of Hakluyt and Samuel Purchas, a rather careless Cambridge clergyman whose *Purchas His Pilgrimage* was published in 1612, 1614, 1617, and 1626, there was set forth clearly the idea of these geographically minded clergymen that the expansion of England and the extension of British commerce was part of a divine mission. Many men, besides ships' captains and company preachers, doubtless held the same unquestioning belief that if they sought first to extend the kingdom of God many material blessings would be theirs. The outburst of maritime activity in Elizabeth's reign also arose from the hope of gain by plundering the hated Catholic Spaniards; from profits in trade; from a very human desire for adventure; from patriotic pressures; and often from a combination of all of these motives.

Peaceful commerce continued steadily to expand. The English and the Dutch, unlike the Spaniards, learned how to trade with all the world. English ships carried many kinds of cargoes over the European sea lanes. For example, Richard Newman of Worcester "sailed as a supercargo in a ship bound to Lisbon with wheat and flax, where they took in a cargo of sugars and other things and returned therewith to England; and from England they went to Antwerp where they loaded with linen stuffs for the city of Oporto in Portugal, where they took in a cargo of sugars, cotton, and Brazil wood which they carried to Antwerp. From Antwerp they proceeded to London, with hops for beer; and from London they went to Leghorn in Italy with flax, stuffs, copper, and lead; and from Leghorn to Civita Vecchia, where they took in a cargo of stone alum for cloth, and brought it to London."

One of the first of the great traders and buccaneers was Sir John Hawkins; he was the son of the Plymouth merchant William Hawkins, who had carried on trade with Brazil and West Africa, dealing in Guinea pepper and dyewoods. Sir John Hawkins shared the resentment of his fellow Englishmen at the claims of the Catholic Portuguese and Spaniards who had set up trading monopolies in America and Asia. The "papal line of demarcation" of 1493 was considered by many Englishmen to be an insolent and unjustified affront. Hawkins began the practice of selling Negroes from Guinea to the Spanish colonists in the West Indies. The Spanish planters were forbidden to trade with Englishmen; but they were glad to buy the human cargo Hawkins had to sell. Hawkins' slave fleet, led by the queen's ship *Jesus of Lubeck,* did a lucrative trade. One voyage yielded a profit of sixty per cent.

In 1568, the Spanish viceroy of Mexico treacherously attacked Hawkins at Vera Cruz. Hawkins lost four ships and many men; but he and his cousin Francis Drake escaped. The incident added to Drake's hatred of Spain. He never tried again to trade with the Spaniards, but became a privateer. Queen Elizabeth secretly supported him, as she backed all the Devon sea dogs who harried the Spanish Main, and collected her share of the plunder. Piracy, of course, could not be officially countenanced. Lord Burghley condemned it as "detestable."

Francis Drake, and many others, sought to part the Spaniards from their wealth. In 1572, for example, Drake captured a large consignment of Spanish gold from the mines of Peru. Drake, a violent daredevil, soon became a terror to Spain. In 1577 he passed from the Atlantic through the Strait of Magellan and sailed up the Pacific coast of South America. The hold of his ship, the *Golden Hind,* was soon filled with treasure seized from startled Spaniards.

Drake pushed north to the Vancouver region, seeking a northern route to the Atlantic. Failing to find it, he dropped back to San Francisco, claiming the territory for England. Then he crossed the Pacific, sailed round the Cape of Good Hope, and reached Plymouth harbor three years after his departure. He was the first Englishman to circumnavigate "the whole globe of the earth." The value of his booty was about five hundred thousand pounds. Elizabeth took forty per cent of the loot and, despite the protests of Spain, knighted Drake on the deck of the *Golden Hind* in the presence of the French ambassador.

Meanwhile Englishmen were seeking new routes of commerce to the near and far East. In 1578 trading privileges were obtained from the Sultan of Turkey; a Turkish company was set up by London merchants. This enterprise was united with the Venice Company in 1592 to form the Levant Company, which carried on trade for two hundred years. In 1583 John Newberrie and Ralph Fitch started together from Syria and travelled to the western coast of India. Fitch went on to Bengal and down the eastern coast. Anthony Jenkinson, an agent of the Muscovy Company, opened up a land route to Persia. In 1591 James Lancaster sailed around the Cape of Good Hope to Ceylon and Malacca. The Yorkshireman Martin Frobisher made three voyages (1576–1578) in search of the Northwest Passage. Captain John Davis searched again for the Passage, without success.

In 1600 there was added to the ranks of the Merchant Adventurers, the Muscovy Company, the Levant Company, and the rest, a new business venture. This was the East India Company, formed by a group of London merchants as a joint stock enterprise. They could not have dreamed of the mighty organization they were beginning when the charter was granted by the crown on December 31, 1600.

In 1578 Sir Humphrey Gilbert, half brother of Sir Walter Raleigh, received a patent for "the planting of our people in America." In 1583 Gilbert founded the first colony in British North America on the dreary coast of Newfoundland. On the return voyage his ship went down in an Atlantic storm and he was lost. Gilbert, who had written a pamphlet to prove the existence of the Northwest Passage, had seen the possibility of colonization on a fairly large scale in America. "We might inhabit some part of those countries and settle there such needy people of our country, which now trouble the commonwealth."

Two years later the versatile Sir Walter Raleigh obtained Elizabeth's permission to send out another colonizing expedition. Under the command of Sir Richard Grenville a hundred pioneers sailed over the Atlantic to settle on Roanoke Island off the coast of what is now North Carolina. The colony was not a success. A second group of one hundred and fifty colonists disappeared completely. Thus ended England's first attempts to set "plantations" overseas. In 1595 Raleigh made a voyage in search of the fabulous city of El Dorado, a voyage that gave England her claim to British Guiana. Meanwhile, he was credited with bringing both the potato and tobacco to the attention of Europeans.

Such were a few of the many expressions of the vigorous energies of the Elizabethan adventurers. England was indeed upon the highway of the world. The achievements of her mariners made an enormous impression upon their contemporaries. Men like Drake, Gilbert, Grenville, Hawkins, and Raleigh, pushing forward England's water frontiers, stood forth as symbols of the daring spirit of a new age.

ELIZABETHAN GOVERNMENT

During the golden age of Elizabeth there were also major developments in the practice of government. These were years of apprenticeship for the house of commons. The greatest Parliamentarian of the reign was the queen herself. "Sure she did play well her tables," wrote Sir John Harington, "to gain obedience thus without constraint." Elizabeth was well aware of the greatness of her position. She was aware also that the house of commons "out of a reverent regard" would be unwilling to pursue policies and adopt attitudes "offending the Queen's Majesty very much." If, as happened on occasion, they meddled with matters of state or ventured to discuss the prerogative, Elizabeth "left no doubting whose daughter she was."

Early in the reign of Elizabeth several petitions from the house of commons requested her to marry. A large pamphlet literature arose. To pamphlets and petitions the queen had one answer: "It is unfitting and unmeet for you to require them that may command, or to frame my will to your fantasy." In such cases conciliation was always mingled with reproof. Part of a subsidy might be remitted or monopolies cancelled. Often the commons were soothed by sentences that made them for the moment forget the reprimand: "I will never conclude anything that shall be prejudicial to the realm." It was otherwise with her successor, a Scotsman whom they neither loved nor admired.

The interests of the queen were also served in the commons by an able and devoted group of councillors. In 1539 a statute had provided that no councillor should have a vote in the house of commons solely because of his office under the crown. Under Elizabeth several councillors who were commoners got themselves legally elected to the house of commons. Then they had a vote in the house and they were able to influence and frequently to dictate the policies and attitudes of the members. The canny Cecils "sate near the chair," together with Sir Francis Walsingham, who thought "the proper position of Parliament was to serve the interests of the Crown." Sir Francis Bacon also had his place. It is not surprising that many in the commons feared to challenge the will of the councillors and to bring upon themselves the frown of the queen. The way to preferment lay in conciliation and submission.

To the direct intervention of the queen and the pervasive influence of the council in the house and in committees may be added the importance of the speaker. His position and prestige assisted further in preventing the growth of opposition to the policy of the government. The speaker was always a royal nominee. He was indeed the important link between the crown and the commons. It was he who recognized those who desired to speak from the floor. He determined the course of business and what subjects were to be discussed.

There was neither increase in authority nor change in form in the house of commons under Elizabeth. The development that occurred was a development in a manner certainly unintended, and perhaps unobserved, by the queen and her council. The increase in the competency of the house of commons during the later years of Elizabeth's reign was chiefly dependent upon two changes. The first was a distinct growth of self-consciousness, the self-consciousness of a corporate body. The second was an increase of enthusiasm and interest sharpened by experience in parliamentary procedure and practice. There was no idea of constitutional advantage in the movements of the house of commons during the reign of Elizabeth. And yet heightened interest and increased experience prepared the way for a generation of men who knew not fear of the royal prerogative and were not coerced by the dread of a sovereign's wrath.

The literary, patriotic, and religious ferment that marked the coming of the Renaissance to England was concomitant with an increased interest in political affairs. A new upper middle class had arisen, and its younger members had gained at the universities more than an education in the classics. By interlocking family connections and by association with other students of the upper middle class they had become aware of a feeling of unity and understanding and sympathy. With this class-consciousness fully awakened, young men turned to literature, to religion, and to politics. The sense of unity filtered far beyond the immediate circles of university students and graduates to become, in this powerful middle class, a significant force in thought and action throughout the nation. No longer was attendance at the house of commons a duty; it became a privilege.

The experiences of the university were often carried into the political sphere. Young men of this new and powerful class frequently looked forward to a career in Parliament. At Westminster they felt themselves bound to their fellows by friendship, common background at the universities, social connections, and the possession of wealth. So it was that this important sense of unity was carried into the house of commons. At the same time, many justices of the peace took their private and local wisdom to Westminster. By association with other representatives in the commons men who had little experience in state questions sought eagerly the "coyners of news" and the opinions, experiences, and prejudices of their fellows. Frequently they developed an interest, an enthusiasm, an earnest desire for experience in politics and state-craft. In 1601 Sir Robert Cecil was "glad to see the Parliament so full, which towards the end used to grow thin." Many members were returned for several Parliaments.

There arose also in the commons an increasing care and courtesy in debate and new modes of procedure and practice. Such developments were accompanied by a heightened watchfulness to safeguard precedent and privilege through the preparation of parliamentary *Journals*. It was fortunate, indeed, for the *Journals* were to be of high importance under the Stuarts in the consolidation of many new or disputed powers. On the threshold of the Stuart age the house of commons differed little in debate and procedure from a modern legislative body. It needed nothing more than the occasion and the necessity to demonstrate its skill, ability, and power. The day was at hand when the winning of the initiative could be undertaken in the certainty of triumph.

The power of the crown was further strengthened by the introduction of small councils into local areas. Subsidiary councils, such as the council of Wales, established earlier by Edward IV, and the council of the north, were given wide powers of administration and criminal jurisdiction. Controlled by the central council of the queen, these local councils had the authority and power to keep order and peace far from London.

The source of the criminal jurisdiction of all local councils was the power of the queen's council itself. Likewise, as described earlier, the court of star chamber was a prerogative court. Also developed to meet special circumstances was the court of requests, created to deal with the civil cases of men too poor to sue in the ordinary common law courts. There was also the court of high commission, designed mainly to enforce the Acts of Supremacy and Uniformity. These arbitrary prerogative bodies encroached on the provinces of the common law courts. Many of their procedures were unknown to the common law. They depended solely upon the crown and the council. Nevertheless, these local councils and courts were not often used as tools of despotism under Elizabeth. The general discretion and wisdom of the officials of the councils and courts usually prevented grave abuses of power. It remained for the Stuarts and their servants to transform these bodies into arbitrary and unjust instruments of the royal will.

Under Elizabeth there was a considerable increase in the functions of local government officials, particularly in the parish, where the church officials assumed many civil duties. In the counties the sheriff had been progressively deprived through the centuries of most of his importance, and the country gentlemen who were the pivotal justices of the peace now saw their judicial and administrative tasks steadily mount in number. Under "stacks of statutes" their powers became very extensive; they were judges in the local courts; they directed the administration of the poor laws; they licensed beggars and forced the physically fit to work; they determined local wages and prices; they supervised the building and maintenance of public works, roads, and prisons; they enforced the laws against the Puritans and Roman Catholics. In scores of ways they helped the central crown authorities in the government of England.

The justices of the peace were appointed by the crown. In the local government system under the Tudors only the constables of the parish and the coroners were elected. The remaining officials, such as the surveyors and overseers, were appointed by the justices of the peace or by the superior agents of the queen in Westminster. All the local royal officials, except the lords-lieutenants of the counties, were in fact responsible to the justices of the peace. They, in turn, were responsible to the privy council of the queen.

The importance of the justice of the peace in Elizabethan England was very great. In their local areas these officials were men of property and prestige; they knew their neighbors and they understood the needs and nature of their communities. There was much truth in the proud words of Sir Thomas Smith written in his *De Republica Anglorum*: "Never in any commonwealth was there devised a more wise, a more dulce and gentle, nor a more certain way to rule the people, whereby they are kept always, as it were, in a bridle of good order."

END OF AN AGE

As the Tudor age neared its end several major social developments were slowly changing the face of England. Although the accepted philosophy continued to be that of degree, priority, and place, many ambitious yeomen, the freeholders of common rank, were passing into the ranks of the gentry. The medieval isolation of the peasant was being broken down still more as rural society became more fluid. The medieval position of the yeomen was giving way to the situation when the Elizabethan agricultural poet Tusser could write "men may be bold of their own." Indeed, in words of some concern and some inaccuracy a contemporary remarked that "the toe of the peasant comes near to the heel of the courtier." Local variations were, of course, numerous. The advance of the yeomen was more marked in the Midlands, in regions closer to the great population centers.

The impact of commercial expansion, rising prices, and the advancing tide of population was on the whole advantageous to the yeomen, particularly in the fact that they were often able to consolidate and extend, at least by a few fields, their acreage. With their small copyhold, leasehold, or freehold farms they became increasingly important in the rural economy. The acquisitive tendency of the large landowners of the eighteenth century was not yet manifest and the yeomen were more than the freeholders in the narrower sense of Arthur Young. The free individual initiative given to the yeomen farmers was apparently an advantage to them and to everybody else. By enclosing modest portions of the domain and of open village fields the employment and wealth of the humble was increased. Despite the clauses of the poor laws of 1597 and 1601 it would appear that Gregory King's "paupers and cottagers" and the nomadic "rogues and sturdy vagabonds" were decreasing by the end of Elizabeth's reign. To an increasing extent community of trade was helping to draw the whole nation together. Often, indeed, the yeomen who invested their capital in land were doing so with an eye on the national market and the universal demand for wool, grain, and cattle. And often, too, yeomen began to try new things, to care for and improve their lands. Turnips appear in time for Shakespeare to mention them, and hops were already changing the face of Kent.

In the unpaid offices of the parish the yeomen were becoming increasingly important; their responsibility and position trained them towards habits of individual initiative and judgment long before England approached democracy. Gentry and yeoman power in local government steadily rose after the defeudalizing of local government began in the reign of Edward III. The parish made its appearance as a civil unit after the Reformation, and poor relief, as noted earlier, became largely a civil rather than a religious function. Then the yeomen grew more active in quarter and petty sessions in regard to the settlement of cases involving the care of paupers, often the cause of bitter interparish quarrels.

While the parish helped the yeomen to learn habits of self-government in a narrow sphere a quite different development was occurring in the boroughs. There close corporations of burgesses were being formed. These centralized oligarchies were never to make stout stands against the municipal policy of the Stuarts. The strongest currents of militant localism were to come from the parish and shire. The long conflict between localism and centralization, so evident in the seventeenth century, was less marked in the Tudor age. "The unity and married calm of states" was in part the result of a flexible and frequently unprincipled Tudor policy based on a perception of the temper of the people.

When the old sanctions tilted and cracked under the Stuarts the prevalent flux was to bring a hankering after rigidity, a search for finalities in a weakening social fabric. As the next chapters will show, the Civil War was not purely a social or local division. The real problem of the Civil War was first of all a legalistic one: how to define fundamentals and where to find authority. Many of the difficulties of the early seventeenth century had their origin in religion, in trade, in the decay and decline of the guilds, in Elizabeth I's failure to devise a sound taxation system. Important also was the fact that the decline of privy council power had helped a strong middle class to win the initiative in Parliament. One key to the social and political changes of the Tudor and Stuart centuries was the rise of the power of the gentry reinforced from the richer townsfolk.

Many other wide areas of national life showed the slow and relentless waves of transition as England passed into the seventeenth century. A new scientific spirit, a new tide of literature, new philosophies and arts of design merged in a restless age to produce a climate of opinion that the Tudor generations would have found strange and often unintelligible. Many of these changes are discussed below in Chapter 20.

Meanwhile, too, the clergy, whose intellectual contributions to English life in the sixteenth and seventeenth centuries need further investigation, were shortly to begin new activities as an unfamiliar breeze was added to the ancient winds of doctrine. The clergy labored to convert the heathen and thus "enlarge the bounds of heaven." As has been earlier suggested, they labored also to obtain tangible rewards; to checkmate Spain; to answer the problem of overpopulation; to be real estate promoters for stock companies; to popularize by propaganda the notion of imperial manifest destiny and to underline the words of the promoters of colonies and commerce.

The mingled themes of salvation and profit ran clear and strong. In another age, the sweet showers of April had impelled men to go on pilgrimages. Now, for divers reasons, the treasure of England was seen to be by foreign trade, by colonies, and by the increase of Christian souls.

The economic achievements of the Tudor period prepared the way for the next two centuries when England was to become a great colonizing power and the center of an expanding empire. Under Elizabeth the national finances, so shattered in the reign of Henry VIII, were soundly repaired. As noted earlier in this chapter, the debased currency was replaced by gold and silver coins of standard quality. Under the shrewd guidance of Sir Thomas Gresham, founder of the Royal Exchange, England paid off most of the heavy government debts accumulated by Henry VIII, Edward VI, and Mary. The budget was balanced and England's national credit steadily rose in Europe. Nursed and protected by a powerful and stable Tudor government, the economic advance of England was steady and sure.

As the guilds declined there arose several new and large-scale capitalistic enterprises aided and controlled by the central government. Mills, shops, and works, sometimes employing hundreds of men, were built: sugar refineries; gunpowder plants; paper mills; alum plants;

brass, saltpeter, and cannon works. The discovery and use of new production techniques in manufacturing and mining proceeded apace with the concentration of industrial capital. In the so-called "domestic system" of manufacturing there was a considerable increase in capital investment. Under the domestic system the workers lived in their rural cottages. These workers usually obtained their raw materials, such as cotton, wool, and metals, from a capitalist; they took the material home and manufactured the finished product; then they brought back the article and were paid for the work they had done. Sometimes the worker bought a small amount of raw material for himself, manufactured and sold it, and made a profit. Often capitalist merchants distributed the raw materials and collected the completed product. In most cases the workers were completely dependent upon the capitalist employers. As industry and capitalist organization expanded in the later Tudor period there were more workers needed. Consequently the number of men dependent upon capitalist employers increased.

The Statute of Apprentices and the poor law legislation illustrate the increasing interest of the state in general social welfare and the improvement of working conditions in England. Industry and commerce were stimulated by grants of monopolies, mentioned earlier. These patent monopoly grants gave to the holders the exclusive right to sell certain articles for a definite number of years. It is true, as suggested elsewhere, that the monopoly system became abused and unpopular late in Elizabeth's reign. Nevertheless, before that time, the monopoly grants were invaluable in affording needed government protection and encouragement to old and new industrial enterprises.

Thus domestic industry flourished and more capital steadily became available for investment in production, trade, and commerce. England was prosperous. Even though wages did not keep pace with the general price rise, the average worker still found his lot more comfortable than it had been hitherto. Most of the new wealth, of course, went to the capitalists, not to the workers. Meanwhile, trading companies increased in number and size. In competition with the traders of other nations, particularly France and the Netherlands, the merchants in these English chartered companies sent their ships to trade with the remote edges of the known world. Upon the numerous ships of the British merchant marine thousands of sailors served. The merchant marine was then, and remained, a valuable source of experienced men for the manning of the British navy in time of war.

The great and expanding gains in commerce and industry during the Tudor age had significant results for England and the world. When James I became king of England in 1603 his new kingdom was on the highway of the world's affairs. Her social fabric, her very institutions, were changing. The events of the next hundred years were to cause her people to be regarded as the most volatile and turbulent in Europe. A century of national revolution was at hand.

James I
Issues
Divine Rt of Kings &
Parliament
Puritans
Relig.
Puritan
Cath.
Protestants
Taxation

Chapter 16

FIRST OF THE STUARTS

THE HEIR OF ELIZABETH

WHEN Queen Elizabeth died the only claimants to the throne were the descendants of Margaret and Mary, sisters of Henry VIII. The will of Henry VIII, approved by his Parliament, had stated that the crown should go to Mary's descendants. In 1603 the privy council ignored Henry's will and the decision his Parliament had made. They proclaimed James VI of Scotland James I of England. He was the great-grandson of Margaret and offspring of the tragic marriage of Darnley and Mary, Queen of Scots. Thus the union of the crowns of England and Scotland was accomplished. James had been steered by the English council into "the right harbour without cross or tide." No more would he know the fogs and troubles of Edinburgh.

In Shakespeare's *Measure for Measure* a speech of the Duke Vincentio is supposed to represent James in his dislike of crowds: "I do not relish well their loud applause and Aves vehement." Thousands of his new subjects pressed about him in his progress from Edinburgh to London. They had been accustomed to Elizabeth, and the Scottish accent of James grated on their ears. They saw a shambling figure, unsteady in gait and unkingly in appearance. His physical disabilities were many: there are several contemporary references to his ill health. "Owing to want of teeth he does not chew his food but bolts it. Fruit he eats at all hours of the day and night. In drink he errs as to quality, quantity, time and order. He has the strongest antipathy to water and all watery drinks." To his English subjects, as to his Scottish, he was fond of "unbuttoning his royal store of wisdom." James was garrulous, generous in self-praise, and dogmatic. He enjoyed learned conversation, particularly if it was largely a monologue.

The pen of James, as well as his tongue, was frequently used. His large literary output, prepared with considerable assistance, touched upon many subjects from demonology to tobacco. The political writings included the famous *Trew Law of Free Monarchies* (1598), the

283

Basilikon Doron (1599), *An Apologie for the Oath of Allegiance* (1608), and *A Premonition to All Most Mighty Monarchies* (1609). Had this first Stuart been more a practical man of action than of words, less careless in the tasks of kingship, the royal will might have been blunted early enough to have prevented the crisis that was to cost Charles I his life. But the chief interests of James I were hunting and hawking, eating and drinking, the searching out of witches and "counterfeit wenches," and the parading of his ideas of kingcraft and prerogative.

James had left the feuds of the Scottish factions, the Presbyterian pulpits, and the poverty of the Scottish court. In the new Canaan of England he would find, he hoped, peace, pleasure, and respect. Public life pleased him so long as the duties did not prove too onerous. James had not expected to encounter difficulties in England. Nor was he prepared for the English reaction to his lack of tact and his gaucherie. Talkative and vain, he believed himself to be a wise ruler of full experience, a king divinely appointed by God. It irked him to be opposed by squires and lawyers in the house of commons and the law courts. And yet, indeed, the difficulties James met were not all of his own making. New forces were abroad. If James did not understand them, neither did anyone else.

THE DIVINE RIGHT OF KINGS

The measure of "free awe" and loyalty accorded Henry VIII and Elizabeth by their subjects was largely the secret of a family. These Tudors fingered the pulse of public opinion. They frequently created the kind of sentiment they wanted. They "tuned the pulpits"; they spread rewards judiciously; and they chose able servants. To a great extent their popularity was a personal thing. Stooping to conquer, avoiding excessive taxation, girt with unique political talents, ruthless and shrewd, the resplendent Tudor strong monarchy brought England prosperity and peace.

There was a wide gap between the kind of world Henry VII had found in 1485 and that left by the passing of the great Queen in 1603. The need for a centralized Tudor monarchy to hammer a nation state into shape was gone. The apprenticeship of Parliament had been long and thorough; the house of commons was ready to win the initiative in the face of Stuart obstruction and incompetence. The gentry, squires and merchants all, were prepared to encroach upon the royal prerogative if the interests of England, and their own, seemed to demand it. This came about because the sixteenth century had changed the whole balance of English society. As explained in previous chapters, a new nobility and a new middle class had appeared. Their economic strength was immense. They wanted more political power, and from their places in Parliament they reached out to grasp it.

In these endeavors they were aided by the ineptitude and incompetence of the first two Stuarts. Then, too, into the great council Elizabeth had made there soon came dissension and weakness. When personnel deteriorated and fissures steadily widened the prestige of the council declined. It lost control of policy; it was placed, and remained, on the defensive. In the midst of such centrifugal and disintegrative forces a blundering crown and an anemic council could not control the house of commons. The rise of favorites about the court contributed still further to executive indecision and paralysis. Finally, the problem of the decreasing financial resources of the crown, now that nearly all the church lands had been sold by the Tudors, burst upon the Stuarts in the very years that the expenses of government were mounting. This development also helped to put the crown on the defensive. In return for grants of money by Parliament the king had to promise to make concessions, to redress grievances. "Every shekel that he doth receive Doth cost a limb of his prerogative."

This developing situation was complicated by other factors. James was not evil, a harsh and strong enemy of mankind; he was a kindly man, and he had good intentions. Only because destiny called him to be a king were his follies more important than those of his subjects. It was unfortunate that among the chief interests of James was his royal prerogative. The Tudors had neither inquired into nor defined the origin and nature of sovereignty. With James it was otherwise. He had clear theoretical ideas about monarchy. He believed in "the divine right of kings." According to this theory a king was appointed by God and responsible only to Him. His subjects might not resist the king's commands, for resistance was a sin. To his son, James wrote: "The state of monarchy is the supremest thing on earth; for kings are not only God's lieutenants upon earth and sit upon God's throne, but even by God himself they are called gods." The people were a "headless multitude" who owed active obedience to the king who conferred organization, at God's command, upon the nation. "Majesty is made to be obeyed and not inquired into."

Under such a theory the king, as deputy of the Lord, was above Parliament, above the laws of England, above the people. It was his duty to see to the welfare of his subjects, for God would one day hold him accountable for his stewardship. But beyond that he had no responsibility. Whatever privileges Parliament possessed, or any individual possessed, were theirs by grace of the king, and were not held by any right. Faced by these assertions, it was not surprising that in the Apology of 1604 Parliament spoke of "the ancient rights of the subjects of this realm" and stated that "our privileges and liberties are our right and due inheritance, no less than our very lands and goods." In that Apology appeared sentences pregnant with warning. "What cause we your poor Commons have to watch over our privileges is manifest in itself to all men. The prerogatives of princes may easily and do daily grow. The privileges of the subject are for the most part at an everlasting stand. They may be by good providence and care preserved, but being once lost are not recovered but with much disquiet."

To James, however, the degree of the royal authority was unlimited and indisputable. "As it is atheism and blasphemy to dispute what God can do, so it is presumption and high contempt in a subject to dispute what a king can do or to say that a king cannot do this or that." It was clear that when quarrels arose between king and Parliament on questions of national policy there would be heavy trouble. Their two points of view could never be reconciled. As disputes increased in number and violence the nation became alarmed. Such was the situation that led ultimately to the Civil War.

THE PURITANS

Over the whole seventeenth century looms the vexed question of religion. Elizabeth's famous Anglican compromise had endured throughout her reign despite heavy assaults upon it. The hammering vehemence of dissent was mounting when James I came to the throne. Throughout the century men were to dispute loudly about the proper road to Jerusalem. The Puritans, called rightly by Elizabeth "dangerous to kingly rule," were searching out the Scriptures and asking for God's guidance in sweating sermons and "a tedious mile of prayer." For various reasons these Puritans were increasing in number. During Elizabeth's reign, for example, the dwindling revenues of the bishoprics had ceased to tempt the aristocracy. Hence more bourgeois clergymen came into the church; they were often much more reform-minded than their aristocratic superiors in the hierarchy. Through them, and also by other channels, the essentially Puritan outlook of the businessman was hallowed and consecrated by Puritan religion.

All Puritan elements moved about so easily in the seventeenth century that it is impossible to define the word "Puritan" with precision and brevity. The term was usually applied to those left-wing Protestants within the Church of England who wanted less ritual and more touches of Calvinism. A few even departed entirely from the Anglican fold and were called Separatists. Nevertheless, men came to be named Puritans for so many different reasons that the anonymous author of a tract published in 1622 explained that any honest man was termed a Puritan if he opposed the government for constitutional or religious reasons. It is also hazardous to seek to describe succinctly much more than the generally blurred lines of demarcation among the various Puritan groups.

The largest number of Puritans were contained in the "Broad Church" element within the Church of England. They wanted to establish a "broader" Anglican Church to include more varieties of

Puritanism. Some wanted relief from ceremonies; others wanted a reformation of the 39 Articles; still others wanted all kinds of changes and "tempering" of Anglican practices. Few of these "Broad Church" elements wished to break completely with the church. They were anxious to "reform" it from within. Indeed, many were really unadmitted Presbyterians, out to recast episcopacy altogether and to build a doctrinal bridge all the way over to Presbyterianism. They knew nothing of "the infelicity of meddling with consecrated places."

Thus the "Broad Church" groups in fact shaded into the organized and formidable Presbyterians, spiritually the Calvinist sons of Geneva. To the merchants and businessmen the Calvinist Presbyterian appeal was usually greater than all the others. The mercantile and financial classes had acquired wealth. Now, as explained above, they were seeking other kinds of power in the church and state. Calvinism had widespread non-Calvinist but anti-Catholic support. Moreover, Calvinism showed its adherents that they had been chosen by God; their legitimate business enterprises would not be restricted by religious considerations. Did not the Scripture say that a man diligent in his business would stand before kings and not mean men? As religion moved with the rise of capitalism the race would be to the swift and the battle to the strong. Geneva, like Rome, gave categorical answers to every question; there was no denial or doubt among the prosperous elect. So the Presbyterians grew in number and strength.

A third Puritan group was formed by the Independents, or Brownists. They had separated completely from the Church of England; they wanted nothing to do with state supremacy in religion. Thus they were opposed both to Anglican and Presbyterian doctrines. They did not approve of a church "system" or of prelates or presbyters. Instead, they stood for full democracy in religion, each congregation governing itself and free from outside interference.

Added to these large bodies of dissent, often inextricably mingled together, were numerous smaller sects, such as the Family of Love, the Ranters, the Muggletonians, and so on. In an age of spiritual excitement men found satisfaction by different means. Emmanuel College, Cambridge, founded by Sir Walter Mildmay in 1584, became a "mere nursery of Puritans" and through its gates passed scores of men to battle against the prelates and the High Churchmen.

Fantastic pictures were painted of the pomp, gluttony, and lechery of the Anglican clergy. "From plague, pestilence, and famine, from bishops, priests, and deacons, Good Lord, deliver us!" In later years many Puritans, such as John Bastwick, Henry Burton, and William Prynne, were to be severely punished for denouncing episcopacy. A cheap and prolific press published a spate of polemical pamphlets, written with pens dipped in vitriol on all sides of the urgent problems of religion and politics. Across the centuries still crackle the imagery and insults of such works as Prynne's *Histriomastix,* the *Hidden Workers of Darknesse,* and the *New Discoverie of Prelates Tyranny.* Here, at least, the Puritans displayed little sour austerity. They sought "to prove their doctrine orthodox By apostolic blows and knocks." John Milton wrote in *Lycidas* of the "scrambling" clergy who "for their bellies sake, creep and intrude, and climb into the fold" while "the hungry sheep look up and are not fed."

In the seventeenth century religion was far more than a set of personal beliefs. An individual's profession of religion was the outward sign of a political and social attitude. The Anglican point of view was enforced, so far as possible, by the state. Dissenters were persecuted. Religion's business was held to be with social, economic, and political affairs as well as with the condition of heaven. Few could say with John Donne "I have never fettered the word religion, not immuring it in a Rome or a Wittenberg, or a Geneva; they are all virtual beames of one sun." Anglicans would adhere to the rocklike certainties of George Herbert, who asked why Rome "hath kiss't so long her painted shrines" and did not stay for an answer. Sir John Eliot in 1625 asserted that "Religion it is that keeps a subject in obedience." The Parliament of 1628 declared that "whosoever shall bring an innovation in religion, or . . . seek to introduce Popery or Arminianism shall be reputed a capital enemy to this kingdom and commonwealth." To attempt a reform of the English church in the seventeenth century was to attempt the reorganization of English society.

Through the years before the Civil War the various arguments advanced for religious toleration supplied ideas for supporting democratic political theories. Most of the writings of the age are both religious and political; they could not well be otherwise. Men who pleaded for religious liberty and church government reforms often pleaded also for civil liberty and political revolution. Theological and Scriptural arguments are frequently merged with those that were political, secular, nationalistic. In the years of growing middle class self-expression this was particularly useful to the opponents of Anglicanism and to men of ambition. Amidst the battles of later years, described below, Lord Strafford shrewdly wrote to Archbishop Laud: "These men do but begin with the church that they may have free access to the state."

THE HAMPTON COURT CONFERENCE, 1604

On his progress from Edinburgh to London, King James was presented with the Millenary Petition, said to have been signed by 1,000 Puritan clergymen of the Church of England. They asked for toleration of certain Puritan practices; they protested against the use of the sign of the cross in baptism and the wearing of the surplice; they objected to declaring their belief in the absolute truth of the Prayer Book; they wanted a better observance of the Sabbath and more stress placed on effective preaching. Despite wide Puritan objection to the use of music in religious worship, that issue was not pressed in the Millenary Petition. To some stark and rigid Puritans it was an important cause for reproof. "Sweete Musick at the first delighteth the eares, but afterwards corrupteth and depraveth the minde, making it weake and quasie, and inclined to all licentiousness of lyfe whatsoever." Shakespeare's lonely Puritan preferred to sing psalms to hornpipes.

King James arranged for a conference between the Puritans and the bishops under his own chairmanship at Hampton Court palace. There he missed an opportunity of securing a comprehensive adjustment in the Church of England. He feared that the growth of Puritanism might spread a democratic temper in the state. Remembering what the Presbyterians had done in Scotland, he resented a suggestion that elements of Presbyterianism be introduced in the framework of the English church. "If you aim at a Scottish presbytery," he exclaimed, "it agreeth as well with a monarchy as God with the devil . . . then Jack, Tom, Will and Dick shall meet and at their pleasure censure me and my Council. . . . How they abused the poor lady, my mother, is not unknown, and how they dealt with me in my minority. . . . I thus apply it . . . no bishop, no king." He concluded his harangue with the ominous statement: "If this be all your party hath to say, I will make them conform, or else will harry them out of the land."

To the seventeenth century it seemed that the alternatives to bishops were presbyters or priests with their ideas about the separation of church and state and limitation of the royal authority. "New presbyter is but old priest writ large." This James I would not have. During later years an increasing number of Puritan groups arose with ideas about democracy and sovereignty of the people. They, too, were often driven outside the church. Some "ran a-madding to New England." Others provided spiritual leadership to the Puritan gentry. By such means was extended the slow growth of Dissent and, ultimately, the diverse shades of modern Nonconformity. Of the 8,600 clergymen in the Church of England in 1604 only about 300 were strongly Puritan; of the total population probably not more than six per cent were of Puritan sympathies. In 1604 the 300 Puritan divines were formally ejected from their livings; attempts were made to obtain a more rigid uniformity. But the rebellious spirit spread; every year the number of Puritans increased; sects multiplied as God revealed himself in many ways; the Scriptures were explained in a Babel of conflicting opinions and the Lord's name was praised in different keys.

Thus the Millenary Petition was almost wholly denied by James I. One request he approved. He appointed a commission to make a new translation of the Bible. The Authorized Version, as it is called, was published in 1611. It is a masterpiece of English prose, the last great achievement of the perfection of Elizabethan richness. To thousands of people, who had no literature but the Bible, the reading of God's word was a constant comfort. The effect of Bible study on the English character cannot be calculated; through three centuries the many-splendored poetry of the Book has been a part of the national life.

THE CATHOLICS

When James I was alienating the Puritans he was faring no better with the Catholics. The later Elizabethan laws against them had been savage. James began by lightening the fines against recusancy and allowing priests to remain unmolested. When Catholics went publicly to mass their numbers appeared so large that the Protestants were alarmed; the Anglican clergy were particularly distressed to see their congregations dwindling. James then reversed his policy; he ordered the priests to leave the country and he renewed the collection of recusancy fines under the Elizabethan code. The Catholics, naturally incensed, hatched the desperate Gunpowder Plot.

The plot was prepared by Robert Catesby, a Midland squire; he was aided by several men from the West Midlands, always a Catholic belt. It was planned to blow up the king, lords, and commons when Parliament assembled on November 5, 1605. In the resulting confusion in London the plotters would establish a Catholic government. One of the plotters warned his cousin to stay away from the opening session. "They shall receive a terrible blow, this Parliament, and they shall not see who hurts them." When the cellars under the house of lords were searched barrels of gunpowder were found hidden under piles of wood. Guarding this gunpowder was Guy Fawkes, who was seized and taken to the Tower. He was hanged; so also were the other conspirators, including the Jesuit Father Garnet. The horror engendered by the Gunpowder Plot revived the old fear of the Catholics. The average Englishman did not like the idea of assassination by gunpowder, stiletto, or sedative. Nor had he forgotten Mary Tudor, the plots against Elizabeth, the Spanish Armada.

JAMES I AND PARLIAMENT, 1604–1614

James at once involved himself in a series of quarrels with Parliament. Believing that his first house of commons would be reasonably subservient, he abandoned the Tudor precaution of ensuring the election of a goodly number of privy councillors and royal officials. The new Parliament was not prepared to yield to the idea of divine right. Early in the session two questions of parliamentary privilege arose. The first was the case of Sir Thomas Shirley, arrested for a private debt. He claimed freedom from arrest as a member of Parliament for Sussex and the king accepted the decision of the house of commons upholding Shirley's contention. The second case was that of Sir Francis Goodwin. Goodwin had been returned as a knight from Buckinghamshire; but he had earlier been outlawed in the process of a civil suit and the royal proclamation summoning Parliament had barred such candidates. Accordingly, a writ of election was refused by the court of chancery. In a new election the defeated candidate, Sir John Fortescue, a privy councillor, was elected. When Parliament assembled in 1604 it insisted that by precedent it had the right to rule on election disputes. The members agreed that Goodwin "was legally elected and returned"; that outlawry did not disqualify him. "The outlawry remained in the hustings; so, as the law could not take notice of it, neither was it pleadable."

King James not only denied that the first election was valid but declared that he was not bound by the precedents set by his predecessors. He informed the commons that "he had no purpose to impeach their privilege; but, since they derived all matters of privilege from him, and by his grant, he expected they should not be turned against him." As the election returns were all made into chancery James held that they should "be corrected and reformed by that court only into which they are returned." After prolonged dispute, James granted the right of the house of commons to be a court of record and the judge of returns of its own members although he did claim a corresponding jurisdiction for chancery. As a compromise he suggested that the elections of both Goodwin and Fortescue should be declared void and a new election held. This proposal was accepted by the commons. The issue of the right of the commons to determine the qualifications of its own members was never again questioned or the claims of chancery asserted. James, of course, did not abandon his position that all the "privileges" of the commons resulted from an act of grace on his part. The Goodwin incident is but one illustration of the king's lack of political sense and tact. He had deliberately raised a storm and then retreated.

James also quarrelled with the house of commons about his hope that the institutions of England and Scotland might be merged and the union of the two nations completed. Because of the long history of Anglo-Scottish hostility the commons refused to pass acts to carry out the king's wishes. When his proposals were rejected James was angry and told Parliament so. In the case of the Postnati (1608), involving actions both in common law and equity, Sir Edward Coke, Chief Justice of the court of common pleas, and Lord Chancellor Ellesmere were among the judges holding that all men born in Scotland after the accession of James I to the English throne were "in natural reason and by the common law of England natural-born subjects . . . of the king of England." Parliament had earlier refused to grant either free trade or English citizenship to Scotsmen. Thus the decision of the court in ruling on the question of citizenship pleased the king more than his recalcitrant Parliament.

When the commons began to debate some reforms of the Church

of England James rebuked them; such matters, he declared, were beyond their proper province. This message of the king was clearly an interference with freedom of speech. The active pressure of Puritan zeal was enough to have forced a demand for liberty of discussion even if there had not been a general tendency on the part of the commons to defend their traditional rights. Meanwhile they had been studying and elaborating parliamentary procedure and marshalling legal precedents for their privileges and powers. They now prepared a cogent statement called the Apology of the Commons which was presented to James on June 20, 1604.

Earlier in this chapter brief passages from the Apology have been quoted. This document explained to James that "the liberties and rights of your subjects of England and the privileges of this House" did not permit acceptance of the principle that the commons were not a court of record and that the return of election writs was due chancery rather than the commons. Thus the disputed points in the Goodwin case were raised again. The Apology also denied that the commons held their privileges by grace of the king; these privileges, it asserted, they held of right. "They cannot be withheld from us, denied, or impaired, but with apparent wrong to the whole state of the realm." By reason of the "misinformation" earlier received by the king "not only privileges but the whole freedom of the parliament and realm have from time to time upon all occasions, been mainly hewed at." The Apology referred to the "troubles, distrusts and jealousy" that had arisen. It reminded James that the commons contained "the whole flower and power" of the kingdom, "the sole persons of the higher nobility excepted"; it asked that James "receive public information from your commons in Parliament" rather than private misinformation; and, finally, it stated that "the voice of the people in things of their knowledge is said to be as the voice of God."

Other disputes arose about taxation. James I had insufficient resources to meet governmental expenses; hence he had to obtain money from Parliament. The costs of government were mounting. Frugal Queen Elizabeth had left a debt of £100,000. Elizabeth's funeral and James's coronation had cost an additional £200,000. James himself was extravagant and the rapacious court favorites about him looted at will. Crown revenues, particularly from land sales and rents, were steadily decreasing. The influx of gold and silver from America and the East had reduced the value of money considerably. James therefore sought to increase revenue by other means. Monopolies were granted lavishly to court favorites and used to increase royal income. James also sought to raise more money from customs. For example, he continued to exact an import duty, called an imposition, earlier levied on currants by Elizabeth. In 1606 John Bates, a merchant trading with the Levant, refused to pay this duty of five shillings a hundredweight. He was brought to trial in the court of exchequer in 1608; the legality of the king's imposition was upheld. Pliable royal judges held that such impositions did not need parliamentary sanction. The opinions of Baron Clark and Chief Baron Fleming were of particular value to the king. "And whereas it is said that, if the king may impose, he may impose any quantity that he pleases. True it is that this is to be referred to the wisdom of the king, who guideth all under God by his wisdom, and this is not to be disputed by a subject." James's Book of Rates (1608) contained still more impositions. Were the arguments of the exchequer court judges to be accepted by the house of commons? If so, Parliament would have no legal control of this kind of taxation. It was fortunate for the parliamentary cause that England's foreign trade was not great enough to render the crown financially independent through the use of impositions alone.

In 1610 James called his first Parliament into the last of its five sessions to ask for a grant of taxes. Once again the commons pressed for a redress of grievances. They objected to the schemes adopted by the king to increase the royal revenue, particularly the collection of feudal dues and the use of purveyance; the first was the revival of a practice almost obsolete and the second, the right of the king to buy provisions for the royal household at a value fixed by royal appraisal, was especially offensive. The commons proposed that James should abandon these revenues in return for a fixed annual parliamentary grant of £200,000. This projected agreement, called the Great Contract, fell through. In the bitter debates the king stated more fully his conception of the divine right of the monarch; the commons, searching for precedents and filled with rising alarm, sought to buttress their claim that James was not only under God, but also under the laws of England. When the house began to discuss the whole question of impositions James ordered them to refrain from debating his right to levy such taxes; the right was his, he declared, because he was the king; it was also his by law and by judicial decision in the Bates case.

Despite this injunction the commons went ahead. "We hold it an ancient, general, and undoubted right of Parliament to debate freely all matters which do properly concern the subject and his right or state; which freedom of debate being once foreclosed, the essence of the liberty of Parliament is withal involved." Without "swerving from the approved steps of our ancestors," the commons declared their intention of proceeding to "a full examination" of the king's alleged prerogative powers regarding taxation; they pointed out that the people, "finding themselves much grieved by these new impositions do languish in much sorrow and discomfort." Weary of acrimonious haggling, irked at the commons' delay in granting money, and annoyed at new discussions about the Puritans, James dissolved Parliament early in 1611.

The royal debts grew larger. The council tried desperately to reduce expenditures. Impositions continued. Forced loans and benevolences were collected. Monopolies and patents of the Elizabethan variety were sold lavishly. Titles of nobility were freely distributed, for a price. Any man with an annual income of £1,000 could buy a title; the new title of baronet, for example, sold for £1,095, payable in three instalments. By such various devices James was obliged to "try the dutiful affections of his loving subjects."

By 1614 the financial position of the crown was so precarious that James was again compelled to resort to Parliament for taxes. He found that his attempts to influence the elections were useless. The rising wind of public anger sent hundreds of hostile members to the new Parliament. When the commons met on April 5, 1614, they were in no mood to grant supplies. At once they turned to grievances. Not a single bill was passed in two months of debate about impositions, the king's prerogative, and a speech of the bishop of Lincoln in the house of lords charging the commons with sedition. "The commons refusing satisfaction from the bishop of Lincoln and growing insolent the king sent them word he would dissolve them unless they attended at once to his wants . . . the house being more like a cockpit than a council." On June I James dissolved this so-called Addled Parliament which had refused to vote him a penny. After the dissolution four members of Parliament were arrested and sent to prison.

On June 16 Sir Ralph Winwood wrote to Sir Dudley Carleton that he "never saw so much faction and passion as in the late unhappy Parliament, nor so little reverence of a King."

THE COURTS OF COMMON LAW

Amidst the clash of interests and disputes regarding religion, taxation, and parliamentary privilege there arose a conflict in another sphere: the courts of common law. Discussions of the legal theory of the English constitution under the early Stuarts have become voluminous. Numerous and difficult problems arise from any scholarly consideration of the nature of the fundamental laws; the absolute and ordinary royal prerogatives; the doctrines of parliamentary trusteeship; the parliamentary repudiation of reasons of state; the contract theories. Limitations of space prohibit any extended discussion here of the wide range of facts and interpretations relating to the constitutional and legal history of the reign of James I.

The strongest resistance opposed to James I came from the common law courts and especially from Sir Edward Coke, Chief Justice of the court of common pleas, the famous author of the comprehensive *Institutes*. Coke and the common lawyers insisted that the common law controlled the province of royal prerogative power. They asserted that the rights of both king and Parliament were derived from and defined by precedent. They were usually determined to enforce these views quite sturdily.

Coke himself asserted that neither king nor Parliament could change the common law. Sir Edward would have been as prepared to fight Parliament as the king had Parliament claimed the powers demanded by James I. In a famous proposition Coke declared that "when an act of parliament is against common right or reason, or repugnant, or impossible to be performed, the common law will control it and adjudge such act to be void." Even among the common lawyers there was not full agreement with this dictum in Bonham's Case (1610) and some modern scholars have concluded that these words of Coke, read in the context in which they were uttered, referred only to a procedural problem of statutory interpretation and not to a substantive constitutional question consciously raised. It is probable, indeed, that Coke's appeals to a higher law were often seen more clearly by later commentators than by Coke himself.

Coke was an obstinate fighter. To him the peculiar wisdom of the common law determined the goods and liberty of the people; the wisdom of the king could not do that. The king, Coke held, was legally limited by the common law; the law was greater than the crown.

It may be argued that the power Parliament possessed after the Revolution of 1688 was more similar to what James I was claiming than to what Coke asserted. In the early seventeenth century all men edged along a road they did not know. In the end the supremacy of Parliament was won; therefore the idea of a fundamental law broke off short in England. In the American colonies that idea was taken up in the eighteenth century. The governmental structure of the United States, including the system of judicial review, would have been more intelligible to Sir Edward Coke than the idea of the sovereignty of Parliament.

From his place in the court of common pleas Coke gave many decisions unfavorable to James. His profound knowledge of the laws of England enabled him to cite strong precedents placing limitations on the crown. The common law itself, as Dr. Cowell stated in the *Interpreter* (1607), was a mixture of the Roman and the feudal laws; the slow contribution of feudal liberties and communities was very great. Thus the English heritage from Roman law is more important than is usually believed. Coke's attempts to limit the prerogative really meant that he was challenging the power of the king to alter this tough common law at his royal pleasure.

The famous arguments in Bonham's Case, the Case of Proclamations, Peacham's Case, and the Commendams Case show Sir Edward Coke battling steadily. James was angered by these events and the assaults of Coke upon the courts of chancery and high commission. There were several rough encounters, in one of which Coke fell "flat on all four" as James threatened to strike him, "looking and speaking fiercely with bended fist."

In 1613 the king tried to hamstring his adversary by appointing him Chief Justice of the court of king's bench where it was thought that the kind of cases would restrict Coke's opportunities of interfering with the royal will. But Coke found means of remaining objectionable. Finally, in November, 1616, he was removed from office. In 1621 he was elected to Parliament where he became a leader in the groups opposed to James.

FOREIGN AFFAIRS

There were other causes of controversy and popular ill-will. Until 1612 Robert Cecil, Lord Salisbury, continued to serve James as he and his father had served Elizabeth. When the shrewd Cecil was gone James turned to Robert Carr, a worthless Scotsman. James had always been addicted to favorites. Most of them had been young men from Scotland and hence regarded as foreign interlopers in England. James often neglected his privy councillors and sought advice from these irresponsible companions. Upon them he lavished money and office. Robert Carr was made Duke of Somerset. Soon the bright and handsome favorite became enmeshed in a series of scandals. When he was convicted of murder James commuted the sentence, thus openly flouting the decision of the court. Public annoyance mounted at this flagrant interference with justice. Somerset was succeeded in the sunshine of royal favor by George Villiers, who was created first Earl and then Duke of Buckingham. Buckingham's power grew apace.

In 1604 James had wisely made peace with Spain. England's ancient enemy was defeated on the seas, but her land armies could not be overcome; so it seemed profitless to keep on with the war. James himself was not hostile to Madrid. He could not appreciate English history and the tradition of anti-Spanish feeling. Nor did he look with strong disfavor upon Catholicism in Spain or at home. His mother had been Catholic; his wife was inclined to Rome. James frequently thought of an alliance with Spain to be cemented by a marriage between his son Henry and the daughter of the Spanish king.

Meanwhile the stage was being set in Europe for a series of religious wars, the great duel of the seventeenth century between Protestants and Catholics. In the German states were two opposing alliances. The leader of the Protestant Union was Frederick, Elector of the Palatine. The Catholic League was under the efficient Maximilian of Bavaria. James gave active support to the German Protestants largely because his advisers urged balance of power considerations and the need of pursuing a more popular foreign policy. In 1612 Elizabeth, daughter of James I, married Frederick, Elector of the Palatine. Thus arose an alliance between England and the vigorous Protestant German state. For this popular arrangement Robert Cecil had been largely responsible.

When Cecil died in 1612 James not only fell under the spell of the feckless Robert Carr; he was also greatly influenced by the new Spanish ambassador, the astute Gondomar. Spain wanted an alliance with England. If a religious war arose in the German states, both the Austrian and Spanish Hapsburgs would champion the cause of the Catholic League. Hence every attempt must be made to weaken England's support of the Elector Palatine and the Protestant Union. The Spanish ambassador therefore suggested that Charles, who had become the heir to the English throne on the death of Prince Henry in 1612, might marry a Spanish princess. Secret negotiations began. The laws in England against Catholics were relaxed. When Spain insisted that any children of the marriage should be educated as Catholics, James paused. He knew that England would never accept such an arrangement.

Already there was popular anger at the influence of Gondomar. For instance, Buckingham had persuaded James to release Sir Walter Raleigh from the Tower. Raleigh was sent on an expedition to Guiana in 1617 to search for gold. The next year he came back to England; he had no treasure; he had been in a skirmish and some Spaniards had been killed. When Gondomar demanded Raleigh's death James sent Elizabeth's stout servant to the block.

In the midst of these events the long threatened religious wars at last broke forth. For thirty years (1618–1648) misery and death marched over Germany. By 1648 thousands of villages had been wiped out. The great city of Augsburg was reduced to 16,000 inhabitants; it had contained 80,000. Incredible atrocities were committed in the name of God. An iron entered into the exhausted German soul.

When the Bohemian Protestants began the struggle in 1618 at Prague against the Emperor Matthias, Spain prepared to follow her sympathies and interests. She would join Austria in the anti-Protestant crusade. Meanwhile she would keep James of England placated and neutral. Hence Madrid hastened to renew the marriage negotiations and suggested that James act as mediator in the German crisis. While James was thus kept inactive Spain pushed war preparations.

In the meantime the Bohemians had offered the kingship of Bohemia to the Calvinist Frederick, Elector of the Palatine, the son-in-law of James. Frederick had accepted. In 1620 his own ancestral territories in the Palatinate were overrun by troops from the Spanish Netherlands. Frederick had neither lands nor funds.

James now saw that he had been duped by Spain and Gondomar. He demanded that the Spaniards restore the Palatinate to his son-in-law and suggested that Charles would marry the Spanish Infanta if they did so. If not, England would intervene to help Frederick recover his lost territories. The waging of war, however, required money. Since the dissolution of the Addled Parliament in 1614 James had reorganized the royal financial system and had collected one benevolence. When he tried to collect a second benevolence he failed. From the privy councillors and the city of London he obtained a few pounds; from other sources he got nothing. The people wanted war with Catholic Spain. Nevertheless, seven years without a meeting of Parliament left them wary. They were unwilling to run the risk of giving money to James. Once James had gold Parliament might not be called at all. England would then continue to be at the mercy of the king and his favorites. Because he could obtain money in no other way James summoned Parliament in 1621.

KING AND PARLIAMENT, 1621–1624

The house of commons was ready for war with Spain. As usual, the Spaniards were accused of manifold sins. For example, Sir Thomas Barrington insisted that the first plague of sheep was brought to England by a Spanish ship. Nevertheless, when the commons were asked for £500,000 to equip an army of 30,000 men they wanted more precise explanations about the war plans, the proposed Spanish marriage, and what was to become of Gondomar. They granted only £160,000 and waited for the royal reaction. They began to debate their grievances. They denounced the excessive granting of monopolies, particularly to royal favorites. Sir Edward Coke, now a member of the house, led the attack on the monopoly holders.

Coke also brought about the impeachment of his old enemy the lord chancellor Francis Bacon before the house of lords. As Bacon was one of the chief defenders of the royal prerogative the commons were striking at the king's claims of absolute power when they impeached Bacon. The lord chancellor was accused of taking bribes from his suitors in court. As the evidence was indisputable, Bacon admitted his guilt. By the judgment of the house of lords it was held "that the lord viscount St. Albans, lord chancellor of England, shall undergo a fine and ransom of £40,000; that he shall be imprisoned in the Tower during the king's pleasure; that he shall forever be incapable of any office, place or employment in the state or commonwealth; that he shall never sit in parliament nor come within the verge of the court." A strong pillar of the king had thus been removed. The weapon of impeachment, unused since the fourteenth century, was to be employed by Parliament against those royal officials and favorites who could not otherwise be reached. Only by proroguing or dismissing Parliament could the Stuarts henceforth protect their servants.

At the second session of Parliament in April, 1621, James announced that the grant of £160,000 had been spent. But the commons made no more appropriations. Instead they talked about their grievances and about foreign affairs. Gondomar took umbrage at the harsh remarks directed against Spain. In a letter to the house of commons James noted that some members of the house had ventured to "argue and debate publicly of the matters far above their reach and capacity, tending to our high dishonour and breach of prerogative royal." He commanded that "none therein shall presume henceforth to meddle with anything concerning our government or deep matters of state; and, namely, not to deal with our dearest son's match with the daughter of Spain." To this James added that he thought himself "very free and able to punish any man's misdemeanours in parliament, as well during their sitting as after."

The commons at once asked for an explanation. It was unsatisfactory. Thereupon the Great Protestation was prepared and inserted in the *Journal* of the house. It declared that the commons' privileges were "the ancient and undoubted birthright and inheritance of the subjects of England." James ripped the Great Protestation from the pages of the *Journal*. "King James in council with his own hand rent out this protestation." He then dissolved Parliament.

James complained that "some ill-tempered spirits" had "sowed tares among the corn." To the commons he declared: "I may truly say with our Saviour, I have often piped unto you and you have not danced. I have warned and you have not lamented. . . . Bishop Latimer said very well: 'the devil is a busy bishop.' If our Church were as busy to persuade the right way as the bold Jesuits and Puritans and other sectaries are to supplant and pervert, we should not have so many go astray on both sides."

Obviously James could not wage war with Spain; he had no army, no supplies. Gondomar now tried to persuade him that Spain would pull her troops out of the Palatinate in return for the marriage alliance so long discussed. In 1623 Charles and Buckingham went to Madrid to view the Infanta. Both were annoyed at their reception. They were refused permission to meet the Spanish princess until they had promised concessions to Catholics in England. This, of course, they could not do. When Charles made an informal approach by climbing over a wall, the Infanta inconsiderately fled. Catholic priests tried to convert the two Englishmen to Catholicism. Charles and Buckingham returned to England hot for war with Spain. The public rejoiced; smoke from bonfires pillared the English skies along the road that took the returning pair to London. Charles and Buckingham forced James to call Parliament. At last, it seemed, there would be war.

Members of Parliament, especially the country gentlemen, pointed out that Spain could be defeated more easily by sea than by land. In a naval war there would be Spanish ships, as of old, to plunder. But James wanted a land war because that was the only way to restore the Palatinate to his son-in-law. Meanwhile Buckingham and Charles silenced Gondomar and persuaded the commons to impeach Middlesex, the only pro-Spanish councillor. James warned his son that he would one day have his fill of impeachments. James saw what Charles did not. To cooperate with the commons against the crown and its councillors was a dangerous business for the heir to the throne. Charles would some day be king. By his actions he had surely shown the commons that he did not believe in the divine right of kings. When he ascended the throne he would find that he himself had helped to arm his foes.

James now attempted to obtain a French alliance. Because France did not want the Spanish and Austrian Hapsburg power to rise too far in Europe, the English proposal was attractive. James suggested that his son Charles marry Henrietta Maria, sister of the French King Louis XIII. The French, in turn, would help English forces push the Spaniards out of the Palatinate. But France wanted English assurance of a greater degree of toleration for Catholics in England. Louis XIII did not wish to despatch French troops to the Palatinate. Despite such major difficulties, a treaty was finally signed. James was bound by a secret clause to allow the English Catholics freedom of worship; those in prison were to be released; recusancy fines were to be returned. Meanwhile Buckingham sent "a rabble of raw and poor rascals" as an army to Holland. The expedition was terribly mismanaged and many men starved to death in the Walcheren region at the mouth of the Scheldt.

In 1625 James died. In his reign, as described earlier in this chapter, the influence of the council steadily diminished. Committees of the house of commons increased the scope and importance of their activities. Parliamentary procedure improved tremendously. Able members of the commons waged skilful battles against the assertions of the royal prerogative. The liberties and privileges of Parliament were defended by shrewd and courageous men. Puritan attacks on the bishops mounted in strength. The abuses of benevolences, monopolies, and impositions took their place beside the other causes of reform urged by the house of commons. Less dramatic and less easily described was the simple fact that the crown was drawing away from the people. The bonds of understanding and sympathy that had meant so much in the years of the Tudors were perceptibly loosening. This James did not see amid his quarrels about liberties, taxation, prerogatives, and all the rest. He was tragically unaware of the currents of social, political, and economic forces, the flood of which no king could stay.

And yet, even if he had been gifted with prophetic insight, James would probably not have bent the knee to those who questioned the divinity of his power. Because he honestly believed what he said he might have become a martyr. His son Charles was prepared to do exactly that. Hard in consequence was to be his fate.

BIRTH OF EMPIRE

Elizabethan seadogs had furrowed waters where no man had been before. Their few attempts at colonial settlement failed. It was in the reign of James that colonial expansion began and the first British Empire was born. The seventeenth century was to be at once more commercial and religious than the sixteenth. There were intimate connections between the Anglican Church and the merchants. Colonizing was at once a high Christian project and an opportunity to profit by the discovery of gold or by trade. "For whatever God, by the ministration of nature hath created on earth was, at the beginning, common among men; may it not then be lawful nowe to atempt the possession of such lands as are void of Christian inhabitants for Christ's sake? Harke, harke, the earth is the Lord's, and all that is therein . . . as it is in the 50 psalme . . . For all is myne that on the earth do dwell, And who shall bar him from his possession?"

It was also argued that the foundation of colonies might drain off surplus population. Contemporary writers complained of the "desolation of counties by enclosures; desolation of the townes for lack of occupation and craftes." Others declared that colonies in America would put "a bit in the mouth of Spain." Those who wished to be unfettered in their religion added to the flow of emigrants seeking to "find refuge in another land for God's oppressed people, where a bulwark might be raised against the kingdom of anti-Christ."

In 1606 James I chartered two companies, the one to trade and colonize the Virginia region, the other New England. The first colony was founded by the Virginia Company (or London Company) at Jamestown in 1606. Slowly the settlers learned that gold and trade profits would not come easily; that "nothing is to be expected thence but by labour." In the first three years there were only 85 survivors out of the 320 that had landed. Between 1606 and 1625 there were 5,649 who came to Jamestown; at the end of the period 1,095 remained. The character of the early emigrants to Virginia was poor. When Sir Josiah Child wrote *A New Discourse on Trade* in 1668 he stated that Virginia was "at first peopled by a sort of loose vagabond people, vicious and destitute of means at home, being either unfit for labour, or such as could find none to employ themselves about." Although the situation was not so dark as this exaggerated comment would imply, there was, nevertheless, a widespread idea that the New World was a fit resort for the failures of the Old. And many failures came.

Slowly the colonists turned to agriculture. There was considerable enthusiasm, particularly after the planting of tobacco about 1612. "What commodities soever Spaine, France, Italy or those parts do yield to us in wines of all sorts, in oyles, in flax, sugar, frankincense

and the like, these parts do abound with the growth of them all."
Tobacco ships sailed back to London. Virginia's economic future was
assured. So far as its political future was concerned, that was foreshadowed in 1622 when "a house of burgesses broke out" to herald
the approaching years of controversy.

In 1609 relief ships with stores and settlers for Jamestown ran
ashore at Bermuda, untenanted except by the descendants of pigs let
loose by Portuguese seamen. Shakespeare's *Tempest* and Andrew Marvell's later *Song of the Emigrants in Bermuda* show the contemporary
interest. "Safe from the storms, the prelate's rage," the colony was
rapidly settled. Other colonies were soon founded in the Leeward and
Windward Islands and in Newfoundland. In 1607 thousands of Presbyterians from Scotland settled in northern Ireland.

In 1620 ships were coasting along the rocky shore of New England. They carried Separatists who had fled to Holland in 1607 and
1608 seeking freedom of worship. Aided by the Puritans of the Virginia Company, they were on their way to found a new colony in
northern Virginia. They never reached their destination. An accidental
landing at Plymouth Rock resulted in the first permanent New England
settlement. "In the name of God, amen; we, whose names are under-
written, the loyal subjects of our dread sovereign King James, having
undertaken, for the glory of God and the advancement of the Christian
faith, and honour of our king and country, a voyage to plant the first
colony in the northern parts of Virginia do by these presents solemnly
and mutually, in the presence of God and of one another covenant
and combine ourselves into a civil body politic . . ." When nearly half
of the *Mayflower* pilgrims had died in the first winter William Brewster
wrote: "It is not with us as with men whom small matters can discourage, or small discontentments cause to wish themselves at home
again."

Other colonies swiftly followed. It is a familiar story. "Here
nature opens her broad lap to receive the perpetual accession of newcomers." Through tidewater, piedmont, and frontier the settlers moved;
the social divisions of later America were being shaped. The impulse
of sanctuary and the impulse of commerce merged in the frontier
stream of continuous movement.

In the reign of James I England was also active in the East. The
Portuguese had been at Ormuz, Aden, Goa and Malacca from early
in the sixteenth century. Englishmen such as Ralph Fitch and Thomas
Stevens reported the wonders they had seen. The English translation
of Linchoten's *Voyage to the East Indies* (1598) hoped that "this poor
translation may work in our English nation a further desire and increase of honour over all countries of the world by means of our
wooden walles." And English ships were already moving in eastern
waters at the turn of the century. On September 22, 1599, an assembly

of London merchants applied to Queen Elizabeth to "incorporate them in a company, for that trade to the Indies being so remote from hence, cannot be traded but in a joint and united stock." On December 31, 1600, Elizabeth granted a charter to the East India Company, the purpose of the undertaking of those trading into the East Indies to be "the Honour of our Nation, the Wealth of our people, the Increase of our Navigation, and the Advancement of lawful traffic for the benefit of our Commonwealth."

The encroaching British interlopers rapidly came into conflict with the Portuguese and Dutch. Because the Dutch defeated the Portuguese in a separate trade and naval war the field of combat was narrowed. In 1623 the Dutch massacred ten Englishmen at the East India Company trading post at Amboina. This event caused deep irritation in England. Thousands of copies of a picture depicting the massacre were distributed by the East India Company. After 1623 the company increased its activities in India. The trading stations at Surat, Madras, and Calcutta increased England's trade and influence later in the century. From these small trading posts was to grow British India. The *Peppercorn* and the *Trades Increase* prepared the way for the argosies of a later age.

Chapter 17

PREROGATIVE LAW AND PARLIAMENT
KING CHARLES I ~ married French Queen Catholic

CHARLES I, who succeeded his father in 1625, is usually described as being kingly in appearance. He was not; he was undersized; he stammered; and he had a red nose. Among the people he was at first popular because he had refused a Spanish bride and had consistently pursued an anti-Spanish policy against the wishes of his father and the Spanish Ambassador Gondomar. His dignity contrasted favorably with the gabbling indecorum of James. The moral level of his court promised to be better than that of his father. Members of Parliament recalled that he had often supported them, particularly in the affair of the impeachment of Middlesex.

England soon discovered that Charles I believed in divine right, as his father had taught him to do. The Puritans found that his artistic nature inclined him to the High Anglican Church ritual and "the beauty of holiness." His whole character was revealed as a curious mixture of weakness and obstinacy. All the Stuarts were obstinate when the fit was on them. Heedless of public opinion, reckless of consequences, Charles defied his opponents. He was, he felt, bound in honor to defend the prerogatives of the crown, even though his own life be forfeit. His royal word was not to be relied upon; he saw no need of keeping it to those who would challenge the anointed of the Lord. Such a ruler, conscientious, unimaginative, obstinate, fishblooded, promised to bring revolution in his train as surely as night follows day.

Charles, like his father, was usually under the influence of stronger personalities. Such was the dashing Duke of Buckingham, long a power in the court. In 1625 Buckingham saw to it that Charles went through with the marriage to the Catholic Henrietta Maria, daughter of Henry IV of France; this was the arrangement earlier agreed upon in the French treaty. The marriage took place before Parliament met, lest they ask unpleasant questions about the Catholic queen, about the treaty with its secret clauses, about Buckingham, whom they disliked. Henrietta Maria was not popular. Her Catholicism made her unsympathetic to the Puritans and Anglicans alike; she was frivolous and frequently swayed by irresponsible and selfish courtiers. Although the nation knew she had no voice at the council table, they feared her diplomatic activities about the court and her influence with the king.

When the first Parliament met late in 1625 much of the early good will towards the new king had been dissipated. The Puritan members were strongly hostile to the High Church Anglicanism of Charles. They felt that there was already far too much emphasis upon ceremony and not enough upon morality and the need for "the inner light." They were angered to see the High Churchmen increasing in number, inclining to uphold divine right, condemning all things Calvinistic. These High Church doctrines, they declared, were moving dangerously close to Rome. The commons were also suspicious of Buckingham and the Catholic queen. They wanted the penal laws against the Catholics more strongly enforced and they petitioned Charles to do it. They disliked the assertions Charles was already making about prerogative power and divine right. They demanded to know more about the war against Spain. They were prepared to insist upon certain Puritan reforms such as salary increases for the clergy so that better men might be attracted into the service of the church.

When Charles asked for money grants Parliament gave him only £140,000 to wage the Spanish war. They made it clear that they intended to debate foreign affairs and religious reforms and they were taking no chances upon Charles dissolving Parliament as soon as adequate funds had been voted to him. Instead of granting tunnage and poundage duties to the new king for life, in accordance with custom, the commons gave them for one year only.

In fact, Charles did not get this income at all because he later dissolved Parliament before the house of lords had passed the bill. Nor was Parliament prepared to vote large sums of money to finance a land war. They still preferred a naval conflict. Charles explained that he wanted to send 6,000 troops to the Netherlands, and an English army into Germany; that he proposed to subsidize heavily the Danish king and the mercenary army of Count Mansfeld then fighting for the German Protestants. The commons not only refused to vote any more money but began to denounce Buckingham because, they said, he wished to set himself up before all men as the Protestant champion of Europe; he was responsible for these costly plans. Did Buckingham not know that the wool trade was in the doldrums? In such circumstances Charles dismissed his first Parliament.

THE PARLIAMENT OF 1626

There now began a year's tale of disaster and folly. Charles and Buckingham arranged to send an expedition under Sir Edward Cecil to Cadiz where it was hoped to seize Spanish treasure ships, laden with gold and silver. Possessed of such plunder, Charles could then go on with the war despite the drawn purse strings of Parliament. But the poorly laid plains went awry. Everything was frightfully mismanaged; those who were incompetent vied with those who were corrupt. The troops that landed at Cadiz drank all the wine they could find and lurched back to the ships in no shape to battle Spaniards. All came home at last; but they brought no Spanish gold. In a complicated arrangement with Louis XIII of France, whom they unsuccessfully tried to outwit, Buckingham and Charles were tricked into sending ships to help Louis against his Protestant Huguenot subjects at La Rochelle. Englishmen were furious to learn that their ships had been used to support a Catholic French king against his rebellious Protestant subjects. In vain Charles and Buckingham tried to explain what had happened. More than a century later Talleyrand remarked that there was only one thing worse than a crime and that was a blunder.

When truculent members of Parliament assembled in 1626 they were in no mood to grant supplies to Charles. Their leaders included such men as John Pym, later the patient, skilful "king" of a moderate group of considerable importance in the Long Parliament; Sir Thomas Wentworth, within two years to become a supporter of the crown and soon, as the earl of Strafford, to die on the block, abandoned by the prince in whom he had put his trust; the fiery Sir John Eliot, a Cornishman, author of the famous *Monarchie of Man,* and destined to die in the Tower of London, a prisoner of Charles. The vindictive king refused to permit the burial of Sir John's body in his native Cornwall. "Let Sir John Eliot be buried in the church of that parish where he died." But in 1626 Eliot was very much alive. To the house of commons he declared: "Our honour is ruined, our ships are sunk, our men perished, not by the enemy, not by chance, but by those we trust." Despite the threats of Charles the debate went on. News came that Cardinal Richelieu had concluded peace with Spain; this was a serious setback to English diplomacy. On May 8, 1626, the commons began impeachment proceedings against Buckingham, charging him with corruption and maladministration.

Earlier Charles had said: "I see you especially aim at the Duke of Buckingham. I must let you know that I will not allow any of my servants to be questioned among you, much less such as are of eminent place and so near to me. I grant you liberty of counsel, but not liberty of control. Remember that Parliaments are altogether in my power for their calling, sitting, and dissolution; and therefore, as I find the fruits of them to be good or evil, they are to continue or not to be." Nevertheless, the impeachment before the house of lords continued. Sir John Eliot led the attack on Buckingham. "He has broken those nerves and sinews of our land, the stores and treasures of the King. There needs no search for it; it is too visible. His profuse expenses, his superfluous feasts, his magnificent buildings, his riots, his excesses, what are they but the visible evidences of an express exhausting of the state, a chronicle of the immensity of his waste of the revenues of the Crown? Must all England be made inferior to this man's will? This only say the house of commons: 'By him come all evils, in him we find the causes, and on him must be the remedies.' "

In an attempt to halt the impeachment proceedings Charles imprisoned Sir John Eliot and Sir Dudley Digges. The commons then resolved to "lay aside all other business until we are righted in our liberties." Thereupon the king released the prisoners but ordered the house to "forthwith bring forth their bill of subsidy to be passed without delay or condition . . . which if they do not, it will force us to take other resolutions. . . . And if by their denial or delay anything of ill consequence shall fall out either at home or abroad, we may call God and man to witness that we have done our part to prevent it." When the commons still refused to consider supply before grievances Charles dissolved Parliament.

GOVERNMENT BY THE KING'S COMMAND

The problem of money supply was urgent. England was at war. Charles pawned the crown jewels and mortgaged crown lands. He tried to collect free gifts from the people. He sought to obtain tunnage and poundage duties by royal ordinance. When nothing was forthcoming he attempted a forced loan in 1627. This was in effect taxation without parliamentary sanction. Many refused to contribute. When a wall of resistance seemed to rise up everywhere Charles arbitrarily imprisoned several who would not pay. A wise man remarked that "the whole nation cannot be consigned to prison, Your Majesty."

Among those imprisoned were five knights who at once sued for writs of habeas corpus from the court of king's bench. The writs were granted by the court but the warden of the Fleet Prison refused to release the prisoners; he declared that he was acting on a warrant from two members of the privy council ordering the knights to be held "by special order of His Majesty." It was pointed out by counsel for the five knights that if no cause were shown for their detention by the king then they should be freed. They asserted that the ancient rights of the subject, set forth in Chapter 39 of Magna Carta, were at stake. "No man shall be captured or imprisoned or disseised or outlawed or exiled or in any way destroyed, nor will we go against him or send against him, except by the lawful judgment of his peers and the law of the land." Freedom from arbitrary arrest was a fundamental English liberty. In the case of the five knights, Chief Justice Hyde declared that "if no cause of the commitment be expressed, it is to be presumed to be a matter of state which we cannot take notice of." The court could find no precedents for delivering prisoners by bail in cases where matters of state were involved, except by order of the king. The whole decision of the court was evasive and weak. "The King hath done it and we can trust him in great matters." The five knights were not released. At the same time, however, Charles found himself blocked by other judges who refused to declare the forced loan a legal levy. The London merchants and the country squires watched in anger while the monarchy strained its resources to obtain the wherewithal to run the government and the war.

The war did not go well. Charles soon quarrelled with his brother-in-law, Louis XIII of France, when Louis asked that relief be granted to English Catholics as called for in the marriage treaty. He also quarrelled with Queen Henrietta Maria and sent her French attendants packing home. The king of Denmark and Count Mansfeld were both defeated by the Catholic forces in Europe. Late in 1627 the peace between France and England gave way to war. Buckingham decided to help the French Protestants and led a fleet to relieve La Rochelle, Huguenot city on the Bay of Biscay besieged by Richelieu. Guarding the harbor was the island of Rhé. The English tried to capture it. Buckingham led the attack. But his troops were poor, spiritless, ill-disciplined; everything was bungled. Buckingham, defeated, came home. The failure was then described as "the greatest and shamefullest overthrow since the loss of Normandy." Would Britain be reduced to a cipher in foreign affairs?

In 1628 Charles called his third Parliament.

THE PETITION OF RIGHT

Amidst debt, disorder, and the extension of a disastrous war the house of commons assembled. Never had Charles or his father faced such public hostility. Twenty-seven members of the new house had been imprisoned for refusal to pay the forced loan. When Charles demanded the money he so desperately needed the commons paid no attention. Almost at once they decided to put their major grievances in a Petition of Right. In it they stated forcefully and clearly a series of principles. This famous document carefully cited precedents and asked Charles to cease actions "not warrantable by the laws and practices of this realm."

Specifically, the Petition asked: (1) that arbitrary taxation should cease and "no man hereafter be compelled to make or yield any gift, loan, benevolence, tax, or such like charge without common consent by act of parliament"; (2) that arbitrary imprisonment should cease, and no man should "be called to make answer, . . . or be confined, or otherwise molested or disquieted" and "no freeman, in any such manner as before mentioned, be impressed or detained"; (3) that compulsory billeting of troops on private citizens should cease; (4) that martial law, except in time of war, should cease; that the king's commissions for proceeding by martial law should be "revoked and annulled"; and that "hereafter no commissions of like nature may issue forth to any person or persons whatever . . . lest by colour of them any of your majesty's subjects be destroyed or put to death, contrary to the laws and franchise of the land."

To this Petition of Right Charles reluctantly agreed. "To avoid all ambiguous interpretations and to show you that there is no doubleness in my meaning, I am willing to please you in words as well as in the substance." This document ranks along with Magna Carta and the Bill of Rights in placing constitutional limits on absolute monarchy. Its historical meaning, of course, was greater than its immediate practical value because its principles, as well as others, were not really won until the physical power of two revolutions made them more acceptable to the Stuarts and their successors.

When Charles granted the Petition of Right the commons voted him taxes. Charles was concerned lest the commons continue their attacks on his ministers, on whom he wanted no "scandal or aspersion." He forbade them to do so. The result was another storm. One member of the house declared: "We sit as men daunted. Let us put on the spirit of Englishmen and speak to purpose." A second asked: "If we must not speak of ministers, what must we do?" Sir Edward Coke quoted precedents to prove that royal advisers misleading the king might properly be attacked in Parliament. "Nothing grows to abuse but this house hath power to treat of it. What shall we do? Let us palliate no longer; if we do, God will not prosper us. I think the Duke of Buckingham is the cause of all our miseries." So the commons refused to heed Charles and debated their grievances about Buckingham.

They also raised another question. Did the king's promise to levy no taxes without parliamentary grant apply only to direct taxes? The decision in Bates Case would seem to have given legal authority for the royal levying of all kinds of indirect taxes. This court decision would take precedence over the Petition of Right, which was not a statute passed by both houses. Indeed, the judicial decision could be overturned only by an act of Parliament or by a court reversal. As tunnage and poundage was an indirect tax Charles held that it was not covered by the promise in the Petition of Right. Although the legal distinction was clear enough, the people of England were not versed in the subtleties of the matter; they felt that Charles was already breaking his word when reports of his speech of June 26, 1628, filtered down to the counties and village greens.

On that day Charles prorogued Parliament. "It may seem strange that I come so suddenly to end this session. Wherefore, before I give my assent to the bills I will tell you the cause: though I must avow that I owe an account of my actions to none but to God alone. A while ago the house of commons gave me a remonstrance—how acceptable every man may judge. And for the merit of it, I will not call that in question; for I am sure no wise man can justify it. Now, since I am certainly informed that a second remonstrance is preparing for me, to take away my profit of tunnage and poundage—one of the chief maintenances of the Crown—by alleging that I have given away my right thereof by my answer to your petition, this is so prejudicial unto me that I am forced to end this session some few hours before I meant it, being willing not to receive any more remonstrances to which I must give a harsh answer."

One grievance, however, was removed. In 1628 the Duke of Buckingham went to Portsmouth to lead another expedition to La Rochelle. There he was murdered by a malcontent lieutenant named John Felton. Felton was cheered as a hero and there was national rejoicing. Charles was overcome with grief. William Laud, then bishop of London, was also saddened. He had long struggled with John Williams, bishop of Lincoln, for the priceless conscience of Buckingham and the loaves and fishes Buckingham provided. "The fountains of my heart," wrote Laud, "will burst their bounds and pour my life away." Later a Genoese agent in London remarked that "The Duke of Buckingham was buried in Westminster Abbey without pomp of any kind, in order to escape any demonstration of public fury." Despite Buckingham's death Charles resolved to continue the war. The expedition to La Rochelle sailed; but the French had built a mole to block the harbor. The English fleet turned back homewards and the Huguenots surrendered to Richelieu.

THE PARLIAMENT OF 1629

The second session of Parliament in 1629 soon protested against the religious policy of the king. Charles, as had James before him, pointed out that matters of religion, as well as trade and foreign affairs, clearly fell within the admitted prerogative of the crown. Those ancient rights would not be renounced without a struggle. By royal proclamation in 1628 Charles had ordered literal acceptance of the Thirty-nine Articles by all laymen; there was to be no discussion whatever. Despite the royal command numerous Puritans in the commons continued to insist upon freedom of discussion and to oppose the small, ritualistic, anti-Calvinist block within the Anglican Church. Members of this High Church group were so favored by Charles that under his royal patronage they were being appointed to many positions of power. Thus they were coming to control and dictate the religious policy of the government.

The virtual leader of this High Church group was William Laud, bishop of London. Laud, the only son of a Reading clothier, had been described, long before in his Oxford days, as "a busy and pragmatical person, at least very Popishly inclined." If his private life was not above reproach, it was certainly less shadowed than that of the Puritan Sir Edward Coke, who had starved and bullied his daughter into a loveless marriage with Buckingham's brother. To the zealous Laud, as to those about him, the appeal of something akin to a Roman church system was particularly strong. Had not the judicious Richard Hooker preached an apostolic English church? Launcelot Andrewes, whose disciple Laud was, also proclaimed an apostolic English church and argued that bishops ruled by divine right and that good works were necessary to salvation. As such High Churchmen saw increasing social anarchy about them they found comfort in a body of doctrine intellectually more complete than that of the Bible alone, of great antiquity, of elevating aesthetic appeal. Crude and uncouth Puritans jarred the tender nerves and sensibilities of those who loved the quiet and ordered beauty of Laudian Anglicanism.

So far as Parliament was concerned Laud subscribed to the ideas of Charles. "I have little hope for good success in parliament until they leave personal persecution; meddling with the church; sit less time, that they might not understand one another too well; remember that the law of God, which gives kings aids and subsidies, may not be broken by them without heinous sin."

There seemed no way to halt Parliament's attacks on royal ecclesiastical policy and Charles's claims to tunnage and poundage except by dissolution. On March 2, 1629, Charles sent an order adjourning Parliament until March 10, intending to declare it dissolved later. The obstreperous house of commons, anxious to get its opinions on record, voted against adjourning. When the Speaker tried to comply with the royal order he was seized and held in his chair. The doors were locked. With the house thus technically in session Sir John Eliot moved three resolutions which were swiftly passed. The first, quoted in the previous chapter, condemned "innovations in religion" and "Popery"; the second and third declared that anyone advising the collection of tunnage and poundage or voluntarily paying it should be considered "a capital enemy to the kingdom and commonwealth." Then the doors were unlocked and the royal messengers, who had been sent to get the mace, were admitted. The commons, declared Charles, had been attempting "to exert a universal, overswaying power which belongs only to me, and not to them." Parliament was dissolved on March 10, 1629.

On April 1, Charles made peace with France and Spain. "He was prepared to be a cipher abroad, so that he might be a king at home." Charles was so heavily in debt that he could not afford to remain at war unless he could obtain money through parliamentary channels. Because Charles's difficult position kept England out of European affairs her international prestige and influence fell. France under Louis XIV was to follow Spain as the predominant power in Europe. Those who recalled the proud position England had held in the days of Elizabeth were shamed and dismayed. They could not know that this withdrawal from Europe would ultimately be a desirable thing. Before England moved strongly abroad again she had completed her domestic revolution and the foundations of limited monarchy and responsible parliamentary government had been laid. France was to have one revolution in the eighteenth century, three in the nineteenth; the results of none of them promised either stability or democratic government.

The sequel of the storm in Parliament came swiftly. Charles arrested nine of his opponents. He accused them of "notable contempts against the king" and conspiracy; Eliot was specifically charged with "raising sedition between the king, his nobles, and people." All claimed parliamentary privilege for what they had said and done. They asserted that they could not be charged before any court except Parliament itself. This was the ancient claim of freedom of speech, advanced again in the Apology of 1604 and in the Protestation of 1621. The judges of the court of king's bench yielded to royal pressure. They held that the parliamentary session had in fact ended with the arrival of the king's messengers and that, in any event, what the defendants had done was "not a parliamentary course." "The Parliament is a high court, therefore it ought not to be disorderly, but ought to give a good example to other courts." All were heavily fined and were to be imprisoned until they confessed their faults and gave surety for good behavior. Six complied and were released. Two, refusing to surrender their claim to freedom of speech in Parliament, were held for ten years. Sir John Eliot, as explained earlier in this chapter, died in the Tower from tuberculosis, probably contracted in the chilling dampness there. Never was the character of Charles less attractive than in this incident. It has been said that Charles held Eliot morally guilty of the murder of his beloved Buckingham and hence would forgive him nothing.

PERSONAL GOVERNMENT: THE PROBLEM OF REVENUE

Charles now decided that he "abhorred the very name of Parliament." He would govern "by those means God put into my hands." For eleven years after 1629 no Parliament was called. Despite the peace with France and Spain Charles found that the financial pressure upon the crown was still heavy. Professor Tawney once rightly remarked that the whole of Stuart social policy was "smeared with the trail of finance." The repercussions of governmental and ecclesiastical economic activities can be traced in the remotest marches of the island, even as the economic bustlings of the merchants and landowners swirled in their own great currents.

Charles saved and skimped and searched for every expedient by which he might keep himself independent of parliamentary grants. But those from whom he asked money were often strong supporters of Parliament, reluctant to aid him. Charles continued his levy of tunnage and poundage; he revived such obsolete customs as the compulsory distraint of knighthood, a practice begun under Henry III, extended after 1278 by Edward I, and largely abandoned in the fifteenth century. Every subject whose income was more than £40 a year was required to accept knighthood or pay a fine. Charles sent out royal commissioners to collect the fines, which were less than the charges involved in accepting a knighthood. Public irritation was also increased by the forest fine. This was imposed upon those who were alleged to have purchased illegally areas of land that had once belonged to the great royal forests. The seventeenth century owners of such forests knew that they could not prove title to the satisfaction of courts controlled by the king. So they paid the fine to keep their lands. The king's commission for levying fines stated that Charles was "pleased for the ease and benefit of our subjects, upon reasonable fines and impositions to be paid into our exchequer for our use, to pardon and discharge them of all encroachments." However, the subjects who angrily paid the fines were not concerned with the application of Henry II's Assize of the Forest of 1184 and Henry III's Charter of the Forest of 1217. They felt that this procedure was all of a piece with the other unjust levies of the king.

Charles also continued his extensive sale of monopolies. Prices of monopoly-controlled goods rose steadily; as the number of monopolies increased the general cost of living rose. "The Crown and the monopoly-holders dip in our dish; they sit by our fire; we find them in the dye-fat, the wash bowls and the powdering tub. They share with the cutler in his box. They have marked and sheared us from head to foot."

Because of the European war neutral England was picking up a considerable amount of commerce. The years from 1629 to 1635 were seven fat years, particularly for the merchants. More and more they saw the disproportion between their wealth and political power. When the revival of forest fines and feudal dues spread resentment this new plutocracy of the merchants often found itself united with the aristocracy in sudden harmony of hatred of the government. This fact was later to be of considerable importance.

There now arose the question of ship money. In earlier centuries this had been a levy imposed in times of national emergency on the port towns of England by which these ports were asked to provide ships for the navy. The collection of ship money by Charles was not the use of an archaic device, as is often supposed. Writs for the collection of it had been issued in 1626 and 1627 when England was in a really critical situation. The money Charles collected was not used to strengthen his financial position; it did go to the building and equipment of ships. Writs were again issued for a levy in 1634. In 1635 the system was extended to all the counties of England and Wales; quotas of ships were demanded from every community, urban and rural. This general levy was defended by Charles on the plausible grounds that the inland counties were protected by the royal navy as well as the outer. Although this money was again actually spent on ships, the collection of it at a time when there was no emergency needed stronger justification than Charles provided. Many declared that ship money had become in fact a tax levied without parliamentary grant, violating the Petition of Right.

Charles addressed a letter to his judges "which, we doubt not, are well studied and informed in the right of our sovereignty." He asked them two questions: May the king compel his subjects to contribute ship money in a national emergency? May not the king decide when an emergency exists? The judges replied in the affirmative to each question. "In such cases your majesty is the sole judge both of the danger and when and how the same is to be prevented and avoided." The collection went ahead; but many declined to pay. In 1637 a test case was made when John Hampden of Buckinghamshire refused to pay twenty shillings assessed upon his land in accordance with the king's writ of 1636.

The name of John Hampden is high on the rolls of those who loved liberty. This cousin of Oliver Cromwell was a country gentleman from Chilterns, where there was a tradition of local freedom; in the thirteenth century the lumbermen of that district had stood for religious liberty and become Lollards; in the eighteenth century Quakers flourished there. Hampden had earlier gone from Magdalen College, Oxford, to the Inner Temple. "He had a great knowledge both in scholarship and the law; he was very well read in history." From 1625 until his death in 1643 Hampden, with his "flowing courtesy," quietly showed that he had more than a lawyer's passion for legal liberties. He had refused to pay the forced loan of 1626 because "he feared to draw upon himself that curse in Magna Carta which should be read twice a year against those who infringe it." The record of his refusal to pay ship money still stands in the village of Great Kimble in Buckinghamshire. "Would 20 s. have ruined Mr. Hampden's fortune? No; but the payment of half 20 s. *on the principle it was demanded* would have made him a slave."

Hampden was a born Parliament man. He worked with John Selden, Sir Edward Coke, and John Pym in the forefront of resistance to Charles. In committees "he had so subtle a way that he left his opinions with those from whom he pretended to learn and receive them." When Charles tried to impeach Hampden and four others in 1642 there rode up to London from Buckinghamshire 4,000 men to support him. He raised a foot regiment in the Civil War, his "green coats." At Chalgrove Field in the summer of 1643 he was mortally wounded. "He was observed to ride off the field before the action was done, which he never used to do, with his head hanging down, and resting his hands on the neck of his horse." When he lay dying, Charles I sent the vicar to inquire how he was.

This was the John Hampden summoned before the exchequer court in 1637 to show cause for the non-payment of the ship money levy. His attorneys declared the charge illegal; they spoke of the sanctity of private property. After twelve days of argument by opposing counsel before all the justices of the central courts in exchequer chamber, judgment was finally given against Hampden by a vote of seven to five. The majority held that the king had the right, absolute and unimpaired, to decide when there was a national emergency. Hence his discretionary power to collect the ship money levy for the national welfare in a crisis could not be challenged. To those who said there was no emergency warranting a ship money levy it was again replied that the king alone was legally judge of what constituted an emergency. On every front, it seemed, the determined Charles had been victorious.

PERSONAL GOVERNMENT:
THE PROBLEM OF THE CHURCH

Meanwhile the religious issue became steadily more bitter as the Laudian High Churchmen, loving ritual, fine music, stained glass, and order, pressed forward against the Puritans within and without the church. As explained above, the High Churchmen wanted no unadorned Puritan buildings, no plain services, no stern preaching of various sectual revelations. Laud himself became archbishop of Canterbury in 1633, when the High Church group was in the full tide of its power and seeking rigid conformity everywhere. Then, as always, Laud hated controversy more than he loved truth. Controversy can sometimes be ended by rigorous suppression. That is exactly what Laud, with his demonic energy, tried to do.

For external support the archbishop and his followers looked to Charles's personal government. Laud was resolved that nothing should thwart his policy of making a single ecclesiastical system prevail throughout England. All must be reduced to uniformity. Public and underground heterodoxy must be wiped away. All publications must be strictly censored. Local compounds of heresy and indifference must be eliminated. The old social harmony must be restored and factions cease. In the opinion of Laud it was not necessary to understand the reasons that wedded Englishmen to their diversity. For example, when he was elected chancellor of Oxford he not only counted the spoons when the induction feast was over; he also decided at once to foster what he called "right learning" and to suppress all other. Oxford would henceforth be an orthodox institution, correct and disciplined. Laud

succeeded very well, for a time. It was the Oxford he made that later
burned Thomas Hobbes' *Leviathan* and expelled John Locke.

The High Churchmen never understood, or saw any need for understanding, the Puritan definition of the church. To Laud and his fellows the church was a visible, separate body and its clergy guided and directed the laity. To the Puritans the clergy were not to be so exclusively and mysteriously separate from the congregation. By Puritan conceptions the ascetic godliness of the clergy was to be demanded of all the people. The whole Laudian idea of a clergy with the right to regulate or to permit indulgences to the laity and to lighten their spiritual exercises was anathema to Puritans. Individual personal effort was the first Puritan commandment. A man might amass a million pounds by personal effort. By personal effort alone could he settle his accounts with God. He needed no mediating clergy.

Many felt that Laud was anxious for a return of the Anglican Church to the fold of Rome, particularly as the recusancy laws were not enforced against the Catholics. The suspicions of Laud's papistical inclinations were not well founded. Because he could not control the court some Roman Catholics did gain favor in high quarters. Queen Henrietta Maria was the center of the Romanizing influence at the court, not Laud. But Laud could not afford to antagonize her. "All that he could do was walk by on the other side and that not too publicly." Fortunately the queen was more interested in dancing than in Catholic propaganda. Her idea of missionary activity was as elementary as most of her thought processes; it consisted of breaking up Anglican services in the royal household with two beagles and interrupting the preacher with hunting calls. Nevertheless, the Puritan suspicions were not easily removed. "The grim wolf with privy paw daily devours apace, and nothing said." So ran a line in Milton's *Lycidas*.

The degree to which Laud antagonized important social groups can be swiftly illustrated. In some areas of England the churches were decaying; the natural consequences of poverty were widely evident. Laud wanted to restore them and to increase the value of the livings. For some time he had opposed enclosures and the consequent depopulation of many rural areas. Now he found that many local landowners had been encroaching on church lands for personal profit. By his vigorous denunciation of the landowners, who were well represented in Parliament, Laud was creating enemies who would one day help to slay him. By offending them he also found that he was reducing the church income. More and more, the prosperous classes refused to contribute to a church that threatened to limit the power and the independence they cherished. Laud misjudged his allies and his enemies. He never appreciated that an expanding commercial and industrial society was creating classes of men who were quite prepared to break through the old coercive toils and sanctions of church and government where they found them inconvenient. The new, dynamic faiths fortified a way of life that Laud could never find intelligible. Nor did he see that the advantages he found in his policy were not such as appealed to the political, parliamentary forces of England. "The honour of the church appealed only to the church." As the external support of Charles's personal government declined, the Laudian cause was also weakened. In that sense Laud is a pathetic figure, a man born out of his time. So, too, was Charles I.

Between 1633 and 1637 Laud arranged a visitation of the parishes of England. All clergymen who differed from the High Church doctrines were forthwith discharged. Laymen were prosecuted on scores of charges. The prerogative court of star chamber inflicted heavy penalties; the ecclesiastical court of high commission harried the clergy who did not conform. Elizabeth had never allowed more than one bishop at a time to sit as a judge in the court of star chamber. Charles I appointed three; they attended faithfully. In the star chamber Laud was "observed always to concur with the severest side." Popular feeling was outraged by the harsh penalties imposed by the persecuting High Anglicans in the hated star chamber court.

Two cases will suffice to illustrate. Alexander Leighton was a fanatical Scotsman who denounced Henrietta Maria as a Jezebel, the bishops as anti-Christian ravens and magpies preying on the state, "knobs and wens of bunchy Popish flesh." The star chamber court sentenced him to pay a £10,000 fine. He was lashed; his cheeks were branded, his ears cut off, and his nose slit. William Prynne, mentioned in Chapter 16, was a man of remarkable learning and absence of judgment. His two hundred books were all bigoted and violent polemics of accumulated scurrility; today they are almost unreadable. He had come down from his home in Shropshire, attended Oriel College, Oxford, and then became a counsel for persecuted sectaries. Sir Christopher Wren said he had "the countenance of a witch." He attacked hundreds of things for as many reasons. The bishops he described as "devouring wolves and lords of Lucifer."

In the thousand pages of *Historiomastix* Prynne proved spicily that stage plays were immoral, with a long glance at Queen Henrietta Maria, who loved drama and dancing. The theatres were "devils' chapels." Pyrnne also denounced long hair, Maypoles, organs, Christmas, and bay windows. The times were so degenerate, he said, that Shakespeare was better printed than the Bible and more widely read than sermons.

In 1632 the court of star chamber dealt with this "libellous, seditious Puritan." He was fined £500, sentenced to the pillory, the loss of his university degree and his membership of the bar, and imprisoned. Both of his ears were cut off. Even among the Puritans he had lost support because of his extreme views. One of John Milton's reasons for writing *Comus* was to dissociate himself from Prynne. Nevertheless, this did not decrease the subsequent (1637) public sympathy at the severity of the sentence imposed upon him. Later released, he died in 1669, a respectable pensioner of the Restoration government of Charles II.

Of the court of star chamber a contemporary said: "It presently became delighted with blood, which sprung out of the ears and shoulders of the punished. Then began the English nation to lay to heart the slavish condition they were like to come under if this court continued in greatness." Thousands of Puritans emigrated to Holland. Hence Amsterdam became the "staple of sects and mint of schism." By such means Laud was driving the moderates over into the ranks of the opponents of his ecclesiastical policy. At the same time his master continued to alienate the moderates who might have supported the royal cause in matters of government.

THE SHORT PARLIAMENT

In England the public hostility to personal rule had deepened and spread more than Charles I and Laud were aware. Their proposal to bring Scotland into line with England was stark insanity. James I had installed bishops in Scotland, but their influence remained negligible. It was now decided to impose upon Scotsmen an appropriate Anglican form of worship. Charles even hoped that he might recover church property for the Scottish episcopal church. Laud prepared a liturgy, similar to the English Prayer Book, to be used in all Scottish churches. He decided that bishops should rule the Scottish Kirk instead of the presbyteries. When Charles ordered the use of the new Prayer Book in 1637 the result was tumult, riots, and a forest of claymores.

The Scots at once seized the Covenant that had been drawn up in 1581 against Roman Catholicism and redrafted it. From "the Tables" at Stirling it was circulated for signature throughout the land. It condemned Laud, "with all the subscribers and approvers of that cruel and bloody band conjured against the Kirk of God." It declared: "We promise and swear by the great name of the Lord our God to continue in the profession and obedience of the Presbyterian religion and we shall defend the same, and resist all the contrary errors and corruptions." To Thomas Wentworth, earl of Strafford, Laud wrote in 1638: "I am sorry to hear it but I doubt it is too true that most of the nation dote upon their abominable traitorous covenant . . . the greatest fear is want of money and minds of all men are mightily alienated and divided. And I fear you will see the King brought upon his knees to a Parliament, and then farewell to Church and ship money and no help but too late."

The Covenanters raised an army and dared Charles to fight. They had 10,000 soldiers under Leslie and Montrose. Charles could obtain no money. Nevertheless, he gathered an army and marched northwards in 1639. The men were such a motley crew that Charles could not hope for any success in battle. By the pacification of Berwick he agreed to leave the Scots alone. This was the first "Bishops' War," a name not given to it by contemptuous Puritans but by a crusading bishop.

Charles now recalled the able Sir Thomas Wentworth from Ireland. Wentworth, who had long before ceased to support Parliament, had been president of the council of the north and, after 1632, lord deputy of Ireland. In Ireland this proconsul had succeeded in his ruthless policy of "Thorough" and the Irish were effectively suppressed. "Black Tom Tyrant" favored despotic methods of government. He had done some good in Ireland; he helped the country prosper by introducing linen manufacture, clearing the sea of pirates, reopening Irish foreign trade and building an effective Irish army. But his methods earned him undying infamy in the hearts of Irishmen. The English and the Scots now feared Wentworth would favor a royal despotism and an efficient "Thorough" policy at home. The king made him the earl of Strafford. "No narrow considerations," said Strafford, "shall fall in my counsels as my own preservation till I see my master's power and greatness above the exposition of Sir Edward Coke and the common law. Let us then in the name of God go on cheerfully and boldly."

Strafford at once advised Charles to call Parliament. He argued that the Scots were rebelling and the English nation, long anti-Scottish, would support the king. "Scottish treason will be overcome by English loyalty." But the Scots had successfully defied Charles and the English applauded. When Parliament met on April 13, 1640, the lord keeper, speaking in behalf of Charles, referred to "some men of Belial" who had "blown the trumpet" in Scotland "and by their insolencies and rebellious action drawn many after them, to the utter desertion of his majesty's government." He asked for an immediate grant of money to put down the Scots. But Parliament was in no mood to vote supplies. It wanted to debate the grievances of the past eleven years. Parliamentary committees enumerated those grievances, one by one, "swarms of projecting canker-worms and caterpillars, the worst of the Egyptian plagues." At last, on May 5, 1640, Charles dissolved Parliament. "Some few cunning and some ill-affected men," said the king, "have been the cause of this misunderstanding." He did not see that the sense of national wrong was now deep and wide. John Pym, the great Somerset squire and successor of Eliot as leader of the commons, observed amidst the ensuing riots: "Things must go worse before they go better. I am wasting and perishing with grief to see how insensibly nigher and nigher draws the catastrophe which must inflict mortal wounds on our country." So ended the Short Parliament. It had lasted for three weeks. The Puritans and the gentry were in full cry after power. Meanwhile Laud was a target of popular displeasure. Six hundred apprentices laid siege to his palace at Lambeth. He stayed at Whitehall, protected by the king's guards.

THE LONG PARLIAMENT

Charles could borrow no money from the London merchants, the kings of France or Spain, the banks of Genoa, or the Pope. He seized the bullion the London goldsmiths had deposited in the mint and the pepper from the warehouse of the East India Company. Financial circles were disrupted; panic threatened. Through the summer of 1640 he planned a campaign against the Scots. But the Scotsmen were hardy and armed; the forces Charles bunched together were not. All the king's attempts to raise money and to obtain military equipment failed. The Scots invaded England's northern counties and the English had to retreat. In October, 1640, came the end of this second "Bishops' War." Charles signed the Treaty of Ripon. The Scots insisted upon staying in England, at the charge of the English government, until a final agreement was ratified by Parliament. Thus Charles had to summon a new Parliament "to buy the Scots out of England." They were costing £850 a day.

On November 3, 1640, the famous Long Parliament assembled. Tempers were hot and revolution was in the air. Charles had to face that fact. Under the leadership of John Pym and John Hampden the house of commons struck first at the king's advisers, the instruments of royal government. Strafford and Laud were arrested. Strafford was first accused of high treason. His bold and resourceful genius must be disposed of. It was alleged that he had attempted "to subvert the fundamental laws and government of England and Ireland, and instead thereof to introduce an arbitrary and tyrannical government against law"; that he had exercised "tyrannical and exorbitant power." He was impeached, "all gazing, and no man capping to him before whom that morning the greatest in England would have stood uncovered." Strafford's courage and defense were magnificent. "We have lived, my lords, happily to ourselves at home; we have lived gloriously abroad to the world. Let us be content with that which our fathers left us, and let us not awake these sleeping lions to our destruction by rattling up of a company of records that have lain so many ages by the wall forgotten or neglected."

No proof that Strafford was technically guilty of high treason could be submitted to the lords at Westminster Hall. Hence the commons adopted an alternative procedure. Recourse was had to the method of an act of attainder, by which no proof of guilt need be offered; such an act simply condemned the accused to death. The commons passed the bill and carried it to the house of lords. John Pym stirred up the London mobs to howl for Strafford's head. The lords passed the bill. Charles had promised that Strafford would not die; but pleading the danger to his wife and children he signed the bill condemning his servant to death. Bitterly Strafford exclaimed: "Put not your trust in princes!"

The Puritans had determined that Strafford should die. From the prison window Laud watched his ally and friend pass by to the scaffold. On May 12, 1641, 200,000 people saw Strafford beheaded on Tower Hill. "I am now petitioning a higher court where neither partiality can be expected, nor error feared."

What fate awaited Laud? Gone was his power; his failure was complete; he had waited for the vengeful talons of his enemies to seize him, an old man who had been too brave to fly and who could not hope to live much longer in any event. On February 14, 1641, the house of commons had impeached him under fourteen charges, accusing him of attempting "to subvert the fundamental laws of the kingdom," of selling justice, of usurping "papal and tyrannical doctrines," of secret communion with Rome, of persecuting "the learned and orthodox," of stirring up an Anglo-Scottish war. On the way to the Tower he had been insulted and abused. "My patience was not moved. I looked upon a higher cause than Shimei and his children."

For nearly three years Laud was not brought to trial. New charges were prepared, among them one of "introducing Popish superstition and idolatry." Laud's old enemy William Prynne was scuttling and prying about for evidence of Laud's treason. When his raids and his inquisitions provided nothing, Prynne tampered with witnesses; he edited Laud's private diary which he had stolen. The judges were apathetic. Laud's end was sure. On a great black scaffold, built high so all could see, he was executed on January 10, 1645.

Meanwhile the Long Parliament swiftly undertook legislation designed to make arbitrary government impossible in the future. To protect itself against a possible "untimely adjourning, proroguing, or dissolving" by the king it passed an act stating that it could not be dissolved without its own consent. A second piece of legislation "for the preventing of inconveniences happening by the long intermission of parliaments" was the new Triennial Act. This act provided that Parliament was to assemble once in every three years whether or not it had been summoned by the king.

The arbitrary prerogative courts of star chamber, high commission, and requests, together with the council of the north and the council of Wales were abolished. Ship money and other arbitrary levies were forbidden. "The said charge imposed upon the subject for the providing and furnishing of ships commonly called ship money . . . and the said writs . . . and the said judgment given against the said John Hampden, were and are contrary to and against the laws and statutes of this realm, the right of property, the liberty of the subjects, former resolutions in parliament, and the Petition of Right made in the third year of the reign of his majesty that now is." Further acts defined forests and forest laws, ended the abuses of forest fines, and abolished fines for distraint of knighthood. The commons also resolved that judges should not hold office at the pleasure of the king but during good behavior. Thus John Pym was leading a united opposition to the royal system of government.

On the issue of religion Pym could find or forge no unity. Was the Laudian system to be destroyed? If so, what would be put in its place? Some thoroughly radical Puritans prepared a "Root and Branch" bill designed to wipe out episcopacy completely. Opposed to them were the conservatives and the moderates who wanted only to purge the church of the Laudian innovations, nothing more. In the Anglican church structure and organization they wanted no change. Debates grew violent; the salvation of souls was at stake. Out of these stormy hours there began to emerge two groups. The more radical element included John Hampden and Oliver Cromwell. The conservative Anglican members were led by Lord Falkland and Edward Hyde, later the famous earl of Clarendon, lord chancellor of England in the reign of Charles II. Standing on the outer edge of the group of radical members was the veteran John Pym. His realistic moderation was later to create the parliamentary machine that finally conquered Charles I. For a few months in 1643 and 1644 he was to hold together about forty members in the commons, a middle group united in vague, tenuous, and fragile fashion by common interests such as Puritanism and family connections.

THE EVE OF WAR

Amid the turmoil Parliament adjourned for four months. Riotous disturbances and strange, fanatical, religious cults sprang up throughout the country. Moderates began to shrink from the visible evidences of a disordered state and to become still more conservative. Meanwhile the Catholic Irish whom Strafford had once restrained burst forth in rebellion to redress their manifold wrongs. Their anger was swiftly turned against the Ulster Protestants, interlopers from Scotland and England. Thousands of the Ulsterites were slain or driven from their homes and lands to die of hunger. Irish Catholic anarchy swept over the fields again.

Soon after Parliament met in October, 1641, news of the Irish rebellion came. The angry commons wanted to crush the rebels at once. At the same time they hesitated to put an army under the command of Charles. The king might use the army to scatter the members of Parliament. Pym and the radicals wanted to have the control of the army in the hands of ministers approved by the commons. But such a step, surely, would make Parliament superior to the king. Pym and his associates argued that an even balance in government between Parliament and crown could never be maintained. It was necessary, they declared, to go further and make Parliament superior; it would be folly to stop still where they were. On the other hand, many conservatives and moderates, frequently touched by an anti-Puritan spirit, consented only to support a reduction of the royal power so that the king would be equal to Parliament. Beyond that they would not go.

The Pym group now took the revolutionary road towards parliamentary government, declaring that it was the only practical thing to do. The Grand Remonstrance was prepared in November, 1641. This famous document recited 201 acts of Charles and his servants that had been offensive; it set forth what had been done to remedy national grievances; it also advanced new demands. For example, it asked Charles to use ministers "such as the Parliament may have cause to confide in." It asked him to curtail the powers of the bishops and end "oppressions in religion." The Grand Remonstrance was passed in the house of commons by a majority of only eleven. "Had it been rejected," declared Oliver Cromwell, "I would have sold tomorrow all I possess and left England forever." But the vote showed that the anti-Puritan party was growing. Many men were getting ready to fall in behind the banners of Charles and the church because they wanted no whirlwind of revolution in which the radicals would rise to power. The situation was grave. No compromise was possible. The house of commons was splitting asunder.

On January 4, 1642, Charles I came down to the commons with 400 swordsmen. His purpose was to arrest Pym, Hampden, and three other leaders. "In an hour," he had said, "I will return master of my kingdom." Warned of Charles's coming, the five members had fled by the river. The king asked where they were. The speaker of the commons replied that he had "neither eyes to see nor tongue to speak in this place but as this house shall direct me." Charles, having remarked that "the birds are flown," walked out amid cries of objection to his invading the house. After January 10 he sent Henrietta Maria to France, took up his headquarters in York, and began to gather an army.

Meanwhile the Irish rebellion still raged. To crush it Parliament proposed to call out the militia. Would Charles turn these forces against Parliament? Because the commons thought he might, a Militia Bill was introduced which took control of the military forces out of the king's hands and gave Parliament power to appoint all militia commanders. When Charles refused to sign this bill Parliament made it into an ordinance. The ordinance referred to "this time of imminent danger" and "the bloody counsels of Papists and other ill-affected persons." It appointed militia commanders for each county. On May 27, 1642, the king ordered the people by royal proclamation to disobey the ordinance of Parliament. If they should obey it, "we shall then call them in due time to a strict account and proceed legally against them as violators of the laws and disturbers of the peace of this kingdom." On the same day both houses of Parliament declared that their ordinance must be obeyed.

Four days later Parliament asked Charles to accept the Nineteen Propositions "as the most necessary effectual means, through God's blessing, of removing those jealousies and differences which have unhappily fallen betwixt you and your people." Under the terms of the Nineteen Propositions, the privy councillors, the principal officers and judges of the state, the tutors of the king's children, all were to be appointed only with the approval of Parliament. The king was asked to put all forts and castles under Parliament's control; to dismiss his military forces; to take away the votes of all Catholic peers; to promise that his children would not conclude any marriage not approved by Parliament; to enforce the laws against Jesuits, priests and Popish recusants. Such were the major demands of the Nineteen Propositions. It is doubtful if Parliament really hoped that Charles would accept them. Their acceptance would have left him but a puppet king. In any event, he refused. On August 22, 1642, in the summer green near Nottingham, Charles raised the royal standard on a hill. As it swung to flutter on the breeze the Civil War had begun.

Behind Parliament stood London, containing 500,000 people, a tenth of the population of England, filled with resources of trade and wealth. Out of the south and east came men to support Parliament. They came from the progressive Midlands and East Anglia; from Puritan, middle class towns like Birmingham, Colchester, and Manchester; from trading seaports like Hull and Portsmouth. Parliament thus had strong economic resources. It soon developed an admirable taxation system. It controlled these wealthy regions; it controlled trade and the sea. The navy that Charles had built up with ship money went over to the side of Parliament.

Behind Charles I were ranged wide areas of the north and west. From them came support from the feudal lords; from the Anglican Church and the Catholics; the country squires who loved the land and the church and were proudly untouched by the whirling commercialism of the urban fleshpots; the peasantry, strong to give a rouse for King Charles. Many a country family melted down its plate for him. The colleges of Oxford did, and some at Cambridge. Land was not an immediate, liquid asset. The Royalist supporters had much land. On the other hand, the Parliament men had much money, easily available to finance a war.

Except in a general way, the Civil War was far from being a cleavage between geographical areas or classes. Many of the gentry, for reasons earlier suggested, supported Parliament. On the other hand, many townsmen fought in the Royalist ranks. Even those who really disliked episcopacy often fought for Charles because they opposed the extreme pretensions of Parliament. Classes and families were shot through with divisions. Several refused to desert the king because they thought it a dishonorable thing to do. Sir Edmund Verney, Charles's standard bearer at Edgehill, wrote: "I heartily wish the King would yield to the Parliament's terms. But I have eaten his bread and served him well nigh thirty years, and I will not do so base a thing as to forsake him; I chose rather to lose my life—which I am sure to do—to preserve and defend those things which are against my conscience to preserve and defend." To many men the instinct of loyalty to the king was a powerful force.

Of the house of commons 300 supported Parliament; 175 sided with Charles I. Of the house of lords 30 were for Parliament, 80 for the king. On both sides many entered upon the war with reluctance and sadness, for they were fighting no foreign foe, but Englishmen. Many, too, feared the results. One said: "I would not have the king trample on the Parliament, nor the Parliament lessen him so much as to make a way for the people to rule us all."

Chapter 18

CIVIL WAR AND REPUBLIC

CAVALIER AND ROUNDHEAD

LONG before the war began Charles I was gathering money. "Trusty and well beloved," he had written to Sir Rowland Egerton on February 8, 1642, "we desire you forthwith to lend us the sum of 2,000 pounds for our necessary support and the maintenance of our army, which we are compelled to raise for the defence of our person, the Protestant religion, and the laws of the land." At the same time the leaders of Parliament, as described in the previous chapter, were seeking out gold and silver. In June, 1642, they published proposals for bringing in money and plate "for the defence and peace of the kingdom." Despite the order of Charles that no citizen should lend money to Parliament, his opponents collected large amounts during the early years of the war. Many gifts were small. In Tonbridge, for example, Thomas Horn, who was a schoolmaster, gave £1; Mary Bartlet, a widow, lent £10 in plate. It was from the wealthy merchants and tradesmen of the cities that the large donations came.

Despite its considerable financial resources Parliament was handicapped in the early stages of the war by lack of efficient fighting men. Many of the Royalists were gentlemen of birth, used to the sword. Their great strength lay in their cavalry power; hence the whole group were called Cavaliers. The Parliamentarians, on the other hand, had few troops of horse; their power was at first in the London militia, in the footsoldiers recruited in the counties. Only a few officers in both groups had served in the armies of Sweden or Holland in the Thirty Years' War; the rest had had no military experience. At first neither side had good generals. The earl of Essex, son of Elizabeth's favorite and a respectable mediocrity, commanded the forces of Parliament. Outstanding in the Royalist armies was the king's nephew Prince Rupert, dashing cavalry officer, inventor of Rupert's drops, and holder of the great grant of Rupert's Land in North America. The overall command of the Royalist armies was in the hands of Charles himself.

Hostilities began with a series of skirmishes all over England. There were no major engagements. Essex, with 20,000 troops, stood athwart the road to London. Charles, seeking to enlist more men, particularly Welsh horsemen, before he struck into Middlesex, moved westward; at Shrewsbury he turned to march on the capital. At Edgehill Essex awaited him. There the first battle was fought. Rupert's cavalry routed the horsemen of the Puritan Roundheads; but the Parliament's infantry closed its ranks and the battle was indecisive. Then Charles marched on to the sprawling outskirts of London. There he was blocked by the London militia and turned back to take up winter headquarters at Oxford.

In the spring of 1643 Charles had three armies in the field with which he planned to mount a three-pronged offensive on London. One Royalist army would strike down from Yorkshire in the northeast; a second would attack from the southwest out of Cornwall and Devon; a third would move in from Oxford. The earl of Newcastle won victories for Charles in the northeast and forced Parliament's Lord Fairfax to retreat into fortified Hull. When Newcastle advanced southward out of Yorkshire into Lincolnshire he was stopped by two obstacles. The first was the fact that his forces did not want to march down to London and thus leave the Parliamentarians behind them to plunder their lands and homes. The current of strong local feeling is a constant factor throughout the Civil War. Secondly, Newcastle was checked by the northeastern Puritan armies organized by Oliver Cromwell, whose home was in nearby Huntingdonshire. So Newcastle turned back to besiege Hull.

The same pattern of events was repeated in the southwest. Sir Ralph Hopton, the local Royalist commander, led the troops of Cornwall and Devon towards London. As they marched, they looked back to Plymouth, supplied by Parliament's navy and garrisoned by Roundheads. They finally decided that they did not want to expose their home counties to these Puritan forces. So they turned back to lay siege to Plymouth.

Charles's main army was held up by the parliamentary defense of Gloucester. Here, as in the case of Hull and Plymouth, Gloucester was in the rear of the Royalist armies. Again, the king's forces were reluctant to continue their advance towards London without reducing Gloucester and thus sparing their countryside the ravages of Puritan raids. So Charles laid siege to this town. Essex rushed out of London to relieve Gloucester; he did so, and slashed his way back to London after fighting the battle of Newbury. Thus, at the end of 1643, the Royalists had not taken London; they had not seized any of the fortified cities held by the Parliamentarians. Nevertheless, they had widely extended their occupation of territory; they had won several victories. The outlook for the parliamentary cause seemed black if the relentless Royalist pressure continued in 1644.

Two events were changing the military scene. The first was the Solemn League and Covenant, the work of John Pym. Indeed, it was his last achievement, for he died three months later. In December, 1643, after "mature deliberation" this treaty was concluded with the Scotsmen. Under its terms the Long Parliament practically agreed to establish a Presbyterian church in England and to give the Scots a subsidy in return for the promise that 20,000 men would be sent from Scotland to fight against Charles. As a result, a joint executive Committee of Both Kingdoms was established to prosecute the war. In January, 1644, a Scottish army invaded England to join parliamentary forces under the earl of Manchester.

The second event of major importance was the extension and reorganization of the Roundhead armies. Local regiments had been undergoing basic training for several months, particularly in the eastern counties. One cavalry regiment under Oliver Cromwell became outstanding for its efficiency, strict discipline, and morale. Cromwell recognized the importance of obtaining an army of enthusiasts. To do that he began to use the strong moral force of uncompromising Puritanism. He wanted "such men as had the fear of God before them and made some conscience of what they did." Conscious of their divine mission, his Ironsides went forth to battle for the Lord. The influence and example of these "men of religion" spread by osmotic process throughout the parliamentary forces.

In July, 1644, a Scottish-Roundhead army of about 27,000 met 17,000 Cavaliers led by Prince Rupert on Marston Moor, eight miles from York. Cromwell's Ironsides broke through Rupert's cavalry on the Royalist right wing, then wheeled to assault the Royalist infantry from the rear. "God made them as stubble to our swords," wrote Cromwell. Newcastle's infantry, the Whitecoats, were nearly wiped out by the Ironsides and the Scottish pikemen. York surrendered; the northeast was lost to the king.

Elsewhere Charles fared better. Highlanders came down from Scotland to fight for him. Parliament's earl of Essex was badly defeated in Cornwall. The earl of Manchester's leadership had been inept. Many Roundheads felt that some cautious and dilatory commanders like Essex and Manchester were anxious to come to terms with the king, to reach a compromise. Hence they had waged war half-heartedly. Those who insisted upon unconditional surrender from Charles now demanded a change in command and a thorough reorganization of the parliamentary armies.

To end the reign of lukewarm and incompetent commanders Parliament passed the Self-Denying Ordinance in December, 1644. This required all members of Parliament to resign their military commands. As a member of Parliament, Cromwell gave up his commission. At the end of forty days he was appointed Lieutenant-General of Horse and second in command of the parliamentary armies. The commander-in-chief was Sir Thomas Fairfax, hero of Yorkshire. Thus, by the Self-Denying Ordinance, all members of Parliament resigned their military posts. Those whom the Roundheads wanted back again were later re-appointed; the others were not. The procedure avoided vicious bickering and recrimination about who should retire and why.

THE NEW MODEL ARMY

The Committee of Both Kingdoms now completely reorganized the armies of Parliament along the lines of Cromwell's Eastern Association. On February 17, 1645, an ordinance was passed providing for the formation of the New Model Army. Under the earlier system there had been frequent desertions, laxity of discipline, difficulties about pay, and a general unwillingness on the part of local troops to cross the boundaries of their own shires. All these defects were also found among the Royalist armies throughout the war. The ordinance founding the New Model Army was intended to create a force paid directly by Parliament; this "constant pay" was to be charged against national taxation. By this time Parliament was making great strides in organizing taxation devices to tap the great wealth of the territory under its control.

The three existing parliamentary armies, formerly commanded by Essex, Manchester, and Waller, were now united into a single force comprising eleven regiments of horse, twelve of foot, and one of dragoons. The nominal strength of these three armies had been about 30,000; but wastage resulting from casualties and desertion in 1644 had been so heavy that hardly half of the 14,400 infantry needed for the foot regiments could be supplied. When the New Model Army assembled in April at Windsor for its first campaign it was still below its fixed establishment.

The battlefields of the seventeenth century were dominated by the cavalry. Horsemen of the New Model Army got two shillings a day, but they had to look after their horses and part of the pay was held back by Parliament as security against desertion. It was "a good employment for a gentleman." The tone of the New Model Army was set by Cromwell's Ironsides, and it was now Cromwell's main task, as Lieutenant-General, to train all the cavalry regiments "armed only with swords and pistols, taught to reserve their fire until they came to close quarters with the enemy, their heavy horses charging 'at pretty round trot.' "

The foot soldiers were armed with either muskets or pikes. There were usually about two musketeers to every pikeman. Each musketeer carried a few ready-made charges in a bandolier over his shoulder; bullets in a small pouch with one or two ready for use in his mouth; about three or four inches of tow to be lighted when action began. When the ready-made charges were exhausted, powder had to be poured down the muzzles of heavy matchlock muskets. The loading and firing of a musket took a long time. Musketeers also carried swords to be used when they had no time to shoot. They wore red coats; regiments were distinguished by facings of the colonel's color. They were given protection by the pikemen. When the bayonet was later invented, pikemen and musketeers, of course, became one. The pikes, about sixteen feet long, were difficult to handle on a windy day. Pikemen also carried the weight of defensive armor. To bear all the awkward heaviness of their equipment the pikemen had to be robust; to manage the clumsy and dangerous matchlocks the musketeers had to be agile.

The New Model Army became a formidable and efficient military machine, the first national standing army. It had strict discipline; violations of it were punished by penalties similar to those today. The regular payment of soldiers helped to reduce plundering and desertion. Late in 1645 there were 80,000 troops in the ranks of this parliamentary force. Cromwell told Parliament that he wanted good soldiers, not necessarily sound Presbyterians. No religious test of any kind was put on the men. Only in later days was the army leavened and committed to certain political views and the maintenance of limited religious tolerance by force.

The purpose of the New Model Army was soon to be served. It had been created in February, 1645, for "a more speedy, vigorous and effectual prosecution of the war." That task it was to perform, fearing God and keeping its powder dry.

The first opportunity came in June, 1645. Fairfax and Cromwell gave battle to Charles's main army at Naseby, northeast of Oxford, in Northamptonshire. The religious fervor of the New Model Army united with its training and discipline to wreak havoc on the Royalists. At Naseby the army of Charles was routed. "I could not but smile out to God in praises, in assurance of victory," wrote Cromwell later. "God did it and it is wonderful in my eyes." The Lord was mightily visiting His people. The war was becoming a holy war, a crusade against the forces of darkness.

Charles had lost the Midlands. In July Fairfax defeated a smaller Royalist army in Somerset. In September the Scottish Highlander Montrose was crushed by the Covenanters near Selkirk. The king had no more armies. For nearly a year there were scattered skirmishes. Loyal Oxford fell in June, 1646. Charles had earlier fled, and surrendered to the Scots.

PARLIAMENT VERSUS ARMY

Now that the controlled momentum of the New Model Army had brought the king to surrender, what was to be done with the victory? What new arrangements should be made in the church and state? The victors swiftly fell into dispute. Indeed, from 1642 onwards there had been strong signs that the only bond holding various groups together was a common opposition to Charles. When war had begun in August, 1642, Parliament had divided; some had gone to the king's standards; some to the army of Parliament; and a few had just gone home. Those of the Long Parliament who were united against Charles had rapidly disagreed about other things. In 1646 they were still divided.

The religious problem was most explosive. All remaining in Parliament generally opposed episcopacy. The majority, Presbyterian in sympathy, wanted a Presbyterian state church. But would the Presbyterians be any less intolerant than the Catholics or the Anglicans? Knox was surely as rigid in his views as Laud. And there were thousands of Anglicans in England, increasing thousands of Independents, uncounted adherents of other sects mushrooming through the counties. What of them? Would the Presbyterians ever incline to toleration for them? The parliamentary party, within and without Parliament, was bitterly split. The Independents, of course, hated presbyters as much as they did bishops. And the army, winning victories for Parliament, contained thousands of these Independents as well as representatives of most other sects. It was politically wise to heed the army.

In 1643 Parliament had accepted the Solemn League and Covenant and practically agreed to set up a Presbyterian Church in England. When Charles surrendered to the Scots in 1646 this Parliament calmly went ahead with its Presbyterian projects. It presented the Propositions of Newcastle to Charles in the summer of 1646 demanding the establishment of a Presbyterian Church in England; the control of the army and navy by Parliament for twenty years; the enforcement of the anti-Catholic penal laws. Charles deliberately delayed his answer. He would balance the Presbyterians against the Independents. At last he declared that he would accept the Covenant for three years. He did not want to enforce the anti-Catholic code. He wished to reduce the period of parliamentary control of the army to ten years. The Scottish Covenanters, angered by Charles's opposition to Presbyterians, handed him over to Parliament after they had been paid £400,000 to cover their expenses.

With the king in their hands Parliament passed bills establishing a Presbyterian church system. It insisted, as Laud had done, on a uniform religion throughout England. It began a bludgeoning persecution of all who were not Presbyterians, particularly the Baptists and Independents. It expelled 2,000 Anglican clergy from their parishes and forbade the use of the Prayer Book. It imposed crippling fines on the Royalists, calling them "rebels." These merciless Presbyterian attacks cemented a political alliance between parsons and squires that has persisted up to our own time. Early in 1647 the New Model Army, already infuriated by arbitrary persecution and denial of religious liberty, was ordered to disband. No provision was made for paying the soldiers' back wages. This was a dangerous thing for Parliament to do.

Their medicine was not one for the distempers of the age. The Presbyterians possessed faith and hope, but not charity, prudence, or pliable common sense.

The New Model Army did not go home. Calculations of justice and safety said otherwise. The soldiers prepared to mutiny. Faced by this prospect, Parliament undertook another maneuver. Charles had long hoped to profit by the breach between the Presbyterian Parliament and the Independents; that was the reason why he dallied so long over the Newcastle Propositions. Now, it seemed, his hope was realized. Parliament, seeking to join forces with the king and the Royalists, offered to restore Charles with his royal authority unimpaired if he would establish a Presbyterian church in England for only three years.

The army proceeded to take a hand in torpedoing the reactionary Presbyterians by kidnapping Charles in the summer of 1647. It was then clear that for a time there could be no Royalist-Presbyterian conspiracy against the Independents or anyone else. Oliver Cromwell, who had long tried to effect a compromise between the New Model Army and Parliament, declared that he would support his soldiers. In doing so, he perhaps hoped that his influence in the army might prevent the threat of war from becoming a reality. With their former leader back among them the soldiers might be more amenable to discipline. At the same time Parliament might shrink from further disputes with a New Model Army led once again by Oliver Cromwell.

THE CRISIS OF DEMOCRATIC IDEAS

Meanwhile radical democratic political theories had been developing in the lower ranks of the army and, to a lesser extent, elsewhere in England. Through the long months of war the common soldiers had debated their policies and attitudes. Having found much wrong in the country, they began to talk about ways of setting things right. In doing so, it was natural that they should find agreeable answers in the radical proposals of the Levellers.

These Levellers, of whom there were probably 10,000 in London, were mostly Independents in religion. Because they were Independents they opposed a national church with appointed officials and ecclesiastical hierarchies. They would ordain their own clergy in congregations relatively independent and self-sufficient; they would conduct their own form of worship without authority from ecclesiastical powers or civil magistrates. A democratic set of ideas such as these, arising from religious causes, easily became political in their direction and consequences. Thus many Independents, within and without the army, wishing no "classic hierarchy" to "ride our consciences that Christ set free," also found themselves politically democratic Levellers.

The Levellers were not only common soldiers; they were artisans, small tradesmen, and farmers interested in maintaining human rights, the rights of Englishmen as persons. Behind legal rights of property and station they saw natural rights and natural justice. Political equality, they declared, should have no economic implications. Parliament should represent the people, not property. "Sovereignty lies only in the people and parliament governs only by their consent." Thus came into prominence the Leveller ideas of the inalienable rights of the individual, of law having authority by the "consent of the people," of the origin of government in an original compact, and, finally, the opinion that the powers of the government should be limited by a fundamental law emanating from the people. "The laws of the land are only valid when they are a statement of higher laws." Through all the later period of the Civil War runs the pervasive influence of the Levellers, weakening reverence for social distinction and dignity of office.

In these years of ferment there were others who held radical political and economic ideas. Some, such as the Fifth Monarchy Men, nursed strange and mystical notions. One group asked a question that has not yet been answered. It was a question about economic democracy. This group, known as the Diggers, asserted that the moral justification of all political institutions was to be found in the well-being of the common people. "God has created the earth a storehouse and a common treasure for all mankind."

The Digger movement began in 1648 in Buckinghamshire. The prophet Everard, who had been cashiered from the army, led a band who attempted communism in land, declaring that political freedom had its condition in economic arrangements. They proposed to take and cultivate unenclosed land and distribute the produce to the poor. "All men are free by God's franchise," asserted the *Light Shining in Buckinghamshire*. The Diggers claimed that no individual was intended to exercise rule over his fellow men. They "sowed the ground with parsnips, carrots, and beans," and gave the crops away. They insisted that the hungry must be fed, the naked clothed. There must be no buying or selling. There must be no unequal wealth, for wealth gives power over others. "Break to pieces the bonds of property, for it is property that made men slaves." Landlords and magistrates were tyrants. "Freedom is to be found only in the unimpeded enjoyment of the land. Property there must be, but all men must possess it." These extremely radical and communistic theories of the Diggers were not widely accepted. The council of state and other authorities interfered with their activities. This episode of their appearance is at once interesting, pathetic, and an indication of the restless seas of the Civil War spirit.

When the officers of the army were confronted with the Leveller ideas of the common soldiers they could not agree with Rainborough that "the poorest he that is in England" should rank with "the greatest he." The dissatisfied soldiers might believe in Leveller doctrines, in equal opportunity for all, in universal suffrage, and so on. But officers, such as Cromwell and his son-in-law Henry Ireton, felt that "nobody has a right to a share in disposing the affairs of this kingdom unless he has a permanent fixed interest in this kingdom." The temperate Cromwell did not base his opposition to the Levellers solely on grounds of the importance of property-holders in a society. He felt that the pro-

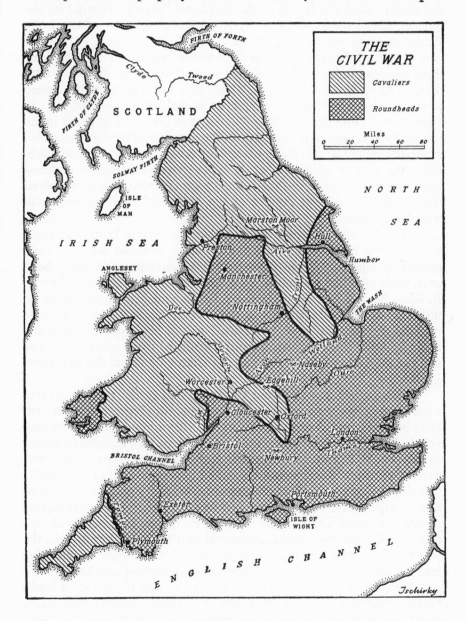

posals of the Levellers marked too radical a departure from previous English practices in government. He believed that England would not go along with such extreme theories and that it was the duty of the officers to induce the common soldiers to moderate their demands.

Against this background Cromwell persuaded the army to offer the king a final settlement. This was done in the long and detailed document called the Heads of the Proposals, largely prepared by the officers. Charles was asked to agree to the dissolution of the Long Parliament and the election of a new one. In the future a Parliament was to be called every two years; each Parliament was to sit at least three months "unless adjourned or dissolved sooner by their own consent." The Heads of the Proposals also asked that plans be developed to ensure "more perfection of equality in the distribution" of seats in Parliament, a broader franchise, "freedom in the election, order in the proceeding thereto, and certainty in the returns." The document also requested religious toleration, except for Anglicans and Roman Catholics; the redress of a number of other grievances regarding forest laws, monopolies, excise taxes, and so on. Finally, it was proposed that Parliament assume control of the army and the great offices of state for ten years.

Had Charles accepted these rather reasonable terms the royal power would have been reined and checked; it would not have been essentially changed. From the intractable king's point of view, however, there could be no sharing or diminution of the prerogative royal. Besides, he felt that by playing off Parliament against the army he might do better still, perhaps in the end set his foot upon both. He rejected the Heads of the Proposals. Nor did he scruple to negotiate again with the Presbyterians. About himself he wove a net of intrigue and deceit. To save the throne and the church he found any deception justified.

The soldiers now did what Cromwell had earlier tried to prevent them from doing. Suspicious of their officers, who represented different class interests, and distrustful of Charles, they drew up their own proposals. Filled with the doctrines of the Levellers, they decided to appeal to the people, from whom came all authority. Accordingly, they prepared their draft of a constitution, called the Agreement of the People. "Having, by our late labors and hazards, made it appear to the world at how high a rate we value our just freedom, and God so far having owned our course as to deliver the enemies thereof into our hands, we do now hold ourselves bound, in mutual duty to each other, to take the best care we can for the future to avoid both the danger of returning into a slavish condition and the chargeable remedy of another war."

The Agreement abolished the monarchy and the house of lords. Government was to be in the hands of a single-chamber Parliament elected by universal manhood suffrage, with the provision that those who had supported Charles in the war might not vote or be elected for seven years. The ninth clause of the Agreement provided for wide religious toleration. "Such as profess faith in God by Jesus Christ, however differing in judgment from the doctrine, worship, or discipline publicly held . . . shall not be restrained from, but shall be protected in, the profession of their faith and exercise of religion according to their consciences." The democratic form of government set forth in the Agreement was limited by an exact and written statement of a bill of rights setting forth certain fundamental liberties, based on the laws of reason and nature, of which the subject could never be deprived.

At first the soldiers demanded a referendum on the merits of their draft constitution. It must be accepted or rejected by "the sovereign people." After long debates, Cromwell, Ireton, and other officers finally persuaded the soldiers to temper their document into a less revolutionary condition and then to submit it to Parliament instead of holding a popular plebiscite. Ireton called the Agreement "political moonshine." The moment the soldiers agreed to do this the immediate political fate of their proposals was sealed. Parliament, of course, would have nothing of what they considered the chimeras of wild and revolutionary spirits.

The Agreement of the People, stating so many of the Leveller theories, grew out of the religious ideas of the Independents and the old concept of a constitution as a statement of fundamental law. Here was evolved the idea of a written constitution with paramount laws limiting the powers of government; this constitution, as all law, was to be enforceable through the courts. Here, too, appears sharply and vividly the idea that there are individual, inalienable rights possessed by all men. Mankind has been endowed by the Creator with rights such as those later more precisely defined as life, liberty, and the pursuit of happiness. And finally there appears the idea of the overwhelming sovereignty of the people. The Leveller and Independent ideas of democracy in seventeenth century England united with the angry and robust voice of Sir Edward Coke to exert a profound influence on later democratic institutional development in the United States. Some of these consequences flowed directly, as in the case of Independent colonists and their descendants; others were channelled through the works of such men as John Locke and the French philosophers to Thomas Jefferson and his contemporaries who were concerned with the state and dignity of man.

THE FALL OF THE KING

In November, 1647, Charles escaped from Hampton Court and fled to the Isle of Wight, where he was again made prisoner. In December, after long negotiations with the Scots, he agreed at last to establish Presbyterianism in England for three years. A large Scottish army then invaded England; they were keeping their bargain with the king. English Presbyterians and Royalists gave scattered support. Charles apparently never understood what a desperate gamble he was making. If the Scots lost, he was lost. From the Ironsides, implacably and poisonously hostile, he could expect no mercy. He had dallied in negotiations with both sides; he had played a waiting game, writing to the queen in Paris, hoping for foreign intervention. And he had also betrayed almost all with whom he parleyed. That was his darkest sin, his duplicity. To treat with him was idle; to trust him would be suicide.

Early in 1648 Cromwell met the leaders of the New Model Army at Windsor. The officers and soldiers patched up their differences. Together they came to "a very clear and joint resolution that it was our duty, if ever the Lord brought us back again in peace, to call Charles Stuart, that man of blood, to account for the blood he has shed and the mischief he has done to his utmost against the Lord's cause and people in this poor nation." So the redcoats of the New Model Army went forth to war again.

The second Civil War lasted only a few months. On August, 1648, the Scottish cavalry were routed at Preston in Lancashire and all their infantry captured. Meanwhile General Fairfax took the Presbyterian town of Colchester. Many of the captives were transported to the Barbadoes. The blaze of a small revolt in Wales was quickly snuffed out.

When the New Model Army was in the north, Parliament had been negotiating again with Charles. Cromwell and Fairfax marched back to London determined to settle both with Charles and the intolerant Parliament. The Independents wanted an absolute Parliament no more than they had wanted an absolute king. Disgusted and alarmed at the maneuvers of the Presbyterians in the commons, Cromwell dealt with them swiftly. On December 6, 1648, he stationed Colonel Pride and some musketeers at the door of Westminster Hall. They prevented about a hundred Presbyterians from entering and haled about fifty more off to prison. When "Pride's Purge" was over only ninety members were left to form the so-called "Rump" of the Long Parliament. They were all Independents, representing the army. The galling knot of Presbyterian opposition had been cut by the sword of Cromwell.

The king must now be brought to book. On January 6, 1649, despite the opposition of a dozen peers left in the house of lords, the members of the commons passed, on their own authority, an "act" erecting a High Court of Justice "for the trying and judging of Charles Stuart, king of England." Charles, this prolix document declared, "hath had a wicked design totally to subvert the ancient and fundamental laws and liberties of this nation and in their place to introduce an arbitrary and tyrannical government . . . he hath prosecuted it with fire and sword, levied and maintained a cruel war in the land against the parliament and kingdom." Charles was to be tried for these crimes, and for treason against the people of England. In this, as usual, Cromwell saw the finger of God.

Could the charge of treason legally be brought against the king? Under the new theory of popular sovereignty such a procedure might have been theoretically arguable had the "Rump" represented a sizeable portion of the people. Legally, however, Charles could not be tried for treason. He was still the king, and treason against himself the king could not commit. The court was illegal. Charles told them so. "No earthly power can justly call me, who am your king, in question as a delinquent. . . . How can any free-born subject of England call life or anything he possesseth his own, if power without right daily make new and abrogate the old fundamental laws of the land? . . . What hope of settlement is there so long as power reigns without rule or law, changing the whole frame of that government under which this kingdom hath flourished for many hundred years?"

The outcome of the trial, made more unseemly by the prosecuting Puritan lawyer John Bradshaw, was never in doubt. To put the king to death seemed the expedient thing to do. It was, in the words that Cromwell is supposed to have uttered, "cruel necessity." The court found the king guilty. "Charles Stuart, as a tyrant, traitor, murderer, and public enemy to the good people of this nation, shall be put to death by the severing of his head from his body." On January 30, 1649, Charles was executed in front of his palace at Whitehall. He died nobly, in the manner of a king. A measureless shock ran through the stunned nation. Even some of the regicides were temporarily appalled at what they had done. In the moment of his death Charles prepared the way for the failure of his foes and the triumph of his son. As the ivy covered the memory of his sins he was widely regarded as a martyr and a saint.

There was now no turning back for the makers of revolution. The Presbyterians had brought Charles to the steps of the scaffold; the Independents had cut off his head. The sword had won the war and had executed the king. The words of Andrew Marvell's ode to Cromwell were fitter than he knew: "the same arts that did gain a power, must it maintain." The sword, then, was to maintain the new republic. It did so, for eleven years.

COMMONWEALTH PROBLEMS: IRELAND AND SCOTLAND

The Rump Parliament was still sitting, all that was left of the Long Parliament summoned by Charles I eight years before. Purged of the Cavaliers and Presbyterians, it numbered only about fifty-six members. It was this Rump assembly, dominated by the army, that proclaimed the monarchy and the house of lords abolished, passed a new Treasons Act, and declared England a "commonwealth and free state." The executive power of the new commonwealth was fixed in a council of state whose members were to be appointed annually by Parliament. "A most happy way is made for this nation, if God see it good, to return to its just and ancient right of being governed by its own representatives or national meetings in council." The council of state at first numbered forty-one individuals; about thirty of these were members of Parliament. Freedom of public worship and toleration was granted to all except Anglicans, Catholics, and Unitarians. A new great seal was made with the inscription "In the First Year of Freedom by God's Blessing Restored."

The chief support of the new republic was the army, not the people. The mass of the people were still monarchists. Englishmen did not generally approve of the execution of the king, of Puritan tactics, of veiled military despotism. The national dislike of a standing army can be traced, in part, to the years of the republican experiment. Even the army was not wholly satisfied. General Fairfax, for example, disapproved of the execution of Charles. The rank and file of the army wanted the Rump dissolved and a national election held. John Lilburne, leader of the green-ribboned Levellers and mighty prophet of England's liberties, denounced the new government as a tyranny and usurpation. Brought to trial for treason, he was acquitted by the jury, and the tumultuous shout of the people made the judges "for fear turn pale and hang down their heads." Later, in 1653, the Rump put him on trial for his life. Again he was freed, and the soldiers beat their drums and blew their trumpets. Cromwell had shouted in anger to the Speaker of the Rump: "I tell you, sir, you have no other way to deal with these men but to break them or they will break you." It seemed that it might be so.

The military despotism that had seized power had acted in the name of the people. Now they found active champions of democracy against them, the people themselves generally hostile. Nevertheless, their opponents were so divided among themselves that the fall of the Rump and the army would certainly have resulted in anarchy. England was held together by force, and force alone. The rule of the Independent saints and the New Model officers could not yield to anything like popular government until some order emerged from the threatened chaos. Only Cromwell and the army, it seemed, could defend the Commonwealth and give it some temporary stability. Meanwhile the maintenance of the Rump avoided the necessity of proclaiming undisguised military rule.

Domestic discontent was heightened by economic problems. During the later years of the war the Royalists had controlled cloth manufacturing regions from which Puritan London merchants obtained their cloth for export. Royalist privateers had plundered the ships of the trading companies. The costs of war had absorbed capital that otherwise would have gone into investment channels in industry and trade. Money was scarce. Standards of living went down. High taxation and unemployment added to the threat of economic disaster.

Imperial and foreign problems pressed heavily. The sovereigns of Europe refused to recognize the new government, whose principles they feared and hated. The Scots, angered by their defeat in the second Civil War and the loss of England for Presbyterianism, decided that Charles II, son of the martyred king, would be their ruler. The Irish proclaimed Charles II king of Ireland. Prince Rupert, with a Royalist fleet, including eleven ships that had gone over to him from the navy, held the Channel and Scilly Islands and the Isle of Man. He swept unchallenged along the eastern English coasts. The Barbadoes and Virginia turned towards Charles II.

Cromwell moved first against the Irish. The London merchants had given odds of twenty to one that he would never sail across to Ireland. But in August, 1649, he landed at Dublin and hastened to attack Drogheda and Wexford, two strongholds of rebel resistance. In an orgy of vengeance the garrisons were massacred. The slaughtered Protestant saints of Piedmont, whom Milton mourned, had their Catholic counterparts in Ireland. Of Drogheda Cromwell reported: "I think that night they put to death about two thousand men." The brutality of Cromwell's terror is still a cursed memory in Ireland. For the Irish Catholics the English Puritans had no mercy. Cromwell himself said that this was "a righteous judgment of God" upon "these barbarous wretches."

Within nine months the hopes of Charles II in Ireland were broken. Another chapter of Irish history had been inscribed in blood. Cromwell, and Ireton after him, so devastated Ireland that one-third of all the people were killed in the welter of havoc and carnage or died of starvation. The inhuman clauses of the final Cromwellian settlement in Ireland, passed by the Rump Parliament in 1652, cannot be read today without horror. Godly ex-Ironsides were given the estates of Irish aristocrats. Two-thirds of all Irish land changed hands. Thousands of Irishmen were transplanted into the unfertile wilderness west of the Shannon and elsewhere. Thousands more were transported to the colonies. The "curse of Cromwell" dates from these months of terror. Cromwell slaughtered and maimed in the conviction that the Lord was avenging Himself; to the Irish Catholics that could not be.

In May, 1650, Cromwell left Ireland to begin the task of subduing Scotland. Young Charles II, who seemed all things to all men, was there. Never easily disturbed by scruples, he had accepted the Covenant and had been crowned king by the Presbyterians at Scone. Meanwhile, in tragic irony, the same Scottish Covenanting Lowlanders seized and hanged the gallant Royalist Highlander Montrose, who had been betrayed by the master he served. "The king," wrote Bishop Burnet, "wrought himself into as grave a deportment as he could; he heard many prayers and sermons, some at great length. I remember in one fast day there were six sermons, preached without intermission." When Cromwell arrived he sought to persuade the Scots that if Puritanism fell in England the Presbyterian Kirk would fall in Scotland too. "I beseech you in the bowels of Christ," he wrote, "think it possible you may be mistaken."

On September 3, 1650, the Scottish general David Leslie foolishly descended with his army from his good position on the hills of Dunbar and thus delivered himself into the hands of Cromwell. Before Leslie could arrange his men Cromwell attacked. The Scottish cavalry was smashed, then the infantry. Three thousand men were slain. Ten thousand prisoners were taken with all the baggage and guns. Edinburgh was captured. From a military point of view the battle of Dunbar was Cromwell's greatest triumph. To Cromwell it was again God's victory. "Let God arise and His enemies be scattered . . . Like as the mist vanisheth, so shalt Thou drive them away." At a halt in the battle Cromwell led in the singing of a psalm. The spirit of Joshua prevailed over the spirit of Jesus. Europe was impressed by Dunbar. Holland suddenly offered England an alliance. Spain accorded the Commonwealth formal diplomatic recognition.

A year later Charles II led the first of the four Stuart invasions of England. Englishmen did not rally to him partly because he was accompanied by Scotsmen. At Worcester the invaders were crushed. Charles II reached the coast in disguise and escaped to France. The bloody battle of Worcester Cromwell called "the crowning mercy." For nine years General Monk efficiently ruled over Scotland. The Scots were given representation in the English Parliament; the Presbyterian church in Scotland was left untouched.

THE DUTCH WAR, 1652–1654

At the same time the Commonwealth government doubled the size of the navy, increasing the number of ships from forty-one to eighty-two. Robert Blake, once a Bridgewater merchant and later a Roundhead soldier, hunted down the Cavalier fleet of Prince Rupert. In doing so, Blake took the British Navy into the Mediterranean; it has been there since that day. The Channel and Scilly Islands, the Isle of Man, Virginia and the Barbadoes were all swiftly persuaded to return to the Empire. The genius of Robert Blake on the sea perhaps matched that of Oliver Cromwell on the land; he was one of England's greatest naval commanders. It was fortunate that the need to protect England against Europe's hostility and to reconquer the lost colonies had produced such a fleet and such an admiral. England was soon established again as the world's greatest naval power.

When the Commonwealth was born, the lawyers and business-men of Parliament were vividly aware of England's treasure by foreign trade and the national importance of vigorous trade and colonial policies. In the first half of the seventeenth century the colonists in America had not been tightly controlled. Despite various royal attempts at direct rule from London, James I and Charles I had found that home affairs had kept them busy. There had also been a few attempts to control colonial commerce, but no effectively enforced and uniform plan for trade regulations had resulted. After 1649 the aggressive Puritans in England persuaded the aggressive Puritans in America that the situation had changed. Blake's navy was a strong argument. The revival of England's commercial power is heralded by the Navigation Act of 1651.

This famous Navigation Act "for increase of shipping and encouragement of the navigation of this nation" provided that no goods from Asia, Africa, or America should be imported into England, Ireland, or the English colonies except in English or colonial ships "whereof the master and mariners are also for the most part of them of the people of this commonwealth." No goods from Europe were to be imported into England or the English colonies except in English ships, the majority of the crews in each case being English. To this rule there was one exception: goods might be shipped to England or her colonies in vessels belonging to an exporting European country provided that the cargoes were produced in the country from which they were exported. The Navigation Act was thus designed to give England and the colonies a larger share of the carrying trade, to help English shipping and increase the number of English seamen. It was aimed particularly at the Dutch, who had been carrying cargoes to and from India and the English colonies; the lobbyists of the East India Company helped to pilot the Navigation Act through Parliament.

In the years of the Spanish decline at sea the Netherlands had made great progress. They had established themselves in the East Indies and the Cape of Good Hope. Battles between Dutch and English sailors increased in number as the maritime rivalry mounted. The Dutch had driven the English from the East Indian islands. They had almost expelled Englishmen from the North Sea herring fisheries; they had a monopoly of the rich spice trade; they had sheltered Royalist refugees. Their astounding commercial expansion and merchant marine activity was now challenged by the militant English Commonwealth.

The passage of the Navigation Act in 1651 did not make war with the Dutch inevitable. War actually came because the English commercial world, whose views were mirrored in Parliament, had decided upon a showdown. There were old scores to settle against the Dutch and the English Navy was strong again. Much of the Dutch trade might profitably be wrested from them. A cause for conflict was shortly at hand. Early in 1652 when a Dutch fleet under van Tromp refused to lower its flag in salute to an English fleet under Blake a battle broke out and war began.

Seven-eighths of the people of Holland lived by commerce and industry; they depended on foreign trade much more than an England still mainly agricultural. The Dutch sadly remarked that their land was "a mountain of gold" and England "a mountain of iron." The merchant fleet of Holland was large. As her ships had to pass through the Channel or go through the North Sea they had to be heavily protected against the English. The Dutch and English navies were about equal in size. The seamanship of their commanders was superb. The great Dutch admirals van Tromp, de Witt, and de Ruyter were evenly matched with England's Blake. Within two years there were nine sea battles, still a subject of study in naval colleges. In 1652 van Tromp defeated Blake and convoyed nearly 500 Dutch merchant ships safely to port. Holland persuaded Denmark to close the Baltic to English ships; the Dutch seized uneasy control of the Mediterranean.

In 1653 the prospect altered. Twice the Dutch were badly handled in major engagements. The English now resorted to the familiar weapon of a blockade. Desperately the Dutch tried to break it. Their merchant fleets rode useless on the Zuyder Zee or nervously probed to find a gap through the watching English warships. Late in 1653 starvation forced the Dutch to make peace. By the terms of the peace arrangements in 1654 the Netherlands government agreed to compensate England for the massacre at Amboina in 1623; to salute the English flag in the narrow seas; to give no refuge to the Stuarts; to see that England was paid for the damage Denmark had done to English ships.

Despite the terms of the treaty the war had really been rather barren of results. The Dutch still had a large merchant marine; so the commercial rivalry went on. English naval supremacy was again unchallenged; but the Dutch began to build new warships apace. During the war the English Navy had cost £1,000,000 a year. The sale of confiscated Royalist estates covered a part of the expenditure, but not all. The rest was paid by taxation; and wealthy Puritan merchants liked heavy taxes no more than their Anglican neighbors.

THE PROTECTORATE

Before the Dutch peace came the Commonwealth ended. The soldiers disliked the war with Holland. They shouted for reforms in the church; they were weary of the lawyers' profitless debates in Parliament. The radical army demanded a dissolution and a new election.

The Rump Parliament replied to military pressure by introducing a bill providing that no one should be elected to the next Parliament unless approved by the members of the Rump. Cromwell tried to reduce the rising frictions and to compromise because he saw that the Rump alone prevented open military rule. Despite the promises of Rump leaders they continued to push through the bill providing for the perpetuation of their power. Cromwell summoned musketeers and went to the house of commons.

"Your hour is come," he informed the Rump; "the Lord hath done with you . . . I will put an end to your prating. You should give place to better men. You are no Parliament!" The musketeers drove out the members and the doors were locked. There was no protest in England. "Not a dog barked," said Cromwell. But what was now to be done? Open force had routed the merchants and lawyers from Westminster Hall. Could there now be a free election? The army publicly declared they wanted one. Nevertheless, all were aware that a freely elected Parliament would probably restore the monarchy and certainly end toleration for the Independents. The army, largely composed of Independents, knew that a democratic election was impossible.

Cromwell and the council of state now decided to select their own Parliament, or almost so. They asked the Independent congregations to submit nominations; from this list the army officers chose men "faithful, fearing God and hating covetousness." The nominated Parliament, later nicknamed the Barebone Parliament after one of its members, Praise-God Barebone, contained 140 members. They were pious men, better men, surely, than the crafty jugglers of the Rump; but they had too many ideas about reform. Saints have usually a passion for setting things right. "Nothing was in the hearts of these men," said Cromwell, "but overturn, overturn." They wanted to set up a voluntary church system; to abolish the chancery court; to abolish patronage and the tithe. So alarmed were the moderates in the assembly that in December, 1653, they carried a vote in a scattered house bringing the Barebone Parliament to an end. Another experiment had failed.

The army officers now drew up a new written constitution called the Instrument of Government. By its terms there was to be a Lord Protector, chosen for life; a perpetual council of state; a Parliament elected every three years by limited suffrage. Power was apparently distributed among these three parts of government. The legislative power was supposed to rest with the elected Parliament of some 460 members, of which 60 were to be sent from Ireland and Scotland. The Instrument of Government stated that Parliament could pass a measure over the Protector's veto by a simple majority vote. The Protector was given revenues to provide for an army of 30,000, a navy, and other expenses of government. There was to be religious liberty for all but those who believed in "popery or prelacy." The first Lord Protector was to be Oliver Cromwell, captain-general of the forces of England, Scotland, and Ireland. Despite the terms of the Instrument the actual power of government was in his hands. Backed by the army, he was really the dictator of England. Cromwell tried to bring peace, but he had to carry a sword. The saint would have to be a warrior saint. How else could order be maintained?

When the new Parliament met England's dilemma was clearly revealed, even to many who had not perceived it before. There was no united national opinion. Half of England was Royalist; the Puritans were irreconcilably divided among themselves. Cromwell at once purged his new Parliament of almost a hundred members. He wanted conservative Puritans. That is what he got; but they were not pliable. Cromwell said his task was "healing and settling." The new Parliament differed from him as to how the "healing and settling" was to be achieved. When it was asked to ratify the Instrument of Government it rejected two "fundamentals." Claiming that it represented the nation as against the army, Parliament declared itself opposed to religious toleration; it wanted to take over control of the army and the navy.

The new Parliament was thus making the same bid for power that the Long Parliament had made. It wanted to end military despotism. Cromwell, on the other hand, wanted to prevent the factions from bringing anarchy and intolerance. "I am as much for government by consent as any man," he said, "but where will you find that consent?" To maintain order, to keep religious toleration, to prevent an "irresponsible assembly" from becoming the prey of bitter parties, the Protector waved the sword and the members of Parliament went home in January, 1655. Cromwell, like Robespierre, found it hard to establish a republic of virtue.

Another experiment was now attempted. When Cavalier and Leveller conspiracies threatened, England was divided into twelve districts, each ruled by a Major-General. The Major-Generals, through stern control of the justices of the peace, enforced their arbitrary will and the Protector's moral "blue laws." Military police and censors poked and pried everywhere. Cockfighting, horse racing, bear baiting, drunkenness, and swearing were prohibited. Stage players were banned in the interests of morals and the public good. "Profaneness and ungodliness" were discouraged. All merry England felt the grim constraints of godly zeal. "The mind is the man," said the Protector; "if that be kept pure, the man signifies somewhat; if not I wish I would very fain see what difference there is between him and a beast."

Meanwhile Cromwell had gone into an aggressive war against Spain. The Protector, like John Pym, was at heart an imperialist. England was no longer weak. Puritan nationalism reached its peak when Catholics were the enemy. The Elizabethan and Protestant quarrel with Spain must be continued, particularly because the sails of the now large English navy should not be permitted to flap idly in the breeze. An excuse was easily found. One expedition to seize undefended Santo

Domingo failed. A second captured Jamaica for the Empire and settlers went out to hold it. At Vera Cruz Blake destroyed a Spanish treasure fleet. As Spanish galleons went down English naval traditions increased. Later, in 1658, after an alliance had been formed with France, an Anglo-French army took Dunkirk from Spain; it was added to the lengthening list of British overseas possessions.

All of this cost money. Special taxes were again imposed on those who had been Cavaliers. The rural Royalists were most heavily hit and they did not forget these harrying Puritan raids when the tables were later turned. Meanwhile expenditures were increased threefold over the average of Charles I's reign. Foreign trade was severely hampered; domestic trade slumped. If victory abroad meant war taxes and a commercial depression, the propertied classes, especially the merchants, wanted peace.

Faced by the dark economic situation, the need for money, and popular outcries against the Major-Generals, then called "the swordsmen," Cromwell called another Parliament in September, 1656. About a hundred were again excluded because they opposed the government. This Parliament prepared the Humble Petition and Advice, a new constitution that would have set up Cromwell as king with power to nominate his successor. It also provided for a second chamber in Parliament containing members appointed by Cromwell for life. This chamber was not to be called the house of lords, but rather the "other house." On the one hand the principles of religious toleration were slightly extended; on the other, those who profaned the Sabbath, frequented taverns, were cursers, drunkards, atheists, or revilers of religion were forbidden to vote or hold office. The purpose of the Humble Petition and Advice was to end military rule, to avert the "blood and confusion" that might follow Cromwell's death, and to make a constitution similar to the old royal one.

Cromwell, under pressure from General Lambert and other republican army officers, refused the crown. The rest of the Humble Petition and Advice he accepted. Forty of the members of the commons were appointed to the "other house." Presbyterians and republicans were now admitted to the commons, from which they had been excluded earlier. At once they began to plot with Royalists and Levellers to oust Cromwell. Meanwhile the commons violently attacked the "other house." Cromwell angrily dissolved his last Parliament. He had moved far along the same road the Stuarts had travelled before him. "I think it high time that an end be put to your sitting, and I do dissolve this Parliament. And let God judge between you and me."

On September 3, 1658, the anniversary of his victories at Dunbar and Worcester, Oliver Cromwell died. Destiny had mocked his dream. He had not pleased many men. In the wreck of religion and parties that had strewn England's way through the years of the first two

Stuarts probably no human being could have done what Cromwell failed to do. He did save the Empire from division. By his armies and mastery of the seas he raised England's international prestige higher than it had been since Elizabeth's day. By force he kept as much toleration as he could. With the sword he maintained order and marched indefatigably on where war and fortune led him. Others perfected the work in which he seemed to fail. The next century answered the eager question of James I, Charles I, and Cromwell: "How can parliamentary government be combined with personal rule?"

Cromwell had brought a king to the scaffold. He had hewn to pieces the enemies of Jehovah. The words of his last prayer may serve for the epitaph that was never written: "Thou hast made me, though very unworthy, a mean instrument to do Thy people some good and Thee service; and many of them have set too high a value upon me, though others wish and would be glad of my death. Pardon such as desire to trample upon the dust of a poor worm, for they are Thy people too; and pardon the folly of this short prayer, even for Jesus Christ's sake, and give us a good night, if it be Thy pleasure. Amen."

Chapter 19

FRUITS OF THE RESTORATION
THE RETURN OF CHARLES II

THE successor of Cromwell was his eldest son, Richard. The new Protector was amiable enough, but weak. In January, 1659, he called a Parliament which at once proceeded to quarrel with the army. In April, the army officers compelled Richard to dissolve Parliament. They then began to dispute among themselves. With the strong hand of Oliver Cromwell removed England was thus threatened with social anarchy.

In such a turmoil the propertied classes at last shelved their quarrels. Royalists, businessmen, and landed Parliamentarians stood together against the army, the challenge of the sects, and the levelling radicalism of the lower classes. In May the old Rump Parliament assembled at Westminster. Richard retired from Whitehall to France.

The once unconquerable army in England was hopelessly divided. The nation was sick of military rule. Against this background, General George Monk, the Ironside commander of occupation forces in Scotland, marched south from Edinburgh and occupied London in February, 1660. Monk was patriotic, wise, and closely connected with both Royalist and Parliamentary landowners. Allying himself with the fearful landowners and businessmen, Monk declared for a "free Parliament." All England caught up the cry.

In March the restored Long Parliament dissolved itself; an election was held; the new "Convention" Parliament at once ended the danger of another civil war by declaring that "according to the ancient and fundamental laws of this kingdom the government is, and ought to be, by Kings, Lords, and Commons." This, at least, was something upon which most Englishmen now agreed. There were a few scattered revolts, the last flickers of the once flaming Independents; but they soon guttered out. Samuel Pepys, most magnificent of diarists, wrote: "The whole design is broken, and every man begins to be merry and full of hope." The stern reign of republican virtue was ending. The epitaph of Puritanism was to be written in John Milton's *Paradise Lost*, the epic of a broken hope and a fallen cause. The demobilized Ironsides were shortly to become sober farmers and workmen again. Cromwell's men laid down the sword. It had not sufficed to bring to earth the Heavenly City, clean and bleak, of the Puritans.

From Breda, in Holland, Charles II issued a declaration promising that all rebels against his father should be pardoned, except those designated for punishment by Parliament; that questions regarding the restoration of Royalist lands should be left to Parliament; that the army should be paid its arrears in wages; that Parliament should grant "liberty to tender consciences" in the practice of religion and "no man shall be disquieted or called in question for differences in opinion in matters of religion, which do not disturb the peace of the kingdom." Charles asserted that he wanted as little "blood and damage" as possible.

On May 25, 1660, Charles II landed at Dover. He declared that the English Bible was "the thing he loved above all things in the world." The exile had come home; he did not propose to go on his travels again. Shrewd, good-humored, witty, affable, he deceived many men who mistook the appearance for the full reality. Behind the dark king's smile and easy charm there was a cynical and calculating astuteness that never left him, even in the whirling debauchery of his court. In his famous and often unreliable *History of His Own Time* Bishop Burnet penned a shrewd description of Charles II: "He had a very ill opinion both of men and women, and did not think there was either sincerity or chastity in the world out of principle, but that some had either the one or the other out of humor or vanity. He thought that nobody served him out of love; and so he was quits with all the world and loved others as little as he thought they loved him."

From Dover Charles proceeded to London. An anonymous diarist recorded that the king was met on the edge of the city by "a kind of rural triumph, expressed by the country swains in a morrice dance" and "a hundred proper maids of Deptford" with "baskets full of flowers and sweet herbs." Not long before Samuel Pepys had written of the "great joy" in London. "At night more bonfires than ever, and ringing of bells, and drinking of the King's health upon their knees in the streets, which methinks is a little too much."

The king was restored and the Convention Parliament began its work. Ten of those who had taken part in the trial and execution of Charles I were themselves executed, as was later the republican Sir Henry Vane. The bodies of Cromwell, Ireton, and Bradshaw were dug up, hung from gibbets and later beheaded. Later those of Pym and Blake were tossed out of Westminster Abbey into St. Margaret's Churchyard. John Milton and many another were for a time "with darkness and with dangers compassed round." Charles, less vengeful than his Parliament, soon had enough of blood and bade the violence cease.

The work of restoration involved a long body of legislation and to that task the Convention Parliament soon turned. Crown and church lands were restored immediately to their original owners. This hit heavily many Independents who had purchased church land. The Presbyterians saw to it that nothing was done to help Royalist citizens who had been compelled to sell parts of their property, very often to Presbyterians, to pay taxes to the Puritan government. The army was paid and disbanded; only three foot regiments, called guards, were kept. A regular annual income of £1,200,000, made up of the port duties added to hereditary excise, was granted to the king; this was to be raised by taxes. However, as the promised revenue was never forthcoming, Charles still had to ask Parliament frequently for more money.

Progressive legislation undertaken by the Convention Parliament included an act abolishing feudal tenures, especially welcome to the landed class; an act for erecting and establishing a post office; and a new Navigation Act which extended still further government control of the carrying trade to and from English ports. The Convention Parliament also declared that the reign of Charles II had legally begun in January, 1649, on the execution of Charles I. All parliamentary actions between that date and the restoration of Charles II were invalidated. Almost all the great reforms carried through by the Long Parliament before 1641 were left unchanged. Hence the prerogative courts of star chamber, high commission, and the council of the north remained at an end; the king might not collect taxes without parliamentary consent; there were to be no forced loans or benevolences; ship money was not revived.

No method had as yet been devised to secure the responsibility of the king and his ministers to Parliament. The constitutional devices of the cabinet system were not developed until the next century. The Civil War had made it clear that government could not be carried on against the demands of the classes represented in parliament. At the same time it was not clear which constitutional power, the executive or the legislative, had the larger say. Until the location of final authority was determined the jostling and bickering that characterized the latter seventeenth century was inevitable.

At the end of 1660 the Convention Parliament of Anglican Cavaliers and Presbyterians was dissolved. It was succeeded in the spring of 1661 by the so-called Cavalier Parliament, filled with young men, Cavalier and Anglican, men who believed in peace and order and ranged themselves behind the church and the king. These individuals represented the conservative interests of the landed gentry who wanted some compensation for the lean years since 1649. From them, in time, was born the great Tory party.

Opposed to this massive body of interest in the state was a second element, strong and progressive, containing the men of business, the merchants and kings of commerce. Of this second group was soon to grow the Whig party, entering into a mighty conflict with the Tories and the king. Nursed in the ruthless world of business and rocked to the tune of Puritan, Nonconformist, Dissenting lullabies, the doughty champions of the cause of parliamentary sovereignty and religious toleration were to prove strong and stubborn. The excesses of these two groups largely account for the feverish political instability of the later seventeenth century.

THE RELIGIOUS SETTLEMENT

The Cavalier Parliament, so pleasing to Charles II, was not dissolved for eighteen years. Soon after it assembled it turned to the question of the church, a problem the Convention Parliament had been unable to settle because the Presbyterians and Anglicans could not agree. The election tide of loyalty had run so high in 1661 that the Cavalier Parliament contained nearly all Anglicans, zealous for church and king. They brought with them no hope of compromise with the Presbyterians or any other Dissenters; against them the fifty Presbyterian members stood stanchly but in vain. At the order of Parliament, the Solemn League and Covenant was burned by the public hangman. In 1662 a Licensing Act required the printing trade to prevent "the frequent abuses in printing seditious, treasonable, and unlicensed books and pamphlets" which "many evil-disposed persons" had printed and sold "to the high dishonour of Almighty God."

The bishops came back to their places in the house of lords. There could now be no broad church established, acceptable to Anglicans and Presbyterians alike. John Williams, a founder of the Royal Society, warden of Wadham College, and bishop of Chester, wanted the Church of England to "take in the Dissenters so that then it would stand on a broad basis." But few were then disposed to follow his advice or to heed the earlier words of John Milton: "A little generous prudence, a little forbearance of one another, and some grain of charity might win all these diligencies to join, and unite in one general and brotherly search for Truth." Few understood that something of the character of Nonconformity had worked itself into the abiding fiber of England. Below the high society of the landed Cavalier folk Nonconformity was to remain a strong cement of the middle and lower middle classes.

One of the leaders of the Cavalier group was Sir Edward Hyde, earl of Clarendon and lord chancellor. Before the Civil War he had quarrelled with John Pym and had turned to become an adviser of Charles I. After 1649 he had been tutor to the exiled Charles II. For seven years after 1660 Clarendon was the most important man in

England after the king. His daughter Anne was married, not without scandal, to James, Duke of York. Clarendon believed in restoring the church and the king; but he did not want the royal prerogative too highly exalted; his ideal was a monarchy working in harmony with Parliament. As a lawyer he had great respect for the law; that was the reason why he had opposed Pym's claims to parliamentary supremacy as much as he opposed the idea of the divine right of kings. Now he had returned to England. He found his country altered. After his long exile he felt like an alien. Because of his disapproval of Charles's licentious debaucheries and seraglio he gradually lost favor at court. At the same time his name became odious to the Dissenters because it was attached to the new religious settlement.

This religious program was in accord with the Anglican inclinations of the Cavalier Parliament. The persecuting acts of the so-called "Clarendon Code" ended toleration and imposed a narrow Anglicanism upon the nation. The severe Municipal Corporations Act of 1661 placed the boroughs, strongholds of Dissent, under Anglican control by requiring that all municipal office holders must renounce the Solemn League and Covenant; take communion according to the rites of the Church of England; and make a declaration under oath that it was unlawful to resist the king. Thus Dissenters of all sects were banished from political office in the borough.

A new Act of Uniformity of 1662 required every minister of the Anglican Church to give his unfeigned assent and consent to everything contained in the Book of Common Prayer; the use of the Prayer Book was enforced in all public worship. This was done because "great mischiefs and inconveniences during the times of the late unhappy troubles have arisen and grown and many people have been led into factions and schisms, to the great decay and scandal of the reformed religion of the Church of England and to the hazard of many souls." Both Charles II and Clarendon felt that the Act of Uniformity was too harsh; but the Anglican zeal of the Cavalier Parliament could not be stayed. Toleration ended. Nearly two thousand rectors and vicars, a fifth of the whole body of the clergy, were forced to resign from their parishes as Nonconformists. The loss to the Church of England was irreparable. Many dissenting elements were now to stand forever outside Anglicanism. Nor could the zeal and learning of the dissenting clergy easily be replaced. The cause of religious liberty suffered serious damage.

The Cavalier Parliament was not finished with its grim work. Under the Quaker Act of 1662 more than five thousand Quakers were imprisoned. The Nonconformist John Bunyan spent twelve years in Bedford Gaol. Here he wrote his *Grace Abounding,* his *Holy City,* and a large part of *The Pilgrim's Progress,* one of the finest products of Puritanism. The balanced power of Bunyan's simple prose touched thousands of readers who followed the travails of Christian from his flight out of the City of Destruction until all the trumpets sounded on the other side to welcome him at the end of his journey. Bunyan showed that all things were possible to God's true servants; they could not be overcome. "But as God would have it, while Apollyon was fetching of his last blow, thereby to make an full end of this good man, Christian nimbly reached out his hand for his sword, and caught it, saying, Rejoice not against me, O mine enemy! When I fall, I shall arise; and with that, gave him a deadly thrust, which made him give back, as one that had received his mortal wound. Christian perceiving that, made at him again, saying, Nay, in all these things we are more than conquerors, through Him that loved us. And with that, Apollyon spread forth his dragon's wings, and sped him away, that Christian saw him no more." Ten editions of *The Pilgrim's Progress* had been sold by 1688.

The Conventicle Act of 1664 made punishable by fine, transportation, or imprisonment all those who attended meetings or "conventicles" of more than five persons, other than the members of any one household, for "any exercise of religion in other manner than is allowed by the liturgy or practice of the Church of England." By the terms of the Five Mile Act of 1665 Nonconformist ministers who had been driven out of their living by the Act of Uniformity were required to swear that they held it unlawful to resist the king and that they would not "endeavour any alteration of government in Church or State." Those who refused to do so were forbidden to go within five miles of any borough or of any parish where they had earlier preached, lest they "distil the poisonous principles of schism and rebellion into the hearts of his majesty's subjects, to the great danger of the church and kingdom." This harsh act was widely denounced by the dissenting clergy. Thomas Woodcock, for example, described it as "a pestilent act made in pestilent times, by men that were esteemed the pest of the nation; who for pensions sold out liberty."

The execution of this "Clarendon Code" was to be carried out by the justices of the peace. Many of them were anxious to crush the Puritans who had once oppressed them. Until the revolution of 1688 the chapters of persecution of dissenters in England are filled with violent and bitter passages. The Puritan gentry usually took the unheroic course of conforming publicly to Anglicanism because they did not wish to surrender their political and social position; it was from these men that the leaders of the Whig party later came. In the middle and lower classes, the persecution was endured and the large body of dissent remained unbroken. Middle class merchants and shopkeepers, apprentices and workmen of the poorer levels were usually still dissenters; many yeomen only waited for a brighter tomorrow to cast their votes for the Whigs and toleration.

Even among those who now conformed to the Established Church the marks of Puritanism remained. The home study of the Bible, the habit of family prayers, the uncomfortable sober Sundays—these were essentially gifts of the Puritans to the Anglican Church. Despite attempts to restore the Anglicanism that once had been in England, the heritage of the years of dissent had slowly passed into the Church itself; nothing could ever remove it.

The modern rivalry of Church and Dissent grew partly out of the unsuccessful attempt of the Cavalier Parliament and the Clarendon Code to dragoon all Englishmen along the gentlemanly, Anglican road to God. Today scores of religions are practiced in England because mutual toleration has proved to be in the interests of national welfare. Events showed that reasonable peace could not be obtained by the dangerous imposition of one state church on the people. The alternative was the granting of freedom to all religions provided that their methods of operation were not too explosive, fanatical, or bloody. Tolerance in England also grew as attitudes changed, particularly as new secular and scientific ideas spread slowly through the land. A humanizing spirit of nationalism and a new sanity gradually prepared the road for the eighteenth century. A part of these many-splendored achievements is discussed in Chapter 20.

FOREIGN AFFAIRS, 1660-1670

The new reign began by the marriage of Charles II to Catherine of Braganza, sister of the king of Portugal. The king's English advisers had favored an alliance with Spain because it would help to redress the balance of power which his cousin Louis XIV was beginning to tilt. But there was no Spanish match available; the only unmarried princess, the second daughter of the Spanish king, had to be united with an Austrian Hapsburg for dynastic reasons. Louis XIV then suggested that Charles II marry the Portuguese princess because Portugal was in revolt against his rival Spain and needed help. The weaker Spain became, the better for the developing designs of Louis XIV.

Portugal offered liberal marriage terms and Charles accepted. Catherine of Braganza brought a dowry of £800,000; her brother the king ceded the naval station of Tangier and the Indian trading center of Bombay to Charles II. Charles provided 10,000 soldiers to support Portugal against Spain. In 1662 he took Catherine out of a nunnery and married her.

Charles soon sold Bombay to the East India Company. He also sold Dunkirk to his cousin Louis XIV. This was a very unpopular act because the memory of the victory of Cromwell's soldiers in seizing Dunkirk from Spain was still vivid among Englishmen. Public reaction to these recent events was summed up in the doggerel lines: "Three sights to be seen, Dunkirk, Tangier, and a barren Queen." It was also noted that the royal sales helped to decrease Charles's dependence upon money grants from Parliament.

In March, 1665, England and Holland again entered into a war born of commercial rivalry. Earlier the English had seized the Dutch colony of New Amsterdam in America and renamed it New York in honor of the king's brother James, Duke of York. The Restoration navy was less successful than Cromwell's ships commanded by Blake had been. Maladministration, corruption, and conflicts between Charles and Parliament combined with the mutinies of unpaid sailors to limit English achievements in the war. Late in the conflict a Dutch fleet sailed up the Thames and destroyed sixteen naval ships in the Medway. By the terms of peace in July, 1667, England obtained Delaware, New Jersey, and New York from the Dutch. In return, the English claims to the Spice Islands in the East were abandoned and Surinam in South America was handed over to Holland.

Meanwhile Louis XIV was seeking steadily to extend the territory of France to her "natural boundaries": the Alps, the Pyrenees, the sea, and the Rhine. By four wars he endeavored to achieve this object. In 1667 he asserted on behalf of his wife an outrageous claim to the Belgian Netherlands which had been inherited in 1665 by his half-witted brother-in-law, Charles II of Spain. By diplomacy Louis had earlier obtained assurances of benevolent neutrality from Holland, Sweden, and the Protestant States of Germany. However, as soon as war broke out between France and Spain and the Anglo-Dutch trade war had ended the whole prospect altered. Because of balance of power considerations England, Holland, and Sweden suddenly formed a Triple Alliance to stop Louis XIV. The architect of it was England's Sir William Temple. Thereupon Louis wisely concluded the Treaty of Aix-la-Chapelle with Spain in 1668 by which Spain retained the larger part of the Belgian Netherlands but gave up three fortified cities. Louis then set about to end the causes of his diplomatic defeat. He saw that the Dutch would always resent the French absorption of the Belgain Netherlands; they did not want a dangerously powerful France on their borders.

For this reason, and because Holland was a strong commercial rival, Louis sought to smash the Triple Alliance and to isolate Holland, preparatory to making war upon her. Liberal pensions persuaded the Swedes to desert the Dutch. There remained England. In 1670 Louis negotiated with Charles II the secret Treaty of Dover. Charles hoped one day to establish both absolute government and Catholicism in England. With the aid of French gold and French-trained army veterans he thought that it might be done. By the top secret Treaty of Dover, known to only three of his Catholic aides, Charles agreed to support France against Holland in return for an annual pension to keep him independent of Parliament and French troops when Charles wanted them. Behind the idleness and frivolity of the English court and the assumed indifference of Charles these dark designs went forward.

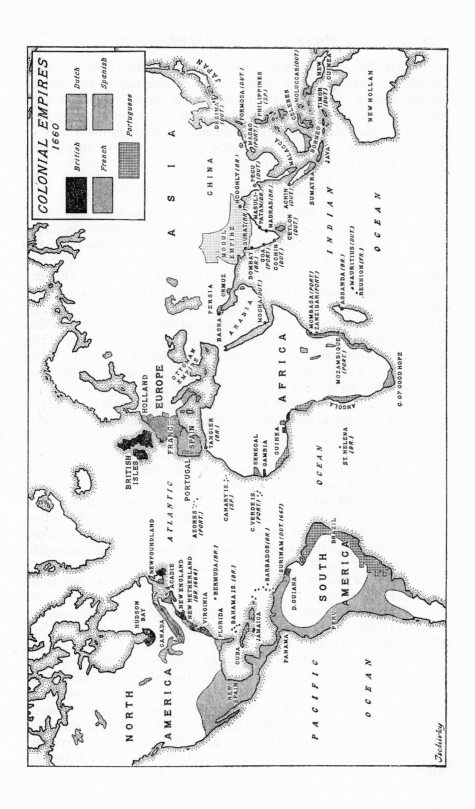

COLONIAL EMPIRES
1660

Dutch   Spanish

British   French   Portuguese

JAPAN

A S I A

CHINA

DESIMA (DUT.)
FORMOSA (DUT.)
PHILIPPINES (SP.)
MOLUCCAS (DUT.)
NEW GUINEA
MACAO (PORT.)
BORNEO
CELEBES
MALACCA
TIMOR (DUT.)
PEGU (DUT.)
HOOGHLY (BR.)
MASULI-
PATAM (BR.)
MADRAS (BR.)
SURAT (BR.)
ACHIN (DUT.)
SUMATRA
JAVA
NEW HOLLAN

MOGUL
EMPIRE
GOA (PORT.)
BOMBAY (BR.)
COCHIN (DUT.)
CEYLON (DUT.)

PERSIA
ORMUZ
BASRA
ARABIA
MOCHA (DUT.)

I N D I A N

O C E A N

ASSANDA (BR.)
MAURITIUS (DUT.)
REUNION (FR.)

MOMBASA (PORT.)
ZANZIBAR (PORT.)

EUROPE
HOLLAND
OTTOMAN
EMPIRE
FRANCE
SPAIN
PORTUGAL

MOZAMBIQUE (PORT.)

A F R I C A

ANGOLA

C. OF GOOD HOPE

BRITISH
ISLES

TANGIER (BR.)

SENEGAL
GAMBIA
GUINEA

ST. HELENA (BR.)

A T L A N T I C

O C E A N

AZORES (PORT.)
CANARY IS. (SP.)
C. VERDE IS. (PORT.)

NEWFOUNDLAND
ACADIE
NEW ENGLAND
NEW NETHERLAND (BR. 1664)
VIRGINIA
BERMUDA (BR.)
BAHAMA IS. (BR.)
CUBA
JAMAICA
FLORIDA
SURINAM (DUT. 1667)
BARBADOS (BR.)

HUDSON
BAY

CANADA

NORTH

A M E R I C A

NEW
SPAIN

PANAMA
D. GUIANA

BRAZIL
PERU

SOUTH

A M E R I C A

P A C I F I C

O C E A N

Jachinsky

Nevertheless, all of Charles's schemes were tentative and irregular; he had no steadily settled plans; his one resolve was to stay on the throne. Such a king would not quarrel about power, religion or anything else unless the disputes promised good results for him. It seemed to Charles that his great Catholic scheme set afoot in the Treaty of Dover might be successful. His policy, therefore, was to attempt the project, but to discard it swiftly if danger threatened.

DOMESTIC AFFAIRS, 1660–1672

As England moved through the Dutch war and the diplomatic intrigues leading to the Treaty of Dover important events occurred on the domestic stage. Two great disasters fell in 1665 and 1666, the plague and the great fire of London. The plague struck again, as it had since the fourteenth century, though not with its earlier fury. This was the last time it came. The resulting scenes of horror can only be imagined by those who are familiar with the great descriptions of Thucydides or Defoe. In its wake came the fire, which raged for five days through the residential and business quarters in the heart of the City. Eighty-nine churches, including old Gothic St. Paul's, were burned. But Christopher Wren had long before come down from Wadham College, Oxford, and his masterpieces soon began to rise over London, where their beauty reigned unchallenged until Nazi bombs destroyed so many in the Second World War. On September 2, 1665, John Evelyn wrote in his diary the sentence: "This fatal night, about ten, began the deplorable fire, near Fish Street, in London." The next night "we beheld that dismal spectacle, the whole City in dreadful flames near the waterside . . . the conflagration was so universal, and the people so astonished, that from the beginning, I know not by what despondency, or fate, they hardly stirred to quench it; so that there was nothing heard or seen, but crying out and lamentation, running about like distracted creatures, without at all attempting to save even their goods . . . Thus, I left it this afternoon burning, a resemblance of Sodom, or the last day . . . London was, but is no more! Thus, I returned."

When the plague, the fire, and the Dutch war had passed, Charles II decided that his old ally Clarendon should be sacrificed. Clarendon was so exalted in his position as lord chancellor and intimate of the king that he had few friends and many rivals. Charles himself was weary of Clarendon's obnoxious fretting about the evils of too many mistresses and too much wine. Like Wolsey and scores of others before him, Clarendon fell easily. He was blamed by an ill-informed and unjust Parliament and public for the king's Catholic marriage, for the Medway disaster, for the religious persecutions, even for the plague and the fire. No doubt he was besmirched, like Bacon, by living too long among mean men; but he was probably less stained than those about him at the court. Rottenness and vice reigned everywhere at Whitehall. Clarendon, relieved of office by Charles, was impeached by the house of commons. Then he fled to France, where he wrote his famous *History of the Great Rebellion*. In England there was general satisfaction that the pilot had been dropped.

With Clarendon gone Charles renewed the custom of consulting with an inner circle of ministers. The privy council, with its fifty members, was too large for business. This smaller group was often called by the sinister word "Cabal" and was a step towards the later cabinet. The members were chosen solely by the king and were not dependent upon Parliament in any way. It so happened that the initials of five ministers closest to Charles after Clarendon's fall in fact spelled out the word "Cabal": Clifford, Arlington, Buckingham, Ashley Cooper, and Lauderdale. Two were Catholic and three Protestant. They were agreed on only one thing: religious toleration, to which Parliament was opposed. None was Anglican. Intriguing knavishly together, the members of the Cabal and the king planned to end the Anglican monopoly and to restore toleration. Only the Catholics Clifford and Arlington knew that Charles plotted to use toleration for Dissenters as a wedge to bring toleration for Catholics.

In 1672 Louis XIV invaded Holland, and England supported him by declaring war. On the eve of hostilities Charles issued a Declaration of Indulgence ordering that "all manner of penal laws on matters ecclesiastical against whatever sort of nonconformists or recusants" should be suspended. To his surprise the Dissenters refused to have any toleration that was also extended to Catholics. Public panic about the dangers of Popery rose again. In the public mind the Catholics were vaguely associated with power and with fire; the ancient and unmuted antipathy to Rome rolled strongly through the counties and boroughs. Especially was the court suspect. James, the Duke of York, was an avowed Catholic; he commanded the English fleets. The union of England and France against Protestant Holland was unpopular. Many of the officers of the army were believed to be Catholics. In a frenzy of dismay, distrust, and anger Parliament assembled. Were the war and the Declaration of Indulgence parts of a plot to establish Catholicism and royal tyranny? Parliament refused to grant supplies until the Declaration of Indulgence was withdrawn. Charles withdrew it, insisting that he had meant no harm. To him perjury was but a peccadillo.

A Test Act was now swiftly passed through both houses of Parliament without opposition. This law excluded from civil or military office all who refused to swear the oaths of allegiance and supremacy, to deny transubstantiation, and to take the sacrament according to the rites of the Anglican Church. Charles and his advisers were startled at the storm which thundered over the land. The Duke of York had to resign as lord high admiral; Clifford resigned as treasurer;

hundreds of Catholics followed. Ambitious Anthony Ashley Cooper, the Cabal member and lord chancellor, who had been made earl of Shaftesbury in 1672, had grown suddenly suspicious of the king's Catholic designs. Shaftesbury believed in civil liberty and religious toleration; so far as his own religion was concerned he was a sceptic. When he was ousted from office by Charles II he realized that he had been tricked. Angered both by Charles's perfidy and the fact that he had been deceived by it, Shaftesbury prepared for revenge; it was a risky thing to dupe Shaftesbury.

The Cabal was finished. Charles, who had sold the interests of his country to Louis XIV, now discovered that the promised golden fruit of all his Catholic plots had turned to ashes in his hands. He never forgot the lesson. His brother James never learned it.

In 1674 Parliament insisted on making peace with Holland. It compelled Charles to join the expanding anti-French alliance. The Dutch gallantly struggled on, cutting the dykes to stop the armies of Louis XIV. By 1678 Louis was halted. He had failed to subjugate the iron Dutch. Under the terms of the Treaty of Nimwegen of July, 1678, it was Spain, not Holland, that ceded territory to France.

WHIGS AND TORIES

In the last decade of Charles II's reign were formed the two great historic parties of Whigs and Tories. After the hasty dissolution of the Cabal Charles turned to Thomas Osborne, earl of Danby, an intolerant Anglican, tainted by the pervasive depravity of the age. As the king's chief minister and lord treasurer, Danby used lavish bribery and judicious distribution of patronage and office to win and hold support. His Court party was based on the old Cavalier principles of devotion to the royal prerogative and the Church of England. These Tory principles were particularly popular among the rural gentry and the clergy. Danby restored the statue of Charles I at Charing Cross. He married Mary, daughter of James, Duke of York, to William, Prince of Orange, thus rendering an immense service to the Protestant cause in England and Holland. Soon his followers came to be called Tories, an insulting epithet long before bestowed on Catholic Irish bandits.

Opposed to Danby's followers were those in the Country party led by Shaftesbury. They believed in toleration for Protestant Dissenters, in the old Roundhead idea of parliamentary supremacy, in commercial development, in the liberty of the subject. These liberal members of the Country party gathered at the Green Ribbon Club in Chancery Lane. The Green Ribbon men organized a real political party; they distributed propaganda; they sent out missionaries; they built bonfires and held street parades. Their appeal was strong among middle class Dissenters, the commercial classes, and certain groups of nobles. They were later called Whigs, a nickname once given to covenanted Scotsmen who murdered bishops.

In Shaftesbury the Country party had a nimble and diligent leader. Long before, as a member of the Short Parliament, he had supported Charles I. He had then passed over to support Cromwell; he had sat on Cromwell's council of state. He had intrigued with Monk and helped to recall Charles II. After this Talleyrand career Shaftesbury was well fitted to lead a political party. In *Absalom and Achitophel* John Dryden later described him with mingled precision and cruelty:

> "Of these the false Achitophel was first
> A name to all succeeding ages curst;
> For close designs and crooked counsels fit,
> Sagacious, bold, and turbulent of wit,
> Restless, unfixed in principles and place,
> In power unpleased, impatient of disgrace;
> A fiery soul, which, working out its way,
> Fretted the pigmy body to decay
> And o'er-informed the tenement of clay."

Readers of Dryden's famous poem will do well to recall that it was published in November, 1681, four months after Shaftesbury was arrested and charged with treason; that Dryden was a Catholic when he wrote it; that the Duchess of Monmouth was his patroness and he feared her.

In the late 1670's Shaftesbury had a chance to advance his political cause. One of the foundation pillars of his party was the widespread fear and dislike of Roman Catholicism. Released from the Tower, where he had been held for several months, Shaftesbury seized and fanned the popular distrust and panic. "Popery is breaking in upon us like a flood!" He cried out against "popishly infected" persons in high places. He corresponded with William of Orange. He spread the alarming truth that Charles had an army of 20,000 men and thousands of pounds doled out by Louis XIV.

Amid the general clamor Titus Oates, a renegade Baptist preacher, used his fertile and febrile brain to invent one of the most colossal lies in history. Oates told of a Jesuit plot to murder the king, seize the government, and set up the Roman Catholic Church. He made a deposition to that effect before Sir Edmund Berry Godfrey, a London magistrate. A few days later Godfrey was found murdered. In 1678 a frightened public at once held the Jesuits responsible. Wild and monstrous stories spread: the Jesuits were going to kill the king and put the Catholic Duke of York on the throne; they were going to burn London with mysterious "fireballs"; they had betrayed England to Louis XIV; and so on.

Parliamentary committees were appointed to investigate. Shaftesbury wanted to force Charles to dissolve the Cavalier Parliament. He was certain that the Country party would fare well in a new election. He hoped to compel the king to abandon France and the French alliance. As a result of the public hysteria about 2,000 Catholics were sent to prison. Every Catholic was ordered to leave London. Five Catholic peers were locked up. Parliament passed a second Test Act excluding Catholics from both houses of Parliament; this act was not repealed until 1829. Meanwhile Titus Oates and his gang were making wilder and wilder charges. The queen herself was accused of being party to the plot to murder Charles. The secretary of the Duchess of York was executed; his case was unusual because the evidence clearly proved his guilt. Many innocent Catholics lost their lives as the demented and perjured Oates dramatically testified against them.

In January, 1679, Louis XIV, who wanted to see Danby ousted, bribed the English ambassador to reveal that Danby had signed a dispatch pressing for a cash payment by Louis XIV to Charles. Although Danby had acted on the king's order he was impeached. Charles was eager to prevent the trial. As was earlier explained, Shaftesbury was anxious to have an election because he thought the Whigs might carry the country and control the new house of commons. So the Whigs were pleased when Charles dissolved the Cavalier Parliament in March, 1679. It had sat for eighteen years.

Shaftesbury and his Whigs won the election. Charles had only thirty supporters in the new house. By dissolving the Cavalier Parliament he had indeed saved Danby, but now he was faced by the Whigs. They immediately introduced a bill to exclude the Catholic James, Duke of York, from the throne. Between 1679 and 1681 Charles summoned three Parliaments. In each assembly the Exclusion Bill was hotly debated. Each time Charles dissolved Parliament to save his brother. Out of the fierce confusion came one celebrated law, the Habeas Corpus Act of 1679. It guaranteed that no British subject should be imprisoned without being speedily brought to trial. This Habeas Corpus Act was rightly entitled "An act for the better securing of the liberty of the subject." The subject was to have early need of such security.

Shaftesbury now proposed that the Duke of Monmouth, illegitimate son of Charles II and Lucy Walters, be recognized as heir to the throne. Most of the Whigs would not support him because they wanted the throne to go to the next in line after James. This was James's Protestant daughter Mary, wife of William of Orange. As the split in the Whig party widened Charles was strengthening his position. Louis XIV was subsidizing him again and he was relatively independent of Parliament. Public excitement about the Popish plot was dying down. The Whigs were growing unpopular. Among various reasons the most important was that many Englishmen feared that Whig policies would provoke an outbreak of civil war.

Through all the excitement Charles appeared indolently cool. Asserting that Shaftesbury had conspired to assassinate him and to raise a rebellion in support of Monmouth, Charles tried to obtain a conviction in the courts. Shaftesbury was acquitted. Fearing for his life, he fled to Holland. A few months later this founder of the Whig party died in exile. Leading Whigs he left behind him were tried for their share in the Rye House and insurrection plots. Lord Russell and Algernon Sidney were condemned by packed juries and died by the headsman's axe. Lord Essex cut his throat in the Tower. Monmouth fled terror-stricken over the sea. Because its leaders had been unscrupulous and violent the Whig party was broken for a time. The revenge of the king was complete.

The Tories shared the king's triumph. As Englishmen realized their narrow escape from civil war addresses of loyalty were sent forward to Charles. He lost no time in striking at the roots of Whig power. By *quo warranto* proceedings he routed out the Whigs who had been successful, despite the Corporation Act, in controlling certain borough governments. The procedure was simple. Charles directed a *quo warranto* writ to Whig-controlled boroughs requiring them to show that their charters granted them the right to exercise specified liberties. Many boroughs could not prove to the courts' satisfaction that they held these liberties under precise and detailed charter provisions, particularly as Charles had seen to it that the judges in the courts were carefully selected. In such cases the original charters were forfeited and the king granted new ones, so written as to insure Tory control of the borough governments. In the counties, Tories were put in the places of Whig justices of the peace. Such steps helped to guarantee future Tory control of the house of commons as well as destroy local self-government.

Everywhere Charles and the Tories were victorious. The ancient liberties of England were again in jeopardy. Nevertheless, the new power of Charles was based on the support of the Anglican Tories. If a royal attempt were ever made to raise the Catholics and depress the Anglicans, then Tory support would be withdrawn.

In February, 1685, Charles suddenly became ill. As he lay dying, there was furtively brought to his bedchamber Father Huddleston, a priest who was said to have saved his life after the battle of Worcester. From him Charles received the last rites of the Roman Catholic Church.

JAMES II

The new king was James II, the Duke of York whom the Exclusion Bill would have proscribed. Charles, with his swift intelligence, had known how to stay politically secure. He had consciously avoided going beyond the edge of safety. With James it was otherwise. He had no tact, no political sense. Fervently Catholic, he heard mass at once in Whitehall, something that Charles II had never dared to do. Anglicans thought that James would treat his religion as a private matter. James thought that the Anglicans would favor Catholicism because they hated Protestant Nonconformists. Both were mistaken.

In May, 1685, the Tory Parliament met, in a passion of loyalty, and granted James £400,000 more than had ever been given to Charles II. It was then that a rising of the Scottish earl of Argyle was crushed and the Duke of Monmouth landed on the southwest coast of England. In Dorset, Wiltshire, and Somerset Monmouth gathered about 5,000 supporters, a smaller force than he had expected. He had fatuously hoped that the Protestant Dissenters would rise to proclaim him king. John Churchill, later the great Duke of Marlborough, was swiftly gathering the royal troops. On the night of July 5, 1685, Monmouth's ill-disciplined peasants, armed with scythes, pitchforks, and swords, bravely sallied forth to attack the royal camp at Sedgemoor. Blocked by an impassable ditch they were exposed to the steady fire of Churchill's veterans. The result for them was disaster.

Myths and legends still cling about the magic name of Monmouth in Somerset. But the man himself died no hero's death. Grovelling on his knees, he vainly begged for his life from James. The new king sent his nephew to die at Tyburn. There followed a hideous slaughter of misguided peasants. Then came the Bloody Assize, conducted by the polluted and cruel Chief Justice Jeffreys, who was later paid for his massacres by the lord chancellorship. More than three hundred individuals were hanged; seven hundred were scourged, fined, or exiled to the Barbadoes. Recent research has tended to show that in some cases the cruelty of Jeffreys has been exaggerated; but enough indisputable evidence remains to convict him still of callous butchery.

The removal of Monmouth ended the schism in the shattered Whig party. All the Whigs now had to stand behind the legitimate claims to the English throne of Mary, elder daughter of James, and her husband, William of Orange. There was nobody else for the English Protestants to support. James had pledged that he would maintain the laws inviolate and protect the Anglican Church. In the bright dawn of his reign the royal word was accepted. It was believed that he would not attempt to impose Catholicism upon England. Moreover, the heirs to the throne, his daughters Mary and Anne, were both Protestant. Although James's second wife, Mary of Modena, was a Catholic, no children at first resulted from this marriage. A Protestant succession to the daughter of James and Anne Hyde seemed assured.

The victory of the royal forces over Monmouth seems to have hastened James's decision to bring England back to Rome. The regular army had been increased from the three foot regiments left after the great demobilization of the Ironsides. It now numbered nearly 30,000 men. James relied on this army completely. He brought 13,000 men to camp on Hounslow Heath to threaten, if need be, London and Parliament. James forgot that these soldiers were also Englishmen. When he sent priests among them there were no conversions. Although many of the soldiers were not very good Protestants they knew what they did not like; they did not like Popery. It was James's folly to think that he could erect a royal and Catholic despotism upon a military basis.

When Parliament met in the winter of 1685 several events had made the members suspicious of the king's intentions. Even the Tories were alarmed at the standing army officered by so many Catholics. Catholic intrigues in the court and government were common gossip. Parliament wanted the army reduced, the Catholics removed from key positions. On the other hand, James wished the Test Act repealed. When both Lords and Commons refused to change the laws, James prorogued Parliament. He never summoned it again.

THE NEW DESPOTISM

James II now proceeded swiftly along the road to his own ruin. Determined to impose Catholicism upon an alienated people, he defied the law and appointed Roman Catholics to the privy council. He established an arbitrary court of ecclesiastical commission similar to the earlier court of high commission; this body suspended anti-Catholic bishops. At the same time James recklessly dismissed judges opposed to his wishes. He increased the appointments of Catholic officers in the army. A test case was made of Sir Edward Hales, a Catholic colonel in the royal forces. Hales was indicted for failure to comply with the provisions of the Test Act. Before the court of king's bench he pleaded that he had the king's letters patent dispensing with the oaths required by the law. In the judgment delivered by Chief Justice Herbert the court upheld James's power to dispense with the law, as the packed courts had sometimes done in the reigns of the first two Stuarts. The judges voted eleven to one that the dispensing power was "the ancient remains of the sovereign power and prerogative of the kings of England, which never yet was taken from them or can be."

Catholic chapels were opened in London. The Jesuits began a school in the Savoy. In Scotland and Ireland a similar pattern of arbitrary interference developed. The antagonism to the royal will steadily mounted and a flood of unlicensed pamphlets, as in the days of the Civil War, poured from the presses as the national alarm increased. Upon the universities, particularly Oxford, James obstinately attempted to foist Roman Catholics. Magdalen and Christ Church were headed by a Catholic dean and president. Objecting fellows were dismissed. In their places were appointed twenty-five Catholics. At Cambridge the vice-chancellor was dismissed when he refused to bestow a degree upon a Benedictine monk. The papal nuncio was received in state at Windsor. James heeded no warnings. The ghost of Mary Tudor stalked through the corridors of Whitehall. James's supporters, Anglican and Tory, fell away. The Anglicans, for example, were furious at the attacks upon the universities. Whigs and Tories, landowners and merchants, churchmen and Dissenters, all drew together in overwhelming force. They welcomed the Protestant Huguenot refugees after Louis XIV revoked the Edict of Nantes in 1685. A final battle with James was at hand.

Popular resistance led the king to hope that he might gain the backing of the Dissenters for his Catholic program by allowing them freedom of worship. He reckoned without the fact that the Protestant Nonconformists, anxious as they were for a relief from odious persecution, were yet unwilling to sacrifice the national cause. In 1687 the king issued a Declaration of Indulgence suspending the laws against all Dissenters and Roman Catholics. The Tory Lord Halifax, who had been dismissed from office, wrote a pamphlet called *Letter to A Dissenter*. He warned the Dissenters: "You are therefore to be hugged now, only that you may the better be squeezed at another time." Twenty thousand copies of this pamphlet were sold within a month. But the warning was unnecessary. All England was already alarmed. There was talk of deposing James and placing his eldest daughter Mary on the throne. Many English leaders were discussing the matter with Mary and her husband, the great Dutch Protestant champion William of Orange.

On April 27, 1688, James issued a second Declaration of Indulgence and ordered that it be read in all churches on two successive Sundays. It was read in only four churches in London. Meanwhile seven bishops, led by Sancroft, archbishop of Canterbury, petitioned James against the Declaration as illegal: "Your petitioners therefore most humbly and earnestly beseech your majesty that you will be graciously pleased not to insist upon their distributing and reading your majesty's said declaration."

The king, declaring the petition to be a "standard of rebellion," sent the petitioners to the Tower, prosecuted them for seditious libel. Amid fierce public demonstrations the bishops appeared on June 29 at the bar of the court of king's bench. The fury of the people overawed the judges and the jury. The judges were divided. To the jury Justice Powell declared: "I can see no difference, nor know of one in law, between the king's power to dispense with laws ecclesiastical and his power to dispense with any other laws whatsoever. If this be once allowed of, there will need no Parliament; all the legislature will be in the king—which is a thing worth considering, and I leave the issue to God and your conscience." On July 30, 1688, the jury found the bishops not guilty. A roar of approval rolled over England. Bonfires were lit in the streets of London. Swiftly the news spread along the country crossroads into the remotest hamlets.

Meanwhile, on July 1, the queen, the Italian Mary of Modena, gave birth to a son. The heir to the throne was now a Catholic. Across the English Channel the march of Catholicism was evident to all Englishmen. "Heresy is no more," declared the great Bishop Bossuet of France. The prospect of Catholic rule in England induced the chief Whig and Tory leaders to act without delay. They had long been in communication with William of Orange and Mary. On July 30, the day of the bishops' acquittal, seven prominent Whigs and Tories despatched a formal invitation to William to come with an army to England to aid in the restoration of English liberties. The Tory doctrine of non-resistance was laid on the shelf. King James stood alone in his realm.

THE GLORIOUS REVOLUTION OF 1688

Louis XIV had earlier planned to aid James by attacking Holland. But James refused the proffered French alliance, and in September, 1688, Louis declared war upon the League of Augsburg and struck at the Rhenish Palatinate. For the invasion of England William had made thorough naval and military preparations. The dockyards and army camps of Holland were hives of activity. On November 5, 1688, the anniversary of the Gunpowder Plot, William reached England with the aid of a "Protestant wind." At Torbay in Devonshire he landed 15,000 men and 600 transports. His forces included 4,000 English and Scottish soldiers who had served in Holland together with Dutch, Germans, and Swedes. When James still refused to call a free Parliament the Tory Danby led a rising in the north. Everywhere men hastened to serve under the banners of rebellion.

The royal army, having gathered at Salisbury, was soon without a commander. John Churchill wrote a decorous letter of farewell to James and rode off to join William, as he had earlier arranged to do. Other officers followed him; the royal forces were demoralized. James II's hopes collapsed. His daughter Anne and her husband, Prince George of Denmark, had joined Danby at Nottingham. The rest of his family James had sent out of England. In early December he fled to find refuge at the court of Louis XIV. That he might leave anarchy behind him he burned the writs for the new Parliament, wrote an order for the disbandment of the army, threw the great seal of England into the Thames. He never saw England again.

The house of lords, all who had sat in the commons during the reign of Charles II before the house had been packed by James, and the aldermen and councillors of London met in an informal assembly to decide what steps should be taken to create a legal government. They requested William to take over the provisional government and to issue writs to borough and county electors asking them to elect representatives to a Convention. This Convention assembled on January 22, 1689. Whigs and Tories mingled their principles in the famous resolution that James II, "having endeavoured to subvert the constitution of the kingdom by breaking the original contract between king and people, and having, by the advice of Jesuits and other wicked persons, violated the fundamental laws and withdrawn himself out of the kingdom, has abdicated and the throne is thereby vacant."

In the Convention the Whig majority was so strong that the outcome of the debates on principles of government was inevitable. Many of the Tories wanted to reconcile events with their theories of the royal power, divine right, and hereditary succession. They shrank from acceptance of the Whig principles of contract, religious toleration, and the superiority of Parliament. They first proposed a regency in the name of James II; then they held out for Mary as sole sovereign, the successor by hereditary right. Mary refused to reign alone; William told Danby that he did not intend to be prince consort, merely his wife's gentleman usher. So William and Mary had to be proclaimed joint sovereigns, the actual administration resting with William alone.

The Tory minority could not escape the consequences of James's departure. William and Mary were clearly rulers by act of Parliament. By no exercise of Tory dialectics could they be proved the rightful sovereigns according to hereditary principle.

A small Tory group clung to the theory of divine right. In later days these men were called Jacobites, from the Latin Jacobus, meaning James. About four hundred High Church Anglicans felt compelled by their adherence to the doctrine of divine right to refuse to take the oath of allegiance to William and Mary because they were not in the direct line of succession. These Nonjurors seceded from the Anglican Church to become tutors or chaplains to Jacobite squires. As the years passed their numbers dwindled. All the rest of the Tories and Anglicans bowed with ill grace to the pressure of inexorable circumstance. Hereditary right, divine and indefeasible, and religious persecution ended in England when James embarked in the darkness for France. Charles II, despite his known immorality, touched thousands for the "king's evil." So far as is known, none were brought to be healed by William III, who was not the Lord's anointed. When Anne, last of the Stuarts, came to the throne the custom was revived. One of those touched by Queen Anne was Samuel Johnson.

SCOTLAND AND IRELAND

In Scotland the revolution followed a different road. Despite considerable loyalty to the ancient Scottish house of Stuart, many Scotsmen recognized that the Calvinist William would look kindly upon Presbyterianism. Accordingly, a Convention held at Edinburgh prepared a "Claim of Right" similar to the English Declaration of Right and offered the crown to William and Mary under terms which included recognition of the Presbyterian Church as the state church of the nation. The offer was accepted.

At once the Highlanders, always loyal to the Stuarts, rose in rebellion. Led by Viscount "Bonny" Dundee, they defeated the Lowlanders and the English in a minor engagement at Killiecrankie in 1689. Nevertheless, when William offered reasonable terms several Highland clans accepted. The oath of allegiance to William was to be taken by January 1, 1692. All the Highlanders took the oath except the Macdonalds of Glencoe, who delayed six days beyond the deadline date. Acting on the advice of an enemy of the Macdonalds William ordered the clan to be punished. Soldiers of the Campbell clan were despatched to carry out the command; they were received as guests by the unsuspecting men of Glencoe. After twelve days the Campbells fell upon their hosts at daybreak on February 13, 1692. The chief and thirty-seven of the Macdonalds were slain. The rest escaped in a snowstorm. This savage crime was denounced, particularly by the Jacobites, and William was widely blamed for it. In fact, he had not known that his order would be so brutally executed. In his ignorance of the Highland situation he had accepted evil advice. He did not know that feuding Scottish clansmen had always been inclined to butchery, swift and thorough.

Scotland soon faced an economic crisis. A trade war had developed between English and Scottish interests. The Scots wanted to increase their foreign trade and to establish colonies overseas. When Scottish merchants in London tried to form trading companies they were blocked by the hostile English Parliament and the monopoly-gorged East India Company. Not only were the English able to stop Scottish competition in English and colonial markets; they were also prepared to make great efforts to keep the Scotsmen out of all foreign markets. There was natural resentment on the part of Scottish businessmen.

Persuaded by Edinburgh merchants, the Scottish Parliament issued a charter to the Darien Company, formed to found a settlement on the Isthmus of Darien which, it was hoped, would be the center of the overland trade route across the isthmus to the Pacific. Three expeditions were sent out in 1698 and 1699. William III refused to support the Scottish enterprise because he was then negotiating a partition treaty with Louis XIV and the Emperor Leopold providing for the maintenance of the balance of power by settling the vexed problem of the succession to the Spanish throne. Spanish hostility in Darien united with the abominable climate to drive the Scotsmen out. In the disastrous scheme they lost thousands of pounds.

As Anglo-Scottish disputes about the succession to the Scottish throne increased it was decided to negotiate as to the possibility of uniting the two nations. Finally, in 1707, an agreement was reached.

England and Scotland were to be "united into one kingdom by the name of Great Britain." The Scottish Parliament came to an end. Scotland was given a representation of sixteen peers in the house of lords and forty-five members in the house of commons. It assumed a small part of the public debt. It kept unchanged all its own institutions, such as the law courts and the Presbyterian Church. It received full free trade with England and the colonies and henceforth shared in English enterprise throughout the world. The economic and political arrangements under the Act of Union were a good bargain for both countries. England no longer had an enemy on her northern border. Scotland began to prosper and to make a massive contribution to the national and imperial life of the new Great Britain.

In Ireland the Catholics remained bitterly resentful of the Cromwellian confiscations that had put three-quarters of the Irish land into the hands of Protestants. Because Charles II and James II were Catholics they had permitted the Irish Catholics to worship freely and thus had won some good will. In 1689 James asked for their support and got it. When he landed in Ireland in the spring of 1689 he brought money, men, and supplies from his ally Louis XIV. At once the Irish Parliament confiscated all Protestant lands; the Irish Catholics, forming eighty per cent of the population, marched with James against the Protestant Ulsterites. The Ulster stronghold of Londonderry was besieged for fifteen weeks.

William III landed in Ireland with an Anglo-Dutch army in 1690. The Irish Protestants, called Orangemen through the centuries because of their alliance with William of Orange, immediately joined William's forces. At the battle of the Boyne on July 12, 1690, the army of James was defeated. James himself did not wait to see the battle through; he went back to France. The Irish Catholics kept up the war until the fall of 1696. Then they agreed to surrender Limerick in return for assurance that they would be given as much religious liberty as they had possessed in the reign of Charles II. However, the Irish Protestants objected, and the English Parliament refused to ratify the Treaty of Limerick. A series of cruel acts was passed against the Irish Catholics. Catholics were excluded from the Irish Parliament. They were forbidden to sit on juries, on town councils, to serve in the army, or to teach in Irish schools. No Catholic was allowed to buy land. When a Catholic landowner died his estate had to be divided among all his children.

In the reign of Charles II the export of cattle from Ireland to England had been prohibited. Now, in the reigns of William and Mary and Anne, further restrictive laws were enacted by the English Parliament. All Irish imports from the colonies were required to pass through England. This increased the purchase price so greatly that trade with the colonies swiftly became unprofitable. The export of Irish woolens to any country other than England was forbidden and the English placed such high import duties on woolen goods that the Irish trade was ruined. As a result of these harsh acts the Irish Protestants suffered as much as the Irish Catholics. Thousands of both groups emigrated to America. The English had wrung the utmost value from their opportunities. Another bloody and bitter chapter had been written in the tragic history of Ireland.

Thus the Revolution of 1688 had profoundly changed the flow of events in the three kingdoms of England, Scotland, and Ireland. When William and Mary came to the throne certain important consequences followed at once. These, usually called the "revolution settlement," will be described in a later chapter. Before the tale of the heirs of the revolution is told, however, we must look at the intellectual and social mosaic of the seventeenth century. The tense and formidable Stuart age was immensely creative. Although the giants of the Tudor century had departed, their successors were men of no mean stature. They achieved excellently, each in his own fashion.

Section III

THE STUARTS AND THEIR FALL

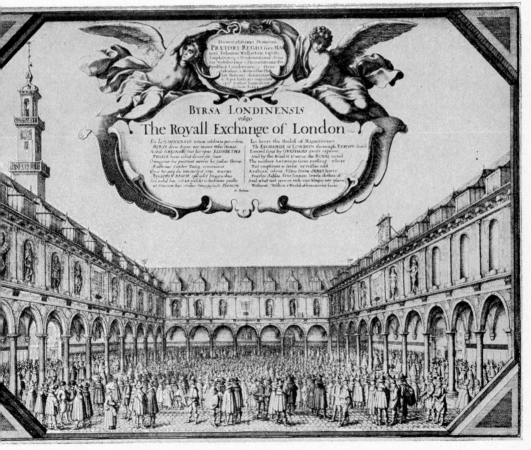

The Royal Exchange, London, A.D. 1644.

James I.

Crest of James I, showing Scotland incorporated with the English arms.

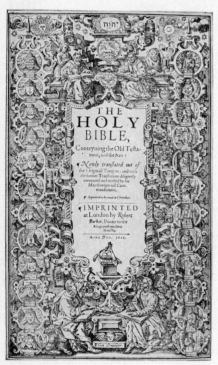

"King James's" Bible, A.D. 1611.

William Laud, Archbishop of Canterbury.

Charles I and Queen Henrietta Maria.

The royal ship *Sovereign of the Seas,* A.D. 1637—the same year in which John Hampden refused to pay "ship-money."

The Battle of Naseby—a contemporary plan.

Soldiers of the "New Model" Army.

Troopers of the King.

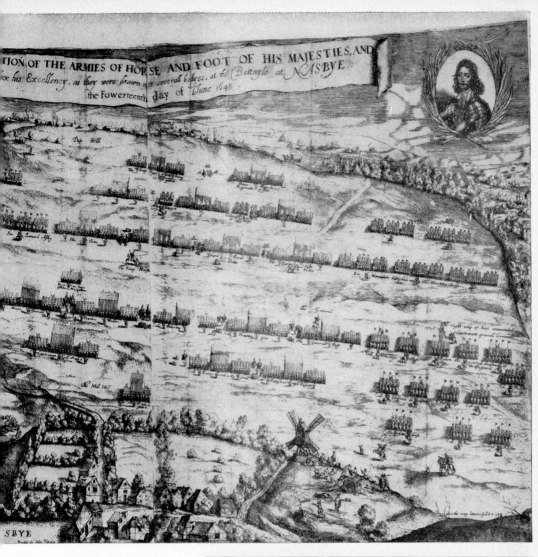

ITION OF THE ARMIES OF HORSE AND FOOT OF HIS MAJESTIES, AND
his Excellency, as they were drawn into severall bodies, at the Battayle at NASBYE
the Fowerteenth day of June 1645

Oliver Cromwell.

Hollar's view of London after the Great Fire.

The battle of Sole Bay, May 28, 1672, in which the Dutch under DeRuyter crippled the combined French and English fleets.

St. Paul's Cathedral, London, designed by
Sir Christopher Wren.

51. Belins gate. 54. Leadenhall.   57. Basinghall,
53. Custome house. 55. Royall Exchange 58. Ludgate.
55. Tower wharfe. 56. Guildhall.

James II.

Contemporary broadside of *Lilliburlero*—the song that whistled a King off his throne.

Chapter 20

THE AGE OF NEWTON

THE NEW SCIENCE

IN ENGLAND the seventeenth century was the age of revolt against authority. Political history has as its central theme the defiance of royal despotism. Ecclesiastical history marks the slow emergence of ideas of toleration. Intellectual history traces the new challenge to the authority of scholasticism. For several centuries the rational synthesis of St. Thomas Aquinas of the Scriptures and Aristotelianism had limited freedom of investigation of the physical world. Shortly after 1600 Francis Bacon began to advance the standards of free inquiry by denouncing scholasticism and its "letters of opium on tablets of lead." Of conditions in the English universities he wrote: "Everything is found adverse to the progress of science. The lectures and the exercises there are so ordered that to think or speculate on anything out of the common way can hardly occur to any man." The new spirit of science was creating a climate of opinion sceptical and derisive, corroding the ancient fetters of authority. At the end of the century Sir Isaac Newton presented the world with an exact demonstration that the universe was one harmonious machine. Between the appearance of Bacon and Newton lamps of aspiration had been lit in innumerable laboratories.

Francis Bacon himself was not nearly such a great scientist as is often supposed; he was too busy with politics, law, and philosophy. Nevertheless, what Bacon did accomplish was of tremendous importance. Despite the fact that as a scientist he was far behind many of his contemporaries, he was much more articulate than any of them. His writings were prolific, his gift of exposition admirable. Thus he performed a great service by lending the weight of his prestige to support those who were arguing for the inductive and experimental method in science. He was indeed the "trumpeter of the new age," heralding the advance of the practical and utilitarian science that would, as he claimed, "extend more widely the power and greatness of man."

In a great series of books which included *The Advancement of*

Learning, The New Atlantis, and the *Novum Organum* Bacon proclaimed a basic change in scientific attitude and method. His teaching had wide results in persuading men of the importance of scientific inquiry. Among the upper classes, for example, the rising intellectual curiosity brought the emergence of hundreds of virtuosi whose wealth and leisure permitted them to indulge their fancies. From the study of nature's wonders they obtained considerable subjective pleasure. Observing the majestic marvels of God's handiwork, such men of sensibility were often filled with a passion to discover more about the mysterious workings of His universe. At the same time, admiring the strange and the rare, they began to collect unusual items of all kinds. John Evelyn sought rarities such as "eggs in which the yoke rattled, a pear, a piece of beef with the bones in it." The dramatist Shadwell mocked at "a Sot, that has spent £2,000 in Microscopes, to find out the Nature of Eels in Vinegar, Mites in Cheese, and the Blue of Plums which he has subtilly found out to be living creatures."

Of course, the virtuosi were not real scientists like Sir Isaac Newton, Robert Boyle, or Robert Hooke. They were not trained in research methods; their energies were scattered; they had no principles of selection in their investigations; and they discovered very little of value to science. Nevertheless, as a part of a society increasingly sympathetic to science and its methods, they helped to prepare the way for further advance. It was such men, for example, who denounced the study of grammar, logic, rhetoric, and metaphysics in the universities; they wanted practical, scientific, utilitarian courses. Unfortunately, their number decreased as culture declined among the aristocracy. The coffee house was soon to take the place of the laboratory, the library, and the art gallery. The gentleman scholar of the seventeenth century was to become the gentleman of the "fashionable, illiterate world" of the eighteenth century, denounced by Swift and Shaftesbury; in the nineteenth century he was to become one of Matthew Arnold's "barbarians."

Meanwhile the scientific spirit resulted in a number of important achievements by the real scientists or "natural philosophers." In the field of medicine, for example, small progress had been made in sixteenth century England. As was earlier explained, there were only a few skilled and competent physicians under the Tudors. The ferment caused on the Continent by the work of Vesalius on the structure of the human body raised but feeble echoes in Oxford and Cambridge although the great Thomas Vicary, physician to Henry VIII and Elizabeth, plagiarized Vesalius' book within five years of its appearance in Europe. Vicary was one of a restricted circle where the ancient authority of Galen had been weakened. To most English physicians, Galen still remained the "prince of physic" and the "lantern of surgeons." Except in the field of preventive plague medicine, England took small part in the medical renaissance of Europe until the seventeenth century.

Padua, home university of Vesalius, was Europe's greatest medical school. At the turn of the century William Harvey went from England to Padua to study. He returned to continue his dissections of animals and his examination of the human anatomy. By observation and without the aid of a microscope Harvey discovered that the blood, pumped by the heart, circulated within the body. He could not see that the blood moved through capillaries between the arteries and the veins; but he knew that somehow the circulation was accomplished. In 1628 he published his *De Motu Cordis* which described his discovery, a massive achievement in the history of physiology.

There were few other advances. In sixteenth century England the best medical work had been done by men who had clinical experience on the battlefield. But under the early Stuarts there were few writings by any surgeons. Medical practice lagged behind medical theory. Unlicensed salesmen with significant bottles took advantage of the fear and ignorance of the sick. Recipes for salves and potions were held in high esteem. Even after Mayerne and Gilbert the great Evelyn could write in praise of the healing qualities of "rain water of the autumnal equinox, exceedingly rectified, very volatile." A contemporary could comment learnedly upon the virtues of the mysterious "lohock in the pot." Although no outstanding medical achievements occurred, later in the century there was a general improvement in medical treatment and sanitation. Research continued, and the work of such men as Richard Lower in anatomy and Thomas Sydenham in diagnostic methods contributed to the advance of medicine in the continuing battle against disease and death.

One of the major contributions to mathematics was made by a Scotsman, John Napier. Napier was an enthusiastic amateur in many fields of endeavor. He invented a machine to force water out of mines; he anticipated the interest of the eighteenth century landowners in improving their land and breeding better cattle; he crusaded against Roman Catholicism. All these activities were insignificant when placed beside the fact that Napier, without advice or aid, developed the theory of logarithms in 1614. He found out how to construct them; he calculated a table; he invented devices similar to the modern slide rule and calculating machine. Henry Briggs, mathematician at Cambridge, continued Napier's work. Edward Wright applied mathematical principles to navigation. John Wallis prepared the way for Sir Isaac Newton by his discovery of some of the essential elements of differential calculus. These men pioneered, others followed.

Botanical study advanced. John Ray of Cambridge spent much time in the collection and systematic classification of plants. English naturalists travelled in Asia and America. In astronomy, Edmund

Halley charted the position of a number of fixed stars; he studied the orbits of comets and calculated the periodicity of the one that bears his name; he investigated tides and terrestrial magnetism. The work of William Gilbert on magnetism confirmed the Copernican hypothesis of the earth's rotation. One of the most versatile scientists of the age was Robert Hooke, who invented the balance wheel for the watch, improved the compound microscope, the reflector telescope, and the barometer. In physics, the Irish Robert Boyle discovered the relation between the volume, density, and pressure of gases. The resulting "Boyle's law" was an important step in the investigation of the physical properties of the atmosphere. As the founder of experimental chemistry Boyle also did much to separate alchemy from chemistry, to the dismay of those who had long sought a way of transmuting base metals into gold. It was Boyle who advanced the view that all matter was composed of minute particles, thus anticipating the later atomic theory.

Most learned men were concerned with the practical application of their discoveries and inventions. Thomas Sprat, bishop of Rochester, wrote that "while the old philosophy could only bestow on us some barren terms and notions, the new shall import to us the uses of all the creatures and shall enrich us with all the benefits of fruitfulness and plenty." Not for a hundred years were men to achieve the conquest of power that brought the Industrial Revolution; but the extension of scientific methods of discovering truth prepared the way for the achievements of a later age. The marriage of science and industry was not yet; but it was soon to come.

There was now a method of obtaining truth that was divorced from theology. Would the character of religious belief be altered? The questioning and experimental spirit of science was shortly to have a mighty effect on English religious thought. Was reason or tradition to be supreme in matters of faith as well as in matters of physical research? On the one hand Englishmen continued to persecute those suspected of witchcraft; on the other, they debated those problems of the absolutes in faith that have never ceased to haunt the souls of men.

"To increase the power of all mankind and to free men from the bondage of errors" the Royal Society was founded in 1662. Early members included Robert Boyle, Abraham Cowley, John Evelyn, Isaac Newton, John Ray, and Christopher Wren. The first curator of the Society was Robert Hooke. Learned men of several professions united in scientific experiment, discussion, and publication. The founding of this Royal Society, which grew out of Robert Boyle's earlier Invisible College, reflected the spirit of the age. So, too, did the new national observatory that rose at Greenwich.

Above all his contemporaries stood Sir Isaac Newton. To his age it seemed that Newton had settled all the chief problems of astronomy, mathematics, optics, and physics. His impressive epitaph in Westminster Abbey speaks of his "vigour of mind almost supernatural." Of him Alexander Pope wrote:

"Nature and Nature's Laws lay hid in Night.
God said 'Let Newton be!' and all was Light."

William Wordsworth thus described Newton's statue at Trinity College, Cambridge:

"The marble index of a mind forever
Voyaging through strange seas of thought, alone."

Son of a Lincolnshire yeoman, Newton studied theology at Cambridge, then became interested in astronomy, physics, and mathematics. When he was twenty-seven years old he was made professor in mathematics at Cambridge. As a mathematician he established the binomial theorem, developed a large part of the theory of equations, invented simultaneously with the German Leibnitz the theory of differential calculus. He investigated the properties of light, showing that the prismatic colors were caused by the different refrangibilities of light rays. He prepared mathematical tables showing how the future position of the moon with reference to the stars could be determined, a calculation of tremendous value to navigation.

In 1697 Newton published his immortal *Mathematical Principles of Natural Philosophy,* usually called the *Principia.* Here he set forth, by precise demonstration, the laws of motion and gravitation. "Every particle of matter in the universe attracts every other particle with a force varying inversely as the square of the distance between them and directly proportional to the product of their masses." This achievement, one of the greatest in the history of pure thought, provided explanation and confirmation of the theories of Galileo and Copernicus. The genius of Newton, it seemed, had discovered a "universal law of nature." He had apparently banished mystery from the world. The universe was obviously a vast mechanism, intelligible, harmonious, uniform, and thoroughly rational. God the Mathematician had made it so. Newton "asserted in his Philosophy the Majesty of God and exhibited in his conduct the simplicity of the Gospel."

Popular expositions of Newton's philosophy were published in many languages. The idea of the immutable, inexorable rule of law in the universe seized upon men's minds. It prepared the way for the eighteenth century, the age of enlightenment and reason, when it was hoped that the discovery of the laws of Nature and Nature's God would in due course make all things new.

POLITICAL PHILOSOPHY: HOBBES, HARRINGTON, LOCKE

It was inevitable that there should be attempts to make terms between the new scientific movement and theological ideas about the nature of the universe. There was an increasing tendency, closely allied to currents of Deism, to defend orthodox Christianity because it was reasonable rather than because it was divinely revealed. When the eighteenth century came it was to be an age of sceptical toleration, of the sceptical idealism of Bishop George Berkeley, of the general scepticism of David Hume and Edward Gibbon. The Latitudinarians in the Anglican Church became particularly undogmatic and liberal. The Cambridge Platonists found in Plato a system of thought which they wedded to Christian theology. They stressed the essentially spiritual nature of Plato's philosophy; they admired his use of reason. Whatever is reasonable, they asserted, should be taken as authoritative in religion as well as in science. God was a reasonable being, and His truth could be apprehended by the tools of man's reason as well as by revelation.

The confirmed Deists held that God was an impersonal Deity and they would not accept revelation at all. John Toland's *Christianity Not Mysterious* (1696) gave new impetus to controversy. Unitarian and Trinitarian disputes multiplied, foreshadowing the doubts and hesitations of the next age. The synthesis between science and theology that the philosophers of earlier centuries had achieved was now quite unacceptable. There were no successors to St. Thomas Aquinas in seventeenth and eighteenth century England.

Meanwhile the masses of the public were untroubled by the clouded relationships between scientific rationalism and the old theology. The minds and hearts of most people, then as now, moved upon a humble and simple level. After the Restoration many Englishmen felt that they had had enough of Puritan idealism; they turned to prosaic common sense as their standard of action. Christian conduct, so far as the welfare of the state and the individual was concerned, might be more important than Christian dogmas. Such a view might not be exciting; but it was comfortable. To this rising attitude may be traced the beginning of new kinds of norms and moral sanctions that have never departed from the fiber of English society.

It was from the field of political philosophy that the most abundant harvest came. As has been shown in earlier chapters, a massive body of books, tracts, newsbooks, printed sermons, and the like streamed from the printing presses in the turbulent Stuart century. The importance of many did not transcend the occasion of their writing; others rose above the political and doctrinal ardors and excesses of their time to make major contributions to the intellectual life of the nation. The most outstanding of these were the works of Thomas Hobbes, James Harrington and John Locke.

Thomas Hobbes of Malmesbury (1588–1679) was the most important English political philosopher of the seventeenth century. His *Leviathan* is the greatest political treatise in the English language. The life of Hobbes was a quiet one until the Civil War broke out; then he turned his attention from mathematics to politics and that was almost his undoing. Had he remained a mathematician he would have been soon forgotten. But because he wrote the *De Cive*, the *Behemoth*, and the *Leviathan* his fame and his influence have continued until the present time.

What is the nature and origin of civil society? To that question political philosophers have given many answers. It is clear that there must exist a state if men are to live in any order with one another. The state, called by Thomas Hobbes the Leviathan or "mortal god," alone stands between man and the state of nature. Hobbes declared that the state of nature existing before civil society was created was a war "of every man against every man." Then the life of man was "solitary, poor, nasty, brutish, and short." To Hobbes all men are filled with "a perpetual and restless desire of power after power, that ceaseth only in death." The result in the state of nature was fear and insecurity. That is the reason why men came together to form a civil society. "Unless there is a power to keep us in awe we are in a state of war."

According to Hobbes, civil society was created when every man made a covenant with every other man and all agreed in conferring their power upon a sovereign. By the theory of Hobbes, men obey their self-imposed sovereign because he gives them protection and security. If the sovereign fails to provide protection, then Hobbes holds that the obligation to obedience and dependency on the part of the subject is ended. Thus Hobbes rejected the theory of divine right. To him a de facto government was also a de jure one; he who succeeded in ruling was the legitimate ruler. Hence Hobbes and the Stuarts both stood for absolutism but not on the same grounds. In fact, Hobbes was supplying the general principles of a legal position. In Hobbes' state there is created a circle of dependency: the law depends on society; society depends on the king; the king depends on the law.

The basis of Hobbes' theory of politics was a materialist theory of human nature which was a rather crude system of behaviorism. Hobbes declared that all of man's conscious life is based on sensation; all sensation is a form of motion; the mechanics of the laws of motion govern everything because nature is a vast machine and all events are motions. In a civil society events happen because of the way people act and everybody acts for his own advantage. The sensations that bombard individual men are good or bad according to whether those individuals like them or not.

Thus Hobbes' whole system is based on individualism. He thought that if all the laws of man's being were once discovered the result could be an explanation of all phenomena by deductive and synthetic methods. His laws of psychology asserted that all people are loyal to governments only if they find it profitable to be so. Individuals are held together in any group by two forces, a sovereign power and their own self-interest. Governments are instruments of self-protection. Hence it pays to be a social and political animal. Only to preserve the state do people obey the law. The only laws of nature Hobbes accepted were the laws of self-preservation and self-interest. He was the first political theorist to try to found the state, not on what men ought to do, but on what they wanted.

What, then, is morality to Hobbes? He turns upside down the idea that law depends on morality; to him there is no morality apart from law. Morality rests on law; it is only the dictate of reason. "Conscience is a form of indigestion." What is justice? Justice is made by the sovereign. In Hobbes' system of government it is irrelevant to speak of right or wrong outside of positive law. As a consistent materialist Hobbes eliminates any concept of justice or natural law coeval with the mind of God and to be apprehended by mankind. To Hobbes the essential fact in civil society is law. The essential motive for creating a state is fear. Man hath "his heart all the day long gnawed on by feare of death, poverty, or other calamity and has no repose; nor pause of his anxiety, but in sleep." And to Hobbes the essential force in the state is the sovereign behind the law.

In the nineteenth century the Benthamite philosophical radicals were to take over into their philosophy the Hobbesian ideas of self-interest and individualism. Bentham was not interested in a dialectical system of sovereignty. He was concerned, as Stammler later, with law as it ought to be. Austin, also deeply indebted to Hobbes, was concerned, as Blackstone earlier, with law as it was. Hobbes would not have approved the later use of his doctrines by bourgeois liberalism. But under the liberal ideology the state was to assume the properties Hobbes and Bentham had put into sovereignty.

Far removed from Thomas Hobbes stood James Harrington, who published in 1656 his almost unreadable *Oceana.* Despite the fact that Harrington missed greatness of thought, he stood out among speculative thinkers in the seventeenth century as a man who had a definite plan. In his *Oceana* he described an ideal state where there would be an attempt to maintain an equal division of landed property; his constitution provided that no man might own land to a value of more than £2,000 a year. Only property owners might vote. Harrington was thus one of the few men in his century who saw the importance of economic forces in politics. Hence in his constitutional republic the power was placed where the balance of property lay. "The wisdom of the few may be the light of mankind, but the interest of a few is not the profit of mankind or of a commonwealth."

The ideal state of Oceana (England) also possessed a republican government based on a system of rotation of office, election by secret ballot, and separation of powers. Harrington's plans were very detailed and complicated; the executive power, for example, was to lie in four executive councils, carefully described. Everywhere he drew upon such varied sources as Plato, Aristotle, Machiavelli, Plutarch, the example of Genoa, Switzerland, and Holland. In presenting the bloodless and unexciting blueprint of his republican Utopia Harrington faced almost every question, except trade. Only a few of his answers can be stated here. For instance, Oceana possessed religious toleration. There was to be a national church, but it was not to possess coercive power. The clergy were not to interfere in politics. There were to be free endowed schools for the whole population and foreign travel for all the youth of the nation. "Home-keeping youth have ever homely minds."

All government, declared Harrington, results from "an act whereby a civil society of men is instituted and preserved upon the foundation of common right or interest; or, to follow Aristotle and Livy, it is the empire of laws and not of men." The principles of government are twofold: first, it must seek to obtain for the people the goods of the mind such as prudence, wisdom, and courage; second, it must attempt to obtain the goods of fortune, prosperity, and riches. "A legislator who can unite in one government the goods of the mind with the goods of fortune comes closest to the work of God." The constitution and the rule of law Harrington ingeniously constructed was capable of expansion "to embrace the world in a federation of liberty."

The long pages of *Oceana* set forth many mechanical details in a mass of turgid prose. Harrington's well was wide but not deep. He was really an engineer; his blueprints are interesting; but he knew little about the nature and spirit of liberty. In the 1650's there was much discussion of his schemes. The Rota Club was founded to study them. They were frequently debated in the Green Ribbon Club. Some of his views found a place in the colonial constitutions of North America. In England they had small effect.

At the end of the century the full tide of polemical pamphlets and newsbooks abated. England's greatest age of propaganda was over. As a result of the revolution of 1688 the Whigs and their principles were for the time triumphant. The great defender of the Whig settlement was John Locke, who sought "to establish the throne of our great Restorer, our present King William, and make good his title in the consent of the people." In pursuing this object Locke set forth his theory of a government based on popular approval.

John Locke was born in 1632 and died in 1704. He attended Westminster School and Christ Church, Oxford. His early years at Oxford were unpleasant and unproductive; later he became interested in metaphysics, medicine, and science. One of his friends was Robert

Boyle, whose *History of the Air* Locke later edited. In 1666 Locke entered the service of Anthony Ashley Cooper, soon to be the earl of Shaftesbury. Thus the road that led to Whiggism lay open ahead. Locke worked by Shaftesbury's side; he was elected to the Royal Society; he held many government posts. But even before Shaftesbury fell from power Locke had found it desirable to leave England; he could not return until 1689 when the Revolution of 1688 had placed William and Mary on the throne.

When Locke returned from exile he published his famous *Letters on Toleration*. Here were expanded the ideas on religious liberty for which Locke had been partly responsible in the *Fundamental Constitutions for the Government of Carolina* which had appeared in 1669. In 1690 Locke also published the *Essay Concerning Human Understanding* which he had begun about 1671. His object was "to inquire into the original, certainty and extent of human knowledge, together with the ground and degrees of belief, opinion, and dissent."

It was the conclusion of Locke that man possesses no innate ideas; all knowledge is a construction of ideas that come from the senses as a result of experience or reflection. To this sensationalist theory of the origin of ideas Locke attached a rationalist explanation of scientific knowledge that could not be reconciled at all with the sensationalist point of view. In Locke empiricism and rationalism were woefully intermixed. The French philosophers had earlier developed the rationalist theories; in this aspect of his work Locke added nothing. It was the sensationalist section of his theory that had such a great influence upon later ethical and political thought.

Locke also held that all motives are a construction from the knowledge obtained through the senses. Pleasure is a group of positive motives; pain, a group of negative ones. Thus Locke shared the honor of influencing Jeremy Bentham's utilitarian philosophy with Condillac, Helvetius, Hobbes, and Hume.

The political theories of Locke are contained in his *Two Treatises of Government*. The first is of small importance. In it Locke attacked the royalist theories of Sir Robert Filmer, whose *Patriarcha* had been published in 1680. Filmer had argued for absolutism and divine right. He had derived the title of the Stuarts from the patriarchal authority of Adam. "Kingship is natural and God, the author of nature, must have ordained it." The whole confused argument between Locke and Filmer was of interest chiefly to contemporaries and it had no result in the realm of action. It is Locke's *Second Treatise* that stands as his great contribution to political thought and practice.

Locke differed from Hobbes in asserting that all men were born free and rational, and lived in a state of reason before the appearance of the state. But men were confused about the laws of reason; there were at first no laws about property, no "known and indifferent judges," no sufficient power to back their judgments and to give them execution. Men therefore agreed to contract with one another to surrender to the sovereign community their individual natural rights of enforcing the law of reason. "Whenever therefore any group of men are so united into one society as to quit everyone his Executive Power of the law of Nature and to resign it to the public, there and there only is a political or civil society." Men did not surrender any other natural rights, of which they possessed several, such as life, liberty, and property. From the point of view of strict logic Locke's political theory is a compromise with his theory of knowledge. In his *Treatise* knowledge about the origin of the state comes from alleged historical events, not from sensation.

When, "for the enjoyment of their properties in peace and safety," the people created a civil society by voluntary union and mutual agreement the legislature became the superior power in the constitution. But the powers of Locke's legislature are limited; they bear no resemblance to the absolute powers of Hobbes' sovereign. Indeed, the word "sovereign" never appears in the *Second Treatise*. The power of Parliament is limited by the natural rights men possessed antecedent to government and never surrendered. The basis of parliamentary strength is popular consent. "All peaceful beginnings of Government have been laid in the consent of the people." Although the authority of Parliament, or of any legislature, is superior, "their power in the utmost bounds of it is limited to the public good of the society. It is a power that hath no other end but preservation, and therefore can never destroy, enslave." Parliament must "govern by promulgated, established laws." What Locke called the federative power had authority, under the law, over the international relations of the state. All authorities were to move under delegated power from the people. "Despotical or arbitrary power . . . neither nature gives, nor compact can convey."

The crown has a real part in Locke's system of government. He does not think of the crown as possessing only a derivative power. The ministers of the government are the ministers of the king. At the same time, the king's power, as the executive branch of the government, is also limited. It is a fiduciary trust, placed there by the people. "For the king's authority being given him only by the law, he cannot empower anyone to act against the law or justify him by his commission in so doing." If kings or Parliaments violate their trust, the people have a right to resist. "The freedom and preservation of all men, that is the natural law that is the command of reason." The voluntary union of independent men should tolerate no interference with law and freedom. "He who threatens liberty, threatens all."

The old tradition of a mixed constitution had never been absent from European political thought. In Tudor England Sir Thomas Smith had explained that the customary constitution was valid because it was a going concern; the only authority needed was custom. Sir Edward Coke had held that the rights of the parts of government "went back forever." The common law provided for everything; it assigned "certain powers and certain rights to all Englishmen including the king." Locke's political philosophy was important for bringing into focus with the Revolution of 1688 many facts that were not acknowledged facts. By the revolutionary settlement, to be described in the following chapter, Parliament obtained legal superiority. On the one hand, however, the powers of the crown were not made negligible. On the other, only a small part of the people were represented in Parliament; there was no democracy. Locke's philosophy was a conservative defense of a conservative revolution.

The theories of Locke reached back through Richard Hooker to maintain the continuity with the Middle Ages. His philosophy, despite some revolutionary qualities, was less discontinuous with the past than is sometimes believed. Hobbes' complete egoism was far more revolutionary than anything in the philosophy of Locke. The idea of fundamental law never snapped completely in England and America, although some of the strands parted slowly. Into Locke's writings, of course, later readers read much that Locke had not intended. His discussion of property, for example, was quite casual. It was much more important to those who followed him in England and America. Montesquieu was to find in the separation of powers the secret of liberty. This theory is much more clearly stated by Harrington than by Locke. In fact, Locke only remarks it; he makes no principle from it. So far as Locke himself was concerned such a position could not have held such force as it did with Montesquieu; Locke had insisted that Parliament had a right to be consulted; with him there could be no effective separation of powers.

Despite the fact that Thomas Hobbes was himself a most irreligious man about one-half of the *Leviathan* was concerned with a religious dispute that had extended backwards through several centuries. In that sense the *Leviathan* was the last chapter of medieval political theory. The character of John Locke, on the other hand, was a distillation of many of the best elements of Puritanism. Yet religion was almost eliminated from Locke's political philosophy. This was not the result of, but it illustrates, the tremendous secularization evident in the late seventeenth century.

John Locke is often considered to be the father of psychology, the father of theoretical liberalism, and godfather at least of the political system of the United States. Had his mind been more profound it might have been less influential. Restive in his orthodoxy and timid in his heresies, Locke foreshadowed in his life, his work, and his attitudes the prudent intellectual morality of the English Whigs and Liberals and their American counterparts. He was the mighty prophet of the wisdom of compromise and polite moderation.

.   .   .   .

ART, MUSIC, ARCHITECTURE

The political and scientific revolutions were not parallelled by any abrupt changes in seventeenth century English art. The Stuart age produced several portrait painters and miniaturists but no landscape artists of consequence. Waves of foreign influence, particularly from the Low Countries, gave directional thrusts to all English artistic endeavor. Foremost among the artists who came from abroad to live in England early in the century was Anthony Van Dyck, whose influence extended through several decades. His easy ability in arrangement and his use of rich colors combined to strengthen the Flemish tradition. Van Dyck himself lived in England from 1603 to 1632 and it was in those years that the magic of his brush won acclaim and provoked imitation. The work of England's own William Dobson and Cornelius Johnson showed the happy influence of Van Dyck.

In the special technique of painting miniature portraits Nicholas Hilliard, "the prince of English limners," Samuel Cooper, and Thomas Flatman surpassed all others. Flatman, a versatile individual, published his *Poems and Songs* in 1674; the songs were particularly good. During the reign of Charles II the art of miniature painting reached a height unequalled elsewhere. Apart from this miniaturist work most English painting lacked the sureness of touch of the Continental masters. In England the seventeenth century produced few pictures of the highest rank; it was not a great period. The aristocracy and the Stuart kings collected large numbers of paintings. Foreign painters continued to come to England from the Continent. Amateurs of all kinds worked vigorously. All of this helped to lay the foundations for further advance. Then, too, capable men such as John Riley, Peter Lely, Robert Walker, and their fellows, under the patronage of the aristocracy, were slowly creating a distinctively native English art.

Although the currents of domestic art development flowed smoothly, the sharp European changes in music deeply affected England. Early in the Stuart period the compact body of English court and ecclesiastical musicians produced together a considerable amount of religious and secular music. For example, there were eighty-eight collections of music published between 1587 and 1630. The madrigal still remained popular and the masque began to offer new themes for composers, especially during the 1630's.

Through long centuries the national life had been characterized by a lively enthusiasm for songs, for dancing, and for musical instruments. Among the lower classes the small drum called the tabor and the pipe were used for the morris dances. Folk songs spread from county to county and generation to generation. The gentry preferred the harpsichord, the lute, and all the various keyed and stringed instruments. The polyphonic madrigal vocal music was gradually superseded by the vocal solo. Late in the century public concerts were held.

Organ building increased. And late in the century, too, a fresh and new musical outlook came from Europe to add to the English tradition of devotional choral singing and secular madrigal development.

One current of the new influence came from Italy. There, early in the century, opera was invented. This was secular, dramatic, melodic, human. In Cromwell's day it began to invade England. One opera, *The Cruelty of the Spaniards in Peru,* had considerable success in 1658. In the reign of Charles II the popularity of opera continued, although the full tide of its early appeal slowly diminished. Henry Purcell wrote his *Dido and Aeneas* in 1680. For many aspects of the European influence Charles II was particularly responsible because he had returned from exile in France with strong tastes for what he had heard there. New interest in Italian, French, and German achievement was everywhere manifest.

The music of England did not fall entirely under European influence. There persisted a distinctly national school of music until the reign of Queen Anne. Then it ceased. Purcell left no successor. In the eighteenth century the matured and massive harmonies of Continental music became the confidently accepted standard of solid Georgian England. Opera was fully naturalized and Georg Friedrich Handel came to live and reign in England while Johann Sebastian Bach presided in solemn dignity over the musical kingdoms of the Continent.

Meanwhile English architecture was undergoing significant changes. John Evelyn praised the Renaissance because it freed architecture from "a night of ignorance and superstition." He did not like the medieval "mountains of stone, vast and gigantic buildings indeed but not worthy the name of architecture." The early experimental Renaissance architecture, described in Chapter 15 as characteristic of the Tudor period, continued well into the seventeenth century, gradually displacing the enfeebled Gothic. The men who finally brought the foreign classical style completely into England were Inigo Jones, the disciple of Palladio, and Sir Christopher Wren. "Being naturally inclined in my younger years to study the arts of design," wrote Jones, "I passed into foreign parts to converse with the great masters thereof in Italy, where I applied myself to search out the Ruins of those ancient buildings, which, in despite of Time itself and the violence of Barbarians are yet remaining." The first fully classical building in England was the Banqueting Hall built in Whitehall by Inigo Jones for James I. This magnificent structure began a new age of English architecture. Before the Civil War interrupted ambitious building the Queen's House at Greenwich and St. Paul's Church, Covent Garden, had been completed.

In place of the vertical Gothic lines, the traceries, the pointed arches, and the buttresses, the revived classical or Palladian style was regular and symmetrical, with a tendency to earth-clinging horizontal lines. It had pillars with low pediments, square or rounded windows and doors. Meanwhile French and Dutch influence continued to aid the great English architects in developing new ideas. Despite these major changes the Gothic tradition was not entirely extinguished. For example, Inigo Jones himself built a Gothic chapel at Lincoln's Inn. Wren put Gothic steeples on some of his churches.

Domestic architecture and interior decorating also underwent considerable change. Tapestries, hangings, and wall paintings no longer remained the chief interior decorations. Carving of balustrades, cupboards, beds, cornices, and wall panels was the new fashion. Decorative arts of all kinds flourished. There developed elaborate plaster decorations in the ceilings, framed pictures, and marble sculptures. The rushes which had been used in Tudor times to cover floors gradually disappeared and carpets and matting took their place. The old trestle tables were yielding to solid tables with carved legs held together by stretchers. Stools replaced benches, but chairs were still reserved for honored guests. Buffets and cabinets, exquisitely carved, stood about the houses of the gentry. Later in the century walnut began to replace oak; foreign experts began to show Englishmen how to use walnut as a veneer with what results the modern world knows. Cane-seated chairs were developed and the solid, square, and heavily upholstered armchairs went out of style, not to return until the twentieth century. Slowly the solid heaviness of seventeenth century furniture yielded to the elegance of the curved lightness of Queen Anne's reign.

It was also in the seventeenth century that the central courtyards of the old manor-house type began to disappear. To the Stuart age the modern world owes the practice of having a "back yard." Seventeenth century Englishmen also became tremendously interested in gardens, especially flower gardens; the modern English insistence upon the importance of a garden plot, however small, is in part traceable to the enthusiasm of Stuart days.

Most Englishmen, of course, continued to live in houses built in earlier centuries; these were usually wooden or half-timbered. Few houses were made of stone unless there happened to be plenty easily available. In some poorer rural regions the cottages were made of mud and straw. When the Civil War ended there was much public and private building to be done. Country squires, the universities, innkeepers, noblemen, borough officials, and so on, all clamored for building supplies and builders. Then the fire of London came. There were thousands of commissions to execute. In such circumstances it was inevitable that purely practical considerations should determine the kind of buildings that were constructed.

After the London fire neither too much time nor too much money could be spent in rebuilding. So plain and cheap houses were built by the hundreds; many were set up in squares, and this practice helped to develop the modern habit of putting houses in city blocks. For reasons of safety only stone and brick were used in the rebuilding of London. Because of the sudden demand for bricks their quality became poorer. All over England brick and stone were used to a far greater extent. Few wooden or half-timbered houses were built after the late seventeenth century. Many houses of an earlier date were now covered up with brick or stone.

Sir Christopher Wren, England's greatest architect, was the son of a rector and nephew of a bishop. He attended Westminster School and Wadham College, Oxford, but had no formal training as an architect; his earlier interests were entirely in science and medicine. When he was about thirty years of age he became assistant to the surveyor-general of works and began to design buildings. Then he visited Paris. Later he wrote: "Bernini's Design of the Louvre I would have given my skin for, but the reserv'd Italian gave me but a few minutes View; it was five little designs in Paper for which he has received as many thousand Pistoles; I had only Time to copy it in my Fancy and Memory." Wren soon became professor of astronomy at Oxford and a founder of the Royal Society.

After the Great Fire of London Wren was appointed surveyor-general of the royal works. He was at once commissioned to rebuild St. Paul's Cathedral, and the result was his masterpiece, the shrine of England and one of the greatest cathedrals in the world. He also designed fifty other London churches including St. Martin, St. Mary-le-Bow, and St. Clement Danes. The Monument commemorating the Great Fire was the work of Wren. It stands on Fish Street Hill about a hundred feet from the spot where the Fire began. At Oxford, Wren designed the Tom Tower of Christ Church College, Queen's College Chapel, and the Sheldonian Theatre; at Cambridge, the Emmanuel and Pembroke Chapels and Trinity College Library. The list of his prodigious achievements is long. "Architecture aims at eternity," he wrote. "Beauty, firmness, and convenience are the principles." Perhaps no more need be said of Sir Christopher Wren than is stated in algebraic brevity over the door of the north transept of St. Paul's: "Si monumentum requiris, circumspice" ("If you seek [his] monument, look around.")

LITERATURE

In the seventeenth century the concepts of Renaissance humanism were being laid aside. Forces of disintegration, pervasive and powerful, were at work. For example, Protestantism paraded its numerous sects, each believing in predestination, or mysticism, or the individual priesthood of men, or something else. Naturalistic philosophy and the new science challenged the authority of the classics and the synthesis of the custodians of the great tradition of Christian humanism. The religious view of life was now not one, but many. The idea of the universe as a battlefield for forces of good and evil, heaven and hell, was giving way before the assaults of the new thinkers in a new age. The last mighty expression of the humanist view is seen in John Milton's *Paradise Lost* and *Samson Agonistes*. In all areas of literature remarkable changes in attitudes and values are clearly revealed. Here, too, is the revolt against authority characteristic of the seventeenth century. It appears alike in drama, prose, and poetry.

Elizabethan drama did not end with the great queen's death in 1603. It really stopped in 1642 when the Puritans closed the theatres. The tragedies of Shakespeare and the publication of his first folio both belong to the reign of James I. The best works of Ben Jonson appeared early in the Stuart age. His comedies of humor, a new type of drama, helped to displace the chronicle play. Jonson was a careful worker; his plays are characterized by meticulous craftsmanship and close observance of the classical rules of the drama. His tragedies, *Sejanus* and *Catiline,* were not popular. His fame rested upon his masques and the great comedies: *Volpone, The Alchemist, Silent Woman,* and *Bartholomew Fair.*

More popular and more facile than Jonson were Francis Beaumont and John Fletcher, whose famous partnership resulted in a long series of plays that provided many difficult problems of authorship for later students of the drama. It was they who were largely responsible for the development of new and rapidly moving tragi-comedies, such as *Philaster.* They also wrote several comedies about London life and manners. Many of the plays of Beaumont and Fletcher, as well as those of men like John Webster and Philip Massinger, were shot through with passages that revealed a public taste, especially in the court, of a somewhat depraved level. This decadence of the drama was accompanied by a rather strict censorship imposed by the court. Playwrights, trying to catch public interest by writing about contemporary events, often found that their plays were suddenly stopped by the privy council. So the stage gradually satisfied the public less and the court more. Puritans like William Prynne attacked the theatre vehemently. The dramatists replied by ridiculing the Puritans from the stage. In September, 1642, the Long Parliament closed the theatres. Throughout the following years, however, plays were still presented at the Cockpit, the Fortune, and the Red Bull. Parliament tried various means of suppression without success; neither raids, arrests, nor wrecking parties won the battle of the Puritans against the social habits of their less godly fellow Englishmen.

With the return of Charles II began the body of plays called Restoration drama. In tragedy only a few Restoration playwrights, such as Thomas Otway, Nicholas Rowe, and Thomas Southerne, had success, and that was limited. The work of the rest was too artificial, stiff, and literary; the cleavage between art and life was too wide. The Restoration years were rather a period of achievement in the flexible comedies of wit, repartee, intrigue, and manners. As in the plays of Molière, the characters were not sharply drawn; there were easily recognizable types: the fop, the fool, the charlatan, the wild debauchee, the gallant lover, the bemused and cheated husband. The Restoration dramatists, such as the witty and elegant William Congreve and the gross William Wycherley, often mocked at virtue, decency, and morality. Self-consciously naughty, they seemed to take a kind of adolescent pleasure in shocking people. Restoration society was not, so to speak, inhibited. Nevertheless, the widely held idea that the age of Charles II was darkly immoral and that London was a Sodom of obscenity and vice is false. As Jeremy Collier pointed out in his *Short View of the Immorality and Profaneness of the English Stage* (1698) the theatre was considerably debauched; but it was not England; nor was the court of Charles II.

At the turn of the century the public taste and mood were changing. Addison's *Cato*, which appeared in 1713, was popular and the fact has been cited to illustrate the veering of public opinion. Such a change it does indicate, although the popular reception and praise resulted in part from the fact that the Whig Addison got the Tory Alexander Pope to write the prologue; the Whig Dr. Garth to write the epilogue. Addison dined with the Tory Bolingbroke and wrote nothing offensive to either party in *Cato*. No expense was spared in presenting the play. Steele undertook to pack the house with spectators; he did. *Cato* was widely hailed as a masterpiece, which it was not. Meanwhile, as the eighteenth century advanced, the theatre was moving further away from court influence. It was becoming a national institution.

In the first part of the seventeenth century there were many prose literary craftsmen, among them such giants as Francis Bacon and Abraham Cowley. The plastic, "daily changing tongue" of the Elizabethans was successfully taken in hand by the Jacobean age and the result was very important in the history of the English language. In the later years of Elizabeth's reign the influence of John Lyly's *Euphues* and Sir Philip Sidney's unfinished *Arcadia* had often resulted in a strained literary style, cumbersome and artificially balanced. Witness a sentence from the *Arcadia:* "And the boy fierce though beautiful; and beautiful, though dying, not able to keep his falling feet, fell down to the earth, which he bit for anger, repining at his fortune, and as long as he could, resisting death, which might seem unwilling too; so long he was in taking away his young struggling soul."

At the same time, amidst great social changes, the middle classes were becoming eager for more books to read. Bored by the heavy, rhetorical products of literary circles, they welcomed books that were simply written. They liked the new translation of *Don Quixote* and the *Decameron* and, above all, the vivid, dignified power of the King James version of the Bible. In the new Bible there were few Latin forms; over ninety per cent of the words used were of English derivation. The overwhelming influence of the Authorized Version (suggested in Chapter 16) is evident in most writing of the early Stuart age.

Meanwhile the printing presses were rolling forth thousands of books, serious and light. Thomas Fuller's *Church History of Britain* and Izaak Walton's *Lives* shared public interest with new translations, with fiction, with reprints of Elizabethan works, with diaries, memoirs, and essays. Writers sought to appeal to the multitude. The forerunners of the modern newspaper appeared. England's first daily newspaper was to be printed in London in 1702. Propaganda pamphlets, tracts, and ballads by the thousands rained praise and abuse over England. All these products were written in plain and simple English because they were designed to be read by people who would not have lingered over ornamental and tortuous prose. At the same time the eloquent and polished pulpit oratory of John Donne and his fellow divines was giving way to the homely and passionate exhortations of the great Puritan preachers. These men spiced their paragraphs with no Greek quotations; they tried to explain God's word in simple terms to ordinary men. In the next century they were to be followed by John Wesley and George Whitefield, greatest of evangelists.

All these tendencies towards simplicity, this revolt against ornateness, continued strongly in the later Stuart years. The new men of science had to explain and describe with clarity and precision. England was becoming more and more a business and trading nation; men of business had little patience with writers who wasted words or could not plainly state their business. Meanwhile, too, the growth of clubs and coffeehouses created new social conditions. Literary men, as well as merchants and politicians, gathered in such places to discuss and debate in a sociable environment. The practice of reviewing books in printed journals began. Literary periodicals published critical essays. Early in the eighteenth century Richard Steele and Joseph Addison marked perhaps the height of the new prose style by writing their unembellished, lucid prose in the *Tatler* and the *Spectator*. Neither had great book-learning but each had considerable acquaintance with men and the world. They wrote naturally, with great charm and humor. The reader was immediately put at his ease. For example, one of Addison's essays about Sir Roger de Coverley begins in this simple, direct, and flexible way: "I am always very well pleased with a country Sunday, and think, if keeping holy the seventh day were only a human institution, it would be the best method that could have been thought of for the polishing and civilizing of mankind. It is certain that country people would soon degenerate into a kind of savages and barbarians, were there not such frequent returns of a stated time in which the whole villages met together in their best faces, and in their cleanest habits."

Thus the usage of language had undergone tremendous changes by the early eighteenth century. Daniel Defoe, for example, probably knew nothing about the classics. Nevertheless, he was one of England's greatest writers. Like William Cobbett in the nineteenth century, Defoe had something to say and he said it. He said it in words everybody understood. "I was born in the year 1632 in the city of York of a good family." So begins *Robinson Crusoe*. Nothing could be plainer than that beginning. The great effects of Defoe's descriptive prose are achieved simply. For instance, he conveys a sense of death and desolation when he writes: "I never saw them afterwards, or any sign of them except three of their hats, one cap, and two shoes that were not fellows." The enduring magic of *Robinson Crusoe* still stands as a monument to a skilled craftsman, even though the author himself was a scoundrel.

Prose had accommodated itself to the public demand that pens be sure and sharp and bring order from chaos. Between the prose of Defoe and Swift on the one hand and Bacon and Cowley on the other there is a wide gulf bridged by the great transition of the seventeenth century.

In non-dramatic poetry the Petrarchan and Spenserian sonnet and pastoral tradition began to give way to the lyric during the Jacobean and Caroline period. There also developed early in the seventeenth century a much greater attention to formal rules of poetic structure than was evident in the Elizabethan age. Patriotic poetry, often written in long verses and weighted with erudition and classical references, found its best expression in Michael Drayton and Samuel Daniel. Throughout the century large numbers of poets also produced satires and epigrams, a form of poetry in which the age took considerable delight. For example, about fifty collections of epigrams were published between 1600 and 1620.

Ben Jonson and "the tribe of Ben," which included Thomas Carew, Sir John Suckling, and Robert Herrick, were prolific writers of epigrams, epistles, odes, and songs. Carew's graceful, racy, and amorous poetry was especially popular about the court; he was the unofficial poet laureate. Some of his lines, though frequently marred by extreme conceits, are among the best of the century. "Ask me no more where Jove bestows, When June is past the fading rose." "I saw fair Chloris walk alone When feathered rain came softly down." The Cambridge Sir John Suckling, versatile prince of the Cavalier poets, wrote several pieces in which the court delighted. His songs are his best work, especially "Why so pale and wan, fair lover?" His most amusing poem is "A Ballad upon a Wedding." The Devonshire vicar Robert Herrick wrote some of the finest short poems in the English language. It is perhaps a sad comment upon our present age that Herrick's poetry is now so little read. Those who admire Herrick will recall the charming beauty of "A Child's Grace"; the lilt of "Cherry Ripe," "Upon Julia's Clothes," "To the Virgins to Make Much of Time"; and the impressive humility of "A Thanksgiving to God for His House."

Revealing a different aspect of a many-splendored age were the sacred poets, led by George Herbert, Richard Crashaw, and Henry Vaughan. Herbert, a Cambridge man and friend of John Donne and Izaak Walton, forsook the court for the Anglican Church. The popularity of his poems reflects the intensely spiritual attitude of his age. Superior to Herbert in his brilliance and technique was Crashaw; his poetry is more rhapsodical, ecstatic, intense. An excellent illustration of these qualities is "A Hymn to the Name and Honour of the Admirable Saint Teresa." The Welsh Henry Vaughan filled his poems with a characteristic romantic and mystical whiteness that caused him to be called "the poet of dawn and early morning." Vaughan, more than Herbert or Crashaw, was a spiritual forerunner of the nineteenth century romantic poets. Some readers will remember the sense of magic casements in "My soul, there is a country Far beyond the stars" and "I saw Eternity the other night." Upon all the sacred and metaphysical poets, of course, the influence of the great John Donne, famous Dean of St. Paul's, was pervasive and strong.

Unfortunately, it is not possible here to discuss the work of such men as Thomas Campion, Abraham Cowley, William Drummond of Hawthornden, Richard Lovelace, Edmund Waller, and Sir Henry Wotton. The songs of Ben Jonson, the satires of Samuel Butler and John Dryden, the odes and lyrics of Andrew Marvell, must likewise be passed with a side glance, a reference, and the hope that readers of this book will travel in realms of gold beyond the regions carefully mapped by professors who prescribe readings. The cross currents of seventeenth century literature are many. On the one hand there is the supreme achievement of Milton's *Paradise Lost* and the stirring lines of Dryden's *Alexander's Feast*. On the other, one may find the stumbling epigram of an amateur whose name has long since perished. Between these two poles in Stuart literature there stand forth the everlasting themes of love, death, the vanity of human wishes, the last judgment, honor, courage, and the eternal follies and hopes of man.

Chapter 21

HEIRS OF THE REVOLUTION

THE REVOLUTION SETTLEMENT

WHEN James II fled, the Convention Parliament offered the vacant throne to William and Mary. It was agreed that the crown should pass to the new rulers under certain conditions clearly stated and understood. There must be no doubt, no ambiguity. Hence Parliament prepared the Declaration of Rights. This document, in the tradition of Magna Carta and the Petition of Right, specifically listed most of the arbitrary acts of which the Stuarts had been guilty and declared them all contrary to the laws of England. "The pretended power of suspending of laws or the execution of laws by regal authority without consent of parliament is illegal . . . the commission for erecting the late court of commissioners for ecclesiastical causes and all other commissions and courts of like nature are illegal and pernicious . . . levying money for or to the use of the crown by pretence of prerogative without grant of parliament, for larger time or in other manner than the same is or shall be granted, is illegal . . . it is the right of the subjects to petition the king . . . for redress of all grievances and for the mending, strengthening, and preserving of the laws, parliaments ought to be held frequently."

This long and exact Declaration of Rights also provided for freedom of speech in Parliament; for fair jury trial; for the ending of excessive bail and unduly heavy fines; and so on. No standing army was to be maintained in time of peace without the consent of Parliament. The crown was to be settled on William and Mary and their heirs; if there were no heirs, the succession rights were to pass to Anne, Mary's sister, and then to her children. The Declaration of Rights was accepted by William and Mary on February 13, 1689. They were then proclaimed king and queen. On December 16, the Declaration was incorporated into a statute entitled the Bill of Rights. This famous Bill of Rights added a number of clauses to the original Declaration, notably one providing that no Roman Catholic, or anyone married to a Roman

Catholic, should ever succeed to the throne of England. "It hath been found by experience that it is inconsistent with the safety and welfare of this Protestant kingdom to be governed by a popish prince."

By these events the power of Parliament and the liberty of the subject were at last secured. There would never be absolute monarchy again. The crown rested upon a parliamentary title. Although several further steps in the revolutionary settlement were necessary the essential constitutional principles of limited monarchy, often enunciated earlier, were finally established by the Bill of Rights. The "glorious revolution" marked the end of the long struggle that had begun with James I. The rule of the nobles, the country gentry, and the merchant classes who sat in Parliament was now assured.

This bloodless revolution brought in its train further important legislative enactments bulwarking the Bill of Rights. William III was a Calvinist and therefore shared the objections of the Whigs to the persecution of Dissenters. The Toleration Act of 1689 allowed all but Catholics and Unitarians to worship in their own way. Nonconformists were still legally excluded from participation in municipal or national government. Soon, however, Dissenters began to hold governmental positions when they practiced "occasional conformity," which meant taking the Anglican sacrament once a year. Annual indemnity acts also helped to nullify the effects of the Corporation and Test Acts. The latter were not formally repealed until 1828. In 1689, however, the Toleration Act was viewed as a great charter of religious liberty.

The Bill of Rights had forbidden the maintenance of a standing army in time of peace without the consent of Parliament. A supplementary statute called the Mutiny Act permitted the raising of an army and use of martial law for a period of six months. Since 1689 Mutiny Acts, now called Army Acts, have been regularly passed, usually at yearly intervals, to enable the crown to keep the British Army in being with the consent of Parliament. A new Triennial Act of 1694 provided that elections must be held at least every three years. The Treasons Act of 1696 protected the accused in treason trials by requiring that he must be permitted to see a true copy of the whole indictment at least five days before his trial; that he should have legal counsel, learned in the law; and that nobody should be indicted or tried for treason but by the testimony of "two lawful witnesses." Censorship acts and licensing rules giving the crown authority over the press were allowed to lapse.

Finally, the Act of Settlement of 1701 was passed to guard against the restoration of the old Stuart line. Queen Mary died in 1694 and hence the heir to the throne was Mary's sister Anne. But the Duke of Gloucester, the last of Anne's thirteen children, had died in 1700. With Anne's death, therefore, the line of Protestant Stuarts would end. The Catholic son of James II and Mary of Modena and the

Catholic Savoy descendants of Charles II's sister Henrietta had hereditary claims stronger than any Protestant rival despite the fact that the Bill of Rights had specifically excluded all Catholics from the throne. The Act of Settlement declared that Anne should succeed William and that if she died without direct heirs the throne should pass to the Electress Sophia of Hanover and her issue. Sophia was the daughter of James I's daughter Elizabeth and Frederick the Elector Palatine, whose lands had been overrun by Spain early in the century. The succession of the Hanoverians thus seemed assured.

The Act of Settlement also confirmed the action of Parliament in the Danby case by providing that the king's pardon would not be a bar to any further impeachment. By another important provision judges were to hold office for life instead of at the king's pleasure. They could be removed or their salary altered only on the address of both houses of Parliament as a result of charges of misconduct proved in Parliament. The Act of Settlement further provided that the sovereign must be a member of the Church of England; that if he were a foreigner England was not obligated to defend his foreign possessions; that he might not leave England without the permission of Parliament. A new rule, later of great importance, declared that "all matters and things relating to the well governing of this kingdom, which are properly cognizable in the privy council by the laws and customs of this realm, shall be transacted there, and all resolutions taken thereupon shall be signed by such of the privy council as shall advise and consent to the same." Finally, it was provided that "no person who has an office or place under the king or receives a pension from the Crown shall be capable of serving as a member of the House of Commons."

With the passage of the Act of Settlement the mixed and clever legislative arrangements following the conservative revolution were complete. England stood on the threshold of the eighteenth century: the age of reason, toleration, moderation, common sense, the growth of capital and industry, and the dignified rule of the aristocracy. A brilliant period of new intellectual achievement was dawning as the great figures of Samuel Johnson, Alexander Pope, David Hume, Edward Gibbon, Adam Smith, and their contemporaries approached the English stage. The settlement of the internal struggle had paved the way for a balanced social order and economic prosperity. The position of the squirearchy was to be marked by the steady intake of land by enclosures and purchase; men with a sense of property can seldom be fanatical. The Anglican Church sank into the deep slumber of a decided opinion. In 1684 Lord Halifax had written in *The Character of A Trimmer* that "Our Church is a Trimmer between the phrenzy of Platonic visions and the lethargick Ignorance of Popish Dreams." In the centuries that followed the Anglican dislike for exclusive and explicit doctrinal statement was to contrast sharply with the Nonconformist passion for exactness of definition. There has always been a lucid quality in Puritan and Dissenting thought, perhaps fostered by adherence to each sentence of the Bible.

Abroad, new English thrusts of energy were soon to push forward colonial expansion from India to Quebec; the sinews of British commerce were to grow stronger, tougher, more resilient. Freed from the shackling effects of domestic conflict, England now moved to lead Europe against the aggressiveness of Louis XIV. Under William III, the deadly and persistent enemy of Louis, the English subservience to France was ended. The results were to be over twenty years of warfare, the eclipse of France, and the emergence of Britain as the first among European powers.

WAR OF THE LEAGUE OF AUGSBURG

After the flight of James II the tide of Bourbon gold no longer flowed across the English Channel to bribe the Stuarts. No coins clinked into the palms of Englishmen to persuade them to remain friendly to France. England had settled her internal conflicts. Now her new king was the stolid, stubborn, dwarfish, and asthmatic William III, captain-general and stadholder of the Dutch nation, long the chief adversary of Louis XIV. The aggressions of Louis and the threat to England, as to Protestant Europe generally, made it easy for the energetic William to range his new kingdom on the side of the enemies of France. This William had long hoped to do.

In the War of Devolution and the Dutch War Louis had pushed French frontiers towards the Rhine. By the procedure of his "chambers of reunion" courts, Louis then began ruthlessly and methodically to absorb further pieces of territory into France under pretense of invoking ancient feudal usage and obligations. Behind the juridical claims of Louis stood the power of the French military forces. All the neighbors of France were alarmed. Louis seized the great imperial free town of Strassburg, the larger part of the Saar valley, the remainder of Alsace (which brought him to the Rhine in 1681), twenty cities of the Holy Roman Empire, and areas of land owing allegiance to Sweden, Spain, and several German princes.

In 1686 the Emperor Leopold formed the League of Augsburg which included Spain, Sweden, the Netherlands, and various German states. Savoy and the Pope entered later. The powers that adhered to the League undertook to resist further French encroachments. In 1688, heedless of warnings, Louis XIV sent a large army into the Rhenish Palatinate. The resulting struggle was the War of the League of Augsburg, a conflict in which the battling nations carried their hostilities to colonial and commercial fronts all over the world.

In his first two wars Louis could rely upon England's neutrality. In this, the third war, the implacable William III brought the might of England to bear against his archenemy. Catholics and Protestants stood together to stop the belligerent, trampling power of France. So England entered the longest, bloodiest, and most costly foreign war she had fought since Elizabeth's day. This was in May, 1689. In the sixteenth century England had joined the nations arrayed against a Catholic Spain anxious to upset the balance of power in Europe. Now, as throughout the eighteenth century, the enemy to that balance of power was France; later it was to be Germany.

England's Whig Parliament did not declare war merely because William III wanted it. Englishmen generally were annoyed at the French persecution of Huguenots following the revocation of the Edict of Nantes in 1685. There was also the long tide of ill-will against France. English hostility and anger were increased when Louis XIV sheltered James II and helped him to mount his ill-fated Irish offensive ending in the battle of the Boyne. And there was an English awareness, which Louis XIV never appreciated, of the commercial and colonial side of the conflict. England began with high hopes of what might be done by naval pressure, by the throttling of French commerce, by hacking at the French Empire. The War of the League of Augsburg was in fact the first of the modern wars in which England fought simultaneously as a member of a European land coalition; as a great sea power fighting a naval war and maintaining an economic blockade; and as a colonial nation adding to her economic and imperial holdings abroad at the expense of hostile rivals.

The theories of mercantilism made it inevitable that all nations should attempt to advance what they believed were their economic interests by increasing their national wealth faster than it increased in other countries. The mercantilists did not absolutely identify wealth with gold and silver, but they attributed to all precious metals very important functions such as that of capital, a state treasure, a source of private wealth, and a circulating medium. Therefore a nation should seek to control as large an amount of bullion as possible. The mercantilists, in brief, often tended to confuse capital and specie. The only way the national supply of gold and silver could be increased was by keeping an excess of exports over imports. In his *England's Treasure by Forraign Trade* Thomas Mun asserted an essential principle of mercantilist theory: England's exports to foreign lands must exceed her imports. "We must ever sell more to them yearly then we consume of theirs in value." His words were later echoed by the *British Merchant:* "If we buy more goods than we sell, we must pay the balance in money and that is so much loss to the nation."

The general fall of money value and the increased strength of nation states had aided in the growth of a general protectionist sentiment in Europe. Every nation tried to be self-sufficient, providing for its own needs from its own resources. After the Navigation Act of 1651

England maintained intricate and elaborate royal, parliamentary, and board of trade regulations about trade and commerce. A "favorable" balance of trade must be maintained by tariff controls of all kinds; the home manufacturers and the home market must be protected. For example, exports from the colonies were controlled; certain "enumerated commodities" were to be shipped only to England. It was always easier to regulate trade than to define constitutional relations between the motherland and the colonies. Commercial treaties were made to encourage trade with countries that exported goods not produced in England or the colonies, such as the timber, tar, pitch, and hemp from the Baltic countries, so important to the English ships.

Meanwhile, as the business economy rose steadily in England the desire to be independent of other nations stimulated the growth of colonies; the Empire was considered as a unit in which the colonies would produce stocks of raw materials. Britain would manufacture them. Manufacturing in the colonies was discouraged by statutes and regulations. "You have sought to raise up a nation of customers in the colonies," remarked Adam Smith later. "Britain would, if she could," said Benjamin Franklin, "manufacture and trade for all the world, England for all Britain, London for all England, and every Londoner for all London."

After the Revolution of 1688 there were about 350,000 British colonists in the mainland colonies of America and the West Indies, all trading with one another and with the mother country. From the East, the East India Company was importing spices, calico, raw silk and indigo into England. It was piling up profits and thrusting English goods, such as textiles, lead and tin, farther into India from its three great stations at Bombay, Calcutta, and Madras.

In both America and India, Britain found a formidable colonial and commercial rival in France. In America Louis XIV controlled all of "New France" as a royal province. Here was a colony tightly united under a centralized government. The British colonists to the south were divided by bitter rivalries. Colbert, great minister of Louis XIV, increased the number of colonists in New France about 300 per cent in twenty years. As French traders, explorers, and missionaries ranged west and southwest from the St. Lawrence valley many English settlers saw a danger that the French might confine the English to the Atlantic seaboard. Colbert told Talon, the Intendant at Quebec, that he wished to see friendship prevail between the French and "the English of Boston." But such intercolonial friendship was impossible in the face of mounting colonial and commercial rivalry between France and England. In India the vigorous French East India Company had trading posts at Chandarnagar, near Britain's Calcutta, and at Pondicherry, near Britain's Madras. In both America and India, then, the stage for a world struggle for empire was set.

The English trading and commercial class, firmly ensconced in the Whig Parliament, were alarmed at the obviously aggressive challenges of France in building up her colonial power, in pushing French trade activities, in strengthening the French navy. Protective measures of the French mercantilist Colbert had hit the English as well as the Dutch. French commercial progress was a particular dread of the merchant classes in the English Parliament. Earlier English feeling against the Dutch commercial power now began to shift towards France. From 1678 to 1685 all imports from France were prohibited; between 1685 and 1704 a heavy tariff was kept on French goods. An act of 1704 forbade the importation of "commodities of the growth and production of France." The act asserted that it had been found "by long experience that the bringing in of French wines, vinegar, brandy, linen, silks, and other commodities of the growth, produce or manufacture of France or dominions of the French king hath much exhausted the treasure of this nation, lessened the value of the native commodities and manufacturers thereof, and greatly impoverished the English artificers and handicrafts and caused great detriment to the kingdom in general."

British economic jealousy of France and the pervasive power of the mercantilist theory made the attitude of vested commercial interests of particular importance in 1689. Thus England went into the war of the League of Augsburg for many reasons, including not only the preservation of Protestant Europe and the balance of power, but also the protection of English commercial, maritime, and colonial interests. This remark is true of all the wars of the eighteenth century in which Great Britain participated.

In the war of the League of Augsburg, England, the Netherlands, the Holy Roman Empire, Spain, Sweden, Bavaria, Saxony, the Palatinate, Savoy, and the Pope waged war against Louis XIV of France until 1697. In America the French and English colonists engaged in "King William's War." So far as England was concerned the early part of the conflict in Europe involved only the campaign in Ireland against James II. The French navy never interfered seriously with the movement of English troop transports ferrying men to Ireland.

Off Beachy Head on June 30, 1690, the ships of Louis XIV defeated the English and Dutch in a minor naval battle as a result of which the English commander, the earl of Torrington, was court-martialled. In 1692 the French gathered an army on the Cotentin Peninsula and prepared to invade England. When the forty-four ships of the French fleet set out to clear the English Channel they encountered nearly a hundred Dutch and English ships. In the six-day battle of La Hogue, fought close along the coast of Barfleur, the French lost fifteen ships, a blow from which they did not soon recover. The allies held command of the sea, except for the limited effect of the raids of French corsairs on English merchantmen.

The next immediate problem was to secure control of the Low

Countries; it has always been a cardinal principle of English policy never to let Holland and Belgium fall under the hegemony of a major European power. In the Spanish Netherlands Louis XIV was winning victories. Until our own day these fields and mud of Flanders have been a frequent battleground; strategy and tactics are still in part determined by the river and fortress systems of that unhappy region. In 1691 William crossed the Channel with his British redcoats. These soldiers were well trained. Some of them had no doubt been drilled from the first English drill book for infantry, issued in 1686. The English army administration was as corrupt and inefficient as the French, particularly in areas of ordnance, transport, pay, and supply. In 1692 the French defeated William in a pitched battle where the English lost two generals, seven colonels, and two peers. In 1693 and 1694 the allies again suffered a series of reverses.

By 1695 the tide turned at last against Louis XIV. After three months of siege the massive fortress of Namur fell to William. In his sixteen campaigns William had not achieved so great a victory. A British fleet moved into the Mediterranean to harass French trade with the Levant and to aid Spain. It blocked a French fleet in Toulon and deprived the French armies in Spain of naval support. Meanwhile all the combatants were feeling the military and economic drain of the protracted war. In 1696 Savoy made a separate peace with France and thus released a French army for operations in Flanders. England bombarded Calais and thwarted a French and Jacobite plan to invade England. Louis XIV was influenced to make peace by the military stalemates, by his unhappy financial position at home, and by the serious illness of Charles II, last of the Hapsburg kings of Spain. Louis wanted an end of the war with Spain before the question of the succession to the Spanish throne arose.

In October, 1697, peace was signed at Ryswick, near The Hague. France restored all territories taken over after 1678, except Strassburg. Louis XIV recognized William III as king of England. All colonial conquests were to be restored to the original holders. Under this provision Port Royal, the French fortress in Acadia (Nova Scotia) that had been captured with the aid of New England colonists, was now returned to France; Fort Albany went back to England's Hudson's Bay Company. Finally, Louis agreed to allow the Dutch to maintain garrisons in the barrier fortresses of the Spanish Netherlands.

Of this peace of Ryswick the Englishmen Ralph Palmer wrote in 1697 to Sir John Verney: "Long may it last, for peace and quietness is best." It was to last for only four years.

THE BANK OF ENGLAND - National Bank

The war between England and France marked the beginning of a new era of public finance. Earlier in the seventeenth century the increased business and trading activities of Englishmen had clearly revealed the need for <u>a national bank</u>. Demands for credit and deposit facilities could not be adequately met by London goldsmiths as trade steadily increased in volume and value. This pressure for the creation of a national bank was made greater by the financial results of the war.

With the coming of large-scale warfare the national expenditure leaped to new levels. The conflict with France was to cost England nearly £40,000,000. New taxes were devised, including heavy taxes on foreign trade. The land tax bore heavily upon the squires. Nevertheless, such expedients could not raise anything like the sums needed for financing the war. Government credit was weak. Interest rates sometimes ran up to fourteen percent. It seemed to the public that it was safer to invest money in business and joint stock companies rather than with governments whose members were often neither able nor honest.

In 1694 the government needed money badly. A new Whig finance company succeeded in raising £1,200,000 from subscribers. Then it lent the money to the government at an interest rate of eight per cent. This Whig finance company was thereupon incorporated as the first English joint stock bank and authorized by charter to issue notes, make loans, receive deposits, discount bills, and so on. The new institution, the Bank of England, owed much to the experience of the goldsmiths and merchants; all its directors and other officers had different duties of their own in mercantile houses or in other banks. Opposition rose from many sources: from the existing rival banks; from landlords fearful that possible merchant control of the Bank of England would result in increased mortgage interest rates; from Tories who said the moneyed interests would now tend to support the Whigs.

The early years of the Bank of England were difficult and dangerous. Some serious mistakes were made, such as the issuing of notes in excess of deposits (1696), the risky business of lending money on stock (1720), and the failure to formulate a reserve policy until the late eighteenth century. Nevertheless, the Bank of England rode out all gales. The credit of the government advanced; the money market grew steadier. Public confidence facilitated the growth of capital for expanding business. More and more financial interests came to feel that the Bank was a national institution. A national institution it has since remained.

EUROPE'S DILEMMA: THE SPANISH SUCCESSION

Meanwhile the Spanish puzzle was still unsolved. The drums of Europe's armies were soon to roll again. Charles II of Spain was childless. Who should be the next king of Spain? What was to happen to the Spanish Empire? Charles II had two sisters. The elder was married to Louis XIV of France. She had renounced her rights to the Spanish throne at the time of her marriage. Was her renunciation legally binding upon her descendants? The younger sister of Charles had married the Emperor Leopold. If either the French Bourbons or the Austrian Hapsburgs succeeded to the Spanish throne, the whole European balance of power would be badly upset. The union of France and Spain, or of Austria and Spain, would be particularly dangerous to the interests of England.

In 1698 a partition treaty was arranged providing for the eventual division of the Spanish Empire. When a Bavarian prince who was to have received a share of the inheritance died of smallpox in 1699 this treaty was invalidated. Then the Austrian Emperor Leopold obstinately refused to sign a second partition treaty, claiming the whole Spanish inheritance for his son. Nor would Spain agree to it, insisting that the Spanish Empire should not be divided.

In his last days, the wretched cretin Charles II shuddered in his restless bed guarded by three friars against devils and witches. He was easily persuaded that the Spanish Empire should remain undivided, easily induced to leave all his dominions to Philip, a grandson of Louis XIV. When Charles died, the king of France accepted the will, occupied Spain, and put Philip on the throne at Madrid. The Emperor Leopold, head of the Austrian Hapsburgs, angrily declared the will of Charles II invalid. His armies moved into Italy and seized Spain's Milan. Leopold also sent missions to obtain the support of England against France. It was true that Philip had renounced his right to succeed to the French throne; but all Europe knew that no Bourbon was precise in promise-keeping.

William III was prepared to go to war with his ancient enemy France if the Parliament and the public approved. The Tories, then in power, were busy trying to impeach Whig politicians. Representing interests mainly agricultural, most Tories were not gravely concerned about the accession of Philip to the Spanish throne. They also recalled that the war concluded in 1697 had meant high taxes on land. On the other hand, those who raised sheep were interested in the Mediterranean cloth market and feared that French power in Spain might bring high protective tariffs against English cloth. These Tories were quite prepared to fight for the cloth market.

The Whigs and all the commercial classes were alarmed at the French menace. If France indirectly controlled Spain through Philip, then Spanish and French commercial and colonial policies would become merged into one. French and Spanish maritime power would be united. The Spanish Netherlands, great channel of commerce with central Europe, would be blocked to English trade. Financial circles interested in England's commercial, trading, and colonial activities abroad also looked to the possibility of sharing in trade and investment developments in Spanish America. Were they to be cut off from the wealth of Spanish colonial trade as France moved towards that banquet table? The answer was swift and clear. The Whigs stood for war.

Louis XIV seized the seven barrier fortresses in the Spanish Netherlands. He publicly declared that his grandson Philip had a right to the throne of France if he should ever fall heir to it. Rumors came to England that French companies were being formed to trade with Spanish colonies. On September 7, 1701, the representatives of England, the Netherlands, and the Emperor Leopold formed a Grand Alliance. They agreed that the French and Spanish thrones must never be united; that the French were to have no share in the Spanish colonial trade. The question as to the disposal of the Spanish colonies and the Spanish Netherlands was left in abeyance. Nor did England and Holland acknowledge that Leopold had clear claims to the Spanish throne.

Before Louis XIV could have known the details of the Grand Alliance he angered England further by two hostile steps. He prohibited all imports from England, Scotland, and Ireland. It seemed logical that Philip would take similar action in Spain. Secondly, when James II died in France, Louis caused James II's son to be proclaimed James III, king of England, thus breaking his treaty promise of 1697. The British ambassador was recalled from Paris and in December a new Parliament voted the taxes necessary for the inevitable conflict. The war officially began in the spring of 1702.

Meanwhile, in March, 1702, William III died as a result of a hunting accident. Mary had died in 1694. William was succeeded by Queen Anne, Protestant daughter of James II and Anne Hyde. Pious, prejudiced, dropsical, and of limited intellect, the last of the Stuarts was to preside over the destinies of England for twelve years.

THE WAR OF THE SPANISH SUCCESSION

Thus England, "moved by her two main nerves, iron and gold," went into a conflict that was to last over eleven years. In the early part of Anne's reign there were good harvests and cheap food, always an important bulwark in time of war. As allies England had the Emperor Leopold, no longer harassed by the Turks, the Netherlands, Prussia, and several other German states. Against them stood France, Spain, Bavaria, Portugal and, for a time, Savoy. England was also fortunate in having as commander-in-chief of her forces John Churchill, who became Duke of Marlborough in 1702. Marlborough, son of Sir Winston Churchill, a country squire, had risen slowly. For thirty years he had been accumulating military and political experience. Despite the sordid alloys that were mingled in his character, he was a superb military strategist and tactician. He never fought a battle that he did not win or besieged a place that he did not take. He was also an excellent diplomat, for the purposes of the war "the executive arm of the state."

The War of the Spanish Succession was fought on three fronts: in Europe, in America, and on the sea. When England came into the conflict the Austrians, under Prince Eugene of Savoy, were already battling the French in southern Italy. Everywhere, except on the sea, Louis XIV had an early advantage in military power. Prince Eugene was in a precarious position, especially when the Hungarians revolted against the emperor and precipitated civil war in Austria. The operations of Marlborough in the first two years were confined to limited campaigns along the Meuse and the Rhine. When the Emperor Leopold appealed for aid early in 1704 Marlborough decided that the French must not be permitted to overrun Austria. He lunged swiftly over four hundred miles towards the Danube to meet the combined forces of France and Bavaria. In the heart of the Empire he was able to link up with the Imperial army under Prince Eugene. The allied forces now numbered about 52,000; the French and Bavarian about 54,000.

At Blenheim the French general anchored his right flank on the Danube, his left on a forest. Before him lay a stretch of marsh. In his good textbook position he thought himself secure; Marlborough would never try to cross the marsh. But Marlborough built bridges, leaped over the marsh, and on the afternoon of August 13, 1704, the battle of Blenheim began. Cavalry smashed the French center. The French and Bavarian attacks were blunted. Thousands were killed or drowned in the Danube. The French commander, all his guns and baggage, and over 10,000 demoralized soldiers were captured. More than half the French and Bavarian troops were casualties. Germany was soon freed of the French. Vienna was saved. Marlborough, at a cost of about 700 men, had won England's most famous land victory between Agincourt and Waterloo. The military star of France was sinking. Europe was no longer the pedestal of the Grand Monarch.

In 1703 Portugal abandoned France, joined the allies, and concluded the Methuen Treaty with England. This treaty, named after the English ambassador John Methuen who was the son of England's greatest cloth merchant, was not abrogated until 1836. It provided for the importation of Portuguese wines into England at a third less duty than those paid by France; this was a reason why Englishmen drank so much port in the eighteenth century. English woollens, core of England's export trade, were to be admitted into Portugal at a low duty. Included in the agreement was a defensive and offensive alliance between Portugal and England. This famous Methuen Treaty strengthened and extended a long tradition of Anglo-Portuguese friendship.

In 1704 Sir George Rooke captured Gibraltar from Spain. Here was one of the cardinal events of the war, an important step in the building of Britain's lifeline to the East. In 1708 the future naval station of Minorca was taken from Spain's Balearic Islands and added to England's Mediterranean holdings. Meanwhile Marlborough had returned to the Spanish Netherlands, the strategic hub of Europe. Lack of support from the Imperial forces caused the campaigns of 1705 to bog down badly. Anglo-Dutch tension rose as a result of English charges that the Dutch were doing less than their share in the war, Dutch charges that the English were deliberately attempting to gain commercial advantages out of the war at Dutch expense. In 1705 the Emperor Leopold died and his successor had to cope with a number of internal revolts. Such events delayed effective action.

In 1706 the allied prospects brightened. Marlborough met the French at Ramillies, near Namur, on May 22 and routed them. Brussels fell and Antwerp surrendered. Within a few months Louis XIV had lost most of his territories in the Netherlands. At the same time Prince Eugene defeated the French at Turin and flung them out of northern Italy. Except in Spain, all went well for the allied cause. In Spain an expedition under the knight-errant earl of Peterborough and the Archduke Charles landed at Barcelona. A British army advanced from Portugal. The archduke, son of the Emperor Leopold, was crowned Charles III of Spain when the allies reached Madrid. But the proud Castilians wanted Charles III as king no more than the people of Aragon and Catalonia wanted Philip V. The allied armies, weakened by lack of wholesome food, ill-disciplined and poorly trained, were no match for the rallying French and the men of Castile. The French commander was the able Duke of Berwick, illegitimate son of James II and Marlborough's sister Arabella Stuart. In April, 1707, the allies were defeated at the battle of Almanza. Spain was lost.

In 1708 the French tried to seize Oudenarde, near Ghent. Marlborough scattered and crushed them in a surprise attack. A few months later Lille fell; Ghent and Bruges surrendered. The French border defenses were broken and the first stretch of the road to Paris was open. In the south the Emperor had finally suppressed the Hungarians; his forces had thrust southward all the way to Naples. France was tottering and, worst of all, famine was clutching at her throat. Peace feelers began to come out of Paris. At the same time, however, dissensions within the Grand Alliance had strained the coalition to the breaking point. If the Dutch and the English fell apart, then Louis XIV might not fare so badly after all. But they could not be split. All the allies held together and their collective demands compelled Louis XIV to fight on.

As Louis fought, he lost still more. In September, 1709, Marlborough won the bloody battle of Malplaquet. Mons surrendered. In 1710 Acadia fell to the English in America. Meanwhile the Whigs in England were drifting out of power. They wanted the war to go on; the Tories wanted peace. In 1711 the Tories at last obtained the dismissal of Marlborough and opened peace negotiations with France. Two years later the general peace of Utrecht ended the War of the Spanish Succession.

The Treaty of Utrecht of April, 1713, is a landmark in history.

It established an uneasy balance of power and a reasonable equilibrium in Europe until the Seven Years' War. By the treaty settlement Philip V was recognized as king of Spain and the Spanish Empire in America on condition that the thrones of Spain and France should never be united. Austria was to have the Spanish dependencies in Europe: Milan, Naples, Sardinia, and the Spanish Netherlands. Sicily went to the Duke of Savoy. The Dutch secured control of the barrier fortresses. Great Britain obtained Acadia, Gibraltar, Minorca, and St. Kitts. Louis XIV abandoned French claims to the Hudson Bay region and Newfoundland. He recognized the Protestant succession to the English throne as arranged by Parliament.

The famous Asiento (contract) clause of a separate commercial treaty made at Utrecht gave Britain the monopoly of the importation of Negro slaves into the Spanish colonies for thirty years. One British ship per year, not exceeding 620 tons gross tonnage, was also permitted to trade with the Spanish colonies. The further chance of an Anglo-French tariff and trade agreement was lost when the proposed arrangements were rejected by a majority of nine votes in the British Parliament.

Thus Britain's colonies were increased. In naval power she stood supreme. Her merchant marine was the greatest on the seas. Her business and commercial strength was advancing beyond immediate challenge. The menace of Louis XIV had been met and shattered. France was nearly bankrupt. The Netherlands were exhausted and would never again achieve the economic heights of the seventeenth century. The decline of Spain had been accelerated. Britain had emerged from the war the foremost of European nations.

CONFLICT FOR POWER: WHIGS AND TORIES

Such was the tide of events abroad in the wake of the silent Revolution of 1688. At home the ebb and flow of political strife had significant consequences. When William and Mary came to the throne many of the levers of power were in Parliament, not in the royal palace. Thus the political party that obtained a majority in the house of commons could control men, money, and at least a part of government policy. William III was not a popular king. He was a foreigner among the islanders; his natural surly and cold personality was accentuated by ill-health. He had little interest in England, except as an aid in the main object of his life, which was to defeat Louis XIV. To defeat Louis he must have efficiency in government. To obtain efficiency he must have parliamentary support.

The parties of Tramecksan and Slamecksan in Jonathan Swift's Lilliput, described in *Gulliver's Travels,* were distinguished only by the high and low heels on their shoes, marking them as high churchmen or low churchmen. "The animosities between these two parties run so high," wrote Swift, "that they will neither eat, nor drink, nor talk to each other." When William discovered the jarring factions and treacheries within the Whig and Tory parties he refused to recognize party at all and made up his government of Whigs and Tories combined. The Whigs, who held a majority in the commons after the revolution, wanted to revenge themselves upon the Tories. They refused to pass the bill of indemnity proposed by William. William, on the other hand, desired no vengeance or persecution. He did not want distraction in his councils or confusion in Parliament, only full national support of the war.

In 1690 William dissolved Parliament. Before doing so he announced a general pardon, called an Act of Grace, for all political offenses. Several of his Whig ministers resigned, piqued by their failure to get revenge. In the election the Tories won a majority of the seats in the commons because the electorate had been angered at the violent Whig intolerance. The house of commons, of course, was now the superior power in the state. It alone could tax the country; it alone could grant supplies to the crown. Its sittings could not be suspended or its will successfully opposed. Nevertheless, the machinery of government was such that the will of the commons could not be brought to bear directly upon the privy council. The ministers were servants of the crown, answering to the king alone. How could they be made immediately responsible to Parliament? The solution was eventually to be found in the simple and effective cabinet system; but for many years England stumbled unawares towards that goal.

The Tories soon began to complain about the cost of the war. They could not remove the king's ministers except by impeachment so they simply carried out a policy of obstruction. The Whig earl of Sunderland advised William to call to his councils men from one party alone, the party that had a majority in the commons. He asserted, and rightly, that such a plan would ensure both unity of administration and the continued support of the party controlling the commons. Sunderland and the Whigs, believing that the balance of political power was really on their side, were seeking a monopoly of office. In that sense they were a modern political party several years before the Tories. The Whigs resolutely supported the war; the Tories resolutely opposed it after 1694. Slowly William was persuaded by events to follow Sunderland's advice.

In 1695 the Whigs were returned with a majority in the commons. William, most deeply concerned with the progress of the war, replaced his Tory ministers with powerful Whig members of the so-called "junto." These men were closely united in thought and action and possessed considerable administrative talent. Because the Whigs controlled the commons the new Whig ministers were less frequently harassed by objections from below.

After the Peace of Ryswick was signed the interparty strife went on, a civil war of intrigue and calumny. The Tories were borne to an election victory by the incalculable and violent political oscillations of 1698. At once the question of the size of the army arose. William III informed his Parliament that he thought England needed an army of 30,000 men in view of the dangerous world situation. Louis XIV of France usually kept about 180,000 under arms. Parliament thought otherwise; it provided William with 7,000 men in England and 12,000 in Ireland. It also ruled that all these troops were to be native Englishmen; there were to be no Irish, no Scots, and no Dutch. The navy was reduced from 40,000 sailors to 8,000. Was the trident to slip from the nerveless fingers of Britannia? Disputes also arose between William and his Parliament about the grants of land in Ireland that William had made to his supporters, including several Hollanders. Despite his objections William's Dutch guards were sent home. It seemed that every member of Parliament who had a complaint, every schemer and intriguer, every enemy of the royal prerogative, woke up and began to speak. Swayed to and fro between the parties, sinking beneath disease and toil, the hitherto indomitable William threatened to leave England forever.

The Continental skies darkened in 1701. Parliament, strongly Tory, opposed England's entrance into a European conflict. The English people were weary of war and laden with debt. But when Louis XIV attacked the Netherlands and recognized the son of James II as England's king the pressure of English public opinion first forced the Tories to enter the war and then elected a majority of Whigs to a new Parliament. In 1702, as England moved behind the trumpet calls into full warfare with France, William III was succeeded by Anne. The new queen had defects of temperament and personality, but she was a good woman, sincere, honest, and deeply religious; above all, she was not a foreigner. In her first speech from the throne she said, "I know my heart to be entirely English." Among her deep prejudices were some of considerable consequence. For example, she distrusted and disliked the Whigs. "The Queen had from her infancy imbibed the most unconquerable prejudices against the Whigs," wrote the Duchess of Marlborough. "She had been taught to look upon them all, not only as republicans, who hated the very shadow of regal authority, but as implacable enemies to the Church of England." The Whigs, for their part, recognized and deplored the importance of the queen's personal feelings and the influence of her likes and dislikes upon royal decisions and political judgments. The situation is summed up neatly in a sentence from a letter written in February, 1714: "Her Majesty, God be praised, is wonderful well in health, tho' the Whigs won't believe a word of it."

All of Queen Anne's many children died in infancy; her husband,

Prince George of Denmark, was an amiable toper; she herself was an invalid. It was therefore natural that Queen Anne should rely heavily upon her friends for advice, especially in affairs of state. Her reign was filled with plots and counterplots, with intrigues in the palace household, with rivalries and jostlings among those who sought to whisper in her ear.

MARLBOROUGH AND GODOLPHIN

Queen Anne could seldom be bullied; but she could be persuaded. Her personal emotions and preferences influenced her choice of friends and ministers. These, in turn, sometimes persuaded her to act in accordance with their wishes. Soon after Anne came to the throne she dismissed many of the Whig ministers. The man she liked best was the Tory Duke of Marlborough. He received the Order of the Garter and high military offices. His brilliant wife, the imperious termagant Sarah, was soon the queen's inseparable companion. Sidney Godolphin, a moderate Tory, became lord treasurer and head of the ministry. Godolphin's son married Marlborough's daughter. The chief policy of Marlborough and Godolphin was to carry on the war and keep down the convulsions of party politics. In 1706 the Tory Henry St. John wrote to Marlborough: "France and faction are the only enemies England has reason to fear, and your grace will conquer both; at least while you beat the French, you give a strength to the government which the other dares not contend with."

Godolphin's government provided the money for war and subsidies for hungry European allies. For a time the extreme Tories in Parliament were willing to go along with Marlborough and Godolphin in fighting the war, partly because they themselves were so busy battling the Whigs. These Tories had always insisted that a land war fought in Europe was expensive and English victory was less certain than in a war fought on the seas and in the colonies. Thus the pattern of strategy conceived by Marlborough did not commend itself to them. As irreconcilable conflicts flamed in the commons Marlborough and Godolphin gradually dropped strong Tories, such as the earl of Nottingham, and took in moderate ones, such as Robert Harley, later the earl of Oxford, and Henry St. John, later Viscount Bolingbroke. —moderate Tory

Harley and St. John were the two outstanding Tory figures in the reign of Queen Anne. Stolid and clerkish, "Robin" Harley was famous for his gifts of conciliation and for the fact that he was a most skilful parliamentarian. Recognizing the value of political propaganda and a lover of letters he became the patron of Swift and Defoe. Always involved in petty intrigues, Harley failed lamentably as a party leader. The queen soon complained that "he neglected all business; that he was seldom to be understood; that when he did explain himself, she could not rely on the truth of what he said." Harley's associate was the fiery, elastic, and knavish adventurer Henry St. John. Much controversy has gathered about his name. Was he a great statesman and philosopher? Or was he a superficial and handsome charlatan, charming the unwary by his eloquence? St. John was certainly a restless, ambitious and free-thinking debauchee. About the rest the Tories had one answer, the Whigs another. There is considerable evidence to support several points of view, so numerous were the facets in St. John's enigmatic character. His influence over the eighteenth century was very great, especially in the realm of political philosophy.

In the election of 1705 the Whigs obtained a majority in the commons. Marlborough and Godolphin set a new course through the crosscurrents; they turned to the Whigs for support in the war. Despite the remonstrances of the queen many Tories in the government were replaced by Whigs. "I have worn out my health and almost my life, in the service of the Crown," wrote Godolphin in 1706 as he attempted to explain to Anne the reasons why the Tory ministers, all but the indispensable Godolphin, would have to go. Harley and St. John were forced to resign. Early in 1708 the ministry was in fact composed entirely of Whigs supporting Marlborough and Godolphin.

One by one the members of the directing Whig junto had climbed into office. There was Charles Spencer, the third earl of Sunderland, disagreeable and intelligent son-in-law of Marlborough; Wharton, the unscrupulous party manager of the Whigs, called by Jonathan Swift the most universal villain that he ever knew and lampooned by one writer as

> "A monster whom no vice can bigger swell
> Abhor'd by Heaven and long since due to Hell."

There was Charles Montague, the adroit earl of Halifax, founder of the Bank of England and a financier equal to Godolphin; the turbulent and self-seeking earl of Orford, earlier Edward Russell, the victor of La Hogue; the incorruptible John, Lord Somers, described by Macaulay as in most respects the greatest man of his age, a lawyer-statesman, a man "who dispensed blessings by his life and planned them for posterity."

Harley and St. John at once plotted the overthrow of the Whigs, of Marlborough and Godolphin. Queen Anne patiently bided her time. She knew that the Whigs were republicans and atheists; she was also certain that the tide would turn. Then she would have her Tories back again.

FALL OF THE WHIGS

Despite Marlborough's victories the weary months of the protracted war brought public dissatisfaction and muttered questions.

Were the Whigs deliberately prolonging the conflict? Did the French have to be forced into unconditional surrender? Were the English being duped and used by the Dutch and the Germans for their own purposes? Late in 1707 the Duchess of Marlborough fell from the queen's favor. Into her place came Abigail Masham, cousin of Harley and willing instrument in his plots to tunnel under the government. "The fortunes of Europe have been changed by the insolence of one waiting woman and the cunning of another."

In November, 1709, Harley's opportunity came; he was prepared for it; his backstairs schemes and his subterranean methods had been carefully developed. A political bombshell exploded when the High Church Dr. Henry Sacheverell preached an inflammatory sermon in St. Paul's on the dangers of toleration and the duties of non-resistance. Sacheverell denounced Godolphin as an enemy of the church; he violently condemned the Whigs and the Dissenters. He liked self-advertisement and excitement and that is what he got. England was nervous and tired after seven years of war. Church agitation was always apt to set off popular currents of unreasoning reaction in which the first casualty was common sense. When the Whig government foolishly impeached the delighted Sacheverell for apparently questioning the legality of the Revolution of 1688 the storm began.

London mobs roared through the streets. Sacheverell was hailed as a martyr; there were cries that the church was in danger; houses were wrecked and the chapels of Dissenters burned; the troops were called out. Forty thousand copies of Sacheverell's polemical sermon were printed; the Whigs ordered it burned by the public hangman. Pamphlets rained over the country. Then the house of lords reached its decision on the impeachment. Sixty-nine, including seven bishops, found Sacheverell guilty; fifty-two, including six bishops, found him innocent. The sentence was not harsh; the light-headed Dr. Sacheverell was forbidden to preach for three years.

The government had received such a jolt that it disintegrated. Godolphin and the Whigs were dismissed. There followed the fourth general election of Queen Anne's reign. The Tories were returned with the large majority of nearly three to one. Queen Anne had her Tories about her once more. Robert Harley, trickster extraordinary, was made the earl of Oxford. The brilliant profligate Henry St. John became Viscount Bolingbroke. Marlborough, Godolphin, and Sarah Churchill had been put outside; Harley, St. John, and Abigail Masham now proudly took their places in the vacated chairs by the side of Queen Anne. "I am afraid we came to court in the same disposition as all parties have done; that the principal spring of our actions was to have the government of the state in our hands; that our principal views were the conservation of this power, great employments to ourselves, and great opportunities of rewarding those who had stood in opposition to us. It is, however, true that with these considerations of private and public interests, there were others intermingled which had for their object the public good of the nation, at least what we took to be such." These were the words of Bolingbroke.

The chief task of the Tories was to make peace. Without consulting England's allies, Bolingbroke came to a separate understanding with the French before the formal peace conference at Utrecht. Charged with accepting bribes and other offenses, Marlborough was dismissed in 1711. Godolphin died in 1712. Jonathan Swift's virulent *Conduct of the Allies* pointed out that there was no need for Britain to continue the war. The Emperor Joseph had died and had been succeeded by Charles VI. If the allies did succeed in dislodging Philip V from Spain, they would then be faced with the demands of Charles VI to be put on the throne of Spain, thus uniting Spain and Austria. That, declared Swift, would be contrary to Britain's interests. Through these years the pen of the Tory Swift served his party well. The Whigs boasted the genius of Addison and Steele. Daniel Defoe served both parties, often at the same time and always at a price.

After the peace of Utrecht was concluded the Tories set out to revenge themselves upon the Whigs. They turned against Marlborough and the great duke had to flee to the Continent where he remained until the death of the queen. They sent young Robert Walpole, future Whig prime minister, to the Tower on a charge of corruption. Later they ousted Richard Steele from Parliament on the flimsiest of charges. Such was the nature of party malice.

In 1711 the queen had created twelve new Tory peers so that the majority in the house of lords might be of the same party as the majority in the commons. Thus the bills passed by the commons were less likely to be blocked by the veto of the lords. By this event the power of the Tories was increased. They used this power to pass several party measures odious to the Whigs. These enactments also illustrate the feverish and bitter political intolerance of the age. The Property Qualification Act required a member of Parliament to have a landed estate of £300 annual value if he represented a borough, of £600 if he represented a rural riding. Most of the Whigs were merchants, financiers, and so on; many were therefore landless and thus could not stand for election. A second act required a penny stamp to be placed on newspapers and a duty of two shillings to be paid on every political pamphlet over half a sheet in size. A third law was the monstrous Schism Act which required all teachers to be licensed by a bishop, to teach nothing but the Anglican catechism. This act, had it been enforced, would have suppressed all schools run by Dissenters and taken away from Dissenters the education of their children.

Another measure was the Occasional Conformity Act which required all individuals who held public office to take communion in the

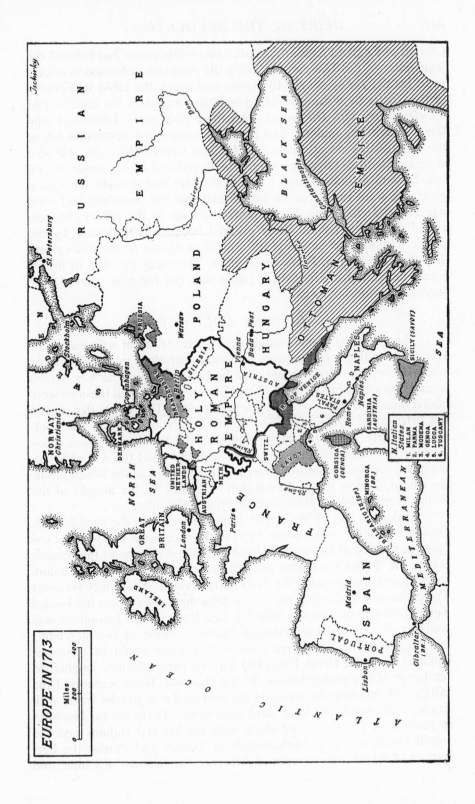

EUROPE IN 1713

Miles
0   200   400

Church of England regularly. Earlier many Dissenters had fulfilled the legal letter of the Test Act by taking the Anglican communion once a year. Daniel Defoe sought to expose and mock the rabid intolerance of the Tories by writing several pamphlets including the famous *The Shortest Way with Dissenters*. "All these phlegmatic Dissenters who fancy themselves undone, and that persecution and desolation are at the door again, are mistaken," Defoe had written ironically. He also suggested that all toleration should be ended and all Dissenters wiped out. Several orthodox High Churchmen who had thought the idea a good one were furious when they found that the pamphlet had been written by Defoe. The Tories sentenced him to the pillory; but the crowd drank his health. They ordered his pamphlet burned by the public hangman so he wrote his caustic *A Hymn to the Pillory* and *The Shortest Way to Peace and Union*. Then they put him in prison where he started his *Review*, a paper that ran for nine years. Defoe stayed in prison for a year.

THE TORY COLLAPSE

The glittering Tory triumph was short. St. John was jealous of Harley. "Nothing could appease a restless, ambitious man." He fretted when Harley was made an earl and he but a viscount; he was piqued when Harley became a knight of the Garter. To personal tensions were added divergent opinions on matters of policy. The Whigs denounced the betrayal of England's allies in the Treaty of Utrecht, the commercial treaty, the apparent surrender on the Spanish question. They also spread rumors that the Tories were out to upset the Act of Settlement and restore the Stuarts. Were not the Whigs, and the Whigs alone, the true upholders of the Revolution of 1688? To the attacks of the Whigs Harley and St. John reacted quite differently.

Under the Act of Settlement Anne's heiress was the aged Sophia, Dowager Electress of Hanover. Next in the succession line was her son George, Elector of Hanover. If Sophia or George came to the English throne the Tories knew that the Whigs would rise triumphant again. In this precarious position the Tory party divided. About fifty Hanover Tories decided to stand by the Act of Settlement. They were not landed Tories but men of business who felt that Francophile Jacobitism was contrary to England's commercial interests. Some of the merchants of London asserted that free trade with France would be a greater calamity than the Great Fire. The fury of party disputes heightened the terror of the protectionists. So the Hanover Tories supported the Whigs and, incidentally, wrecked the proposed commercial treaty with France. The words of Defoe went unheeded: "There are no Jacobites in matters of trade . . . we trade with the bigoted Italians and the stupid Portuguese; the Mohametans in Turkey and Persia; the barbarians of Africa; the savages of America: the heathen of China; and

in general with everybody and every nation whom we can trade with to advantage."

Not many of the remaining Tories were really Jacobites; but because they were anxious to be on the safe side they were in correspondence with the Old Pretender "James III." Bolingbroke certainly wanted to build up a strongly forged Tory party on the traditional foundation of loyalty to the royal prerogative and the church. At the same time, he worked too closely with the Jacobites for his own reputation. How far he would have gone towards supporting a Jacobite restoration is still a matter for conjecture.

Bolingbroke was impatient; and he was bold and dangerous. He wanted to purge the Tory party of the Hanover Tories, of all lukewarm elements, so that his followers would be united, strong, and indispensable to the new ruler. On the other hand, the irresolute, conciliatory, and shifty Oxford preferred a waiting game. Bolingbroke persuaded Queen Anne, who was very ill, to dismiss Oxford. Many offices had gone to High Tories; the commands of regiments had been given to suspected Jacobites. Bolingbroke was now in a position to press his plans. What could he do in the dramatic hours left to him? He had no time to act, for the queen died on August 1, 1714, a week after Oxford had been ousted. "What a world is this," wrote Bolingbroke, "and how has Fortune bantered us!"

The Hanoverian succession was saved. The Electress Sophia had died shortly before Queen Anne, and her son George was now the new king of England. When he landed in England he took the Whig view that most Tories were Jacobites. The game was in the hands of the Whigs. The road was open for their oligarchic reign, a reign that was to last fifty years. George I dismissed the completely broken Tory party and called the Whigs to sit upon his right hand. The Whigs, as the prophets had foretold, turned to impeach Oxford and Bolingbroke. Oxford stayed and fought through a protracted trial to acquittal. Bolingbroke deemed it discreet to forego the rewards of valor. He fled to France to become the secretary of state of the Old Pretender. "His fortune had turned rotten the moment it turned ripe."

MEN AND MANNERS

The England that accepted the first Hanoverian without enthusiasm was entering an oligarchic calm in government, contrasting sharply with the tempests and reefed sails of the Stuart age. Ahead were years of general allegiance to the ideals of compromise, moderation, humanity, and cooperation that had held an increasing appeal through the last years of Queen Anne's reign. The population of England and Wales numbered about 5,500,000. London had nearly 675,000 inhabitants; the port and mart of London was growing, "sucking the vitals of trade to herself." England's harbors bristled with masts; her rivers were filled with traffic. Daniel Defoe's *Tour Through Great Britain* describes the sheep-farming, the cloth trade, the rise of traders and middlemen, the ideas of agricultural improvement, the importance of grain. Eighteenth century England was to be a land of decent harmony and quiet strength.

Before the smoke-pall of the industrial revolution crept over woodland and meadow the English freehold yeomen numbered one-eighth of the population of the country; the tenant farmers about one-tenth. Country gentlemen ruled England in the interests of Empire, trade, and commerce. The Church of England held its privileged position and the squires and parsons continued their alliance; the good vicar of Wakefield sat cheek by jowl with the parish clergyman acidly described in Swift's *Tale of a Tub*. Common sense became a new keynote of society. When Jane Wenham was charged in 1712 with witchcraft and accused of flying, the doubting judge remarked that there was no law against flying and refused to sentence her.

In the age of the three Georges a Frenchman found England "a drunken Gothic nation that loves noise and bloody noses." Gambling with cards and dice "brought footmen into coaches and hath made them walk on foot that before kept them." Cheap spirits carried drunkenness not only into Hogarth's Gin Lane. Fox hunting, snaring and shooting, horse racing, cockfighting, cricket, and duelling brought riotous variety. There were over five hundred cheap and informal coffee houses in London, ancestors of the modern clubs. The dramatists, nearly all Whigs, created a new sentimental drama early in the century. Most writers sought and found wealthy patrons. Many earned good fees by political pamphleteering. A few, such as Ned Ward of Grub Street, made a living out of journalism. Alexander Pope, who pilloried the gossipy Ward in the *Dunciad*, said that Ward's books sold better in foreign "ape and monkey lands" than in England. At the same time, the work of any able prose craftsman could be assured of a reasonably good market in England. This was an age of great literary achievement and many readers. "The only end of writing," remarked Dr. Samuel Johnson, "is to enable the readers better to enjoy life or better to endure it."

Charitable and missionary societies multiplied: the Society for the Promotion of Christian Knowledge; the Society for the Reformation of Manners; the Society for the Propagation of the Gospel in Foreign Parts. The tendency to good works grew strong again. It was remarked, too, that more was heard from Anglican pulpits about Charles the Martyr (Charles I) than about Jesus Christ.

Meanwhile the slow pace of life in the rural regions was not easily quickened. The culture of cities grew slowly and, as it grew, millions of human beings were denied relief from smoke, from noise, and from the illogical improbabilities that spatter the lives of street-bred men.

From his country home at Houghton Sir Robert Walpole wrote to Major-General Churchill in 1743: "This place affords no news, no subject of amusement to fine Gentlemen. Men of wit and pleasure about town, understand not the language, nor taste the charms of the inanimate world. My Flatterers are all Mutes. The Oakes, the Beeches, the Chestnuttes seem to contend which shall please the Lord of the Manor. They cannot deceive, they will not lie. I in return admire them."

From his country home at Houghton Sir Robert Walpole wrote to Major-General Churchill in 1743: "This place affords no news, no subject of amusement to fine Gentlemen. Men of wit and pleasure about town, understand not the languages, nor taste the charms of the inanimate world. My Flatterers are all Mutes. The Oaks, the Beeches, the Chestnuts seem to contend which shall please the Lord of the Manor. They cannot deceive, they will not lie, I in return admire them."

Chapter 22

THE FIRST TWO GEORGES

GEORGE I AND THE WHIGS

E NGLAND was not pleased by George I, first of the Hanoverians. This German princeling was cold, stingy, sensual, and a bully. He had quarrelled with his wife, and kept her locked up for thirty years; he had even become involved in the murder of her lover. The relations between the new king and his son, the Prince of Wales, were consistently hostile; their public battles were venomous and degrading. Several German courtiers came with George I; two mistresses followed him.

Although he knew almost nothing about politics George had sense enough to see that he could not be an absolute ruler in England as he had been in his beloved Hanover. He also saw that the Whigs had brought him from Germany for political and religious reasons. They alone could hold the house of Hanover safely upon the throne. Hence George I threw himself into the arms of the Whig party. They were indeed his friends and he trusted them. He did not like the Tories. But even the Whigs could not easily spare affection for George I.

The new king at once appointed a predominantly Whig cabinet under Viscount Townshend and an election in 1715 gave the Whigs a substantial majority in the commons; they already had a majority in the lords. The previous chapter has described how these Whigs proceeded to display the usual political malice of the age by impeaching Robert Harley, Lord Oxford, and other Tories for treason. When this had been done and Bolingbroke had fled to France the Tories, desperate and bitter, saw their party shattered and leaderless. Some joined in Jacobite plots to place the Old Pretender on the throne.

In September, 1715, a Jacobite rebellion burst out of Scotland, led by Highlanders who hated the English and embraced a chance to raid the Whiggish Lowlander Campbell clan. This rebellion resembled a comic opera affair; it fizzled out. James, the Old Pretender, chilly, incompetent, and sturdily Catholic, could rally few followers except

421

the doughty, warlike Highlanders. France withdrew her support. When Louis XIV of France died his successor was a small child, Louis XV. The Duke of Orleans, who thereupon became regent of France, discovered that the Bourbon Philip V of Spain was scouting hungrily for support in his plans to seize the crown of France for himself, despite the provisions of the Treaty of Utrecht. Thus the Duke of Orleans was not prepared to antagonize Britain by giving the Old Pretender or the Jacobites any aid. The spiritless Old Pretender wandered forlornly about Europe. His hopes slowly died and the Jacobite cause withered.

Meanwhile the English public was growing restive. Were England's interests being subordinated to Hanover? Was an English fleet sent to maneuver in the Baltic to threaten Sweden, a nation with whom Hanover was at war? Riots and other disturbances against the king and his German loyalties became so frequent, especially in the Midlands, that the Whigs passed the stringent Riot Act in 1715. This famous enactment "for preventing tumults and riotous assemblies" is still on the statute books; it states that "any persons to the number of twelve or more being unlawfully, riotously, and tumultuously assembled together" may be ordered "to disperse themselves and peaceably to depart to their habitations or to their lawful business." The command to disperse may be given by a justice of the peace, a sheriff, a mayor, or certain other specified officers. One of these officers "shall, among the said rioters or as near to them as he may safely get," loudly make the brief proclamation set forth in the Riot Act and order the crowd to scatter. Under the terms of the act, if the assembly has not broken up within an hour all individuals remaining become thereby guilty of a felony.

Thus the country grew into general turmoil. To the Whigs it seemed that the carnival of corruption and riot accompanying a general election might be dangerous. In 1716 they passed the Septennial Act to take the place of the Triennial Act, thus extending the life of Parliament from three years to seven. The Septennial Act remained in force until the Parliament Act of 1911. By such steps the Whigs strengthened their power still more. The rule of "the Venetian oligarchy of the Whigs" was becoming firmly established. This time they would not, surely, be wrecked by a Tory and High Church typhoon such as that of 1710.

So firmly were the Whigs fixed in their places that they soon fell into disputes among themselves. Viscount Townshend and Sir Robert Walpole were anxious to avoid being entangled in any European difficulties arising from the fact that George I was Elector of Hanover. They wanted to keep the advantages of England's naval power and her insular position. On the other hand, Earl Stanhope and Lord Sunderland were prepared to support extensive British participation in Continental affairs.

Europe was getting disordered again. The brilliant and furious career of Charles XII of Sweden had resulted in the Great Northern War. Philip V of Spain yearned for the French throne and still thought the Treaty of Utrecht had made Austria too strong in Italy. Charles VI of Austria wanted Sicily, then possessed by Savoy; he also coveted the throne of Spain. In 1716 Great Britain and Austria concluded a defensive alliance. At the same time the regency government in France arranged a treaty with England by which France promised to help England against the Stuarts and England agreed to support France against the pressures of Philip V of Spain. Townshend insisted that the treaty could not last long because the Anglo-French commercial and colonial rivalry was too strong. Stanhope, for his part, asserted that Britain would lose more by not being friendly with France and stood to gain support against the Jacobites by the terms of the treaty.

In 1717 Stanhope, backed by George I, succeeded Townshend as leading cabinet minister. Townshend was soon dismissed and carried Robert Walpole with him into opposition. In 1718 the Quadruple Alliance of Britain, Austria, France and Holland was formed after Spain struck at Austria in Italy. France invaded Spain and Britain destroyed a Spanish fleet in the Mediterranean. Spain at last gave way before the power of the Quadruple Alliance and a European peace congress met in 1722. Meanwhile Britain had joined in the Great Northern War. Sweden, enfeebled, weary, and badly defeated, accepted in 1721 the terms dictated by the victorious coalition of Brandenburg, Britain, Hanover, Prussia, Poland, Russia and Saxony. From Stockholm to Naples peace prevailed, for a time.

THE SOUTH SEA BUBBLE

As Britain's difficult role in foreign affairs was thus played successfully the domestic scene was darkened by a spectacular financial crash known as the South Sea Bubble. The mania for gambling and speculation, so rife in the early eighteenth century, in this case had black results. It was the counterpart of the Mississippi scheme in France and the tulip madness in Holland.

The South Sea Company had been organized by Robert Harley in 1711; after the Treaty of Utrecht it received a monopoly of the British trade with Latin America. It took over about £31,000,000 of the national debt. Despite fundamental weaknesses, noted by such men as Sir Robert Walpole, the company won public confidence. Then it proceeded to pay for the privilege of taking over the whole national debt and agreed to reduce the rate of interest to be paid by the government. It advertised its business and its stocks soared fantastically. It promised grasping hands gold without labor; it would conjure away the laws of economics.

Hundreds of smaller companies were formed in the months of

speculative insanity. " 'Change Alley became a roaring hell-porch of insane and dishonest speculators." The shares of the South Sea Company were sold only in multiples of £100; but stocks of the smaller companies were within the reach of all; shares nominally priced at £50 and £10 were quoted at £305 and £105 respectively; some half crown shares were sold at £8 apiece. Promoters and subscribers raced to speculate and to sell shares at substantial profits to greater fools than themselves. Common sense gasped and expired as the prices and paper profits rose to dizzy peaks.

A few of the schemes and projects, such as mining, fishing, and colonizing were sound and reasonably practicable. Most of the smaller companies were based on ideas best described as sheer lunacy or brazen swindling: the importation of Spanish jackasses to breed large mules; the manufacture of a gun that fired square bullets against infidels and round bullets against Christians. There was a conspiracy for "improving malt liquor" and an undertaking whose purpose was to be disclosed only when the first instalment on the stocks had been paid; the purpose was indeed disclosed by the disappearance of the projector with all the money from the stock sales. A clergyman proposed a company "to discover the land of Opir and monopolize its gold and silver." There were companies founded to promote the growing of silkworms, walnuts, hemp, flax, and so on; to extract oil from poppies, salt from sea water.

> "While some build castles in the air
> Directors build them in the seas."

The directors of the South Sea Company were alarmed at the sensational rise of the stocks of other companies; they feared the prices of rival stocks might prevent the South Sea shares going up still higher. So they persuaded the government to prosecute several of the smaller enterprises on the ground that they were not chartered and had no legal status. This was a foolish step for the South Sea Company to take. Speculators were suddenly frightened; they started a panic nobody could control. All stocks, including that of the South Sea Company, thumped and bounded downwards. Hundreds of companies failed; thousands of people were ruined. Desperately the South Sea Company tried to restore confidence. They promised a fifty per cent dividend guaranteed for twelve years. Nobody was impressed. The foundations of public credit were crumbling.

In June, 1720, the £100 shares of the Company had stood at £1060; on September 20 they were at £410 and on September 30 £150; there were no buyers. Colonel James Windham sadly wrote: "The Directors have brought themselves into Bankruptcy by being cunning artful knaves and I am come into the same state for being a very silly fool. . . . Almost all one knows or sees are upon the Brink

of Destruction, and those who were reckoned to have done well yesterday are found stark naught today. Those Devils of Directors have
ruined more men's fortunes in this world than I hope old Beelzebub
will do souls for the next." The South Sea Bubble had burst.

Most of the victims shouted for revenge. The directors of the
South Sea Company and the Whig politicians who had accepted bribes
and backed the company must be punished and disgraced. A cabinet
minister committed suicide. Only Sir Robert Walpole, who had cannily
made a fortune and then withdrawn to a well-calculated retirement,
was held to be free of blame. Had Sir Robert not opposed the South
Sea Company and publicly deplored the whole sorry affair? Had he
not warned the crazed speculators that they would reap the whirlwind?
Reputed to possess the shrewdest financial mind in England, Walpole
was summoned from his home at Houghton to save the threatened
Whig party and to salvage the wreckage left by the exploding Bubble.
He took charge of the exchequer and urged Parliament to "proceed
regularly and calmly, lest by running precipitately into odious inquiries
you should exasperate the distemper to such a degree as to render all
remedies ineffectual." His measures were sagacious and bold. The
government was reorganized. The long rule of Walpole began.

SIR ROBERT WALPOLE

When Walpole's two elder brothers died he succeeded to the
family estates in Norfolk and became a country gentleman. He had
earlier been educated at Eton and King's College, Cambridge, when
it had been expected that he would enter the church, a path frequently
followed by younger sons of upper class families. But Robert Walpole
was in fact well fitted to be a squire and a member of Parliament in
the eighteenth century. He was a hale, lusty, coarse-grained and sensual
materalist, interested in hunting, the game of politics, the pleasures of
the bottle. At the same time he was a master of debate, a superb manager of men with a sagacious business sense. Holding a low view of
human nature, Walpole believed that most men had their prices. By
unscrupulous patronage, by bribery, by interest pressures of all kinds,
and by hard work, he managed and controlled his own Whig party and
often inveigled some Tories into supporting him, for a price.

Above all, Sir Robert Walpole wanted to maintain the internal
equilibrium of the nation; he wanted to keep the Hanoverians on the
throne; he wanted peace, appeasement, and prosperity; he was anxious
to let sleeping dogs lie; to provoke no disputes, no public fuss. "I am
no reformer," he once said. So long as things went on in that way Walpole knew that he would not have to increase the land tax on the
squirearchy and so drive some of the gentry over to the shattered Tory
party. However lowering politically and morally these tactics might be
Walpole gave England twenty years of quiet government in an age

that respected moderation, reason, compromise and common sense. The voice and the hand of the cynic and sceptic had succeeded the ardors and the faiths of the Stuart age.

In external affairs Walpole's policy as diplomatic helmsman was much the same. Why should England's treasure be spent in war or Englishmen pass their time cutting Frenchmen's throats? "The most pernicious circumstances," Walpole said, "in which this country can be are those of war; as we must be losers while it lasts and cannot be great gainers when it ends." He felt that the house of Hanover could best be made secure by peace at home and abroad; prosperity was born of peace and England needed a pause for prosperity and economic adjustment after nearly eighty years of intermittent and distracting revolution and foreign war. France and Spain were dangerous colonial and commercial rivals but Walpole believed that violence was not yet the answer; he would keep on good terms with France and Spain. England would not take part in Continental wars or wranglings. During the War of the Polish Succession Walpole noted with pride that 50,000 men had been killed in Europe in one year and not one was an Englishman.

Perhaps, indeed, Walpole did go too far in appeasing the Bourbons. But after him came Pitt and the balance was adjusted then. Meanwhile Walpole wisely guided and reined his Whigs. Probably he did not in fact control George I "by bad Latin and good punch" but he won the affection of George I and the result was the same. He also obtained the friendship of George II's adroit wife, Caroline of Anspach. If more royal support were needed Walpole got it by adding £100,000 to the revenue provided for the private use of George II.

THE CABINET SYSTEM

Walpole remained the leading minister from 1721 to 1742. In those twenty years important steps were taken in the development of the cabinet system of government, by which the executive is today rendered answerable to Parliament. In preceding chapters it has been pointed out that even after the Revolution of 1688 the house of commons had no legal way to enforce their will upon the king or his ministers in wide areas of policy. There were, of course, the limiting facts of the Revolution settlement legislation and the awkward and violent impeachment process; but the former contained largely general principles and the latter could not be invoked whenever the majority in the commons wanted the king's minister to resign.

It was true that the third article of the Act of Settlement had provided that the king's ministers in the privy council should sign the measures they supported and thus their responsibility could easily be proved by the evidence of their signatures. The object of this provision had been to keep the legislative and executive separate and distinct because the makers of the Act of Settlement had feared the corrupting influence of the crown. Nevertheless, impeachment was still an unwelcome, inadequate, and cumbersome process. Nor was it sensible to withhold the grant of supplies every time Parliament had a grievance.

Under William III it had been found that the machinery of government worked better when the ministry was of the same party as the majority in the commons. What happened under William III has been described in some detail above. All was haphazard. Expediency ruled the councils of the king. His advisers were still his personal servants and he was not responsible to Parliament. There was as yet no idea that any permanent harmony between the executive and the legislative could be achieved by having the king's ministers chosen from the party controlling the house of commons and by steadily keeping the personnel of the cabinet in consonance with the party balance in the lower house.

Queen Anne was persuaded by Godolphin and Marlborough to change her ministers when the Tories lost their majority in the commons. It was becoming increasingly obvious that the monarch could no longer choose ministers or advisers solely as a result of personal inclinations. As the impulses of Queen Anne frequently overrode her reason her ministers often talked over questions before they met her formally. For example, Godolphin wrote to Harley that they should meet with Marlborough "regularly at least twice a week if not oftener, to advise upon everything that shall occur." When her advisers took a united stand Queen Anne seldom refused to yield. Here is the germ of the later custom that the cabinet must be publicly unanimous. Legislative changes in the Act of Settlement also helped further cabinet development because they provided that the principal officers of state might sit in the house of commons if they stood for re-election after being appointed to office.

Another illustration of the fact that the cabinet was carrying on the legislative program of Parliament to an increasing extent is seen in the last exercise of the royal veto in 1707. If the cabinet functions successfully then the veto is not needed; if it fails then a new cabinet is clearly necessary. The mounting cabinet power over Queen Anne is also indicated by her creation of twelve Tory peers in 1711 to make the majority of the house of lords of the same party as that of the majority of the house of commons. The Whig-controlled lords had been blocking too many bills sent up by the Tory-controlled commons and deadlock threatened. Because what happened in the lower representative house was deemed more important than what happened in the upper hereditary house Anne created the Tory peers.

Under the first two Georges and Walpole the cabinet government assumed some of its modern characteristics. George I rarely attended cabinet meetings because he was indifferent to English politics and he did not understand English. Walpole did not understand German. George I thus left his ministers free to debate and to compromise their differences in much the same way as in Queen Anne's day. The king's opportunity to influence cabinet decisions was greatly reduced. George II seems to have accepted the action of George I in staying away from cabinet meetings as setting the precedent that the king should not attend.

Meanwhile, during the twenty years of his power, Walpole came to be called the prime minister, although the title was repudiated by him and widely denounced as suggesting a flavor of arbitrary government. After 1721 Walpole was first lord of the treasury and chancellor of the exchequer. In 1741 he said: "But while I unequivocally deny that I am sole and prime minister, and that to my influence and direction all measures of government must be attributed, yet I will not shrink from the responsibility which attaches to the post I have the honour to hold; and should, during the long period in which I have sat upon this bench, any one step taken by government be proved to be either disgraceful or disadvantageous to the nation I am ready to hold myself accountable." The prime minister has been called by Lord Morley "the keystone of the cabinet arch." Today he is usually the leader of the party that controls the house of commons. He chooses his colleagues from that party unless there is a coalition government in which case the ministers are selected from all the parties that form the coalition.

In his day Sir Robert Walpole was coming to recognize the necessity of keeping his majority in the commons; that is the reason why he used so much bribery, corruption, and wise management. Walpole himself would probably have been reluctant to accept fully the modern idea that in all cases the cabinet is answerable immediately to the house of commons; but as soon as he was defeated in the commons, even though it was upon a minor issue, he resigned. Cabinet government was coming to mean what it means today: party government. Walpole saw that if his cabinet's policies did not command the approval of the majority in the commons he could not carry on for long. Theory always lagged behind practice; but Walpole's successors never violated the basic principles of his system without inviting, and sometimes suffering, disaster.

Another feature of the modern cabinet system is collective responsibility. Walpole insisted that his ministers work both with him and under him. When his brother-in-law Townshend objected, Townshend had to go (1730). Walpole saw the cabinet as a unit, both with respect to the sovereign and to Parliament. He therefore insisted that the members of the cabinet must publicly support the policies agreed upon in private. When they refused to defend cabinet decisions in Parliament Walpole compelled them to resign. To Walpole the solidarity of the cabinet came first; the services of such Whigs as John Carteret, William Pulteney, and Charles Townshend came second.

THE EXCISE BILL (1733)

Walpole had many enemies. After 1725 they tended to gather about Viscount Bolingbroke who returned to England in that year. Bolingbroke, in partnership with the malcontent Whig Pulteney, published a paper called the *Craftsman* in which Walpole was attacked regularly. Other disloyal Whigs, such as Carteret, also joined in hurling invective at Walpole. Frederick, the son of George II, supported Bolingbroke because his royal father, whom he hated, stood by Walpole. The tone of political controversy in these years is revealed in the following sentences, said to have been written by Walpole himself, furious at an anonymous and fiercely malignant article from the pen of Bolingbroke: "Though you have not signed your name I know you. . . . You are an infamous fellow who makes a principle of doing mischief. . . . You are of so profligate a character that in your prosperity nobody envied you, and in your disgrace nobody pities you. . . . You are a fellow who has no conscience at all. . . . You have no abilities. You are an emancipated slave, a proscribed criminal, and an insolvent debtor. . . . You have been a traitor and should be used like one. . . . I would rather have you my enemy than my friend."

When Walpole turned to economic questions there were none in England who could deny his excellence as a reformer of acknowledged and proved abuses. He fully justified the confidence the bankers and trading interests placed in him. He reduced the land tax and the interest on the national debt. In an effort to encourage domestic industry he undertook to simplify the customs levies. For example, he removed in one year over a hundred export duties on manufactured articles so that British manufactured products would be in a better position to compete in foreign markets. He reduced or eliminated in one year thirty-six import duties on raw materials essential to British industry. He introduced the system of warehousing foreign goods duty free. As a part of his commercial policy he planned to check smuggling by collecting excise duties on imported spirits and tobacco from the retailers who sold these goods rather than customs duties from the importers at the ports of entry.

The word "excise" was odious from the days of the Long Parliament. Popular opposition, diligently fanned by the factious Bolingbroke and the smuggling interests, blew up a quite unreasonable storm. It was asserted that the new tax proposed in Walpole's Excise Bill of 1733 would require the employment of large numbers of officials who would raid private houses to collect the tax. The slogan "No slavery, no excise!" was shouted in the streets. Faced by such implacable opposition Walpole withdrew his proposal. "I will not be the minister to enforce taxes at the price of blood." Walpole's deference to public opinion was frequently remarked: it occurred again when he yielded to the ferment occasioned by Swift's *Drapier's Letters;* and again when he took England to war against Spain in 1739. There were to be no serious national discords if Walpole could help it. Meanwhile trade and commerce flourished; wealth was made for Walpole's successors to spend in war.

Bolingbroke soon retired from his closet leadership in the political scene to write *The Idea of A Patriot King* (1738) an unreasonable but brilliant denunciation of the Whig theories of government, a plea for a reconstructed and resplendent Toryism abandoning all theories of divine right, an appeal to the monarch to destroy party government by coming forward as a patriot and choosing his own ministers solely for their fitness. No party, asserted Bolingbroke, would be able to challenge a king who bulwarked his power by popular support. The throne would be securely based on the people's affection; government would be efficiently conducted and free of the evils of party and factional strife. Bolingbroke wrote his *Patriot King* for the edification of Prince Frederick, son of George II. When Frederick died the "patriot king" turned out to be George III, who tried to follow Bolingbroke's advice with disastrous results.

Henry St. John, Viscount Bolingbroke, adroit, ambitious, unscrupulous, and vehement, really contributed little to social or political theory. His voluminous writings were the results of practical political circumstances and his principles of action were always based on his conceptions of political expediency. His influence on his contemporaries was limited by his notorious depravity, his lack of political principles, his restless violence, and his doubtful attitude towards Christianity. Lord Chesterfield, Alexander Pope, and Jonathan Swift applauded the brilliance of Bolingbroke's gifts. Later in the eighteenth century Dr. Samuel Johnson's judgment was severe: "Sir, he was a scoundrel and a coward." Edmund Burke found him "presumptuous and superficial." Thomas Carlyle described his writings as "lacquered brass" and Macaulay called him "a brilliant knave."

Towards the middle of the nineteenth century Benjamin Disraeli and the young Tories looked upon Bolingbroke as the unacknowledged prophet of a New Toryism, the founder of the Tory democracy of a united crown and people as opposed to a Whig oligarchy of united nobles and financiers. In his *Vindication of the English Constitution* Disraeli's rehabilitation of Bolingbroke pointed the way to new concepts of Toryism to be held later by such men as Lord Randolph Churchill and Lord Birkenhead. Thus Bolingbroke's political damnation was not so complete as it appeared to his great contemporaries.

THE FALL OF WALPOLE

In 1735 several younger men joined the volatile Carteret, the unstable Pulteney, and the cynical and able earl of Chesterfield in virulent opposition to Walpole. One was the "boy patriot" William Pitt, who had been educated at Eton and Oxford and had obtained a commission in a cavalry regiment. He then sat in the commons for the pocket borough of Old Sarum which his family controlled. His first speech in Parliament roused so much comment that Walpole is reported to have remarked: "We must muzzle this terrible cornet of horse." But Pitt was not to be muzzled. His oratory, perhaps the greatest heard in the house of commons before that of Winston Churchill in the twentieth century, won immediate acclaim. One of England's greatest sons had come upon the stage. The quiet years of Walpole's reign were over.

Meanwhile, in 1733, the year of the Excise Bill, two important events occurred in Europe. Spain and France formed a secret Bourbon family compact under which they agreed to act in concert against Austria; there was also included in the compact reference to the possibility of united action against Great Britain so far as commercial and colonial policies were concerned. Secondly, a European war developed over the question of the succession to the throne of Poland. France and Spain supported Stanislaus, father of the French queen. Russia and Austria backed Augustus, elector of Saxony.

Despite heavy pressure from England's ally Austria, from George II, and from the English public, Walpole refused to enter the war. His tenacious efforts to effect a compromise settlement contributed greatly to the arrangements that ended the conflict in 1735, the year that William Pitt, Walpole's persistent foe, entered Parliament. Two years later Queen Caroline died and Walpole's steady bulwark at court was gone. Meanwhile the opposition to Walpole increased as more and more of his Whigs deserted to support the Tories in factious attacks upon the government. "The principles of the opposition," said the earl of Chesterfield "are the principles of very few of the opposers."

In such circumstances Walpole could not hold his political fortresses against new and stronger assaults. These came swiftly, born of his policy regarding Spain. Under the Asiento agreement of 1713, Britain had been allowed to supply Spanish America with slaves and to send one ship a year for other trade. For some time Britain had been violating this agreement by sending unlicensed ships to Spanish America, particularly to West Indian ports. The South Sea Company was guilty of many infringements; private British smugglers rolled thousands of tons of goods into ports on the Spanish Main. The Spaniards, naturally enough, resented such activities. They set up coastal patrols to search British ships found in Spanish waters and to seize them when evidence of smuggling was discovered.

Nobody could deny the right of Spain to take such steps. The British certainly did not; but they complained that the Spaniards were seizing ships that were not engaged in illicit trade; that British subjects were being tortured and imprisoned; that Spanish patrols were stopping and searching British vessels outside Spanish territorial waters. In vain the Spaniards rightly pointed out that Britain, alone of all European powers, took no steps to stop her nationals smuggling goods into Spanish America. The Anglo-Spanish disputes might have been settled by negotiation had not political and emotional storms in Britain risen to such furious heights that intelligence and common sense were swamped. The splenetic opponents of Walpole actively encouraged the public hysteria because they hoped the jingoistic hurricane would sweep Walpole from office.

In the commons, with an eye to the popular effect, gentlemen from the heterogeneous and energetic opposition groups spoke movingly of the plight of British sailors in chains and slavery. A sea captain named Jenkins told how the cruel Spaniards had cut off one of his ears. Contemporaries are not agreed as to whether he carried his withered ear about in a tin box, a bottle, or in his pocket. In any event, he produced it frequently and told his story. "I commended my soul to God and my cause to my country." This silly remark, probably quite unlike the one the sailor Jenkins uttered, caught the public fancy. The maddened popular imagination was too strong for Walpole to resist. Even before the tales of the Spanish atrocities, he was preparing to yield slightly. "I endeavoured to show him," wrote Lord Chancellor Hardwicke, "that his difficulties arose chiefly from a fixed opinion in many, and from a suspicion in some of his friends, that nothing would be done against Spain. . . . I really think he is determined to act with vigour to a certain degree."

So Walpole gave way before the martial clamor and reluctantly declared war against Spain in 1739. The galaxy of his talented and venomous opponents shone brightly. Many Englishmen thought the conflict would be a profitable and easy affair. Spain was weak; her treasure ships were numerous; she was popish. "They are ringing their bells now," Walpole is said to have remarked; "they will be wringing their hands soon." This war with Spain was to lead into a war with France; the war with France was to be followed by the revolt of the American colonies; and this, in turn, by the long struggle with Napoleon. After twenty years of peace and prosperous fatness Britain was now entering upon a series of wars destined to last intermittently for nearly seventy-five years.

Thus the age of Walpole's lenient spirit of compromise was passing. He had opposed the war and he wanted to resign; but George II demurred. In the early months of conflict Britain captured Porto Bello in the West Indies; the public was jubilant. But the notes of jubilation were soon stilled. The promise of Porto Bello faded. Patronage had corrupted the armed services Everything was rusty and out of gear. British naval expeditions to the West Indies had no good results. The attack on Cartagena failed. Combined operations on the Spanish Main were ill-conducted and uniformly unproductive. Walpole was unjustly charged with thwarting and starving the British war effort. Then, in 1740, arose the question of the Austrian succession.

At the beginning of the struggle between Hohenzollern Prussia and Hapsburg Austria Frederick II of Prussia had taken advantage of the death of the Emperor Charles VI and the succession of the young Maria Theresa to the throne in Vienna. He plotted with Bavaria and France to dismember her inheritance. France would get the Austrian Netherlands; the elector of Bavaria would be made Holy Roman Emperor; Frederick II would obtain the fertile and prosperous Austrian duchy of Silesia. He invaded Silesia as France and Bavaria prepared to strike at Austria and Bohemia. The War of the Austrian Succession began.

The part of British public opinion that was politically effective saw an old danger emerging. If France took over the Austrian Netherlands then Britain's liberal trading arrangements with the Austrian provinces would be ended. France would control territory dangerously close to the shores of England. The rival French commercial power would be increased. These possibilities Britain did not like. Economic and political interests seemed to demand that she support Austria with men and money. Spain, anxious to recover her former possessions in Italy ceded to Austria in 1713, supported France, Prussia, and Bavaria. Thus Britain became involved in the conflict although she did not formally declare war until 1744.

Meanwhile the elections of 1741 went against the Whigs supporting Walpole and his majority in the commons after dwindled to three or four. He fought hard against the many enemies his long monopoly of power had made. In the end they beat him by one vote on an election petition. This was on January 28, 1742. Three days later Walpole resigned, thus doing much to establish the principle that he who cannot command a majority in the house of commons should make way for one who can.

On February 9, Walpole was created earl of Orford. "All cry out," wrote Horace Walpole, "that he is still minister behind the curtain." But that was not true. Walpole knew what translation to the house of lords meant. To another new peer he said: "Here we go, my lord, the two most insignificant men in the kingdom." What power Walpole still exerted was used at court and on occasion it proved to be considerable. Nevertheless, this political influence was now largely a personal thing; it had little to do with Walpole's earldom and he had no official position at all. At the same time, until his death in March, 1745, his conduct justified Lord Hervey's comment: "Walpole, understanding the fluctuation of human affairs, never built on certainty, and so instead of worrying about possible contingencies always applied himself to the present occurrence, studying and generally hitting upon the properest method to improve what was favourable, and the best expedient to extricate himself out of what was difficult."

THE HEIRS OF WALPOLE

Although the prudent and practical Walpole was gone, the Whigs, under the nominal leadership of the earl of Wilmington, remained in power, supported by a few fox-hunting Tories "fat with country ale." The real leader was Lord Carteret whose government was called "the Drunken Administration," partly because of Carteret's predilections to claret and partly because of his reckless foreign policy. Under Carteret England formally entered the War of the Austrian Succession. A year later the earl of Wilmington died. Carteret was soon forced to resign on the grounds that he was subordinating British to Hanoverian interests and England was getting too deeply involved in the Continental war.

Carteret, now Earl Granville, was succeeded by Henry Pelham, younger brother of the Duke of Newcastle. With the aid of Newcastle, a consummate artist in corruption and greatest political manager of his age, Pelham floated carefully among the rocks. His government was supported by powerful cliques, although it was weakened by the fact that William Pitt was left out. Pitt was a commoner, soon to be known as "the Great Commoner." He lacked the support of a powerful Whig family. George II disliked him because he was a friend of the Prince of Wales and had opposed the king's concern for the welfare of Hanover. To overcome one difficulty, Pitt soon married into the great Whig Temple family. Then he served as paymaster of the forces until Pelham's death in 1754. Despite a strong attempt by Pelham in 1746 to obtain Pitt's admission to the cabinet George II stubbornly kept him out. In his other demands, however, Pelham had his way. When the cabinet resigned in a body to force the king to yield to their wishes George II tried to form another government. He did so, with unhappy results. "Thus far," wrote Horace Walpole, "all went swimmingly; they had forgotten one little point, which was to secure a majority in both houses." So, after a few days, Pelham came back because only he commanded a majority and could carry on a government.

Before Pelham died in 1754 there were few important events in domestic affairs. Three measures may be noted here. The Tippling Act of 1751 was designed to reduce the alarming consumption of spirits. It abolished distillers' licenses and prohibited illegal distilling. Lord Hardwicke's Marriage Act provided that no marriage should be valid unless the banns had been published in the parish church on three successive Sundays or a special license had been obtained. This diminished the number of hasty and irregular "Fleet marriages" and clandestine arrangements. Finally, in 1752 the Gregorian calendar, introduced on the Continent by Pope Gregory XIII in 1582, was substituted for the old Julian calendar introduced by Julius Caesar.

Abroad, the War of the Austrian Succession continued. In 1743 Britain sent an army under the command of George II himself to fight the French. George won the battle of Dettingen; he was the last English king to lead his troops into battle. Two years later the British were defeated at Fontenoy in Flanders. In the summer the Young Pretender, Charles Edward, grandson of James II, landed in the west Highlands of Scotland to attempt once more the recovery of the English throne for the Stuarts. The Highland clans, as usual, flocked to his banners. A motley army invaded England. "Bonnie Prince Charlie" was a good leader. He won the battle of Prestonpans with a single charge of his clansmen; he took Carlisle and Manchester; in early December he lunged as far south as Derby. Consternation reigned in London. Meanwhile the British navy silently kept the French from sending help; the English Jacobites were apathetic and would not rise to support the king from over the water.

The five thousand Highlanders retreated. In April, 1746, they were beaten at Culloden Moor by a British army commanded by the Duke of Cumberland, George II's brother. The last Stuart stand was broken. Bonnie Prince Charlie became a fugitive, sheltered for months by the Highlanders. Finally, after strange adventures, he escaped to France. Forty years later he died, a pathetic sot. His younger brother, usually called "Cardinal York," lived until 1807. With his death the direct Stuart line came to an end.

Meanwhile the European war dragged wearily. Henry Pelham was not a good war minister; almost everything was badly mismanaged. Pelham wanted the war to stop. He had "never any opinion of the success of the war and was always preaching up peace." In 1748 complex peace treaties were concluded at Aix-la-Chapelle. Their terms provided for a return to the situation existing before the war except for the fact that Frederick II's possession of Silesia was confirmed. Great Britain handed back Louisburg to the French; it had been taken by the English colonists. France, for her part, returned Madras which had been seized from the British in India. In none of the treaties was the right of the Spaniards to search British vessels mentioned at all, although this had been the ostensible cause of Britain's entry into the first instalment of the war in 1739. So far as Britain and France were concerned the whole conflict was an indecisive chapter in their long commercial and colonial struggle. The peace of 1748 was merely a truce. The great war was still to come.

NEWCASTLE AND PITT

When the mediocre Henry Pelham died in 1754 George II is reported to have said "Now I shall have no more peace." He was right.

Pelham's elder brother, the Duke of Newcastle, succeeded as prime minister. Newcastle had been a secretary of state since 1724; he was one of the richest men in England and he used his fortune to keep himself and the Whigs in power. His name is recorded in history as that of the greatest boroughmonger of his age; it is said that he knew how much it would cost to buy the vote of any member of the house of commons. In many ways Newcastle was an able politician and administrative officer, but his gifts in that direction were offset by vacillation, timidity, and ignorance. In Tobias Smollett's *Humphry Clinker* there is a description of Newcastle's reaction when he was informed that Cape Breton was an island. Its essential truth is beyond dispute. "Cape Breton an island! Wonderful—show it to me on the map. So it is, sure enough. My dear sir, you always bring me good news. I must go and tell the king that Cape Breton is an island."

Equally revealing is Horace Walpole's famous description of the conduct of Newcastle at the funeral of George II. "This grave scene was fully contrasted by the burlesque Duke of Newcastle. He fell into a fit of crying the moment he came into the chapel, and flung himself back in a stall, the Archbishop hovering over him with a smelling bottle—but in two minutes his curiosity got the better of his hypocrisy, and he ran about the chapel with his glass to spy out who was or was not there, spying with one hand, and mopping his eyes with t'other."

As an individual Newcastle was eccentric to the point of grotesqueness. "He always lost half an hour in the morning and spent the rest of the day running after it." Fussy and spluttering, he rushed about mending his great parliamentary machine by gold and corruption. He loved the game of politics. In playing it he spent three-fourths of his ducal fortune.

There were other weaknesses in Newcastle's administration. He craved power and would not share his authority with anybody else. His political management and his use of patronage contaminated and debauched almost all he touched. Because he would not agree to the policy proposals of the Whig Henry Fox he had to rely upon weak men to lead the debates in the house of commons. Newcastle could tightly control his supporters in the lords but he looked with alarm upon the assaults of Henry Fox and young William Pitt in the lower house. In 1755 Newcastle finally dismissed Pitt from his post as paymaster of the forces. Had he taken this step earlier the result might have been to his advantage. But he struck too late. Corruption in politics often has incompetence as its twin. In time of war the state cannot afford to be piloted by the incompetent or the feckless. There were too many of both about Newcastle.

The war that came in 1756 was preceded in Europe by a remarkable diplomatic revolution. After the War of the Austrian Succession Maria Theresa cast about for allies in the hope of recovering Silesia from Frederick of Prussia. Frederick, fearing a formidable alliance against Prussia, turned for support to his uncle George II of England. Austria's great diplomat Count Kaunitz bound France in alliance with Austria. England's Newcastle and George II, anxious to protect Hanover, abandoned Austria and concluded an alliance with Prussia. Thus, early in 1756, Austria and France stood ranged against Prussia and England. War was inevitable.

Sporadic outbursts between French and English colonists and traders had been frequent in India and America. In India the French were led by the patriotic and able Joseph Dupleix, governor of the French East India Company with his headquarters at the great French post of Pondicherry. Since long before the Indian chapter of the War of the Austrian Succession Dupleix and the French had intervened in the affairs of the native states with a view to increasing French commerce, influence, and political power through all southern India. In 1746 Dupleix had taken Madras but the Treaty of Aix-la-Chapelle had forced him to hand it back. Then he succeeded in setting up a puppet ruler in the Carnatic, a native state in which Madras stood.

The British decided to checkmate the French. Their Robert Clive had come out to India as a clerk in the East India Company. He had stayed to be a soldier. Under Clive British soldiers seized Arcot in 1751, forced a French army to surrender at Trichinopoli in 1752, pulled down the nabob of the Carnatic installed by the French and in his place put a native loyal to the British. In 1754 the French East India Company recalled Dupleix because he was spending too much money; the French directors of the company were more interested in trade profits than in empire. They dismissed Dupleix and he died in poverty. The new governor made a treaty of peace with the British which was ended when the Seven Years' War broke out.

In America the French power extended through the St. Lawrence and Great Lakes region and down the Mississippi valley. Their mighty fortress of Louisburg, built in 1720, looked out from Cape Breton Island across the waters of the southern entrance to the Gulf of St. Lawrence. All through their great belts of territory the French built forts in much the same fashion as the Norman and Angevin kings had built their guardian castles in the Middle Ages. At strategic points stood such citadels as Quebec, Fort Frontenac, Fort Ticonderoga, and Fort Niagara, bastions against the English and the Indians. At the mouth of the Mississippi the French held Louisiana. From missions, forts, and trading-posts floated the flag of France. The English were apparently to be held in their coastal colonies behind the Appalachians while the unexplored West was to be left to the French.

In the Ohio valley the conflict burst forth first. Virginian traders had long had considerable difficulty there. The French intended to keep all Englishmen out. The War of the Austrian Succession produced several skirmishes. In the North, as described above, the English colonists took Louisburg but under the terms of the Treaty of Aix-la-Chapelle they returned it to the French. To offset French influence in Nova Scotia the British founded Halifax in 1749. They also deported several thousand Frenchmen from Nova Scotia to reduce the danger of French revolt in the event of war with France.

In 1749 George II had given the newly chartered Ohio Company 200,000 acres of land in the Ohio valley. As the French attempted to extend their chain of forts to the southwest they were warned to keep off British territory. All these conflicting claims could have but one result. In 1753 France built Fort Duquesne on the Ohio. When George Washington, acting under the orders of the governor of Virginia, tried to take Fort Duquesne in 1754 he was forced to retreat. The French started to move soldiers across the Atlantic. Two of their troop transports were seized by the British; the rest escaped. In 1755 Newcastle sent General Braddock to America with two regiments of British troops to push the French out of the Ohio valley.

In July, 1755, Braddock's advance guard, numbering about 1,400 men, was ambushed eight miles from Fort Duquesne by some 900 Frenchmen and Indians. Over half the British force was killed or wounded. Braddock, shot in the lungs, died four days later. Those who escaped went back to Virginia with George Washington. The traditional view that Braddock was defeated mainly because he adhered to the column formation prescribed by British army manuals has been proved incorrect. The British authorities who ordered Braddock to take Fort Duquesne left him hampered by lack of money, supplies, transportation, and labor forces. His soldiers were wearied by the task of cutting a road westward from Fort Cumberland. He had no friendly Indian allies. It was not just to hold Braddock, an excellent general, wholly responsible for the disaster that fell upon his arms.

Such was the situation in Europe, India, and America when the Seven Years' War officially began in 1756. The first hostilities in Europe occurred when Frederick of Prussia learned that the elector of Saxony had made a secret alliance with Austria. Frederick suddenly lunged into Saxony and seized Dresden. This was the signal for the explosion of more armed conflict on three continents. For nearly two years Great Britain suffered a series of reverses. In April, 1756, the French sailed from Toulon and landed forces on the British island of Minorca. Britain's Admiral Byng came out of Gibraltar but did not effect a landing to aid the defenders of Port Mahon. Because Newcastle had to blame somebody, Admiral Byng was tried by court-martial for failing to relieve Port Mahon and shot on his own quarter-deck "pour encourager les autres." It was a disgraceful episode. In America Fort Oswego fell to the French under Montcalm. In India the British lost their post at Calcutta. Surajah Dowlah, the native ruler of Bengal, was responsible for the tragedy of "the Black Hole of Calcutta" where several British subjects died as a result of his wanton and callous cruelty. The French occupied Hanover. The forces of Russia, Austria, and France closed in upon Frederick of Prussia.

Newcastle and his helpers had blundered and failed. Military operations had been misconducted. National indignation roared about the rooftops. Newcastle, fighting desperately, tried in vain to save himself by a union with Henry Fox. His political machine collapsed under the sheer weight of public rage. The frantic duke turned at last to his deadly enemy William Pitt, the Great Commoner. To keep power Newcastle would do anything. He knew that the country trusted Pitt. Perhaps, with Pitt's aid, he could ride out the storm.

But Pitt refused to serve with Newcastle. Enraged, filled with self-pity, Newcastle at last resigned. Long years of bungling were ended. The nominal head of the new ministry was the Duke of Devonshire, chief of the great Whig house of Cavendish. Secretary of state and real leader of the government was William Pitt. With the new man came a new spirit. Pitt once said: "I am sure I can save this country and nobody else can." He now had the chance to make good his boast.

THE YEARS OF VICTORY

Pitt was very distasteful to the irascible and pompous George II because he had so often denounced the Hanoverian policies of the king and his friends. He had opposed "the changing of an illustrious kingdom into a mere appendage of a miserable electorate." The Whig leaders were jealous of him. Many found his theatricality and arrogance offensive. Genius often dwells with infirmity. Pitt's virulent and histrionic attacks upon Newcastle echoed far beyond the house of commons. He reminded a startled house that he was not beholden to them. "It is the people who sent me here." His arguments were powerful, his invective deadly. "We have provoked before we can defend, we have neglected after provocation, and in every quarter of the world we are inferior to France." Now, in December, 1756 Pitt had been placed in power by forces surging outside both houses of Parliament and stronger than either. "The corrupt and Philistine house of commons trembled beneath his glance."

Pitt acted at once. A huge naval construction program began. Large additions were made to naval personnel; new regiments were raised. In defiance of routine and seniority rules young men of vigor and ability were given command; old men were sent home to nurse their gout and reminisce. A new enthusiasm stirred about Britain. At the same time, a combined navy and army operation against Louisburg was planned in considerable detail. Arrangements were made to give greater effective support to Prussia, England's only ally. "England has been a long time in labor," Frederick of Prussia is said to have remarked later, "but she has at last brought forth a man." Meanwhile the war raged furiously in Europe, and death and sorrow entered thousands of peasant homes.

Faced by such a challenge Pitt's political enemies swiftly closed their ranks. George II complained that Pitt "made him long speeches which possibly might be very fine, but were greatly beyond his comprehension." Pitt did not make much headway in the commons. Newcastle still controlled enough votes to sabotage any plans other than his own. And the king, suddenly growing brave, dismissed Pitt five months after he had come into office.

It was a foolish action. Instantly the flame of public enthusiasm blazed again. When George II negotiated with all possible candidates for office, eighteen cities offered Pitt their freedom. England rang with his name. After three months Pitt came back into power. Every expedient had failed to keep him out. The result was the unexpected Pitt-Newcastle coalition. Newcastle, who knew nothing about war, would produce the votes. Pitt would carry on the war. Pitt, with his genius, his oratory, his patriotism, was back. "I want to call England out of that enervated state into which twenty thousand men from France can shake her." He was supercilious, priggish, affected, passionate, egotistical, irritable; but he was the architect of victory; he was Britain's greatest war minister before the hour of Winston Churchill.

The plan of Pitt was twofold. In the first place England would keep France occupied in Europe by solidly supporting Frederick of Prussia with men and with subsidies. Secondly, by combined operations overseas England would isolate and overwhelm the French outposts of empire. "We shall win Canada on the banks of the Elbe." The reorganization of the army and navy went forward. Able and energetic young officers, such as James Wolfe and Robert Clive, were chosen for important commands. Efficiency became the watchword. Naval squadrons were sent to prevent French reinforcements from reaching America and India. The French coasts were raided. Cherbourg was captured and its forts destroyed. British and Hanoverian troops fighting on the Rhine stopped the French from leaving to join the Russians and Austrians in a concerted attack on Prussia.

Frederick of Prussia, son of a military maniac, was battling desperately against almost insuperable odds. He won some victories, notably that of Rossbach, over the French. But four major enemies stood ranged against him: France, Austria, Russia, and Sweden. Frederick's armies were being cut down; his money was slipping away; every month his position worsened.

In 1759 Britain's Admiral Hawke won a naval victory at Quiberon Bay on the coast of Brittany and nearly wiped out the French Atlantic fleet. In the same year Admiral Boscawen crushed the French Mediterranean fleet off Lagos. The war at sea gave England naval supremacy;

ninety per cent of the French navy was destroyed by 1760. In America and India the tide was everywhere flowing in Britain's favor. The French colonial empire was collapsing. The French slave trade fell when Britain took Senegal and Goree in West Africa. In the West Indies Britain seized Guadaloupe. A great attack in North America shattered French power in Canada. In these years of victories Horace Walpole, son of Sir Robert, wrote: "It is necessary to enquire every morning what victory there is, for fear of missing one."

In 1758 Louisburg was taken by Admiral Boscawen and Generals Amherst and Wolfe. The gate to the St. Lawrence was open. British soldiers, kilted Highlanders, and American colonists pushed forward to take Fort Oswego and Fort Frontenac on Lake Ontario. The French abandoned Fort Duquesne which was appropriately renamed Fort Pitt and later Pittsburgh. In September, 1759, the army of General James Wolfe was ferried down the St. Lawrence to Quebec. The soldiers climbed at night to the Plains of Abraham and defeated Montcalm, the French governor, in a pitched battle. Both Montcalm and Wolfe were mortally wounded.

The key to French Canada was in the hands of the British. Wolfe's skill and daring had made certain that Britannia's flag would be planted firm in a domain forever lost to France. When Montreal fell in 1760 the last spark of French hope was extinguished. To the south the British colonists needed no longer to rely on Britain for aid and protection against France. "England," remarked a Frenchman, "will soon repent of having removed the only check that could keep her colonies in awe."

In India the pugnacious Robert Clive began and carried through a vigorous campaign against the French and their degenerate lackey Surajah Dowlah, the ruler of Bengal whose infamous orders had been responsible for the Black Hole of Calcutta. In 1757 Clive met Surajah Dowlah north of Calcutta at Plassey. Clive's army numbered about 3,200 British and native troops and Surajah Dowlah's about 50,000. The result was a rout, not a battle. Clive won vast Bengal at a cost of twenty men. Meanwhile French naval units had been forced to abandon French forces in India. In 1760 the Comte de Lally was defeated by Sir Eyre Coote at Wandewash halfway between Pondicherry and Madras. The next year Pondicherry surrendered and the French empire in India was no more.

Everywhere Britain had been victorious. In Europe Britain's ally Prussia was weakening fast before the onslaughts of Russia, France and Austria. Part of her territory was occupied by each of her enemies. Pitt had promised to stand by Prussia to the end, to make no separate peace. Despite Britain's victories on the sea, in America and in India, Pitt determined to continue the war to help Prussia. This was not a popular policy; many Englishmen were quite prepared to desert Frederick.

Meanwhile France was trying to persuade the new king of Spain, Charles III, to enter the war. When France demanded certain concessions to Spain Pitt suspected a revival of the old Family Compact. He finally learned that some understanding did exist between Paris and Madrid. The terms of that agreement, which Pitt did not know, provided that Spain would come into the war in 1762 if peace terms had not been agreed upon by that time. Convinced of Spanish intentions Pitt asked his cabinet to declare war against Spain. His colleagues refused.

They refused because some feared it would be harder to defeat the Continental strength of France and Spain on land than at sea; some were jealous of Pitt's achievements and his power; some disliked Pitt personally because of his intransigence and dictatorial ways; and some fell under the influence of the new king, George III. George III wanted to take advantage of the disintegration of the Whig party and the cabinet division to recover the power his predecessors had lost. He thought that with Pitt out of the way his road would be smoother. The interests of the king came first; the welfare of Britain second. George III decided against war with Spain. Pitt resigned. Soon Newcastle was dismissed by the king. The old jobber fell honorably and refused a royal pension.

THE PEACE OF PARIS, 1763

The man who supplanted Pitt was the Scotsman Lord Bute, famed for his fine legs and solemn elocution, a former tutor and close friend of George III. He and his king soon found that Pitt had been right in foreseeing the coalition of France and Spain. Because Pitt had prepared for that event his plans were carried out after Britain declared war on Spain in 1762. From Spain British forces took Havana, the capital of Cuba. A British expedition from India seized Spain's Manila in the Philippines. Meanwhile the prospects of Prussia were brightening. Russia's new Tsar Peter III so admired Frederick the Great that he took Russia out of the war before he was deposed by his wife Catherine. Frederick's Prussian armies defeated Austria. When France proceeded to negotiate with Britain Maria Theresa saw that Austria could not struggle on alone. So Frederick, his obstinacy at last rewarded, kept Silesia.

Peace was made by the Treaty of Paris in 1763. Had George III and his ministers been less concerned with political affairs at home, more of the harvest of the war's victories might have been garnered in by Britain's representatives at Paris. But nothing could upset the chief triumphs of the Seven Years' War. In America Britain obtained from France Canada and all territory east of the Mississippi; Spain ceded Florida to Britain in exchange for Havana and Manila; as further compensation for her losses Spain received Louisiana from France. Britain kept Senegal, Minorca, and Grenada which had been taken from France. Guadeloupe, Martinique, and several smaller islands were returned. France was granted fishing rights off Newfoundland and given the two islands of St. Pierre and Miquelon.

In India all conquests made since 1749 by either Britain or France were mutually restored. France agreed to refrain from any political acts in India, to maintain no fortifications or armed forces there. French possessions in India were to be used only as commercial stations. The future lay in the hands of the powerful and eager British East India Company.

Spain in the sixteenth century and the Netherlands in the seventeenth had been defeated by Britain. In neither case had the disaster been so overwhelming as that of France. The French surrendered most of their colonial possessions, much of their overseas trade. Only the names on the land in India and America bespeak the pride and glory that once was Imperial France. The French navy had almost entirely disappeared. The nation was bankrupt and disconsolate.

Britain, for her part, had a national debt of £132,000,000; it had been about £72,000,000 before the war. But she now stood forth as the world's first colonial power. The Peace of Paris was a milestone marking the apogee of British strength in the eighteenth century and the height of the First British Empire. At the same time this moment in British history brought grave dangers. Before 1763 Britain had always been able to rely on at least one of the Continental powers to act as her partner in the prolonged dance of European discord. After 1763 Britain herself was so powerful that she was no longer the natural center of coalitions against the aggressive designs of overmighty states. She had become so dangerously strong that the balance of power in Europe was upset. She had no friends on the Continent and no hopes of obtaining any. Meanwhile France and Spain discussed with other nations the possibility of redressing the balance of power should a convenient opportunity arise. There were other problems such as the defense and administration of the Empire. England was now vulnerable in every part of the globe.

These things, and many more, provided a challenge for the highest statesmanship. But England had only one great statesman after 1763 and William Pitt was ill and out of power. The rest were petty men, fumbling men, second rate men without imagination or vision. The drums that had beat the parades of triumph in 1763 soon lay silent by the barrack walls. The Royal Navy was neglected; in an hour of shame and folly it could not meet the demands put upon it. The British state was now to be piloted by the young and obstinate George III whose anxiety to rule was surpassed only by his unfitness to do so.

Chapter 23

THE AGE OF JOHNSON
MAN AND SOCIETY

EIGHTEENTH century England was ruled by the aristocracy and landed gentry. Those who possessed land had social prestige and political power. Upon the country house the whole flourishing aristocratic society was riveted. If gentlemen went into trade they lost caste; for them only the church, the army, or the law were suitable professional fields. On the other hand, men from lower social ranks made fortunes in trade in business. Then they sought to have others forget how they made their money. They bought land as a passport to high society. They usually tried to marry their sons and daughters into the aristocratic families or at least into the landed gentry. The "nabobs," returning newly rich from India, vied with the opulent businessmen and traders in buying broad acres. Great estates were built up to rival the hereditary holdings of the proud landed peers.

The lords and the gentry designated most of the members of Parliament and shamelessly influenced elections by bribery, pressures, and other forms of corruption. In the middle of the century fifty-one peers and fifty-five commoners made or effectively influenced the return of over 190 members of Parliament. Freeholders alone had the vote in the counties; leaseholders, copyholders, tenants-at-will, and cotters had none. In many cases there were no elections because the great landowners controlled the rotten and pocket boroughs. The local administration of England was in their hands; they were the lords-lieutenant; they were the sheriffs; they were the justices of the peace. Local oligarchies multiplied. Seats in Parliament were bought and sold without disguise. And yet, although the legislation of the era was class legislation in behalf of land and commerce, there remained among the aristocrats and business magnates a sense of public responsibility. They were not utterly estranged from the people even in a sordid night of harsh criminal laws, game laws, child labor, slave trade, and barbarous jail conditions.

Immediately below the nobility and gentry were the yeomen in the country and the numerous middle class merchants and professional men in the towns. The yeomen, whose importance in Tudor and Stuart days has been described above, were declining in number long before the economic revolution of the later eighteenth century. Some were rising into the class of squires; others were dropping down into the ranks of the tenant farmers. The merchants and professional men were increasing in importance. As this happened, the social prejudice against people who made money in business gradually declined. When society became more fluid later in the century many deplored the levelling of social distinctions. "The crest of noble or illustrious ancestry has sunk before the sudden accumulation of wealth in vulgar hands." As "the low, the illiterate, and unfeeling" seized opportunities to make money in trade the successful among them played an increasingly powerful part in political and social life.

At the same time England's foreign trade steadily increased. "Our ships are laden with the harvest of every climate," wrote Joseph Addison in the *Spectator* in 1711. "Our tables are stored with spices, oils, and wines. Our rooms are filled with pyramids of china, and adorned with the workmanship of Japan. We repair our bodies by the drugs from America and we repose ourselves under Indian canopies." Addison could not know how the volume of England's overseas trade was to soar later in the century. Between 1720 and 1802 the annual value of imports increased from about £6,000,000 to £31,000,000; the value of exports from more than £7,000,000 to over £41,000,000. With every increase of trade England prospered; and the merchants prospered most.

Thus the reign of the aristocracy and the gentry was in time to be ended by the successful challenge of the middle classes. That event did not occur until the nineteenth century; but throughout the eighteenth century the foundations were slowly being laid for a redistribution of political and social power. Most of the impetus came from the urban merchants and professional men. As the yeomen in the country decreased in numbers their social and political importance declined accordingly. Below these yeomen stood the rural wage earners. Until the latter part of the century their position did not change appreciably. And in the towns the artisans and day laborers followed much the same pattern of life as their ancestors in the Stuart age.

Later in the century the great social and economic strifes profoundly altered the whole character of English life. Through the flux and confusion of those years, described in Chapter 25, the voice of a troubled landed aristocrat clearly suggests his awareness that he lives at the end of an age; that the foundations of the England he has known are crumbling; and that, to him, there is nothing to take its place. "It is from neglect and despair that Democracy, that Anarchy, spring

. . . . Being born, being bred a gentleman I feel I always was and that I ought to be an aristocrat; but, in good fact, they won't let me continue one . . . I respect government; but let the Government respect and cherish me . . . Whilst the unaided paupers of the country will look at a dog-kennel with envy; and the starvers of the town are to peep down without hope upon the blazing display of cookery I will say something *is rotten in the state of Denmark!* Hope is lost in despair; and honesty is engulfed in misery . . . Hence the few grave men, the many ruined men, and the multitudinous poor cry out 'Reform, reform!' "

Over the roads of the early eighteenth century the pack horses and coaches moved slowly. The parishes, whose duty it was to keep the highways in repair, failed to do so. Few hard roads had been built after the Romans left England. The whole society moved as slowly as the coaches. Municipal government was as corrupt and oligarchic as that at Westminster. Public organization was as inefficient as the powerful local justices of the peace. Then, slowly, commerce made new demands upon England's transportation system. Turnpikes made the users pay for the upkeep of roads. It was all symbolic of a mighty revolution. Industrial advance continued. Smoke spread over the fields. Cottonopolis was built on coal. The pace of society quickened, and never again slowed down.

Behind the solid walls of the country houses vague fears began to stir. Long before, the Romans had fled from their villas before the advancing Anglo-Saxons. But the landed aristocrats of the eighteenth century had no place to flee. So, in the nineteenth century, they turned to stem the march of the middle classes. When conquest proved impossible, the lords and gentlemen joined the merchants, the shop-keepers, and the lawyers. Then, together, the great property interests were to stand against the urban and country workers who were clamoring for political and economic reforms.

NATIONAL HABITS

Many other aspects of the social scene were slowly changing. For example, the increased importance of foreign goods profoundly altered the national diet. The new diet, in turn, perhaps helped to change what is often described quite vaguely as "the British character." Early in the century potatoes were becoming more widely used except in the southern counties where a long invincible prejudice kept them out. The tomato was grown as an ornament in English gardens; it was seldom eaten. New kinds of spinach and asparagus became popular. The squash and vegetable marrow were accepted much more swiftly than the pumpkin. Wealthier Englishmen enjoyed such fruits as figs and dates. In most cases the middle and lower classes were reluctant to experiment and prejudiced about using new things or eating unfamiliar foods. Nevertheless, lemons, oranges, limes, and bananas swiftly became popular among all classes. When large Chile strawberries were crossed with Virginia strawberries and native English varieties the results were excellent.

Other commodities streamed through English ports. Chocolate became a common beverage. The consumption of sugar steadily increased; late in the century England imported from the West Indies an annual average of over 250,000,000 pounds. Tea became available in larger quantities. Pipe smoking continued and the taking of snuff increased. Coffeehouses multiplied; for many years this famous social institution remained a center for the discussion of politics, philosophy, fashion, and news of all kinds.

Coarse and vicious tastes and habits extended down from the indecent royal court. Heavy drinking was more widely practiced than in the days of Charles II. Spirits totalling 527,000 gallons were distilled in England in 1684; in 1714 the figure was increased to 2,000,000 gallons; in 1735, to 5,394,000 gallons; in 1750, to 11,000,000 gallons. Among the lower classes the consumption of gin and rum was tremendous. Gin was cheap and poisonous, a "liquid fire by which men drink their hell beforehand." Vast fortunes were accumulated by the purveyors of liquor. Gin shops offered to make the drinker drunk for a penny, dead drunk for twopence. Eighteenth century books and papers were filled with comments about drinking; it was an important part of life. In Benjamin Franklin's *Autobiography* are recorded his experiences in 1725 among the "great guzzlers of alcohol" in a London printing shop. Joseph Addison remarked that "in this thirsty age, the honor falls upon him who carries off the greatest quantity of liquor, and knocks down the rest of the company."

Gambling was rife through all levels of society. The South Sea Bubble is an excellent illustration of the mania for speculation evident everywhere. In an age when Oliver Goldsmith described contemporary novels as "instruments of debauchery" society was "one vast casino." Some men, such as Charles James Fox, lost huge sums at cards or dice. The great clubs of Whites and the Cocoa Tree made fortunes for their owners. The "malice, rapine, accident" of which Dr. Johnson wrote in his *London* (1738) united with the fates of the gambling tables to part fools, hopefuls, and desperate men from their gold. Government lotteries raised large sums. For example, such methods were used to finance the building of Westminster Bridge (1736) and the founding of the British Museum (1753). Despite all efforts to reform gambling the fever did not abate until the end of the century. New forms of betting were invented. In the reign of George III it became popular to make wagers on horse races, a custom which has continued.

This, then, was a century of heavy drinking, lawlessness, gambling, and immorality. An age that insisted on the hardness of its common sense was often very foolish. Nevertheless, there were moral and sober people, even in London. In the country the standards were higher, especially among the working classes. In the midst of such humble people the ancient folkways were not easily abandoned for new paths. Thus debauchery was not quite universal. In that fact lay hope for the future.

Much of the brutality of the period, especially among the gin-inflamed poor of the cities, was the result of ignorance. The courtly gentlemen were themselves usually Squire Westerns rather than Sir Roger de Coverleys. They spent their days with their hounds and horses, their nights with their drunken and sensual companions. The poor could not afford an education even if they had wanted it. The gentry often felt that study at the universities was unnecessary when all that a man had to do was manage his estates. A tutor at home could teach a youth how to read, write, and do simple sums. Sometimes a son was also sent to tour Europe for a year or two. The merchants and professional men, on the other hand, usually sent their children to one of the few endowed schools. The state, of course, maintained no schools at all. "Ignorance is the opiate of the poor" wrote an Englishman in 1757, "a cordial administered by the gracious hand of providence." The writer hoped that nobody would presume to deprive the poor of their opiate "by an ill-judged and improper education."

THE AGE OF REASON

In the meantime the eighteenth century was considered by the philosophers who lived in it to be the Age of Reason. Because their ideas were generally in accord with what many individuals wanted to believe the "climate of opinion" became one in which the magic and pervasive words "reason," "common sense," "compromise," "nature" and "nature's laws" were accepted and made respectable. God the Heavenly Father tended to become God the Mathematician, Architect, or Engineer. Once again, as so often in human history, man boldly ventured to equip the Almighty with attributes that man thought He should possess.

The universe fashioned by the Great Architect was not disordered. Nor should society be disordered. The eighteenth century held that the customs, ideas, and institutions of mankind should be shaped to conform with Nature's immutable and harmonious logic. The "Newtonian philosophy" dominated the age of the enlightenment. It was believed that if men employed the tools of Reason they might add cubits to their stature. The Heavenly City might be built on earth. It was agreed that the universal natural order could not be defied or scorned without inviting black disaster. Hence it was the task of men to recast all human institutions according to the laws of Nature and of Nature's God. This would breathe a new life into the thought, the imagination, and the social ideas of the civilized world.

All eighteenth century Utopias were therefore the headquarters of Reason. In 1792 Thomas Paine spoke for his age when he remarked that "the insulted German and the enslaved Spaniard, the Russ and the Pole all began to think. The present age will hereafter merit to be called the Age of Reason." In 1714 Dean Swift said that "God hath given the bulk of mankind a capacity to understand reason when it is fairly offered; and by reason they would easily be governed, if it were left to their choice." Swift also noted that "the Goths of ignorance, pedantry, pride and corruption were ever ready to swarm from their frozen north and bury all in universal darkness." Dean Swift was really saying more than his words at first suggest. He was admitting that behind the shield of brave words many men of his age were secretly afraid, not so much of "ignorance, pedantry, pride and corruption," as of being caught without any understanding of the nature of God or man's relations to Him. The eighteenth century, of course, adolescently courageous about so many things, preferred to call God something else, something to them more descriptive, such as the "Great Original."

Long religious controversies had so dimmed the divine simplicity of primitive Christianity that it is not surprising to find weary men turning to discover if Nature might supply the answer to their questions. "We have got reason enough," said the deist John Toland early in the century, "if we will only take the trouble to be reasonable." So the pilgrims of the age of enlightenment set out to find some principles to unify the moral world.

Newton's principles of "attraction" had unified the physical world. Might there not be some similar law of "moral Newtonianism" to rule the actions of men and society? Could this be discovered by Reason? Is Nature's universe really a system that works together for good? In the midst of a solid aristocratic and bourgeois social order some individuals speculated as to whether the materialism and "common sense" of the age in fact provided any answer to their gnawing doubts. Others were satisfied to become sceptics or atheists. In the eighteenth century, man became very much concerned about himself, about such problems as empiricism, the association of ideas, benevolence, self-love, sensationalism, the laws of psychology. Scores of treatises on moral philosophy and human understanding came from the pens of those who were once held as gods for their wisdom. "The illumination became dark with excessive light."

Such was the search for new and undiscovered laws of nature and man, the preoccupation with the cult of Reason. Amid all this debate and exploration what was the condition of the Church of England? In an age of scepticism and immorality was it entirely without spiritual influence?

THE CHURCH OF ENGLAND

Towards the middle of the eighteenth century Bishop Berkeley declared that morality and religion had collapsed "to a degree never known before in any Christian country." The anti-Puritan purges of the Cavalier years had driven over two thousand Puritan clergymen out of the Church of England. Under William III about four hundred Nonjuring divines had been expelled. When the devout Queen Anne came to the throne she tried to strengthen her beloved Anglican Church, so weakened and anemic.

Her first step was a financial one. From the days of Henry VIII the crown had collected large revenues from the clergy. Anne turned all these revenues back to the church. This gift, called Queen Anne's bounty, was primarily intended to increase the salaries of underpaid clergymen. But more was needed than money. The Anglican Church contained many inferior men. Political patronage considerations impelled Whig governments to give bishoprics and deaneries to Whigs without regard for learning or piety. Tory governments gave them to Tories. Many ecclesiastical preferments went to the highest bidders, especially to the younger sons of nobles; such men were usually neither godly nor intelligent. Pluralism and sinecurism prevailed everywhere.

The poorer positions were opened to individuals who were incapable of making better livings elsewhere. Nevertheless, many of the humbler clergy were pious and capable. "Six thousand of your clergy," wrote Sydney Smith, "the greater part of your whole number, had at a middle rate, one with another, not £50 a year." Henry Fielding's famous Parson Adams drew £23 a year. Oliver Goldsmith's father was one of those who were "passing rich with forty pounds a year." The annals of the starveling curates were often sad as well as short and simple.

In 1717 the Whigs saw an opportunity to muffle the Tory High Churchmen and persuaded George I to prorogue convocation, the legislative body of the church and long the cockpit of clerical warfare. Convocation was not permitted to transact business until the middle nineteenth century. Bereft of competent pilots in an age of moral drifting the Church of England found her course uncharted. Amidst public corruption and dim ideals venal primates and prelates arrogantly lived like princes; hard-drinking, fox hunting and pluralist parsons usurped the name of clerics. Why should Christianity interfere with the pleasures of the world? "The pulpit," said Daniel Defoe, "is daily profaned with invectives instead of sermons." Beneath the surface of early eighteenth century prosperity the springs of spiritual life were running dry. It was not proper, in this polished society, "to teach one's haggard and unreclaimed reason to stoop unto the lure of faith." The orthodox, on the whole, were more pessimistic than the heretics.

There were, of course, many stalwart, virile, and hard-working Christians in the Anglican Church; but their voices were unheeded in the streets. In the churches of London Sir William Blackstone did not hear "a single discourse which had more Christianity in it than the writings of Cicero." Bishop Watson saw "the generality of the bishops polluting Gospel humility with the pride of the prelacy." Later in the century William Pitt, earl of Chatham, rose to defend the Dissenting ministers. "Their ambition is to keep close to the college of fishermen, not of cardinals; and to the doctrine of inspired apostles, not to the decrees of interested and aspiring bishops." The cumulative effect of the expulsion of the Puritan and Nonjuring clergy, the suppression of convocation, and the political rise of the church as a reservoir of patronage was an unprecedented degree of spiritual decadence. The church-dominated and decaying universities were seldom concerned with scholarship. The tutor of Edward Gibbon "remembered he had a salary to draw but forgot he had duties to perform." Over three centuries before Geoffrey Chaucer had asked: "If gold rust, what shall iron do?"

For some time, as described earlier in this chapter, there had also been growing a widely diffused, indolent scepticism through the upper classes. Many who were willing that faith should perish wanted the Church of England to survive because it helped to keep the lower classes subservient to the governing aristocracy. The origin of much scepticism about the truth of Christianity was in deism. The deists denied the supernatural in religion and insisted that revelation was contrary to reason. Nothing, they said, was above the comprehension of man's reason. By taking thought man could lay bare the secrets of heaven as well as of earth. The spiritual senses were dulled. Why should there be awe, gratitude, or reverence for God the Mathematician?

"Natural religion" sometimes moved on a high level of argument, as in Matthew Tindal's *Christianity as Old as the Creation*. Usually, however, the "reason" invoked was a weak weapon. The clergy gave hundreds of answers to the deists. So far as logic and argument were concerned the divines won easily. Against such clerical antagonists as Bishop Butler, the deists seemed as children, dabblers in ideas, innocent of speculative ability.

In all this controversy about natural and revealed religion the clerics made no appeal to the hearts of men. The chief object of sermons seemed to be to shun enthusiasm. Deism merged into the historical scepticism of Gibbon and the philosophical scepticism of Hume. From France came the chants of philosophers enthroning Reason and pulling down Christian faith. But the Church of England continued to fight with intellectual arguments about such things as moderation, compromise, rational progress, and common sense. The sermons were often saltless, pedantic, prosaic, chilling discourses about abstractions. There was no appeal to the emotions. The masses found small comfort in polished and reasoned equations proved from the pulpit. "Stomach well alive, soul extinct" was the later verdict of Thomas Carlyle.

Wesley

THE METHODISTS

Often in the history of mankind sudden movements have swirled across the planet's face to darken or cleanse societies. Over the arctic spiritual barrenness of the eighteenth century swept the Methodist movement led by John Wesley. When Wesley was a fellow of Lincoln College, Oxford he was a leading member of the small "Holy Club." Many Oxford jests were made; one scoffed at the methodized discipline of the club by calling the members "Methodists." These young men followed the pattern of the religious societies of Queen Anne's reign. They visited the sick and the poor; they prayed; they fervently tried to quicken the embers of emotional awareness about God and His teaching. With John Wesley was his brother Charles; there was also George Whitefield, erratic, eccentric, but one of the greatest evangelists of all time. These three were all trained for the priesthood in the Church of England. They began their work as ordained ministers.

In 1735 John Wesley went as a colonial missionary to Georgia. He was quite unpopular there. Continuous friction arose. Wesley's domineering ways, his discipline and High Church formalism annoyed the people. "We know that we are Protestants; but as for this man we know not of what religion he is!" When Wesley came home to England in 1738 he fell under the influence of the Moravian Peter Bohler, who talked to him of justification by faith. "How can I preach to others," said Wesley, "when I have not faith myself?"

Then, suddenly, on May 24, 1738, Wesley obtained the faith he sought. "I felt my heart strangely warmed. I felt I did trust in Christ, Christ alone, for my salvation." The conversion promised by the Moravians had come. At once John Wesley sought to save others. He preached on the text "This is the victory that overcometh the world, even our faith." In his *Journal* he wrote: "And I saw more than ever that the Gospel is in truth but one great promise, from the beginning of it to the end." The Methodist movement had begun and "the glad tidings of salvation" were now to be declared.

John and Charles Wesley and George Whitefield set forth to preach salvation by faith. Their revival crusade was obviously at odds with the caste system and the chartered stagnation of the early eighteenth century. To stir the emotions was unseemly. To declare that all immortal souls were equally precious to God was offensive to the upper classes. "These doctrines are most repulsive," wrote the Duchess of Buckingham. "They are strongly tinctured with impertinence and disrespect towards their superiors in perpetually endeavouring to level all ranks and do away with all distinctions. It is monstrous to be told that you have a heart as sinful as the common wretches that crawl upon the earth." The itinerant Methodist preachers were often excluded from the pulpits of the frigid Anglican Church despite the fact that they were ordained ministers. Many proud and orthodox clergymen thought the Methodists fanatical and vulgar. Abuse for the new doctrines came from many quarters.

Meanwhile, over all England, John Wesley and his disciples preached to the masses, to the colliers, the impoverished rural workers, and "the wild, starving blasphemers" of Newcastle. Mobs often assailed them in open air meetings. "In Cornwall the war against Methodism was carried on with far more vigor than against the Spaniards." Methodist chapels were built and many were as promptly torn down by angry rioters. John and Charles Wesley and George Whitefield narrowly escaped with their lives on several occasions. Anglican clergymen asked popular support for "the defense of the Church of England." The Epworth rector said: "Pray tell Mr. Wesley that I shall not give *him* the sacrament as he is *not fit*." Whitefield left the Church of England. John Wesley stayed in.

There was no essential conflict between the teachings of Methodism and the Anglican Church. It was a question of spirit, of emphasis. Even after separate chapels were built and a government for the Methodists established they insisted that they were still within the Church of England. Only gradually did they become a separate sect. Through the early years of the movement its strength grew swiftly among the middle and lower classes. George Whitefield, for example, was one of the greatest of pulpit orators. He preached 18,000 times in thirty-four years, often to thousands of people. His Napoleonic energy was perhaps equalled among the Methodists only by that of John Wesley. These evangelical preachers were bringing a religion of uplifting enthusiasm with an exciting moral fervor in contrast to the heavy dignity of the established church.

The New Testament preaching of brotherly love, of social righteousness, held a particular appeal for the masses. The leaders of the Methodist movement always stressed the brotherhood of all men. For example, John Wesley denounced slavery in direct, graphic, vehement language. "Can human law turn darkness into light or evil into good? Notwithstanding ten thousand laws, right is right and wrong is wrong still." He spoke against the liquor traffic. He joined the Quakers in condemning the insanity of war. On the eve of the American Revolution he wrote to Lord North: "Waiving all considerations of right and wrong, I ask, is it common sense to use force against the Americans?" In a famous treatise he asked the people of England: "But what are they going to do? To shoot each other through the head or heart, to stab and butcher each other? . . . Why so? . . . What an amazing way of deciding controversies! . . . What a flood of folly and madness has broken in upon us!" Wesley also denounced the abuse of money and privilege. Wealth was to him a curse if it became an end in itself. "Gain all you can. Save all you can. Give all you can." To the commissioners of excise Wesley wrote: "I have two silver spoons at London and two at Bristol. This is all the plate I need at present, and I shall not buy any more while so many around me want bread."

Throughout the teachings of Methodism there was the constant stress upon the need for social reform. "The Gospel of Christ knows of no religion but social, no holiness but social holiness." The appeal to the human conscience, to sympathy, to moral imperatives was always in the Methodist sermons. Multitudes up and down the land heard these messages about the brotherhood of man, the immortality of the soul, and the trumpet of faith. And through the years the great hymns of the Wesleys rolled over the world: "Jesus, Lover of My Soul"; "Love divine, all love excelling"; "Christ the Lord is risen today"; "Hark, the herald angels sing." Regardless of social status, men who sang such hymns must have felt themselves close to God.

In the late eighteenth century the Methodist movement had a strong effect upon the Church of England. An evangelical revival within the church developed to sweep away much of the earlier lethargy and sterile incompetence. Methodism also had an important part in the movements for education reform, the abolition of slavery, prison and criminal reform, the improvement of labor conditions, and world missionary activity. Men such as William Wilberforce and John Howard were deeply indebted to the Methodists. "I look upon all the world as my parish," John Wesley had said.

The Methodist Church has remained pre-eminently the church of the working classes in Britain. Its greatest strength is still in the industrial counties. Its steadying influence on the side of the king and the constitution helped to forestall any political revolt during the shaking years of the French Revolution. Had there been no religious revolution in the middle eighteenth century England might have been more deeply touched by the European revolutions of 1848. Among other reasons, the Chartists failed because there was a Methodist Church. From the early nineteenth century Methodism has given much impetus to trade unionism. Its influence touched almost every aspect of English life. It united with the great thrusts of Puritanism to produce the important "Nonconformist conscience."

THE ARTS

The solid and secure eighteenth century knew its own mind; it had its own standards. There was, in many ways, a certainty we are now without. The aristocratic men of the country houses, small and great, presided over the destinies of England. Few were aware that incalculable forces were already working to shape a society that was not to be aristocratic at all, a world in which they and their kind would be most uncomfortable. Some of these forces, such as the Methodist movement, were dramatic and intense. Others rolled quietly along, causing no sudden social lurches. In the end, all these trends and currents, or whatever the sum total of the actions of men may most properly be called, merged into the nineteenth century. The society of Victorian England, in turn, underwent its own chameleon changes.

The age of Johnson was a time when the press grew steadily in range and power. The uses of posterity were recognized in a mounting volume of memoirs, diaries, and letters carefully packed away in trunks and boxes. Some diarists, such as Parson James Woodforde, did not write for the eyes of later generations. Woodforde's diary measures the settled and ordinary life of a very ordinary Norfolk parson. Little incidents stand out sharp and clear, as they do in the famous Torrington diaries.

In Sir William Blackstone's *Commentaries* was published the most complete statement of English law that had yet appeared. "Lawyers know life practically," said Dr. Johnson. "A bookish man should always have lawyers to converse with. They have what he wants." Meanwhile medicine advanced with long strides. The plague was defeated. Sir Edward Jenner stayed the terror of smallpox. Famous philanthropists increased the number of hospitals. Public health improved. Chemistry, physics, and optics enlarged their bounds. A new era in surgery began with John Hunter, father of modern surgery. On the other hand, with the advent of new methods of advertising, patent medicines and irregular practices multiplied. "Dr. James's Fever Powder" probably hurried Oliver Goldsmith to his grave. Sir Robert Walpole is said to have become so addicted to one popular treatment that he consumed 180 pounds of soap and 1,200 gallons of lime water before he died.

A great change in manners occurred. The graces of social refinement, so lacking in the reign of Queen Anne, became very important as the century advanced. Dr. Johnson noted that "every man of any education would rather be called a rascal, than be accused of deficiency in the graces." The impeccable common sense of the urbane Lord Chesterfield's letters to his son shows how diligently the precepts of proportion and controlled politeness were to be followed. In that looking-glass world the alphabet of the art of pleasing must be studied with care. In time good manners were often exaggerated into affectation; but then the pendulum swung back again and extreme elegance was usually recognized as the refuge of snobs and charlatans. These polished refinements in the polite world did not extend to improve the manners of the laboring poor in town and country. Workers in rural England were usually less vulgar and gross than their city cousins; but many travellers found them boorish and rude enough.

There were significant developments in drama and music. The early decades of the eighteenth century brought violent attacks upon the theatre. Many playwrights did try to pitch their plays at a high moral level. They usually succeeded only in writing what William Hazlitt called "homilies in dialogue" filled with "sickly sensibility that shows as little hearty aversion to vice as sincere attachment to virtue." Before the middle of the century English drama was poor; it was far outstripped in appeal by the variety stage, by the ballet, tight-rope dancing, magicians' tricks, and pantomine. Later there arose a decorous drama, innocent of the sensationalism of earlier days, calculated to amuse rather than startle or offend. The sophisticated gentlemen preferred to have no horseplay, no crudities, nothing unbecoming.

It remained for Oliver Goldsmith in *She Stoops to Conquer* to introduce a whimsical and human element into the comedy of manners. Sheridan's *The Rivals, The School for Scandal,* and *The Critic* carried on the work so splendidly begun by Goldsmith. Great actors, such as David Garrick and Sarah Siddons, helped to save Shakespeare from those who had tried to rewrite him. It was Garrick, for example, who began the Stratford-on-Avon Festival (1769).

At the same time John Gay's *Beggar's Opera* (1728) showed England what could be done in a musical comedy. Italian opera was not widely popular until after Handel came to England in 1710. Although Handel wrote thirty-six operas his fame rests upon his oratorios. *The Messiah, Saul,* and *Samson* would alone have made his name immortal.

Meanwhile Thomas Chippendale and Thomas Sheraton were creating new types of furniture that were to be the envy of later generations. Josiah Wedgwood led the way in a new age of pottery making. And meanwhile, too, England for the first time had a school of native English painting. The arrogantly original painter and engraver William Hogarth caricatured the common people of England. His grim "Gin Lane," the "Harlot's Progress," and the "Rake's Progress" are the finest satirical products of the age. A native school of portraiture was headed by Sir Joshua Reynolds, the most fashionable portrait painter of the day. Statesmen, beauties, soldiers, actors, and men of letters sat for him. He was first president of the Royal Academy, founded in 1768. Ruskin later called him one of "the utmost masters." Certainly no artist rivalled his consummate skill in placing upon canvas the great figures of eighteenth century aristocracy.

A third artist, Thomas Gainsborough, painted both landscapes and portraits. In some respects he was greater than Reynolds. His most famous portraits are those of Mrs. Siddons, the younger Pitt, and "A Young Gentleman," usually called the "Blue Boy." In landscape painting Gainsborough was particularly effective in his use of light and color. In 1777 an Italian painter wrote of Gainsborough's "The Watering Place" that the large landscape was inimitable. "It revives the coloring of Rubens in that line. The scene is grand, the effect of light is striking, the cattle very natural." Most of Gainsborough's inspiration came from nature rather than from Italy.

Reynolds and Gainsborough shared the stage with a third great portrait painter, George Romney. Romney's most famous pictures are not so dignified as those of his great contemporaries; but what they lack in dignity they possess in charm and freshness. His delightful portraits of Lady Hamilton and Charles Grey place him in the first rank of English artists. It is a pity that his life was a long personal tragedy; he died a madman.

A brilliant and luminous landscape painter was Richard Wilson who produced some of his best work before Gainsborough turned away from portraiture to paint landscapes. Hence Wilson is often called "the father of English landscape painting." In his own day he was not widely recognized among his own countrymen; his works were seldom mentioned by reviewers. However, Wilson did found a real landscape school in England. In water colors the four most successful landscape painters were Paul Sandby, who was also an engraver and originated the aquatint process, John Robert Cozens, Thomas Girtin, and J. M. W. Turner. Both Girtin and Turner were born in 1775. Girtin died in 1802. Turner, one of England's greatest exponents of nature in color, did most of his work in the nineteenth century. Public appreciation of landscape art grew steadily; a real impulse to popularity was given by the engravers, who sold thousands of landscape engravings.

How far actual appreciation of art did extend cannot now be known. A vigorous age is often insatiable in its curiosity; but curiosity is not appreciation. It was characteristic of the eighteenth century that men searched for novelty. In 1779 Horace Walpole found that "the rage to see public exhibitions is so great that sometimes one cannot pass through the streets where they are. But it is incredible what sums are raised by mere exhibitions of anything." In an orgy of spending, tradesmen who wanted to be "genteel" bought pictures; sometimes they bought forgeries. "Persons of all ranks set up for connoisseurs and even the lowest people tell familiarly of Hannibal Scratchi, Paul Varnish, and Raphael Angelo." Sir Joshua Reynolds was amazed at the Englishmen in Rome. "Instead of examining the beauties of the works of fame, and why they are esteemed, they only inquire the subject of a picture and the name of the painter, the history of a statue and where it is found and write that down."

As money fertilized the taste of a more numerous leisure class the mania for collecting things increased. The sale of antiques, real and fake, became a lucrative trade, although the English virtuosi had "no value for statues without hands." At the same time the English sculptors were busily employed by men who had seen or heard of the classic wonders of the antique world. Portrait busts were in great demand. Other kinds of busts were valued as household decorations. Sir Robert Walpole ordered them in dozen lots to place about the rooms and gardens of Houghton.

The architecture of the eighteenth century was mainly concerned with the construction of town and country houses, town halls, churches, and colleges. Although Sir Christopher Wren died in 1723 the Renaissance or classical architecture that he had helped to bring to England remained popular until the romantic revival of the nineteenth century. The result was a fine school of classical brickwork and the apogee of English domestic architecture. The followers of Wren were influenced by both Italian and French models and thus created a predominantly baroque style. The disciples of Inigo Jones, on the other hand, relied almost solely upon the Italian Andrea Palladio for their inspiration. Examples of the mellow classical style in an English idiom can best be seen in Chelsea Hospital, Hampton Court Palace, and in the livable houses with their white-painted sash windows and rubbed brick "arches." Early in the century Daniel Defoe remarked on the increase of building, especially about London. "This is most visible at Stratford in Essex . . . in which place above a thousand new foundations have been created, besides old houses repaired, all since the Revolution."

Discussions of Georgian art and architecture tend easily to become a catalogue of names. Among the best architects of the eighteenth century were Sir John Vanbrugh, Nicholas Hawksmoor, James Gibbs, the versatile William Kent, the Adam brothers, and Sir William Chambers. These are only a few of the outstanding figures. Perhaps mention should also be made of the earl of Burlington, great patron and battling champion of the Palladian style, of "Capability" Brown, the famous landscape gardener. The work of such men is still found in England and eastern America, portraying in brick and stone the vanished symmetry of another age.

Sir John Vanbrugh, poet, playwright, soldier, and architect was a student of Wren. His large masterpieces included the exuberant Castle Howard in Yorkshire and the gigantic Blenheim Palace, built for the Duke of Marlborough by a grateful nation. Blenheim had four acres of lead roof. Its exterior appearance was dramatic and effective. The interior, however, was divided into many small rooms; it was said that the kitchen was a hundred yards from the dining room. Many found Blenheim Palace pompous as well as comfortless. It was suggested that Vanbrugh's epitaph, with apologies to Martial, might read: "Lie heavy on him earth, for he Laid many a heavy weight on thee."

Nicholas Hawksmoor, the pupil of Sir Christopher Wren, was much influenced by Vanbrugh, with whom he often worked. Hence Hawksmoor's buildings were sometimes a characterless pastiche of Wren and Vanbrugh. His best achievements are in the quieter designs of the Clarendon Building, Oxford. He was also in part responsible for the main quadrangle of Queen's College, Oxford and the curious perversity of the northern quadrangle of All Souls, where twin "Gothick" towers stand strangely blunted, as if the architects and builders both were weary. James Gibbs, most of whose work was in the Inigo Jones tradition, designed the churches of St. Martin's-in-the-Fields and St. Mary-le-Strand in London, the Senate House at Cambridge, and the Radcliffe Library at Oxford. Gibbs also published two books on architecture; they were as elegant and scholarly as his designs.

William Kent built Holkham House in Norfolk and the Horse Guards, Whitehall; the latter is a splendid example of the Palladian style in the hands of a sensitive architect. Kent was also a pioneer in landscape gardening in a great gardening age. The brothers Robert and James Adam built the screen and gate of the Admiralty and Lansdowne House; they also designed many beautiful homes in London, and filled them with their famous masterpieces, fireplaces, painted panel and oval ceiling designs, expressive of the taste of their age. Sir William Chambers designed Somerset House where he took full advantage of the river frontage in his plans; a later generation built the Embankment and the full glory of Somerset House has since been hidden. Chambers also helped to introduce the mania for Oriental decorations that were used along with the popular Greek temples and statues; to him England owed the Pagoda in Kew Gardens.

As the century ended the ubiquitous John Nash was beginning to contribute his easy charm to Regency London. The age of brick was passing. Soon a deluge of stucco was to lead to the accusation that Nash "finds us all brick and leaves us all plaster."

LITERATURE

The great age of the coffee house and tavern was a period in which the world of letters flourished. At one level were the hack writers and journalists of Grub Street who usually wrote for party politicians newly aware of the value of press and pamphlet propaganda. Those who were fortunate enough to find wealthy patrons ate more frequently than their struggling fellows. As the habit of reading became more widely diffused among the population it was easier to make a living out of journalism. Some of the greatest writers of the age lent their pens, for a price, to political causes. The reader will recall the satire and invective of Addison, Steele, Defoe, and Swift early in the eighteenth century. The genius of their tracts is often forgotten. Thus the early decades of the century, usually called the "Augustan Age," brought food and money to those who had patrons or could sell their controversial manuscripts to political periodicals.

The "Augustan Age" was happy to think that it had much in common with the Romans and, to a lesser extent, the Greeks. Some of the aspects of culture and society in these years have already been described. Had not the substantial "Augustan Age" of Rome been secure, prosperous, stable? So, too, was the England of Queen Anne and George I. As cultivated interest in the Roman models of civilization increased, literary men turned to the classics, certain that they would find an earlier age of Reason. The Romans had eschewed emotion; they had formalized their literary style and language; they had been concerned with mankind and nature in the abstract. Such an attitude and method suited eighteenth century England very well. Indeed, all European literature in this period was moving away from the particular to the universal. "Man" meant the abstract qualities of all men, not a particular human being. "Nature" usually meant universal law, not particular streams or trees or sky. "Sky" meant Newton's astronomy rather than the deep blue over the parish steeple. "God" often meant a passionless Mathematician, not a Heavenly Father. It is easy to see why such a pervasive spirit of cold rationalism and the seeking out of abstractions and formulas followed in the wake of the new laws of Newton and Locke. The pendulum swung away from the fervors and emotions that had shot through so many chapters of the seventeenth century.

Many of the ideas of the Augustan Age are clearly illustrated in the work of Alexander Pope. Pope was a tormented and bitter genius. "The weakness of his body continued throughout his life," wrote Dr. Johnson, "but the mildness of his mind perhaps ended with his childhood." He took pains to conceal a humble birth; he could not conceal his physical deformities or his ill-health. "His life was a long disease." His Roman Catholicism jarred on some men. His methods were devious and often offensive. "He hardly drank tea without a stratagem." He was irascible, troublesome, capricious, egocentric. "Next to the pleasure of contemplating his possessions, seems to be that of enumerating the men of high rank with whom he is acquainted."

Despite such characteristics Pope surpassed all his contemporaries in his technical craftsmanship. He had been twelve years old when Dryden died in 1700 and, after Dryden, Pope took up and appropriately polished the classical regulations about writing and criticism. At the age of twenty he wrote his *Essay on Criticism,* carefully setting forth the authorized rules for literary composition. Dr. Johnson felt that "it exhibits every mode of excellence that can embellish or dignify didactick composition, selection of matter, novelty of arrangement, justness of precept, splendour of illustration, propriety of digression." Pope's translation of Homer, the mock heroic *Rape of the Lock,* the *Windsor Forest,* all represent, in admirable fashion, the spirit of his time.

In 1733 he published his *Essay on Man,* "a work of great labour and long consideration." It is a poem divided into four epistles and written in the usual heroic couplets. In such a poetic form the distinction between Pegasus and a rocking-horse is often not clear to a modern reader accustomed to the jagged lines of the present age. In the *Essay on Man* Pope is concerned with some philosophic problems that confront mankind in the abstract. What is man's relation to the universe? "Is Heaven unkind to man, and man alone?" What can man learn about himself? "Know then thyself, presume not God to scan; the proper study of mankind is man." What is man's relation to society? What is happiness? Much of the early eighteenth century is summed up in the famous words: "Whatever is, is right." Man will be happy if he accepts the fact that "Reason's whole pleasure, all the joys of sense, Lie in three words, health, peace, and competence." The aristocracy approved of such sentiments. The patrons, accustomed to the "Grand Tour" of Europe, helped to link English culture more closely to the Continent than it had been for several centuries. Alexander Pope was speaking the cosmopolitan language of cultured and sophisticated men in search of the fruits of reason and clearness of thought and expression.

The most characteristic literary figure of the age was Dr. Samuel Johnson. His father was a poor Lichfield bookseller. Johnson could not afford to complete his studies at Oxford and left to teach in a private school. He later became a hack writer in London. For three years he wrote up the parliamentary debates. In doing so he virtually composed the speeches recorded there, taking care "that the Whig dogs should not have the best of it." In 1755 he completed his famous *Dictionary*. His articles in *The Idler* and *The Rambler*, his novel *Rasselas*, and his *Lives of the Poets* are not read today except by the professed historian or student of literature. His literary work, great as it was, would not have brought him everlasting fame. Yet he is still quoted and discussed a hundred and sixty-five years after his death as no other writer except Shakespeare. Why is this so?

Dr. Johnson was incomparably one of the best talkers that the world has known. The greatest of English biographies was written about him; the author was James Boswell, a Scot. When his strong friend died Boswell's life ended in vice and shame. But he left the *Life of Johnson*. It is the work of a superb artist, full of wisdom and laughter and the human, sane, and roaring honesty of his great subject. Robert Louis Stevenson once said: "I am taking a little Boswell daily; I mean to read him now until the day I die."

Boswell, and Macaulay after him, described almost everything about the rugged Johnson: his huge and slovenly figure, his scrofulous face, his shrivelled and unpowdered wig, his St. Vitus' dance, his arguments at midnight, his bearish growls, his insolence, his temper, his habit of saving pieces of orange peel, his insatiable thirst for tea. What happened to those hardy enough to oppose him is admirably told in Max Beerbohm's essay "The Clergyman."

Johnson's deeply religious nature, carefully revealed by Boswell, stands forth in his own *Prayers and Meditations*. His piety was constant and fervent. He had little patience with the Methodists, whose principles he found "utterly incompatible with social or civil security."

When a lady talked to him of republicanism, he asked her to permit the footman to sit down and eat with them. "I, thus, Sir, showed her the absurdity of the levelling doctrine. She has never liked me since." A staunch Tory, he hated Whigs. "Sir, I perceive you are a vile Whig." Whiggism he defined as "a negation of all principle." He did not like Americans and Scotsmen. "The noblest prospect which a Scotsman ever sees is the high road that leads him to England." When Boswell told him that he had heard a woman preach at a Quaker meeting Johnson replied: "Sir, a woman's preaching is like a dog's walking on his hinder legs. It is not done well; but you are surprised to find it done at all." Boswell records that when Johnson had once "uttered an explosion of High Church zeal he had come close to my chair, and his eyes flashed with indignation. I bowed to the storm and diverted the force of it."

Dr. Johnson was more than a respected literary dictator, a Tory bulwark of the established order in society, church and state. The genius of Boswell has shown many other reasons why Johnson was held in high esteem by distinguished contemporaries such as Oliver Goldsmith, Sir Joshua Reynolds, David Hume, Adam Smith, Horace Walpole, and Edward Gibbon, greatest of English historians. He was not usually harsh or stern. His warmth and kindness were often shown. His common sense, his integrity and his sterling independence never wavered. "Sir, clear your mind of cant." Once Boswell wrote: "My reverence and affection for him were in full glow. I said to him 'My dear Sir, we must meet every year, if you don't quarrel with me.' *Johnson*: 'Nay, Sir, you are more likely to quarrel with me, than I with you. My regard for you is greater almost than I have words to express; but I do not choose to be always repeating it; write it down in the first leaf of your pocket book, and never doubt of it again."

On another occasion Boswell asked Johnson if he "really thought a knowledge of the Greek and Latin languages an essential requisite to a good education." The reply of Johnson was characteristic. "Most certainly, Sir, for those who know them have a very great advantage over those who do not. Nay, Sir, it is wonderful what a difference learning makes upon people even in the common intercourse of life, which does not appear to be much connected with it . . . a desire of knowledge is the natural feeling of mankind, and every human being, whose mind is not debauched, will be willing to give all that he has to get knowledge." When Johnson died in 1784 Boswell recorded the abrupt felicity of a friend: "He has made a chasm which not only nothing can fill up, but which nothing has a tendency to fill up. Johnson is dead. Let us go to the next best. There is nobody; no man can be said to put you in mind of Johnson."

As the years passed, some men of letters began to rebel against the exact and formalized coldness of expression prescribed by the

Augustan rules of composition. This happened for several reasons. For instance, the rising middle class was not much interested in neatly chiselled blocks of epigram; they wanted to read something that would appeal to their emotions as well as challenge their wits. This vague attitude was sharpened by the emotional tide of the Methodist movement running over the dykes of the Anglican Church. Perhaps, after all, the true "nature" of man might not be his "reason" but rather his emotions and his instincts. Inner sentiments and feelings are usually incapable of analysis by the tools of logic. Hume and Shaftesbury had said that man's moral and aesthetic judgments were not the offspring of reason. The road to Rousseau was opening and many men were ready to walk upon it. Impassioned appeals to the heart now began to replace the icy darts of classical satire or the rather thinly monotonous and conventional descriptions of nature. In religion the methods of rational ethical suasion were yielding to the heat, the zeal, the uncompromising ardor of Wesley and Whitefield. Later in the century Edmund Burke declared that "politics ought to be adopted, not to human reason, but to human nature, of which reason is but a part, and that by no means the greatest part."

The new cult of sentimentalism, sensibility, tenderness and compassion grew steadily. In 1759 Lawrence Sterne, that remarkable cleric, published his *Tristram Shandy*. At once he was famous. In 1768 he published the *Sentimental Journey*, filled with tears, love, and always laughter. The hypersensitive William Cowper decided that he would not include among his friends the man "who needlessly sets foot upon a worm." On the eve of the Romantic movement self-aware poets such as Thomas Gray, William Collins, and Christopher Smart found inspiration in country churchyards, ancient mythology, the Middle Ages, and the pure and simple lives of primitive and noble savages across the sea.

As the century neared its end the Romantic Age of literature began. Robert Burns and his fellows prepared the way for the *Lyrical Ballads*, for Wordsworth and Coleridge, for Keats and Shelley and Byron and all who felt the beauty and the slow stain of the world in the blood and along the heart. In these years the primal energy of William Blake burst forth. "A cistern contains: a fountain overflows." Blake overflowed. All but the most impudent of critics approach his engravings and his poems with an uneasy humility. Blake's poetry was written for those who felt and saw beyond the physical senses that "distort the heavens from pole to pole." He hated the "mind-forg'd manacles" of man, the evils brought by the "chartered Thames" and the "dark, satanic mills." In his *Marriage of Heaven and Hell* it is fitting that Hell is a type factory. The prophetic fury of his Preface to *Milton* every reader knows. Like so many of the romantic poets, Blake was a rebel. But philosophers and poets are not kings or unacknowledged legislators, and the New Jerusalem that Blake foresaw has not yet been built in England or anywhere else.

THE NEMESIS OF MATERIALISM

Thus the tides of taste in philosophy, religion, art and literature rolled towards the nineteenth century. Meanwhile, the floods of politics and war were removing many ancient landmarks. Men who were eager for adventure, profit, and glory explored and traded far from the coasts of England. The result was an expansion of the British Empire. Captain James Cook, for example, made three voyages to the Pacific between 1768 and 1779 and thus opened the way for British claims to Australia and New Zealand. Missionaries went forth to save the souls of savages. Explorers probed into Africa and Canada, minor prophets of the golden Victorian Age of Empire.

Meanwhile, too, new problems were brought by more effective attempts to apply the mercantile theory to England's colonies in America. The principle had long been held that by various acts of trade the commerce of the colonies could be controlled in the interests of the whole Empire. The colonists, for their part, viewed with mounting antagonism the numerous restrictions placed upon them. Because no really rigorous control of commerce had been undertaken in the seventeenth and early eighteenth centuries the American colonists evaded and defied the restrictive aspects of the navigation laws and the acts of trade with impunity. Trouble began when the British government finally decided to enforce the laws and tighten trade controls, as well as to tax. The colonists refused to obey the commands of London. The gates to revolution were unbarred.

The general values held by the majority of men at any given moment in the time-scale can usually be described with reasonable accuracy. It is not possible to do very much more. He who tries to embrace all individuals and events in easy patterns of description inevitably fails. Historians, philosophers, and economists have made many laws and carved many categories; it is a pity that the ideas and actions of human beings do not lend themselves to neat classifications. The rules of the game are various. There is no uniformity; only the deceptive semblance of it. Thus, in the eighteenth century, as in any age, multitudes of men pursued their individual hopes and ambitions down a labyrinth of many roads. The gap between the ideal and the actual remained wide, even among the enlightened sons of the Age of Reason. Dr. Johnson once said of a sceptic "If he really does think that there is no distinction between virtue and vice, why, Sir, when he leaves our houses let us count our spoons."

The country homes and coffee houses were comfortable places, symbols of an age of materialism, of a general ordered calm and outward conformity. As the century wore on, however, new winds chilled the aristocrats; their domestic empire began slowly to crumble about them. Part of the colonial empire in America was about to slip from their vainly clutching fingers. He who listened could hear the drums and fifes in America as the sparks flew upward. From across the English Channel was soon to come the sound of the rumbling tumbrils of Robespierre. The reign of virtue and the brotherhood of man was at hand. It was to be achieved by legislation, by the bayonet, by the poised and relentless knife of the guillotine.

Chapter 24

THE AMERICAN REVOLUTION
THE AIMS OF GEORGE III

O N OCTOBER 25, 1760, George II dropped dead in the act of dressing. His grandson, George III, succeeded to the throne. In recent years there has been much scholarly controversy about the history of this new king's reign. Is the familiar Whig interpretation of the age of George III warped and wrong? Or is it essentially correct? Several leading historians, particularly Sir Lewis Namier and Professor Herbert Butterfield, have stated, with strength and skill, their differing points of view.

"Born and bred in this country I glory in the name of Briton," declared George III in his first speech to Parliament. He considered Hanover "a horrid electorate." High Tories found it easy to attach their famished loyalties to him. The middle classes, remembering the moral weaknesses of the first two Georges, were pleased to have a monarch who was both a faithful husband and a pious Christian. At the beginning of his reign George III was the popular "Farmer George" of whom Lord Byron later wrote: "A better farmer ne'er brushed dew from lawn, A worse king never left a realm undone."

George III soon revealed several undesirable qualities. He was a bundle of complexes; he was arbitrary, petty, and obstinate. Compromise was a word he uttered with the utmost reluctance. He worked hard to fulfil the duties of kingship as he understood them. His mistakes and his tragic fate resulted from ill-directed ability, from obtuse stubbornness, from a set of perverted ideas, and from the incompetence of futile, pompous, and unimaginative ministers. Many of those ministers, contrary to the well-born assumption, did possess some qualities well above the ordinary; it was unfortunate that they were seldom employed in the service of the state.

The first clear purpose of George III was to destroy the system of cabinet government. He had been educated by his mother and carefully chosen tutors to believe in a strong monarchy. He had read Sir William

Blackstone's *Commentaries* in manuscript. In the first book of this famous work Blackstone wrote: "The King of England is not only the chief, but properly the sole magistrate of the nation. . . . He governs the kingdom. Statesmen who administer affairs are only his ministers." George III had also studied Bolingbroke's *The Idea of a Patriot King,* the importance of which has been described in Chapter 22. Bolingbroke had written that the king "must begin to govern as soon as he begins to reign. . . . He will put himself at the head of his people in order to govern or, more properly, to subdue all parties."

With such training the young ruler came to the throne in 1760 at the age of twenty-two. He was determined to be a "patriot king," to crush the cabinet system which placed limitations upon him, to rule as a king above parties in accordance with what he, and he alone, considered to be the national welfare. He would be, in effect, his own first minister of state. As a result George III was fated to do his country considerable mischief. He opposed the reform of Parliament, the emancipation of Roman Catholics, the relaxation of the Irish commercial laws, and concessions to the American colonies. He supported the slave trade. He wanted subservient "placemen" about him rather than ministers responsible to Parliament.

Before a royal non-party government could be created, the Whig oligarchy had to be overthrown. The Whigs were unpopular; they were weakened by their division into irreconcilable cliques and factions. George III began his attack upon them by telling the Whig Duke of Newcastle that he intended to take the patronage of the crown into his own royal hands. The "placemen" henceforth looked no longer to the Whig ministers for pensions and jobs but to George III himself. Thus the king soon had a solid body of personal supporters in the commons bound to him by ties of interest in their political and financial futures. This party was shortly called the "King's Friends."

The Scottish Tory sporting grandee, Lord Bute, as we have seen, served in the Pitt-Newcastle government as secretary of state because George III put him there in defiance of the chief principle of cabinet government. Bute told his personal friend the king what went on in the secret sessions of the cabinet. It will be recalled that Pitt was forced to resign in October, 1761; Newcastle left a few months later. Bute thereupon became prime minister and negotiated the Treaty of Paris that left England friendless in Europe. The house of commons approved the treaty for several reasons. Chief among them was the fact that Lord Bute paid cash for numerous votes; the "golden pills" of George III were a useful vaccine against opposition.

Newcastle had made bribery and jobbery the basis of Whig strength. George III was using the same means to advance the royal power. He used royal revenue to buy parliamentary seats as well as votes; the price of seats rose to £4,000. He scrutinized the lists of votes in Parliament and distributed rewards and punishments accordingly. Parliament would grow, he hoped, into the instrument of his will. It was a rather serious set-back when Lord Bute became the target of a venomous newspaper campaign. Bute was widely detested for his part in the shaping of the Treaty of Paris. Wincing under a barrage of insult and harassed by several public disturbances, Bute resigned. For the moment George III was baffled, but not subdued.

The Whigs still held a majority in the commons. They were divided into two major groups. The first was led by the Marquis of Rockingham, who leaned towards William Pitt and strongly supported the commercial classes. The second large section of the Whigs was commanded by George Grenville and the Duke of Bedford. Because they both really hated Pitt the king thought kindly of them. In 1763 a ministry was formed under the leadership of Grenville; the Duke of Bedford drummed his followers into line to support the new government. Grenville became prime minister; Bedford came into the cabinet. Grenville, a narrow-minded, diligent, constitutional formalist, remained in power until 1765.

THE WILKES CASE

The Grenville years are chiefly remembered because of the famous struggle between the government and John Wilkes. This individual published a journal called the *North Briton*. He used his paper as a mouthpiece for the popular hatred of the Treaty of Paris. Although Wilkes himself was a scoundrel his bitter denunciation of the treaty was widely applauded. In number forty-five of the *North Briton* Wilkes published a blunt and anonymous comment on the king's speech about the peace arrangements, declaring that George III had given "the sanction of his sacred name to the most odious measures and to the most unjustifiable public declarations from a throne ever renowned for truth, honour, and unsullied virtue."

George III insisted on the prosecution of Wilkes, and the cabinet acceded to his demand. A "general warrant," so called because it did not specify the person to be arrested or the property to be seized, was issued by the secretary of state against the "authors, printers and publishers" of the *North Briton*. Under this warrant John Wilkes and forty-five other persons were arrested. Under the same warrant the house of Wilkes was searched and some papers taken away. Wilkes claimed that the general warrant was "illegal and ridiculous." He asserted that as a member of the house of commons he was exempt from arrest except on charges of treason, felony, or breach of the peace.

Chief Justice Pratt decided that a general warrant was "a practice in itself illegal, and contrary to the fundamental principles of the constitution." Wilkes was released under a writ of *habeas corpus*. In 1765 Chief Justice Pratt, then Lord Camden, rendered a decision in the case of *Entick v. Carrington* that ended the use of general warrants for all time. "If it is the law, it will be found in our books. If it is not to be found there, it is not the law. . . . The silence of the books is an authority against the defendant and the plaintiff must have judgment." As a result of this decision Wilkes collected heavy damages in 1769.

Nevertheless, the cabinet controlled a majority in the house of commons. The commons, accordingly, voted that parliamentary privilege did not extend "to the case of writing and publishing seditious libels," ordered the forty-fifth number of the *North Briton* to be burned by the public hangman, expelled Wilkes from the house. The commons also resolved that the article in the *North Briton* contained "expressions of the most unexampled insolence and contumely towards his majesty, the grossest aspersions upon both houses of parliament, and the most audacious defiance of the authority of the whole legislature; and most manifestly tending to alienate the affections of the people from his majesty, to withdraw them from their obedience to the laws of the realm, and to excite them to traitorous insurrections against his majesty's government." Wilkes was seriously wounded by a crack shot who forced a duel upon him. He fled to France. When he did not return to face the main charge of libel filled against him by the government, he was outlawed by the Court of King's Bench.

George III had won a costly victory in the fray. The arbitrary methods used by the government to suppress freedom of speech had roused London. Members of Parliament were mobbed. The cry "Wilkes and Liberty!" rolled over England. Six years later the failure of the prosecution against the mysterious "Junius" for his *Letter to the King* established the right of the press to criticize the king himself. Popular opposition to the rough interference with a freedom long held inviolate created an ominous atmosphere. However, as the masses of the people had no vote the immediate political consequences of the widespread hostility to the king and his government were negligible.

THE COLLAPSE OF CABINET GOVERNMENT, 1765–1782

The cabinet was unpopular both for its position in the Wilkes combat and its colonial policy. In 1765 Grenville gave way to the sensible and second-rate Rockingham. The king disliked Rockingham and his old Whig and Newcastle party connections. Pitt declined to join the cabinet or support it. When Rockingham refused to yield to the royal wishes the "King's Friends" voted against him and his majority in the commons dwindled. George III finally decided to appeal to William Pitt. In 1766 Pitt agreed to become the head of a non-party ministry. He had slowly reached the conclusion that the party system was undesirable because it was so corrupt. In his attitude towards party government he was thus at last in agreement with his king.

The new cabinet of Pitt contained Whigs, Tories, and "King's

Friends." Internal dissension was inevitable among such heterogeneous groups. Pitt knew the dangers he faced in attempting to control this "diversified mosaic, a tessellated pavement without cement." He seemed to think that he could rule both George III and his colleagues. In this he was mistaken, for he was no longer the flashing comet of 1756; he was gouty, old, and ill. The old magic was gone, and the king worked steadily against him.

When Pitt went to the house of lords as earl of Chatham his influence in the commons further declined. His cabinet got into difficulties for arbitrarily using an order-in-council to prohibit the export of grain; it was defeated on a money bill; it was divided on the question as to whether conciliation or coercion should be used in America. Amidst this confusion and disorganization Pitt collapsed and retired, a sick lion. George III had called him "the trumpet of sedition." Then the young Duke of Grafton became nominal head of a weak and divided cabinet in 1768. The leader in the commons was the chancellor of the exchequer, the frothy and capricious Charles Townshend. It was clear that the maladies of the state were not soon to be cured.

Meanwhile the influence of George III and the "King's Friends" grew apace. The mounting power of the crown provoked Edmund Burke's *Thoughts on the Cause of the Present Discontents* (1770) and the anonymous *Letters of Junius* (1769–1772). The personal system of the king and the unrepresentative Parliament was dangerously at odds with the manifest will of the people.

It was to such a disturbed scene that John Wilkes returned from France in 1768. He stood as a candidate for Parliament in Middlesex and was elected. George III then wrote to Grafton: "I think it highly expedient to apprise you that the expulsion of Mr. Wilkes appears to be essential and must be effected." Parliament therefore expelled Wilkes as an undesirable libeller. Huge mobs milled through London demonstrating their support of the hero of the cause of liberty and the symbol of opposition to the personal rule of the king and a corrupt Parliament. Wilkes was again elected. The commons quite illegally proceeded to resolve that "Mr. Wilkes having been in this session of Parliament expelled the House, was and is incapable of being elected as a member to serve in the present Parliament." In a third election Wilkes was once more elected by a four-to-one majority. The commons again defied the choice of the electors by declaring that his opponent "ought to have been returned."

A tempest of riot mounted in fury. The scandalous Wilkes had become a martyr, an unseemly champion of popular rights. Clubs and societies were formed to promote the cause of parliamentary reform. The searing invective of the *Letters of Junius* declared that the house of commons did not represent the people. But the king was obstinate. He had beaten Wilkes again by arbitrary and illegal methods. Reckless of results, George III failed to see that a radical spirit was rising against the king and the royal creatures in the cabinet and the commons. He had played the king but not the patriot.

Meanwhile Charles Townshend had died and George III put Frederick, Lord North into the cabinet as chancellor of the exchequer. North was a Tory, an able political manager, and a man of considerable ability. In the preface to the last volume of the *Decline and Fall of the Roman Empire* Edward Gibbon remarked that North had many political opponents but was almost without a personal enemy. This judgment would seem to be in accord with the facts. The exact role of Lord North in the king's system of government and in the years of the decline of the first British Empire has yet to be determined by competent historians. In his later days, as blindness approached, North insisted that the actions of George III were misunderstood. In 1779 he said: "An honourable gentleman has talked much of the influence of the Crown. I do not know if such influence exists, that it has lately increased. For my part I can say with truth that I never endeavoured to exert it or make an improper use of it." In 1783 he wrote: "I have heard much in my time of secret influence. I never saw anything like it. Otherwise, I should have undoubtedly relinquished my situation."

In any event, there is no doubt that Lord North yielded to the wishes of his king. In 1770 George III accepted Grafton's resignation and Lord North became prime minister. The Tories and the "King's Friends" in Parliament provided an apparently unshakable majority. The king at last had obtained a subservient cabinet, a corrupted and pliable majority in Parliament. The Whigs were no longer a threat. George III was the real prime minister. For twelve years (1770–1782) he ruled as he pleased through Lord North. For a time cabinet government was at an end. These years marked the rise and advance of the American Revolution. To the Tories there was something darkly sinister in the American claim "which supposes dominion without authority and subjects without subordination." Across the Atlantic General Thomas Gage raised another question. "Surely the people of England," he said, "can never be such dupes as to believe the Americans have traded with them so long out of pure love and brotherly affection."

COLONIAL GRIEVANCES

When the French power in North America had ended, the American colonies found the imperial tie less necessary. The French had ceased to threaten them, and they no longer needed Britain as a shield against their enemy. At the same time the territorial arrangements in America resulting from the Treaty of Paris had made a thorough revision of colonial policy imperative. Apart from the Indian problems and difficulties about boundaries there were the long-standing colonial grievances regarding defense, trade, and colonial administration. The attempt to solve these problems led directly to the disruption of the Empire.

It seemed to the British authorities that there should be permanent garrisons in America to defend the colonists against the Indian tomahawks and a possible French renewal of the war. They proposed a standing British army of 10,000 men, of which 2,500 would be sent to the West Indies, the remainder to the thirteen colonies. Britain had always paid naval expenses; except for a few British troops the colonies had earlier supplied men for their own defense. But the colonies had never been a homogeneous area with identical interests. Common action to provide colonial troops, even in the Seven Years' War, had not been successful. It was extremely difficult to get the colonies to take any kind of united action. Troops had to be despatched from England because the colonies refused to fill the quotas of men required of them.

The British government felt that a standing British army in America would obviate the difficulty of gathering local military forces. This problem is only one illustration of the fact that before the coming of the American Revolution the thirteen colonies were divided by distance, by political, social, and economic differences, by mutual jealousies, and provincial attitudes. Only gradually were they willing to band together to oppose Britain. This happened in part because the loud and uncompromising radicals, led by Samuel Adams, knew what they wanted and made many converts. When the loyal American "Tories" made no adequate effort to obtain the support of numerous moderate men their cause was lost.

In matters of trade the protectionist mercantilist policy had kept the colonies in "firmer dependence" upon the mother country. The Empire was considered to be a single, consolidated economic unit. All European powers who held overseas possessions treated their colonial markets as a monopoly. The universally prevalent system by which trade was regulated and British colonies imported British industrial goods and exported raw materials to the mother country was more than a century old; it needed considerable adjustment.

Meanwhile, too, the stream of Britain's export trade had shifted. In the early eighteenth century the markets of the colonies had supplanted those of Portugal and the Netherlands. In 1700 one third of all British exports had found markets in the Netherlands. By 1760 this had been reduced to one seventh. In 1700 one seventh of Britain's exports had gone to Portugal. By 1760 this had fallen to one twelfth. In 1770 about three quarters of all the export manufactures of Manchester went to the thirteen colonies. The colonial market, therefore, was steadily mounting in importance. On the eve of the American Revolution one third of all Britain's exports found a market in the American colonies. The exports to Jamaica in 1764 equalled the total exports to all the English plantations in 1704. International trade rivalry, as has been shown in earlier chapters, relentlessly increased. In the *Wealth of Nations* (1776) Adam Smith deplored the rising conflict: "Commerce, which ought to be among nations as individuals a bond of union and friendship, has become the most fertile source of discord and animosity. The capricious ambition of kings and ministers has not, during the present and preceding century, been more fatal to the repose of Europe, than the impertinent jealousy of merchants and manufacturers."

The whole question of general imperial policy was further complicated by the fact that the colonial administrative machinery in England was both corrupt and inefficient. The greatest single weakness was divided power and responsibility. The privy council, the lords of the treasury, the customs commissioners, the secretaries of state, and the board of trade all shared in colonial administration. There was no central executive organ or controlling authority. Widespread indifference often prevailed about colonial affairs; important reports from the colonies frequently remained for weeks unopened and unread. The board of trade, for example, frequently fell in a slough of almost complete inactivity. Only sporadic attempts were made to stop illegal trade. Indeed, one of the reasons why the colonies grew so swiftly towards economic maturity was the lax enforcement of the acts of trade.

Across the Atlantic in the colonies the representatives of the crown suffered from this muddled and divided authority at home. In battles with the colonists the royal agents could not be certain of constant or firm support from Westminster. Controversies in the colonies were frequent. Not only did they arise out of questions of principle and policy but also from purely personal issues, sometimes of a ridiculously petty nature. British upper class governors and colonels did not usually mix well with raw democratic colonists. Thus class sympathies and antagonisms merged with the warp and woof of economic conflict. In the face of intermittent, inefficient, and often lax control from London, the colonists had in fact progressively become masters of their own internal affairs. Whatever the law might be, they tended to regard themselves as possessing the substance of independence.

When George Grenville succeeded Lord Bute as prime minister in 1763 several unfortunate steps in colonial policy were immediately undertaken. Many colonists, especially in Virginia and Pennsylvania, had looked forward to extensive operations in the Ohio valley. Hence they were angered when the British government decided temporarily to close the country west of the Alleghenies to settlement. Under the terms of a royal proclamation of 1763 a frontier "proclamation line" was established along the crest of the Alleghenies. West of this line further settlement was for the time being forbidden. The immediate British purpose was to conciliate the Indians through protecting them from any exploitation by greedy land-grabbers or traders. Satisfied

Indians would help to thwart any French effort to recover lost territory. This British reasoning did not appeal to the colonists concerned. They were aggrieved at what they deemed selfish and injurious restrictions.

A general tightening up of the whole imperial organization seemed in prospect. Strenuous efforts were made to increase British customs revenue by enforcing the acts of trade. The British taxpayers had a heavy burden of debt and it seemed reasonable that the colonists should be asked to lighten the load. There was considerable replacement and shuffling about of customs officers. Minor dependents of the Grenville tribe were hungry for jobs. The courts of admiralty were strengthened. Ships of the royal navy were sent out to hunt down smugglers. Colonial commercial interests began to suffer.

In 1764 Parliament passed the Sugar Act. Charles Townshend "did dazzle them by playing before their eyes the image of a revenue to be raised in America." This Sugar Act placed new customs duties on several articles, including Madeira wine, sugar, and molasses. The duty on molasses required under the Molasses Act of 1733 was cut in half. It was felt by the British authorities that this reduction of duty would make smuggling less profitable; therefore more molasses from the foreign West Indies would flow through legitimate channels; and hence the total revenue collected would be larger than when a higher duty prevailed.

The colonial merchants of the Atlantic seaboard loudly pointed out that this act was in fact designed to increase revenue, not to control trade. They had been in the habit of selling their products in the West Indies and buying sugar and molasses. They had smuggled the latter into the colonies, made cheap rum, and exchanged the rum for Indian furs and slaves from Africa. When Britain reduced this trade the colonists ran short of hard money with which to purchase British goods. They ran up large debts in London. Then they tried to issue more paper currency to make up for the hard money shortage. The British Parliament blocked that plan by the Currency Act of 1764, an act mainly designed to check the enormous issues of legal tender paper money earlier required to finance the war. Such were the immediate results of British efforts to suppress smuggling and increase the customs income. Meanwhile, as the north coastal cities angrily denounced the endorsement of trade and revenue controls, the tidewater south continued to demand more liberal bankruptcy laws; the Scotch-Irish of the foothills, who had no love for England, still noisily pressed for the removal of the galling frontier "proclamation line" of 1763. Land speculators were also incensed at the blocking of their opportunities beyond the Alleghenies.

Meanwhile Grenville went ahead with the British plans to station 10,000 British troops in North America. The home government was also anxious to have the colonists help defray the expense of this new military program. Could the British taxpayer be aided by a colonial contribution of somewhat less than one half of the cost of the standing army? In discussions with colonial representatives in London Grenville suggested that a sum of approximately £100,000 might be raised by a light stamp tax on certain articles. Benjamin Franklin proposed that the British government should trust to requisitions upon the colonial governments as in the past. Asserting that he was prepared to consider any colonial proposals, Grenville then asked if the colonists could agree on the proportion each colony should raise. The colonial agents could not promise any such united action. The colonists could only agree to protest against an imperial tax. Grenville then proceeded to carry through the Stamp Act in 1765 which required stamps purchased from the government to be placed on such articles as legal documents, calendars, advertisements, newspapers and pamphlets.

To the colonists, of course, there were many more implications in the Stamp Act than the obvious one of taxation to help maintain a standing army in America. British colonial officials had long desired to be "independent of the factious will and caprice of an assembly." Would the British "scheme of government new in many things" weaken the strength of colonial assemblies? If the British Parliament proceeded to extend its taxation system would that fact decrease the "power of the purse" in the hands of the assemblies? Would twenty battalions of British troops be used solely for "defending, protecting, and securing British colonies in America"? Or might they be used to coerce the colonists? Unlimited parliamentary power was dangerous. If Parliament could tax the colonists for one thing, it could tax them for anything. "Power to tax is power to destroy."

The result of the Stamp Act was a widespread disturbance in America. London was astounded at the unexpected speed and violence of the reaction. James Otis of Massachusetts said that the act did more "to stir opinion" in the colonies than all that had gone before. Most of the earlier grievances had been sectional. The Stamp Act was now a focal point for disaffection, especially among lawyers and men of business; their pride and their pockets both were touched. The Grenville policy was launched at a most inopportune time; it levied taxes when the colonies were in an economic depression; it called for money to redeem outstanding colonial bills of credit in addition to the stamp taxes. Hard money was not in the colonies because it was being sent to England. England, it seemed, wished to regulate commerce to the disadvantage of the colonists and then to tax the colonies in addition for revenue. The colonies slowly came towards a new degree of unity as they banded together to oppose the mother country. A new Radical group began to act as a leaven in colonial society; more and more loudly, the Radicals raised a chorus of general infidelity.

THE FAILURE OF BRITISH POLICIES

It was clear that no consistent imperial policy could be expected in the midst of the swift cabinet changes between 1765 and 1770. Even if such a policy had been agreed upon, the lack of coordination between the various governmental departments charged with ill-defined responsibility for colonial administration would have made impossible any unified pattern of effective change. The result of disputes, disorganization, and inefficiency was vacillation. Westminster was far from the colonies. There was a wide gap, wider than English statesmen knew, between their ideas about the colonies and the facts of the American situation. The colonists, rising in wealth and population, many of them living in the independent Puritan tradition of resistance, could be very formidable. It was natural that they should be irritated by the swiftly changing policies of London. It was natural, too, that as the British cabinets moved from one mistake and subterfuge to another, the minority of Radicals in the colonies increased in numbers and vehemence.

The stamp tax could not be collected. Royal officials were attacked. British goods were boycotted. Colonial merchants signed nonimportation agreements. Earlier opposition to British trade regulations had been entirely on the grounds that such controls harmed colonial trade. The challenge of the colonists to the Stamp Act rested on the basis of the new claim that it was beyond the legal right of Parliament to legislate for the colonies. The nine colonies represented in the Stamp Act Congress of 1765 insisted that the Parliament at Westminster had no power to impose "internal" taxes. They declared that the colonial legislatures were not subordinate to Parliament but equal in status to it. Most of the legal arguments advanced by the colonists were unsound; but what mattered, in a purely practical sense, was that the conditions in the colonies made the famous constitutional issue of "taxation without representation" inevitable.

The Stamp Act Congress was quite right in pointing out the distinction between taxation to regulate trade and taxation to raise revenue. Almost all the legislation of Parliament before 1763 had been concerned with either the regulation of trade or the establishment of post offices, the control of currency, and the like. If, in terms of strict legality, Parliament did have the right to tax the colonies the fact remained that Parliament had not done so for many years. Meanwhile the colonial situation had altered. Measures such as the Stamp Act, however legal, were widely regarded in America as offensive and arbitrary. Reinvigorated officialdom often strikes out blindly.

When Rockingham succeeded Grenville in 1765 British industrial and commercial interests were complaining heavily about the effect of the American boycott. Rockingham was further influenced by Edmund

Burke who sympathized with the colonists. William Pitt also spoke against the Stamp Act. Nevertheless, both Pitt and Burke supported Parliament's legal claim to sovereignty; they opposed the Stamp Act on the grounds of expediency. Pitt also insisted that taxation was no part of legislation. In such circumstances the act was formally repealed by Parliament in 1766 because it was "attended with many inconveniences" and likely to be "productive of consequences greatly detrimental to the commercial interests in these kingdoms."

A minority of the house of lords objected to the total repeal of the Stamp Act because "it would make the authority of Great Britain contemptible hereafter." The lords also pointed out that the Stamp Act had originally been passed by the commons "with very little opposition, and in this house without one dissentient voice . . . which, we presume, if it had been wholly and fundamentally wrong, could not possibly have happened." The dissenting lords were perhaps partly mollified by a Declaratory Act that was added to the repeal. It stated that Parliament "had, hath, and of right ought to have, full power and authority to make laws . . . in all cases whatsoever."

Grenville and his friends regarded the repeal of the Stamp Act as an affront to them as well as an error in imperial policy. When Rockingham was replaced by Pitt the controversy as to whether the colonies should be coerced or conciliated again burst forth in the cabinet. Pitt was for conciliation; most of his colleagues were not. Charles Townshend, chancellor of the exchequer, was faced with a deficit of about £500,000. To him the remedy seemed clear. He decided to revive the policy of taxing the colonies to pay for imperial administration. He also carried out another reform of the American customs service.

It seems that British statesmen never properly understood the distinction made by the colonists between taxes imposed to raise revenue and taxes imposed to regulate commerce. They apparently thought that the Americans were drawing a distinction between taxes levied internally on the colonies, as in the Stamp Act, and those levied externally, as in the acts of trade. This was the reason why Townshend's Revenue Act of 1767 levied new import taxes on such articles as tea, glass, paper, lead, and paint. Similar taxes had been in effect since the first part of the eighteenth century. The British felt that the colonists could have no sound grounds for objection to the new levies.

But the colonists did object. A half-healed wound was ripped open. They asserted that the earlier import duties had been levied to regulate trade; the new ones were imposed to raise a revenue. "How is this mode," asked John Dickinson of Pennsylvania, "more tolerable than the Stamp Act?" The non-importation agreements in the colonies were revived. British trade slumped once more. There were riots throughout the New England colonies, particularly in Boston. Four thousand British troops were quartered in that restless capital of

Massachusetts. Meanwhile, as usual, the members of the British government were not united in their views. Pitt spoke against the taxation of the colonies. "America is obstinate. America is almost in open rebellion. Sir, I rejoice that America has resisted." Burke again warned the cabinet of the dangers of its policy.

In March, 1770, during the last phase of the Grafton regime, the British cabinet decided after bitter debate to repeal all the Townshend duties except the tax on tea. Many hoped for a quiet return to normal conditions. This proved impossible. British soldiers in Boston got into quarrels with the citizens. The publication of letters in which some British officials had expressed disagreeable opinions of the colonists increased American indignation. After Lord North came into power his cabinet contained many men who were hostile to America. "The Tories," said Burke in 1772, "universally think their power and consequence involved in this American business." Pitt had warned the house of lords of the possible fatal consequences of a mistaken policy. No longer was Britain "the envy and terror of its neighbours." Many agreed about "the impudence, the absolute madness" of the attitude towards America of "weak, uninformed ministers and an irresponsible monarch."

Members of the house of commons with interests in the East India Company pointed out that the company had about 22,000,000 pounds of tea in British warehouses. The financial position of the company compelled it to ask the government for aid. Lord North replied by extending a government loan of £1,400,000. A new Tea Act in 1773 allowed the East India Company to send its tea directly to America and to sell it there without paying British export duties. Hitherto the tea had been sold at public auction in England and private English and American merchants had then shipped it abroad. The new Tea Act thus threatened to ruin most of the private merchants and put the East India Company in a monopoly position through its selected colonial agents. Despite the fact that the retail price of tea in America was cut in half the company monopoly alarmed the colonial merchants from Boston to Charleston. The colonists said: "If Parliament can give a monopoly of one article to the disadvantage of individual trade, then Parliament can grant other dangerous monopolies." It was a tragic mistake to use the colonies as an attempted means of solving the problems of a corrupt and nearly bankrupt East India Company.

In Charleston the merchants stored the tea in damp cellars. In Philadelphia and New York they compelled ships' captains to take it back. In Boston they had a mighty ally in Samuel Adams, a man who had failed in his brewing business but who proved to an excellent organizer and popular leader. In 1773, some of his followers, disguised as Indians, boarded ships of the East India Company in Boston harbor and threw overboard about 350 chests of dutiable tea valued at £15,000.

This invasion of sacred private property rights was received with rage in England. Lord North declared: "We are now to establish our authority or give it up entirely; when they are quiet and return to their duty we shall be kind." Britain must "subdue the insolent violence of those men who have so grossly violated public authority." Another chapter had been written in the history of American taxation. "What variety of schemes have been adopted," said Edmund Burke, "what enforcing and what repealing; what bullying, and what submitting; what doing and undoing; what straining and what relaxing; . . . what shiftings, and changes, and jumblings of all kinds of men at home."

AN EMPIRE LOST

William Pitt pleaded for "mutual confidence" and "something to trust to." Edmund Burke begged Britain to restore "the former unsuspecting confidence of the colonies in the Mother Country." Nothing of the sort occurred. A fatal and miserable policy of alternate coercion and vacillation was tried again. In 1774 George III and Lord North first attempted coercion. The charter of Massachusetts was suspended; the port of Boston was closed; the capital was moved to Salem; new provisions were made for quartering British troops in Boston; the right of public meeting was restricted. British officials accused of crimes in the thirteen colonies were to be tried in Halifax or in Great Britain.

The Quebec Act of the same year gave further offense to the colonists, although it was not intended in any sense to be punitive. The act extended the boundaries of Canada to the Ohio; this cut off the western lands coveted by Massachusetts, New York, Pennsylvania, and Connecticut. The French Canadians were generously allowed to retain French civil law and to keep and practice their religion; this concession to the French Roman Catholics was especially offensive to Puritan New England.

George III dismissed a petition from Massachusetts as "frivolous and vexatious." He wrote to Lord North: "The die is cast. The colonies must either triumph or submit . . . If we take the resolute part, they will undoubtedly be very meek." In England there were a few Englishmen who stood with the colonists, especially those who felt that George III wanted to fix tyranny on both England and America. In the colonies large sections of the mercantile, professional, and landowning classes strongly desired to keep the British connection, particularly in the southern and middle colonies. The ignorance and ineptitude of the British government and the obstinacy of the British king resulted in a handling of the situation that drove many of the moderates to rally to the side of the Radicals and Samuel Adams. This the conservatives and moderates had not wanted to do; but they had no alternative. The Radicals wanted revolt; and revolt it would be.

The opinion of the average Englishman, who was also a taxpayer, was not generally favorable to America. He felt that the colonies should be subject to taxation and control by the mother country. He asked why the colonists refused to contribute to their own defense. He did not understand what the Americans meant by the phrase "no taxation without representation." The colonists meant, of course, that the taxation should be imposed by a body, such as a colonial assembly, in which they felt that they were somehow more directly represented than in the British Parliament. Englishmen who thought about the problem at all remarked that almost every adult male in England paid some taxes, but only about ten percent had the vote. The rest were really not represented in Parliament to a much greater extent than the colonists across the Atlantic.

In 1774 the First Continental Congress was held in Philadelphia. Representatives from all the thirteen colonies except Georgia attended. The British government was asked to repeal the recent "Intolerable Acts." Until grievances were redressed there was to be a complete boycott of trade with Britain. Soon British regulars and colonial militiamen began to exchange shots around Concord and Lexington. The conservative classes wanted the threatening struggle avoided. The Radical element wanted it carried on; some saw shining brightly a final goal of full independence from Great Britain.

In 1775 a second American Congress made a feeble gesture towards peace by sending the Olive Branch petition to London. As this petition explicitly denied the legislative power of the British Parliament there was little hope of its success. The Congress also appointed Colonel George Washington Commander-in-Chief and General of the American Army. Washington was a conservative and aristocratic Virginian planter descended from a Norfolk county family. Able, quiet, and infinitely patient, George Washington moved slowly towards the final victory that brought the First British Empire to an irreparable end.

The British army sent out to reconquer rebellious America was commanded by Sir William Howe. British forces totalled about 60,000 men, widely distributed over long and vague fronts. They were aided by colonial Loyalists, who supported the British cause; thousands of these United Empire Loyalists later moved to Canada, especially to regions now in the provinces of New Brunswick and Ontario. British problems of supply were tremendous. The theatres of war were widely spread; sailing vessels had to carry much food and equipment across the Atlantic from England. The towns on the coast could easily be occupied but not the vast spaces back from the sea. Colonial armies might be beaten; but they often melted away to fight again later. Britain's General John Burgoyne was not optimistic in 1775: "After a fatal procrastination, not only of vigorous measures but of preparations for such, we took a step as decisive as the passage of the Rubicon, and now find ourselves plunged at once in a most serious war without a single requisition, gunpowder excepted, for carrying it on."

Of course the colonial armies had difficulties, familiar to every American student. It was often hard to get and keep troops. The paper money issued by the Continental Congress became worthless. Some colonists preferred to sell supplies to the British who paid in gold. Many were reluctant to go out of their own counties to do battle with the British; if the British came to them, then they would fight; but they did not want to march long distances to aid colonists in other areas of conflict.

In January, 1776, Thomas Paine's explosive pamphlet *Common Sense* was published. "The fate of Charles the First," wrote Paine, "hath only made kings more subtle, not more just!" He demanded complete separation from Britain. Over 120,000 copies of his pamphlet were sold in America within three months. The ideas of Locke and Montesquieu and Sir Edward Coke were widely quoted and discussed; what the eighteenth century philosophers said about natural rights and fundamental laws filled many a notebook besides that of Thomas Jefferson.

Across the Atlantic the despairing voice of Edmund Burke had firmly warned of events to come. "If intemperately, unwisely, fatally, you sophisticate and poison the very source of government, by urging subtle deductions, and consequently odious to those you govern, from the unlimited and illimitable nature of supreme sovereignty, you will teach them by these means to call that sovereignty itself into question . . . If that sovereignty and their freedom cannot be reconciled, which will they take? They will cast your sovereignty in your face. Nobody will be argued into slavery." In March, 1775, during his famous remarks on conciliation with America Burke had said: "The question with me is not whether you have a right to render your people miserable; but whether it is in your interest to make them happy." Many of his sentences are famous still. "Magnanimity in politics is not seldom the truest wisdom." "A great Empire and little minds go ill together."

Early in 1776 Sir William Howe was compelled to evacuate Boston, carrying off his troops by sea to Halifax. In the summer he came south and captured New York. In July, the third American Congress met at Philadelphia and drew up the Declaration of Independence, asserting "that these United Colonies are, and of right out to be, Free and Independent States; that they are absolved from all allegiance to the British Crown." Thus the Declaration of Independence broke the ties that had become progressively so frayed and weak.

The British defeated Washington on Long Island, captured New York, and drove the dwindling colonial army into Pennsylvania. During the following winter Washington crossed the Delaware, captured Trenton and won a victory at Princeton, New Jersey. Then, in 1777, the

British made a serious miscalculation. Military operations were as ill-conducted as the political. According to the British plans, Burgoyne was to move down from Canada to join Howe at Albany. Thus communication would be established between Canada and New York and New England would be cut off. But Howe sailed away to fight the battle of Brandywine Creek and captured Philadelphia. The operation took longer than he had expected. Thus he was not in a position to put pressure on the Americans who were gathering to oppose Burgoyne's northern army advancing down the Hudson. In October, 1777, Burgoyne's position had become hopeless; he was forced to surrender at Saratoga with his army of 3,500 men. This was the turning point of the war.

French despotism was now emboldened to come to the aid of liberty. Early in 1778 France allied herself with America and entered the conflict on the side of the colonists. Here was an opportunity to reverse the decision of the Seven Years' War. In 1778 the French attacked the West Indies and began to hamper British communications with the American mainland. American privateers, led by the famous Paul Jones, harassed British shipping. French financial aid helped to bolster the colonial cause.

In 1779 Spain joined France and attacked Britain in the Mediterranean. France sent a fleet to strike at British power in India. The Netherlands were added to Britain's foes in 1780. Disputes about the rights of neutral ships led to the formation of the League of Armed Neutrality. This League included Russia, Prussia, Sweden, Denmark, and Holland who asserted their right to trade with the belligerents. They threatened to declare war upon Great Britain if the British continued to seize ships of neutral northern maritime powers trading with Britain's enemies. All these developments weakened Britain's offensive power in America. Could she stand alone against half the world?

As the war mounted in violence Britain captured St. Pierre and Miquelon and the French posts in India. Her foes stirred up a rebellion in India, seized British territory on the west coast of Africa and the West Indies, and laid siege to Gibraltar. Meanwhile British foreign trade was heavily hit across the seas and in Europe. With the spread of the conflict the maritime insurance rates went up, reaching a height of thirty percent. In 1781 the government of Lord North floated its last war loan; Lord North's cabinet said that British credit could stand no more loans. Scores of British merchant ships were being captured by the enemy. The long tale of disaster promised to be longer still.

Only in the southern colonies after 1778 did the British achieve some success. Sir Henry Clinton captured Charleston. Lord Cornwallis won several battles in North and South Carolina. Nevertheless, Cornwallis could not profit from his victories. Stubborn guerrilla warfare in the interior compelled the British to hug the coast. Slowly Cornwallis advanced to Yorktown with 7,000 men. There, in October, 1781, disaster fell upon him. A sudden advance of Washington enabled an American and French army to blockade the British by land at a moment when a French fleet in Chesapeake Bay held mastery of the sea. The position of Cornwallis was hopeless. He surrendered.

The great civil war in America was virtually ended by the military catastrophe at Yorktown. Lord North exclaimed: "It is all over!" Even George III reluctantly conceded that further hostilities against America would be useless. Popular clamor for an early end of the war had risen steadily after 1778. Upon George III had fallen an increasing public condemnation for his share in the conduct of military affairs. Demands for the reform of Parliament had multiplied. The war must be ended. The personal power of the king must be reduced. The constitution must no longer be subverted by an obstinate and maladroit monarch.

A debate in the house of commons about Lord North's government in 1779 had revealed a bitterness of temper reminiscent of the seventeenth century. References were made to the "most calamitous and disgraceful effects" of Lord North's administration. "If anything can prevent the consummation of public ruin, it can only be by new counsels and new counsellors without further loss of time." The Whig Charles James Fox reminded Parliament and the nation that "the present sovereign's claim to the throne of this country was founded only upon the delinquency of the Stuart family—a circumstance which should never be one moment out of his majesty's recollection." In 1780 George Dunning's famous resolution declared "that the influence of the crown has increased, is increasing, and ought to be diminished." The commons carried Dunning's resolution by a vote of 232 to 215. Was what Dunning had called a "most corrupt and unconstitutional influence" now to be diminished?

Lord North had wanted to resign in 1779. George III, aware that North's departure would lead to the collapse of the royal experiment in personal government, had refused to let him go. After Yorktown the house of commons accepted without a division a motion demanding peace with America. North insisted on resigning; he left the side of his king in March, 1782. Yorktown ended the attempt of George III to regain political power for the crown. Since the day of North's resignation England has been governed by a cabinet responsible to the house of commons. Parliamentary and party government were restored. George III talked of abdicating and going to Hanover. His political and mercantile Empire had been broken asunder. A new nation had come into existence in America. Bolingbroke's prescription had failed.

THE RETURN OF THE WHIGS

George III could do nothing but call in the Whigs, long his open

Section IV

THE EIGHTEENTH CENTURY

An Experiment with the Air Pump—an 18th Century engraving showing the popular interest in natural science.

Sir Isaac Newton.

Sketch of Napier's "Bones"—a computing machine devised by the inventor of logarithms.

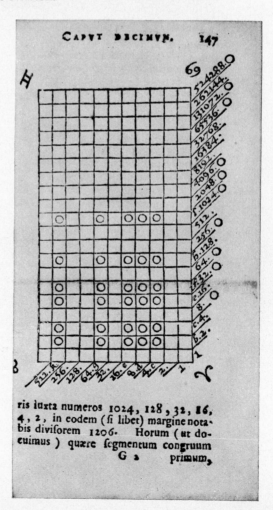

ris iuxta numeros 1024, 128, 32, 16, 4, 2, in eodem (si libet) margine notabis divisorem 1206. Horum (ut docuimus) quære segmentum congruum

G 2   primum,

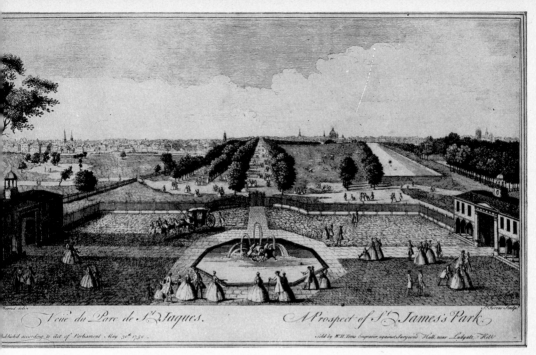

St. James's Park, London, in mid-18th Century.

An 18th Century country-house—Bradbourne, near Maidstone, Kent.
Photograph, copyright *Country Life*.

" 'Change Alley became a roaring hell-porch of insane and dishonest speculators" during the days of the South Sea Bubble. Here is a group of contemporary satiric prints on the subject, including playing-cards.

Sir Robert Walpole (*left*) and Speaker Onslow in the House of Commons.

Tea Time,
A.D. 1720.

"Canvassing for Votes"—one of Hogarth's contemporary satires on British election methods.

Alexander Pope.

Samuel Johnson by Sir Joshua Reynolds.

Thomas Gainsborough, a self-portrait.

David Garrick and his company in the Green Room at Drury Lane.

An Exhibition at the Royal Academy of Arts, A.D. 1771.

Specimens of Wedgwood ware, *circa* 1780.

John Wesley.

The Tree of Life, a graphic presentation of Methodist doctrine.

Adelphi Terrace, London, in which the brothers Adam strove for unity of design in a street facade.

A general view of London in the mid-18th Century.

George III.

The battle of Quiberon Bay, November, 1759. In the center, the *Royal George* leads the British fleet in pursuit of the French under Admiral Conflans.

Quebec, *circa* 1760.

An 18th Century British caricature of George III, satirizing the employment of Indians in war.

A View of the Year 1765 by Paul Revere, expressing an American view of the Stamp Act.

The siege of Yorktown—a painting after a sketch by Berthier who was present with Rochambeau's army.

Parliamentary Reforms

enemies. During their exile the Whigs had advanced some distance from the days of the corrupt Newcastle oligarchy. Exasperated by the methods of George III they intended to undertake internal parliamentary reforms by decreasing graft and corruption. Despite their aristocratic leadership the Whigs were also prepared to look beyond the walls of Parliament and to be more sensitive to public opinion than in earlier days. The Whig and Tory parties had been born in the seventeenth century as a result of one major question: should the king be coerced? With the French Revolution was to come a second question: is the gospel of democracy inimical to the English system of government? The Tories were to stand for a time united against any democratic extension of the franchise. The Whigs were to divide into two groups: the conservative Whigs, led by Edmund Burke, and the liberal Whigs, headed by Charles James Fox.

In 1782, Edmund Burke was in his early career and his emphasis was therefore still liberal. His glittering and unreliable oratory bulwarked his patron Lord Rockingham, leader of the old Whigs and now called by George III to be prime minister. Before Rockingham took office he demanded and received the king's assurance that he would agree to the recognition of the American colonies as independent states and would not oppose new laws designed to cleanse Parliament of corruption.

The first step of the Whigs was to pass Burke's Economic Reform Bill. This legislation drastically reduced the number of sinecures and places that could be given by a government to placemen in the house of commons. Never again would it be possible to bribe Parliament wholesale in the manner of Walpole, Newcastle, and George III. Charles James Fox wanted to reform the system of representation and abolish rotten boroughs; but his fellow Whigs would not go along with him on such a revolutionary proposal.

To George III Rockingham had long been obnoxious. When the king discovered rifts in the Whig party he tried his familiar gambits again. The Whig faction once commanded by Pitt was now led by the enigmatic Lord Shelburne, home secretary in the Rockingham cabinet. Shelburne, called by his foes "The Jesuit of Berkeley Square," was an unusually able man. The royal attempts to divide the prime minister and his home secretary were succeeding when Rockingham died in July, 1782.

Then a quarrel between Shelburne and Charles James Fox, the foreign secretary, flamed into the open. Shelburne was technically responsible for negotiations with the colonies; Fox was responsible for concluding peace with France. The two could not agree about their functions or their respective powers. They fought about the negotiations in Paris. They deliberately kept each other misinformed. Their representatives in Paris were bewildered at the varieties of instructions crossing the Channel from Westminster. The split in the cabinet widened; what was worse, it was soon discovered by the Americans and the French. They used their knowledge to get all they could.

The remarkable Charles James Fox, the greatest of the Whigs and "the eternal schoolboy," led a notorious and vicious private life; many moral men were alienated from him despite his kindly nature, his abilities, and his Whiggism. Fox had stood forth as a champion of the colonists between 1776 and 1780, an unpopular cause. He had wanted to recognize American independence long before Yorktown; what he said appeared to many to be close to treason or sedition, or both. Now, in July, 1782, he resigned when his colleagues refused to call Shelburne's representatives home from Paris. George III was pleased at the turn of events. He gave the prime ministership to Lord Shelburne. It was now Shelburne's task to make peace with all the enemies of England.

THE TREATIES OF PEACE

In May, 1782 Admiral Rodney restored British naval power in the Atlantic by defeating France's Admiral De Grasse in the West Indies. Gibraltar, long assaulted by Frenchman and Spaniard, was at last relieved. Britain's position at the peace conference was therefore improved. Meanwhile Benjamin Franklin learned that the French minister, Vergennes, was carrying on secret negotiations with Great Britain with a view to limiting the new United States to the territory east of the Alleghenies. In the French-American alliance of 1778 the two powers had agreed not to negotiate separately. Faced by French duplicity Franklin likewise entered into secret discussions with the British government.

The peace arrangements were finally concluded at Versailles in 1783. To France was returned St. Pierre and Miquelon, her West African settlements, the islands of Tobago and St. Lucia in the West Indies, her trading posts and privileges in India. To Spain was returned Florida, which she had lost in 1763; and Minorca, which she had lost in 1713. Spain handed over the Bahamas to Britain. The Dutch and the British mutually restored all conquests, except in one minor case.

The thirteen colonies were given their independence as the United States of America. The territory of the new nation was to extend west to the Mississippi and north approximately to the Great Lakes and the St. Lawrence; the boundary west of the Great Lakes was left to be settled at a later date. To Americans was granted the right to fish off Newfoundland. Private debts contracted before the war were to be paid. The British and Americans were to have the right to navigate the Mississippi. The United States promised that Congress would recommend to the various states the restoration of property taken from the Loyalists. This recommendation of Congress that justice should be done to the Loyalists was never heeded by the state governments. Thousands of United Empire Loyalists fled persecution and sought safety and happiness in Canada and over the seas. Across the tracts of time many descendants of the Loyalists returned to live in the United States. The grass grows swiftly over the battlefield. Harsh and bitter memories have been blurred and softened by the mist of the years.

To Canada, so effectively British during the Revolution, there was thus added forty thousand Loyalists, "abhorrers of Republicanism." In 1791 the Canada Act created two British provinces north of the Great Lakes and the St. Lawrence: Upper Canada, largely English, now the province of Ontario; and Lower Canada, mainly French, now the province of Quebec. Each was given a legislative assembly; the road towards self-government stretched ahead for sixty years. What happened in the Canadian development of responsible government, her greatest political gift to the Commonwealth and Empire, is described below in Chapter 30.

ENGLAND IN 1783

When George III rejoiced at the resignation of Charles James Fox and called Lord Shelburne to be prime minister he thought that Fox would stay out in the political wilderness. But Fox thought otherwise. Late in 1783 he outraged the nation's sense of decency by forming an unexpected and shocking political alliance with the Tory Lord North against whom he had shot his venomous shafts for so many years. George III was astounded by the "desertion" of North and furious at the success of Fox, whom he hated. The Fox-North union, said the king, was "the most unprincipled coalition the annals of this or any other nation can equal." Fox was the leader of the detested Whigs; he was an intimate friend of George, the Prince of Wales, and George III blamed Fox for corrupting his son. In the eyes of the king, North was an ungrateful traitor. Fox and North controlled a majority in the house of commons. They stood together and defeated Shelburne in April, 1783. Then they formed a cabinet. George III could not keep them out of power; but he angrily determined to have his revenge.

The king's chance soon came. Through the house of commons Fox passed a bill to extend government control over the East India Company. George III called the bill "a monster of graft and iniquity," which it was not. In December, 1783, he authorized Earl Temple to make the statement among the peers that "whoever voted for the India Bill was not only not his friend, but would be considered his enemy." The house of lords rejected the bill.

A motion was at once passed in the commons protesting that "to report any opinion or pretended opinion of his majesty upon any bill or other proceeding depending in either house of parliament, with a view to influence the votes of its members, is a high crime and misdemeanour derogatory to the honour of the crown, a breach of the fundamental privileges of Parliament, and subversive to the constitution of this country." This "midnight conspiracy against the constitution" by "an infamous string of bedchamber janissaries" gave George III the opportunity he sought. He at once dismissed Fox and North. They had held power for only eight months.

Who could now command and hold a majority in the commons? George III called young William Pitt, the second son of the deceased Pitt the Elder, earl of Chatham, to form a cabinet. The precocious Pitt was the leader of a reviving Tory party. He had been elected to

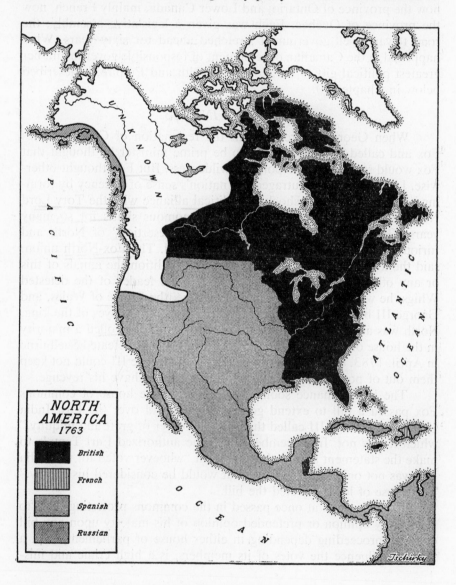

NORTH
AMERICA
1763

British

French

Spanish

Russian

Tschirky

Parliament at the age of twenty-one and had been chancellor of the exchequer under Shelburne. At the age of twenty-five he was now prime minister. "A kingdom trusted to a schoolboy's care," laughed his political foes. Fox and North were experienced and wily. How could Pitt cope with them?

By their voting power in the commons Pitt's foes held up supplies. They defeated Pitt on every measure; still he would not resign. At last, when the opposition once sank to a majority of one, he asked for a dissolution of Parliament. The nation had watched Pitt struggling with the old politicians. For several reasons, some of which have been

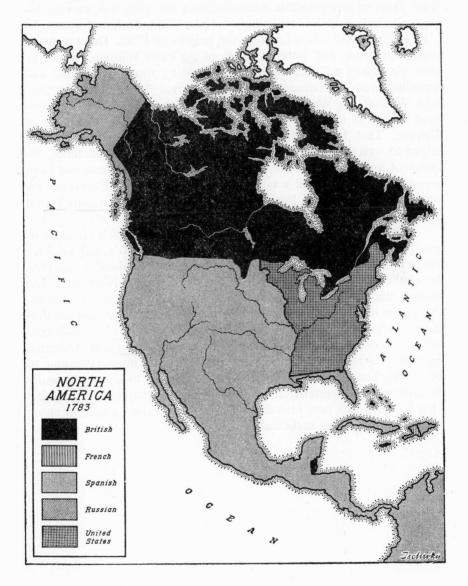

NORTH
AMERICA
1783

British

French

Spanish

Russian

United
States

Tschirky

earlier described, North and Fox were not popular. Were they seeking only the spoils of office? Were they ruthlessly spurning the rules of fair play in the methods they were using against Pitt?

In the general election of 1784 the supporters of North and Fox lost seat after seat. Pitt came back into power with a working majority. George III, who preferred the Tory Pitt to the hated Whigs, also found that Pitt would have his way, even against the king. Soon Pitt's position was as powerful as Walpole's had been. He was the master of the house of commons; he was the master of the king.

The long assaults of George III on cabinet government had ended. After years of irresponsible administration the king was moving towards those dark valleys when he was to be blind, deaf, and insane. In 1783 England had fallen far from the heights of 1763. There were no longer the strong and intrepid hands of the elder William Pitt at the helm, despising political corruption, deriding rotten boroughs, and appealing from Parliament to what he called "The Great People." John Wesley and William Pitt, earl of Chatham, had been the two great leaders of idealistic reaction from the materialism of the age of Walpole. That brightness had departed by 1783. George III had helped to wreck the first Empire by low cunning, by his methods, his choice of agents. To him, at least, the Whig historians have not been unjust. In 1783 England was unpopular and defeated. Everyone saw that an empire had been lost. Not everyone realized that a constitution had been saved.

When the younger William Pitt became prime minister in December, 1783, a new era was opening for England. Pitt's first ministry was to last for seventeen years. There was to be a decade of peace, then the challenge of the Jacobins and the challenge of Napoleon. The French, underestimating England's power, received a serious shock. One of the reasons for it had almost passed unnoticed. Amidst the dramatic years of war and rebellion in the last half of the eighteenth century there occurred a less dramatic economic revolution. Defeated England was rapidly becoming the workshop and financial center of the world. These economic changes were destined to alter profoundly the course of all western civilization. The next chapter will describe what happened as new instruments of power hurried mankind along new roads of progress and catastrophe.

Chapter 25

THE ECONOMIC REVOLUTION
PROGRESS AND POWER

THROUGHOUT his history man has added to the strength of his hands new instruments of precision and power. In the beginning there were a few crude hand tools, primitive agriculture, the use of fire. Nature surrendered her secrets slowly. During a few thousand years men succeeded in making strong states and empires. They created systems of religion and philosophy. They deliberately sought to conquer the physical world. They changed their ways of living in proportion as they discovered new ways to master the external world of things. This conquest of nature forms a large part of what is usually meant by the word "progress." Over three hundred years ago Francis Bacon observed that there was "much ground for hoping that there are still laid up in the womb of nature many secrets of excellent use . . . which have not yet been found out."

In recent centuries there came a swift improvement of tools, the rise of strange technical skills, the broadening achievements of science. An increasing part of the outer world of nature has been subdued to human use. All the diverse activities of men and things have been altered. Speed, power, mass production, intricate patterns of government, business, industry, all these have emerged in the sudden acceleration of man's ability to create material wealth in an age of scientific and social revolution. Not long ago robust and poetic enthusiasts proclaimed the coming of a new Golden Age: they were then unaware that western civilization might in fact be past its zenith.

Disputes about the proper distribution of the expanding production of wealth have led to furious class conflicts, to discordant political and economic battlecries, to general confusion and frequent despair. Everywhere men discuss the world economic disturbance and the haphazard social arrangements. Into the equations of human society science and its machines have thrown new terms. In the whirlpool of changing conditions the nature, spirit, habits, and ideas of man have

491

remained but clumsily adjusted. Science has remained passive, unprejudiced, and indifferent in the presence of the complex and unstable society it has helped to create. On every hand the brute realities show the failure of man to achieve a rational control of his social relations. The problems created by the release of atomic energy give added point to the proverb that it is easier for man to take a city than to govern himself.

The last major surge in mankind's industrial advance began in eighteenth century England and still continues. The consequences of this famous and frequently described economic revolution profoundly altered the lives of Englishmen and, through them, affected the larger part of the world.

THE REVOLUTION IN AGRICULTURE

Few really sudden shifts take place in economic history. The movements of economic progress and change are much slower than melodramatic writers might think. Economic historians see the rapidity of developments in the eighteenth century; they also note that the old industrial and agricultural order had begun to crumble long before Erasmus Darwin wrote his poem in praise of steam, Adam Smith his *Wealth of Nations,* Jethro Tull his *Horse-Hoeing Husbandry,* Richard Rolt his new *Dictionary of Trade and Commerce,* or John Payne his *New Tables of Interest.* Economic tides are constant, strong, and often almost imperceptible.

The torrent of creative energy and variety of achievement characteristic of the late eighteenth century changed the face of England. Two movements, inextricably mingled together, went on in an increasing flood to give English society its contemporary form. The first is usually called the "Agricultural Revolution"; the second the "Industrial Revolution." Before the modern industrial civilization was well under way in England there occurred two silent rural changes of vast significance: a revolution in the methods of farming and the enclosure of the common fields.

"I love agriculture," wrote the earl of Bristol to Arthur Young, famous for his vivid accounts of travels in England and France, "because it makes good citizens, good husbands, good farmers, good children; because it does not leave a man time to plunder his neighbour, and because by its plenty it bereaves him of the temptation." The general state of things before the eighteenth century revolution in agriculture may not have been exactly as the honest earl of Bristol described them. Nevertheless, the slow pace of English rural life had obviously much to do with producing the kind of men who harrowed clods and drove stunted cattle over the heath.

Few improvements in farming methods had been made in England since the Middle Ages. The conservative temper of English farming past and present united with communication difficulties to prevent the spread of the few new agricultural techniques that were developed in some localities. The medieval three-field system, characterized by the age-old strip-farming custom, still was the common practice. England in 1700 was mainly a land of agriculture. Large open fields without fences or hedges surrounded each village. Farm production kept pace with the growing population; the people were fed. Until the latter part of the century there was usually a little grain left over for export. Large areas of England were left untilled; heaths and forests blanketed wide acres of such counties as Lancashire, Nottinghamshire, and Northumberland.

Despite this widespread stagnation and lethargy there were a few men, not content with things as they were, who began to experiment and invent. Some were obscure individuals; others were rich farmers whose names are now usually associated with the steps that marked the famous innovations in eighteenth century agriculture. One of these scientific farming pioneers was the irascible and wealthy Oxford graduate Jethro Tull. He began to experiment on his land and verified some conclusions he had reached while watching the European wine-growers frequently stirring the soil about the roots of the vines. As a result Tull asserted that the ground prepared for most crops should be well broken up before seed was planted and well cultivated by horse-drawn cultivators after growth had begun.

Obviously these cultivators, or "horse-hoes," could not be used if the seed had been sown broadcast by a human sower. It was necessary to plant the seeds in rows. After the plants came up the cultivator could pass up and down between the rows. To plant the seed Tull invented a drill. In his *Horse-Hoeing Husbandry* (1733) he claimed that his machine "makes the channels, sows the seed into them, and covers them at the same time with great exactness and precision." Tull showed England that he could use less seed and grow more grain by his new methods.

A second pioneer was Lord Charles Townshend, Walpole's brother-in-law. Townshend, like Tull, borrowed some of his ideas from Continental countries such as Holland. On his Norfolk estates Townshend began experiments in crop rotation. Under the prevailing system farmers allowed one third of their land to lie fallow each year because no adequate grain crops could be produced from land used more than two years in succession. Townshend showed rural England that fields did not have to lie fallow one year in three. By planting root crops and clover the fertility of the soil would be restored by replacing the lost nitrogen. The roots and clover could then be fed to the livestock, ending the practice of killing off most of the cattle in the autumn. With winter food for livestock fresh meat and milk would be available throughout the year. All the land could be kept under cultivation because the root crops and clover had these beneficial effects on the soil. "Turnip" Townshend, who had plenty of leisure after his retirement from politics in 1730, made several other contributions to agriculture. For example, much of his estate was sandy heath. He spread large quantities of fertilizing marl, lime and manure over it; the results were demonstrably good.

A third leader in agricultural experiments was Robert Bakewell of Leicestershire; his chief interest was in the improvement of sheep, cattle, and horse breeding. Now that sheep and cattle could be wintered over, the problem of breeding had become very important. Bakewell saw that the increasing and shifting population meant that England would soon face a heavier demand for food. If better cattle and sheep could be developed, the beef and mutton supply would be increased. Formerly farmers had paid scant attention to breeding. Cattle and sheep had not been used mainly for food. Sheep had been grown for wool; cows to produce butter and milk; oxen to pull loads. The gaunt, long-legged cattle were "more like ill-made black horses than an ox or cow."

In 1750 Bakewell, with a shrewd eye to the future meat demand, began to experiment with longhorn cattle. He wanted animals "shaped like a firkin and with as short legs as possible." In this cattle breeding Bakewell was not very successful but his imitators later developed the Durham shorthorns and the Herefords. Bakewell did succeed in raising a new breed of fat and chunky sheep. The Leicestershire sheep that he developed from inbreeding large and compact animals were deservedly famous.

Slowly, aided by such influential men as Arthur Young and the enthusiastic Squire Coke of Holkham, the knowledge of these advances in farming methods spread over England. The interest of the landed aristocrats steadily increased. When George III opened his Parliament of 1770 he was speaking as "Farmer George" to the large agricultural interests of England: "It is with much concern that I find myself obliged to open the session of Parliament with acquainting you that the distemper among the horned cattle has lately broken out in this kingdom." It was these great landowners who were in the van of agricultural progress. They wanted to benefit by the discoveries of Tull and Townshend. Improved agricultural methods promised to bring more profit. The owners of broad acres were always interested in profits.

Among the small farmers in the villages local prejudice and a deep affection for the old ways often held back the adoption of the new techniques. Some felt that the great meat markets were so far away and transportation so difficult that there would be no profit in raising shorthorn cattle or Leicestershire sheep. There were other obstacles. Under the communal open field system the whole village had to be convinced that the proposed changes would be desirable. To do that was not easy; the conservative small farmers were disinclined to try novelties. A few men could not go ahead on their own initiative and disrupt the whole communal management of the great fields. Nor could much be done about improving the breed of sheep and cattle when all the animals of the village were pastured in a common field. Many leaseholders were reluctant to spend money to improve the land because their leases might suddenly be terminated by their landlords.

In the last part of the eighteenth century the old system of English agriculture changed swiftly. It has already been explained that the great landlords were usually anxious to introduce the improved agricultural methods. They saw that the new ways produced rich crops and thus increased manyfold the rental value of their lands. Shrewd men noted that the rising population would put a heavy pressure on England's food supply. That demand would drive food prices upwards. More people were moving into the cities to engage in business and industry. Obviously agriculture was more profitable than ever before.

In these circumstances it was inevitable that the landlords would try to put more land under cultivation; to produce as much as they could; to obtain high rents and high prices. So it came about that the open fields and the ancient common lands were enclosed to a far greater extent than before. In Tudor days, and earlier, the enclosures had been made to raise more sheep for wool. In the eighteenth century the land was enclosed to grow grain, cattle, and sheep for the hungry markets of England's cities. Thus great areas of the common or waste land were now broken up by the plow. The open fields were enclosed and split up into modern farms separated by fields or hedges.

Usually special private acts of Parliament were necessary to enclose the open fields and the common lands. The chief landowners of a parish would prepare a bill calling for parliamentary commissioners to survey the parish lands and to redistribute them in individual holdings. After examination by a parliamentary committee the bill would be submitted to Parliament. With the passage of the bill those who had scattered strips in the open fields and rights in the common land by indisputable title would be given single allocations of land in the parish. Very small landowners were usually given money payments in return for the surrender of their titles. As the landlords controlled Parliament the enclosures progressed steadily from about 1750 to 1850, when all the open fields had been swallowed up. Between 1700 and 1750 about 100 enclosure acts were passed; between 1750 and 1800 there were about 2,500. In the eighteenth century nearly 3,000,000 acres of open fields and over 1,000,000 acres of common waste land were enclosed. A General Enclosure Act of 1801 made the whole process much easier for the landlords. "They converted barren heaths into smiling cornfields."

Thus the agricultural system of England was improved. The new system was less wasteful than the old. Production mounted steadily. Large landowners added field to field and laid up great profits. The increasing industrial population was more adequately fed as more foodstuffs became available under the impetus of the new methods of scientific farming. All England benefited from the tide of agricultural production.

To the small owners and the leaseholders the enclosures usually meant disaster. In the villages of England the small yeomen farmers, owning their acres by copyhold or freehold, frequently found that they could not afford to enclose by fence or hedge the single farms now given them in return for their rights in the open field and the common land. To fence in their new farms, to pay for such things as roads, drainage, and commissioners' surveys was expensive. Hence the yeomen farmers often had to mortgage their farms to raise enough money to pay the costs of enclosure. Then they could not borrow money on mortgage to buy the new livestock and machinery essential to carry out successful scientific farming.

When wheat prices fell early in the nineteenth century the yeomen found their position even more difficult. To pay their debts they had to sell their farms, usually to large landowners. Some rented land and became tenant farmers. Some drifted to the cities and entered industry. A conservative English country gentleman wrote that the cities "have sucked up the villages and the single cottages. Birmingham, Manchester, and Sheffield swarm with inhabitants; but look at them, what a set of mean, drunken wretches! Are they of the make, or honesty, or the use of the husbandman?" Sometimes the dispossessed yeomen emigrated to the colonies; others stayed on the land as hired laborers.

The very small landholder, as earlier explained, received either a compact allotment of land too small to support himself and his family or a sum of money. Usually it was not long before land and money were both gone. Those who had been cottagers or small leaseholders became hired men on the great estates or sought to better themselves among the unsorted masses of the cities. Some of the great English business firms of the present day were founded by such men. Those who could show no legal title to the land they had always held by village custom in the open fields were summarily evicted. They lost their right to till the soil and grow food; they lost the right to pasture animals and gather fuel on the common land.

> "A sin it is in man or woman
> To steal the goose from off the Common
> But what then is his excuse
> Who steals the Common from the goose?"

These men, too, became rural wage-earners or city workers. They were no longer their own masters. Often, as William Cobbett was to show in the next century, their resentment led to crime and dissatisfaction. "All I know is that I had a cow, and an act of Parliament has taken it from me."

Such changes in rural economy did contain within themselves the means by which the landless laborer was one day to have his revenge. The industrial capitalist farmer producing to supply a market may be ruined by a fall of prices. Every agricultural depression since the eighteenth century has thrown many large landowners into bankruptcy. New taxation methods in the twentieth century hastened the division of the great landed estates. Slowly the rural workers, the old-style laboring farmers, invaded thousands of acres of land. For them farming was a way of life as well as an investment. But this was far in the future; the immediate problem was the suffering created by the enclosures.

The independent yeomanry was extinguished; the healthy and self-sufficient old village system of England was departing. Stern and bitter poets like George Crabbe, who took a sordid view of the daily human village drama, probably viewed these events with no regret. The enclosures meant efficiency and modern production methods. The bulk of the English fields had been enclosed to increase productivity and profit; bread must be found for the new towns. The village had meant inefficiency and old-fashioned farming. But the lesser folk had probably been happier in the village than they were ever to be again in a mysterious and bewildering world. The England of the yeoman and the ale house was gone forever. The village green might now be plowed up. No longer was it true that "every rood of ground maintain'd its man." Now "one man had better steal a horse than another look over a hedge." There has been no greater change in English history than this.

The famous lines of Oliver Goldsmith's *Deserted Village* find a place in every anthology: "Ill fares the land, to hast'ning ills a prey, Where wealth accumulates and men decay." Another contemporary described the scene in prose that is almost poetry: "How wisely did the fostering hand of ancestry provide for the poor, by an allotment of a cottage right of common in the open fields; the village green before their door; the orchard adjoining the house and the long close behind it!—these two latter being seized by the greedy farmer, and the two former being forced from them by the hand of power (upon some inadequate infamous bargain) has driven away the poor, has levelled the cottage, has impoverished the country, and must, finally, ruin it."

THE NEW MACHINES

Meanwhile Englishmen were applying mechanical power to industry on a scale never known before. Production was increased. New economic, social, and political problems were created for all western civilization. Into every phase of English industry came new inventions, improvements, more efficient power machinery to take the place of human hands and muscles. For example, many pages could be written about the shifts and revolutions in the pottery industry as Josiah Wedgwood made his products an important branch of English commerce; about the linen manufacturers of Belfast; about the tin-plate of South Wales.

It is always difficult, and frequently tedious, to cite a long list of the names of inventors unless their achievements are described in some detail. The meaning of the activities of such men will be swiftly illustrated here by reference to certain cardinal inventions that transformed England's basic industries: wool, cotton, iron, and steel.

The wool industry had been England's most important since the later Middle Ages. Farmers were forbidden to export wool to feed the foreign looms of Flanders or any other country. High duties were imposed on foreign cloth so that the English clothier would be adequately protected. The import of cotton was discouraged. Englishmen were encouraged to drink port so that the Portuguese and Brazilian markets would remain open for English wool textiles. Although war and tariffs sometimes did check England's export trade in wool there still remained through the years a considerable expansion. In rough figures the export of wool textiles probably rose from a value of £300,000 in 1720 to £5,000,000 in 1790. Some of the first inventions were, naturally enough, applied to the old woolen industry, then to the new manufacture of cotton in Lancashire.

In 1733 John Kay of Lancashire invented the "flying shuttle," which doubled the output of the hand weaver. Both woolen and cotton weavers soon discovered that the spinners with their spindles could not keep up with the larger demand for spun yarn and cotton thread. What could be done to increase yarn and thread production? An answer was found in 1764, when James Hargreaves invented his multiple "spinning jenny," a machine that was in fact a large spinning wheel lying on its side and turning from eight to a hundred spindles at a time. Despite violent objections by the hand spinners, who feared that Hargreaves' invention would take away their jobs, the new machine was soon widely used. Then, in 1771, Richard Arkwright devised the water frame, in which a number of rollers prepared tougher threads than the "spinning jenny." In 1779 Samuel Crompton combined the merits of Arkwright's frame and Hargreaves' "jenny" in his "mule," a machine that spun a thread both fine and tough. By such mechanical developments, requiring the use of water power, the manufacture of cotton was concentrated in the factories and the old system of domestic manufacture in the homes of the spinners and weavers rapidly declined.

The production of thread and yarn was soon larger than the hand looms could handle. In 1785 the Reverend Edmund Cartwright developed a power loom. Water supplied the power needed to run the new machine. New mills sprang up by the swift streams and waterfalls on the Pennine slopes of Lancashire. But the balance between spinning and weaving was not fully restored because Cartwright's loom was not entirely successful; not until after 1820 were power looms perfected.

Meanwhile an adequate supply of raw cotton seemed to be assured when Eli Whitney invented his cotton gin in the United States in 1793. This machine swiftly separated the fibers from the seeds and was of tremendous importance in the economic history of the cotton belt of the United States. In 1760 Lancashire imported nearly 8,000 tons of raw cotton; in 1800 the total had risen to about 25,000 tons; in 1861, to about 300,000 tons. The damp climate of Lancashire suited the cotton thread. Huge exports of cotton cloth rolled through the ports of England.

Another major step in cotton and woolen manufacture was completed by the development of a steam engine. Captain Thomas Savery had invented a steam pump in 1698. In 1705 appeared Thomas Newcomen's immense fire engine. The piston of his upright machine was about five feet in diameter. The engine delivered about twenty horsepower and burned about thirteen tons of coal a day. Steam was shot into the cylinder to push the piston up; then the cylinder was sprayed with cold water to condense the steam and create a vacuum inside. This enabled the atmospheric pressure on the outside of the piston head to force it down. Five-sixths of the steam energy was consumed by the alternate heating and cooling of the cylinder. This engine was used mainly to pump water out of mines.

In 1769 James Watt of Glasgow, after repairing a model of Newcomen's engine, took out a patent on a horizontal steam engine in which the steam not only pushed out the piston but also pulled it in. Aided by Matthew Boulton, a hardware manufacturer near Birmingham, Watt finished a fairly efficient engine in 1775. Later improvements were made, and in 1785 the first steam engine was used to supply power for a cotton factory. The age of the steam factory began. The new source of power was now not water, but coal. England had vast supplies of coal. That fact was, and remains, of major importance.

The first development of the iron and steel industries had been delayed in the early part of the eighteenth century because of the difficulty of obtaining an adequate fuel supply. The only known fuel for smelting purposes was wood and England's forests were becoming exhausted. In 1739 there were about seventy blast furnaces in England producing about 17,000 tons of iron annually. The advance of the iron industry had to wait the discovery of new smelting methods.

Up in Shropshire three generations of Abraham Darbys used coke made from coal to make their cast iron and copper kettles and pans. Their chief difficulty was in getting a sufficient combustion of the coke to make a temperature high enough to produce high-grade iron. Several methods, including the use of a steam engine to increase the blast, were developed to improve the results obtained by using coal. In the end the Darbys were able to produce cast iron in large quantities with their new blast furnaces. After 1770 coke was used by other ironmasters.

In 1783 Henry Cort found a way to convert pig or cast iron into malleable or wrought iron bars by a process known as puddling and rolling. The wrought iron possessed much more tensile strength than the carbon-heavy cast iron and hence could be used for a much larger number of industrial purposes. Foundries multiplied and by 1800 England was producing 250,000 tons of iron annually. Puddled iron and small amounts of blister and crucible steel were used in 1855 when Sir Henry Bessemer patented a famous process for making steel in large quantities cheaply. By the end of the eighteenth century England led the world in heavy industries. It was a happy accident that her coal was so close to her iron deposits in the "Black Country" of the midlands and the north.

Such were the inventions of major importance in the manufacture of textiles, iron and steel. The pattern of inventive conquest was much the same in the other basic industries such as pottery manufacturing. Through years of hastening change nimble hands and quick brains made machines do things that human beings had always done before. Men drove bargains and smashed obstacles. They seized unimagined opportunities. They made things of beauty and beastliness. The wens of England's great cities sprawled ugly and dark; they enslaved the workers and the factory owners at the same time. Industrial capitalism became huge, efficient, and impersonal. Between the sweating laborer and the industrialist the gulf was fixed and wide. The main connection between the two was a wage check, what John Ruskin called the "cash nexus." Was the worker worthy of his hire? Was the capitalist worthy of his profit? Around these twin questions was to turn many of the later disputes about the unsolved riddle of social justice.

THE REVOLUTION IN TRANSPORT

The new age of the machine could not prosper without an improvement in the British transportation system. In the latter part of the eighteenth century startling advances were made in methods of moving goods and people from one part of the country to another. Earlier, as described in Chapter 24, the roads in winter were usually quagmires in which the heavy, springless, four-horse coaches stuck unmoved by imprecations or petitions to the house of commons. The deep clay areas of the Midlands were particularly bad. For example, about 1750 it took four and a half days to cover the distance between

Manchester and London, a week to travel from York to London. Teams of pack horses, as in the Middle Ages, still carried such commodities as wool throughout England and coal sacks over the passes of the Welsh hills. Most heavy goods, such as Newcastle "sea coal," were shipped by sea. If Britain had been a larger island her roads would probably have been improved earlier.

By the end of the eighteenth century better transport increased the pace of travel. One coach was called the "Balloon Coach" because of "its travelling so fast, making it a point to be before the Mail Coach." John Palmer's famous competitive instinct brought a sixteen-hour service between London and Bristol; his rivals had to try to keep up or go bankrupt. Private turnpike companies, earlier praised in Defoe's *Tour*, built good roads and charged fees to those who travelled over them; parish and county authorities often agreed that the roads must be fixed so that the business of living could be speeded up on the road as well as at home. "Dispatch, which is the very life and soul of business," declared a contemporary, "becomes more and more attainable."

Famous road engineers made it easier to bring producers and markets together. John Metcalfe designed many roads in Yorkshire, Lancashire, and Cheshire. Thomas Telford built the Holyhead Road and a suspension bridge over the Menai Straits. Early in the nineteenth century John Macadam invented a new way of laying roadbeds using small stones to form a smooth road surface. Thus land travelling conditions were transformed on the eve of the railway age and a century before the truck and automobile.

Meanwhile a network of canals was being dug. In 1761 the Duke of Bridgewater, a colliery owner, had a canal constructed from his mine at Worsley to Manchester, a distance of twelve miles. When "Bridgewater's folly" became a success the freight cost between Worsley and Manchester was cut in half. Soon Hull, Manchester, Birmingham, Bristol, Leeds, Liverpool, and London were all connected. By 1790 over 3,000 miles of canals helped to knit the country together. Coal, building material, wool, pottery, foodstuffs, and most other products of industry and agriculture could now be moved cheaply about the land. The cost of canal carriage was usually one third to one half of the cost of land carriage. By such transportation developments the isolation of areas was being further broken down. Almost everywhere there was evident a broadening of horizons, a quickening of pace, a feeling of wonderful changes afoot.

POPULATION MOVEMENTS

Simultaneously with the changes in agriculture, the multiplication of machines, the transformation of production methods, and the advances in transport and communications there occurred an unprecedented growth and shift of population. Some idea of what this development meant for England as a part of an agricultural and industrial revolution that still continues may be gained by citing a few statistics.

Late in the seventeenth century slightly more than 5,000,000 people lived in England. From 1700 to 1750 the population rose at a rate of about 18 per cent; from 1750 to 1800 it climbed at a rate of 52 per cent. In 1801, the year of the first census, the population of England totalled 8,600,000. The death rate dropped sharply because Englishmen had more milk and fresh meat, cheaper bread, more hospitals, improved medical techniques. As the eighteenth century drew to its end fewer people drank gin. Another major cause of the population rise was the great shift from farming to manufacturing. Industry can maintain a denser population than agriculture.

In 1700 about 4,000,000 Englishmen depended on their farms for a living and about 240,000 depended on industry. By 1801 over 3,000,000 were busy in manufacturing. On the other hand, there had only been a negligible increase in the number of those engaged in agriculture. Thus the occupations and general life patterns of the people had undergone tremendous changes during the hundred years from 1700 to 1800. Meanwhile the supply of producers and consumers was growing and Thomas Robert Malthus was provided with new bases for his pessimistic principles of population.

Not only did population and industrial enterprise increase but the centers of population shifted. Areas such as East Anglia and the Cotswolds declined; some once heavily populated places became "ghost towns" and rotten and pocket boroughs multiplied. Northern and western England, rich in iron ore, coal, water power, and good ports, were rapidly deluged with migrating waves of workers, with mushrooming industries of all kinds. For example, the fuel famine due to the using up of English timber had hit such areas as Sussex and Surrey rather heavily; so the ironmongers moved nearer to coal and new wood supplies in the west and north. The population of Lancashire was about 160,000 in 1700; it was about 700,000 a century later. New towns were born; old towns expanded. As England moved into the nineteenth century the "Black Country" in the Midlands was made. A blanket of factory smoke spread haphazardly over the area; the jerry-builder grew fat and vast slums sprawled, dirty and indecent. Cities such as Birmingham, Leeds, Glasgow, Manchester, Liverpool, and Sheffield became larger every year, filled with grimy alleys and ugliness. A nation of farmers and village craftsmen was becoming a nation of factory workers.

Into the overcast cities came thousands of men and women. The new frontier was in the factory. Industry and commerce were hungry for workers. A Manchester man remarked in 1792 about "the wonderful importation of children purchased in London at so much the half score (nine sound and one cripple) by those merchants, the most forward against the slave trade." The new machines stepped up the pace of production with untiring efficiency and power. Human hands could now do more by pulling a lever than by working long hours over a cottage loom. Dr. Samuel Johnson, understanding little and caring less about the economic destinies of the factory system, was happy that Lichfield had few factories and Birmingham so many. "Sir, we are a city of philosophers; we work with our heads and make the poor boobies of Birmingham work for us with their hands."

ADAM SMITH

With all these changes over a vast sphere of economic life there came a new economic theory. It seems natural enough, when one looks back, that the Glasgow professor Adam Smith should have published his *Wealth of Nations* in 1776. Adam Smith, like the French Physiocrats, opposed the controlled economy of a mercantilist system designed to increase national wealth, industry, and trade. That system, indeed, had been decaying long before the days of Adam Smith. Governmental regulations had remained longest in the areas of foreign trade; but there also, as Professor Conyers Read has pointed out, "the steady drift was towards greater freedom in economic matters." By the time of the American Revolution, restraints were "relaxed in fact before they were relaxed in theory." Although the old laws remained on the books it has been said, and rightly, that England really had no economic policy at all for perhaps fifty years before the revolt of the American colonies.

Adam Smith agreed with the national rights philosophers and utilitarian reformers who asserted that an enlightened self-interest realizes both public and private welfare. Governmental control was an obstacle to the "natural order" of society; laws of nature, discoverable by human reason, should govern all, or almost all, the political, social and economic relations of men.

Hence Adam Smith stated that the natural economic laws fixed two things as the main features of a sensible economic system: private property and free competition. Any eighteenth century English industrialist would agree with that. All through the nineteenth century the classical economists who followed Adam Smith asserted that the important task of any national economy is to produce consumable goods. The "natural economic man" assumed by the classical economists would of course produce what other men want. This "economic man," self-seeking, well-informed, and intelligent, would always want to buy his goods and services in the cheapest and sell them in the dearest markets. Competition would result from the actions of a "natural economic man" living in a natural economic order. Competition and the natural economic laws, asserted the classical economists, always work together for the welfare of all. External controls interfere with the natural laws of free enterprise. Each man, pursuing his own interests, will at the same time serve best the interests of the whole community. A system of full liberty, said Adam Smith, would release tremendous economic powers.

Of course no classical economists ever held completely to the principle of non-interference in economic affairs. They agreed, for example, that the government should administer public works, education, and so on. Nevertheless, they did insist that the problems of an industrial society could best be met in the long run under a system of freedom of exchange and association. This is the famous economic system proposed by the sagacious Adam Smith and called the doctrine of *laisser faire*. The following sentences from the *Wealth of Nations* clearly state the essential principles of *laisser faire:* "All systems either of preference or of restraint, therefore, being thus completely taken away, the obvious and simple system of natural liberty establishes itself of its own accord. Every man, as he does not violate the laws of justice, is left perfectly free to pursue his own interest his own way, and to bring both his industry and capital into competition with those of any other man, or order of men."

This *Wealth of Nations*, the Bible of Free Trade, had tremendous influence. The new capitalist industrialists liked the ideas of free enterprise and the prospects of unrestricted initiative and open competition. Government interference with liberty and trade was now denounced by a respectable and sober Glasgow economist; the successful business men of England welcomed his words. Adam Smith soon had many disciples, including William Pitt the Younger. Early in the nineteenth century the government began to repeal many of the statutes regulating trade, commerce, wages, conditions of apprenticeship, and so on. For many years the economic doctrines of *laisser faire* were unchallenged by any important voice. The prophet of Free Trade had triumphed. Then, slowly, questions began to be asked very loudly about the results of this unimpeded exercise of individual liberty. The answers were not reassuring.

RESULTS OF THE REVOLUTIONS

"There are few ways in which a man can be more innocently employed than in making money," wrote Dr. Johnson in 1775. As a pioneer of a mighty revolution in industrial production England opened a road to greater national wealth and power. In this she was aided by technical skills, by vast deposits of coal and iron, by the fact that she was already the first commercial and maritime power. She could produce and export more cheaply than any nation on earth. The whole world was her market, and she made the most of it. The products of her indefatigable machines were exported over the seas and across the continents. From every corner of the planet she sucked up the raw materials needed by the hungry maws of her factories. In 1700 the annual value of export-import trade was roughly £10,000,000. In 1800 the figure was approximately £73,000,000. The precise real value of Britain's export-import trade is difficult to determine because before 1854 import values were calculated in official values, based on a scale of prices prevalent in 1696; exports were listed at their declared value. Nevertheless, the approximate figures quoted above illustrate well enough what was happening.

Such immense production meant huge wealth. But the profits born of expanded production and trade brought no immediate rewards to the workers in the form of higher wages. On the other hand, the enterprising owners and managers of industry became modern capitalists; and they used their capital to produce more capital. The merchants grew richer; so did the bankers, the shopkeepers, the professional men, the middlemen. Thus the great class of the "bourgeoisie" grew strong and rejoiced in its strength. "The merchant," said Dr. Johnson, "is a *new* kind of gentleman."

For several decades aristocratic landowners continued to control the government of England. Then, in 1832, the bourgeois middle class ended that aristocratic monopoly of political power. In 1846 the middle classes also showed their strength and suggested their intentions by repealing the Corn Laws that had protected the landowners so long. The rest of the nineteenth century was to mark the reign of the bourgeoisie, the new aristocracy of commerce. Then the twentieth century heralded the final emergence of the laboring class as a political force of broadening power.

The surplus of capital was invested in many ways. Millions of pounds went to stimulate and support experiments with new inventions; to expand production capacity; to develop new industrial processes. The thud and beat of pistons and hammers became louder as more money made more machines, and better ones. The golden stream of surplus British capital also poured into foreign fields. Huge international loans were extended to other nations. London succeeded Amsterdam as the center of the international money market. Accumulated capital disposable abroad would go anywhere for profit. It was "exported" to backward countries to open up natural resources and to create new markets. The rate of interest was usually high.

Behind the private investors stood the British government. The constant pressure brought upon the governments of all countries by industrial capitalists, anxious for the political protection of their foreign investments, was to be a major impulse towards imperialism and "manifest destiny," particularly in the nineteenth century. With the increasing industrialization of many nations there arose a ruthless competition among the great powers for raw materials, for markets, for colonies. The life blood of empire is trade and commerce. International economic competition helped to bring diplomatic crises and war.

Thus, by fertilizing investment and re-investment all over the world the United Kingdom prospered still more. It has been estimated that by 1875 Britain had holdings abroad worth about £1,200,000,000. Industrial capitalism had become a giant, in some ways a blind and irresponsible one. No man knew how big it would grow. The new world meant speed, efficiency, wealth; it also meant a sudden acceleration of man's power to destroy as well as to create.

With the rapid rise of the new industrial capitalists came also the rise of the industrial proletariat. Not until the middle of the nineteenth century, as later chapters will show, were the propertyless wage earners able to combine into groups or unions to agitate for shorter hours, higher wages, or better working conditions. Although England's restrictive Combination Acts were repealed in 1825 effective labor organization did not appear until the 1850's. Meanwhile the depressed classes, unorganized and often dumb, lived in the dingy, unsanitary, and congested cities amidst the humming factories belching smoke and noxious fumes. Disease and misery stalked through the fetid alleys and the crowded tenements of the slum. The worker had to sell his labor in the available markets or starve. Industrial lords bound "a host more numerous and more dependent than were ever sworn to the bear and ragged staff of a Neville." It is not surprising that the new cities were to be the seed ground of a new democracy.

Men, women, and children often worked under appalling conditions for long hours. Here was fertile ground for seeds of agitation and rebellion. Modern industrialization was usually soulless and hard, not measurably sweetened by human sentiment. Later chapters will describe the rise of radical movements and the efforts of nineteenth century crusaders to protect the workers from the most hideous legacies of the industrial revolution. Some social progress was made when the state and voluntary societies began their task of grappling with the demands of social welfare. Meanwhile the full divorce and widespread antagonism between capital and labor characteristic of our contemporary society had been born. The makers of modern history include not only the statesmen, warriors, diplomats, physicians, inventors, and capitalists but also the great labor organizers who have harnessed and directed the power of the industrial masses.

The infinitely complicated process that we call history had given rise to another shift in equilibrium and new social problems. The bourgeoisie were acquiring power and were becoming conscious of their virtues and their interests. Unfortunately, their political and economic interests were often in conflict with the interests of the men who worked in their factories. In recent times this conflict of class interests has become more obvious, more dangerous, and more productive of profound social discords. Under a system of private property in the means of production of wealth and the price system in the means of distributing it the larger part of the wealth produced goes to those who own or control the machines. Those who do not own or control the machines but only work them, receive what they can command on a labor market with or without the support of their trade unions or other labor organizations.

The urgent problem of the distribution of economic power has therefore resulted in a dilemma for modern democracy: Is there a way in which democratic societies can use the democratic method to correct the obvious inequality of possessions and the distribution of opportunity? Would a democratic nation be greatly weakened by too many government restrictions of the national economy? If so, how can comparatively unrestrained private economic enterprise be made to function effectively and at the same time for the common welfare?

To such questions many answers have been given, most of them incompatible with democratic institutions. The world of human relations has not yet been shaped to rational and humane purposes. Man has tremendous physical power at his disposal. Upon his capacity to make good use of it depends the future of his world. At the end of the Second World War a British Labor government embarked upon a policy that would, it was hoped, bring to the United Kingdom a greater degree of economic democracy. The achievements and defeats of Britain's post-war cabinet are discussed in the final chapter of this book.

Chapter 26

THE CHALLENGE OF THE JACOBINS

WILLIAM PITT THE YOUNGER

WILLIAM PITT came back to undisputed power in 1784 after a desperate election contest filled with the usual evils of beer, bribery, and riot. It was expected that his term of office would be short. How could this "schoolboy" of twenty-five years of age hope to defeat the blows and plots of his foes? The events that followed his election gave the answer. Pitt remained England's prime minister continuously for eighteen years, longer than any man except Sir Robert Walpole.

The second son of the Great Commoner, the younger Pitt had inherited his father's mental powers. He was born in 1759, the year of England's massive victories in the Seven Years' War. After studying classics and mathematics at Cambridge he had entered Parliament when he was twenty-one years of age. Haughty and serious, Pitt had worked hard to prepare himself for a political career. His private life was pure; his only bad habit was an excessive consumption of port wine. His talents were of the first order. Despite his icy austerity he was a better tactician and party manager than his father had ever been.

Pitt was patriotic, hungry for power, Napoleonic in his energy. He cared little about money; in an age of corruption and graft Pitt died a poor man. His rise to fame was swift, swifter than any statesman before or since. It will be recalled that Pitt was chancellor of the exchequer under Shelburne, a vehement opponent of the Fox-North coalition, a parliamentary debater almost, but not quite, the equal of his father. After Pitt had delivered a maiden speech of precocious skill in the house of commons a wit had declared: "It is not a chip off the old block; it is the old block itself." Such was the man who was to reorganize the Tory party; to re-establish the authority of the prime minister; to maintain cabinet solidarity on a level never achieved before; and to fight a great war with the dauntless heart, though not the skill, of his father.

Pitt's great capacities were particularly evident in finance; there he was a genius. His command of this field enabled him, like Walpole, to obtain the support of both the business classes and the landed gentry. By the American Revolution England's debt had been doubled; in 1783 it stood at £266,000,000. Exchequer bills were at a twenty per cent discount. Pitt held the post of chancellor of the exchequer himself and his successive budgets and other shrewd measures swiftly raised the public credit. In 1786 Pitt established the Sinking Fund by which £1,000,000 was to be set aside annually to accumulate at compound interest. The time would come, Pitt said, when the sum thus accumulated would pay off the national debt. He did not foresee the approaching Continental war that would cost the nation millions of pounds.

Pitt also tried to balance the budget by increasing government income and reducing expenditures. The huge and lucrative smuggling traffic, especially in tobacco, tea, and wine, had resulted in a large customs loss. In 1784 Pitt made contraband trade less profitable by reducing the high tariff on articles usually smuggled. The tea duty, for example, was reduced from 50 to 12.5 per cent. To offset the loss in revenue Pitt introduced a variety of new excise taxes on such luxury items as race horses, ribbons, servants, candles, hats, hair powder, and windows. Travellers today may see Georgian houses where windows were bricked up long ago to avoid payment of the tax imposed on windows.

At the same time the energetic chancellor of the exchequer wiped out the vicious system of keeping numerous separate government accounts, a practice encouraging graft and manipulation. In place of these special accounts Pitt put a new Consolidated Fund; all government money was paid into the Fund or drawn from it. As government bonds were secured against this Consolidated Fund they became known as "Consols." Meanwhile many sinecures were abolished. Partly because of these reforms England was put on such a sound financial footing that she was soon able once again to be "paymaster of the allies" in the titanic struggle against France.

The first ten years of Pitt's able administration were years of peace. Besides his financial achievements Pitt, carrying the gospel of Adam Smith in his hand, tried to apply a part of the principles of free trade to foreign commerce. "What an extraordinary man Pitt is," wrote Smith, "he understands my ideas better than I do myself." As a step towards breaking down the barriers of mercantilism denounced in *The Wealth of Nations* Pitt proposed a commercial union between England and Ireland. The mercantile interests, not without avarice and failing to see that Irish prosperity and better Anglo-Irish relations might be to England's advantage, bitterly opposed Pitt's plan. His opponents were organized into an efficient lobby called the Chamber of Manufacturers. They felt that the admission of Irish goods into

English markets would hurt their business. Faced by such opposition Pitt abandoned his proposals.

In his scheme for lowering trade barriers with France, Pitt was more successful. In April, 1786, Sir William Eden, Britain's ambassador in France, reported from Paris that France was "eager to promote a commercial intercourse between the two countries, as the best means of maintaining a pacific system." The Eden Treaty was finally negotiated, providing for a mutual reduction of tariffs, except on a limited list of imports. France, for example, reduced her duties on English cotton, steel, and woolen goods. England lowered her duty on French claret so that it could compete in English markets with Portuguese wine. This commercial treaty provoked wide debate in England; the adoption of the doctrine of Adam Smith was not pleasant to those who still knelt at the mercantilist shrines. In the end Pitt triumphed. "A market of so many millions of people," he declared, "a market so near and so prompt, a market of expeditious and certain, of necessary and extensive consumption, is an object which Englishmen ought to look up to with eager and satisfied ambition."

Pitt thus took a pioneer step in the direction of free trade. The treaty with France was to last only three years; then it was shattered by the French Revolution. In England, meanwhile, the ancient suspicion of France could not easily die. Pitt himself wrote: "Though in this commercial business I think there are reasons for believing the French may be sincere, I cannot listen without suspicion to their professions of political friendship." A Tory peer was pessimistic. "That France is a natural enemy and that she will remain so long as envy and jealousy are attributes inseparable from the human mind I am fully persuaded." Edward Gibbon said that "as a citizen of the world" he must rejoice "in every agreement that diminishes the separation between neighboring countries, which softens their prejudices, unites their commerce and industry, and renders their future hostilities less frequent and less implacable. I hope both nations are gainers; since otherwise the treaty cannot be lasting, and such double mutual gain is surely possible in fair trade, though it could not easily happen in the mischievous amusements of war and gaming."

These were years marked by several reform proposals. For some time a popular agitation had been growing for the reform of the system of representation in Parliament. The franchise was limited; the shifts of population since the Middle Ages had resulted in the existence of a large number of rotten and pocket boroughs. About half the members held their seats by nomination or purchase. Representation of the people was so inadequate that they had to express their opinions largely by extra-parliamentary means, sometimes by violence and rioting. Propaganda for electoral and franchise reform was steadily spreading, especially through the cities. Before reaction closed in with the French

Revolution the reform movements were gaining momentum. It was events on the Continent that hardened conservative hearts against reform.

The liberal position of William Pitt is shown by such facts as his commercial policies and his friendship with the evangelical Anglican William Wilberforce, leader of the campaign against the slave trade. And yet Pitt's sympathy with Wilberforce was never sufficiently strong to break the shackles of commercial and political considerations. Pitt spoke in the house of commons for the abolition of the slave trade; but he would not put forward the full power of his government against it. Likewise Pitt's attitude towards Parliamentary reform was tempered with caution. True, he never resorted to direct bribery in Parliament as a means of keeping a majority; but he did discreetly use the un-representative electoral system for political purposes. Many a man who controlled a rotten borough found himself made a peer on the recommendation of the prime minister. To such men the bribes of vanity were more important than the temptation of money.

In 1785 Pitt mildly asked leave to introduce a bill to disfranchise some of the rotten boroughs; their owners were to be compensated. Under Pitt's scheme the seats that were thus made available would be redistributed to the counties and heavily populated boroughs. Fearing to alienate a powerful block of his borough-mongering supporters in Parliament Pitt did not press for approval of his plan. He dropped the question, wise enough to know that many Tories agreed with Lord North's remark: "Begin with innovation and there is no knowing where you will stop." All measures tending towards parliamentary reform flowed against a rampart of corruption, religious exclusion, and the wishes of a privileged minority. Soon England went to war against the intractably republican France. In those dark years, Pitt and his followers were too busy grappling with the fleets and armies of the Jacobins to give much sympathetic thought to domestic reform.

INDIA

The younger Pitt was also responsible for the partial settlement of urgent problems in India. The peace of 1763 had not ended French activities hostile to British interests in that divided land. The French were aided by the fact that many British agents of the East India Company had been guilty of corruption, graft, and robbery. As a result several Indian native princes were ready to attack the British and to drive them out of the country. In 1770 a devastating famine, corruption among the British agents, the assaults of rebelling native princes, and the collapse of court and police administration all joined to produce heavy problems for the East India Company. One result was the seriously defective Regulating Act, passed by Lord North's administration in 1773. Under this piece of legislation the Governor of Bengal was made Governor-General of all the company's possessions in India. He was to rule with the aid of a resident council of four whose vote could limit his actions.

The first Governor-General was Warren Hastings who had started his Indian career in 1750 as an employee of the East India Company. Hastings was hard-working, energetic, and efficient. It was his misfortune that three members of his council were his personal enemies, determined to oppose and thwart him at every turn. The forceful Hastings did what he could in the circumstances. He had high ideals for British government in India. At the same time the ceaseless demands of the East India Company for money compelled Hastings to take it where he found it, often ruthlessly and without justice. In order to maintain the frontiers of Bengal and to block the French plots Hastings frequently disregarded the protests of his recalcitrant council. To wage wars in defense of Bengal Hastings had to find money to maintain forces in the field. Sometimes he used methods that he felt were justified at the time but which could not stand unfriendly scrutiny later.

After France entered the war in support of the American colonies Hastings concluded that the native Indian princes hostile to Britain must be kept from successful rebellion. Hyder Ali, the Mohammedan ruler of Mysore, attacked British territory. Hopeful of French aid he joined with the Mahrattas in an attempt to push the British out of India. In 1783 one well-informed Englishmen wrote: "Foreigners in general think we are in danger of losing our East Indian possessions entirely by the intrigues of the French and the strength of their allies in Hindostan." In 1787 another noted that "there is scarcely an Indian prince who has not a French emissary at his court." It was mainly due to the rare administrative skill and spirit of Warren Hastings that India was not lost.

Charles James Fox had been defeated on his policy of Indian reform. In 1784 Pitt passed his India Act which settled the way in which India was to be governed until the Indian Mutiny in 1858. By this act the British government accepted its responsibility for the welfare of the natives in the territories of the company. The act set up a governmental board of control in London, comprising the chancellor of the exchequer, one of the secretaries of state, and certain other privy councillors. This was the forerunner of the India Office.

To this board of control, headed by an unsentimental Scotsman, the company directors were required to submit proposals about political and military matters. The officers of the company resident in India could be removed by the board. Under the terms of Pitt's act, the company would continue to direct matters of commerce. The Governor-General was to be appointed by the British government and the functions of his resident council were in future to be merely advisory. At last, it seemed, a workable system of government for India had been developed.

Hastings returned to England in 1785. Under an impeachment listing twenty-two charges the Empire's weary proconsul was accused of misgoverning India. His trial, with several postponements, lasted for seven years (1788–1795); it cost Hastings over £70,000, the whole of his fortune. Were his acts in India arbitrary and wicked? Did he deserve to be punished? About the answers to these questions there will always be controversy. Macaulay's famous and unjust essay did not close the case.

The leaders of the attack on Hastings were Edmund Burke and Richard Brinsley Sheridan. All the vehement invective of Burke's Irish tongue was evident in his oratory. He was not noted for his practical wisdom; that is one of the reasons why he never held a high government post. In this case, Burke knew next to nothing about India. Nevertheless, his warm fancies were excited as he reflected upon the tale of wrongs and misrule reported to him by the enemies of Hastings.

"Do you want a cause, my lords?" he asked. "You have the cause of oppressed princes, of undone women of the first rank, of desolated provinces and of wasted kingdoms. Do you want a criminal, my lords? When was there so much iniquity laid to the charge of anyone? . . . I impeach Warren Hastings, Esquire, of high crimes and misdemeanours. I impeach him in the name and by virtue of those eternal laws of justice which he has violated. I impeach him in the name of human nature itself, which he has cruelly outraged, injured and oppressed, in both sexes, in every age, rank, and condition of life." To such words Sheridan, then thirty-six years old, added a few of his own. It was his opinion that "the condemnation we look for will be one of the most ample mercies accomplished for mankind since the creation of the world."

Hastings was acquitted; he lived to the age of ninety-three. One of the results of his trial was an increase of England's sense of responsibility for affairs in India and the rest of the colonial empire. This fact, however, should not be stressed unduly. The peaceful reign of an inefficient colonial administration was still to continue for more than half a century. Through succeeding years in India Lord Cornwallis (1786–1793) and the marquis of Wellesley (1793–1798) crushed the pro-French elements; the greatest of these was Tippo, the ally of Napoleon and ruler of Mysore. By conquest, consolidation, and annexation these Governors-General and their successors began the territorial advances that laid the foundations of British India.

EVE OF THE FRENCH REVOLUTION

After the defeat of 1783 Great Britain cast about for allies on the Continent. The opportunity to end Britain's isolation came when

France extended her influence in the Netherlands by forming an alliance in 1785 with the Dutch republicans who were seeking to overthrow the stadholder. Into a divided Netherlands France thus thrust her power. London feared the French might obtain effective control of Antwerp and use it as a naval and trading port to threaten England. In 1784 Austria had asserted that the Treaty of Westphalia had provided that the Scheldt river, on which Antwerp stood, should not be opened to navigation. Britain wanted the Scheldt kept closed and out of the control of France. As the stadholder of the Netherlands was related by marriage to the king of Prussia it was possible in 1786 for William Pitt to form the Triple Alliance by which Britain, the Netherlands, and Prussia guaranteed the territories of one another. The designs of France in the Netherlands were thus blocked and England had gained two Continental allies.

At the same time Pitt concluded that Russia's successive attempts to compel Turkey to surrender control of the Black Sea, the Straits of the Dardanelles, and Constantinople were a threat to Britain's position in India and the Mediterranean. When Austria and Russia combined to attack Turkey in 1788 Sweden attacked Russia in the rear. Then Russia persuaded Denmark to strike at Sweden. Pitt was able to use the Triple Alliance power to compel Denmark to cease supporting Russian policy. In 1791 Parliament refused to permit Pitt to threaten Russia directly by intervening in the Near East; but the foundations of Britain's later attitude were being laid. Throughout the nineteenth century Britain seldom departed from her policy of supporting Turkey against Russia's expansionist tendencies in the Near East.

Across the Channel, France, the home of imposing despotism, was heading for the first of her great revolutions. The French Revolution had its origins deep in the past. France was not really a unit, even in the eighteenth century. There were many divisions: territorial, military, financial, legal, and ecclesiastical. There were regional tax differences. The feudal stratification of classes into the clergy, the nobility, and the third estate still continued rigid and irritating. The clergy comprised about 1.8 per cent and the nobility about 1.6 per cent of a total population of 25,000,000. These two small upper classes lived at the expense of the mass of the people, the third estate. In fact, the regular and secular clergy formed a state within a state. Upper ranks of the church were pervaded by ignorance and immorality. The lower clergy, the 60,000 parish priests, had much more in common with the third estate than with their ecclesiastical superiors. Part of the "godlessness" of the Revolution can be traced to the nature of the church in the old regime.

The nobility of the gown and sword possessed "the best of manners and the worst of morals." They held the best offices in the government, the army, the church; and they usually performed few services to earn their incomes. Characterized by politeness and exquisite taste, these nobles strutted at or near the royal court in luxury and frequently in debt. They held a monopoly of the profitable positions in France, paid few taxes, enjoyed their own feudal taxes and rights, battened on the state treasuries. "The nobles," wrote Arthur Young, "ate and drank and sat and walked, loitered and smirked and smiled and chatted, with an easy indifference that made one stare at their stupidity." The poorer nobles, the "sparrow hawk" nobility, possessing little more than "a rusty sword and a genealogical table," scornfully lorded it over the lower classes in their own communities, usually longing to get to the court at Versailles. The lower classes, for their part, moved with silent malignity about their accustomed tasks.

The middle class did what they could to creep into the ranks of the blooded and insolent nobility, often trampling on those below, grasping for the profits of trade and industry. At the same time, they resented a system that denied them the rewards of energy and intelligence. They felt themselves the equals of the titled parasites about the king. As business men they were appalled at government abuses and inefficiency. The bourgeoisie were usually busy, aggressive, and wealthy, in contrast to the disdainful, indolent, and frequently impecunious nobles. Nevertheless, the prevailing mania for speculation pulled money away from productive industry and thus weakened the economy of France. The nobility, of course, disdained trade. That, surely, was for their social inferiors. "On one point the king was adamant; he would kiss no green grocers' wives."

The France of 1789, then, was infected with the plague of rigid class lines, lack of opportunity, despotic government in which the masses of the people had no share. The third estate was plundered by taxes and all the feudal demands of privilege. The courts were slow, costly, unjust. The royal administrative system, heavily staffed by sycophants and drones, sprawled over the country, confused and inefficient. Justice was supposed to flow in a clear stream from the king; but it did not. "All had been made dependent on one fountainhead, yet every channel was stopped up." There was confusion in the capital, chaos in the provinces.

Privilege and poverty had long confronted each other across the class lines. Indeed, conditions in France were improving in the late eighteenth century. The miseries of the third estate have frequently been exaggerated. In many neighboring states the lot of the underprivileged was worse than in the land of Louis XVI. But the people of France were becoming more enlightened than those who lived elsewhere in Europe. Outside of Paris a restless population stirred. "We are only the small provincial towns; we will wait until we see what Paris will do." The sense of injustice had long been at war with the acceptance of discipline. Now a desire for reform was soon to goad the middle class into action. Later the power was to slip from the faltering bourgeois hands and the cry of Liberty, Equality, and Fraternity was to rise from the throats of the masses.

Besides the forces of events and the conditions of the third estate there were the forces of thought. As explained in Chapter 23 this was an age of fermenting ideas, an enlightenment, an intellectual upheaval of the first magnitude. The eighteenth century French philosophers believed in universal natural laws, a new golden age in the future that would be achieved when man succeeded by reason and experiment in bringing himself into general harmony with "the laws of Nature and of Nature's God." Mankind, these philosophers declared, must be freed from the shackles of ignorance and superstition. The "laws" revealed by the use of Reason showed that a Heavenly City could be built on earth. The good life could be achieved if existing evils, which were contrary to the "natural order," were removed.

Over the western world swept the words of such men as Condorcet, Diderot, Montesquieu, Voltaire. The object of another, Jean-Jacques Rousseau, was "to inquire if, in the civil order, there can be any sure and certain administration taking men as they are and laws as they might be." He finally based his system on human freedom, and made the will of the members the sole basis of every society. "I should have wished to be born in a country in which the interests of the sovereign and that of the people must be single and identical; to the end that all the movements of the machine might tend always to the general happiness."

The intellectual revolution helped to create a new point of view; and this, in turn, helped to bring the French Revolution. Many of the criticisms of the philosophers scorched and burned through France, probably reaching in some form most of the humble peasants and city workers. The new ideas were not for minds kept free from thought by dead patterns of platitudes and undigested slogans. They were seized by men who were ready to set society on fire by the four corners. So widely did the words of the philosophers spread that it has been said that "the French Revolution was accomplished before it began."

THE COURSE OF THE REVOLUTION

To this perilous sum of conditions on the eve of the Revolution was added the fact that in 1789 France was bankrupt. Attempts to reform the financial system had failed. Louis XVI reluctantly agreed to summon the ancient representative body known as the Estates-General; it had not been called for 175 years. On May 5, 1789, the Estates-General met. It consisted of 1,200 deputies of which 600 represented the third estate. If the three estates voted "by order" the privileged minority of clergy and nobility would always unite to defeat the third estate by a vote of two to one; in a vote taken "by head" the third estate, aided by a few friendly nobles and priests, would hold a safe majority. When the deputies of the masses stood resolutely against the king and the upper classes a prolonged struggle resulted. In the end Louis XVI yielded. The new "National Assembly" would vote "by head."

Soon the Revolution was at hand with the dismissal of the popular Necker, the fall of the Bastille on July 14, 1789, and the famous events of the night of August 4. In the fervor and enthusiastic excitement of that night the way was opened for the destruction of the political and social fabric of France. Amidst the tide of reform then and later the Declaration of the Rights of Man and the Citizen was designed to be the preface to a new French constitution. What Edmund Burke called "paltry and blurred sheets of paper about the rights of man" contained heavy hints of the semi-religious symbolism so important later when St. Just could say: "Even the indifferent are to be punished, all those who are passive in the republic."

On November 2, 1789, the landed property of the church was placed "at the disposal of the nation." On February 13, 1790, monasteries, convents, and religious orders were abolished. On July 12, 1790, one of the leaders of the Revolution declared that "the service of the altar is a public function." Thus the ancient church was mutilated. To help the economic plight of the government the Assembly at once issued assignats, or paper notes, for which the newly confiscated church lands served as security.

By the terms of the Civil Constitution of the Clergy the church became a department of government designed to promote morality, a civil institution served by elected and salaried civil servants. The clergy were to have the status of ordinary citizens, nothing more. All but seven of the bishops and two thirds of the parish priests opposed the Civil Constitution of the Clergy. On April 13, 1791, the Pope denounced the action of the Assembly in confiscating the church property and condemned the Revolution. Roman Catholics were now faced with the choice of abandoning the Revolution or their faith.

At the same time the National Assembly completed the self-imposed task of providing a new constitution. The Constitution of 1791 transformed France from an absolute into a limited monarchy. This document was a product of middle class planning. Under its terms the middle class would control the government. Apparently the proletariat were to be excluded from political power. "The veil that hides the dazzling figure of Liberty," declared one of the bourgeois makers of the Constitution of 1791, "must not be torn away too suddenly." Was the revolution to be stabilized at this point? For several reasons the bourgeois settlement failed. The people of Paris wanted equality. A radical minority in the assembly did what they could to bring about the collapse of the whole middle class movement. The apprehensive counter-revolutionaries, within and without France, were the unrelenting enemies of the makers of change in the National Assembly.

Outside of France the enlightened despots did not see the dangerous expansive forces inherent in the nature of the French Revolution. They thought they saw in a weakened France a new Poland to partition. Frederick William of Prussia declared: "France is hopelessly lost." Then, on June 21, 1791, a new chapter of the French Revolution began. Louis XVI tried to escape from France. He was detected near the frontier at Varennes and brought back to Paris. A proclamation ordered that "whoever applauds the king will be flogged. Whoever insults him will be hanged." The republicans in Paris grew more vociferous. The strength of the radical Jacobin Club increased.

By the summer of 1791 the kings and conservatives in Europe were becoming aroused to the dangerous character of the Revolution. Might not the doctrines of the French radicals spread across the borders to Austria, Prussia, and beyond? Stirred by these vague fears and urged on by those who had fled from France the Austrian Emperor, brother of the French Queen Marie Antoinette, joined Prussia in a series of declarations and measures designed to check the contagious virus spreading out of Paris. In April, 1792, France declared war on Austria; six days later Prussia joined Austria. The Jacobins wanted to "consolidate the Revolution" by war. A Jacobin leader proclaimed: "We must declare war against all kings and peace with all peoples." The radical groups were getting power because the moderates had failed to hold it, a familiar aspect of the character of most revolutions.

In August, 1792, the French monarchy fell. A month later came the "popular justice" of the "September Massacres." Although the objective truth about these events seems buried beyond monographic recovery it is clear that thousands of Royalists, priests, and nobles were killed. The Jacobins demanded that loyal revolutionaries "treat as enemies the people who, refusing liberty and equality, or renouncing them, may wish to preserve, recall, or treat with the princes and the privileged classes." Maximilien Robespierre said: "Virtue has always been in a minority on earth." In September the "one and indivisible" French Republic was established; it was to be a great "Republic of Virtue."

On the same day the French stopped the Prussians at Valmy in "the victory of humanity." Then a French decree stated that France was prepared "to accord fraternity and aid to all peoples who desire to recover their liberties." In November, "having consulted the archives of Nature," the French annexed Savoy. They overran Belgium and several Rhine regions. The new France was obviously going to expand French boundaries in the manner of Louis XIV.

In January, 1793, Louis XVI was sent to the guillotine. England was filled with horror and aversion at what was called "the most odious and atrocious crime ever known in history." At the end of January the French marched on Holland, proclaimed the Scheldt river open, declared war on England on the grounds that "the king of England has not ceased, especially since the Revolution of August 10, 1792, to give the French nation proofs of his ill-will and attachment to the coalition of crowned heads." Soon there stood against Revolutionary France the First Coalition of Prussia, Austria, England, Russia, the Netherlands, Sardinia, Spain, Naples, Portugal, Tuscany, and the Holy Roman Empire.

In July, 1793, the twelve members of the Committee of Public Safety were given broad powers of revolutionary government. The Convention, scornfully described by a Jacobin as a body of 300 scoundrels and 400 imbeciles, continued to debate and legislate; but the real power was in the hands of the Committee of Public Safety. They assembled and used the machinery of the Terror. "We must establish the despotism of liberty in order to crush the despotism of kings." At first the fanatic "revolutionary justice" was directed against real enemies of the Revolution, later against imaginary ones. "No one feels safe; no one is safe. If not a suspect one may be suspected of being a suspect."

Against the increasing enemies without the nation was called to arms. The flames of the Terror played against the dark background of foreign and civil war. The essentially theological political theory of the Jacobins stood for salvation by grace; the regeneration of the race was to be effected by extermination and conversion. "The men who made the Terror were the compeers of the First Crusaders, Savonarola, Calvin."

In the summer of 1794 the extremes of revolutionary justice abated. Many of the makers of the Terror were sent to their deaths. The cult of Reason, the four great festivals of the Revolution, and the smaller ones "to love, filial affection, misfortune, posterity, disinterestedness" lingered on; but the nation was weary of bloodshed. After Robespierre was executed "government fell into an open sewer." In 1795 the Republic was reorganized and the executive power was given to a Committee of Five, called the Directory. The Directory was weak and corrupt. France, back in the hands of the moderates, became increasingly ready to "accept any master who knows how to bind them by their hopes and fears." The man who could do this was Napoleon Bonaparte.

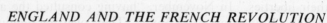

ENGLAND AND THE FRENCH REVOLUTION

During the years when these events in France were running their violent course English public opinion had undergone several changes. In the first peaceful phase of the Revolution there was wide approval of its aims among the English middle and working classes. Was France, the home of oppression and tyranny, to achieve a constitution at last? The work of the National Assembly was watched with sympathy by most liberals. Until the summer of 1790 it seemed to be a constructive imitation of the English Revolution of 1688. The Duke of Dorset, British ambassador in Paris, hailed "the accomplishment of the greatest revolution in history." Charles James Fox rejoiced at the fall of the Bastille: "How much the greatest event it is in the history of the world and how much the best!" William Wordsworth, whose magnificent *Prelude* sums up the spirit of these years, later wrote: "Bliss was it in that dawn to be alive; but to be young was very heaven."

And yet the early achievements of the National Assembly were not universally approved. One of the early opponents of the Revolution was Edmund Burke, who published his denunciatory *Reflections on the French Revolution* in October, 1790. Burke condemned the Revolution as a "foul, impious, monstrous thing, wholly out of the course of nature, a wild attempt to methodize anarchy." He wrote as the indignant and inspired prophet of conservatism, piety, and tradition. He rejoiced that he was far removed from the contamination of the slow stain of the Jacobin sympathizers. He declared that men must remember the value of continuity in human affairs, "without which men would become as flies in summer."

Across the Channel rose the embodiment of all Edmund Burke hated, a Revolution founded on a scorn of history, threatening with ruin the whole social fabric that the past had reared. "The age of chivalry is gone," declared Burke, "and that of sophisters, economists, and calculators has succeeded and the glory of Europe forever extinguished." In France the ordered structure of classes and ranks crumbled before a doctrine of social equality. The ancient state was rudely demolished and reconstituted. In a night the church and nobility were swept away.

To Burke any rapid and complete change was analogous to the decapitation of the body social and politic. For him the body politic was a complex organism, a sublime mystery, the product of centuries of corporate life in society. "I set my feet in the footprints of my ancestors, where I may neither wander nor stumble. The words of the law are my words; I have no organ but her voice. If this be not ingenious, it is at least safe." This organic conception of society saw the state as the embodiment of the idea and ideal of continuity, with a vital connection with the past, present, and future. "People will not look forward to posterity," declared Burke, "who never looked backward to their ancestors."

Burke, who owed much more to Bolingbroke and Montesquieu than to Locke, virtually abandoned the individualist concepts of the Whigs and the ideas of contract and natural law. He really recognized no law but the eternal laws of God and of organized society.

In Burke's philosophy civil society rests upon spiritual foundations, being nothing less than the product of the divine will. The semi-secular Locke would have found nothing to approve in this, or in the idea that the established Church of England was the appropriate symbol of the "consecration of the state." Nor would he have approved any conclusion that "history is the known march of the ordinary Providence of God."

Burke warned Englishmen that the course of the Revolution would become more and more extreme. He asserted that an attack on property and aristocracy in France might easily spread to England. As the Revolution advanced in violence English liberal approval of its aims and achievements turned to general distrust, suspicion, and, finally, to aversion and hostility. Soon the armies of the tricolor began to campaign where the lilies of Louis XIV had been advanced. Then Englishmen no longer refused to join the reactionary European powers against France. Once again, as so often in history, the English felt that the French had challenged their security. It was to take twenty years to free Europe from the domination of Revolutionary France and Napoleon.

There were about thirty-five printed replies to Burke's *Reflections*. Among his opponents was Shelley's mother-in-law Mary Wollstonecraft, whose *Vindication of the Rights of Man* went through several editions. A second challenge to Burke was from the pen of Tom Paine, crusader and pamphleteer extraordinary in America, France, and England. In 1791 Paine issued the first part of his *Rights of Man*. He declared that hereditary government was "an imposition on mankind." It was his view that all power was derived from the people and he demanded that a representative government should be established at once. When Paine praised republicanism and urged the abolition of monarchy he became unpopular. By that time most Englishmen were becoming alarmed at the excesses in France. They denounced the proposals of Paine with a torrent of invective that seems unmerited to men of a later age.

Another individual of some importance was William Godwin, husband of Mary Wollstonecraft, son of a Calvinist minister, author of novels, plays, children's stories, and political studies. Godwin attacked the moral and social ills resulting from public government and private property. With some accuracy, Godwin has been called the first modern utopian anarchist. In 1793 he published *An Enquiry Concerning Political Justice*. This book held that private property was the world's greatest evil. The influence of *Political Justice* was not very strong in Godwin's own day; the book cost three guineas, a price few men could afford to pay.

More and more conservative Whigs, including Burke and the Duke of Portland, began to desert their liberal leader Charles James

Fox. They went over to support Pitt and the Tories. Thus the political party balance was badly upset. Late in 1792 most of those who stood for the repression of dangerous liberal tendencies and wanted to defend the coasts of England against any invasion of French doctrines were united under the leadership of the Tory Pitt. Most were convinced that the triumph of French ideas meant the destruction of order, religion, and the class system. Revolutionary propaganda and reform movements must be suppressed. In the eyes of alarmed conservatives the September Massacres showed the insane results of hysterical radicalism and the meaning of the regime of the guillotine. Exaggerated tales of the horrors in France were brought by thousands of refugee priests and nobles. It was estimated that over 15,000 Frenchmen were living in London at the end of 1792. "There are so many priests in the streets that with their sable appearance and the help of the fogs our pavement is totally darkened."

In its early stages the French Revolution had stimulated English reform movements. New societies mushroomed up alongside old associations; a large pamphlet literature advocated various reforms. Members of the Corresponding Society, founded in 1792, corresponded with French leaders. Despite the fame achieved by the Corresponding Society it seems that its total influence was inconsiderable. In most of these new societies there were some radical revolutionaries; but the number was certainly small. However, the fact that a few revolutionists and French secret agents were loose in the land served to increase popular apprehension. Even the rather respectable Society of the Friends of the People became suspect. The Tory government seized the chance to keep public opinion excited so that legitimate reform movements would be temporarily stifled and national feeling would be ready to support, if need be, a war against France.

In the spring of 1792 a proclamation was issued against "seditious writings." After the war with France began in 1793 the fear of "Jacobins" increased. A large number of trials brought injustice from prejudiced judges and juries. In 1794 an act was passed suspending *habeas corpus* in certain cases, which made imprisonment possible without trial. The act stated that "a traitorous and detestable conspiracy has been formed for subverting the existing laws and constitution and for introducing the system of anarchy and confusion which has so fatally prevailed in France."

In 1795 the passage of the Treasonable and Seditious Practices Act and the Seditious Assemblies Act gave further evidence of the panic caused by events across the Channel. There was now no chance to agitate for reform. So far as the government was concerned reform meant the same thing as revolution. This harsh series of repressive acts took away from a large part of the population its only way of expressing an opinion; because it was not represented in Parliament it could say nothing without being liable to punishment under the new muzzling legislation. Both labor and capital had a difficult time in abiding by such laws as these during the successive economic crises between 1793 and 1797.

Meanwhile the series of bad harvests and worsening industrial conditions resulted in one attempt to relieve the working classes. In 1795 the Berkshire magistrates began the so-called Speenhamland system by which wages were to be supplemented out of the parish rates. A scale was drawn up providing that the parishes would make up a worker's wages to 3s. a week for himself, and 1s.6d. for each member of his family. If the cost of bread rose the scale of aid was to rise with it. After 1795 the employers paid lower wages because they knew the parish authorities would make up the deficiency. The evil consequences of this Speenhamland system continued far into the nineteenth century. Some of the later results are explained in Chapter 28.

The repressive spirit of the times is again shown by the passage of the Combination Acts of 1799 and 1800. These measures made trade unionism illegal. They made it a punishable offense for workmen to combine with one another "to obtain an advance in wages." Workers were also prohibited from "wilfully and maliciously" endeavoring to prevent any person from hiring himself to a manufacturer or business man. They were forbidden "to decoy, persuade, solicit, intimidate, influence, or prevail" upon a worker to quit his job. If any man "without just or reasonable cause" refused to work he could be imprisoned "for any time not exceeding three calendar months." A government fearful of Jacobinism looked upon tradesmen's unions as a potential danger. It was also the opinion of Parliament that industry should be based upon a system of free enterprise and therefore the workers should not be permitted to combine for any purposes that would alter the free competition of employers in a labor market.

Such were a few of the measures passed by Parliament during these years of war and fear. The counter-revolutionary point of view was in full flood. Many liberal Foxite Whigs retired to their country houses. Fortunately their leaders remained. Charles James Fox, Lord Holland, and Charles Grey, later Earl Grey of Reform Bill fame, kept firmly fixed their Whig ideals of liberalism and parliamentary reform. They sturdily held remnants of the Whig party together. If the Whigs had collapsed during their long exile the story of the nineteenth century might not have been one of parliamentary reform; it would probably have been a French tale of armed revolution and reaction. A great British historian has referred to the gallant Foxites as "a bridge, however slender and insecure, still hanging across the gulf that divided classes in the new era." It was England's good fortune that this was so; amidst the unreason of war her conscience was kept alive by men like Fox and Wilberforce.

THE FIRST COALITION

When France opened the navigation of the Scheldt River, Pitt replied that "England will never consent that France shall arrogate the power of annulling at her pleasure, and under the pretence of a pretended natural right, of which she makes herself the only judge, the political system of Europe, established by solemn treaties and guaranteed by the consent of all the Powers." When France declared war on Britain on February 1, 1793, the event surprised nobody. Five years earlier an English diplomat had written: "We suppose the French are looking out for an opportunity of commencing hostilities against us, and the French think that Great Britain is seeking for pretences to begin a war against them." To the British horror of Jacobin excesses was now added the French threat to the Netherlands and Antwerp. "The Low Countries," said Britain's foreign secretary, "form the chain which unites England to the Continent, and the central knot of our relations to Austria and Russia. It would be broken if they belonged to France."

George III found the declaration of war "highly agreeable." He hoped that England would "curb the insolence of those despots and be the means of restoring some degree of order to that unprincipled country, whose aim at present is to destroy the foundation of every civilized state." Not all Englishmen were so hopeful. "I think I see," wrote one, "the end of King, of Government, and indeed of all rule, approaching." He saw England "hastily and unthinkingly plunged into war; discontent will increase with taxes and we shall double our stakes like ruined gamesters."

The tenacious and formidable Pitt lacked the war skill of his father; he could not plan so brilliantly the massive combined operations that had won the Seven Years' War; nor was he wise in selecting the ministers who were responsible for the naval and military forces; his friend Henry Dundas was useless in an army post; his elder brother made a poor First Lord of the Admiralty. But for twelve dark and desperate years Pitt was an able, inspiring, and brave political leader. Until his death he was the soul of every coalition against France.

In the first stages of the war Pitt began the familiar British policy of helping the European allies by direct cash subsidies. It was hoped that British gold would keep the coalition in being against France. The European powers of the coalition would then hold the enemy on land. British naval strength would whittle down French sea power, attack French ports, seize French colonies. Early in 1793 a small British army was sent over the Channel and the Austrians, Prussians, Dutch, and English forces combined to drive the French out of the Netherlands. Several allied forces penetrated the French frontiers. Meanwhile, however, the French were raising huge forces by national conscription.

The Republic was organizing the armies which were to be Napoleon's tool of conquest. The blazing enthusiasm of the revolutionary spirit and the sheer weight of numbers united to force the invaders out of France. Then the French, by a stroke of luck, captured the Dutch navy.

Meanwhile the acquisitive rulers of Prussia, Russia, and Austria became preoccupied with the second (1793) and third (1795) partitions of unfortunate Poland. Napoleon Bonaparte, an artillery lieutenant, laid siege to Royalist Toulon and forced the British to withdraw from the harbor. In the West Indies the British schemes were going badly. In June, 1794, Lord Howe won a long sea battle with the French; he captured six battleships, but let a grain convoy slip through his blockade.

Elsewhere the allies of the First Coalition were in retreat. Early in 1795 the French occupied the Netherlands. The Dutch had to change sides. Then the British seized the Dutch colonies of Ceylon and the Cape of Good Hope. Prussia, bankrupt and deeply concerned about the Polish situation, made peace with France. European coalitions have usually been plagued by intrigues, greed, and apathy. Spain also made peace; in 1796 she was to come into the war again, this time on the side of France.

Behind her tutelary winds and waves Britain stood obstinately impregnable; but she stood now with only three important members of the First Coalition left by her side: Austria, Sardinia, and Russia. It was in such circumstances that the challenge of the Jacobins was replaced by the challenge of Napoleon Bonaparte. To defeat Napoleon was a heavy task. It took nearly twenty years of unrelenting struggle.

Chapter 27

THE CHALLENGE OF NAPOLEON

WAR AND PEACE, 1796–1802

FOR fifteen years the biography of Napoleon Bonaparte and the tempestuous history of Europe were almost the same thing. Napoleon knit the Continent together in a vast partnership of strife and subjugation. The whole Napoleonic era possesses the cohesive unity of a great drama. This chapter is about the years of England's relentless conflict with Napoleon until the final disaster fell upon him in 1815. "All the ills and curses which afflict mankind come from London," Bonaparte said, "England should be an appendix to my France. Nature has designed her, like Corsica, to be a French island."

Napoleon was born in Corsica in 1769. He was educated in France, received a commission in the French army, won recognition by assisting in the capture of Toulon from the English and the French Royalists (1793), and later by defending the Convention against a mob attack in Paris (1795). In the spring of 1796 he was placed by the Directory in command of the French army in Italy. With this appointment his astonishing military career began.

Napoleon faced the combined armies of Austria and Sardinia. He split his two enemies by marching north from Savona, forced the Sardinians back upon Turin, and compelled them to conclude a truce. Then he struck against the Austrians. He outflanked them, forced them into Mantua, besieged them, accepted their surrender. By April, 1797, Napoleon approached Vienna. The Austrians signed a peace by which Austria ceded to France the Austrian Netherlands, recognized the French frontier on the Rhine, and acknowledged the dependent republics the French had established in Holland, Switzerland, and North Italy. Napoleon, declaring that the French nation needed a head who had been "rendered illustrious by glory and not by theories of government," now set out to be master of the French Republic. He was utterly unscrupulous; he plotted and awaited the day to strike for power.

England now stood alone against the victorious French Republic.

527

A few years before, Frederick the Great had said: "England is a ruined and undone country, crippled by an unfortunate war, and unable ever again to become a formidable rival of France." Early in 1797 Englishmen faced heavy taxation, rising prices, a financial crisis, and rebellion in Ireland. Against England stood the fleets of France, Holland, and Spain. There were two serious mutinies in the British fleet at Spithead and in the North Sea. England's command of the sea was in jeopardy. Then the naval scene brightened. In July, 1797, the Spaniards were defeated off Cape St. Vincent. Later the Dutch were beaten at Camperdown; nine of the sixteen Dutch ships were captured.

Meanwhile Napoleon persuaded the Directory that England could best be ruined by striking at her empire and trade. He proposed an attack on British commerce in the Mediterranean and an invasion of Egypt. The Mediterranean would become a French lake. The road to the annexation of Turkey would be open. Bonaparte, dreaming of the career of Alexander the Great, also foresaw the French conquest of India. "This little Europe," he once said, "is too small for me."

In May, 1798, Napoleon transported a French army from Toulon to Alexandria, eluding in the darkness a British squadron under Admiral Horatio Nelson. Napoleon easily defeated the Turkish forces in the Battle of the Pyramids. On August 1, Admiral Nelson, who had looked in vain for the French along the Syrian coast, discovered Napoleon's fleet in Aboukir Bay, one of the mouths of the Nile. All but four French ships were sunk. Napoleon's troops were completely cut off from Europe. "Had I been master of the sea," Napoleon later said, "I should have been lord also of the Orient."

Despite his broken communication lines Napoleon decided to continue his land campaign against the Turks. Early in 1799 he marched into Syria; but the Turks, aided by an English fleet, held him back at Acre. He returned to Egypt; his army was suffering badly from the numerous diseases that slay and cripple in the Near East. Napoleon now learned that the corrupt, inefficient, and demoralized Directory in France had lost northern Italy to the armies of the Second Coalition; France herself was threatened with invasion. It seemed that the time for Napoleon to seize power had come; he deserted his army and returned to France in October, 1799. The conquest of Egypt was barren. India was secure. Napoleon's oriental vision had faded.

The Second Coalition was largely the creation of William Pitt. In December, 1798, he had been able to join England with Russia, Austria, Turkey, and Naples in a common front against the Directory. Then an Austro-Russian army had swept the French out of northern Italy and driven deep into Switzerland. The royalists in Naples began a violent compaign against the Neapolitan republicans. Elsewhere the arms of the Second Coalition were also successful against the nerveless Directory.

Such were the circumstances when Napoleon arrived from Egypt. He was greeted as a hero by the enthusiastic French people who had the idea that he had conquered widely in the Near East. It was easy for him to overthrow the Directory. In its place he set up a new government of three consuls, with himself as First Consul. He was, in fact, virtual dictator of France. Most people in France, after nearly a decade of revolution and war, wanted a stable government and peace more than an ineffective republican regime.

Napoleon at once began to "consolidate the Revolution" by establishing a strong French government on the basis of the social and economic changes effected by the Revolution. He organized a new plan of government; centralized the administrative system; stabilized the currency; arranged a Concordat with the Pope (1801); and pushed through the Civil Code (1804) which embodied the basic changes brought about by the Revolution in the legal status of persons and property. Meanwhile he set about the "pacification of Europe" by endeavoring to end the war with Austria and England. Russia, at odds with Austria, had left the allied camp. To accomplish his ends Napoleon had to break the Second Coalition. He swiftly raised new armies. These, he trusted, would establish the prestige of France abroad and increase his own at home. Those who believed in his genius were not disappointed.

Napoleon secretly collected an army near Dijon and took it over the Alpine pass of St. Bernard to strike at the surprised Austrians in the rear. On June 15, 1800, the Austrians were defeated at Marengo, near Genoa. A truce was signed next day. The "freed" Cisalpine Republic was compelled to pay a monthly tax of 2,000,000 francs. The profits of foreign wars also helped to fill the French state treasuries. Napoleon knew that a regime that hopes to be popular must try to hold the tax level down. Austria was defeated again at Hohenlinden in southern Germany. Early in 1801 she agreed to make a separate peace with France and crept out of the war.

Again Britain stood alone. Napoleon made overtures for peace but Pitt refused to negotiate. "That Bonaparte has an interest in making peace," he said to Parliament, "is at best but a doubtful proposition, and that he has an interest in preserving it is still more uncertain." Pitt, strongly opposed by Charles James Fox, declared that Napoleon "united in his own person everything that a pure republican must detest; everything that a sincere and faithful royalist must feel as an insult. . . . If we are ultimately disappointed of that complete success for which we are at present entitled to hope, the continuance of the contest, instead of making our situation comparatively worse, will have made it comparatively better." By this time Britain had taken Malta, which has remained a British island, and many French, Spanish, and Dutch possessions in various parts of the world. The British fleets were victorious; the French had been stopped everywhere on the seas. On the other hand, the Second Coalition had fallen. The French had triumphed on the land. Once again, the British had to find European allies.

Meanwhile Napoleon profited by the British searchings and seizure of neutral vessels. As in the days of the American Revolution, the Baltic powers grew resentful. In 1800 the half-crazy Tsar Paul I revived the Armed Neutrality of the North under which Russia, Sweden, and Denmark opposed the British insistence that neutrals should not supply France with goods by sea. As a matter of economic warfare, Britain could not abandon the advantages given her by naval supremacy. In 1801 a British fleet under Nelson bombarded Copenhagen for four hours; the Danes surrendered. When Paul I of Russia was murdered his son Alexander I came to terms with Britain. The League of Armed Neutrality fell and the Baltic stayed open.

Napoleon could not challenge the strong sea walls of England's navy. England could not make headway against Napoleon on land because she had no allies after the collapse of the Second Coalition. The war of "the whale and the elephant" had reached a stalemate.

Under these circumstances haggling negotiations for peace began. The result was the hollow Treaty of Amiens signed in March, 1802. This agreement provided for "peace, friendship, and intelligence" between Great Britain and France. Under its terms Britain kept Trinidad and Dutch Ceylon. She agreed to return the Cape of Good Hope to the Dutch, and all of the French colonies to the French. Britain further promised to hand back Malta to the Knights of St. John. The territorial integrity of Portugal and Turkey was guaranteed by both powers. It was also agreed that "the contracting powers shall use the utmost efforts to preserve a perfect harmony between their respective countries, without permitting any act of hostility whatever by sea or by land for any cause or under any pretext."

The Treaty of Amiens was important especially for what it did not say. For example, no reference was made to the status of the Low Countries, "the pistol pointed at the heart of England," which was one of the reasons why Pitt had gone to war in 1793. There was no guarantee that the French controlled European markets would be opened to British trade. There were other omissions. Had England conceded too much? Severe criticism of the settlement spread swiftly. About the whole arrangement there were several opinions. The always hopeful Henry Addington declared: "This is no ordinary peace. It is the actual reconciliation of the two foremost nations of the world." George III did not agree. "Do you know what I call this peace? An experimental peace—for it is nothing else." Napoleon said: "At Amiens I achieved the moral conquest of Europe." There could be no lasting peace with Napoleon. After one year the two weary nations were to turn again to war.

THE DOMESTIC SCENE, 1793–1802

As the war moved forward to the uneasy peace of 1802 the English national debt had been increased by £135,000,000. "We have a revenue equal to all Europe," said Pitt, "a navy superior to all Europe, and to make us quite gentlemen, a debt as large as that of all Europe." High taxes bore harshly on all classes. The currency was heavily inflated as a result of war loans, the shipments of gold to subsidize England's European allies, and the overissue of paper money. In 1797 the Bank of England suspended specie payments. Prices rose swiftly and food outpaced all other commodities in the price spiral. Between 1790 and 1815 there were only five good harvest years. Grain had to be imported throughout the war period. Because shipping was scarce and insurance rates high the total freight costs leaped upwards. The result of these facts of war and weather was an increase of the price of wheat from about nine shillings a bushel to a maximum of about fifteen shillings a bushel. Hence the price of bread, the workers' staff of life, was forced steadily higher. Some aspects of this grim situation have been described in the preceding chapter.

Added to these causes of economic dislocation were the fluctuations in business. In one year there would be unemployment and depression; in another, a boom, high employment, good wages. Part of this was due to the variation in the volume of government war orders. The demand for such things as cloth, cannon, shoes, and uniforms rose and fell. At the same time, however, there was a fairly large and constant domestic industrial development with the creation of new and ill-distributed goods and capital. For example, the imports of raw cotton totalled 31,000,000 pounds in 1790; in 1799 the total was 43,000,000 pounds; in 1801, 56,000,000 pounds. In 1788, 68,000 tons of pig iron were produced; by 1796 the total was 125,000 tons. A similar increase occurred in the volume of exports. Meanwhile, as noted earlier, the Speenhamland system of poor relief and the repressive Combination Acts helped to block the road to reform agitation.

During these fateful years the volcano of the Irish problem erupted violently. "England's difficulty is Ireland's opportunity." Earlier in the century Ireland was quiet but discontented and ill-governed. It was true that many of the cruel statutes against the Catholics were not harshly enforced in an age of reason. The Irish were able to develop new commercial activities and to increase their incomes by smuggling. Nevertheless, in the south the Catholic Irishman was excluded from political office; no Catholic might vote or sit in Parliament. In Protestant Northern Ireland the Test Act kept the Ulster Presbyterians from taking part in the government. Thus the majority of Irishmen had no political rights, and few economic ones. They were ruled by a few Anglican families. Even the Irish Parliament in Dublin, unrepresentative as it was, was dependent upon England because it could pass no legislation without the approval of the English government.

The revolt of the American colonists had stirred the Irishmen to renew their demands for free trade and a free Parliament. The leader of the Irish national revival was the moderate Protestant Henry Grattan, a landowner, a statesman of vision, a magnificent orator. After France entered the war in 1778 the Irish Catholics and Protestants joined to raise Irish volunteer regiments to defend Ireland against a threatened French invasion. Grattan used the hour of danger to force a fearful English Parliament to wipe away many obnoxious restrictions on Irish trade. In 1782 the short-lived Rockingham administration repealed Poyning's law, which since 1494 had made the Irish Parliament subordinate to the privy council in London. Thus Ireland received a considerable degree of legislative independence. No longer did the acts of the Irish Parliament have to be "certified into England."

Despite these concessions there were still major Irish grievances. The Irish boroughs were as "rotten" as those in England and the Irish landlords really controlled parliamentary majorities in Dublin. The English cabinet still appointed the executive officers in Dublin Castle. Westminster could veto the acts of the Irish Parliament. A small minority of non-Presbyterian Protestants, virtually all of them Anglicans, still held tightly to the reins of power in Ireland. Soon the penal code was modified and the Catholics were given the vote (1793); but they were not permitted to sit in the Irish Parliament.

With the outbreak of the French Revolution the clouds darkened. The Society of United Irishmen corresponded with French republicans who promised to help them. Catholic peasants in the south burned hayricks and attacked their landlords. Radical Irish leaders like Wolfe Tone preached violence and outrage. Then the Catholics and Protestants began to fight among themselves. An ugly civil war broke out as Orangemen and Catholics battled passionately about the ancient questions of religion. A Catholic revolt in 1798, inadequately supported by the French, was swiftly crushed by British forces. Both sides were guilty of horrible excesses. The British, as the famous Irish song relates, hanged men and women for "wearing of the green." The Irish, for their part, burned and massacred without mercy or justice.

Pitt decided that the arrangements with Henry Grattan were unsatisfactory. He now proposed a legislative union between the English and Irish Parliaments, similar to that which had been made between England and Scotland in 1707. Pitt promised that if the Irish agreed to send representatives to Westminster instead of to Dublin the Irish Catholics would be given full political rights and the laws against them would be repealed. This promise of Catholic emancipation helped to carry the bill for the legislative union through the Irish Parliament, although there was also needed the bribery of gold, pensions, and

Section V

REVOLUTIONS, ECONOMIC AND POLITICAL

A view of Leicester, A.D. 1743, showing common land still unenclosed outside the town.

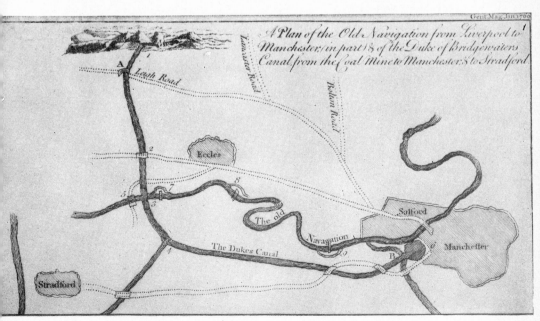

The Manchester Canal—a contemporary plan.

Jethro Tull's grain-drill "makes the channels, sows the seed into them, and covers them at the same time."

A spinning jenny.

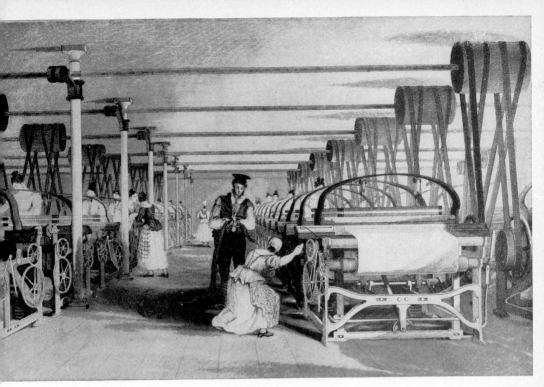

A power loom.

Thomas Newcomen's
atmospheric
steam engine.

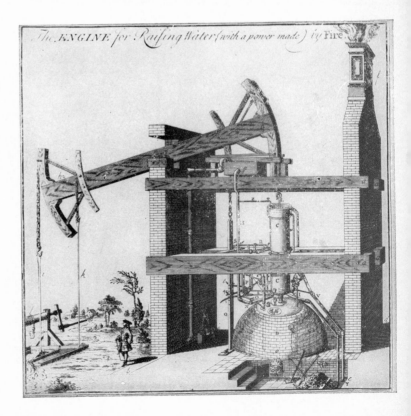

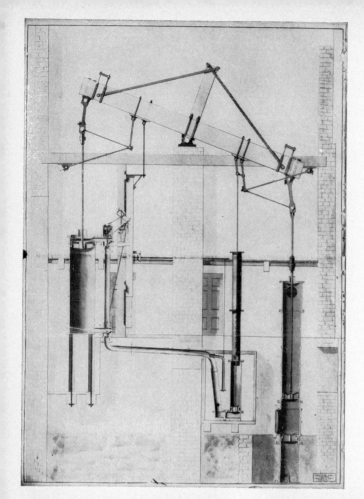

A Watt single-acting
pumping engine.

William Pitt, 1759–1806.

Edmund Burke.

Adam Smith.

The POLITICAL BANDITTI assailing the SAVIOUR of INDIA.

A contemporary cartoon defending Warren Hastings. The "Political Banditti" are Burke, Fox and Sheridan.

One of James Gillray's many satires on the activities of English sympathizers with the French Revolution. Note the Mamelukes with the bowstrings waiting to enforce the Rights of Man.

The French line broken at Trafalgar.

MENE MENE, TEKEL, UPHARSIN

The Hand-Writing upon the Wall.

An English view of Napoleon's situation in 1803.

Waterloo—a contemporary print.

peerages. Despite Henry Grattan's eloquent opposition, the Act of Union passed both Parliaments and the separate Dublin Parliament ceased to exist on January 1, 1801. After that date Ireland was represented at Westminster by 100 members in the house of commons and 28 peers and 4 bishops in the house of lords. There was to be full free trade between the two countries. The kingdom of Great Britain, formed in 1707, became the United Kingdom of Great Britain and Ireland.

The solution of the Act of Union might have been made real and workable had the Catholics been emancipated or enfranchised. The intermittently insane George III stubbornly refused to give the Irish Catholics their political freedom because he claimed that in doing so he would violate his coronation oath. Pitt worked vainly to convince the obstinate king of the practical wisdom of removing the disabilities of the Catholics. George III's anti-Catholic prejudices were too deeply rooted; he was secretly encouraged by Pitt's enemies to persist in his refusal; he threatened to go mad if the Catholics were enfranchised. Pitt felt that he had given his promise to the Irish and must see the measure through Parliament or, as a matter of honor, surrender his office. In 1801, he resigned. Although Pitt did not make his resignation a party issue, a number of his colleagues followed him out of the cabinet. In Ireland a disillusioned people prepared to travel a long road of conflict and misunderstanding.

The new Tory prime minister was Henry Addington, later Lord Sidmouth. Addington, a student and friend of Pitt, had decorously filled the speaker's chair in the house of commons. He was handicapped by lack of ability and imagination. "Pitt is to Addington as London is to Paddington," said a contemporary wit. It was generally felt that the mediocre Addington was only "Pitt's warming pan." His most conspicuous achievement was once held to be the recommendation of a hop pillow to the king as a soporific. About him were many weak and inexperienced ministers. It was this government that made the Treaty of Amiens in 1802. The period of peace lasted only a year. Soon after the war with Napoleon was renewed Addington's majority dwindled and popular demand brought Pitt back into office.

THE THIRD COALITION

English business and industrial interests were irked that the markets controlled by France remained closed to English exports. French commercial interests, on the other hand, rejoiced at a state of affairs so prejudicial to the economic welfare of their English rivals. The provisions of the Eden Treaty, declared Napoleon, were abrogated. Moreover, the French still stayed in Belgium. Napoleon was feverishly building naval ships; he obtained Louisiana and laid robber hands on Santo Domingo in the West Indies; he sent a secret mission to India; he kept troops in Holland and the British feared he might try to control the Cape of Good Hope, athwart the road to India, which had been returned to the Netherlands under the terms of the Treaty of Amiens.

Napoleon also declared himself president of the Cisalpine Republic, annexed the Piedmont in northern Italy, proclaimed a new constitution for Switzerland. It seemed to the apprehensive British that France was using the months of peace to prepare for further conquests. "France needs glorious deeds, and hence war," said Napoleon to his council of state in 1802. "She must be the first among states or she is lost. I shall put up with peace as long as our neighbors can maintain it, but I shall regard it as an advantage if they force me to take up my arms again before they rust."

Under the terms of Amiens England had agreed to give up Malta. But Malta was an excellent naval base and Minorca had been lost in 1783. Suspicious of Napoleon's plans, the British cabinet refused to surrender Malta, and this was the technical cause of the resumption of hostilities in 1803. In terms of naval power Britain was in a safe position to go to war when peace failed. In 1793 she had 135 ships of the line and 133 frigates; France had 80 ships of the line and 60 frigates. In 1802 Britain had 202 ships of the line and 277 frigates. In that year, despite Napoleon's naval building program, France had only 39 ships of the line and 35 frigates. Before the Treaty of Amiens the British army strength stood at about 250,000; after the peace arrangements it fell to about 125,000; then it was swiftly increased as war threatened. By January, 1803, there were over 190,000 Englishmen under arms.

England was also strengthened by the fact that there was no longer any national disunity as there had been earlier in the war. Almost all Englishmen were at last convinced that their liberty was threatened by the ambitious aggressions of Bonaparte. It was in 1803 that William Wordsworth wrote his famous sonnet about "the flood of British freedom" that must not perish in the bogs and sands of slavery.

In 1804, when Addington and his colleagues proved unequal to the conduct of the war, Pitt came out of retirement. A month later Napoleon was crowned Emperor Napoleon I. Already he had in mind the creation of a "Grand Empire" extending far beyond the frontiers of France. Talleyrand later said that "the extension of France to the Rhine, the Alps, and the Pyrenees was the work of the Revolution; everything else was the work of Napoleon." A contemporary English pamphleteer wrote: "After the noble line of kings had been brought to an end, after the oratory of the Republicans, and the hysterical violence of the Jacobins, France's originality in the choice of her rulers surpasses herself. A puny little soldier man sits upon her throne." Napoleon, much more wisely, said: "Power is never ridiculous."

Against France stood the Third Coalition, in which Russia and Austria were England's chief allies, persuaded by "Pitt's gold" as well as by their own interests. Napoleon may have concluded that to make his projected "Grand Empire" safe he must first subdue England; Austria and Russia could be disposed of later. In any event, he assembled a large army at Boulogne; he gathered transports and naval fighting ships. Nearly eight hundred years before, William the Conqueror had moved against England from the Somme estuary, near St. Valery. Julius Caesar, Napoleon Bonaparte, and Adolf Hitler all assembled invasion forces at Boulogne; only Caesar sailed.

Across the Channel Englishmen were preparing their defenses as they had in 1588. If Napoleon could gain control of the Channel for twenty-four hours, his armies might soon be in London. But two British naval squadrons watched off Brest and Toulon; smaller forces blockaded French and Spanish ports. Lord St. Vincent declared in the house of lords: "I do not say, my lords, that the French cannot come. I only say, they cannot come *by sea*."

After several attempts to escape the watchful Admiral Nelson, one of which took them to the West Indies, the French and Spanish fleets still found the British guarding the Channel. Finally, the French ships from Toulon did succeed in joining the Spanish ships at Cadiz. Napoleon was at Boulogne, apparently impatient for his vessels to cover his crossing to England. Did he really intend to sail against the British Isles? Or was he in fact planning an unexpected attack upon Austria? To these questions many answers have been given, most of them worthy of respect, none of them final and certain. In August, 1805, Napoleon acted on reports that the Austrians were mobilizing and suddenly shifted his Grand Army from Boulogne towards Austria.

A few weeks later the combined French and Spanish fleets sailed out of Cadiz to meet Nelson. The result was the battle off Cape Trafalgar, the last great naval battle fought with sailing ships. On October 21, 1805, Nelson won the battle and lost his life. A week earlier he had written: "May God Almighty give us success over these fellows and enable us to get a peace." Now England's security at sea was confirmed. It was to be left unchallenged for a hundred years. "I cannot be everywhere," said Napoleon. On November 9, 1805, William Pitt was hailed at a banquet as the "saviour of Europe." His reply was characteristic: "Europe is not to be saved by any single man. England has saved herself by her exertions and will, I trust, save Europe by her example."

Meanwhile Napoleon's legions were marching away from the useless camp at Boulogne. He forced one Austrian army to surrender at Ulm. Then, in December, 1805, he completely smashed the combined Austrian and Russian armies at Austerlitz. Austria toppled, and signed the humiliating Peace of Pressburg by which she recognized all Napoleon's changes in Italy and lost her possessions in south Germany. It seemed that the Third Coalition was crumbling. Information also came that Berlin had accepted Napoleon's proposal that Prussia should take England's Hanover as a reward for co-operation with France.

Although he was only forty-seven years old, William Pitt was already weary and ill in 1805. "The truth is," wrote a contemporary, "that he was entirely worn out by his constant attendance upon his parliamentary duties from a very early age, and from the unwholesome life that he led, seldom eating anything until the house had adjourned, which was frequently not before three or four in the morning." Pitt had also been heavily buffeted by the disloyalty of some cabinet colleagues and the outright defection of others. He had earlier wanted to make a broad-bottom coalition war cabinet of the best men of both parties; but George III was opposed to such an arrangement because it might give too much power to Charles James Fox; the king abhorred Fox.

Such difficulties had steadily dogged Pitt. He had to fight political foes at home and the French abroad at the same time. It is possible that the news of Napoleon's shattering triumphs hastened his death. "Roll up that map of Europe," he is supposed to have said; "it will not be needed these ten years." His last words were: "My country, how I leave my country!" This was in January, 1806.

THE CONTINENTAL SYSTEM

After the death of Pitt there was a succession of mediocre prime ministers. George III was at first compelled to accept a coalition government called "the Ministry of All the Talents." This administration, headed by Lord Grenville, included several Whigs. Chief among them was Charles James Fox, who became foreign secretary. For many years Fox had worked with men like Wilberforce against slavery in the Empire. Shortly after coming into office he helped to introduce a bill for the abolition of the slave trade. Fox died in September, 1806, but the bill was passed and the slave trade was made illegal in 1807.

The death of Fox resulted in the disintegration of the coalition cabinet. The king threw his ministers out when they proposed to complete the military emancipation of the Catholics by admitting them to the higher grades of the army. Early in 1807 a new ministry was formed, headed by the second-rate and decrepit Duke of Portland. In 1809, after Portland had resigned and died, another cabinet was formed by the ultra-Tory and Protestant lawyer Spencer Perceval, who was murdered by a maniac in 1812. His successor was Lord Liverpool, who held office until 1827. Liverpool's great strength was his mediocrity, which excited no jealousy and under which rival ambitions might unite.

Meanwhile Napoleon was remaking the map of Europe. Part of his scheme for a Grand Empire by which he would "fuse all nations into one" was the creation of dependent kingdoms ruled by various members of his family. In 1805 the Cisalpine Republic became the kingdom of Italy, ruled by Napoleon's stepson. In 1806 southern Italy became the kingdom of Naples under his brother Joseph and the Batavian Republic became the kingdom of Holland under his brother Louis. In 1806 Napoleon formed the Confederation of the Rhine as a dependency of France and forced Francis II of Austria to abdicate the title of Holy Roman Emperor. Thus the famed Holy Roman Empire, founded by Charlemagne and since the fifteenth century a possession of the Austrian Hapsburgs, came to an end.

Late in 1806 Prussia learned that Napoleon had offered to hand Hanover back to George III despite the fact that he had earlier promised it to Prussia. This fact, coupled with Napoleon's alarming aggressions, drove Prussia into war, in which she was joined by Russia and Great Britain.

Napoleon's smashing victories at Jena and Auerstadt left Prussia prostrate before his armies. In 1807 Napoleon turned against Russia and defeated her at Friedland. He thereupon arranged treaties with Prussia and Russia which together constituted the Peace of Tilsit. By its terms Russia became an ally of France. The possessions of Prussia west of the Elbe, together with other German principalities, were gathered into the kingdom of Westphalia under Napoleon's brother Jerome. The Polish possessions of Prussia became the Grand Duchy of Warsaw, nominally ruled by the king of Saxony, but in fact controlled by Napoleon. Almost all of Continental Europe was now dominated by France.

Sea-girt Britain was once more alone, but still undefeated. Napoleon now decided to strike at British political, naval, and economic power by destroying her commerce and industry through a vast embargo which was called the "Continental System." England, he felt, might be ruined commercially and industrially by excluding her manufactured and colonial goods from the continent of Europe. Napoleon reasoned that an interruption of England's export trade would reduce government revenues from taxes and customs; national income would shrink; national credit would fall; unsold goods would glut English warehouses. England must buy some goods, such as certain foodstuffs, abroad. If those imports could not be paid for by exports then England would have to pay in specie and her gold reserves would soon be exhausted. Then, surely, the fragile structure of British credit would finally collapse and the national power would be submerged in a sea of inflation.

It was also noted that England's national debt, which had alarmed Adam Smith in 1775, was still rising. In 1793 it had stood at £230,-000,000; in 1802 it was £507,000,000. In 1793 the annual budget was £27,000,000; in 1802 it was £100,000,000; and in 1813 it was £174,000,000. Continental observers could not understand how the English public could be persuaded to accept irredeemable bank notes or how the government could borrow so much to aid in financing the war. More astounding was the fact that foreigners shipped capital for investment in England. British credit stayed sound and her trade balance remained reasonably favorable. Nevertheless, Napoleon's Continental System bore hardly upon Britain's strained economy, particularly in the dark years of 1810 and 1811. The domestic effects of this economic warfare will be described in the following chapter.

Napoleon began his new attempt to break the stalemate and end British resistance by issuing his famous Berlin Decrees on November 21, 1806. These decrees declared Great Britain to be in a state of blockade. They forbade all commerce between Britain and France or the states allied with France. Neutral ships that entered British ports and later came into any French-controlled ports in France, Germany, Holland, Italy, or Spain were liable to seizure.

On January 7, Great Britain replied by her Orders in Council declaring a blockade of all the states of Europe that submitted to Napoleon. However, neutrals might call at British ports for licenses to proceed to French ports. The president of the board of trade explained the British policy with precision and brevity: "France by her decrees has resolved to abolish all trade with England. England now says that France shall have no trade but with England." Napoleon stated in his Milan Decree (1807) that any ship sailing to or from a British port was lawful prize. Thus a new phase of economic warfare began. The question was: which would break first, France or Britain?

Napoleon's plan could not succeed without the full support of all Europe. So long as a few leaks remained in his economic dyke Napoleon could not hope to triumph. On the edge of Europe he failed to obtain the cooperation he needed. British commerce flowed under neutral flags, under British licenses, under licenses issued by European authorities, even with the permission of Napoleon himself. French industry staggered before the demands suddenly thrust upon it. France had to buy British goods. Many soldiers of the Emperor were shod with British shoes and dressed in British uniforms. In 1807 over 50,000 of the French troops engaged in the campaign against Russia wore British overcoats. British tea, coffee, tobacco, and chocolate could not be excluded from Europe; the demand was too great, the agents of France too corruptible. British goods were smuggled through the ports of Greece, Dalmatia, Portugal, Holland, and northern Germany. As European prices mounted the profits to be made by smuggling overbalanced the risks involved. There was bribery, carelessness, and frequently calculated negligence on the part of customs officials.

Under the terms of the Treaty of Tilsit Russia had agreed to join the Continental System and to support Napoleon in forcing it upon Sweden, Denmark, and Portugal. George Canning, foreign secretary in the Portland administration, learned that Napoleon intended to seize the Danish navy. Britain at once demanded the surrender of the Danish fleet and bombarded Copenhagen until the Danes yielded. Denmark, naturally incensed at this unfriendly performance, now adhered to the Continental System. Two years later Sweden also joined Napoleon's blockade. But the British fleet kept the Baltic open.

Meanwhile Napoleon sought to stop the flood of British goods through Portugal. His attempts to do so involved him in the conquest of Spain. In 1808 he shamelessly turned against his ally and forced the Spanish king to abdicate. Napoleon's brother Joseph was put on the Spanish throne. Proud Spain revolted. There had never been much sympathy in conservative and Catholic Madrid or Lisbon for the liberal and irreligious doctrines of the French Revolution. And Spain rebelled as a united nation, not as a weak and divided Italian or German state. Against Napoleon the Spaniards waged an irregular guerrilla warfare with which his generals could not cope. A national spirit had helped France conquer her neighbors; the rise of national spirits over Europe was to turn the tables and wreck the Grand Empire.

Events in Spain gave Britain an opportunity to invade the Continent and to restore the prestige of the British army. An alliance was made with Spain and a British army of about 30,000 men was sent to Portugal under the command of Sir Arthur Wellesley, later the Duke of Wellington. London and Madrid saw to it that Napoleon never escaped from the net of the Spanish entanglement. At first the British waited behind the fortified lines of Torres Vedras; their army was anchored on Lisbon; and Lisbon was supplied from the sea. By 1811 the ill-fed French had been forced to retreat from Portugal with heavy losses; their supply and communication lines were too long. The hard facts of the Peninsular War drained French troops from other parts of Europe. The sniping guerrilla tactics of the Spaniards never slackened. Wellesley and Sir John Moore fought relentlessly and with superb strategy, inflicting major defeats on the proud armies of France. Napoleon's Grand Empire was becoming too large and cumbersome.

In 1809 Austria, heartened by Spanish resistance, entered the war again. "The conduct of the Austrians," said Napoleon later, "upset all my plans." The battle of Wagram saw Austria defeated once more. Then Napoleon tried to tighten up the Continental System by annexing Holland and the north coast of Germany up to the Elbe, by establishing prohibitive duties on colonial commodities, and by setting up special courts to deal with smugglers. It was all to no avail. The whole Continent was stirring behind the barriers.

By 1811 England was reacting to the pinch of the Continental System; but Napoleon's Europe, feeling keenly the loss of British trade, was slowly moving towards revolt. Recently annexed Holland was still bounding out of control. Russia was finding that the policy of Napoleon was having disastrous results for Russia's commerce and finance. Why should the Muscovites be deprived of luxuries and comforts for the sake of Napoleon? At the same time Alexander I was suspicious of Napoleon's intentions in Poland and his alliance with Austria (1810). Meanwhile Wellington was going from victory to victory in Spain. Alexander took heart and defied Napoleon. Napoleon replied by invading Russia in 1812. The Russian war ended the Continental System and was the beginning of the end of Napoleon's power.

NAPOLEON: THE LAST PHASE

At the same time as Napoleon invaded Russia the United States declared war upon Great Britain. Americans were angered at the restrictions placed upon neutral commerce and the carrying trade by the British blockade and resentful of Britain's exercise of the right of search. A few American leaders desired to conquer Florida and Canada. From a naval and military point of view the War of 1812 was not important. It contained some dramatic chapters, usually described with more patriotism than accuracy in Canadian and American accounts. The American invasion of Canada failed; the British descent upon Washington was useless; the brilliant American victory at New Orleans in 1814 came after peace had been signed at Ghent on the basis of the status quo.

Meanwhile Napoleon had embarked upon his Russian campaign. He crossed into Lithuania with an army of about 450,000 men. He expected to defeat the Russian army and force upon Russia the cession of Lithuania. But the Russians retreated. Napoleon followed them to Smolensk, to Borodino, to Moscow. He remained in deserted Moscow six weeks in the hope that Alexander I would make peace. At last he retreated with the Russians fighting on rear and flank and reached Germany with an army of about 100,000 men. It was one of the most appalling military disasters in history.

While these events were taking place Wellington was holding large French forces in Spain and moving up towards the Pyrenees. Napoleon hastened to Paris and raised additional forces to maintain his control of Germany. Russia and Prussia entered into a new alliance against him. In May, 1813, Napoleon twice defeated them. Then he agreed to a truce in the hope of separating Alexander I from Prussia by promising to give him Poland. Alexander refused the offer and Austria entered the alliance against Napoleon. In the decisive four days' battle of Leipzig in October, 1813, Napoleon's army was forced back into France. When his power in Germany collapsed almost all Europe rose against him. In the spring of 1814 the allies invaded France. Despite the masterly skill of Napoleon in fighting magnificent rearguard actions against overwhelming odds, he was overwhelmed and forced to capitulate.

The allies now compelled Napoleon to abdicate and he agreed to retire to the Mediterranean island of Elba off the coast of Italy. The stodgy Bourbon Louis XVIII, brother of the executed Louis XVI, was placed upon the throne of France. On May 20, 1814, Louis signed with the allies the first Treaty of Paris, according to the terms of which the boundaries of France were to be virtually what they had been before the Revolution.

In March, 1815, Napoleon escaped from Elba and returned to France. He restored the Empire and made his last play for power at the battle of Waterloo in June, 1815. There he hurled his infantry and cavalry against the stubborn wall of the British army under Wellington. When the Prussian forces entered the battle the cause of Napoleon was lost. He was banished to St. Helena, Britain's bleak island in the Atlantic. There he died in 1821.

Napoleon was conquered. England's new industrial achievements had made the conquest possible. The battle of Waterloo was won in the "dark, Satanic mills" as well as on the playing fields of Eton. Europe was at peace for the first time in more than twenty years. Louis XVIII was once more restored to the throne of France. "If they are wise, the Bourbons will only change the linen on my bed," said Napoleon. From the capitals of Europe the peacemakers gathered at Vienna. The Napoleonic era had ended.

Chapter 28

THE YEARS OF REACTION

THE CONGRESS OF VIENNA

B Y 1815 it was clear that the French Revolution had not yielded the dividends of felicity foreseen by the eighteenth century philosophers. Apparently there was to be no brotherhood of man or triumph of reason and the laws of nature. Certainly there were no signs of a Heavenly City in this world. In the wake of the French Revolution came bitterness, exhaustion, and disillusionment. Napoleon had not succeeded in pacifying and consolidating Europe. Now he was an exile on St. Helena. Weary after twenty years of war, Europe wanted peace and security. When the Congress of Vienna ended its labors in June, 1815, there seemed reason to believe that peace and security had been guaranteed. The empire of Napoleon had been liquidated; a new map of Europe had been shaped; steps had been taken to ensure European stability against the dangers of liberalism and destructive revolution. In the arrangements at Vienna the governing consideration was the necessity, as the Congress saw it, of maintaining this stability.

It is not to be concluded that the all-embracing formula of the Congress of Vienna was simple reaction. The peacemakers of 1815 did not expect to make their new Europe in the image of the old order before 1789. They were practical men. They realized that some things had happened which they could never undo. The world they had known before the Revolution had shattered; but they resolved to gather together as many of the fragments as possible and build anew on the old foundations.

The French Revolution and Napoleon had helped to spread nationalism and liberalism. These two forces, now in disrepute, must be suppressed. The imbalance of power created by Napoleon's Grand Empire must be destroyed and the old balance of power system revived for the good of the European body politic. Strong and legitimate governments must be created. France must be weakened so that her armies could not pour over Europe again. Finally, England, Austria, Prussia, and Russia must be compensated for the losses and sacrifices they had made to save Europe and to humble Napoleon. To the victors belonged some reward.

A hard task faced the Congress. Representatives of every European country except Turkey were there. Behind the pomp and pageantry the real decisions were made by the four great powers: Austria, Prussia, Russia, England. The hand of Prince Metternich of Austria reached everywhere. Talleyrand of France, who was to serve thirteen masters in his long life, matched, or almost matched, the suave and calculating Metternich. Talleyrand moved with celerity and skill. He was soon able to obtain a seat for France at the councils of the victorious powers. The "Big Four" became the "Big Five." Talleyrand insisted that the common foe had been Napoleon, not France. He presented the welcome idea of "legitimacy" to the Congress and sponsored Louis XVIII, the Bourbon brother of martyred Louis XVI, as king of France. So Louis XVIII crept out from exile and returned to Paris. Acting upon the principle of "legitimacy," the Congress put legitimate monarchs back upon their thrones, except where it was inconvenient to do so.

Talleyrand also insisted that it would be a criminal act of folly to dismember France or to punish her too heavily. With this position the Anglo-Irish aristocrats, Lord Castlereagh and the Duke of Wellington, were in full agreement. They had come to Vienna chiefly interested in two things: restoring the balance of power and obtaining strategic colonies to protect trade routes and the Empire. To aid in achieving the former they supported Talleyrand: a strong France would contribute to the maintenance of equilibrium in Europe. Castlereagh said he wanted "to bring the world back to peaceful habits." His chief purpose was to contribute to that end by seeing to it that no nation became too strong among the European states. For centuries this had been a cardinal point in British foreign policy. It was to remain so.

Despite the annoyance of Prussia, which wanted revenge and more territory, the boundaries of France were left substantially as they had been in 1789. England returned most of the French overseas possessions seized during the war. France was to pay an indemnity for supporting Napoleon after his return from Elba. Until this indemnity was paid an allied occupation force was to be stationed within her territories. When France had borrowed the money from England the indemnity was paid and the occupation army withdrew. It was also agreed that the art treasures looted from the rest of Europe by Napoleon were to be returned. These were the only penalties placed upon France, apart from the loss of a few square miles of land. It was a lenient treatment of a defeated nation.

But France must not be too strong. Hence it was decided to create two buffer states as guarantees against possible French aggression.

Austria gave up the Austrian Netherlands (Belgium) and they were united with Holland to form the United Kingdom of the Netherlands. A friendly nation across the Channel added to English security. England also restored Java and the Dutch East Indies to the Netherlands. To create a strong state to guard the mountain passes on the southeastern frontier of France the states of Genoa and Sardinia-Piedmont were joined under the house of Savoy. England and Russia saw that this independent Italian state would also serve to check and balance Austrian power in Italy.

The fantastic Holy Roman Empire was not revived. In Germany Napoleon had ousted about seventy princes, dukes, and counts. He had taken away the autonomy of over forty free cities. At the same time he had strengthened states like Bavaria and Prussia. Thus Napoleon helped to stimulate German nationalism and heightened the hopes of those who dreamed of a united Germany. At Vienna such hopes were disappointed by the creation of an imperfect and impotent confederacy of thirty-nine states in which each state remained almost independent. This was done because Metternich saw that an efficient German Confederation would weaken Austria and strengthen her rival Prussia.

As compensation for the loss of the Austrian Netherlands Austria was given Lombardy and Venetia, thus adding four million Italians to the polyglot population of the Hapsburg Empire. Otherwise no changes were made. "Austria" said Castlereagh, "is the great hinge upon which the fate of Europe must ultimately depend." The autocratic rule of the Hapsburgs remained undisturbed. In Italy the Pope received back the states of the church. The Bourbon Ferdinand III went to the kingdom of Naples and the Bourbon Ferdinand VII to the throne of Spain. Russia obtained the larger part of Poland. Because Denmark had supported Napoleon, Norway was taken from her and granted to Sweden in compensation for Finland, earlier conquered by Russia.

As an important part of the Vienna settlement Castlereagh claimed for England a number of small but important colonies, the strategic value of which was considerable. In the North Sea there was Heligoland; in the Mediterranean, Malta and the Ionian Islands (later given to Greece); in the Indian Ocean, Ceylon and Mauritius, strategic outposts of the eastern Empire. At the foot of Africa there was Cape Colony, conquered and later purchased by the British from the Dutch after Holland had been seized by Napoleon. In the West Indies Tobago and St. Lucia were taken from France, not because they were desirable as defense posts for the Empire but because they could supply sugar in abundance to the United Kingdom.

England was now the foremost power in the world. As unchallenged mistress of the seas she controlled the sea lanes of trade. Her colonies had steadily increased in number and importance. No foreign competitor was yet in a position to threaten her industrial and commercial supremacy. London was becoming the financial center of Europe. Peace with victory had been secured. England's postwar position seemed impregnable.

THE QUADRUPLE AND HOLY ALLIANCES

To safeguard the agreement reached at Vienna England, Russia, Austria and Prussia organized the famous Quadruple Alliance. Under Article 6 of the agreement it was provided that from time to time representatives of the four nations would hold "reunions devoted to the common interests and the examination of measures judged salutary for the repose and prosperity of the peoples." These diplomatic conferences were intended to facilitate cooperation in suppressing any liberal or revolutionary movements in Europe. In the triumphant age of Metternich's diplomacy the Quadruple Alliance prevented political changes and, in order to do so, frequently interfered to employ coercion in the domestic affairs of lesser states. Intervention, in Spain and Naples, for example, brought reaction and uneasy peace. Until 1848 the Metternich "system" remained in a position to defend the autocratic values which Metternich called "the eternal laws of the moral world."

The Quadruple Alliance was a definite and practical agreement. Far different was the Holy Alliance, the product of the unstable and cloudy mind of Alexander I, Tsar of Russia. Probably under the influence of Madame de Krudener, a mystic and seer, Alexander drew up a document which he hoped would lead the rulers of Europe to "live in true and indissoluble fraternity" and to "take for their rule of conduct only the Christian religion." Metternich said it was a "sonorous nothing"; Castlereagh said it was "a sublime piece of mysticism and nonsense." There had certainly been nothing like this document in European history before. Francis I of Austria was polite and signed. Prussia signed. Great Britain did not sign, explaining to Alexander that His Majesty's government regretted that the British constitution forbade it.

PEACE AND ECONOMIC DISLOCATION

Despite the advantageous position of England in 1815 the situation at home was generally unsatisfactory. Immediately obvious was the difficulty of suddenly transforming the economy of a nation which had been at war for twenty years into a peacetime system. At the same time, and quite apart from the difficulties created by war, England was moving through the continuing transition brought by the agricultural and industrial changes of the economic revolution. As has been explained in Chapter 25 this steady flood of physical, social, and economic alteration was shortly to destroy the eighteenth century social harmony and to create new classes of labor and capital, hostile to each

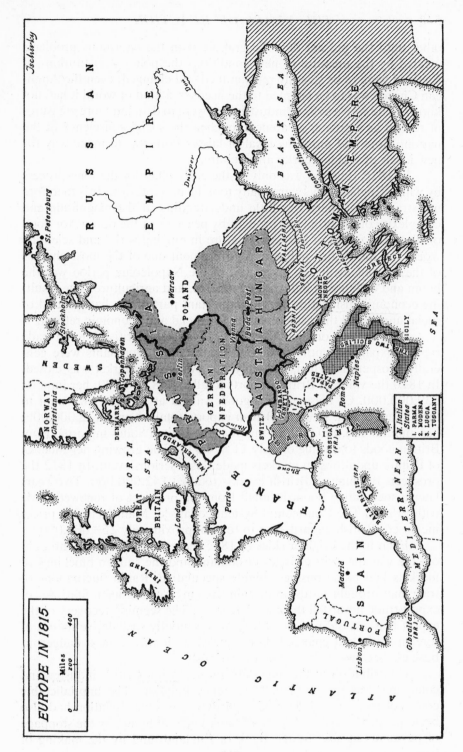

EUROPE IN 1815

Miles
0   200   400

ATLANTIC OCEAN

NORWAY
Christiania

SWEDEN
Stockholm

St. Petersburg

RUSSIAN   EMPIRE

Tschirky

Dvina

Dnieper

POLAND
• Warsaw

DENMARK
Copenhagen

NORTH SEA

GREAT BRITAIN
London •

IRELAND

NETHERLANDS

PRUSSIA
Berlin •

GERMAN CONFEDERATION

Rhine

SWITZ.

FRANCE
Paris •

Vienna •

Buda • Pest

AUSTRIA-HUNGARY

LOMBARDO-VENETIA
SARDINIA

PAPAL STATES
Rome •

TWO SICILIES
Naples •

SICILY

BLACK SEA

OTTOMAN EMPIRE
Constantinople

WALLACHIA
Danube
SERVIA
BOSNIA
MONTE NEGRO
MACEDONIA
GREECE

MEDITERRANEAN SEA

Rhone

CORSICA
(FR.)

BALEARICS (SP.)

SPAIN
Madrid •

PORTUGAL
Lisbon •

Gibraltar
(BR.)

N. Italian
States
1. PARMA
2. MODENA
3. LUCCA
4. TUSCANY

547

other until the present day. To grapple with the enormous problems
created by the pressure of new conditions the political institutions of
England were to be steadily re-examined and changed; even the Anglican Church was to be adapted to the needs of a kind of world it had not
known. The worse evils of industrialism were to demand more measures
of reform as a greater awareness touched the social conscience of the
nation. More and more the ideal of laissez faire was to make way for
new ideals of social security and welfare.

In 1815 England was only in the early phase of the long process
by which English society gradually took its present form. It is therefore
not strange that there was little understanding of the magnitude and
complexity of the problems brought by peace or of the power, for good
or ill, of the forces of harnessed nature in our industrial and scientific
world. To the British public and government one of the most obvious
of these problems in the latter part of the Napoleonic period was the
boom and collapse in industry, commerce, and agriculture. The resulting economic dislocation was an important part of the background of
social unrest and the rising pressure for social and economic reform.

Despite the Continental System of Napoleon British foreign trade
rapidly expanded until 1810. Industrialists and merchants were generally prosperous. Then, suddenly, the American market was closed.
In 1810 the value of British exports totalled £48,000,000; her imports
£39,000,000. Of these exports goods valued at £11,217,685 went to
the United States. In 1811 British exports totalled only £32,000,000;
her imports £26,000,000. In this year the United States imported from
Britain goods to a value of only £1,874,917. The growing dependence
of Britain upon foreign markets made this a serious event. In 1812 the
prospects brightened. British exports totalled £42,000,000. Two years
later a speculative boom resulted from the prospect of renewed trade
with France. The Continental System collapsed. Manufacturing prices
increased. British exports rose to total approximately £50,000,000.

Even in the brighter skies of 1815 there were shadows. Throughout the war the swift changes of demand and the sudden blockings of
markets had made business highly speculative. Rapid fluctuations of
trade had brought hardship or ruin to many businessmen. Statistics of
export trade never tell the complete story. The seeming recovery of the
export markets did not mean that the essentially speculative nature of
foreign trade had changed. For some years it was to be a dangerous
business because its basis was precarious.

Contributing to the uncertain future facing British industry and
commerce was the problem of currency inflation. The unpredictable
course of foreign trade had been partly responsible. Inflation had also
been speeded by the expansion of bank paper at home; by the stoppage
of payments in gold by the Bank of England; and by the making of
paper currency legal tender.

It can thus be seen that although the volume of British manufacturing and merchant business grew through a series of pauses and leaps in the years before 1815 the bases of prosperity were decidedly unstable. In agriculture the situation was similar. Early in the war period the British farmers had been generally prosperous. During the war years, in view of shipping and other difficulties, foodstuffs were often in short supply. As no modern devices of subsidies or price ceiling controls had been used by the government prices were forced upwards by the pressure of demand.

High prices stimulated production. Farmers were persuaded by prospects of profit to raise unusually large quantities of grain, often on poor land and at considerable cost. There was great enclosure activity "to increase the crop of bread and meat." Over three million acres were enclosed between 1800 and 1820. In such circumstances many farmers would inevitably suffer heavy losses in the event of a sudden collapse of grain prices. At the same time, the swift enclosure of this large amount of land added to the social dislocation by accelerating the migration of those who were being remorselessly evicted so that the nation could march to a new order through the wreckage of the old.

In 1809 the harvest season was bad, almost as bad as it had been in the wet summer of 1799. The next three harvests were poor. A large tonnage of grain had to be imported. It must be remembered that nearly forty per cent of the population was still engaged in agriculture in the early years of the nineteenth century. Crop failures were therefore serious events. The main currents of life were still local ones. Population was increasing at the rapid rate of about fifteen per cent every decade; but this increase added more to the rural population than to the urban. The population of London did not rise above 1,000,-000 until 1819; only Manchester and Liverpool had more than 100,000 inhabitants; only Birmingham, Bristol, and Leeds had more than 60,000. Hence a series of four years in which the crops were very small brought considerable suffering and hardship to a large part of the people. In these years, too, the farmers who had invested too heavily and mortgaged their futures in the hope of continuing high prices were in very great difficulty. The good harvest of 1813 gave only a small measure of relief. England's ills in the world of commerce and industry were matched by the depression in agriculture.

FURTHER CAUSES OF DISCONTENT

Against this background of dislocation in industry, trade, and agriculture there arose a widespread social disturbance in the early nineteenth century. Most producers in agriculture and industry had been reasonably prosperous during the war; but all individuals with a fixed income, especially wage earners, faced a period of rising prices which in many cases brought real distress as prices rose and paper

money depreciated. The cost of living, particularly in food, continued
to spiral long after the war was over. Meanwhile the balance of economic activity in the north and Midlands was shifting. As a result of
the new and rising industrial life the slow movements of people from
the country to the city steadily continued.

> "And Birmingham grew so big, so big,
> And Stratford stayed so small."

This added to the confusion of the labor market. So, too, did the increased burdens brought by the maladministration of the poor law.
Under the so-called Speenhamland system the parish rates made up to
the laborers the deficiencies in wages. The increased local taxes to pay
for poor law costs added to the weight of a steadily rising national
taxation. Even then parish relief was wretchedly inadequate. Meanwhile the national taxation level was over £4 per head.

There were other factors which contributed to the gathering
momentum of depression and discontent. In 1799 an income tax was
levied for the more effective prosecution of the war. On incomes over
£200 a year the tax was a shilling to the pound. All incomes over £60
a year were taxed. This new income tax was difficult to assess and hard
to collect. Defaulting parish collectors frequently played havoc with
the administrative system. The tax was also very unpopular. Lord
Holland said it was prepared by an "unscrupulous economist" at the
Treasury. An anonymous writer to the London *Times* in 1816 viewed
the future with alarm: "There is the despotic spirit of this inquisitorial
impost, its horde of petty tyrants! A government exercising inquisitorial
powers may easily extend them. A single root will throw out suckers
on all sides." For Pitt the income tax was "a stop-gap, a temporary
visitant." But the tax was not easy to discard, widespread as was the
reaction against "measuring loyalty in hard cash." A chancellor of the
exchequer, "seated on an empty chest, by a pool of bottomless deficiency, and fishing for a Budget" could not be expected to omit the
income tax from his calculations. It was painfully clear that the cost
of obtaining victory over Napoleon had been very great. The national
debt was over £850,000,000. The prospect of tax reduction seemed
remote.

In the summer of 1815 nearly half a million men were swiftly
demobilized. There were few jobs for them. War contracts were cancelled. Clothiers, steel and iron workers, gunsmiths, and scores of other
laborers and artisans found themselves unemployed. No markets could
be found for many manufactured goods. Tons of commodities were
available for export to liberated Europe; but the people of Europe had
little money to pay for them. When these goods were suddenly dumped
on the English market the result was a rapid glutting and stagnation;

demand declined and prices fell abruptly. Many companies went bankrupt.

Such was the shadowed scene of 1815. During the next three years the darkness of a great postwar depression spread over all England. Two grain crops failed; factories closed; poverty, dirt, disease, ignorance, and a widespread feeling of disillusionment and frustration united to produce bitter complaints and violence.

SOCIAL UNREST

For over a century the English landed aristocracy had been content with a state of society that had given them power and prosperity. It was natural that they should not welcome new ideas or the prospect of change. They were angered by any challenge to order, discipline, or to their monopoly of power. They had been frightened by the excesses of the French Revolution and still thought it possible that Jacobinism or some radical plague equally unpleasant could come to England. The economic maladjustments resulting from the successive depressions, the progress of the agricultural and industrial changes, the transition from war to peace, found the Tory cabinet under Lord Liverpool without any important ameliorative or remedial legislation to offer. When popular dissatisfaction brought widespread popular disturbances the answer of the Tories was usually repression, not relief.

A few measures calculated to do some good were passed in the years from 1815 to 1820. The first was a new Corn Law. As soon as the Continental System of Napoleon had been completely broken German and other foreign grain flowed into England. Since the late seventeenth century Corn Laws had given some protection by tariff to English grain producers. Nevertheless, the tariff wall had not been high enough to stop the importation of foreign grain. Hence this grain came into England during the years of bad English harvests and helped to depress the domestic price level and to ruin many farmers. The Parliament of landowners in part depended on tenant farmers who could pay their rent fully and on time. And so, despite many protests, the Corn Law of 1815 was passed to protect English grain against the competition of foreign producers. The duty was raised to prohibitive heights. No grain was to be admitted until the domestic price reached eighty shillings a quarter (eight bushels). Soon the price of grain rose; the home market was kept for English landowners; and they had their rents again, at least more frequently than before. The price of a loaf of bread now rose from 10d. to 1s. 2d. when the usual wage of a farm laborer was about eight shillings a week.

As the middle classes paid a large part of the income tax they had long been objecting to it. To satisfy them the income tax was reluctantly abolished in 1816. Three years later the Bank of England resumed payment in specie; this action resulted in a healthy deflation of the currency and made a minor contribution to economic recovery.

Here the Tory government of Lord Liverpool stopped. No further steps were taken to deal with a mounting economic crisis or to attempt by legislative means to cushion the impact of the mysterious disruptive forces at work in England. The Liverpool cabinet had been successful in war, or at least the war had been won under them. In peace they were inexperienced. After the defeat of Napoleon the ministers, most of the Tory party, and many Whigs were dismayed and bewildered. The fruits of victory had turned sour. There was neither peace nor prosperity, only turbulence and depression. These men did not understand what was happening to the England they had known. They had no answers for those who demanded political and economic reform. So they stood together to protect themselves, their property, and their way of life. They sought security in repression. In the unreformed Parliament the English freedom that Montesquieu had pictured was not to be found. Eighteenth century minds and hearts were dealing with nineteenth century problems.

During the depression years following 1810 there arose numerous disorders. In an age of transition the workers are usually the first to suffer. The so-called Luddite Riots took their name from Ned Ludd, a half-witted Leicester apprentice who was said to have smashed machines to revenge himself on his master. The Luddites destroyed and damaged probably £100,000 worth of property. It is unlikely that they would have wrecked the new labor-saving machinery or burned hayricks had they not been the victims of unemployment and low wages. In their acute misery and bitterness they accepted the simple explanation that the coming of the machines was responsible for their troubles. The answer seemed equally simple: the machines must be destroyed. It has been explained that the depression of 1810–1813 was due more to the breach with the United States than to new machinery, Jacobin doctrines, or any other single cause. Similarly in the post-war years what mattered most was not the spread of sedition but the impact of the great depression upon the workers. However, neither the Tories nor the Luddites were aware of the hidden causes behind the visible and unpleasant facts.

BENTHAM, COBBETT AND SHELLEY

Meanwhile the cry for reform slowly became more insistent. The reformers were of many kinds. At least they agreed upon two things: their opposition to the power of the aristocracy and their desire to reform Parliament. It was felt that once parliamentary reform was accomplished many other reforms would swiftly follow. The apostles of Wilberforce would see slavery abolished. Sir James Mackintosh would see the criminal code amended. Francis Place would speed the departure of the iniquitous Combination Acts.

In 1817 Jeremy Bentham (1748–1832) published his *Catechism of Parliamentary Reform*. In this book he explained, with the precise legal logic for which he was famous, that the existing representative system was absurd. He insisted that a more democratic form of government would aid in bringing "the greatest happiness of the greatest number." By thinking men Bentham's work was read with interest and often with approval.

More to the liking of the masses was the radical leader William Cobbett (1762–1835) chief propagandist of the first working-class movement in modern politics. Cobbett had discarded his peasant smock in Surrey to join the army. There he stayed until he was a sergeant-major. Later, under the name of "Peter Porcupine," he began to write articles in praise of Pitt and the Tories, who paid him for it. About 1806 he changed his mind and wrote as a bitter enemy of the government and the aristocrats. His newspaper, the *Political Register,* was soon read and quoted by thousands of workers.

Cobbett was a violent man, with a remarkable command of language. His exploding prose style was simple, muscular, direct, and terrific in its strength. He did not think calmly, this champion of causes. But when he wrote, his skill was magic. He was probably the greatest of all popular journalists.

Cobbett's prejudice against the government was unreasoned, unwearying, and fierce. In 1810 he was sent to Newgate prison for two years; his papers were confiscated. "The sons and daughters of corruption openly chuckled at what they thought my extinguishment. Almost everyone stood aloof except my creditors." In 1816 Cobbett reduced the price of the *Weekly Register* to 2d. He avoided the stamp tax on newspapers by omitting all news items. The *Register* had a circulation of 50,000 copies. The poorest peasant or artisan could buy it.

To William Cobbett, once called "the last of the great yeomen," the aristocratic system was an evil and fraudulent conspiracy against the people. He hated the whole social system. In his view the landlords and church made the people poor by rents and tithes; the manufacturers were ruining rural England and creating the cities, bloated and poisonous, like "the Great Wen" of London; the financiers were swindling the workers; the rotten boroughs were utterly damnable because through them omnipotent privilege exploited the whole state of England. Cobbett condemned collectively all the things he loathed by calling them "The Thing." The sadness and savagery of Cobbett is perhaps best revealed in his *Rural Rides,* the description of journeys on horseback through his beloved southern England.

How mighty was the flood of Cobbett's prose and how strong his passion can be illustrated by brief passages quoted almost at random from his writings. The first is self-explanatory: "Things have once been merry for the English poor and, by God, they will be merry again despite this whole army of ministers, judges, pensioners, squires, financiers, clergy, spies and magistrates, who are the authors and maintainers of England's shame."

The second quotation is from one of Cobbett's numerous onslaughts upon paper money: "This vile paper money and funding system! This system of Dutch descent, begotten by Bishop Burnet and born in hell! O cursed paper money, is there a torment surpassing the wickedness of thy inventor?"

Such a champion as Cobbett generated heavy emotional excitement among the workers. The masses accepted his easy explanations of the reasons for the condition of England and, obeying his voice and their own inclinations, agitated for the reform of Parliament. There were, of course, many other journalists fighting for various reform causes. There were also the public agitators like Henry Hunt. It is important to remember that the years following the Napoleonic Wars showed a remarkable development of the newspaper press, the public meeting, and the popular orator. The factory and factory towns provided increasing facilities for mass action and the workers, slowly seizing upon that discovery, were to unite and struggle with a new power and a new hope as the nineteenth century progressed.

The aristocrats and industrialists were also attacked by another enemy, the poet Shelley. "Shelley believed mankind had only to will that there should be no evil, and there would be none." Much of his poetry of dissent is filled with a passionate protest against the inhumanity of man. This is particularly true of *The Revolt of Islam, Queen Mab, Peter Bell the Third, Prometheus,* and the *Masque of Anarchy.* His advice to the workers of England was to revolt against their masters:

> "Rise like lions after slumber
> In unvanquishable number
> Shake your chains to earth like dew
> Which in sleep had fallen on you—
> Ye are many—they are few."

Shelley, like Blake and Cobbett, saw only evil in the great cities born of a money exchange and industrial system:

> "Hell is a city much like London—
> A populous and a smoky city;
> There are all sorts of people undone,
> And there is little or no fun done;
> Small justice shown and still less pity."

There were many other crusaders, great and small, for the cause

Tories were aware of the new strength of those reformers who sought to achieve a political reform of Parliament by peaceful means.

The refusal of the Whigs to accept parliamentary reform as a party policy was a costly political mistake. If the Whigs had allied themselves with the less disreputable radicals after Peterloo or in the early 1820's in a campaign for an extensive reform of Parliament the Tories could not have clung to power long. This is exactly the course that the Whigs decided to follow ten years later. Only then was the mutual suspicion between Whigs and radicals in part removed. It was of course difficult in 1820 for the old Whig families to adopt a people's program designed to change the very basis of society. It was easier for the younger Whigs to do so. However, the Whig leaders felt that the espousing of parliamentary reform would break up their party. Any union with the radicals seemed so fraught with danger that it was decided to delay a decision and to wait and see. That delay gave the Tories an opportunity to change their cabinet and their policy. They did both, and remained in power for another ten years.

Chapter 29

THE RISE OF THE MIDDLE CLASS
THE NEW TORYISM

FOR several years the friction between the extreme Tories such as Liverpool, Castlereagh, Eldon, Sidmouth, and Wellington and the younger and more liberal Tories such as Canning, Peel, and Huskisson had been growing steadily greater. This internal stress was more than merely the result of differences within a political party regarding general problems of principles or action. It was a part of the important story of the mounting struggle between the landowning aristocrats and the middle class industrialists, merchants, and professional men. This struggle began long before the 1820's and in some respects is not ended yet. Only the first long chapter was to be concluded in 1832 when the first Reform Bill gave the franchise to the middle class.

In the early nineteenth century both the Tories and the Whigs contained two groups shading into each other: the ultra-conservatives or reactionaries, and the liberals. The names of the political parties remained unchanged; but more and more the real division in England came to be between conservatism and liberalism. The conservative groups in each of the two parties had more in common with each other than with the left wing elements of their own parties. The conservatives usually included the landowning aristocrats and gentry who wanted as little change and as few new ideas as possible. The liberal groups usually included those who were sympathetic to the middle class point of view and who understood much more of the meaning of the economic revolutions in industry and agriculture than the old-line Tories and Whigs. It will be noted later that about the middle of the nineteenth century England's political parties gradually changed their names from Whig and Tory to Liberal and Conservative. By that time the conflict between the middle class and the aristocracy was slowly declining. At the same time, however, the struggle for the independence of the workers from the social, political, and economic controls of both the aristocracy and the middle class was rising throughout the world.

561

The coming of the new liberal Toryism as an effective political instrument really began with the suicide of Lord Castlereagh in 1822. Castlereagh had been widely unpopular. His funeral procession was hooted as his body was borne to Westminster Abbey. However, the passing of Castlereagh meant more than merely the death of a hated minister. It meant that the Tory party had a further chance to save itself from the consequences of its weakness and its policy. So long as Castlereagh had lived the grip of the extreme Tories had been slipping only gradually. Now that he had gone the liberal Tories were more optimistic about the future of their party and themselves.

One of the important steps in the needed reconstruction of the cabinet was the return of the brilliant and ambitious George Canning. Canning had long been disliked by the king and by his colleagues for his liberal tendencies and his energetic opposition to the extreme Tories. He had resigned from the cabinet because he could not go along with the prosecution of Queen Caroline. He had then been appointed Governor-General of India and was about to sail as an exile to his new post when his rival Castlereagh died. Lord Liverpool at once offered him the secretaryship of foreign affairs and the leadership of the Tories in the house of commons. When Canning accepted and re-entered the cabinet he was at the height of his popularity. The middle classes and the workers acclaimed him. In both parties he was supported by young men, who looked upon him as a new Pitt, a man destined to be the saviour of England.

By the side of Canning stood two able men. The first was Sir Robert Peel, who had succeeded the reactionary Sidmouth as home secretary shortly before the return of Canning to the cabinet. Peel was not a landed aristocrat. He was a product of the industrial revolution, the son of a Lancashire manufacturer who had made a huge fortune in cotton. Trained for a political career at Harrow and Oxford he came to the house of commons in 1809 as member for an Irish borough. Later he sat for his own university. Slowly he found it necessary to abandon many Tory opinions because he preferred to reach his own conclusions without reference to party doctrine. In that sense Peel was never a strictly party man. His more party-minded and less liberal associates soon found that he was not entirely dependable in an old-line Tory sense because his principles came before his party.

The second friend and follower of Canning was William Huskisson, who entered the cabinet early in 1823 as president of the board of trade. Huskisson, like Canning, was a disciple of William Pitt. Both recalled that Pitt had been a reforming minister before the French Revolution and the war with Napoleon had checked his liberalism. Huskisson was particularly concerned with carrying on the economic policy of Pitt in the direction of freer trade and away from Tory protectionism.

The coming of this able triumvirate of Tory reformers to the cabinet resulted in an immediate and decisive change in government policy. Between 1822 and 1830 the old, inelastic Toryism was compelled to yield on many fronts. The new spirit permeated a large area of the party. Many of the younger Whigs cooperated with the enlightened Tories rather than with their own chieftains. At the same time trade continued to increase; harvests were good; with better times tempers and passions subsided. The road was open for a series of moderate and progressive reforms supported and carried through under the banners of liberal Toryism.

LAW REFORM

Sir James Mackintosh, Sir Samuel Romilly, and other able advocates of criminal law reform had long urged a careful and sane revision of the criminal code. The whole system of criminal law was cumbersome and honeycombed with injustice. Nothing had been done because successive cabinets had not chosen to do anything. Time and circumstances through the centuries had accumulated much criminal law and, for those who violated it, provision for drastic punishment. In the early nineteenth century the statute books were disgraced by a large number of laws providing heavy penalties for offenses once serious, later trivial.

For instance, the game laws set forth the harsh punishment to be inflicted on poachers who took partridges, rabbits, or pheasants from the estates of the wealthy landowners; a law of 1816 stated that even the possession of a net for catching rabbits was punishable by transportation for seven years, in such cases usually to the convict settlements of Australia. Over two hundred so-called crimes were punishable by death. In 1818 Sir James Mackintosh told the house of commons that 101 persons had been hanged for forgery in the preceding seven years. It was a capital offense to steal fish or five shillings worth of goods from a shop. The theft of a cow or sheep was rather less dangerous. That crime was punishable only by transportation.

Many draconic penalties were so far from fitting the crimes that juries frequently refused to convict men charged with lesser offenses. In 1819, for example, of 14,000 committed for trial only 9,500 were convicted. The inevitable result was an increase in crime because the chances of being punished had so markedly decreased. In the midst of man-made hunger and poverty a repressive penal code was not enough to curb the violent and reckless habits born of hatred and despair. In 1812 Lord Byron had warned of the dangers: "If your land divides against itself and your dragoons and your executioners must be let loose against your fellow-citizens will you erect a gibbet in every field, and hang up men like scarecrows? Are these the remedies for a starving and desperate population?"

Sir Robert Peel began his work as home secretary by consulting Jeremy Bentham and Sir James Mackintosh about law reform. Within four years he had secured the passage of five statutes abolishing the death penalty for over a hundred offenses. Nearly three hundred acts providing harsh punishments for minor crimes and misdemeanors were removed from the law books. The result was a steady decrease in crime. Reason and humanity demanded this kind of legislation. However, despite steady progress, it was some time before all the barbarous enormities were excised from the criminal code. As late as 1837 a workman was sentenced to transportation for life for stealing a Bible and Prayer Book from a local church. In 1838 three men received the same sentence at the Monmouthshire assizes for stealing a colt.

Peel was also successful in a number of further reforms. He stopped the Tory use of government spies and agents provocateurs among the workers. He ended the foolish public prosecutions of the radical agitators and the press. In the Gaol Act of 1823 provisions were made for greater cleanliness and sanitation in the prisons of England; it was also recommended that the prison authorities regularly employ chaplains and schoolmasters. The laws concerning juries were consolidated. In 1829, after being out of the home office for a year, Peel returned to establish the metropolitan police force in the growing London district. It was his idea that an efficient police system would do more to curb crime than the multiplication of capital felonies by statute law. Within the next quarter century Peel's plan was adopted throughout England. His "new police"—sometimes called "Bobbies" or "Peelers" after him—carried no guns and were armed only with truncheons or night sticks. Efficient and impartial, the London civilian police were soon widely respected, except by a few low-type radicals. These police could deal with London mobs; and all mobs knew it. The metropolitan police force and similar police units elsewhere in England brought a decrease in crime, a greater respect for the law, and more ordered liberty.

FREER TRADE

William Huskisson was a man whose ideas and outlook were wide as the poles asunder from those Whigs and Tories whose interest was in landed wealth and whose confidence was in agriculture. This new president of the board of trade believed that England's future was in commerce and in industry, not in the land and its products. He saw England as a great trading nation, the clearinghouse in a rolling flood of trade between Europe and America, with London as the financial center of the western world.

As a disciple of Adam Smith and William Pitt it was natural that Huskisson should carry on the liberal work abandoned by Pitt when England had gone to war in 1793, particularly in the reduction and simplification of tariffs. At the same time it was fitting that Huskisson succeeded his friend Canning as member for Liverpool in the house of commons, for Liverpool was the great center of mercantile interest. That interest was swiftly served by Huskisson, for he turned at once to the task of removing as many of the fettering controls of mercantilism as possible. His changes in the direction of free trade helped to prepare the way for final victory under Peel and Gladstone.

Because so little had been done for so many years, Huskisson found his tasks formidable. The high protective tariffs largely established by the Whigs in the eighteenth century had not been altered for the better by the indiscriminate additions made in the war years. Despite the fact that the chief purpose of such tariffs was not protection but revenue the levies on raw materials were often larger than those on manufactured articles. There was no sound or scientific policy. Moreover, when the income tax had been abolished at the behest of the middle classes the general maladjustment of the whole haphazard taxation system had been worsened.

In the budgets from 1823 to 1825 Huskisson proclaimed a complete revision of tariff theory and practice. He abolished many restrictions completely. He reduced the import duties on a large number of articles, especially on foreign products used in England such as iron, cotton, wool, silk, sugar, and coffee. For example, the import duties on cotton were reduced from 50 per cent to 10 per cent, on iron by £5 a ton. These changes were significant as a step and influence towards free trade. They were also significant in themselves: before 1823 the tariff ranged from 18 to 40 per cent; after 1825 the range was from 10 to 30 per cent.

Huskisson and Canning now proceeded to overturn the foundations of the old British colonial and commercial system by making important changes in the Navigation Acts, passed under Cromwell and Charles II. At a time when Europe's purchasing power was recovering from the ill effects of war various European nations were following the example of the United States and passing navigation laws of their own, thus closing their markets and ports to English goods and ships. Huskisson saw that these developments, logical enough in themselves as part of a general world policy of protection, were fraught with danger for England. After the revolt of the Spanish colonies in South America the Spanish monopoly of trade had been broken and other nations began to trade with the new republics. Huskisson decided to permit all foreign countries to trade with English colonies provided that reciprocal concessions were given to England. Reciprocity treaties were negotiated with other countries in order to insure free exchange of port facilities. Trade between England and her colonies was still to be carried by English ships. These measures were clearly an important departure from the essential principles of the Navigation Acts and mercantile theory. Although the Navigation Acts were not abolished until 1849 the most important single step towards abandoning control of the carrying trade had been taken by Huskisson. In this he went beyond Adam Smith who had thought the Navigation Acts harmful to English wealth but necessary for English security because the great mercantile marine trained seamen, always an important shield of England.

A temporary industrial dislocation in 1825 stopped Huskisson from carrying out further modifications of tariff policy. Then came a poor harvest in 1826. The resulting distress again raised the explosive question of the Corn Law of 1815. In the decade following its passage it had been violently denounced by the middle class factory owners and the working class wage earners totalling nearly two thirds of the nation. It has earlier been explained that the Corn Law had been passed to keep the price of grain artificially high, and it had done that. But when grain was scarce the Corn Law had brought widespread misery and havoc. England was fiercely and bitterly divided on the question of maintaining high tariffs to protect grain growers.

Even the agricultural interests suffered because they expected the Corn Law to keep the price above 80 shillings a quarter (8 bushels). With the idea that the high price was always sure they did not raise much poultry, meat or vegetables, but repeated their procedure of the war boom days and planted all the grain they could, even using sub-marginal land. In some years the inevitable result was overproduction. Prices fell. Landlords did not get the high rents they expected and some went broke. What was to be done? The Corn Law, sacred ark of the covenant of the aristocracy, could not be tampered with unless he who meddled was prepared to split the Tory party and to bring screams of fury from the landlord keepers of the temple. "Corn was King."

In 1825, however, the difficulty was not overproduction but the reverse. The wide distress brought by the poor harvest of 1825 caused Huskisson to propose that the tariff on foreign grain should vary more directly with the domestic price. The duty should be high when the domestic price was low; low when the price was high. A new sliding scale of duties would then permit grain to be imported easily when the domestic market price was high and long before the famine price of 80 shillings a quarter required by the Corn Law was reached. Canning also wanted to reduce the level at which foreign grain could be imported into England without duty payments from 80 shillings to 60 shillings a quarter.

In 1827 Lord Liverpool suffered a stroke of apoplexy and was succeeded by Canning. The restive Wellington and Eldon at once resigned rather than serve under a liberal Tory. Although Canning did not possess the diplomatic skill and gyroscopic controls of the sure-footed Liverpool he was able for a time to carry on his government with the aid of a few Whigs. Amidst rising division in the Tory party the proposed revisions in the Corn Law were passed by the house of commons, thrown out by an angry house of lords led by the Duke of Wellington. The general principle of the sliding-scale of duties had been accepted but a fierce battle arose about the rate and incidence. The house of commons stood out for a lower rate; the house of lords for a higher. The Tory party and cabinet were hopelessly divided.

In August, 1827, Canning died, only five months after taking office. The incapable Lord Goderich tried to carry on the Whig-Canningite ministry and failed. So the Duke of Wellington became prime minister. He dropped the Whigs. The liberal Tories were unhappy but stayed in the cabinet long enough to compel the duke to introduce Huskisson's Corn Bill again with minor changes. This time it passed both houses. The new law permitted grain to be imported at any time. If the English market price was 73 shillings a quarter or above the grain would be admitted free of duty. Any duty was to be on a sliding scale to begin when the market price was under 73 shillings. The scale was so devised that the duty would be greater or less as the price in the English market fell or rose shilling by shilling under the duty-free entrance ceiling of 73 shillings. It was hoped that this price thermometer system of tariff control would prevent the soaring or plummeting of domestic prices. The hope was not realized. For land-owner, mill-owner, and worker the Corn Law question remained unsolved until 1846.

REPEAL OF THE COMBINATION ACTS

One important event of the 1820's was largely the result of the skill and organizing power of Francis Place, a wealthy tailor of Charing Cross, whose work as a social and political reformer has been well described in the famous biography written by Graham Wallas. Place was a private citizen who collected evidence of the evil results of the Combination Acts passed by Pitt in 1799 and 1800. These unfair acts forbade any combinations of laborers for the purpose of obtaining higher wages. Thus for twenty-five years trades unions had been illegal; the heavy penalties of the law had been used by employers and magistrates to blackmail the workers into accepting whatever wages were offered. Often employers dealt directly with labor groups despite the law, but Place was able to show that in a large number of cases savage and unjust penalties had been inflicted on offenders, as in the case of the London *Times* compositors in 1810. In 1824 his ally Joseph Hume, a radical member of Parliament, obtained the appointment of a house of commons committee to investigate the operations of the Combination Acts.

With the assistance of Hume the shrewd Place picked and coached the witnesses who were to appear before the committee. As a result the abolition of the Combination Acts was recommended and carried through, with the support of a group of enlightened employers who felt that the repressive laws were prejudicial to good labor relations. Unfortunately the workers at once launched into strikes and general disturbances. In the resulting panic the government limited the activities of trades unions to combinations on questions of wage levels and hours of employment. As these were the two most important reasons for the existence of organized trades union groups the gains were important. Nevertheless, great handicaps to union development remained, such as the matter of effective collective bargaining power.

FOREIGN AFFAIRS

When Canning succeeded Castlereagh as foreign secretary in 1822 he brought to the field of foreign affairs the new liberalism that was to be expected. Castlereagh was fundamentally a cautious aristocrat in general sympathy with the ideals of Metternich. It is true that Castlereagh did not favor the Metternichian policy of repressive intervention in the domestic affairs of European states but neither did he wish to disturb the rayless expanse of reaction that was then synonymous with European peace and equilibrium. Canning, on the other hand, was ready to oppose the reactionary program of the Quadruple Alliance. Whenever it seemed feasible he openly championed the cause of liberalism and nationalism. His methods and his reliance upon English public opinion to support him disturbed the European diplomats and startled some of his colleagues. Canning did not hope for too much. "Let us not in a foolish spirit of romance suppose that we alone could regenerate Europe." Nevertheless he was determined to do what he could to advance the cause of liberalism abroad.

In 1822 the Congress of Verona considered the problem of intervention in Spain to suppress a liberal revolt and to restore the despicable but legitimate Bourbon Ferdinand VII to his throne. On Canning's instructions the English representatives at Verona opposed the conquest of the liberal Spanish regime by joint action of the Quadruple Alliance. The remaining allies decided to go ahead without the aid of England. French armies, acting in the name of the Quadruple Alliance, invaded Spain and restored Ferdinand VII who at once took a ferocious revenge on the Spanish rebels. It was then suggested that a congress should be held to discuss ways and means of reconquering the Spanish colonies in South America that had revolted and declared their independence of Spain during the rule of Napoleon.

The disgusting actions of Ferdinand VII stirred and angered the English public. At the same time English merchants had by the 1820's obtained a solid grip in Latin American markets. English interests there would suffer a serious blow if the new republics were broken and restored to Spain. Then Spanish and French Bourbons would unite to keep English goods away from South and Central America. English trade and English power would be threatened as in the eighteenth century. The balance of power in Europe had been upset. That imbalance must not be increased by the extension of French and Spanish power to the New World.

To the discomfiture of the European powers Canning bluntly refused to send representatives to the Congress proposed by Spain. He would not agree to European interference in the domestic affairs of the nascent states of Latin America. The British fleet stood between the allies of Metternich and Ferdinand VII and the reconquest of the lost empire. Canning thus broke England loose from the alliance with Austria, Prussia, Russia, and France which Castlereagh had helped to forge. The Latin American revolutions had been fostered and aided by British skill, arms and money. Now the British foreign office lent a hand.

Nor could the United States approve either the proposed extension of reaction to the New World or the possible threat to American trading interests. In 1822 the United States gave diplomatic recognition to a few of the new states. Canning then sent British commercial consuls to some South American ports and threatened war if the European allies despatched expeditions to recover Spain's colonies. In December, 1823, President Monroe stated the position of the United States in a famous message to Congress. This "Monroe Doctrine" asserted that any European intervention would be regarded as "the manifestation of an unfriendly disposition towards the United States" and "dangerous to our peace and safety." The President added a general statement of principle declaring that the American continents were "henceforth not to be considered as subjects for future colonization by any European powers."

In 1824 England formally recognized the governments of the Latin American republics, including that of Brazil, former colony of Portugal. Said Canning: "I have called the New World into existence to redress the balance of the Old." Throughout this series of diplomatic efforts in the Spanish American question Canning was upheld by the liberal feelings of the British public and by middle class business interests who were anxious to provide exports and investment capital for the new Latin American states.

Meanwhile Canning warned Spain that England was bound by treaty to Portugal and would resist any Spanish attempt to invade and control that country. When Spain disregarded the warning Canning sent 40,000 British soldiers to Lisbon. Henceforth Spain left Portugal alone. Liberalism in British foreign policy had reached a new high point. Even non-intervention was repudiated.

At the same time Canning helped to make it politically possible for Greece to achieve independence from Turkey. Lord Byron was the tragic hero of the public mind; Canning worked through the less dramatic channels of diplomacy towards the same end. When war had first arisen in 1821 between Greece and Turkey England had been chiefly concerned with the possible Russian intention of pressing towards Constantinople at Turkish expense and thus threatening British interests. When it became clear that Russia intended to enter the war it seemed that joint action by Britain and Russia against Turkish despotism might best serve the twofold purpose of checking Russian ambition and of satisfying the pressure of English public opinion for intervention on the side of the Greeks. Canning visited Paris and persuaded the reactionary Charles X to cooperate with England and Russia as champions of the Greek insurgents. The Treaty of London of 1827 provided the formal basis for this cooperation.

As Austria and Prussia were fiercely opposed to the Greek cause the Quadruple Alliance was now torn apart through the middle. It was never to be mended again. So far as the independence of Greece was concerned that event was only slowly realized. Canning did not live to see the final chapters of the struggle. Two months after his death in 1827 the English, Russian and French fleets blasted the Turkish ships in the "accidental" encounter at Navarino. Then the new policy, if policy it could be called, of the Wellington government left the final liberation of the Greeks to other hands.

CATHOLIC EMANCIPATION

Reference has earlier been made to the brief attempt of Lord Goderich to carry on the government after Canning's death. His incompetence would have made it difficult enough in any case; his unpopularity with George IV made it impossible. In 1828 the Duke of Wellington became prime minister. When the Whigs were sent packing and the saddened liberal Tories resigned, only the narrow Tories were left.

The hybrid policy of the ministries of Liverpool and Canning was now, it seemed, to be abandoned. However, events showed that it was not in fact easy to abandon very much of that policy. Liverpool and Canning, who had violated the "High Toryism" of Wellington and Eldon, had held their cabinets together by remarkable feats of compromise with various groups willing to support "improving" legislation. Wellington and his followers could understand that evidence of political skill. Holding stoutly to their principles, the narrow Tories could also see how the flexible Canningites had taken advantage of the growing friction between landed and commercial interests and had allied themselves with hard-headed and efficient business men against the landed aristocracy. It is doubtful, however, if the old-line Tories ever reached a semblance of understanding as to the importance of the steadily increasing influence of public opinion on administration. Peel called this rising force "that great compound of folly, weakness, prejudice, wrong feeling, right feeling, obstinacy, and newspaper paragraphs." Nevertheless, the liberal Tories recognized the value of public opinion, helped to shape it, called upon it as an ally in both domestic and foreign policy.

Failure to grasp the importance of public opinion contributed greatly to the decline and fall of the Wellington government. As has been described above, the last act of the liberal Tories before they resigned had been to force the Duke of Wellington to support a Corn Bill only slightly different from the one of Canning which he had earlier defeated in the house of lords. The passage of the Duke's bill did him no good. Everyone knew that Canning had been really responsible for it. There was also the question of the Greek revolution. Within a few months after Canning's death Wellington had bungled badly. As a few of his narrow Tory group were pro-Turkish the Duke took no further steps to support the Greek insurgents. At the same time he remained deaf to Turkey's demands for reparations. Thus the purely negative policy of the Wellington government lost England good will in both Turkey and Greece. Russia finally rolled an army towards Constantinople and forced Turkey to recognize the independence of Greece by the Treaty of Adrianople in 1829. Russia also obtained a large degree of effective control in the two Turkish provinces of Moldavia and Wallachia. Canning's hopes for Greece had been realized; but Russia, not England, had profited most. It was obvious to all England that Wellington had blundered in reversing Canning's policy and substituting for it nothing at all.

The ultra-Tory cabinet was also confronted by the question of religious inequalities in England and civil disabilities imposed on various Protestant dissenting groups. Since the reign of Charles II the Test and Corporation Acts had forbidden Nonconformists to hold national and municipal public offices. In practice, however, a yearly Indemnity Bill had been passed to exempt non-Anglican Protestant office-holders from the necessity of taking the oath to conform to the religion of the Church of England. It was therefore not difficult to secure the passage of a bill introduced in 1828 by the Whig Lord John Russell to repeal the Test and Corporation Acts. This action merely recognized a state of affairs already existing. The Anglican Church monopoly was not in fact seriously challenged. It could be challenged only by a revision of the whole municipal and national system of representation which would give greater effective political power to the Nonconformist classes, by the 1820's numerous and wealthy.

Far more important in its implications was the explosive issue of Catholic emancipation facing the weakened cabinet of Wellington and Peel. Roman Catholics in England and Ireland were still refused admission to Parliament, to the law courts, and to the universities. Before the passage of the Act of Union in 1801 the Irish had been given cause by Pitt to hope that these and other grave restrictions upon the Catholics would be repealed. When George III had refused to agree to any change Pitt had resigned and the Irish Catholics were left where they had been before. Not until 1823 did an organized movement for Catholic emancipation called the Catholic Association arise in Ireland. Its leader was Daniel O'Connell.

O'Connell was a Dublin lawyer who was convinced that the only way to win political justice for Catholics was to bring immediate and heavy pressure to bear upon the British government. The familiar method of agrarian protest by rick burning, cattle maiming, and scattered sniping had not proved successful in the past. It seemed that what was needed was united and ordered action. Hence came the formidable force of the Catholic Association, well-organized and backed by the appeals of the parish priests.

In 1828 the expected trial of strength between the Wellington government and the Irish Catholics was finally joined. Wellington had appointed a Mr. Vesey Fitzgerald, an Irish Protestant landlord, as president of the board of trade. When Fitzgerald stood for re-election in his constituency of County Clare the Catholic Association herded its enthusiastic supporters to the polls and elected his opponent Daniel O'Connell. Because he was a Catholic the new member could not take his seat in the house of commons. The issue was clear: either the law must be changed or O'Connell would be expelled from Parliament and there would be a general rebellion in Ireland.

Wellington and Peel both opposed Catholic emancipation. However, they were now convinced that the law must be changed. Always they stressed the fact that the Irish had extorted the concession. After long debate the cabinet agreed to undertake the unpleasant task of relieving the Irish Catholics of their civil disabilities. The Tories in Parliament were bludgeoned into line by the Iron Duke. King George IV finally approved, seeing surrender as a preferable alternative to civil war in Ireland and a Whig government at Westminster. After the languid fears of George IV had been overcome Parliament reluctantly accepted Catholic emancipation. The Roman Catholic Emancipation Act of 1829 provided, among other freedoms, that any persons professing the Roman Catholic religion might sit and vote in either house of Parliament upon taking an oath of allegiance to the crown. The required oath included the following declaration: "I do swear that I will defend to the utmost of my power the settlement of property in this realm as established by the laws. . . . And I do solemnly swear that I will never exercise any privilege to which I am or may become entitled, to disturb or weaken the Protestant religion or Protesant government in the United Kingdom." This capitulation to Catholic demands was in part cushioned by a new law requiring voters in Ireland to possess £10 freeholds. Nearly 200,000 forty shilling freeholders were thus disfranchised. The Catholic Association was suppressed. The government also took a petty revenge by snubbing and insulting O'Connell, who remarked bitterly that the smile of Peel was like "the silver plate on a coffin." Nevertheless, no currents of ill-will could alter the inescapable fact that Catholic emancipation had been granted. A new precedent had been established; an important breach with the past had been made.

The older Tories were outraged and furious at what they considered a flagrant betrayal by their leaders. The Oxford dons, the high and dry squires, and the Anglican parsons loosed a torrent of invective. The old cry of "No Popery" was heard in the streets again. Whirlwinds of passionate unreason silenced the voices of forbearance and common sense. It was true that Wellington and Peel had abandoned one of the sacred laws of the Tory party but they had done so because they had become convinced that such a step would alone suffice to prevent dangerous and shameful tragedy in Ireland. But in the uncontrolled floods of prejudice and recrimination that rolled over England the old Tory party was swept away. In driving through the Catholic Emancipation Act Wellington not only alienated the Canningites still more but added to his enemies the High Tories led by Lord Eldon. All these stood together and prepared to pull Wellington down even if it meant putting the Whig Lord Grey into the prime minister's office. The long eclipse of the Whigs was soon to be ended.

STEAMSHIPS AND RAILROADS

The year 1830 marked the eve of the greatest battle of the long campaign for parliamentary reform and the first major political triumph of the middle class. Because of the drama of these events it is easy to ascribe to them a greater significance in the vast and complicated process of English history than in fact they may merit. The importance of the silent and shifting social and economic forces in the years after Waterloo contributed as much as past politics to the growth of modern England. For example, it was in these years that steamboats and railways heralded the birth of the age of speed.

The steamboat came first. In 1786 the American John Fitch first demonstrated his "water beetle" at Philadelphia. In 1787 a Scotsman named William Symington invented a marine engine and in 1802 his boat the *Charlotte Dundas* travelled twenty miles down the Clyde. Five years later the American engineer Robert Fulton ran a passenger steamboat on the Hudson River. Regular service across the English Channel began in 1818. The following year the *Savannah* crossed the Atlantic using steam power for part of the voyage. In 1833 the Canadian *Royal William* travelled from Nova Scotia to London using steam engines all the way. A few years later the *Great Western* crossed from Bristol to New York in thirteen days. Within a short time the great British and American ocean steamship lines were established.

A second event of tremendous significance in the history of human technical achievement was the development of the railway. Those who soberly considered this new invention were unaware of its meaning for England and the world. Men who live in the midst of revolutions know less about them than historians later. In the England of the 1820's there were heavy doubts and some perturbation about the railway steam engine and its importance as a step in man's conquest of distance.

American and English pioneers had been experimenting with "steam carriages" as early as the 1780's. Among the many inventors at the dawn of the railway era may be mentioned the American John Stephens who in 1811 saw the possibility of using steam engines running along rails by means of flanged wheels. In 1814 the Englishman George Stephenson made an engine which pulled a load of thirty tons along a road at a speed of four miles an hour. He then conceived the idea of an engine with cars attached travelling along rails. Here, as in the case of steamship development, American and British inventors often independently came to similar conclusions. In 1825 the Stockton and Darlington Railway began operations. In 1830 Stephenson's famous *Rocket* reached a speed of thirty miles an hour on the day the Liverpool and Manchester Railway was opened. The ceremonies attending this event were shadowed by tragedy when William Huskisson was fatally injured by the *Rocket*.

The canal, stagecoach, and toll-bridge operators feared the competition of the railways and the country gentlemen did not want their estates disfigured. Their opposition was strong, but not strong enough. A number of small companies soon were founded to serve local areas. These were all later absorbed into the four great railway systems of England. Huge amounts of money were invested, particularly in the "railway mania" of 1845 when over £150,000,000 was placed for profit in railway stock.

The early doubts about the future of the railway are well illustrated by the recorded reaction of Thomas Creevey. A member of the railway committee of the house of commons, in 1825 Creevey wrote of "this infernal nuisance—the loco-motive Monster, carrying *eighty tons* of goods, and navigated by a tail of smoke and sulphur, coming thro' every man's grounds between Manchester and Liverpool." In 1829 Creevey took a trip of five miles on the railway, once reaching a speed of twenty-three miles an hour. "It is really flying, and it is impossible to divest yourself of the notion of instant death to all upon the least accident happening. It gave me a headache which has not left me yet." By 1842 Sydney Smith could write in a different vein: "Man is become a bird; he can fly longer and quicker than a solan-goose. The early Scotchman scratches himself in the morning mists of the north and has his porridge in Piccadilly before the setting sun. . . . Time, distance, and delay are abolished."

THE CASE FOR RECONSTRUCTION

Meanwhile the demands for political reform continued. Early protests of the eighteenth century about the condition of parliamentary representation in England had resulted from numerous forces, such as the beginnings of the economic revolution, the successful revolt of the American colonies, wide impatience with evident corruption and injustice, and the reasonably liberal sentiments of men like William Pitt. To these must be added the importance of a chapter in the history of ideas. Even while lip-service was still being given to John Locke his followers were massaging the doctrine of "natural rights" into something different from the original idea. Through the eighteenth century there was an increasing tendency to stress, as in Leveller days, the "right" of all Englishmen to participate in government, whether or not they were property-holders. Hence the Lockian and Whig argument of property as a sacred "natural right" became steadily less important when used to defend political and economic inequalities. The idea of the "pursuit of happiness" often replaced the idea of property-holding as a "natural right." One aspect of the way in which this new attitude was translated into something politically effective is illustrated by the rise of the political clubs of eighteenth century England dedicated to the cause of parliamentary and suffrage reform.

The violence of the Jacobins in later years gave the English government greater apparent reason to suppress those who openly supported change in England. A number of laws sharply restricted reform agitation. Immediately after 1815, as described in Chapter 28, the gospel of liberalism was heard again. By 1830 it was widely agreed that before any steps could be taken to solve the riddle of social and economic justice in England the reform of Parliament must be achieved.

There was no doubt that the High Tories of Wellington's ministry did not intend to retreat very swiftly or very far or to undertake anything more than a few sedative legislative compromises. In 1828 the cabinet had decided against giving any representation in Parliament to Manchester and Birmingham. At the same time Wellington, heedless of popular opinion, had sharply reversed Canning's foreign policy. This kind of closed-door reaction was no more welcome to the middle class than it had been to the workers. Moreover, the crops of 1829 were poor and the winter which followed very severe. Trade was bad and thousands were out of work in the cities. Suffering was widespread. Workers drilled for revolution; southern England was terrified by rick-burning. This economic blight and sense of class injustice helped to increase the number of recruits and volunteers in the cause of parliamentary reform. In 1830 Thomas Attwood founded the Birmingham Political Union, an association of both middle and working classes, to agitate for the reform of Parliament. As in 1817, William Cobbett preached to large crowds, including people of different social and economic groups: merchants, farmers, clerks, dark-collar workers, grim and inflexible Nonconformists. The old system was challenged by almost all classes, except the landowners and the Anglican clergy, for a time the black soldiery of reaction.

The reformers were not united in knowing precisely what they desired when they demanded a reform of Parliament. Some wanted household suffrage; some wanted socialism; others wanted a currency reform; still others felt only vaguely that a dose of social equality was needed to temper the gentlemanly tradition; and some knew only what they did not want. Despite the wide dissidence of opinion among the reformers their "constant and active pressure from without" upon cabinet and Parliament was a constructive historical force. Hence it follows that any explanation of political or economic reform conceived largely in terms of cabinet or parliamentary personalities is inadequate.

It should now be made clear that Parliament was in fact quite unrepresentative in 1830; the operation of the franchise was irregular and restricted; corruption and bribery had not greatly decreased from the high level of the eighteenth century. The whole system of representation, flagrantly unfair, was based upon a population distribution and a national economy that belonged to an age long past. There had been no redistribution of seats since the early seventeenth century. No new boroughs had been made after 1677. Because the population had been largely concentrated in southern and eastern England when boroughs were being created in the period from the Middle Ages to the seventeenth century these areas contained 115 of the 203 boroughs; there were 21 in the corrupt nest of Cornwall alone. Borough members of Parliament were of course more numerous than county members; 203 boroughs returned 483 members; 40 counties or shires returned 82 members. Although great changes had taken place in England the remains of medieval boroughs were still sending burgesses to Parliament in 1830.

The general situation can be indicated succinctly by a clear statement of specific cases. For the boroughs a table showing parliamentary representation would reveal the following: 35 places with scarcely any voters at all returned 70 members to Parliament; 46 places with not more than 50 voters sent 90 members; 19 places with not more than 100 voters sent 37 members. The old Suffolk borough of Dunwich was falling into the North Sea. Old Sarum, a notorious example usually cited by reformers in 1830 and by historians later, was a Wiltshire meadow, deserted save by livestock. Gatton was an ancient wall. In 1830 each of these still sent two representatives to Westminster. The cities of Manchester, Leeds, and Birmingham had no representation in Parliament, although the population of Manchester was about 130,-000 and of Leeds and Birmingham about 80,000 each. The corresponding disparity in county representation can be seen in the fact that populous Yorkshire sent two members to Parliament; but so also did the tiny shire of Rutland. The county of Galway in Ireland had a larger population than Worcestershire, but the latter had four members and Galway only two. The county of Cork had nearly as large a population as Wales; but Wales had twenty-eight representatives and Cork had two.

The result of this chaotic and anomalous situation was that a large proportion of the members of the house of commons were in fact nominated and controlled by a few great landowners: 85 men nominated 157 members; 70 patrons returned 150 members by recommendation; the Duke of Norfolk controlled eleven seats; Sir James Lowther, nine; Lord Darlington, seven. About seventy-five interrelated families really controlled the house of commons. In some cases the great landowners owned whole boroughs. Thus they had the right to choose the representatives for these "pocket" boroughs, so called because the landowners carried the nominations "in their pockets." In other cases the population of the boroughs was so small that it was easy for a wealthy landlord to control the elections by influence or bribery. These were the "rotten" boroughs.

The unrepresentative character of the house of commons was increased by the haphazard and narrow franchise requirements. It has been estimated that there were about 160,000 individuals legally entitled to vote in the United Kingdom before 1832; the total population was then about 16,000,000. In the counties the franchise was granted only to individuals with freehold property worth forty shillings annually. This rule had been declared by statute in 1430. In the boroughs where there was any voting at all the most chaotic and diverse conditions prevailed. In some boroughs the right to vote was given to all who paid local taxes; in others only to the hereditary "freemen"; in still others, only to individuals who owned or occupied certain houses.

The whole political structure was shot through with corruption. Voters were widely bribed; traffic in seats was considered quite in order and was certainly normal. A seat in the house of commons could usually be bought for £7,000 or £8,000. It was natural that men who paid so much for places in Parliament would attempt to recoup themselves for their expenses in one way or another. When elections were contested they were often bitter and costly. For example, in one election of 1802 the poll was kept open for fifteen days. The expenses of the unsuccessful Whig candidate amounted to more than £15,000. This sum included payments to innkeepers for over 11,000 breakfasts, 36,000 dinners, 700 suppers, 25,000 gallons of ale, 11,000 bottles of spirits, 8,000 bottles of porter, and so on.

DEFEAT OF THE TORIES

When George IV died in 1830 a new Parliament was necessary on the accession of his brother, William IV. In the election the Whigs supported moderate parliamentary reforms, such as the abolition of the "rotten" boroughs and the extension of the franchise, not to the workers but to the propertied middle class. For the first time reform became a party issue. Against the background of Tory weakness and unpopularity, the rising agitation outside of Parliament, and the general state of ferment and emotion, the two political parties fought the election campaign. Meanwhile, in July, 1830, the French overthrew the reactionary Bourbon Charles X and put the bourgeois Louis Philippe on the throne of France. This July revolution, unlike many French experiments, was neither long nor bloody. In France, it seemed, the bourgeoisie had triumphed rather easily over the aristocrats. The English middle class took note. Over fifty seats changed hands in the August election, most of them passing to liberal candidates. At a time when many seats were tightly controlled this marked an important shift in the composition of the house of commons.

Before Parliament met in early November the strength of the Whigs and Tories was not known. Many members of the house were joined together in groups, cliques, and compacts. These men were not necessarily loyal supporters of either party, or united by a set of political principles in which they were all agreed. Hence the Duke of Wellington could be certain of commanding a majority in the house only by taking certain steps, politically wise in the circumstances. The Whigs had already adopted reform as a policy; they had also done much to reconstruct their party. If Wellington gave some better answer to the advocates of reform than the usual sophistries of chartered right, he might then rally sufficient support to weather the Whig and Radical attacks.

At the same time the nation was seeking some assurance about British policy towards the new France and the newly created Belgium. It was clear that the remaining members of the Quadruple Alliance intended to wipe out Belgian independence. It was also clear that the France of Louis Philippe would fight by the side of Belgium. If France and Belgium won such a war, how independent would Belgium be? England had never welcomed French influence, however disguised, in areas so important to England's safety as Belgium and the Netherlands. On the other hand, if Austria, Prussia, and Russia defeated France and Belgium, the interests of England would still be in jeopardy. In either case, England might become involved in war. To many Englishmen it seemed the course of self-interest and of wisdom for England to co-operate with Belgium and France in defying Metternich and his allies. If England ranged herself with liberal and independent France and Belgium at once, then Austria, Prussia, and Russia might be reluctant to strike and war would be prevented.

The Duke of Wellington chose to challenge the people on both questions. He had reversed Canning's policy in Greece; he did not like the tricolor back in France; he did not approve the Belgian revolution. Accordingly, he did not propose to adopt a liberal foreign policy. In the matter of parliamentary reform, he took the offensive. He declared that the existing British system of government was the most perfect ever devised by the hand of man. He was convinced that the Parliament answered "all the good purposes of legislation, and this to a greater degree than any legislature ever has answered in any country whatever." The Duke went still further and asserted that "the Legislature and the system of representation possess the full and entire confidence of the country."

The result of this speech was certain. Wellington had said too much. Within two weeks every liberal reforming group in the house came together to support Earl Grey and the Whigs; the High Tories, who hated Wellington for betraying them on Catholic emancipation, girded themselves to vote against him. On a minor civil list question the Wellington government was defeated, and resigned.

THE REFORM BILL

Earl Grey created a composite and strange cabinet. However, despite the charge that it was too aristocratic because all but two of its members were peers or the sons of peers, this cabinet was wisely chosen. In such a crisis Earl Grey saw that he needed able men; because the most able men were aristocrats they entered his government. For a second reason it was wise to have a cabinet of aristocratic reformers: any bill to reform the system of parliamentary representation would have to pass the house of lords; the upper house would look with a less jaundiced eye upon a bill prepared and sponsored by aristocrats. It is also important to note that Earl Grey was bringing into the Whig party not only Radicals but also Canningites and other reforming Tories. With this fused power behind him he could easily control the house of commons together with a large area of the house of lords. Thus all shades of liberal opinion were in this remarkable cabinet. At the end of one wing was the troublesome Radical Whig Henry Brougham. At the other was the moderate Grey himself. The ministry and cabinet also included Durham and Holland in the house of lords; Russell, Althorp, Stanley, Palmerston, and Macaulay in the house of commons.

The new government began its career with a series of mistakes. Its repressive policy towards the rebellious laborers in the southern counties caused widespread disapproval. There was also the usual Whig weakness in financial matters. When in opposition the Whigs and their supporters had talked too loosely about "retrenchment" and tax reduction. Once in office, they discovered that the public hopes they had roused could not be fulfilled. The first budget had to be recast; the second did not provide for any appreciable tax reductions.

It was fortunate that in March, 1831, the early errors of Earl

Grey's ministry were forgotten in the outburst of popular enthusiasm that hailed the Whig Reform Bill introduced in the house of commons by Lord John Russell. Regarding the "perilous question" of parliamentary reform Earl Grey had earlier written: "With the universal feeling that prevails on this subject, it is impossible to avoid doing something, and not to do enough to satisfy public expectation (I mean the satisfaction of the national public) would be worse than to do nothing." Consequently this bill was a bold and unexpected proposal, much more of a departure from the existing system than the earlier cautious program planned by the Whig party caucus. It had been framed by a four-man committee of the cabinet which included Grey's son-in-law, Lord Durham, and Lord John Russell.

The debate on the first reading took seven nights; on the morning of March 10 the bill passed this first reading without a division of the house. The vote on the second reading came on March 23. "It was like seeing Caesar stabbed in the Senate-house or seeing Oliver taking the mace from the table; a sight to be seen only once, and never to be forgotten." The bill was carried by a majority of only one. After considerable difficulty in the house and a defeat in committee Earl Grey recommended the dissolution of Parliament. "Your Majesty's confidential servants have arrived at the painful conclusion that there is no reasonable hope of the ultimate success of the Reform Bill in the present house of commons." In the election campaign the slogan of the reformers was "The Bill, the whole Bill, and nothing but the Bill." On September 22 the new house carried the bill by a majority of 109. On October 7 the house of lords rejected it by a majority of 41.

When the newspapers, edged in black, announced and mourned the defeat of the Reform Bill by the recalcitrant lords an explosion of popular anger swept over the country. A mob at Bristol controlled the city for three days, looting and burning at will. They burned and sacked the Mansion House and the bishop's palace, and the constables watched helplessly. The jails at Derby were opened and the prisoners loosed. A castle belonging to the Duke of Newcastle was burned. There were numerous riots in Scotland and Ireland. In many areas social order almost gave way to anarchy. The windows in the residence of the Duke of Wellington were smashed. For years the iron shutters at Apsley House remained a mute rebuke to the people. Francis Place began his direction of a run on the Bank of England: "To stop the Duke, go for gold."

Meanwhile the bill, with slight changes, was passed again by the house of commons in the third reading on March 26, 1832. In this direct collision with the commons and the people, the house of lords seemed adamant. The lords wanted to amend and to mutilate the bill. "The Bill once passed," said the Tory John Croker, "good night to the Monarchy, the Lords, and the Church." In view of the attitude of the upper house the cabinet decided to recommend to William IV the creation of fifty or sixty new peers to force the bill through the house of lords. This device had not been used since the reign of Queen Anne. The king found the large number of peerages proposed a "fearful" prospect and refused to agree. The cabinet thereupon resigned. In these days public temper was boiling and England was close to civil war. In hundreds of English towns, political clubs and unions rose to new heights of power, arming and drilling for popular action. On May 10, 1832, the king sent for the Duke of Wellington; but the Duke could not form a government. Five days later Earl Grey's cabinet was back in office and the king promised that he would create enough Whig peers to pass the Reform Bill "unimpaired in its principles and in its essential provisions." In the face of the threat of a deluge of new Whig peers a sufficient number of Tory lords absented themselves to give the Whigs a majority in the house of lords. The Reform Act at last took its place among the statutes.

This great Reform Act did not equalize electoral districts. It did deprive many inconsiderable places of the right of returning members to Parliament. By schedule A it disfranchised fifty-six boroughs with less than two thousand inhabitants. By schedule B it took away one member each from thirty boroughs having less than four thousand inhabitants. There were other reductions in representation. From the seats which thus became available for redistribution two each were given to forty-three urban areas; large, well-populated counties were given additional representatives. Scotland obtained eight more members, Ireland five. Thus the reform in the representative system was considerable.

The worst evils of the narrow franchise controls were also removed. In the boroughs the franchise was extended to all occupiers of property with an income value of £10 a year, subject to certain residence requirements and the payment of local taxes. Nearly all the old anomalous qualifications for the borough franchise were eliminated. In the counties the famous forty-shilling freeholder, residing on his freehold, kept the right to vote. Holders of long-term leases (sixty years or more) and copyholders paying £10 annual rent were admitted to the franchise. So also were the short-term leaseholders and tenants-at-will who paid at least £50 annual rent. Finally, the Reform Act helped to decrease election evils by reducing the voting period from fifteen days to two; by providing for a more adequate list of legally qualified voters; and by limiting election expenses.

Among the Whigs who had appealed to the house of commons to extend the franchise to the middle class was Thomas Babington Macaulay. "The voice of great events is proclaiming to us, reform, that you may preserve. Renew the youth of the state. Save property, divided against itself." With the Reform Act of 1832 the monopoly power of aristocracy was broken. About one half of the propertied middle class was enfranchised, but none of the working class. In the following decades the shift from landed aristocratic control to control by the commercial and industrial classes continued steadily. Land accounted for 66 per cent of the economic interests represented in the house of commons in 1832. By 1865 land accounted for only 44 per cent and industrial and commercial interests for 56 per cent. Meanwhile the laboring classes found that the middle class and the aristocracy were united, as men of property, in making common cause against the pressure of working-class movements and demands. Property was no longer divided against itself.

Chapter 30

THE YEARS OF REFORM

DECLINE OF LAISSEZ-FAIRE

[handwritten marginal notes: Capital, Labor, classes]

D URING the early nineteenth century another process of tremendous significance proceeded at an accelerated pace. The accumulation of capital in industrial and commercial nations relentlessly increased. This development slowly resulted in the financial aristocracy of the great corporate systems. In democratic states this new aristocracy in fact lay largely beyond the control of government. Opposing the economic power of centralized finance there gradually emerged the organized power of labor, also largely outside government control. Not only in England, but also in the United States and other democratic states where the economics of revolution have not prevailed, one of the major functions of government has been the limited successive attempts to achieve reasonable compromises between capital and labor groups.

These attempts at compromise have not been successful in answering many of the fundamental problems of privilege and poverty arising from the growth of organized and ordered finance. Consequently, to an increasing extent democratic governments have been compelled to intervene and to make a steadily expanding series of laws to provide a greater degree of protection and social security for the laboring classes. It is well to note this trend in England in the first half of the nineteenth century. The natural law of Adam Smith and the power and influence of the doctrine of laissez-faire slowly began to decline. In the years following the Reform Bill of 1832 Parliament carried through a body of reforming legislation that was not at all in accord with the theory that natural laws of economics and politics would make their own inevitable and automatic adjustments to the ultimate advantage of the state.

ROADS TO UTOPIA: BENTHAM, MILL, AND OWEN

In the eighteenth century Adam Smith had said that business prospered best when let alone. According to the classical economists,

583

the intelligent, self-seeking, natural economic man who pursued his own welfare under the immutable laws of economics would best achieve his own interests and, at the same time, the true interests of the whole community. To some the steady growth of British industry showed the wisdom of a free enterprise policy. The defenders of laissez-faire asserted that the natural laws of economics, leading capital and labor as if by an invisible hand, had decreed that certain men must grow wealthy and others must starve. In 1798 Thomas Malthus had declared that population constantly tended to increase beyond the subsistence level; war, disease, and the food supply limited that increase. David Ricardo had added that if wages were lifted above the subsistence level the workers would raise more children. Thus the labor supply would be increased, and, by the iron laws of economics, wages would be forced down again to the subsistence level. Hence there was no advantage to anybody in raising wages. All of these theories were usually quite acceptable to the wealthy industrialists and to the governing classes because they appeared to provide a moral sanction for profits and for existing conditions generally. Inexorable laws had decreed that it was right that things should seem to be wrong in this world. And yet, despite the arguments of economists and vested interests, nobody could deny the wretched consequences resulting from the combination of laissez-faire and the economic revolution. Thomas Carlyle declared that to say "button your pocket and stand still" was a policy which he would "by no manner or means believe in, but pronounce at all times to be false, heretical, and damnable if ever aught was!"

It has already been explained that working class opinion, often fierce and wild, was not convinced of the absolute and eternal validity of the doctrine of laissez-faire. The impulses behind the legislative reform activity in the 1830's were complex and numerous. There was, of course, no recession of the economic, political, and social pressures underlining the demands for various reforms. At the same time, the general climate of opinion was influenced by a number of more imponderable forces. The most significant of these was the impact of the philosophy of Jeremy Bentham (1748–1832). The ideas of Bentham, often roughly translated, permeated very large areas of English thought and feeling. For example, there were the "philosophical radicals" who were Benthamites because they had been intellectually convinced of the validity of Bentham's conclusions. There were also those who became aggressive and diligent reformers because the utilitarian creed appeared so simple and sane. It was not necessary to move upon the highest intellectual level to follow the widely publicized logic of Bentham or to agree with at least a part of his teaching. Consequently, many reformers, touched by Benthamism in various ways, demanded changes in the representative system, in the economic and political policy of the government, in the criminal laws, in legal procedure, and so on.

Jeremy Bentham had declared that every individual acts in a way that he thinks will give him most pleasure. Pleasure, said Bentham, is a calculable thing; all pleasures are qualitatively the same because "pushpin is as good as poetry." Each individual, then, follows the dictates of self-interest and pleasure. Because all pleasures are equal in value the purpose of society is to make as many people happy as possible, "each to count as one and none as more than one." Bentham therefore claimed that the chief purpose of government was to see to it that all institutions, laws, and customs were in fact "useful" to men living in a society. Where they could not be proved "useful" they should be reformed or discarded. To Bentham and his followers the foundation of value and morals was this principle of utility, defined as "the greatest happiness of the greatest number." "The happiness of a people is made up of the happiness of single persons." Institutions and actions were held to be right as they tended to promote happiness, wrong as they tended to deprive men of pleasure. "The multiplication of happiness is, according to utilitarian ethics, the object of virtue." This pleasure-pain calculus was not fully accepted by all the philosophical radical followers of Bentham; but much of it was. They all agreed that there could be no rational basis for defending proved abuses or evils on grounds of tradition or natural law. Law, they asserted, should be an instrument of social welfare; the end of all law and all institutions is the happiness of the many rather than the few.

John Stuart Mill (1806–1873), educated by Jeremy Bentham and his father, James Mill, claimed that there was a qualitative distinction among pleasures. "It is better to be Socrates dissatisfied than a fool satisfied." Nevertheless, Mill retained many of the essential principles of Bentham in the same way that they have been accepted in varying degrees by numerous philosophers and politicians up to the present day. For example, Mill maintained that society could be greatly improved by education and political machinery. "The present wretched education, and wretched social arrangements, are the only real hindrances to its [happiness] being attainable by almost all." Human care and effort, said Mill, could conquer "all the sources of human suffering." It is easy to understand how doctrines such as these shook the deep foundations of the laissez-faire structure created by Adam Smith. The utilitarian questions stressed all kinds of problems resulting from the slowly rising conflict of capital and labor. For instance: to what extent did the wealth that dripped into the coffers of the financiers contribute to the greatest happiness of the greatest number? In these years the questions and answers of the utilitarians profoundly influenced the whole approach to legislation. The pert spirit of Bentham challenged reaction and inertia everywhere.

The popular attitude of the hour was questioning, reforming, humanitarian. Vigorous and able royal commissions were appointed to investigate and report to the cabinet about various reform proposals. Popular agitation continued apace. The Whig Dr. Thomas Arnold of Rugby echoed many who were weary of the disturbance brought by the radical missionaries when he wrote unkindly of "the brazen, shallow, and insolent speakers; the ignorant, lying and malignant writers, known for nothing but their turbulence and their libels." Yet it was these men who were largely responsible for the fact that the idea of the state as an instrument of human welfare began to supersede the conception of the state as a power existing chiefly to protect the "natural rights" of the eighteenth century.

In opposition to the reactionary and conservative appeals to tradition, to natural law, to precedent, and to authority the progressive reformers of the early nineteenth century also appealed to the past, with different results. They found in history the proof they sought of the possibility of continuous and beneficent progress. This idea of progress had been a part of the gospel of those eighteenth century philosophers who hoped for the ultimate perfectibility of man. Although the nineteenth century had considerable doubts about the final conquest of all disharmonies by the use of reason alone, the idea of progress was still a pivotal and prevalent idea in the nineteenth century. "Better fifty years of Europe than a cycle of Cathay." The whole century proclaimed its hope, and sometimes its certainty, that the final goal of ill would be good. In this, at least, the Utopian Socialists, most of the great poets, and men like Carlyle and Matthew Arnold were in agreement. Late in the century Herbert Spencer declared that the evolution of human society was a part of "the whole movement towards perfection."

One of the pioneers working for the regeneration of society was Robert Owen (1771–1858), the father of the factory laws and the cooperative movement. "Wealth," said Owen, "has accumulated in the hands of what are called the monied class, who created none of it, and who misused all they had acquired. This misdirection of the rational faculties of humanity has led all nations and peoples through all manner of insane absurdities." Owen had risen from the ranks of the workers to become the owner of the great cotton mills at New Lanark in Scotland. When he had achieved success he was able to put some of his benevolent and humanitarian ideas into practice. His generous social experiments included the reduction of working hours and improvement of factory conditions. As early as 1816, with the assistance of Sir Robert Peel, he brought this question to the attention of Parliament and the public; but nothing effective was done. Because he believed that labor was the basis of value Owen favored a paper note currency representing hours of labor. He also proposed to eliminate poverty and unemployment by setting up model communities, the

greatest of which was in his mills at New Lanark. These were cooperative and self-governing units, working and sharing profits, "looking
back to the monasteries and forward to the Soviet." In Owen's Utopia
the machines would serve all men; life would be sane and beautiful.
His vision of a great and clean society was born of an uncritical and
guileless heart and mind, and a mighty faith in his fellow men. Although nearly all of Owen's schemes failed, his precepts and practice
influenced most of the social legislation of the nineteenth century and
his contribution to the cooperative and trades union movements was
immense. To the end of his career his confidence in the future remained
secure: "The change is now before us, and will be the revolution of
revolutions. It will secure the permanent well-doing and happiness of
the human race."

Philosophers and planners like Bentham, Mill, and Owen and
popular agitators like William Cobbett, Richard Oastler, and Michael
Sadler were supported by many people who had no general theory of
the aims and purpose of government. These individuals knew only that
they were repelled by the unhappy results of laissez-faire. The appeals
of popular pamphlets and the revelations of parliamentary reports
united with the protests of the agitators to influence the house of commons. Then, too, famous writers such as Thomas Arnold, Thomas
Carlyle, Charles Dickens and Mrs. Gaskell appealed to the Christian
and decent humanitarian sentiments of the English people. Christian
Socialists, such as Charles Kingsley, attempted, with some success, to
apply Christian ethics to the reform of the state. Throughout these
years, thousands of leagues and societies, including the great Mechanics'
Institutes, were founded for all kinds of causes and purposes. These
voluntary associations spread through society as arteries of public discussion and agitation. By propaganda and dissemination of facts they
helped adult education and aided the growth of a more alert and informed public opinion.

Thus a variety of forces united in the extraordinary and dynamic
early nineteenth century to assist in the molding of modern England.
Old and new elements existed simultaneously. In some aspects of life
the new overlapped the old. In others, the old and the new mingled in
a common stream. In still others, the old ways yielded only slowly, or
not at all.

1833: FACTORY ACT AND END OF NEGRO SLAVERY

Shortly after the passage of the Reform Act a strong agitation
developed in the industrial north about the hard and distressing conditions of factory labor. From the late eighteenth century vigorous
humanitarian crusades had urged Parliament to do something about
these deplorable conditions, particularly the appalling exploitation of
child labor by factory owners and by bad parents. In 1830, as in 1816,

a select parliamentary committee reported that children often began to work when eight or nine years of age; they usually worked from twelve to fourteen hours a day; they were frequently beaten and starved; immoral and unsanitary conditions were common. The result was profit to the mill owner but blighted and unhappy lives for the children, deprived of good food, education, medical care, sleep, and recreation.

In 1833 Lord Althorp, Whig leader in the house of commons, succeeded in obtaining the passage of a Factory Act which applied to most textile mills (except silk mills). This act provided that no children under nine years of age could be employed in the factories; children between the ages of nine and thirteen might not be worked more than nine hours a day; those between the ages of thirteen and eighteen might not be worked more than twelve hours in one day or more than sixty-nine hours in one week. All children and "young persons" were entitled to the following holidays: Christmas Day, New Year's Day, and eight half-days besides. The law also provided for medical examinations for children employed in factories and for somewhat improved sanitary conditions. It was wisely decided to make the act really operative by taking the responsibility for enforcement out of the hands of careless local magistrates. Hence four paid inspectors were appointed who were to report twice a year to the government. Such was the "children's charter." Despite the bitter opposition of many factory owners, the state had intervened to protect the youth of England in the interest of national welfare. This Factory Act, supported by the public conscience, was an important chapter of a steady record of triumph.

The strenuous efforts of the Evangelical philanthropist Lord Ashley (later the earl of Shaftesbury) and his followers resulted in further ameliorative measures. After a royal commission had revealed the abominable conditions in the mines of England the Mines Act of 1842 forbade the employment of women and children under ten years of age in underground work. An act of 1844 restricted the hours of labor for children between nine and thirteen years of age to a half-day, or to alternate days; the remaining half-time was to be spent in school. This measure also provided for greater safety precautions to decrease the number of industrial accidents. The Ten Hours Act of 1847 made it illegal to require women and "young persons" to work more than ten hours a day. As the men in the factories could not carry on alone, the act really reduced their hours of labor. By such slow steps as these the working conditions of the industrial laborers of England were gradually transformed.

The year 1833 marked the end of slavery in the British Empire. The slave trade had been abolished in 1807. After long years of agitation by reformers like William Wilberforce, about 750,000 Negro slaves were at last emancipated by the action of Earl Grey's government. So that the transition might be less difficult for both masters and slaves the emancipating law provided that the slaves were to remain as apprentices for seven years, owing a portion of their time to their former masters until they became entirely free. At the same time, all slave owners, mostly West Indian planters, were compensated for their losses by a parliamentary grant of £20,000,000.

The abolition of the slave trade in 1807 had contributed to the decline of the West Indies. The act of 1833 hastened the relative economic stagnation because the old-line West Indian planters apparently could not prosper without the aid of slaves. However, at a time when England admitted free of duty slave-grown sugar from Brazil and Cuba and a competitive beet-sugar industry was already rising in Europe and elsewhere in the Empire a rather derelict future for the British West Indies seemed in any event assured.

1834: THE POOR LAW AMENDMENT ACT

From the late eighteenth century the number of paupers, underfed and miserable, had steadily increased among the distressed laboring classes. "What is a pauper?" asked William Cobbett. "Only a very poor man." Few problems before the Whig government demanded more urgent consideration than the state of the poor. There was no effective central government control over the magistrates and the parish overseers who were charged with administering relief under the Elizabethan act of 1601. The result was widespread incompetence, lack of interest, and general maladministration by the local officials. The Speenhamland decision of the Berkshire justices in 1795, described in Chapter 26, produced haphazard administrative practices of giving relief. The only uniformity was systematic abuse of common sense relief principles. Usually definite scales of relief allowances were based upon the size of an applicant's family, the price of bread, and the wages earned. If the wages were considered by the local magistrate to be too low to maintain life, the difference was made up by relief grants from the parish poor rates. The unemployed received still more assistance. Identical treatment was therefore given to able-bodied loafers and to honest men who were really prepared to work. As a result there was little incentive to find or to keep jobs because it was just as profitable to be idle. The employers, aware that the local magistrates would not let men starve, lowered wages; though the wages fell, the birth rate was kept up. In forty years the local taxes to pay the poor rates had tripled. The morale of the working classes in "the little, hard parishes" sank low.

The Poor Law of 1834 "for the amendment and better administration of the laws relating to the poor in England and Wales" brought the rather drastic but effective surgery of the workhouse system. The new law succinctly stated that relief was being distributed "in modes productive of evil." To end the evil it was provided that no relief was to be given by the parishes to able-bodied men unless they entered the workhouses. By stern, utilitarian logic it seemed wise to make life in these workhouses less attractive than the life of the lowest paid worker outside. Families were often divided by the grim clauses of the unpopular law. In *Oliver Twist* (1838) Charles Dickens described the choice of an unemployed poor man as one "of being starved by a gradual process in the workhouse, or by a quick one out of it." In the violent prose of *Past and Present* Thomas Carlyle denounced the evils of the "poor law Bastilles." "Fatal paralysis spreading inwards, from the extremities, in St. Ives workhouses, in Stockport cellars, through all limbs, as if towards the heart itself. Have we actually got enchanted, then; accursed by some God?"

To ensure the reasonably effective operation of this Poor Law Amendment Act the administration of relief was completely reorganized. Control was placed in the hands of three Poor Law Commissioners for England and Wales. These Commissioners, later called the Poor Law Board, were to become the Local Government Board in 1871; the Local Government Board became the Ministry of Health in 1919. The actual administration of the act was given to various Boards of Guardians, each in charge of a group of parishes, or "unions." In each parish the local administrative officers were to be elected by the taxpayers.

Despite widespread objection and bitterness the act of 1834 did result in a reduction of the taxes for poor relief. Many employers were forced at last to pay sufficient wages to enable their workers to live. However, the decrease in the number of paupers was very slow. In 1840 there were almost two million individuals listed on the pauper rolls of England and Wales; the total population was about eighteen million.

1835: MUNICIPAL CORPORATIONS ACT

The Grey Reform Ministry now turned to remedy the deplorable situation in local government. A royal commission revealed that the control of most municipal governments was actually in the hands of small local rings and family compacts. For example, in Portsmouth, a town of 46,000, there were only 102 freemen eligible for office. In these inefficient and unrepresentative systems, corruption and jobbery of all kinds were rampant. Officials often used and manipulated municipal property to their advantage. Large salaries, banquets, and bribes absorbed tax money. Meanwhile, in the midst of this inert incompetence, public works were neglected as the towns grew into cities.

To remedy these evils the Municipal Corporations Act was passed in 1835. It was one of the most far-reaching reforms of the Whig government. The preamble explained that as it could no longer be hoped that the cities and towns "might forever be and remain well and quietly governed" under the old system, certain alterations were desirable. These alterations touched all the large centers except London, where a reasonably democratic government already existed. Elsewhere the act abolished the charters of a number of small boroughs. In all remaining boroughs there was established a uniform type of town council to be elected by male taxpayers who had been resident within seven miles of the borough for at least two years prior to the election. Careful provision was made for the election of "fit persons" to be councillors. To ensure a continuity of experience in each council a system of rotation was established. Two thirds of the council was to serve for three years, one third retiring each year. The remaining third of the council was to serve for six years, one third retiring every two years. The mayor of each borough was to be elected annually by the council. The council was also to appoint the town clerk and all other officials. Finally, the council was to make such by-laws "as to them shall seem meet for the good rule and government of the borough." In summary, then, the councils were responsible for local town and city government, strong and popular centers of authority.

The Municipal Corporations Act of 1835 still remains the basis of the English municipal government system, though later legislation has expanded the duties and powers of the borough councils. Thus local government was reformed in the towns and cities; it was not reformed in the country until 1888. Hence the countryside remained subject to the squires; in the counties the justices of the peace continued to carry on rural administration and justice. This fact helps to explain why the power of the Labor and Liberal parties is today in the towns and cities and the strength of the Conservative party remains in rural England.

DECLINE OF THE WHIGS

In July, 1834, Lord Grey had retired following a series of cabinet quarrels about the collection of tithes from Irish Catholics for the maintenance of the established Anglican Church in Ireland. Grey's successor was the moderate, wealthy, popular, and cynical Lord Melbourne. The new leader was able to balance against each other the radicals who wanted more reform and the standpat conservatives who thought there had been too much already. It was a difficult task, made no easier by the knowledge that William IV disliked his ministry. When Althorp went to the house of lords a considerable group thought that Russell should be the new Whig leader in the house of commons. "Lord John Russell," said the king, "would make a wretched figure." Such language bred no confidence or harmony between William IV and his cabinet. Melbourne feared that the government might break up and founder on the rock of the Irish Church question; he said as much to the king. At once William IV dismissed the Whigs and called Sir Robert Peel to form a Tory government. There is considerable mystery about the circumstances of Melbourne's dismissal; but none about the fact. Lord Palmerston summed it up: "We are all out; turned out neck and crop." William IV had rid himself of the Whigs. He was the last English ruler to dismiss a government without the direct advice of the prime minister.

Peel did not expect to hold office long; he remained for only five months. In the election of 1835 the strength of the Tories increased from 150 to 232; but they lacked a clear majority even with the additional support of about forty renegade Whigs. Accordingly, after a formal defeat on the Irish tithes question, Peel resigned. The Tories had no opportunity to do more than proclaim that they had ceased to be a party of reaction and henceforth would support the cause of moderate progress at a gentle pace. Peel accepted the Reform Bill of 1832 as "a final and irrevocable settlement of a great constitutional question." In the famous Tamworth manifesto he prepared the way for the later democratic Toryism of Benjamin Disraeli. "If by adopting the spirit of the Reform Bill it be meant that we are to live in a perpetual vortex of agitation; that public men can only support themselves in public estimation by adopting every popular impression of the day, by promising the instant redress of anything that anybody may call an abuse . . . I will not undertake to adopt it. But if the spirit of the Reform Bill implies merely a careful review of institutions, civil and ecclesiastical, undertaken in a friendly temper, combining with the firm maintenance of established rights the correction of proved abuses and the redress of real grievances—in that case I can for myself and my colleagues undertake to act in such a spirit and with such intentions."

Lord Melbourne found his second ministry no stronger than his first. Despite the king's displeasure, Lord John Russell became Whig leader in the house of commons and home secretary. Lord Palmerston went back to the foreign office; Charles Grant (later Lord Glenelg) became colonial secretary; Lord Lansdowne returned to the presidency of the council. This cabinet was so weak that it could not afford to offend any of the diverse groups that gave it support in the commons. For example, the Irish followers of O'Connell sometimes held the balance of power; their votes could have defeated Melbourne. Hence the frail government had to avoid the introduction of new reform proposals that might alienate support; this explains the paucity of reform measures in the years of the doldrums immediately following the passage of the popular Municipal Corporations Act.

The Whigs also had to cooperate fully with the Irish members in the terms of the "Lichfield House Compromise" by which O'Connell was promised that the Whigs would try to appropriate the surplus revenues of the Anglican Church in Ireland for Irish national purposes; that the tithe would be reduced and changed to a land tax paid by the landowners; that part of the Irish patronage would be handed over to

O'Connell to permit some Irish Catholics to replace a few English officials in Ireland. This explains why the Melbourne Ministry, otherwise lethargic, was so much concerned with Irish affairs. Both the Whigs and the Irish kept their compact despite the fact that the house of lords stood grimly athwart the path of Irish conciliation. The Tithes Commutation Bill, long delayed by the lords, finally became law in 1838; it reduced the tithes by 25 per cent and transformed them into permanent rent charges so that a tenant no longer paid his tithe directly to the Anglican Church. In the same year the Irish Poor Law was passed, similar in form to the English law of 1834. In 1840 Catholics were admitted to a limited share in Irish municipal government; as a result of this concession O'Connell was to become mayor of Dublin.

Meanwhile, in 1837, William IV had died. He was succeeded by his niece, Victoria, a girl of eighteen who swiftly obliterated much of the cloud that had fallen darkly over the throne when George IV and his brothers lived. From the election which followed the accession of Victoria the Whigs again emerged with a dangerously narrow majority. When a division of 1839 sustained Melbourne in a full house by a margin of only five votes he decided at last to resign.

The young queen, given to strong likes and dislikes, had been captivated by the charming and fatherly Lord Melbourne. From him she learned valuable political and constitutional lessons useful through a reign of sixty-four years. Many of her other friends were also Whigs. At first the inexperienced Victoria did not fully understand that a monarch must have no politics. When Melbourne departed from office in 1839 she viewed his going with some apprehension and doubted whether she would like the austere Peel. The incoming prime minister rightly felt that the Whig backstairs influence about Victoria had been too great. He therefore asked that the queen dismiss two Whig ladies of her bedchamber and replace them by Tories. Victoria refused, with Hanoverian obstinacy, on the grounds that these ladies were her personal attendants.

Peel, who was not at all anxious to take office until he had stronger support in the house of commons, insisted that the bedchamber attendants should be regarded as holders of political offices and therefore changed with changing ministries. As the queen proved adamant, Peel refused to form a government. Thereupon Lord Melbourne reluctantly agreed to return to office. For two uneasy years after this curious episode the Whigs sucked the last dregs of power. England was weary of them. There had been no important reforms since 1835. Trade was stagnant. Whig budgets, as usual, were unbalanced. England was on the eve of the terrible "hungry forties." In 1841 a new general election gave Peel a clear majority. Melbourne resigned again. This time the Whigs stayed out of office for five years.

COLONIAL REFORM

In these years of Whig rule a series of important colonial problems arose to add to the burden of domestic affairs. The roots of these questions were deep in earlier days. After the American Revolution the English were usually indifferent or timid in their colonial policy. If Lord Castlereagh had considered colonies as great assets, England would have retained more of her conquests in 1815; but Castlereagh thought a pacified France and a peaceful world more important. At the same time, it was becoming clear that the abandonment of mercantilism meant in reality the jettisoning of the idea that the main purpose of colonies was to provide a monopoly of trade for the mother country. Had not the practice of this idea helped to bring revolution in America? Now the disciples of Adam Smith were claiming that even the theory was false. Of what value were colonies? Would it not be well and wise to give them their independence?

Colonies, it was argued, were costly; the expense of defense and maintenance offset any gains resulting from mere physical possession. Minor prophets asserted that it was in the logic of things that England's colonies would drop away into independence like ripe fruit from a tree; no harm would be done, for possessions abroad were perhaps an evil, certainly a useless and costly encumbrance. Jeremy Bentham and the utilitarians thought so; the new economists, who looked to free trade and European markets, agreed; the politicians and statesmen were busy with foreign policy and domestic reform problems. This "loose the bond and go" attitude, particularly among liberal groups, continued until the 1860's and beyond. In the early nineteenth century there were few who spoke against the prevailing hostility and indifference to colonies and empire.

Nevertheless, various individuals were actively discussing the evils and weakness of colonial administration. In 1798 William Knox had written: "Behold two secretaries of state who cannot write a sentence of English. . . . Since the Heptarchy we do not believe the offices were so ill-filled." In his *Book of Fallacies* (1824) Jeremy Bentham pilloried the civil servants in the colonial office, as well as the "deaf auditors of the exchequer" and the "blind surveyors of the melting-irons." Charles Buller's famous description of "Mr. Mother Country" contains the following picture of the "back room" at the end of the corridor: "Here, if perchance you shall some day be forced to tarry, you will find strange, anxious-looking beings who pace to and fro in feverish impatience or sit dejected at a table . . . These are men with colonial grievances . . . No experienced eye can mistake their faces, once expressive of health and energy, now worn by hopes deferred and the listlessness of prolonged dependence." Of course, the colonial office was not entirely filled with functionless drones; but divided authority, corruption, patronage, incompetence, and indifference generally prevailed in colonial administration.

Meanwhile, the second British Empire continued to grow, without settled pattern and often without intention. In 1787 the English government had begun to send out to Australia large numbers of convicts sentenced to transportation under the harsh criminal laws. This movement continued for several decades. In such fashion the settlement of the great southern colony began. Soon the tide of free settlers was to increase with the discovery of the great grasslands where sheep could be raised on a scale never before known. In the middle of the nineteenth century, the discovery of gold drew thousands, like a mighty magnet, to the new frontiers of Australia. In India and Africa the power of England advanced. The missionary societies expanded their activities. The Bible, the flag, the gunboat, and the trader moved on their relentless ways.

In the pessimistic years after 1815 many Englishmen began to wonder if emigration and colonization might help to ease economic distress and painful social dislocations at home. Between 1815 and 1830 about 23,000 persons left the United Kingdom annually; between 1830 and 1840 about 100,000 annually; after the Irish famine of 1846 the yearly total was about 280,000. The whole subject of emigration and colonization was made more intelligible by the work of the colonial reformers. These men, often called "the theorists of 1830," were at once reformers, idealists, empire-builders, and sometimes sound business men. Their recognized leader was Edward Gibbon Wakefield, who published his celebrated *Letter from Sydney* under rather peculiar circumstances in 1839 and his *View of the Art of Colonization* in 1849. In these books and elsewhere Wakefield set forth his theories of "systematic colonization." He argued that land in the colonies should be sold at a "sufficient price." New settlers who could not buy land at once would work for hire before they became landowners. This would help to solve the problem of labor supply. Part of the capital obtained from the sale of the crown lands should be used to bring out selected emigrants who were not paupers. Each colony would be largely self-governing; socially it would be a replica of England, except that there would be few poor people.

Wakefield, William Molesworth, Charles Buller, Lord Durham, and their fellow colonial reformers infused a new spirit into public and government consideration of colonization, emigration, administrative reform, imperial expansion and the form of colonial government. They believed in the future of a British Empire of free men and the "new majesties of mighty states" beyond the seas. It was fortunate that the leaven of their teaching had worked among the Whigs before the Canadian challenge to the outworn colonial system rolled across the Atlantic in 1837.

In 1837 two rebellions, led by William Lyon Mackenzie and the French-Canadian Louis Joseph Papineau, broke out in Upper and Lower Canada (now the provinces of Ontario and Quebec). This Canadian challenge to an anomalous colonial policy exploded at the same time that distrust of that policy was welling up in England. The Canadians demanded responsible government, by which they meant that Canadian ministers responsible to the Canadian legislative assemblies should have executive authority. The Governor-General in Canada, as the representative of the king, should have a position similar to that of the king in England; he should reign but not rule; his Canadian cabinet should rule. Disputes had long been multiplied. How could colonial self-government be reconciled with control by the crown? How could the Governor-General take commands from both the British and Canadian governments?

The Whig cabinet, its hand forced by events, sent to Canada as high commissioner the brilliant and radical Lord Durham. With the aid of Charles Buller, another colonial reformer of the Wakefield group, Lord Durham studied the Canadian situation. In his famous and long *Report on the Affairs of British North America* of January 31, 1839, Durham made two important recommendations. Despairing of a federal union that would embrace the eastern colonies of Nova Scotia and New Brunswick, he proposed the fusion of Upper and Lower Canada. He hoped that the French-Canadians and the English in these provinces would merge into one people and would cease to be "two nations warring in the bosom of a single state." The two provinces were joined by the Union Act of July 23, 1840; but the hope of Lord Durham remains unfulfilled.

The second major suggestion of the *Report* was that complete self-government should be granted in all matters that were the sole concern of the Canadian colonies. The Imperial government would retain control of all powers considered necessary for Imperial unity, such as foreign affairs and commerce. Lord Durham felt that it was nonsense to suppose that "Englishmen would renounce every political opinion and feeling when they enter a colony, or that the spirit of Anglo-Saxon freedom is utterly changed and weakened among those who are transplanted across the Atlantic." In his opinion the attempt of the Governors to extend the executive powers was "totally incompatible with the principles of constitutional liberty." He therefore proposed that "the Colonial Governor be instructed to secure the cooperation of the Assembly in his policy by entrusting its administration to such men as could command a majority."

The interpretations placed upon Durham's *Report* have varied considerably, both in his own time and later. As a document in the history of Canadian self-government it shares the importance of Joseph Howe's trenchant letters from Nova Scotia to Lord John Russell. There continued to be differences of opinion as to the meaning of "responsible government" through the regimes of successive Governors-General: Sydenham, Bagot, and Metcalfe. In 1847, however, Lord Elgin, son-in-law of Lord Durham, came to Canada. With the support of Earl Grey and the Canadians Louis Lafontaine and Robert Baldwin, Elgin established the principle of responsible government in domestic affairs by the simple act of signing the Rebellion Losses Bill on April 25, 1849. This was a bill to compensate those who had suffered damage in the rebellion of 1837; it was opposed by the British government and by the Canadian Tories. Nevertheless, it had passed the legislative assembly by a large majority. The Tories, angered by their defeat and by Elgin's approval of the bill, burned down the Parliament buildings; they insulted and stoned the Governor-General who had yielded to the will of the majority. Elgin's robust faith in British institutions would not permit him to retreat. The first step towards self-government had been taken; the precedent was established. Later in the nineteenth century the Canadians progressively obtained more control of their fiscal and foreign affairs in the gradual extension of self-government into new areas. In Canada, Australia, New Zealand, and South Africa the foundations were slowly laid for the development of the autonomous communities which today form the British Commonwealth of Nations.

THE OXFORD MOVEMENT

While England and her colonies were being steadily disturbed by numerous waves of unrest arising from unsolved riddles of political and social justice, the tide of reform agitation swept over the Anglican Church with results of profound importance. From its center in Oxford University the influence of the strong and passionate Oxford Movement radiated over all England and in time over most of the Christian world. Its leaders were a group of able and zealous individuals who wished to lift the Anglican Church from "the morass of stupid ease" into which they felt it had fallen. Men such as John Henry Newman, John Keble, and E. B. Pusey not only wished more religious enthusiasm and less lethargy but they also feared that unless the clergy was aroused the state might make too many secular reforms and thus weaken the church. Laymen who wanted to undertake reform could point to manifest evils of corruption, non-residence, and outworn procedure in the Anglican system. Nonconformists disliked the tithe and disputed the exclusive right of the Church of England to solemnize marriages. Many thought that the church should stand on its own feet, unsupported by the state; that it should be "disestablished." The Anglican Church, on the other hand, asserted that such questions were outside the proper purvieu of parliamentary reform. Nevertheless, the Whigs, acting on the recommendation of an ecclesiastical commission, did enact some reforming legislation between 1836 and 1840. That they did not do more was the result of the Oxford Movement.

The Oxford men disliked the close connection between the Anglican Church and the state. They wished to return, in spirit and usage, to the doctrines and rituals of the Middle Ages. They reasserted the principle of continuity and insisted that it must not be forgotten that the Anglican Church was really a part of the Catholic Church. Nearly 200,000 copies of Keble's *Christian Year* were published. The *Tracts for the Times,* written by Newman and Keble, went all over the Western world. Newman thus stated his own position: "I felt affection for my own church, but not tenderness. I felt dismay at her prospects, anger and scorn at her do-nothing perplexity. . . . I was confident in the truth of a definite religious teaching—that there was a visible church with sacraments and rites which are the channels of invisible grace. I thought this was the doctrine of Scripture, of the early Church, and of the Anglican Church."

By 1837 the vigorous propaganda of the movement had spread over England, bringing with it much good. However, in January, 1841, Newman questioned the practice of the Anglican Church. In 1845 he joined the Church of Rome, an action which caused wide excitement. When he published his famous *Apologia pro Vita Sua* in 1864 he explained the reasons why he had sought salvation in the Roman Catholic road to God. Meanwhile many other Anglo-Catholics followed him.

As a result of the Oxford Movement the Anglican Church was improved and enlivened. Nevertheless, the conversions to Roman Catholicism of so many prominent Anglicans caused reverberations heard for decades. Particularly among Nonconformist groups the popular suspicions of Catholicism and ritualism continued to be loudly and strongly expressed.

The deeper significance of the Oxford Movement is to be found in the fact that it was primarily a protest against the widespread materialism of the age. In this aspect of its history, the Oxford Movement is closely connected with the literary protests of Thomas Carlyle, Matthew Arnold, and John Ruskin.

THE CHARTISTS

Meanwhile there arose new demands for political reform. Shortly after 1832 it became clear to the working class that the passage of the Reform Bill had not brought much improvement in their lot. New streams of disappointment and bitter impatience found the familiar channels of agitation in clubs, in press and pamphlets, and in public demonstrations. One such movement was the early attempt to develop and extend trade unions as a method of improving industrial conditions. Robert Owen's Grand National Consolidated Trades Union, formed in 1834, had about half a million members.

Owen demanded the abolition of individual competition in industry and the creation of "National Companies." These socialistic proposals, of course, shocked both Whigs and Tories. When a wave of strikes and violence swept over England the Whigs reached out and throttled them. The workers catalogued the action of the government under the same heading as the unpopular Poor Law: no trust could be placed in the "base, bloody and brutal" Whigs and the middle classes. "Don't be deceived by the middle classes again. You helped them to get their votes. . . . But where are the fine promises they made you? Gone to the winds! They said that when they had gotten their votes they would help you to get yours. But they and the rotten Whigs have never remembered you." By adopting repressive measures the Whigs were following the road the angry and frightened Tories had stumbled down twenty years before. The results were almost the same.

The depression of 1837 produced the challenge of the Chartists. Several forms of agitation coalesced into a demand for a share in political power for the workers. The Chartists drew up a "People's Charter" embodying their demands in six points: universal manhood suffrage; payment of members of Parliament; abolition of property qualifications for members of Parliament; equal electoral districts; annual Parliaments; and vote by ballot. The Chartists proclaimed, and widely believed, that if their demands were met the causes of their misery could then be wiped away by acts of Parliament. Theirs was a robust faith in the efficacy of legislation.

The basic causes of Chartism were economic and social. Earlier figures in the movement were more interested in social reform than in political agitation. There were some who believed in moral persuasion; others advocated physical force. As Chartism developed the voices of demagogues and journalists became louder. Those who hoped for economic remedies talked about trade unions, factory reforms, and cooperatives; the political reformers demanded the Charter; some dreamed of political rebellion. The Charter, they declared, would bring relief from social distress. Beyond the Charter they had no political philosophy. The pressure of events hurried them along.

Nor was there any solidarity or full agreement on policy and method. The arch-opportunist Feargus O'Connor, William Lovett, and their associates gave weak leadership. Because the Chartists made no attempt to conciliate the middle class they alienated those upon whose good will and whose votes in Parliament success depended. One Whig asserted that payment of members of Parliament was "too absurd for an idiot to be the author of it." At the same time the influence of the Anglican Church was brought to bear against the movement. The Anglicans tried to associate Chartist riots in Birmingham and elsewhere with Nonconformity. One preacher declared that Chartism was diametrically opposed to the will of God; men were only equal in the sense of being equally sinful by nature; poverty was part of the everlasting purpose of God. Through pulpit, platform, and pamphlets a bitter campaign was waged. The theater, as usual, was used as a vehicle for propaganda.

Chartist petitions were circulated at thousands of mass meetings. In 1839 a petition said to contain 1,200,000 signatures was presented to the house of commons and rejected. Riots and small armed rebellions multiplied. In 1842 a general strike was called. Over five hundred Chartists went to jail. In 1848, the year of European revolutions, a last attempt was made to bring parliamentary action on the Charter. Another petition was prepared; it was said to have been signed by 5,706,-000 persons. The Chartist leaders planned a monster procession to carry the petition to Parliament. O'Connor boasted that half a million men would march. But the government forbade the parade; the petition was taken to the house of commons in an old cab. When it was examined it was found to contain less than two million signatures. Many were fictitious, such as Queen Victoria, the Duke of Wellington, Snooks, and Pugnose. The Chartists claimed these names were maliciously added by their opponents. But the resulting ridicule was a death blow. Soon Chartism disappeared. The working class began to move towards middle class liberalism and to rely on existing political parties within Parliament and on trade union power outside. The collapse of Chartism was hastened by two other events. The first was the return of prosperity after 1850. The second was the successful middle class agitation against the Corn Laws which distracted public attention from the Chartists.

THE REPEAL OF THE CORN LAWS

In 1841 Sir Robert Peel became prime minister at the head of a remarkably able cabinet. His first problem was fiscal; the Whigs, who had seldom balanced their budgets, had left a deficit of £2,000,000. To repair the inherited damages of shaky Whig finance Peel's masterly budget of 1842 reorganized the whole system of taxation. In the first place, Pitt's income tax was revived. A tax of 7d. on the pound was imposed on all incomes over £150 a year. Although this tax was declared to be a temporary three-year emergency measure, it was never abandoned. Secondly, Peel walked in the footsteps of Huskisson and altered the tariffs in the direction of free trade. In 1840 there were about 1,200 articles subject to import duties. All imports were now divided into three classes. On manufactured goods a tax of 20 per cent was levied; on partly manufactured goods, 12 per cent; on raw materials, only 5 per cent. These tariff revisions were partly based upon the report of a commission headed by Joseph Hume in 1840. This report claimed that most of the import duties were not in fact sources of profit to the government but only added to consumer costs. In 1842 Peel's reductions were experimental. He felt that the increased revenue from the income tax would offset any government losses resulting from tariff reduction. After a three-year period of testing, Peel renewed the income tax and extended his free trade policy: most raw materials were admitted free of duty; the tax on manufactured goods was reduced to 10 per cent. In one respect, however, Peel had not advocated free trade. He did not dare to touch the sacred Corn Laws, which kept a high duty on imported grain. The Tory landowners who sat behind him in the house of commons would not permit it.

Meanwhile the demand for cheaper grain grew more insistent. In 1836 the Anti-Corn Law League had been founded in London by some radical members of Parliament. Two years later John Bright and Richard Cobden, the calico king, began to campaign in Manchester. Their purpose was to rouse the public against the evil tariff which protected the producers, but not the consumers, of grain. One of the opponents of the League remarked that their vast educational crusade was launched "for the purpose of uniting all in a common enthusiasm for a proposition in economics." In 1843 the Anti-Corn Law League published over 9,000,000 tracts; the central offices in London had a staff of 800 persons. Robert Smith Surtees wrote in *Handley Cross* that "every house-end and every dead wall was covered with their Blue Bills." The Anti-League, founded by the landed squires, used few of these propaganda methods and had little effect. Cobden, Bright, and their followers explained how the landlords were able to charge more for their wheat because the Corn Laws cushioned them against foreign competition; how the price of bread was thus kept up; how the tenants did not really profit from the high prices of grain because they handed over most of their profits to the landlords in high rents; how Britain's foreign trade would increase if other countries were permitted to pay for British manufactured goods by shipping grain, now kept out by the Corn Laws. Cobden and Bright, both members of Parliament, carried the campaign into the house of commons itself. After Peel came into office in 1841 the crusade mounted in strength and violence and gained an increasing hold upon public opinion.

Then came 1845. The English harvest was bad. A blight destroyed the Irish potato crop. Because nine tenths of the Irish peasants depended on potatoes for their chief food supply the result was disastrous. "Go where you would, in the heart of the town or in the suburbs, there was the stillness and heavy pall-like feel of the chamber of death. You stood in the presence of a dread, silent, vast dissolution. An unseen ruin was creeping around you." From 1830 to 1841 the population of Ireland had risen from 5,000,000 to 8,000,000. From 1841 to 1850 it fell to 6,500,000. Nearly 2,000,000 emigrated. About 700,000 died.

The hand of Peel was forced. The logic of facts converted him. Food must be made cheap. The protectionists in his party must be ignored. Peel therefore proposed the repeal of the Corn Laws. When his cabinet, heedless of popular clamor, refused to support him he resigned. Lord John Russell failed to form a government, ostensibly because Earl Grey refused to serve so long as Lord Palmerston insisted on being foreign secretary. So Russell "handed back with courtesy the poisoned chalice to Sir Robert." With a reorganized cabinet Peel came back, pledged to repeal. In 1846 he introduced a bill providing for the gradual reduction of import duties on grain over a period of three years until only a one shilling registration tax per quarter would remain. As the Corn Laws were the last redoubt of protection the passage of Peel's proposals meant a virtual free trade policy.

By taking this step Peel wrecked his political career, split the Tory party and kept it out of any long spell of power for nearly thirty years. The landlords felt that Peel was a traitor. They had no leader; but they found one in Benjamin Disraeli, to whom Peel had refused office in 1841. Disraeli had entered Parliament in 1837. At first he had been rather radical in his tendencies. Then he had moved to support Peel. He was ambitious, brilliant, confident, and eccentric. The squires cheered the gifted Hebrew as he denounced Peel's "betrayal" in heights of magnificent invective where none could follow him. "Protection to native industry is a fundamental principle. It may be vain now, in the midnight of their intoxication, to tell them that there will be an awakening of bitterness . . . but the dark and inevitable hour will arrive. Then, when their spirits are softened by misfortune, they will recur to those principles that made England great and which, in our belief, will only keep England great." Spears of epigram found their mark and wounded. Peel, said Disraeli, was "a political burglar of other men's ideas." Peel, he declared, "caught the Whigs in bathing and walked away with their clothes."

The Whigs, the Irish, the independent Radicals, and some Tories voted for repeal. The bill was passed, and the cause was won. "I shall leave a name execrated, I know, by every monopolist," said Peel. He was not mistaken. Disraeli and the landowners were less concerned about bread being "no longer leavened with a sense of injustice" than about obtaining their revenge. Because he had kept Disraeli out of office and had betrayed the Protectionists Peel must be punished. The same night that the repeal bill passed its third reading in the house of lords the Whigs, the Irish, and the Protectionist Tories voted in the house of commons against an Irish coercion bill designed to suppress the disturbances that the famine had caused in Ireland. So Peel was broken and turned out of office; the cabinet resigned. The Whigs came in under Lord John Russell. They carried on the policy of free trade, repealing the Navigation Acts in 1849.

The Tories remained divided into Peelites and Protectionists. Most of the Peelites slowly travelled with the Whigs to form the Liberal party, of which the greatest leader in the nineteenth century was the former Peelite William Ewart Gladstone. Under the leadership of Lord Derby and Benjamin Disraeli the Protectionist Tories waited out their long exile. Meanwhile they gathered strength and gradually created the new Conservative party with a new political philosophy.

The industrial interests had supported the Anti-Corn Law League partly because they saw that cheaper wheat meant cheaper bread, which in turn meant that the workers would require less wages to live. The defeat of the Protectionists was a great victory of the industrial interest of the middle class over the agricultural interest of the squire-archy. In fact, however, free trade was a less severe blow to agriculture than had been feared. Prices steadily rose, stimulated by increased trade, the gold discoveries in California and Australia, and the Crimean War. Agriculture shared in the general prosperity which continued for twenty years.

Chapter 31

THE MARCH OF PALMERSTON

FOREIGN AFFAIRS, 1830–1846

LORD PALMERSTON was born in 1784. He was educated at Harrow and Cambridge. In 1807 he entered the house of commons as the representative of a rotten borough. He was to remain in Parliament for nearly sixty years. Under Perceval he became secretary-at-war and held that office for nineteen years under five Tory prime ministers (1809–1828). When Huskisson seceded from the Duke of Wellington in 1828, Palmerston followed him and gradually drifted into the Whig party. The true heir of Canning's foreign policy, Palmerston was in sympathy with liberal movements everywhere. In 1830 he joined the Whig cabinet of Earl Grey and went to the foreign office.

To Palmerston life was an adventure. His energetic and audacious conduct of British foreign policy was peculiarly his own. In method, certainly, he did not follow his master Canning. Profoundly aware of England's place in the world, Palmerston recklessly blustered, insulted, and scolded. He astounded the public; he frightened his colleagues; he disturbed and dismayed other nations. Queen Victoria called him "that dreadful old man." Lady Cowper remarked that he would be "a source of mischief to Europe as long as he lives." One wit observed that "Europe depended on which leg he put out of bed first." But among the people Palmerston was popular. Here, it seemed, was John Bull incarnate; he could drive Britannia's chariot close to the edge of the cliff; he could navigate the shoals; his jaunty and aggressive independence touched the national pride. That was the chief reason why Palmerston, ready "to knock the heads of the kings of Europe together," commanded such strong support. No Whig government could long afford to leave him out of the cabinet.

When Palmerston came to the foreign office Europe was disturbed by the revolutions of 1830, the first major challenges to the Metternich system. Liberalism and nationalism were straining against the fetters of reaction hammered out by the Congress of Vienna. The French revolt of 1830 not only ousted Charles X; it also lit the powder train to revolution in Belgium, Italy, Portugal, Poland, and Spain. Palmerston intervened in Spain, Portugal, and Belgium. It was in Belgium that his diplomatic victory was greatest, much to his delight.

The Belgian revolt arose as a result of the union of Holland and Belgium arranged by the Congress of Vienna. By this step a barrier state had been erected to prevent French expansion. What had seemed a wise step to Castlereagh in fact roughly ignored national feelings. The Belgians and Dutch differed in language, culture, religion, and economic interests. When the Belgians rebelled, demanding independence, Wellington was still prime minister. He felt, as Castlereagh earlier, that a strong Dutch-Belgian state protected Britain's flank. Nevertheless, the French sympathy for Catholic and French-speaking Belgium made it almost certain that France would resist any attempt by a third power to compel the Belgians to adhere to the Vienna settlement. Therefore Wellington agreed that the question should be discussed by Great Britain, France, Prussia, Austria, and Russia at a conference in London.

This conference had not been held when Palmerston came to the foreign office in November, 1830. Palmerston, of course, wanted a strong coast bastion friendly to Britain across the Channel; unlike Wellington, he sympathized with the Belgians. His task was to work with France against Russia, Austria, and Prussia, who wanted to crush the rebels and to restore the Vienna arrangement. At the same time Palmerston feared a possible extension of French influence in Belgium. The first task was easily discharged. The conference agreed to the independence of Belgium because a refusal to do so would probably have meant a general European war. However, when the terms of separation were found by the Belgians to favor the Netherlands they refused to accept them. After prolonged discussion the terms were altered. The Dutch, in turn, found the proposals unsatisfactory and marched 50,000 soldiers into Belgium. The Belgians appealed to Louis Philippe for aid, which he gave. Unless France withdrew from Belgium a general European war seemed inevitable.

Palmerston prevented that war. He obtained an armistice; made it clear that Britain would fight to compel France to withdraw from Belgium; succeeded in having the separation terms revised. When the Dutch rejected the new terms Britain and France united to drive them from Belgium. In 1832 both France and Britain withdrew. Belgium was left independent under a constitutional monarchy. Not until 1839 was a treaty finally signed between Belgium and Holland establishing Belgian independence and perpetual neutrality. This treaty was guaranteed by Britain, France, Austria, Russia, and Prussia. It was the "scrap of paper" torn up by Germany in 1914.

Thus neither France nor any other great power had obtained control or influence along the Belgian coast. It was Palmerston's first diplomatic victory. "The French hate us as a nation," he wrote. "They can never forget Aboukir, Trafalgar, Waterloo, and St. Helena." When Richard Cobden suggested a gesture of friendship to France Palmerston replied: "These letters of Mr. Cobden are like his speeches, illustrative of the saying that shallow streams run with the most noise." When Cobden wrote of concessions to Ireland Palmerston answered: "Ireland is the abode of ruffians; the Irish have no grievances not of their own making." The Irish were furious; the queen was annoyed; his colleagues were stupefied. When Lord Aberdeen objected, Palmerston replied: "I consider Lord Aberdeen a specimen of antiquated imbecility." On many subjects the foreign minister expressed himself with equal vehemence. In some respects it was fortunate that he took little interest in domestic affairs. He was opposed to universal suffrage, to feminism, and to temperance movements.

In 1839 there arose a second international crisis. Mehemet Ali, the Albanian adventurer who ruled Egypt, again attempted to make himself completely independent of the Sultan. Encouraged by France, he successfully attacked Turkey. Britain and the rest of the European powers had no desire to see the break-up of the Ottoman Empire or to support French influence in Egypt. When France refused to unite with Britain in pressing Mehemet Ali to relinquish his attempts to dismember a weak Turkey Palmerston decided to challenge directly the policy of Louis Philippe. "If the French attempt to bully us the only way of meeting their menaces is by quietly telling them we are not afraid, and by showing them first that we are stronger than they are and, secondly, that they have more vulnerable points than we have." He instructed the British ambassador in Paris to inform the French government "in the most friendly and inoffensive manner possible" that in the event of war "France will to a certainty lose her ships, colonies, and commerce before she sees the end of it; that her army in Algiers will cease to give her anxiety and that Mehemet Ali will just be chucked into the Nile." Palmerston then proceeded to arrange the Treaty of London of July 15, 1840, by which Britain, Austria, Russia, and Prussia guaranteed the integrity of Turkey. France, isolated and angry, talked of war. But Palmerston knew that for the sake of his dynasty and the welfare of France Louis Philippe wanted no European conflict. Sir Charles Napier was sent to Syria, where he defeated the Egyptians, captured Acre, compelled Mehemet Ali to restore the Turkish fleet and to agree to the terms of the Treaty of London. In the end France accepted diplomatic defeat and signed a second Treaty of London with the other four powers.

Thus Palmerston achieved a second victory. In the first place, France had been kept out of Egypt. Secondly, Russia's ambitions in Turkey had for a time been thwarted and British interests protected. Palmerston, always suspicious of Russia's designs, had seen to it that the integrity of Turkey was guaranteed by all the great powers and hence not protected by Russia alone. The second Treaty of London also provided that the Dardanelles should be closed to all foreign warships while Turkey was at peace. Russia's plans of controlling Constantinople and the Dardanelles were again upset. Palmerston's anti-Russian policy was generally followed by Britain throughout the rest of the nineteenth century.

A third crisis had meanwhile arisen in the Far East. To understand this crisis it is necessary to survey swiftly the history of the English beginnings in China. During the seventeenth century England had developed a trade with China of considerable economic importance. Anglo-Chinese commercial relations were always handicapped by the hostility of the Chinese to foreign intercourse and by differences in religion, culture, government, and language. Trading activities were also restricted by periodic civil wars. Nevertheless, the East India Company extended its operations and exchanged woolens, lead, and gunpowder for sugar, quicksilver, silks, alum, china, tea, and camphor. In the early years of the eighteenth century English trade lines seemed to be soundly anchored at Canton and Amoy.

Soon, however, in an atmosphere of bribery, corruption, trickery, anti-foreignism, and high prices the English merchants found their position increasingly irksome and precarious. In 1757 a Chinese imperial edict restricted trade to Canton and created Chinese merchant monopolies. This action prevented the expansion of British trade to other areas of China. Chinese merchants were frequently hostile. Many Chinese feared concessions to Europeans would ultimately lead to the European control of China. Notwithstanding these difficulties the volume of Anglo-Chinese trade increased. Fortunes were made in commerce with China, and Englishmen drank more tea.

In the early nineteenth century Britain pushed farther towards the East. In 1819, for example, Stamford Raffles obtained Singapore for England. Singapore, lying at the southern tip of the Malay Peninsula, controlled the shortest route to China from India and Europe. In 1824 more than 35,000 tons of shipping cleared the active port of Singapore. By 1850 the population reached 60,000. The interior of the Malay Peninsula was swiftly penetrated and in 1867 Singapore, Penang, and Malacca became a crown colony under the title of Straits Settlements.

Until 1833 the British share of European trade with China was controlled by the East India Company. The company also regulated the trade in India-grown opium by virtue of its vested monopoly rights. But the company's charter lapsed in 1833 and when it was renewed the opium monopoly was abrogated. The opium trade was now open to other British traders who moved into China and became smugglers. When the British government sent officials to aid the Chinese in their efforts to curb the drug traffic the Peking government resented alien interference and received the British rudely. At the same time they jailed some British traders and seized their goods.

To protect the status of the British diplomatic officials Palmerston sent gunboats up the Canton river. In 1839 a representative of the Peking government demanded the surrender and destruction of all opium in the hands of British traders in Canton. On the order of the British superintendent, who promised them indemnity, the traders complied. The Chinese then proceeded to demand that all vessels engaged in smuggling should be confiscated and all smugglers executed. Thereupon the British diplomatic officials and traders withdrew from Canton. Shortly afterwards war began. It was ended in 1842 by the Treaty of Nanking. The Chinese ceded Hong Kong to England, paid an indemnity, opened five ports to world trade, and accorded diplomatic status to British representatives. However, as China still refused to legalize the opium trade a huge smuggling traffic arose to plague the relations between China and the world outside.

Before the Treaty of Nanking was concluded the Whigs had given place to the Tories and to Peel. Palmerston was out of office until he returned with Lord John Russell in 1846. In the interval the foreign policy of Peel's government was in the hands of the mild and diplomatic Lord Aberdeen. Aberdeen's methods were far different from those of Palmerston. Relations with France improved, partly because of the personal friendship of Peel and Guizot. European chancelleries generally were relieved to see the pacific and correct Aberdeen replacing the aggressive and interfering Palmerston.

Under Aberdeen's administration two important treaties with the United States were concluded. The first was the Webster-Ashburton Treaty of 1842, which ended a bitterly disputed boundary question between the United States and Canada. This agreement gave to the United States territory claimed by Canada north of Maine and Vermont, and yielded to Canada a small area claimed by Maine. Secondly, the Oregon Treaty of 1846 established the boundary between British Columbia and Oregon at the forty-ninth parallel on the mainland and along a line running through the middle of the channel between Vancouver Island and the mainland to the Pacific Ocean. The water boundary was later to cause disputes about the ownership of San Juan Island but the major points at issue had been settled. Canada was left in full possession of Vancouver Island. The valuable fishing areas of the Columbia River were within the territory to which the United States now had clear title.

THE DOMESTIC SCENE, 1846–1852

For many reasons the repeal of the Corn Laws was the most important event in mid-Victorian politics. Among other results, it helped to throw the whole party system of government into a state of disequilibrium that lasted for over twenty years. Of course, the growth of radical, liberal, and conservative groups in both the Whig and Tory parties had been evident long before. But the Corn Law crisis opened a chasm within the Tory party wider than had ever existed between democratic and old-line Tories. After 1846, as has been described above, there were in fact three major elements in the house of commons: (1) the Peelites, or free-trade Tories, led by Peel until his death in 1850, and by Lord Aberdeen later; (2) the Protectionist Tories, generally resenting the idea of being shepherded and charmed by the outlander Benjamin Disraeli, but able to find nobody else; (3) the Whigs, led by Lord John Russell of the great Whig house of Bedford, able, respected, and courageous.

These three elements were themselves divided. For example, the old divisions persisted within the Whig party. The progressive groups, including the Manchester School led by Bright and Cobden, could not be relied upon to vote with the conservative Whigs solely to preserve party strength and unity. From all these fluctuating factions the two strong and homogeneous Liberal and Conservative parties were only slowly to emerge. Meanwhile, the divergent groups within each party usually prevented the passage of important domestic legislation. Thus the prosperous middle years of the nineteenth century appear pale and barren when contrasted with the early or later period; in years of prosperity there is seldom strong agitation. Such political weakness was inherent in internal party divisions that it was difficult for any government to maintain a working majority except by compromise or coalition. Cabinets rose and fell. Between 1846 and 1868 there were eight different ministries.

It was fortunate that the Whig cabinet of Lord John Russell contained men rich in ability and political experience because their task was difficult. They had to keep the support of the Peelites and almost every other group except the Protectionist Tories and the Irish members. Hence they were compelled to compromise and to move circumspectly. Only when there was not strong opposition were they able to carry out a few important measures. Among these may be noted the Ten Hours Act of 1847, described in the previous chapter; the repeal of the Navigation Acts in 1849; and the Australian Colonies Act of 1850, passed under pressure from the colonial reformers of the Manchester School and enabling the Australian colonies to determine their own form of government. Between 1854 and 1859 New Zealand, New South Wales, Queensland, South Australia, Tasmania, and Victoria made new constitutions and followed Canada in gaining responsible government.

Often overlooked is the significance of a further reform measure: the first Public Health Act of 1848. This act was largely due to the

energetic efforts of Edwin Chadwick in behalf of the "cellar population" of England. As a poor law commissioner in the 1830's he had
seen the deplorable housing conditions common in the depressed areas.
He had been appalled by the contaminating filth resulting from lack
of sanitation. Factories spreading across the green fields had often
turned trout streams into sewers. In *Bleak House* Charles Dickens had
written of "a hemmed-in churchyard, pestiferous and obscene, whence
malignant diseases are communicated to the bodies of our dear brothers
and sisters who have not departed . . . a shameful testimony to future
ages how civilization and barbarism walked this boastful island together." The government, said Chadwick, must wage ceaseless war
against poverty, disease, and dirt. His stubborn and deadly criticisms
of a laissez-faire policy where the national health was concerned
brought the setting up of a Public Health Board in London and local
Boards of Health where there were no municipal bodies to enforce the
law. The need for health reform had also been emphasized by a royal
commission report in 1845. Scattered cases of cholera gave further
impetus to remedial legislation. Chadwick's act was the first step in a
long series of reforms. It marked the beginning of governmental concern with the health of the nation.

Meanwhile the general advance of trade and enterprise was
broken by the brief commercial crisis of the fall of 1847. This acute
disturbance resulted from a collapse of credit induced by general over-
speculation and the railway mania. When the smash came at the end
of the "boom" years there were numerous business failures as stocks
fell. The government restored confidence by temporarily authorizing
the Bank of England to issue notes without the legal gold reserves.
When the panic of 1847 had been checked and the Chartists finally
defeated, England moved along a broad road to a roaring prosperity.
The growth of the railways continued to provide a stimulus to employment. Conditions of the working class improved as wages rose and
employment became more regular. Trade unions swiftly increased in
numbers and power. This "new model" of highly organized trade
unions was not welcomed by giants in the manufacturing world like
Richard Cobden. "Depend upon it," said Cobden, "nothing can be got
by fraternizing with trade unions. They are founded upon brutal
tyranny and monopoly. I would rather live under a Dey of Algiers than
a trades committee." But henceforth trade unions were to be a part of
the British industrial system. So too were the cooperatives, designed to
share the profits of business among their customers. The cooperative
movement, founded in 1844 by about two dozen Chartists and Owen-
ites known as the Rochdale Pioneers, began the enormous development
which has continued to the present day. At the same time that the
principle of state interference was being enlarged the workers were
developing the idea of self-help by peaceful cooperation.

Most serious was the Irish problem. The great famine had brought suffering, death, and an upsurge in crime. It will be recalled that a bill for the "coercion" of Ireland had been used to push Peel out of office. The Irish were glad to see Peel go. Daniel O'Connell, hating Peel and the Tories, had earlier hurled himself into a campaign for the repeal of the Union. In the battle for Catholic emancipation in 1828 O'Connell had achieved success by the same methods. This time he failed. He failed because Peel knew that O'Connell did not want bloodshed or open rebellion. When Peel forbade a mass meeting O'Connell had to rebel or submit. O'Connell submitted, and lost much Irish support by doing so.

Such had been the situation when the famine struck. After Peel's defeat the Whigs faced the twin problems of relief and coercion. In the summer of 1847 government rations were feeding over 3,000,000 Irish people. By shipments of seed, by assistance to fishermen, and by loans at easy interest rates, the Russell government aided Ireland. To reduce the waves of crime and violence a stringent coercion act was passed. Although the disorder then abated, thousands of bitter Irishmen still attributed the catastrophic famine to the policy of the British government. Even before the moderate O'Connell's death in 1847 the "Young Ireland" movement, violent and nationalistic, had been gaining ground. When the European revolutions of 1848 broke out, the "Young Ireland" groups plotted armed rebellion and prepared to declare Ireland a republic. But the British government arrested the leaders, tried them under the new Treason-Felony Act of 1848, transported some to Australia and Bermuda. The rebellion ended in a small fight, at once ludicrous and pathetic.

The Irish policy of the Whigs did not add to their decaying strength. They remained weakly in power simply because there was no united desire to oust them. Peel and his followers continued to support Russell because the Whigs stood for free trade. When Peel died in 1850 the situation changed. The Whigs were soon defeated on a motion for the extension of the county franchise. This happened because the Radicals voted against the Whigs and the Peelites abstained from voting at all. So the cabinet resigned. However, the Protectionist Tories could not obtain or hold a majority in the house. Russell then attempted to form a coalition between the Whigs and Peelites. The negotiations collapsed because the Peelites refused to share responsibility for the Ecclesiastical Titles Bill.

In 1850 Pope Pius IX had issued a bull dividing England into twelve territorial dioceses. Thus English territorial titles were given to Roman Catholic archbishops and bishops. Hitherto the Roman Catholic church in England had been governed by vicars apostolic whose titles were derived from abroad. To many Englishmen, already excited by the Oxford Movement and the alleged drifting of the High Church towards Rome, this appeared to be another step towards the union of

Section VI

REACTION AND REFORM

London in the Regency. A view of Hyde Park.

Industrial landscape, Yorkshire, 1814.

PAPER AGAINST GOLD

AND

GLORY AGAINST PROSPERITY.

OR,

An Account of the Rise, Progress, Extent, and
Present State of the Funds and of the Paper-
Money of Great Britain;

AND ALSO

Of the Situation of that Country as to its Debt and
other Expenses; its Navigation, Commerce, and
Manufactures; its Taxes, Population, and
Paupers; drawn from authentic Documents,
and brought down to the end of the Year 1814.

IN TWO VOLS.

BY WILLIAM COBBETT.

VOL. I.

LONDON:
PRINTED BY J. M'CREERY, BLACK-HORSE-COURT.

1815.
Retail Price, 20s. in Paper-Money.

In William Cobbett's view, paper-
money had ruined England.

Jeremy Bentham.

John Stuart Mill.

The yeomanry cavalry ride down a Reform meeting at Manchester, August, 1819. "Orator" Hunt is seen protesting at the upper right in this satirical print by Robert Cruikshank.

George Canning, a portrait by Sir Thomas Lawrence.

The Duke of Wellington.

Sir Robert Peel.

Henry John Temple, Viscount Palmerston.

Child Labor in the 1840's.

A collier. Note in the background a colliery tram engine; and on the top of the hill a Blenkinsop steam engine at work.

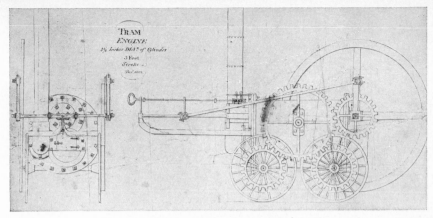

Sketch of Trevithick's tram engine, 1803.

A railroad locomotive of the 1830's.

The steamship *Enterprise* shown entering Madras Roads after a successful passage to India, A.D. 1825.

The young Queen Victoria.

the Anglican and Roman Catholic churches. Lord John Russell declared the action of the papacy to be "insolent and insidious." The Ecclesiastical Titles Bill, introduced by the Whigs, declared the papal bull null and void and forbade the Roman Catholic clergy to assume any of the proposed territorial titles. This, then, was the bill that prevented the proposed coalition. The Peelites would not accept it and Russell rather ridiculously came back to office at the head of the same Whig ministry which had resigned. The Ecclesiastical Titles Bill was passed but remained pigeonholed until it was quietly repealed in 1871.

Meanwhile it was clear that the Whig cabinet could not long survive. What finally toppled it over was the quarrel between Lord John Russell and his masterful and ebullient foreign minister, Lord Palmerston.

PALMERSTON AND FOREIGN AFFAIRS

In 1840 Queen Victoria had married her cousin Prince Albert of Saxe-Coburg-Gotha. The Prince Consort was a hard-working, sober, bookish man, interested in many things. He had a German passion for order, neatness, protocol, and precedent. He scrutinized the royal household expenses; he advised the queen; to him life was a serious business. He was naturally pained to perceive that Lord Palmerston was going far beyond what the Prince Consort thought were his proper functions as foreign minister. Confident in his knowledge of foreign affairs, assured of his steady popularity among the English people, careless of the opinions of his colleagues, Palmerston often behaved as though he could do as he pleased without consulting anybody. Lord John Russell repeatedly warned him that he must consult the queen and the cabinet on matters of policy. It seemed to Russell, and to others, that Palmerston's diplomatic methods were dangerous. Nevertheless, Palmerston made it clear that he did not welcome intruders into his domain of the foreign office. He considered himself a national institution, perhaps not indispensable to England, but certainly indispensable to any Whig government that wanted to stay in office.

The personal feelings and value judgments of Lord Palmerston sometimes led him into alarming words and deeds. For example, in 1847 he advised the Italian rulers to avert revolution by making reforms. In 1848, without telling the cabinet, he authorized the Woolwich Arsenal to supply the rebelling Sicilians with arms. He instructed the British ambassador in Vienna to inform the Austrians of the "disgust" their repressive vengeance against the liberals had excited in England. "The Austrians are really the greatest brutes that ever called themselves by the undeserved name of civilized man." About the same time Palmerston impetuously ordered the British fleet to the Dardanelles to support Turkey when the Sultan was threatened with war by Austria and Russia because he had refused to surrender Louis Kossuth and other refugees. Palmerston also instructed the British ambassador at Madrid to tell Queen Isabella of Spain that England did not like her illiberal domestic policies. As the Spanish queen felt that the internal affairs of Spain should not be England's business, she dismissed the ambassador. When the exiled Louis Kossuth came to London it took a special meeting of the cabinet to stop Palmerston from inviting him to his house. Palmerston reluctantly yielded. Usually, however, he ignored the remonstrances of the queen and the prince consort and was quite untroubled by the qualms of his colleagues. Early in 1850 Russell had decided that, no matter what the cost in political strength to the government, Palmerston would have to be removed from the foreign office.

But the pace of events was swift. Before Russell could act the Don Pacifico incident occurred. Don Pacifico was a rather undesirable Gibraltar Jew who had gone into business in Athens. When a mob broke into his house and damaged his property he complained to the British government that the Greeks paid no attention to his demands for redress. When Palmerston's diplomatic representations in behalf of Don Pacifico also failed he cut the knot by sending Sir William Parker with a British fleet to seize Greek vessels lying off Athens. The Greeks then dealt with the claim of Don Pacifico.

Palmerston's headlong action offended both Russia and France. The sensitive Louis Napoleon recalled the French ambassador from London when his offer of mediation was refused. In the house of lords Palmerston was censured by a formal vote. The shocked lords regretted "that various claims against the Greek government, doubtful in point of justice or exaggerated in amount, have been enforced by coercive measures directed against the commerce and people of Greece and calculated to endanger the continuance of our friendly relations with other powers." In the house of commons, however, Palmerston won a vote of confidence by a majority of forty-six. This verdict was largely the result of Palmerston's speech of defense, masterly in its effectiveness, huge in its success. He spoke of principles and aims rather than methods. At the end he triumphantly likened an Englishman to a Roman "who in the days of old held himself free from indignity when he could say 'Civis Romanus sum.'" When Palmerston spoke of the "watchful eye and strong arm of England" protecting British subjects wherever they might be the English public applauded and were proud.

The queen was unconvinced. She had earlier urged Palmerston's removal and Russell, as we have seen, had agreed; but the vote in the house of commons showed Palmerston's power; the people proclaimed it on every side. If Palmerston went out, it seemed probable that the whole Whig government would shortly follow. Russell vainly attempted to persuade Palmerston to exchange the foreign office for another cabinet post. The queen sent a formal memorandum demanding that her foreign secretary let her know precisely what he proposed to do before he acted "in order that the Queen may know as distinctly *to what* she has given her Royal sanction." The queen also insisted that Palmerston's dispatches be submitted to her before they were sent off and not arbitrarily altered after she had approved them. Palmerston agreed. He was penitent. The queen had made her point. Soon, however, the incorrigible foreign minister returned to his old ways again.

In December, 1851, Palmerston made a mistake which cost him his post. Louis Napoleon had carried out a carefully planned coup d'état and had overthrown the Second French Republic. Palmerston, who never liked republicans, was delighted. Without waiting to ascertain the wishes of the queen or the cabinet he indiscreetly expressed his personal approbation of the coup to the French ambassador. He also neglected to show the queen or the prime minister a dispatch to the same effect sent to the British ambassador in Paris. Meanwhile the British government decided, for the time being, to follow a policy of strict neutrality. In England the French coup d'état was not popular and this time Palmerston could not rely on public support. Russell was certainly justified in requesting Palmerston's dismissal. "The real question now," said Russell in the house of commons, "was whether the secretary of state was entitled, on his own authority, to write a dispatch as the organ of the Queen's Government in which his colleagues had never concurred and to which the Queen had never given her royal sanction." So Palmerston was dismissed.

The queen and the prince consort were delighted. The wiser members of the cabinet neither cheered nor wept, but waited. After two months Palmerston brought about the defeat of the Russell government on a militia bill. As he phrased it, he had "had his tit for tat" by turning out Russell and the Whigs.

TORIES, WHIGS, AND PEELITES

Under the spirited leadership of Lord Derby the Tories nervously rallied to take office. Derby's position, like Russell's before him, was unhappy. He had no majority in the house of commons and could only stave off defeat by placating his opponents, usually through the avoidance of controversial subjects. To be thus politically hamstrung was awkward and annoying. Derby also found that he could not find experienced cabinet material. The long Whig rule had prevented the Tories from having many men with administrative training. The best of these had been drained off by the Peelites; and the Peelites would not join the government.

Derby did his best. He made Benjamin Disraeli chancellor of the exchequer and Tory leader in the house of commons. Of the rest, only two had ever held cabinet office before. Obviously this kind of government could not accomplish much or remain in power long. In anticipation of an early general election Derby decided to avoid controversial issues until the people indicated whether or not they wanted to substitute protection for Peel's free trade. The election came in the summer of 1852. Unfortunately it did not change the balance of parties in the house. But it did show beyond doubt that England wanted free trade. Indeed, many Englishmen attributed the new prosperity to the new free trade policy.

The Tory leaders, politically shrewd, decided that the protection plank of their platform should be torn out and discarded. In November, 1852, Disraeli announced that his party would abandon protection, which was, in his words, "not only dead but damned." Thus quietly ended the dispute which had divided the Tories in 1846. Would the wandering Peelites now return to the fold? There were many reasons why that was impossible. Gladstone's personal dislike of Disraeli was alone a major obstacle. Then, too, the Peelites as a group were moving towards the Whigs and away from that Toryism to which they had given full loyalty in 1846. The old Tory party was dead. The new Conservative party, to which Derby and Disraeli were to contribute so much, was not yet born.

On December 3, 1852, Disraeli brought up his budget to the house of commons. It was an ingenious budget, especially in its proposal to remit half the malt tax and tea duty and to reduce the farmers' income tax. But the Whigs and the Peelites both vehemently opposed the plan to increase the tax on houses. So they stood together and defeated the budget. On December 20, 1852, Lord Derby's first ministry resigned. It had been in power about nine months.

No party possessed a majority in the house of commons. Therefore the new cabinet was a coalition of Whigs and Peelites. Although Lord John Russell and the Whigs formed the largest single group in the house, the queen decided to summon the Peelite Lord Aberdeen. Despite his sixty-eight years the veteran Scottish peer consented to lead the coalition. His cabinet was composed of six Whigs, six Peelites, and Lord Palmerston, usually called a Whig, but not in fact a party man at all. Palmerston once said that this remarkably able cabinet contained every man of first rank in the house of commons, except Disraeli. But the brilliance of Russell, Palmerston, Gladstone, and their colleagues was not enough. "England," said Disraeli, "does not love coalitions." In this case, at least, Disraeli appeared to be right.

At once there were disputes within the cabinet. Palmerston, who always objected to parliamentary reform, resigned and came back after a quarrel about Russell's pet reform project. When Russell felt that he was not obtaining sufficiently vigorous support from his colleagues he too resigned; he also came back later. Athwart these currents were the divergent views of Aberdeen and Russell on foreign policy.

Amid all these confusions and bickerings William Ewart Gladstone, in a magnificent speech five hours long, presented his budget of 1853, one of the most important financial measures of the middle century. Meanwhile Aberdeen and his divided cabinet were moving towards the Crimean War. The period of the great peace (1815–1854) was ending.

THE CONDITION OF ENGLAND: ECONOMIC AND SOCIAL

Through the years from Waterloo to the Crimean War important changes had come over the face of England. For fifteen years in the middle of the century the confused political situation called a halt to the progress of political and social reform. In the 1860's that progress was to be resumed. Meanwhile, however, no obstacle was placed in the way of England's march to world industrial supremacy. It is well, now, on the eve of the Crimean War, to consider briefly the economic and social position of England, the prevailing climate of opinion, and the great expectations of the people.

The tide of the great mid-Victorian industrial and commercial expansion submerged almost everything else beneath its waves of prosperity. The dramatic performances of Lord Palmerston must not obscure the less spectacular economic forces working together to make England more than ever before the "workshop of the world." In these fat and comfortable years it was inevitable that the domestic facts of pain and poverty which had caused so much disturbance earlier seemed to retreat into the background and to become less ugly. The main political interests of the nation lay in foreign affairs and the achievements of Lord Palmerston. Because the economic developments were long-continuing and not pin-pointed as dramatic facts in the time-scale they did not catch or hold the popular interest in the same fashion as political or military events. Yet for England and the world their consequences were of tremendous significance.

The Great Exhibition of 1851 marked the beginning of international trade advertisement on a grand scale. The world was invited to contemplate the results of the era of progress in England, her industrial power, and her inventive genius. Every year the factories turned out larger supplies of goods. Larger amounts of surplus capital were being directly invested or lent abroad. For example, in 1825 British foreign loans totalled about £100,000,000; in 1870 they were about £800,000,000. British ships furrowed the world sea lanes, still the highways to empire. British re-export trade steadily mounted. Throughout all the rest of the century, with but few pauses, this process of creating wealth went on. England was able to use her enterprise, her strategic location, and her natural resources to become the world's greatest producer, exporter, shipper, and banker.

A more vivid idea of what is actually meant by these general statements can perhaps be given by the listing of a few statistics. British foreign commerce increased fourfold in the years between 1846 and 1872. Even as late as 1889 English foreign trade still exceeded that of France and Germany combined and was more than double that of the United States. The national income rose from £515,000,000 a year in 1841 to about £650,000,000 in 1852 and about £1,000,000,000 in 1872. In 1840 England exported £2,524,000 worth of iron and steel; in 1850 the value totalled £5,350,000; in 1860 it reached £12,154,000. The Bessemer process for making steel, patented in 1856, reduced the price from £40 to £5 a ton; but England continued to lead the world until the latter part of the century, when American and German production exceeded that of England. By the 1850's England was exporting nearly three billion yards of cotton cloth a year. For many years the production of British coal was double that of Germany, France, and Belgium combined. Almost everywhere in central England the smoke of the mills belched forth to mar the soft horizons. The railways, throbbing arteries of the new body economic, spread their networks into all but the remoter shires. Between 1850 and 1880 the mercantile marine more than doubled in tonnage.

In the midst of this mighty advance the trade unions added the weapon of strikes to the arsenal of labor combinations. For example, a Preston strike involved 15,000 workers and lasted for nine months. At the time, however, this development was but a small cloud in the general brightness. The English people, particularly the middle classes, were more concerned with the new wealth and the new worlds made possible by it. These were years of revelling and conspicuous consumption. The middle class built large and ugly houses; they often filled them with tasteless bric-a-brac and furniture. It was an age of display and parade, of respectability and the discipline of the Victorian Sunday, and of Babbitt vulgarity. England was rich, optimistic, and discreetly enthusiastic about the material benefits of Progress.

It is easy, however, to stress unduly this aspect of Victorian life. An accurate and just portrait of the age must not be confined to a chastisement of the barbarians and philistines of the upper and middle classes. Despite all the materialism, profit-seeking, and narrowness of the Victorian compromise there remained deeper value currents within English society. From these came the great body of Victorian literature; the humanitarian movements; the philosophy of men like Mill and Green, Bagehot, and Spencer; and the scientific achievements of Darwin, Huxley, and Sir Charles Lyell. The pride and delight in material things that characterized Victorian England was matched by the deep and profound consciousness of the importance of imponderables and moral absolutes in the life of man. Through all the Victorian age there flows a stream of publications whose titles tell their own story of the interest in the substance of things hoped for as well as the certainty that in this world the battle would probably be to the strong and the race to the swift.

THE CRIMEAN WAR

As the Aberdeen cabinet strove to remain united and in power the international skies steadily darkened. Russia had long been interested in the decline of the Turkish Empire and determined to take advantage of it. England and France were both equally determined to resist Russian advance in the Near East. Confident of the approaching demise of Turkey, the Tsar Nicholas I declared that he wanted an agreement with England "lest the old man should suddenly die upon our hands and his heritage fall into chaos and dissolution." Twice, in 1844 and in 1853, he had proposed that Turkey should be divided. England, he suggested, might annex Egypt, Crete, and Cyprus. Russia might perhaps occupy Constantinople. Although the English cabinet had not acted on this immoral suggestion, Nicholas I knew that Lord Aberdeen was a stanch supporter of peace. He felt certain that England would not attempt to block his plans by taking up arms against him.

Nicholas I was mistaken. The English people disliked him. To them he appeared as the pillar and prop of sinister despotism. He had cruelly suppressed the popular revolutions in Poland and Hungary. Now he wanted to dismember Turkey, to overthrow the European balance of power, and to threaten English interests in doing so. Nor had the English public forgotten their old suspicion of Russian designs in the Middle East and in India. Clashes between England and Russia in Persia and Afghanistan added fuel to that suspicion. Palmerston and Russell stood for war if Russia committed any act of aggression. So also did Gladstone. As events moved rapidly a fevered press raised the cry for battle. England had lived in peace for forty years. Now the belief was honestly held that once again the English people were fighting for the ancient cause of liberty.

In 1852 the situation had been worsened by the outbreak of a paltry dispute about the guardianship of the holy places in the Turkish province of Palestine. In 1740 Turkey had given France the right of guardianship of these Christian shrines in behalf of the Roman Catholics. By the mid-nineteenth century, however, the Greek Orthodox Catholics had effective control over the holy places, largely because so many Greek Catholics made pilgrimages there. Nicholas I considered himself the keeper of the interests of the Greek Orthodox Church, the national church of Russia. When Napoleon III, seeking by adventure and glory to buttress his regime in France, proceeded in 1852 to revive the French guardianship claim under the concession of 1740 Nicholas I hotly opposed the demand. This was the ostensible, but not the real, cause of the Crimean War.

Early in 1853 the Tsar took a further step. Through the special mission of Prince Menschikoff he demanded a general Russian protectorate over all Greek Orthodox Christian subjects of the Sultan in European Turkey. This exceeded all previous claims. The Turkish government explained in a formal note to all the major European powers that Turkey could not agree to such a proposal "without compromising gravely her independence and the most fundamental rights of the Sultan over his subjects." Lord Stratford de Redcliffe, the powerful British ambassador at Constantinople, advised the Sultan to refuse and encouraged him to believe that England would support him in the event of war.

In June, 1853, the armies of Nicholas I occupied the Turkish Danubian provinces of Moldavia and Wallachia. A conference held at Vienna by England, France, Austria, and Prussia attempted to effect a peaceful settlement. The proposals of the four powers were accepted by Russia, rejected by Turkey. On the refusal of Russia to withdraw her forces Turkey declared war in October, 1853. A month later the Russian Black Sea fleet sank a Turkish naval squadron in the Bay of Sinope. Because the Russians had declared that they would take no offensive action at all, this event became known as the "massacre of Sinope" and aroused wide indignation in western Europe. In March, 1854, England and France demanded the withdrawal of Russia from Moldavia and Wallachia. Despite all Lord Aberdeen's efforts for peace, Russia refused. Thereupon England and France declared war. Austria remained at peace, "astonishing the world" by her ingratitude to Russia. Prussia also remained neutral. Truculent diplomacy and febrile spirits had made war inevitable.

The allies mounted an offensive in the Crimea and attacked the fortified city of Sebastopol. In these operations the allied generals were distinguished by their incompetence. Their methods were criminal and their objectives insane. The siege of Sebastopol lasted for twelve months. The Russians, with shorter supply lines than the allies, increased their troops in Sebastopol from 40,000 to 100,000 men. Other Russian forces launched strong counterattacks, particularly at Balaclava and Inkerman. During the winter the English troops suffered horribly from the Russian cold and storms; from cholera; from hunger; from lack of shoes, tents, overcoats, medical supplies, and doctors; from breakdowns in transport and supply; from gross maladministration all along the perverse and collapsing chain of command. In the army nothing had been changed since Waterloo. Nor had anyone but the Duke of Wellington given strong support to any proposals to increase the army budget during the years of peace. At one time there were 20,000 English troops in action and 20,000 in hospitals.

At home the *Times* roused public indignation by printing news dispatches from the front. William Howard Russell, their special correspondent, vividly described the horrors resulting from a chaotic and blundering campaign. Even the genius of Florence Nightingale came too late to save thousands of lives which had been needlessly sacrificed. In the early months of the war the mortality rate at the Scutari hospital had been 50 per cent.

The Aberdeen government could not survive the shock of these disclosures and the pressure of public fury. Aberdeen himself, long a pacifist, had become increasingly unpopular as the war dragged on. He was often wildly blamed for events with which he had no connection whatever; but the public had need of a scapegoat. When Parliament met on January 23, 1855, a motion was introduced for the appointment of a select committee to inquire into the Crimean muddle. Russell at once resigned, amid a hail of abuse from his colleagues, who stood together until the motion was carried. Then they resigned. The coalition ended.

Three times Queen Victoria attempted to find someone other than Lord Palmerston to form a cabinet. At last she was forced to accept Palmerston, in whom alone the people now had confidence as a fighter who "stood forth in the tempest of doubt and disaster." Palmerston easily made his cabinet, composed of a coalition of Whigs and Peelites. It did not include either Aberdeen or Russell.

Led by Palmerston, who was "never better than when the gale rides high," the new cabinet at once undertook a series of administrative reforms, particularly in the War Office, pointing towards the removal of the worst causes of inefficiency. The coming of spring helped matters in the Crimea. In September, 1855, Sebastopol fell. Meanwhile Tsar Nicholas had died. With his successor, Alexander II, the allies, now joined by Sardinia, made peace. The preliminary peace negotiations had been long and bitterly contested. Under Palmerston, England was ready to continue the war; but Napoleon III was eager to quit, having "consolidated" his empire and reaped all the "glory" possible. France had lost 97,000 men; of these only 20,000 had died in action. The Congress of Paris (February 25 to March 30, 1856) therefore ended "the one perfectly useless modern war."

The Treaty of Paris was perhaps as futile as the war. By its terms the "integrity" of the Turkish Empire was guaranteed; this clause was kept for twenty years. Turkey and Russia mutually restored to each other all conquests. Turkey declared "generous intentions" towards her Christian subjects; the Sultan soon overlooked this promise. There were to be no warships or fortified coastal zones in the Black Sea or in the Dardanelles; Russia tore up these clauses in 1870. Moldavia, Wallachia, and Serbia were given autonomy in domestic affairs under Turkish suzerainty rights guaranteed by the powers; this, too, was discarded as the old disorder in the Balkans continued. An international commission was to control the navigation of the Danube.

A document separate from the treaty, known as the Declaration of Paris, marked an important forward step in the development of international law. This Declaration provided that privateering was to be abolished; blockades could not be merely theoretical but had to be effective in practice; neutral flags would cover any enemy goods not contraband under the laws of war. At the Congress Count Cavour of Sardinia seized the planned opportunity to denounce Austrian suppression in the Italian peninsula and extended the widening sympathy for the unification dreams of Italian liberals. This was one of the most significant results of the whole sordid havoc of the Crimean War. Sardinia had lost twenty-eight men in action at the front. The chance to raise the wrongs of Italy at an international conference was a fair return.

PARTIES AND POLITICS, 1856–1859

At home the road of party politics was still winding and rocky. Palmerston's first ministry had been weakened by the early departure of the Peelites. In February, 1857, Gladstone, Russell, and Disraeli supported Richard Cobden's motion of censure which passed the house of commons by a majority of sixteen. This motion was politically foolish because Palmerston was then the public hero. In the ensuing election his enemies were scattered; Cobden and many others lost their seats in the house. Palmerston returned with a majority of eighty-five, the largest held by any government for several years. However, it is important to note that this majority was not a party one; it was Palmerston's personal following that had been increased, nothing more. The party instability remained. A personal majority can melt away, and Palmerston swiftly found his triumph empty.

In January, 1858, Felice Orsini, an Italian exile, vainly attempted to assassinate Napoleon III. It was soon discovered that the plot had been prepared in England and the bombs made in Birmingham. Although the French public reaction was violently hostile to England the formal French note of protest was not offensive. It merely stated that the French government hoped for effective guarantees against the repetition of such outrages. To appease the French Palmerston introduced a Conspiracy to Murder Bill to amend the law so that conspiracy to murder would no longer be a misdemeanor but a felony punishable by imprisonment. The language used in France against England had so angered the English public that they resented the apparent readiness of the cabinet to meet the French wishes. So Palmerston's majority vanished. He was defeated and resigned. Derby and Disraeli formed their second cabinet. They held office for about a year. Then Lord Palmerston returned, bringing into his cabinet Gladstone. The Peelites and the Whigs were ending their long trek towards the goal of a new Liberal party. When Gladstone joined Palmerston the Peelites really ceased to exist as a separate element in the house. The evident hardening of party lines during the years now permits the use of the new terms "Liberal" and "Conservative" to describe the two major political groups.

The second Palmerston ministry lasted until his death in 1865. Palmerston has been described as "the last of the Whigs." His successor was the Liberal William Ewart Gladstone, later mighty opponent of the Conservative leader Benjamin Disraeli.

BRITISH EXPANSION IN INDIA

Within two years after the end of the Crimean War in Europe the British government was faced by the outbreak of a serious native mutiny in India. One of the major causes of this unhappy event was the swift expansion of British power. Pitt's India Act of 1784 had placed revenue, civil, and military affairs under a board of control headed by a Secretary of State for India. The cabinet was to appoint the Governor-General. Full control over political patronage was kept by the East India Company until about 1813. Then, slowly, the British government began to pry many prerogatives from the company's weakening grasp. Meanwhile, several serious attempts were made to develop a more satisfactory administrative system within British India. As always, these efforts were blunted by inertia, ignorance, corruption, and bureaucracy. Warren Hastings had conscientiously attempted many more reforms than he was able to carry through. His failures, and the failures of those who followed, were largely made inevitable by the native situation.

When Hastings was impeached in 1788 the numerous charges against him included that of conquering too much territory by dubious methods. "Nations had been extirpated for a sum of money, whole tracts of land laid waste by fire and sword to furnish investments . . . the British Government exhibited in every part of Hindustan holding a bloody sceptre in one hand and picking pockets with the other." Lord Cornwallis, fresh from disaster in America, succeeded Hastings as Governor-General. He received elaborate instructions as a result of which numerous reforms were carried out, particularly in the areas of revenue and justice. Because Hastings had been accused of levying too many wars of conquest, Cornwallis was forbidden to declare war without permission from London except to defend British or friendly territory. He soon discovered, however, that it was sometimes impossible to avoid interference in the affairs of independent native states.

The marquis of Wellesley, whose younger brother was later to become the Duke of Wellington, was Governor-General from 1798 to 1805. He made the same discovery as Lord Cornwallis. Despite the disapproval of the distant British government and the East India Company, Wellesley could not remain aloof from Indian politics. He felt that as a policy of non-intervention could not be consistently pursued it was better for the honor and safety of the British to adopt a more aggressive procedure. For example, the intriguing French encouraged Tipu, the ruler of the southern state of Mysore, to believe that he could expel the British and become master of India. Thereupon Wellesley defeated Tipu, and annexed a large part of Mysore. The remainder was at first a subsidiary state under an alliance with the British and later a protected state more completely under British control. Meanwhile Wellesley extended the British system of alliances with native princes, notably with Hyderabad. In 1801 he annexed the Carnatic and Tanjore regions along the southeast coast. In northwest India the native state of Oudh was compelled to cede a part of its territory which included Delhi, the capital of the old Mogul Empire. Having established British power in all southern India, Wellesley took advantage of civil war to extend the sway of Empire into the center of the Maratha confederacy in the west. In the midst of his campaigns he was recalled. But the policy of intervention could not be ended.

It is not possible here to describe in detail the unrelenting pressure of British expansion northward. Much depended upon the abilities and desires of the various Governors-General or upon the weight of circumstances. When the British wished to keep order or to prevent attacks on British territories the only effective way of doing so was often by conquest and annexation. Russian plans in Afghanistan and northern India caused the British to move more swiftly. Defense seemed to demand more expansion. Sind was annexed in 1843. Most of the Punjab was taken over in 1846 and the rest in 1849. Kashmir became a protected state in 1846. The part of lower Burma that had not been taken in 1826 was annexed in 1852. Lord Dalhousie, who became Governor-General in 1843, annexed the province of Oudh in 1856 and ended the insufferable rule of an imbecile despot and his harpies. Dalhousie also introduced the "doctrine of lapse" which stated that childless chiefs of subsidiary states might not adopt successors. Consequently the annexations were increased, substituting British for native rule. Dalhousie honestly felt that the British had a heavy responsibility for the welfare of the peoples of India. In these circumstances he felt justified in arbitrarily extending British control to ensure for the natives, so far as was possible, the benefits of British rule. At the same time, the British government progressively reduced the power of the East India Company by the three acts of Parliament of 1813, 1833, and 1853. As the government extended its control, the number of social, economic, and administrative reforms steadily increased.

Under Dalhousie many rapid changes had taken place, some of them very offensive to the natives. They found British law and order an inadequate compensation for their own customs, institutions, and religion which they feared they would be forced to abandon. To Hin-

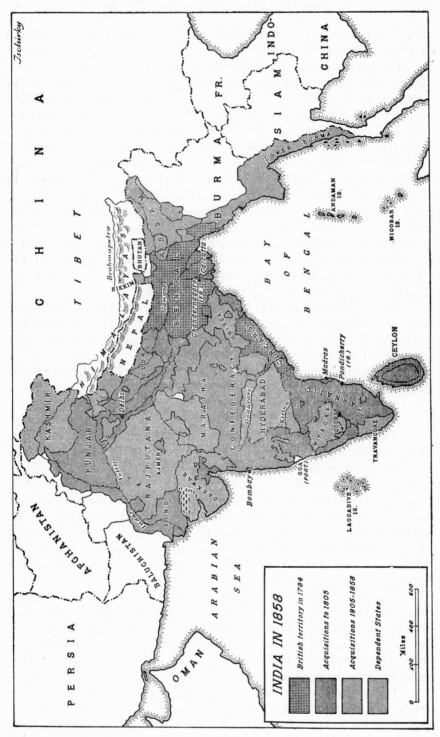

INDIA IN 1858

British territory in 1784
Acquisitions to 1805
Acquisitions 1805-1858
Dependent States

Miles

625

dus, Moslems, Sikhs, and all of the other racial, religious, and cultural groups there were different reasons for bitterness and objection. Causes of irritation also varied from region to region. About such a vast country as India general statements are easily made and as easily disproved. There was no doubt, however, that the Crimean War had fostered rumors found throughout India and decidedly injurious to British military and political prestige. Discipline in the native army was lagging. Many native troops were idle, restless, troubled, ready for mischief. An old Hindu prophecy had told of the end of the rule of the East India Company in 1857. Hindus feared that they would lose their caste if they served outside of India; a recent East India Company order had said that no volunteer should be accepted who would not serve overseas. A new cartridge, encased in paper and greased with mutton fat, had recently been introduced into the army. Suspicious Hindus, fearful of losing caste, became excited when rumor said that the grease was from the fat of the sacred cow. Moslems were terrified when they heard that the fat was from the unclean pig.

In 1857 there were 233,000 native troops or sepoys in India and only 46,000 British soldiers. Tales began to float that Britain intended to force all India to become Christian. Discontent in the army and throughout the civilian millions prepared India for the mutiny which crept among the sepoys and roared like a jungle fire through the central and northern states.

THE INDIAN MUTINY

The mutiny began at Meerut and spread to Delhi. Flames of disorder swiftly licked out from the ancient capital. The natives often reverted to primitive and savage bestialities. At Cawnpore all Europeans were massacred. In Lucknow the desperate siege of the British residency lasted three months. Had the British authorities moved with greater despatch and had more troops been available the whole disturbance might soon have been quelled. Indeed, the dramatic nature of the violent convulsion tends to obscure the fact that the Indian Mutiny was not an all-India uprising. In fact, it was limited almost entirely to the Bengal army.

The British had been caught off guard; their troops were widely scattered. Only slowly were they able to abate the disorder. Supporting troops were sent from England and Persia. Not until the end of 1859 was India normal again. As the British soldiers regained control they took a bloody revenge on the sepoys. There were no further mutinies in India, only the needling pertinacity of native discontent.

The Indian Mutiny ended the dual control of company and crown established by Pitt's India Act of 1784. All the remaining political powers of the East India Company now passed into history; they were transferred to the British government. Henceforth India was to be ruled in the name of the queen. Thus, by the India Act of 1858, the British government assumed complete control of Indian administration. The Viceroy of India was to be responsible to the Secretary of State for India, who, as a member of the cabinet, was in turn responsible to Parliament.

FOREIGN AFFAIRS: CHINA, EUROPE, AMERICA

Meanwhile England had become involved in another war with China (1856–1858.) The Chinese authorities had boarded the schooner *Arrow*, a ship flying the British flag and under British registry, and had arrested the Chinese crew on charges of piracy. England demanded reparations and also insisted that the "treaty port" clauses of the Treaty of Nanking of 1842 be kept by the Chinese. Following the Chinese defeat the Treaty of Tientsin (1858) provided that a permanent British embassy should be established at Pekin; the Chinese would set up an embassy in London. Christians in China were to be protected. The Yangtse River and five more ports would be opened to foreign trade.

In Europe Palmerston and Russell, his foreign secretary, slowed the pace and pressure of British diplomacy. Russell was now old and sapless. Palmerston, as prime minister, had much to do besides manage foreign affairs, and he was an aging lion. In a few cases, however, something of the earlier energy was displayed. For example, Palmerston and Russell left no doubt of England's position with respect to the movement for Italian unification. In 1859 Austria had dragged her weakening armies to wage war against Sardinia. Because Napoleon III had then fulfilled his promise to aid Count Cavour the usurping Austrians had been driven from Lombardy. Although Napoleon deserted his ally at the critical moment because he really did not wish to see Italy united from "the Alps to the Adriatic," the cause of Italian unification had been advanced considerably. When England firmly declared that the problem of Italian unification should be left to the Italians themselves other powers were reluctant to intervene. All through the struggle for unification under the house of Savoy the Italians were aided by liberal England. Meanwhile the Poles were supported in their revolt against a ruthless Tsar. The Ionian Islands were given to Greece because the inhabitants wished it so.

In 1864 Prussia and Austria declared war upon Denmark to settle the knotted diplomatic question of the possession of the duchies of Schleswig and Holstein. It is not surprising that Palmerston and Russell had attempted to prevent the two great states of the German Confederation from despoiling the weaker Denmark. When they failed, Palmerston and Russell threatened war. But the wily and determined Bismarck overrode the threat. He was certain that the feeling of the English people, and their queen, was not inclined to support a war over the Schleswig-Holstein problem. After this event the diplomatic power and prestige of England began to wane in Europe. The years when Palmerston could berate and trounce the foreign ministers of the Continent were over. A moderate and often vacillating policy, harmful to British prestige, soon prevailed.

Meanwhile the United States was engaged in a great civil war. The British government, and still more the upper and middle classes, viewed the secession of the South with friendly eyes. The lower classes, including the cotton workers who depended on the South for their supply of cotton, were solid supporters of the North. Palmerston's silence and Gladstone's oratory helped to increase the tension between the two nations. Resentment in the Northern states was quickened and extended by such men as Charles Sumner and his apostles, to whom England was a "soulless monster of Frankenstein" and who assured excited audiences that "not to blast was to bless."

When England permitted the Confederacy to obtain cruisers such as the *Alabama* from English shipbuilders to ravage Northern commerce the bitterness was heightened. In Northern states there were demands for the annexation of Canada. Fenian raiders invaded Ontario to shoot quiet settlers. A series of events, including the famous "*Trent* affair," brought the two nations to the edge of conflict. When the Civil War ended, the Northern states did not forget the unfriendly attitude of England in the hour of American division and peril. Only in 1871 did the representatives of the United States, Great Britain, and Canada end the major causes of friction. The result of their conference was the Treaty of Washington, an important chapter in the history of the three nations which form the "north Atlantic triangle." Its happy terms included provision for the settlement of boundary and fishery problems and the *Alabama* claims. The latter question was submitted to a tribunal at Geneva. In accordance with its decision England paid the United States $15,500,000 in full payment for the damage inflicted by the *Alabama* and other Confederate vessels obtained from British sources.

Chapter 32

DISRAELI AND GLADSTONE

THE HEIRS OF PALMERSTON

LORD PALMERSTON died in October, 1865, at the age of eighty. With his death came the "strange doings" he had predicted. "Palmerston," said a contemporary, "held a great bundle of sticks together; they are now unwound, and there is nobody to tie them up again." No more would the dual alliance of Russell and Palmerston bulk large on the political stage. Russell was now in the house of lords, old and alone. Although he became prime minister for the second time to head a tottering administration, he was not the real leader of the Liberal party. The real leader and champion of the Liberals was William Ewart Gladstone, chancellor of the exchequer. A similar situation existed in the Conservative party. There the titular head was Lord Derby. The actual power was slowly dropping into the waiting hands of Benjamin Disraeli.

Between Gladstone and Disraeli there arose a personal and political duel. For many years they divided the loyalties of Englishmen between them. When Disraeli and the Conservatives were elected a shadow like a funeral pall often fell over Liberal households. When Gladstone and the Liberals were returned to power Conservatives frequently felt that a national catastrophe had occurred. To some, indeed, the battle of the giants assumed the character of a cosmic struggle between good and evil forces fighting for the souls of men.

Gladstone was born in 1809, the fourth son of Sir John Gladstone, a wealthy corn merchant of Liverpool, a baronet and a member of Parliament. He was educated at Eton and Oxford. At Oxford he was president of the Oxford Union and took a double first-class degree. His enormous vitality, his debating skill, and his energetic morality rapidly marked him as a man eminently fitted for a career either in the Anglican Church or in politics. He preferred the church; his father was determined to make him a politician. In 1833 he sat as a High Tory member for Newark in the first reformed Parliament. For over sixty years he was to remain in the house of commons.

629

In the years between 1833 and 1846 Gladstone held many offices. Under Peel he was successively a junior lord of the treasury, under-secretary of state for the colonies, vice-president of the board of trade, and secretary of state for the colonies. In 1846, as explained in Chapter 30, he followed Peel in the great division of the Tory party and slowly broke his original ties with the Tories. In 1847 he began to sit as the Peelite representative of Oxford University. Under Aberdeen he became chancellor of the exchequer, and his budget speech of 1853 proved that he was a brilliant economist and financier as well as a master of burnished rhetoric. Under Palmerston too, Gladstone served as chancellor of the exchequer. Always he was conspicuous, able, brilliant. However, as he moved toward Liberalism he lost the confidence of Tory Oxford University. Defeat came in 1865. After Gladstone was thus "unmuzzled" he represented the industrial district of South Lancashire, a district much more in sympathy with his advancing liberal ideas. Thus, when Palmerston died, Gladstone had already behind him a distinguished parliamentary career characterized by hard work, patience, weighty and involved eloquence, and high moral fervor.

Benjamin Disraeli was born in 1804. At the age of thirteen he was baptized in the Anglican Church when his father quit the tents of his people and took his family with him. Ambitious, self-confident, and diligent, he set out to educate himself. For three years he worked in a solicitor's office. In 1824 he began to study for the bar at Lincoln's Inn. Five years later he published his clever and insolent novel *Vivian Grey*. Soon he decided to become a writer and a politician; the idea of a law career was abandoned. While he proceeded to write a series of books and pamphlets he tried three times to get into Parliament. Not until 1837 was he finally returned as Tory member for Maidstone.

The early career of Disraeli in the house of commons was rather too dazzling and erratic to impress that august assembly favorably. Slowly, however, his political brilliance, his wit, and his debating power dissipated much of the earlier prejudice roused against him by his affectations, his theatricality, and his race. The story of his dramatic part in the battle of the Corn Laws has been told above. Through the dull, dark, locust years of opposition after 1846 he had worked patiently with Lord Derby and others to rebuild the shattered Tory party. Now, in 1865, as Disraeli faced Gladstone across the house of commons, the new Conservative party was slowly rising to match the new Liberal strength and stature.

These, then, were the rivals who were soon to captain the Liberal and Conservative teams. As masters of politics and statecraft they were to hammer out and squarely fashion coherent policies and principles. Party lines became more tightly drawn and political vagabonds were sorted out and sent packing home. Meanwhile, in the three years between the death of Palmerston in 1865 and the formation of the first

Gladstone ministry in 1868 two significant events occurred. The first was the reversal of British foreign policy. The second was the revival of the controversy about parliamentary reform.

The reversal of foreign policy was complete and swift. Immediate changes were made in the textbook of diplomatic tactics and external affairs. A cold policy of non-intervention abroad succeeded the full-blooded warmth of Palmerston's coursing frontal assaults. This negative British tendency to isolation was heightened by the results of the Schleswig-Holstein dispute from which British prestige had suffered so considerably. Moreover, the Manchester School of Bright and Cobden advocated a policy of laissez-faire in foreign relations. Then, too, the thoughts of an increasing number of Conservatives were turned overseas to distant posts of Empire; they were more concerned with British than with foreign lands. It seemed that Britain would return to the councils of Europe only if British interests were directly challenged.

In domestic affairs, the Russell ministry was faced with difficult problems. For example, there was a serious Fenian conspiracy in Ireland. In England a cattle plague was killing thousands of animals weekly. Public opinion was excited over the unduly severe repression of a Negro rising in Jamaica. Overshadowing these questions there was the mounting pressure for further parliamentary reform. After Chartism collapsed in 1848 there had been little agitation for a greater extension of the franchise. Lord John Russell, always prone to entertain reform ideas, had three times put forward a bill: in 1851 to his cabinet, which opposed him; in 1852 to the house of commons, which defeated him before the bill was passed; in 1853 to his colleagues in the Aberdeen coalition and later to Parliament, where tepid enthusiasm forced him to drop it. In 1859 Disraeli had proposed a bill to extend the suffrage in the rural areas where the Conservatives were strong. Russell claimed it did not go far enough because the vote should be given to the city workers who would vote for the Liberals. After the Conservatives were defeated Russell advanced his fourth bill. Widespread indifference within and outside Parliament again persuaded him to withdraw his proposals.

After the death of Palmerston, who had viewed all these reform projects with a basilisk eye, the prospects seemed fairer. In 1866 Gladstone introduced a bill to extend the franchise to certain classes of city workers. This bill was of course opposed by the Conservatives. It was also denounced by some rebels within the Liberal party who were more Whig than Liberal. Their leader, the imprudent Robert Lowe, said that he did not trust the moral and intellectual competence of the working classes. Lowe claimed the bill was revolutionary and dangerous because it would lead to the dread end, as he saw it, of pure democracy. John Bright pointed out that these malcontents were gathering about Lowe in the same way as the outlaws once rallied to King David in the

Cave of Adullam. So Lowe's followers came to be called Adullamites.

These Adullamites were a rather talentless group, wavering and trimming among themselves; but they stood together long enough to aid the Conservatives in smashing Russell's bill. Because war was impending between Austria and Prussia the queen was reluctant to change her ministry. So Russell delayed a week. Then he resigned. This was in June, 1866. Gladstone felt that the Liberals could not long remain out of office. "You cannot fight against the future; time is on our side."

THE SECOND REFORM BILL

Thus the Russell government was overturned by the kind of squall that sprang up so often in the middle nineteenth century. Russell himself now retired from public affairs. His had been a long career; he had first been elected to Parliament in 1813. Derby and Disraeli reluctantly tried to form a cabinet, negotiating with all the nomadic tribes in the house in an attempt to obtain a majority. The class-conscious Adullamites, still angry and in their war paint, would have no dealings with either Conservatives or Liberals, both of whom they suspected of wanting to give the vote to the "impulsive, unreflecting and violent" lower classes. But hardly had the third Derby-Disraeli ministry been patched together than John Bright and Gladstone began to trumpet the Liberal reform notes again. This time there was considerable public excitement. The American Civil War had shown the strength of a democratic state, something in which many of the English upper classes had never believed. So far as liberal reforms in England were concerned it was quite clear that the former apathy was gone. Parliament and people were "very hot for reform without delay."

The adroit Disraeli at once decided to make capital for his own party out of the reform tumult. "Of all the possible hares to start," he remarked, "I do not know a better than the extension of household suffrage." The decision was not entirely his own. Both the queen and Lord Derby realized that the hour for a settlement had come. Thus the Conservatives proposed to introduce a reform bill. It was expected that the Liberal gladiators, then in the midst of their loud reform campaign, would be nonplussed by such a step. Aware that the Conservatives were associated in the popular mind with Tory reaction and exclusion, Disraeli wanted to show that his party did not in fact distrust the people; that there could be an association between the aristocracy and the workers; that the Conservatives had a historical title to deal with reform and were but embracing again the traditions of Bolingbroke and the younger Pitt. In brief, the narrow Tory policies of Lord Liverpool and his successors were to be discarded, and for them substituted the broad and comprehensive program of what was to be called "Tory democracy."

To do all this was not easy. Disraeli later said: "I had to prepare the mind of the country, and to educate—if it be not arrogant to use such a word—to educate our party." Meanwhile, with his usual histrionic skill, Disraeli introduced the new reform proposal, declaring that the Conservatives wished to establish the character and functions of the house of commons "on a broad, popular basis" and to undertake a prudent and practical redistribution of seats in the house of commons.

All happened as Disraeli foresaw, or almost so. The more Conservative groups in both parties wanted no reform. So Disraeli withdrew his first bill and put forward a second, designed to appeal to all liberal and radical elements, regardless of party. Gladstone, fighting hard, declared that the bill still did not go far enough. Disraeli, regretting that Gladstone "gets up and addresses me in a tone which, I must say, is very unusual in this House," nevertheless was forced to accept a series of radical and liberalizing amendments. However, the premature amendment of John Stuart Mill for the enfranchisement of women was defeated by a vote of nearly three to one. In its final form the bill went far beyond anything proposed before. The old High Tories grumbled, but came to heel. Outside Parliament some radicals pressed for Gladstone's suggested £5 qualification; Disraeli called them "spouters of stale sedition" and "obsolete incendiaries." Amidst such national excitement the bill passed into law.

Earlier Lord Derby had admitted that the Conservatives were "making a great experiment and taking a leap in the dark." He had also sardonically remarked: "Don't you see how we have dished the Whigs?" It now seemed that Gladstone and his party were "dished" indeed. Gladstone, his followers divided by dissension and plots, denounced the "diabolical cleverness of Dizzy" and his "revolting cynicism." The splenetic Thomas Carlyle described the reform bill as "shooting Niagara" and compared the people of England to "mesmerized, somnambulant cattle." Coventry Patmore, the great Catholic poet, was so horrified that he wrote bitterly of the treachery of the Conservatives "and their Jew." Robert Lowe commented: "We must now at least educate our new masters."

The Representation of the People Act of 1867 brought almost universal manhood suffrage to the boroughs of England. In the boroughs the act enfranchised two classes of adult males: (1) those who for at least a year had been inhabitant occupiers, as owners or tenants, of dwelling houses on which the poor rates had been paid; (2) those who for at least a year had occupied, as sole tenants, unfurnished lodgings worth £10 annually. Likewise two classes of adult males were admitted to the franchise in the counties: (1) those who were property owners or long-term renters (sixty years or more) of lands or tenements of an annual value of at least £5; (2) those who were occupiers of lands or tenements of an annual ratable value of £12 or more. Finally, there was a small redistribution of seats. Towns with populations of less than 10,000 were allowed only one member of Parliament instead of two; a few boroughs were disfranchised. This gave twenty-five new seats to the counties and nineteen to the towns and cities.

The important result of this act of 1867 was that the artisans and other small householders, who formed the largest part of the English working class, now had the vote. The rural county laborers were not yet enfranchised; their turn was to come in 1884. Meanwhile the rule of the middle classes, which had begun so brightly in 1832, seemed now at an end.

In its short term of office the Derby-Disraeli government also passed the British North America Act of 1867. This act created the Dominion of Canada, a federal union with the British parliamentary system of government. In this union the provinces were specifically given fifteen powers in addition to their exclusive control over purely provincial matters. All other powers, twenty-nine of which were listed, remained with the Dominion government. To the Canadian fathers of Confederation it seemed that the American Civil War might not have happened had the residual powers in the United States been vested in the federal government rather than in the separate states. In 1867 the new Dominion consisted of four provinces: Nova Scotia, New Brunswick, Quebec, and Ontario. British Columbia and Manitoba joined in 1871; Prince Edward Island, in 1873; Alberta and Saskatchewan, in 1905; Newfoundland, in 1949.

About Canada and the Canadian question there was little debate in the British house of commons. No more interest was shown than if the Confederation proposal had been "a private bill uniting two or three English parishes." Both Conservatives and Liberals were apathetic; the Liberals because they had slight regard for the Empire and thought that most of the colonies would ultimately become independent; the Conservatives because they had not yet reached the years of their surging interest in Britain's imperial destiny. "The Dominion of Canada was born in a period of mid-Victorian gloom."

In February, 1868, Lord Derby retired and Disraeli became prime minister. "I have climbed," said Disraeli, "to the top of the greasy pole." But meanwhile the Liberals had recovered from the shock tactics of the Conservatives in the parliamentary reform battle. Gladstone now challenged Disraeli upon an old problem: British policy in Ireland. A Fenian rebellion in 1865 had repeated the Young Ireland failure of 1848. Yet British repression had done nothing to relieve the pain of the Irish ulcer. Bitter Irishmen burned and murdered; from behind Irish hedges the snipers' bullets hummed. Gladstone felt that his mission was to pacify Ireland. This could never be done, he asserted, by violence and coercion. To the end of his long career he tried to find a peaceful solution. It is not ultimately to be counted against him that he failed.

In the spring of 1868 Gladstone proclaimed a policy of sweeping Irish reforms. On these proposals the divided Liberals closed their ranks; former Peelites, Whigs, Radicals, Adullamites, and nondescript stragglers stood together. In the house of commons the Conservatives were defeated. In the general election which followed the householders that Disraeli had enfranchised voted for Gladstone. England found it hard to believe that the Conservatives really wanted to come to terms with the new democracy. Gladstone, then fifty-nine years old, formed the first and greatest of his four ministries. Under the new impulse for reform the constant Liberal assaults on outworn institutions and vested privilege gathered momentum. The domestic scene became busy and uproarious. Victorian England began to doubt still more the value of the legacies of laissez-faire. Domestic political activity resulted, on the whole, in the gradual adaptation and change of old institutions and laws to fit new conditions. More and more the state intervened to promote social welfare. Energy and conscience increased their scope and area.

IRELAND: THE CHURCH AND THE LAND

Gladstone earnestly tried to pacify Ireland. As a first step in this hard task he proposed to disestablish and disendow the Anglican Church of Ireland, thus dissolving its connection with the state and putting it on a voluntary basis. Of every ten Irishmen, nine were Roman Catholics; to require them to pay tithes to the alien Anglican Church, even in the form of a rent charge, was clearly rather iniquitous. Nevertheless, both Irish and English Anglicans opposed Gladstone's bill: the former because they stood to lose by it; the latter because they were afraid the same arguments might one day be applied to England and the Anglican Church be disestablished there. Disraeli once remarked: "There are few great things left in England, and the Church is one." The house of lords fought the proposal stubbornly. In the end, partly because Queen Victoria wished to avoid a constitutional crisis on a religious question, a compromise was reached by which the new voluntary Anglican Church in Ireland was to get considerably more than half of all the church property. Parliament was to appropriate the remainder, worth about £7,000,000, which was to be earmarked for Irish relief. Thus, in 1869, the first obnoxious branch of what Gladstone called "the Irish upas tree" was lopped off.

Gladstone now turned to the land problem, a cause of fierce anger among the Irish. In 1841 about 8,000,000 people had lived in Ireland; in 1871 there were only 5,000,000. Death and emigration had taken a heavy toll. The Irish farmers were hard put to avoid starvation. For example, over 1,000,000 people lived upon 200,000 farms, each of which contained less than fifteen acres of poor land. The usual form of tenancy in Ireland was tenancy at will, subject to six months' notice. Rent in southern Ireland was a "rack rent" based upon competitive bidding; in Ulster a more equitable scheme based rent charges on valuation of land. In Ulster, too, a tenant could not be evicted without compensation for any improvements or repairs he might have made. In southern Ireland, however, unpopular and dishonest agents of absentee English landlords continued to evict tenants without compensation or to raise rents whenever tenants had made repairs or improvements increasing the property value of their holdings. In 1870 Gladstone's Irish Land Act compelled the landlord to pay compensation to a tenant evicted for no fault of his own. But the purpose of this act was never fully realized because it gave Irish tenants no protection against increased rents. Any unscrupulous landlord could take profit from a tenant's improvements by raising the rent; he could also raise the rent to an unreasonable sum and then evict the tenant. In such cases, of course, the evicted tenant would get no compensation. Why should he? He was being evicted because he had not paid his rent.

THE EDUCATION ACT, 1870

Meanwhile Gladstone proceeded with a series of reforms in England. Probably his greatest achievement was the passage of the Education Act of 1870. Before 1870 there was no system of education in England providing for the masses of the people. The new Education Act created a national system of elementary education. A national system of secondary school education came in 1902. The step of 1870 meant that the working classes would no longer have to rely on the voluntary Anglican and Nonconformist church schools, with their religious bias, or the private schools, some of which were like Charles Dickens' "Dotheboys Hall." Despite the small assistance given by the British government after 1833 to Anglican and Nonconformist voluntary schools the teaching was usually poor and the buildings inadequate. Almost everything was woefully mismanaged. More than 2,000,-000 children of school age were not attending school at all. Over 1,000,000 were in schools of such low standard that they could get no government grants.

The Education Act of 1870 is sometimes called the Forster Education Act because W. E. Forster, vice-president of the council, a Quaker and a Bradford woolen manufacturer, was largely responsible for it. The task of Forster and his colleagues was ticklish. For example, the Birmingham Education League, led by Joseph Chamberlain, wanted free universal education without denominational religious instruction. The Anglican church resented government interference. The Nonconformists were equally suspicious of the government and the Anglicans. It was therefore clear that the existing voluntary schools could not be suppressed without a rather vicious hubbub. Further, it would be a costly business to duplicate existing schools. So it was decided to divide England into school districts, controlled by local school boards.

By the act of 1870, the school boards were authorized to build and maintain schools where the voluntary schools were not already in existence and answering community needs. Expenses would be met by national grants, local taxes, and pupils' fees. Not until 1891 was elementary school education free in England. Each school board might require attendance of all children between five and thirteen years of age; but not until 1880 was such attendance made compulsory by an act of Parliament. The famous Cowper-Temple clause of the Education Act of 1870 provided that "the time or times during which any religious observance is practised or instruction in religious subjects is given at any meeting of the school shall be either at the beginning or the end." Thus the parents could easily withdraw their children if they did not wish them to be present at a non-sectarian session. The existing voluntary church schools, their grants increased, of course continued to give their own religious instruction.

Whatever may be said in adverse criticism of this Education Act it was probably about as satisfactory a piece of legislation as could have been devised in the circumstances. In 1870 male illiteracy was nearly 20 per cent; at the turn of the century it had fallen to less than 2 per cent. In 1874 Lord Esher commented on the first results of the new law: "It is pleasant to see the small and dirty boys reading labels in the shop windows. It is one of the signs of a happier future." Only slowly, however, was there acceptance of the idea that an opportunity to acquire an education should be available to the sons of nobles, millionaires, and paupers alike.

CIVIL SERVICE, ARMY, COURTS OF LAW

Gladstone's first ministry passed a number of other important reform measures. It boldly opened almost all posts in the civil service to competitive examination and thus helped to form a public-spirited class of permanent administrative servants who would remain at their posts, aloof from politics, while governments rose and fell. Although the dangers of a spoils system were thus avoided in 1870, another weakness unfortunately remained and later spread to the British dominions. Because of the inelasticity of the civil service system it seldom bred men of audacity and vision; the usual behavior of the old Whitehall hand emphasized the negative sides of his character rather than imagination and enterprise. Many dull and disciplined civil servants became content with an adequate performance of routine tasks. A reputation for "soundness" was often obtained only when the zest for experiment had departed.

In the army, significant reforms were achieved. Edward Cardwell, Gladstone's war secretary, decided that the system by which army officers bought their commissions should be ended. Promotion, he felt, should depend on merit. To this proposal there was strong opposition, particularly in the house of lords, where many peers had bought, or intended to buy, army careers for their younger sons. Although the lords vetoed Cardwell's bill, the queen abolished the purchase of commissions by issuing a royal warrant. About the same time short term enlistments were permitted, providing for six years in the regular army and six years in the reserve.

In 1873 the Supreme Court of Judicature Act began a general reconstruction of the procedure and organization of the central courts. Under the terms of this act and the Appellate Jurisdiction Act of 1876 a Supreme Court of Judicature was created. These acts, and supplementary ones, simplified procedure, ended conflicts of jurisdiction, removed many anomalies, helped speed the administration of justice, and made it less expensive.

The main branch of the new Supreme Court was called the High Court of Justice and consisted of three divisions: (1) Chancery; (2) King's Bench; (3) Admiralty, Probate, and Divorce. The judges of any one division might serve in another. Law and equity were applied in all divisions; in cases where the rules of law and equity conflicted the law of equity was to prevail. The second branch of the Supreme Court of Judicature was the Court of Appeal, created to hear appeals from the High Court of Justice. Beyond the five judges of the Court of Appeal still lies the house of lords, the highest court in the British judicial system. In order to strengthen that house in exercising its appellate jurisdiction provision was made by the Appellate Jurisdiction Act of 1876 for the crown to appoint two lords of appeal in ordinary, learned in the law. Each of these men bears the title of baron during his lifetime and sits and votes in the house of lords. His dignity as a lord of Parliament does not descend to his heirs.

These, then, were the chief reforms of the first great Gladstone ministry. There were still others. In 1869 imprisonment for debt was abolished. In 1871 the religious tests which had kept Nonconformists out of Oxford and Cambridge were removed. Steps were taken to increase facilities for the education of women. In 1872 the Australian secret ballot replaced open voting. This was particularly useful after 1867 because it protected the newly enfranchised city workers from undue influence or intimidation by their employers.

DECLINE OF LIBERAL POWER

By the end of 1873 it was clear that the country was weary of such a deluge of reform measures. Somebody is usually annoyed or hurt by any reform; when the number is large, any government must think about the practical political consequences of losing too many votes, however desirable from a national point of view the projected reforms may be. So it was with Gladstone. As he progressed, the mordant words of Disraeli followed him. In 1871 Disraeli spoke of Gladstone's Irish policy: "He persuaded the people of England that with regard to Irish politics he was in possession of the philosopher's stone. . . . Under his influence and at his instance we have legalized confiscation, consecrated sacrilege, condoned high treason; we have destroyed churches; we have shaken property to its foundations." In a famous speech of April, 1872, Disraeli continued the attack: "Extravagance was being substituted for energy by the government. The unnatural stimulus was subsiding. Their paroxysms ended in prostration. Some took refuge in melancholy, and their eminent chief alternated between a menace and a sigh. You behold a range of exhausted volcanoes. Not a flame flickers on a single pallid crest. But the situation is still dangerous. There are occasional earthquakes, and ever and anon the dark rumbling of the sea."

The mounting unpopularity born of Liberal domestic policy and the weight of Conservative condemnation would doubtless have served alone to scuttle the Gladstone cabinet. The process was aided by difficulties within the Liberal party and by public impatience with Gladstone's handling of foreign affairs.

FOREIGN AFFAIRS

Despite all shifting national moods and tempers, England can not long remain aloof from the affairs of Europe. Whenever Englishmen have retreated behind the Channel moat and failed to heed signals of warning from the Continent the results have invariably been unhappy. Even before Gladstone came to power the prestige of England abroad had declined. European states did not understand why Palmerston's policy had been reversed and the lion roared no longer. Although Gladstone had sincerely and vaguely assured the world that England would defend her interests his ideas about those interests differed from the ideas of Palmerston and Disraeli. In foreign affairs the Liberals had promised a cautious policy. To some it appeared that these retreats, hesitations, and apparently weak surrenders went far beyond the demands of caution.

On August 2, 1870, the Franco-Prussian War began. One month later, on September 2, the battle of Sedan was fought. The British government had vainly attempted to prevent Bismarck's legions from marching against France. A renewal of the Treaty of 1839 guaranteeing Belgium's neutrality was obtained; but nothing more. France fell. Defeat brought revolution. The French Empire ended and the German Empire began. With the approval of Bismarck, Russia took advantage of the war to denounce and tear up Article XI of the Treaty of Paris of 1856 which had declared the Black Sea neutralized. The Russians cynically stated that the law did not then retain "the moral validity which it may have possessed at other times." At a conference in London the powers agreed to give Russia what she had already taken. It was clear that England would not fight to preserve the neutrality of the Black Sea. When it also became obvious that Russia was once more probing in the direction of Afghanistan the English suspicions were quickened again.

Public dissatisfaction was increased still more by the final settlement of the *Alabama* dispute with the United States, described above in Chapter 31. To many Englishmen it seemed very important that energy in domestic reform should not be combined with an apparently inept and spineless handling of external affairs. Harassed by attacks from every quarter the Gladstone cabinet fought on. In March, 1873, the Liberals were finally defeated by a majority of three on the Irish University Bill, a proposal to reform the whole system of higher education in Ireland. Gladstone at once resigned; he was annoyed when Disraeli refused to form a government. Disraeli, usually a shrewd party politician, wanted to see the Liberal oaks go down with a resounding crash before he took office. He wished no quiet entry through the gates to power but rather a national election. Then he would have an opportunity to describe and denounce the Liberal failures from the public platform. Gladstone would be soundly trounced and the revived Conservatives would return in triumph. Reasoning thus, Disraeli waited. Gladstone's difficulties increased. The English harvest failed. Foreign trade declined and business depression began. In January, 1874, the Liberal cabinet asked for a dissolution, and got it.

THE ELECTION OF 1874

Gladstone made a number of election promises, including one to abolish the income tax. But the domestic and foreign measures of his party were cruelly examined by Disraeli and the Conservatives. In the election battle the Liberals were both out-maneuvered and out-gunned. In his six years as leader of the Opposition Disraeli had completely reorganized the Conservative party. He had created an entirely new system, a party organization that was the forerunner of the great modern political machines. A comprehensive National Union had been formed in 1867. Later a Conservative party manager and a large staff had been established in London. Numerous local Conservative associations and workingmen's societies formed a chain of stout political outposts.

It was inevitable that the Liberals should follow the Conservative example. They extended their Birmingham caucus system throughout Britain. Later in the nineteenth century the Liberals, who believed so much in freedom, found that these Liberal and Conservative political machines were in many respects the enemies of freedom and true parliamentary democracy. They also discovered that their insistence upon free trade had spurred the development of a capitalist and industrial system often inimical to the growth of economic democracy and effectively fettering the freedom of individual choice. The Liberals were soon to face another paradox. Their doctrine of free markets in labor, land, and money had as its necessary corollary the familiar idea of the self-regulating market. However, the Liberals also believed in advancing public welfare by legislation. Thus they were confronted by a sharp and vivid contrast between theory and practice. Nobody could deny that state intervention, as in the case of the factory laws, checked and altered not only the self-regulation of markets but also the free operation of many other things. Hence the Liberals talked about individualism long after they had in fact ceased to be individualists. The later decline of Liberalism was partly the result of the Liberal failure to swallow the consequences of what they had done. For example, their creation of an impersonal and efficient party machine was certainly expedient. Nevertheless, it could never be defended or explained in terms of declared Liberal ideals.

To command confidence and to win elections a party must have both organization and a program. In 1872, at Manchester in April and at the Crystal Palace in June, Disraeli defined the principles and program of the New Toryism. The first object of the Conservatives, Disraeli declared, would be to maintain the historic institutions of England. Gladstone and the Liberals had tampered with almost everything in their reforming zeal. Disraeli asserted that the Conservatives had no destructive program "to despoil churches and plunder landlords," no policy "which assails or menaces every institution, every class, every interest, and every calling." The Conservative party, said Disraeli, felt that its duty was "to maintain the Constitution of the country." There would be none of the Liberal alarums and excursions; but simple, ordered progress that would never threaten the church, the house of lords, or the monarchy. In view of public disapproval of the spate of Liberal reforms, this decision was popular.

The second object of the Conservatives, and the most important, was the maintenance of the British Empire. To the end of the century this was to be the first article of the Conservative creed. The Empire and Imperial affairs had always been of minor importance to Liberals. For the Conservatives Disraeli recalled an ideal almost forgotten since the days of Burke: an Empire bound together by sentiment. Thoughts of Empire had long been simmering in Disraeli's mind; they are found, for example, in his novel *Alroy*; in 1859 he had spoken of "those great states which our own planting and colonizing energies have created by ties and interests that will sustain our power." Now, in 1872, Disraeli declared that to consider the affairs of the British Empire, as the Liberals had done, largely from the economic point of view, was to overlook "those moral and political considerations which alone make nations great and by the influence of which alone men are distinguished from animals." He would not subordinate the interests of the Empire, as Gladstone had done. "If there be any object which, more than another, ought to engage the attention of the statesmen of this country, it is the consolidation of our colonial Empire." With some justification, Gladstone could later denounce the new Imperialism as immoral and cold-blooded, "a vague and boundless adventure of annexation"; but in 1874 Disraeli's words were not demanding an expansionist Imperialism. They were restrained, rather sentimental, and popular.

The third object of the Conservatives was social reform. Gladstone's reforms had alienated many; the speed with which he had undertaken them had probably offended more. Disraeli, on the contrary, promised a gradual approach to economic and social legislation designed to aid the workers. He had earlier proclaimed his sympathy with working-class legislation, and the laboring class were more inclined to heed his political promises in 1874 than earlier. "Sanitas sanitatum," said the phrase-maker at Manchester, "omnia sanitas." Workers turning towards "Tory democracy" were assured that the Conservatives would not ignore the new impulse to reform.

The election of 1874 resulted in a conspicuous victory for the refounded Conservative party. Disraeli, now seventy years old, became prime minister; he had already been in Parliament as long as the queen had been upon the throne. His greatest ministry, like Gladstone's, was to stand for six years.

THE DISRAELI GOVERNMENT, 1874–1880: DOMESTIC POLICY

After the election of 1868 it was clear that the faltering and disorderly leadership of both parties so evident in the preceding twenty years had ended. Gladstone, and after 1874 Disraeli, gave England more political stability, more coherent policies, and hence better government. The manufacturing interests, especially in the north and west of England, increased their power in both parties at the expense of the landed aristocracy. The skilled working classes, particularly the organized factory workers, shared in the mid-Victorian tide of wealth. They represented about ten per cent of the industrial population; protected by their trade unions they got higher wages and shorter hours. The remaining ninety per cent of unskilled and semi-skilled labor got little. They suffered severely in the great depression which began in 1873.

The factory workers, who had obtained the franchise in 1867, voted for Gladstone in 1868; six years later they helped to oust him. In 1874 their votes were as much against Gladstone as for Disraeli;

the Liberal cause might have been aided considerably had Gladstone not been hostile to trade unions. For the moment, however, the voting workers voted for the Conservatives, pledged to "Tory Democracy." Disraeli had promised that there would be no radical Gladstonian innovations at home; his reforms, he said, were to be of an "honest humdrum" kind.

The first slow and unheroic steps of Disraeli in internal reforms resulted in some useful ecclesiastical and land law legislation. The Artisans' Dwellings Act of 1875 tackled the problem of the housing of the poor. It gave the local authorities of London and certain other large cities the power to condemn and demolish buildings declared unfit for human habitation and to build new and improved dwellings. There was also a considerable body of labor legislation, the broad results of which were twofold. The first was a marked advance in trade union status. The second was a codification of the laws regarding working conditions and hours by the Factory and Workshops Act of 1878. Local taxation was reduced. A new sinking fund was established. A Merchant Shipping Act of 1876 increased the powers of the board of trade to deal with ships made unseaworthy by age, damage, or overloading. With much of this social reform legislation Disraeli had a genuine concern. After all, he had written *Sybil*. */Empire* +Suez/

THE ROAD TO THE EAST

To external and imperial affairs Disraeli turned with even greater interest. One of his most masterly achievements came in 1875. Ismail, khedive of Egypt, was forced to sell his 177,000 shares of Suez Canal stock to meet the coupons on the Egyptian public debt. The French, to whom the shares were first offered, held out for exorbitant terms. Taking advantage of the French delay, Disraeli moved swiftly. Parliament was not sitting; there was no time to obtain its consent to the terms of any agreement with Ismail. With the sanction of the urgently summoned cabinet Disraeli borrowed £4,000,000 from his friends the Rothschilds and bought the shares.

The Suez Canal, opened in 1869, controlled the shortest route to India and formed a valuable link in Britain's fortress chain to the East. Eighty per cent of the shipping that passed through it was British. Disraeli's purchase gave Britain control of nearly half the stock. The remaining shares were divided among several powers. Had France been successful in purchasing Ismail's holdings the control of the Canal would have been exclusively in French hands. The English public was delighted. "The highway to India," said Disraeli, "is now secure."

In 1876 Disraeli sought to bind India more securely to the British crown by asking Parliament to confer upon Queen Victoria the title "Empress of India." Some Liberals remarked that the Empire idea had recently suffered shocks in France and Mexico. Others said that the

She asked for the bill (see Maurois Book on Disraeli)

older title "Queen of England" might be submerged in the new. Despite their opinions, on January 1, 1877, Victoria was proclaimed empress of the land where Baber, mighty descendant of Tamerlane, had founded the Mogul Empire, three hundred and twenty years before. It was natural that Disraeli should have pressed for the passage of the Royal Titles Bill. His shrewd recognition of the political value of the new title in India was joined with his romantic loyalty to the throne and his desire to please his sovereign. The mystery and grandeur of the "gorgeous East" touched his artistic imagination. The queen was delighted as the rococo flattery of Disraeli passed from words to action. She was displeased at the heated debate caused by the Liberals in the house of commons. Gladstone, as usual, gravely offended her. So, too, did Liberal pamphlets such as "How little Ben, the innkeeper, changed the sign of the Queen's Inn to the Empress Hotel Limited and what was the result." To Disraeli the queen gave a confidence not granted to any other prime minister during her long reign.

FOREIGN AFFAIRS

Meanwhile, on the flank of the road to the East, the uneasy Balkans once more sought by the sword to hurl the Turks from Europe. In 1875 the provinces of Bosnia and Herzegovina revolted against Turkish misgovernment and tyranny. In 1876 Bulgaria rebelled; soon Montenegro and Serbia followed. England had earlier refused to join Austria, Russia, and Prussia in an attempt to force Turkey to fulfill the promise she had made in 1856 to treat with decency the Christians in her empire. However, when the Turks committed sickening atrocities in Bulgaria a shocked English public forced Disraeli to press the Turkish government to grant reforms and stop the slaughter. The Turks, certain that England would never ally herself with Russia, Austria, and Prussia, refused Disraeli's demands.

Disraeli insisted that the figures about the Bulgarian atrocities were exaggerated. He spoke of froth and faction and "coffee house babble." It was not expedient for England to oppose the Turks when Russia was ready to creep nearer to the Suez Canal, Egypt, the Persian Gulf, and the road to India. "What our duty is at this critical moment is to maintain the Empire of England." Gladstone believed otherwise. He denounced Disraeli for substituting expediency for conscience. He demanded that the Turks be expelled "bag and baggage from the provinces they have desolated and profaned." His pamphlet *Bulgarian Horrors* sold over 200,000 copies. With bitter words he described "the fell, satanic orgies" of the Turks, who were "the one great anti-human specimen of humanity." He asserted that "God's law should override the calculations of political expediency." Once he declared: "The sense of sin, there is the great want of modern life. Do not blunt your sense of sin." But Disraeli, who saw that the Balkans would be Russian pawns once the Turks were pushed from Europe, felt it was no sin to guard the national interest of England. Gladstone, he said, was an "unprincipled maniac."

Russia declared war on Turkey in 1877 to free the Serbs and the Bulgars from Turkish control and, in the doing so, to draw near to Constantinople. Austria and Prussia took no action. Bismarck could not see in the whole Eastern question "any interest for Germany which would be worth the healthy bones of a single Pomeranian grenadier." By 1878 the Russians had leaped close to Constantinople and Turkey sued for peace. Russia imposed the Treaty of San Stephano. By the terms of this treaty Turkey retained only a narrow strip of land in Europe. The size of Bulgaria, now autonomous under nominal Turkish suzerainty, was greatly increased, especially by the addition of a slice of Macedonia, stretching nearly to Constantinople. Bosnia and Herzegovina were declared autonomous states, also under nominal Turkish rule. Montenegro, Rumania, and Serbia were to be independent. In fact, the heavy hand of Russia was slowly descending upon the Balkans. Turkey was almost out; Russia was moving in.

Disraeli, now Lord Beaconsfield, declared that the Treaty of San Stephano altered the terms of the treaties of 1856 and 1871. It must therefore be submitted to all the powers that had signed the earlier treaties. For this purpose a European Congress was necessary. Meanwhile Parliament appropriated large sums for armaments. The grey ships of a British fleet lay off Constantinople. British public opinion showed itself quite ready for war. Russia reluctantly agreed to the holding of a Congress at Berlin where the Treaty of San Stephano would be revised.

The most important points in dispute were settled through diplomatic channels before the Congress met. Bismarck, as president of the Congress, was ostensibly the "honest broker." But Bismarck saw beyond Berlin. He saw the rivalries of Austria and Russia in the Balkans, their bitterness and their overlapping ambitions, especially in Serbia, Bosnia, and Herzegovina. He saw that the frail Three Emperors' League, formed in 1873 by Germany, Russia, and Austria as a counterweight to a France that might one day revive, was in fact broken. Germany would have to choose between Austria and Russia. Bismarck turned to Austria. Usually he supported Disraeli at Berlin. Thus, despite his later methods of reinsurance, he gained for Germany the long ill-will of the Russians. In 1879 Germany and Austria formed the Dual Alliance. Russia was isolated on the east; France was alone in the west. It was Bismarck's policy to keep them apart and friendless.

The Congress of Berlin changed the Treaty of San Stephano. Macedonia was returned to Turkey, despite the objection of Macedonians and their fellow Slavs and Christians in the Balkans. Bulgaria was divided into two autonomous parts. Although Bosnia and Herze-

govina remained nominally Turkish the administrative control of these
two provinces was given to Austria, ancient enemy of the dismayed and
angry Serbs. Russia agreed not to fortify Batum. By a treaty with Turkey Britain guaranteed the defense of the Sultan's Asiatic territories
and took control of Cyprus, the isle of Venus and the city of Aphrodite.

The Congress of Berlin was an important step towards the First
World War. The frictions to which its settlements gave rise mounted
steadily in importance during the following thirty-six years. At the time,
however, the veil of the future concealed this fact. If men are a little
lower than the angels, they are also a little less reliable than the minor
prophets. Disraeli returned to England in triumph. He had protected
the interests of England and avoided war. He had brought, he said,
"peace with honor." "High and low," wrote Queen Victoria, "the country is delighted, except Mr. Gladstone, who is frantic."

IMPERIAL POLICY

John Stuart Mill once described the British Empire as "a vast
system of outdoor relief for the upper classes." He meant that one main
function of the Empire was to provide jobs for the aristocrats. But by
the last quarter of the nineteenth century it was clear that this Liberal
idea of Empire was yielding before the trumpets of the new Imperialism
of Disraeli and the calculations of the merchants and financiers. The
long depression (1873–1885) helped to turn the eyes of bankers, industrialists, and commercial men towards the colonies. Prosperity might
be restored, they felt, by the expansion of markets within the Empire.
Colonies, surely, were profitable fields for investment capital; sources
of raw material for Britain's factories; export markets for British goods.
The idea was old, much older than the Liberal opinion that the colonies
might well be encouraged to go their own way to early and complete
independence. To this cold economic approach to Imperialism Disraeli
added the romantic and emotional appeal of the new Toryism. He spoke
of the destiny of the British race and "the sublime instincts of an ancient
people." His aggressive steps to protect the life line to India were the
translation into action of a philosophy he had held for a long time. England was almost ready to support him in his vigorous and spirited
imperial policy; almost, but not quite.

Disraeli's methods pushed England into several minor wars. In
Afghanistan, for example, the old fear of Russian pressure and infiltration impelled Disraeli, always mindful of the importance of the northern bastions of India, to demand that the Afghans accept a British
resident agent who would in fact control the external affairs of their
country. When the proposal was refused, British troops compelled its
acceptance. After the troops returned to India the Afghans murdered
the British agent and his companions. Thereupon the British sent a
punitive expedition northwards. To many Englishmen the whole pro-

cedure appeared to be rather unscrupulous. Gladstone said: "Remember that the sanctity of life in the hill villages of Afghanistan, among the winter snows, is as inviolable, in God's eyes, as your own." The weapon of moral indignation was Gladstone's greatest. In these years of Bismarck's cynical activities it seemed to the Liberals that the same virus was insidiously infecting British policy. The threat to Liberal idealism was clear; more than that, the unhealthy sullying of England's soul must be stopped.

In South Africa England became involved in one war with the Dutch settlers, or Boers, and a second with the Zulus. There had been a long tale of friction between Briton and Boer after the British acquired Cape Colony in 1815. Shortly after the abolition of slavery in 1833 many Boers began to trek northward and westward out of Cape Colony. They founded the Transvaal and Orange Free State, which they claimed were beyond British control. In 1852 the Transvaal and in 1854 the Orange Free State were recognized by Britain as virtually independent states. However, in 1876 Lord Carnarvon, colonial secretary, decided that difficulties between the British colonies and the Transvaal could easily be ended if the Boers would agree to come under the British flag. Sir Theophilus Shepstone went beyond his orders and declared the annexation of the Transvaal despite the objections of the Boers. "If Cyprus and the Transvaal were as valuable as they are valueless," said Gladstone, "I would repudiate them because they are obtained by means dishonorable to the character of this country."

By 1879 the support at first given to Disraeli was being withdrawn. The English public was not yet convinced of the wisdom or utility of this ranging interference and these costly wars. Gladstone, who had retired from the leadership of the Liberals, could not resist an opportunity made for his talents. He took to the platform. This imperialism, he declared, had been carried too far. "The annexation of the Transvaal," he asserted, "is the invasion of a free people." Through the Scottish constituency of Midlothian he went. Thousands came to hear the "Grand Old Man." He spoke of the opposing moralities of the Liberals and Conservatives. Like a prophet of old, he called upon Britain to return from what he insisted was an evil path. In speeches of evangelical fire he implored the people to break the idols in the temple of Baal and to vote for the Liberal party. "The end of this Government has arrived. Our great Liberal party will then turn its eyes from the hills of Afghanistan and act to remove the sorry grievances that trouble our domestic scene."

To Gladstone, "the social forces moving on in their might and majesty" made certain the triumph of middle class Liberalism. To Disraeli, ill in London with asthma, bronchitis, and Bright's disease, it was all "drenching rhetoric." But the Liberals won the election of 1880. Disraeli at once resigned. Gladstone returned from retirement to become prime minister for the second time. On April 19, 1881, Disraeli died. He had won and wielded great political power; his name is probably the greatest of the undisputed chiefs of the Conservative party. Two years after his death the Primrose League was founded in his honor as a social cult and a Conservative political association. The founders of the League employed an elaborate and romantic symbolism, a hierarchy of medieval titles, a complexity of machinery. There were the Knights, singing the "Song of the Primrose Knights," and the Dames (the Liberals called them "filthy witches").

The purposes and program of the League were clear and simple. Its members followed the ideals of Conservatism, the principles of Disraeli. They organized Conservative opinion for election purposes. A barrage of pamphlets rolled from their central depots. All through England these preaching friars of the Conservative faith investigated and reported local sentiment. Exuberantly they spoke of the eternal and splendid Empire that had smote a pathway to the world's end. Into the counties they brought lectures, magic lanterns, wax works, dancing, tableaux, community singing, travelling libraries, and talks on health followed by a fruit supper. Beams of bright light came into the slow dullness of village evenings. The Liberals might denounce these "Primrose League orgies" but they were powerful instruments of Conservative propaganda.

Meanwhile the task of Gladstone was to reverse the foreign and Imperial policies of Disraeli. The new Liberal government was apparently to be a government of social reform, of international morality, of idealism. How singularly unsuccessful Gladstone was in changing the methods of Disraeli the following chapter will show. Gladstone, most reluctantly, was to become an Empire builder.

Chapter 33

THE IMPERIAL ADVENTURE

THE ENGLISH SPIRIT, 1880–1900

IN late Victorian England the minds of Englishmen turned with enthusiasm towards expansion. Nearly a million square miles of territory were added to the British Empire between 1880 and 1900. Bound to their humble tasks at home, the miner, the clerk, and the tenant farmer shared a vicarious satisfaction in the success of their fellow Britons abroad. Although personal ambitions might be frustrated there was emotional consolation in the collective Imperial adventure. England would take up the burden imposed upon the white man to bring civilization and the lamp of Christianity to benighted natives in distant lands. To the service of this lofty ideal all men could come. The romantic and mystical elements in the growth of Imperialism should never be lightly regarded. Symbols are always important to man whatever the cause may be. In this case they were the Queen, the Flag, the Fleet, and the Empire.

Armies of journalists wrote romantic tales of the adventures of the builders of Empire in the far-flung posts beyond Suez. "The fiction filling our monthly magazines," complained Herbert Spencer, "has been mainly sanguinary." The patriotism of the press was unrestrained. Nor were the pens of the scholars and the statesmen idle. Sir Charles Dilke published his *Problems of Greater Britain*; Sir John Seeley, his *Expansion of England*. Men of letters wrote of the Imperial destiny. The books of Robert Louis Stevenson were eagerly read by thousands. A greater multitude read and quoted the works of Rudyard Kipling. Because the motives of literary criticism are often obscure and combative the achievements of Kipling have not been adequately or objectively measured. Often he expressed his emotions with a stucco music-hall facility; he relied heavily on the Jacobean translation of the Psalms and the simple litany of the blaspheming soldier; he wrote with gusto of the laws of the pack and the craft; he displayed his class feeling; he praised extravagantly efficiency and authority; his Toryism was

649

partly swank and swagger; blood was more important than intellect. For his contemporaries the important fact was that he carried the public imagination to the outer edges of Mercator's projection. It became his high mission to convince Englishmen that those who knew only the little island of England knew little of England's glory. From Canada to Mandalay there was the long trail of Empire.

In 1887 further impetus was given to the tide of emotion when Queen Victoria presided over a jubilee held to celebrate the completion of her fiftieth year on the throne. In that year, too, an Imperial Conference of Empire statesmen was held in London. Ten years later there was another great jubilee. As European nations moved forward in competition for colonies and empire the Conservative Joseph Chamberlain declared: "The day of small kingdoms with their petty jealousies has passed. The future is with great Empires and there is no greater Empire than the British Empire. . . . You cannot make omelettes without breaking eggs; you cannot destroy the practices of barbarism, of slavery, of superstition without using force. . . . I maintain that our rule does bring happiness and prosperity and peace to those that never knew those blessings before."

At the same time there arose other Imperial ideas and movements. There was, for example, the Imperial Federation League (1884) whose offshoots ran all over the Empire. The Royal Colonial Institute, founded in 1868, began to grow strong and to flourish only later in the century. Some of these movements "dissolved like Canadian ice and blew away like Australian sand." Although others remained their glory swiftly dimmed in the twentieth century. When the great queen died the Imperial adventure ended, or almost so. It ended because the world in which Imperialism had been possible and desirable was rapidly passing. As later chapters will show, the chastening effects of the Boer War, the demands for social reform at home, the clouds prophetic of war, all joined with other forces to give a new thrust to the directions of the new century.

Inextricably united with pressures of sentiment, prestige, politics, and missionary zeal is the economic aspect of Imperialism. European powers grasped for colonial possessions in the late nineteenth century because they wanted more raw materials, more open markets, and more opportunities to invest and protect surplus capital. The demands of industrialism were inexorable; men of business knew what they wanted and why. Cecil Rhodes stated his opinion quite precisely: "These islands can only support six millions out of their thirty-six millions. We cannot afford to part with one inch of the world's surface which affords a free and open market to the manufactures of our countrymen." To some other nations, especially envious Germany, it seemed that England wanted to bring the whole of the unclaimed world into the British Empire. "They say Christ, but they mean cotton." Thus a German author wrote: "Greedily as an octopus, the Briton spreads his merchant fleet, and would close the realm of Amphitrite the free as if it were his own house." Such suspicion cast its weight into the scales to add to the causes of the First World War.

At the same time, the Empire became more significant as a frontier for thousands of Englishmen. Because this was so, the course of Imperial history was changed. Unowned property in Australia and Canada waited for the paupers of Lancashire; when they could emigrate they left England; with them they took their "God Save the Queen" and their memories of "the Old Country." Their sons were born far from England and their first loyalties were to the homes their fathers found. As the British Commonwealth developed the new worlds were again called in to redress the balance of the old.

These, succinctly stated, are the major themes in the complex mosaic of the years of Imperialism. Not all Englishmen, certainly not Liberals, agreed that the methods or ends of Imperialism were desirable. For example, Sir William Vernon Harcourt scorned the idea of "occupying deserts peopled by savages" and confessed that he "never contemplated a large map without feelings of dismay." The Irish regarded the Empire as the result of fraud, force, and exploitation. For most Englishmen, however, the definition given by Cecil Rhodes was sufficient: "Imperialism is philanthropy, plus five per cent."

THE GLADSTONE GOVERNMENT, 1880–1885

In the beginning of the new chapter of Imperialism Britain advanced with reluctance and hesitation down the road of Empire. When strategic and economic interests were clearly challenged steps had to be taken against defiant pressure and outright blackmail. The result was a series of British political annexations of territories that otherwise would have been seized by Germany, Belgium, France or other powers. During the second ministry of Gladstone this process was foreshadowed by the fact that the Liberals were harassed by urgent problems in South Africa, Egypt, the Sudan, Afghanistan, and Ireland. To none of these problems did they find an answer satisfactory to themselves, the Conservatives, or the British public.

Gladstone had been elected in 1880 on his indictment of Disraeli's policy. He had denounced the annexation of the Transvaal. But after he came to power he did nothing. The angered Boers revolted. General Colley and a hundred British troops were killed at Majuba Hill. This disaster, and other defeats, brought a public cry for vengeance. Gladstone refused to yield to popular pressure. In 1881 he gave the Transvaal internal independence under British suzerainty. Three years later Britain abandoned her claim to suzerainty and insisted only that the external affairs of the Transvaal should be under British control. Despite the mandate of 1880 this apparent retreat in the face of Boer recalcitrance galled the public. Gladstone's political position was badly undercut. The Boers regarded his action as surrender, not magnanimity. Soon the search for diamonds brought more outlanders to dig in the blue clay. Other invaders came to toil along the fifty-mile length of a great gold reef. It was no wonder that the Boers, mindful of Majuba Hill, stubbornly clinging to the Bible, the oxcart, and the ancient ways, were ready to take up arms again at the end of the century.

Thus the Liberals had reversed Disraeli's policy in South Africa. It was less easy to do likewise in Egypt. The spendthrift khedive Ismail, who had earlier been compelled to sell his Suez Canal shares, continued to spend swiftly all the money he could borrow abroad. When he could not pay the interest on his debts the British and French took charge of the national finances to protect their bondholders. In 1881 an Egyptian named Arabi headed a rebellion against the invertebrate khedive Tewfik who had replaced Ismail and the foreigners who had assumed financial control. Many Europeans were killed, especially in Alexandria. France at first agreed to help Britain subdue the rebels but later refused to do so. In 1882 Britain completed the task alone. Over a thousand Egyptians were killed. There was fire and looting. Arabi was banished to Ceylon. Gladstone said that when order was restored British troops would be withdrawn.

But order was not restored. In 1883 the Arabs in the Egyptian province of the Sudan revolted against the tyrannical misrule of their khedive and his agents. Led by wild dervishes and a theologian who called himself the Mahdi, or prophet, they carved a bloody road through Egyptian forces. At Shekan ten thousand Egyptians and their British officers were wiped out by forty thousand tribesmen. British authorities in Cairo informed the British cabinet that the Sudan would be lost unless help was sent from England. The cabinet hesitated. Gladstone had strong opinions: "I look upon the possession of the Sudan as the calamity of Egypt. It has been a drain on her treasury; it has been a drain on her men. It has been estimated that 100,000 Egyptians have laid down their lives in endeavouring to maintain that barren conquest."

In 1884 General Charles "Chinese" Gordon was sent to Khartum, the capital of the Sudan, to speed the evacuation of the British and Egyptians. Gordon, who had earlier been governor of the Sudan under the khedive, declared that "the Sudan is a useless possession; ever was and ever will be so. I think Her Majesty's Government are fully justified in recommending the evacuation inasmuch as the sacrifices necessary towards securing a good government would be too onerous to admit of any such attempt being made. Her Majesty's Government will now leave the Sudanese as God has placed them." But after Gordon reached Khartum he exceeded his orders, for reasons which are obscure. He delayed his return to Egypt. Khartum was cut off by the forces of the

Mahdi. The vacillating Gladstone government, anxious to avoid further responsibilities in Africa, delayed a decision too long. When a British relief expedition reached Khartum on January 28, 1885, it found a silent city. Two days before the forces of the Mahdi had flooded through the gates. Gordon and his garrison were dead.

When the dark news reached England the government was formally censured in the house of lords for their failure to support Gordon soon enough; in the house of commons they escaped a similar reprimand by a narrow margin. The shadow of procrastination and alleged negligence dimmed the prospects of a Liberal victory in the next election. In 1885 British troops were withdrawn from the Sudan. They were not long absent. Eleven years later the khedive decided to use his reorganized Egyptian army to reconquer the lost province. Under the command of the British General Kitchener an expedition accomplished this task with the victory at Omdurman in 1898.

Meanwhile in Afghanistan Gladstone honored the spirit of the Midlothian campaign. The Liberals said that the Afghans must be kept in friendly alliance with Britain. Then Afghanistan would be a buffer state protecting India from Russian designs. To those who argued that even a strong Afghanistan could not block Russia Gladstone replied that the alternative would be British conquest of Afghanistan in an immoral, difficult, and costly war. So British troops withdrew in 1881. Afghanistan was to be independent. Three years later, when Britain was busy in the Sudan, Russia began to occupy strategic points in northern Afghanistan. The Gladstone cabinet, acting with unusual speed and unity, forced Russia to submit her claims to the arbitration of the king of Denmark. The fact that Russia obtained but little territory as a result of the arbitration decision did not decrease British fears about what the Russian plans for tomorrow might be. Was the Gladstonian diplomacy as wise as it was apparently moral? Could Afghanistan continue indefinitely to exist as a buffer state, as an arena in which British and Russian agents sat cheek by jowl to advance the opposing interests of London and Moscow?

The clouded problems of South Africa, Egypt, the Sudan, and Afghanistan were only briefly of importance to Gladstone. Far different, and more difficult, was the continuing Irish question, with all its complicating factors. Weltering in bitterness, poverty, and turmoil, Ireland had cause for grievance; but the responsibility for Irish woe was not entirely English. Between the English and Irish people there had always been a great gulf fixed; through several centuries' history each had been too stern in its judgment of the other. In his second ministry Gladstone was challenged, not by rick burnings or land legislation proposals, but by a blunt demand from southern Ireland for Irish self-government. Since the union of 1801 the imperial Parliament had passed laws for Ireland, often without seeking Irish advice or consent. The hundred Irish members in Parliament were powerless except when their votes were needed by Liberals or Conservatives. Despite their insistence on Ireland's claims they found that words were not enough. And to no avail the Irish at home bayed across the Irish Sea. O'Connell had earlier demanded that the union be repealed. In 1871 the Home Government Association, later called the Home Rule League, was formed to press for the control of Irish domestic affairs by the people of Ireland. Soon there were Home Rule advocates elected to Parliament. In the election of 1880 they carried sixty of the hundred Irish seats.

The first leader of the Home Rule party was Isaac Butt; he died in 1879. The second was the enigmatic and unsociable Charles Stewart Parnell, president of the Land League and soon to be "the uncrowned king of Ireland." Parnell was a Protestant Irish landowner; his father was of English ancestry; his mother was the daughter of an American admiral. Parnell hated England. He embodied the Irish traditions of dreams and rebellion. He believed that force, and force alone, would gain for Ireland the freedom so long denied. Talk should be helped by dynamite and guns. His strictly disciplined followers adhered to the letter of his cold and military instructions. They must, he declared, paralyze Parliament by obstructing its normal procedure. To the exasperation of Gladstone, the ordered progress of debate was frequently disturbed by long delays or interrupted by Parnell's stentorian motions for adjournment. The formidable Parnell also called for agrarian disturbances in Ireland; for the payment of what the tenants thought was a fair rent, no more. In 1880 the potato crop was only about one-third the normal yield; nevertheless the Irish tenant farmers who could not pay their rent were often evicted by English landlords or their agents. Under the aegis of the Land League crimes and outrage increased; there was wild disorder. The currents of charity were frozen.

The Liberal government passed a coercion bill. Then it passed a new Land Act based upon the Irish Land League's demand for "the three F's": fixity of tenure; free sale of tenants' interests to other tenants; and fair rent, to be decided by the courts. Despite this concession to "the agrarian greed of the peasantry" the Irish disorders continued. The Gladstone cabinet then decided that "the resources of civilization were not exhausted" and arrested Parnell. After long negotiation the government made a compromise agreement called the "Kilmainham treaty." The terms provided that all Irish suspects would be released from prison on condition that Parnell and the Irish Land League would try to abate Irish violence. There were also some ambiguous and general utterances about future cooperation between Home Rule Irishmen and the Liberals. It was hoped that compromise might kill conspiracy.

But this agreement never came into effect. In May, 1882, the implacable hostility of southern Ireland was given all the emphasis of atrocity. Lord Frederick Cavendish, the newly appointed chief secretary for Ireland, and Mr. Burke, the undersecretary, were both murdered in Phoenix Park in Dublin by a gang calling themselves the Invincibles. Parnell had no hand in this crime. Gladstone had earlier freed him from prison and amended the Land Act in accordance with Irish suggestions. The coercive terms of a new Crimes Act, rigorously enforced, cut down disorders. Nevertheless, it was quite clear that Irish society could not be made into a model of peace and contentment by changes in the land laws, by coercion or strenuous rule, or by the middle road of compromise. The southern Catholic Irish were determined to have Home Rule. But the six Protestant counties of Ulster in northern Ireland, fearful of the southern Catholics, obstinately insisted on maintaining the Act of Union; hence they were called unionists. Thus the legacy of the past, the internal divisions of Ireland, the obstructions of the land-owning, Anglican house of lords, the Liberal schisms and Conservative doubts combined to bring deadlock. Home Rule, disputed and postponed, remained to convulse society and politics with passion and intensity.

In domestic affairs the second Gladstone ministry carried through a considerable body of legislation. The titles of some of the acts of Parliament will suggest their content: the Bankruptcy Act, the Electric Lighting Act, the Agricultural Holdings Act, the Employers' Liability Act, the Ground Game Act. In 1884 the Representation of the People Act provided for a further reform of Parliament by giving the vote to the agricultural workers. This was done by extending to the counties the "household qualification" established for the boroughs by the Act of 1867. About two million voters were added to the register. After 1884 almost all males who possessed or occupied property had the right to vote.

The Redistribution of Seats Act of 1885 provided that all boroughs with fewer than 15,000 inhabitants ceased to elect members to Parliament and were merged with the counties. Two-member constituencies with a population of less than 50,000 were deprived of one member. Only the universities and twenty-two boroughs retained two members each. The rest became single-member constituencies, approximately equal in population. County and borough boundaries were changed considerably. Although representation in proportion to population was not completely achieved the act of 1885 was a significant step in that direction.

About most of the foreign and domestic policies of the government there had been tempestuous dissension in the cabinet. Some members resigned; others threatened to do so. From 1880 to 1905 the Liberals were to be continuously weakened by disunion. Thus Gladstone was faced by the danger of rupture within his party and by attacks from his opponents outside. In June, 1885, his ministry was defeated on the budget, and resigned. No government, united or not, could have stood the blows to national and imperial prestige suffered by Gladstone's second administration.

THE DEFEAT OF HOME RULE

The successor of Disraeli as leader of the Conservatives was Lord Salisbury, an able and resolute representative of the great Cecil family. After the resignation of Gladstone, Salisbury reluctantly took office pending the registration of the voters enfranchised under the recent Representation of the People Act and the holding of a general election. In the election of December, 1885, the Liberals carried 335 seats, the Conservatives 249, and the Irish Nationalist or Home Rule party 86. Thus the Irish Nationalists held the balance of power. Meanwhile Gladstone had finally decided to grant Home Rule if he could carry the Liberals with him. Hence Parnell and the Nationalists supported Gladstone when he became prime minister for the third time at the age of seventy-seven.

The consequences of Gladstone's decision were deplorable; for his own party they were tragic. He introduced a bill proposing to exclude the Irish members from the Parliament at Westminster and to set up a bicameral, elective, Irish parliament at Dublin. Ireland was to contribute about seven per cent of the cost of Imperial expenditure. Control of foreign and colonial affairs, the army and navy, coinage, trade and navigation, customs and excise, and certain other matters was to be retained by the Imperial parliament. The right of veto was reserved to the crown. Upon this Home Rule Bill the Liberals split completely. Some opponents of Home Rule said the Irish were not fitted for self-government. Others said the Catholic majority would persecute the Protestant minority. "Home Rule meant Rome Rule." Still others said an independent Ireland might betray England in time of danger.

 Ninety-three Liberals, including Joseph Chamberlain, John Bright, and Lord Hartington, voted against their leader's proposals. At the same time Lord Randolph Churchill helped to fan the flames of opposition to Home Rule in Protestant northern Ireland. The slogan of the Ulstermen was "Ulster will fight and Ulster will be right." Gladstone's bill was rejected by a vote of 343 to 313. His faithful followers never forgave the defection of those Liberals who had abandoned the ship when all were needed to man the guns. These Liberal Unionists, so called because they supported the union of England and Ireland, left the Liberal ranks forever. Most of them, including Joseph Chamberlain, later joined the Conservatives. Gladstone's decision had shattered his party and, except for one interval, the Liberals remained out of power for twenty years. Forty years before Peel had divided the Tories with similar consequences on the bitter question of the Corn Laws.

Another national election in the summer of 1886 decisively proved that England was against Home Rule. Gladstone's third government then resigned and Lord Salisbury and the Conservatives returned to hold office for six years. So far as Irish affairs were concerned the turbulence continued. Arthur James Balfour, Salisbury's nephew, became Irish secretary. With the approval of his colleagues he secured the passage of a repressive Crimes Act to check Irish violence. "What Ireland wants," said Balfour, "is government, a government that does not flinch, that does not vary, a government that she cannot hope to beat down by agitations at Westminster."

At the same time Balfour extended earlier plans to transfer ownership of land to the tenants. By the Ashbourne Act of 1885 the British government had earmarked £5,000,000 as a loan fund from which tenants could borrow money for the purchase of land, repaying the loan at four per cent interest over a period of forty-nine years. Balfour increased the amount of the loan fund. Within six years over 25,000 tenants borrowed nearly £10,000,000. By 1912 loans totalling about £75,000,000 had been made and nearly 7,000,000 acres had been purchased by the tenants from their landlords. Further successful steps were taken to improve economic conditions generally. But Home Rule was not to be killed by either coercion or kindness.

Meanwhile the Irish Nationalists were indefatigable. In 1887 the *Times* published a series of articles entitled "Parnellism and Crime" which included letters alleged to have been written by Parnell. These letters implicated him in the Phoenix Park murders. A special judicial commission cleared Parnell of the charge. The letters were forgeries. Thus vindicated, Parnell's credit rose. But it did not rise for long. There were revelations about his private life and his relations with Mrs. O'Shea. He was named in a divorce suit and his guilt was clear. His Catholic party angrily divided. The Nonconformist conscience of the Liberals was offended. Gladstone could no longer work with the Irish leader. Although Parnell, humiliated and powerless, died in 1891, the breach in his party was not fully bridged until 1899 by his successor, John Redmond.

Although the six years of Salisbury's second ministry were rather barren in domestic legislation there were a few important internal reforms. One was the passage of the Local Government Act of 1888. This act entirely changed the basis of local government by transferring the administrative authority from the justices of the peace to elected county councils. The justices of the peace kept their judicial functions: "Nothing in this act shall affect the powers, duties, and liabilities of justices of the peace as conservators of the peace." The Technical Instruction Act of 1889 authorized local councils to provide technical education facilities. By these measures, as well as others involving social reforms in agriculture and industry, the Tory democracy of Disraeli continued.

The first section of this chapter explained that the last years of the nineteenth century were particularly important in the history of the British Empire. While the islands at home were disturbed by the Home Rule battles and pleased by the onward march of domestic reform the Imperial idea was shooting through the national consciousness. In the decade from 1880 to 1890 Disraeli, Carlyle, Matthew Arnold, and Anthony Trollope died; Newman and Tennyson were soon to follow. Whistler's butterfly and Oscar Wilde's lily in one sense marked the last chapter of an age that was passing. Likewise the emergence of Imperialism at the end of the century prepared the way for a new era in a mutable world.

THE PARTITION OF AFRICA

It was in Africa that the European powers fought their most dramatic battles for empire in a kind of closed international experiment. This continent had long remained untroubled by invading Europeans. Africa has almost no natural harbors; there are few bays or gulfs except the Gulf of Guinea. The rivers are seldom navigable. There are no continental crossroads; the wastes of the dividing Sahara stretch wide and formidable. Through great areas no pack animals can go because the tsetse fly brings death.

In the late eighteenth century Portuguese Jesuits discovered the source of the Blue Nile; several men probed into the northern interior from the Red Sea, Somaliland, the Nile, and Zanzibar. In the south the Dutch moved into the land about the Cape of Good Hope. Mungo Park discovered and explored the Niger. But exploration advanced only slowly until the nineteenth century. In 1823 Hugh Clapperton discovered Lake Chad; he and Major Dixon Derham explored parts of West Africa. The Scotsman Alexander Mackay scouted through the long miles of the Uganda country. About 1856 John Speke and Richard Burton found Lake Tanganyika.

Earlier, in 1841, David Livingstone had come out from Scotland as a medical missionary. He was shocked to find that Africa was still a human reservoir for slave labor. So far as the British Empire was concerned the slave trade had been "utterly abolished, prohibited and declared to be unlawful" in 1807; in 1833 slavery had been ended throughout the Empire. But Livingstone found that a stream of slaves flowed from the Lakes area through the great slave depot at Zanzibar to the markets of the world outside. "All I can add in my loneliness," Livingstone wrote, "is may Heaven's rich blessings come down on everyone, American, English, or Turk, who will help to heal the open sore of the world." Besides the abolition of slavery Livingstone sought to bring Christianity to the people; to open good trade routes; to develop trade with the natives. Wide interest was roused when the journalist Henry Morton Stanley searched and found the famous missionary whom the world thought lost. But Livingstone remained at his tasks in Africa. When he died the natives carried him 1,500 miles to the British consul at Zanzibar; from there his body was brought to lie in Westminster Abbey. This was in 1874.

A jealous competition for colonies in Africa now began among the European powers. The speed of this colonial scramble can best be described by pointing out how and when Africa was divided. In 1878 King Leopold II of Belgium created an international company to de-

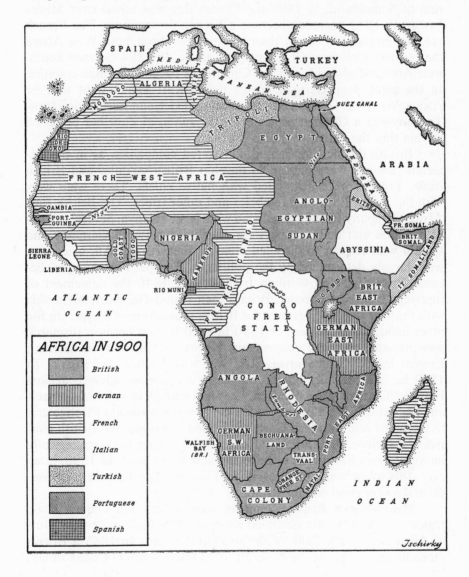

velop the Congo basin. Leopold was quite unscrupulous. The native Bantus were so cruelly degraded and massacred that the civilized world protested. In 1879 the Congo Free State was created; in 1908 it became a Belgian colony. Meanwhile the Portuguese enlarged their holdings into the protectorates of Mozambique and Angola. In 1885 Italy occupied Eritrea; in 1892, a part of Somaliland.

France and Germany entered the contest with energy and skill. In 1880 the French took over a portion of the Congo; in 1881 Tunis was added to Algiers as a protectorate; in 1888 France occupied a section of Somaliland; in 1896 the French flag was raised over Madagascar; in 1912 Morocco became a French protectorate. The French colonial empire was larger than all Europe. Throughout West Africa the German Colonization Society was active. In 1884 German Southwest Africa, Togoland, and the Cameroons became German colonies. In the same year German agents under Karl Peters went to East Africa. When the German emperor declared German East Africa (now Tanganyika) a German protectorate the sultan of Zanzibar protested in vain that the natives were his subjects.

Britain did not lag behind. Chartered companies, as in the sixteenth century, were formed to develop British colonies and British trade. Treaties were negotiated with native chiefs. There were wars with the Zulus, Basutos, Matabeles and other tribes. The British East Africa Company (1888) developed what is now Kenya. Several treaties of partition and delimitation were concluded between Germany and Britain with respect to disputed areas in East Africa. All, of course, were largely determined by the politics of Europe. For example, because Britain wanted German friendship in 1886 the agreement of that year favored Germany. Britain then feared Germany might side with France, who was pressing for British evacuation of Egypt. On the other hand, the agreement of 1890 favored Britain because Bismarck was prepared to make concessions. He was afraid that the German Empire might become involved in war with France and Russia. In 1889 he had formally offered Salisbury a defensive alliance against France. "Germany," he declared, "has had enough of colonial quarrels and flag-hoisting." So Britain ceded the North Sea island of Heligoland to Germany and in return Germany ceased to dispute the British control of Zanzibar. For Germany Heligoland was later to be strategically important as a naval base close to the new Kiel Canal. In 1890, however, this event was not foreseen in London. The bargain was considered a very good one for Britain.

Meanwhile a British company moved into the Guinea coast region. In 1884 Britain occupied a section of Somaliland on the Gulf of Aden and on the flank of the road to the East. In 1885 a British protectorate was established over Bechuanaland, north of Cape Colony.

The Royal Niger Company (1886) extended its control of Nigeria. In 1894 Uganda became a protectorate. Thus the number of Britain's tropical colonies increased. They increased not only in Africa but also in the East. The conquest of Burma was completed in 1886. Many Pacific islands came under the British flag. A protectorate was established over the Malay peninsula, north of Singapore. British New Guinea was annexed; colonies were developed in Borneo. In the meantime the French were in Indo-China, Cochin China, Tonkin, Annam, and part of Cambodia. New Guinea was recognized as a German protectorate in 1884; the two largest Samoan islands became German in 1899; other islands were purchased by Germany from Spain.

In South Africa the greatest of British Empire builders was Cecil John Rhodes (1853–1902). In the Kimberley diamond mines he had made a fortune; he was a member of an international syndicate that controlled the gold mines. Rhodes had a remarkable faith in the future of the British Empire. He dreamed of a belt of British territory stretching from the Cape to Cairo and bound together by a great railway. Because he was more than a dreamer he organized the British South Africa Company for quite practical purposes in 1889. One purpose was to occupy the territory north of Bechuanaland and the Transvaal which was soon known as Rhodesia. By this northward stride the Boer republics of the Orange Free State and the Transvaal were surrounded. Thus British imperial impatience moved another step towards the conflict with Dutch obstinacy which came in the Boer War at the end of the century.

GLADSTONE AND LORD ROSEBERY

Lord Salisbury ended his six dramatic years of power in 1892. The Liberals and Irish Nationalists emerged from a national election with more seats than the Conservatives. Defeated by a majority of forty in the house, Salisbury resigned. Gladstone, now eighty-three years of age, became prime minister for the fourth time. He was handicapped by an unstable majority divided into different groups with different wishes. Few toes could be trodden upon. Hence the members of the new cabinet, perforce selected from these groups, contained men of widely separated views. They disputed about the long series of reform proposals in the so-called Newcastle program proclaimed in 1891 by the Liberal party caucus. What reforms were desirable? The cabinet agreed upon a few. Which of these should be attempted first? They could not decide.

Under pressure from the Irish Nationalists the new ministry immediately suspended the operation of Balfour's coercive Crimes Act by royal proclamation. Five months later Gladstone, indomitable as ever, entered the lists to battle for the old cause of Home Rule. He introduced a second Home Rule Bill, similar in its terms to the first except for the provision that eighty Irish members would sit in the Imperial Parliament with the right to vote only on Imperial isues. Debates and amendments continued through eighty-five sittings of Parliament. For example, it was agreed that the Irish members should have the same status as other members and vote on all questions. In its final form the bill passed the house of commons. The house of lords rejected it by a vote of 419 to 41. Gladstone then wanted to fight another election at once on the issue, but his colleagues convinced him that the Liberals would be defeated. A strong mandate would be needed to override the mighty power of the house of lords. It might be given one day by the people, but not in 1893 and not on the question of Home Rule. To these strong arguments Gladstone yielded. His last crusade had failed.

In March, 1894, the Grand Old Man resigned as leader of the Liberal party. Local fights were springing up among his supporters in the house. Ambitious young Liberals were restive; some were impatient of discipline; the long years of apprenticeship served by Gladstone were not for the young men of a later age. Some of his colleagues wanted naval expansion; others were becoming more Empire-minded than their leader thought they should be. And Gladstone was eighty-five years old; his sight was darkening; his deafness increased; he was weary. With slow steps he left the house of commons which he had entered at a faster pace sixty-two years before. In 1898, on the eve of a new age that he had helped to make possible, William Ewart Gladstone died. He would not have understood the twentieth century. In it his values have found but narrow room.

Lord Rosebery now became prime minister and Sir William Harcourt led the Liberals in the house of commons. Rosebery was the chief of those imperialist Liberals who had been the bane of Gladstone. Because Rosebery inherited Gladstone's difficulties but not his personal influence the task of holding a majority together was very heavy. Gladstone had been able to obtain only one important piece of legislation in the previous two years: the Parish Councils Act of 1894 which introduced the elective principle into the small parish units of government. Likewise Rosebery was able to pass but one significant measure: the Budget of 1894 which applied the graduation principle to succession duties and provided for identical legacy duties on real and personal property. His government promised licensing reform, the abolition of plural voting, the disestablishment of the Anglican Church in Wales; but these reforms, and others, would never have been carried through; the Rosebery government was no stronger than its most lukewarm supporters. At last Rosebery, slowly discouraged, took advantage of a minor defeat on a snatch vote to resign. In the circumstances he saw that no good would come of clinging to precarious power. This was in

June, 1895. The Conservatives now returned. Their gaze, as usual, turned abroad.

SALISBURY AND THE UNITED STATES

The first serious problem in foreign affairs came swiftly. An undetermined boundary between British Guiana and Venezuela gave rise to the Venezuelan Affair of 1895. Venezuela, claiming wide regions near the mouth of the Orinoco and much of the backlands where undiscovered gold was believed to lie, refused to submit the boundary dispute to arbitration lest a compromise be reached that would give her less than half of British Guiana. Diplomatic relations with England were broken off and a clever campaign invoking the Monroe Doctrine was launched in the United States. President Cleveland, pressed by elements in both American parties, approved a ten-thousand-word note to the British government asserting that Britain was violating the Monroe Doctrine and requesting the submission of the case to the United States for arbitration.

After four months' delay Salisbury replied that the Monroe Doctrine of 1823 was not applicable to the situation of 1895; that the Doctrine was not international law; that it could not be invoked for "the determination of the frontier of a British possession which had belonged to the Throne of England long before the Republic of Venezuela came into existence." In December, 1895, President Cleveland urged Congress to appoint a boundary commission and to defend its decision "by all the resources of the United States." In vain it was pointed out that the United States could not protect Venezuela against British naval power. Indeed, at that time, the United States was almost defenseless along her own coasts. But stock markets crashed and war with Britain threatened.

Salisbury did not want war; nor did the English public. Soon the counsels of steadier minds prevailed in the United States. Both Britain and the United States stood alone. The Continental powers were unfriendly to each; the larger Latin American republics were angered by what they regarded as interference by the United States in their domestic affairs. To the relief of thoughtful realists Britain accepted the United States' proposal to arbitrate. "Is there to be no forgiveness?" asked Lord Randolph Churchill. "Are we never to cancel old scores and begin our international bookkeeping, if I may say so, on a clean page? Let us call a truce to petty and malignant carping." In the arbitration decision the main British contentions were upheld.

From Salisbury's surrender to Cleveland's threat came a new Anglo-American understanding, filled with imponderable ingredients. It stood several strains and stresses as American manifest destiny unfolded in the next decade. It grew stronger when Britain stood forth alone in Europe as the champion of the United States in the Spanish-

American War. The British government "did not propose to take any steps which would not be acceptable to the Government of the United States." It progressed still further as the United States, committed to empire in the Pacific and the Caribbean, sought to build the Panama Canal. In 1901 Britain signed the second Hay-Pauncefote Treaty which provided for exclusive American construction of a canal and jettisoned the Clayton-Bulwer Treaty of 1850 which had stipulated that any canal would be a joint British-American enterprise; that neither would exercise exclusive control; that it would never be fortified. In the twentieth century both Britain and the United States moved more confidently towards fuller cooperation in their own interests and often in the interests of the whole world.

THE FAR EAST

England's Asiatic policy has always been largely determined by her interest in the protection of India. This governing factor was present in the decision to control the Suez Canal; to enter Egypt, Somaliland, Cyprus, Baluchistan, Burma, Malaya, and the rest; to hold Russia back from Constantinople; from Afghanistan and the approaches of the Khyber Pass; from Tibet; from the Persian Gulf. In China and the adjacent areas British power did not usually grow by outright annexations but rather by trade controls, by loans, and by various economic pressures varying from place to place in degree and in kind. This policy increased trade and influence; and it, too, helped to protect the British territorial and economic empire in the East, including India.

In the late nineteenth century 70 per cent of China's foreign trade was with Britain; British influence reached into every port and far from the coast, especially down the Yangtse River. There was no desire to annex Chinese territory; British interests were commercial. When the Sino-Japanese war (1894–1895) for the possession of Korea revealed to the world the inner weakness of the sprawling hulk of China the first object of British policy was to keep the European powers out. If they came, seeking the kind of colonial banquet table they had found in Africa, Britain would be hard put to avoid embarking on a series of annexations to hold her own. When Russia, Germany, and France demanded a revision of the Treaty of Shimonoseki (1895) which had ended the Japanese war with China Britain refused to join them. Thus she kept Japan's good will.

Nevertheless British diplomacy was heavily pressed to avoid the partition of China. Russia probed in from the north; France from the south. These countries lent money to China in return for appropriate concessions such as the right to build railways. They forced Japan to return her conquests on the mainland. When two German missionaries were killed in China Germany grasped the event to justify a step planned months before. Kaiser William II, as usual preaching the gospel of his hallowed personality, talked alternately of the "yellow peril" and the sanctity of his mission in China. Under pressure China leased the port of Kiaochow in the Shantung peninsula to Germany in 1898. Russia seized Port Arthur, earlier surrendered by Japan when Germany, France, and Russia, reluctant to see a new power in the Far East, had deprived her of the spoils of victory, insisting that China must not be dismembered.

It was now clear that British diplomacy could not stop the European invaders. So Salisbury secured Kowloon, a territorial cushion for Hong Kong, and Weihaiwei, a port strategically as well located in relation to Pekin as Kiaochow or Port Arthur. Meanwhile France obtained Kwangchow. Hoping to prevent any further territorial encroachments, Britain joined with the United States in 1899 to gain from the European powers a recognition of the "open door" policy in China. This policy was in fact applicable only to commerce; but it helped to reduce the desire for territorial aggression. The anti-Western Boxer rebellion of 1900 brought an international police force to Pekin when the "Boxers" threatened to slay all foreigners. That China was not then divided was mainly due to the deplorable areas of suspicion and envy which were increasing among the European nations. For example, the construction of the Trans-Siberian railway by Russia caused wide alarm. In 1902 Britain, fearful of Russian influence in China and desiring to strengthen her position throughout the Far East, concluded a defensive alliance with Japan. The alliance provided that if Japan were attacked by a third power as a result of her interests in Korea, Britain would remain neutral; if Britain were attacked because of her interests in China, Japan would stay neutral. If either partner should be attacked by two or more powers, the other would immediately come to the aid of her ally.

Thus, in these dramatic years, Salisbury and the Conservatives were troubled by problems from Venezuela to Pekin. One major crisis arose midway between China and Latin America: at the desert station of Fashoda in the Sudan. This time the dispute was with France.

THE FASHODA INCIDENT

When General Sir Herbert Kitchener reconquered the Sudan for the Anglo-Egyptian government at the battle of Omdurman in 1898 the value of the whole upper Nile basin was more fully recognized than in 1886. Rhodes had pushed British holdings in the south up to Rhodesia. British control of the Sudan would mean that only German East Africa blocked fulfilment of the dream of a red belt of British territory from the mouths of the Nile to Table Mountain. Rumors of French ambitions in the Sudan area had persuaded the Salisbury cabinet to act swiftly. The French were pressing eastward across French

West Africa from Lake Chad, some five hundred miles from the Sudan. About the time of the battle of Omdurman a small French expedition under Captain Marchand reached Fashoda, a key point on the White Nile about midway between Khartum and the northern boundary of British Uganda and standing athwart the north-south route. The nation that controlled Fashoda controlled the whole upper Nile region. Marchand had hoisted the French flag.

Kitchener claimed Fashoda for England. The English public, already inflamed over the Dreyfus case, were in a dangerous mood. "Who speaks of pardon? Nay, for France there's none." The French, angered by English interest in the fate of Dreyfus, which they felt was a purely domestic affair, refused to order Marchand to withdraw. When the French government delayed meeting Salisbury's formal request for the recall of Marchand both nations came close to war. Although the Irish Nationalist members of Parliament proclaimed their sympathy for France their voices were lost in the general tumult denouncing the Third Republic. After six weeks the crisis ended when France finally agreed to withdraw. The Sudan became a protectorate under Anglo-Egyptian government. The incident was closed. It was soon realized that in the face of the European situation only Germany would rejoice if Britain and France drifted into conflict. In 1904, as a part of the entente cordiale between Britain and France, France recognized the British position in Egypt and the Sudan; Britain in return acknowledged the French claims to interest in Morocco. The swift partition of Africa was drawing to a close.

PROBLEMS OF EMPIRE

At home the deep currents of English life were not visibly changed by these alarms abroad. In 1897 Queen Victoria celebrated her Diamond Jubilee; it was sixty years since she had been Lord Melbourne's pupil; it was thirty-six since she had become Prince Albert's widow. To the great Jubilee came representatives and contingents of troops from all the Empire; the French-Canadians from Quebec mingled with Dayaks from Borneo; there were eleven colonial premiers; the colorful spectrum of Empire flashed in the Jubilee processions. In 1897 the swelling tide of Imperial sentiment was in full surge, not only in England but also in the Dominions and the colonies. The Imperial bond was growing strong and tight.

The Diamond Jubilee was also the occasion of the second Colonial Conference. In this meeting, as in those of later years, discussions among the statesmen ranged over wide areas. As colonial secretary, Joseph Chamberlain explored ways to check centrifugal forces within the Empire. He proposed the creation of an Imperial Council "to which the colonies would send representative plenipotentiaries." The colonial premiers were cool to this proposal and to any idea of Imperial federation. They were content to approve the continuance of periodic conferences to discuss problems of Imperial defense, commerce, and other matters of common interest. There was, it seemed, small prospect of any new political arrangements to draw the Empire more closely together. The Dominions and colonies remained satisfied with the existing system despite the hopes of Joseph Chamberlain and the Imperial Federation League that a formal federative polity might be developed. About the problems of defense there was more agreement. Australia increased her naval contributions to £200,000 per annum; Cape Colony promised an annual contribution of £30,000. Thus the Empire helped to forge the Imperial shield. These questions of Imperial defense were discussed at length; the Empire, sprawling over a quarter of the earth's surface, has always tempted mighty robbers. Finally, careful consideration was given to a series of Imperial economic problems, particularly the important question of preferential tariffs pointing towards a greater degree of economic unity within the Empire. In 1907 it was agreed that Imperial Conferences should be held regularly every four years. Thus the Victorian period ended with a considerable advance in the realm of Imperial policy.

Meanwhile the Dominions were moving towards complete self-government. Canada had achieved responsible government in domestic affairs fifty years earlier and her stature in foreign affairs was steadily increasing. In January, 1901, the self-governing Australian colonies were united in the Commonwealth of Australia. This new federation embraced the six states of New South Wales, Victoria, Queensland, Tasmania, South Australia, and West Australia. So the new Dominion of the antipodes was created, half a world away from Britain but bound to her by the "silken ties" of language, race, culture, institutions, and sentiments. New Zealand, twelve hundred miles from Australia, retained her separate identity. As a Dominion today New Zealand is one of the most democratic nations in the world.

While these events of orderly progress were unfolding and the pride of Empire touched the lives of the British people everywhere the first great challenge to their Imperial glory was rising in the veld of South Africa. The golden age of Victoria closed in three leaden years of war. From disaster, defeat, and final triumph Britain learned an Imperial lesson: even the mightiest Empire on earth might crumble if it stood alone, without allies and friends in an hour of peril.

THE BOER WAR, 1899–1902

When the Boers had trekked from Cape Colony earlier in the century they had hoped they could live undisturbed, their republics of the Transvaal and the Orange Free State uncoveted. Events had shown their hope was vain. Soon the Transvaal had about 250,000 European inhabitants, many of them seeking Witwatersrand gold; thousands were unassimilable non-Boers. The city of Johannesburg grew into a Babel of 100,000 people; aggressive mining interests sank shafts and invested capital, indifferent to the inevitable disharmonies that were arising between a hasty society of money, machinery, and initiative on the one hand and a becalmed society of land, cattle, tradition, blood, and the Bible on the other.

Cecil Rhodes controlled two Johannesburg newspapers, the *Leader* and the *Star*, which he used to increase discontent among the foreigners, or "outlanders," in the Transvaal. The Boers were suspicious of his efforts, and those of Lord Carnarvon and Jan Hendrik Hofmeyr, to create a South African federation under the British flag in all the regions south of the Zambezi. They resented the political encirclement of the Transvaal and the necessity of finding an indirect outlet to the sea through the Portuguese harbor of Delagoa Bay. Fearful of the outlanders who came as birds of passage or as settlers the Boers refused them the franchise, taxed them heavily, subjected them to military service, made it impossible for them to become citizens until they had been residents for fourteen years. State aid to English schools was withdrawn. Dutch was the only official language. High import duties were placed on all goods used by gold miners and the state created a monopoly on the sale of the dynamite necessary for mining operations. There were also quarrels about railways and telegraph lines. The outlanders protested and invoked the aid of Britain. Interest and emotion led them to overstress their hardships and to consider how the Transvaal law might be circumvented.

The leader of the Boers was Paul Kruger, president of the Transvaal from 1882 to 1900. He remembered the Great Trek; and he believed that all South Africa belonged to the Boers. The specter of British dominance angered him. And now the Boers had gold and gold was power. To the south, Cecil Rhodes was impatient to consolidate all South Africa within the Empire before he died; and his physicians said he would die soon. In 1895 he entered into a conspiracy against Kruger and the Transvaal. The plot was this: some outlanders in Johannesburg would revolt; they would demand protection against the Boers; then forces of the British South Africa Company from Rhodesia would sweep into the Transvaal. But the plan went awry. The foreigners failed to rebel. When Dr. L. S. Jameson led five hundred raiders into the Transvaal in December, 1895, all were captured. This was the tragic farce known as the "Jameson Raid." Kruger was shocked; his views hardened; he was not entirely wrong in believing the British government was a party to the plot. The Boers vigorously commenced to arm; soon they had weapons for about 80,000 men; the outlanders began to smuggle arms into the Transvaal.

Angry winds blew from England when Kaiser William II sent Kruger a New Year's greeting stating that he was glad the Boers had been successful "without appealing to the help of friendly powers." But the British imprisoned the leaders of the raid for short terms; Jameson was sentenced to fifteen months in prison. Rhodes resigned as premier of Cape Colony; although he was censured by the British Parliament he was never brought to trial. The strangers in the Boer republics were treated more harshly than before.

A series of conferences was initiated by Sir Alfred Milner, the new high commissioner. They extended through nearly three years and finally revealed that no agreement could be reached. On several occasions compromise was nearly achieved; but the complex points of dispute blotted out a simple answer. Nor can a simple answer be found by historians. The usual explanations of the causes of the Boer War, as Professor C. W. de Kiewiet and others have explained, are glibly false. Events and characters were alike complex. Neither the Boers, the capitalists, nor the British were entirely to blame. The great cause, so to speak, was gold. And beyond that point, in the narrow compass of these pages, it would be vain to attempt to go.

Paul Kruger knew that Britain was reluctant to go to war. The international situation was grim and might easily become critical; he knew that British forces in South Africa were not strong; he thought that Cape Colony might revolt. Above all, he had an Old Testament faith. Like Oliver Cromwell, he believed that the God of his people would arise and scatter the enemy.

On October 9, 1899, the last frail thread of negotiations snapped. An ultimatum from the Transvaal demanded the withdrawal of British troops from the frontier within forty-eight hours. The British government did not comply, and war began. The Orange Free State joined the Transvaal. Together they invaded Natal and Cape Colony. Some Englishmen called the action of Kruger infatuated and wanton. Others feared the conflict might be long and costly.

The spectacle of a great Empire warring with two tiny republics brought waves of anti-British feeling in Europe. The Tsar of Russia, himself a symbol of despotism, called for a general European alliance against Britain. The vigorous and volatile Kaiser William II observed with delight the numerous weaknesses of the British Army. So far as Europe was concerned, however, nothing could be done. The British Fleet ruled the seas. Meanwhile many Englishmen were not enthusiastic about the war. Viscount Haldane said: "We must support our government in the position into which events even more than their own want of foresight have driven them." David Lloyd George, in opposing the war with Celtic fervor, asked a question: "What shall it profit a nation if it annex the gold fields of the whole world and lose its own soul?"

For more than three months the war went well for the Boers. A British army was defeated and later besieged in Ladysmith. Others were hemmed in at Kimberley and Mafeking. The British leaders were Sir Redvers Buller, Lord Roberts, and Lord Kitchener. The Boers were led by General Joubert, General Christian de Wet, and General Louis Botha. From Canada, Australia, and New Zealand came contingents to swell the British forces to more than 300,000 men. Slowly the tide of battle turned. The Boers had no reserves to fall back upon. The British blockade cut off supplies from outside. In March, 1900, Lord Roberts occupied Bloemfontein, the capital of the Orange Free State; in May he entered Pretoria, capital of the Transvaal. Both the Boer republics were annexed. But guerrilla warfare continued. General Kitchener advanced slowly, establishing camps to take care of the wives and children of the Boers. Because it was impossible to maintain adequate health conditions in these camps the mortality was high and the memory of this unhappy aspect of the war was never obliterated. At last, on May 31, 1902, the Treaty of Vereeniging was signed.

The provisions of the treaty were generous. The Boers were permitted to use their language in schools and courts of law. They were promised that "representative institutions leading up to self-government" would soon be introduced. The treaty also provided that a commission in which the local inhabitants would be represented would be appointed in each district "for the purpose of assisting the restoration of the people to their houses and supplying those who, owing to war losses, are unable to provide themselves with food or shelter, or the necessary amount of seed, stock, and implements." The British government gave £3,000,000 as a gift to the commission. It also made advances of loans for rehabilitation purposes, free of interest for two years and afterwards repayable over a period of years at three per cent interest. In 1906 the Transvaal obtained responsible government; the first Prime Minister was Louis Botha, the former Boer general. In 1908 the Orange Free State also gained responsible government and the first prime minister was likewise a former Boer leader: General Christian de Wet.

Before the chastening Boer War had ended, the death of Queen Victoria closed the longest reign in English history. The queen and her ministers had travelled far together to advance the interests of England at home and abroad. The great age of progress and liberalism upon which the curtain was now falling had clearly marked a diminution of the constitutional power of the monarch. At the same time the personal influence of the beloved queen had steadily increased. So it was to be with her successors. As a symbol of the continuing British traditions of freedom and ordered law throughout a united Empire and Commonwealth the crown has assumed a greater importance in the twentieth century then it ever possessed in the years of its highest prerogative power.

When Edward VII ascended the throne in 1901 immensely significant changes were being set in train. A multitude of forces born of the ever-rising demands of an industrialized society and a dangerous international situation deranged the structure of Victorian England. The complacency of Britannia had been shaken by the Boer War; isolation might be dangerous as well as splendid. Hence British diplomatic policy altered its course. Widening discussion of working class conditions, sociological investigations, and the rise of political gospels of dissent captured public attention as eyes withdrew from contemplating the Empire. Hence came the great era of social reform in the early twentieth century. The sanctions of Victorian morality began to slip slowly into discard, cherished chiefly by aging men who lived into a new world the equations of which they did not understand. Those who recalled with nostalgia the days of the great queen frequently declared that England, and with England the world, was selling its soul to Mars and to Mammon.

The directions of the winds of change can best be explained by describing the decline of Conservative power at the end of the century; the growth of socialism and the development of the Labour party; the rise of a new spirit of liberalism; and the successive steps in the road to the First World War. It was to be the task of anonymous millions in the twentieth century to struggle with sweat and blood to defend the accumulated freedoms of the centuries; and to seek new gates to a world where economic democracy, decency, and social justice might one day prevail.

cant changes were being set in train. A multitude of forces born of the ever-rising demands of an industrialized society and a dangerous international situation deranged the structure of Victorian England. The complacency of Britannia had been shaken by the Boer War; isolation might be dangerous as well as splendid. Hence British diplomatic policy altered its course. Widening discussion of working class conditions, sociological investigations, and the rise of political gospels of dissent captured public attention as eyes withdrew from contemplating the Empire. Hence came the great era of social reform in the early twentieth century. The sanctions of Victorian morality began to slip slowly into discard, cherished chiefly by aging men who lived into a new world the equations of which they did not understand. Those who recalled with nostalgia the days of the great queen frequently declared that England, and with England the world, was selling its soul to Mars and to Mammon.

The directions of the winds of change can best be explained by describing the decline of Conservative power at the end of the century; the growth of socialism and the development of the Labour party; the rise of a new spirit of liberalism; and the successive steps in the road to the First World War. It was to be the task of anonymous millions in the twentieth century to struggle with sweat and blood to defend the accumulated freedoms of the centuries; and to seek new gates to a world where economic democracy, decency, and social justice might one day prevail.

Chapter 34

THE RISE OF LIBERALISM
DECLINE OF THE CONSERVATIVES

Conser [handwritten annotation]

Lord Salisbury to ELIST [handwritten annotation in left margin]

L ORD SALISBURY was the last prime minister to come from the house of lords. He was a landed aristocrat, descended from the great minister of Queen Elizabeth, William Cecil. Intellectually and morally he maintained at a high level the standard of English public life. Bismarck once said Salisbury was "a lath painted to resemble a lion." In this the German chancellor was wrong. The prestige of Salisbury has steadily grown as more evidence of his achievements has become available. In the closing chapter of the long Conservative reign he led his party through the Boer War and beyond the edge of the new century. In 1902 he retired; a year later he died. He was succeeded as Conservative chief by his nephew, the brilliant and fastidious Arthur James Balfour. Balfour carried on until the Liberal triumph of 1906.

Because the Salisbury government had been confronted by so many foreign and Imperial problems its achievements in domestic legislation were few. In 1897 a Workmen's Compensation Act made employers liable for compensation to workmen for accidental injuries suffered in the course of their employment unless such injuries were proved to be the result of their own "serious and wilful misconduct." This act at first applied only to railways, factories, mines, and similar fields of labor; in 1900 it was extended to cover agricultural workers. Apart from a few local government reforms in Ireland and the founding in 1899 of an Irish Department of Agriculture under Sir Horace Plunkett there was no other important legislative activity in internal affairs under Salisbury.

Despite the few reform proposals of the Conservatives the Balfour government was responsible for the great Education Act of 1902. This act abolished the local school boards. Henceforth local county and borough councils, under the minister of education, were to control secular education in all schools, including those established by county councils under the act of 1870 and the voluntary schools founded by religious groups. Thus was taken a long step towards a uniform and compulsory system of education. There nevertheless remained difficult problems of religious education. For example, because the minister of education appointed only one third of the managers of voluntary schools, these schools continued to teach religion as they pleased. The Education Act also contained provisions for secondary and technical education. The new science had increasingly tended to subdue nature and to mold society. Hence men of industry and commerce called for reform of the British educational system. Utilitarian considerations were becoming a national necessity. Technical schools would provide young men with training in useful skills. Highly practical people often took the view that students emerging from new "utilitarian" universities like the University of Birmingham could serve themselves and an industrial society more efficiently than Oxford or Cambridge products. In Britain, as in the United States, the rise of the weapons and disciplines of "utilitarian" training in schools and universities has increased to the present day.

Meanwhile, by the Licensing Act of 1904 the temperance cause was advanced in England. This act reduced the number of places licensed to sell liquor and at the same time provided that compensation, out of a liquor tax, should be given to those whose licenses were withdrawn. The Conservatives also established the Committee for the Coordination of Imperial Defense. With these measures the Balfour government stopped. It had neither the time nor the inclination to do more. Heavy squalls were blowing up. The conduct of the Boer War brought adverse criticisms. Commissions produced voluminous reports on the state of the British army; several reforms were proposed; long disputes arose; a suspicious public clamored for less debate and more results. The Liberals also noted that because of labor shortages in South Africa a number of Chinese and Hindu laborers had been imported. These workers had complained of labor conditions. Here the Liberals saw an excellent source for election propaganda. Rather startling pictures of Chinese coolies in chains shortly appeared on Liberal election posters. Meanwhile the decision of the house of lords in the Taff Vale case had alienated thousands of workingmen from the Conservatives. The house of lords, acting in its capacity as the highest appeal court, handed down a decision which in effect made trade unions financially responsible for any acts committed by their agents. Employers might now sue trade unions for any damage resulting from trade disputes.

Then the heavily buffeted government was wrecked on an uncharted reef. Startling proposals came from the colonial secretary, the Imperialist ex-Liberal Joseph Chamberlain. He advocated an Imperial preferential tariff. He urged that a high protective barrier be established against Europe and the United States and that a preference in duties be given to all Dominions and colonies provided that they were willing to give similar tariff preferences to Great Britain. Thus the Empire would be strengthened by new economic bonds; customs revenue would be increased; Great Britain would be less dependent upon foreign nations for food; British manufacturers would be assured of Empire markets; the colonies and Dominions would have sure markets for their wheat, meat, and other foodstuffs. Chamberlain declared: "We have an Empire which, with decent organization and consolidation, might be absolutely self-sustaining. There is no article of your food, no raw material of your trade, no necessity of your lives, no luxury of your existence, which cannot be produced somewhere or other in the British Empire."

At once the Conservative party divided. Many wanted a tariff on agricultural products that would protect British landowners; but not one that would give a preference to Australia, Canada, or South Africa. These Dominions were as much competitors with British agriculture as foreign countries. For once Balfour was shaken from his Olympian detachment. When his adroit dialectics failed he fought passionately to hold his party together. At last Chamberlain resigned from the cabinet, taking some followers with him. The Liberals, always historically a free trade party, hastened into the controversy. They created the slogan "Your food will cost you more!" In the face of such defection and intense opposition Balfour could not carry on. On December 4, 1905, his collapsed cabinet was forced to resign. The Liberal leader, Sir Henry Campbell-Bannerman, remarked unkindly that the Conservatives had "lived on tactics for some years. Now they have died of tactics." In the election of 1906 Balfour and his party suffered a heavy defeat. The Liberals won 379 seats; the Conservatives, 132; the Irish Nationalists, 83; and the new Labour party, 51. Thus the Liberals, pledged to a policy of vigorous social reform, came to power with a majority over all other parties combined.

THE GROWTH OF THE LABOUR PARTY

In this election of 1906 a new political party had appeared, dedicated to the cause of reorganizing society in the interests of all the people, poor and rich alike. Those who had represented labor interests in the nineteenth century had always allied themselves with either the Conservatives or the Liberals. As early as 1869, however, some held the idea that the workers should form an independent party and seek representation in Parliament. In 1874 two workingmen, officials of the Miners' Union, were elected; they were considered left wing members of the Liberal party. By 1885 there were twelve labor representatives in Parliament. They had no organization and voted with the Liberals. Gladstone called them "very good men but very ignorant." In 1893, however, there appeared three members who were not, as were the earlier labor representatives, "the most stable and reliable element of the Liberal party." They were members of Keir Hardie's Independent Labour Party, with no Liberal affiliations. All their candidates were defeated in 1895 although ten "Liberal-Labourites" were elected. Increasing objection to Liberal patronage and condescension helped to push labor groups towards independence. "We are only guys to them all the time," wrote Keir Hardie. "We must not lose touch with our own folk." There was also an increasing labor awareness of fundamental differences between their aims and those of the Liberals. Philip Snowden, once a Liberal, declared in 1893 that he was a Liberal no more. "Like St. Paul on the road to Damascus I suddenly saw the light and knew myself to be a socialist."

Through these years there was a steadily mounting public interest in the economic conditions of the poor. In 1883 William Reaney, a Nonconformist clergyman, wrote his *Bitter Cry of Outcast London.* In 1889 Charles Booth began his *Life and Labour of the People of London;* it was finished in 1903 and numbered seventeen volumes. These were the years of Henry George's *Progress and Poverty;* of the founding of social settlements such as Toynbee Hall; of careful sociological investigation; of Charles Booth's *In Darkest England and the Way Out.* It was claimed that 30 per cent of the population lived at the subsistence level. A million were on poor relief. Eighty per cent of the children were in poor physical health. Was poverty beyond the reach of legislation?

The hatred of injustice and pauperism resulting from the unequal distribution of wealth and other aspects of an industrial society touched the social conscience of England to a greater extent than ever before. In such an atmosphere considerable support arose for the cause of social reform and for labor societies formed with the intention of achieving it. All kinds of individuals, including teetotallers, secularists, Christian Socialists, and State Socialists, found a place in such movements. Their purpose, though not the means for attaining it, was clear. H. M. Hyndman, founder of the Social Democratic Federation (1884) declared: "From the misery around us there is necessarily arising a glorious future, the Golden Age that all the greatest sons of men from Plato to More onward have desired and foreseen, in which men will cooperate for the greater advantage and enjoyment of all."

One of the most important of the numerous socialist societies founded in these years was the famous Fabian Society (1883). In the tradition of Fabius Cunctator the Fabians were prepared to await the slow coming of socialism. They were usually devoted and competent people with orderly minds. They believed not in violent revolution but in "the inevitability of gradualness." These Fabians, about five thousand in number, carried through a great deal of research into social problems. By tracts and by lectures they influenced public opinion. Their members included George Bernard Shaw, H. G. Wells, Sidney and Beatrice Webb, Philip Snowden, Graham Wallas, and Ramsay MacDonald. Before 1899 many Fabians were closely associated with the Liberal party. Fabian speakers were constantly addressing Liberal clubs and spreading their socialist doctrines. Advanced Liberals often considered socialism to be the logical completion of the ideas of Mill and Gladstone.

In 1899, however, the Fabians and Liberals split on the Boer War question. The advanced and keen young Liberals were mostly pro-Boer; so too were the older Campbell-Bannerman and Lloyd George. The Fabians, on the other hand, issued an indiscreet Imperialistic manifesto about the war, partly because Sidney Webb worshipped the Imperialistic Liberal Lord Rosebery. Those who disagreed with the manifesto resigned from the Fabian Society; one was Ramsay Mac-Donald. The irritated Liberals were further put out of patience when the Fabians opposed them on free trade and education. For example, the Fabians issued an Ishmaelitish manifesto about free trade. Sidney Webb supported the Balfour Education Act of 1902; this added to the distrust of the Nonconformist Liberals who hated the Education Act. Graham Wallas left the Fabians on the issue. It was therefore quite natural that after the election of 1906 the Liberals were inclined to keep the Fabians at arm's length.

It was fortunate that the refined and intellectual Fabians informed and advised the leaders of labor movements. They were what H. G. Wells called the "brain-workers." He once remarked: "It is our brains and their feelings that will do the trick." Yet in the early days of labor political development many stalwarts of the trade unions regarded the new socialism with disfavor. "It was too highbrow and too foreign for their shrewd liking." By 1906 the unions had over two million members. New unions for unskilled workers had rapidly increased after 1880. The Labour party has always contained two branches. The first is the poor man's labor movement, born of trade unionism. From it came candid, intelligent, balanced men like Ernest Bevin and Herbert Morrison. The second is the labor movement of the rich and the middle class. It is to the latter group that the Fabians really belonged. For example, Beatrice Webb was the daughter of a railway magnate. Her husband, Sidney Webb, was made Lord Passfield by a Labour government. Her nephew was Sir Stafford Cripps, son of Lord Parmoor; here the landed gentry family line is very old.

In 1899 it was decided that the cause of labor could be more swiftly advanced if all labor groups would cooperate. In 1900 a conference was held of representatives of the Trades Union Congress, the Independent Labour Party, the Social Democratic Federation, and the Fabian Society. A permanent Labour Representation Committee was formed. Fifteen candidates ran in the election of 1900 under the auspices of the new committee; two were elected. Before the election of 1906 the Labour Representation Committee became the Labour party. Meanwhile new impetus was given to the political organization of labor by the Taff Vale decision of the house of lords, so harmful to the strength of trade unions for the reasons set forth above. In 1906 twenty-seven socialist nominees of the Labour party were returned to Parliament, including James Ramsay MacDonald, Philip Snowden, and Arthur Henderson. There were also twenty-four new labor members who were more or less allied to the Liberals. Indeed, all of the labor representatives announced that they would vote with the Liberals because the latter had promised a series of great social reforms that would go far towards marking the demise of nineteenth century individualism and laissez faire.

Both Liberals and Labourites realized that any cooperation could only be temporary. The difference in political ideals prevented anything more. The Liberals have always believed that private initiative is the source of all human progress; that the power of the state should be used to emancipate private enterprise and to create competitive conditions where all individuals will be stimulated to put forth their best efforts. The economists had shown that English wealth, industry, and commerce were the children of free competition. The Darwinians had said that man himself was the child of free competition, laissez-faire, and chance rather than of divine design. So the principle of the survival of the fittest seemed to agree with Ricardian economics. Any socialist state interference might therefore retard the onward march of man. These reasons and this atmosphere are of the essence of the nineteenth century Liberal habit of thought. That is the reason why Liberals in the twentieth century moved into a greater dilemma and conscience-stricken state of mind in proportion as they moved away from the tenets of Gladstone and laissez-faire.

The Socialist Labour Party, on the other hand, does not believe in private enterprise as the motive power of progress. Labourites do not believe in the social or moral justice of the private ownership of "the means of production." They do believe in organized state action in place of private initiative. And they also believe that state ownership or "nationalization" of national resources, public utilities, key industries, and other "means of production" would remove many of the evils born of ruthless private enterprise in an industrial age. Socialism, said the Labour party, would inevitably come by gradual stages in the natural evolution of society. By the slow transition towards a "planned economy" the wealth and other advantages created by science and industry would be more equitably diffused with a resultant social regeneration. By such processes the relation between the state and the individual would be entirely changed. Free enterprise would yield to collectivism. The Liberals, of course, wisely saw that the existing system of English local government was hardly adequate to administer very many new policies of regulation. The local officials of parish, county, and town could do only so much in the absence of a centralized administrative system. This was to be one of the major problems faced by the advocates of regulative measures in advancing state controls.

THE LIBERAL REFORMS, 1906–1908

The Liberal cabinet of 1906 was one of the ablest of modern times. The prime minister was Sir Henry Campbell-Bannerman, a tactful, courageous, honest, and shrewd Presbyterian. During his thirty-six years in Parliament he had been Irish secretary and war secretary; he hated war and Imperialism. The chancellor of the exchequer was the erudite Henry Herbert Asquith, a Nonconformist product of Yorkshire and Balliol. The secretary of war was Richard Burton Haldane, famous lawyer and philosopher, pugnacious Liberal Imperialist, and probably the greatest war secretary in English history. He created the General Staff of the British Army; he began to prepare the Expeditionary Force; he reorganized the voluntary services to create the Territorial Army and the Officers Training Corps. The secretary of state for India was John Morley, celebrated author and critic. The president of the board of trade was David Lloyd George. He had exploded into politics from Wales where he had been a solicitor and editor of a newspaper called *The Trumpet of Freedom*. He was the ideal of the radicals; the Celtic fervor and magic of his oratory won many votes; his life was a long crusade. The foreign minister was Sir Edward Grey (later Lord Grey of Fallodon), a Liberal Imperialist. The minister of education was the author and critic Augustine Birrell. This was indeed, as it has been called, "the Ministry of All the Talents."

Campbell-Bannerman had earlier stated that the policy of his government would be social reconstruction "looking towards a greater equalization of wealth and a destruction of the oppressive land and liquor monopolies." Asquith had declared that "property must be associated in the minds of the people with reason and justice." In such circumstances the Conservatives contemplated the cabinet and Parliament with considerable misgivings. One of them described the house of commons as "the most hysterical and ill-informed Parliament that has ever, at a critical moment, determined the fortunes of the nation." From the Conservative point of view it was fortunate that their party controlled the house of lords. The veto power of the lords still remained. The lords had fought the Whig Reform Bill of 1832; they had scotched Home Rule; they would now protect England from the threatened bruising excesses of the Liberal and Labour zealots in the lower house. Balfour, detached and tranquil, was prepared to lead the Conservatives in the commons and to win what he could with his subtle and sinewy dialectic. But all Conservatives looked to the house of lords to do the needful in checking the comprehensive Liberal social reform program. The reform measures that the Conservatives approved were passed by the Conservative majority in the house of lords. The Liberal bills they did not approve were blocked, despite the mandate given to the Liberals by the nation in the election of 1906.

The first dispute between the lords and commons arose on the question of education. The Balfour Education Act of 1902, as described above, had provided that the minister of education could appoint only one third of the managers of denominational voluntary schools. There were one hundred and twenty-seven Nonconformists in the house of commons, most of them Liberals, who objected to the fact that in voluntary schools the control and choice of teachers through religious tests remained with the denominations, especially the Church of England. They asserted that as the voluntary schools were largely supported by public taxes they should be put on the same basis of public management as any other schools; there should be no religious tests for teachers. A Liberal Education Bill of 1906 accepted the Nonconformist principle and included clauses providing for non-denominational religious education, whereupon Anglican bishops met at Lambeth and angrily declared that "the whole cause of religion" was at stake. When the bill passed the house of commons the Lords mutilated it by amendments and returned it to the commons. The commons rejected all the amendments and sent the bill back to the lords. As the lords insisted on their amendments the Act of 1902 remained unchanged. Later governments were reluctant to stir the controversy anew and little was done to settle the religious problem until 1936. The house of lords asserted that the election of 1906 had not been fought on the issue of education; that the people did not favor the Liberal proposals; that they were using their ancient powers of amendment in the public interest. The Liberals, on the other hand, declared that the Conservative party was again attempting to rule England through its huge majority in the house of lords.

The Trades Disputes Bill was more successful. The Taff Vale decision of 1901, described above, had exposed to ruin any trade union that undertook or sanctioned a strike. The lawyers of the cabinet now supported a complicated bill to restrict the laws of agency so far as trade unions were concerned with a view to giving the unions exemption from liability for damages caused by striking workers provided that the damaging acts were not authorized by the unions. The Labour party introduced another bill which stated flatly that trade unions were not suable; that an action against a trade union "in respect of any tortious act alleged to have been committed by or on behalf of the trade union shall not be entertained by any court." After three months' debate the cabinet accepted the Labour bill. Many Liberals, including

Campbell-Bannerman, preferred it to the involved bill of the Liberal lawyers laying down in industrial combination a whole new code of the law of agency. In its final form the Trades Disputes Bill granted the unions the right "peaceably to persuade." This meant that unions might boycott and picket if these activities did not involve violence. "It shall be lawful for one or more persons . . . to attend at or near a house where a person resides or works or carries on business or happens to be, if they so attend merely for the purpose of peacefully persuading any person to work or abstain from working." This bill was less clearly associated with Liberal policy than other bills sent to the lords. The workers supported it and the workers had votes. Hence it passed the upper house.

Meanwhile the house of lords vetoed the Plural Voting Bill designed to prevent individuals from casting ballots in more than one place. They passed the Workmen's Compensation Bill which extended the provisions of the earlier acts of 1880 and 1897. Under the new act of 1906 most workers receiving less than £250 a year were entitled to compensation from their employers in cases of industrial accidents and occupational diseases. During the period of illness or injury the compensation equalled about one half the usual wages. In the event of a worker's death resulting from injury or occupational disease his dependents received a sum approximately equal to three years' wages. Nearly six million workers were protected under this Workmen's Compensation Act.

The pace of the controversy between lords and commons was soon accelerated. Its spirit grew bitter. Some Liberals declared that they would not "act as caretakers for the party that the country has rejected." Others proclaimed that the time for "compromise and temporizing and verbal expostulations" had gone. Balfour asserted that the Liberals had "deliberately picked a quarrel with the house of lords and deliberately framed bills to get them rejected." Lloyd George replied that the house of lords was not "the watchdog of the British Constitution. It is Mr. Balfour's poodle." There were several proposals as to how the power of the lords might be curbed. The Liberals finally decided to press for the abolition of the absolute veto of the house of lords, substituting a suspensive veto power.

By 1908 the house of lords had rejected a Liberal bill for land reform in the United Kingdom. Secondly, they had killed a Liberal Licensing Bill which provided for the revocation of nearly 30,000 licenses for the sale of liquor in the following fourteen years, after which local option would come into operation. There were, of course, powerful land and brewing interests in the Conservative party. On the other hand, the Nonconformist elements in the Liberal party were usually supporters of temperance and scornful of the Anglican-Conservative alliance between "beer and the Bible." Thirdly, the lords had mauled the Agricultural Holdings Bill and the Irish Town Tenants Bill. Fourthly, they had almost rejected the Old Age Pensions Bill. This bill provided for the payment of five shillings a week to all over seventy years of age who had no other means of support, who were not criminals or common loafers, and who had been British subjects for twenty years and British residents for twelve. Smaller weekly sums were to be paid to those whose incomes were very small. Lord Lansdowne and others were troubled by a scheme "so prodigal of expenditure" but the bill finally passed the lords in 1908. Its cost was expected to be between six and seven million pounds a year. This fact, however, was to be set against the decline of the parish rates resulting from the exodus of thousands of elderly people from the parish workhouses. Within a few months about 620,000 persons were receiving old age pensions. Despite the early lamentations of the Conservatives and the *Times* the "destructive scheme" of old age pensions did not bring the "general bankruptcy" the dark prophets foresaw. Thus the controversy between the lords and commons moved toward the final crisis. The lords, said the Liberals, were "filling up the cup."

Meanwhile, Campbell-Bannerman resigned as leader of the Liberals in April, 1908; he died within a month of his resignation. Asquith became prime minister. David Lloyd George became chancellor of the exchequer. The new president of the board of trade was Winston Churchill, then thirty-four years of age. Churchill, like his father a rebel, had broken with Balfour and the Conservatives in 1905 on the tariff question and had impetuously brought his talents to the Liberals.

SOUTH AFRICA AND INDIA

Although the Liberals were immediately occupied with domestic reforms they were responsible for two important Imperial measures. The first concerned South Africa. Responsible government had been granted to the Transvaal in 1906 and to the Orange Free State in 1908. In 1909 the Imperial Parliament passed the Union of South Africa Act which united Cape Colony, Natal, the Orange Free State, and the Transvaal into a centralized state. The Union was not a federation in the Canadian or Australian sense. Each of the four South African units kept its political identity and certain local administrative powers exercised by provincial councils. The legislative capital of the Union is at Capetown; the executive capital is at Pretoria; the judicial capital is at Bloemfontein. On May 31, 1910, the Union Act came into operation; this was the eighth anniversary of Vereeniging. Thus the self-governing British Dominion of the Union of South Africa was created. Its first prime minister was Louis Botha, earlier commander-in-chief of the Boer armed forces.

The second significant action in the area of Imperial affairs concerned India. Among its masses strong native nationalist movements had arisen. Over half of the territory and about eighty per cent of the population were contained in the fifteen British provinces. The remainder was divided among the native states, each of which was in rather close treaty relationship to the British Indian government. The major nationalist movements were two: one was Hindu, the other Moslem. In each group the moderates wished an increased native share in the government leading eventually to autonomy. The more deeply irritable and extreme elements wished to expel the British from India.

Britain felt that it was impossible to yield to demands for self-government until the people of India had fitted themselves for democratic institutions. The language problems, the illiteracy, and, above all, the bitter religious divisions, combined to prevent any solution acceptable to all Indian groups. The basis for parliamentary government simply did not exist. Viscount Morley, secretary of state for India, tried to give the moderate and educated natives places in the government. As a part of the Morley-Minto Reforms the Indian Councils Act of 1909 extended the elective principle of the Indian Councils Act of 1892. It provided for the admission of natives to the legislative councils of the viceroy and the governors of the provinces. Native council members were to be elected by the small number of natives permitted to vote under the restricted franchise. The British government took the position, then and later, that the vote should be given only to those who possessed some education and who understood something of what was meant by a system of representative government.

The native councillors had great influence, particularly in the provinces; but they did not control the government. All governments in British India were still ultimately responsible to the British parliament, through the chain of command of the viceroy and the secretary of state for India. The Morley-Minto Reforms of 1909 satisfied the demands of the Hindu National Congress and the All-India Moslem League for only a short time. Riots, seditious literature, garbled history, and all the familiar Indian tools of irreconcilable agitation soon appeared again. Concessions only slackened outrages. The general situation continued formidable and obscure.

1909: EMPLOYMENT AND HOUSING

In 1905 a parliamentary committee had been appointed to investigate poverty and poor relief. Its report, submitted in 1909, was embodied in forty volumes containing much valuable statistical material. For example, it showed that one-eighth of the population held half the wealth of the nation; a third of the employed workers received wages of less than twenty-five shillings a week; less than a fourth received more than thirty-five shillings a week; the annual cost of poor relief was about £15,000,000. Several important pieces of legislation followed this report. Three came in 1909. The first was the Labour Exchanges Act which established three hundred and fifty labor exchanges in eleven districts as clearinghouses for information about vacancies. This reduced the wanderings of the unemployed. The government agreed to lend travelling expenses to those seeking jobs listed as being available. Skilled technical workers found the labor exchanges of special value. With the machinery thus created for directing labor to the places where it was most needed one cause of unemployment was reduced.

The second important law of 1909 was the Trade Boards Act which dealt with the problem of sweated labor, particularly serious among unskilled workers. A number of trade or minimum wage boards were now established, composed of representatives of the government, the employers, and the workers. These boards were to fix minimum wages for certain specified trades, especially the textile and box-making industries. Women, who often did only piece work in such industries, found this law a bulwark against exploitation; with no unions to protect them their position had usually been worse than that of the men.

The third significant piece of reform legislation in 1909 was the House and Town Planning Act which consolidated and extended earlier legislation. The census of 1901 had showed that millions of Englishmen were living in dingy, squalid tenements, crowded in cellars, unhealthy victims of dampness, disease, and cold. The report of the parliamentary committee in 1909 sharply confirmed what the census had indicated in 1901 and what Charles Booth, William Reaney, and their fellows had so often described. The House and Town Planning Act made landlords legally responsible for the condition of their property; forbade the construction of back-to-back houses; provided for the demolition of condemned buildings by the municipal authorities and state aid for the construction of new ones.

By such slow steps the condition of England's workers was to be lifted above the level permitted by uncontrolled competition. The strong arm of the state was reaching to afford a greater protection to the poor, the unskilled, the sick, and the old. The acts described above and others of a similar nature were designed to remove many of the causes of poverty and its attendant national evils. Poverty itself was partly the result of economic conditions produced by a system which gave different returns to capital and to labor. With the money and labor exchange system itself the Liberals were not prepared to interfere. At a later hour the Socialist Labour Party was to undertake the task of altering economic relationships among Englishmen.

LORDS VERSUS COMMONS

All these unexampled reforms paled beside the Lloyd George

budget of 1909. The epochal budget proposals were probably more revolutionary than any ever submitted to Parliament. In preparing the financial estimates Lloyd George had to meet an enormous deficit of about £14,000,000. The cost of the expanding naval program together with the financial demands of the new social reforms meant a huge tax increase. "Democracy," Gladstone had said, "will prove a very costly mistress."

As one of the avowed ends of the new Liberalism had been to redistribute the national income, Lloyd George prepared "the People's Budget" with a view to invading a promising field of taxation. The capitalists and landlords would pay both for social reform and for battleships. They would discover what democratic finance really meant. In his remarkable budget proposals Lloyd George increased all death duties on estates over £5,000. This included a ten per cent death duty on all estates valued at £200,000 or more. He placed a super-tax on all incomes of over £3,000 a year. He placed a tax of twenty per cent on all increase of urban land values. A tax of a half-penny per pound was put on "undeveloped" land, by which was meant land intended for building purposes but held up until its value increased. Thus the Liberals decided to carry out the Henry George idea of taxing unearned increment. There were also advances in liquor and tobacco duties. After forty-two days in committee the Budget Bill passed the house of commons on November 4, 1909, by a vote of 379 to 149. Throughout England controversy mounted. The Budget League and the Anti-Budget League arose, reminiscent of the Corn Laws battles of sixty-three years before.

Although the house of lords had already vetoed important Liberal measures it was an entirely different matter to quash a budget. By constitutional tradition finance was outside the province of the house of lords. Usage dictated that the lords could not initiate or amend any money bills. Theoretically, of course, they had the right to throw out the budget altogether. If they did that, Asquith would certainly demand an election. The people might then support the Liberals. In that event, the lords would be in for heavy trouble. On the other hand, this budget struck at wealth in general and land-holding in particular. For centuries the lords had been England's greatest land-holders; their ranks included the wealthiest men in the country. Under the budget they were liable for heaviest taxes. Most of them believed in the old order. This budget, they said, was socialistic revolution. Both their pockets and their pride were challenged. Heedless of consequences, they rejected the Liberal budget by a vote of 300 to 75.

Lloyd George had already started a bitter campaign in his famous Limehouse and Newcastle speeches. "The landlords," he said, "are not in business, but in blackmail." He described the house of lords as "five hundred men, ordinary men, chosen accidentally from among the unemployed." He pleaded for the workers and "the wounded soldiers of humanity." The function of a duke, he declared, was "a stately consumption of the wealth produced by others." With the rejection of the budget by the lords it was felt that the time had come for a final reckoning. Asquith asked for a dissolution. A national election was held in January, 1910. By the election results the Liberal power was greatly reduced. For a majority in the commons the government was dependent upon Irish Nationalist and Labour votes. The Irish agreed to support the Liberals only on the understanding that the Liberals would support Home Rule. When the Irish obtained that assurance the new house promptly passed the budget again. This time the lords accepted it.

Meanwhile the commons had turned once more to the task of devising legislation to whittle down the powers of the lords. Violent disputes arose. On May 7, 1910, the death of Edward VII resulted in the accession of his son, George V. The new king vainly attempted to effect a settlement. In the autumn of 1910 Asquith brought in a Parliament Bill "for regulating the relations between the Houses of Parliament." It provided that the house of lords could not delay by more than one month any measure certified by the speaker of the house of commons to be a money bill. Any other bill passed by the commons in three consecutive sessions would become law without the assent of the lords provided that two years had elapsed between the introduction of the bill and its final passage. The life of Parliaments was to be limited to five years instead of seven. Scenes reminiscent of the days of Pym and Hampden occurred in both houses. Opponents of the Liberals accused them of trying to "revise at ten days' notice the constitution of eight hundred years." King George V arranged secret conferences at Lansdowne House between Liberal and Conservative leaders. In November Asquith admitted "an apparently irreconcilable divergence of opinion." When the lords rejected the Parliament Bill a national election was held in December. The Liberals won 272 seats, the Conservatives, 272. The Irish and Labour groups again held the balance of power.

In February, 1911, the commons passed the Parliament Bill again. By July the lords had drawn its teeth by amendments. Asquith then announced that the king had agreed to create about five hundred Liberal peers to force the Liberal bill through the upper house. In vain the lords raged as waves of excited public clamor beat against the walls of Parliament. In the house of commons Asquith faced his tormentors, his speech punctuated by screaming denunciations. When Balfour rose to reply the speaker was compelled to adjourn the house, "a state of grave disorder having arisen." At last, under the revolutionary threat of the creation of hundreds of peers, the lords yielded. Most Conservative peers absented themselves and the bill passed by a vote of 131 to 114. The Parliament Bill became the Parliament Act. The house of lords had been forever shorn of a part of its powers. No longer could it thwart the will of a majority of the house of commons.

THE REVIVAL OF LABOR UNREST

Despite the controversy attending the difficult passage of the Parliament Act in 1911 the government was able to carry through a number of other important measures. One of these provided for a yearly salary of £400 to all members of the house of commons. Although a gloomy prophet of the *Times* foresaw the flooding of constituencies by an inrush of adventurers the Labour party rejoiced because the act opened the doors of the commons to those who did not possess independent means. In the Osborne Case of 1909 the house of lords had forbidden trades unions to use their funds to help Labour members of Parliament. The lords had held that members paid by unions were not free to vote as they pleased and the liberties of Parliament were thereby violated. Several Labour members were now relieved of the heavy burdens imposed upon them by the Osborne judgment.

A second law of profound importance was the National Insurance Act which began the great experiment of compulsory insurance against sickness and unemployment. Nearly 15,000,000 workers earning less than £160 a year were insured against sickness. To provide for sick benefits the worker, the employer, and the government each contributed a few pence a week. In the event of illness a worker received free medical care from physicians whose names were on a panel and who had contracted with the government to serve the insured workers. Free hospital care and medicine were also provided together with a specified sum for the support of the worker's family and a smaller weekly allowance thereafter. The unemployment insurance section of the act was designed to cover those trades where the seasonal nature of the work increased the danger of unemployment. Within the engineering and building trades the insurance was compulsory; over two million workers were covered. The employer, the government, and the worker each contributed a few pence weekly. Unemployed workers received six or seven shillings a week for a certain number of weeks, depending upon the length of time they had contributed. The law provided that no benefits would be paid to workers in cases of strikes, misconduct, or lockouts. All contributions, less the amount received in benefits, were to be returned with 2.5 per cent compound interest when a worker reached the age of sixty. From this act of 1911 was to rise the "dole" system of the years following the First World War. In 1920 the percentage of unemployed was 2.4; in 1924 it was 10.3; in 1926 it was 12.5. The "dole" then supported millions of idle men.

Despite the obvious benefits brought to the working classes by the series of Liberal reforms culminating in the National Insurance Act, they remained dissatisfied. They saw that the gains which they had made were offset by other factors. For example, the rise of prices, general throughout Europe, meant a drop in real wages. The cost of living rose and production increased; but wages did not rise proportionately. Miners in South Africa and Alaska increased the world's gold stock. The swelling tide of gold accelerated the general price rise; by 1910 the purchasing power of the pound declined about 15 per cent below the 1900 level. Unaware of the economic reasons for this price increase, the workers knew only that they were in fact poorer than they had been in 1900. They did not understand the interacting significance of the decline of the small entrepreneur, the migration of British capital to foreign investment fields, the concentration of wealth in fewer and fewer hands, the challenge of foreign tariffs, the growth of cartels and trusts, the sinister warfare for world markets with Germany and the United States. It seemed to the workers that the Liberal and Labour parties had not really tried to remove their grievances. They felt that the mass of social reforms had been designed to soothe, but not to cure, the economic ills of the lower classes. In such a state of mind they turned for aid to their trade unions; by 1910 these unions had over four million members.

Thus began a great social unrest, marked by a series of strikes and outbreaks of violence. In many respects the manifestations of discontent were the result of a curious mass psychological irritation. Miners, railwaymen, dock workers, textile workers, canal workers, and carters joined firemen and boilermakers in striking for higher wages, shorter hours, better working conditions, and so on. Often their grievances were never clearly stated at all. Throughout the islands stoppages multiplied. In August, 1911, London was threatened by famine as the transport workers refused to carry on. In 1911 nearly a million men were involved in strikes; ten million working days were lost; trade unions increased their membership by 600,000. The events of 1911 were repeated in the next two years. In 1912, for example, there were 857 disputes; nearly forty million working days were lost. In the first half of 1914 there were 937 strikes; forty million working days lost.

By the spring of 1914 the three great unions of miners, railwaymen, and transport workers formed a triple alliance and prepared for a general strike to be called in September, 1914, to demand "a wage, a living wage, for all." In vain the Liberals tried to focus the attention of the workers on the problem of land reform in England, the Welsh Disestablishment Bill, and other such questions. Meanwhile the repercussions of the Marconi scandal dogged the footsteps of Liberal ministers. Lloyd George himself was accused of being "a capitalist on the sly." On the eve of the First World War the condition of England caused alarm to many conservatives. The threat of a general strike was not calculated to reassure them. German observers, taking note, concluded that England was not in a position to enter a European war.

THE SUFFRAGETTE MOVEMENT

The redoubtable energy of the combatants in the battle of the budget in 1909, the Parliament Act, and the labor unrest was matched by the firebrand tactics of the militant suffragettes. Votes for women had been proposed early in the nineteenth century. John Stuart Mill had cogently argued for such a step at the time of the second Reform Bill in 1867; in 1869 he had written his work on the *Subjection of Women*. Queen Victoria spoke of the "mad, wicked folly of women's rights." Asquith asserted that votes for women were contrary to the laws of nature. Not until the twentieth century, however, did a strong suffragette movement arise. In England it was a strange, melodramatic, and unlovely phenomenon.

The Women's Social and Political Union was formed in Manchester in 1903. In 1907 it moved its headquarters to London and began its campaign against convention and prejudice. By 1910 it had an annual income of about £32,000 and a large staff of workers. Leaders in the militant movement were Emmeline Pankhurst and her two daughters, Christabel and Sylvia. They and their associates undertook a hysterical campaign of dubious outrages to obtain for women their proper place in the world. They cut telephone wires; broke porcelain in the British Museum; threw stones and wielded knives and hatchets; put jam and tar in mailboxes and wreaths on a statue of Joan of Arc; they set fires and planted bombs. Sylvia Pankhurst sought to dissuade women from marriage by writing *The Great Scourge*. Emily Davison hurled herself in front of the horses at the Derby and was killed. The government adopted the so-called "cat and mouse" tactics to deal with hunger-strikers. They were kept in jail until they were exhausted; then they were released; after they recovered they were taken into custody again.

Within the suffragette movement there were many moderates who did not approve of these methods of violence. The militant group were already losing ground when war came in 1914. In an England at war there was a greater cause than before for those who had been valiantly battling for votes for women. Christabel Pankhurst, for example, became very much concerned about the patriotic duty of all British subjects to resist the German menace. The resourceful Sylvia Pankhurst took a different road. She opposed conscription and became the socialist editor of the *Workers' Dreadnought*.

IRELAND: DUBLIN AND BELFAST

The confused domestic scene in England was further disturbed by the Irish Home Rule problem. When Gladstone's first Home Rule crusade had failed in 1886 Ireland was a country of bitterness, starvation, and violence. By 1912 the situation had changed for the better. Agricultural prices had risen. Emigration had declined. The Conservative policy, described above, had brought excellent results. Irish land was being returned to the Irish people. Increasing self-government in local affairs had increased native self-reliance. Sir Horace Plunkett had taken steps to reorganize the economic life of southern Ireland. To John Redmond, successor of Parnell as leader of the Irish Nationalists, Asquith had promised that the Liberals would embrace Home Rule in return for Irish support in the disputes with the house of lords. Accordingly, in 1912 Asquith introduced the third Home Rule Bill.

The new Liberal bill was based on the formula of Gladstone. It provided for a bicameral Irish Parliament in Dublin which was to have full control over all Irish matters not reserved to the British government. Important constitutional and administrative functions were to be retained by Westminster. These included control over the army and navy, foreign affairs, old age pensions, land settlement, the administration of the National Insurance Act, and the collection of taxes. The British government guaranteed religious liberty. The royal veto remained. Forty-two Irish members were still to sit in the English Parliament. The Liberals insisted that these safeguards were necessary. Britain had many investments and many liabilities in Ireland. British interests must be protected. The southern Irish were willing to support the bill as a first instalment of freedom. "It is a great measure," said John Redmond, "and we welcome it."

From the Protestant industrial Ulster counties of northern Ireland came loud and strong objections. They feared domination by the Catholic and agricultural south. Proud of the progressive north, they viewed with anger the prospect of being linked with a south they regarded as economically backward. The Ulster leader was the great lawyer Sir Edward Carson, once the prosecutor of Oscar Wilde. Carson called the third Home Rule Bill "the most nefarious conspiracy that has ever been hatched against a free people." In the mounting crisis Lloyd George saw "the gravest issue since the days of the Stuarts." Largely for partisan political reasons the Conservatives strongly supported Ulster against the Liberal bill and stirred the Ulsterites to action. On September 19, 1912, Ulster's resistance was formally declared by the signing of the Solemn League and Covenant. "Being convinced in our conscience that Home Rule would be disastrous to the material well-being of Ireland, subversive of our civil and religious liberties, destructive of our citizenship and perilous to the unity of the Empire, we, men of Ulster, . . . do hereby pledge ourselves . . . to defeat the present conspiracy to set up a Home Rule Parliament in Dublin." Meanwhile John Redmond declared that the division of Ireland into two nations would be "an abomination and a blasphemy."

In January, 1913, the house of commons passed the third Home Rule Bill. Despite its rejection by the house of lords the bill would become law, under the terms of the Parliament Act, if passed by the commons three times within two years. Guns and ammunition were smuggled and distributed in Ireland. Ulsterites armed and drilled. In the south the Nationalist Volunteers did likewise. "We shall fight the Ulsterites if they want fighting, but we will never let them go, never!" Serious difficulties arose in the British army. General Paget's officers preferred "to accept dismissal" if ordered north against the men of Ulster. In May, 1914, the bill passed the house of commons again. A conference between Carson and Redmond held at Buckingham Palace in July, 1914, failed completely. British troops fired on National Volunteers in Dublin. Civil war seemed inevitable. It was prevented only by the coming of the First World War. A Suspensory Act was passed by the British Parliament providing that Home Rule should not become operative in Ireland until hostilities with Germany had ceased. John Redmond pledged Irish Nationalist cooperation, if necessary even with Ulstermen, in the defense of Ireland. "We ourselves will defend our coasts." But the influence of Redmond on the tides of Irish opinion was not the planetary influence of Parnell. Not all southern Irishmen accepted the Redmond principle of peaceful cooperation pending the end of the European war. The result was confusion and plotting and, finally, the small-scale Irish rebellion of 1916. Meanwhile, however, the United Kingdom and the Empire were locked in the titanic struggle of the First World War.

Chapter 35

THE FIRST WORLD WAR
BRITAIN AND EUROPE, 1871–1904

AFTER the empire of Napoleon III crashed in 1871 Bismarck determined to keep France powerless and isolated. His first step was taken in 1873 when he was architect of the Three Emperors' League of Germany, Austria, and Russia. But this League lasted only five years. It died at the Congress of Berlin when Britain opposed Russian designs of expansion towards the Dardanelles and Austria battled the extension of Russian influence in the Balkans. Because Bismarck did not support Russia at the Congress the cordiality between St. Petersburg and Berlin was chilled. Bismarck turned at once to Austria and formed with her the secret Dual Alliance in 1879, an arrangement that became the Triple Alliance in 1883 with the adherence of Italy.

Meanwhile by a series of secret reinsurance treaties Bismarck attempted to retain the lukewarm support of Russia. The constant factor at the root of his policy was the resolve to prevent Russia and France from forming an alliance against Germany. In 1890 the new kaiser William II dismissed Bismarck. With the dropping of the pilot and the jettisoning of his charts the German course was altered. France and Russia began at last to come together. In 1894 they formed a defensive alliance; the way to agreement was smoothed by French loans to Russia. Hence, at the turn of the century, there were two so-called defensive alliances in Europe. The first embraced the central European bloc of Germany, Austria, Italy, and Rumania; the second, Russia and France. Great Britain stood outside; but her position was clearly less safe than in Palmerston's day. The complacent isolation policy of Salisbury had been based on the exceptional British security of the nineteenth century. That security was now challenged.

It was challenged in many ways. The militarist spirit was rising again in Germany, spurred on by the visionary ranting of the young kaiser and the more sober tones of the professors who explained that war was a "biological necessity." Great financial houses of England,

Germany, and France intensified their rivalry in seeking fields for profitable investment. In 1890 England exported £82,600,000 of surplus capital, in 1912 £226,000,000. Bitter disputes arose between competing financial interests in Siam, China, Persia, and Turkey. Sprawling and gigantic international cartels and trusts thrust tentacles into nearly all countries. Industrial capital and monopoly controls served the economic interest of organized finance. Meanwhile the relative strength of Britain's financial, industrial, and commercial power, as compared with that of Germany and the United States, was steadily declining. For example, in 1860 the total value of United Kingdom exports had been £135,000,000; of German exports £40,000,000; of United States exports £74,000,000. By 1913 the margin had narrowed. The value of exports from the United Kingdom then totalled £525,000,000; from Germany £509,000,000; from the United States £362,000,000. Previous chapters have described how colonial rivalries produced tension and bickering with Russia in the Middle and Far East; with France in Africa and the Pacific; with blustering and envious Germany in Africa and elsewhere. William II wanted more colonies. Germany had not been given her rightful "place in the sun." All these events combined to disturb Britain. Moreover, the Boer War helped to underline the deplorable consequences that might follow a policy of isolation too long continued.

Even before the Boer War Joseph Chamberlain had proposed an alliance with Germany. "There is something more that I think any far-seeing Englishman must long have desired, and that is that we should not remain primarily isolated on the continent of Europe; and I think it is evident the moment that aspiration is formed—it must have appeared evident to everybody—that the natural alliance is between ourselves and the great German nation." It seemed to Chamberlain, and to others, that it would be easier to come to an agreement with Germany than with either France or Russia. Negotiations looking towards an Anglo-German alliance continued until 1901. In the end they failed. Berlin feared an agreement with England might bring Germany into war with Russia or France or both. Confident that England would never mend her differences with France and Russia, the German government insisted that England join the Triple Alliance. England refused.

Friction also developed over the proposed construction of the Bagdad railway by Germany and the increasing German influence in Turkey. Meanwhile British misgivings increased as a stream of hostile statements came from the German press, from German statesmen, from the neurotic Emperor. German naval construction threatened to make her capable of challenging Britain at sea. The preamble to the German naval bill of 1900 stated that "Germany must have a battle fleet so strong that, even for the adversary with the greatest sea power, a war against us would involve such dangers as to imperil her position in the world." The Kiel Canal was opened in 1893; Heligoland was fortified. In 1899 representatives of twenty-six nations attended a peace conference at the Hague; a second was held in 1907.

In such circumstances England turned in 1902 to conclude the defensive alliance with Japan described earlier; this alliance was dictated in part by Anglo-Russian conflicts in the Far East. At the same time momentous steps were taken to reach an understanding with France. In 1903 Edward VII made a visit to Paris, the importance of which is usually exaggerated. Soon President Loubet visited London. Delcassé, the French minister of foreign affairs, and Lord Lansdowne, the British foreign secretary, held exploratory conversations. A series of later conferences resulted in the agreement of April, 1904, known as the Entente Cordiale. The French surrendered all claims in Egypt; Britain recognized the predominant French interest in Morocco. Conflicting claims elsewhere were reconciled, such as the problem of Newfoundland fishing rights, joint control of the New Hebrides, colonial boundaries in Africa, the French possession of Madagascar, and spheres of influence in Siam. Both France and England made considerable concessions to secure the understanding each desired. No formal military alliance was signed. Nevertheless the settlement of outstanding issues marked a significant diplomatic revolution. When Berlin, disagreeably surprised, determined to challenge the new Entente the result was a diplomatic defeat for Germany and a hardening of the Anglo-French arrangements into something very close to an actual alliance. England had reversed her policy; the years of political isolation were ended. Germany, on the other hand, complained of being "encircled" by the Franco-Russian alliance and the Entente Cordiale.

THE TRIPLE ENTENTE

The Anglo-German rivalry in colonial, commercial, and naval affairs had forced England to assume again her historic role of the balance wheel of Europe. For centuries England had resisted the attempt of any nation to establish a hegemony on the Continent or to control the Lowlands against the narrow seas and the approaches to her shores. By coalitions, by armies and fleets and gold, England had fought and defeated Philip II, Louis XIV, and Napoleon. William II and Adolf Hitler were to follow the same road to disaster.

The Russo-Japanese conflict (1904–1905) revealed to the world the weakness of Russia. France noted that her Russian ally might be of small account in a grapple with Germany and was glad of her new understanding with England. London saw that her fear of St. Petersburg had not been fully warranted. When Russia had earlier rejected Salisbury's offer of friendship the Conservative government had tried to balance Muscovite power in the Far East by the alliance with Japan. Now Czarist Russia was defeated, her armies disorganized, her national debt tremendous, and a part of her people in rebellion. Fearful that Nicholas II might turn towards Germany and cheered by his promises of liberal reforms after the small-scale revolution of 1905 the British Liberal government once again took the initiative and approached Russia.

This time the Russians welcomed the British gesture. An Anglo-Russian entente was signed on August 31, 1907. By the terms of the new entente Russia and England agreed to stay out of Tibet; the Russians promised to plot and incite no more in Afghanistan; Persia was divided into Russian and British spheres of influence separated by a neutral zone. All of these agreements were achieved by an informal exchange of letters; there were no naval or military commitments. In 1908 the new relations between Russia and England were strengthened by a meeting of Edward VII and Nicholas II at Reval, the base of the Russian Baltic Fleet. The bonds uniting England, France, and Russia in the Triple Entente were slowly tightening. Confronted with this unpleasant fact, the suspicious and truculent Germans attempted to break the Entente by direct diplomatic attacks. In each case the international crisis provoked by Berlin forced the members of the Triple Entente closer together, which was exactly what Germany did not want.

ALGECIRAS, BOSNIA, AND AGADIR

The first major crisis had passed before the Anglo-Russian accord. When the Entente Cordiale was established in 1904 Germany felt that a counter stroke was imperative. France, with the tacit consent of England, Spain, and Italy, went ahead with her designs in Morocco, whereupon the German government pointed out that an international convention of 1880 gave Germany certain commercial rights in that country. William II went to Tangier and delivered a bellicose harangue, congratulating the sultan upon his independence and insisting that the question of Morocco concerned Europe as a whole and that a conference of the signatories of the convention of 1880 should be held to discuss Moroccan problems. France yielded to German pressure; her ally Russia had been defeated by Japan; the entente with England was as yet untried. So Delcassé, who had loudly insisted that England would fight for France, resigned. In 1906 an international conference met at Algeciras, in Spain.

Germany wished to show France that the Entente Cordiale was useless. But the Algeciras conference proved otherwise. England backed France at every point. Spain and Italy ranged themselves on the side of France and England. Italy had made a secret agreement with France as early as 1900. France had then agreed to place no obstacle in the way of Italian advances in Tripoli and Cyrenaica; Italy, for her part, stated that she would not object to French penetration in Tunis and Morocco. In 1902 Italy had also promised that she would not join her partners in the Triple Alliance in an aggressive war on France. At Algeciras, then, Germany and Austria stood alone. The powers formally guaranteed the integrity and independence of Morocco. Behind the solemn guarantee were clauses providing for an international police force to protect foreigners and keep order; this police force was to be under the control of France and Spain; it was in fact used for the extension of their own political and economic power in Morocco.

To browbeat France had been a stupendous German blunder. The Entente Cordiale stood unshaken. Under Campbell-Bannerman and Sir Edward Grey the British and French general staffs continued and extended the conversations that had begun in 1905 under Balfour and Lord Lansdowne. The experts discussed military plans in the event that Germany attacked France and England came into the conflict to support the French. The British government made no formal commitments of any kind. Only four or five members of the cabinet knew of the discussions. The Parliament and public were not informed because it was felt that publicity might be alarming, and perhaps dangerous. From 1906 until 1914 these secret conversations proceeded. Although no commitments were made, some degree of moral obligation on the part of England was certainly incurred. Arrangements were made so that England could land 100,000 men in France within twelve days after the outbreak of war; the British fleet would keep the watch in the North Sea; the French fleet would move into the Mediterranean. Such were the results of the first German attempt to split asunder the Entente Cordiale.

The second international crisis came in 1908. It arose out of the continuing struggle between Austria and Russia in the Balkans. Turkey, shaken by the Young Turk revolution, could do nothing to stop the sudden Austrian annexation of Bosnia and Herzegovina, the Turkish provinces placed under Austrian protection by the terms of the Treaty of Berlin. Isvolski of Russia, a tireless intriguer, had earlier indicated to Vienna that St. Petersburg would not oppose the Austrian seizure of Bosnia and Herzegovina provided that Austria did not obstruct Russian action to open the straits of the Dardanelles. Austria, ignoring this "Buchlau bargain," went ahead with the annexation without informing Russia. Austria then refused to have the seizure discussed by a conference of the powers signatory to the Treaty of Berlin. Germany's menacing language in support of Austria forced Russia to yield. The Austro-German victory, won by diplomatic roughness, dimmed Russian prestige in the Balkans. As the inhabitants of the annexed Turkish provinces were chiefly of Slavic stock the adjoining state of Serbia resented their incorporation into the polyglot Austro-

Hungarian Empire. Lacking support from her protector, Russia, Serbia had to bow with bitterness before the Austrian demand that she cease to agitate for an outlet to the sea and that she stop stirring up trouble for Vienna among the Slavs in Bosnia and Herzegovina. Nevertheless, Serbian secret societies operated silently across the borders. Pan-Slav movements, guided by Russia, grew stronger.

A third crisis arose in 1911. A palace revolution in Fez had given France occasion to send French troops into Morocco on the grounds that endangered Europeans needed protection. Spain and Germany insisted that the French step violated the Algeciras agreement. So Spain took the Moroccan areas to which she felt entitled under a secret treaty of 1904. Germany acted in accordance with the idea of a revealing memorandum submitted to William II by his advisers: "It will do us no good to protest against the French absorption of Morocco. We must therefore secure an object which will make the French ready to give us compensations. Just as the French protect their subjects in Fez, we can do the same for ours at Agadir by peacefully stationing ships there. We can then await developments and see if the French will offer us suitable compensations. If we get them, it will make up for past failures and have a good effect on the coming elections to the Reichstag."

Germany therefore sent the gunboat *Panther* to Agadir, an obscure seaport on the Moroccan Atlantic coast, claiming a strong desire to protect "German interests." The British government, unaware of the ulterior German purposes, feared German occupation of Agadir and the creation of a German naval base on the flank of British sea lanes. Sir Edward Grey protested. Lloyd George, then chancellor of the exchequer, warned the Germans in his famous Mansion House speech. If peace could be preserved only "by allowing Britain to be treated where her interests are vitally affected as if she were of no account in the Cabinet of nations," then "peace at that price would be a humiliation intolerable for a great country like ours to endure." The German government was impressed. It seemed that Britain could also threaten. In the end it was agreed that Germany would accept as compensation for French advances in Morocco a portion of the French Congo which would be added to the Cameroons. This territory, about 100,000 square miles in area, was mostly desert, economically valueless. The *Panther* blackmail had not been very successful.

NAVAL RIVALRY

Meanwhile Germany, militant, restless, and fearful of the "encircling ring of enemies," added to her military and naval strength. In 1908 William II declared that the English were "mad, mad as March hares" to suspect the German navy. It was being built to protect German commerce, not to attack England. Nevertheless, the British were in considerable doubt about German intentions. Sir John Fisher's "all big gun" battleship, the 17,000 ton *Dreadnought,* had been launched in 1906. This ship was superior to all its predecessors; it mounted ten twelve-inch guns; it had an eleven-inch armor belt; its speed was twenty-one knots; its cost was £1,600,000. Anglo-German naval rivalry was heightened because each nation was starting from near equality so far as dreadnought construction was concerned and neither wished to be left behind. The year after the Bosnian crisis, Mr. McKenna, first lord of the Admiralty, had a heavy battle with the Treasury watchdogs about the expenses involved in his new navy bill. Despite the cries of "We want eight and we won't wait!" and the demands of Lloyd George and Winston Churchill that construction of eight dreadnoughts should begin immediately, it was decided to compromise: four British dreadnoughts were to be laid down at once and four more early in 1910 if it proved necessary. In the four years from 1910 to 1914 England increased her dreadnought strength from five to eighteen; the German advance was from two to thirteen.

To England the naval challenge was the most serious event of all. "Without a superior fleet," said Balfour, "Britain would no longer count as a power. Without any fleet at all Germany would still remain the greatest power in Europe . . . . If Germany had a bigger fleet she could not only defeat us at sea, but could soon be in London with her army. If our fleet is once defeated we are at the mercy of every plunderer." In 1912 Lord Haldane, the secretary of state for war, went on a mission to Berlin to find out if Germany would agree to slow down her naval building if Britain did likewise. Haldane had limited hopes of success. He and Admiral Tirpitz fought stiffly; Tirpitz insisted that commercial competition caused Anglo-German antagonism. Bethmann-Hollweg, the German chancellor, was very agreeable and apparently willing to retard German construction if a "general and comprehensive agreement" could be reached with England, by which was meant a political arrangement that would limit England's freedom to intervene to aid France and Russia in the event of a European war. If Britain refused to make any promise about neutrality Germany wanted a ratio of three keels to two in naval building; Britain wanted two to one.

Haldane was given the German naval estimates for 1913. These, it was said, would remain unchanged unless Britain met the German demands for a political agreement. The British Admiralty was shocked at the German figures, which provided for a huge construction program. When the Haldane mission failed Britain began to build in haste; there was a first-class naval scare. It was grimly agreed that if a war should come Britain's floating bulwark must be ready, as of old, to defend the shores of the islands and to destroy the enemy at sea.

WAR IN THE BALKANS, 1912–1913

Italy had seized the Turkish province of Tripoli in 1911. Urged on by Russia, the Balkan states of Serbia, Montenegro, Greece, and Bulgaria attacked Turkey in 1912 with the declared intention of liberating Macedonia from Turkish tyranny. When these allies had achieved a swift victory the great powers stepped in to arrange a peace settlement at the London Conference. Austria wanted to create the new state of Albania to keep Serbia from growing too large and formidable. Serbian insistence on an outlet to the Adriatic was stubbornly opposed by Austria for two reasons. A Serbian Adriatic port might be used as a Russian naval base. Secondly, the possession of such a port would strengthen the Serbian economic position. As a result of the mediation of Germany and England the danger of a general European war was temporarily avoided. When Serbia, seeking compensation, turned to seize a large section of Macedonia her former ally Bulgaria started a second Balkan War which involved Greece, Rumania, Serbia, and Turkey. The Turks recaptured Adrianople. Bulgaria was defeated and the Treaty of Bucharest of August, 1913, forced her to surrender some of the territory she had taken in the first Balkan War. The weakened Bulgarians were anxious to be revenged on Serbia. Bulgaria had always been supported by Austria. Now Bulgarian strength and Austrian prestige had declined together in the Balkans. The Serbs, inflamed by victory, increased their "Greater Serbia" agitation among their fellow Slavs in Bosnia and Herzegovina. Disorders in those two provinces of Austria grew in number and violence. Two million patriotic Slavs passionately desired to join their blood brothers in Serbia and to leave the Austro-Hungarian Empire.

On June 28, 1914, the Archduke Franz Ferdinand, heir to the Austrian throne, and his wife were assassinated in Sarajevo, the capital of Bosnia. The murderers were Bosnians. There is no doubt that they received aid from Serbian sources; that the Serbian government knew of the plot has not been proved. Austria obtained blanket assurances from Germany in support of any steps she might take against Serbia. Germany gave these assurances despite the fact that any strong Austrian course would clearly lead to dispute and possible war with Russia. Thereupon the Vienna government despatched an ultimatum to Belgrade. Confident now of Germany's full backing, the Austrians framed their ultimatum on July 23, 1914, so that Serbia could not possibly have found it agreeable. Its extreme terms, if accepted, would have ended Serbia's independent existence. For example, the note demanded the wiping out of the whole "Greater Serbia" movement and listed the steps which were to be taken, some of them under Austrian supervision, to that end. Austria required a reply within forty-eight hours.

On July 25 Serbia met nearly all the Austrian demands. The only ones she refused to accept were those which violated her sovereignty. She offered to submit the whole question at once to arbitration. No nation could have been expected to do more. Despite these tremendous concessions Austria found the Serbian reply unsatisfactory. Serbia and Austria mobilized. Three days later Austria declared war on Serbia. Behind Serbia stood Russia. "If Austria gobbles up Serbia," the Russian Sazonov had said, "we shall make war upon her." On the evening of July 29 Czar Nicholas II signed the order for general Russian mobilization. The First World War was beginning.

DIPLOMACY AND WAR

Sir Edward Grey had earlier striven desperately to prevent hostilities. He tried to get Berlin to persuade Vienna to lengthen the time limit attached to the ultimatum. He urged Russia not to mobilize at once. He proposed mediation between Austria and Russia by the four neutral powers of Great Britain, France, Germany, and Italy. France stated that she could not agree, lest it appear she was not supporting Russia; nor could Germany agree, because she had promised to back Austria. England and Russia then wanted direct discussions between Austria and Russia and mediation between Austria and Serbia. When Grey proposed a London conference of neutral powers, Germany feared that too much time might thus be given for Russian mobilization. Meanwhile Germany urged Austria to agree to negotiations with Russia. By that time, however, Austria had declared war on Serbia; Russia had begun to mobilize.

Time is a commodity of war. No nation can afford to delay in hours of crisis because delay increases the danger of being outpaced by the enemy in the first hours of conflict. To be strategically unprepared is the first military sin. The huge double mobilization plan of Russia called for the movement of troops and supplies towards the German as well as towards the Austrian borders. Germany therefore prepared for mobilization and demanded that the Russians cease their mobilization within twelve hours. To Russia's ally France Berlin sent an ultimatum demanding an unconditional promise of neutrality within eighteen hours. On August 1, Germany declared war against Russia. On August 3 she declared war against France.

Such were the European events born of aggressive nationalism, international anarchy, and the terrifying myopia of men. Would Great Britain be drawn into the expanding rings of the war whirlpool? The Liberals had long been protagonists of peace. Their great newspapers, such as the *Manchester Guardian,* the *Nation,* and the *Daily News,* spoke with one voice in favor of neutrality. Neutrality committees were formed in several cities. But the cabinet was divided. In the last week of July, 1914, a crisis faced the Liberals. A majority, including

Viscount Morley and Sir John Simon, were against intervention. A strong minority, including Sir Edward Grey, Winston Churchill, and Prime Minister Asquith, were in favor of moving at once in support of France and Russia. "If we are engaged in war," said Sir Edward Grey, "we shall suffer but little more than we shall suffer even if we stand aside." Only the skilful handling of the cabinet by Asquith prevented disorder or dissolution.

To the urgent requests of France and Russia for an assurance regarding British support Sir Edward Grey was compelled by his colleagues to reply that Britain would make no commitments. At the same time the British government refused to give Germany any guarantee that she would remain neutral. On July 31 Grey asked both France and Germany to respect the neutrality of Belgium. France agreed; Germany sent an evasive reply. On August 2, after considerable debate, Sir Edward Grey was authorized to assure the French government, subject to the consent of Parliament, that "if the German fleet comes into the Channel or through the North Sea to undertake hostile operations against the French coasts or shipping, the British fleet will give all the protection in its power." It was held that Britain could do no less, as the French fleet was in the Mediterranean as a result of arrangements reached earlier in the British and French naval conversations. At noon on August 2 the Conservative party sent a message to the cabinet stating that, in their judgment, "it would be fatal to the honor and security of the United Kingdom to hesitate in supporting France and Russia" and offering "unhesitating support in any measures the government may consider necessary for that object."

The decisive event was a German ultimatum to Belgium demanding the unopposed passage of the German armies through Belgium to invade France at her least fortified boundary. Prussia had guaranteed Belgian neutrality in 1839 along with Great Britain and France. Would Britain go to war because Germany had torn up "a scrap of paper"? In addition to the impulse of moral obligation there was the important fact of vital and immediate British self-interest. It had long been a pivotal point of British policy that no great power should menace or control the Belgian coast. Opinion in cabinet, Parliament, and press swiftly hardened. Where there had been division there was soon almost unanimity. The degree of British obligation to France and Russia, never clearly defined, was no longer a question for debate. The important thing was the indisputable treaty commitment to Belgium and the threat to British national security in the German thrust towards the coast and the narrow seas.

On August 3 the British government sent an ultimatum to Germany demanding the immediate withdrawal of her forces across the Belgian borders. Attached to the ultimatum was a time limit expiring at midnight. When Germany sent no reply Britain was at war. "We

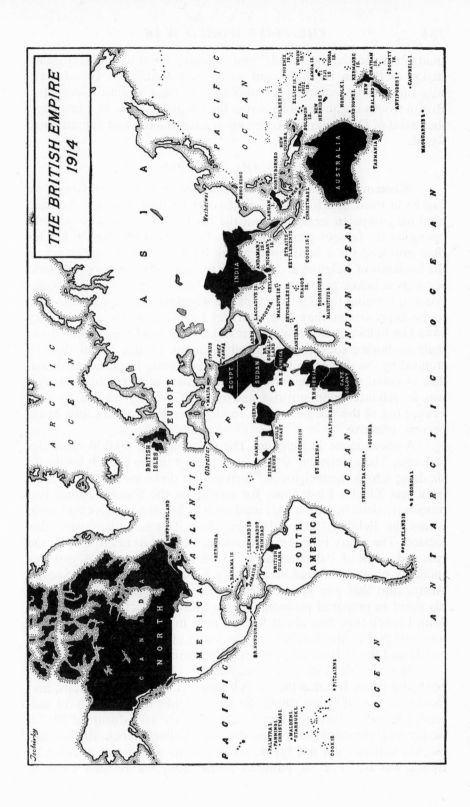

shall never sheathe the sword," said Asquith, "until the military domination of Prussia is wholly and finally destroyed." The British navy
was ordered to "commence hostilities at once against Germany."
British troops began to move across the Channel. Thus, in a few days,
the sword of Damocles had fallen upon a bewildered and apprehensive
world.

THE WAR: 1914–1916

"Remember," William II had twice said to Sir Edward Grey, "we
can be in Paris in a fortnight." When war resulted from the Austrian
punitive campaign against Serbia the Germans immediately put into
operation the famous plan designed by Count Schlieffen in 1906. This
plan provided for a hard, swift attack by five German armies across
the lowlands of Belgium and northern France; two more armies would
serve as a heavy pivotal anchor about Metz. The First and Second
Armies, forming the right wing of the wheeling German forces, were
to be kept strong; they had to travel farther than the others; they
would be fighting hard. It was their task to tear the French flanks from
their anchoring sockets and to roll them up. France would then be
stunned by the savage and unexpected hammering from the northeast.
The essential and distinguishing characteristic of this Schlieffen plan
was its reliance upon surprise and speed. Germany wanted to blast
France out of the war before the cumbersome Russian machine could
become effective.

A check came in Belgium. The Germans had 40,000 casualties
at Liege. Their timetable called for a plunge to the French border in
six days; it took them eighteen. Then several divisions were withdrawn
from von Kluck's First Army for service on the Eastern Front; two
more were detached from that weakened right wing to mask Antwerp,
where the Belgians had withdrawn. Thus German plans were dis-
located. The weary First Army hesitated, reduced its arc to loop to the
east and south of Paris instead of to the west and south. A gap was
suddenly opened between von Kluck's First and von Bulow's Second
Army. Into that gap poured British and French troops. Joffre took
his stand in prepared positions on the Marne. The British under Sir
John French now had about 90,000 men in the field. The Germans
were stopped in the butchery of the battle of the Marne (September
5–10) and thrust back thirty miles to the Aisne.

At once "the race to the sea" began. The Germans took Antwerp and drove towards the French seaports of Dunkirk, Calais, and
Boulogne. Had they got round the Allied flanks they might have succeeded in rolling them up; they would certainly have disrupted British
supply and communication lines. But the bending French, British, and
Belgian defenses did not break. So began the exhausting attrition of
trench warfare. For six hundred miles, from the Belgian coast to

Switzerland, the immense and dreary front became an almost rigid line, marked by twisting trenches and barbed wire, churned by shells, cursed by mud, cold, and rats. It was now clear that the war would be long. New tactics and new weapons were to be developed as further chapters were added to the history of man's achievements in the art of organized demolition, homicide, and mayhem. Tanks and poison gas joined with the submarine and new artillery to contribute to the rising slaughter.

As the first phase of the war ended, the British Fleet had bottled up the German navy at Kiel and elsewhere. By 1915 the seas were swept clear of all their prowling warships. Because the Germans were able to send no aid over the seas to their colonies all except German East Africa were captured early in the war. South Africa took German South West Africa; New Zealand seized Samoa, and Australia, German New Guinea; France and Britain overran Togoland and the Cameroons; Japan, who had entered the war under the terms of the Anglo-Japanese alliance of 1902, took Kiaochow and several Pacific islands. British control of the seas also kept troops, equipment, and food flowing to the United Kingdom and the war fronts from all the world. Economic warfare and blockade controls began the slow throttling process so important in the First and Second World Wars. Only the German merchant ships that remained moored to their docks stayed afloat; the rest were sunk. Britain extended the list of contraband goods and resolutely stopped and searched all ships bound for Germany or neutral states from which Germany might get supplies. All contraband, including foodstuffs, was seized.

In the field of economic cooperation the Allied nations achieved a degree of mutual assistance hitherto unknown. There developed financial alliances; cooperation in the purchase and allocation of food, war supplies, and transport facilities; committee and conciliar control in the creation of inter-Allied bodies with executive powers. Devices used within the British Empire in the First World War forecast the emergence of intra-Imperial committees and conferences of experts: the Imperial Economic Committee; the Empire Trade Board; the Imperial Shipping Committee; conferences on education, air communication, government statistics, and many other subjects.

In Europe the German Empire alone had 4,300,000 fully trained men. The French army was badly shaken. Before the end of the year 1915 over 3,000,000 volunteers had come into the British forces, with 30,000 additional men needed each week. In January, 1916, the first Military Service Act conscripted all unmarried men between the ages of eighteen and forty-one; later all between the ages of eighteen and fifty were called up. Canada, New Zealand, and Newfoundland passed similar acts. Conscription was repugnant, but necessary. By the end of the war the British Empire had 8,654,000 men under arms. From the United Kingdom came 5,704,000; from India, 1,100,000; from Canada, 641,000; from Australia, 417,000; from New Zealand, 220,-000; from South Africa, 136,000. Of these over 2,000,000 were wounded; about 950,000 were killed.

On the Eastern Front the German High Command had made another miscalculation. The Russians, mobilizing with unexpected speed, had lunged out of Russian Poland in a two-pronged offensive into East Prussia and eastern Galicia. It was then that the Germans had to withdraw troops from their western assault forces. At the battle of Tannenberg (August 26–September 1) General Paul von Hindenburg routed the Russians advancing through East Prussia. Meanwhile the Russian attack in the Austrian sector rolled unchecked to the forts of Cracow, in western Galicia. In May, 1915, the Germans and Austrians mounted a huge counteroffensive. The Russians were driven out of Galicia. Hindenburg captured Warsaw. Russian armies, staggering before a series of crippling onslaughts, fell back behind their own borders. The Allies of the west now realized that as a military factor the power of Russia was rapidly becoming a negligible quantity. The Russian army system was mired in bogs of corruption and incompetence; training and equipment were poor; troops grew demoralized as hope fell away; the whole state, it seemed, was beginning to disintegrate.

Meanwhile in October, 1914, Turkey entered the war on the side of the central powers. This event brought a threat to the southern bastions of Russia and to the British in Egypt and the East. If Germany and Austria could establish a direct bridge to Turkey through Bulgaria, Greece, and Rumania, that challenge would be reinforced. Because of the stalemate on the western front the Allies probed for strategic and important soft spots to attack elsewhere. It was decided to make an attempt to force the entrance to the straits of the Dardanelles with a view to removing the Turks from the war, opening up the Black Sea, and funnelling aid to Russia. In March, 1915, a naval bombardment failed. In April 29,000 British and Anzac troops were landed on six cruel beaches at Gallipoli; but the Turks could not be driven from their prepared positions on the dominating slopes. Not until the end of the year were the surviving men withdrawn. Nothing had been gained by the costly blunder.

To the dark Russian and Gallipoli chapters of 1915 was added a third. Bulgaria joined Germany and Austria in the conquest of Serbia. About 100,000 Serbian soldiers escaped to Albania and were picked off the Adriatic coast by Allied naval forces. The rest remained in enemy hands. Albania and Montenegro were also overrun by Austro-German armies. The pro-Ally Premier Venizelos of Greece had arranged for the landing of a British force at Salonika. But the Greek King Constantine, who was prevented from allying his country with

Germany only by fear of British naval power, decided to remain neutral. These Balkan developments had created a bridge for the central powers to Turkey. Meanwhile Italy, bargaining for territorial gains Austria was not prepared to grant, joined the Allies. Because France and Britain misjudged the value of Italian military aid they promised her parts of "unredeemed Italy" such as the Istrian Peninsula, a part of the Dalmatian coast, and the Brenner Pass.

On the Western Front the carnage of trench warfare continued. Great frontal attacks, such as the German thrust in the second battle of Ypres (February, 1915) where Germany used poison gas, failed at tremendous cost. Major British and French offensives were halted. After the Germans had disposed of the Russian threat they moved thousands of troops back to the west where determined attempts were made to break through the Allied lines, especially at Verdun (February–June, 1916) where the French and Germans each lost about 350,000 men. In July the British and French in turn began a great drive on the Somme salient. The British under Sir Douglas Haig held fifteen miles on the twenty-five-mile line of attack. In the first day the British lost 60,000 men; it was the blackest day in British military history. In the first week they gained five miles and lost 170,000 men. They moved only slowly over the tortured earth; they fought desperately from trench to trench; then they stopped. The Germans fell back on their heavily defended rear positions. Their casualties totalled 500,-000; the British suffered 410,000; the French, 190,000. In the two battles of Verdun and the Somme the Allies had 950,000 casualties and the Germans 850,000.

At the same time the Germans crushed Rumania and occupied Bucharest. The British had been halted in Mesopotamia. An entire army under General Townshend was forced to surrender at Kut-el-Amara after a defense of 147 days without reinforcements. British prestige was shaken throughout the Moslem world. A cataract of disaster had fallen upon the Allied cause. In these months the chief grounds for dispassionate and restrained optimism lay in the fact that the strength of the Austro-German surge had been reduced by the terrific attrition; the Allies had a greater reservoir of manpower; the silent blockade was having its effect; industry was being deliberately organized for war production.

Meanwhile the main sea battle of the war was fought at Jutland on May 31, 1916. For the first time out of port and on the prowl the German fleet was discovered by a squadron of British cruisers under Admiral Beatty. Behind Beatty was the main British fleet commanded by Admiral Jellicoe. The German Admiral von Hipper tried to lead Beatty towards the German High Seas Fleet under Admiral Scheer. When Jellicoe and Scheer came into the action late in the day the British vainly attempted to cut off the German retreat. In the fog and the gathering darkness the German fleet escaped. By gun and torpedo they had inflicted on the British heavier losses than they had suffered themselves; but the Germans knew that they had been saved from destruction only by darkness and fortune. They did not emerge again from their home bases until the war ended.

THE COALITION GOVERNMENTS

In the first two years of conflict several important political developments had occurred in England. The position of Asquith, in 1914 apparently unassailable, had been steadily undermined. A major explosion had shaken the cabinet in May, 1915, when Admiral Sir John Fisher, the eccentric genius who was first sea lord, quarreled with Winston Churchill. Churchill supported the British assault in the Dardanelles. "In the East take Constantinople. Take it by ships if you can. Take it by soldiers if you must. But take it; take it soon; take it while time remains." Fisher, on the other hand, wanted a sudden descent on the Baltic coast of Germany. Both Churchill and Fisher resigned.

Asquith was also harassed by the mounting feeling against Lord Kitchener, who had succeeded Haldane as secretary of state for war. Although the name of the conqueror of Khartum had been magic the public confidence in him was shaken by the revelations of the powerful Northcliffe press regarding the shocking shell shortage and Kitchener's obstinate opposition to the creation of a separate ministry of munitions. Despite Kitchener's protests Lloyd George became minister of munitions, surrendering the post of chancellor of the exchequer to Reginald McKenna. There the torrent of his activity resulted in a production of shells earlier deemed impossible by the war office and the industrialists. These events combined with the alarming casualty lists and restlessness of the Conservatives to produce the first coalition cabinet. The Conservative Bonar Law became colonial secretary; Balfour went to the admiralty. In the new government were twelve Liberals, eight Conservatives, one Labourite, and Lord Kitchener. When Kitchener was drowned in the *Hampshire* in the summer of 1916 Lloyd George succeeded him as war secretary.

By the end of 1916 the drag and darkness of the war scene increased the impatient assaults upon Asquith. Public and press were often cruelly unjust. There were demands that Asquith be replaced as prime minister by Lloyd George, who seemed better fitted to play the part of war leader. The efficiency of Lloyd George as minister of munitions, his great reputation as an individual who could inspire public enthusiasm, won him wide support. He had preached the need of doggedness. "I feel that we are not waging this war in the way wars alone can be waged. I hate war; I abominate it . . . but once you are in it you have to go grimly through it, otherwise the causes which hang upon it will all perish." He had pointed out the evils of delay.

"Too late in moving here. Too late in arriving there. Too late in coming to this decision. Too late in starting that enterprise . . . In this war the footsteps of the Allied forces have been dogged by the mocking spectre of 'too late.' " His was a hurrying spirit that contrasted strongly with the calm and judicial Asquith. The English public felt the need of a lively organizer of victory, a new Pitt. That fact accounted for the fall of Asquith more than any political intrigues. In December, 1916, several resignations from the cabinet forced Asquith to resign himself and thus to end the longest premiership since that of Lord Liverpool.

Lloyd George immediately formed the second coalition cabinet. In it the Conservative element was stronger than before, although party lines were becoming blurred at this stage of the war. New ministries of air, labor, and pensions were created. A food controller and a shipping controller were appointed. Winston Churchill returned as minister of munitions. Accompanying these political shifts were other important developments. Government power and responsibility had been temporarily increased during the war. The Defense of the Realm Consolidation Act of 1914 and later legislation had given to the king in council vast authority "to issue regulations for securing the public safety." It was in the national interest that individual liberties should be restricted where such restriction contributed to the successful prosecution of the war. Famous judicial decisions, as in the case of the King *v.* Halliday (1917) and the Attorney General *v.* De Keyser's Royal Hotel (1920) made it clear that in time of war a great nation could not be governed on the principles of Magna Carta.

The burden of increasing domestic and war business and the importance of speed and efficiency made a large cabinet cumbersome and unwieldy. Moreover, the twenty-nine ministers who were heads of departments had much more departmental work than before the war. Lloyd George therefore created a small, flexible, inner "war cabinet" of three Conservatives, one Liberal, and one Labourite. Bonar Law, chancellor of the exchequer, was the only one who held a portfolio and had departmental duties. The rest were completely free to devote their full time and to reach swift decisions in matters of policy. The other ministers were outside the regular meetings of the inner circle of the war cabinet. They carried on their heavy administrative duties and came to the war cabinet only when the interests of their departments were intimately concerned. For the first time in history minutes of these cabinet meetings were kept and later published. The flexible nature of the British system was clearly demonstrated by the emergence of this new institution. It was further illustrated by a second innovation, simple in operation and important in its implications.

On three occasions in 1917 and 1918 the war cabinet expanded into a wider Imperial war cabinet. To "special and continuous meetings" of the British war cabinet came the Dominion prime ministers, the secretary of state for India and Indian representatives, and the secretary of state for the colonies. These men were full members of the British cabinet for questions of Imperial world policy. The Dominion prime ministers were not members of the same Parliament; they were not responsible to the same Parliament. They sat in the Imperial war cabinet for no other reason than that the interests of the Empire demanded it.

Although the main task of the coalition government was the vigorous prosecution of the war two important measures in the field of domestic legislation were passed in 1918. The first was the Representation of the People Act, or fourth Reform Bill, which gave the vote to all men over twenty-one years of age who occupied either a residence, or business premises of a yearly value of not less than £10, or held a university degree. The franchise was also extended to include all women over thirty years of age who occupied property of a yearly value of not less than £5 or whose husband met that occupation qualification. Women over thirty years of age were also permitted to register as parliamentary electors if they had passed university residence and examination requirements which would have given them university degrees had they not been barred from receiving them by reason of their sex.

The act of 1918 also provided that no person might vote in more than two of the constituencies where he might be properly qualified and registered. No person was to be disqualified from voting because he had received poor relief. Election expenses of candidates were to be limited. Finally, the ninth schedule to the act contained a complete amended list of all constituencies in the United Kingdom setting forth the number of members to be returned by each. By a redistribution of seats thirty-seven new members were added to the house of commons. This redistribution recognized more completely than before the principle of representation by population. There was now to be one member of Parliament for every 70,000 persons in Great Britain and one for every 43,000 in Ireland. This act added about 8,000,000 voters to the electorate, including 6,000,000 women. By another law of 1918 women over twenty-one years of age were made eligible for election to the house of commons. The Sex-Disqualification Removal Act of 1919 further advanced the banners unfurled by the suffragettes earlier in the century.

The second important domestic measure of 1918 was an Education Act which increased the educational benefits available to the working classes. All children between the ages of five and fourteen were required to attend school regularly; children between the ages of fourteen and eighteen were to spend a certain number of hours a week in continuation schools. The act also established nursery schools and schools for mentally defective children. More adequate provision was made for free medical care. Several sections of the act dealt with the problem of raising standards in the training of elementary school teachers and in guaranteeing a higher scale of salaries throughout the teaching profession.

THE WAR: 1917

At the end of 1916 the Germans made proposals for a peace conference. They had recently conquered Rumania. Victory sat on their banners almost everywhere. Nevertheless, their losses had been terrible; they did not want the war prolonged. The Allies, however, had no desire to accept German terms. Lloyd George declared: "To enter, on the invitation of Germany, proclaiming herself victorious, without any knowledge of the proposals she has to make, is to put our heads into a noose." The war continued.

After the sinking without warning of the British liner *Lusitania* in February, 1915, Germany had relaxed her submarine activities partly because of her fear of bringing the United States into the war. In 1917, however, the Germans decided to remain on the defensive on land and to use the submarine ruthlessly to starve Great Britain into surrender. On February 1 the German government announced the beginning of unrestricted submarine warfare. Any ship, Allied or neutral, was to be sunk at sight if found within a certain distance of Great Britain, France, or Italy. At once British shipping losses shot upwards; the situation became very serious. In April, for example, 875,000 tons of shipping went down. Only a few weeks' supply of food remained in Britain; the ration allowances were reduced and reduced again. Then the British began to use the convoy system, with excellent results. Depth bombs often found their targets beneath the surface of the seas; "Q-boat" decoys and mines added to the German list of overdue submarines. By no great margin, but by enough, the challenge was beaten off. Late in 1917 it was certain that submarines would not win the war and that Britain would be fed.

As the Germans had feared, the unrestricted submarine attacks added the United States to the ranks of the Allies in April, 1917. To defeat Germany the United States was prepared, in the words of President Wilson, to "dedicate our lives and our fortunes, everything that we are and everything that we have." It was a formidable foe that Germany's prowess in brutality had brought against her. British and American shipyards were soon producing twice as many ships as the submarines were sinking. American warships at once helped to convoy supplies to the United Kingdom. Before April, 1917, the Allies had been anxious to avoid straining or rupturing friendly relations with the United States by enforcing the blockade against Germany too vigorously where American goods or interests were concerned. After the

United States entered the war it was possible to close sluices that had hitherto been open. Blockade controls were tightened everywhere. The doctrine of freedom of the seas was abandoned. The want of balance in German food resulting from the blockade, and particularly the deficiency in fats and oils, helped to undermine the health and powers of resistance of the German people.

A month before the United States joined the Allies, Russia collapsed as a result of a bloody domestic revolution. The ancient Tsarist government was overthrown; Nicholas II abdicated and was later murdered. But the provisional government of Prince Lvov and Kerensky was in turn destroyed by Nicholas Lenin, leader of the radical Bolsheviks. Lenin, an apostle of Karl Marx, was determined and merciless in his methods. His end was the achievement of a Communist state under the unquestioned control of the leaders of the Communist party until the inevitable withering away of the state and the emergence of a classless society and the dictatorship of the people. Lenin and his comrades stood together and killed their enemies, then and later. Some, like Leon Trotsky, once the close associate of Lenin, were stalked abroad for years and finally slain by Communists far from Moscow. With the progress of the Bolshevik revolution the Russian army dissolved. In the spring of 1918 the Russians signed the severe treaty of Brest-Litovsk imposed upon them by Germany. Over 600,-000 German soldiers were released for service in the west.

On the western front the battle lines swayed back and forth and the murderous losses continued. The Germans had retreated to the apparently impregnable defenses of the Hindenburg Line and against that obstacle the waves of French troops broke in vain at the center of the front. The British renewed their attacks in Flanders' fields. The battle of Passchendaele was fought in a horrible sea of mud. This struggle, which lasted from July until November, 1917, cost the British 300,000 casualties. It was followed by the battle of Cambrai where tanks were used on a large scale for the first time. There a German counterattack changed British victory into defeat. On the southern front a part of the Italian line at Caporetto collapsed under pressure from Austro-German forces transferred from Russia. The routed Italian Second Army was forced back all the way to the Piave River.

Only in the Near East did the Allies find comfort. There General Maude recaptured Kut-el-Amara, seized Bagdad, and chased the enemy northward. In Palestine General Allenby and T. E. Lawrence brought the Turks nearer defeat. Beersheba and Gaza fell. In December, 1917, Allenby took Jerusalem in the last of many Christian crusades. The Allied morale was also strengthened by the deposition of the pro-German King Constantine of Greece. Premier Venizelos was then able to bring Greece into the war against Germany.

THE LAST PHASE

Early in 1918, with about forty divisions released from the eastern theatre, the Germans determined to stake all on three great blows in the west. If these offensives had succeeded the war would have been over before any large numbers of Americans had arrived in France. Through a heavy fog on March 21 Ludendorff uncoiled his first attack on the British near the old Somme battlefield. The numerical superiority of the Germans was nearly two to one. Ludendorff used a creeping and intense barrage along a forty-three-mile front followed by flame-throwers, machine gunners, and infantry. A break through the British lines would have meant the fall of the great railway center of Amiens. The French and British armies would then have been separated and the British hurled back to the Channel. In two black weeks the Germans drove a salient bulging forty miles deep to within ten miles of Amiens. General Sir Douglas Haig ordered his forces to retreat no more. "There is no course open to us but to fight it out. Every position must be held to the last man; there must be no retirement." The bending British lines did not break. Meanwhile the evils of divided command in the hour of terrible danger resulted in the selection of General Ferdinand Foch as supreme commander of all Allied forces in the western front.

In the middle of April Ludendorff suddenly struck a second blow on the northern front immediately south of Ypres. Armentières fell; the road seemed open to Ostend, Dunkirk, Calais, and Boulogne. But the Allied gaps were sealed over. Against the obstinate lines the Germans made no progress. A third attack was then begun against the French between Rheims and Soissons. In seventy hours the Germans advanced thirty miles to Chateau Thierry on the Marne; they were within fifty miles of Paris. But again they were stopped; two American divisions had arrived to bolster the French. Twice more Ludendorff tried to break through. The Allied lines were solid.

By this time the nightmare of the German High Command had become a reality. American troops were arriving at the rate of 250,000 a month. Ludendorff made a last effort on July 15, though desperately short of reserves. When the German thrust was stopped Foch began a counteroffensive on July 18. This second battle of the Marne marked the beginning of the end. The German Chancellor, Bethmann-Hollweg, later said: "We attacked on the 15th. By the 18th even the most optimistic among us understood that all was lost. The history of the world was played out in those three days." On August 8, using nearly 500 tanks, the British, Canadians, and Australians wiped out the German bulge in the Amiens area. "This," said Ludendorff, "was the black day of the German Army."

Even as the tide of military fortune began to go against the central powers the adroit paper offensive of British propaganda increased in scope and intensity. In 1917 Lord Northcliffe had become "director of propaganda in enemy lands." The Germans called him "a forger, falsifier, assassin, and the most thorough-going rascal of the Entente." At Crewe House Northcliffe assembled a group of distinguished writers including Wickham Steed, Professor Seton-Watson, and H. G. Wells. Under his direction leaflets, pictures, weekly newspapers, and millions of pamphlets were prepared. In the unflagging campaign of paper Northcliffe tried to induce the Austrians and Germans to end the war. Pamphlets and newspapers were dropped from airplanes, thrown in dummy hand grenades, shot into the enemy trenches in rockets. Hundreds of thousands of subversive leaflets were dropped daily to aid in the destruction of German confidence. "The soldier thought it could not be all enemy lies," said Hindenburg later. "He allowed it to poison his mind."

In September and October, 1918, the Americans, Belgians, British, and French continued to advance against stubborn German resistance. One by one Germany's allies crumpled. The Allied army that had earlier been sent to Salonika now leaped upon Bulgaria and forced her to sign an armistice on September 29. The Turks, hamstrung by the slashing attacks of Allenby on the long roads from Bagdad, Damascus, and Aleppo, followed suit. In October the British and Italians struck at Austria on the Piave front with swift success. The British moved through the Tyrol into Bavaria; the Italians seized Trent and Trieste, and thus achieved two of their major aims in the war. On November 3 Austria signed an armistice. Revolution shook Vienna. A mutiny in the German navy flamed into a general German revolt. William II abdicated and sought security in flight. On November 11, 1918, Germany signed an armistice in a railway dining car in a French forest.

Had Germany been lured to final ruin by the doctrines of Bismarck, Moltke, and Treitschke? Her starving, defeated, and embittered population now awaited the dictates of the victors. In the cities of the Allied nations people danced and sang in the streets. On November 18 Lord Curzon declared in the house of lords: "The Armistice is not only the precursor, but it is the sure guarantee of peace. . . . The armies have already won peace; it will remain for the statesmen to see that it is honourable and lasting."

Chapter 36

THE PROBLEMS OF PEACE

PEACEMAKING, 1919

WHAT Lloyd George had called "the blood-stained stagger to victory" was finished. In December, 1918, the coalition government carried 485 seats in a national election. This was a landslide victory. In the new house the Labour party had sixty-one members. The independent Asquith Liberals who continued to oppose the government obtained only twenty-eight seats; Asquith himself was defeated in his own riding. The indefatigable cabinet that had been in at the winning of the war was thus rewarded and given an overwhelming mandate to win the peace.

In the election campaign Lloyd George and his colleagues, aware of the bitter public temper, did nothing to moderate popular demands for the punishment of Germany. "Who is to foot the bill?" asked the prime minister. "By the jurisprudence of any civilized country the loser pays. It is not a question of vengeance; it is a question of justice . . . I have always said that we will exact the last penny that we can out of Germany up to the limit of her capacity to pay. With regard to the Kaiser, there is absolutely no question but that he has committed a grave crime against international right. There is absolutely no doubt that he ought to be held responsible for it." Beyond such general election statements about the making of peace with Germany there were many promises regarding the creation of a new and happier England. For example, it was asserted that a swift surge of national prosperity could be expected; the returning soldiers would find "homes fit for heroes to live in."

In January, 1919, amid national passions inflamed by propaganda and suffering, the representatives of twenty-seven nations met at Versailles to make a victors' peace. Allied occupation forces were in Germany. The German fleet that had failed to seize the trident of Neptune was scuttled by its German crews at Scapa Flow. No representatives of the four defeated nations were invited to participate in the peace conference. The humiliation of the conquered enemy was complete. After the Adriatic ambitions of Italy were thwarted and she withdrew from Versailles the terms of peace were largely determined by the leading spokesmen of the United States, Great Britain, and France: Wilson, Lloyd George, and Clemenceau. These men, aided by their staffs of experts, labored to produce treaties that would establish some kind of reasonable settlement.

Clemenceau fiercely insisted that Germany must be punished and kept too weak to be dangerous; that was his chief concern. It was realism, he said, to recognize that France must have hard and firm guarantees against the resurgence of German power. President Wilson feared that the kind of peace terms for which Clemenceau clamored would provoke another war. He placed his trust in general principles of justice bulwarked by the League of Nations. But Clemenceau saw a great gulf fixed between the ideal and the actual. He wanted international guarantees, backed by political and economic sanctions and, if need be, by the sword. Lloyd George, always shrewdly aware of the watching eyes of the British voter, took a strong line only when the interests of Britain were directly concerned. In all else he urged moderation. The result was an unsatisfactory compromise.

By the Treaty of Versailles Germany returned Alsace-Lorraine to France. To France she also surrendered the Saar coal mines. For fifteen years the whole Saar basin was to be under the control of the League of Nations. Both banks of the Rhine were demilitarized. An Allied army was to occupy the left bank of the Rhine for at least fifteen years. To the new Poland, which appeared on the map of Europe for the first time since the third partition of 1795, Germany also lost West Prussia, a section of Silesia, and a part of Posen. Danzig, at the end of the "Polish corridor to the sea," was made a free port under the control of the League of Nations. As a result of a plebiscite Germany also yielded the northern half of Schleswig to Denmark.

All German colonies were surrendered to the Allies. These were to be held by various nations as mandates from the League of Nations. Under the rules governing the administration of mandates the League was to receive annual reports from the holding powers. The mandates were to expire when the occupied colonies were considered fit for independence.

Most of the German colonies were not ready for self-government. Japan took over the German concessions in the Shantung peninsula and the German Pacific islands north of the equator; Australia and New Zealand administered all but one of the German islands south of the equator. The Union of South Africa virtually absorbed German South West Africa. Great Britain obtained as mandated territory German East Africa (Tanganyika) and divided Togoland and the Cameroons with France.

As partial compensation for the damage done by their submarines the Germans were required to surrender all shipping over 1,500 tons as well as half of their ships between 500 and 1,500 tons and a fourth of their fishing trawlers. New shipping to a total of 1,000,000 tons was to be built by Germany and handed over to the Allies. The Germans were also asked to surrender 30,000 freight cars, 5,000 locomotives, thousands of trucks, agricultural implements, horses, hogs, and cattle; they gave up all their ocean cables; they promised to deliver annually thousands of tons of coal to the Allies. Germany had surrendered her fleet. She was also required to reduce her army to a maximum strength of 100,000 men, as a prelude to general disarmament.

The Austro-Hungarian Empire was broken up by the treaties of St. Germain and Trianon. Rumania obtained Transylvania from Hungary, on the famous principle of nationality or "self-determination." Serbia became the kingdom of Jugoslavia and took the southern Slav provinces of Austria. Czechoslovakia was created out of Bohemia, Moravia, and the Slovak part of Hungary. Poland took Galicia. Italy took Istria and Trent. Bulgaria surrendered her Aegean coastline to Greece. As an anchor of protection against Germany in eastern Europe France soon made an alliance with Poland and with the "Little Entente" powers of Jugoslavia, Czechoslovakia, and the enlarged Rumania.

Out of the Russian provinces surrendered to Germany by the Treaty of Brest-Litovsk were created independent republics: Finland, Esthonia, Latvia, and Lithuania. By the Treaty of Sevres (1920) with Turkey the non-Turkish provinces of Syria and Lebanon were given as mandates to France, and Iraq, Transjordania, and Palestine as mandates to Britain. Smyrna and a section of the Anatolian coast went to Greece. Constantinople and the Dardanelles were placed under international control. The Turks under Mustapha Kemal later forced a revision of this arrangement. By the Treaty of Lausanne (1923) they kept Constantinople and the whole of Asia Minor.

Thus the Allies made over the map of Europe. There remained the question of reparations to be paid by Germany. By the terms of the Treaty of Versailles Germany undertook to "make compensation for all damage done to the civilian population." The prolonged insistence on excessive reparations brought infinite mischief and confusion to the whole world. The Allies demanded that one billion pounds be paid immediately. A Reparations Commission was established to decide the total sum that might be expected from Germany. It was first suggested by the Hughes-Cunliffe Committee of 1918 that Germany should pay a total of £24,000,000,000 in annual installments of £1,200,000,000. The Boulogne Conference figure of June, 1920, was £13,450,000,000. In March, 1921, the Germans offered £1,500,000,-000. In April, 1921, the Reparations Commission recommended the collection of £6,600,000,000. There were twelve international conferences about reparations. Thirty-nine cabinets in central and western Europe fell as a result of reparations controversies. All of these discussions accelerated the economic collapse of Germany that came with despair, bankruptcy, inflation, and the ruin of the middle class. They delayed the restoration of normal business and trade in Europe and the world. Likewise the prolonged and abortive disarmament debates were to retard the development of reasonable stability in international relations. The old disorder in Europe had not abated.

THE LEAGUE OF NATIONS

At Versailles the Allies created the League of Nations, an international body that was superseded by the United Nations Organization in 1946. The Covenant that created the League was made an integral part of the peace treaties. Hence the defeated nations did not consider it as a foundation stone of a new order but rather as an instrument of ruthless victors to maintain their peace settlement. Neither the beaten central powers nor Communist Russia were at first permitted to become members. The structure of the League was further deranged by the withdrawal of the United States. At the same time Britain soon made it clear that she was reluctant to enter into any further agreements for the preservation of the status quo in Europe. As a member of the League she was bound to support the peace settlement, but not too strongly. Her domestic troubles seemed sufficient in their weight and urgency.

Successive British governments were also keenly aware that the Dominions shared, to a large degree, the apathy of the United States; Britain could not rely upon their support in any forthright Continental policy. Only in 1925, the bright year of Locarno, did Britain repeat and extend her guarantee of the frontiers established in Western Europe by the Treaty of Versailles. Beyond that she did not travel far. British representatives attended disarmament conferences; her ambassadors and statesmen preached the virtues of moderation and goodwill. Meanwhile strong and evil forces were going about their corrosive work. Soon the Germans openly challenged the settlement of 1919. Then, with a new sense of Teutonic destiny, they removed the shackles hammered out at Versailles and prepared for the day of revenge.

In the Covenant of the League of Nations the members pledged themselves "to promote international cooperation and to achieve international peace and security." In Article Ten of the Covenant the League undertook "to respect or preserve as against external oppression the territorial integrity and existing political independence of all members." By Article Sixteen it was the duty of the League to punish aggression on the part of any of its members by "financial and economic measures" and by "armed forces." Nevertheless Japan invaded China in 1931; Italy, invading Ethiopia in 1935, was not deterred by the imposition of weak "economic sanctions" by fifty nations. The League also undertook to labor for the limitation of armaments "to the lowest point consistent with national safety." All future international treaties were to be published; all earlier treaties incompatible with the Covenant were to be abrogated.

The Assembly of the League, in which each member had one vote, was to meet annually at Geneva to "confer, advise and deliberate." The Council, or executive of the League, contained five permanent members, representing the leading powers and four (later nine) non-permanent members chosen by the smaller powers. All international disputes likely to cause war were to be submitted by League members to arbitration or judicial investigation. The permanent Court of International Justice was to meet in the Palace of Peace at the Hague. The administrative Secretariat formed an international civil service. The International Labour Office was to investigate and report upon world labor conditions and problems and to recommend desirable labor legislation. There were also numerous committees established to deal with specific questions, such as the supervision of mandates, plebiscites in disputed regions, child welfare, arms and narcotics traffic, slavery, general health problems, and international transport.

Such, briefly stated, was the purpose and the constitution of the League of Nations. In the beginning it was a reasonable, earnest, and intelligent attempt to achieve collective security. The essential principle of the League was that the members composing it, while surrendering none of their sovereign independence, should recognize that they were partners in the greater unity of the human whole. The retreat of the world from this high hope is explained in the following pages.

GREAT BRITAIN: THE ECONOMIC PROBLEMS

"The nations have bled at every vein," said Lloyd George, "and this restlessness you get everywhere today is the fever of anaemia." Britain, however, did not suffer so much as Germany or France; she had been neither defeated nor invaded. Immediately after the war there was a short, swift boom. British coal, for example, was exported to Europe at £5 a ton. Then the wheel turned. Many former Continental customers, now exhausted, could not buy. Russia and Germany were no longer trade rivals; but neither were they purchasers of British goods. Disabled Germany had been Britain's best customer before the war. Japan had invaded many British markets in the East. The United States had increased her export trade to Latin America, at Britain's expense. Economic nationalism in Europe and America resulted in higher tariff barriers restricting the entrance of British products. With deflation of wages in Britain the workers found themselves with reduced purchasing power.

The importance of these factors is evident when it is recalled that Britain's population is the most highly industrialized in Europe. Of the total occupied population seven work in industry for every one that works in agriculture. Naturally Britain is very highly dependent on imported foodstuffs. Between 1919 and 1929, Britain produced only fifteen per cent of the wheat needed by her people; forty-four per cent of the meat; twenty per cent of the vegetables; sixty per cent of the fish. She imported fruit to an annual value of about £54,000,000; and produced about £8,500,000 worth at home. About a quarter of Britain's imports usually come from the Empire, the rest from foreign countries. Despite considerable annual variations, about forty per cent of her imported goods come from Europe and twenty-nine per cent of her total exports go there. About thirty-eight per cent of Britain's working population are normally engaged in producing for export markets. Foreign trade has always been the pillar of Britain's prosperity. The shipping used in overseas trade and commerce is another valuable support. By the summer of 1920 the total of international trade was shrinking swiftly. The interlocking cogs of the world economic machine had been thrown out of gear. The value of Britain's imports, for example, totalled £1,932,000,000 in 1920; £1,320,000,-000 in 1925; £1,043,000,000 in 1930; £703,000,000 in 1932. The value of her exports totalled £1,557,000,000 in 1920; £927,000,000 in 1925; £657,000,000 in 1930; £416,000,000 in 1932. The value of re-exports fell from £222,000,000 in 1920 to £50,000,000 in 1932.

More than 10,000,000 men were killed in the First World War. Of these over 700,000 were from the United Kingdom. Almost a whole generation of human natural resources had been lost. The British cost of financing the war had been about £9,593,000,000. Despite heavy taxation only £2,733,000,000 or about twenty-eight per cent had been defrayed out of revenue; the rest had been borrowed. Thus the national debt had been tremendously increased and the interest alone was a heavy burden upon the taxpayers. The First World War, like almost all modern wars, left behind an increase in debt and budget which years of peace were not likely to wipe out. Before the war British annual national expenditure stood at about £197,000,000. For 1920–1921 the budget was £1,195,000,000; for 1921–1922 it was £1,097,000,000. This meant a total of about £26 a head for Great Britain, as compared with £16 for France and £11 for the United States. Parts of Britain's wartime industrial system had to be converted to peacetime production. Much of that system had been greatly expanded to meet war demands. The coal industry, for example, had been over-stimulated; and coal is the only important raw material exported from Britain. By 1920 Germany, under the terms of the Treaty of Versailles, was delivering free coal to the Allies, especially to Italy. Hence British coal exports declined.

Great merchant ships reddened from rust as they lay idle in the shipyards. All countries had increased their merchant marines; then Germany had been required to surrender her ships. Because international commerce and the carrying trade were at a low ebb the world, it seemed, had too many merchant vessels. Cheap labor had enabled the Japanese to undersell England in Eastern cotton markets; by 1934 British cotton exports to India totalled only twenty per cent of her exports in 1913. The great iron and steel industries were shaken. Soon the monetary systems of most of the world were to undergo frantic adjustment. Thus the burden of debts, trade depression, tariffs, depreciated currencies, and taxation increased.

Unemployment in Britain rose like a demoralizing tide. In 1920 the percentage was 2.2 of the employable population; in 1924 it was 10.3 (or nearly 2,000,000); in 1926 it was 12.5; in 1929 it was 10.4. Between 1919 and 1924 more than £525,000,000 was provided for unemployment relief; about £300,000 was allocated to assist emigration. Social security legislation with respect to housing, unemployment insurance, and pensions lightened the hardships but slightly. The Labour party, growing in numbers as the economic skies lowered, demanded the socialization of industry; angry workers went on strikes, the railway men in 1919, the coal miners in 1921. But the hard core of unemployment was untouched; discontent seethed as capital and labor renewed the conflict halted by the war against Germany. And added to all these economic woes were the shadows of frequent political ineptitude. Less easily described was the creeping advance of crime and social degeneracy, inevitable companions of anger, doubt, and despair.

FOREIGN AND IMPERIAL PROBLEMS

As bright hopes waned it was not surprising that the Lloyd George ministry lost public support. The Conservatives, long restive under the Liberal Lloyd George, were anxious to go back to regular party government. Thousands of workers marched into the Labour party as the post-war boom glided into a slump. The Labourites, who had deserted the coalition, made golden promises. In vain Asquith, still the leader of the anti-Lloyd George Liberals, warned that "nationalization would sap the free-flowing life blood of British industry" and "enthrone the rule of the bureaucrats." The Labour party relentlessly gained ground, usually at the expense of both the Lloyd George and Asquith liberals. Besides these political shifts, chronic unemployment, strikes, and general economic instability were other causes for the decline of the coalition led by Lloyd George and supported by the Conservatives under Bonar Law.

The cabinet at once encountered difficulties in foreign affairs. One was Bolshevik Russia. For a time Anglo-American forces, supporting the counter-revolutionary "White" Russians, operated in frozen futility about Archangel. But Lenin triumphed at last. In a nervous England fears and suspicions of Russia, rumors of her conspiracies and her secret agents, often shadowed the Socialist Labour Party. What should British policy be towards Moscow? A second problem was Poland, established at Versailles to atone for an ancient wrong and to provide a buffer state against the red plague of Bolshevism. In the spring of 1920 the Russians crossed the "Curzon" line and pushed the Poles to Warsaw. Thereupon France sent General Weygand to Poland, where his victories enabled the Poles to dictate peace to the Russians. Many Englishmen were troubled to note that the "Council of Action" of the Labour party had openly opposed the government's plan to send military aid to Poland. All Europe, including Great Britain, was inclined to doubt that Poland would be an effective dyke against the molten lava of Leninism.

Trouble also arose in Egypt and India. Although Egypt nominally remained a Turkish province after 1882 the British possessed effective control. When Turkey entered the First World War on the side of Germany, Britain formally made Egypt a British protectorate. During the war the nationalism of Zaghlul Pasha and his Wafdist party spread among the Egyptians. With peace came Egypt's demand for full independence urged upon the British by oratory, riots, and murder. Although the British government abolished the form of the protectorate it was difficult to reconcile Imperial necessity with Egypt's unqualified independence. Certain restrictions were set up which were to be the subject of later treaty negotiations. Britain was to continue to protect the Suez Canal and foreign interests in Egypt. To this end, and to protect Egypt against aggression, British armed forces were to be stationed there. This temporary settlement caused considerable friction which was not reduced until the Anglo-Egyptian Treaty of 1936, described in the following chapter.

In India native agitation for autonomy had mounted in the latter part of the First World War. For example, the Indian National Congress and the All-India Moslem League agreed in principle on a "scheme of reforms" at Lucknow in December, 1916. The Imperial War Conference of 1918 discussed the question of Indian self-government. In the same year Edwin S. Montagu, secretary of state for India, and the viceroy, Lord Chelmsford, submitted their Report on Indian Constitutional Reforms. Upon their report and subsequent discussions was based the Government of India Act of 1919.

This act set up a national government for India consisting of a legislative assembly and a council of state. A majority of representatives in both central bodies was to be elected and the franchise was extended to admit about 5,000,000 voters. In the provinces, by a division of power upon the principle of dyarchy, the Indian ministers responsible to the provincial legislative councils were responsible only for the administration of certain "transferred services," including education and public health. The "reserved services," such as the police, law courts, army, and external affairs, remained under British control. In the central government the principle of dyarchy was not adopted. There was no responsible government. If the legislative assembly or council refused to pass legislation or approve grants of supplies the viceroy could impose taxation or make laws despite their opposition. In succeeding years many native leaders demonstrated that the new constitution provided excellent opportunities for obstruction, particularly in the council of state.

IRELAND

During the First World War southern Ireland was disturbed by the rise of the bitter, militant, and secret Sinn Fein (ourselves alone) movement seeking not Home Rule but complete independence from Britain and the absorption, by force if necessary, of northern Ireland. The Sinn Feiners, plotting with the Germans throughout the war, rebelled with the promise of German aid in Easter week, 1916. The center of the revolt was in Dublin, where the rebels seized a number of key public buildings. The Germans sent no help and the Sinn Feiners had to yield to British troops. After long negotiations with the southern Irish and the Ulsterites the Lloyd George government admitted that there seemed no way in which opposing demands could be met. When conscription was extended to Ireland only Ulster approved. Southern Ireland, inflamed by Sinn Fein agitation, was not satisfied when the British decision to impose conscription was withdrawn. In the election of December, 1918, the Sinn Fein party obtained 73 seats; the Ulster Unionists, 25; the Irish Nationalists, only 7. The Sinn Fein members would not attend the British Parliament. All Sinn Feiners refused to pay taxes. Boycotting British courts, they set up their own and enforced their decisions. In 1919 they met in Dublin and declared Ireland a republic.

Faced by civil war, murder, and looting, the British government declared martial law and introduced the "Black and Tans" as an auxiliary police force. Meanwhile, Eamon De Valera, the selfless and frosty Sinn Fein leader, kept his two thousand secret assassins busy sniping; they were aided and screened by the whole population; the way of an informer was hard. When the "Black and Tans" answered violence with violence the British public demanded that the competition in crime be stopped. At this stage Lloyd George, always swift to sense popular sentiment, called for a conference with the Sinn Fein rebels.

An Irish delegation came to London. Headed by Arthur Griffith and Michael Collins, it included the strange Englishman Erskine

Childers, who was later hanged as a rebel, Gavan Duffy, Robert Barton, and Eamon Duggan. After long negotiations Articles of Agreement were signed between the British and the Sinn Fein representatives. As a result of this treaty the virtually independent Irish Free State was established early in 1922 as a British Dominion in southern Ireland. The six counties of Ulster remained aloof. Although the "Irreconcilables" under the intransigent De Valera refused to accept anything short of absolute independence, the Dail Eireann ratified the treaty by the narrow vote of 64 to 57. The new Irish government put 12,000 of its extreme opponents, including De Valera, in jail. In 1923 De Valera announced that he would one day become head of the government, tear the treaty to shreds, and force Ulster into union with the south. Meanwhile he and his followers would cease armed resistance. So the moderates at last achieved a temporary victory. Under President William Cosgrave, capable and steady, the Irish Free State had eight years of quiet reconstruction and progress. The storm was to blow up again with diminished violence when De Valera was elected president in 1932.

ARMAMENTS AND REPARATIONS

In the midst of all the world economic problems, the challenges to foreign and Imperial policy in Poland, Russia, India, Egypt, and Ireland there developed a series of events that resulted in the Washington Naval Conference of 1922. After 1919 Britain almost completely suspended naval construction because of her indisputable superiority in European waters. In the Pacific, however, British naval power was less than that of the United States and Japan. The earlier British policy of maintaining a fleet equal to any two other navies combined was now abandoned. Britain was not troubled by the naval building of the United States because war with America was considered impossible. But the United States and Britain took a dim view of the new position of Japan.

Having obtained Germany's North Pacific islands, Japan was now two thirds of the way to Australia; she was athwart the sea-lanes to the Philippines; her policy with respect to the banquet-table of China was becoming clearer; her emigrants were moving to the American west coast areas; she was becoming a serious commercial rival; she was building steadily a powerful fleet. Tension increased in the Pacific. In 1922 the United States called a naval conference at Washington to consider limiting naval construction. After long debates it was agreed to stabilize the battleship strength of Great Britain, the United States, Japan, France, and Italy in the respective proportions of 5:5:3:1.75:1.75.

No agreement was reached with respect to cruisers and smaller craft. The United States, Great Britain, and Japan did agree to refrain from extending their fortified areas in the Pacific. In place of the abrogated Anglo-Japanese alliance of 1902 a four power pact to preserve the status quo in the Pacific was signed by Great Britain, the

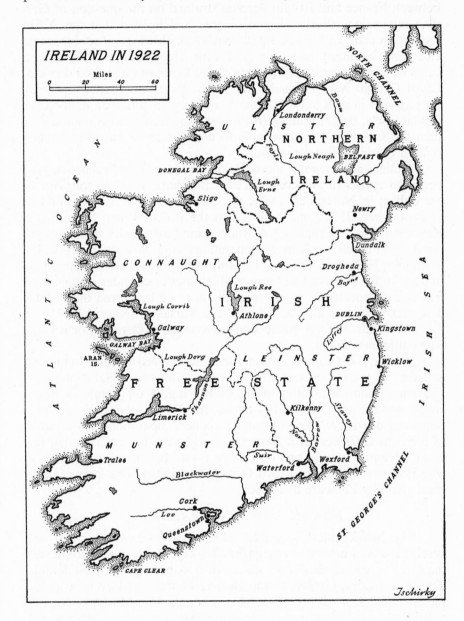

IRELAND IN 1922

Miles

0   20   40   60

United States, Japan and France. The Washington Conference, although discussions broke down in wide areas, was at least a step towards the limitation of armaments. In 1922 it was felt that future meetings, as the world moved slowly to a new stability, might be even more hopeful events.

In Europe the prospect was not at all hopeful by 1922. Relations between France and Britain became strained on the question of German reparations. Earlier Lloyd George had insisted that the Allied reparation claims would be rigidly enforced. However, it soon became clear that Germany had little gold with which to pay. Britain then came to fear the competition of proffered German goods and services. Lloyd George was genuinely anxious to moderate French demands for payment in gold to the last mark, or if not in gold then in goods or capital assets. Britain wanted to aid Germany to recover economically; then the Germans would be able to export and to buy. But France refused to reduce her demands.

Under such pressure the walls of the German financial structure began to crack. In November, 1918, the mark stood at fourteen to the dollar; in November, 1921, the rate was fifty-two to the dollar; in September, 1922, one hundred to the dollar. When the militant Raymond Poincaré replaced Aristide Briand as premier the prospects for Anglo-French harmony on reparations were dark. Poincaré was a Lorrainer; he hated Germany; he obstinately refused to have anything to do with the Geneva Conference which met to consider problems of European reconstruction and rehabilitation; he instructed the French delegates to permit no discussion of the Versailles treaty; he ordered them to withdraw if any concessions were made to Germany or Russia. The conference failed.

Russia and Germany, both friendless, agreed on a mutual cancellation of their war claims and a restoration of normal diplomatic relations. Benito Mussolini would shortly march on Rome. Poincaré would soon launch his armies across the Rhine to occupy the rich industrial district of the Ruhr and to collect reparations at the point of a bayonet. Critics throughout the world were to prophesy that the Ruhr adventure would one day prove a bad business for everybody. The European policy of Lloyd George had failed. The last veto had been given by Poincaré of France.

BONAR LAW AND BALDWIN

The heavily bludgeoned Lloyd George government could not survive the final blow that came from Turkey. By the Treaty of Sevres the Greeks, whom the Turks despised, had been given considerable Turkish territory. Greece, to the chagrin of Italy, had even occupied the town and district of Smyrna. Meanwhile the iron Mustapha Kemal, a brilliant Anatolian patriot, was building up a new life for the Turkish people in the Kemalist movement. In the summer of 1920 Turkish armies moved towards the Dardanelles and the Bosphorus but were driven back by Greek forces sent by Premier Venizelos of

Greece. Soon, however, Premier Venizelos was ousted and King Constantine returned to Athens. Because Constantine had once opposed the Allies Britain and France now sent no further aid to Greece. When Constantine tried to crush Kemal the Turks withdrew and waited.

In the summer of 1922 Kemal struck hard at Smyrna. Italy and France, fearful of war, retreated from the scene. In vain Britain canvassed the Balkans for support against the Turks, a procedure to which Premier Poincaré of France took venomous exception. But a small British force remained at Chanak on the Asiatic side of the Dardanelles, supported by the guns of British ships. Kemal's forces advanced, then stopped. Swift diplomatic developments resulted in an agreement at Lausanne, late in 1922, by which areas predominantly Turkish in population, including Constantinople, were returned to Turkey. British prestige was lifted throughout the East because Britain alone had seemed prepared to fight. At the same time the British public was not pleased at having been brought so close to war by Lloyd George.

Meanwhile the Conservatives under Bonar Law decided to withdraw from the coalition and operate on the old separate party basis. Lloyd George at once resigned. Bonar Law and the Conservatives were returned in a national election with 344 seats; the Labour party obtained 142; the Asquith Liberals 60; the Lloyd George Liberals 57. Bonar Law had been elected on the slogan of "tranquillity"; in the United States, the slogan of President Harding was "normalcy." In Britain, too, it seemed that a disillusioned public was demanding "not surgery, but serenity."

Thus the Conservatives came into power for the first time since their defeat in 1906. As soon as the new government under the Canadian-born Bonar Law was operating smoothly Stanley Baldwin, head of a vast coal, iron, and steel empire and chancellor of the exchequer, went to Washington to discuss the British debt to the United States. The total British indebtedness was over £850,000,000 and no arrangements had been made for a method of payment. Not long before Baldwin crossed the Atlantic Great Britain had addressed the famous "Balfour Note" to France, Greece, Italy, Portugal, and Rumania. This note explained that Britain had total claims on Europe of about £3,400,000,000. There seemed small prospect of collecting the £650,000,000 due from Bolshevik Russia or the payment owed by Germany. But Britain had advanced about £1,300,000,000 to her allies during the First World War. The Balfour Note stated that as Britain recognized her obligation to pay the United States she wanted to receive from her former allies at least enough to enable her to clear her account with America. "Our undoubted rights as a creditor nation cannot be left wholly in abeyance. . . . In no circumstances does Great Britain propose to ask more from her debtors than is necessary to pay her creditors—not more, but not less." This in fact meant that Britain was prepared to cancel a part of the debt owed her by Europe.

Against that background of British policy Baldwin went to Washington to negotiate. In February, 1923, an agreement was ratified by Congress providing that British bonds for the total sum owed the United States were to be issued to the United States government. These bonds, maturing over a period of sixty-two years, were to bear interest at three per cent for the first ten years, and three and one half per cent after that. At the time it seemed a sound and business-like agreement. Britain thought five per cent interest was too much; so the rate was reduced. The United States did not want payment in goods and services; so the British agreed to pay in gold.

Meanwhile, however, the German reparations were not coming forward. The French, led by Poincaré, were determined to collect. In January, 1923, Bonar Law journeyed to Paris to ask Poincaré to "allow Germany a breathing-space to restore her shattered credits before pressing her for payments she cannot at the moment make." But Poincaré was adamant. Despite British disapproval, he ordered French armies to occupy the Ruhr in the hope of seizing German coal and other products. The passive German resistance frustrated French aims and accelerated the German domestic collapse. The prestige of Poincaré and the hopes of France went down together. So far as France was concerned there were no profits in the dramatic Ruhr adventure; it was all loss, especially when the franc began to slither downward like its neighbor the mark.

In May, 1923, Bonar Law retired; the cancer in his throat raced on with long and malignant strides. Who would succeed him as prime minister and leader of the Conservative party? The names most frequently mentioned were Sir Austen Chamberlain and Lord Curzon. Chamberlain, however, had lost much reputation because he had wanted the Conservatives to continue in the Lloyd George coalition. Curzon, although shadowed by his part in the Irish controversy, seemed a more likely choice. Majestic, proud, erudite, and industrious, this ex-viceroy of India, Conservative leader in the house of lords, and secretary of state for foreign affairs was unfortunately not an adaptable man; his colleagues often found him too hectoring and superior. Perhaps, too, it would not be desirable to have a prime minister in the house of lords; there had been none since Lord Salisbury. And was Lord Curzon temperamentally suited to a democratic age? To the end Curzon expected that he would be summoned by the king to succeed Bonar Law. When he learned that Stanley Baldwin had been called instead, he collapsed in an agony of disappointment. Rallying swiftly, he carried on with dignity and good-will under Baldwin's leadership.

Stanley Baldwin, shrewd and sound, delighted in being considered "the supremely ordinary man," a soil-rooted Saxon farmer.

For political purposes, he window-dressed this aspect of his character. His speeches in the house of commons or his little book of essays *On England* will show, however, that there was another Stanley Baldwin less well known to the voting public. When Baldwin succeeded Bonar Law the economic situation had temporarily improved. Neville Chamberlain, new chancellor of the exchequer, began to attack the bottleneck in housing construction; over 2,000,000 new houses were to be built between 1919 and 1933. Unemployment was down slightly, although the jobless still numbered over 1,000,000. Both the cost of living and the general taxation level were now lower. Nevertheless, Stanley Baldwin felt that unemployment could be further reduced by giving the Dominions tariff preference in British markets provided the Dominions gave similar preference to British products. As foreign markets were more and more closed to British goods by high tariff walls, should not everything possible be done to encourage trade within the Empire? This was the rock upon which Joseph Chamberlain had piloted the Conservatives at the turn of the century. But Bonar Law had promised that no steps towards increased protection would be taken. Baldwin therefore felt that he could not act until he had obtained public approval.

In the national election of December 6, 1923, Stanley Baldwin learned too late that he had not been wise to hazard his safe majority on a single toss. All his enemies drew together and made common cause against him on the bitter question of protection. As solid for free trade as in the days of Bright and Cobden stood the industrial north. Several of the great press barons opposed protection. In the election the Conservatives won 257 seats; the Labour party 192; and the Liberals, 152. At once the Liberals and Labourites voted Baldwin out of office.

As the Socialist Labour party was now the second largest group in the house of commons the king asked their leader, Ramsay MacDonald, to form a Labour government. This MacDonald did in January, 1924. Many Conservatives felt that as Britain's first Labour cabinet came into being revolution was indeed at hand. Some were pleased to reflect that the great trade unions had never been strongly socialistic. There was also consolation in the fact that the Labourites depended upon Liberal support for a working majority.

THE LABOUR GOVERNMENT, 1924

The new cabinet contained Ramsay MacDonald as prime minister and foreign secretary; Philip Snowden as chancellor of the exchequer; Sidney Webb as president of the board of trade; Arthur Henderson as home secretary; J. H. Thomas as colonial secretary.

In several respects Ramsay MacDonald was a strange leader for a democratic party. He was an honest, humorless, rather aristocratic

and aloof Scotsman, respected by all his followers but really understood by few. He was not a doctrinaire socialist. Nor was his chancellor
of the exchequer, Philip Snowden. Snowden disliked militant socialists
as much as he did the Tories, Imperialism, war, and the vested interests
of the upper classes. His economic views were rigid and orthodox. He
believed in sound finance. He stood for high taxation, the gold standard, free imports, and the repayment of the British debt to the United
States. In him and his policies there was no threat to the existing structure of society. He would champion the interests of the masses, but not
to the extent of upsetting the political or economic bases of the state.
Sidney Webb, later Lord Passfield, was a famous Fabian. Arthur
Henderson was a powerful trade union leader from the north, with
strong support in his native Glasgow. J. H. Thomas was a Welshman,
once an oil-wiper of locomotives and now a railway union leader. All
had long been associated with the Labour party in its hard struggle
up the grade to power.

In domestic policy the Labour government surprised its enemies
and disappointed many of its friends. Before the Labourites had
entered office they had promised many things, none of which they
now delivered, partly because of their dependence upon Liberal votes
in the house of commons. The first Labour budget was no more
startling than a Liberal product might have been; there were no capital levies, no confiscatory raids on wealth. Nor did Ramsay MacDonald
and his colleagues solve any domestic problems. Unemployment continued to rise; labor disputes multiplied. The only step of significance
taken by the Labour government at home was the abolition of a large
number of protective and preferential tariffs, a step in which the
Liberals rejoiced.

It was in foreign affairs that MacDonald and his colleagues had
their most outstanding success. Shortly after the Labour cabinet entered
office the French admitted that the Ruhr adventure of naked violence
had not worked out according to Poincaré's blueprints. All French
calculations had been upset. Her muddled budgets were unbalanced;
the franc was bounding downwards; no reparations could be extracted
from Germany. How could Germany be made to pay at least enough
to help France weather the financial storm? How could Germany be
kept weak enough so that France would not have to fear a resurgence
of her military power? Edouard Herriot, who had succeeded Raymond
Poincaré as premier, was more amenable to suggestion than his predecessor; he consented to an investigation into Germany's capacity to
pay by an international commission of financial experts. This commission, headed by General Charles G. Dawes, prepared a report,
mainly written by Sir Josiah Stamp of Great Britain and Owen D.
Young of the United States.

The "Dawes Plan" which was formally accepted by Great Britain,

France, and Germany, provided that with assistance from the United States and Great Britain Germany should create a national bank, return to a stabilized currency based on gold, and balance her budgets. It was felt that a Germany financially dependent on the Allies, particularly the United States and Great Britain, might be less inclined to think upon revenge. The Allies therefore subscribed to a German loan of $200,000,000. American controls in German industry and commerce were extended swiftly as Americans found a place to invest surplus capital. The Dawes Plan also provided that Germany would pay enough to balance the budgets of France and help France to pay Britain and the United States. In brief, this "milk-cow method" of the Dawes Plan meant that the United States would lend Germany money. Germany, in turn, by payments beginning at $250,000,000 annually and rising to $625,000,000 in 1929, would pay France and Britain, who would then pay the United States. It was agreed that the French would withdraw from the Ruhr within one year after the Dawes Plan went into effect.

This, then, was an apparently bright achievement in foreign affairs. It remained to be seen how long such an arrangement would continue to be acceptable to a resentful Germany. Meanwhile there were heavy clouds elsewhere. Italy, defying the League of Nations, had appealed to arms in the Corfu dispute with Greece. The ideal of disarmament was slowly fading. France, fearful of a Germany that might one day rise again in the full panoply of Mars, refused to reduce her armaments. Ramsay MacDonald, who stopped defense work on Singapore to soothe Japan, strained every resource for peace, for security, stability, disarmament. "Preparedness is not the best weapon in diplomacy," asserted one of his colleagues. "The best weapon in diplomacy is to have a sound and righteous cause. If we continue to put fear at the helm and folly at the prow we shall steer straight for the next war."

But how could safety be secured? Not by disarmament, surely, for who would disarm unless the security of each had been effectively guaranteed by all? And how could any nation, in an age of duplicity and possible secret armament, be assured that guarantees and treaties were really effective? For example, the Draft Treaty of Mutual Assistance of 1923 was designed to transform the League of Nations into a great defensive alliance. France was willing thus to implement the Covenant, which had said: "A nation embarking on aggressive war in defiance of the League has committed an act of war on all its members." But the British Dominions were no more prepared than the United States to enter into blanket commitments that might entangle them in war far from their shores and for causes of no immediate concern to them.

Again, in September, 1924, at the Fifth Assembly of the League of Nations, MacDonald of England, Herriot of France, Politis of Greece, and Benes of Czechoslovakia joined with others to prepare the Geneva Protocol, a document that carefully set up machinery for arbitration; abolished the right of nations to go to war except when ordered to do so by the League; made compulsory the submission to the World Court of cases that might lead to war. Partly because the Geneva Protocol threatened to make the League a superstate and so fettered the cherished freedom of action of Great Britain and the Dominions it was rejected. In any event, its validity had earlier been made dependent upon the success of a disarmament conference scheduled for 1925. All disarmament conferences failed because the first problem of security, often discussed, was never answered.

Meanwhile the tide that had swept the MacDonald Government into power was now fast ebbing. Votes fell away from the Labourites by hundreds of thousands. Little had been done to improve the domestic situation. Labor problems daily worsened; trade was down again and unemployment was up. Trouble stirred in Ireland. MacDonald added to these causes of discontent by proposing to resume normal trade relations with Soviet Russia and to lend her £30,000,000. On October 25, 1924, the *Daily Mail* published the Zinoviev letter, allegedly sent by the Russian President of the Third International in Moscow to the British Communist Party. The letter urged British Communists to "stir up the masses of the British proletariat to organize and foment mutiny in the Army and Navy and rebellion in Ireland and the colonies."

The importance of this Zinoviev letter is often exaggerated. Many reasons combined to cause a steady withdrawal of support from MacDonald. When at last the Liberals refused their votes to him, the Labour government could not carry on. Had not MacDonald and his colleagues obstinately refused to denounce the Zinoviev letter for the forgery it was then the fall of the Labourites from office might possibly have been delayed, but not for long. In the election the Conservatives returned with a large majority; they won 415 seats. The Labour representation was reduced to 152. At the same time, disaster sat upon the Liberal banners; they obtained only 42 seats.

Thus, late in 1924, Stanley Baldwin began his second ministry. This time he avoided the rocks and shoals of the tariff problem. Shortly afterwards, the Labour party, anxious to reduce public fears and suspicions of the rumored connection between British Labourites and Russian Bolsheviks, officially declared: "No member of the Communist Party shall be eligible as a Labour candidate for any office, or be entitled to become a member, or remain a member, of the Labour Party."

LOCARNO

The problems of peace increased at home. Stanley Baldwin, in an unexpected step, appointed Winston Churchill chancellor of the exchequer. Because Churchill's own ideas and principles always took precedence over party policies he never remained a very reliable supporter of any political group. He was an Imperialist; he was critical of the idea of the League of Nations; he did not approve of a wide extension of social services. Thus he could not be a good Liberal. But because he did believe in free trade he could not be a constant Conservative. Any competent biography of Churchill will explain his varied course as a brilliant wandering star in many political constellations. Before he agreed to enter the cabinet he obtained from Baldwin the assurance that the Conservatives would not pursue a strong protectionist tariff policy. Many sturdy, cautious, and protectionist Tories were not pleased to be joined by the dashing and volatile Imperialist free trader who had held eight portfolios in seventeen years.

On April 25, 1925, Churchill opened the first of his five budgets. He proposed a small reduction of the income tax. He promised an annual decrease in his future budgets of about £10,000,000 a year. He asked that Britain return to the gold standard. In vain the industrialists pointed out that British trade would suffer by a return to the pre-war gold standard because 10 per cent would be added to the cost of British exports. Churchill's predecessor, the Labourite Philip Snowden, called the budget "the worst rich man's budget of recent years," the work of "a profligate and a bankrupt." Mr. J. M. Keynes denounced Churchill's plans in a book entitled *The Economic Consequences of Mr. Churchill*. But the budget passed both houses. So far as the public expressed any opinion at all it was generally favorable. There was less complete approval about six months later when Britain's export trade declined. Late in 1925, however, public attention was directed to other problems. Hints of serious domestic trouble were brewing. Discontent was boiling up in the coal mines, backbone of British industrial power.

Meanwhile a significant event occurred abroad. The prestige of the League of Nations was waning. International bickering and tension shadowed the eyes of disillusioned men who had seen the contrast between shining hopes and the travail of sordid experience. Under Stanley Baldwin, whose foreign secretary was Sir Austen Chamberlain, there came a swift departure from the "peace by pacification" methods of Ramsay MacDonald. Declaring that the security of Britain must not be placed in jeopardy, the Conservatives proceeded with an ungentle policy in Egypt; heedless of Japanese rumbles, they resumed work on the defenses of Singapore; because they did not like the Bolsheviks they abruptly refused to ratify the treaty MacDonald had negotiated with Moscow. It was Sir Austen Chamberlain who finally announced to the Assembly of the League of Nations that Great Britain rejected the Geneva Protocol. So the Protocol was sent to lie on the shelf by the Draft Treaty of Mutual Assistance. This was in March, 1925.

In many ways, however, the Conservatives had a realistic foreign policy. They wanted, as MacDonald had wanted, friendly cooperation with France. Beyond this, they hoped to bring about better relations between France and Germany. The German Republic was being steadily weakened by hostile thrusts in Berlin and Munich. Vast subterranean conspiracies were born of reviving German nationalism. In these days Hindenburg succeeded Ebert; Erzberger and Rathenau died because they did not put Germany first; Hugenberg and Hitler snarled and plotted. But for those in Germany who did want peace and goodwill the conciliatory Gustav Stresemann seemed an appropriate spokesman. With Aristide Briand of France and Sir Austen Chamberlain of Great Britain Stresemann began long negotiations that culminated in the signing of a series of eight security pacts at the Swiss town of Locarno in October, 1925.

To Locarno came the representatives of seven powers: Great Britain, France, Germany, Belgium, Czechoslovakia, Poland and Italy. Of the eight agreements the most important was the Treaty of Mutual Guarantee, signed by Great Britain, Belgium, France, Italy, and Germany; this was the only pact to which Great Britain was signatory. The five powers involved agreed to settle all their disputes without resorting to war. They guaranteed the borders set up at Versailles between Germany, France, Belgium, and the Netherlands; they guaranteed the demilitarized zone established on the left bank of the Rhine in 1919. This pact meant that France, Belgium, and the Netherlands on the one hand and Germany on the other were protected against any attempt to alter their frontiers. Great Britain had pledged herself to go to war to defend the Versailles territorial settlements in the West. Austen Chamberlain declared: "Great Britain has confirmed her friendship with France and sealed her reconciliation with Germany." Only thirteen members of the house of commons opposed this Treaty of Mutual Guarantee. The Imperial Conference of 1926 approved it as "a successful contribution to the peace of the world." The seven subsidiary treaties of Locarno extended the areas of protection and agreement. For example, France guaranteed the territorial integrity of Czechoslovakia and Poland. All pledged assistance in the event of an "unprovoked attack" by Germany. All agreed to carry out fully and in good faith any future agreements reached between themselves and Germany.

Germany, admitted for the first time since 1919 to an international conference, guaranteed the frontiers of nations touching both her eastern and western borders. At Locarno she voluntarily accepted the demilitarized zone and the loss of Alsace-Lorraine. Fearing a possible alliance of Great Britain, France, and Belgium, dreading a long French occupation of the Ruhr, and recognizing that immediate chances of recovering Alsace-Lorraine were small, Germany thus renounced all intentions of disturbing the Versailles arrangements. So, too, did satisfied France. British prestige rose in Europe. Here, surely, was compensation for the English rejection of the Geneva Protocol. At the same time, Britain had taken a further step towards securing the territorial integrity of France, Belgium and the Netherlands. "In guaranteeing those frontiers," said Austen Chamberlain, "we insured our own."

The Locarno pacts were widely applauded as a landmark in European history, a "splendid act of reconciliation," a vindication of man's will for general peace. Had international solidarity at last been achieved with the new safety curtains between Germany and her neighbors? Some doubting individuals such as Alfred Fabre-Luce, French author of *Locarno the Reality,* challenged the general optimism. At the moment, however, most observers were inclined to agree with Aristide Briand: "Peace for Germany and for France; that means we have done with the long series of terrible and sanguinary conflicts which have stained the pages of history. . . . The League is not going back; its future will be one of constant expansion." Of the Briand-Chamberlain-Stresemann achievements were born the new "spirit of Locarno." Soon, however, the shadows were to return. One of the darkest came out of Germany.

The swelling tide of bitter German nationalism was not checked by the new pacts. In 1926 Germany entered the League of Nations in accordance with the decisions reached at Locarno. Even as she did so vocal German nationalists declared that the League stood for a prolongation of the hated terms of Versailles. Germany, they asserted, had a score to settle with France, and with other authors of her humiliation. The League of Nations and the Locarno agreements, said German nationalists, were useful only insofar as they afforded Germany time to achieve economic and military power. If Germany one day repudiated the disarmament provisions of Versailles and began to arm what would France do? Or Italy? Or Britain? If France crossed the Rhine into Germany and thus violated the Treaty of Mutual Guarantee would Britain then support Germany against France?

Slowly the Germans came to believe that they could tear up the disarmament clauses of the Versailles "Diktat" with impunity. They could begin to arm again, secretly or openly, and France would do nothing but protest. Great Britain would do nothing. Because the Germans guessed rightly, the way was prepared for a holocaust of barbarism and hideous terror. Meanwhile, unaware of the next chapter of the destiny of western man, the leaders of many nations continued the desperate search for security. The "spirit of Locarno" was to become dead and brittle, swept away by the rising wind.

Chapter 37

THE SEARCH FOR SECURITY

THE GENERAL STRIKE, 1926

IN DECEMBER, 1925, there were 1,500,000 unemployed in Great Britain. Under the government of Ramsay MacDonald and the Labour party there had been widespread hope that some remedial measures could be undertaken by parliamentary action. When MacDonald had given way to the Conservative Stanley Baldwin that hope had flickered and guttered out. In its place came a demand for direct and violent action by the powerful trade unions. The first step was taken by the Miners' Federation, whose secretary was Mr. Arthur Cook, a neurotic and febrile Bolshevik who had been committed to prison on several occasions for inciting to unlawful assembly or riot.

A royal commission on the coal industry stated that British exports of coal in 1924 had totalled 3,000,000 tons less than the annual average from 1909 to 1914; in 1925 coal exports had decreased by 12,000,000 tons below the 1924 level. In May, 1924, there were 38,000 unemployed miners; in May, 1925, there were 199,000; in June, 1925, the total had risen to 301,000. The mine operators declared that if they maintained the existing wage and hour levels they would swiftly become insolvent. On June 30, 1925, they announced their intention to terminate on July 31 the national wage agreement of 1924. When the Miners' Federation refused to negotiate they had behind them the formidable threat of a general strike, similar to that which had been planned for September, 1914, and much more extensive than the ill-coordinated effort that had failed in 1921.

Before this fighting alliance of bitter trade unions the government retreated. To avoid industrial warfare the Conservative cabinet agreed to extend a subsidy to the coal industry for nine months. This grant of about £20,000,000 enabled the operators to maintain the existing wage scales. Headed by Sir Herbert Samuel, another royal commission investigated the coal industry. In its full and impartial report, issued on March 10, 1926, the commission recommended a complete reorganization of the coal industry. They proposed that all existing private properties be forced to coalesce into larger units to facilitate production and distribution. They declared that the issue was clear: either there must be a contraction of the coal industry or a prompt reduction of production costs. A lowering of costs would obviously have involved an increase of working hours or a reduction of wages, perhaps both. On the other hand, any contraction of the coal industry would have forced additional thousands of workers into the ranks of the unemployed.

New negotiations between the operators ran into the sands. Meanwhile the government prepared carefully to deal with the threatened emergency of a general strike. Arthur Cook shouted "Not a minute on the day, not a penny off the pay." Baldwin declared that there would be no extension of the subsidy. The government could not use tax money to subsidize the coal industry. On May 1, 1926, the General Council of the Trades Union Congress called for a general strike involving all railwaymen, all workers in the building, iron, and steel trades, all printers, and large groups of other workers. The prime minister, backed strongly by those of his Conservative colleagues who did not love trade unions, declared that the general strike was an attempt to set up "an alternate government," a plot to hold England to ransom, a blackmail of society. He asked the nation to resist. "The general strike is a challenge to Parliament, and is the road to anarchy and ruin." In vain the Trades Union Congress declared that "the General Council does not challenge the constitution nor is it desirous of undermining our Parliamentary institutions." The government marshalled its forces to smash the strike.

Was a general strike lawful? Sir John Simon held that it was not. "Once you proclaim a general strike, you are, as a matter of fact, starting a movement of a wholly unconstitutional and unlawful character." Here, then, was one of England's greatest legal minds stating that "the decision of the Council of the Trade Unions Executive to call out everybody, regardless of the contracts which these workmen had made, was not a lawful act at all. Every workman who was bound by a contract to give notice before he left work, and who, in view of that decision, has either chosen of his own free will or has felt compelled to come out by leaving his employment without proper notice has broken the law. . . . Every trade union leader who has advised and promoted this course of action is liable in damages to the utmost farthing of his personal possessions." This opinion of Sir John Simon was upheld by a decision of Mr. Justice Astbury, who also pointed out that British labor legislation protected nobody from the consequences of illegal acts.

Meanwhile the government dramatically succeeded in maintaining vital services. Thousands of upper and middle class amateurs co-

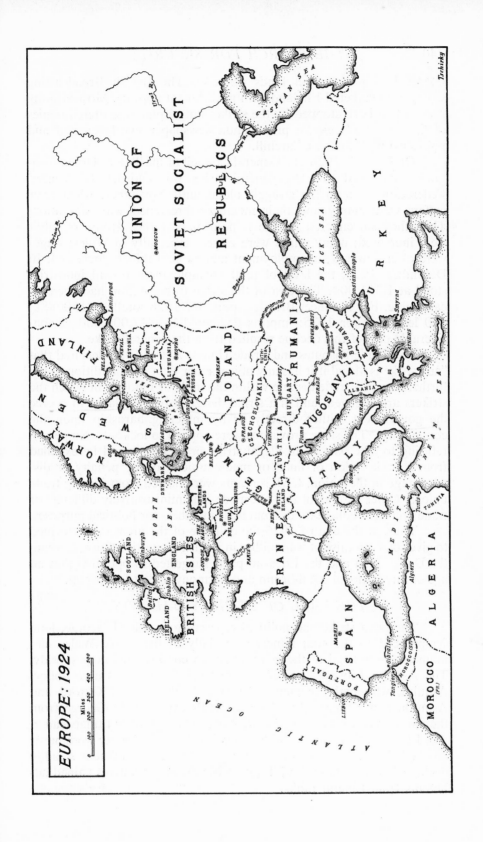

EUROPE: 1924

operated to perform all kinds of tasks. The British Broadcasting Company blanketed England with government appeals. Most printing presses had been stopped by the strike; but airplanes scattered copies of the *British Gazette,* a propaganda newspaper swiftly created and published by Winston Churchill.

On May 12, 1926, the General Council of the Trades Union Congress announced that the general strike was ended. The Miners' Federation kept up the struggle alone until November, when their coffers were empty and their members threatened with starvation. Then they surrendered on the mine-owners' terms. Hours of labor were increased; many mines were closed, especially in Wales; wages were often lowered; unemployment among coal miners increased. In December, 1926, the level of total unemployment for all industries stood at 1,351,000. The cost of the strike to the nation had been incalculable. For instance, British exports for 1926 totalled £150,000,-000 less than for 1925; imports decreased by £77,000,000; a considerable part of this decline resulted from the general strike.

The Trade Disputes and Trade Unions Act of 1927 declared that "any strike is illegal if it has any object other than or in addition to the furtherance of a trade dispute within the trade or industry in which the strikers are engaged, and is a strike designed or calculated to coerce the government, either directly or by inflicting hardship upon the community." The same provisions were applied to lockouts. No person refusing to take part in an illegal strike or lockout could be expelled from a trade union or fined or made subject to any penalty or disadvantage in the union. Civil servants were barred from joining trade unions. Other clauses of this act made it administratively difficult for trade unions to collect funds from their members for political purposes.

Thus, at the end of 1926 the collapse of the great strike seemed to give some promise of tranquillity in British domestic affairs. Abroad, the Dawes Plan and the Locarno pacts suggested to optimists that an age of international equilibrium and harmony had at last begun.

THE FALL OF STANLEY BALDWIN

The great strike had political repercussions. Lloyd George, long sympathetic to the coal miners, especially of his native Wales, denounced the refusal of the government to continue the coal subsidy. The Asquith Liberals, however, supported the Conservative policy. Asquith, who had accepted a peerage as the earl of Oxford and Asquith, now demanded that the Liberals expel Lloyd George from the party. When they refused, Asquith resigned as their titular leader. The Lloyd George and Asquith wings of the Liberal party were never reconciled. The number of Liberal members of Parliament steadily declined. In these years both Labourites and Conservatives gained adherents from Liberal ranks.

In the midst of these events, the Russian problem suddenly leaped forth again. In May, 1927, a raid by Scotland Yard officials on the London headquarters of the Russian trade delegation gave proof of Russian espionage and subversive activities in England. The Baldwin government, never friendly to Communist Russia, now terminated the Anglo-Russian Trade Agreement of March, 1921, and recalled British diplomatic representatives from Moscow. Russia was condemned for her alleged "network of malignant activity" in Britain. In Conservative quarters the break with the Soviet was hailed as "putting an end, once for all, to a sterile and irritating sham." Baldwin himself observed that "diplomatic relations, when deliberately and systematically abused, are themselves a danger to peace."

In home affairs two important events occurred. The first was the passage in 1928 of the Equal Franchise Act described in the preamble as "an act to assimilate the franchise for men and women in respect of parliament and local government elections." By this act about 5,000,-000 women were admitted to the vote on equal terms with men. At long last the cause of the emancipating suffragettes was blessed with victory.

The second significant event was a part of Baldwin's general policy of soothing labor and union groups. In 1928 his chancellor of the exchequer, Winston Churchill, brought down a less dramatic budget than that heralded by the Conservative trumpets in 1925. Churchill paid no attention to the loud disputes about wages and hours. The Conservatives in 1928 were certain that the existing British labor and industrial maladjustment would soon cease; that world trade would improve; that a reasonable prosperity would arrive very shortly. The budget of 1928 was limited to a few improvements; a new tax was placed on gasoline, the proceeds of which were to be used to reduce the burden of poor relief on the parishes; the tax on tea was removed completely. To the Conservatives it seemed unnecessary to do more in view of the apparently brightening skies. The significance of their budget of 1928 lies largely in the fact that it did so little. That large part of the British voting public who had hoped for more resented the little they received.

By the terms of the Parliament Act of 1911 the legal life of Parliament had been reduced to five years. Hence a national election was due in 1929. The Conservatives, loud prophets of a bright tomorrow, asked the British public to return them to power. "Trust Baldwin!" said one slogan. "Safety First!" said another. Lloyd George and his Liberals tried desperately to overcome the handicap of a divided, dwindling party. They promised to abolish unemployment by keeping hundreds of thousands of men busy on government work projects, the cost of which would be paid by public loans. But rumors born of the Marconi scandal still pursued Lloyd George; the wizard magic had departed. The real battle, then as later, was between the Conservatives and the Labourites. The Labour party had been steadily moving towards the right in the late 1920's; even the Conservatives no longer thought of Ramsay MacDonald as wild and subversive; he was now adorned with the top hat of respectability. The Conservatives, for their part, were becoming more flexible as more of their "die hard" and reactionary leaders left the political scene.

In the election of 1929 the Labourites won about 287 seats; Baldwin's Conservatives held 260. With the support of some 50 Liberals Ramsay MacDonald formed the second Labour government.

REPARATIONS: THE YOUNG PLAN

The main achievements of the First Labour ministry of 1924 had been in foreign affairs. In 1929 it appeared that the process was about to be repeated by the second Labour cabinet. At the Hague Conference on Reparations Great Britain was represented by Philip Snowden, once again chancellor of the exchequer, Arthur Henderson, and William Graham. As the Dawes Plan for reparations payments clearly needed change there was submitted to the Hague Conference a new proposal prepared by a commission headed by Owen D. Young of the United States. The Young Plan recommended the creation of a new Bank of International Settlement to take over the functions of the Reparation Commission; to watch over the interests of creditor nations; and to receive and allocate reparation payments. By the removal of foreign controls such as the Reparation Commission the Germans were thus left free to run their own national economy.

Under the terms of the Young Plan Germany was to make annual reparations payments from 1929 to 1988. Until 1966 Germany was to pay out of the national budget or the German Railway Company an average annuity of about $474,000,000. After 1966 the payments were to be much lower. In fact, if the Allies had paid all their debts to the United States by 1966 Germany would not be asked to make any further payments. France was to receive 52.7 per cent of each payment; the British Empire, 20.6 per cent; Italy, 10.8 per cent; and so on. In this, briefly stated, consists the essential features of the Young proposals.

Philip Snowden objected that the British share in the payments was too small. "An alteration of the percentages to England's disadvantage is a thing to which England will never consent, as the sacrifices she has made are great enough." Despite Britain's displeasure at the projected distribution of the annuities and some proposed deliveries in kind it was felt that the conference should not be permitted to drift into crisis or to end in failure. So Snowden did not finally press his point. Some concessions were made to the British arguments but they were only minor deviations from the original Young program.

As soon as the Young Plan was finally ratified in 1930 the Allies evacuated the Rhineland as an act of conciliation to Germany. The occupation therefore ended more than four years before the date set by the Treaty of Versailles. Germany had thus been freed of financial control by the adoption of the Young Plan, particularly the proposals setting up the international bank. She was now also free of military control as a result of the departure of foreign troops from German soil.

The Young Plan was the last serious attempt to settle the reparations problem. In the midst of the great depression President Herbert Hoover of the United States proposed a one-year moratorium on payments of international debts. This proposal, made in 1931, was accepted by all countries. When it became clear that Germany could not keep up her annuity payments under the Young Plan the representatives of the creditor powers met in 1932 at Lausanne. At Lausanne the Allies agreed to cancel the German debt if Germany would put up $750,000,000 in bonds at once. These bonds would be held for three years, then sold, and the proceeds distributed among the Allies.

The nations represented at Lausanne expected the United States to cancel the war debts owed at Washington when it was seen that the debtors of the United States were not receiving any reparations from Germany. But the United States refused to write off the war debts. Hence the Lausanne agreements were not ratified by the creditors of Germany, although Germany paid no more in reparations after the Weimar Republic foundered in the Nazi storm of 1933. The French stopped paying the United States. Soon nearly all foreign debtors followed suit. The British continued instalments and token payments during the crippled years of the early thirties.

Then Britain, too, ceased to pay. Britain had lent the Allies £2,312,000,000; she had received in payment £71,000,000. Britain had borrowed from the United States £945,000,000; she repaid £278,000,000.

THE LONDON NAVAL CONFERENCE, 1930

As the fire of the reparations controversy fell into embers the MacDonald ministry moved into two other areas of foreign affairs. In the first place, officially friendly relations were once again established with Soviet Russia. There were two British conditions: Russia was to cease her Communist agitation in Britain and the Empire; Moscow would negotiate regarding the possible payment of Russian debts to Britain. To these conditions Stalin agreed.

Secondly, an international naval conference was held in London in 1930 looking towards a possible limitation of naval armaments. It will be recalled that a 5:5:3:1.75:1.75 ratio for the battleship strength of Great Britain, the United States, Japan, France and Italy had been agreed upon at the Washington Conference eight years earlier.

At that time no success had attended attempts to extend this ratio principle to other types of naval craft. In 1930 the mounting rivalry of France and Italy in the Mediterranean prevented agreement regarding smaller vessels. Nearly all the lesser naval powers insisted on freedom to construct submarines because submarines cost little and could do great damage. The only major agreement of the conference was between Britain and the United States. The parity of Great Britain and the United States in battleship strength was extended to apply to all classes of warships. Before the representatives departed they also agreed to hold a naval conference in 1935.

In these cold years of rising apprehension, confusion, and cynicism the sands of hope were running out fast. At the London Conference of 1935 the Japanese insisted on naval equality with Great Britain and the United States. When their demand was refused they withdrew from the conference. The United States, Britain, and France signed a treaty limiting the maximum tonnage of battleships to 35,000 tons and agreeing to exchange naval information. This was the last naval conference before the Second World War.

THE FINANCIAL CRISIS, 1931

In the midst of the darkening scene, when Philip Snowden found things "just as bad as a hundred years ago," an unprecedented economic and financial crisis was shaking America and Europe. The stock market crash in the United States had global repercussions. According to available indices the world output of raw materials was rising more rapidly than population; it is probable that the output of the manufacturing industries increased even more than raw material production. The world as a whole was therefore richer than before the First World War. The destruction of wealth in that conflict had more than been made good by 1930. In this sense the world as a whole was not poor; but because of the financial, economic, and political arrangements of modern civilization a state or an individual can be financially poor in the midst of plenty. The British financial crisis of 1931 is a case in point.

Following the First World War there had been a considerable increase in the adverse balance of Britain's export-import trade accompanied by a decline in British capital available for overseas investments. In 1925, for example, the export-import adverse balance was nearly £400,000,000; the average for the years 1920–1930 was approximately £350,000,000. As opposed to this adverse balance such credit items as revenue from British shipping, overseas investment income, and financial services resulted in a total credit balance of £54,-000,000 in 1925, £114,000,000 in 1927, and £137,000,000 in 1928. In the abnormal general strike year of 1926 the credit balance fell to £9,000,000. When the great world depression came in 1929 all revenues from overseas investment, shipping, and financial services fell sharply. At the same time, the export-import adverse balance increased with the decline of British exports. In 1930 the credit balance fell to £23,000,000. In 1931 the loss of revenue resulted in a net adverse balance of £75,000,000.

This serious situation with respect to currency payments contributed to the financial crisis of September, 1931. At the same time industrial prices in Britain declined still more with the deepening slump. The price of tin was £267 a ton in 1924; it was £117 in 1931. Welsh coal sold for 27 shillings a ton in 1924; it sold for 20 shillings in 1931. The price of pig iron was 81 shillings a ton in 1924; it was 63 shillings in 1931. More directly important was the loss of confidence in the pound caused in part by the government's unbalanced borrowings to meet a deficit in the Unemployment Insurance Fund. Unemployment was creeping upwards towards the 3,000,000 mark. In 1911 the cost of the social services was £63,000,000; in 1929 it was £341,-000,000. The effects of the United States collapse had already shaken Europe. Would the British pound ride out the storm? Was the British banking system stable? The doubtful answers to these questions helped to precipitate panic among foreign depositors and an incipient flight from the pound.

In May, 1931, it was admitted that "the solidarity of the British financial system" was in danger. "Drastic measures will have to be taken if the budget equilibrium is to be maintained and industrial recovery made." In June a government commission reported that the budget would show a deficit of at least £120,000,000. The Austrian Credit Anstalt had failed. Hindenburg had appealed to President Hoover and Hoover proposed the one-year moratorium on international debts described above. France and the United States, no longer in receipt of money directly from Germany, withdrew gold more heavily from Britain. Loans from New York and Paris temporarily bulwarked the pound sterling; but the gold reserves of the Bank of England were shrinking with alarming speed.

How could the country be kept solvent? In the face of dwindling revenues drastic financial economies must be effected. The only obvious means of reducing government expenditure and reassuring the world was to restrict the social security program, especially unemployment insurance. But the whole conceptual ideology of the Labour party was based on social security. The Labourites divided. Philip Snowden, always a sound, rigid, orthodox financier, insisted that the budget must be balanced, no matter what was sacrificed. He complained that the succession duties were not bringing in sufficient revenue. "The rich are not dying up to expectation." Nevertheless, he asserted that the unsatisfactory condition of British finances could only be remedied by strict adherence to the principle that the government must pay its way. MacDonald and ten other cabinet ministers agreed. Eight of the cabinet, however, together with the trade union leaders, opposed any economy in the social services. "Don't let foreign money magnates stampede you into a course so treacherous to the working classes." They refused to sacrifice or decrease unemployment insurance, or reduce other social security benefits. Although Parliament was not in session most faithful Labourites would have viewed with repugnance the proposals of MacDonald and Snowden. "We must not abandon benefits to the worker gained with such difficulty in past generations."

Lacking sufficient support to carry on, MacDonald resigned in late August. Together with fourteen supporters he was read out of the Labour party and Arthur Henderson was elected its new leader. Thus MacDonald and a small group of followers stood alone. King George V, after consulting with the Conservative and Liberal leaders Baldwin and Samuel, commissioned MacDonald to form a "National Government" containing members of all three major parties "to deal with the financial emergency." The new cabinet included four Labourites, four Conservatives, and two Liberals, one of whom was Sir John Simon. The flexibility of the British governmental system is shown by the fact that MacDonald, who was really a man without any party at all when he accepted the king's commission, became prime minister at the king's request and with the support of those who had opposed him earlier. The Conservatives, a few days before his strong enemies, were now, in the National government, his constant and chief support. Arthur Henderson and the anti-MacDonald Labourites were furious at what they deemed the "betrayal" of MacDonald.

The new National government at once reduced the unemployment insurance by 10 per cent. All pay rates in the armed services and all salaries of crown servants were temporarily cut. Taxes were raised on tobacco, beer, gasoline, and amusements. The income tax was increased by about 25 per cent. Education grants were decreased. When the Nationalist government met Parliament on September 8, 1931, it received a majority of sixty in a vote of confidence. A new budget lopped £70,000,000 from the anticipated government expenditure for the following year and added £81,500,000 to anticipated revenue. But even these drastic measures were not enough to stop the hurricane of gold withdrawals. The Stock Exchange closed.

On September 16 the Bank of England, whose gold holdings were reduced to about £130,000,000 and whose foreign credits raised in the summer were exhausted, asked the government to relieve it from the provisions of the Gold Standard Act of 1925 requiring the sale of gold at a fixed price. Parliament, on the motion of Philip Snowden, suspended the fixed price and purchase obligation by a vote of 375:112. Thus Great Britain abandoned the gold standard. It was

expected that the fall in the exchange value of the pound would have
the usual result of restricting imports and stimulating exports. Australia, Canada, India, Ireland, and the Scandinavian bloc soon followed the British step. Shortly afterwards Winston Churchill declared:
"I accept my share of the blame for restoring the gold standard in
1925. We were promised reality and stability by our financial experts.
We have had neither. The price of gold has increased by 80 per cent.
That is as though the foot rule had become twenty-two inches and
the pound weight twenty-eight ounces. Think what that means in terms
of debt—the extra production demanded to satisfy existing mortgage
indebtedness. This financial condition amounts to a hideous oppression."

On October 27, 1931, the National government went to the country in a general election, asking for "a doctor's mandate" to bring
economic recovery. The inflated level of British prices would have to
be lowered; Britain's foreign trading accounts would have to be balanced swiftly to prevent the exchange value of the pound from declining too far in the direction of the franc and the mark. MacDonald and
the few National Labourites who followed him stood with the Conservatives led by Baldwin and the Liberals led by Sir Herbert Samuel.
Against the National government were the Lloyd George Liberals
and the Labour party under Arthur Henderson. The opponents of the
government won only 56 seats: the Henderson Labourites 52; the
Lloyd George Liberals 4, consisting of Lloyd George himself, his son,
his daughter, and his son-in-law, all returned from Wales.

The National government thus won the largest majority in modern British history. The Conservatives were returned in 473 ridings;
the MacDonald National Labourites won 13 seats; the Independent
Nationalists 2; the Samuel and Simon Liberals 68. The National government therefore held 556 seats. Because of the number of parties
competing in this election, however, those who follow the doctrines
of the Proportional Representation Society (1884) may point to the
fact that the Conservatives obtained about 75 per cent of the seats but
only about 50 per cent of the votes cast. The Labour party under
Henderson obtained about nine per cent of the total seats but polled
about 30 per cent of the total vote.

Thus the National government was returned to power. At the
exchequer was Neville Chamberlain, son of Joseph Chamberlain and
half-brother of Sir Austen Chamberlain, once described by David
Lloyd George as "not one of my lucky finds." Stanley Baldwin was
lord privy seal; Sir John Simon was foreign secretary; Sir Herbert
Samuel was home secretary. Under various leaders and in various
forms the National government was to carry on through fifteen
troubled years to the end of the Second World War.

THE STATUTE OF WESTMINSTER, 1931

Meanwhile significant events were occurring throughout the British Empire. The First World War pointed to the fact that the principles first conceded in the granting of responsible government to the British Dominions contained within themselves the basis of a new Imperial unity implying the final growth of the Dominions into independent nations. In external affairs the Dominions had slowly assumed almost full responsibility. Canada, for example, signed the Treaty of Versailles. She was a non-permanent member of the Council of the League of Nations. In 1926 the Imperial Conference stated that "Equality of status, so far as Britain and the Dominions are concerned, is the root principle governing our intra-imperial relations." This famous Imperial Conference also declared that the self-governing Dominions were to be regarded as "autonomous communities within the British Empire, equal in status, in no way subordinate one to another in any aspect of their domestic or external affairs, though united by a common allegiance to the Crown, and freely associated as members of the British Commonwealth of Nations."

As a result of the reports of the Imperial Conferences held in 1926 and 1930 and the recommendations of legal experts the decisions regarding Dominion status were embodied in the Statute of Westminster, passed by the Imperial Parliament in December, 1931. This statute recognized the sovereign right of each Dominion to control its own domestic and foreign affairs. For example, it was provided that "Any law touching the succession to the throne or the royal style and titles shall hereafter require the assent as well of the Parliaments of all the Dominions as of the Parliament of the United Kingdom." It was also stated that "no law hereafter made by the Parliament of the United Kingdom shall extend to any of the said Dominions as part of the law of that Dominion otherwise than at the request and at the consent of that Dominion." It was expressly provided that "no law and no provision of any law made after the commencement of this act by the Parliament of a Dominion shall be void or inoperative on the ground that it is repugnant to the laws of England, or to the provisions of any existing or any future act of Parliament of the United Kingdom or to any order, rule, or regulation made under any such act, and the powers of the Parliament of a Dominion shall include the power to repeal or amend any such act, order, rule, or regulation insofar as the same is part of the law of the Dominion." The great bond of the Commonwealth remains the common allegiance to the crown, the imponderables of tradition and sentiment, the recognition of the Dominions that they have a common interest in freedom, cooperation, and Imperial defense.

Thus the remarkable British experiment in developing political organisms abroad resulted in this unique Commonwealth of "autonomous communities, in no way subordinate one to another." These freely associating Dominions, daughters of the slow and unspectacular changes of time, again revealed their essential unity in the storm of the Second World War. Professor Chester Martin has somewhere likened the Commonwealth to an oak tree planted long ago; it is not easily torn up by the roots.

IRELAND

Meanwhile many shadows lay across the map of Empire. In South Africa the steady, volcanic pressures of racial and economic problems rumbled deep and strong. There the Boer "Irreconcilables" under General Hertzog strained against the power of Jan Christian Smuts and the pro-British South African Party. In many ways the Union of South Africa has proved more nationalistic than Australia, Canada, or New Zealand, insisting proudly upon her status as "a sovereign, independent state."

In another quarter of the Empire, Ireland remained ulcerous and fitful. After the Irish Free State Agreement Act of 1922 the Sinn Feiners, led by De Valera, refused to sit in the Dublin Parliament, or Dail Eireann. When their bitter revolt, described in the previous chapter, had halted in mid-career they followed a different course. In 1927 the Sinn Feiners bowed to a new law requiring all candidates to sit if elected. They went to the Dail, calling themselves by the political party name of Fianna Fail; and they took the repugnant oath of allegiance to the king, declaring it to be but an "empty formula." By unaccustomed parliamentary methods they fought William T. Cosgrave and the moderates in the government. In the election campaign of 1932 De Valera's party declared that they stood for the abolition of the oath of allegiance, the retention in Ireland of the land annuities owed to England, and the end of unemployment. Such a platform appealed to Irishmen touched by patriotism and the world depression. Fianna Fail won the election, defeating Fine Gael, Mr. Cosgrave's party.

Now the granite De Valera attempted to carry out his extreme policies. He demanded "a united Irish Republic." Under a republican system, of course, southern Ireland would be no freer than as a British Dominion. De Valera and his followers wished to see a self-sufficient, united, republican Ireland standing alone for purely ideological reasons. Finally, in 1933, De Valera did succeed in getting the oath of allegiance to the king abolished as a requirement for members of the Irish Parliament. The office of governor-general remained, but was virtually ignored. The lord lieutenant soon departed from Dublin Castle.

Very difficult was the problem of the land annuities, involving repayment of money earlier advanced by the British government to enable Irish tenants to purchase land. Although an Anglo-Irish agreement of 1923 provided for the payment of these annuities, De Valera refused to honor the pledge. Britain then collected the money by imposing tariffs on goods coming into England from southern Ireland. This bore heavily upon Irish farmers accustomed to sending their produce across St. George's Channel and the Irish Sea. The economic dependence of southern Ireland upon England never muffled the claims of Fianna Fail to independence; but before 1949 it helped to prevent an actual and complete separation of southern Ireland from Britain and the Empire.

The 3,000,000 southern Irishmen have never been prosperous. Before its defeat in February, 1948, De Valera's government increased public services and social security protection. There was an advance in gross industrial output. Despite these steps in De Valera's New Economic Policy the national economic position did not improve; the public debt steadily increased. Ireland still remains, in an economic sense, the "Deep South" of the British Isles.

In 1937 the De Valera Constitution was ratified by plebiscite. It declared Ireland an "independent and sovereign state" to be called Eire. It asserted that its territory included all Ireland; but for obvious reasons the writ of De Valera ran only through the twenty-six counties of the south. The new constitution abolished the office of governor-general; it omitted all reference to the crown. The king was retained only for purposes of external affairs, especially within the Empire Commonwealth. The constitution also established a president to be elected by a direct vote every seven years. There remained two houses: the dail, or assembly, and the senate. Through the president, the dail was to appoint the prime minister, who, in turn, was to appoint his ministers. A large number of electors voted against this constitution; it evoked but limited enthusiasm.

In April, 1938, the economic battle between England and Eire was ended by the payment by Eire of £10,000,000 to settle in full the annuity land payments account due to England. Tariffs were reduced on both sides; especially important was the British removal of the penal tariff on cattle, earlier imposed as a part of Britain's method of collecting the equivalent of the unpaid annuities. In June, 1938, largely because of this agreement, Fianna Fail was returned to power with an overall majority of sixteen seats.

The outrages of the Irish Republican Army pointed to their disapproval of De Valera's partial reconciliation; they also showed that many still desired to end the Irish partition and to weld Ulster and Eire forcibly into one republic. Protestant and industrial Ulster, containing forty per cent of Ireland's population, wanted union with Eire no more now than in 1920. Ulster was determined to remain an integral part of the United Kingdom.

Meanwhile, safe behind Britain's power and with effective independence under Dominion status, De Valera's Eire remained neutral in the Second World War. Her ports were closed to Britain, despite the British hope that they might be made available as bases for naval and merchant marine operations. In the days of Hitler's steady submarine toll of Allied shipping the lack of Irish ports was a handicap pregnant with danger.

Chapter 40 will describe how all links between Eire and the British Commonwealth were finally severed in 1949. The Celtic tendency to brood over the shadowed and cruel chapters of a long history cannot easily be overcome. By slow steps it may be possible to reach the uplands of reconciliation. This can happen only if the necessary incentives to good-will, now still tragically lacking, are found.

PALESTINE, EGYPT, INDIA

In the Near East there were two danger zones: Palestine and Egypt. It will be recalled that strategically important Palestine, with 1,200,000 inhabitants, had become a mandate of Great Britain after the First World War; with British aid, it had prospered. Behind the economic advance, however, the bitter Arab-Jewish hostility spread its malignant strength. In 1917 Arthur Balfour, then British foreign secretary, had stated that Britain viewed with favor "the establishment in Palestine of a National Home for the Jewish people." The Jews in Palestine, especially in Jerusalem and Tel Aviv, clashed frequently with the Arabs. The Arabs regarded Palestine as their own; for religious, social, and economic reasons they despised and hated the Jews. No Jewish home, they declared, would be made on the land that the Moslem Arabs had helped to seize from the Turks. The Arabs, left alone, would have massacred the Jews, whom they outnumbered. Only the restraining hand of Britain prevented that. British authorities continued to balance and mediate. In the end, they pleased neither Jew nor Arab.

Because of the religious and racial antipathies, bitter and violent, Palestine's problems were in many respects similar to those of India. Despite passionate propaganda to the contrary, it is difficult to see how Britain, acting in justice and good faith, could have yielded to the wishes of either group. As a result of German persecution of the Jews the British government permitted an unusually large number to enter Palestine. The Arabs loudly protested. In 1939 Britain closed the doors again. With the end of the Second World War demands arose throughout the world for Britain to permit unrestricted Jewish immigration to Palestine. Arab leaders declared they would resist, by force if necessary, the entrance of more Jews. Behind the Arabs of Palestine stood all the Arab world. Despite international conferences and detailed proposals it was not easy to find an acceptable answer to the dilemma. The very terms of the difficult Palestine equation did not permit an easy explanation or a simple answer. The answer that was found in 1948 is discussed in the final chapter of this book.

A further Imperial problem had arisen in Egypt. The agreement of 1922, described in the previous chapter, was not popular. In 1923 the first Egyptian Parliament elected under the new constitution renewed the demand for complete British withdrawal from Egypt. After Sir Lee Stack, governor-general of the Sudan, was murdered in Cairo in 1924 the stern measures taken by the British government maintained an uneasy peace. In 1928 there were further difficulties. Two years later a treaty creating an Anglo-Egyptian alliance was rejected by the Egyptian Nationalists.

In 1936, under the terms of a new treaty, Great Britain withdrew British troops from Cairo and Alexandria. Only British forces required for the defense of the Suez Canal were to remain in Egypt. It was also agreed that a twenty-year Anglo-Egyptian alliance should be established under the terms of which Egypt and Britain agreed to support each other in the event of war. Egypt was not bound to enter a war by Britain's side unless she desired to do so; she did promise to place her ports and transportation facilities at Britain's disposal and to allow British forces and supplies free passage through her territory. The Egyptians were also to share in the government of the Sudan. In the Second World War Egypt did not declare war upon the Axis powers; but she fulfilled to the letter every clause of the treaty of 1936.

In the years before the Second World War the pervasive spirit of nationalism seeping through the East touched not only Egypt, Palestine, and the Arab lands. Patterns of nationalism became more distinct in India; some individuals demanded responsible government and Dominion status; some wanted complete independence and the driving out of the British Raj. In previous chapters reference has been made to the successive instalments of political liberty granted to India and to the baffling problems of race and religion, caste and culture, education, language, and economic advance. Between the two World Wars there were about 250,000,000 Hindus in India; there were 75,000,000 Moslems and 6,000,000 Christians; the rest were Parsees, Jains, Sikhs, and so on. India had over 2,000 castes of Hindus. Many Moslems looked upon the Hindus with dislike, and not only for religious reasons. Moslem political power was greater than their numbers suggested and they did not intend to submit to the numerically superior Hindus. Each of the six hundred native states, officially not a part of British India, differed in its relation to the British crown. The affairs of some were handled by British agents; others, usually the larger areas, dealt directly with the Viceroy. Some sat in the Chamber of Princes; some did not.

After the appearance of the Montagu-Chelmsford Report and the passage of the Government of India Act in December, 1919, the saintly and subtle Mahatma Gandhi, later leader of the National Congress party, became angered by British attempts to suppress nationalist agitation. In 1920 Gandhi headed the "swaraj" or home rule group and formulated the policy of peaceful non-cooperation with the British, a policy soon adopted by the National Congress. By this passive resistance program the followers of Gandhi agreed never to resist the British by violent means. They would silently boycott British schools and law courts; they would not take part in political life; they would not buy British goods. Gandhi persuaded thousands to take up hand spinning and weaving as a protest against western industrialism. But passive resistance was not enough for many of Gandhi's followers. There were riots; bolts of British cloth were seized and burned; British troops were guilty of several errors of judgment and common humanity, especially at Amritsar; Indian Nationalists continued to snipe and to beat unguarded Englishmen to death. Gandhi was jailed.

In 1924 the Indian assembly threw out the budget when the British would not agree to grant India immediate home rule. The Viceroy, under the Act of 1919, thereupon put the budget into effect without legislative support. In 1927 the British government appointed the Simon Commission to report on the problem of stabilizing the rupee, the working of the governmental system, the growth of education, and the affairs of India generally. The Simon Commission contained only British members; it was stated that the inclusion of any Indian representatives might have prejudiced the impartiality of the report. The National Congress, the larger part of the Moslem League, and the Liberal Federation boycotted the Commission. In 1929 Gandhi began his famous "march to the sea" to defy the British government by making salt out of sea water. By law the making of salt was a government monopoly. At the end of his long pilgrimage Gandhi broke that law. The result was another outburst of violence and riots.

In 1930 the Simon Report was issued. It advocated the creation of a federation of all Indian states, except Burma and the Northwest Frontier Province. Thus, if the native states wished to enter this federation they were to be permitted to do so. In the separate Indian provinces responsible government was to be established but not in the All-India Legislature. Following the Simon Report two Round Table Conferences were held in London in 1930 and 1931 for the purpose of framing a new constitution. The Conferences agreed on the federation of the Indian native states and British India. Gandhi himself attended the Conference of 1931. Shortly afterwards he began an alarming "fast unto death" to gain political recognition for the "untouchables." In London the Moslems and Hindus discovered many difficulties in all proposals regarding representation, law, finance, and so on. Their disagreement with one another was usually greater than with the British. Soon disaffection rose to new heights; economic distress increased; taxes were left unpaid; tongues of flaming terrorism licked through the Deccan and Bengal.

After a third Round Table Conference the British undertook the herculean task of framing a new governmental system for India. The Government of India Act of 1935 set up an Indian federation with limited responsible government in both the bicameral federal government and in the provinces. The British government retained control of finance, foreign affairs, and the military services. Although the dyarchy system of 1919 was thus fortunately ended the British retention of important powers meant that India had not yet been given Dominion status.

At the same time the door was left open for the entrance of the native states under their princes into the federation. Negotiations to that end were proceeding at the outbreak of war in 1939. In some Indian circles it was said that the British were thus attempting to influence the central government because Britain could rely on the co-operation of the princes. Nevertheless, no longer did the Viceroy control the composition of the upper house in the central legislature; its members were now to be appointed by the provincial legislatures or, in the case of a native state, by the ruling prince. The Government of India Act of 1935 also separated Burma from India. In April, 1937, Burma became a crown colony with a bicameral legislature.

In India the new act was unpopular. It did not grant Dominion status; it did not grant independence. Amidst ignorance and poverty, cultural and religious divisions, new leaders rose beside the old. On the eve of the Second World War Jawaharlal Nehru of the predominantly Hindu All-India National Congress Party demanded independence, socialism, and a strong central government for India. On the other hand, Mohamed Ali Jinnah of the Moslem League insisted that the Moslems should have an independent state, separate from the Hindus. This famous doctrine of Pakistan always took first place among Moslem demands. Could the gulf fixed between Hindu and Moslem elements ever be bridged? Would the British be willing and able to devise a concrete plan to satisfy Indian aspirations towards freedom? The answer, described in the final chapter of this book, was to come in 1946 from the Labour government of Clement Attlee.

THE OTTAWA CONFERENCE, 1932

Meanwhile, as these forces moved relentlessly across the face of the Empire, the problems of British, Imperial, and world trade grew heavy and urgent.

Throughout the years following the First World War and at a speeded pace during the great depression British exports had fallen, partly because other countries were raising their tariff barriers. The

United States, for example, imposed the Smoot-Hawley tariff in 1930, stopped lending abroad, and devalued the dollar with a view to raising domestic prices in the United States; this devaluation temporarily ended any chance of a general exchange rate stabilization. The fall of British exports made necessary the reduction of British imports. But because these imports were largely essential foodstuffs and raw materials any major reduction would have involved a large decline in total British money income with consequent deflation, bankruptcies, and more unemployment.

When Britain abandoned the gold standard in 1931 the situation was altered. The exchange value of the pound could then be permitted to fall, thereby giving British exporters a competitive advantage in world trade. This would have been satisfactory if other countries in the sterling area had not remained on the gold standard and linked to sterling at the old level. To them the fall of the pound was a heavy blow, implying severe deflation. Meanwhile, "refuge capital" moved from countries outside the sterling area because they feared their own currencies would fall in value; as sterling had already fallen, it was reasonably safe. The new British Exchange Equalization Account operated to cushion fluctuations in the exchange value of sterling and to keep "refuge capital" from pushing it up. Thus the restrictive British policies combined with those of the other great powers in contributing to economic instability and peril.

Great Britain took a second step of great significance in virtually abandoning free trade and adopting a general protective tariff, supplemented by import quotas. The Conservatives, who had long demanded protection, rejoiced. As Britain had previously bought about one sixth of all goods entering world trade these tariff quotas imposed hardship on foreign countries. When foreign tariffs were raised Britain sought to extend her Imperial markets. At the Ottawa Conference in July, 1932, the Dominions declared their determination to develop their own industries. At the same time they wanted preference in British markets, particularly for their raw materials and foodstuffs, in return for the preference they had long been giving to goods coming from Great Britain. Mutual trade should be stimulated by mutual preferences.

As a result of seven separate agreements the Dominions increased their overall preference to British exports by raising duties on foreign goods above the earlier levels. Britain took similar action, so far as her long-term commitments to Russia and Argentina permitted. The Import Duties Act of 1932 imposed a general ad valorem tariff of ten per cent on almost all goods except those imported from British countries. Additional duties were later placed on some commodities. On luxuries such as furs and jewelry the ad valorem duty rose to 30 per cent. On automobiles, bicycles, and motor cycles it was increased to

33.3 per cent. Tariffs were placed on imports into non-self-governing British colonies, hitherto open to world trade. In order to protect the British farmer against Imperial competition the British government resorted to subsidies. In 1937–1938 duties under the Import Duties Act yielded £29,700,000. After 1938 the tariff income steadily declined as numerous trade arrangements, such as the Anglo-French agreement of 1934 and the Anglo-American agreement of 1938, reduced the number and weight of duties.

What was the effect on intra-Imperial trade? It is true that British imports from the Empire increased from a level of 29 per cent in 1930 to 40 per cent in 1938. Nevertheless, this fact taken by itself could be misleading. Total British imports rose steadily after 1930. Exports from the United States to Britain, for instance, rose from 44.5 per cent in 1929 to 50 per cent in 1938. Despite all arguments in favor of Imperial cohesion and economic unity the operation of the Ottawa agreements showed the great difficulty of obtaining any sizeable expansion of intra-Imperial trade. In 1938, for example, only one third of the total trade of all British countries was with one another. In that year British countries took 42 per cent of all United States exports. In turn, 32 per cent of all United States imports came from British sources.

The preferential tariff concessions and mutual trading arrangements agreed upon at Ottawa were expedients made desirable by European and United States tariffs. They also enabled Britain to bring pressure on other countries to concede advantages for British exports. Thus Britain obtained trade treaties from countries to which the British markets were of a special importance. This "most favored nation" policy increased the difficulties of Britain's rivals in attempting to sell to those countries with which Britain had made bilateral trading arrangements. However, despite the advantages resulting from the depreciated pound and from protection, the tide of British exports, throughout the decade before the Second World War, was about 25 per cent below the 1929 level. More than by her trade and financial policies Britain was aided by the domestic building boom and by the relatively low price of imported food.

THE LOCUST YEARS: 1932–1935

Heavy clouds rolled over the international scene. The feeble pulse of disarmament conferences failed at last. Public opinion grew weary and sceptical of the value of the meetings of diplomatists and statesmen. Slowly the world came within practical distance of almost measureless calamity. Ramsay MacDonald spoke of "reconciliation, collaboration, justice." But in July, 1932, when MacDonald had returned from the Lausanne Conference, Winston Churchill asked a question: "What has become of Versailles? There has been no Carthaginian peace. Neither has there been any bleeding of Germany white by the conquerors. The exact opposite has taken place. The loans which Great Britain and the United States particularly, and also other countries, have poured into the lap of Germany since the firing stopped, far exceed the sum of reparations which she has paid." It has been explained above how reparation payments by Germany were in fact abandoned after Lausanne. Armaments began to increase, army and naval plans to multiply. "We have steadily marched backwards since Locarno," said Churchill. "Fears are greater, rivalries are sharper, military plans are more closely concerted, military organizations are more carefully and efficiently developed. Britain is weaker and Britain's hour of weakness is Europe's hour of danger. . . . And all this has been taking place under Governments whose statesmen and diplomatists have never ceased to utter the most noble sentiments of peace amidst the cheers of the simple and the good."

Successive events marked the rising peril. Late in 1932 Japan left the League of Nations when the Lytton Report condemned her aggression in Manchuria. In January, 1933, Germany passed under the iron control of the National Socialist German Labor party led by Adolf Hitler. The London Economic Conference, held in the early summer of 1933, accomplished nothing towards removing the obstructions to international trade. British and American representatives could not agree about the cause of the great depression. Britain's Neville Chamberlain asserted that the chief reasons were low prices and war debts; Cordell Hull of the United States blamed high tariffs and economic nationalism. For several reasons, the United States refused to cooperate in any plan to stabilize the world's currency.

In October, 1933, Germany withdrew from the League of Nations and secretly began to rearm. As a matter of fact, the Allied Control Commission had never succeeded in completely disarming Germany. What, indeed, had now become of Versailles? "Do not forget," said Churchill in speaking of the inadequate defenses of Britain and the Empire, "that Germany is ruled by men who have no restraint of public opinion. . . . The German power is in their hands, and they can direct it this way or that by a simple gesture. No nation has a right to permit itself to be blackmailed by such a government. Far away are the days of Locarno. The hope is gone and we must act." British Army estimates for 1933 were £1,462,000 more than for 1932; Navy estimates were £3,093,000 more; but Air Force estimates were £340,000 less. Only with hesitation and reluctance did elder statesmen and military authorities in many lands come to understand the importance of the air in the shape of things to come.

Meanwhile the warning words of Churchill and his few supporters rang more loudly. Of Ramsay MacDonald Churchill said: "The Prime Minister's interventions in foreign affairs have been remarkably unsuccessful. His repeated excursions have not led to any solid, good result. His four years of control of foreign relations have brought us nearer to war, and have made us weaker, poorer, more defenceless." Some men, like Lord Grey of Fallodon, could find meagre solace in the fact that "the great security for peace at the present moment is that Germany is not armed and not in a position to go to war."

The tide of grim events swept on. On June 30, 1934, over sixty of Hitler's suspected opponents were shot without trial. Already uncounted Marxian Socialists and Jews were being slaughtered in Germany. On July 19 it was announced that the British Royal Air Force would be increased by forty-one air squadrons. On July 25 the anti-Nazi Austrian Chancellor Dr. Engelbert Dollfuss was assassinated by National Socialists in Vienna. Hitler, who wanted an anschluss with Austria, was preparing the way by dividing the Austrian people and slaying those who rejected his friendship. On August 3 President von Hindenburg died; Hitler became president of the Reich as well as chancellor. On October 9, King Alexander of Yugoslavia and Alexander Barthou of France were murdered.

In January, 1935, the Saar basin was returned to Germany as a result of a plebiscite. In February Great Britain announced a 40 per cent increase in her defenses, especially in the Air Force. In March Hitler publicly denounced the Treaty of Versailles and told the world what it already knew, that Germany was arming again. Sir John Simon stated that his discussions with Hitler disclosed considerable divergences of view between the British and German governments. Sir John told the cabinet that Hitler had no interest in a collective system of peace and security; that he would give no guarantee with respect to Austria; that Hitler would not withdraw his conscription order; that Germany had achieved parity with Great Britain in the air. In April, 1935, representatives of Great Britain, France, and Italy met at Stresa to discuss the German defiance. Despite the so-called "Stresa front" no action was taken, beyond the formal statement that the independence of Austria must be observed. Few commitments were made.

In June, 1935, an Anglo-German Naval Pact provided that Germany might build battleships and cruisers up to 35 per cent of Britain's strength and submarines up to 45 per cent of the British level. France, Italy, and Russia protested. But Britain felt this agreement might check the kind of Anglo-German naval rivalry that had preceded the First World War. And, far beyond the circle of Cato's "Guilty Men," there were those in Britain and America who hoped that a prosperous and satisfied Germany would assist in restoring world trade and that profitable business could be done with Hitler. Others, lacking the French fear of Germany, knew only that they hated war and that peace was an absolute good to be sought above all other values; still others felt that Nazi Germany was a dyke against Communism; and, finally, some believed that it was better to balance the budget and eat well than to spend too much in rearmament. Of these opinions was the policy of appeasement born. Meanwhile Churchill spoke of "the woeful miscalculations of which we are at present the dupes and of which there are those who hope we may some day be the victims." He joined with others to demand that the government hasten to rearm. "Let us free the world from the reproach of a catastrophe carrying with it calamity and tribulation beyond the tongue of man to tell."

Meanwhile the Silver Jubilee of King George V for the moment pushed fear into the background of the public consciousness. In the economic situation there was a small improvement. The British departure from the gold standard had helped her to sell more cheaply abroad; this early advantage only gradually diminished when other countries went off gold and the cost of imported foods and raw materials rose. The tariffs had prevented the dumping in Great Britain of surplus products from other countries. A continuing conversion of the public debt and reduction of the bond interest rate saved money for the government and helped to send capital into more profitable private enterprise fields. The extensive building boom, the development of new enterprises, the housing program, government financial aid to industry, and rearmament united to reduce unemployment and increase income. In 1931 there had been about 3,200,000 unemployed; by January, 1937, the total had fallen to approximately 1,830,000. Moreover, agriculture had been aided by subsidies; some land settlement projects had been used to relieve unemployment. It was planned to spend about £2,000,000 to help "depressed areas" in the basic coal, cotton, steel, and shipping industries.

As the National government had been in power for four years a national election was due in 1936. In view of the brightening domestic scene the government considered that it might be politically wise to call an election in the spring of 1935. Ramsay MacDonald, however, was exhausted, disillusioned, and ill. On June 7, 1935, he resigned as prime minister and took a minor post in the cabinet. Stanley Baldwin, the Conservative leader, became prime minister for the third time.

Baldwin found things otherwise than in his first two ministries. The road to war was broadening. Japan had entered the game of world politics and aggression. Britain's isolated possessions in the Pacific seemed admirably suited to the Japanese policy of "nibbling" even before the days of heavy propaganda about an Asiatic co-prosperity sphere dominated by Japan. Germany was shedding the encumbrances, physical and moral, that had manacled her dangerous will to make war. Coming over the horizon of time was a war born of the aggression of Italy in Ethiopia. Mussolini wanted Ethiopia to add to Eritrea and

Italian Somaliland; this, he hoped, might be the first step in building a new Roman Empire and in turning the Mediterranean into an Italian lake. Although the opiate of the Locarno spirit was clearly gone, no man then knew that the unprovoked Italian attack on Ethiopia in fact marked the hour when the methods of European diplomacy were beginning to yield to those of war. Weakness and ineptitude had made their inevitable invitation to tyranny. International anarchy had returned. And another war, the war between science and morals, was about to burst forth with such demonic fury that the whole destiny of man depended upon its outcome.

Chapter 38

THE SECOND WORLD WAR

ETHIOPIA, THE RHINELAND, SPAIN

A CLASH between Ethiopian and Italian forces occurred in the desert at Wal Wal in December, 1934. Mussolini boldly asserted that the Ethiopians under their Emperor Haile Selassie must be punished for deliberate raids upon Italian territory. As a weak member of the League of Nations Ethiopia at once sought protection. When Japan had attacked Manchuria in 1931 no effective steps had been taken to check her aggression. Now Japan and Germany were no longer members of the League. Would Geneva act against Italy? Fearing Germany, France wanted Italian support. Hence Pierre Laval and the French government agreed to raise no objection when Italy moved against the Lion of Judah. Great Britain decided to support Ethiopia. Anthony Eden hastened about Europe in an attempt to obtain aid for Britain and the League. On June 24, 1935, he visited Mussolini. His visit was in vain. Mussolini wanted Ethiopia.

British interests were at stake. Ethiopia bordered on the Anglo-Egyptian Sudan. Out of Lake Tana, in Ethiopia, rose the Blue Nile, source of much water used in irrigating areas of the Sudan. The Suez Canal was not far distant from Italian bases. Britain also remembered the proud boasts of Mussolini about the future of the new Roman Empire and England's fate in the Mediterranean. Moreover, a recent "peace ballot" in Britain had showed strong public support of the League. Yet despite Britain's attitude Geneva failed in its attempt to bring agreement between Rome and Addis Ababa.

In early October, 1935, when the summer rains had ended, Mussolini's armies marched. Britain immediately sent great naval strength into the Mediterranean. Following the advice of its Sanctions Committee, the League imposed economic sanctions upon Italy. Nevertheless, the League members approved no measures of naval blockade; they did not close the Suez Canal. They were not running any risks for collective security or the Covenant. In the words of Pierre Laval,

761

they were "ruling out everything that might lead to war." Economic sanctions against Italy meant the banning of bank loans, credits, and all imports from Italy. But no embargo was placed on oil; France opposed any such stern measure because Italy was perhaps a future ally against Germany. Nor was any embargo imposed on pig iron or steel billets. No biting sanctions, no crippling or effective measures to halt Italy were ever applied. "Leadership," remarked Winston Churchill, "cannot exist on the principle of limited liability." The *Morning Post* found that "sanctions and disarmament are bats which lodge in the same belfry."

Stanley Baldwin seized the opportunity to hold a national election in November, 1935. All parties supported sanctions against Italy. All wanted accelerated rearmament. The National government of Baldwin obtained 431 seats; most were won by Conservatives. "They had ridden in on sanctions." Only 185 members now sat on the Opposition benches. There the Labour party far outnumbered the weakened Liberals.

On December 13, 1935, Sir Samuel Hoare, the British foreign secretary, came to an agreement with Pierre Laval. The two agreed that about two thirds of Ethiopia was to be surrendered to Italy. In Britain a tidal wave of public anger swept Hoare from office. His successor was Anthony Eden. Both Baldwin and Eden hesitated to stand against Italy without French support; and that France would not give. Meanwhile Italy marched on. On May 7, 1936, Ethiopia was annexed and formally made a part of the Italian Empire. Britain's policy had failed. Italy had defied the League; and the League, no more courageous than its individual members, had not taken up the challenge. Diplomacy is the art of the possible. When there was no wide support for collective security measures then collective security could not be.

In March, 1936, when other powers were actively concerned in the problem of Italian aggression, Hitler occupied the demilitarized Rhineland, thus tearing up another clause of the Treaty of Versailles and a large section of the Locarno pacts. So long as the Rhine valley was unfortified Germany had been vulnerable to French attack. France now wanted the British support promised at Locarno as Britain had earlier wanted French support against Italy. Would France move alone against Germany? Would Britain and France move together? Peace hung in the balance. Hitler stated that the Rhineland was German territory; that he had no territorial claims to make in Europe. Slowly the crisis passed. Many Englishmen felt that, after all, the terms of Versailles were perhaps excessive and certainly humiliating to a proud state like Germany. Would Hitler be less dangerous in the Rhineland than out of it? Might a satisfied Germany, justly treated, cease to be a threat to peace? In any event, it was clear that there would probably be small chance of securing collective security through the firm and united action of the members of the League of Nations. On the other hand, were there limits to the ambitions of Germany, Italy and Japan, the three great militaristic, anti-democratic, and unsatisfied powers?

In the summer of 1936 a civil war, hard and bloody, broke out in Spain. Germany and Italy actively supported the rebel and reactionary General Francisco Franco. They sent men and materials to place him in power. Russia stood behind the Loyalist forces and likewise sent men and materials to keep a liberal government in Madrid. France and Britain officially adopted a policy of non-intervention although men from France, Britain, and the United States enlisted to fight for the Spanish Loyalists. But Franco won the long war. He proceeded to dispose of thousands of his political opponents, who were swiftly shot, tortured, or jailed. Once again anti-democratic forces had prevailed.

In the midst of the Spanish civil war Italy and Germany entered into an alliance, forming the so-called Rome-Berlin Axis in October, 1936. In November, 1937, the Japanese joined the Fascists and Nazis. Almost at once Japan, without a declaration of war, started a great invasion of China beyond her earlier Manchurian conquests. British interests, especially in Shanghai, suffered heavily. The hour that Churchill, Eden, and others had forecast was almost come.

THE NAZI PESTILENCE, 1936–1939

With every crisis British rearmament proceeded more rapidly. Even for those who believed in appeasing the Axis, there was satisfaction in feeling that Britannia's strength was rising. Large appropriations were made for the Royal Navy. The size of the Army was to be increased. The expanded Air Force was to number 10,000 airplanes, including several types of fast fighters. Planning of new production proceeded apace although a famous "shadow factory" scheme, by which each of several factories was to make one part of a product, was abandoned; Lord Nuffield and others pointed out that if one factory in the projected chain should be destroyed the whole flow of production would be blocked. The budget of 1936–1937 provided for an expenditure of £160,700,000 for national defense, an increase of 30 per cent over the allocation for 1935. A slight business boom in 1936 and 1937 was followed by a serious recession; the adverse trade balances in 1937 and 1938 were the largest in British history. In 1938 the public debt was £8,000,000,000; taxes rose still higher.

In 1937 Winston Churchill proposed a new five-year rearmament plan under which Great Britain would spend £300,000,000 annually for national defense. On the eve of war, the 1939–1940 budget provided for an expenditure of £580,000,000. By January, 1940, the war was costing the United Kingdom £6,000,000 daily. In September, 1939, income taxes were raised by 37.5 per cent and estates duties by 10 per cent. In March, 1940, the first war bond issue was announced; it totalled £300,000,000, bearing three per cent interest redeemable at par in 1959. The defense of democracy was again to prove a costly business.

Meanwhile, in January, 1936, Britain was saddened by the death of King George V. His eldest son succeeded to the throne as Edward VIII. The new king had many qualities that might have made him a great constitutional monarch. He was popular, conscientious, and genuinely interested in the condition of the poor. All would have judged him worthy of the throne if he had never ascended it. In December, 1936, to the distress of the British people, Edward VIII made his "final and irrevocable decision" to marry a twice-divorced woman. By an Instrument of Abdication he renounced the throne. The Declaration of Abdication Act, giving effect to his wishes, was passed by both houses of Parliament in less than three hours. The cabinets of the Commonwealth, consulted earlier, were unanimous in their approval. On the night of December 11, 1936, the king who had suddenly become the Duke of Windsor went out into exile. "In the darkness," said the archbishop of Canterbury, "he left these shores." Fortunately the catastrophe was personal, not public. The new king, George VI, came to the throne prepared to maintain in the highest degree the traditions of his family and position.

After the coronation of George VI and Queen Elizabeth, Stanley Baldwin resigned as prime minister and went to the house of lords. His successor as head of the National government was Neville Chamberlain, who had been chancellor of the exchequer. Chamberlain was at once confronted by tasks with which he was not by ability or temperament fitted to cope. The new prime minister was an excellent business man and an admirable financier. In areas of diplomacy and statesmanship he was less successful. As a business man, he had deep faith in the value of negotiation and discussion with the German and Italian governments. Reasons for international friction, he felt, could be largely removed by frequent conferences conducted in an atmosphere of frankness and honesty. In this he was mistaken.

Hitler now moved towards Austria. In March, 1938, German pressure forced the resignation of Chancellor Kurt von Schuschnigg. A German army occupied Austria; Hitler annexed it. Italy, now the ally of Germany, approved. France, caught by a cabinet crisis, did nothing. Britain denounced the gangster methods of Berlin; but Hitler was not distressed by words alone. The policy of appeasement thus prevailed. Anthony Eden had already resigned from the cabinet in protest against continued British retreat.

Czechoslovakia was the next victim of Nazi aggression. Hitler felt grave concern about some 3,000,000 Sudeten Germans who were within the Czechoslovakian frontiers. Besides, Czechoslovakia was allied with France and Russia. Berlin insisted that the borders of Czechoslovakia established in 1919 must be altered. Led by Conrad Henlein, the Sudeten Germans of Bohemia were to be brought into Germany.

The crisis came in September, 1938. Twice Neville Chamberlain went to talk with Hitler at Godesberg and Berchtesgaden. Then, with Edouard Daladier of France, he went by airplane to Munich to confer with Hitler and Mussolini. Neither the Russians nor the Czechs were invited to attend the conference. Heavy pressure was put upon the Czechs by France and Britain to accept the German demands. The final "Munich Award" gave one-fifth of Czechoslovakia to Germany. Hitler declared before the world that the revisions of the Czechslovakian borders were his final territorial demands in Europe.

Earlier it had been agreed that areas where the total population was clearly more than half German would be ceded forthwith to Germany. An international commission would then hold plebiscites in regions where it was not certain that the Germans were in a majority. At Munich it was decided that the German army might occupy certain zones and that the international commission would decide where plebiscites should be held. Germany, Italy, Britain, and France guaranteed the new frontiers of Czechoslovakia. When Chamberlain returned to England he dramatically declared that he had obtained "peace for our time." Peace had indeed been kept, but not for long. Many Englishmen were shamed and shocked at the terms of the Munich agreement, even though they were relieved that the immediate threat of war had been turned aside.

In March, 1939, Hitler seized the remainder of Czechoslovakia. Britain and France at once declared that Germany would proceed further at her peril. Soon Hitler demanded the return of Danzig to Germany and a German road across the Polish corridor. At once Britain and France promised the Poles "all support in their power" in the event of "any action which threatened Polish independence." When Italy, on April 7, moved across the Adriatic to seize Albania, Britain and France also gave an unconditional promise of aid to Greece and Rumania in the event of Axis aggression. At the same time they sought an agreement with Russia.

On August 21 Russia suddenly made a non-aggression pact with Germany. Of the great powers, Britain and France thus stood alone. Hitler at once sent an ultimatum to Poland. But the Poles were given no time to consider it; the Nazis did not intend that they should. On September 1, 1939, German armies moved over the Polish borders.

Britain had made a pledge to Poland. Chamberlain warned Berlin that only Nazi retreat would save the peace of the world. "Unless the German Government are prepared to give His Majesty's Government satisfactory assurances that the German Government are to suspend all aggressive actions against Poland, and are prepared promptly to withdraw their forces from Polish territory His Majesty's Government will without hesitation fulfill their obligations." Berlin did not reply.

The Royal Navy, the Army, and the Air Force had been mobilized on September 1. On September 3 the British government informed Hitler that "unless not later than 11 A.M. British Summer Time, today, September 3, satisfactory assurances have been given by the German government and have reached His Majesty's government in London a state of war will exist between the two countries as of that hour." Berlin did not reply. The French government declared war. Australia, Canada, New Zealand, South Africa, and all the British Empire moved together to battle again their enemy of the First World War.

THE FALL OF POLAND, DENMARK, NORWAY

Appeasement had ended. War had begun. Within a few days Hitler showed the world how mighty a power was his. Three highly mechanized armies hurtled across the Polish borders. In support of the land forces the proud Luftwaffe of Marshal Goering blasted rail centers and air fields. To bring with terror the conviction that resistance was useless the Nazis bombed the cities and towns and strafed the fleeing inhabitants. Forced beyond Warsaw, remnants of the Polish forces encountered Russian armies that had invaded Poland from the east. On September 28, 1939, Russia and Germany divided the conquered country. At once Russia forced Esthonia, Latvia, and Lithuania to allow Russian air fields and naval bases within their borders. The following spring Russia annexed these republics outright; she also took over the Bessarabian section of Rumania. When Finland refused a Russian demand for unusual concessions war broke out on November 30, 1939. In March, 1940, Finland surrendered and Russia seized several regions of strategic and economic value.

The Germans swiftly undertook a savage extermination of the Jews. The Poles, an inferior people by Nazi standards, saw many of their political and intellectual leaders taken to concentration camps. Few came back. It was not long, however, before the Germans were plagued in Poland, as they were to be elsewhere later, by a secret underground movement of stubborn and silent resistance and sabotage. Guided by patriots through the darkness, many Poles escaped to Britain to find a chance to renew the war against Hitler. Later, over all Europe, the vast underground system grew stronger, more efficient, an invisible secret state with which the Nazis could not cope.

The following winter was a period of little activity. The British Navy scoured German shipping from the seas. In December, 1939, the first of Germany's "pocket battleships," the *Graf Spee,* was badly damaged and forced to flee into Montevideo by three British cruisers in the dramatic Battle of La Plate. There she was scuttled by her German crew; her captain committed suicide. During these quiet months intricate weapons of economic warfare came slowly to support the naval blockade. Meanwhile Nazi submarine commanders sank Allied and neutral ships, often with such wanton inhumanity that President Roosevelt called them the "rattlesnakes of the Atlantic." Behind the forts of the two-million-dollar Maginot Line the French and British armies preferred to fight a war of defense, their artillery shelling the German Siegfried Line. The Germans, on the other hand, did not intend to be starved by the Allied blockade.

When suitable weather came with the spring Hitler ordered his armies to thrust without warning into Denmark and Norway. This was on April 9, 1940. Although Denmark was swiftly overrun, Hitler's Germans found that the conquest of territory was not enough. The Danish spirit was not broken. After the land of the Danes was taken they continued to resist; at night and in secret places the men of the underground struck silently and hard. After Denmark had fallen, Norway was invaded at several points along her coast. Despite the aid of some 12,000 British troops the Norwegians finally had to yield before the German attacks. Their king escaped to Britain; thousands followed, often bringing valuable ships with them. Once more the Nazi power had been demonstrated. By conquering Denmark and Norway, Hitler had protected his northern flank; he had practically isolated Sweden with her rich ore resources; he had increased his available supplies of food and other commodities; he had obtained new and strategically valuable bases for air operations against Britain and for attacks by submarine and surface raiders on the sea supply lanes to British ports.

The German "blitzkrieg" had now struck down three nations with terrible speed. This was clearly to be no slow war of fixed trenches and siege guns but a conflict of swift mobility in scores of important theaters from Narvik to New Guinea and the Coral Sea. In these long six years the world saw a steady flood of weapons undreamed of in the First World War or in the taut years of peace. Speedy fighters planes streaked through the skies from Dover to the Celebes; mighty bombers ranged from the "Happy Valley" of the Ruhr to Tokyo, each dropping bomb loads totalled in tons. Heavily armed tanks pushed about like giant beetles; huge gliders and transport planes decanted paratroopers; the intensive "flak" of anti-aircraft guns curtained about important targets; huge searchlights probed through the night skies, their beams blunted against the clouds in phosphorescent discs. Radar, rockets, magnetic mines, new types of land mines and "booby traps," all combined with the miracle of the atomic bomb to make the Second World War quite unlike any previous chapter of the long world disorder.

. . . .

THE FALL OF THE NETHERLANDS, BELGIUM, FRANCE

As Poland, Denmark, and Norway toppled, Britain prepared her defenses. In anticipation of heavy air raids millions of civilians volunteered for new duties as air raid wardens, fire watchers, demolition experts, plane spotters, hospital workers, transport drivers. The lights went off to conceal the cities from the dark raiders flocking overhead. Thousands of women and children were evacuated from the large cities and sent to safer billets in the country. In January, 1940, food rationing began; many other commodities were soon rationed as Britain sought to save shipping space and to strengthen her foreign exchange position abroad in order to increase her purchase of war tools.

On May 10, 1940, Hitler struck without warning at Luxembourg, Holland, and Belgium. Their fall would mean the outflanking of the Maginot Line. Hitler would have new air and sea bases close to England. On the same day Neville Chamberlain fell from power in Britain. He had long been associated in the public mind with "appeasement"; his competence as a war leader was doubtful. Faced by Allied disasters Britain turned to Winston Churchill. A new National government was formed, which now included Conservative, Labour, and Liberal ministers. On May 13 Churchill told the British people that he had "nothing to offer but blood, toil, tears, and sweat." The democratic world was appalled by the tornado of German power. How long would Britain survive? The defiant words of her new leader reminded all that the cause of freedom was not yet lost. "You ask, what is our aim? I can answer in one word: victory—victory at all costs, victory in spite of all terror, victory however long and hard the road may be; for without victory there is no survival."

An hour after the invaders crossed the frontiers of Luxembourg, Holland, and Belgium Nazi parachute troops showered down in Dordrecht, Rotterdam, and near the Hague. They seized strategic airports and bridges. Supported by dive-bombing Stukas German armies forced a crossing of the Yssel and Maas rivers and turned the flank of the southern Dutch line. The Great Belgian fortress of Eben Emael was swiftly taken. Upon Rotterdam descended a hail of Nazi bombs bringing widespread death and destruction. When the Germans crossed an undestroyed bridge at Maastricht they were able to roll up the main defenses of the Albert Canal line, to encircle Liege, to push swiftly across the Ardennes region, and to engulf defenses down the Meuse from Namur. On May 13 German mechanized units erupted about Sedan, crossed the Meuse and thrust behind the Allied lines. Meanwhile British and French forces had moved up to meet the enemy.

On May 4 Holland capitulated. Queen Wilhelmina and her government fled to London. The German advance units swirled closer to Brussels. On May 16 Brussels fell. Meanwhile Nazi panzer divisions, supported by bombers, ripped through broken French defenses towards Soissons on the Aisne. When they were held at Rethal they swept down the Somme valley, intent on thrusting northwest to Peronne, Cambrai, Arras, and the coast. Upon capturing Amiens and Abbeville they turned north towards Boulogne and Calais. Thus the main French forces were separated from British, Belgian and French units operating in the north. The German drive also cut athwart the communications of Allied armies holding the Scheldt line. When Leopold, king of the Belgians, suddenly surrendered on May 28 the northern Allied flank was exposed and the Nazis were able to exert pincer pressure from three sides. It seemed that the constricting German onslaughts would cut off the retreat of British and French forces to the one open port of Dunkirk. Britain was prepared for "hard and heavy tidings." The beach was exposed; the jaws of the Nazi trap were closing.

Protected for a few hours by fierce and admirable rearguard fighting most of the British and French troops reached Dunkirk. The Royal Air Force and the Fleet Air Arm destroyed 350 enemy aircraft about Dunkirk in eight days. Over 200 ships of the Royal Navy were assisted by a motley volunteer fleet of some 600 small boats manned by fishermen, tugboat captains, yachtsmen, and amateurs of all kinds. They rescued 337,130 British and French soldiers. This continuous operation lasted from May 29 to June 3. The weather stayed fair and the sea calm. Guns and tanks were left behind; all but 30,000 of the British troops came home. This was the "miracle of Dunkirk."

At once the Germans wheeled to strike at French defenses along the Somme and the Aisne. Under the assaults of massed tanks and infantry the French staggered backwards. On a ninety-mile front between the Oise and the Bresle the Nazis used about 4,000 tanks and 500,000 men. The Maginot Line was soon to be smashed from the rear as the Weygand Line, defended by thirty-seven French divisions, collapsed and plans for defenses in depth failed. The rapid development of German attacks paralyzed French forces; with their communication lines slashed they ceased to resist. Shattered French armies fled southwards, their retreat checked by desperate civilians who clogged the highways. All roads were regularly sprayed by the bullets of low-flying German aircraft.

On June 10, as France writhed before the lashing German armies, Italy declared war on France and Britain. Mussolini thought that "the hour marked out by destiny" had arrived at last. The jackal joined the pack and leaped to the kill. Under the arrogant Mussolini Italy had developed an army, war industries, an air force, and a navy. Because of the mounting strategic importance of the Mediterranean and Middle Eastern theatres in the Second World War the decision of Italy to join the Nazis was soon to alter the whole character of the conflict.

On June 13 General Weygand declared Paris an open city. The

French government moved to Bordeaux. On June 15 the Germans entered the French capital. "Generals are now commanding battalions," wrote French Premier Paul Reynaud to President Roosevelt. Meanwhile Great Britain had discussed the request of Reynaud that France be released from her obligation not to make a separate peace. Britain agreed to permit Franco-German armistice negotiations if the French fleet, the second largest in Europe, would move to ports not under German control until arrangements between France and Germany were concluded. But before any further steps could be taken Paul Reynaud was overthrown and the aged Marshal Pétain became premier. He rejected Churchill's offer of a Franco-British union under a single cabinet and with united economic, foreign, and defense policies. Instead, he turned to Hitler. On June 16 he asked for an armistice. He betrayed Britain; and he betrayed his own country.

France had suffered particularly from the lack of close cooperation between her political and military leaders. Some of the former were contaminated by a blighting moral plague that placed self-interest before the national welfare. On the military side, generals like Gamelin and Weygand obviously failed to understand the importance of the changed time factor brought about by the use of mechanized forces. The French High Command did not fortify the line between Sedan and Givet on the line of the Meuse. They did not expect the German panzers to advance along the southern road from Luxembourg to Sedan, close to the Maginot Line. Nor did they take into account the problem of air attack on communication arteries and the consequent effect on French morale. The Germans, on the other hand, had a clear plan of strategy. They had subdivided their armies into groups suitable to the efficient use of mechanized power. They avoided the mistakes they had made in 1914. They had superior numbers. Thus the French lost the first battles, and surrendered. Marshal Pétain, the arch-bellwether of all safe men, concluded his armistice with Hitler.

The clever and cruel armistice terms were signed at Compiegne in the same railway carriage where Marshal Foch had granted Germany an armistice in 1918. By these terms the northern and western French coasts and all territory north of a line drawn from Tours through Bourges and Moulins to Geneva were to be occupied by the Germans. Italy was to hold a small area in the southeast. Thus three fifths of France was under direct German and Italian control, including Paris and the industrial north. France was to pay occupation costs at a rate of $8,000,000 a day. All French armed forces were to be demobilized; all artillery, munitions, tanks, aircraft, naval yards, and fortifications were to be surrendered intact. Two million French prisoners of war were to be held in Germany as hostages of Hitler. At the southern resort town of Vichy Marshal Pétain and Pierre Laval set up a government for unoccupied France. This government, its path stained with dishonor, cooperated closely with Berlin.

In treacherous repudiation of France's pledge to Britain the armistice terms provided that the powerful French navy should be placed under German and Italian control. Hitler promised that the French ships would be disarmed and interned; that they would not be used against Britain. But confidence in Hitler's word was no longer a British weakness. The loss of French naval support was costly enough; the addition of it to German and Italian strength might prove disastrous. Hence the British moved swiftly. When French warships in ports controlled by Britain refused to cooperate with the British Navy they were interned. Those that wanted to fight Hitler joined the British. The French commander in the Algerian port of Oran insisted that he would not support the British or permit his ships to be interned in British or neutral ports. His declaration led to what Churchill called "this melancholy action"—the British naval attack on Oran and the subsequent crippling and sinking of many French ships; a few escaped to the French port of Toulon where other French vessels had already found an uneasy haven. At Dakar the British were repulsed by a Vichy force, but the stern of the French battleship *Richelieu* was blown out in the engagement. At Alexandria French naval units were interned.

The Vichy government had already broken diplomatic relations with Britain. The Churchill cabinet recognized the new "Free French" forces headed by the patriot General Charles de Gaulle, a cold, ambitious, and difficult man, but a brave one. De Gaulle, who had escaped the Germans, declared that France had lost a battle but not the war. Under the Cross of Lorraine he rallied Frenchmen who had neither been stunned by disaster nor lost the will to resist. Thus, over all the world, the diplomatic, military, and naval servants of France had a chance to decide whether they would serve Pétain or de Gaulle.

France had fallen. Britain stood at the beginning of her year alone against the Nazi might. The situation was desperate. The nine divisions of soldiers were too few. No weapons had been saved at Dunkirk and the supply of arms was meagre. In all Britain there were fewer than a hundred tanks. Twenty-two miles from the fortress shores of England stood Hitler's army, the mightiest in history. Supported by the great German air force, the submarine wolf packs, the surface navy, the industrial power of all Europe, the Italian ally, the fawning men of Vichy, Hitler could be confident. From Berlin came a peace offer. If Britain would agree to leave the German conquests intact then Hitler would not attempt to dismember the British Empire.

London rejected the proposal. Hitler paused. He prepared to conquer the English skies as the first step towards invasion. "The whole fury and might of the enemy must very soon be turned on us," said Churchill. "Hitler knows that he will have to break us in this island or lose the war. If we can stand up to him all Europe may be free. . . . Let us therefore brace ourselves to our duty and so bear ourselves that, if the British Empire and its Commonwealth last for a thousand years, men will still say, 'This was their finest hour.' "

THE BATTLE OF BRITAIN

In August and September, 1940, occurred the battle of Britain. Then the British Fighter Command that had earlier demonstrated its talents and resources in Flanders and had given the Germans a drubbing at Dunkirk dimmed forever the glories of the Luftwaffe. The eventual perdition of the German Air Force was foreshadowed by this intensive bloodletting in the skies over Britain in the summer of 1940. There is no doubt that the Germans underestimated the ability of the Royal Air Force to keep adequate single-engined fighters in the air. They also miscalculated the time British airfields could be kept unserviceable by German attacks. Marshal Goering used his aircraft extravagantly and the wastage was too high. The Germans did not employ sufficient fighter strength to nurse their bombers. Nor was their armament adequate. In preparation for the invasion of Britain Hitler was also building too many transport aircraft while his bomber strength slipped downwards. Moreover, the Germans spent too much time attacking shipping and seaports; they were thus diverted from their main task of striking at British fighter air fields.

The Royal Air Force, on the other hand, husbanded its power. Radio-location devices made it possible to detect the height and strength of German attacks. Thus the British used their fighters economically. In ten days the Junkers 87 lost nearly one half of their first-line strength. On August 8, 1940, there were at least a hundred German aircraft lost or put out of action.

In early September Hitler expected that Britain would soon be well softened up for a seaborne and airborne assault. He therefore gathered 3,000 invasion barges at Antwerp, Boulogne, Calais, Flushing, and Ostend. This was "the Armada that never sailed." On September 7 about 400 German aircraft attacked London. Approximately 25 per cent were destroyed. On September 15 the Luftwaffe lost about 200 planes. On September 27 the Germans sent over probably 800 aircraft. It was their last appearance in major force. Night attacks continued for many months, inflicting heavy damage and casualties in British cities. In the long weeks of the Blitz 40,553 individuals were killed; 46,850 were seriously injured.

The battle of Britain was over. It has been estimated that from August to October Germany had lost or put out of action more than half of its total first-line air strength which was engaged in combat. This was particularly serious in the days of the later multiple demands on German air power. When it was clear that Britain would not yield and could not be conquered Hitler turned south to the Mediterranean, east to the Balkans, still farther east to Russia. As the theatres of combat increased, the burdens on the German war machine multiplied in number and mounted in weight. At the same time the opportunities for error and miscalculation were extended.

THE YEAR ALONE

The Royal Air Force Bomber Command continued its attacks on enemy railways, docks, airfields, factories, oil refineries and tanks in occupied Europe, in Germany, and in Italy. In British skies newly developed techniques of night fighting discouraged the Germans. The silent wastelands made by Nazi bombs in the midst of Coventry, Birmingham, Bristol, Glasgow, Hull, Manchester, Plymouth, and other cities made the British more dogged in their defiance. Secret preparations were made for the first Commando raids on Europe. Seventy-six per cent of all manufacturing industries were soon working on government orders. Farm production was doubled. Salvage squads recovered valuable rubber, iron, and other materials. The starchy diet made necessary by severe rationing did not slacken factory output; Britain slowly became a mighty arsenal. British factories, for example, were to produce 70 per cent of the total munitions placed in the hands of her own forces and those of the British Dominions and colonies during the whole war period. Ten per cent came from the Commonwealth and Empire. Twenty per cent came from the United States. Meanwhile the silent economic warfare continued. The German deficiency in oilseeds, copper, wool, cotton, oil, and asbestos was never made up by her European conquests; an adequate supply of these commodities was beyond Hitler's clutch. He had obtained Scandinavian iron ore; but he still remained deficient in tungsten and chrome. In France he had seized bauxite; but he found little else of long-term value.

Meanwhile, however, the blockade was challenged by Germany. Nazi aircraft leaped from Continental bases to wound and destroy British shipping; submarines prowled from their lairs along the coasts. British destroyer strength had fallen; hence the convoys were often weakly guarded. In June, 1940, Britain lost nearly 540,000 tons of shipping. In September, 1940, the British government leased to the United States, rent-free for ninety-nine years, sites for air and naval bases in Newfoundland and Bermuda. For six other sites in the Caribbean area the United States paid rent in the form of fifty overage destroyers which were transferred to the Royal Navy. The addition of these destroyers helped the British in the vital battle of supplies. Canadian corvettes aided at the western end of the Atlantic run; British aircraft of the Coastal Command often nursed the convoys to harbor at the eastern end. Soon, too, the German surface raiders were further reduced in number by the destruction of the mighty *Bismarck*.

As the months passed the public opinion of the United States altered profoundly. In 1939 American neutrality legislation, amending the Neutrality Act of 1935, had provided that arms and munitions exported from the United States must not be carried on American ships and must be paid for in cash before shipment. This "cash and carry" law also prohibited American vessels from entering the war zone. Later, with the dramatic victories of the Axis forces set vividly before the world, the United States began soberly to consider the position of America in the event that Britain fell. Did the first defense line of American democracy lie across the Atlantic?

In August, 1941, President Roosevelt prepared with Winston Churchill the Atlantic Charter. From the great factories of the United States rolled more guns, more aircraft, more munitions for Britain. When British dollar resources were exhausted, including all British private investments in the United States which were taken over by the British government and paid for in sterling, the United States Congress on March 11, 1941, passed the famous Lend-Lease Act. This Act enabled "the government of any country whose defense the President deems vital to the defense of the United States" to obtain raw materials in the United States without cash payment. Before the war ended the United States was to supply about fifty billion dollars' worth of goods and services to the Allies. Under "reverse lend lease" the British Empire and Commonwealth provided supplies and services to United States forces abroad. By this convenient means Australia and New Zealand returned to the United States almost as much as they had obtained. Under their own Mutual Aid program the Canadian government gave without charge several billion dollars' worth of goods and services to the United Nations. Soon American ships ferried goods to Britain; American aircraft patrolled the western end of the Atlantic shipping lanes; American vessels and airplanes were ordered to fire upon any German raiders or submarines. "All aid short of war" was being given in full measure by the late summer of 1941.

Meanwhile the Italians were hacking at Britain's life line in the Mediterranean. Although Mussolini's navy was new and large it did not long remain a formidable threat. After their cruiser the *Bartolomeo Colleoni* was sunk the Italian ships huddled in their harbors. On November 11, 1940, the British aircraft carrier H.M.S. *Illustrious* sent 21 Royal Navy aircraft to Taranto. Bombs and torpedoes disabled three Italian battleships, two cruisers, two fleet auxiliaries. On March 28, 1941, Admiral Cunningham met the Italian fleet at sea. Off Cape Matapan one Italian battleship was badly damaged; three 10,000-ton Italian cruisers and two 1,500-ton destroyers were sunk. Italian gunnery was inadequate; not one British ship was hit.

In August, 1940, the Italians had seized British Somaliland. In September, forces under Marshal Graziani invaded Egypt; they advanced sixty miles; then, for nearly three months, they waited. On December 9 General Wavell's small Army of the Nile attacked. The

British numbered 30,000; the Italians, 260,000. Within two months Mussolini's troops were driven out of Egypt and Cyrenaica. The British captured 133,295 prisoners, including six senior generals. Wavell lost 600 men. In December, 1941, Sudanese and Ethiopian forces, aided by a British army totalling 70,000 men, inflicted 289,000 casualties on the Italians; they conquered Italian Somaliland and Eritrea and they freed British Somaliland and all Ethiopia. On October 28, 1940, Mussolini's Roman legions had attacked Greece; the Greeks spanked them back into Albania.

The Nazis moved into Bulgaria, Hungary, Rumania and Slovakia. This was another step towards cutting British communications to the Far East. On April 6, 1941, they invaded Jugoslavia and Greece. About 75,000 British troops were at once drained from Africa to help the Greeks in fulfilment of the British pledge of 1939. In ten days Jugoslavia was conquered, although guerrilla fighters battled on. Soon the British had lost 30,000 men in Greece. The rest were forced to withdraw under terrible air bombardment. The Germans than invaded Crete. Again the British were compelled to withdraw; their losses in men, equipment, and ships had been heavy.

When British naval and military forces had been thus diverted to Greece and Crete the Germans poured crack Nazi troops into Libya to help the Italians. The famous Afrika Korps drove the British out of Libya except for the port of Tobruk, held grimly for eight months by Australians. The way seemed almost open for a final drive on Suez, Syria, and the Near East oil fields. There was an Axis-inspired revolt in Iraq. Free French forces joined with the British to squash the Vichy-controlled government in Syria, briskly spinning Nazi plots.

For a year Britain had stood valiantly alone. Then, suddenly, on June 22, 1941, Hitler attacked Russia. His left flank must be protected in the drive to the East. The "world island" of the Nazi geopoliticians must be seized; and Russia, as well as the Middle East, possessed oil. The grain fields of the Ukraine awaited German reapers. Britain at last had an ally. Winston Churchill called the event the "fourth climacteric." He declared: "Any man or state who fights on against Nazidom will have our aid. Any man or state who marches with Hitler is our foe." Supplies began to move from Britain and America to Russia through southern routes and over the freezing hell of the arctic seas to Murmansk and Archangel.

THE UNITED NATIONS

The logic of war is relentless. Some strategic blunders can be remedied; others never. The fatal tendency of the Germans was to overtax their strength by extending the theatres of war too widely. It was one thing to make tactical gains; it was quite another to exploit properly the implacable logic of geography, strategy, production, transportation, and communication. In a global war one cogent rule remains: "the excessive expenditure of effort in one direction influences adversely the potential maximum that can be exploited in another." This military commandment the Germans did not obey. The great Clausewitz had said: "Lost ground is a standard of lost moral force." But wars are not won by the seizure of territory alone. There are also the rigid laws that govern the tensile strength of communication lines, the immutable factors that limit land transport facilities, the fixed and changeless terms in the equations of economic endurance. The danger of deep penetration into Russia had been stressed by von Falkenhayn, von Leeb, von Schlieffen, and von Seeckt. Hitler ignored the warning.

The Russian war was a war of distance. The front was 1,600 miles long. German supply problems were appalling. When the interior lines of German land communication in Europe began to deteriorate all the other terms in the equation of Nazi defeat fell easily into place.

On the sea the Germans never had an opportunity to study Admiral Mahan's maxim that "communications dominate war." Even at the darkest hours the Allies kept the ocean channels open. The Axis had lost over six millions tons of shipping in the first three years of the war. Aware that North Africa was the easiest approach to the East, the Nazi High Command tried to seize and to hold it; they lost one third of all their Tunis-bound shipping in the last stages of the North African campaign. At the same time Admiral Sir A. B. Cunningham was able to bring up supplies by sea as he cleared the ports along the Mediterranean. The Germans could not do that. Again, in the "water war" of the Pacific the Japanese were inferior to the United States in tonnage afloat and in capacity to replace their losses. In terms of distance Japan had a supply problem comparable to that of the Allies in the European theatre; but the total shipping tonnage at her disposal in 1941 was only about one seventh that of the Allies. The road to Berlin and to Tokyo was strewn with Axis miscalculations.

The Nazi campaign in Russia was planned according to a timetable that was swiftly upset. Indeed, the British intervention in Greece had thrown Hitler's plans off balance even before he turned upon Russia. When Marshal Stalin's armies were not annihilated the Nazis had to grapple with two foes of constant vigor: distance and cold. Late in 1941 German forces were still held back from Leningrad and Moscow. In the next three years, as Churchill later declared, the Russian armies were to "do the main work of tearing the guts out of the German Army."

On December 7, 1941, Japan bombed the United States naval base at Pearl Harbor in Hawaii. Britain had pledged that if the United States ever declared war on Japan the British Empire would follow "within the hour." Without waiting for American action the Churchill government added Japan to its list of enemies. In a truly global war, the United States and Britain became formal allies. It had long been obvious that Japan, like her European partners in aggression, had broad ambitions for a dominant position in the Far East. Hitherto thwarted by Britain and the United States, Japanese expansionists believed that the hour for the creation of a new empire had at last arrived.

Japan seized Hong Kong, Malaya, and Burma. The great British naval base at Singapore fell. Small British forces suffered severe reverses. Off Malaya the battleship *Prince of Wales* and the cruiser *Renown* were sunk. The Philippines, the Dutch East Indies, and hundreds of Pacific islands were occupied by the Japanese. They swarmed into New Guinea and threatened to attack Australia. By grasping the Burma Road they blocked the sending of supplies to China; they threatened India; they grabbed a huge supply of rubber, oil, and all the vast resources of Borneo, Java, Malaya, and Sumatra.

In the naval battles of Midway, the Coral Sea, and the Solomon Islands the Japanese suffered hard damage from the United States Navy. The British sent reinforcements to India. On May 5, 1942, they overcame brief Vichyite resistance and seized the French island of Madagascar to protect the route to the East around the Cape of Good Hope. American, Australian, and New Zealand troops went into action against the Japanese on the islands of Guadalcanal and New Guinea. Slowly the Allies began a relentless drive northwards.

Meanwhile, the British Commonwealth and the United States developed careful long-range plans to coordinate their war efforts. With Russia and China they formed the spearhead of the Allies, large and small. At different times major conferences were held at Cairo, Casablanca, Potsdam, Quebec, Teheran, Washington, and Yalta. The armed forces of the United States, the British Commonwealth and Empire, China, and Russia carried out the massive undertakings agreed upon by Roosevelt, Churchill, Chiang Kai-shek, and Stalin in consultation with their chiefs of staff and other experts. In each major theatre of war one man was placed in command of the land, sea, and air forces of all nations. For example, the Southwest Pacific Area was commanded by General MacArthur; the Pacific Ocean Areas by Admiral Nimitz; the Southeast Asia Command by Admiral Lord Louis Mountbatten; the Middle Eastern Area by General Sir Harold Alexander; the later European Theatre of Operations by General Dwight Eisenhower. On January 1, 1942, twenty-six countries, henceforth called the United Nations, signed the "Declaration of Washington" which created a huge military alliance pledged to wage unrelenting war against the common enemy.

Slowly the months of grim jeopardy passed. On October 23, 1942, the British in North Africa leaped upon the Germans from behind the sixty-mile defense line stretching from El Alamein on the Mediterranean coast to the Quattara Depression. This mighty attack, carefully planned by General Sir Bernard Montgomery, was preceded by a heavy artillery barrage. On the northern end of the front there was one gun every twenty-three yards for six miles. After the battle of El Alamein and the tank battle of El Aqaqqir of November 2 the Afrika Korps began its long 1,750-mile retreat chased by the triumphant Montgomery's British Eighth Army. The coastal road was crammed with fleeing German vehicles and blasted by the Royal Air Force. Montgomery captured 75,000 prisoners, 500 tanks, 1,000 guns, and the ports along the Mediterranean up to Tunisia.

On November 7, in a great amphibious expedition, the Americans and British landed a large force in North Africa at Algiers, Oran, and Casablanca. General Rommel and the Nazis were caught between these Anglo-American troops and the advancing forces of Montgomery. Tunis and Bizerte were captured in May, 1943. Over 250,000 Germans and Italians were made prisoner, including seventeen Axis generals; among them was General von Arnim, the German Commander-in-Chief. From the battle of El Alamein to the final defeat at Cape Bon the Axis had lost 427,000 men in Africa, including twenty-six generals. They also lost 1,000 tanks, 3,779 airplanes, and 70,000 trucks. The "soft underbelly" of Europe was now exposed to Allied attack.

On July 10, 1943, Allied ships carried 140,000 men to Sicily; that Italian island fell in thirty-eight days. On July 25 Mussolini resigned and the Fascist regime ended. It had lasted for twenty-one years. On September 3 the Italian mainland was invaded. Then Italy surrendered unconditionally; it was the penalty of guilt, defeat, and folly. The Germans in that unhappy land continued to offer powerful resistance. On October 1 Naples was captured; but the Allied advance was bitterly contested past the Gustav line and Cassino, past Rome and the Anzio beachhead, all the way to the Apennines; there the Germans defended the strong Gothic line for many months. Not until April, 1945, were the Allied forces able to move into the Po valley.

Meanwhile, in January, 1943, the Russians won the battle of Stalingrad. They had repelled a terrific onslaught and captured 300,-000 Germans. They had already killed or permanently put out of action far more men than Germany had lost during the whole of the First World War. Along the whole vast front from the arctic to the Crimea the Russians moved into a continuous offensive. Never again was Hitler able to seize the initiative. Over two hundred Axis divisions

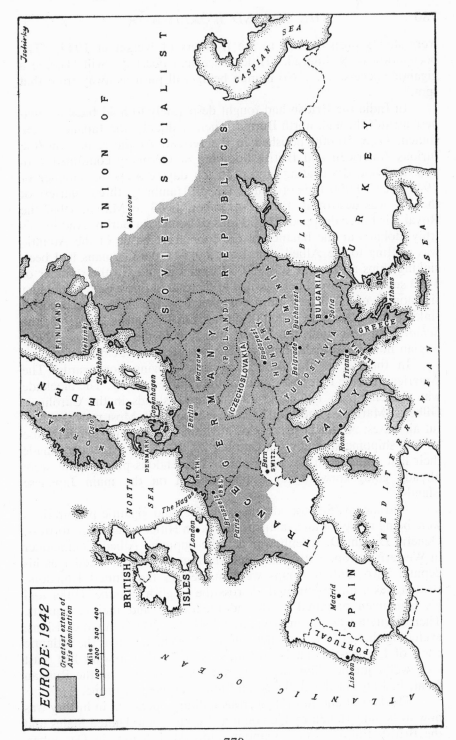

EUROPE: 1942

Greatest extent of
Axis domination

Miles
0   100 200 300 400

were slowly pushed back to the frontiers of Russia in 1944. "The occupation of Stalingrad," Hitler once had boasted, "will become a gigantic success. . . . No human being will push us away from that spot."

In India the British had fought desperately to hold back a Japanese assault through north Burma. Then, suddenly, the Japanese were routed. Over 50,000 perished in the retreat. At the same time the furious American and British bombing of Germany continued with unabated and devastating power. In ten days during the summer of 1943 over 10,000 tons of bombs fell on Hamburg; three quarters of the city was destroyed. From November, 1943 to March, 1944 the Royal Air Force dropped 33,000 tons of bombs on Berlin. And in this truly global war the balance of the submarine battle in the Atlantic was shifting to the Allied side. Late in 1941 the Germans had been sinking ships at the rate of 485,000 tons a month. In the summer of 1943 submarines were being killed at the rate of one a day. In the first six months of 1943 new ships completed by the Allies exceeded all sinkings by more than 3,000,000 tons. On December 26, 1943, the *Scharnhorst* was sunk; the *Tirpitz* was sent to the bottom of a Norwegian fiord by British bombers. The sea peril was being broken.

In the Pacific the Americans were moving northwards. The American Pacific Fleet was mauling the Japanese badly. The blockade was tightening. In 1943 and 1944 several islands in the Carolines, Gilberts, Marianas, and Marshalls were recovered. Most provided useful air bases. A steady process of attrition was wasting the Japanese air and shipping strength. On October 20, 1944, the Americans made their first landings in the Philippines. Tremendous preparations were already going forward for a final assault on the main Japanese islands.

And meanwhile, too, detailed, precise, and gigantic preparations were being made for an avalanche attack on Hitler's European fortress. General Dwight D. Eisenhower became Supreme Allied Commander in Western Europe with Air Chief Marshal Sir Arthur Tedder as his deputy. Two million troops were massed in the United Kingdom. Britain was a mighty arsenal. Across the English Channel Hitler and his henchmen prepared to defend themselves and their conquests. Their strength was still massive; they had over 300 German divisions, excluding those of the satellite states. Hitler claimed that the Atlantic coast of Europe was an impregnable wall. Behind it waited at least sixty well-equipped divisions. The rest were scattered on the Russian front, in Italy, in the Balkans, and about enslaved Europe.

The largest and most dangerous military operation in history was now to be undertaken by the combined arms of the United States and the British Empire and Commonwealth. At Teheran, in December, 1943, Marshal Stalin of Russia had been promised that an Anglo-

American invasion of France would be mounted at the end of May or the beginning of June, 1944. The promise was kept.

THE END OF THE SECOND WORLD WAR

On D-Day, June 6, 1944, over two thousand tons of shells hurtled from Allied battleships and cruisers towards German installations on the Normandy coast. A thousand tactical air force bombers opened their bomb bays and dropped their loads. British and American troops had been ferried from Britain by a mighty armada of 800 warships and 4,000 landing craft. They landed in force on five beaches along a sixty-mile stretch of the Cotentin peninsula. Eleven thousand Allied aircraft protected the invaders. Airborne troops parachuted down behind the German lines. Beachheads were won and held. Within twenty days 1,000,000 troops had landed, despite the fact that stormy weather twice interrupted the flow of men and supplies. Great breakwaters were built. Artificial ports, fabricated long before in England, were set up within two weeks after D-Day. Miracles of engineering were accomplished.

Shortly after the landing in Normandy the Germans directed against England a 400-mile-an-hour robot, jet-propelled, gyroscopically balanced bomb, with a wingspread of sixteen feet and guided by a magnetic compass. These V-1 (Vengeance Number One) bombs were launched in salvoes from about one hundred camouflaged concrete ramps along the French coast above Calais. Over 5,000 people were killed and 16,000 injured, chiefly in London and Kent; 1,104,000 homes were wrecked or damaged. Barrage balloons, aircraft and anti-aircraft guns firing proximity fuse shells accounted for large numbers of the robots. Later the Germans sent over their V-2 bombs. These were twelve-ton monsters, reaching a speed of fifty miles a minute. Forty-six feet long, they carried an explosive charge of one ton. Because of their speed they could not be intercepted.

In the savage battle of Normandy the Germans stubbornly held the British and Canadians around Caen, the coastal hinge of the gateway to Paris. After capturing the ruined port of Cherbourg the Americans swept down the west side of the peninsula. The British Second Army and the Canadians finally took Caen on July 18 and the armored divisions of the American Third Army broke through the German left flank at Avranches, ripped into Britanny, swung northeast on the Seine, and outflanked Paris from the south. The Allies freed Paris on August 25. Most of western France was liberated. The battle of Normandy had been a bloody affair.

Meanwhile the Franco-American Seventh Army had landed on the Riviera on August 15. It moved up towards the Rhine in southern France against the weakened German Nineteenth Army. Despite resistance at Toulon and Marseilles the Americans, aided by French Maquis, swept through the Rhone Valley, and swung round the Swiss border towards the Belfort Gap between the Vosges and Jura mountains. By September it was pressing towards Alsace and the Rhine at the southern end of the Allied line. Immediately to the north the American Third Army was advancing towards Metz and Nancy. Beyond lay Saarbruecken and Strasbourg.

Meanwhile, too, the British Second Army and the Canadians advanced up the Channel coast into Belgium. On August 31 the Canadians liberated Rouen and the British freed Amiens. On September 1 the Canadians took Dieppe, and the British, Arras. On September 3 the British moved into Brussels and on September 4 into Antwerp. There still remained the German guns dominating the Scheldt estuary to be wiped out before the port could be used by Allied shipping; that was a formidable task. On their right, now the center of the advancing Allied line, the American First Army stormed Sedan on August 3, and captured it on September 7. By the end of August the Germans had lost 400,000 men, of whom half were prisoners. Allied armies were pressing against the Rhine and the Ruhr. The Russians were storming against East Prussia, against the whole German eastern front from the Baltic to the Balkans. In September, however, the lightning advance of the Allies was halted; they had to wait for supplies.

The first stages of the battle of Germany were slow. On September 11 American First Army units leaped off into Germany from Luxembourg; four days later they were surrounding Aachen where the fighting was prolonged and bloody. On September 17 large Allied parachute and glider forces landed in the Netherlands about Arnheim to turn the German right flank and the Siegfried Line. The Germans swiftly contained these troops; after nine bloody days only about 2,800 of the original 8,000 escaped to join the British Second Army. Allied progress on all fronts slowed down. An unexpected German assault in the Ardennes sector launched by General von Runstedt resulted in the "Battle of the Bulge." For a time the Germans threatened to break through to Liege and to Antwerp. Allied forces were rushed to stem the armored Nazi tide. At last, with tremendous effort, American and British pressure levelled out the bulge. It was the last major effort of the defiant Nazis.

As the Germans were thrust back on the west and east the British landed forces in Greece. When the Germans withdrew they completed the destruction that had already proceeded so far. Throughout the latter stages of the war the Greek people had been aided by the Swedish-Swiss Relief Commission. Millions of dollars had been given to the cause of Greek relief, particularly in the United States and Canada. A fleet of Swedish ships, protected by safe conduct agreements, had sailed regularly between St. John, New Brunswick and the Piraeus carrying wheat, fish, medical supplies and clothing. Without this aid, millions of Greeks would have perished. When Greece was free again the incidence of disease and malnutrition was fully revealed.

After the British restored the exiled Greek government civil war broke out. Political animosities, long pent up, flamed across the nation. The radical Greek forces of ELAS and EAM attempted to oust the government by force. Largely as a result of British efforts, a truce was achieved. The civil war was ended, at least for a time, by the creation of a regency under Archbishop Damaskinos and a comprehensive cabinet embracing all political parties. Greece then turned to the sad task of reconstruction.

In February the British and Canadians were clearing the west bank of the Rhine. On March 6 a part of the American First Army reached Cologne. On March 7 other units of the First Army crossed the Ludendorff railway bridge at Remagen before the Germans were able to blow it up. The Americans rolled over the Rhine. In five days the bridgehead was nine miles long and four miles deep. On March 23 British Second Army and American Ninth Army troops crossed the Rhine at Rees and Wesel. British troops could now operate on the north German plain. While the Canadians cleared the Nazis out of the remainder of Holland the British rushed ahead. By early April American and British forces were rolling through the rich Ruhr industrial areas. The Russians were swirling into Germany from the east. On April 25, near Torgau, patrols of the Ukrainian First and American First Armies met. Germany was split in two.

On May 1 Nazi Admiral Doenitz announced that Hitler had died in Berlin in the holocaust of terror that had swept through the heart of the Nazi Reich. In Italy, Mussolini and his mistress were shot by Italians and hanged by the heels in Milan. On May 2 the British Second Army took Lubeck and encircled Hamburg. They met a Russian armored squadron moving up from Rostock. Devastated Berlin surrendered to the Russians. The Germans in Italy gave up the struggle and a million German soldiers surrendered unconditionally to Field Marshal Montgomery on the British and Canadian fronts. There were further collapses on May 4 and 5. On May 7 the Germans made a complete and unconditional surrender at Rheims. The war in Europe had ended.

The Allies turned with single-minded purpose to the defeat of Japan. In February, 1945, the Fourteenth British Army captured Mandalay, encircled large Japanese forces, swept down towards Rangoon and the many mouths of the Irrawaddy. Before the monsoon came in May Rangoon fell and the Japanese fled. Burma was free again.

Meanwhile the island of Iwo Jima, 770 miles from Japan, had fallen to American arms. After desperate fighting Okinawa was taken in May, 1945. Britain had two powerful battle fleets in the Far East. With Germany out of the way, the United Kingdom and the British

Dominions turned to range their combined forces by the side of the United States. Vast preparations were being made for the final push against Japan.

Then, suddenly, on August 6, 1945, the industrial city of Hiroshima was struck by a new and fearful atomic bomb. This weapon unleashed a tremendous destructive power with the release of atomic energy. It had been developed by the cooperation of American, British, and Canadian scientists after long labors in closely guarded plants. The secret of the method by which the fissionable material was used in the construction of the atomic bomb was held by the United States. The atom had been split. Mighty power, for good or ill, was released to mankind. Again man had conquered nature, unless it should turn out that nature had conquered man.

Russia declared war upon Japan and at once attacked Manchuria. A second atomic bomb was dropped on the port city of Nagasaki. Japan needed no more evidence that the prolongation of the war meant her utter destruction. The wages of Pearl Harbor had been paid. Japanese leaders sued for peace. On board the battleship *Missouri* in Tokyo Bay Japan surrendered unconditionally. The date was September 1, 1945. "The mills of the gods grind slowly, but they grind exceeding small."

Chapter 39

TODAY AND TOMORROW

REVOLUTION BY BALLOT

D URING the Second World War the Conservative and Labour parties had cooperated in the coalition government. When the conflict in Europe ended, that coalition, once so harmonious and effective, began to fall apart. In July, 1945, the British people went to the polls and the Conservatives, led by Winston Churchill, suffered a heavy defeat. They obtained about 10,000,000 votes and 216 seats in the house of commons. With slightly more than 2,000,000 votes the Liberals carried 11 constituencies. The Communists obtained about 100,000 votes and 2 seats. The Independent and other groups gathered 677,000 votes and won 17 seats. All remaining support went to the Labour party. Nearly 12,000,000 ballots were cast to return 393 Labour members to the house of commons.

A strong Labour cabinet was created under the leadership of the sixty-two-year-old Clement Attlee, an Oxford graduate who had lectured for nine years at the London School of Economics and had held several political posts. Included in the cabinet was Herbert Stanley Morrison, Lord President of the Council and Deputy Prime Minister. Morrison was a policeman's son who had become an authority on local government and had been a member of the second MacDonald Ministry and Home Secretary during the Second World War. The Foreign Secretary was the vigorous Ernest Bevin, a farmer's son who became a famous labor organizer and head of the central council of the trade unions. The Chancellor of the Exchequer was Hugh Dalton, one of England's most brilliant economists. Dalton was later succeeded by Sir Stafford Cripps, who left the presidency of the Board of Trade to become both Chancellor of the Exchequer and Minister of Economic Affairs.

With a clear mandate from the people the Labour cabinet embarked upon an experiment to change the battle-scarred British Isles

785

into a "Socialist Commonwealth." A steady stream of remarkable legislation began to transform the face of Britain.

HOUSING AND EDUCATION

In 1901 Britain spent £36,000,000 on social services; in 1921, £206,000,000; in 1937, £455,000,000. These services included old age pensions, health insurance, housing, unemployment insurance, and various other aids. Between two World Wars one-third of the population of England had been rehoused. Ninety per cent of the workers were protected by insurance against sickness and unemployment. Nine years had been added to life expectancy as a result of improved national health. During the Second World War the pace of this social reform legislation increased.

In February, 1942, the Ministry of Town and Country Planning was established. The Town and Country Planning Act of 1942 enabled the new ministry to undertake a long-term housing program. It was hoped that more than 3,000,000 houses could be built by 1955. The planning authorities set up under the act were put in a position to purchase all land in reconstruction areas so that overall building schemes could be carried through.

Despite the steps taken during the war the new Labour government faced a complex and difficult problem in 1945. More than 25,000 dwellings had been completely destroyed; 300,000 had been made uninhabitable; 4,000,000 had been damaged. Manpower and materials were in acute short supply. At the end of 1946 nearly 300,000 families had been rehoused; 48,000 permanent and 80,000 temporary houses had been built.

In January, 1947, a new Town and Country Planning Act forbade landowners to build upon their land "unless the building is in accord with the proper planning requirements." The act, said a cabinet minister, "for the first time makes practical such projects as reconstruction and development of old towns, preservation of green belts, provision of open spaces in overcrowded areas, and allocation of space for factories." Meanwhile the government took steps to improve conditions in the "distressed areas," long plagued by decaying industry and mining, by slums, disease, unemployment, and other results of what Hugh Dalton called "political neglect and private unenterprise."

A further major advance was in education. The Education Act of 1944, superseding all previous acts, went into operation on April 1, 1945. It provided for comprehensive reforms in the British public system of education and for the inspection of all the voluntary schools outside the system. Under the provisions of the act the central authority for education for England and Wales was to be the Ministry of Education. The 145 Local Education Authorities were made responsible for seeing that there was a full range of educational provisions in their areas through the three stages of primary, secondary, and further education. After April, 1947, all children were required to attend school until they were fifteen years old. "County Colleges" were to be established for young people who had left school before reaching the age of eighteen. Facilities for technical and vocational training and adult education were extended.

Between 1945 and 1964 about 3,500 new schools were constructed and thousands of additional teachers were trained. In 1919 there were thirteen state-aided nurseries; by 1964 there were nearly 3,000. At the other end of the education process thousands of university students were aided out of public funds. An extensive re-shaping of educational aims and methods is still under way. In 1963, for instance, an eleven-man committee headed by Lord Robbins recommended a great expansion of Britain's system of higher education to give more students access to a university education and thus "help the nation meet the competitive pressures of the modern world."

EMPLOYMENT POLICY

In June, 1941, the British government asked Sir William Beveridge to recommend changes in the existing programs for social insurance and allied services. Sir William was the director of the London School of Economics from 1919 to 1937, when he went to University College, Oxford. His comprehensive and imaginative report, presented in November, 1942, outlined a social security plan for "all citizens without upper income limit, all-embracing in scope of persons and needs" based on the assumption that the government would take other measures to prevent mass unemployment, establish comprehensive health services, and provide children's allowances. Sir William proposed that the government, employers, and employees should pool annually millions of pounds for pensions, unemployment and health insurance, death benefits, and birth and marriage bounties.

Almost all workers in the United Kingdom were to be covered by the Beveridge plan of insurance. They would make weekly contributions which would entitle them to full benefits under the plan. Old age benefits would be doubled. Unemployment and disability rates would be equalized except for industrial ailments in hazardous occupations. Comprehensive medical care would be provided for all members of workers' families. Thus Sir William Beveridge proposed the elimination of the tangle of services resulting from the earlier legislation providing for workmen's compensation, health insurance, unemployment insurance, and old age pensions. Everything would be administered by the government in a single, coordinated program.

In May, 1944, the government issued a White Paper on Employment Policy. The White Paper proposed a plan to maintain a high and stable level of employment in normal times by controlling the volume of the national expenditure, both public and private. Private investment was to be partially controlled by the regulation of rates on interest. The government would "encourage" private enterprise to plan its capital expenditures in accordance with a general stabilization policy. The government would also vary its own investment expenditures to compensate and counteract unevenness in private investment. A threatened depression would be met by expanding instead of contracting capital expenditures. Thus the public purchasing power would be raised. Such were some of the steps designed to keep the volume of capital investment on an even keel and, in the words of Ernest Bevin, to "insulate it against slump."

In November, 1944, Sir William Beveridge followed the government's White Paper on Employment Policy by publishing his *Full Employment in a Free Society*. Here Sir William insisted that one condition was essential to full employment in peacetime: "There must be a common objective with finance subordinated to that objective." The "common objective" was the social conscience of the nation deliberately directed to the abolition of want, squalor, ignorance, ugliness, and disease.

In addition to the "common objective" of the collective will of the nation there was a second condition necessary for the achievement of full peacetime employment. This was a "centrally planned economy" in the sense of the expansionist economics of Lord Keynes. The Beveridge scheme required at all times an adequate total outlay, public and private, on goods for immediate consumption or for investment. Such an outlay, said Beveridge, could be maintained only by a long-term government program for spending on capital equipment and social reforms and for balancing British accounts abroad. The chief instrument of Sir William's centrally planned economy was to be a new type of budget in which the total national outlay would be equated with the estimated money value of the estimated production of the nation under conditions of full employment. This outlay, said Beveridge, should be estimated by a National Investment Board in terms of private investment and consumption, the balance of payments, and the loan and revenue accounts of local and central governments. The direction of public outlay would be determined by the demands and driving force of the social conscience.

Acceptance of the thesis of Sir William Beveridge depended on deciding that it should be a function of the state to protect its people against large-scale unemployment. It involved the rejection of the orthodox dogma that employment could not be created by state borrowing and state expenditure. Sir William declared that the government's program did not provide remedies at all adequate for the cure, largely because of financial considerations as seen by orthodox economists. The new Beveridge proposals were as important as his original social insurance scheme. All of the principles underlying the Beveridge program rapidly became a fundamental issue in British politics, in some respects more important than private enterprise versus socialism, controls versus liberties, or even social insurance.

SOCIAL SECURITY

At the same time as the government issued its White Paper on Employment Policy it rounded out its comprehensive social and economic program by a second White Paper outlining government proposals for family allowance, national assistance, social insurance, and workmen's compensation. This document embodied much of the Beveridge plan. Under the new government system it was hoped that "provision will have been made against every one of the main attacks which economic ill fortune can launch against individual well-being and peace of mind."

Built on existing programs which had grown steadily in scope and thoroughness since the nineteenth century, the new government scheme extended, in a unified plan, the benefits and coverage of social insurance. By its provisions insurance payments were to comprise unemployment, sickness, maternity, invalidity benefits, survivor bene-fits, retirement pensions, and death grants. Outside the insurance system but an integral part of the plan were family allowances to help meet the economic burden of rearing children, similar to the system already operating in Canada. There were also to be training allowances for young people of working age. Added to these were provisions for retirement on a national scale and for compensation in cases of disability or loss of life resulting from industrial injury or occupational disease. None of these proposals was presented as an employer's liability but as a social service. Although both employers and workers were to contribute, the benefits, paid weekly at fixed rates, were not to depend upon the length of time contributions had been paid.

By similar National Health Service proposals everyone in the population, regardless of income, insurance status, or occupational class was to have access, without charge, to any needed maintenance or care in a hospital, to medical services, to special or "national" assistance, as in the case of the blind. It was planned that this Health Service would be a combination of socialized medicine and private medical practice.

The novelty of all these British plans was apparent. The scheme was to be extended to the entire community. The whole population was to be insured. The scale of payments was to be unusually high. There were several other entirely new features, such as retirement pensions. The various benefits were to be included under a single system financed out of a single fund and administered by a single authority.

Several acts of Parliament soon extended and reorganized the whole system of social welfare. For example, the National Insurance Act of 1946 provided almost everyone in Great Britain with a large measure of personal protection from childhood to old age. Major clauses of the act included provisions for sickness and unemployment insurance, widow's benefits, maternity benefits, guardian's allowances, death grants, and retirement pensions. A Family Allowance Act provided five shillings for all children after the first under fifteen years of age. An Industrial Injuries Act extended workmen's compensation so that all persons employed under contract are protected.

Early in 1946 Parliament passed the National Health Services Act, which went into effect in July, 1948. This act was based upon the government proposals described earlier and was designed to provide "a universal health service without any insurance qualifications of any sort." There was no limitation placed upon the kind of medical assistance to be given. All medical aid was to be free. Patients were permitted to choose their own physicians and surgeons. The country's 80,000 doctors were left free to decide whether or not they desired to practice under the act. Each doctor who entered the plan was to be paid a basic salary, or retaining fee, of £300 annually. In addition, all participating physicians and surgeons were to receive "capitation fees" according to the total number of patients voluntarily registering for treatment with them. Since 1948 several minor alterations have been made in the British health services. The main principles and procedures remain unchanged.

It is impossible to describe in detail the large body of legislation designed to carry out the main proposals of the earlier White Papers and the general policies of the Attlee government. The acts of Parliament now in operation are important milestones in the history of social security. The three basic principles of the Beveridge plan, the nation's responsibility in the matter of health, of employment, and of children's allowances, have been fully accepted. Lord Keynes' motto: "What we can do we can afford" has had its truth stressed to such a degree that few in Britain question the principle of social security.

THE NATIONALIZATION PROGRAM

In the election platform of 1945 the Labour party pledged itself to the nationalization of the "commanding heights of industry" so that the principal citadels of economic power would be under public ownership. The Labour party also declared its intention to subject the entire British economy to careful direction by public authorities.

In the new "mixed economy" it was intended that several sectors of private enterprise would be left untouched by the Labourites. The case for the socialization of each industry "must stand or fall," asserted Herbert Morrison, "on its own merits." What was deemed most appropriate or efficient for each industry would be done, whatever might happen to the profits of private capital investment.

In carrying out the first stages of its nationalization plans the Attlee government moved swiftly. A series of major alterations in the British economic structure began when the Bank of England passed under public control. The former shareholders received government stock at the same yield as their former holdings. The governor of the Bank of England was reappointed as an official of the British government and sixteen directors were selected from industry and finance to assist in administering the bank's affairs.

There was also the problem of the coal mines. For several years the Labour party had been insisting that the coal mines must be transferred to public ownership for the sake of efficiency, fundamental reconstruction, and the miners' morale. As a result of the nationalization of the whole coal industry in January, 1947, the National Coal Board, a public corporation responsible to the Minister of Fuel and Power and representing industry, science, labor, and finance, took control of coal production in Britain. The Board was to own, work, develop, and supply the nation's coal. It controlled more than 1,000 collieries, 1,000,000 acres of land with farms, hospitals, power stations, and villages. Its employees numbered about 800,000; its annual business turnover was more than £400,000,000. The main task of the National Coal Board was to increase the output of coal. If Britain did not produce more coal, her industrial recovery would be retarded, thus placing in peril the whole structure of her economy.

In January, 1947, the Transport Act nationalized the railways, the London Passenger Transport Board (the whole public transport system of London), 18 canals, 100 steamships, 20,000 motor trucks, 50,000 houses connected with the transport industry, and a number of other transport and haulage facilities. Under the act the four great British railway systems became the "British Railways." About 1,000,000 private shareholders, holding stock worth over £1,000,-000,000, received for each share of private company stock a British Transport 3 per cent guaranteed stock, 1978 to 1988, issued at par and redeemable at par, pound for pound to the value set by the Transport Act for the old securities. The magnitude of the whole transaction can be suggested by citing the fact that the British railways have about 635,000 employees, 52,000 miles of track, 1,252,000 freight cars, 45,000 passenger coaches, and 20,000 locomotives.

In addition to the Bank of England, the coal mines, and the railways, the British Labour government also nationalized civil aviation. Three public corporations under the control of the Air Ministry were given authority to manage civil air services and air fields. All telephone communications, including the world-wide facilities of British cable and wireless companies, passed under public ownership in 1947. The Labour party also renewed the monopoly charter under which the government-subsidized British Broadcasting Company operates. Although the electricity industry had long been largely controlled by the Central Electricity Board, complete nationalization was effected in 1947. In addition to the great fuel industries of coal and electricity more than 1,000 gas companies, including nearly 300 operated by municipal governments, were marked for public ownership. After payment of about £200,000,000 in compensation to private owners the government's Central Gas Council took full control on May 1, 1949.

In May, 1946, the house of commons approved a vague motion of the Minister of Supply to transfer "appropriate sections" of the iron and steel industry to public ownership. Considerable discussion at once arose in Labour ranks about the total nationalization of the iron and steel empire, or even a part of it, such as the rolling mills and the sectors producing pig iron and steel ingots. In October, 1948, the government introduced its controversial nationalization bill under which it proposed to take over 107 iron and steel plants, employing 300,000 persons, at a cost of £300,000,000.

Clement Attlee and his colleagues were aware that their projected iron and steel nationalization bill might weather the debates and votes of the house of commons only to be vetoed by the house of lords. Under the terms of the Parliament Act of 1911 the lords had a suspensive veto of two years on all measures not certified as money bills. Hence the lords could obstruct the passage of any Labour iron and steel nationalization bill until the next general election in 1950.

To end that danger the government introduced a new Parliament bill designed to reform the house of lords. This bill proposed to reduce the upper house to 300 members; to trim its veto power to one year; to change the ancient system of hereditary succession to allow greater representation through the election of men and women who had made outstanding contributions to the nation.

The radical changes in the powers and constitution of the upper house proposed by the Labour bill were acceptable neither to the lords nor to the Conservatives and Liberals in the commons. The opponents of Labour revived the arguments, old and powerful, against tampering with the upper house. They repeated the warning that the lords had stood for centuries as an obstacle to the accumulation of power in the hands of a single authority, including the house of commons. They called attention to a second important fact: many lords were leaders in various professions and their opinions were those of highly gifted and expert men, possessing unusual stores of wisdom and experience, and representing a wide section of the British community. Against this background an all-party conference collapsed in April, 1948. The prospect of open war between the government and the house of lords emerged to cast another shadow upon an already darkening and confused political scene.

Meanwhile the Labour government took major steps to increase the agriculture output. A crop and livestock program announced in August, 1947, was designed to advance the net production of British agriculture by 20 per cent (£100,000,000) within five years. Under the details of the program farmers, workers, and large landowners were to be provided with all possible government aid, including additional workers, new machinery, buildings, the advisory services and "supervision" of the Agricultural Research Council and its agents, loans, and subsidies. Minimum farm prices for meat and dairy products were established by the Ministry of Agriculture four years in advance of production. Prices of cereals, sugar beets, and potatoes were set up eighteen months in advance.

To increase agricultural efficiency and production the government obtained wide authority over land use and development. For the future, the words of a cabinet member gave promise and warning: "The Labour party believes ultimately in land nationalization and is pledged to work towards it."

It was not surprising that the Conservative party denounced most of the measures of the Labour government. Some Conservatives asserted that the deep foundations of British liberty were endangered by Labour policies. Winston Churchill accused the Labourites of "tyranny, deceit, and incompetence," and stated his belief that the "liberties and free life of Britain" were " in great danger." This apprehension was increased as the Labour government examined the possibility of nationalizing certain other sectors of the economy, such as water, the vast chemical industries, and the oil companies.

As the members of the government prepared to defend themselves in the election of 1950 they were faced by the unpleasant fact that their nationalization program had been heavily buffeted by an economic crisis. For instance, steel could not be spared to improve the railways. The government had hoped to show the millions of travelers, most of whom were voters, how superior the nationalized "British Railways" were to those earlier operated by private companies, and this they could not do. The British government had become the employer of railway workers and coal miners. But there was no decline in the rate of absenteeism. Strikes did not stop.

The workers who had voted to put the Labour party in power were not wholly cooperative when they felt their interests assailed.

In the disturbing economic crisis certain controls had to be imposed upon the workers of Britain. One of the critical hurdles in Britain's production line was the shortage of manpower. The "manpower budget" of the government, designed to place every worker where he was needed to serve Britain best, doubtless alienated many voters. Harmony between the Labour party and the Trades Union Congress, which had 8,500,000 members, was frequently strained.

FINANCE AND EXPORT TRADE

Heavy economic burdens were imposed by the war upon Britain's economy. To defeat Hitler the British turned away from their normal export trade. They tripled their public debt. They suffered heavy losses of capital, totalling £7,300,000,000, and including the destruction of 18,000,000 gross tons of shipping, damage to some 4,000,000 houses, deterioration of industrial and commercial property, and the like. About 25 per cent of Britain's prewar capital was consumed by war losses. To pay for the purchase of war supplies, foreign investments totalling about $4,500,000,000 were liquidated. By sacrificing so many of her financial assets abroad Britain lost almost all of her invisible imports.

Meanwhile, Britain's need for imports was far greater than in prewar years. Millions of houses had to be built and the task of financing the new social security program demanded funds in unprecedented volume. The strain placed upon the British economy by military commitments did not end with the cessation of hostilities. In 1946–1947 the cost of Britain's defense forces was £1,737,000,-000. Moreover, Britain gave large-scale relief to European countries. To Germany alone Britain sent £140,000,000 worth of civilian supplies; her occupation costs for the British zone of Germany in 1947 were £79,000,000. To numerous countries Britain lent sums totalling nearly £300,000,000.

To the dark facts of wartime losses, accumulation of debt, defense, and European relief charges was added the problem of crippled and unbalanced trade. Britain is more dependent upon world prosperity and peaceful trade than any other nation. Many raw materials for manufacture and much food must be brought in from abroad. Every ton of goods imported must be paid for by exports or by income from foreign investments or services. In the years after World War II the problem of paying for these imports became acute and urgent.

Despite enormous difficulties, the production and export drive went on. Thousands of men were removed from less essential and personal services and channelled into essential industries. Foreign exchange had to be earned not only to pay for needed imports, the cost of which had increased with world price rises, but also to meet high expenditures overseas, including Britain's heavy responsibilities in Europe. The British government set high export targets for British trade, particularly in manufactured goods. The results were encouraging. Largest increases were in metals, metal products, especially machinery and vehicles, and textiles. For the home markets there were only trickles of many commodity supplies.

In June, 1946, the United States loaned $3,750,000 to Britain. It was hoped that this loan would offset Britain's unfavorable balance of interest and trade until 1950 when Britain's economy would perhaps be stabilized. For several reasons this hope was not fulfilled. The world was short of dollars. British expenses soared as she paid the high world commodity prices. The result was an unexpected drain on the new credits. By the middle of 1947 the adverse and menacing gap in Britain's export-import income and outlay was still running at a rate of about £675,000,000 annually. In August, 1947, Mr. Attlee announced that Great Britain would have to make drastic reductions in her purchases of goods requiring payment in dollars or other "hard currencies."

In October, 1947, Sir Stafford Cripps, newly appointed Minister of Economic Affairs, announced a series of emergency programs designed to increase exports into hard-currency areas, to advance production still further, and to reduce imports for the conservation of dollar holdings. Despite difficulties with the trade unions and its own followers the government continued its wage, price, and profit-pegging policy. A White Paper in February, 1948, declared that there should be no further wage increases without a corresponding increase in production. It was obvious that no such wage-control policy was workable without the support of the Trades Union Congress. Although the support was reluctantly given, most workers recognized that only by an acceptance of a radical reorganization of industry, a lowered standard of living, and a period of grim austerity could Britain successfully make port through the storm.

The determination of the Labour government to battle with every resource was clearly shown when Sir Stafford Cripps submitted the annual budget on April 6, 1948. Cripps planned for a large and deflationary surplus. To decrease inflationary pressure the budget employed several devices, among them a non-recurring levy on investment income, an increase in taxes on alcohol and tobacco, a 20 per cent tax on "sports pools," Britain's most popular form of gambling. The income tax allowances were made more generous, thus freeing about 500,000 low-paid workers entirely from income tax payments. The purchase tax was reduced on several items. There was to be an increased expenditure of £143,000,000 for the new health services, £30,000,000 for education, £14,000,000 for housing. The demands for national defense were to cost £693,000,000.

In May, 1948, as the giant European Recovery Plan of the

United States began to make millions of dollars available for Europe, Britain's Ernest Bevin believed that he could see "the light at the end of the tunnel" and the approaching end of a difficult passage to economic survival.

THE FALL OF THE LABOUR PARTY

The hopes of the optimists were not realized. In September, 1949, the pound was devalued by about 30 per cent (from $4.03 to $2.80). The reduction of the overseas deficit combined with a high level of investment at home created a situation that required careful handling if inflation was to be braked, governmental expenditures cut, and unrequited exports to soft-currency countries kept within bounds. Many shrewd men asserted that Britain needed new and improved technical processes, new machinery, greater managerial skill and inventiveness. They also urged the making of more goods for export that would be effectively competitive in world markets. Meanwhile, despite the best efforts of a skilled and wary government, British prices stayed dangerously high. The total balance of overseas payments did not markedly improve. The critical problem of bridging the dollar gap and dealing with long-range terms of trade was reflected not only in the policies of the government but in the lives of the most humble citizens.

In February, 1950, the British nation went to the polls. The Labour party's manifesto "Let Us Win Through Together" carefully listed the new areas of the economy that were to be nationalized. It declared that the Labourites stood for "full employment." It made vague pledges about foreign policy. The Conservative party's manifesto "This Is the Road!" promised direct and indirect tax reduction, more housing, the setting free of the nation from hampering controls. The Labour Party obtained 13,246,957 votes; the Conservatives 12,450,403; the Liberals 2,634,482; and the others 1,338,113. The result of the election was nearly a stalemate. In the virile Parliament of 1945–50 the Labour party had an overall majority of 140. After the election of 1950 the Labour majority was only 7. The Labourites held 315 seats, the Conservatives 296, the Liberals 9, the other groups 3.

There were several reasons for this erosion of Labour popularity. For instance, it seemed to many citizens that the Parliament led by Clement Attlee had been the instrument of an economic revolution too hastily pressed at a time when the nation's economic and financial circumstances were unfavorable to such a change. The unrelenting rhythm of nationalization, hailed by Labour as a sovereign specific for most ills, had shaken the state too much. The drastic economic measures of the government, often ably defended and explained, were widely unpopular. After a long and crippling war it was hard to endure with forbearance the continuing pressures and crises made necessary by economic dislocation and experiment. Now, in 1950, it was widely felt that the internal economy was too rigid. Some urged the further devaluation of the pound. Others said that the income tax should be lowered.

When Sir Stafford Cripps presented his third budget in April, 1950, he made a reduction in the lower rates of the income tax, increased the petrol taxes and the purchase taxes on commercial vehicles, and claimed inflationary pressures were declining. Meanwhile, however, the gold reserves were still falling. Sales at home were sluggish. British economic prospects were not hopeful.

The Labour party, shaken and shrunken, held on with its tiny majority. In April, 1951, Hugh Gaitskell, the new Chancellor of the Exchequer, presented his budget. He estimated that the British government would spend £939,000,000 more than in 1950. The income tax, the distributed profits tax, and several purchase taxes were increased. Health service patients were to be required to pay half the cost of such items as dentures and spectacles. Meanwhile the dollar deficit problem dragged its dull length along. Soon, it seemed, the appalling situation of 1947 and 1948 would be repeated. Britain would be down to the danger gold reserve line of £2,000,000,000. In such circumstances, how could Britain's money be protected? How could she be the broker of the sterling area?

There were dark hours for the Labour party. Sir Stafford Cripps became ill. Ernest Bevin died, the biggest trade union figure of his generation. Herbert Morrison, sometimes at odds with his chief, Clement Attlee, was not successful at the Foreign Office. The rebellious and aggressive Aneurin Bevan objected to the budget of his colleague Hugh Gaitskell and asserted, among other things, that the rising cost of Britain's armament was a threat to the civilian economy. Bevan obviously could not take the position he did and remain in the Cabinet as Minister of Labour. He resigned. The Labour ship, lacking ballast, rode high and unsteadily.

In October, 1951, a general election showed that throughout the country there was a small and remarkably uniform swing to the Conservatives. In the election campaign, the official Labour party manifesto was designed to allay public anxiety. It made no specific mention of new nationalization schemes. It said nothing about Labour's Aneurin Bevan and his militant followers, nothing about rearmament. The impetus of the Labour party, it seemed, had fallen off.

Winston Churchill and the Conservatives campaigned under a policy statement entitled: "Britain Strong and Free." In damaging language the Conservatives condemned the "lamentable eighteen months of Socialist minority rule." Winston Churchill denounced a

Labour government "responsible for growing disunity at home and loss of respect abroad, a government warped by faction and class prejudice and hampered by extraordinary incompetence." England, asserted the Conservatives, needed a period of steady, stable administration. Such a government, they also insisted, could not be provided by the tired and stumbling Labourites. The Conservatives were careful not to promise the voters too much. For instance, they stated that if they were returned to power they would denationalize iron and steel but not railways and coal. The "unscrambling process," they said, would be too hazardous in times of economic strain.

When the votes were tallied in the election of 1951 the Conservatives held 321 seats; the Labourites, 294; the Liberals, 6; the others, 3. Clement Attlee was out and Winston Churchill was in.

A cabinet of sixteen members included Winston Churchill, Prime Minister and Minister of Defence; Anthony Eden, Deputy Prime Minister and Foreign Secretary; Richard Austen Butler, Chancellor of the Exchequer; Oliver Lyttleton, Colonial Secretary; Harry Crookshank, Minister of Health; Lord Salisbury, Lord Privy Seal. These men and their colleagues formed an able team. The tasks laid upon them were hard and heavy.

TURNING A CORNER

In February, 1952, George VI died. He had been "a model to guide constitutional sovereigns throughout the world." This decent and kindly man was sincerely mourned from Canberra and Capetown to the Tyne and the Tees. In June, 1953, the Archbishop of Canterbury presented Elizabeth II, daughter of George VI, to the people as their "undoubted Queen" in the ancient rites of the coronation.

The first budget of the new government was placed before Parliament in March, 1952. It was clear that although the pressures on the pound sterling had been slightly eased there had been little progress towards balancing the overseas accounts. The negative device of import restrictions had not made much impression on the total import bill. Sales abroad were slow and the prices of several main export commodities were falling. Industry at home was not increasing its output. Richard Austen Butler, Chancellor of the Exchequer, estimated that in the first half of 1952 imports would exceed exports by £250,000,000. There had been an unusually large expansion of the floating debt. New monetary weapons were needed to combat inflation. New steps must be taken to rehabilitate British credit. Some of these were provided in Mr. Butler's budget. A series of drastic measures reduced the overload on the economy. The Conservatives could rightly claim credit later for a marked improvement in the national finances. Wages and prices soon were rising far more slowly than in 1951. By 1953, as a result of complex control instruments, sterling became stronger and wages and prices more stable. There was a striking improvement in the earned surplus even with the world outside the sterling area.

Within the Labour party the controversial Aneurin Bevan led a strong movement against his leader Clement Attlee and defied the moderate men who attempted to pour oil on stormy seas. Bevan declared that rearmament would bankrupt Britain and would give no protection in the terrors of a Third World War. He insisted that Britain's money should be spent in a vast extension of nationalization and welfare. In October, 1952, the Bevanites defeated and displaced the moderate Herbert Morrison and Hugh Dalton in the election of members to the National Executive of the Labour party on a carefully limited franchise framed to keep out the trades union vote. Early in 1953 the Trades Union Congress informed the Labour party that it was opposed to any plans for further nationalization in the early future. In 1954 Bevan widened the gulf in the party by resigning from the "shadow Cabinet" and declaring his opposition to German rearmament, the projected South East Asia Treaty Organization, and Britain's support of United States' foreign policy. In March, 1955, Bevan defied the rules of the Labour party and was barred from the party's parliamentary organization.

Meanwhile the Conservative government was united and busy. Under the Steel Act of 1953 the state corporation controlling the iron and steel industry was dissolved and a private agency was entrusted with the disposal of shares to private investors. The Town and Country Planning Act of 1954 extended the provisions of the legislation of 1947, especially in the widening of land-use control and the powers of local authorities or other agencies to buy land for disposal to private developers for approved purposes. The government set up as a target the yearly construction of 3,000,000 houses. At the same time, despite crises in the coal fields, Mr. Butler and his colleagues continued to check inflation. In the spring of 1954 the Exchequer was able to report a monthly increase of £45,000,000 in gold and dollar reserves, a fall of 40,000 in unemployment, a 7 per cent increase in industrial production in real terms, a new high point in the index. Exports in 1954 reached a record level of £2,500,000,000. Metals and engineering products took the export place once held by textiles and coal. Automobile exports exceeded those of all European countries combined. Chemicals to the value of £186,700,000 were sold overseas. A perennial trade deficit had been at last transformed into a surplus.

Early in 1955 Mr. Butler stated that real wages had risen 6 per cent in the three and one half years of Conservative government; industrial earnings were up 9 per cent; production had increased 10 per cent. The Treasury had a surplus of about £34,000,000. The

1955 budget reduced taxes by about £125,000,000. Nevertheless, the old dangers of a perilous drain of the sterling area's gold and silver reserves still remained. At any time the terms of world trade could lurch and shift unfavorably for Britain. The dollar gap could widen once more. It did widen, for instance, in the summer and autumn of 1955 and again the watchful government moved to impose more rigid controls. The margin of safety was thin indeed.

In April, 1955, Sir Winston Churchill, eighty years old, resigned as Britain's forty-second Prime Minister and leader of the Conservative party. Churchill had lived and served under five sovereigns. His retirement marked the end of an epic span of history. The free world perhaps owed its life to this tough and dauntless Titan. From that free world tributes volleyed and thundered to Westminster when the incomparable Churchill departed in glory. On January 24, 1965, he died at the age of ninety, the greatest Englishman of his time.

After the resignation of Churchill the "doom-laden responsibility" of leadership passed to Sir Anthony Eden, long-time Conservative Foreign Secretary and widely respected for his character, courage, moderation, and diplomatic skill. Sir Anthony led his strong Conservative government into a dull and demure national election in May, 1955. The liberal-minded Conservatives were able to say, and they did say, that they had staved off an economic crisis without panic and brought new forces of expansion into play. They pointed to the fact that their spring budget gave concessions to men with small incomes. In the election campaign the Conservatives made no extravagant promises. They spoke genially of a new "Tory democracy" and welfare capitalism, of tax cuts to stimulate investment, of slum clearance, better roads and railways.

Many voters were aware that the earlier Labour nationalization experiments had had only a limited success. Some citizens feared the maximum of bureaucratic interference if the Labourites came back to power. Still others were convinced that the followers of Aneurin Bevan were refusing to face economic realities. The Bevanites believed in nationalization as a sacred principle and said that they wanted to nationalize such things as chemicals and machine tools. True, the right wing of the Labour party, led by Clement Attlee and Herbert Morrison, turned against extremism. They relied heavily upon the trades union members who were not committed to nationalization for its own sake but who did think in terms of wages, conditions and hours of work, social security and bread. Even Labour's right wing, however, was steadily losing the support of the unions. The Labour party in the spring of 1955 was thus both divided and bogged down. Its election manifesto was deliberately lavish in vague promises, filled with bits and pieces of platforms of the past. Old slogans contained no new ideas.

The final results of a lack-lustre campaign were decided on May 26, 1955. The Conservatives obtained 13,336,182 votes and 344 seats. The Labourites won 12,405,130 votes and 277 seats. The Liberals held 6 seats, the others, 2. Sir Anthony Eden and the Conservatives had triumphed indeed.

Early in 1956 the structure of the cabinet was changed. Mr. R. A. Butler left the Exchequer and became Deputy Prime Minister and Lord Privy Seal; Sir Walter Monckton went to the Defence Ministry; Mr. Harold Macmillan became Chancellor of the Exchequer; Mr. John Selwyn Brooke Lloyd was the new Foreign Secretary.

There were also changes on the other side of the house of commons. In December, 1955, Mr. Clement Attlee resigned as leader of the Labour party and became Earl Attlee. As his successor the Labour party chose Mr. Hugh Gaitskell, a moderate, skilled, and vigorous leader. Gaitskell, a Winchester College and Oxford man, was a lecturer in political economy at the University of London before the Second World War. In 1945 he entered Parliament. Two years later he became Minister of Fuel and Power and in 1950, as mentioned earlier, he succeeded Sir Stafford Cripps as Chancellor of the Exchequer.

During these years, and later, Hugh Gaitskell had many clashes with his less moderate colleagues, especially the mercurial Aneurin Bevan, that remarkable Welshman whose death in July, 1960, made poorer the political life of Britain. Despite Gaitskell's skills in argument and diplomacy bitter disputes about political and economic policies continued to divide and harm the Labour party. Men who had risen through the ranks of the trade unions frequently looked with suspicion upon middle-class socialist intellectuals, such as Mr. Gaitskell, who came from the university world.

MACMILLAN VERSUS GAITSKELL

In 1956 the Conservative government was confronted by a series of economic and financial problems. Prices and wages continued to increase. The level of unemployment rose and inflationary pressures were strong. Imports increased and exports declined. Gold and dollar reserves were low. As the skies darkened, the government placed restrictions on imports from dollar areas and the bank rate was raised. Within a few months, there was a modest advance in the rate of industrial production and an increase in the speed of economic expansion.

Meanwhile, there were other problems. Early in 1957, Sir Anthony Eden was firmly told by medical specialists that he must resign. The new leader of the Conservative party and Prime Minister was Mr. Harold Macmillan, an Eton and Oxford man. Mr. Macmillan had fought and been wounded in the First World War. Then he had been associated with his family publishing house and later had entered the world of diplomacy and politics. As a leading member of the Conservative party he had been successively Minister of Defence, Secretary of State for Foreign Affairs, and Chancellor of the Exchequer.

The Suez Canal crisis of 1956, described in the next chapter, had damaged Anglo-American relations. Mr. Macmillan, with his diplomatic skills, helped to speed the growth of a new confidence between the United States and Britain and a revival of strength and unity in the Conservative party.

The prestige and power of the Conservatives were also increased by the fact that in 1957 and 1958 the economic and financial conditions in Great Britain rapidly improved. The bank rate was gradually lowered to 4 per cent and sterling was soon made freely convertible to dollars. There was a great increase in British exports, particularly in chemicals, machinery, and small automobiles. Meanwhile large investments from abroad, especially from the United States, strengthened still further the financial position of Britain. Mr. Macmillan asserted that "the country is better off today—better fed, better clothed, better housed—better off in every way than ever before in history." It seemed to him and his Conservative colleagues that a general election, fought in the midst of such prosperity, would give the Conservative party their third straight victory. A Conservative election slogan declared: "You never had it so good."

The Labourites were not able to find a major issue upon which to base their election campaign. Some Labourites asserted that the Tories had been in office too long. Others vaguely attacked "the few" who were said to be obtaining most of the profits from Britain's prosperity. The Labour party issued an election manifesto "Britain Belongs to You" and called for such things as a capital gains tax and a tightening of the inheritance tax laws. Mr. Gaitskell and his followers promised to construct new schools, hospitals, and houses if they were returned to power. They promised to abolish the sales tax on such "essential goods" as furniture and clothes. They said that they would provide a 20 per cent increase in old age pensions and some other welfare services, the costs of which would be paid by "planned expansion." The Conservatives denounced these "lavish and irresponsible" promises of the Labourites and asserted that they would result in a "high increase of public expenditure, a sharp rise in taxation and a return to inflation."

The general election of October, 1959, brought a tremendous victory for the Conservatives, a staggering defeat for Mr. Gaitskell and the Labour party. The Conservatives won 365 seats, the Labour party 258, the Liberals 6. The Conservatives obtained 13,750,935 votes, the Labourites 12,216,166, and the Liberals 1,640,761.

In December, 1959, Mr. Gaitskell told Labourites attending a conference at Blackpool that several old Labour party slogans had no appeal in a changing world. He asserted that the Labour party must drop its demands for widespread nationalization or be content "to remain in permanent opposition." It was clear, said Mr. Gaitskell, that Labour's loudly proclaimed nationalization plans had frightened many prosperous middle-class people. Again and again he asserted that only if the Labour party brought its ideas and policies up to date could it arrest its own decay.

Opposed to the point of view of Mr. Gaitskell and his moderate followers were the dedicated socialists, particularly several older men and some militant trade unionists, who vehemently insisted that any abandonment of the ideal of nationalization was "a betrayal of socialist interests." They pointed to clause four of the Labour party constitution which stated clearly the principle of "common ownership of the means of production, distribution, and exchange."

Late in 1960 a Labour party conference held at Scarborough was divided by bitter feuds and violent controversies. After prolonged dispute, it was finally agreed that "both public and private enterprise have a place in the economy." A majority of the thirteen hundred delegates to the Scarborough conference also voted to scrap Britain's nuclear weapons. About one hundred Labourites, then and later, supported the Campaign for Nuclear Disarmament and took part in protest marches and attended mass meetings in Trafalgar Square. A majority at Scarborough also agreed to oust Britain's allies from air bases in Britain and pull Britain out of the North Atlantic Treaty Organization. A majority of the Labour party, after much acrimonious controversy, refused to accept the decisions of the Scarborough conference about nuclear weapons, foreign air bases in Britain, and Britain's relations with the North Atlantic Treaty Organization. At the Blackpool Labour party conference of 1961 Mr. Gaitskell declared that a neutral and unilaterally disarmed Britain would encourage Russia and be "profoundly dangerous to world peace." This time his point of view was supported by a vote of 4,526,000 to 1,756,000. Despite this victory it was clear that recurring divisions among the Labourites, so sharp and bitter, increased their political weakness.

BRITAIN AND THE COMMON MARKET

After the end of the Second World War several Western European states created new organizations such as the Organization for Economic Cooperation, the Western European Union, the European Coal and Steel Community, and the European Atomic Energy Community. Upon a political, economic, and military level Western Europe seemed to be moving steadily toward some kind of unification and integration.

Several European leaders, particularly France's President Charles de Gaulle, who came to power in 1958, wanted a loose alliance of sovereign nations. Others, such as Belgium's Paul-Henri Spaak, France's Jean Monnet, and Joseph Luns of the Netherlands were eager for a federation of European states under a single parliament. There was, then, a marked lack of agreement about the nature of the political arrangements that might exist in the united Europe of the future. On the other hand, it was generally agreed that some form of European economic organization was an indispensable step toward any kind of effective European political system.

In 1956 France, West Germany, Italy, the Netherlands, Belgium, and Luxembourg signed the Treaty of Rome which created the European Economic Community or the Common Market with headquarters at Brussels. These six nations, with a combined population of 168,000,000, agreed to build and maintain around the whole group a wall of tariffs on imports from states outside the Common Market. They also agreed to take away all duties on iron and steel within the Common Market and to reduce and finally eliminate in three easy stages all customs barriers and restrictions on trade among themselves.

It seemed to some shrewd observers that if Britain stayed outside of Europe she might become an offshore island with a diminished influence in the affairs of the Western world. Foreign investments in Britain would dwindle. She would have to cut her living standards and either raise her tariff walls or enter into free trade arrangements with European states outside the Common Market and perhaps with the United States. On the other hand, if Britain did decide to join the Common Market, the large European market would be increasingly open to her goods as tariffs were wiped away. She would be a source of strength to Europe and part of a powerful economic bloc with a population of about 225,000,000. Foreign investments in Britain would rapidly increase. It seemed certain that the United States, for instance, would find in Britain a door to the Common Market and London would be a magnet drawing millions of dollars across the Atlantic.

Yet the British knew that entrance into the Common Market meant that they would no longer be protected against European imports into the United Kingdom. Some trade union leaders feared that British wages might be reduced to European levels. How successfully could British industries compete, at home and abroad, with those of Europe? Certainly many British industries would need to be reorganized and provided with new equipment. Many Britons also appreciated the fact that Britain, once inside the Common Market, would be only one of several nations and her wishes would not always prevail. Her special tariff arrangements within the Commonwealth would come to an end. She would probably find that she could no longer follow an independent foreign policy.

Once Britain entered the Common Market she would not be a strong partner of the United States and a major prop and pillar of Commonwealth power. It was difficult to persuade a traditionally insular people that they should enter into close relationship with European states or surrender any part of their national sovereignty, something that they must do if the Common Market ever grew into a political union. A hasty decision to join the Common Market might be unwise. On the other hand, Britain could not hesitate too long.

Meanwhile, the expanding power of the Common Market did not go unchallenged. Several nations outside of the Market decided that they, too, might cooperate for their mutual advantage. In July, 1959, the Finance Ministers of Britain, Sweden, Norway, Denmark, Switzerland, Portugal, and Austria set up a new and loose arrangement called the European Free Trade Association (EFTA). This group, with a combined population of about 90,000,000, came to be known as the "Outer Seven" and the Common Market nations were called the "Inner Six." Although the "Outer Seven" pursued a policy of lowering their tariffs at about the same pace as the nations in the "Inner Six," they could not offer a formidable economic threat to the Common Market. The "Outer Seven" was not a natural economic bloc. It had less geographical cohesion and industrial strength than the "Inner Six." The members of EFTA did more trading with the Common Market than they did among themselves.

In the summer of 1961 Mr. Macmillan announced that Britain had decided to apply for full membership in the European Economic Community "if satisfactory arrangements can be made to meet the special needs of the United Kingdom, the Commonwealth, and the European Free Trade Association." Mr. Macmillan asserted that if Britain stayed outside the Common Market she would be "a pygmy in a race of giants." Mr. Reginald Maudling, Chancellor of the Exchequer, pointed to the familiar fact that Britain had "not yet succeeded in achieving an adequate and steady rate of economic growth." British productivity had continued to rise more slowly than wages. On the other hand, the Common Market nations had leaped forward.

The Liberal party, slowly growing in strength, enthusiastically supported the plan to bring Britain into the Common Market. The Labour party did not. In October, 1962, Mr. Hugh Gaitskell delivered a fiery speech at a Labour party conference. "Are we forced to go into Europe? No. Would we necessarily be stronger economically if we go in and weaker if we stay out? No." A month earlier Mr. Gaitskell had asserted that if Britain entered the Common Market it would mean "the end of the Commonwealth and a thousand years of history."

In September, 1962, the Prime Ministers of the Commonwealth met in London for the eleventh postwar Commonwealth Conference. Prime Minister Macmillan, Mr. Duncan Sandys, Secretary of State for Commonwealth Relations, and other British government leaders explained that Britain would face economic and political decline if she stayed out of the Common Market. They pointed to the fact that Britain's exports to the Commonwealth had steadily gone down. In 1954, 49 per cent of her export trade had been with Commonwealth nations; in 1961 it had fallen to 36 per cent. Several Commonwealth nations had placed tariffs on British goods. Meanwhile, about 30 per cent of Britain's overseas sales were to the Common Market countries and the total was rising every year.

Several Commonwealth Prime Ministers, particularly Mr. Robert G. Menzies of Australia, Mr. John Diefenbaker of Canada, and Mr. Kwame Nkrumah of Ghana, spoke vigorously against the entry of Great Britain into the Common Market. They complained that in many cases the terms stated by the European Economic Community for Britain's admission were ambiguous and they asked for definite assurances and commitments. It was certain that if Britain joined the Common Market then she would have to adopt the full Common Market tariff which was designed to protect European markets. Thus Britain's tariff exemptions and other concessions to Commonwealth goods would end.

The possible loss of their special trading privileges and preferential tariff arrangements in the United Kingdom alarmed and dismayed the Commonwealth nations. Canada, Australia, and New Zealand continued to proclaim their strong objections. The representatives of India, Pakistan, and Ceylon stressed their fears that if the existing trade arrangements with Britain were ended their export industries, especially in cotton textiles and jute goods, would be badly hurt by the progressive application of duties. Many of their plans for new projects, several of them essential to continued national development, would have to be abandoned, curtailed, or delayed. Nigeria's Prime Minister Sir Abubakar Tafawa Balewa stated the fear of several African leaders that the Common Market might try to hinder Africa's advance and keep her a producer of raw materials for Europe's hungry factories.

To the representatives of the European Economic Community the British explained that they were concerned about the Common Market tariff levels for tropical goods such as cocoa, bananas, and coffee imported from Commonwealth areas in Africa and the West Indies. They also pointed to the large agricultural exports of Canada, Australia, and New Zealand (especially dairy products, wool, fruits, grain and meat) for which adequate and continuing markets must be found. In 1962 Great Britain took 62 per cent of New Zealand's exports, including 91 per cent of her butter and 94 per cent of her mutton, lamb, and cheese. About 25 per cent of Australia's export trade was with the United Kingdom. Twenty per cent of Canada's sales abroad, mostly raw materials and foodstuffs, was to Great Britain. India sent about 30 per cent of her exports to Britain, Pakistan about 20 per cent.

It was not surprising that Prime Minister Robert G. Menzies of Australia said that Britain's entry into the Common Market would mean a "loosening of Commonwealth relations" and that Prime Minister Jawaharlal Nehru of India asserted such a step would "weaken the Commonwealth." On the other hand, France's President Charles de Gaulle and several Common Market leaders insisted that Europe's farming industry must be protected and no special concessions should be made to the agricultural interests of the Commonwealth. It was natural that France, Western Europe's largest wheat producer, should have opposed concessions to Commonwealth wheat growers.

After long discussions it was agreed that if Britain entered the European Economic Community then a part of the Common Market preferences would be extended until 1970 to Commonwealth goods that enjoyed tariff preferences in the United Kingdom. It was also widely hoped that world-wide commodity agreements might be negotiated within a few years as the nations of the world sought to abolish their commerce-throttling trade barriers. Some of these hopes were realized in May, 1963, when the Ministerial Conference of the forty-four-member General Agreement on Tariffs and Trade (GATT) made preparations for the multilateral negotiations which began in 1964. In the United States, a new Trade Expansion Act enabled the government to make 50 per cent "across-the-board" tariff reductions on a reciprocal level.

During the long negotiations between Great Britain and the Common Market it became increasingly obvious that many of the major issues were more political than economic. France's President de Gaulle opposed Britain's entry into the Common Market. He hoped that the Western European nations would gather around France to create a "third force" that would be independent of both the United States and Russia. On the other hand, Belgium and the Netherlands wished to have Britain inside the Common Market, partly to act as a check on the growing power of a France that desired to be the leader of Western Europe.

In January, 1963, the negotiations that had been carried on for fourteen months suddenly came to an end. Maurice Couve de Murville, the French Foreign Minister, asked for "the adjournment of the conference on the entry of Great Britain into the Common Market." President de Gaulle asserted that "England is insular, she is maritime. . . . She has in all her doings very marked and very original habits and traditions. . . . The very nature and structure of Great Britain differ profoundly from those of the Continental countries." He also said: "One day, perhaps, England will be admitted to Europe after it has detached itself from its ties with the Commonwealth and the United States."

France's abrupt veto of Britain's admission to the Common Market was greeted in several European capitals with dismay and anger. The North Atlantic Alliance was shaken. "What happened at Brussels," said Prime Minister Macmillan, "was bad, bad for us, bad for Europe, bad for the whole world."

Many of those who had looked upon the growth of the Common Market as a step towards freer trade throughout the world were disillusioned and displeased. They disapproved of the tendency of the Six, particularly under French influence, to be increasingly concerned with the internal problems of their organization and apparently less aware of the needs and interests of the wider world beyond. The optimism and energy that had marked the early history of the Common Market seemed to be slowly ebbing away in 1964 and 1965. There were signs of internal strain, especially in agricultural policy. National interests and rivalries among the Common Market members were a persistent challenge to its success and survival. Meanwhile, Great Britain remained outside.

THE POLITICAL SCENE

In 1959 the financial position of Great Britain seemed healthy and strong. At the height of a wave of prosperity and satisfaction the Conservatives had won the election of October, 1959. Then the British economy became sluggish again. True, a deceptive prosperity continued at home. Wages were high and unemployment low. At the same time, the per capita production had only increased by about 2 per cent a year. By 1960 the British were once again living beyond their means. They were spending more money than they were earning. Manufacturers, finding it easy to sell in their home markets, were careless about the prospects of foreign trade.

Mr. Macmillan urged the British businessmen to be "merchant adventurers" abroad once more. He reminded them that they must get into a position to compete effectively with the products of other industrial nations. They must reduce costs, improve their products, sell aggressively. To reduce domestic consumption numerous restrictions were placed on instalment buying. Higher excise taxes were imposed on foreign imports, higher sales taxes on consumer goods. To increase pressures against the inflationary spiral the bank rate was raised to 5 per cent, then to 6, then to 7. To stabilize the pound Britain borrowed $2,000,000,000 from the International Monetary

Fund. The "austerity program" of the Macmillan government included a freezing of wages in all of the nationalized industries. This rigid "pay pause," designed to hold down wages and prices, was widely unpopular and there were several strikes.

In May, 1962, the British gold and foreign currency reserves had increased considerably. There had been a substantial expansion of long-term investments in Britain and a sudden surge in industrial output. Meanwhile it was clear that the prestige of the Macmillan government had fallen far and fast. Several bye-elections had brought defeat to the Conservatives. Mr. Macmillan, always an astute politician, saw the danger signals and concluded that drastic action must be taken to stop the decay of Conservative support among the rank and file of the electors.

In July, 1962, Mr. Macmillan suddenly removed seven senior members of his cabinet and several other holders of major appointments. Mr. Selwyn Lloyd, the Chancellor of the Exchequer who had administered the anti-inflationary "pay pause," was dismissed and replaced by Mr. Reginald Maudling, former Colonial Secretary. Mr. Richard Austen Butler, formerly Home Secretary, became Deputy Prime Minister and was also appointed to the newly created post of First Secretary of State with continuing responsibility for the Common Market and African Affairs. Defence Minister Harold Watkinson was replaced by Mr. Peter Thorneycroft, former Minister of Aviation. Mr. Duncan Sandys, already Secretary of State for Commonwealth Relations, became Colonial Secretary as well. Mr. Henry Brooke, formerly Postmaster General, became Home Secretary.

Mr. Macmillan hoped that his dramatic changes would turn the attention of the British public to the new men in the cabinet who had not been associated with unpopular Conservative policies in the past. Would the voters of Britain be favorably impressed by the "new faces" in a government that had been more than eleven years in office? The voters alone could answer that question. Mr. Gaitskell called the Prime Minister's action "a political massacre which can only be interpreted as a gigantic admission of failure." Nevertheless, Mr. Macmillan and the Conservatives remained in power.

In the summer and autumn of 1962 Britain's financial and economic situation improved once more. Mr. Reginald Maudling, the new Chancellor of the Exchequer, announced (November, 1962, and January, 1963) that the government would make generous tax allowances to industry. He promised that interest rates would be lowered; government spending in depressed areas, particularly the northwest, would be increased; there would be more building of roads, factories, and houses; taxes would be cut on many consumer goods. Mr. Maudling said that the Conservative party's theme was "Modernize—not Nationalize."

In January, 1963, Mr. Hugh Gaitskell died of a virus infection at the age of 56. For seven years, with shrewdness and skill, he had led the Labour party. He had tried to weld together its disparate elements, insisting that unity alone gave strength and the promise of political victory. He had supported the North Atlantic Treaty Organization and the Commonwealth. He had opposed the socialists who had demanded widespread nationalization. He had stood against the plans of the Conservative party to bring Great Britain into the European Economic Community, the Common Market. Now, suddenly, a fine political career had ended.

After the death of Mr. Gaitskell the Labour party chose as its leader Mr. James Harold Wilson, a pipe-smoking, intellectual, affable, calculating, and cautious Yorkshireman. Mr. Wilson had obtained first-class honors in politics and economics at Oxford. During the Second World War he had served in the Ministry of Fuel and Power and in 1945 he was elected to Parliament. In 1947 he became President of the Board of Trade at the age of thirty-one, the youngest cabinet minister of the century. Four years later he resigned from the Attlee cabinet along with Aneurin Bevan because he thought that Attlee and Ernest Bevin had accepted a rearmament program that would bankrupt the nation. In 1960 he had been defeated by Hugh Gaitskell in the contest for the leadership of the Labour party. Now, at the age of forty-six, he began to lead the Labour forces against Mr. Macmillan and the Conservatives. He tried to bring to an end some of the personal quarrels and doctrinal squabbles in his party, especially among the unstable elements in the left wing. He insisted that he would follow the moderate policies of Hugh Gaitskell and he was emphatic in his support of NATO, strong in his opposition to the left wing Labourites who demanded unilateral nuclear disarmament.

The Labour party was aided by the fact that the Conservatives were already in political difficulty. The Labourites were winning control of local governments where earlier elections had given the Conservatives comfortable majorities. Although the pace of inflation declined in 1963 and 1964 and taxes were reduced, there was still widespread unemployment, particularly in Scotland, northern England, and northern Ireland. There were investigations and court cases that suggested the possibility of weakness in the British security system. One particularly sordid sex and security scandal involved a cabinet minister who resigned in disgrace. In foreign and Commonwealth affairs the Macmillan government had suffered a series of reverses. Problems of defense policy multiplied.

In October, 1963, Prime Minister Harold Macmillan suddenly became ill and entered a London hospital for surgery. He decided to relinquish the leadership of the Conservative party. After a fierce struggle for power among the Conservatives, Queen Elizabeth II visited Mr. Macmillan and accepted his advice. She called upon the fourteenth Earl of Home, formerly Foreign Secretary in Mr. Macmillan's cabinet, to form a government.

Under the provisions of the Peerage Act of July, 1963, Lord Home renounced his peerage and became Sir Alec Douglas-Home. He was then elected to the house of commons from the Scottish constituency of Kinross and West Perthshire. His new cabinet contained Mr. Richard Austen Butler, Foreign Secretary; Mr. Reginald Maudling, Chancellor of the Exchequer; Lord Hailsham, Lord President of the Council and Minister for Science; Mr. Duncan Sandys, Commonwealth and Colonial Secretary; Mr. Peter Thorneycroft, Minister of Defence; Mr. Selwyn Lloyd, Lord Privy Seal and Leader of the House of Commons; Sir Edward Boyle, Minister of Education; and Mr. Ernest Marples, Minister of Transport. Mr. Edward Heath went into a newly created senior post as Secretary of State for Industry, Trade, and Regional Development.

The Conservatives immediately began a massive campaign to stop the anti-Conservative trend. They called for the modernization of British industry to obtain the full benefits of the age of automation. They promised that if they remained in power there would be a rapid advance in health, housing, trade, education, regional development, science, and transport. The defense structure would be improved. The Conservatives said that they intended to retain the long-range nuclear forces and later the Polaris submarines under Britain's full control. Of high importance, in the words of Sir Alec Douglas-Home, was "a steady expansion of our national wealth."

The new Labour symbol was "Thumbs Up" and the slogan was "Let's Go With Labour." The Labourites announced a two-year "crash program" to start a social, economic, and industrial renovation of Britain. Mr. Harold Wilson demanded an expanded scientific program and reforms in industry and agriculture, including the nationalization once more of the steel industry and heavy road transport, the levy of a new profits tax, and the creation of a national land commission to place land for development purposes in the hands of municipal councils. In the fall of 1963 and the spring and summer of 1964 Harold Wilson and the Labourites continued to assert that the Conservatives had no plans to stimulate the economy and no answers to the formidable problems of industry and trade. Britain's industries, they said, must become more inventive; manpower must be more freely used; exports must grow more rapidly; and British goods must be priced so that they could compete successfully in foreign markets. As the British political parties prepared for a general election, the Labourites claimed that the prestige of the Conservatives was at a low ebb. They said that the British people had become fatigued and bored during "the thirteen wasted years" in which Conservative governments had promised so much and done so little.

Election day was October 15, 1964. The Labour party obtained 12,205,576 votes and 317 seats in the house of commons. With 12,002,407 votes the Conservatives won 304 seats. The Liberals got 3,093,316 votes and 9 seats. Britain's Labour party was back in power for the first time in thirteen years. The victory was narrow and the future uncertain.

Almost at once some plans of the Labour leaders went awry. Harold Wilson had expected that the Secretary of State for Foreign Affairs in the new Labour cabinet would be Patrick Gordon Walker, formerly an Oxford don, friend of Hugh Gaitskell, and Commonwealth Relations Secretary in the Attlee government. That hope was ended when Walker suffered a surprise defeat in a bye-election at Leyton. It was necessary to find someone else to be Foreign Secretary. The choice was Michael Stewart, an efficient and eloquent man who had earlier been appointed as Minister for Education and Science.

Alfred George Brown, the loyal and turbulent trade unionist who had been defeated by Harold Wilson in the contest for the leadership of the Labour party, became First Secretary of State and Minister for Economic Affairs. Herbert Bowden, another shrewd and skilful Labourite, was appointed Lord President of the Council and Labour leader in the house of commons. Leonard James Callaghan, a moderate Labourite, was the new Chancellor of the Exchequer. Denis Winston Healey, a Liverpool Irishman and Oxford graduate, became Minister of Defence. The Lord Chancellor was Lord Gardiner, the spirited advocate of many law reforms who was said to have "a greater knowledge of common law than any other man alive." Fred Cousins, the general secretary of the Transport and General Workers' Union, was the Minister of Technology. The Home Secretary was Sir Frank Soskice. Anthony Greenwood became the Colonial Secretary and Arthur Bottomley the Secretary of State for Commonwealth Affairs. These members of Harold Wilson's new Labour cabinet were strong and competent men.

Despite a razor-thin Labour majority that fell to three in the house of commons in February, 1965, Harold Wilson insisted that his party had obtained a mandate from the people. He said that the Labourites would press ahead with the major points in their bold and controversial program. What, for instance, could be done about soaring land prices and higher public and private housing costs? The Labour government's plans to cope with these urgent problems included the restoration of rent controls, the establishment of commissions to acquire land for urban housing, the rebuilding of large areas in the cities, and similar measures. Other government plans to deal with problems of social security included new social welfare legislation to help the aged, the disabled, and the sick. "Nothing could be worse," asserted Harold Wilson, "than failing both at home and abroad because of the parliamentary balance of power."

Shortly after the new government was formed, the Prime Minister disclosed plans to tighten Britain's economy and to make it more productive and competitive. Corporate mergers were restricted. Laws against monopolies were made more stringent. Well-advanced plans for the production of several types of military aircraft were abandoned because, said the government, other excellent military planes could be purchased abroad at less cost. Despite measures such as these, the economic and financial clouds that hung over Britain remained black and threatening. The shipyards, for instance, were ailing, badly hurt by Japanese and Swedish competition.

The British steel industry had been nationalized in 1951, denationalized in 1953. The Labour party had promised that if it regained power it would nationalize steel once more. After the election of October, 1964, the Labour government decided to nationalize ten or twelve of the largest steel companies and operate them through a central agency similar to the coal and railway boards. The shareholders were to be compensated on the basis of stock values. On November 9, 1964, the house of commons supported the Labour government's plan to renationalize the steel industry by a majority of seven (307:300).

Still other problems continued to harass Prime Minister Harold Wilson and his Labour government. In 1964 there was an increase of about 5 per cent in Britain's gross national product. Wage increases had not been pegged to production and British consumers, pleased with rising wages, bought a large part of the mounting flow of goods. Consequently there was only a small increase in sales abroad. Meanwhile, purchases from foreign countries grew in volume and cost. Government and business spending overseas steadily expanded. There was a widening gap between Britain's total foreign expenditure and her income from abroad. The balance of payments question became once more a dismal part of the economic and financial scene.

Britain's gold and convertible currency reserves decreased rapidly. In December, 1964, they fell by £10,000,000. International pressure against the pound sterling reflected the widespread belief that the British government had not taken sufficiently bold and effective action when confronted by the alarming export-import ratio and the resulting balance of payments deficit. It was estimated that there would probably be a deficit of about £800,000,000 in Britain's balance of payments, the largest in British history. Meanwhile currency speculators helped to increase the pressure on the pound.

On October 27, 1964, the British government tried to curb imports and trim the deficit in British payments by placing a temporary

15 per cent tariff surcharge on most imports. This short-term measure was bitterly opposed by some foreign governments. From the nations of the EFTA trading bloc there were angry protests. The leaders of the Outer Seven were not satisfied with the British statement that the surcharge was an essential defense of sterling.

In November, 1964, the British government acted to curb international speculation against her currency by raising from 5 to 7 per cent the bank rate, the key interest rate that controls the flow of credit in the country. Meanwhile, the Bank of England arranged to obtain a credit of $3,000,000,000 from central bankers in eleven countries to defend sterling and re-invigorate the British economy. The government deferred payment of $175,000,000 owed to the International Monetary Fund. Under stand-by arrangements with the Fund more money was withdrawn to pay short-term currency advances earlier made by foreign central banks.

"Our future is heavily mortgaged," said the *Manchester Guardian*. "The efficiency with which we work must be increased and the prices we charge for our goods and services (which include wages and salaries) must be held in restraint." Between 1958 and 1965 British export prices rose 12 per cent, those of the United States 7 per cent, of France 4 per cent. The leaders of Britain's industries had to modernize their plants, increase their productivity, and reduce their production costs per unit. Leaders in commerce had to compete for world markets as they never had before. In the long term, the dangerous gap that existed between Britain's imports and exports could best be closed by a considerable rise in exports. Prime Minister Wilson warned British industrialists and businessmen that both their techniques and attitudes must be changed. "To resist change," he said, "is to spur decline."

In 1965, many men agreed with Mr. Wilson. Some men also asked this question about the plans and policies of the Labour government: "Can the Labour program inspire confidence when it seeks, all at the same time, monetary stabilization, wage increases, a 4 per cent growth rate, a vast state plan of housing construction, the costly nationalization of the steel industry?" The Labourites believed that they could keep their promises and reach their goals. The Conservatives were convinced that they could not.

Chapter 40

HOPES AND PERILS

TWILIGHT OF EMPIRE: INDIA AND PAKISTAN

AFTER the Second World War the masses of many lands, filled with a seething nationalism, stumbled and raced from passivity and impotence to belligerence and power. Old empires, such as those of France and the Netherlands, were shivered and broken. In many parts of the British Empire men and events proclaimed that the old Imperial order was ending. Swift thrusts of change made nonsense out of old dogmas and habits of thought. In a series of dramatic steps successive British governments attempted to guide and direct the forces they could no longer fully control. "In changing conditions," Clement Attlee once remarked, "one has got to change one's mind."

In earlier chapters of this book some of the major problems of India have been swiftly described. The running steps of modern history did not change those problems; but they did change the answers given to them by Britons, Hindus, and Moslems alike. It is a comment upon the advance of Indian leadership to record the fact that before the Second World War both the Congress party and the Moslem League recognized the importance of raising the standard of living of India's masses. Hindus and Moslems prepared impressive plans to deal with the formidable challenge of poverty, disease, illiteracy, the low standards of Indian agriculture and industry, the problems of finance, water and electrical power development, transportation, irrigation, and soil erosion. In July, 1944, the government of India announced the creation of a new Department of Planning and Development. An Indian leader wisely remarked: "Economic events cannot indefinitely wait upon politics."

Meanwhile there were increasing Indian demands for political independence. In 1939 Hindu leaders had expressed their sympathy for the Allied cause. At the same time, they repeated their earlier assertions that the British should quit India. Late in 1940 there was

815

widespread resistance to British authority, with results that threatened to lame the war effort. In 1942 a British mission, headed by Sir Stafford Cripps, offered India eventual Dominion status. This offer was refused by both Hindus and Moslems. When the Second World War ended it was clear that the British could stay in India only with difficulty.

The new Labour cabinet of Clement Attlee was prepared to make startling concessions. On May 16, 1946, a British cabinet mission issued from New Delhi a White Paper proposing an independent federated union of India's provinces and states. Immediately the British proposals met with passionate Indian opposition. The predominantly Hindu National Congress wanted a strong central government for all India. Mohammed Ali Jinnah's Moslem League insisted that the Moslems should have an independent state of Pakistan separate from Hindu India.

The British were determined to grant India what India had so long demanded. "Let no one doubt our intentions," said Sir Stafford Cripps. He asserted that the policy of the Labour party was "to transfer power quickly and smoothly and as cooperatively as the difficulties of the process admit."

On August 15, 1947, a second British plan, acceptable to the Indian leaders, went into effect. By the provisions of the new arrangement, India was divided into two independent British dominions. The one dominion, predominantly Moslem, was to be called Pakistan, with its capital at Karachi. Moslem Pakistan was to include Sind, most of Baluchistan, the Punjab region, and a large part of Bengal. Kashmir, the Northwest Frontier Province, and Jammu were unable to reach a decision about entering Pakistan, and, for a time, there was serious danger of civil war in Kashmir, which was governed temporarily by an emergency administration.

The second independent British dominion was India, predominantly Hindu. Its capital was established at New Delhi and its first prime minister was the Hindu leader Jawaharlal Nehru. Most of the southern princely states entered India. The main exception was the great central state of Hyderabad. The Nizam of Hyderabad, a Moslem ruler, refused to sanction the merging of his predominantly Hindu state with India, despite the fact that it was surrounded by Indian territory.

The creation of the two dominions did not bring immediate satisfaction or peace in India. There were numerous problems, such as the division of money balances, debts, and military stores between India and Pakistan. Nearly 6,000,000 Moslem refugees fled from Hindu India to join the 70,000,000 already contained in Moslem Pakistan. More than 4,000,000 non-Moslems, especially Hindus and Sikhs, were forced to flee Pakistan territory. Roaming armed bands killed thousands of people, looting and burning without restraint. In the midst of great migrations there were widespread massacres, particularly in the Punjab areas. Refugees from Pakistan demanded revenge. In India there were mass riots against the Moslems. In Pakistan there were mass riots against the Hindus and Sikhs. In vain the frail and emaciated Mahatma Gandhi pleaded for "communal peace."

Early in January, 1948, Gandhi began to fast to end the savage fighting. Gandhi had been the engineer of the passive resistance movements in India and had endured twelve years in prison and many fasts in the cause of Indian freedom. Without rank or post, he had won the devotion of millions of followers. He had made the spinning wheel the symbol of India's economic independence. He had undertaken the famous "march to the sea" in 1930 to protest against the British salt tax. A London-educated lawyer, Gandhi had shown, in South Africa and India, his unquenchable faith in civil disobedience campaigns and passive resistance. He had battled against child marriages, untouchability, and suttee. Always he had sought, as a political and spiritual leader, a united and independent India. Fellow Hindus looked upon him as a saint on earth and an architect of freedom. No emperor or mogul ever held greater power in India than the remarkable Mahatma Gandhi.

In behalf of peace between Hindus and Moslems Gandhi, seventy-eight years old, began his fast, demanding that the Hindus in Pakistan and the Moslems in India should be guaranteed freedom to worship, to travel, to keep their own houses, and to earn a livelihood. Millions of India's inhabitants were alarmed at the aged Gandhi's decision. Stock markets were closed. Rioters paused. The fast ended after six days, when India and Pakistan agreed to negotiate upon the basis of Gandhi's terms. As the fighting subsided Gandhi was resting at Birla palace. There, on January 30, 1948, when he was walking to his evening prayers, Gandhi was assassinated by the editor of an extremist newspaper.

In September, 1948, Mohammed Ali Jinnah, the governor-general and founding father of Pakistan, died in Karachi. There seemed to be no leader in Pakistan to succeed Jinnah as chief of the Moslem state. At the same time, soldiers of the new dominion of India invaded the state of Hyderabad. Jawaharlal Nehru, prime minister of India, showed that the policy of non-violence had died with Gandhi. Nehru was determined to force Hyderabad to join the dominion of India, claiming that the Nizam was defying the will of his people. Pakistan denounced India's "open aggression." In the end the Nizam was compelled to yield to Nehru. The forging of a new India had brought no peace, but the ancient appeal to the sword.

In 1950 India became a "sovereign independent republic" within the Commonwealth. In 1956 Pakistan followed the same road. Meanwhile, in the north, the struggle between India and Pakistan for the possession of Kashmir continued. A cease-fire order imposed by the United Nations ended more than a year of fighting. India, in control of about two-thirds of the disputed area, ignored three resolutions of the United Nations calling for a plebiscite because Nehru's government feared that the predominantly Moslem population of Kashmir might choose to unite with Moslem Pakistan. Steps were taken to integrate Kashmir more fully into India. Under Nehru's leadership India tried to force Portugal to surrender Goa, a Portuguese colony since 1510. In 1954 India placed a trade embargo on Goa and in December, 1961, she invaded Goa and seized it.

In October, 1958, Pakistan's President Mohammed Ayub Khan overthrew the parliamentary government in Pakistan by a military coup, asserting that only martial law would save his country from political and financial chaos and corruption. He also insisted that Western institutions, including democratic government, are unsuited to developing nations in other lands. A limited electorate of about 80,000 members of town and village councils was established. The result was stability and steady economic progress. In January, 1965, President Mohammed Ayub Khan retained power in Pakistan's first presidential election.

India, in contrast, maintained a democratic system of government. The national election of February, 1962, was the largest free election in the world. Of the 210,000,000 eligible voters, about 126,-000,000 went to the polls to choose 494 members of the lower house of Parliament and 2930 in the local assemblies of the 13 states.

In the years following the forging of a new India the government pushed ahead with its plans for progress and reform. More than $24,000,000,000 was spent in two successive five-year plans. Industrial production nearly doubled. Agricultural production increased. Electrical power grew. At the same time, sober and serious men realized that although much had been achieved the tasks ahead were many and difficult. There was a serious failure of a third five-year plan to meet its goals. In 1964 the population of India was about 490,000,000 and steadily increasing. But India's economic growth had fallen to 2 per cent a year. The problems of poverty, disease, and illiteracy still remained.

There were difficulties and dangers. A serious challenge came from the People's Republic of China, the recent conqueror of Tibet. The Chinese government said that the northern boundary of India was not the McMahon Line, drawn on a map along the Himalayan peaks from Bhutan to Burma by Sir Arthur McMahon at a conference with Tibetan and Chinese officials in 1914. True, the Tibetan and Chinese delegates had initialed the map, but the government of Sun Yat-sen's Chinese republic had refused to ratify the agreement.

In the early 1960's Chinese armies occupied about 9,000 square miles in Kashmir around Ladakh and claimed 42,000 more. After long discussions between China's Premier Chou En-lai and India's Jawaharlal Nehru, China suddenly attacked India in October, 1962.

The armies of India were out-gunned and unprepared. Prime Minister Nehru said: "We were out of touch with reality." In response to Nehru's appeal for military aid, the United States, Great Britain, and Canada sent arms. Soviet Russia, in the midst of a bitter dispute with China, delivered planes earlier purchased by India.

On November 30, 1962, China suddenly ordered a cease-fire on all fronts and announced that Chinese troops would retire twelve and one half miles behind the lines of actual control (as of November 7, 1959) by December 1. If the Indian soldiers did not withdraw the same distance from the lines the Chinese would "reserve the right to strike back." All along the Sinkiang-Ladakh border area the Chinese and Indian troops pulled back. A tense peace prevailed.

In May, 1964, Jawaharlal Nehru died. One of the great men of his age, he had embodied the aspirations of millions of the people of India. His successor, chosen by the ruling Congress party, was Lal Bandur Shastri. Shastri and the men who followed him were faced by formidable problems. Could they keep the nation of India united and stable? What could they do to meet the swelling challenge of illiteracy, poverty, disease, and the rising birth rate?

PALESTINE

When Turkey joined the Central Powers in 1914, Great Britain and France encouraged the restless subject peoples of Asia Minor to revolt against their Turkish masters. To the insurgent Arabs were supplied money, arms, and technical assistance. At the end of the First World War Turkey was weakened by the territorial losses described in an earlier chapter. The surge of Arab nationalism was not checked; it rolled on. Moreover, the years between the two World Wars saw strong movements for unity in the Arab lands. In 1944 the Arab League came into formal existence. The League embraced the seven independent states of Egypt, Iraq, Lebanon, Saudi Arabia, Syria, Transjordania, and Yemen. These states covered an area of 100,000 square miles and contained a population of about 37,000,-000. If they could develop their resources and combine their strength they could build a massive bloc of Arab power in the Near East.

Beneath the sands of Asia Minor lie huge reservoirs of oil. Modern times have seen the relentless pressure of oil-hungry nations to obtain a portion of their oil supply from the Arab lands. Many important chapters of diplomatic and commercial history have been written by events that arose from the demands for oil, so important in peace and war.

Russia obtained concessions in northern Iran. Great Britain secured similar oil concessions in wide stretches of land from the Persian Gulf to Bagdad. Oil companies from the United States gained the right to exploit many rich fields in Saudi Arabia. French and Dutch companies likewise extended their power and increased their dividends. Great pipe lines carried their profitable liquid freight down to empty tankers waiting in the hot harbors of the Middle Eastern seas.

It has been the consistent aim of the Western powers to maintain friendly relations with the Arab states. The Arabs, fierce, proud, and independent, have bargained shrewdly. For the concessions they have granted the Arabs have received large returns in money, commerce, and military assistance. Some Arab leaders have used the money provided from the deep exchequers of Western oil companies to begin the modernization of their kingdoms, often with limited success. They also used the money they got from the Western countries to purchase military power. Suitable alliances with Western nations further strengthened several Arab states.

Of rising importance to the Moslem lands, to the interests of Great Britain and the United States, and to the peace of the world were the problems of turbulent Palestine. In 1917 the famous Balfour Declaration had stated that "His Majesty's Government view with favour the establishment in Palestine of a national home for the Jewish peoples, and will use their best endeavours to facilitate the achievement of that object, it being clearly understood that nothing shall be done which may prejudice the civil and religious rights of existing non-Jewish communities in Palestine or the rights and political status enjoyed by Jews in any other country." In 1918 there were about 50,000 Jews in Palestine. In 1946 the Jewish population stood at nearly 600,000. The Arabs numbered about 1,000,000. These Arabs, alarmed at Jewish expansion, claimed that the British were discriminating against them in favor of the Jewish immigrants. They feared that the Moslems might become a religious minority in a Jewish state. They demanded that the flow of Jews into Palestine should be stopped at once.

The British were aware that the entire Moslem world was sympathetic to the claims of the Palestine Arabs. Within the British Empire and Commonwealth there were more than 100,000,000 Moslems. It was clear that Great Britain could not afford to prejudice the peace of her Moslem peoples or provoke a holy war by an anti-Arab policy in the mandate of Palestine. Despite strong and vociferous objections throughout the world Britain proceeded to restrict the further entry of Jews into Palestine by the establishment of a quota system of immigration.

In the welter of intense and angry propaganda, claims and

counterclaims, the British government insisted that the free immigration of Jews into Palestine would bring open war between the Jews and the Arabs, with consequences impossible to foretell. Zionist leaders throughout the Western world gathered funds and arms to aid the Jewish cause. Jewish underground groups in Palestine engaged in sniping and blowing up British and Arab strong points. Arab irregular fighters replied in kind as British forces tried desperately to keep the Holy Land a land of peace.

In 1947 the British government grimly announced its intention to surrender the mandate of Palestine, to withdraw completely from that divided land, and to transfer to the United Nations the thankless task of finding and imposing a solution of the Arab-Jewish dispute. Many of those who had condemned Great Britain for finding no solution were now challenged by the task of finding a solution themselves. The British government stated that they would officially withdraw from Palestine on May 15, 1948. Until that day they would attempt to maintain order. When that day had passed the peace of Palestine was no longer to depend upon the policy of Britain but upon the policy and power of the United Nations.

On November 13, 1947, the representatives of six Arab states in the United Nations walked out of the Assembly when that body voted to partition Palestine into two sovereign Arab and Jewish states. Under the plan of the United Nations Palestine was to be divided into eight regions. The Jewish state was to contain three parts, two of which did not touch each other. The Arab state was to contain three parts, two of which did not touch each other. The city of Jaffa was to belong to the Arab state but would be surrounded by the Jewish state. Jerusalem was to be under the international control of the United Nations. Such an arrangement, asserted the Arabs, was unworkable. They asked such questions as these: Why were almost all of the citrus groves in the Jewish state, although the Arabs owned about half of them? Why did the Arabs outnumber the Jews in two of the three parts of the Jewish state? Meanwhile hundreds of Jews and Arabs died as new waves of violence swept over the Holy Land. It seemed that the vacuum created by British withdrawal might have lamentable results throughout the important strategic and economic areas of the Near East.

When Britain officially terminated her thirty-one-year rule of Palestine on May 15, 1948, the Jews proclaimed at Tel Aviv the independence of the new Zionist state of Israel. Over the buildings of Tel Aviv rose the Zionist flags bearing two pale blue stripes and the blue star of David. For the first time in nearly two thousand years the Jews had a state of their own.

The Arab states now prepared to challenge the new nation of Israel. King Abdullah of Transjordania moved with his Arab Legion into the valley of the Jordan towards Jericho. In southern Palestine Egyptian troops marched along the road to Gaza and Egyptian airplanes bombed Tel Aviv. In the north, Syrian and Lebanese forces thrust a few sharp prongs over the border. Against the Jewish Hagana troops the Palestine Arabs fought at Haifa, Jaffa, Jerusalem, and Acre. The Security Council of the United Nations was not prepared to impose either military or economic sanctions upon the battling Jews and Arabs. Repeatedly they ordered the troops to cease fire and observe a truce. Despite spasmodic periods of uneasy armistice the prospects of immediate and settled peace in the Holy Land grew daily more remote. Later in this chapter appears the tale of recent dark events in the history of the contending peoples of the Near East.

THE BIRTH OF MALAYSIA

Major changes in postwar policy were not confined to India, Pakistan, and Palestine. In January, 1948, after more than a hundred years of British rule, Burma, with a population of 17,000,000, was given absolute independence. In February, 1948, strategically located Ceylon, after 351 years under successive Portuguese, Dutch, and British colonial rule, became a sovereign part of the Commonwealth. In the same month, nine Malay states and two former straits settlements, Malacca and Penang, were established as the Federation of Malaya. In the interests of "efficiency and democratic progress" a unified administration was created to offer "the means and prospect of developing Malaya's capacity in the direction of self-government." The 4,300,000 people in the Malay peninsula, rich in rubber and tin, were to have full authority over most domestic affairs. Only external affairs, defense, and appeals to the privy council remained under British control. The fortress island of Singapore remained outside the federation, a crown colony governed by a separate administration. In 1959 considerable powers of self-government were given to Singapore. Only the control of external affairs and defense remained in British hands.

The Federation of Malaya was soon plagued by Communist attempts to overthrow the government by subversion, violence, and terror. In 1952 Sir Robert Templer was appointed High Commissioner in Malaya. Under his command, British and Malay soldiers, skilled in jungle warfare, slowly pushed back the Communists, cleaned out their jungle nests, and brought to the Malayan villages a new security.

In the late 1950's discussions began about the possibility of creating a large union of territories in Southeast Asia. After the favorable report of the Cobbold Commission (November, 1961), long and intensive negotiations began. On July 9, 1963, representatives of Britain, Malaya, Singapore, and the British territories of North

Borneo and Sarawak signed an agreement to form a new nation to be called Malaysia.

Indonesia and the Philippines, important neighbors of the proposed new federation, objected to the merging of Singapore, Sarawak, and Sabah (North Borneo) with the eleven states of Malaya. Indonesia's President Sukarno pointed out that the four component parts of Malaysia were all formerly British colonies and asserted that the proposal to form a federation was the result of a "neocolonial plan" by the British to extend and prolong their power and influence in Southeast Asia. Sukarno, for his part, wanted to annex North Borneo as he had earlier annexed West New Guinea. The Philippine government based its objections upon its claims to North Borneo, claims that the British had steadily denied and rejected.

Indonesia and the Philippines agreed at a Manila meeting that if a survey by the United Nations showed that Sarawak and North Borneo wanted to join Malaysia then they would "welcome" the decision. The proposed Malaysian federation was originally scheduled to come into being on August 31, 1963, but it was decided to await the outcome of the United Nations survey in Sarawak and Sabah (North Borneo). The survey showed a "sizable majority" for the federation proposal. On September 16, 1963, the Federation of Malaysia was formally created.

Indonesia's President Sukarno continued to claim that Malaysia was a British puppet state. Excited and angry mobs sacked and burned the British embassy in Jakarta, capital of Indonesia. Other British property was attacked and seized. Guerrillas, spies, and saboteurs were sent from Indonesia into Malaysia. A trade embargo was imposed against Singapore. Britain sent troops to help defend the new state. Australia strengthened her defenses and promised aid if Malaysia needed it. Meanwhile it seemed to President Sukarno that the United Nations was supporting the cause of Malaysia. On January 21, 1965, Indonesia withdrew from the United Nations.

The first Prime Minister of Malaysia was Tunku (Prince) Abdul Rahman of Malaya, a British-educated and pro-Western man of energy and imagination. Kuala Lumpur, capital of Malaya, became the capital of the new federation. The financial and commercial center is, of course, Singapore. Malaysia contains about 10,000,000 people and covers an area of 130,778 square miles, stretching in a great arc along the lower edge of the South China Sea. Two great cultures, the Chinese and the Malay, exist side by side in the new state. Despite the divisions within the federation and the threats of foes outside, the architects and supporters of Malaysia continued to hope that it might become a stable and prosperous nation, standing firmly against the challenge of communism and the southward thrust of the People's Republic of China.

AFRICA

The postwar years also marked the beginning of a new era for Africa. Between 1954 and 1966 millions of Africans won their independence. From the collapsed ruins of old empires were built new states, unstable groupings of tribes and peoples faced by an alarming shortage of capital and skills, their survival threatened by rivalry and disorder.

Many British colonies became free and independent states. In 1956 the Sudan, with a population of 12,000,000, decided by a plebiscite to become an independent republic outside of the Commonwealth. Egypt, long anxious to possess the Sudan, was not pleased. In 1960 British Somaliland united with the territory that was formerly Italian Somaliland to form the independent republic of Somalia outside of the Commonwealth.

In 1957 the Gold Coast, with a population of about 7,000,000 became the dominion of Ghana. In 1960 it became a republic within the Commonwealth. The President of the new republic was the ambitious Kwame Nkrumah who hoped to lead a movement to build a vast United States of Africa. Unfortunately, President Nkrumah did not display the qualities necessary for effective leadership. In his own state of Ghana he frequently interfered with the law courts in order to get the verdicts he wanted. It soon became increasingly clear that many Africans did not approve of the words and deeds of the autocratic Kwame Nkrumah.

In October, 1960, the British colony of Nigeria, with a population of 42,000,000 and rich in pepper, ivory, and palm oil, became an independent member of the Commonwealth. Its first Prime Minister was the astute, able, and conservative Sir Abubakar Tafawa Balewa.

The Federal Republic of Nigeria has a fine capital at the coastal city of Lagos, five universities, and a people earlier trained by Britain in the principles and practices of political democracy. Nevertheless, there are still deep cleavages and dangerous tensions in Nigeria. Much of the wealth and talent is concentrated in the south and east, a fact resented by many people in the northern and western areas. There are problems of tribalism: the Yorubas of the west fear domination by the aggressive Ibos of the south, and both fear the numerous Hausas of the north. When the first national election was held in January, 1965, it seemed that Nigeria might splinter into separate states. Despite the clashes and bitterness, there was no revolution, no collapse of the central government. For a time, at least, fears about the future of the new Federal Republic of Nigeria were allayed.

In 1962 Uganda joined the ranks of the independent states of Africa and its black, red, and yellow flag floated proudly over the land. Uganda has a population of nearly 7,000,000. The stability of its economy depends heavily upon the price of its primary products: coffee and cotton. Under the leadership of Apollo Milton Obote, the first prime minister, the new state of Uganda tried to cope with the problems brought by the deep decline of coffee and cotton world market prices in the 1960's. The difficulties of Uganda were similar to those of several undeveloped countries whose economic health— and sometimes survival—depends upon a few products.

Meanwhile the postwar years brought increased tribal tensions and mounting conflict between African and non-African interests in the British colony of Kenya. The Europeans wanted to keep their dominant position. They held valuable farm areas in the "White Highlands" of Kenya and resisted African attempts, born of land hunger and nationalism, to oust them. The whites, their hearts often heavy with fear, did not forget that there were about 65,000 whites in Kenya and nearly 8,000,000 non-whites. Did the Swahili word "uhuru" (freedom), so often heard, portend disaster for the whites on the green highlands, in Nairobi, on the great southern plains?

In central Kenya the combination of land and race problems brought the turbulent and disaffected elements of the Kikuyu tribesmen into the Mau Mau organization, a secret underground of terror and dark magic determined to drive the Europeans out of Kenya. Intensive police and military operations crushed the revolt. Slowly a new era of gradual political and economic change began.

In 1954 a multi-racial government was formed. Large grants from Britain spurred agricultural development. New African leaders elected under a limited franchise in 1957 and 1958 dreamed and spoke about the future of Kenya as an independent African state. A constitutional conference in London in 1960 resulted in a new constitution for Kenya and a broadened franchise. National political parties now appeared. One of the large parties was the Kenya African National Union (KANU), representing the Kikuyus, the major tribe, and supporting urban nationalism and centralized government. Another was the Kenya African Democratic Union (KADU) which looked mainly to the rural areas for support and represented the tribes that feared the Kikuyus might take away their lands and destroy their tribal traditions.

A fully democratic one-man one-vote election in March, 1961, gave the KANU party a majority but the leaders refused to form a government until Jomo ("Burning Spear") Kenyatta, once a leader of the Mau Mau terrorists, was released from the prison where the British had put him in 1953. The British government finally set Kenyatta free. With his silver-topped tribal cane and his famous whisk, symbol of power, Jomo Kenyatta led his Kenya African National Union party to a landslide victory in the eight-day election that began on May 18, 1963. KANU won 66 of the 117 seats in the House of Representatives, 19 of the 41 seats in the Senate. One of the members of the new government was Tom Mboya, the popular and competent labor leader.

In December, 1963, Kenya obtained full control of her domestic affairs and a new constitution giving much political power to local authorities. In December, 1964, Kenya became an independent republic within the Commonwealth. Under the new constitution, Kenya passed almost completely under the control of the central government and KANU. Mr. Ronald Nyale, leader of KADU, dissolved his party and thus Kenya became a one-party state.

Elsewhere in Africa the demands for freedom and independence continued. Tanganyika became a republic within the Commonwealth in December, 1962. In 1963 a series of discussions was held about the future of the British protectorates of Basutoland, Swaziland, and Bechuanaland. Zanzibar became an independent state in December, 1963, but the new government was overthrown by a revolution in January, 1964. On April 22, 1964, President Julius K. Nyerere of Tanganyika and President Abeid A. Karume of Zanzibar signed articles providing for the union of their two countries. In October, 1964, the new state was named Tanzania.

In 1963 the British government took steps to dissolve the crumbling Central African Federation. This Federation had been built in 1953 by the union of Northern Rhodesia, Southern Rhodesia, and the protectorate of Nyasaland. There were about 8,300,000 blacks and 305,000 whites in the Central African Federation, and the British hoped in 1953 that their experiment in uniting these peoples would succeed and be a model for later multi-racial partnerships. The dream soon faded. There were many points of view about the rights and claims of blacks and whites. Bitterness grew, tensions increased, and the hopes of harmony and compromise collapsed.

In April, 1963, Northern Rhodesia asked permission to secede from the ill-starred Central African Federation and join the Commonwealth as an independent state. Despite the vehement objections of Sir Roy Welensky, the Northern Rhodesian Prime Minister of the Federation, and others who feared the end of white supremacy the British government gave Northern Rhodesia the right to secede from the Federation (August, 1963). On October 24, 1964, Northern Rhodesia became the Republic of Zambia. The first President was Dr. Kenneth Kaunda, fiery head of the United National party.

In 1961 the protectorate of Nyasaland obtained an all-black government under the leadership of Dr. Hastings Kamuzu Banda. The blacks in Nyasaland asserted that the whites in Northern and Southern Rhodesia dominated the Central African Federation. They asked the British government for permission to secede. Sir Roy

Welensky, militant leader of the whites, opposed the request of Nyasaland as he opposed the similar request of Northern Rhodesia.

Despite the objections of Sir Roy Welensky and his associates in Salisbury, the British government decided that it was Britain's duty to accede to the wishes of the elected leaders of Nyasaland. In July, 1964, Nyasaland became the independent African states of Malawi, a full member of the Commonwealth, the thirty-seventh country to achieve independence in restless, emerging Africa.

The tide of African nationalism also surged into Southern Rhodesia, the third territory in the Central African Federation and the least prosperous part of it. There taxes were high. Unemployment was increasing. The public debt steadily mounted. The 3,616,000 blacks who lived in Southern Rhodesia had virtually no political rights. Hunger and disease were their constant companions. About 221,000 whites ruled the land.

For many years Southern Rhodesia depended for economic survival upon the markets of Northern Rhodesia and Nyasaland. When the black governments were established in Northern Rhodesia and Nyasaland, the white rulers of Southern Rhodesia feared the results. Would the black governments cut their economic and financial ties with Southern Rhodesia? What then might happen?

Meanwhile the blacks in Southern Rhodesia became increasingly militant. There were frequent riots against a constitution that denied the franchise to most Africans. The whites in Southern Rhodesia were determined to maintain their minority rule and the doctrines of white supremacy. Their leader was Winston Field, Premier of Southern Rhodesia, a man who was outspoken and unyielding in his opposition to the claims of the Africans. Those who supported Premier Field agreed with him that Southern Rhodesia should try to obtain independence before Britain drafted a new constitution for Southern Rhodesia that would give the blacks majority rule. Premier Field moved swiftly. He tried to suppress the Africa Peoples' Union and Joshua Nkomo, the African Nationalist leader. He formally requested the British government to permit Southern Rhodesia to secede from the Central African Federation and to become an independent state at the same time as Northern Rhodesia and Nyasaland.

In April, 1963, the British government rejected the request of the all-white government of Southern Rhodesia. Other members of the Commonwealth agreed that Britain should take no steps that might tend to perpetuate white minority rule in Africa. Mr. Harold Wilson, leader of the British Labour party, said that Southern Rhodesia should not be given independence until it had "a constitution which enables the mass of the people in Southern Rhodesia to govern themselves."

When the Central African Federation was formally ended on

December 31, 1963, no answers to the problems of Southern Rhodesia had been found.

Premier Winston Field was soon succeeded by Ian Douglas Smith, leader of the Rhodesian Front party and a white supremacist. Joshua Nkomo, the popular African leader, was arrested and banished. Smith insisted upon independence for Southern Rhodesia and continued white domination throughout the country.

Among those opposed to Premier Smith was Sir Roy Welensky, former Prime Minister of the Central African Federation. Welensky saw ultimate disaster for Southern Rhodesia if Smith and his supporters persisted in their policies. In a special election (October, 1964) Sir Roy was defeated. During the long months that followed there seemed to be little chance of reaching a satisfactory settlement between embattled whites and Africans in Southern Rhodesia.

In the Union of South Africa the government of Jan Christian Smuts was defeated in 1948 and the new premier was Dr. Daniel F. Malan, leader of the Afrikaner Nationalist party. Dr. Malan and his followers were fearful that their white civilization might be engulfed by the blacks. They were determined to maintain and extend the policy of *apartheid,* a policy based upon a belief in white supremacy and the wisdom of separating the whites from the blacks and the colored non-Europeans.

In 1953 Dr. Malan was elected for a further term. He died in 1954 and the next two premiers were Dr. Johannes Strijdom and Dr. Hendrik Verwoerd. These leaders continued to uphold and defend the harsh doctrines of white supremacy in a land where there were about 3,000,000 whites and 11,000,000 non-Europeans.

The Population Registration Act of 1950 had said that all non-Europeans in South Africa were required to carry a fifty-page "pass" so that they could be readily identified. On March 21, 1960, several blacks at Sharpeville, a town near Johannesburg, refused to carry passbooks. In a demonstration organized by the militant Pan-Africanist Congress about 20,000 Africans marched to the local police station. From behind wire fences the police force fired into the crowd, killed about 72 men and women, wounded about 200. The "Sharpeville Massacre" was denounced in many parts of the world. In some countries South African goods were boycotted. South Africa was asked to withdraw from the International Labour Organization. Between March and July, 1960, foreign exchange reserves fell from $405,000,000 to $321,000,000. Foreign investments declined. Premier Verwoerd was wounded by a white South African who believed that the policies of the Nationalist party would bring disaster to South Africa. In May, 1960, a new security act was demanded by Dr. Verwoerd to meet "a crisis of survival."

Violence continued, especially in Capetown, Durban, Johannes-

burg, and Pretoria. Knots of passive resistance were tightened. Ignorant and embittered masses became more restless. It was clear that
the attitudes and policies of Dr. Hendrik Verwoerd and his fellow
white supremacists would not be changed by the words and deeds of
the blacks. Nor would the Nationalist government be swayed by the
opposition of the anti-*apartheid* United Party of English-speaking
whites or the strong condemnation of Ambrose Reeves, Anglican
Bishop of Johannesburg, Joost de Blank, Anglican Bishop of Capetown, and other liberal white Christian leaders. The African National
Congress and the Pan-Africanist Congress were banned. Almost all
the top leadership of liberal white, Asian, and African groups, about
1600 people, were arrested.

A resolution of the Security Council of the United Nations
called upon South Africa to "abandon its policy of *apartheid* and
racial discrimination." Dr. Verwoerd's government ignored the resolution. When Britain's Prime Minister Macmillan visited South Africa
he said: "We reject the idea of any inherent superiority of one race
over another. . . . There are some aspects of your policies which make
it impossible for us to support you without being false to our own
deep convictions about the political destinies of free men." Again,
Dr. Verwoerd's government was unmoved. The Nationalists refused
to change the repressive policies of *apartheid,* policies later described
by Adlai Stevenson, United States' Ambassador to the United Nations,
as "calculated retrogression." In November, 1963, Paul Martin,
Canada's Secretary of State for External Affairs, called the policies
of South Africa's government "ill-advised and repugnant."

In October, 1960, a national referendum was held in South
Africa to decide whether or not that country should become a republic. Only whites were allowed to vote. Those who desired a republic got 52 per cent of the votes and thus won the referendum.

Dr. Verwoerd and his followers wanted South Africa to become
a republic. They also wanted to keep South Africa inside the Commonwealth. Their formal request to remain in the Commonwealth
was submitted to the tenth Commonwealth Conference in London in
the spring of 1961. There Dr. Verwoerd was challenged by hard
attacks upon the *apartheid* policies of his government. Many Commonwealth statesmen, including representatives from Canada, Ceylon,
Cyprus, Ghana, Malaya, Nigeria, India, and Pakistan, stated clearly
and strongly their distaste for *apartheid*. Britain's Prime Minister
Harold Macmillan later declared that South Africa's racist policy was
"a tragically misguided and perverse philosophy . . . abhorrent to the
ideals towards which mankind is struggling in this century."

Confronted by such opposition, Dr. Verwoerd decided to withdraw the application he had made for continuing membership in the
Commonwealth. In March, 1961, South Africa left the Common-

wealth. On May 31 she became an independent republic. The new Republic of South Africa stayed inside the sterling area. Several bilateral agreements were made so that some of the Commonwealth trade preferences were granted to her. The *Cape Times* said: "Now we are a lonely little republic at the foot of turbulent Africa!" Meanwhile, the General Assembly of the United Nations censored South Africa's *apartheid* policies by a vote of 95 to 1 (Portugal).

The Nationalist government of the new republic continued to tighten the chains of coercion and control. The Group Areas Act of 1952, for instance, had provided for racial zoning and the movement of millions of blacks into eight special Bantu reserves, all-black "states" called Bantustans to which were allotted about 14 per cent of South Africa's land. The rest, containing the richest farm areas and virtually all of South Africa's mineral and industrial wealth, was to be left to the whites. The first "state," called Transkei, was established in May, 1960. It was about the size of Denmark and had a population of 1,500,000. It held its first election in November, 1963. Over Transkei and the other projected Bantustans the South African government retained all effective power, including control of the police, defense, and foreign affairs. The Bantustans were to be little more than reservations for cheap labor. "This solution," said the *New York Times,* "is immoral, self-defeating and highly dangerous."

The Sabotage Acts of 1962 provided the death penalty for any citizen who received training in subversion abroad or who urged intervention by force in South African affairs. Other legislation gave the government further control over native education. The General Law Amendment Acts of 1962 and 1963 increased the police powers of Dr. Verwoerd's government. The government was given authority to detain without trial for successive ninety-day periods any individual suspected of committing certain political offenses or any person deemed likely to have information of value to the government, information "which need not be related to a crime." Under the General Law Amendment Acts about 5,000 persons were detained, some of them in solitary confinement, for alleged political activities against the state. Many others, especially professional men, left the country to seek happier homes elsewhere. Still others, placed under house arrest or denied exit permits, were compelled to remain in South Africa. Many of the control measures were extended and tightened by the Bantu Amendment Act which went into force on January 1, 1965. Throughout the land there was much tension and terror, little hope.

IRELAND, THE WEST INDIES, CYPRUS

As the Commonwealth and Empire moved towards the last quarter of the twentieth century there were several lights and shadows in areas far distant from India, the Near East, and Africa. In southern Ireland, for instance, Eamon de Valera's sixteen years in office were abruptly ended when his Fianna Fail (Soldiers of Destiny) party lost control of the thirteenth Dail after an election early in 1948. John A. Costello, a fifty-six-year-old lawyer and leader of the Fine Gael (United Irish) party, was able to form a coalition government.

In November, 1948, the Dail passed the Republic of Ireland Bill and on Easter Day, 1949, the anniversary of the rebellion of 1916, southern Ireland became a republic and left the Commonwealth. Soon Eamon de Valera and the Fianna Fail party returned to power.

Successive governments of the Republic of Ireland agreed that the partition of the island must be ended and Ulster brought into union with the southern Republic. The men of Ulster, for their part, showed no sign of swerving from the paths of their fathers. They would, it seemed, stay adamantly aloof from the southern counties, whatever storms might blow from the land of Fine Gael.

In August, 1956, after eleven years of negotiation, the Caribbean Federation of Jamaica, Trinidad, the Barbados, and the Leeward and Windward Islands was created. This flexible federation, containing 3,000,000 people, began to function in March, 1958. Beset by economic ills and plagued with sharp disputes, the West Indies Federation gradually moved towards collapse. Jamaica seceded in September, 1961. Trinidad and Tobago also dropped out. The Federation was formally dissolved on May 31, 1962. Jamaica obtained her independence on August 9, 1962, and Trinidad and Tobago became an independent state on August 31. Thus Britain's federation experiment in the West Indies failed. In British Guiana, meanwhile, successive British governments were increasingly troubled by a bitter and bloody struggle between the rural East Indian and urban Negro groups and the activities of Cheddi B. Jagan, an aggressive and anti-British Marxist who had become Prime Minister in 1962 (the British had forced him out of office in Georgetown in 1953) and demanded independence for British Guiana. Jagan was defeated in December, 1964, by James Burnham, leader of the Negro-dominated People's National Congress. Hopes for independence faded.

There were also changes and problems in the Mediterranean area. The island of Malta became independent on September 21, 1964. Meanwhile, on the island of Cyprus demands had arisen among the Greek part of the population for the cession of Cyprus to Greece. In 1956 the toll of death and destruction mounted as underground movements of violence, encouraged by the Greeks, were directed against the British, the Turks, and many native Cypriots. The British attempted by stern measures to stem the tide of terrorism. In March,

1956, the British government deported and exiled Archbishop
Makarios because of his "direct incitement to violence." In 1960
Cyprus became an independent republic and Archbishop Makarios,
restored to power, became the first president. It was agreed that
Britain would retain her military base on Cyprus and the Turkish
minority would be protected. In 1961 Cyprus was admitted to the
Commonwealth. At the end of 1963 the Greeks and Turks on Cyprus
began to fight again. After the summer of 1964 an uneasy peace prevailed. Peace did not come easily to Cyprus.

ECONOMIC AID TO UNDERDEVELOPED LANDS

After the Second World War successive British governments
were increasingly aware of the wisdom of helping the peoples of
underdeveloped countries. Those governments served Britain's long-
term interests by providing gifts, technical assistance, loans, and sterling releases to many lands long starved for money and skills. Britain
has also been the second largest contributor of money to the technical
assistance activities of the United Nations and its specialized agencies.

After 1945, Britain's Labour government decided to begin a
rapid and extensive development of Africa's vast resources. As a result of the Economic and Welfare Act of 1945, £120,000,000 was
allocated to assist the colonial authorities in carrying out a series of
large-scale programs. In 1948 a Public Development Corporation
was created with borrowing powers up to £100,000,000. Surveys,
reports, and various other research programs were undertaken in
Tanganyika, Kenya, Uganda, Rhodesia, Aden, Sierra Leone, and
elsewhere. The British planned extensive operations to increase the
production of gold, copper, iron, palm oil, tobacco, sisal, tin, and
cocoa. In many areas, the largely untapped potential economic power
of Africa was to be systematically developed by big plantation enterprises and by the building of several industries on the spot, such as
textile factories in Uganda and chocolate, soap, and margarine proc-
essing plants near the numerous sources of supply. Extensive projects
were swiftly planned to hasten the increase of hydro-electric power
development, railways, highways, airport facilities, social services,
education, water supplies, housing facilities, soil conservation, and
improved mechanical equipment for factories.

In 1955, the sum of £6,000,000 was allocated to help the
growth of colonial colleges and universities, especially in Africa.
Throughout the Empire and Commonwealth went technical experts
in such fields as flood control, health, and agriculture. Locust survey
and control teams moved into Kenya. Between 1945 and 1963
Britain paid £1,367,000,000 in grants and loans to underdeveloped
areas. In 1962–63, for instance, Britain made available £148,000,-
000 in grants and loans, including about £15,000,000 to non-

Commonwealth countries such as the Cameroon Republic, Senegal, South Korea, and South Viet Nam. In 1963–64 the British increased the sum to about £200,000,000.

THE COLOMBO PLAN

It is 2,000 miles from the Himalayas to the Indian Ocean, more than 4,000 miles from the Persian Gulf to the South China Sea. This large area contains more than 600,000,000 human beings. Economic resources are not developed. Poverty stalks and kills. There the agents of communism work to "lure the hungry with promises of food, the sick with promises of health, the dependent with the promise of equality, and the weak with promise of power."

In January, 1950, the Foreign Ministers of the United Kingdom, Canada, Australia, New Zealand, South Africa, Pakistan, India, and Ceylon met at Colombo, capital of Ceylon. They hoped to decide there upon an economic aid policy that would help to combat ignorance, poverty, and disease, a policy designed to strengthen the free peoples of Southeast Asia, and to keep them from rallying to communism. At the Colombo Conference it was agreed that the participating nations of the Commonwealth would pool their resources in a project of mutual aid in which each member nation would give according to its ability. Further arrangements were made two months later at Sydney, Australia, and later still at London. Technical committees were established. By November, 1950, there had been completed a detailed analysis of the main economic needs and problems of Southeast Asia. Seven carefully planned programs had been prepared, each for a specific area.

These programs were expected to cost about £1,868,000,000. India was to receive £1,379,000,000; Pakistan, £280,000,000; Ceylon, £102,000,000; Borneo and Malaya, £107,000,000. Transport facilities and communications were to be improved. Agriculture was to be further developed. Health, housing, and education were to be aided. Industry, mining, hydro-electric power, and highway building were to be expanded. In 1954 Thailand, Japan, and the Philippines joined the Colombo Plan. Within a few years much work had been done and substantial progress achieved.

In 1965 there were twenty-one nations that were cooperating in the Colombo Plan. The donor nations were the United States, Britain, Canada, Australia, New Zealand, and Japan. The nations receiving aid were Bhutan, Burma, Cambodia, Ceylon, India, Indonesia, Laos, Malaysia, Nepal, Pakistan, the Philippines, South Korea, South Viet Nam, the British protectorate of the Maldive Islands, and Thailand. By 1963 the donor nations had given or lent £13,800,-000,000 for technical training, the building of new factories, hydroelectric plants, and highways.

An earlier White Paper of the British government, wisely conceived and written, had said: "Speed is necessary. In a world racked by schism and confusion it is doubtful whether free men can long afford to leave undeveloped and imprisoned in poverty the human resources of the countries of South and Southeast Asia which could help so greatly not only to restore the world's prosperity, but also to reduce its confusion and enrich the lives of all men everywhere."

The Commonwealth is one of the great bridges that span the gulf between the East and West. The Colombo Plan does much to increase the tensile strength of that bridge. It is an important political, military, and humanitarian fact of the twentieth century.

EUROPE: A NEW TIME OF TROUBLES

In December, 1943, Anthony Eden rose in the house of commons to make his report upon the results of the Teheran Conference. In the course of his speech he said: "More than once before allies have stood together in war and fallen apart in peace. . . . The recurrent threat of war can only be met if there is an international order firmer in strength and unity than any enemy that can seek to challenge it." In June, 1945, following a series of international meetings at Moscow, Cairo, Teheran, Dumbarton Oaks, and Yalta, the Charter of the United Nations was adopted at San Francisco. It was hoped that the world, scarred and armed by experience, would end a long age of predatory exploitation and nationalistic ambitions.

The United Nations Charter contained 111 articles defining the aims of the United Nations and establishing a constitution. In the General Assembly of the United Nations each member state was given one representative and one vote. The Assembly was to meet once a year. Special sessions might be called at any time. Members of the Assembly were to discuss any problems not under consideration by the Security Council. They were to make recommendations to the Council. They were to elect the six nonpermanent members of the Security Council, the members of the Economic and Social Council, and the fifteen members of the International Court of Justice. They were to admit or expel members. In all important decisions of the Assembly a two-thirds majority was necessary.

The Security Council contained eleven members. The United States, the USSR, Great Britain, France, and China held permanent seats; six others were elected for a two-year term by the Assembly. Each of the permanent members possessed the power of vetoing almost any proposed action by the Council, except on procedural questions. The major task of the Security Council was to investigate and discuss international disputes, to seek to prevent war, and to punish aggressor states by economic sanctions and military force.

An Economic and Security Council, consisting of eighteen members selected by the Assembly, was empowered to study and make recommendations about world social and economic conditions, particularly those that might be basic causes of international hostility and conflict. Other important bodies within the organization of the United Nations included the Secretariat, the international civil service of the United Nations, responsible for administration and research; the International Court of Justice; the International Monetary Fund; the Educational, Scientific and Cultural Organization, designed to promote understanding and cooperation among the world's peoples; the World Bank; the Food and Agriculture Organization; the Civil Aviation Organization; and the Atomic Energy Commission, which contained the eleven members of the Security Council.

In later conferences held in 1945 at Potsdam, London, and Moscow it became apparent that the divergent views of the wartime allies were placing the new peace in jeopardy. The London Conference, for example, became deadlocked as Russian diplomats clashed with representatives of the United States, Great Britain, and France upon several issues: the Soviet claims to dominance in the Dardanelles region; the peace treaties with Italy and the disposal of the Italian colonies; the control of the Ruhr Valley; the war crimes trials; the reconstruction of the Eastern European states; the problem of reparations and rehabilitation loans; the control of the atomic bomb secrets; and numerous other questions. In the Security Council of the United Nations considerable strife arose between the representatives of Russia and the spokesmen of the United States and Great Britain. When Iran twice complained about Russian interference in Iranian affairs, Russia tried to block consideration of the controversy by the Security Council. Although defeated in this attempt, the Russian delegates repeatedly thwarted and vetoed proposals and policies they considered inimical to their interests. Between 1945 and 1960 Russia used her veto power one hundred times. The other four permanent members of the Security Council resorted to the veto a total of seven times.

As the international controversies increased in number and gravity, the Soviet Union stood firmly against Great Britain and the United States on many major issues. Successive conferences of foreign ministers resulted in further grave disappointments. The breach widened as differences in national ideologies and interests became clearer. Under the terms of the Potsdam agreement, for instance, Germany had been divided into four administrative zones under the control of Great Britain, the United States, France, and Russia. It soon became clear that the zonal experiment was a failure as Russia and the Western powers clashed and daily disputes multiplied. In September, 1946, Britain and the United States merged their zones and prepared with France to consider plans for setting up a government for Western

Germany. The Russian zone remained isolated from the rest of Germany as the Russians tightened their army and press controls.

In the Far East the Indonesians battled to win freedom from Dutch control. The Chinese Communists surged relentlessly past Mukden and Suchow towards Nanking and the Yangtze valley. The Nationalist government of Chiang Kai-shek seemed unable to stem the Communist advance. In Eastern Europe the Soviet Union proceeded to extend the network of her political and economic power. Beyond the borders of her satellite states, particularly Hungary, Rumania, and Poland, Russian pressure was felt from Iran to Greece and the Mediterranean shores. Early in March, 1948, free Czechoslovakia fell as a result of Communist internal aggression. Finland's freedom of action was definitely limited by the fact of Russian power.

Meanwhile the Western powers moved to check the Russian advance. In 1948 the United States Congress approved the European Recovery Plan (the Marshall Plan). As a result of the Economic Cooperation Act, a decision of "inspired and generous diplomacy," United States aid began almost immediately to move to Europe on a gigantic scale. Sixteen European nations were to participate in sharing the benefits made available by the United States to assist in European reconstruction. It was not surprising that Russia and her satellites spurned American aid and denounced the European Recovery Plan as "imperialism" and "intervention" in the affairs of Europe.

There were numerous signs of hardening resistance to Moscow among the powers of Western Europe. Late in 1948, for instance, Russia increased her attempts to force the Western nations out of Berlin, surrounded by the Soviet zone. Despite the menacing risk of war with Russia, airplanes of the American and British "airlift" supplied food and fuel to Berlin and the Russians finally lifted their blockade. In March, 1948, Britain, France, Belgium, the Netherlands, and Luxembourg concluded a fifty-year military, economic, and political alliance in Brussels. This "Benelux" agreement was unprecedented in the history of Europe. It provided for automatic joint defense and mutual aid against attack in Europe; for consultation in case of attack in colonial areas; for the harmonization of production, standards of living, legal systems, trade practices, and the like. Russia claimed that the Brussels pact was a "plot against the peace of Europe." Others hoped that this regional alliance might be the forerunner of an eventual Continental federation. In January, 1948, Britain's Foreign Secretary Ernest Bevin had said: "The time is ripe for the consolidation of Europe."

Meanwhile the "Benelux" countries of Western Europe negotiated with the United States and Canada for an unprecedented North Atlantic military alliance. Within a few months, the North Atlantic Treaty Organization was formed, based upon a treaty signed by thir-

Section VII

VICTORIA TO ELIZABETH II

Queen Victoria,
A.D. 1887.

News-correspondent's sketch of the siege lines before Sevastopol.

The Allied High Command in the Crimea. From *left* to *right*, Lord Raglan, Omar Pasha, General Pelissier.

William Ewart Gladstone.

Benjamin Disraeli.

Salisbury Cathedral from the Bishop's Garden, a painting by John Constable.

Sir Galahad, a painting by D. G. Rossetti.

Alfred, Lord Tennyson,
a portrait by G. F. Watts.

View over a pottery town, Staffordshire.

Winston Churchill in 1900 after his escape from a Boer prison.

Inspector Rolfe reasoning with Mrs. Pankhurst during a 1914 Suffragist riot.

Submarine E-11 surfacing after a scout—Dardanelles campaign.

Support troops moving up to attack near Ginchy, September 9, 1916.

Lawrence of Arabia,
a portrait by Augustus John.

John Maynard Keynes.

Stanley Baldwin.

Dockers walk out during the General Strike, 1926.

The second Labour Cabinet, 1929. Ramsay MacDonald is at center of the first row, flanked to left and right by Philip Snowden and Arthur Henderson. Sidney Webb is third from the right in the first row.

Gandhi and Followers, 1938.

Winston Churchill as
Prime Minister during
World War II.

Back safe from Dunkirk.

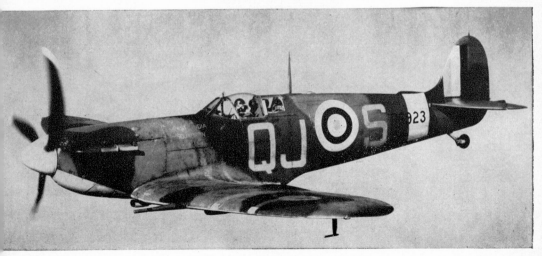

A Spitfire.

Sir William Beveridge.

Clement Attlee.

The Bank of England (left) and the Royal Exchange after an air raid. Below are the same buildings and the area of Threadneedle Street and Cornhill as they are today.

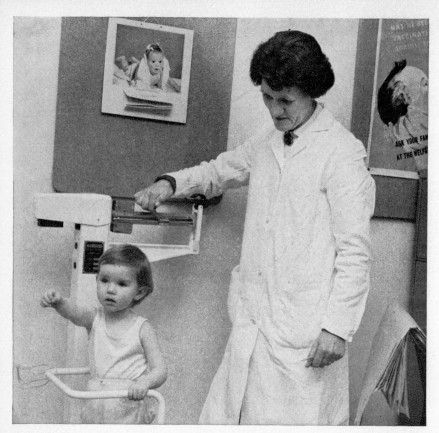

The Burney Street Welfare Center which operates under the National Health Services Act.

Harold Macmillan.

Harold Wilson.

Members of the British Royal Ulster Rifles searching for Indonesian infiltrators in Borneo, 1964.

The coffin of Sir Winston Churchill in Fleet Street, January 30, 1965, being drawn toward St. Paul's Cathedral.

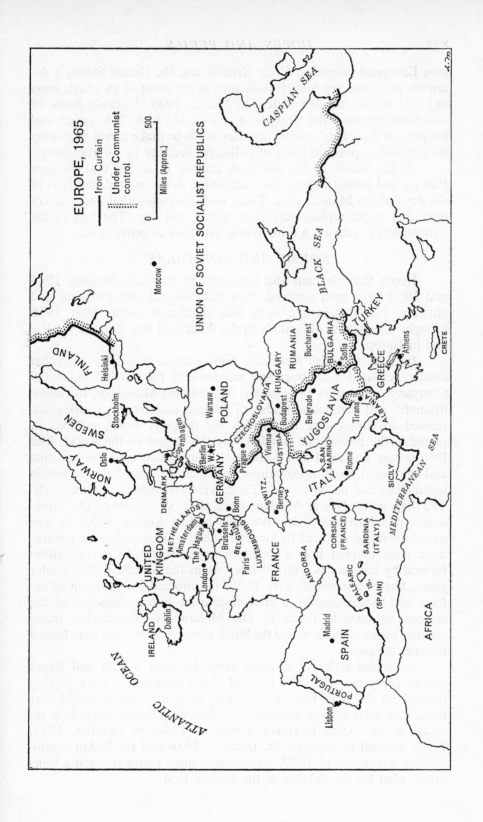

EUROPE, 1965

Iron Curtain
Under Communist control

Miles (Approx.)
0   500

UNION OF SOVIET SOCIALIST REPUBLICS

teen European countries, Great Britain, and the United States, a defensive pact pledging mutual assistance in the event of an attack upon any one of the member states. In March, 1949, Britain's house of commons approved the treaty by a vote of 333 to 6. "The object and purpose of this pact," said Ernest Bevin, "is to make a real beginning on the widest possible basis of collective security in its true sense."

At the middle of the twentieth century it seemed that Western Europe had passed beyond the vacillation, delusion, and paralysis of the days of the Munich pact. There were also signs that peaceful cooperation might replace suspicion, abuse, and war. The task of the nations was to prevent a third World War, not to provoke it.

FORMS AND FORMULAS

Hopes that gleamed and beckoned in the years between 1945 and 1950 were soon dimmed. New facts shaped new problems and answers. For Britain the swift and significant events after 1950 brought unexpected difficulties in the Near and Far East, in Africa, and in Europe.

In 1951 a foolish and futile dispute arose with Iran when that country violated a contract and nationalized the Anglo-Iranian Oil Company's properties in Iran. Dr. Mohammed Musedegh, the melodramatic and venomous leader of flushed and fervent nationalists, refused to compensate the British for property worth millions of pounds—the refinery at Abadan was the largest in the world. The British case was legal and economic. The Iranian case was spiritual and emotional. Long negotiations were fruitless. Iran failed to obtain technicians and no oil flowed. There were no customers, no exports. The dials and valves at Abadan stayed still. An erosion of Dr. Musedegh's popularity inevitably occurred and in August, 1953, he was overthrown and replaced by General Zahedi. The new Iranian government soon entered into a long-term agreement with a consortium formed by companies with oil interests in the Middle East. In later years, Shah Mohammed Riza Pahlevi continued his program of reform and modernization in Iran despite the bitter opposition of the zealous nationalists (such as Dr. Mohammed Musedegh), many wealthy upper-class men, and the Shiah clergy, whose faces were turned towards the past.

A second series of disputes arose between Britain and Egypt during the years when the tides of Arab nationalism were surging throughout the Near East. Immediately after the Second World War there had been several abortive negotiations pointing towards a revision of the Anglo-Egyptian Treaty of 1936. In October, 1951, Egypt decided to abrogate the treaty of 1936 and the Sudan condominium agreement of 1899. At the same time, Egypt rejected a four-power plan for the defense of the Middle East.

Egyptian governments had long insisted upon two things: a political and military union of Egypt and the Sudan and an immediate and complete evacuation from the Suez Canal Base of all British military personnel. Egypt refused to consider these as separate issues. They were, said the Egyptians, parts of the total questions about "the unity of the Nile valley." Britain, on the other hand, said that the British forces could not be pulled abruptly out of the Suez Canal Base when they were holding a point of high strategic value in the defenses of the entire free world against major aggression. Secondly, Britain stated that Egypt would not be given the Sudan without reference to the wishes of the inhabitants.

In July, 1952, King Farouk of Egypt was compelled to abdicate, thus ending a scandalous rule of corruption and greed. A military junta under General Mohammed Neguib came to power and stayed there until Neguib, in turn, was ousted in February, 1954, by the forces of Colonel Gamal Abdel Nasser. Egypt became a republic in June, 1953. Against a background of ugly riots and skirmishes, Anglo-Egyptian talks, so often broken off, were renewed after Farouk was deposed.

In 1953 Britain and Egypt reached an agreement "concerning self-government and self-determination for the Sudan." It was agreed that there was to be: (1) an election of a wholly Sudanese parliament; (2) the Sudanization of the administration and police system and the creation of a Sudan Defence Force; (3) the decision by the inhabitants of the Sudan within three years as to whether they wished to enter into some sort of federation with Egypt or move under British protection or become a completely independent state. In another context in this chapter it was noted that the Sudan became independent in 1956.

In October, 1954, a seven-year Anglo-Egyptian treaty was signed in Cairo providing for the future of the Suez Canal Base. It was agreed that there would be a complete evacuation of British forces from the Suez area by June, 1956. Egypt and Britain would join in maintaining the Base at a high level of efficiency—the British contribution to stores and installation maintenance was to be carried out by civilians and commercial firms. "In the event of an armed attack by an outside power on Egypt or any other country which at the date of signature of the present agreement is a party to the Treaty of Joint Defence between the Arab League states or on Turkey, Egypt will afford to the United Kingdom such facilities as may be necessary in order to place the Base on a war footing and to operate it effectively. . . . In the event of an attack on any of the above-mentioned countries there shall be immediate consultation between the United Kingdom and Egypt."

During these years Britain steadily extended the network of her alliances and obligations. As a part of her contribution to the North Atlantic Treaty Organization Britain agreed in October, 1954, to keep four divisions of troops in Europe, including three armored divisions, plus the Tactical Air Force, provided that the Nine Powers of the London Conference formally admitted Germany and Italy into the North Atlantic Treaty Organization. Emergency air bases in Malta, Cyprus, Aden, Singapore, and Hong Kong were built at a cost of more than $40,000,000. Britain sent about 35,000 men to battle the Communists in Malaya, a force second only to that of the United States to fight the Communists in Korea. Britain kept forces in Austria, Germany, and Trieste, contributed fifteen hundred tactical aircraft to the North Atlantic Treaty Organization, sent equipment to ten NATO countries, made treaty commitments to the defense of Belgium, Denmark, Egypt, France, Greece, Iceland, Iraq, Italy, Jordan, Luxembourg, the Netherlands, Norway, Portugal, Turkey, the United States, and Western Germany. An Anglo-Libyan Treaty of Friendship in July, 1953, provided for common defense and mutual assistance. Libya made military facilities available to British troops and the United Kingdom furnished financial aid to Libya.

There were, of course, other alliance arrangements between certain Commonwealth countries and other nations. For instance, in April, 1954, Pakistan and Turkey concluded a treaty of friendship. Early in 1955 Turkey and Iraq made a five-year treaty of mutual defense to help strengthen the shield of stability and security in the Middle East. This treaty bound both countries to resist aggression whether from within or without the region. Syria and Egypt naturally objected to an arrangement which seemed to drive a wedge into the Arab League. Israel, for obvious reasons, was alarmed to see Turkey signing a treaty of alliance with a state of the Arab League, a vehement and bitter foe of Israel. Britain later entered into the Turkish-Iraqi pact and in the Bagdad agreement of March, 1955, extended commitments were made by Britain to Iraq. Meanwhile Britain was also extending her special responsibilities to Kuwait and other states on the Persian Gulf. Meanwhile, too, Pakistan and the United States, despite objections from India's Prime Minister Nehru, concluded a Mutual Defense Assistance Agreement which provided that the United States would give military equipment and training assistance to Pakistan. Pakistan did not provide military bases for the United States; this was not a military alliance.

These examples of treaty arrangements indicate one aspect of the pace and breadth of Britain's role in the complicated and dangerous world of the second half of the twentieth century. "Let us not chop logic," said Sir Anthony Eden in 1954, "let us face realities." If there is to be coexistence between Russia and the West there has to be balance of power.

Of particular importance to Great Britain, of course, is the protection of her long and vulnerable communication lines. That is one reason why the whole Near and Middle Eastern areas have long been an object of British concern. The lands of the Arab League—Egypt, Iraq, Jordan, Libya, Lebanon, Saudi Arabia, Syria, and Yemen— are strategically the most important land bridge of the world, linking three continents, providing the shortest air and sea traffic routes linking Europe and Asia, containing 40 per cent of the world's known reserves of oil. Even though the rise of nuclear weapons makes necessary the re-thinking of all military strategy, the Near and Middle East still remain vital defense areas. One of the substantial deterrents to hydrogen bomb attack is of course the known probability that counterattacks will be launched from many angles and from widely dispersed bases. Forewarned is forearmed.

Because the Near and Middle East are such important areas, the major powers of the West, particularly the British, view with dark concern the malevolent tension and the disputes between the Arab states and the land of Israel. In 1950 the United Kingdom, the United States, and France declared that they would take action both within and without the United Nations to prevent either the Arab countries or Israel violating the existing frontiers on the armistice lines resulting from the Palestine conflict of 1948–1949. Later, however, the raids continued; the sniper's bullet hummed. There was no agreement on the problem of the poverty-stricken and desperate refugees, the frontier question, the riddle of the Jordan waters. Border raids continued; mutual accusations and recriminations multiplied. Despite the censures of the United Nations Egypt defiantly barred the use of the Suez Canal to ships carrying cargoes to Israel. In 1956 President Nasser of Egypt declared that Israel must be destroyed.

In July, 1956, a critical situation arose in a dramatic dispute about the Suez Canal. Egypt's President Nasser suddenly seized the famous waterway from the Suez Maritime Canal Company, a private stock company that had controlled the canal for many decades. President Nasser then nationalized the canal, insisting that no international agreements could be created or maintained if they limited Egypt's sovereignty. Nasser also wanted to collect the tolls of Suez— amounting to about $45,000,000 annually—and put them in Egypt's treasury. Several nations, including Great Britain, the United States, and France, asserted that the international control of the canal must be continued, particularly since President Nasser had not in the past been precise in keeping his pledges. By seizing the Suez Canal President Nasser broke agreements of the Suez Canal Convention of 1888 by which the Suez Canal Company was to have been liquidated in 1968. Egypt was to have obtained the Canal then, not before. Moreover, it had never been contemplated that Egypt would get the canal unconditionally, even in 1968.

Was a single Arab nation under the leadership of one man to

control a waterway of such international importance? The Western nations drew together in defense of common interests placed in jeopardy. Numerous conferences put forward proposals for international supervision. Heavy pressures, including the threat of military force and the silent throttling power of economic strength, were used to persuade Egypt to accept international control of the Suez. On the other hand, Egypt's challenge roused the Arab world against the West.

In October, 1956, discussions were held in New York by the Foreign Ministers of Britain, France, and Egypt, in the presence of Dag Hammarskjöld, Secretary-General of the United Nations. In the Security Council, the Soviet Union vetoed a proposal that sought to make effective several proposals agreed upon by the Foreign Ministers. As the security and freedom of shipping through the Suez Canal was in growing danger, the situation became more explosive. Jordan complained to the Security Council about the border raids of Israel. Israel, for her part, said the sorties were retaliatory. She had long complained about Egyptian "fedayeen" (commando) raids in the Gaza Strip region. Egypt, despite several rulings by the United Nations, refused to permit Israel's ships to use the Suez Canal. Egypt, Syria, and Jordan placed their armed forces under a unified command. Israel mobilized, attacked Egypt on October 29, and rapidly advanced halfway to the Suez Canal.

Britain and France requested the belligerents to stop fighting and permit an Anglo-French force to occupy temporarily key spots at Port Said, Ismailia, and Suez. Egypt refused. Britain and France at once attacked Egypt and sent paratroops and seaborne forces into the Port Said area on November 5 and 6.

Meanwhile, Britain, France, and the United States had brought the matter before the Security Council. Resolutions of the Soviet Union and the United States called upon Israel to withdraw her forces immediately and upon all United Nations members to refrain from the use of force or the threat of force in the area. Both resolutions were vetoed by Britain and France on the ground that they failed to take full account of all aspects of the situation. Egypt filed a formal complaint of "aggression" by Britain and France. The Assembly of the United Nations called for an unconditional cease-fire and withdrawal behind armistice lines. A United Nations Emergency Force, proposed by Canada, was created to maintain the uneasy peace after the cease-fire was accepted by Britain, France, Israel, and Egypt. By the end of December Britain and France had withdrawn their forces. Israeli forces, which had occupied all of the Sinai peninsula, were withdrawn by March, 1957. The Suez Canal, blocked by Egypt, was cleared by April.

John Foster Dulles, the American Secretary of State, strongly opposed and condemned the British and French invasion of the Suez Canal area. On the other hand, Britain's Sir Anthony Eden felt that swift action had been necessary. Egypt had said that Israel must be destroyed. Egypt and Syria had unified their military command. Large supplies of military aid were being sent by the Soviet Union to several Middle Eastern lands. When Israel had invaded Sinai the Suez Canal traffic flow was endangered. It seemed possible that a great conflagration might sweep through all of the Middle East if Britain and France did not act rapidly.

Robert Menzies, Prime Minister of Australia and an "unrepentant supporter" of Sir Anthony Eden, called the Suez Canal trouble a "disagreeable affair." It certainly damaged Anglo-American relations at a critical time when the Russians were brutally crushing a revolt in Hungary. Meanwhile Egypt's President Gamal Abdel Nasser survived. Egypt took over the Suez Canal. Nasser continued to dream of a Pan-Arab nation with himself as its leader. His words continued to disturb the minds and rouse the hearts of Arab nationalists throughout the Middle East. Agitators followed him. Plots increased. His prestige rose steadily in the Arab world.

Early in 1958 Egypt's President Nasser created the United Arab Republic consisting of Egypt and Syria, later joined by the little state of Yemen at the southwest corner of the Arabian peninsula. Nasser hoped that this new union might be the beginning of a great Pan-Arab state. Among those opposed to Nasser's dreams and plans were King Hussein of Jordan, King Saud of Saudi Arabia, and King Faisal of Iraq.

No peace or order came to the Near East. On May 13, 1958, Lebanon accused the United Arab Republic of "massive interference" in Lebanese internal affairs. A United Nations observer group was sent to Lebanon. On July 14, the Iraqi government was overthrown by a military *coup d'état*. The United States, in response to an appeal from Lebanon, sent a force to protect that unhappy country. On July 16, King Hussein of Jordan asked Britain to send soldiers to guard his country against attack by the United Arab Republic. When King Hussein sent his appeal to Britain, Syrian forces were already moving towards the borders of Jordan. On July 17 British soldiers were flown to defend Jordan, and on the same day formal complaints were made to the United Nations about the interference of the United Arab Republic. Russia vetoed any action by the Security Council. On August 8, 1958, an emergency session of the General Assembly called upon all members of the Arab League to refrain from actions calculated to change the system of government in any of their member states. The Assembly stressed the principles and purposes of the Charter of the United Nations in relation to Lebanon and Jordan and began to make arrangements for the withdrawal of foreign troops. Slowly the American and British forces were pulled out of Lebanon and Jordan.

The sudden, bloody revolution of July, 1958, in Iraq brought death to King Faisal and his prime minister. The army officers who had led the revolt gave the presidency of the new republic to General Abdel Karem Kassem. General Kassem, an erratic and incompetent man, soon became a dictator. He withdrew from the Bagdad Pact, a treaty organization formed by Britain, Turkey, Iran, Iraq, and Pakistan for mutual protection against a possible attack by Russia. After Iraq's withdrawal the remaining Bagdad Pact countries formed the Central Treaty Organization (CENTRO). Meanwhile General Kassem rapidly became embroiled with most leaders of other Arab states. His quarrel with Egypt's President Nasser was particularly violent and dramatic.

In February, 1963, General Kassem was deposed and killed by a *coup d'état*. The new president of Iraq, chosen by young officers and intellectuals, was Colonel Abdel Salem Arif, a man who declared himself an admirer of President Nasser and dedicated to the cause of Pan-Arab unity.

Meanwhile there were upheavals in the United Arab Republic. In September, 1961, Syria angrily declared that its union with Egypt was ended. What was left of the United Arab Republic consisted of Egypt and the tiny state of Yemen. A year later a civil war in Yemen brought death and chaos. Saif al-Badr, the ruler of Yemen, was overthrown and replaced by General Abdullah al-Salal who was called the President of the Yemen Arab Republic. King Hussein of Jordan and Crown Prince Faisal of Saudi Arabia feared the spread of revolution and championed the cause of Saif al-Badr. President Nasser, on the other hand, sent about 18,000 troops to support General Abdullah al-Salal, and by 1965 had increased the number to about 40,000. For a time, Yemen's civil war threatened to engulf the whole Middle East. After Saif al-Badr's forces were driven back, he escaped to Saudi Arabia. In October, 1964, a truce and cease-fire agreement between the royalists and republicans was reached. In January, 1965, it collapsed. The war went on. Plots and counterplots multiplied.

In March, 1963, the anti-Nasser government of Syria was overthrown. The Ba'ath party, stressing the importance of the unity of all Arabs, seized and held power. The three key states of Egypt, Syria, and Iraq were now, for a time, on friendly terms. A new United Arab Republic was formed, a loose political and military alliance. Soon, however, the Syrians and Egyptians began to quarrel. On the other hand, President Nasser, who had long fomented revolt in Jordan, became friendly with Jordan's King Hussein.

Israel stood aloof and hostile, remembering that the Arab states were agreed upon the necessity of eliminating Israel and regaining the former Arab property in Palestine. In January, 1964, leaders of the thirteen Arab League states met in Cairo and agreed upon measures designed to prevent Israel from diverting waters from the Jordan River to irrigate the Negev desert. In 1964 and 1965 there were several clashes between the soldiers of Syria and Israel in the area north of the Sea of Galilee.

Meanwhile there were many doubts, suspicions, and rivalries among the Arab states. There were also some significant changes in governments. For instance, on November 2, 1964, King Saud of Saudi Arabia was deposed. He was succeeded by the 58-year-old Crown Prince Faisal, a man determined to use the oil royalties to modernize Saudi Arabia.

In the vast spaces of Africa there were other dreams and problems. In that great continent there swirled the floods of nationalism, anticolonialism, ignorance, fear, and hope. The old hunger of poverty was often matched by the new hunger for power.

When Portugal refused to grant independence to her "province" of Angola, the result was rebellion, mercilessly crushed by the Portuguese under their dictator Antonio de Oliveira Salazar. When Spanish and French Morocco obtained independence in 1956, there were plots and mutterings but no revolution. When Belgium suddenly gave independence to the people of the Congo early in 1960, the whole country was suddenly filled with anarchy, violence, and terror. The Belgians had taken no steps to prepare the Congolese tribesmen for self-government. As soon as the Belgian officers had relinquished command, the Congolese soldiers did as they pleased, looting and killing at will. There are about two hundred tribes in the Congo, many of them hostile to one another. Upon such a basis it is not easy to build a unified and civilized state. The Congo has few competent leaders, few doctors and lawyers or other professional men, few skilled workers.

Patrice Lumumba, the eccentric premier of the Congo, asked the United Nations to send forces to bring peace and stability. It was decided that the United Nations would send a police force but no troops would come from any of the big nations that might be accused of being "colonial" powers. Most of the soldiers came from African or Asian states (India, Pakistan, Ghana, Malaya, Nigeria) and from Sweden and Ireland. It was unfortunate that the police force of the United Nations did not have authority to take full control in the Congo.

Meanwhile Patrice Lumumba, a man not to be trusted, began to intrigue with Soviet Russia. Congo's President Joseph Kasavubu dismissed the excited and fumbling Lumumba and Lumumba's foes murdered him in January, 1961.

President Kasavubu and Cyrille Adoula, the new premier, hoped to hold the Congo together. On the other hand, the erratic and crafty Moise Tshombe, leader of Katanga province, insisted that

Katanga should be independent. Katanga seceded from the Congo in July, 1960. About 40,000 Europeans and 1,750,000 Congolese lived in Katanga province. In the years before the Congo became independent Katanga supplied about 65 per cent of the Congo's exports, including copper, cobalt, and uranium. About 60 per cent of the income of the Belgian Congo came from Katanga.

In these days of fear and confusion, Leopoldville and Elisabethville, the capital of Katanga province, became cities of terror. The power of the central government rapidly declined. Many white people fled from the country.

In September, 1961, Dag Hammarskjöld, Secretary-General of the United Nations, tried to bring Moise Tshombe back under the authority of the central government of the Congo. In the midst of negotiations, Hammarskjöld was killed in a plane crash in Northern Rhodesia.

The Security Council directed Tshombe to dismiss the 500 European officers leading the 11,600 soldiers of the Katanga army. When Tshombe resisted, he was defeated and compelled to agree that Katanga would not secede from the Congo. In June, 1963, the parliament at Leopoldville forced Moise Tshombe out of his position of leadership in Katanga. In June, 1964, Cyrille Adoula resigned as premier in the central government and Moise Tshombe succeeded him. In November, 1964, rebel tribesmen slaughtered several white people. They continued to defy the weak central government. Poverty, ignorance, fear, and disunity stand athwart the paths that lead to freedom in the Congo.

More than 2,000 miles from the Congo Basin lies Algeria, until recently a colony of France. There a bitter and bloody war divided and scarred the land in the early 1960's. When France's President de Gaulle decided to grant independence to Algeria, he was opposed by many Frenchmen, some of them living in Algeria and fearful that they might lose their property and perhaps their lives if the Moslem Algerians obtained control of the country. Many other Frenchmen stood against President de Gaulle because they did not like to see another part of France's empire slip away. Several of the men who opposed the granting of independence to Algeria formed a secret army organization to carry out a campaign of terror. Plastic bombs exploded and bullets whined in the summer sun. Some units of the French army in Algeria revolted. Plots were made to murder President de Gaulle. At last, in 1962, Algeria became independent. The plotters and rebels lost their cause. Under a new leader, Mohammed Ben Bella, the people of Algeria hoped that a respite from battles and bloodshed had come at last.

No prospects of peace and stability appeared in the Near East. Shrewd and informed observers saw new plots and rivalries. In the

Far East, too, the skies were confused and dark. Early in 1949 the Nationalist government of China was finally engulfed by a great wave of revolution. Chiang Kai-shek, the successor of Sun Yat-sen, had ruled China for twenty-five years. His Kuomintang party had slowly become a body of conservatism and reaction opposed to social change. Now it had fallen. The victorious Chinese Communists, with their doctrines of a "New Democracy," founded a Central People's Government with its capital at Peking. "Power," said the Communist leader Mao Tse-tung, "comes out of the end of a gun." Chiang Kai-shek and the surviving Nationalists fled to Formosa (Taiwan).

In January, 1950, the British decided that the Nationalist government had ceased to be the effective ruler of the Chinese mainland. Therefore Britain withdrew its recognition of the Nationalists and recognized instead the Central People's Government at Peking. To the British the recognition of Communist China was a policy of convenience, an acceptance of realities. The United States, on the other hand, steadily refused to recognize the People's Republic of Mao Tse-tung. Britain and the United States pursued wholly divergent policies with respect to China.

On June 25, 1950, the Republic of Korea was violently attacked by the Communist government of North Korea. Within twenty-four hours, mainly as a result of the swift action of President Harry S. Truman of the United States, the Security Council of the United Nations branded the attack as a breach of the peace and ordered North Korea to withdraw to the boundary line of the 38th parallel. It called upon the member states of the United Nations to furnish assistance to the Republic of Korea. Fifty-two nations supported the Security Council decision. British land, sea, and air forces, numbering about 20,000 men, were engaged in the Korean campaign.

Thus began the long and costly "police action" in Korea, that unhappy peninsula where 30,000,000 people once lived in peace. Communist China intervened by sending equipment and "volunteers" to aid North Korea and was condemned by the United Nations as an "aggressor nation." The battle lines swayed back and forth. Only in late July, 1953, was an armistice signed in Korea. A bloodless stalemate replaced a bloody one.

During these tense years the relations between the United States and Communist China became steadily more strained. The United States recognized the Nationalist government and protected Formosa. Across the eighty miles of the Formosa Strait, patrolled by the U.S. Seventh Fleet, stretched the 3,800,000 square miles of continental China, the menacing strength of Mao Tse-tung. In February, 1955, the Chinese Nationalists evacuated the off-shore island of Tachen but stayed upon Quemoy and the Matsus. It was not clear whether the United States would aid the Formosan Nationalists in defending these off-shore areas. At the Geneva Conference of July, 1955, Premier Nikolai Bulganin of Russia said: "The Formosan question has become a dangerous hotbed of complication in the Far East." With that statement, all could agree.

Many states held sharply differing views about Communist China's desire to be admitted to the United Nations. In the United Nations the number of states that supported admission of China sharply increased, particularly among the new nations of Africa and Asia.

Mao Tse-tung and Chou En-lai, the able and ruthless leaders of Communist China, believed in the Marxist-Leninist theory that a struggle between capitalist and Communist states was inevitable. The leaders of the Soviet Union, in contrast, approved of the armed truce called "peaceful co-existence." For these and other reasons, a loud and bitter quarrel broke out between Russia and China, the world's two giant Communist nations.

The promise of China's "great leap forward" in industry and commerce soon faded. There were great failures and dislocations produced by incompetence, poor planning, and misfortunes. In the midst of China's economic plight, the Soviet Union called back to Russia thousands of technicians that Russia had sent earlier to help the Chinese. Peking was not pleased.

Meanwhile, the tentacles of communism were stretching forward elsewhere in the East. The agents and disciples of communism were active and dangerous. By guns and plots and pamphlets the Communists pushed ahead. Earlier in this chapter it was remarked that China extended its sprawling empire by conquering Tibet in 1950. Early in 1954 the Communist Vietminh rebels in northern Indo-China, powerful and disciplined, defeated the Viet Nam and French forces in the south. In July, 1954, an armistice was signed in Geneva by which the Indo-China state of Viet Nam was partitioned near the 17th parallel. North of that line the Communists remained in control. South Viet Nam went to Bao Dai's French-backed government. Laos and Cambodia stayed as they were, nominally independent and sovereign states. The truce terms were to be supervised by India, Canada, and Poland.

Soon conflict came again. The little state of Laos, bordering on the four non-Communist countries of Cambodia, Burma, Thailand, and South Viet Nam, was thrown into confusion and civil war as the Communists sought to seize control. In July, 1962, 14 nations signed an agreement at Geneva establishing Laotian neutrality. Meanwhile, too, the Communist Viet Cong forces in Viet Nam continued a jungle warfare against the Viet Nam government in Saigon. They raided, plundered, burned, and killed. Despite military aid and advice from the United States the costly war continued.

Several governments rose and fell in Saigon. Viet Cong guerrillas, relentless and well trained, blew up South Viet Nam barracks, hurled bombs, struck without warning at army camps and villages. In August, 1964, navy vessels of the United States were attacked in the Gulf of Tonkin. Early in 1965 airplanes of the United States and South Viet Nam made several raids on North Viet Nam in reprisal for Viet Cong activities in South Viet Nam. Communist China denounced these raids as acts of aggression. For many months the situation in Viet Nam remained complex and dangerous. No man could tell what might happen if the great powers entered the conflict.

Several years before the struggles in Laos and Viet Nam an attempt had been made to establish security arrangements that would prevent or limit conflict in the East. In September, 1954, Australia, Britain, France, New Zealand, Pakistan, the Philippines, Thailand, and the United States signed the Manila Treaty which brought into being the South East Asia Treaty Organization as a protective shield against aggression. Each nation signing the pact agreed to "act to meet the common danger in accordance with its constitutional principles" in the event of an attack anywhere in the Treaty area—an area from which Formosa and Korea were carefully excluded. The Manila Treaty also obliged the partners to "consult immediately in order to agree on the measures which should be taken for the common defense" in the event of a threat to one of the signatories by subversion or infiltration. In February, 1955, the first meeting of the Council of SEATO was held in Bangkok.

Neither Burma, Ceylon, India, nor Indonesia signed the pact. Prime Minister Nehru of India was sharply hostile to the arrangements, asserting that they were in conflict with the basic principles of India's foreign policy. Nehru also stated that he could not consider the Manila Treaty either stabilizing or defensive. Obviously the main weakness of the rather shadowy and unsubstantial pact was that it did not include the major Asian nations.

It was also a fact that the undertakings and commitments of the SEATO states were limited. There were no firm guarantees in a fluid situation. The SEATO states had only small forces at hand to support any decisions that called for swift action. Even among the nations that had signed the pact, particularly Britain and France, there was no enthusiasm. In many respects, SEATO was more a diplomatic than a military alliance. When the Communists threatened Laos in 1962, SEATO reacted with strongly worded statements, nothing more.

In many Eastern lands there was the pervasive feeling that an alliance with the West was undesirable. It was felt that the imperialism and colonialism of the West might in fact be revived by such agreements as those reached at Manila. It was said that SEATO might increase hostile action by Communist China and help to lead to a final collision which all feared; that both East and West should avoid taking steps which might lead by design or accident to war; that the results of truculence might be as unhappy as those of appeasement.

A spectacular conference on Asian and African affairs was held at Bandung in April, 1955. Thirty Asian and African nations were represented at the Bandung assembly. Chou En-lai of China proclaimed the philosophy and policy of the People's Republic, of militant communism. Sir John Kotewala of Ceylon spoke for the cause of non-Communist democracy and the dignity of all men. Here, as at many other times and places, the issues that divide so many men were clearly and strongly stated.

During the years since the Bandung Conference and the signing of the Manila Treaty, the Communists have continued to struggle with the democracies for the bodies and minds of many peoples. What paths and policies will the wakening lands of Asia and Africa choose to follow? A watchful world awaits an answer.

THE DIPLOMACY OF SURVIVAL

After 1950 the plans to build an integrated collective defense system for Europe were steadily extended. Russia was stopped from carrying her autocracy and her revolution across the miles to the North Sea. After Greece and Turkey were admitted in 1951 to the North Atlantic Treaty Organization, twelve powers stood together as allies. Under the provisions of the bold and imaginative Marshall Plan billions of dollars flowed from the United States to strengthen the nerves and sinews of the states and peoples who ranged themselves among the allies of the West.

In Europe, as in Asia, a carping and jibing war of nerves continued between the USSR and the West. These were the years of the barren "cold war," a world condition that was neither stability nor strife. Heads of states, foreign ministers, and deputy foreign ministers met in frequent, prolonged, and sometimes futile discussions in Paris, London, and Washington to debate and study a lengthening roll of problems and controversies. The balance of peace was delicate and precarious. In these days, the British course was one of caution; all around lay minefields. Meanwhile the Communist pressure was ruthless and unrelenting on every front. The Kremlin preached peace and at the same time promoted disturbance and war as a part of a calculated long-range policy.

What was to be the future of Germany? How and under what conditions was that state to be united again? Eastern Germany was controlled by the Communists. West Germany, called the German Federal Republic, had limited sovereignty under the Bonn Convention of May, 1952, signed by the United States, Great Britain, France, and West Germany. At a four-power conference in 1952 Russia made it clear that she wanted a united Germany forbidden to join any military alliances, an unreal neutral defenseless against Communist armies. The Western powers insisted that they must have unambiguous assurances that a new united Germany would have full sovereign rights and would be "free" in a Western sense, not in a Russian. All discussions then were futile.

In March, 1953, Josef Stalin died and his successors wrangled and wrestled over his mantle. In December, Lavrenti Beria, the Georgian Chief of the Soviet Secret Police, was executed. For a time, Georgi M. Malenkov, President of the Soviet Council of Ministers, seemed to emerge as the Russian leader. In February, 1955, after another upheaval in the Kremlin, Malenkov resigned and the control of Soviet policy appeared to pass into the hands of Premier Nikolai Bulganin, Communist party Secretary Nikita Khrushchev, and Foreign Minister Vyacheslav Molotov.

Two months after the death of Stalin, Winston Churchill proposed a conference between the leaders of the USSR and the Western powers. He repeated the proposal in October, 1953. Soviet replies were chilly and discouraging. The early months of 1954 gave no hope that any high-level conference would bring either profit or pleasure. Russia was quite unaccommodating. Molotov had nothing new to say.

In the fall of 1954, after the collapse of a proposed European Defence Community Plan, formal agreements were signed at the Nine Power Conference at London and Paris by Belgium, Britain, France, Italy, Luxembourg, the Netherlands, and West Germany. These agreements stated that almost all of the special armed forces in Europe were to be under a Supreme Allied Commander. No country was permitted to take independent action or move its forces operationally within the system of his command. At the end of each year there was to be a ministerial review by all NATO members of the size and scope of all national defense efforts and an examination of each country's proposed allocation and use of its national resources for defense. A maximum level was laid down for the armed forces which each member was to contribute; these were ceilings, not commitments. Elaborate control arrangements were to apply to all countries in Europe. The London and Paris agreements were designed to assure that all national forces in the area of the allied command in Europe could be welded into one organization capable of operating as an effective fighting unit.

It was also agreed that the occupation of the Federal Republic of West Germany was to be ended. The German Federal Republic and Italy were to join the Western European Union by acceding to the Brussels Treaty. The German Federal Republic was to join NATO and to contribute twelve divisions to the defense of Europe. She was not to manufacture certain types of weapons. In this way Western Germany assumed once more the functions of a sovereign state and took full membership in the Western European Union and the North Atlantic Treaty Organization.

It was inevitable that the USSR should have made many attempts to undermine NATO—an organization denounced by the Russians as "an aggressive military alliance." In spite of many Russian threats and pressures the agreements reached at the Nine Power Conference in 1954 were ratified. The Western nations had taken a further step towards the building of a system of joint defense. It was hoped that Russia would now be convinced that a swift attack could not succeed before a counterattack would be effective. "Western unity has been massively reinforced," said Anthony Eden to the British house of commons. In November, 1954, Winston Churchill remarked that "we might even find ourselves in a few years moving along a broad, smooth causeway of peace and plenty, instead of roaming and peering around the rim of hell."

In July, 1955, the meeting "at the summit" first proposed by Winston Churchill was held at Geneva. To a six-day conference came President Dwight D. Eisenhower of the United States, Prime Minister Anthony Eden of Great Britain, and Premier Edgar Faure of France. Russia was represented by Premier Nikolai Bulganin, Nikita S. Khrushchev, Vyacheslav Molotov, and Georgi Z. Zhukov.

The Russians again asserted that the "main obstacle" to German unification was the integration of Western Germany into the Western alliance system. It was clear that the Russians wanted to see NATO abolished and the rearming of Germany prevented. The discussions at Geneva showed that the problems of European security and German unification were not capable of swift and easy solution. They were menacing questions, signs of the strange and sinister climate in which all men lived. And yet it was clear that the statesmen who came to Geneva did want peace. The atmosphere was cordial although on some issues the hearts were cold. The watching world, so sensitive to intangible forces, felt cause for careful hope. Meanwhile, in a "new epoch of trust and truth," the successors of Stalin tried to blacken his name. Upon scores of occasions, the Russian leaders also insisted that "a new order" had indeed dawned and chilly diplomacy was usually replaced by surface smiles. The frequent informality of Dmitri Shepilov, Russia's new Foreign Minister in 1956, was in happy contrast to the icy Molotov. Changes in immediate tactics and strategy did not mean that the long-range plans and purposes of the Soviet Union had been laid aside.

In these tense and hostile years the makers of British policy decided to end their heavy reliance on manned aircraft for the defense of the nation. They began instead to depend to an increasing extent upon nuclear weapons and guided missiles. Meanwhile, British naval forces were reorganized and much emphasis was placed upon equipment and skill in anti-submarine warfare. The government also reduced the total of British soldiers stationed outside of Britain and established a mobile reserve force from which highly trained troops could be sent by air to handle military problems anywhere in the world.

Important and difficult questions arose in what Prime Minister Macmillan called the "special relationship" between the United States and Great Britain. For instance, the United States planned to develop the "Skybolt," a forty-foot, two-stage solid fuel weapon equipped with a nuclear warhead and designed to ride under a bomber's wing. This weapon promised to be superior to Britain's "Blue Streak," and the United States government said that the British might have the new "Skybolt" if they paid the production costs of the missiles they obtained. Britain therefore abandoned her "Blue Streak" and put her hopes in "Skybolt." But the "Skybolt" proved to be costly. There were several failures. Production lagged behind schedule. Meanwhile the United States was producing a new intercontinental ballistic missile—the silo-protected "Minuteman"—and the need for "Skybolt" declined. Therefore the United States decided that work on "Skybolt" would be stopped. The British were naturally displeased.

In December, 1962, President John F. Kennedy of the United States and Prime Minister Macmillan met in Nassau. The United States offered to sell Britain another deterrent, the special proved "Polaris" second-strike weapon, for her nuclear submarines. In an attempt to meet Europe's desire for a greater voice in nuclear strategy the United States proposed the creation of an eight-nation NATO fleet of twenty-five ships armed with two hundred Polaris missiles and manned by mixed crews from the participating navies. The West German government supported the American proposal. Norway, Belgium, and Denmark opposed it. France vigorously insisted that she must keep her independence and denounced the giving of West Germany a share in nuclear weapons through membership in the projected force.

In November, 1964, President Lyndon B. Johnson of the United States won a landslide victory in the Presidential election. In December, he met in Washington with Prime Minister Harold Wilson of Britain. Britain did not approve of the American plan for a multi-national manning of twenty-five Polaris surface vessels and suggested instead a NATO force in which ten or twelve surface ships manned by international crews would be only one element in a considerably broadened force, including most of Britain's long-range V-bombers and a multi-national component made up by the non-nuclear nations.

When the thirty-fourth session of the NATO ministerial Council was held in December, 1964, there was considerable danger that NATO unity might be splintered. Although the United States ceased to press for the acceptance of its plan for the mixed-manning of a Polaris-armed fleet, there still were difficulties. There was no doubt that the time was at hand for a revision of NATO policy regarding the management, collective or otherwise, of its nuclear resources. About what that revision should be or how it was to be achieved there was no agreement.

There were other problems. For several years France's President de Gaulle had not approved Britain's "special relationship" with the United States. Less than a month before France had brought the Common Market negotiations to an end, President Kennedy had made the Polaris missile available to Great Britain but had not offered to share any of the nuclear secrets of the United States with France. President de Gaulle was displeased. France, he said, would soon have her own nuclear striking force. In June, 1963, France withdrew her fleet from the command of NATO. "France," asserted de Gaulle, "intends to remain its own master."

The intransigent and sensitive President Charles de Gaulle, conscious always of the past glories of France, was convinced that he could lead his country to a new era of greatness. He looked forward to the day when France would be the leader of a third force of nations not allied with or dependent upon either the United States or Russia. This was his hope, this his dream. After France's release from her Algerian difficulties, President de Gaulle speeded his pace, increased his pressures, and challenged more sharply those at home and abroad who disagreed with his policies.

As the policy gap widened between the United States and France, President de Gaulle took another step. In April, 1963, he declared that the investments of the United States in France had become excessive and demanded that those investments should be curtailed. France also stressed her independence by declining to share the expenses incurred by the United Nations in the Congo and the Middle East. Russia also refused to pay.

President Charles de Gaulle wanted a nuclear force of bombers and atom-powered submarines, both armed with nuclear missiles. In October, 1963, the French government announced that the cherished symbol of independence had been obtained. An undisclosed number of French planes were armed with forty-kiloton bombs. France had become the world's fourth nuclear power.

It was clear that the challenging decisions and achievements of President de Gaulle were progressively loosening the ties with NATO and with the United States and Britain. It was also clear that the words and deeds of France had their influence upon other nations.

In the semi-annual meeting of the NATO Council in Ottawa in May, 1963, several member states declared that they, too, wanted to have their own nuclear defenses which they alone would control.

The challenge which President de Gaulle made to NATO, especially to the United States and Great Britain, was not supported by West Germany. A Franco-German treaty of friendship was signed, but it had few tangible results. Chancellor Konrad Adenauer wished to strengthen NATO and President Charles de Gaulle did not. In October, 1963, the austere and paternalistic Dr. Adenauer retired. He was eighty-seven years old and had been Chancellor of the Federal German Republic for fourteen years. Dr. Adenauer was succeeded by the vigorous sixty-six-year-old Dr. Ludwig Erhard, the Christian Democratic party's Economic Minister who had been the outstanding architect of West Germany's postwar prosperity. Chancellor Erhard supported NATO and shared Konrad Adenauer's distrust of President de Gaulle's ambitions.

Several unhappy incidents and threatening crises darkened the international scene. In May, 1960, an American plane flew about 1400 miles on an intelligence mission into Russia before it was downed and the pilot captured. This event occurred eighteen days before Russia's Premier Khrushchev was scheduled to meet at a summit conference in Paris with President Dwight D. Eisenhower of the United States, President Charles de Gaulle of France, and Prime Minister Harold Macmillan of Britain. At Paris Premier Khrushchev made a truculent and insulting speech attacking the United States, recalled an invitation to President Eisenhower to visit Moscow, broke up the conference, and went home. Britain's Harold Macmillan later wrote to Khrushchev: "I simply do not understand what your purpose is." In October, 1960, Premier Khrushchev astounded and alarmed members of the United Nations Assembly by making a violent speech and angrily pounding his shoe upon a desk. John F. Kennedy, elected President of the United States in November, 1960, met and talked with Premier Khrushchev at Vienna late in 1961. The atmosphere was one of doubt and distrust and President Kennedy said that the conversation was "sombre." The sense of urgency and deep concern increased.

Meanwhile the nations of the world were spending about $120,-000,000,000 annually for military purposes. Britain, for her part, had built a powerful nuclear striking force. A set of military bases spanned the globe and mobile integrated task forces, mentioned earlier, were prepared to respond swiftly to danger signals. Britain placed increasing stress upon these mobile, hard-hitting units. At the same time, she reduced her conventional forces and committed about 85 per cent of her naval strength and about 50 per cent of her air power to NATO.

Again and again controversies arose between Russia and the Western world about the divided city of Berlin. The West asserted that troops of the United States, Britain, and France must remain in Berlin to guard against hostile attack or subversion. They also insisted upon the free use of the access roads and air corridors to and from Berlin. Thirdly, they declared that West Berlin must have political and economic freedom. These basic demands, said the statesmen of the West, were not negotiable. The Russians, on the other hand, wanted the Western states to recognize the government of East Germany. Then the East Germans would control the access routes to Berlin. Besides, the East German government would not be bound to adhere to the earlier agreements signed by Russia with the United States, Britain, and France. Premier Khrushchev frequently said that he would sign a separate treaty with East Germany and hand control over to Walter Ulbricht, the Communist leader of East Germany.

East Germany was kept in a dependent status as an industrial satellite of Russia. Many East Germans resented Communist political controls and economic dependence upon the USSR. In 1953 there were violent anti-Communist uprisings in East Berlin. The revolt was crushed but bitter memories remained. More than 2,000,-000 people moved from East to West Germany between 1953 and 1961. About 52,000 men and women in East Berlin went daily to jobs in West Berlin. The East German government decided that the exodus must be stopped.

On August 13, 1961, Walter Ulbricht closed the border between the two parts of Berlin, forbade any further movement of people westward, built a twenty-five-mile wall through the city. The East-West frontier was also guarded by barbed wire, soldiers, tanks. In the world's press there were frequent reports of the shooting of men and women who were trying to escape to the West. Behind the East German government and police was the armed power of the USSR. "There are 20 Russian divisions there to say that Socialism has not failed in East Germany."

In 1962 the peace of the world was threatened by a crisis in Cuba. Photographs taken by reconnaissance planes of the United States in October, 1962, showed that the Soviet Union had shipped and installed several deadly long-range and medium-range missiles in Cuba. Such steps had obviously been taken with the consent and assistance of Premier Fidel Castro, Cuba's leader. On October 22, 1962, President John F. Kennedy informed the people of the United States and the world that he had told Premier Khrushchev that Russia must halt missile shipments to Cuba and dismantle and remove all missiles already there. He added that any aggressive action from Cuba would be regarded by the United States as an attack by the

Soviet Union and the United States would retaliate with nuclear power. President Kennedy also informed the world that a partial blockade or quarantine procedure had been set up to stop all shipments of offensive weapons considered a threat to the United States. A vast mobilization of ships, planes, and submarines showed that behind the strong and precise warning of President Kennedy stood the massed power of the United States.

Premier Nikita Khrushchev agreed to dismantle the missile bases, crate and ship the missiles back to Russia. In October, 1962, there were about 22,000 Russians in Cuba, many of them soldiers. Although several thousand Russians were withdrawn a large number still remained. Some of them were technicians. Others were experts in sabotage, demolition, and underground warfare, men taught to destroy and kill. It was their task to train Cuban soldiers and secret agents how to spread violence and revolution throughout Latin America. Russia provided considerable non-military aid to Cuba to bolster the island's sagging economy. In contrast, the United States continued to apply economic and political pressures to hasten the fall of the Communist regime in Cuba.

In October, 1964, Nikita Khrushchev was suddenly ousted from power by his comrades in Moscow. He lost his seat in the Praesidium, or Central Committee, of the Communist party. He resigned as Premier and First Secretary. After his removal, his failures and errors were described and denounced by his former associates. During the years of his leadership Russia had lost her former primacy in the Communist world. The unity that had once prevailed wherever the writ of Moscow ran was now broken. In the dramatic months of the Cuban crisis the Soviets had suffered a humiliating defeat. Premier Khrushchev had made damaging miscalculations about China and the leaders in Peking. The Chinese Communists refused to recognize Moscow's leadership in the Communist world and differed from the Russians in several important matters of ideology. They asserted that the Russians had departed from the right teachings and true standards of communism. Premier Khrushchev had planned to hold an anti-Chinese meeting of world Communist parties on December 15, 1964. It seemed probable that several Communist states would not send delegates.

Khrushchev's opponents also pointed to his mistakes in domestic policies, especially to the frequent failures in agriculture. He had promised an improvement in the standard of living in Russia. This promise he had not kept. Some of the party members who shelved Khrushchev so rapidly also denounced his "cult of personality" and his "bragging, phrasemongering, and armchair methods." These qualities, they said, they had found undesirable and offensive.

After Nikita Khrushchev's swift eclipse and fall he was replaced by other leaders in the Kremlin. The new Premier was Aleksei N. Kosygin. The First Secretary of the Communist party was Leonid I. Brezhnev. Their words seemed to promise no significant departure from the patterns of earlier Russian policy. These men, together with all the statesmen of the world, knew that the affairs of the planet were in a state of grave disarray.

THE CONDITION OF MAN

In the latter part of the twentieth century the world was divided intellectually and, to a large extent, geographically by contending political, economic, and religious creeds. Modern science had given mankind the obliterating weapons of a nuclear age. Against thermonuclear instruments there was, and could be, no absolute defense. All nations lived under the fear of bombs, nuclear submarines, and ballistic missiles, of blast and heat and the fallout of radioactive particles bringing terrifying genetic mutations and malignant genes and death. The United States, Russia, and Great Britain continued until 1963 to test their atomic weapons before a fascinated and fearful world. It was clear that global war probably meant mutual destruction. Science does not give man moral wisdom. There are no equations for that.

In 1963 the United States, Russia, and Great Britain signed an eight-hundred-word nuclear test ban treaty. They agreed "to prohibit, to prevent, and not to carry out any nuclear test explosion or any other nuclear explosion in the atmosphere, outer space, or under water." France and the People's Republic of China did not sign this pact because they were both eager to become nuclear powers. President John F. Kennedy of the United States said that the test ban treaty was "an important first step, a step towards reason, a step away from war."

In these years, too, atomic energy authorities in several countries had their budgets for works and services in producing "atoms for peace." Radioactive isotopes were available on an increasingly larger scale. Industrial plants for making atomic energy soon passed the blueprint stage. Steadily Britain's work went on with cyclotrons, synchrotons, linear accelerators, experimental atomic piles and the like at the atomic research center at Harwell under the direction of Sir John Cockroft. The scientists of other nations, particularly those of the United States and Russia, probed and challenged the secrets of matter and energy and continued to seize more of the basic powers of the universe.

Meanwhile there appeared several man-made capsules that streaked around the globe. In April, 1961, Russia's Yuri Alekseevich Gagarin circled our planet in 89 minutes. In August, 1961, Gherman Titov made 17 orbits in the five-ton capsule Vostok II. In March, 1962,

Major John Glenn of the United States traveled three times around the world at a speed of more than 17,000 miles per hour. In August, 1962, one Russian astronaut made 64 orbits and traveled 1,663,000 miles in Vostok III and another made 48 orbits and covered 1,247,-000 miles in Vostok IV. In later years more space flights were made by American and Russian pioneers. Scientists in Russia and the United States designed space ships in which it was hoped that men might be able to journey to the moon.

In these exciting years, so filled with tumbling events and brave and brilliant ideas, men applauded the new electronic microscopes, the increasing wonders of radar, the transistors, the differential rectifiers, the solar batteries, the feed-back mechanisms of automation, the new cogs, valves, and circuits, all mileposts marking progress towards a goal no man can know. Meanwhile other scientists, seeking the secrets of life and bases of living matter, were studying the mysteries of the polymer molecules called proteins and the amino acids. In 1962 the Nobel Prize for medicine was awarded to Dr. James D. Watson of the United States, and his British colleagues Dr. Francis H. C. Crick and Dr. Maurice H. F. Wilkins for their discovery that the secret of the heredity mechanism resides in the architecture of the enormous molecule of deoxyribonucleic acid (DNA), that submicroscopic "coil of life." The scientist may yet write more history than the politician. Perhaps he may do it in a calmer and kinder age.

This book began with a description of the powers of nature that carved out the seas and made the British Isles. Through the mists of the centuries we peer at the strange half-enigmatic figures of the men who first settled upon those islands and stood, though they did not know it, at the portals of British history. The descendants of successive invaders developed laws and customs. They battled for power among themselves and against their enemies across seas narrow and broad. They created things of delicate beauty and sprawling beastliness. In their domestic quarrels they shaped the mother of parliaments. They furrowed the seas to win wars and build empires. They helped to erect systems of philosophy, religion, and science that lift the eyes of the beholder above the ages' inheritance of pain and degradation. From the innumerable biographies of generations of British people has grown the Britain of today.

As the world moves towards the last decades of the twentieth century, many men have shielded their eyes from the shape of things to come. They have declared that the crumbling of the world's moral cornerstones marks the deterioration of organized society; that the new technological advances and the terrible power of atomic energy have unleashed forces so crippling and destructive that unimaginable stretches of collapse and barbarism rush upon us out of the darkness ahead. It has been asserted that the appalling complexity and con-

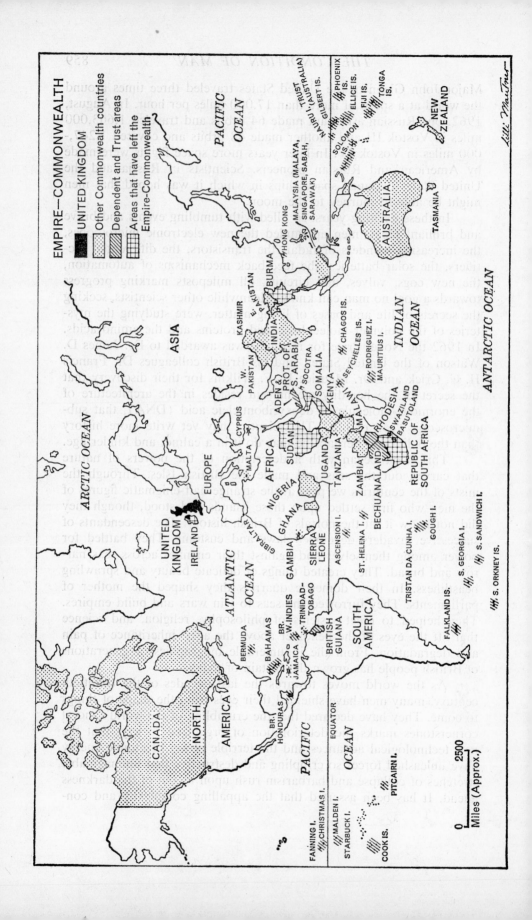

EMPIRE—COMMONWEALTH

UNITED KINGDOM
Other Commonwealth countries
Dependent and Trust areas
Areas that have left the Empire-Commonwealth

Lilli Mautner

PACIFIC OCEAN

NEW ZEALAND

TASMANIA

AUSTRALIA

PHOENIX IS.
ELLICE IS.
TONGA IS.
FIJI IS.
SOLOMON IS.
NAURU (AUSTRALIA), TRUST
GILBERT IS.
MALAYSIA (MALAYA, SINGAPORE, SABAH, SARAWAK)

INDIAN OCEAN

ANTARCTIC OCEAN

ASIA

BURMA

PAKISTAN
E. PAKISTAN
W. PAKISTAN
KASHMIR
INDIA

HONG KONG

CHAGOS IS.
SEYCHELLES IS.
RODRIGUEZ I.
MAURITIUS I.
SOCOTRA
S. ARABIA
ADEN & PROT. OF
SOMALIA
KENYA
UGANDA
TANZANIA
MALAWI
RHODESIA
ZAMBIA
SWAZILAND
BASUTOLAND
REPUBLIC OF SOUTH AFRICA
BECHUANALAND
GOUGH I.
S. GEORGIA I.
S. SANDWICH I.
S. ORKNEY IS.

EUROPE
CYPRUS
MALTA
SUDAN
NIGERIA
GHANA
AFRICA

ARCTIC OCEAN

UNITED KINGDOM
IRELAND

ATLANTIC OCEAN

SIERRA LEONE
GAMBIA
GIBRALTAR
ASCENSION I.
ST. HELENA I.
TRISTAN DA CUNHA I.

BERMUDA
BAHAMAS
BR. HONDURAS
JAMAICA
TRINIDAD-TOBAGO
BR. W. INDIES
EQUATOR
BRITISH GUIANA
SOUTH AMERICA
FALKLAND IS.

CANADA

NORTH AMERICA

PACIFIC OCEAN

FANNING I.
CHRISTMAS I.
MALDEN I.
STARBUCK I.
COOK IS.
PITCAIRN I.

0   2500
Miles (Approx.)

fusion created by conflicting sovereign states will result in economic and political competition, isolation, and anarchy, all mileposts on the road back to the jungle: "This is the way to the Natural History Museum where European man, Western man, will take his silent place, in the dust and shadows beside the dinosaur."

The historian is aware that the best qualification of a prophet is to have a good memory. The memory of the historian, groping back through the centuries, recalls that man has survived many dark chapters of disaster, folly, and crime. In the chances of time and space the inhabitants of this planet have moved slowly sunward to new knowledge and new horizons. Long ago, Marcus Aurelius remarked that "the man of forty years, if he has a grain of sense, in view of this sameness, has seen all that has been and shall be." Despite our heavy political and social storms, it is not merely facile optimism to hope that the destiny of mankind once more may be to rise above the hazards of the present hour. Disasters now, as in the past, may be avoided by deliberate acts of intelligence, will, and faith.

It is not for historians to draw aside the veil of the future. They are a little lower than the angels, a little less reliable than the minor prophets. They are wise to recall, now and then, the words of the philosopher who said: "History never begins a new chapter. Only historians do."

APPENDICES and INDICES

Kings

ANGLO-SAXON KINGDOMS
Northumbria
Ethelfrith, 593–617
Edwin, 617–633
Oswald, 635–642
Oswy, 642–670
Ecgfrith, 670–685

Mercia
Penda, 626–655
Ethelbald, 716–757
Offa II, 757–796
Cenulf, 796–821

Kent
Ethelbert, 560–616

Wessex
Ine, 688–726
Egbert, 802–839
Ethelwulf, 839–858
Ethelbald, 858–860
Ethelbert, 860–866
Ethelred, 866–871

ENGLAND
Alfred, 871–899
Edward, 899–924
Ethelstan, 924–939
Edmund, 939–946
Edred, 946–955
Edwig, 955–959
Edgar, 959–975
Edward, 975–978
Ethelred, 978–1016
Edmund, 1016
Canute, 1017–1035
Harold, 1035–1040
Harthacanute, 1040–1042
Edward, 1042–1066
Harold, 1066

NORMANS
William I, 1066–1087
William II, 1087–1100
Henry I, 1100–1135
Stephen, 1135–1154

ANGEVINS
Henry II, 1154–1189
Richard I, 1189–1199
John, 1199–1216
Henry III, 1216–1272
Edward I, 1272–1307
Edward II, 1307–1327
Edward III, 1327–1377
Richard II, 1377–1399

LANCASTRIANS
Henry IV, 1399–1413
Henry V, 1413–1422
Henry VI, 1422–1461

YORKISTS
Edward IV, 1461–1483
Edward V, 1483
Richard III, 1483–1485

TUDORS
Henry VII, 1485–1509
Henry VIII, 1509–1547
Edward VI, 1547–1553
Mary, 1553–1558
Elizabeth I, 1558–1603

STUARTS
James I, 1603–1625
Charles I, 1625–1649
Commonwealth and Protectorate, 1649–1660
Charles II, 1660–1685
James II, 1685–1688
William III and Mary, 1688–1702
Anne, 1702–1714

HANOVERIANS
George I, 1714–1727
George II, 1727–1760
George III, 1760–1820
George IV, 1820–1830
William IV, 1830–1837
Victoria, 1837–1901
Edward VII, 1901–1910
George V, 1910–1936
Edward VIII, 1936
George VI, 1936–1952
Elizabeth II, 1952–

Prime Ministers

Sir Robert Walpole, 1721–1742

Lord Wilmington and John Carteret, 1742–1744

Henry Pelham, 1744–1754

Duke of Newcastle, 1754–1756

Duke of Devonshire and William Pitt, 1756–1757

Duke of Newcastle and William Pitt, 1757–1761

Duke of Newcastle and Lord Bute, 1761–1762

Lord Bute, 1762–1763

George Grenville, 1763–1765

Lord Rockingham, 1765–1766

William Pitt, earl of Chatham, 1766–1768

Duke of Grafton, 1768–1770

Lord North, 1770–1782

Lord Rockingham, 1782

Lord Shelburne, 1782–1783

Duke of Portland, Lord North, Charles James Fox, 1783

William Pitt, the Younger, 1783–1801

Henry Addington, 1801–1804

William Pitt, the Younger, 1804–1806

Lord Grenville and Charles James Fox, 1806–1807

Duke of Portland, 1807–1809

Spencer Perceval, 1809–1812

Lord Liverpool, 1812–1827

George Canning, 1827

Lord Goderich, 1827

Duke of Wellington, 1828–1830

Earl Grey, 1830–1834

Lord Melbourne, 1834

Sir Robert Peel, 1834–1835

Lord Melbourne, 1835–1841

Sir Robert Peel, 1841–1846

Lord John Russell, 1846–1852

Lord Derby and Benjamin Disraeli, 1852

Lord Aberdeen, 1852–1855

Lord Palmerston, 1855–1858

Lord Derby and Benjamin Disraeli, 1858–1859

Lord Palmerston, 1859–1865

Lord John Russell, 1865–1866

Lord Derby and Benjamin Disraeli, 1866–1868

William Ewart Gladstone, 1868–1874

Benjamin Disraeli, 1874–1880

William Ewart Gladstone, 1880–1885

Lord Salisbury, 1885–1886

William Ewart Gladstone, 1886

Lord Salisbury, 1886–1892

William Ewart Gladstone, 1892–1894

Lord Rosebery, 1894–1895

Lord Salisbury, 1895–1902

Arthur James Balfour, 1902–1905

Henry Campbell-Bannerman, 1905–1908

Herbert Henry Asquith, 1908–1916

David Lloyd George, 1916–1922

Andrew Bonar Law, 1922–1923

Stanley Baldwin, 1923–1924

James Ramsay MacDonald, 1924

Stanley Baldwin, 1924–1929

James Ramsay MacDonald, 1929–1931 (Labour government)

James Ramsay MacDonald, 1931–1935 (National government)

Stanley Baldwin, 1935–1937

Neville Chamberlain, 1937–1940

Winston Churchill, 1940–1945

Clement Attlee, 1945–1951

Sir Winston Churchill, 1951–1955

Sir Anthony Eden, 1955–1957

Harold Macmillan, 1957–1963

Sir Alec Douglas-Home, 1963–1964

Harold Wilson, 1964–

Genealogical Tables
(ABBREVIATED)

I. ANGLO-SAXON KINGS OF ENGLAND

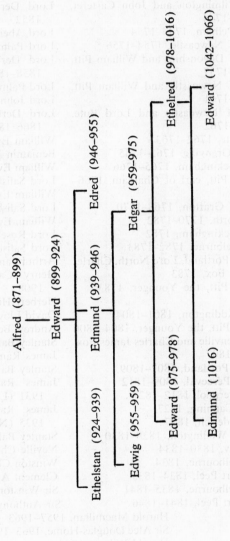

Alfred (871–899) — Edward (899–924)

Edward (899–924) — Ethelstan (924–939), Edmund (939–946), Edred (946–955)

Edmund (939–946) — Edwig (955–959), Edgar (959–975)

Edgar (959–975) — Edward (975–978), Ethelred (978–1016)

Ethelred (978–1016) — Edmund (1016), Edward (1042–1066)

II. THE NORMANS AND ANGEVINS

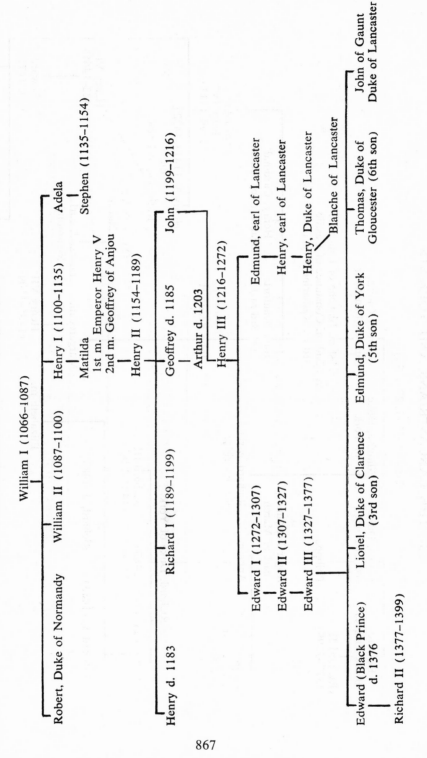

III. THE LANCASTRIANS AND YORKISTS

Edward III (1327–1377)

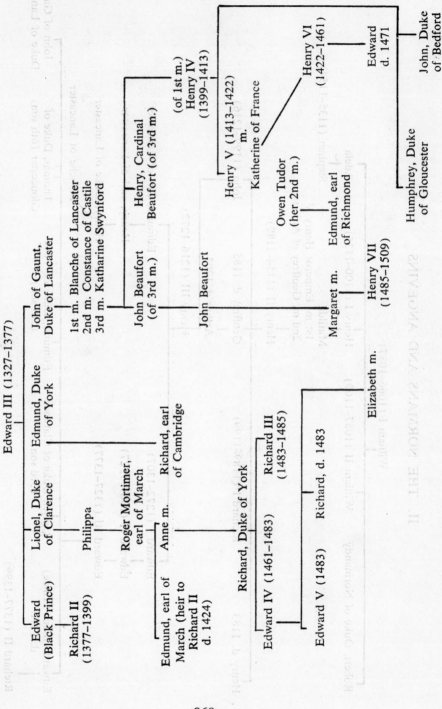

Edward (Black Prince)

Richard II (1377–1399)

Lionel, Duke of Clarence

Philippa

Roger Mortimer, earl of March

Edmund, earl of March (heir to Richard II d. 1424)

Anne m.

Edmund, Duke of York

Richard, earl of Cambridge

Richard, Duke of York

Edward IV (1461–1483)

Edward V (1483)

Richard, d. 1483

Richard III (1483–1485)

Elizabeth m.

John of Gaunt, Duke of Lancaster

1st m. Blanche of Lancaster
2nd m. Constance of Castile
3rd m. Katharine Swynford

Henry IV (1399–1413) (of 1st m.)

John Beaufort (of 3rd m.)

Henry, Cardinal Beaufort (of 3rd m.)

Henry V (1413–1422)
m.
Katherine of France

Owen Tudor (her 2nd m.)

Henry VI (1422–1461)

Edward d. 1471

John, Duke of Bedford

Humphrey, Duke of Gloucester

John Beaufort

Margaret m.

Edmund, earl of Richmond

Henry VII (1485–1509)

868

IV. THE TUDORS AND STUARTS

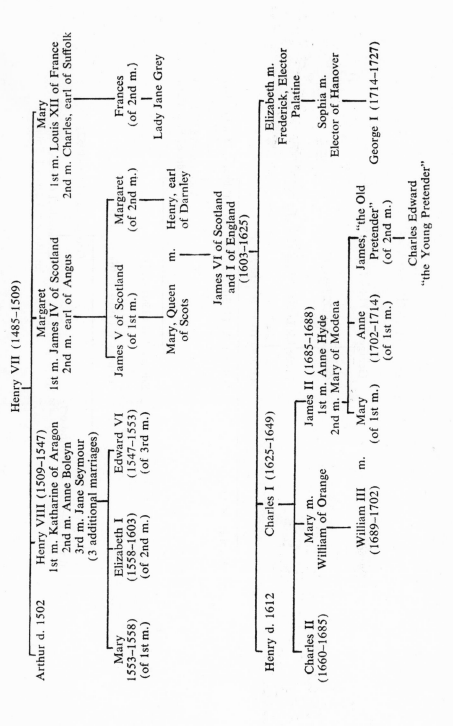

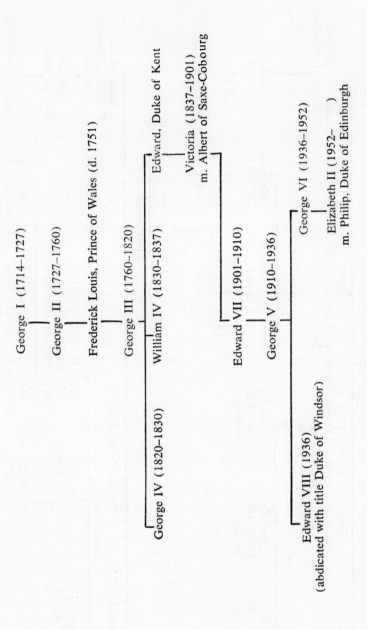

V. THE HANOVERIANS

George I (1714–1727)

George II (1727–1760)

Frederick Louis, Prince of Wales (d. 1751)

George III (1760–1820)

George IV (1820–1830)

William IV (1830–1837)

Edward, Duke of Kent

Victoria (1837–1901)
m. Albert of Saxe-Cobourg

Edward VII (1901–1910)

George V (1910–1936)

Edward VIII (1936)
(abdicated with title Duke of Windsor)

George VI (1936–1952)

Elizabeth II (1952–   )
m. Philip, Duke of Edinburgh

Bibliography

GENERAL WORKS

It is impossible to list all of the important works covering the essential features of the various subjects discussed in the chapters of this book. Bibliographies in many of the volumes listed below will indicate the directions in which more comprehensive studies may be undertaken. There are also valuable bibliographies in Lunt, W. E., *History of England* (4th ed., 1956) and Hall, W. P., Albion, R. G., and Pope, J. B., *A History of England and the Empire-Commonwealth* (4th ed., 1961). The following are useful bibliographical aids: Gross, C., *The Sources and Literature of English History from the Earliest Times to about 1485* (2nd ed., 1915); *British Civilization and Institutions,* a book list compiled by the Books and Periodicals Committee of the British Council and published by the American Library Association, Chicago (1946); Alison, W. H., *et al., Handbook of British Chronology* (Royal Historical Society, 2nd ed., 1961); Frewer, Louis B., *Bibliography of Historical Writings Published in Great Britain and the Empire, 1940–1945* (1947); *International Bibliography of Historical Sciences* (ed. by the International Committee of Historical Sciences, 1930–   ); Milne, A. T., *Writings on British History* (Royal Historical Society, 1937–   ); Grose, C. L., *A Select Bibliography of British History 1660–1760* (1939); Read, C., *Bibliography of British History, Tudor Period 1485–1603* (2nd ed., 1959); Davies, G., *Bibliography of British History, Stuart Period 1603–1714* (1928); Pargellis, S., and Medley, D. J., *Bibliography of British History: the Eighteenth Century, 1714–1789* (1951). See also Howe, G. F., *et al.* (American Historical Association) *Guide to Historical Literature* (1961). Information about individuals can be obtained by consulting the *Dictionary of National Biography,* the *Encyclopaedia of Social Sciences,* and the *Encyclopaedia Britannica.* Always useful are *The Statesman's Year Book* (since 1864); *Whitaker's Almanac* (since 1868); and *The Annual Register* (since 1759). More advanced students will profit by the suggestions frequently found in such sources as the *Huntington Library Bulletin;* the *Bulletin of the Institute of Historical Research;* the special bibliographies in *The Journal of Modern History;* and the book review sections of the reputable historical journals, particularly *The English Historical Review, The American Historical Review, The Journal of British Studies,* and *The Historical Journal* (its predecessor was the *Cambridge Historical Journal,* 1923–1957).

871

The best one-volume survey of English history still remains Trevelyan, G. M., *History of England* (1926), available in a condensed Pelican edition: *A Shorter History of England* (6th ed., 1960). Professor Trevelyan's *Illustrated English Social History* (4 vols., 1949–1952) is also unsurpassed. Worth reading and possessing are Rowse, A. L., *The Spirit of English History* (1945) and Cole, G. D. H., and Postgate, R., *The British Common People 1746–1946* (1947), available in a University Paperback edition (1961). See also Ashley, M., *Great Britain to 1688* (1961). Longer works include Hunt, W., and Poole, R. L., (eds.) *The Political History of England* (12 vols., 1905–1910); Oman, C. W. C., (ed.) *A History of England* (8 vols., 1904–1934); Clark, G. N., (ed.) *The Oxford History of England* (14 vols., 1934–1960); the volumes of the *Oxford History* are listed in the appropriate chapter bibliographies below. Also listed are the volumes of the *History of England* series, ed. W. N. Medlicott and published by Longmans, Green, and Co. in Great Britain and by the David McKay Company in the United States; the eight volumes of the *History of England* published by Thomas Nelson and Sons of Edinburgh. See further the volumes in the Mentor series published in the United States by the New American Library and Morpurgo, J. E., (ed.) *The Pelican History of England* (8 vols., 1950–1955); Churchill, Winston S., *A History of the English-speaking Peoples* (4 vols., 1956–1958); Cam, Helen, *England Before Elizabeth* (1961); Traill, H. D., and Mann, J. S., (eds.) *Social England* (6 vols., 1909); the sections concerned with English history in the *Cambridge Medieval History* (8 vols., 1911–1936); Previté-Orton, C. W., *The Shorter Cambridge Medieval History* (1956); the *Cambridge Modern History* (14 vols., 1902–1912); and *The New Cambridge Modern History* (1958–   ).

MAPS, ATLASES, AND GAZETTEERS. In addition to the standard Shepherd, W. R., *Historical Atlas* (8th ed., 1956), an excellent book is Darby, H. C., (ed.) *A Historical Geography of England Before A.D. 1800* (1936). Also useful are Fox, Edward W., (ed.) *Atlas of European History* (1957); Bartholomew, J., (ed.) *The British Isles Pocket Atlas* (1943); *The Survey Atlas of England and Wales* (1931); *The Survey Gazetteer of the British Isles* (1944); the Ordinance Survey *Maps* and *Atlases* issued by the Ordinance Survey (pub. H. M. Stationery Office); and Stamp, L. D., (ed.) *Land of Britain: The Report of the Land Utilization Survey* (from 1936 to the present; not yet completed).

FOREIGN POLICY. Most of the published works on foreign policy relate to specific periods or particular persons; many of them are listed under the chapter headings below. The only standard work of a broad scope covers the period 1783–1913: Ward, A. W., and Gooch, G. P., (eds.) *Cambridge History of British Foreign Policy*

(3 vols., 1922–1923). See also the numerous volumes published by the Royal Institute of International Affairs including the reports of the Chatham House study groups.

ECONOMIC. A brief and excellent economic history is Birnie, Arthur, *An Economic History of the British Isles* (1935, 1961). Also valuable are Bland, A. E., Brown, P. A., and Tawney, R. H., *English Economic History: Select Documents* (1914); Cunningham, W., *Growth of English Industry and Commerce* (2 vols., 5th ed., 1910–1912); Lipson, E., *Economic History of England* (3rd enlarged ed., 1943; the second and third vols. on the 16th and 17th centuries were reprinted in a 5th ed., 1948–1956); Milner, F., *Economic Evolution in England* (1931). For the modern period nothing is better than Clapham, J. H., *An Economic History of Modern Britain* (3 vols., 1926–1938). See also Clapham, J. H., and Court, W. H. B., *A Concise Economic History of Britain* (1964).

CONSTITUTIONAL AND LEGAL. Useful texts include Smith, Goldwin, *A Constitutional and Legal History of England* (1955); Lovell, C. R., *English Constitutional and Legal History* (1962); Lyon, B. D., *A Constitutional and Legal History of Medieval England* (1960); Marcham, F. G., *A Constitutional History of Modern England, 1485 to the Present* (1960); Adams, G. B., *Constitutional History of England* (rev. ed., 1934). Excellent brief studies are Amos, M., *The English Constitution* (1930) and Bailey, Sydney D., *British Parliamentary Democracy* (1958). More detailed and standard works are Maitland, F. W., *Constitutional History of England* (1926); Keith, A. B., *The Constitution of England* (2 vols., 1940); Anson, W. R., *The Law and Custom of the Constitution* (2 vols., 1935); Stubbs, W., *Constitutional History of England* (3 vols., 1897), which covers the period down to 1485; Petit-Dutaillis, C., *Studies and Notes Supplementary to Stubbs' Constitutional History* (trans. by W. E. Rhodes, Manchester, 1930). For the modern period the best books are Mackintosh, J. P., *The British Cabinet* (1962); Keith, A. B., *The British Cabinet System 1830–1938* (1941); Keir, D. L., *The Constitutional History of Modern Britain Since 1485* (6th ed., 1960); Jennings, W. I., *Cabinet Government* (1936), *Parliament* (1939), *The British Constitution* (4th ed., 1963), and *Party Politics* (3 vols., 1960–1962). A new series, *The History of Parliament* (eds. John Brooke and the late Sir Lewis Namier) began with the publication of *The House of Commons 1754–1790* (1964).

The best one-volume collection of documents, with a valuable bibliography and footnotes, is Stephenson, C., and Marcham, F. G., *Sources of English Constitutional History* (1937). See also the various volumes in the *English Historical Documents* series listed under the chapter headings below. The best books on English constitutional law are Wade, E. C. S., and Philips, G. G., *Constitutional Law* (3rd ed., 1946) and Keir, D. L., and Lawson, F. H., *Cases in Constitutional Law* (3rd ed., 1948). For further references see Cam, H. M., and Turberville, A. S., *A Short Bibliography of English Constitutional History* (History Assn. Leaflet No. 75, London, 1929).

Excellent bibliographies of works in English political philosophy are to be found in Sabine, G. H., *A History of Political Theory* (3rd ed., 1961) and Coker, F. W., *Recent Political Thought* (1934). For English legal history the two finest works are Pollock, F., and Maitland, F. W., *A History of English Law before the Time of Edward I* (2 vols., 2nd ed., 1898), which covers the period up to Edward I, and Holdsworth, W. S., *A History of English Law* (12 vols., 1903–1938). The best brief volume is Jenks, E., *A Short History of English Law* (5th ed., 1938).

MILITARY AND NAVAL. In addition to the books listed under chapter headings below, the standard military history is Fortescue, J. W., *History of the British Army* (13 vols., 1899–1930). See also Lewis, M. A., *History of the British Navy* (1957); Clowes, W. L., *The Royal Navy, a History* (7 vols., 1903).

RELIGIOUS. The most useful brief study of the Church of England is Wakeman, H. O., *Introduction to the History of the Church of England* (rev. ed., 1920). Standard works include Stephens, W. R. W., and Hunt, W., (eds.) *History of the English Church* (9 vols., 1899–1910). The most complete collection of documents is Gee, H., and Hardy, W. J., *Documents Illustrative of English Church History* (1914). Books about religious groups and movements outside the Church of England are listed in the appropriate chapter divisions below.

LITERATURE. In addition to the works mentioned later the following are useful: Ward, A. W., and Waller, A. R., (eds.) *Cambridge History of English Literature* (15 vols., rev. ed., 1933); Legouis, E. H., and Cazamian, L., *A History of English Literature* (2 vols., 1927). The most satisfactory short studies are Grierson, H. J. C., *The Background of English Literature* (1935) and Osgood, C. G., *The Voice of England* (1935). See also Grierson, H. J. C. and Smith, J. C., *A Critical History of English Poetry* (1946). The volumes published in the *Oxford History of English Literature* (eds. Wilson, F. P., and Dobrée, B.) are cited under chapter headings below. Also useful are the volumes of the *English Men of Letters* series; Marriott, J. A. R., *English History in English Fiction* (1941); Arundell, E., *The Sources of English Literature* (1926). Particularly valuable are Bateson, F. W., (ed.) *Cambridge Bibliography of English Literature A.D. 600–1900* (4 vols., 1940) and Ford, B., (ed.) *Pelican Guide to English Literature* (6 vols., 1954–1958).

ARCHITECTURE. The most valuable short works are Gardner, H. B., *Outline of English Architecture* (1946) and Dickinson, P. L.,

History of Architecture in the British Isles (1926). Also useful are Bond, F., *The Cathedrals of England and Wales* (1912); Evans, H., *The Castles of England and Wales* (1912); and Summerson, J. H., *Architecture in Britain 1530–1830* (Penguin ed., 1953); Boase, T. S. R., *Oxford History of English Art* (8 vols., 1949–1957).

SCIENCE AND TECHNOLOGY. In addition to the books cited later the reader is referred to Thorndike, L., *A History of Magic and Experimental Science* (8 vols., 1923–1958); Singer, C., (ed.) *Studies in the History and Methods of Science* (2 vols., 1917–1921); Singer, C., *et al.*, *A History of Technology* (5 vols., 1954–1958).

WALES, SCOTLAND, IRELAND. The two most satisfactory histories of Wales are Lloyd, J. E., *History of Wales* (2nd ed., 1912) and Williams, D. A., *A History of Wales 1485–1931* (1934). The best brief histories of Scotland are Brown, P. H. A., *A Short History of Scotland* (1920) and Terry, C. S. A., *A History of Scotland* (1920). Longer works are Brown, P. H. A., *A History of Scotland* (3 vols., 1902–1909) and Lang, A., *A History of Scotland* (4 vols., 1900–1907). For an excellent treatment of modern Scottish history, see Mackenzie, A. M., *Scotland in Modern Times 1720–1939* (1941). Two of the most objective and competent surveys of Irish history are Curtis, E. A., *A History of Ireland* (1937) and Joyce, P. W., *A Short History of Ireland* (1911). Also useful are Joyce, P. W., *A Social History of Ireland* (2 vols., 1920) and Dunlop, R., *Ireland from the Earliest Times to the Present Day* (1922). See also Macardle, D., *The Irish Republic* (1937); Kohn, L., *The Constitution of the Irish Free State* (1932); and the books listed in the chapter divisions below.

THE COMMONWEALTH AND THE BRITISH EMPIRE. The most satisfactory short histories of the Empire are Mullett, C. F., *The British Empire* (1938) and Robinson, H., *Development of the British Empire* (1936). For the early period the most complete and scholarly book is Newton, A. P., *The British Empire to 1783* (1932). For the later period the best single-volume work is Knaplund, P., *The British Empire 1815–1939* (1942). See also his *Britain, Commonwealth and Empire, 1901–1955* (1957). Several problems and events in modern Imperial and Commonwealth history are discussed in the multi-volumed *Survey of Commonwealth Affairs* begun by Hancock, W. K., and continued by Mansergh, N. See further Toynbee, A. J., *British Commonwealth Relations* (1943); Underhill, F., *The British Commonwealth: An Experiment in Cooperation Among Nations* (1956); Walker, E. A., *The British Empire: Its Structure and Spirit* (1943); Williamson, J. A., *The British Empire and Commonwealth* (1935); Zimmern, A., *The Third British Empire* (1934). Brief and able studies in Imperial political and economic geography include Fawcett, C. B. A., *A Political Geography of the British Em-*

pire (1933) and Buchanan, R. O., *An Economic Geography of the British Empire* (1935). Longer works include the *Cambridge History of the British Empire* edited by Rose, J. H., Newton, A. P., and Benians, E. A., (9 vols., 1929–1959) and Lucas, C. P., *et al., A Historical Geography of the British Empire* (8 vols. in 14 parts, 1887–1923). Many of the volumes listed above contain excellent bibliographies. Other references are contained under the chapter headings below.

CANADA. Best brief histories are McInnis, E., *Canada: A Political and Social History* (1947); Lower, A. R. M., *Colony to Nation* (1946); Creighton, D. G., *Dominion of the North* (1944); and Wittke, C., *A History of Canada* (rev. ed., 1941). The important achievement of responsible government in Canada is described in considerable detail in Martin, C., *Empire and Commonwealth* (1929). Other volumes about men and topics of importance in Canadian history are Wrong, G. M., and Langton, H. H., (eds.) *The Chronicles of Canada* (32 vols., 1914–1916). Useful reference books are Wallace, W. S., (compiler) *The Dictionary of Canadian Biography* (1926) and Wallace, W. S., (ed.) *The Encyclopaedia of Canada* (6 vols., 1935–1937). W. P. M. Kennedy's *Constitution of Canada* is the only constitutional history of Canada that has been published. Detailed and valuable information on many subjects may be found in the *Canada Year Book,* published annually. *The Canadian Historical Review* is an excellent quarterly journal. An outstanding achievement of Canadian-American scholarship is the cooperative work of twenty-five volumes published under the auspices of the Carnegie Endowment for International Peace: *The Relations of Canada and the United States,* edited by James T. Shotwell; the series was completed by J. B. Brebner's *The North Atlantic Triangle* (1945). See also the new *Canadian Centenary Series* (17 vols., 1963–   ).

AUSTRALIA. Excellent books about Australian history are Greenwood, G., (ed.) *Australia: A Social and Political History* (1955); Scott, E. A., *A Short History of Australia* (5th ed., 1927); Hancock, W. A., *Australia* (1930). The first volume of Clark, C. M. H., *A History of Australia* was published in 1962 under the title *From the Earliest Times to the Age of Macquarrie.* Also valuable are Sweetman, E., *Australian Constitutional Development* (1925); Clark, C. M. H., and Pryor, L. J., *Select Documents in Australian History* (2 vols., 1950, 1955); and Ward, R., *The Australian Legend* (1958). *The Official Yearbook of the Commonwealth of Australia,* published annually, contains much useful information.

NEW ZEALAND. Among the best books are Condliffe, J. B., and Airey, W. T. A., *A Short History of New Zealand* (1938); Marsh, N., *New Zealand* (1942); Morrell, W. P., *New Zealand*

(1935); Sinclair, K., *A History of New Zealand* (1959); and Mc-Clymont, W. G., *The Exploration of New Zealand* (2nd ed., 1959). See also Jenks, E., *History of the Australasian Colonies* (3rd ed., 1912).

AFRICA. In addition to the works cited in the chapter bibliographies the most valuable references to the history of South Africa before her departure from the Commonwealth in May, 1961, are vol. viii of the *Cambridge History of the British Empire;* de Kiewiet, C. W., *The Imperial Factor in South Africa* (1937) and *A History of South Africa* (1941); Macmillan, W. M., *Africa Emergent: A Survey of Social, Political and Economic Trends in British Africa* (1938); Walker, E. A., *A History of South Africa* (2nd ed., 1939). See also Carter, G., *Independence for Africa* (1960); Cohen, A., *British Policy in Changing Africa* (1959); Emerson, R., *From Empire to Nation: The Rise to Self-Assertion of Asian and African Peoples* (1960); Oliver, R., and Fage, J. D., *A Short History of Africa* (Penguin African Library, 1962).

INDIA. The most satisfactory works include Griffith, P., *The British Impact on India* (1952); Roberts, P. E. A., *A History of British India* (1938); Spear, P., *The Oxford History of India* (3rd ed., 1958); Ramon, T. A., *India* (1942); Keith, A. B., *Constitutional History of India from 1600 to 1935* (1938). See also Buchanan, D. H., *The Development of Capitalistic Enterprise in India* (1934); Dodwell, H. H., *India* (2 vols., 1936); the *Cambridge History of India* (6 vols., 1922–1937; vols. iv and v of the *Cambridge History of the British Empire* form vols. v and vi of the *Cambridge History of India*). Further references may be obtained in the bibliographies of such works as Knaplund, P., *Britain, Commonwealth and Empire 1901–1955*, cited earlier. See also the references below, particularly those listed for Chapter 40.

CHAPTER 1

GENERAL WORKS: Rostovzeff, M., *Social and Economic History of the Roman Empire* (1926); Keith, Sir Arthur, *The Antiquity of Man* (1925); Childe, V. G., *Dawn of European Civilization.*

ENGLAND AND WALES: The best one-volume survey for this period is the first volume of the *Oxford History of England* series, cited earlier: Collingwood, R. G., and Myres, J. N. L., *Roman Britain and the English Settlements* (2nd ed., 1937). Other excellent and authoritative works are Blair, P. H., *Roman Britain and Early England 55 B.C.–A.D. 871* (1960), vol. 1 in the *History of England* series published by Thomas Nelson & Sons, Edinburgh, cited earlier; Kendrick, T. D., and Hawkes, C. F. C., *Archaeology in England and Wales, 1914–1931* (1932); Haverfield, F. J., *The Romanization of Roman Britain* (4th ed. by Sir George Macdonald, 1923), *Roman Occupation of Britain* (ed., Sir George Macdonald, 1924), and "Roman Britain" in the *Cambridge Medieval History*, vol. 1, chap. xiii. Also valuable are Fox, Cyril, *The Personality of Britain* (2nd ed., 1923); Childe, V. G., *Prehistoric Communities of the British Isles* (1940); Fleure, H. J., *Races of England and Wales* (1923); Clarke, G., *Prehistoric England* (1941); Wheeler, R. M., *Prehistoric and Roman Wales* (1925); Piggott, S., *The Neolithic Cultures in the British Isles* (1954); Macdonald, G., *et al.*, *Caesar to Arthur* (1960).

GUIDES, MAPS, JOURNALS: Of particular value and interest are the British Museum Guides to the Stone Age, Bronze Age, and Early Iron Age; the Ordinance Survey Maps of Roman Britain and Dark Age Britain; and several of the British Office of Works Regional Guides to Ancient Monuments (pub. H. M. Stationery Office). Reports of recent investigations and progress are available in such scholarly publications as the *Proceedings of the English Prehistory Society* (pub. twice a year by the Society of Antiquaries of London); the *Archaeological Journal* of the Royal Archaeological Institute of Great Britain (pub. twice a year); the quarterly *Antiquity* (1927–   ); the Royal Anthropological Institute *Journal* and its monthly publication *Man*.

CHAPTER 2

GENERAL WORKS: Stenton, F. M., *Anglo-Saxon England* (1943); this fine book is the second volume of the *Oxford History of England;* Hodgkin, R. H., *A History of the Anglo-Saxons* (2 vols., 1939); *Cambridge Medieval History*, vols. ii and iii; Laistner, M. L. W., *Thought and Letters in Western Europe A.D. 500–900* (1931); Stephenson, C. and Lyon, B. D., *Medieval History* (4th ed., 1961); Chambers, R. W., *England Before the Norman Conquest* (rev. ed., 1938); Chadwick, H. M., *The Heroic Age* (1912); *The Anglo-Saxon Chronicle* (1934 Everyman edition); Whitelock, D., Douglas, D. C., and Tucker, S. I., (eds.) *The Anglo-Saxon Chronicle: A Revised Translation* (1961); Brooke, C., *From Alfred to Henry III, 811–1272* (1961), vol. 2 in the *History of England* series published by Thomas Nelson & Sons, Edinburgh.

ANGLO-SAXON INSTITUTIONS: Morris, W. A., *The Constitutional History of England to 1216* (1930); Chadwick, H. M., *Studies in Anglo-Saxon Institutions* (1905), still useful; Stephenson, C., *Borough and Town* (1933), a brilliant dissenting comment on several theses of F. M. Stenton, F. W. Maitland, and P. Vinogradoff; Tait, J., *The Mediaeval English Borough* (1936), an able and interesting book that states a series of conclusions about borough origins and development. A prolonged and scholarly controversy has resulted because several historians doubt the validity of the views of Professor Tait. Other valuable works are: Vinogradoff, P., *Growth of the Manor* (2nd. ed., 1911); Pollock, F., and Maitland, F. W., *History of English Law*, chap. ii; Holdsworth, W. A., *History of English Law* I, Book I; Gray, H. L., *English Field Systems* (1915); Stenton, F. M., *The Latin Charters of the Anglo-Saxon Period* (1955).

SPECIAL STUDIES: Jolliffe, J. E. A., *Pre-feudal England: the Jutes* (1933); Plummer, C., *The Life and Times of Alfred the Great* (1902); Duckett, E. A., *Alfred the Great* (1956); Lees, B. A., *Alfred the Great* (1919); Stephenson, C., "The Problem of the Common Man in Early Mediaeval Europe," *A. H. R.*, vol. LI, No. 3 (April, 1946) and "Feudalism and Its Antecedents in England," *A. H. R.*, vol. XLVIII, No. 2 (January, 1943); Larson, L. M., *The Kings's Household Before the Norman Conquest* (1904) and *Canute the Great* (1912).

ART AND LITERATURE: Excellent works are Dale, E., *National Life and Character in the Mirror of Early English Literature* (1907); Leeds, E. T., *Early Anglo-Saxon Art and Archaeology* (1930); Kendrick, T. D., *Anglo-Saxon Art to A.D. 900* (1938); Chambers, R. W., *Beowulf* (2nd ed., 1932); Lawrence, W. W., *Beowulf and the Epic Tradition* (1928).

RELIGION: The best works are Crawford, J. S., *Anglo-Saxon Influence on Western Christendom, 600–800* (1933) and Allison, T., *English Religious Life in the Eighth Century* (1929). Two useful and interesting biographies are Robinson, J. A., *The Times of St. Dunstan* (1923) and Bury, J. B., *The Life of St. Patrick* (1905).

CHAPTER 3

GENERAL WORKS: Several of the volumes listed here are also useful for later chapters. The most adequate narrative surveys of the Norman and Angevin period are Poole, A. L., *From Domesday Book to Magna Carta, 1087–1216* (1951), vol. iii in the *Oxford History of England;* Davis, H. W. C., *England under the Normans and Angevins* (8th ed., 1924) and Adams, G. B., *History of England from the Norman Conquest to the Death of John* (1905). A brief and excellent account of the Normans in England and Europe is Haskins, C. H., *The Normans in European History* (1915). Still useful is Freeman, E. A., *History of the Norman Conquest* (5 vols. and index, 1867–1879); this large work covers the period 975–1087. Two other volumes written many years ago and worth reading are Round, J. H., *Feudal England* (1895) and Vinogradoff, P., *English Society in the Eleventh Century* (1908). A brief summary of some important aspects of Norman rule in England is contained in the *Cambridge Medieval History,* vol. v, chap. xvi. See also Barlow, F., *The Feudal Kingdom of England 1042–1216* (1955) and Douglas, D. C., and Greenaway, G. W., (eds.) *English Historical Documents 1042–1189* (1953). See also Bryant, A., *Makers of the Realm* (1954).

NORMAN INSTITUTIONS: Of the numerous studies about various Norman institutions the best are Richardson, H. G., and Sayles, G. O., *The Governance of Medieval England from the Conquest to Magna Carta* (1963); Maitland, F. W., *Domesday Book and Beyond* (1897) and *Township and Borough* (1898); Stenton, F. M., *The First Century of English Feudalism* (2nd ed., 1961); Morris, W. A., *The Mediaeval English Sheriff to 1300* (1927); Haskins, C. H., *Norman Institutions* (1918); Painter, S., *The Rise and Fall of the Feudal Monarchies* (1951); Adams, G. B., *Councils and Courts in Anglo-Norman England* (1926). The larger part of Domesday Book is translated in the various volumes of the *Victoria History of the Counties of England.* See also Galbraith, V. H., *The Making of Domesday Book* (1961); Finn, R. A. W., *Introduction to Domesday Book* (1963); Loyn, H. R., *Anglo-Saxon England and the Norman Conquest* (1963).

SPECIAL STUDIES: Douglas, David C., *William the Conqueror: the Norman Impact Upon England* (1964); Round, J. H., *Geoffrey de Mandeville* (1892); Stenton, F. M., *William the Conqueror* (1915); Slocombe, G. E., *William the Conqueror* (1959); Macdonald, A. J., *Lanfranc* (1926); Lennard, R., *Rural England 1086–1135: A Study of Social and Agrarian Conditions* (1959).

RELIGION: The best survey of problems of church and state and the development of religion in the Norman period is Brooke, Z. N., *The English Church and the Papacy from the Conquest to the Reign of John* (1931). See also Cantor, N. F., *Church, Kingship, and Lay Investiture in England 1089–1135* (1958).

ARCHITECTURE: The best books about the important contributions of Norman architecture are Clapham, A. W., *English Romanesque Architecture* (2 vols., 1930–1934); Crossley, F. N., *The English Abbey* (1943); Brown, H., *The English Castle* (1943). Gardner, H. B., *Outline of English Architecture,* mentioned earlier, contains an excellent section on the Norman achievements.

CHAPTER 4

GENERAL WORKS: Useful for this and the immediately following chapters are Norgate, K., *England Under the Angevins* (2 vols., 1887); Tout, T. F., *History of England from the Accession of Henry II to the Death of Edward III* (1905). A concise general description of the work of Henry II is contained in the *Cambridge Medieval History*, vol. v, chap. xvii. Two standard biographies of Henry II are Green, A. S., *Henry the Second* (1888) and Salzman, L. F., *Henry II* (1914).

SPECIAL STUDIES: Jolliffe, J. E. A., *Angevin Kingship* (1955); Dark, S., *St. Thomas of Canterbury* (1927); the sections about the reign of Henry II in Plucknett, T. F. T., *A Concise History of the Common Law* (1940); Poole, R. L., *The Exchequer in the Twelfth Century* (1912); Adams, G. B., "The Origin of English Equity," *Columbia Law Review*, XVI, 87 (1916).

CHAPTER 5

GENERAL WORKS: In addition to the books cited earlier the following are useful: Stephenson, C., *A Brief Survey of Mediaeval Europe* (1941); Sayles, G. O., *The Medieval Foundations of England* (2nd ed. rev., 1950); Barrow, G. W. S., *Feudal Britain: The Completion of the Medieval Kingdoms 1066–1314* (1956); Newhall, R. A., *The Crusades* (1927); Munro, D. C., *The Kingdom of the Crusaders* (1935); Poole, S. L., *Saladin and the Fall of the Kingdom of Jerusalem* (1903); various editions of Froissart's *Chronicles*. Excellent biographies are Painter, S., *William Marshal* (1933); Norgate, K., *Richard the Lion Heart* (1924); Dunn-Pattison, R. P., *The Black Prince* (1910). Valuable for this and other chapters are two sound and scholarly volumes: White, A. B., *The Making of the English Constitution 449–1485* (1925); Jolliffe, J. E. A., *The Constitutional History of Medieval England from the English Settlement to 1485* (2nd ed., 1947). See also Sayles, G. O., and Richardson, H. G., *The Governance of Mediaeval England* (1963). See further the *Cambridge Medieval History*, vol. vi, chaps. vii and viii.

SPECIAL STUDIES: Powicke, F. M., *The Loss of Normandy 1189–1204* (1913); Morris, J. E., *The Welsh Wars of Edward I* (1900); Lodge, E. C., *Gascony under English Rule* (1926). Of the many writings about Magna Carta these are best: McKechnie, W. S., *Magna Carta* (rev. ed., 1914); Bémont, C., *Magna Carta*, translated by E. F. Jacob (1930); Painter, S., "Magna Carta," *A. H. R.*, LIII, No. 1; Thompson, F., *The First Century of Magna Carta* (1925). See also Hollister, C. W., "King John and the Historians," *Journal of British Studies* I, No. 1 (November, 1961). Other books that may be read with profit are Powicke, F. M., *Stephen Langton* (1928) and Treharne, R. F., *The Baronial Plan of Reform, 1258–1263* (1932). An important essay is Carl Stephenson's "The Beginning of Representative Government in England" in *The Constitution Reconsidered*, edited by Conyers Read (1938). See also Thompson, F., *Magna Carta 1300–1629* (1948); Painter, S., *The Reign of King John* (1949); Warren, W. L., *King John* (1961); Bémont, C., *Simon de Montfort* (1930); Labarge, M. A., *Simon de Montfort* (1962).

CHAPTER 6

GENERAL WORKS: For the whole period of the Middle Ages the following are excellent background books worth reading and possessing: Holmes, G., *The Later Middle Ages 1272–1485* (1963); Crump, C. G., and Jacob, E. F., *The Legacy of the Middle Ages* (1926); Powicke, F. M., *Mediaeval England* (1931); Poole, R. L., *Illustrations of Mediaeval Thought and Learning* (1920);

Haskins, C. H., *Studies in Mediaeval Culture* (1929) and *The Renaissance of the Twelfth Century* (1927); Coulton, G. G., *Mediaeval Studies* (1921). *Mediaeval Panorama* (1937) and *The Mediaeval Village* (1926); Taylor, H. O., *The Mediaeval Mind* (2 vols., 4th ed., 1930); McIlwain, C. H., *The Growth of Political Thought in the West* (1932).

RELIGION: Outstanding volumes are Deanesley, M., *History of the Mediaeval Church* (1925); Coulton, G. G., *Five Centuries of Religion* (1923–1927); Jessopp, A., *The Coming of the Friars* (8th ed., 1889); Knowles, D., *The Monastic Order in England 943–1216* (1940) and *The Religious Orders in England* (3 vols., 1948–1959); Moorman, J. H. R., *Church Life in England in the Twelfth Century* (1945).

EDUCATION: The best works are Rashdall, H., *Universities of Europe in the Middle Ages* ed. by Powicke, F. M., and Emden, A. B. (3 vols., 1936); Mallett, C., *History of the University of Oxford* (1924); Haskins, C. H., *Rise of the Universities* (1923); Waddell, H., *The Wandering Scholars* (1927); Leach, A. F., *The Schools of Mediaeval England* (1915); this book stresses the history of the Anglo-Saxon schools.

ECONOMIC: In addition to the books cited elsewhere in this bibliography, consult Pirenne, H., *Mediaeval Cities, Their Origin and the Revival of Trade* (1928); Neilsen, N., *Mediaeval Agrarian Economy* (1936); Homans, G. C., *English Villagers of the Thirteenth Century* (new ed., 1941); Carus-Wilson, E. M., *Medieval Merchant Venturers* (1954).

LITERATURE: See books listed for other chapters and also the early sections of Baldwin, C. S., *Three Mediaeval Centuries of Literature in England, 1100–1400* (1932); Schofield, W. H., *English Literature from the Norman Conquest to Chaucer* (1906).

ARCHITECTURE: Useful for this and other chapters are Prior, E. S., *Mediaeval Church Architecture in England* (1912); Bond, F., *Gothic Architecture in England* (1905); and Harvey, J., *Gothic England* (1947).

SCIENCE: In addition to the appropriate sections of Thorndike, L., *History of Magic and Experimental Science* (6 vols., 1923–1941), mentioned earlier, and the general works cited above, see Little, A. G., *Roger Bacon* (1914). Consult also the items listed in the bibliography for Chapter 9.

CHAPTER 7

GENERAL WORKS: For the whole period of the Middle Ages the following are valuable: Pollard, A. F., *The Evolution of Parliament* (1926); White, A. B., *Self-Government at the King's Command* (1933). See also the *Cambridge Medieval History*, vol. vii, chaps. xiv, xvii, xix; Haskins, G. L., *The Growth of English Representative Government* (1948). See especially Powicke, F. M., *The Thirteenth Century 1216–1307* (1953), vol. iv in the *Oxford History of England;* Mitchell, S. K., *Taxation in Medieval England* (1951); Thompson, F., *A Short History of Parliament, 1295–1642* (1953).

The contribution of Edward I is ably described in Tout, T. F., *Edward I* (rev. ed., 1909). Jenks, F., *Edward Plantagenet* (1902), stresses the legal reforms of Edward I's reign. See also Pasquet, D., *Essay on the Origins of Parliament* (1925).

CHAPTER 8

GENERAL WORKS: For this and other chapters, see the *Cambridge Medieval*

History, vol. vii, chap. xv, and vol. viii, chaps. xii, xiv. The best study of medieval warfare and military science is Oman, C. W. C., *History of the Art of War in the Middle Ages* (2 vols., 2nd ed., 1924). See also Bryant, A., *The Age of Chivalry* (1964).

CONSTITUTIONAL AND ADMINISTRATIVE: Useful for the whole medieval period as well as the fourteenth century are Wilkinson, B., *Constitutional History of Medieval England 1216–1399* (3 vols., 1948–1958); Tout, T. F., *Chapters in the Administrative History of Mediaeval England* (6 vols., 1920–1933); Clarke, M. V., *Medieval Representation and Consent* (1936); Baldwin, J. F., *The King's Council in England during the Middle Ages* (1913). Competent and interesting is the brief book of Cuttino, G. P., *English Diplomatic Administration 1259–1339* (1940). See also Stephenson, C., "Taxation and Representation," *Haskins Anniversary Essays* (1929); Chrimes, S. B., and Brown, A. L. (eds.) *Select Documents of English Constitutional History 1307–1485* (1961).

SPECIAL STUDIES: Of outstanding merit and interest are Davies, J. C., *The Baronial Opposition to Edward II* (1918); Tout, T. F., and Johnstone, H., *The Place of the Reign of Edward II in English History* (1914); Armitage Smith, S. A., *John of Gaunt* (1904); Steel, A., *Richard II* (1941).

CHAPTER 9

GENERAL WORKS: Lodge, R., *The Close of the Middle Ages* (1923); Trevelyan, G. M., *England in the Age of Wycliffe* (1909); Vickers, K. H., *England in the Later Middle Ages* (1914); McKisack, M., *The Fourteenth Century 1307–1399* (1959), vol. v in the *Oxford History of England;* Taylor, B. D., *Chaucer's England* (1959).

ECONOMIC AND SOCIAL: The most useful works are Power, E., *The Wool Trade in English Medieval History* (1941); Unwin, G., *Finance and Trade under Edward III* (1918); Gras, N. S. B., *The Early English Customs System* (1918), covers the thirteenth through the sixteenth century; Gross, C., *The Guild Merchant* (2 vols., 1890); Kramer, S., *English Craft Guilds* (1927); Salzman, L. F., *English Trade in the Middle Ages* (1931) and *English Industries of the Middle Ages* (1923); Chadwick, D., *Social Life in the Days of Piers Plowman* (1922); Jusserand, J. J., *English Wayfaring Life in the Middle Ages* (1889); White, L., "Technology and Invention in the Middle Ages," *Speculum,* XV (1940), 141–159.

RELIGION: Coulton, G. G., *Inquisition and Liberty* (1938); Turberville, A. S., *Mediaeval Heresy and the Inquisition* (1920); Workman, H. B., *Wyclif* (1926); Lorimer, P. J., *John Wycliffe and His English Precursors* (1884); Pantin, W. A., *The English Church in the Fourteenth Century* (1955).

SPECIAL STUDIES: Several important books, monographs, and articles have been written upon this period of which only a few can be listed here. Most important are Gasquet, F. A., *The Black Death of 1348 and 1349* (2nd ed., 1908); Putnam, B. H., *The Enforcement of the Statute of Labourers During the First Decade After the Black Death, 1349–1359* (1908); Oman, C. W. C., *The Great Revolt of 1381* (1906); Harvey, J. H., *Henry Yevele* (1944); Clarke, M. V., *Fourteenth Century Studies* (1937); Cam, H. M., *The Legislators of Mediaeval England* (the Raleigh Lectures on History, British Academy, 1946) and Lapsley, G. T., *Crown, Community and Parliament in the Later Middle Ages* (1953).

LITERATURE: Among many valuable books covering various aspects of literature in the later Middle Ages the following are outstanding: Jusserand, J. J., *Piers Plowman* (1894); Kittredge, G. L., *Chaucer and His Poetry* (1914); Coulton, G. G., *Chaucer and His England* (1937); Owst, G. R., *Literature and Pulpit in Mediaeval England* (1933); Root, P. K., *The Poetry of Chaucer* (1922).

CHAPTER 10

GENERAL WORKS: The best surveys of all or part of the Lancastrian-Yorkist period are Jacob, E. F., *The Fifteenth Century 1399–1485* (1962), vol. vi in the *Oxford History of England;* Oman, C. W. C., *History of England from the Accession of Richard II to the Death of Richard III* (1906); Mowat, R. B., *The Wars of the Roses* (1914); Gairdner, J., *History of the Life and Reign of Richard III* (1879); Kendall, P. M., *Richard III* (1955); Scofield, C. L., *Life and Reign of Edward IV* (2 vols., 1923); Wylie, J. H., and Waugh, W. T., *The Reign of Henry the Fifth* (3 vols., 1914–1929). Three good biographies are Vickers, R. H., *Humphrey, Duke of Gloucester* (1907); Kingsford, C. L., *Henry V* (1901); Oman, C. W. C., *Warwick the Kingmaker* (1891). Useful for chapters 10–21 is Dunham, W. H., and Pargellis, S., *Complaint and Reform in England 1436–1714* (1938). For a special study of a chapter in military history see Newhall, R. A., *The English Conquest of Normandy, 1416–1424* (1924). See also Kingsford, C. L., *Prejudice and Promise in Fifteenth-Century England* (1925) and Hastings, M., "High History or Hack History: England in the Later Middle Ages," *Speculum,* XXXVI (1961).

CONSTITUTIONAL AND LEGAL: The important constitutional and legal developments are described in Chrimes, S. B., *English Constitutional Ideas in the Fifteenth Century* (1936); Gray, H. L., *The Influence of the Commons on Early Legislation* (1932), also useful for the fourteenth century; Hastings, M., *The Court of Common Pleas in Fifteenth-Century England* (1948); Scofield, C. L., *A Study of the Court of Star Chamber* (1900); McKisack, M., *Representation of English Boroughs in the Middle Ages* (1932). Excellent articles are Skeel, C. A. J., "The Influence of the Writings of Sir John Fortescue," *Trans. Royal Historical Society,* X; Shepard, M. A., "The Political and Constitutional Theory of Sir John Fortescue," in *Essays in History and Political Theory,* in honor of C. H. McIlwain (1936); Haskins, G. L., "Parliament in the Later Middle Ages," *A. H. R.,* vol. LIII, No. 4 (July, 1947).

SCIENCE: The most complete discussion of the bibliography of fifteenth and sixteenth century science is by Johnson, F. R., and Larkey, S. V., in *Modern Language Quarterly,* II (1941), 363–401. See also Singer, C., *et al.,* *A History of Technology,* cited earlier.

ECONOMIC AND SOCIAL: The most satisfactory works are Postan, M. M., and Power, E., (eds.) *Studies in English Trade in the Fifteenth Century* (1933); Bennett, H. S., *The Pastons and Their England* (1932); Gairdner, J., (ed.) *The Paston Letters, 1422–1509* (4 vols., 1900–1901); this famous collection of letters is also published in an Everyman edition. See also Abram, A., *Social England in the Fifteenth Century* (1909) and *English Life and Manners in the Later Middle Ages* (1913).

CHAPTER 11

GENERAL WORKS: Useful for chapters 11–20 is the brief survey, Feiling, K., *England under the Tudors and Stuarts* (1927); for chapters 11–15 see Innes, A. D., *England under the Tudors* (1905); Read, C., *The Tudors* (1936);

Seton-Watson, R. W., *Tudor Studies* (1924); Garvin, K., (ed.) *The Great Tudors* (1925); Williams, C. H., *The Tudor Despotism* (1935); Zeeveld, G., *Foundations of Tudor Policy* (1948); Oman, C. W. C., *The Sixteenth Century* (1937). See also Stone, L., *The Tudor Age 1485–1603*, vol. 4 in the *History of England* series published by Thomas Nelson & Sons, Edinburgh; Smith, L. B., "A Taste for Tudors," in *Studies in the Renaissance*, vii (1960). For Chapters 11 and 12 see Fisher, H. A. L., *History of England from the Accession of Henry VII to the Death of Henry VIII* (1906). An excellent volume in the *Pelican History of England* series is Bindoff, S. T., *Tudor England* (1950).

The reign of Henry VII is discussed in Pollard, A. F., *The Reign of Henry VII from Contemporary Sources* (1914); Gairdner, J., *Henry the Seventh* (1899); Temperley, G., *Henry VII* (1914); Busch, W., *England under the Tudors*, vol. i (1895); Stubbs, W., *Seventeen Lectures on the Study of Mediaeval and Modern History* (1896), lectures xv, xvi.

POLITICAL THEORY: In addition to the books listed under the "General Works" section of the bibliography the best studies for the whole Tudor period are Allen, J. W., *History of Political Thought in the Sixteenth Century* (1928); Carlyle, A. J., *History of Mediaeval Political Theory in the West*, vol. vi (1936); and Morris, C., *Political Thought in England: Tyndale to Hooker* (1953).

GEOGRAPHY AND EXPLORATION: For this and the immediately following chapters consult Taylor, E. G. R., *Tudor Geography, 1485–1583* (1930) and Williamson, J. A., *The Tudor Age* (1953). See also Burwash, D., *English Merchant Shipping, 1460–1540* (1948) and Williamson, J. A., *Voyages of John and Sebastian Cabot* (1920); Callender, G., "The Evolution of Sea Power under the First Two Tudors," *History*, vol. v, pp. 141–158 (1921); Beazley, C. R., *John and Sebastian Cabot* (1898) and *Dawn of Modern Geography*, vol. ii (1902).

THE EARLY RENAISSANCE: Seebohm, F., *The Oxford Reformers of 1498* (1867); Froude, J. A., *Life and Letters of Erasmus* (1927); Ferguson, W. S., *The Renaissance in Historical Thought* (1948) and the appropriate sections of his *Europe in Transition 1300–1520* (1963); Gilmore, M. P., *The World of Humanism 1453–1517* (1952); Allen, P. S., *The Age of Erasmus* (1914); sections in Cox, T., *The Renaissance in Europe, 1400–1600* (1933); all of the author's illustrations are taken from works of art in London museums and galleries. See also Parks, G. B., *The English Traveler to Italy in the Middle Ages (to 1535)* (1954) and the bibliography for Chapter 15.

LEGAL AND CONSTITUTIONAL: Pickthorn, K. W. M., *Early Tudor Government: Henry VII* (1934); Percy, E., *Privy Council under the Tudors* (1907), early sections; Pollard, A. F., "Council, Star Chamber, and Privy Council under the Tudors," *English Historical Review*, xxxvii, 337–360, 516–539; xxxviii, 42–60; Hughes, P. L., and Larkin, J. F., *Tudor Royal Proclamations: the Early Tudors 1485–1553* (1964).

LITERATURE: Berdan, J. M., *Early Tudor Poetry, 1485–1547* (1920); Reed, A. W., *Early Tudor Drama* (1926).

IRELAND: Bagwell, R., *Ireland under the Tudors* (3 vols., 1885–1890).

CHAPTER 12

GENERAL WORKS: For Chapters 12–14 consult Froude, J. A., *History of England from the Fall of Wolsey to the Defeat of the Spanish Armada* (12 vols., 1865–1870); this work is frequently unreliable. See also Smith, P., *The*

Age of the Reformation (1920); Brewer, J. S., *The Reign of Henry VIII* (2 vols., 1884); Pollard, A. F., *Henry VIII* (new ed., 1951) and *Wolsey* (1929); Ferguson, C. W., *Naked to Mine Enemies: The Life of Cardinal Wolsey* (1958); Lehmberg, S. E., *Sir Thomas Elyot: Tudor Humanist* (1960); Mackie, J. D., *The Earlier Tudors, 1485–1558* (1952), vol. vii in the *Oxford History of England*.

LEGAL AND CONSTITUTIONAL: Pickthorn, K. W. M., *Early Tudor Government: Henry VIII* (1934); Leadam, I. S. (ed.) *Select Cases Before the King's Council in Star Chamber, 1477–1544* (2 vols., Selden Society, 1903–1911); Usher, R. G., *The Fall of the Court of High Commission* (1913); Pearson, A. F. S., *Church and State* (1928); Baumer, F., *The Early Tudor Theory of Kingship* (1940); Elton, G. R., *The Tudor Revolution in Government* (1953); Richardson, W. C., *Tudor Chamber Administration, 1485–1547* (1952) and *History of the Court of Augmentations, 1536–1554* (1961). See also Hughes, P. L., and Fries, R. F., *Law and Parliament in Tudor-Stuart England: A Documentary Constitutional History 1485–1714* (1959).

ECONOMIC: The best works are Tawney, R. H., and Power, E., *Tudor Economic Documents* (1924); Usher, R. G., *Introduction to the Industrial History of England* (1920), particularly satisfactory for this period; Unwin, G., *Industrial Organization in the Sixteenth and Seventeenth Centuries* (1904); Oman, C. W. C., "The Tudors and the Currency," *Trans. Royal Society,* new series, xiv, 213–303.

RELIGION: Grimm, H. J., *The Reformation Era, 1500–1650* (1954); Elton, G. R., (ed.) *The Reformation, 1520–1559* (1958), vol. II in the *New Cambridge Modern History;* Hughes, P., *The Reformation in England* (3 vols., 1951–1954); Smith, L. B., *Tudor Prelates and Politics 1536–1558* (1953); Constant, G., *The English Reformation* (2 vols., 1939–1941); Baskerville, G., *English Monks and the Suppression of the Monasteries* (1932); Merriman, R. B., *Life and Letters of Thomas Cromwell* (1902); Routh, E. M. G., *Sir Thomas More and His Friends* (1934); Gasquet, F. A., *Henry VIII and the English Monasteries* (1902); Mathew, D., *Catholicism in England, 1535–1935* (1937); Powicke, F. M., *The Reformation in England* (1941); Smith, P., "Luther and Henry VIII," *English Historical Review,* vol. XXV, 656–669; Harbison, E. H., *The Age of the Reformation* (1955) and *The Christian Scholar in the Age of the Reformation* (1956).

CHAPTER 13

GENERAL WORKS: The best studies are Pollard, A. F., *England under the Protector Somerset* (1900) and the first part of his *History of England from the Accession of Edward VI to the Death of Elizabeth, 1547–1603* (1910). See also Froude, J. A., *The Reign of Mary Tudor* (1924); Stone, J. M., *History of Mary I, Queen of England* (1901); Hume, M. A. S., *Two English Queens and Philip* (1908); Prescott, H. F. M., *Mary Tudor* (paperback ed., 1962).

RELIGION: Excellent for Chapters 13–15 are Jordan, W. K., *The Development of Religious Toleration in England* (4 vols., 1932–1940); Gairdner, J., *The English Church in the Sixteenth Century* (1904). For this chapter see particularly Smyth, C. H., *Cranmer and the Reformation under Edward VI* (1926); Pollard, A. F., *Thomas Cranmer and the English Reformation* (1904); Ridley, J., *Thomas Cranmer* (1961); Muller, J. A., *Stephen Gardiner and the Tudor Reaction;* Gasquet, F. A., and Bishop, E., *Edward VI and the Book of Common Prayer* (1891); Pocock, N., "The Conditions of Morals and Religious Beliefs in the Reign of Edward VI," *English Historical Review,* vol. x, pp. 417–444. See also Read, Conyers, *Social and Political Forces in the English Reformation* (1953); Hughes, P., *Rome and the Counter-Reformation in England* (1942); and Schenck, W., *Reginald Pole: Cardinal of England* (1950).

ECONOMIC: Tawney, R. H., *The Agrarian Problem in the Sixteenth Century* (1912), useful for other chapters in the Tudor period; sections in Unwin, G., *Industrial Organization in the Sixteenth and Seventeenth Centuries* (1904) and *Gilds and Companies of London* (1925); sections in Bradley, H., *The Enclosures in England* (1918); Gay, E. F., "Inclosures in England in the Sixteenth Century," *Quarterly Journal of Economics,* XVII, 576–597; Thirsk, J., *Tudor Enclosures* (1959).

CHAPTER 14

GENERAL WORKS: The finest biography of Queen Elizabeth I is Neale, J. E., *Queen Elizabeth* (1st ed. 1934, paperback ed. 1957). Less satisfactory is Williams, C. H., *Queen Elizabeth* (1936). Of great value for the period is Black, J. B., *The Reign of Elizabeth 1558–1603* (2nd ed., 1959), in the *Oxford History of England* series. Also useful are Cheyney, E. P., *History of England from the Defeat of the Spanish Armada to the Death of Elizabeth* (2 vols., 1914–1926); Creighton, M., *The Age of Elizabeth* (1876); Rowse, A. L., *The England of Elizabeth* (2 vols., 1951–1955).

RELIGION: Brown, P. H., *John Knox* (2 vols., 1895); Maitland, F. W., "The Anglican Settlement and the Scottish Reformation" in the *Cambridge Modern History,* vol. ii, chap. xvi; Klein, A. J., *Intolerance in the Reign of Elizabeth* (1917); Meyer, A. O., *England and the Catholic Church under Elizabeth* (1916); Birt, H. N., *The Elizabethan Religious Settlement* (1907); Frere, W. H., *The English Church in the Reign of Elizabeth and James I* (1904); Gee, H., *Elizabethan Clergy and the Settlement of Religion, 1558–1564* (1898); Dawley, P. W., *John Whitgift and the English Reformation* (1954).

BIOGRAPHIES: Among several good biographies the following are outstanding: Brook, V. J. K., *A Life of Archbishop Parker* (1961); Hume, M. A. S., *Philip II* (1897) and *The Great Lord Burghley* (1898); Henderson, T. F., *Mary, Queen of Scots* (2 vols., 1905); Rowse, A. L., *Sir Walter Raleigh: His Family and Private Life* (1962); Wallace, W. M., *Sir Walter Raleigh* (1959); Strathmann, E. A., *Sir Walter Raleigh* (1951); Read, C., *Mr. Secretary Walsingham and the Policy of Queen Elizabeth* (3 vols., 1925); *Mr. Secretary Cecil and Queen Elizabeth* (1955); and *Lord Burghley and Queen Elizabeth* (1960).

SPECIAL STUDIES: Notestein, W., *A History of Witchcraft in England, 1558–1718;* Evans, F. M. G., *The Principal Secretary of State . . . 1558 to 1680* (1923); Bindoff, S. T., et al., *Elizabethan Government and Society: Essays Presented to Sir John Neale* (1961). Of importance for the Tudor and Stuart periods is Jordan, W. K., *The Chantries of London 1480–1660* (1960); *The Forming of the Charitable Institutions of the West of England, 1480–1660* (1960); and *Philanthropy in England 1480–1660* (1959). See also the bibliography for Chapter 15.

CHAPTER 15

GENERAL WORKS: See the bibliography for Chapter 14. The following are valuable: Wright, L. B., *Middle Class Culture in Elizabethan England* (1935); Salzman, L. F., *England in Tudor Times* (1933); Hall, H., *Society in the*

Elizabethan Age (1888), still useful; Taylor, H. O., *Thought and Expression in the Sixteenth Century* (1920); Einstein, L., *Tudor Ideals* (1921); Raleigh, W., Lee, S., and Onions, C. T., (eds.) *Shakespeare's England* (2 vols., 1917); Lee, S., *Great Englishmen of the Sixteenth Century* (1904); Byrne, M. St. Clare, *Elizabethan Life in Town and Country* (new ed., 1947); Stephenson, H. T., *Elizabethan People* (1910); Williamson, J. A., *The Age of Drake* (1938).

TUDOR SEAMEN: Corbett, J. S., *Drake and the Tudor Navy* (2 vols., 1899); *Sir Francis Drake* (1894); and *The Successors of Drake* (1900); Raleigh, W., *English Voyages in the Sixteenth Century* (1910); Mason, A. E. W., *The Life of Francis Drake* (1941); Mattingly, G., *The Armada* (1959); Lewis, M. A., *The Spanish Armada* (1960); Unwin, R., *The Defeat of John Hawkins* (1960); Williamson, J. A., *Hawkins of Plymouth* (1949); Quinn, D. B., *The Voyages and Colonizing Enterprises of Sir Humphrey Gilbert* (2 vols., 1940).

ECONOMIC AND SOCIAL: Foster, W., *England's Quest of Eastern Trade* (1933), six studies; Wood, A. C., *A History of the Levant Company* (1935); Parks, G., *Richard Hakluyt and the English Voyages* (1928); Lingelbach, W. E., *Merchant Adventurers of England* (1902); Seeley, J. R., *The Growth of British Policy*, vol. i (1895); Williamson, J. A., *A Short History of British Expansion* (4th ed., 2 vols., 1956); Campbell, M. C., *The English Yeoman under Elizabeth and the Early Stuarts* (1942), a brilliant result of careful scholarship; Gerson, A. J., Vaughan, E. V., and Deardorff, N. R., *Studies in the History of English Commerce in the Tudor Period* (1912); Knappen, M. M., *Tudor Puritanism: A Chapter in the History of Idealism* (1939); Hannay, D., *The Great Chartered Companies* (1926); Scott, W. R., *Joint Stock Companies* (3 vols., 1910–1912); Simpson, A., *The Wealth of the Gentry 1540–1660: East Anglian Studies* (1961); Trevor-Roper, H. R., *The Gentry, 1540–1640* (1953); Tawney, R. H., "The Rise of the Gentry, 1558–1640," *Economic History Review*, vol. XI, No. 1 (1947); Willan, T. S., *Studies in Elizabethan Foreign Trade* (1960).

ASPECTS OF THE RENAISSANCE: Chew, S. C., *The Crescent and the Rose: Islam and England during the Renaissance* (1937); Einstein, L., *The Italian Renaissance in England* (1913); Hearnshaw, F. J. C., (ed.) *Social and Political Ideas of Some Great Thinkers of the Renaissance and Reformation* (1925); Gardner, T., and Stratton, A., *Domestic Architecture of England during the Tudor Period* (2 vols., 1929); Addy, S. O., *The Evolution of the English House* (1933); Boyd, M. C., *Elizabethan Music and Musical Criticism* (1940); Fellowes, E. H., *English Madrigal Composers* (1921) and *William Byrd* (1936); Westrupp, J. A., *Purcell* (1937). See also the appropriate sections of Waterhouse, E. K., *Painting in Britain 1530–1790* (1953) and Mercer, E., *English Art 1553–1625* (1963) vol. vii of *The Oxford History of English Art*. See further the bibliography for Chapter 11.

LITERATURE: Wilson, F. P., *Elizabethan and Jacobean* (1935); Bush, D., *The Renaissance and English Humanism* (1940); Cawley, R. R., *Unpathed Waters; Studies in the Influence of the Voyages on Elizabethan Literature* (1940); Paradise, N. B., *Thomas Lodge* (1931); Davis, B. E. C., *Edmund Spenser* (1933); Chambers, E. K., *William Shakespeare* (2 vols., 1930) and *The Elizabethan Stage* (4 vols., 1923); Adams, J. Q., *A Life of William Shakespeare* (1923); Boas, F. S., *An Introduction to Tudor Drama* (1933) and *Christopher Marlowe* (1940); Lewis, C. S., *English Literature in the Sixteenth Century* (1954), vol. iii of the *Oxford History of English Literature;* Munz, P., *The Place of Hooker in the History of Thought* (1952); Caspari,

F., *Humanism and the Social Order in Tudor England* (1954); Boas, M., *The Scientific Renaissance 1450–1630* (1962).

CONSTITUTIONAL AND LEGAL: Tanner, J. R., *Tudor Constitutional Documents, 1485–1603* (2nd ed., 1930); there is an excellent introductory essay. See also Prothero, G. W., *Select Statutes and Other Constitutional Documents Illustrative of the Reigns of Elizabeth and James I* (4th ed., 1913); Maitland, F. W., *English Law and the Renaissance* (1901); Neale, J. E., *The Elizabethan House of Commons* (1950), *Elizabeth I and Her Parliaments, 1559–1581* (1953) and *Elizabeth I and Her Parliaments, 1584–1601* (1957). See also Elton, G. R., (ed.) *The Tudor Constitution: Documents and Commentary* (1960). This book contains several debatable conclusions and students should also consult other works on the subject.

CHAPTER 16

GENERAL WORKS: Several of the items listed here are valuable for Chapters 16–21. See Trevelyan, G. M., *England under the Stuarts* (1953); Clark, G. N., *The Seventeenth Century* (1929); Davies, G., *The Early Stuarts, 1603–1660* (2nd ed., 1959), in the *Oxford History of England* series; Hill, C., *The Century of Revolution 1603–1714* (1961), vol. 5 in the *History of England* series published by Thomas Nelson & Sons, Edinburgh; Ashley, M., *England in the Seventeenth Century 1603–1714* (1952) in the *Pelican History of England* series; Gardiner, S. R., *History of England, 1603–1625* (1883–1885); Harrison, G. B., *Jacobean Journal* (1941); Havran, M. J., *The Catholics in Caroline England* (1962). Very useful is Taylor, E. G. R., *Late Tudor and Early Stuart Geography, 1583–1650* (1934).

RELIGION AND EMPIRE: Newton, A. P., *The Colonizing Activity of the English Puritans* (1914); Wright, L. B., *Religion and Empire: the Alliance between Piety and Commerce in English Expansion, 1558–1625* (1943) and *The Atlantic Frontier: Colonial American Civilization 1607–1673* (1947); Osgood, H. L., *The American Colonies in the Seventeenth Century* (2 vols., 1904–1907); Innes, A. D., *The Maritime and Colonial Expansion of England under the Stuarts, 1603–1714* (1931); Beer, G. L., *The Origins of the British Colonial System, 1558–1660* (1908); Notestein, W., *The English People on the Eve of Colonization 1603–1630* (1954).

CONSTITUTIONAL: Judson, M. A., *The Crisis of the Constitution* (1949); McIlwain, C. H., *The Political Works of James I* (1918) and sections of *The High Court of Parliament and Its Supremacy* (1910); Gooch, G. P., *Political Thought from Bacon to Halifax* (1915); Allen, J. W., *English Political Theory, 1603–1640* (1938); Figgis, J. N., *The Divine Right of Kings* (1922); Tanner, J. R., *English Constitutional Conflicts of the Seventeenth Century 1603–1689* (new ed., 1961); Wormuth, F. D., *The Royal Prerogative, 1603–1649* (1939); Moir, T. L., *The Addled Parliament of 1614* (1958); Notestein, W., "The Winning of the Initiative by the House of Commons," *Proceedings of the British Academy*, 1924–25; Willson, D. H., *Privy Councillors in the House of Commons 1604–1629* (1940); Aiken, W. A., and Henning, B. D., (eds.) *Conflict in Stuart England: Essays in Honor of Wallace Notestein* (1960); Eusden, J., *Puritan Lawyers and Politics in Early Seventeenth-Century England* (1958).

BIOGRAPHIES: Taylor, A. E., *Francis Bacon* (1924); Williamson, H. R., *King James I* (1935) and *George Villiers, First Duke of Buckingham* (1940); Willson, D. H., *King James VI and I* (1955); Stafford, H. G., *King James VI of Scotland and the Throne of England* (1940); Lee, M., *John Maitland of*

Thirlestane and the Foundation of the Stewart Despotism in Scotland (1959); Bowen, C. D., *The Lion and the Throne: the Life and Times of Sir Edward Coke (1552–1634)* (1957).

CHAPTER 17

GENERAL WORKS: In addition to the volumes cited for Chapter 16 the reader may profitably refer to Gardiner, S. R., *History of England, 1625–1642* (2 vols., 1883–1885); Wedgwood, C. V., *The King's Peace, 1637–1641* (1955) and *The King's War, 1641–1647* (1959).

CONSTITUTIONAL: Relf, F. H., *The Petition of Right* (1917); Pease, T. C., *The Leveller Movement* (1916); Brailsford, H. N., *The Levellers of the English Revolution* (1961); Aylmer, G. E., *The King's Servants: the Civil Service of Charles I 1625–1642* (1961); Pocock, J. G. A., *The Ancient Constitution and the Feudal Law: A Study of English Historical Thought in the Seventeenth Century* (1957); Ashton, R., *The Crown and the Money Market 1603–1640* (1961). See also the relevant chapters in Sabine, G. H., *A History of Political Theory* (3rd ed., 1961).

RELIGION: Tawney, R. H., *Religion and the Rise of Capitalism* (1926); Whiting, C. E., *Studies in English Puritanism* (1931); Hutton, W. H., *The English Church, 1625–1714* (1903), early chapters; Schneider, H. W., *The Puritan Mind* (1930); Hughes, P., *The Reformation in England,* vol. III (1954); Solt, L., *Saints in Arms* (1959).

BIOGRAPHIES: Outstanding among several biographies are Jones, A. S. D., *Archbishop Laud* (1927); Trevor-Roper, H. R., *Archbishop Laud 1573–1645* (1940); Higham, F. M. G., *Charles I* (1932); Wedgwood, C. V., *Strafford* (1935) and *Thomas Wentworth: First Earl of Strafford 1593–1641: A Revaluation* (1961); Traill, H. D., *Lord Strafford* (1899); Stearns, Raymond P., *The Strenuous Puritan: Hugh Peter, 1598–1660* (1954); Hulme, H., *The Life of Sir John Eliot 1592 to 1632: Struggle for Parliamentary Freedom* (1957); Schlatter, R., *Richard Baxter and Puritan Politics* (1961); Wade, C. E., *John Pym* (1912); Brett, S. R., *John Pym 1583–1643* (1940); Hexter, J. H., *The Reign of King Pym* (1941). See also Wedgwood, C. V., *A Coffin for King Charles* (1964). Most of the works cited here are useful for the following chapters.

CHAPTER 18

GENERAL WORKS: For this and the following chapters see Gooch, G. P., *English Democratic Ideas in the Seventeenth Century* (2nd ed., by H. J. Laski, 1927); Zagorin, P., *A History of Political Thought in the English Revolution* (1954); Feiling, K., *Early History of the Tory Party, 1640–1714* (1924). See also Gardiner, S. R. A., *History of the Great Civil War, 1642–1649* (4 vols., 1893) and *History of England, 1642–1656* (2 vols., 1883–1885); Firth, C. H., *The Last Years of the Protectorate* (1909) and *The House of Lords during the Civil War* (1910).

RELIGION: Henson, H. H., *Studies in English Religion in the Seventeenth Century* (1904); Firth, C. H., *Oliver Cromwell and the Rule of the Puritans in England* (1905, 1953); Sykes, N., *Old Priest and New Presbyter* (1956); Haller, W., *Liberty and Reformation in the Puritan Revolution* (1955) and *The Rise of Puritanism* (1957); Scholes, P. A., *The Puritans and Music in England and New England* (1934); Simpson, A., *Puritanism in Old and New England* (1955). See also the bibliographies for Chapters 16, 17.

ECONOMIC: Ashley, M. P., *Financial and Commercial Policy under the Cromwellian Protectorate* (1934); Beer, G. L., "Cromwell's Policy in Its Economic Aspects," *Political Science Quarterly*, xvi, xvii.

CONSTITUTIONAL: Haller, W., *Tracts on Liberty in the Puritan Revolution* (2 vols., 1934); Latham, R. C., "English Revolutionary Thought, 1640–1660," *History*, March, 1945; Haller, W., and Davies, G., *The Leveller Tracts, 1647–1653* (1944); Sabine, G. H., (ed.), *The Works of Gerrard Winstanley* (1941); Wolfe, D. M. (ed.), *Leveller Manifestoes of the Puritan Revolution* (1944); Gardiner, S. R. A., *The Constitutional Documents of the Puritan Revolution* (1899); Keeler, M. F., *The Long Parliament 1640–1641: A Biographical Study of Its Members* (1954); Brunton, D. O., and Pennington, D. H., *Members of the Long Parliament* (1954); Underdown, D., *Royalist Conspiracy in England 1649–1660* (1960).

BIOGRAPHIES: Firth, C. H., *Oliver Cromwell* (1909); Buchan, J., *Oliver Cromwell* (1934); Morley, J., *Oliver Cromwell* (1901); Ashley, M. P., *The Greatness of Oliver Cromwell* (1957). See also Carlyle, T., (ed. S. C. Lomas) *Letters and Speeches of Oliver Cromwell* (1905), and Abbott, W. C., *A Bibliography of Oliver Cromwell* (1929) and *The Writings and Speeches of Oliver Cromwell* (4 vols., 1938–1947). See further Hardacre, P. H., "Writings on Oliver Cromwell Since 1929," *The Journal of Modern History*, vol. XXXIII, No. 1 (March, 1961).

CHAPTER 19

GENERAL WORKS: Of special value for Chapters 19–21 is Clark, G. N., *The Later Stuarts, 1660–1774* (new ed., 1940), in the *Oxford History of England* series. For this chapter see Ogg, D., *England in the Reign of Charles II* (2nd ed., 2 vols., 1955); Lodge, R., *History of England from the Restoration to the Death of William III* (1910); Turberville, A. S., *Commonwealth and Restoration* (1936); Bryant, A., *The England of Charles II* (1935). See also Walcott, R., "The Later Stuarts (1660–1714): Significant Work of the Last Twenty Years (1939–1959)," *American Historical Review*, LXVII, No. 2 (January, 1962).

SPECIAL STUDIES: Feiling, K., *English Foreign Policy, 1660–1672* (1930); Davies, G., *Essays on the Later Stuarts* (1958) and *The Restoration of Charles II 1658–1660* (1955); Beer, G. L., *The Old Colonial System, 1660–1754* (1912); Plum, H. G., *Restoration Puritanism* (1943); Overton, J. H., *Life in the English Church, 1660–1714* (1885). Indispensable is the work of Trevelyan, G. M., *The English Revolution, 1688–1689* (2nd ed., 1946). See also Wilson, C. H., *Profit and Power: A Study of England and the Dutch Wars* (1957).

BIOGRAPHIES: Excellent are Trail, H. D., *Shaftesbury* (1886); Chapman, H. W., *Mary II, Queen of England* (1953); Bryant, A., *King Charles II* (1936); Airy, O., *Charles II* (1901); Kenyon, J. P., *Robert Spencer, Earl of Sunderland 1641–1702* (1958); Cranston, M., *John Locke: A Biography* (1957); O'Connor, D. J., *John Locke* (1952).

CHAPTER 20

GENERAL WORKS: Willey, B., *The Seventeenth Century Background* (1934); Garnett, R., *The Age of Dryden* (1932); Woodhouse, A. S. P., *Puritanism and Liberty* (1938). Readers interested in the architecture and furniture of the Stuart age may consult Webb, G., *Wren* (1937); Summerson, J. H., *Sir*

Christopher Wren (1953); Stratton, A., *The English Interior* (1920); Gloag, J., *English Furniture* (1944). The art and architecture of the later Stuart period are described in vol. viii of the *Oxford History of English Art* (1957). An excellent discussion of science in the seventeenth century is Clark, G. N., *Science and Social Welfare in the Age of Newton* (1937). See also Thorndike, L., vols. vii and viii of *A History of Magic and Experimental Science,* cited earlier; Westfall, R. S., *Science and Religion in Seventeenth-Century England* (1958); Boas, M., *Robert Boyle and Seventeenth-Century Chemistry* (1958); Merton, R. K., "Science, Technology and Society in Seventeenth Century England," *Osiris,* IV (1938), 360–632; More, L. T., *Isaac Newton* (1934).

ECONOMIC AND SOCIAL: Trotter, E., *Seventeenth Century Life in the Country Parish* (1919); Coate, M., *Social Life in Stuart England* (1924); Clark, G. N., "Early Capitalism and Invention," *Economic History Review,* VI (1936), 143–156, and *The Wealth of England from 1496 to 1760* (1946). For this and other chapters see Heckscher, E. F., *Mercantilism* (2 vols., 1935). See also W. K. Jordan's three volumes on British philanthropy cited in the references for Chapter 14.

LITERATURE: Grierson, H. J. C., *Cross Currents in English Literature in the Seventeenth Century* (1929); Lershman, J. B., *The Metaphysical Poets* (1934); Wendell, B., *The Temper of the Seventeenth Century in English Literature* (1904); Tillyard, E. M. W., *Milton* (1930); Bentley, G. E., *The Jacobean and Caroline Stage* (1941); Bryant, A., *Samuel Pepys* (2 vols., 1933–1939); Eliot, T. S., *John Dryden* (1927); Dobrée, B., *Restoration Comedy* (1924) and *Restoration Tragedy* (1929); Nicoll, Allardyce, *A History of Restoration Drama, 1660–1700* (1929); Bush, D., *English Literature in the Early Seventeenth Century, 1600–1660* (1945), vol. v of the *Oxford History of English Literature.* There are many editions of the works of Evelyn, Harrington, Hobbes, Locke, and Pepys. See also Wedgwood, C. V., *Poetry and Politics under the Stuarts* (1960).

CHAPTER 21

GENERAL WORKS: Useful for Chapters 21–27 are Owen, J. B., *The Eighteenth Century 1714–1815,* vol. 6 in the *History of England* series published by Thomas Nelson & Sons, Edinburgh; Lecky, W. E. H., *History of England in the Eighteenth Century* (7 vols., 1878–1890); Oliver, F. S., *The Endless Adventure* (3 vols., 1930–1931); Leadam, I. S., *History of England from the Accession of Anne to the Death of George II* (1909). Of special value for this chapter are Trevelyan, G. M., *England under Queen Anne* (3 vols., 1930–1934); Churchill, W. S., *Marlborough, His Life and Times* (6 vols., 1933–1939); Ogg, D., *England in the Reigns of James II and William III* (1957). The great work of T. B. Macaulay begins with the Whig Revolution: *A History of England from the Accession of James II* (6 vols., 1913–1915; there are many editions). See also Bultmann, W. A., "Early Hanoverian England (1714–60). Some Recent Writings," *The Journal of Modern History,* vol. XXVI, No. 1 (March, 1963).

SPECIAL STUDIES: Petrie, C., *The Stuart Pretenders* (1933); Taylor, F., *The Wars of Marlborough* (2 vols., 1922); Atkinson, C. T., *Marlborough and the Rise of the British Army* (1921); Turberville, A. S., *The House of Lords in the Reign of William III* (1923); Morgan, W. T., *English Political Parties and Leaders in the Reign of Queen Anne* (1920); Ehrman, T., *The Navy in the War of William III 1689–1697* (1961).

CHAPTER 22

GENERAL WORKS: Williams, B., *The Whig Supremacy, 1714–1760* (2nd rev. ed., 1962), in the *Oxford History of England* series; Robertson, C. G., *England under the Hanoverians* (1934); Marshall, D., *The Eighteenth Century* (1962) in the History of England series edited by W. N. Medlicott, mentioned earlier; Green, V. H. H., *The Hanoverians, 1714–1815* (1948); Walcott, R., *English Politics in the Early Eighteenth Century* (1956); Petrie, C. A., *The Jacobite Movement* (2 vols., 3rd ed., 1959); Laprade, W. T., *Public Opinion and Politics in Eighteenth Century England to the Fall of Walpole* (1936). See also *English Historical Documents,* vol. X, 1714–1783, eds. Horn, D. B., and Ransome, M. (1957); Plumb, J. H., *England in the Eighteenth Century 1714–1815* (1954) in the *Pelican History of England;* George, M. D., *England in Transition* (1931). Of interest to many readers will be Wyndham, M., *Chronicles of the Eighteenth Century* (2 vols., 1924); these volumes contain the Sir Thomas Lyttleton correspondence, which gives a typical picture of the part of the community that formed the real government of England in the eighteenth century.

SPECIAL STUDIES: Lodge, R., *Great Britain and Prussia in the Eighteenth Century* (1913); Winstanley, D. A., *Lord Chatham and the Whig Opposition* (1912); Robertson, C. G., *Lord Chatham and the British Empire* (1948); Hoon, E. A., *The Organization of the English Customs System, 1698–1786* (1938); this book includes an account of the organization, administration, and the basic records upon which a statistical knowledge of the mercantile era in England must rest. See also Corbett, J. S., *England in the Seven Years' War* (2 vols., 1907); Brooke, J., *The Chatham Administration 1766–1768* (1961); Williams, B., *Cartaret and Newcastle: a Contrast in Contemporaries* (1943).

BIOGRAPHIES: Williams, B., *The Life of William Pitt, Earl of Chatham* (2 vols., 1915) and *Stanhope: A Study in Eighteenth Century War and Diplomacy* (1932); Sherrard, O. A., *Lord Chatham* (3 vols., 1952–1958); Morley, J., *Sir Robert Walpole* (1921); Plumb, J. H., *Sir Robert Walpole: the Making of a Statesman* (1956); *Sir Robert Walpole: the King's Minister* (1961); and *The First Four Georges* (1957); Stacey, C. P., *Quebec, 1759* (1960); Waugh, W. T., *James Wolfe* (1933); Dodwell, H. H., *Dupleix and Clive* (1929); Forrest, G., *Life of Lord Clive* (2 vols., 1918). See also Lord Macaulay's famous essay on Clive; Stirling-Taylor, G. K., *Robert Walpole and His Age* (1931); Sichel, W. S., *Bolingbroke and His Times* (2 vols., 1901–1902); Robertson, C. G., *Bolingbroke* (1947); Owen, J. B., *The Rise of the Pelhams* (1957).

CHAPTER 23

GENERAL WORKS: For this and other chapters about the eighteenth century the student of ideas will find of particular interest Stephen, L., *History of English Thought in the Eighteenth Century* (2 vols., 1902); the four superb essays in Black, J. B., *The Art of History* (1926); Willey, B., *The Eighteenth Century Background* (1941); and Becker, C., *The Heavenly City of the Eighteenth Century Philosophers* (1932), one of the finest books written about the eighteenth century.

ECONOMIC AND SOCIAL: Andrews, C. B., (ed.) *The Torrington Diaries* (4 vols., 1934–1938); Turberville, A. S., *English Men and Manners in the Eighteenth Century* (1929) and (ed.) *Johnson's England* (2 vols., 1933); Jackson, F. J. F., *Social Life in England, 1750–1850* (1916); Marshall, D.,

English People in the Eighteenth Century (1956); Ashton, T. S., *Economic Fluctuations in England, 1700–1800* (1959) and *Economic History of England: the Eighteenth Century* (1955). See also the bibliography for Chapter 25.

RELIGION: The best books are Sykes, N., *Church and State in England in the Eighteenth Century* (1934); Overton, J. H., *John Wesley* (1881); Abbey, C. J., and Overton, J. H., *The English Church in the Eighteenth Century* (1887); Gill, F. C., (ed.) *Selected Letters of John Wesley* (1956); Mossner, E. C., *Bishop Butler and the Age of Reason* (1936). See also Coomer, D., *English Dissent under the Early Hanoverians* (1946); Every, G., *The High Church Party* (1956); Stromberg, R. N., *Religious Liberalism in XVIIIth Century England* (1954).

ART: Of special value for the eighteenth century are Crundall, H. M., *A History of the British Water Color Painting* (1933); Newton, E., *British Painting* (1943); Gray, B., *The English Print* (1937); Fry, R., et al., *Georgian Art, 1760–1820* (1929).

LITERATURE: Dowden, E., *The French Revolution and English Literature* (1897); Krutch, J. W., *Comedy and Conscience after the Restoration* (1924); Van Doren, C., *Swift* (1930); Bailey, J., *Doctor Johnson and His Circle* (1913); Dobrée, B., *English Literature in the Early Eighteenth Century 1700–1740* (1959), vol. vii of the *Oxford History of English Literature;* Baker, H., *William Hazlitt* (1962); Fisher, P. F., *The Valley of Vision* (1962), a study of William Blake; Smithers, P., *Life of Joseph Addison* (1954); Bateson, F. W., *English Comic Drama, 1700–1750* (1932); Tillotson, G., *On the Poetry of Pope* (1938); Nicoll, A., *A History of Early Eighteenth Century Drama 1700–1750* (1929) and *A History of Late Eighteenth Century Drama 1750–1800* (1927); Cross, W., *The Life and Times of Laurence Sterne* (1925).

SPECIAL STUDIES: Hearnshaw, F. J. C., (ed.) *Social and Political Ideas of Some English Thinkers of the Augustan Age* (1928); Brinton, C., *The Political Ideas of the English Romanticists* (1926); Lecky, W. E. H., *History of Ireland in the Eighteenth Century* (1893); Laski, H. J., *English Political Thought from Locke to Bentham* (1920); Mahan, A. T., *The Influence of Sea Power on History, 1660–1783* (32nd ed., 1928); Maccoby, S., *English Radicalism, 1762–1785* (1955); Robbins, C., *The Eighteenth-Century Commonwealthman* (1959). See also Foord, A. S., *His Majesty's Opposition 1714–1830* (1964).

CHAPTER 24

GENERAL WORKS: There are many competent studies of the background and progress of the American Revolution. Among the best are Namier, L. B., *England in the Age of the American Revolution* (2nd ed., 1961); Andrews, C. M., *Colonial Background of the American Revolution* (1924); Egerton, H. E., *Causes and Character of the American Revolution* (1923); Schuyler, R. L., *Parliament and the British Empire* (1929) and *The Fall of the Old Colonial System: A Study of British Free Trade, 1770–1870* (1945); Rossiter, C., *Seedtime of the Republic: the Origin of the American Tradition of Political Liberty* (1953); Van Tyne, C. H., *The Causes of the War of Independence* (1907); McIlwain, C. H., *The American Revolution* (1923); Osgood, H. L., *The American Colonies in the Seventeenth Century* (3 vols., 1904–1907) and *The American Colonies in the Eighteenth Century* (4 vols., 1924–1925); Becker, C. L., *The Eve of the Revolution* (1918); Morgan, E. S., *The Birth of the Republic 1763–1789* (1956); Ritcheson, C. R., *British Politics and the American Revolution* (1954). See also Beer, G. L., *Commercial Policy of*

England Towards the Colonies (1893) and *British Colonial Policy, 1754–1765* (1907). Always useful is the *Cambridge History of the British Empire*, vol. I. See also the appropriate sections of Fortescue, J., (ed.) *The Correspondence of King George the Third* (6 vols., 1927–1928); Aspinall, A., (ed.) *The Later Correspondence of George III* (5 vols., 1962–) and Watson, J. S., *The Reign of George III* (1960), vol. xii in the *Oxford History of England* series.

SPECIAL STUDIES: Namier, L. B., *The Structure of Politics at the Accession of George III* (2 vols., 1929); Winstanley, D. A., *Personal and Party Government . . . 1760–1766* (1910); Coupland, R., *The Quebec Act* (1925); Albion, R. G., *Forests and Sea Power: the Timber Problems of the Royal Navy, 1652–1862* (1926); Anderson, T. S., *The Command of the Howe Brothers during the American Revolution* (1936); Van Tyne, C. H., *The Loyalists in the American Revolution* (1902); Butterfield, H., *George III, Lord North and the People 1779–1780* (1949) and *George III and the Historians* (rev. ed., 1959); Pares, R., *King George and the Politicians* (1953); Morgan, E. S. and H. M., *The Stamp Act Crisis: Prologue to Revolution* (1953); Dickerson, O. M., *The Navigation Acts and the American Revolution* (1951).

BIOGRAPHIES: Trevelyan, G. O., *The Early Life of Charles James Fox* (new ed., 1908); Lyall, A. C., *Warren Hastings* (1926); Feiling, K., *Warren Hastings* (1954); Bleackley, H. W., *Life of John Wilkes* (1917); Freeman, D. S., *George Washington: A Biography* (7 vols., 1948–1957); Brown, G. S., *The American Secretary: The Colonial Policy of Lord George Germain 1775–1778* (1963).

CHAPTER 25

GENERAL WORKS: For this and other chapters see Clapham, J. H., *An Economic History of Modern Britain* (3 vols., 1930–1938), mentioned earlier; Slater, G., *The Growth of Modern England* (1932); Usher, A. P., *Introduction to the Industrial History of England* (1920). Of special value for a general study of the economic revolution are Hammond, J. L. and B., *The Rise of Modern Industry* (1937); Mantoux, P., *The Industrial Revolution in the Eighteenth Century* (1928), excellent bibliography; Toynbee, A., *Lectures on the Industrial Revolution in the Eighteenth Century in England* (1908); Prothero, R. E., (Lord Ernle) *English Farming Past and Present* (1913); Usher, A. P., *A History of Mechanical Inventions* (1929); Curtler, W. H. R., *The Enclosure and Redistribution of Our Land* (1920). See also Hobson, J. A., *The Evolution of Modern Capitalism* (1904), still useful; Court, W. H. B., *The Rise of the Midland Industries* (1938); Pinchbeck, I., *Women Workers in the Industrial Revolution, 1750–1850* (1930); Thompson, E. P., *The Making of the English Working Class* (1964); Slater, G., *English Peasantry and the Enclosure of the Common Fields* (1907). Consult also the general economic histories listed earlier.

SPECIAL STUDIES: There have been numerous books, monographs, and articles about special phases of the economic revolution. In addition to the general bibliographical sources listed at the beginning of this section the reader may consult Power, E., *The Industrial Revolution, 1750–1850: a Select Bibliography* (Economic History Society, London, 1927). The following studies are excellent: Ashton, T. S., *Iron and Steel in the Industrial Revolution* (1924); Chapman, S. J., *The Lancashire Cotton Industry* (1904); Daniels, W., *The Early English Cotton Industry* (1932); Dumville, J., and Kershaw, S., *The Worsted Industry* (1947); Gras, N. S. B., *The Evolution of the English Corn Market from the Twelfth to the Eighteenth Century* (1915); Heaton, H., *The York-*

shire Woolen Industries (1920); Honey, W. B., *English Pottery and Porcelain* (1933); Jackman, W. T., *The Development of Transportation in Modern England* (2 vols., 1916); Lipson, E., *A History of the Woolen and Worsted Industries* (1921); Nef, J. U., *The Rise of the British Coal Industry* (1924). See also Singer, C., *et al.*, *A History of Technology*, vol. iv. (1958).

CHAPTER 26

GENERAL WORKS: The best survey volumes are Brown, P. A., *The French Revolution in English History;* Laprade, W. T., *England and the French Revolution* (1904); Mathieson, W. L., *England in Transition, 1789–1832* (1920); Bryant, A., *The Years of Endurance, 1793–1802* (1942). An excellent book on the reform currents of these years is Hall, W. P., *British Radicalism, 1791–1797* (1912). A good collection of documents is vol. XI of the *English Historical Documents* series covering the period 1783–1832 (eds. Aspinall, A., and Smith, E. A., 1959). Always useful for the whole European scene are Gottschalk, L., *The Era of the French Revolution* (1929) and Brinton, C., *A Decade of Revolution, 1789–1799* (1934).

SPECIAL STUDIES: Veitch, G. S., *Genesis of Parliamentary Reform* (1908), for this and other chapters; Brailsford, H. N., *Shelley, Godwin, and Their Circle* (1913); Morley, J., *Burke* (1903); Mahoney, T. H. D., *Edmund Burke and Ireland* (1960); Copeland, T. W., *The Correspondence of Edmund Burke* (8 vols., 1958–   ); Taylor, G. R. S., *Mary Wollstonecraft* (1911); Mahan, A. T., *The Influence of Sea Power upon the French Revolution and Empire* (2 vols., 10th ed., 1898). See also the critical introduction and text of F. E. L. Priestley's edition of William Godwin's *Enquiry Concerning Political Justice* (3 vols., 1948). See further Parkinson, C. N., *War in the Eastern Seas 1793–1815* (1954) and *Trade in the Eastern Seas, 1793–1813* (1937); Renwick, W. L., *English Literature 1789–1815* (1963), vol. ix of the *Oxford History of English Literature.*

CHAPTER 27

GENERAL WORKS: Oman, C., *Britain Against Napoleon* (1942); Bryant, A., *The Years of Victory, 1802–1812* (1945); Rose, J. H., *Life of Napoleon I* (1922); Fisher, H. A. L., *Napoleon* (1928). A good survey of the whole European struggle is Gershoy, L., *The French Revolution and Napoleon* (1933). The most brilliant modern discussion of the Napoleonic period is Bruun, G., *Napoleon and the French Imperium* (1935).

SPECIAL STUDIES: Macunn, F. J., *The Contemporary English View of Napoleon* (1914); Webster, C. K., *British Diplomacy, 1813–1815* (1921); Perkins, B., *Prologue to War: England and the United States, 1805–1812* (1961); Cruttwell, C. R. M. F., *Wellington* (1936); Fremantle, A. F., *Nelson* (1933); Guedalla, P., *Wellington* (1931); Wilkinson, C., *Nelson* (1932); Rosebery, Lord, *Pitt* (1892); Coupland, R., *Wilberforce, A Narrative* (1923); Galpin, W. F., *The Grain Supply of England during the Napoleonic Wars* (1925); Heckscher, E., *The Continental System* (1922); Melvin, F. E., *Napoleon's Navy System* (1919). A detailed history of British military operations in Spain and Portugal is Oman, C., *The Peninsular War* (7 vols., 1902–1934).

CHAPTER 28

GENERAL WORKS: Useful for this and following chapters are Fay, C. R., *Great Britain from Adam Smith to the Present Day* (1928); Walpole, S., *The History of England from the Conclusion of the Great War in 1815* (5 vols.,

1878–1886); Slater, G., *The Growth of Modern England* (1932), mentioned earlier; Fremantle, A. F., *England in the Nineteenth Century* (2 vols., 1929–1930); Broderick, G. C., and Fotheringham, J. K., *The History of England from Addington's Administration to the Close of William IV's Reign* (1906); Marriott, J. A. R., *England Since Waterloo* (1913); Beales, D., *From Castlereagh to Gladstone 1815–1885* (1962), vol. 7 in the *History of England* series published by Thomas Nelson & Sons, Edinburgh; Trevelyan, G. M., *British History in the Nineteenth Century and After* (1937); Wood, A., *Nineteenth Century Britain 1815–1914* (1960) in the *History of England* series edited by W. N. Medlicott, mentioned earlier; Rees, F. J., *Social and Industrial History of England, 1815–1918* (1920); Dibelius, W., *England* (1928); Briggs, A., *The Age of Improvement 1783–1867* (1959), in the *History of England* series edited by W. N. Medlicott, mentioned earlier; Thomson, D., *England in the Nineteenth Century* (1950), vol. viii of the *Pelican History of England.* Halévy, E., *History of the English People in the Nineteenth Century* is available in a 6-volume University Paperback edition. See also Bury, J. P. T., (ed.) *The Zenith of European Power 1830–1870* (1960), vol. x of *The New Cambridge Modern History.*

For this chapter see particularly Webster, C. K., *The Foreign Policy of Castlereagh, 1812–1815* (new ed., 1931), his *Foreign Policy of Castlereagh, 1815–1823* (1925) and his *Congress of Vienna, 1814–1815* (new ed., 1937); Perkins, B., *Castlereagh and Adams 1812–1823* (1965); Halévy, E., *The Liberal Awakening 1815–1830* (1961), vol. ii of Halévy's *History of the English People in the Nineteenth Century,* cited earlier; Brock, W. R., *Lord Liverpool and Liberal Toryism, 1820–1827* (1941); Temperley, H. W. V., *The Foreign Policy of Canning, 1822–1827* (1925); Perkins, B., "George Canning, Great Britain and the United States, 1807–1809," *American Historical Review,* LXIII, No. 1 (October, 1957); Nicolson, H., *The Congress of Vienna: A Study in Allied Unity, 1812–1822* (1946). Of considerable interest and value are Knowles, L. C. A., *Industrial and Commercial Revolutions in Great Britain during the Nineteenth Century* (1926); Herford, C. H., *The Age of Wordsworth* (1939); Gooch, G. P., *History and Historians in the Nineteenth Century* (1913); Buckland, C. S. B., *Metternich and the British Government* (1932); Lockhart, J. G., *The Peacemakers, 1814–1815* (1932); Woodward, E. L., *Three Studies in European Conservatism* (1929); Darvall, F. O., *Popular Disturbance and Public Order in Regency England* (1934); Webb, R. K., *The British Working Class Reader 1790–1848* (1955); Read, D., *Peterloo: the "Massacre" and Its Background* (1958).

BIOGRAPHIES: Garrod, H. W., *Keats* (1939); Chesterton, G. K., *William Cobbett* (1926); Cole, G. D. H., *Life of William Cobbett* (1924); Fulford, R., *George the Fourth* (1949); Gray, D., *Spencer Perceval: The Evangelical Prime Minister 1762–1812* (1963).

CHAPTER 29

GENERAL WORKS: In addition to the volumes mentioned in the bibliographies for the immediately preceding chapters the following are standard: Hammond, J. L., and B., *The Town Labourer, 1760–1832* (1911), *The Skilled Labourer, 1760–1832* (1920), and *The Village Labourer, 1760–1832* (new edition, 1929). See also Clapham, J. H., *An Economic History of Modern Britain,* cited earlier, vol. i: *The Early Railway Age, 1820–1850* (1930); Christie, O. F., *The Transition from Aristocracy* (1928) and *The Transition to Democracy* (1934). Two very good books about the course of political thought are Dicey, A. V., *Lectures on the Relation Between Law and Public Opinion*

(1905) and Brinton, C., *English Political Thought in the Nineteenth Century* (1933). Of interest for many aspects of the early nineteenth century is Greville, G. F. C., *Journals of the Reign of George IV, William IV, and Victoria* (ed. H. Reeve, 8 vols., new ed., 1888). See also Fay, C. R., *Huskisson and His Age* (1951).

SPECIAL STUDIES: Aspinall, A., *Lord Brougham and the Whig Party* (1927); Taylor, E. R., *Methodism and Politics, 1791–1851* (1935); Griffiths, G. T., *Population Problems of the Age of Malthus* (1936); Rolt, L. T. C., *George and Robert Stephenson: The Railway Revolution* (1960).

BIOGRAPHIES: Wallas, G., *Life of Francis Place* (1925), detailed, standard; Garratt, G. T., *Lord Brougham* (1935); New, C. W., *The Life of Henry Brougham to 1830* (1961); Petrie, Sir Charles, *Life of George Canning* (1930).

CHAPTER 30

GENERAL WORKS: In addition to the works previously cited the following are useful: Handcock, W. D., and Young, G. M., (eds.) *English Historical Documents*, vol. xii, Part I, 1833–1874 (1956); Woodward, E. L., *The Age of Reform, 1815–1870* (rev. ed., 1962) in the *Oxford History of England* series; Low, S., and Sanders, L. C., *History of England during the Reign of Victoria* (1907); Davis, H. W. C., *The Age of Grey and Peel* (1929); Hammond, J. L., and B., *The Age of the Chartists, 1832–1854* (1930); Young, G. M., (ed.) *Early Victorian England, 1830–1865* (1935). A very valuable book about the rising reform tide is Maccoby, S., *English Radicalism, 1832–1852* (1935). See also Gash, N., *Politics in the Age of Peel* (1953); see also Southgate, D., *The Passing of the Whigs 1832–1886* (1962).

INTELLECTUAL, SOCIAL, ECONOMIC: Murray, R. H., *Studies in the English Social and Political Thinkers of the Nineteenth Century* (2 vols., 1929); Halévy, *The Growth of Philosophical Radicalism* (1928); Davidson, W. L., *Political Thought in England from Bentham to John Stuart Mill* (1927); Stephen L., *The English Utilitarians* (1900); Nef, E., *Carlyle and Mill* (2nd ed. revised, 1926); Benn, A. W., *History of English Rationalism in the Nineteenth Century* (2 vols., 1906); Bury, J. B., *The Idea of Progress* (new ed., 1960); Hovell, M., *The Chartist Movement* (1918); Kent, W., *The English Radicals* (1909); Barnes, D. G., *A History of the English Corn Laws, 1660–1846* (1930); Fay, C. R., *The Corn Laws and Social England* (1932); Topham, E., and Hough, J. A., *The Cooperative Movement in Britain* (1944); Webb, S. and B., *English Poor Law History* (3 vols., 1927–1929); Coker, F., *Recent Political Thought* (1934), chap. 1.

CONSTITUTIONAL: Smellie, K. B., *A Hundred Years of English Government* (1937). See also bibliographies for later chapters.

COLONIAL: Knaplund, P., *James Stephen and the British Colonial System 1813–1847* (1953); Walker, E. A., *The Great Trek* (1938); Morrell, W. P., *British Colonial Policy in the Age of Peel and Russell* (1930); Mills, R. C., *The Colonization of Australia, 1829–1842* (1915). See the bibliography in Knaplund, P., *The British Empire, 1815–1939* (1942) and in his *Britain, Commonwealth and Empire, 1901–1955* (1957).

RELIGION: Wearing, R. F., *Methodism and the Working Class Movements of England, 1800–1850* (1937); Church, R. W., *The Oxford Movement* (1904); Ollard, S. L., *A Short History of the Oxford Movement* (1915).

LITERATURE: Chesterton, G. K., *The Victorian Age in Literature* (1932); Cecil, D., *Early Victorian Novelists* (1934).

BIOGRAPHIES: New, C. W., *Life of Lord Durham* (1929); Hammond, J. L. and B., *Shaftesbury* (1923); Ramsay, A. A. W., *Sir Robert Peel* (1928); Thursfield, J. R., *Life of Peel* (1924); Gash, N., *Mr. Secretary Peel: The Life of Sir Robert Peel to 1830* (1961); Morley, J., *Life of Richard Cobden* (1881); Harrold, C. F., *John Henry Newman* (1945); Ward, W. P., *Life of John Henry, Cardinal Newman* (1937); Podmore, F., *Robert Owen* (1924); Trevelyan, G. M., *Lord Grey of the Reform Bill* (1920) and *Life of John Bright* (1913); Williams, D., *John Frost, A Study in Chartism* (1939) and Read, D., and Glasgow, E., *Feargus O'Connor: Irishman and Chartist* (1961).

CHAPTER 31

GENERAL WORKS: For this and the immediately following chapters see Young, G. M., *Portrait of an Age* (1936); Benson, A. C., Buckle, G. E., and Lord Esher, *The Letters of Queen Victoria* (9 vols., 1907–1932); Bryant, A., *Pageant of England, 1840–1940;* Maccoby, S., *English Radicalism, 1853–1886* (1938) and *The English Radical Tradition 1763–1914* (1952).

THOUGHT AND LETTERS: For this and other chapters on the nineteenth century see Somervell, D. C., *English Thought in the Nineteenth Century* (1949); Willey, B., *Nineteenth Century Studies* (1949) and *More Nineteenth Century Studies* (1956); Hearnshaw, F. J. C., (ed.) *The Social and Political Ideas of Representative Thinkers of the Victorian Age* (1923); Kitson Clark, G., *The Making of Victorian England* (1962). See also the bibliographies for other chapters.

SPECIAL STUDIES: Temperley, H. W. V., *England and the Near East: the Crimea* (1936); Schmitt, B., "Diplomatic Preliminaries of the Crimean War," *A. H. R.,* XXV, 36–57; Costin, W. L., *Great Britain and China, 1833–1860* (1937); Owen, D. E., *British Opium Policy in China and India* (1934); Puryear, V. J., *England, Russia, and the Straits Question, 1844–1856* (1931); Woodham-Smith, C., *The Reason Why* (1953); Webster, C. K., *Foreign Policy of Palmerston, 1830–1841* (2 vols., 1951).

BIOGRAPHIES: The best biography of Lord Palmerston is Bell, H. C., *Palmerston* (2 vols., 1936). See also Guedalla, P., *Gladstone and Palmerston, 1851–1863* (1928) and his *Palmerston* (1926). Also useful is Martin, K., *The Triumph of Lord Palmerston* (1924). Other valuable biographies are Strachey, L., *Eminent Victorians* (1933) and *Queen Victoria* (1921); Benson, E. F., *Queen Victoria* (1935); Longford, E., *Queen Victoria* (1965); Lane-Poole, S., *The Life of Stratford Canning* (2 vols., 1868); Temperley, H. W. V., *Life of Lord Aberdeen* (1921); Packe, Michael St. John, *The Life of John Stuart Mill* (1954); Woodham-Smith, C., *Florence Nightingale 1820–1910* (1954).

CHAPTER 32

GENERAL WORKS: For this and later chapters two excellent works are Ensor, R. C. K., *England, 1870–1914* (1936), in the *Oxford History of England* series, and Somervell, D. C., *Modern Britain, 1870–1939* (1939). See also Clive, J., "British History, 1870–1914, Reconsidered: Recent Trends in the Historiography of the Period," *A. H. R.,* LXVIII, No. 4 (July, 1963). The best biographies of Gladstone are Morley, J., *Life of William Ewart Gladstone* (3 vols., 1903); Hall, W. P., *Mr. Gladstone* (1931); Burdett, O., *Gladstone* (1927); Magnus, P., *Gladstone: A Biography* (1954). The best biography of Disraeli is Monypenny, W. F., and Buckle, G. E., *The Life of Benjamin Disraeli, Earl of Beaconsfield* (rev. ed., 2 vols., 1929). A readable, but less reliable, life of Disraeli was written by J. A. Froude (1890). See also

Jerman, B. R., *The Young Disraeli* (1960). A remarkable study of the two political giants is Somervell, D. C., *Disraeli and Gladstone* (1929).

CONSTITUTIONAL: Schuyler, R. L., and Weston, C. C., *British Constitutional History Since 1832* (1957); Hardie, F., *The Political Influence of Queen Victoria, 1861–1900* (1935); Bagehot, W., *The English Constitution* (new ed. 1961); Barker, E., *Political Thought in England from Herbert Spencer to the Present Day* (1915).

ECONOMIC AND SOCIAL: Bowley, A. L., *England's Foreign Trade in the Nineteenth Century* (1893); Saul, S. B., *Studies in British Overseas Trade, 1870–1914* (1960); Lynd, H. M., *England in the Eighteen-Eighties* (1945); Ausubel, H., *The Late Victorians: A Short History* (1955) and *In Hard Times: Reformers Among the Late Victorians* (1960); Habbakkuk, H. J., *American and British Technology in the Nineteenth Century* (1962). See also the bibliographical notes for other chapters.

IMPERIAL AFFAIRS: Bodelsen, C. A., *Studies in Mid-Victorian Imperialism* (1925); Creighton, D. G., "The Victorians and the Empire," *Canadian Historical Review*, XIX (1938), 138–153; Knaplund, P., *Gladstone and Britain's Imperial Policy* (1927); Smith, Goldwin, *The Treaty of Washington, 1871* (1941); Tyler, J. E., *The Struggle for Imperial Unity, 1868–1895* (1938). See also Willcox, W. B., *Star of Empire: A Study of Britain as a World Power, 1485–1945* (1950); Benians, E. A., Butler, J., Carrington, G. E., (eds.) *The Empire-Commonwealth 1870–1919* (1959), vol. iii of the *Cambridge History of the British Empire;* Burt, A. L., *The Evolution of the British Empire and Commonwealth* (1956). See also Langer, W. A., *The Diplomacy of Imperialism 1890–1902* (2 vols., 1935); Stokes, E., "Great Britain and Africa: the Myth of Imperialism," *History Today*, X (August, 1960); Galbraith, J. S., "Myths of the 'Little England' Era," *A. H. R.*, LXVII, No. 1 (October, 1961); Robinson, R., Gallagher, J., and Denny, A., *Africa and the Victorians: the Official Mind of Imperialism* (1961).

SPECIAL STUDIES: Seton-Watson, R. W., *Disraeli, Gladstone, and the Eastern Question* (1935); Guedalla, P., *The Queen and Mr. Gladstone* (1933); Routh, H. V., *Towards the Twentieth Century: Essays in the Spiritual History of the Nineteenth* (1937); Petrie, C. A., *The Victorians* (1960); Singer, C., *et al., A History of Technology*, vol. v, (1958); Hammond, J. L., *Gladstone and the Irish Question* (1938); Mansergh, N., *Ireland in the Age of Reform and Revolution, 1840–1921* (1941); O'Brien, C. C., *Parnell and His Party, 1880–1890* (1957); Knaplund, P., *Gladstone's Foreign Policy* (1935); Hallberg, C. W., *The Suez Canal: Its History and Diplomatic Importance* (1931); Robb, J. H., *The Primrose League, 1883–1906* (1942); Maccoby, S., *English Radicalism, 1886–1914* (1954); Roberts, D., "Tory Paternalism and Social Reform," *A. H. R.*, LXIII, No. 2 (January, 1958).

BIOGRAPHIES: Hearnshaw, F. J. C., *Prime Ministers of the Nineteenth Century* (1926); Sitwell, E., *Victoria of England* (1936); Ervine, St. J. G., *Parnell* (1935); Carrington, C., *Rudyard Kipling* (1955).

CHAPTER 33

GENERAL WORKS: One of the most detailed and useful volumes for this and later chapters is Spender, J. A., *Great Britain, Empire and Commonwealth, 1886–1935* (1936). Also of value are Gretton, R. H., *Modern History of the English People, 1880–1910* (2 vols., 1913); Clark, G., *The Balance Sheets of Imperialism* (1936).

ECONOMIC: Jenks, L. H., *The Migration of British Capital to 1875* (1927); Imlaw, A. H., *Economic Elements in the Pax Britannica* (1958); Knowles, L. C. A., *The Economic Development of the British Overseas Empire* (1924); Ashworth, W., *An Economic History of England 1870–1939* (1960).

SPECIAL STUDIES: Dicey, A. V., *England's Case Against Home Rule* (1887); Thompson, A. P., *The Imperial Idea and Its Enemies: A Study in British Power* (1959); Raphael, L. A. C., *The Cape to Cairo Dream* (1936); Hoskins, H. L., *European Imperialism in Africa* (1930); Morrell, W. P., *Britain in the Pacific Islands* (1960); Lovell, R. I., *The Struggle for South Africa, 1875–1899* (1934); Galbraith, J. S., *Reluctant Empire: British Policy on the South African Frontier, 1834–1854* (1963); Pakenham, E., *Jameson's Raid* (1960); Pyrah, G. B., *Imperial Policy and South Africa 1902–1910* (1955); Marais, J. S., *The Fall of Kruger's Republic* (1961); Thompson, L. M., *The Unification of South Africa 1902–1910* (1960); Chirol, V., *The Egyptian Problem* (1920); Allen, B. M., *Gordon and the Sudan* (1931); Sanderson, E., *Great Britain and Modern Africa* (1907); Campbell, C. S., *Anglo-American Understanding, 1898–1903* (1960). See also the *Cambridge History of the British Empire*, vol. viii and Grenville, J. A. S., *Lord Salisbury and Foreign Policy: the Close of the Nineteenth Century* (1964).

BIOGRAPHIES: Buxton, E., *General Botha* (1924); Cecil, Lady Gwendolyn, *Life of Robert, Marquis of Salisbury* (4 vols. to 1892, 1921–1932); Kennedy, A. L., *Salisbury, 1830–1903* (1953); Crewe, the Marquis of, *Life of Lord Rosebery* (1931); Garvin, J. L., and Amery, J., *Life of Joseph Chamberlain* (4 vols., 1932–1951); Millin, S. G., *Rhodes* (1933); Williams, B., *Cecil Rhodes* (1921); Elton, G. E., *Gordon of Khartum* (1955); James, R. R., *Lord Randolph Churchill* (1960); Magnus, P., *Kitchener: Portrait of An Imperialist* (1959); Wrench, E., *Alfred, Lord Milner* (1958); Hancock, W. K., *Smuts: the Sanguine Years 1870–1919* (1962).

CHAPTER 34

GENERAL WORKS: In addition to the surveys noted earlier these general books may be read with profit: Marriott, J. A. R., *Modern Times, 1885–1932* (1934); Spender, J. A., *A Short History of Our Times* (1934); Wingfield-Stratford, E., *The Victorian Aftermath* (1933); Dangerfield, G., *The Strange Death of Liberal England* (1935); Somervell, D. C., *British Politics Since 1900* (1950); Havighurst, A. F., *Twentieth Century Britain* (1962); Pelling, H., *Modern Britain 1885–1955* (1960), vol. 8 in the *History of England* series published by Thomas Nelson & Sons, Edinburgh. For this chapter see also Hearnshaw, F. J. C., (ed.) *Edwardian England, 1901–1910* (1933); Monger, G. W., *The End of Isolation: British Foreign Policy 1900–1907* (1964); and Swinnerton, F. A., *The Georgian Scene: A Literary Panorama* (1934).

POLITICAL, ECONOMIC, SOCIAL: McDowell, R. B., *British Conservatism 1832–1914* (1959); MacDonald, J. R., *The Socialist Movement* (1911); Poirier, P. P., *The Advent of the British Labour Party* (1958); Pelling, H., *The Origins of the Labour Party 1880–1900* (1954); Reid, H. S., *The Origins of the British Labour Party* (1955); Cole, G. D. H., *A Short History of the British Working Class Movement* (1927); Slesser, Sir Henry, *History of the Liberal Party* (1944); Shaw, G. B., (ed.) *Fabian Essays in Socialism* (1931); Hayes, C. J. H., *British Social Politics* (1913), discusses social legislation 1906–1911; Cole, M., "The Fabian Society," *Political Quarterly*, July-September, 1944 and *The Story of Fabian Socialism* (1961); McBriar, A. M., *Fabian Socialism and English Politics, 1884–1918* (1962); Beer, M., *History of*

British Socialism (2 vols., 1923); Webb, S. and B., *A History of Trade Unionism* (new ed., 1920); Clegg, H. A., Fox, A., Thompson, A. F., *A History of British Trade Unions Since 1889,* the first volume of which was published in 1964 and covers the period 1889–1910; Pelling, A., *A History of British Trade Unionism* (1963); Hobson, J. A., *The Evolution of Modern Capitalism* (new ed., 1926) and *The Crisis of Liberalism* (1909); see also Laski, H. J., *The Rise of Liberalism: The Philosophy of a Business Civilization* (1936).

CONSTITUTIONAL: Very useful for the background of political and constitutional development are Keith, A. B., *The Constitution of England from Queen Victoria to George VI* (2 vols., 1940); Thomas, J. A., *The House of Commons, 1832–1901* (1939). See also earlier chapter bibliographies.

BIOGRAPHIES: Pankhurst, E. S., *The Life of Emmeline Pankhurst* (1936); Haldane, R. B., *An Autobiography* (1929); Dugdale, B. E. C., *Arthur James Balfour* (1937); Lee, Sir Sidney, *King Edward VII* (2 vols., 1925–1927); Wells, W. B., *John Redmond, a Biography* (1919); Spender, J. A., *Life of the Right Hon. Sir Henry Campbell-Bannerman* (2 vols., 1924); Newton, Lord, *Lord Lansdowne: A Biography* (1929); Maurice, F., *Life of Lord Haldane* (2 vols., 1937–1939).

CHAPTER 35

GENERAL WORKS: The best general surveys of the background and progress of the First World War are Sontag, R. G., *Germany and England: Background of Conflict, 1848–1894* (1938); Schmitt, B. E., *England and Germany, 1740–1914* (1916) and *The Coming of the War* (2 vols., 1930); Albertini, L., *Origins of the War of 1914* (3 vols., 1952–1957); Fay, S. B., *The Origins of the World War* (2 vols., 1928); Gooch, G. P., *Before the War* (2 vols., 1936–1938); Brandenburg, E., *From Bismarck to the World War* (1927); Renouvin, P., *The Immediate Origins of the War* (1928); Langer, W. L., *European Alliances and Alignments, 1870–1890* (1933); Cruttwell, C. R., *A History of the Great War, 1914–1918* (1936); Buchan, J., (Lord Tweedsmuir), *The History of the Great War* (4 vols., 1921–1922); Churchill, W. S., *The World Crisis* (5 vols., 1923–1928). See also Moon, P. T., *Imperialism and World Politics* (new ed., 1932); Seton-Watson, R. W., *Britain in Europe, 1789–1914: A Survey of Foreign Policy* (1937); Gooch, G. P., and Temperley, H. W. V., (eds.) *British Documents on the Origins of the War 1898–1914* (11 vols., 1926–1938); Liddell Hart, B. H., *The Real War* (1930); Wingfield-Stratford, E., *They That Take the Sword* (1924); Falls, C., *The First World War* (1960); Tuchman, B. W., *The Guns of August* (1962).

SPECIAL STUDIES: Moorehead, A., *Gallipoli* (1956); Hoffman, R. J. S., *Great Britain and the German Trade Rivalry, 1875–1914* (1933); Gooch, G. P., *Recent Revelations of European Diplomacy* (4th ed., 1940); Stuart, C., *Secrets of Crewe House* (1920); Churchill, R. P., *The Anglo-Russian Convention of 1907* (1939); Wolf, J. B., *The Diplomatic History of the Bagdad Railroad,* (1936); Gray, H. L., *Wartime Control of Industry, the Experience of England* (1918); Frost, H. H., *The Battle of Jutland* (1936); Chambers, F. P., *The War Behind the War, 1914–1918: A History of the Political and Civilian Fronts* (1939); Marder, A. J., *Anatomy of British Sea Power, 1880–1905* (1940); Schuyler, R. L., "The British War Cabinet," *Political Science Quarterly,* xxxiii, (1918).

BIOGRAPHIES, MEMOIRS, DIARIES: Trevelyan, G. M., *Grey of Fallodon* (1937); Duff Cooper, A., *Lord Haig* (2 vols., 1936); Haldane, Lord, *Before the War* (1920) and *Autobiography* (1930); Nicolson, H., *Portrait of a Diplomatist*

BIBLIOGRAPHY

Hamilton, Sir Ian, *Gallipoli Diary* (1920); Asquith, H. H., *Fifty [Years] of British Parliament* (1926); Spender, J. A., and Asquith, C., *The Life [of He]rbert Henry Asquith, Lord Oxford and Asquith* (2 vols., 1932); Kier-[nan], R. H., *Lloyd George* (1940); Sylvester, A. J., *The Real Lloyd George [194]7); Jones, T., *Lloyd George* (1951); Lloyd George, David, *War Memoirs* [(6 v]ols., 1933–1935); Webb, B., *Diaries 1924–1932* (1956); Pound, R., and [Ha]rmsworth, G., *Northcliffe* (1960); Ervine, St. John, *Bernard Shaw (1905– [19]50): His Life, Work, and Friends* (1956). See the bibliographies for the [t]wo following chapters.

CHAPTER 36

GENERAL WORKS: See the official record of British diplomacy between the two World Wars in *Documents on British Foreign Policy 1919–1939,* eds. Butler, R., and Woodward, E. L., (later by Bury, J. P. T.). The First Series, which deals with British policy in 1919 after the signing of the Treaty of Versailles, contains 6 vols. (1947–1956). Several volumes of the Second Series have also been published. The Third Series (1938–1939) has been completed in 9 vols. See also Brailsford, H. N., *After the Peace* (1920); Fay, C. R., *Cooperation at Home and Abroad* (1920); Masterman, C. F. G., *England After War* (1922); Wingfield-Stratford, E., *The Harvest of Victory, 1918–1926* (1935); Walters, F. P., *A History of the League of Nations* (2 vols., 1952); Hirst, F. W., *The Consequences of the War to Great Britain* (1934), one of the best of the expert analyses, particularly the economic sections.

ECONOMIC AND FOREIGN AFFAIRS: An important and valuable book is Benham, F., *Great Britain under Protection* (1941). Also useful are Plummer, A., *New British Industries in the Twentieth Century* (1937); Bowley, A. L., *Wages and Income in the United Kingdom since 1860* (1937), *Some Economic Consequences of the War* (1930) and *Studies in the National Income* (1942); Orr, J. B., *Food, Health and Income* (1937); Cole, G. D. H., *Labour in the Coal Mining Industry* (1923); Hawtrey, R. G., *The Gold Standard in Theory and Practice* (1939); Lawrence, F. W. P., *The Gold Crisis* (1931); Einzig, P., *The World Economic Crisis* (1931); Francis, E. V., *Britain's Economic Strategy* (1939); Keynes, J. M., *The Economic Consequences of the Peace* (1920); Heaton, H., *The British Way to Recovery* (1934); Robbins, L. C., *The Great Depression* (1937); Salter, Sir Arthur, *Recovery: The Second Effort* (1932); McGuire, E. B., *The British Tariff System* (1939); Beveridge, William, *Tariffs: The Case Examined;* Young, E. H., *The System of National Finance* (1936).

See also Llewellyn Smith, H., *New Survey of London Life and Labour* (9 vols., 1930–1935); Sykes, J., *British Public Expenditure, 1921–1931* (1933); Dalton, H., *The Principles of Public Finance* (1941); Richardson, J. H., *Economic Disarmament* (1931); Bergman, C., *The History of Reparations* (1927); Wheeler-Bennett, J. W., *The Wreck of Reparations* (1933); Auld, G. P., *The Dawes Plan and the New Economics* (1927); the Royal Institute of International Affairs, *Monetary Policy and the Depression* (1933).

POLITICAL: Fyfe, H., *The Liberal Party* (1928); Lyman, R. W., *The First Labour Government 1924* (1957); McHenry, D. E., *His Majesty's Opposition* (1940), a discussion of the Labour Party in the 1930's.

IRELAND: Gwynn, D. R., *De Valera* (1933) and *The Irish Free State, 1922–1927* (1928); Mansergh, N., *The Irish Free State, Its Government and Politics* (1934); Pomfret, J. E., *The Struggle for Land in Ireland, 1800–1923* (1930); Philips, W. A., *The Revolution in Ireland, 1906–1923* (1923); Henry, R. M.,

The Evolution of Sinn Fein (1920); McNeil, R. M., *Ulster's Stand for Union* (1922); Harrison, H., *Ulster and the British Empire* (1939).

SPECIAL STUDIES: Wickwar, W. H., *The Public Services* (1939); Hewart, Lord, *The New Despotism* (1929); Dawson, R. M., *The Development of Dominion Status, 1900–1936* (1937).

BIOGRAPHIES: Nicolson, H., *Curzon, The Last Phase, 1919–1925* (1934); Mosley, L., *Curzon: The End of an Epoch* (1960); Snowden, Viscount, *An Autobiography* (2 vols., 1934); Hamilton, M. A., *Sidney and Beatrice Webb* (1933) and *Arthur Henderson* (1938); Cole, M., *Beatrice Webb* (1946); Blake, R., *Unrepentant Tory: The Life and Times of Andrew Bonar Law 1858–1923* (1956); Postgate, R., *The Life of George Lansbury* (1952); Harrod, R. F., *The Life of John Maynard Keynes* (1951).

CHAPTER 37

GENERAL WORKS: Mowat, C. L., *Britain Between the Wars 1918–1940* (1955); Wolfers, A., *Britain and France Between Two Wars* (1940); Soward, F. H., *Twenty-Five Troubled Years 1918–1943* (1944); Jordan, W. M., *Great Britain, France, and the German Problem, 1918–1939* (1943); Gathorne-Hardy, G. M., *A Short History of International Affairs, 1920–1938* (1939). For studies of shorter periods see Macartney, M. H. H., *Five Years of European Chaos* (1924); Stannard, H., *The Fabric of Europe* (1923); Churchill, W. S., *The Aftermath* (1929); Schwarzchild, L., *The World in Trance: From Versailles to Pearl Harbor* (1942); Birdsall, P., *Versailles Twenty Years After* (1941). See also Simonds, F. H., and Emeny, B., *The Great Powers in World Politics: International Relations and Economic Nationalism* (1937).

On the Paris Peace Conference of 1919 see also Toynbee, A. J., *The World After the Peace Conference* (1925); Nicolson, H., *Peacemaking, 1919* (new ed., 1945); Temperley, H. W. V., (ed.) *A History of the Peace Conference of Paris* (6 vols., 1920–1924); Lloyd George, D., *Memoirs of the Peace Conference* (2 vols., 1939); Tillman, S. P., *Anglo-American Relations at the Paris Peace Conference of 1919* (1961).

INTERNATIONAL AFFAIRS: Webster, C. K., and Herbert, S., *The League of Nations in Theory and Practice* (1933); Highley, A. E., *The First Sanctions Experiment* (1938); Buell, R. L., *The Washington Conference* (1922); Benes, E., Coulborn, R., Feiler, A., *International Security* (1939); Churchill, W. S., *While England Slept* (1938) and *Step by Step* (1939); Miller, D. H., *The Peace Pact of Paris* (1928); Maddox, W. P., *Foreign Relations in British Labour Policies* (1934); Medlicott, W. N., *British Foreign Policy Since Versailles* (1940); Reynolds, P. A., *British Foreign Policy in the Inter-War Years* (1954); Petrie, Charles, *Twenty Years Armistice and After* (1940); Rappard, W. E., *The Quest for Peace Since the World War* (1940); Lee, D. E., *Ten Years: The World on Its Way to War, 1930–1940* (1940); Deane, V. M., *The Struggle for World Order* (1941). Very useful is Langer, W. L., and Armstrong, H. F., *Foreign Affairs Bibliography* (1933) which contains several thousand items with brief critical comments. See also Butler, R., and Woodward, E. L., and Bury, J. P. T., (eds.) *Documents on British Foreign Policy, 1919–1939*, First, Second and Third Series, cited earlier, and the *Survey of International Affairs* published annually since 1925 for the Royal Institute of International Affairs by the Oxford University Press.

DISARMAMENT: Wheeler-Bennett, J. W., *Disarmament and Security Since Locarno, 1925–1931* (1932); Tate, M., *The Disarmament Illusion* (1942);

Engeley, G., *The Politics of Naval Disarmament* (1932); Jacobs, A. J., *World Peace and Armaments* (1931); Shotwell, J. T., *War as an Instrument of National Policy* (1929); Crosby, G. R., *Disarmament and Peace in British Politics, 1914–1919* (1957).

REPARATIONS AND WAR DEBTS: Wheeler-Bennett, J. W., *The Wreck of Reparations* (1933), mentioned earlier; Frasure, C. M., *British Policy on War Debts and Reparations* (1940); Bergman, C., *The History of Reparations* (1927) mentioned earlier; Sedgwick, J. H., *The War Debts* (1929).

SPECIAL WORKS: Angell, Norman, *The Defense of the Empire* (1937); Norton, H. K., *China and the Powers* (1927); Hudson, G. L., *The Far East in World Politics* (1937); Wheare, K. C., *The Statute of Westminster and Dominion Status* (1942); Newman, E. W., *Great Britain in Egypt* (1928); Quigley, H. S., and Blakeslee, G. H., *The Far East* (1938); Foerster, F. W., *Europe and the German Question* (1940); the Royal Institute of International Affairs, *Political and Strategic Interests of the United Kingdom* (1940); Webb, S., and Webb, B., *Soviet Communism* (2 vols., 1935); Cole, G. D. H., *Socialism and Fascism 1931–1939* (1960), vol. v of his *History of Socialist Thought;* Croon, W. H., *The General Strike* (1931); Symons, J., *The General Strike: A Historical Portrait* (1957).

BIOGRAPHIES: Hamilton, M. A., *J. Ramsay MacDonald* (1929); Feiling, K., *The Life of Neville Chamberlain* (1946); MacLeod, I., *Neville Chamberlain* (1962); Petrie, C., *Life and Letters of the Right Hon. Sir Austen Chamberlain* (2 vols., 1939–1940); Gore, J., *King George V* (1941); Buchan, J. (Lord Tweedsmuir), *The People's King* (1935), in British editions entitled *The King's Grace;* Nicolson, Sir Harold, *King George the Fifth* (1953) and Young, G. M., *Stanley Baldwin* (1952). See also the bibliographies for Chapters 38, 39.

CHAPTER 38

GENERAL WORKS: In addition to the books cited for the previous chapters the following are valuable: Thomson, D., (ed.) *The Era of Violence 1898–1945* (1960), vol. xii of *The New Cambridge Modern History;* Bruun, G., *The World in the Twentieth Century* (3rd ed., 1960), a brilliant survey of global economics, politics, and patterns of power; Benns, F. L., *Europe Since 1914* (new ed., 1945); Lipson, E., *Europe, 1914–1939* (1943); Langsam, W. C., *The World Since 1914* (new ed., 1943); Chambers, F. P., Grant, C. P., and Bayley, C. C., *This Age of Conflict* (1943). For France and the French background see Brogan, D. W., *France under the Third Republic* (1940); Werth, A., *The Twilight of France, 1933–1940* (1942). See also Mansergh, N., *Problems of External Policy 1931–1939* (1952) and *Problems of Wartime Co-operation and Post-War Change 1939–1952* (1958) in the *Survey of Commonwealth Affairs* edited by Hancock, W. K., and Mansergh, N., cited earlier; Thornton, A. P., *The Imperial Idea and Its Enemies: A Study in British Power* (1959); Lewis, W. A., *Economic Survey 1919–1939* (1949).

THE ROAD TO WAR: Haines, C. S., and Hoffman, R. J. S., *The Origins and Background of the Second World War* (1947); Eden, Anthony (Earl of Avon), *Facing the Dictators 1923–1938* (1962); Schuman, F. L., *Europe on the Eve* (1939) and *Night Over Europe: The Diplomacy of Nemesis, 1939–1940* (1941); Scott, J., *Europe in Revolution, 1938–1945* (1945); Fisher, H. A. L., (ed.) *The Background and Issues of the War* (1940); this book contains several essays of uneven quality. See also Henderson, N., *Failure of a Mission*

(1940); Chamberlain, N., *In Search of Peace* (1939). Students who read Taylor, A. J. P., *The Origins of the Second World War* (1961), a controversial volume, should also study other works on the subject.

THE WAR, 1939–1945: Professor Edgar McInnis of the University of Toronto began to publish his broad annual surveys of the war in 1940. The six volumes of his work *The War: First Year, The War: Second Year,* etc., remain among the best general descriptive sources for the events of the conflict. Another satisfactory work is Hall, W. P., *Iron Out of Calvary* (1946). See also Elliott, W. Y., and Hall, D. H., *The British Commonwealth at War* (1943); Angell, N., *For What Do We Fight?* (1940); Richmond, Admiral Sir Herbert, *British Strategy, Military and Economic* (1941); Snyder, L. L., *The War: A Concise History 1939–1945* (1960); Falls, C. B., *The Second World War, A Short History* (1948); Roskill, S. W., *White Ensign: The British Navy at War 1939–1945* (1960); Kemp, P. K., *Victory at Sea, 1939–1945* (1958); Churchill, W. S., *Blood, Sweat, and Tears* (1941), *The Unrelenting Struggle* (1942), *The End of the Beginning* (1943), *Onwards to Victory* (1944), *The Dawn of Liberation* (1945); Nickerson, H., *Arms and Policy, 1939–1944* (1945); Martel, G., *Our Armoured Forces* (1945).

See also Brown, F., and Manditch, L., *The War in Maps: an Atlas of the New York Times Maps* (1946). Sir Winston Churchill began in 1948 and completed in 1953 his six-volume history of the Second World War (*The Gathering Storm, Their Finest Hour, The Grand Alliance, The Hinge of Fate, Closing the Ring, Triumph and Tragedy*). The official British *History of the Second World War* will total 84 volumes, consisting of the United Kingdom Military Series edited by J. R. M. Butler (34 volumes, including 6 on grand strategy), the United Kingdom Civil Series edited by W. K. Hancock (29 volumes) and a medical series (21 volumes). A number of volumes have been published by H. M. Stationery Office in London. They are distributed in the United States by the British Information Services. See also Woodward, E. L., *British Foreign Policy in the Second World War* (1962) and the bibliographies for Chapters 36, 37.

See further the books, pamphlets, and papers of the wartime information services of the nations involved in the Second World War. Invaluable for an understanding of the British war effort are the publications of the British Ministry of Information, such as the *British War Blue Book* (1939), *Bomber Command* (1941), *Bomber Command Continues* (1942), and the *Britain Today* series. Most of the important British war publications were released in the United States through the British Library of Information in New York. Other useful publications during the war appeared in the *Oxford Pamphlets on World Affairs* and the *Macmillan War Pamphlets.* See also Woolbert, R. G., *Foreign Affairs Bibliography* (1945); this book contains about 10,000 titles for the 1930's and covers the years up to 1942.

SPECIAL STUDIES: Falls, C., *The Nature of Modern Warfare* (1941); Lee A., *The German Air Force* (1946); Saunders, H. St. G., and Dennis, R., *The Royal Air Force 1939–1945* (3 vols., 1953–1954); Hearnshaw, F. J. C., *Sea Power and Empire* (1941); Buss, C. A., *War and Diplomacy in Eastern Asia* (1941); Sargeant, E., *The Royal Air Force* (1941); Strabolgi, Lord, *Sea Power in the Second World War* (1943); the Royal Institute of International Affairs reports *Abyssinia and Italy* (1935) and *Europe under Hitler* (1941); Guedalla, P., *Middle East, 1940–1942* (1945); Clifford, A. G., *The Conquest of North Africa* (1943); Trevor-Roper, H. R., *The Last Days of Hitler* (1947); Marshall, General George C., *The Winning of the War in Europe and the Pacific* (1945). See also Cairns, J. C., "Great Britain and the Fall of France:

A Study in Allied Disunity," *Journal of Modern History,* XXVII, No. 4, December, 1955.

BIOGRAPHIES AND MEMOIRS: Alexander, Field-Marshal the Earl, *The Alexander Memoirs: 1940–1945* (1963); Montgomery, Viscount, *The Memoirs of Field-Marshal the Viscount Montgomery* (1958); Bryant, A., *Triumph in the West: A History of the War Years Based on the Diaries of Field-Marshal Lord Alanbrooke, Chief of the General Staff* (1959).

CHAPTER 39

GENERAL WORKS: Havighurst, A. F., *Twentieth Century Britain* (1962); Pelling, H., *Modern Britain 1885–1955* (1960), vol. viii in the *History of England* series published by Thomas Nelson and Sons, Edinburgh. See also bibliographies for Chapters 38 and 40.

ECONOMIC: For the years immediately following the Second World War see *Britain and World Trade, a Report by PEP* (Political and Economic Planning, 1947), distributed in the United States by the Macmillan Company. See also the statistics and comments on world trade in the *Commerce Yearbook* and *Commerce Weekly* (Bureau of Foreign and Domestic Commerce, Government Printing Office, Washington, D. C.). See further the Department of State Bulletins. The quarterly bulletins of the London and Cambridge Economic Service provide detailed information about British foreign and domestic trade and the current trends in world trade and commerce. Among the numerous United Kingdom government publications available through H. M. Stationery Office are these: the annual customs and excise and inland revenue reports; the Board of Trade reports, including the *Trade of the United Kingdom* accounts (monthly), the *Navigation and Shipping* statements (annual), the *Journal* (weekly), the *Statistical Abstract of the United Kingdom* (annual) and the *Survey of Industrial Development* (annual); the annual reports of the Home Office, Mines Department, Ministry of Agriculture and Fisheries (containing detailed agricultural statistics), Health, Labour (valuable for labor statistics), the *Labour Gazette* (monthly), Transport (railway statistics), Treasury (finance accounts of the United Kingdom).

Excellent books on contemporary economic patterns and problems are these: Kahn, A. E., *Great Britain in the World Economy* (1946); Kranold, H., *The International Distribution of Raw Materials* (1939); Lippincott, I., *The Development of Modern World Trade* (1936); Staley, E., *Raw Materials in Peace and War* (1937) and *World Economy in Transition: the Conflict between Technology and Politics* (1939); Shonfield, A., *British Economic Policy Since the War* (1958); Youngson, A. J., *The British Economy 1920–1957* (1960); Burns, D., (ed.) *Structure of British Industry* (2 vols., 1958); Allen, G. C., *British Industries and Their Organization* (1959); Worswick, G. N. N., and Ady, P. H., (eds.) *The British Economy 1945–1950* (1952).

RECONSTRUCTION AFTER THE SECOND WORLD WAR: See Robson, W. A., *Nationalized Industries and Public Ownership* (1960); Lewis, B. W., *British Planning and Nationalization* (1952); see also the following publications of H. M. Stationery Office: *Social Insurance and Allied Services* (the Beveridge Report, Command Paper 6404, 1942; published in the United States by the Macmillan Company); *Social Insurance* (Command Papers 6550, 6551), *Report of the Cotton Textile Mission, Employment Policy* (all published in 1944); *Report on Iron and Steel Plans* (1946); *Report on the Iron and Steel Industry* (1946); *Cotton Working Party Report* (1946); *Report of the Royal Commission on the Coal Industry* (1946).

Also important are Abercrombie, P., *Town and Country Planning* (1943) and *Our Towns: a Close-up* (a study made in 1939–1942 and published in 1943). See further the Nuffield College Pamphlets, an excellent series that began to appear during the Second World War. One of the best of these pamphlets is *Employment Policy and Organization of Industry After the War* (1943). The *Political and Economic Planning* (PEP) surveys, published in the United States by the Macmillan Company, are of special interest to the student of the economic policies and programs of the British Labour Party. See also the *Report of the Royal Commission on the Distribution of the Industrial Population* (Barlow Report, Command Paper 6153, H. M. Stationery Office, 1939) and "Second Thoughts on Planning," *Economist*, February, 1947; Dennison, S. R., *The Location of Industry and the Depressed Areas* (1939); Burnham, T. H., and Hoskins, G. O., *Iron and Steel in Britain* (1943); Fisher, A. G. B., *International Implications of Full Employment in Great Britain* (Royal Institute of International Affairs, 1946); Cohen, E. W., *English Social Services* (1949); Titmus, R. J., *Problems of Social Policy* (1950); Marsh, D. C., *The Changing Social Structure of England and Wales 1871–1951* (1958).

Several other major postwar questions are dealt with in the following reports, all published by H. M. Stationery Office: *Rehabilitation and Resettlement of Disabled Persons* (Tomlinson Report, Command Paper 6415, 1944); *Design of Dwellings* (Dudley Report, 1944); *Rural Housing* (Hobhouse Report, 1944); *Private Enterprise Housing* (Pole Report, 1945).

EDUCATION: The following British government papers, all published by H. M. Stationery Office, are valuable: Fleming Report: *Abolition of Tuition Fees in Grant-Aided Secondary Schools* (1944); Wood Committee Report: *Standard Construction for Schools* (1945); McNair Report: *Teachers and Youth Leaders* (1945). See also the various series of pamphlets and reports issued by the Board of Education through H. M. Stationery Office, especially the *Report and Statistics of Public Education,* issued annually. The *Report* for 1935 includes a survey of educational developments, 1910–1935. See further Lindsay, K., *English Education* (1941); Ward, H., *The Educational System of England and Wales and Its Recent History* (1935); Dent, H. C., *Growth in English Education, 1946–1952* (1954) and *Universities in Transition* (1961).

PUBLIC HEALTH: Clegg, H., *Medicine in Britain* (1944); Ross, J. K., *The National Health Service in Great Britain* (1952); Owen, A. D. K., *The British Social Services* (1943). The official report on "A National Health Service" (Command Paper 6502, 1944) was published in the United States by the Macmillan Company. See also Hall, M. P., *Social Services of Modern England* (1952) and Eckstein, H., *The English Health Service: Its Claims, Structure, and Achievements* (1958).

AGRICULTURE: Easterbrook, L. F., British Agriculture (1944); Astor, Viscount, Rowntree, B. S., and others, *British Agriculture* (1938); *Committee on Land Utilization in Rural Areas Report* (Command Paper 6386, H. M. Stationery Office, 1942).

LITERATURE: See Macniece, L., *Modern Poetry* (1938); Reade, A. R., *Main Currents in Modern Literature* (1935); Ward, A. C., *Twentieth Century English Literature, 1901–1960* (1964); Tindall, W. Y., *Forces in Modern British Literature, 1885–1946* (1947).

SPECIAL STUDIES: Of particular interest is the epilogue, *The Bank As It Is,* in Sir John Clapham's *The Bank of England: A History* (2 vols., 1945). Other works of specialized value are Gibson, C. H., *The Spirit of British Administration* (1959); Dale, H. E., *The Higher Civil Service of Great Britain* (1941); Anderson, H., *The British Post Office: A History* (1948); Keith, C., *British*

Police and the Democratic Ideal (1944); Allen, G. C., *British Industry* (1944); Price, J., *British Trade Unions* (1941); Thornton, R. H., *British Shipping* (1939); Zweig, F., *The British Worker* (1952); Rozow, A. A., *The Labour Government and British Industry 1945–1951* (1956); Harrison, M., *Trade Unions and the Labour Party Since 1945* (1960).

See also Bulmer-Thomas, Ivor, *The Party System in Great Britain* (1953); McCallum, R. B., and Readman, A., *The British General Election of 1945* (1946); Nicholls, H. G., *The British General Election of 1950* (1951); Butler, D. E., *The British General Election of 1955* (1955); Butler, D., and Rose, R., *The British General Election of 1959* (1960); McKenzie, R. T., *British Political Parties* (1955); Stout, H. M., *British Government* (1953); Campion, Lord, *et al.*, *Parliament: A Survey* (1952); Lewis R., and Maude, A., *The English Middle Classes* (1950); Maccoby, S., *English Radicalism: the End?* (1961); Broomhead, P. A., *The House of Lords and Contemporary Politics 1911–1957* (1958). For a discussion of British law and government today see Smith, Goldwin, *A Constitutional and Legal History of England* (1955). See also *Harwell: The British Atomic Energy Research Establishment* pub. 1955 by H. M. Stationery Office. See further Winkler, H. R., "Some Recent Writings on Twentieth-Century Britain," *Journal of Modern History,* vol. XXXII, No. 1 (March, 1960).

BIOGRAPHIES AND MEMOIRS: Broad, L., *Anthony Eden* (1955); Eden, Anthony (Earl of Avon), *Full Circle: the Memoirs of Anthony Eden* (1960); Bullock, A., *The Life and Times of Ernest Bevin* (vol. I, 1960, *Trade Union Leader 1881–1940*); Evans, T., *Bevin of Britain* (1952); Foot, M., *Aneurin Bevan* (1963); Wheeler-Bennett, J. W., *King George VI: His Life and Reign* (1958); Morrison, Herbert, *An Autobiography* (1960); Williams, F., *A Prime Minister Remembers: the War and Post-War Memoirs of the Rt. Hon. Earl Attlee* (1961) and *Twilight of Empire: Memoirs of Prime Minister Clement Attlee* (1963); Dalton, H., *Call Back Yesterday: Memoirs 1887–1931* (1953); *The Fateful Years: Memoirs 1931–1945* (1957); and *High Tide and After: Memoirs 1946–1960* (1962). There are numerous biographies of Sir Winston Churchill, including those of Philip Guedalla, René Kraus, Lewis Broad, and Peter de Mendelssohn.

CHAPTER 40

GENERAL WORKS: Of the many books published about the problems of Great Britain and the contemporary world the following are among the best: Bruun, Geoffrey, *The World in the Twentieth Century* (3rd ed. 1960), mentioned earlier; Black, C. E., and Helmreich, E. C., *Twentieth Century Europe* (1950); Harrison, J. B., *This Age of Global Strife* (1952); Dawson, Christopher, *Understanding Europe* (1952); Ward, Barbara, *Policy for the West* (1950) and *Faith and Freedom* (1954); Hoskins, H. L., *The Atlantic Pact* (1949); Kohn, Hans, *World War in Historical Perspective* (1942); Carr, E. H., *The Conditions of Peace* (1942); Reeves, E., *The Anatomy of Peace* (1945); Angell, N., *The Steep Places: an Examination of Political Tendencies* (1947); Mannheim, K., *Diagnosis of Our Time* (1944); McNeill, W. A., *America, Britain, and Russia: Their Cooperation and Conflict* (1953). The British Information Services in New York, Washington, Chicago, and San Francisco distribute a wide range of publications concerning British affairs; these are listed in their regularly published catalogs.

FOREIGN AFFAIRS: Always useful is the *Survey of International Affairs* published annually by the Oxford University Press for the Royal Institute of International Affairs. The publications of the Royal Institute for International Affairs are sound and scholarly. See, for example, *British Security* (1946) and *The*

Pattern of British Security (1946), as well as the volumes cited elsewhere. The Institute also publishes *The World Today* (monthly). In the United States the articles in the quarterly *Foreign Affairs* (Council on Foreign Relations, 1922–   ) are usually excellent. See also the publications of the Foreign Policy Association, New York. The reports and comments of the *New York Times* and the *Christian Science Monitor* are particularly complete and objective. In the United Kingdom the most satisfactory sources for facts and comments are the *Times*, the *Manchester Guardian*, the *Economist*, the *New Statesman and Nation*, the *Spectator*, the *Fortnightly Review*, the *Contemporary Review*, and the *Nineteenth Century and After*. Most of the important documents in foreign affairs are published regularly by the U. S. Department of State, the United Nations, H. M. Stationery Office, the Royal Institute of International Affairs. Many of them are available in *International Conciliation*, published regularly by the Carnegie Endowment for International Peace.

See also Woodhouse, C. M., *British Foreign Policy Since the Second World War* (1961); Windrich, E., *British Labour's Foreign Policy* (1952); Fitzsimons, M. A., *Foreign Policy of the British Labour Government 1945– 1951* (1960); British Information Services, *Britain and the United Nations* (rev. ed., 1962).

IMPERIAL AND COMMONWEALTH AFFAIRS: See Wheare, K. C., *The Constitutional Structure of the Commonwealth* (1960); *The Empire-Commonwealth* (1959), vol. iii of the *Cambridge History of the British Empire;* Knaplund, Paul, *Britain, Commonwealth and Empire 1901–1955* (1957), cited earlier; Mansergh, N., *The Multi-Racial Commonwealth* (1955) and *Commonwealth Perspectives* (1960); McInnis, E., *The Commonwealth Today* (1955); Taylor, D., *The Years of Challenge 1945–1958* (1960); Willcox, William B., *Star of Empire* (1950), especially the latter chapters.

For the background of British policy in Palestine see Sidebotham, H., *Great Britain and Palestine* (1937); *Report of the Royal Commission on Palestine* (Command Paper 5479, published by H. M. Stationery Office, 1937); Hannah, P. L., *British Policy in Palestine* (1942). See also Woodhouse, C. M., *Britain and the Middle East* (1959).

Several important problems and events in India and Southeast Asia are discussed in Thompson, E., and Garratt, G. T., *The Rise and Fulfilment of British Rule in India* (1934); Coupland, R., *Britain and India* (1941) and *The Indian Problem: Report on the Constitutional Problem in India* (1943); Walbank, T. W., *India* (1948) and *A Short History of India and Pakistan* (1958); Spear, T. G. P., *India: A Modern History* (1961); Nanda, B. R., *Gandhi* (1959); Brecker, M., *Nehru* (1959); Hartog, M., *India in Outline* (1944); Nehru, Jawaharlal, *The Discovery of India* (1946); Amery, L. C., *India and Freedom* (1943); Holland, William L., (ed.) *Asian Nationalism and the West* (1953); Mills, L. A., *et al.*, *The New World of Southeast Asia* (1949); Spear, T. G. P., *India, Pakistan, and the West* (1949); Warner, Levi, *Free India in Asia* (1952); Philips, C. H., *The Evolution of India and Pakistan 1858–1947* (1962).

For other aspects of Imperial and Commonwealth history see *South Africa, Rhodesia and the Protectorates* (1936), vol. viii in the *Cambridge History of the British Empire;* Haile, Lord, *African Survey: A Study of Problems Arising in Africa South of the Sahara* (rev. ed. 1957); Bourret, F. M., *Ghana: The Road to Independence 1919–1957* (1960); Carter, G. M., *Problems of Equality* (1958); Patterson, S., *The Last Trek* (1957); Curtin, P. D., *The Two Jamaicas* (1955); Ayearst, M. M., *The British West Indies: the Search for Self-Government* (1961); Stovel, E. A., *Canada in the World Economy* (1959). See also Curtin, P. D., "The British Empire and Commonwealth in Recent Historiography," *A. H. R.,* vol. LXV, No. 1 (October, 1959).

List of Illustrations and Sources

THOMAS GAINSBOROUGH
A self-portrait, *courtesy* the Royal Academy of Arts, London, and Copyright Reserved

DAVID GARRICK READING TO THE COMPANY AT DRURY LANE
Painting by William Hogarth, *courtesy* the British Museum, London

ROYAL ACADEMY EXHIBITION, A.D. 1771
Engraving by Earlom after C. Brandoin, *courtesy* Print Room, New York Public Library

SPECIMENS OF WEDGWOOD, A.D. 1780
Courtesy, Josiah Wedgwood and Sons, New York

JOHN WESLEY
A portrait (*circa* 1766) by Nathaniel Hone, *courtesy*, National Portrait Gallery, London

THE TREE OF LIFE
An Eighteenth Century engraving by J. Doleman and J. Pace, *courtesy*, the Pierpont Morgan Library, New York

ADELPHI TERRACE
From Malton's *Picturesque Tour Through London and Westminster*, London, 1792, *courtesy* Department of Printed Books, the British Museum, London

GENERAL VIEW OF LONDON, A.D. 1751
Engraving by T. Bowles, *courtesy* the British Museum, London

GEORGE III
Portrait from the studio of Allan Ramsay, *circa* 1767. *Courtesy* the National Portrait Gallery, London

THE BATTLE OF QUIBERON BAY
Painting by Dominique Serres, 1759, *courtesy* the National Maritime Museum, Greenwich

QUEBEC
A view drawn before 1760 by Captain Hervey Smyth from *Scenographia Americana*, London, 1768. *Courtesy*, Stokes Collection, New York Public Library

BRITISH CARICATURE OF GEORGE III, 1780
Courtesy, the Print Room, New York Public Library

A STAMP ACT CARTOON
Engraving by Paul Revere taken from a facsimile in *Paul Revere's Engravings* by C. S. Brigham, *courtesy* the American Antiquarian Society, Worcester, Massachusetts

SIEGE OF YORKTOWN
Painting by H. D. Van Blarenberghe after a sketch by Berthier, from the Museé de Versailles. Photograph, *courtesy* Hachette, Paris

SECTION V (*between pages 532 and 533*)

UNENCLOSED COMMON LAND OUTSIDE LEICESTER
From Samuel and Nathaniel Buck's *Views of Castles, Abbeys and Towns*, London, 1743. *Courtesy* the Department of Printed Books, the British Museum, London

THE MANCHESTER CANAL
From the *Gentleman's Magazine*, January, 1766. Photograph, *courtesy* the New York Public Library

TULL'S GRAIN DRILL
From Jethro Tull, *Horse-Hoeing Husbandry*, 1733. *Courtesy* the Museum of English Rural Life, the University of Reading, England

SPINNING JENNY AND POWER LOOM
From G. N. Wright, *Lancashire: Its History, Legends and Manufacture*, London, 1850. *Courtesy* New York Public Library

A NEWCOMEN ENGINE, 1717
Engraving, *courtesy* the Science and Technology Division, New York Public Library

DRAWING OF WATT'S PUMPING ENGINE, 1784
Photograph, *courtesy* The Science Museum, London

WILLIAM PITT, 1759–1806
Portrait by John Hoppner, *courtesy* the National Portrait Gallery, London

EDMUND BURKE
Portrait from the studio of Sir Joshua Reynolds, 1771. *Courtesy* the National Portrait Gallery, London

ADAM SMITH
Medallion portrait, 1787. *Courtesy* the National Portrait Gallery, London

Maps

Index

918

A Royal Academy exhibit where Reynolds was president

Here Keats saw the Elgin marble

Where Browning found Elizabeth Barrett a prisoner to her fathers will

My lady takes a chair to a ball

Soho Sq.

Shelley came here when expelled from Oxford

Lady Mary Montagu and Horace Walpole lived in

HYDE PARK

MAYFAIR

The blue stocking ladies entertain london celebrities in Hill Street

KENSINGTON GARDENS

The Forsytes' houses faced these parks

GREEN PARK

St JAMES'S P

At Holland House Addison wrote his "Spectator" papers

KNIGHTS BRIDGE

THE SPECTATOR VOLUME · FIRST LONDON · MDCCXLVII

Buckingham Palace

Thackeray wrote "Vanity Fair" at 16 Young St. Kensington

Poets corner in Westminster Abb

Fielding was justice of peace for Westminster

WESTMI

The Rotunda

On Cheyne Walk lived George Eliot. Carlyle. Hunt. Rossetti, Swinburne, and Meredith.

in Ranelagh Gardens

Chelsea Bridge

Whistler's picture of Old Battersea Bridge

Hampton Court, Twickenham and Strawberry Hill about 12 miles up the River

STRAWBERRY HILL